S0-ADZ-427

A New Anthology of Canadian Literature in English

A New Anthology of

Canadian Literature in English

Edited by

Donna Bennett
Russell Brown

OXFORD UNIVERSITY PRESS

70 Wynford Drive, Don Mills, Ontario M3C 1J9
www.oup.com/ca

Oxford University Press is a department of the University of Oxford.
It furthers the University's objective of excellence in research, scholarship, and education by publishing worldwide in

Oxford New York
Auckland Cape Town Dar es Salaam Hong Kong Karachi
Kuala Lumpur Madrid Melbourne Mexico City Nairobi
New Delhi Shanghai Taipei Toronto

With offices in
Argentina Austria Brazil Chile Czech Republic France Greece
Guatemala Hungary Italy Japan Poland Portugal Singapore
South Korea Switzerland Thailand Turkey Ukraine Vietnam

Oxford is a trade mark of Oxford University Press
in the UK and in certain other countries

Published in Canada
by Oxford University Press

Copyright © Oxford University Press Canada 2002

The moral rights of the author have been asserted

Database right Oxford University Press (maker)

First published 2002

All rights reserved. No part of this publication may be reproduced, stored in a retrieval system, or transmitted, in any form or by any means, without the prior permission in writing of Oxford University Press, or as expressly permitted by law, or under terms agreed with the appropriate reprographics rights organization. Enquiries concerning reproduction outside the scope of the above should be sent to the Rights Department, Oxford University Press, at the address above.

You must not circulate this book in any other binding or cover and you must impose this same condition on any acquirer.

Since this page cannot accommodate all the copyright notices, pages 1171–5 constitute an extension of the copyright page.

National Library of Canada Cataloguing in Publication Data

Main entry under title:
A new anthology of Canadian literature in English / Donna Bennett, Russell Brown, editors

Previous eds published under title: An anthology of Canadian literature in English.
Includes index.
ISBN–10: 0–19–541687–2 ISBN–13: 978–0–19–541687–9

1. Canadian literature (English). I. Bennett, Donna, 1945– . II. Brown, Russell, 1942– .
III. Title: An anthology of Canadian literature in English.

PS8233.N48 2002 C810.8 C2002–901471–9
PR9194.4.N48 2002

Cover and text design: Brett Miller

3 4 5 6 — 08 07 06 05
This book is printed on permanent (acid-free) paper ♾.
Printed in Canada

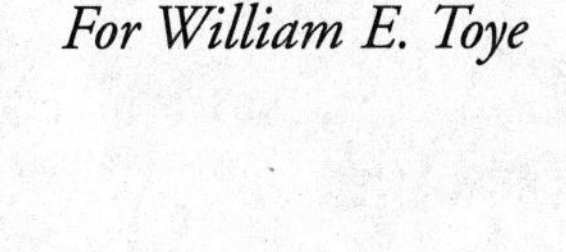

For William E. Toye

Contents

Preface

This book had its moment of origin in a class in English-Canadian poetry, one spring afternoon in 1979. The poems studied that day were filled with allusions unfamiliar to student readers, and a great deal of class time was spent in explanation. Afterwards, a sales representative from Oxford University Press called to discuss possible text adoptions for the following year. That coincidence in timing led to the first collection of English-Canadian literature to use footnotes and substantial headnotes to facilitate the reader's initial engagement with its selections—the first version of this anthology, published in two volumes in 1982–3. In 1990, joined by Nathalie Cooke, we prepared an abridged and updated version of that text, adding some authors who had emerged since 1983.

Now, we find ourselves back at the task, two decades after the original version of this anthology was published. The result is the volume you hold in your hands, a reconsideration of Canadian literature in English at the beginning of the twenty-first century—a moment marked by the kind of contradictions that characterize every era. Although we are acutely conscious of the serious problems now facing Canadian literary publishing and concerned about the future implications of the current inadequacy of arts funding, we can also say that there has never been a better time for Canadian literature. In this volume readers will find new authors and works that accurately suggest the wealth and range of talent that has emerged in the last twelve years. Even a partial list of those new to this volume would include many now seen as defining Canadian literature: Carol Shields, Thomas King, Jane Urquhart, Anne Carson, Tomson Highway, Guy Vanderhaeghe, Rohinton Mistry, Dionne Brand, Anne Michaels, and George Elliott Clarke. These are writers who have changed our understanding of the shape of the English-Canadian literary tradition.

Forces other than the simple passage of time are visible in this flowering. In the past generation, Canadian publishers and readers have expanded their range in a way that reflects the new diversity as well as the continuing vitality of the Canadian literary milieu. Some of the writers who appear for the first time in this edition of our anthology come out of new writing by individuals of Native descent; some are here as a result of the increased impact of Maritime and Western writers beyond their regions; some are shaped by the continued urbanization of Canada, some by the increased presence of immigrants who trace their descent from areas other than Europe; some have found their voice because of the acknowledgement of greater sexual diversity; and some would previously have been visible only in minority communities.

There have also been formal changes in English-Canadian literature that affect anthologists' choices. When Canadian literature first became an object of serious study (around the middle of the twentieth century), it was agreed that—from the Confederation poets, through E.J. Pratt and Earle Birney, to Margaret Avison and P.K. Page—

poetry formed the centre of the Canadian canon, though it was also understood that short fiction had a significant role in the tradition, from the early nineteenth-century sketches of Thomas Chandler Haliburton, through the successful magazine fiction of Morley Callaghan, to the finely crafted tales of Ethel Wilson. In the 1960s and 1970s, the balance began to shift from poetry to fiction. Poetry remained the most important literary form, but the appearance of Alice Munro, Alistair MacLeod, and Mavis Gallant showed that Canadian writers were becoming world leaders in the art of the short story. In the last two decades, fine new short-story writers have continued to appear and there is a revival of interest in poetry, but longer works of fiction and other prose forms have moved to the centre of attention. The result is that there are now many important writers who cannot be represented by poems or stories—and many others who are misrepresented or under-represented by those forms (David Adams Richards, for example, began by publishing collections of poetry and short stories, but is now known as a novelist; Michael Ondaatje has always been important as a poet, but not to read his fiction would be to see a very limited part of his achievement). The novel is now the reigning literary form in Canada, but its length—like that of full-length drama, which we have not attempted to include in either the last edition or the current one—presents a challenge for anthologists.

There have, in the same period, been changes in the way we view literature. The definitions of, and the boundaries of, the 'literary' do not seem as clear as they once were. Our first anthology included some exploration and settlement writing: those forms have become more important since, and their presence here has increased; travel writing (see Anna Jameson's selection, for example) has now become an object of serious attention, as has that amorphous category called 'life writing'. (The clearest example of life writing in this volume is the selection from Adele Wiseman's *Old Woman at Play*, but the presence of other recent works, such as Fred Wah's *Diamond Grill* and Aritha van Herk's *Places Far from Ellesmere*, remind us that generic distinctions have become more difficult in the contemporary age.) To give readers a broad sense of Canadian literature today, we have made more use of excerpts than in previous editions. (The fact that once-dominant organic theories of literature have yielded to other critical schools has made this decision easier.) We have taken care that these excerpts have their own integrity and have often been able to follow the author's own decisions about what will stand on its own, and we have framed such selections in a way that suggests their larger contexts. Omissions are always indicated by three spaced asterisks.

In adding footnotes to the texts in this anthology, we have tried to find a judicious balance, seeking to expedite the informed reading of the selections but not to replace standard reference aids or to document every allusion. To minimize distractions, more than one item is sometimes glossed in a single footnote; in such cases, the superscript is usually appended to the first item and the additional words being glossed are repeated in the note. All quotations from the Bible are from the King James Version (also known as the Authorized Version) except where otherwise indicated.

When more than one version of a text exists, we have chosen the author's most recent revision. We have silently corrected a few obvious typographical errors. The dates appended to the ends of texts are, if single, the date of first book publication. If substantive changes were later made, then the date of the revision follows that date (e.g. '1962; rev. 1968') and the second date is that of the text used in the anthology. When two dates are provided without that other indication (e.g. '1962, 1972'), then the second date is that of first book publication and the first is the date of first journal publication, included because it significantly predates the work's inclusion in a book. When two dates are provided and the first is in brackets (e.g. '[1870], 1984'), the bracketed date indicates the composition of a work that was published at a later date. In a few cases, poets have appended dates to their poems; we have retained these at the end of the poem and placed them to the right.

As with any project of this size and duration our indebtedness is beyond counting. We have often asked our students questions about their needs as readers. And we have frequently been assisted, both in this past year and over many preceding years, by colleagues, friends, and the writers themselves. The extraordinary generosity of the literary and scholarly communities in Canada makes projects like this a pleasure. In addition to those we have thanked in earlier editions, a partial listing of individuals who should be singled out for their assistance or advice this time includes Jesse Bundon, Jack David, Kristina Fagan, Patricia Fagan, Ajay Heble, Bruce Meyer, Carolyn Meyer, Irene Morra, William Toye, Georgia Wilder, and Glenn Willmott. We want to thank Oxford University Press for their assistance over the years: in the preparation of this volume Eric Sinkins was particularly invaluable. We apologize to those we have overlooked.

And as with any project of this size, readers have also contributed significantly in the past and can be expected to in the future. We invite those who have feedback to e-mail us at nacle.oup@utoronto.ca

Donna Bennett
Russell Brown
July 1, 2002

Introduction

There are eighty-five individuals in this anthology, arranged chronologically, from the earliest moments of what we now call Canada to today. Taken together, these selections and the headnotes that introduce them trace out a history of Canadian literature in English. Faced with this large and various offering, readers may want to focus only on a single time period, on one region, or on a particular form. Some may choose to look chiefly at women's writing or to emphasize works that reflect urban experiences or rural backgrounds. Some might seek out themes visible throughout—such as the immigrant experience or the search for home. Others might want begin by investigating major figures such as Charles G.D. Roberts, E.J. Pratt, Al Purdy, Alice Munro, Margaret Atwood, or Michael Ondaatje, and later locate these among their contemporaries, their precursors, and those they influenced. Some readers will be intrigued by the cross-connections that appear (for example, both Robert Bringhurst and Lorna Crozier write poems that rethink the story of Leda and the swan) or will enjoy seeing later writers enter into conversation with earlier ones. (Robert Kroetsch does that in his poem 'F.P. Grove: The Finding', just as Erin Mouré looks back to Al Purdy in the opening lines of 'It Is Only Me'.)

For those who come to this volume for its historical perspective, one way of looking at the development of the Canadian literary tradition found in these pages would be to focus on the issue of representation. Although Canada has its share of fantasists and writers of romances, a recurrent concern among our writers has been to report accurately about experience, with a consequent interest in concrete detail and response to the local, the immediate. English-Canadian letters began with the need to get down the particulars—the details—of experience and to chronicle everyday events: describing the milieu became one way to understand it and to give it value. The earliest descriptions, of the 'bush' or of a northern barren, give way to accounts of an emerging settlement, which in turn are followed by the story of a nation based on a rural economy, and eventually to a record of an increasingly urbanized culture standing between a wilderness and a highly technological and imperial neighbour.

As Canada has changed, so have writers' priorities about *which* details are important to depict, and about what kind of depiction is appropriate, what language to use, what narrative structures will best serve, and what value to assign to these changing circumstances. But an aspiration to report, to document, has remained strong. Perhaps that is one reason the Imagist movement, begun by Ezra Pound early in the twentieth century, became important for Canadian writers: the Imagists' devotion to getting down the telling concrete details that communicate a perception spoke to a desire already present. Later, some members of the West Coast *Tish* school complained about 'realism' having dominated Canadian writing, yet they, too, embraced a poetry that grounded itself in the local and sought to capture the immediate.

At the same time, there has been a countervailing tendency in Canadian literature, one that moves writers away from the everyday world to the realms of myth or that looks for a numinous world within or beneath the quotidian one. The expressions of these impulses can be seen throughout this volume, from Isabella Valancy Crawford, through James Reaney and Margaret Atwood, to Lorna Crozier and Anne Carson. The presence, in the middle of the twentieth century, of Northrop Frye, can be understood as a manifestation of that desire, not just as an influence that explains the use of myth by the writers who came after him. The tension between these two drives, the one leading Canadian writers to value the concrete world of physical experience, the other an idealizing tendency, remains with us still.

Both mimetic and mythic concerns are framed by prior considerations. The way a writer's, or a culture's, conception of what 'reality' is changes over time and will significantly influence the goals and methods of representation, even when the act of recording experience is conceived of as transparent. In the earliest selections contained here, an age of reason was confidently sending out its explorers, colonizers, and colonial administrators to build and oversee empires; that program began to be understood rather differently by the age of romantic idealism that followed, an age more inclined to value intuition over reason, and to look for a transcendent rather than a human plan. In the later nineteenth and twentieth centuries, that transcendental view was challenged by a more mechanistic one, its idealism displaced by a growing confidence in science and a sense that order could be located in political and social realities. Today, many hold some version of one of these earlier views, but a pervasive wariness has arisen about the limitations of human abilities to describe, generalize, or judge with acuity; a belief in Truth has been challenged by a sense that truths must be plural and may be contingent.

It is the way these epistemologies govern a writer's understanding of the world and the way they frame a writer's response to that world that make divisions into periods meaningful. But strong distinctions between periods, with each seen as having characteristic styles and concerns, may work better for the older and established literatures of Europe than for a newer one like Canada's. Literatures of former settler colonies are difficult to divide into eras, partly because an existing indigenous tradition has been disrupted—but not erased—when the imperial power comes into contact with its newly acquired territory, and partly because the immigrant-settler culture, once it has left behind the mainstream of the Old World, rarely develops smoothly or in pace with the world it has left behind. Space itself is a factor: because it takes time for settlers to move into and through the physical space of the colony, different areas and groups may become prominent in the discourse at different times; each may bring to the fore distinct concerns, needs, values, and aesthetics. Moreover, the particular pattern of Canadian settlement—that thin east-west line running alongside the border of another, more populous, nation—challenges national, and therefore temporal, coherences.

Trying to describe the shape of the literary history of Canada remains, nevertheless, a useful hermeneutic exercise. We will attempt one kind of overview here. Although the Aboriginal peoples of Canada did not have written languages, and for a long time had very limited access to print culture except through transcriptions made by the invader culture, the reader of this volume will see the persistence of Native voices. However, the bulk of this anthology is a record of a literary tradition begun by the immigrant-settlement culture of Canada. We can begin by dividing that tradition into two early periods:

(1) *The first stirrings of a literary culture before Confederation.* Often expressing an explorer's excitement of discovery or an immigrant's sense of loss and displacement, pre-Confederation writers responded to their new locations while looking back to the place they were leaving behind. Writing home, they found themselves—sometimes quite consciously—searching for a suitable language and for appropriate forms in which to express and contain their experience of new landscapes and changed circumstances.

(2) *The emergence of a national literature.* The writers who flourished in the era immediately following Confederation—such as Isabella Valancy Crawford, Charles G.D. Roberts, D.C. Scott, and Archibald Lampman—were conscious of living in a time of nation-building. They wanted both to draw on and to transform the Romantic and post-Romantic heritage (chiefly as it came to them from the United Kingdom and the United States), and they longed for an indigenous literature and a sustaining tradition.

In the twentieth century, we become more aware of the difficulties of history. With the emergence of a literary culture in the Canadian west, region challenges period as a way of understanding the shape of Canadian literature. And the lateness of the opening of the west means that a writer like Frederick Philip Grove is responding to the aesthetics of a settlement culture as well as to those of modernism. Nonetheless, we can identify a third literary period in Canada:

(3) *The emergence of literary modernism.* The first half of the twentieth century sees Canadian writers responding to modernism in its various manifestations, perhaps beginning with Sara Jeannette Duncan's desire to blend an urbane Jamesian realism with her own witty, often satirical, responses to her experiences of small-town ways and means. Duncan's western counterpart is Grove, whose version of the new realism tested the bounds of late Victorian propriety. The fiction writers who followed, such as Morley Callaghan and Sinclair Ross, like the poets writing in Montreal and Toronto between the wars, increasingly looked to the standards of 'International Modernism'. But Canadian writers of this period seem less interested in the revolutionary aspects of that modernism—with its desire to shock or astound and its tendency to break sharply with the past—than were their peers outside of Canada. Canadian modernists pursued the formal concerns of the movement, introducing innovations in language and in technique and investigating the relation between authorial voice and text.

The period following the Second World War could be thought of as a fourth period. In the introduction to the 1990 anthology we identified it as

(4) *The fragmented aesthetics of the end of the twentieth century.*

However, that act of naming suggests how problematic we found it then; we find it more so now. 'Postmodernism' has been one serviceable term applied to the age (though definitions of the postmodern have changed with succeeding decades), but period definition has become difficult, and region has also become less significant. From 1950 until around 1980, it looked as if a unitary means of defining a national Canadian literature was possible (which itself produced regional resistances). Many factors encouraged that sense, including the fruition of governmental support for the arts and media with such things as the Canada Council and the CBC; the emergence of a stronger and more autonomous publishing industry; more accessible trans-Canadian travel; an increasingly urban populace; and the expansion of post-secondary education. Whether this era was also a continuation of modernism or the beginning of something else is not clear: some of the most important Canadian writers of those years—including Robertson Davies, Mavis Gallant, Margaret Laurence, David Adams Richards, Alice Munro, and Alistair MacLeod—produced work that could be viewed as remaining within the conventions of modernist aesthetics; others, such as Sheila Watson, Robert Kroetsch, Leonard Cohen, and George Bowering, broke with modernism in innovative and even radically experimental works.

Defining what has happened since is even more difficult. Canadian poets, for example, moved away from modernism by various routes: some, like bp Nichol, by experimenting with forms; some, like Erin Mouré, by destabilizing the text. But many followed the lines opened up by Al Purdy or by the West Coast *Tish* school, choosing a colloquial and highly accessible voice or opting for a stripped diction, creating a plain-style poetry that does not fit easily into either 'modern' or 'postmodern' classifications. Fiction writers similarly have had several modes to choose from—and recently many have embraced a strongly lyrical style that replaces conventional narratives with stories that unfold the way a poem does.

Perhaps because we live in a time when the archives of the past are more available to us in the present than ever before and perhaps because we now move so freely across boundaries both geographical and cultural, period and region will give way to other ways of organizing our discussions, ways no longer structured chiefly by time or by place. As the work of writers from recent years attests, the modes of artistic expression themselves are becoming less clearly defined. The phenomenon in Canada of poet-novelists such as Margaret Atwood, Michael Ondaatje, Dionne Brand, and Anne Michaels has already been remarked upon by many, but increasingly we can see that Canadian writers move across many art forms. P.K. Page turns from expressing herself verbally to expressing herself visually, and back again; Anne Carson paints volcanoes and refuses to distinguish between her scholarly and her creative endeavours and titles her poems as 'essays', 'novels', and 'tangos'; George Elliott Clarke leaps easily from poem to drama to film script to opera libretto to personal essay to critical essay to novel; and a single book by Fred Wah—*Diamond Grill*—seems to partake of the novel, the memoir, the poem, and the essay. Perhaps the anthology of the future will be a multimedia work. While we await that future, the literature we have is richly multiple and various and endlessly fascinating.

Saukamapee

1714?–1791?

Saukamapee was a Nahathaway who left his own people and joined the Peigans to the west. By the time he met David Thompson (in the winter of 1787–8), he had become an elderly chief of a Peigan band. He took great interest in telling the explorer about his past experiences—prompting Thompson to provide a long description of Saukamapee in his journals and to transcribe the account he gave of North American life prior to and just after the first European contact.

Before the Europeans arrived, First Nations tales and beliefs were transmitted chiefly in oral form—now sometimes referred to as 'orature' (to contrast it to written literature). Because most transcriptions of these early oral materials are the product of European pens such as Thompson's, they have been regarded with suspicion by scholars of Native culture as unintentionally distorting, if not explicitly falsifying. More recently, scholars have begun to feel that such records, if used carefully, can provide valuable accounts that might otherwise be unavailable. Thompson's journals have proved especially important because, while not free of cultural biases—especially his feeling that Christianity provided a more enlightened view than Native religious perspectives—he made a conscious effort to record information objectively and sought out the elders of the tribes he visited, hoping that their knowledge of their cultures prior to European contact could be preserved.

Saukamapee is described by Thompson as follows:

He was full six feet in height, erect and of a frame that shewed strength and activity. . . . After a few days the old man spoke to me in the Nahathaway language and asked me if I understood it, and how long since I had left my own country. I ansered this is my fourth winter and the Nahathaways are the people we trade with, and I speak their tongue sufficient for common purposes, upon which, with a smile, he said, I am not a Peeagan of these plains I am a Nahathaway of the Pasquiaw River (a River that joins the Kisiskatachewan about fifty miles below Cumberland House.) . . . He said it is many winters since I last saw the ground where my parents lie. . . . Although erect and somewhat active, and in full possession of his faculties, yet from the events he related, and comparing them with the accounts of the french writers on the fur trade of Canada he must have been near ninety years of age, or more for his relation of affairs went back to near the year one thousand seven hundred. . . . He was fond of conversing in his native tongue, and recounting the events of his life, the number and positions of the different tribes of Indians, how they were allied, and the battles they had fought to gain the country of the Bow River. . . . Almost every evening for the time of four months I sat and listened to the old man, without being in the least tired, they were blended with the habits customs, and manners, politics, and religion such as it was, anecdotes of the Indian Chiefs and the means of their gaining influence in war and peace, that I always found something to interest me.

Since the war between the Blackfoot and the Snake Indians (the Shoshonean) took place around 1730, at which point Saukamapee was around sixteen, Thompson has overestimated Saukamapee's age here.

As well as being a unique source of the history of the Algonkian in the early eighteenth century (the events that Saukamapee recalls include the introduction of firearms and how it affected the mode of fighting around that time, the arrival of the horse on the plains, and the first smallpox epidemic), these tales have an immediacy that gives them continuing fascination.

[Life among the Peigans]

* * *

The Peeagans[1] were always the frontier Tribe, and upon whom the Snake Indians made their attacks, these latter were very numerous, even without their allies; and the Peeagans had to send messengers among us to procure help. Two of them came to the camp of my father, and I was then about his age (pointing to a Lad of about sixteen years) he promised to come and bring some of his people, the Nahathaways[2] with him, for I am myself of that people, and not of those with whom I am. My father brought about twenty warriors with him. There were a few guns amongst us, but very little ammunition, and they were left to hunt for the families; Our weapons was a Lance, mostly pointed with iron, some few of stone, A Bow and quiver of Arrows; the Bows were of Larch, the length came to the chin; the quiver had about fifty arrows, of which ten had iron points, the others were headed with stone. He carried his knife on his breast and his axe in his belt. Such was my father's weapons, and those with him had much the same weapons. I had a Bow and Arrows and a knife, of which I was very proud. We came to the Peeagans and their allies. They were camped in the Plains on the left bank of the River (the north side) and were a great many. We were feasted, a great War Tent was made, and a few days passed in speeches, feasting and dances. A war chief was elected by the chiefs, and we got ready to march. Our spies had been out and had seen a large camp of the Snake Indians on the Plains of the Eagle Hill, and we had to cross the River in Canoes, and on rafts, which we carefully secured for our retreat. When we had crossed and numbered our men, we were about 350 warriors. They had their scouts out, and came to meet us. Both parties made a great show of their numbers, and I thought that they were more numerous than ourselves.

After some singing and dancing, they sat down on the ground, and placed their large shields before them, which covered them: We did the same but our shields were not so many, and some of our shields had to shelter two men. Theirs were all placed touching each other; their Bows were not so long as ours, but of better wood, and the back covered with the sinews of the Bisons which made them very elastic, and their arrows went a long way and whizzed about us as balls do from guns. They were all headed with a sharp, smooth, black stone (flint) which broke when it struck anything. Our iron headed arrows did not go through their shields, but stuck in them; On both

1 The Peigans (US: Piegans) are one of the three allied Algonkian tribes that make up the Blackfoot. They were much feared by trappers.

2 Thompson explains that 'Nahathaway' is a general name for the Natives who inhabit the area south of 'a people who call themselves "Dinnie"' (i.e., the Dene, who, Thompson tells us, were called 'by the Hudson Bay Traders "Northern Indians" and by their southern neighbours "Cheepawyans"'). He further explains that the Nahathaways were referred to by the French voyageurs as the Cree, a name he says they did not use for themselves, adding that the Nahathaways 'are separated into many tribes or extended families, under different names, but all speaking dialects of the same language, which extends over this stony region, and along the Atlantic coasts southward to the Delaware River in the United States . . . and by the Saskatchewan River westward, to the Rocky Mountains'. (In today's terms, he is describing members of the Algonkian language family.)

sides several were wounded, but none lay on the ground; and night put an end to the battle, without a scalp being taken on either side, and in those days such were the results, unless one party was more numerous than the other. The great mischief of war then, was as now, by attacking and destroying small camps of ten to thirty tents, which are obliged to separate for hunting: I grew to be a man, became a skilful and fortunate hunter, and my relations procured me a Wife. She was young and handsome and we were fond of each other. We had passed a winter together, when Messengers came from our allies to claim assistance.

By this time the affairs of both parties had much changed; we had more guns and iron headed arrows than before; but our enemies the Snake Indians and their allies had Misstutim (Big Dogs, that is Horses) on which they rode, swift as the Deer, on which they dashed at the Peeagans, and with their stone Pukamoggan[3] knocked them on the head, and they had thus lost several of their best men. This news we did not well comprehend and it alarmed us, for we had no idea of Horses and could not make out what they were. Only three of us went and I should not have gone, had not my wife's relations frequently intimated, that her father's medicine bag would be much honored by the scalp of a Snake Indian. When we came to our allies, the great War Tent [was made] with speeches, feasting and dances as before; and when the War Chief had viewed us all it was found [that] between us and the Stone [Assiniboine] Indians we had ten guns and each of us about thirty balls, and powder for the war, and we were considered the strength of the battle. After a few days march our scouts brought us word that the enemy was near in a large war party, but had no Horses with them, for at that time they had very few of them. When we came to meet each other, as usual, each side displayed their numbers, weapons and shiel[d]s, in all which they were superior to us, except [for] our guns which were not shown, but kept in their leathern cases, and if we had shown [them], they would have taken them for long clubs. For a long time they held us in suspense; a tall Chief was forming a strong party to make an attack on our centre, and the others [were] to enter into combat with those opposite to them; We prepared for the battle the best we could. Those of us who had guns stood in the front line, and each of us [had] two balls in his mouth, and a load of powder in his left hand to reload.

We noticed they had a great many short stone clubs for close combat, which is a dangerous weapon, and had they made a bold attack on us, we must have been defeated as they were more numerous and better armed than we were, for we could have fired our guns no more than twice; and were at a loss what to do on the wide plain, and each Chief encouraged his men to stand firm. Our eyes were all on the tall Chief and his motions, which appeared to be contrary to the advice of several old Chiefs, all this time we were about the strong flight of an arrow from each other. At length the tall chief retired and they formed their long usual line by placing their shields on the ground to touch each other, the shield having a breadth of full three feet or more. We sat down opposite to them and most of us waited for the night to make a hasty retreat. The War Chief was close to us, anxious to see the effect of our guns.

3 (Also spelled 'pogamagan'): a club consisting of a stone wrapped in leather and fastened to a wooden handle.

The lines were too far asunder for us to make a sure shot, and we requested him to close the line to about sixty yards, which was gradually done, and lying flat on the ground behind the shields, we watched our opportunity when they drew their bows to shoot at us, their bodies were then exposed and each of us, as opportunity offered, fired with deadly aim, and either killed, or severely wounded, every one we aimed at.

The War Chief was highly pleased, and the Snake Indians finding so many killed and wounded kept themselves behind their shields; the War Chief then desired we would spread ourselves by two's throughout the line, which we did, and our shots caused consternation and dismay along their whole line. The battle had begun about Noon, and the Sun was not yet half down, when we perceived some of them had crawled away from their shields, and were taking to flight. The War Chief seeing this went along the line and spoke to every Chief to keep his Men ready for a charge of the whole line of the enemy, of which he would give the signal; this was done by himself stepping in front with his Spear, and calling on them to follow him as he rushed on their line, and in an instant the whole of us followed him, the greater part of the enemy took to flight, but some fought bravely and we lost more than ten killed and many wounded; Part of us pursued, and killed a few, but the chase had soon to be given over, for at the body of every Snake Indian killed there were five or six of us trying to get his scalp, or part of his clothing, his weapons, or something as a trophy of the battle. As there were only three of us, and seven of our friends, the Stone Indians, we did not interfere, and got nothing.

The next morning the War Chief made a speech, praising their bravery, and telling them to make a large War Tent to commemorate their victory, to which they directly set to work and by noon it was finished.

The War Chief now called on all the other Chiefs to assemble their men and come to the Tent. In a short time they came, all those who had lost relations had their faces blackened; those who killed an enemy, or wished to be thought so, had their faces blackened with red streaks on the face, and those who had no pretensions to the one, or the other, had their faces red with ochre. We did not paint our faces until the War Chief told us to paint our foreheads and eyes black, and the rest of the face of dark red ochre, as having carried guns, and to distinguish us from all the rest. Those who had scalps now came forward with the scalps neatly stretched on a round willow with a handle to the frame; they appeared to be more than fifty, and excited loud shouts and the war whoop of victory. When this was over, the War Chief told them that if any one had a right to the scalp of an enemy as a war trophy it ought to be us, who with our guns had gained the victory, when from the numbers of our enemies we were anxious to leave the field of battle; and that ten scalps must be given to us; this was soon collected, and he gave to each of us a Scalp. All those whose faces were blackened for the loss of relations, or friends, now came forward to claim the other scalps to be held in their hands for the benefit of their departed relations and friends; this occasioned a long conversation with those who had the scalps; at length they came forward to the War Chief, those who had taken the trophy from the head of the enemy they had killed, said the Souls of the enemy that each of us has slain, belong to us, and we have given them to our relations which are in the other world to be their slaves, and we are contented. Those who had scalps taken from the enemy that were found dead under the shields were at a loss what to say, as not one could declare he had actually slain the enemy whose scalp he held, and yet wanted to send their Souls to be the slaves of their departed relations. This caused much discussion; and the old Chiefs decided it could not be done, and that no one could send the soul of an enemy to be a slave in the other world, except the warrior who actually killed him; the scalps you hold are trophies of the Battle, but they give you no right to the soul of the enemy from whom it is taken, he alone who kills an enemy has a right to the soul, and to give it to be a slave to whom he pleases. This decision did not please them, but they were obliged to abide by it. The old Chiefs then turned to us, and praising our conduct in the battle said, each of you have slain two enemies in battle, if not more, you will return to your own people, and as you are young men, consult with the old men to whom you shall give the souls of those you have slain; until which let them wander about the other world. The Chiefs wished us to stay, and promised to each of us a handsome young wife, and [to] adopt us as their sons, but we told them we were anxious to see our relations and people, after which, perhaps we might come back. After all the war ceremonies were over, we pitched away in large camps with the women and children on the frontier of the Snake Indian country, hunting the Bison and Red Deer which were numerous, and we were anxious to see a horse of which we had heard so much. At last, as the leaves were falling we heard that one was killed by an arrow shot into his belly, but the Snake Indian that rode him, got away; numbers of us went to see him, and we all admired him, he put us in mind of a Stag that had lost his horns; and we did not know what name to give him. But as he was a slave to Man, like the dog, which carried our things; he was named the Big Dog.

We set off for our people, and on the fourth day came to a camp of Stone Indians, the relations of our companions, who received us well and we staid a few day[s]. The Scalps were placed on poles, and the Men and Women danced round them, singing to the sound of Rattles, Tambours and flutes. When night came, one of our party, in a low voice, repeated to the Chief the narrative of the battle, which he in a loud voice walking about the tents, repeated to the whole camp. After which, the Chiefs called those who followed them to a feast, and the battle was always the subject of the conversation and driving the Snake Indians to a great distance. There were now only three of us to proceed, and upon enquiry, [we] learned a camp of our people, the Nahathaways were a day's journey from us, and in the evening we came to them, and all our news had to be told, with the usual songs and dances; but my mind was wholly bent on making a grand appearance before my Wife and her Parents, and presenting to her father the scalp I had to ornament his Medicine Bag: and before we came to the camp we had dressed ourselves, and painted each other's faces to appear to the best advantage, and were proud of ourselves. On seeing some of my friends I got away and went to them, and by enquiries learned that my parents had gone to the low countries of the Lakes, and that before I was three Moons away my wife had given herself to another man, and that her father could not prevent her, and they were all to the northward there to pass the winter.

At this unlooked for news I was quite disheartened; I said nothing, but my heart was swollen with anger and revenge, and I passed the night scheming mischief. In the morning my friends reasoned with me upon my vexation about a worthless woman, and that it was beneath a warrior['s] anger, there were no want of women to replace her, and a better wife could be got. Others said, that if I had staid with my wife instead of running away to kill Snake Indians, nothing of this would have happened. My anger moderated, I gave my Scalp to one of my friends to give to my father, and renouncing my people, I left them, and came to the Peeagans who gave me a hearty welcome; and upon my informing them of my intention to remain with them the great Chief gave me his eldest daughter to be my wife, she is the sister of the present Chief, and as you see, now an old woman.

The terror of that battle and of our guns has prevented any more general battles, and our wars have since been carried by ambuscade and surprize, of small camps, in which we have greatly the advantage, from the Guns, arrows shod of iron, long knives, flat bayonets and axes from the Traders. While we have these weapons, the Snake Indians have none, but what few they sometimes take from one of our small camps which they have destroyed, and they have no Traders among them. We thus continued to advance through the fine plains to the Stag River when death came over us all, and swept more than one half of us by the Small pox, of which we knew nothing until it brought death among us. We caught it from the Snake Indians. Our Scouts were out for our security, when some returned and informed us of a considerable camp which was too large to attack and something very suspicious about it; from a high knowl they had a good view of the camp, but saw none of the men hunting, or going about; there were a few Horses, but no one came to them, and a herd of Bisons [were] feeding close to the camp with other herds near. This somewhat alarmed us as a stratagem of War; and our Warriors thought this camp had a larger not far off; so that if this camp was attacked which was strong enough to offer a desperate resistance, the other would come to their assistance and overpower us as had been once done by them, and in which we had lost many of our men.

The council ordered the Scouts to return and go beyond this camp, and be sure there was no other. In the mean time we advanced our camp; The scouts returned and said no other tents were near, and the camp appeared in the same state as before. Our Scouts had been going too much about their camp and were seen; they expected what would follow, and all those that could walk, as soon as night came on, went away. Next morning at the dawn of day, we attacked the Tents, and with our sharp flat daggers and knives cut through the tents and entered for the fight; but our war whoop instantly stopt, our eyes were appalled with terror; there was no one to fight with but the dead and the dying, each a mass of corruption. We did not touch them, but left the tents, and held a council on what was to be done. We all thought the Bad Spirit had made himself master of the camp and destroyed them. It was agreed to take some of the best of the tents, and any other plunder that was clean and good, which we did, and also took away the few Horses they had, and returned to our camp.

The second day after this dreadful disease broke out in our camp, and spread from one tent to another as if the Bad Spirit carried it. We had no belief that one Man could give it to another, any more than a wounded Man could give his wound to another. We did not suffer so much as those that were near the river, into which they rushed and died. We had only a little brook, and about one third of us died, but in some of the other camps there were tents in which every one died. When at length it left us and we moved about to find our people, it was no longer with the song and the dance; but with tears, shrieks, and howlings of despair for those who would never return to us. War was no longer thought of, and we had enough to do to hunt and make provisions for our families, for in our sickness we had consumed all our dried provisions; but the Bisons and Red Deer were also gone, we did not see one half of what was before, whither they had gone we could not tell, we believed the Good Spirit had forsaken us, and allowed the Bad Spirit to become our Master. What little we could spare we offered to the Bad Spirit to let us alone and go to our enemies. To the Good Spirit we offered feathers, branches of trees, and sweet smelling grass. Our hearts were low and dejected, and we shall never be again the same people. To hunt for our families was our sole occupation and kill Beavers, Wolves and Foxes to trade our necessaries; and we thought of War no more, and perhaps would have made peace with them for they had suffered dreadfully as well as us and had left all this fine country of the Bow River to us.

We were quiet for about two or three winters, and although we several times saw their young men on the scout we took no notice of them, as we all require young men, to look about the country that our families may sleep in safety and that we may know where to hunt. But the Snake Indians are a bad people, even their allies the Saleesh and Kootanaes cannot trust them, and do not camp with them, no one believes that they say, and [they] are very treacherous; every one says they are rightly named Snake People, for their tongue is forked like that of a Rattle Snake, from which they have their name. I think it was about the third falling of the leaves of the trees, that five of our tents pitched away to the valleys in the Rocky Mountains, up a branch of this river (the Bow) to hunt the Big Horn Deer (Mountain Sheep) as their horns make fine large bowls, and are easily cleaned; they were to return on the first snow. All was quiet and we waited for them until the snow lay on the ground, when we got alarmed for their safety; and about thirty warriors set off to seak them. It was only two days march, and in the evening they came to the camp, it had been destroyed by a large party of Snake Indians, who left their marks, of snakes heads painted black on sticks they had set up. The bodies were all there with the Women and Children, but scalped and partly devoured by the Wolves and Dogs.

The party of their return related the fate of our people, and other camps on hearing the news came and joined us. A War Tent was made and the Chiefs and Warriors assembled, the red pipes were filled with Tobacco, but before being lighted an old Chief arose, and beckoning to the Man who had the fire to keep back, addressed us, saying, I am an old man, my hair is white and [I] have seen much: formerly we were healthy and strong and many of us, now we are few to what we were, and the great sickness may come again. We were fond of War, even our Women flattered us to war, and nothing was thought of but scalps for singing and dancing. Now think of what has happened to us all, by destroying each other and doing the work of the bad spirit; the Great Spirit became angry with our making the ground red with blood: he called to the Bad Spirit to punish and destroy us, but in doing so not to let one spot of the ground, to be red with blood, and the Bad Spirit did it as we all know. Now we must revenge the death of our people and make the Snake Indians feel the effects of our guns, and other weapons; but the young women must all be saved, and if any has a babe at the breast it must not be taken from her, nor hurt; all the Boys and Lads that have no weapons must not be killed, but brought to our camps, and be adopted amongst us, to be our people, and make us more numerous and stronger than we are. Thus the Great Spirit will see that when we make war we kill only those who are dangerous to us, and make no more ground red with blood than we can help, and the Bad Spirit will have no more power on us. Everyone signified his assent to the old Chief, and since that time, it has sometimes been acted on, but more with the Women than the Boys, and while it weakens our enemies [it] makes us stronger. A red pipe was now lighted and the same old Chief taking it, gave three whiffs to the Great Spirit praying him to be kind to them and not forsake them, then three whiffs to the Sun, the same to the Sky, the Earth and the four Winds; the Pipe was passed round, and other pipes lighted. The War Chief then arose, and said Remember my friends that while we are smoking the bodies of our friends and relations are being devoured by wolves and Dogs, and their Souls are sent by the Snake Indians to be the slaves of their relations in the other world. We have made no war on them for more than three summers, and we had hoped to live quietly until our young men had grown up, for we are not many as we used to be; but the Snake Indians, that race of liars, whose tongues are like rattle snakes, have already made war on us, and we can no longer be quiet. The country where they now are is but little known to us, and if they did not feel themselves strong they would not have dared to have come so far to destroy our people. We must be courageous and active, but also cautious; and my advice is, that three scout parties, each of about ten warriors with a Chief at their head, take three different directions, and cautiously view the country, and not go too far, for enough of our people are already devoured by wolves and our business is revenge, without losing our people.

After five days, the scout parties returned without seeing the camp of an enemy, or any fresh traces of them. Our War Chief, Kootanae Appe, was now distressed, he had expected some camp would have been seen, and he concluded, the Snake Indians had gone to the southward to their allies, to show the scalps they had taken and make their songs and dances for the victory, and in his speech denounced constant war on them until they were exterminated. Affairs were in this state when we arrived, and the narrative [of the] old man having given us the above information, he lighted his pipe; and smoking it out said, the Snake Indians are no match for us; they have no guns and are no match for us, but they have the power to vex us and make us afraid for the small hunting parties that hunt the small deer for dresses and the Big Horn for the same and for Bowls. They keep us always on our guard.

* * *

The Chief soon collected his warriors and, having examined their arms and [having seen] that every one had two pairs of shoes, some dried provisions, and other necessaries, in the evening the principal War Chief addressed the Chief at the head of the party; reminding him that the warriors now accompanying him would steadily follow him, that they were sent to destroy their enemies, not to be killed themselves, and made the slaves of their enemies, that he must be wise and cautious and bring back the Warriors entrusted to his care. Among them was the eldest son of the Old Man in whose tent we lived. They all marched off very quietly as if for hunting. After they were gone; the old man said it was not a war party, but one of those they frequently sent, under guidance of those who had showed courage and conduct in going to war, for we cannot afford to lose our people, we are too few, and these expeditions inure our men to long marches and to suffer hunger and thirst. At the end of about twenty days they returned with about thirty five Horses in tolerable condition, and fifteen fine mules, which they had brought away from a large camp of Snake Indians. The old Man's son gave him a long account of the business. On the sixth evening the scouts ahead came and informed the Chief, that we must be near a camp, as they had seen horses feeding: night came on, and we went aside to a wood of cotton and poplar trees on the edge of a brook, in the morning some of us climbed the trees and passed the day, but saw nothing. In the night we went higher up the brook, and as it was shoal, we walked in it for some distance, to another wood, and there lay down. Early the next morning, a few of us advanced through the wood, but we had not gone far, before we heard the women with their dogs come for wood for fuel. Some of us returned to the Chief, and the rest watched the women, it was near midday before they all went away, they had only stone axes and stone clubs to break the wood; they took only what was dry, and cut none down. Their number showed us the camp must be large, and sometimes some of them came so close to us, that we were afraid of being discovered. The Chief now called us round him, and advised us to be very cautious, as it was plain we were in the vicinity of a large camp, and manage our little provisions, for we must not expect to get any more until we retreated; if we fire a gun at the Deer it will be heard; and if we put an arrow in a deer and he gets away, and they see the deer, it will alarm them, and we shall not be able to get away. My intention is to have something to show our people, and when we retreat, take as many horses as we can with us, to accomplish which, we must have a fair opportunity, and in the mean time be hungry, which we can stand some time, as we have plenty of water to drink. We were getting tired, and our solace was of an evening to look at the horses and mules. At length he said to us to get ready, and pointing to the top of the Mountains, [said] see the blue sky is gone and a heavy storm is there, which will soon reach us; and so it did: About sunset we proceeded thro' the wood, to the horses, and with the lines we carried, each helping the other, we soon had a horse or a mule to ride on. We wanted to drive some with us, but the Chief would not allow it; it was yet daylight when we left the wood, and entered the plains, but the Storm of Wind was very strong and on our backs, and at the gallop, or trot, so as not to tire our horses, we continued to midnight, when we came to a brook, with plenty of grass, and let them get a good feed. After which we held on to sun rising, when seeing a fine low ground, we staid the rest of the day, keeping watch until night, when we continued our journey. The storm lasted two days and greatly helped us.

The old Man told his son, who, in his relation had intimated he did not think the Chief very brave; that it was very fortunate that he was under such a Chief, who had acted so wisely and cautiously; for had he acted otherwise not one of you would have returned, and some young men coming into the tent whom he supposed might have the same opinions as his son, he told them; 'that it required no great bravery for a War Party to attack a small camp, which they were sure to master; but that it required great courage and conduct, to be for several days in the face of a large camp undiscovered; and each of you to bring away a horse from the enemy, instead of leaving your own scalps.'

[1846–51], 1916

Frances Brooke

1724–1789

Early English-Language Publications

The first English-language books were, in contrast to the oral expression of First Nations peoples, communications about the experience of an unfamiliar territory directed to readers who live elsewhere—audiences who had never seen and might never see what was being described. Such texts exemplify the deep desire by those who have come from away to 'write home', to convey the news of the New World to those left behind in the Old.

The forms these communications took vary widely. Some books began as actual letters to family members or friends before finding a more general audience through publication; others were the journals of explorers; still others were reports prepared by travellers to communicate their experiences once they were back in their homeland. Early literary writing was also a form of 'writing home', since the literary public remained in Europe. Frances Brooke's *History of Emily Montague* is doubly this kind of communication: not only is the novel aimed at an audience in England but, as an epistolary novel, it dramatizes characters in the act of writing letters, many of them directed to friends and family back in England.

Frances Brooke

The History of Emily Montague, published in London in 1769, is often described as the first Canadian novel (and as the first North American one). Its author was already well established as a writer in England before she travelled to Quebec in 1763 to join her husband, the chaplain of the garrison there. Part of a literary circle that included Samuel Richardson (Brooke adopted the epistolary form of her fiction from Richardson, who is often described as the first English novelist), before leaving England she published a novel (*The History of Lady Julia Mandeville,* 1763), a book of poetry, and a play, and served as editor of a weekly periodical called *The Old Maid.* Her translation of a French romance speaks to an interest in French literature and culture, which helped provide the background and disposition to respond to what had until very recently been New France. Except for one visit home, Brooke seems to have lived in Quebec until 1768, when she and her husband returned to England.

In *The History of Emily Montague,* Canada's relationship to England resembles that of the enchanted woods to the everyday world in Shakespeare's comedies: Canada is a place to escape to for romantic intrigues and the confusions of love, an idyllic interlude from which all the principals eventually return to the orderly world of their origins. The novel's 228 letters are mostly by its young English lovers: Ed. Rivers, a half-pay officer who initially plans to settle in Canada but eventually returns to England; the beautiful Emily Montague, with whom he falls in love; and Emily's best friend, the coquettish Arabella Fermor.

Emily Montague met with a favourable reception in Europe: it was reprinted twice in its author's lifetime and was translated into French. Though her novel seems to have had little direct influence on Canadian writers, it is a valuable work for understanding Canada's literary tradition because Brooke provides one of the earliest imaginative responses to the country. The experience of the immigrant in the New World receives its first literary treatment in this novel, and Brooke uses that topic to comment on, and give some freshness to, the plot of her highly conventional romance—as when Rivers says that if only Emily loves him, 'I know in my own heart, that Canada will no longer be a place of exile' (Letter 83). Brooke describes the garrison-based society at Quebec and the surrounding landscape and the climate, and shows the effect of these upon individuals. In addition, she offers interesting observations about the co-existence of the French and English; examines the Indians and their culture; sees North American society as calling up new questions about the roles of women; and expresses a need for new language, metaphors, and myths to deal with the radically new experiences she encountered in Canada.

At the same time, Brooke's European background is evident. It is especially revealed in her perception of the Indians, which seems to be founded on a reading of Rousseau, and in the way her reactions to the landscape are shaped by the eighteenth-century fascination with the sublime.

From *The History of Emily Montague*

LETTER I

To John Temple, ESQ; at Paris
[From Ed. Rivers]

Cowes, April 10, 1766

After spending two or three very agreeable days here, with a party of friends, in exploring the beauties of the Island, and dropping a tender tear at Carisbrook Castle on the memory of the unfortunate Charles the First,[1] I am just setting out for America, on a scheme I once hinted to you, of settling the lands to which I have a right as a lieutenant-colonel on half pay. On enquiry and mature deliberation, I prefer Canada to New-York for two reasons, that it is wilder, and that the women are handsomer: the first, perhaps, every body will not approve; the latter, I am sure, you will.

You may perhaps call my project romantic, but my active temper is ill suited to the lazy character of a reduc'd officer:[2] besides that I am too proud to narrow my circle of life, and not quite unfeeling enough to break in on the little estate which is scarce sufficient to support my mother and sister in the manner to which they have been accustom'd.

1 Charles I was incarcerated in Carisbrook Castle on the Isle of Wight before his execution in 1649. The sentiments expressed in this passage owe much to the Gothic sensibility of Brooke's period, with its fondness for indulging in the melancholy feelings inspired by ruined castles.

2 One discharged from active service and put on half-pay, subject to recall.

What you call a sacrifice is none at all; I love England, but am not obstinately chain'd down to any spot of earth; nature has charms every where for a man willing to be pleased: at my time of life, the very change of place is amusing; love of variety, and the natural restlessness of man, would give me a relish for this voyage, even if I did not expect, what I really do, to become lord of a principality which will put our large-acred men in England out of countenance. My subjects indeed at present will be only bears and elks, but in time I hope to see the *human face divine* multiplying around me; and, in thus cultivating what is in the rudest state of nature, I shall taste one of the greatest of all pleasures, that of creation, and see order and beauty gradually rise from chaos.

The vessel is unmoor'd; the winds are fair; a gentle breeze agitates the bosom of the deep; all nature smiles: I go with all the eager hopes of a warm imagination; yet friendship casts a lingering look behind.

Our mutual loss, my dear Temple, will be great. I shall never cease to regret you, nor will you find it easy to replace the friend of your youth. You may find friends of equal merit; you may esteem them equally; but few connexions form'd after five and twenty strike root like that early sympathy, which united us almost from infancy, and has increas'd to the very hour of our separation.

What pleasure is there in the friendships of the spring of life, before the world, the mean unfeeling selfish world, breaks in on the gay mistakes of the just-expanding heart, which sees nothing but truth, and has nothing but happiness in prospect!

I am not surpriz'd the heathens rais'd altars to friendship: 'twas natural for untaught superstition to deify the source of every good; they worhsip'd friendship, which animates the moral world, on the same principle as they paid adoration to the sun, which gives life to the world of nature.

I am summon'd on board. Adieu!

Ed. Rivers

LETTER 10

To Miss Rivers, Clarges Street
[From Arabella Fermor[1]]

Silleri, August 24

I have been a month arrived, my dear, without having seen your brother, who is at Montreal, but I am told is expected to-day. I have spent my time however very agreably. I know not what the winter may be, but I am enchanted with the beauty of this country in summer; bold, picturesque, romantic, nature reigns here in all her wanton luxuriance, adorned by a thousand wild graces which mock the cultivated beauties of Europe. The scenery about the town is infinitely lovely; the prospect extensive, and diversified by a variety of hills, woods, rivers, cascades, intermingled with smiling farms and cottages, and bounded by distant mountains which seem to scale the very Heavens.

1 Brooke borrowed this name from the woman to whom Alexander Pope dedicated *The Rape of the Lock* (1712) and who served as a model for its central character, Belinda—the epitome of a mannered coquette. Brooke may also have liked the name because its eighteenth-century pronunciation—'Farmer'—would have made it, like 'Rivers', appropriate to her rustic setting. This letter is addressed to Lucy Rivers, Ed. Rivers' sister, who remains in London.

The days are much hotter here than in England, but the heat is more supportable from the breezes which always spring up about noon; and the evenings are charming beyond expression. We have much thunder and lightening, but very few instances of their being fatal: the thunder is more magnificent and aweful than in Europe, and the lightening brighter and more beautiful; I have even seen it of a clear pale purple, resembling the gay tints of the morning.

The verdure is equal to that of England, and in the evening acquires an unspeakable beauty from the lucid splendor of the fire-flies sparkling like a thousand little stars on the trees and on the grass.

There are two very noble falls of water near Quebec, la Chaudiere and Montmorenci: the former is a prodigious sheet of water, rushing over the wildest rocks, and forming a scene grotesque, irregular, astonishing: the latter, less wild, less irregular, but more pleasing and more majestic, falls from an immense height, down the side of a romantic mountain into the river St Lawrence, opposite the most smiling part of the island of Orleans, to the cultivated charms of which it forms the most striking and agreable contrast.

The river of the same name, which supplies the cascade of Montmorenci, is the most lovely of all inanimate objects: but why do I call it inanimate? It almost breathes; I no longer wonder at the enthusiasm of Greece and Rome; 'twas from objects resembling this their mythology took its rise; it seems the residence of a thousand deities.

Paint to yourself a stupendous rock burst as it were in sunder by the hands of nature, to give passage to a small, but very deep and beautiful river; and forming on each side a regular and magnificent wall, crowned with the noblest woods that can be imagined; the sides of these romantic walls adorned with a variety of the gayest flowers, and in many places little streams of the purest water gushing through, and losing themselves in the river below: a thousand natural grottoes in the rock make you suppose yourself in the abode of the Nereids;[2] as a little island, covered with flowering shrubs, about a mile above the falls, where the river enlarges itself as to give it room, seems intended for the throne of the river goddess. Beyond this, the rapids, formed by the irregular projections of the rock, which in some places seem almost to meet, rival in beauty, as they excel in variety, the cascade itself, and close this little world of enchantment.

In short, the loveliness of this fairy scene alone more than pays the fatigues of my voyage; and, if I ever murmur at having crossed the Atlantic, remind me that I have seen the river Montmorenci.

I can give you a very imperfect account of the people here; I have only examined the landscape about Quebec, and have given very little attention to the figures; the French ladies are handsome, but as to the beaux, they appear to me not at all dangerous, and one might safely walk in a wood by moonlight with the most agreable Frenchman here. I am surprized the Canadian ladies take such pains to seduce our men from us; but I think it a little hard we have no temptation to make reprisals.

2 Sea nymphs.

I am at present at an extreme pretty farm on the banks of the river St Lawrence; the house stands at the foot of a steep mountain covered with a variety of trees, forming a verdant sloping wall, which rises in a kind of regular confusion,

'Shade above shade, a woody theatre',[3]

and has in front this noble river, on which the ships continually passing present to the delighted eye the most charming moving picture imaginable: I never saw a place so formed to inspire that pleasing lassitude, that divine inclination to saunter, which may not improperly be called, the luxurious indolence of the country. I intend to build a temple here to the charming goddess of laziness.

A gentleman is just coming down the winding path on the side of the hill, whom by his air I take to be your brother. Adieu! I must receive him: my father is at Quebec.

Yours,

Arabella Fermor

Your brother has given me a very pleasing piece of intelligence: my friend Emily Montague is at Montreal, and is going to be married to great advantage; I must write to her immediately, and insist on her making me a visit before she marries. She came to America two years ago, with her uncle Colonel Montague, who died here, and I imagined was gone back to England; she is however at Montreal with Mrs Melmoth, a distant relation of her mother's. Adieu! *ma tres chere!*

3 Milton, *Paradise Lost*: 'Cedar, and pine, and fir, and branching palm, / A sylvan scene, and, as the ranks ascend / Shade above shade, a woody theatre / of stateliest view' (IV, 139–42).

LETTER 11

To Miss Rivers, Clarges Street
[From Ed. Rivers]

Quebec, September 10

I find, my dear, that absence and amusement are the best remedies for a beginning passion; I have passed a fortnight at the Indian village of Lorette,[1] where the novelty of the scene, and the enquiries I have been led to make into their antient religion and manners, have been of a thousand times more service to me than all the reflection in the world would have been.

I will own to you that I staid too long at Montreal, or rather at Major Melmoth's; to be six weeks in the same house with one of the most amiable, most pleasing of women, was a trying situation to a heart full of sensibility, and of a sensibility which has been hitherto, from a variety of causes, a good deal restrained. I should have avoided the danger from the first, had it appeared to me what it really was; but I thought myself secure in the consideration of her engagements, a defence however which I found grow weaker every day.

1 More properly Jeune Lorette, where the Hurons settled in 1697, having previously taken refuge from the Iroquois at Lorette a generation earlier.

But to my savages: other nations talk of liberty, they possess it; nothing can be more astonishing than to see a little village of about thirty or forty families, the small remains of the Hurons, almost exterminated by long and continual war with the Iroquoise, preserve their independence in the midst of an European colony consisting of seventy thousand inhabitants; yet the fact is true of the savages of Lorette; they assert and they maintain that independence with a spirit truly noble. One of our company having said something which an Indian understood as a supposition that they had been *subjects* of France, his eyes struck fire, he stop'd him abruptly, contrary to their respectful and sensible custom of never interrupting the person who speaks. 'You mistake, brother,' said he; 'we are subject to no prince; a savage is free all over the world.' And he spoke only truth; they are not only free as a people, but every individual is perfectly so. Lord of himself, at once subject and master, a savage knows no superior, a circumstance which has a striking effect on his behaviour; unawed by rank or riches, distinctions unknown amongst his own nation, he would enter as unconcerned, would possess all his powers as freely in the palace of an oriental monarch, as in the cottage of the meanest peasant: 'tis the species, 'tis man, 'tis his equal he respects, without regarding the gaudy trappings, the accidental advantages, to which polished nations pay homage.

I have taken some pains to develop their present, as well as past, religious sentiments, because the Jesuit missionaries have boasted so much of their conversion; and find they have rather engrafted a few of the most plain and simple truths of Christianity on their ancient superstitions, than exchanged one faith for another; they are baptized, and even submit to what they themselves call the *yoke* of confession, and worship according to the outward forms of the Romish church, the drapery of which cannot but strike minds unused to splendor; but their belief is very little changed, except that the women seem to pay great reverence to the Virgin, perhaps because flattering to the sex. They anciently believed in one God, the ruler and creator of the universe, whom they called *The Great Spirit* and the *Master of Life*; in the sun as his image and representative; in a multitude of inferior sprits and demons; and in a future state of rewards and punishments, or, to use their own phrase, in *a country of souls*. They reverenced the spirits of their departed heroes, but it does not appear that they paid them any religious adoration. Their morals were more pure, their manners more simple, than those of polished nations, except in what regarded the intercourse of the sexes: the young women before marriage were indulged in great libertinism, hid however under the most reserved and decent exterior. They held adultery in abhorrence, and with the more reason as their marriages were dissolvible at pleasure. The missionaries are said to have found no difficulty so great in gaining them to Christianity, as that of persuading them to marry for life: they regarded the Christian system of marriage as contrary to the laws of nature and reason; and asserted that, as the *Great Spirit* formed us to be happy, it was opposing his will, to continue together when otherwise.

The sex we have so unjustly excluded from power in Europe have a great share in the Huron government; the chief is chose by the matrons from amongst the nearest male relations, by the female line, of him he is to succeed; and is generally an aunt's or sister's son; a custom which, if we examine strictly into the principle on which it is founded, seems a little to contradict what we are told of the extreme chastity of the married ladies.

The power of the chief is extremely limited; he seems rather to advise his people as a father than command them as a master: yet, as his commands are always reasonable, and for the general good, no prince in the world is so well obeyed. They have a supreme council of ancients, into which every man enters of course at an age fixed, and another of assistants to the chief on common occasions, the members of which are like him elected by the matrons: I am pleased with this last regulation, as women are, beyond all doubt, the best judges of the merit of men; and I should be extremely pleased to see it adopted in England: canvassing for elections would then be the most agreeable thing in the world, and I am sure the ladies would give their votes on much more generous principles than we do. In the true sense of the word we are the savages, who so impolitely deprive you of the common rights of citizenship, and leave you no power but that of which we cannot deprive you, the resistless power of your charms. By the way, I don't think you are obliged in conscience to obey laws you have had no share in making; your plea would certainly be at least as good as that of the Americans, about which we every day hear so much.

The Hurons have no positive laws; yet being a people not numerous, with a strong sense of honor, and in that state of equality which gives no food to the most tormenting passions of the human heart, and the council of ancients having a power to punish atrocious crimes, which power however they very seldom find occasion to use, they live together in a tranquillity and order which appears to us surprizing.

In more numerous Indian nations, I am told, every village has its chief and its councils, and is perfectly independent of the rest; but on great occasions summon a general council, to which every village sends deputies.

Their language is at once sublime and melodious; but, having much fewer ideas, it is impossible it can be so copious as those of Europe: the pronunciation of the men is guttural, but that of the women extremely soft and pleasing; without understanding one word of the language, the sound of it is very agreeable to me. Their style even in speaking French is bold and metaphorical: and I am told is on important occasions extremely sublime. Even in common conversation they speak in figures, of which I have this moment an instance. A savage woman was wounded lately in defending an English family from the drunken rage of one of her nation. I asked her after her wound; 'It is well,' said she; 'my sisters at Quebec (meaning the English ladies) have been kind to me; and piastres,[2] you know, are very healing.'

They have no idea of letters, no alphabet, nor is their language reducible to rules: 'tis by painting they preserve the memory of the only events which interest them, or that they think worth recording, the conquests gained over their enemies in war.

When I speak of their paintings, I should not omit that, though extremely rude, they have a strong resemblance to the Chinese, a circumstance which struck me the more, as it is not the stile of nature. Their dances also, the most lively pantomimes I ever saw, and especially the dance of peace, exhibit variety of attitudes resembling the figures on Chinese fans; nor have their features and complexion less likeness to the pictures we see of the Tartars, as their wandering manner of life, before they became Christians, was the same.

2 Coins.

If I thought it necessary to suppose they were not natives of the country, and that America was peopled later than the other quarters of the world, I should imagine them the descendants of Tartars; as nothing can be more easy than their passage from Asia, from which America is probably not divided; or, if it is, by a very narrow channel. But I leave this to those who are better informed, being a subject on which I honestly confess my ignorance.

I have already observed, that they retain most of their antient superstitions. I should particularize their belief in dreams, of which folly even repeated disappointments cannot cure them: they have also an unlimited faith in their *powawers*, or conjurers, of whom there is one in every Indian village, who is at once physician, orator, and divine, and who is consulted as an oracle on every occasion. As I happened to smile at the recital a savage was making of a prophetic dream, from which he assured us of the death of an English officer whom I knew to be alive, 'You Europeans', said he, 'are the most unreasonable people in the world; you laugh at our belief in dreams, and yet expect us to believe things a thousand times more incredible.'

Their general character is difficult to describe; made up of contrary and even contradictory qualities; they are indolent, tranquil, quiet, humane in peace; active, restless, cruel, ferocious in war: courteous, attentive, hospitable, and even polite, when kindly treated; haughty, stern, vindictive, when they are not; and their resentment is the more to be dreaded, as they hold it a point of honor to dissemble their sense of an injury[3] till they find an opportunity to revenge it.

They are patient of cold and heat, of hunger and thirst, even beyond all belief when necessity requires, passing whole days, and often three or four days together, without food, in the woods, when on the watch for an enemy, or even on their hunting parties; yet indulging themselves in their feasts even to the most brutal degree of intemperance. They despise death, and suffer the most excruciating tortures not only without a groan, but with an air of triumph; singing their death song, deriding their tormentors, and threatening them with the vengeance of their surviving friends: yet hold it honorable to fly before an enemy that appears the least superior in number or force.

Deprived by their extreme ignorance, and that indolence which nothing but their ardor for war can surmount, of all the conveniencies, as well as elegant refinements of polished life; strangers to the softer passions, love being with them on the same footing as amongst their fellow-tenants of the woods, their lives appear to me rather tranquil than happy: they have fewer cares, but they have also much fewer enjoyments, than fall to our share. I am told, however, that, though insensible to love, they are not without affections; are extremely awake to friendship, and passionately fond of their children.

They are of a copper color, which is rendered more unpleasing by a quantity of coarse red on their cheeks; but the children, when born, are of a pale silver white; perhaps their indelicate custom of greasing their bodies, and their being so much exposed to the air and sun even from infancy, may cause that total change of complexion, which I know not how otherwise to account for: their hair is black and shining, the women's very long, parted at the top, and combed back, tied behind, and often twisted with a

3 That is, to pretend not to be insulted.

thong of leather, which they think very ornamental: the dress of both sexes is a close jacket, reaching to their knees, with spatterdashes[4] all of coarse blue cloth, shoes of deer-skin, embroidered with porcupine quills, and sometimes with silver spangles; and a blanket thrown across their shoulders, and fastened before with a kind of bodkin,[5] with necklaces, and other ornaments of beads or shells.

They are in general tall, well made, and agile to the last degree; have a lively imagination, a strong memory; and, as far as their interests are concerned, are very dextrous politicians.

Their address is cold and reserved; but their treatment of strangers, and the unhappy, infinitely kind and hospitable. A very worthy priest, with whom I am acquainted at Quebec, was some years since shipwrecked in December on the island of Anticosti:[6] after a variety of distresses, not difficult to be imagined on an island without inhabitants, during the severity of a winter even colder than that of Canada; he, with the small remains of his companions who survived such complicated distress, early in the spring, reached the main land in their boat, and wandered to a cabbin of savages; the antient of which, having heard his story, bid him enter, and liberally supplied their wants: 'Approach, brother,' said he; 'the unhappy have a right to our assistance; we are men, and cannot but feel for the distresses which happen to men;' a sentiment which has a strong resemblance to a celebrated one in a Greek tragedy.[7]

You will not expect more from me on this subject, as my residence here has been short, and I can only be said to catch a few marking[8] features flying. I am unable to give you a picture at full length.

Nothing astonishes me so much as to find their manners so little changed by their intercourse with the Europeans; they seem to have learnt nothing of us but excess in drinking.

The situation of the village is very fine, on an eminence, gently rising to a thick wood at some distance, a beautiful little serpentine river in front, on which are a bridge, a mill, and a small cascade, at such a distance as to be very pleasing objects from their houses; and a cultivated country, intermixed with little woods lying between them and Quebec, from which they are distant only nine very short miles.

What a letter have I written! I shall quit my post of historian to your friend Miss Fermor; the ladies love writing much better than we do; and I should perhaps be only just, if I said they write better.

Adieu!

Ed. Rivers

4 Leggings worn to protect the trousers or stockings from mud.
5 A small pointed instrument.
6 Ile d'Anticosti in the Gulf of St Lawrence
7 In fact this is a rather common sentiment in Greek tragedy; the resemblance Brooke has in mind may well be to Theseus' first speech in Sophocles' *Oedipus at Colonus*:

. . . no wanderer shall come, as you do,
And be denied my audience or aid.
I know I am only a man; I have no more
To hope for in the end than you have.

8 Characteristic.

LETTER 49
To Miss Rivers, Clarges Street
[From Arabella Fermor]

Silleri, Jan. 1

It is with difficulty I breathe, my dear; the cold is so amazingly intense as almost totally to stop respiration. I have business, the business of pleasure, at Quebec; but have not the courage to stir from the stove.

We have had five days, the severity of which none of the natives remember to have ever seen equaled: 'tis said, the cold is beyond all the thermometers here, tho' intended for the climate.

The strongest wine freezes in a room which has a stove in it; even brandy is thickened to the consistence of oil: the largest wood fire, in a wide chimney, does not throw out its heat a quarter of a yard.

I must venture to Quebec to-morrow, or have company at home: amusements are here necessary to life; we must be jovial, or the blood will freeze in our veins.

I no longer wonder the elegant arts are unknown here; the rigour of the climate suspends the very powers of the understanding; what then must become of those of the imagination? Those who expect to see

'A new Athens rising near the pole',[1]

will find themselves extremely disappointed. Genius will never mount high, where the faculties of the mind are benumbed half the year.

'Tis sufficient employment for the most lively spirit here to contrive how to preserve an existence, of which there are moments that one is hardly conscious: the cold really sometimes brings on a sort of stupefaction.

We had a million of beaux here yesterday, notwithstanding the severe cold: 'tis the Canadian custom, calculated I suppose for the climate, to visit all the ladies on New-year's-day, who sit dressed in form to be kissed. I assure you, however, our kisses could not warm them; but we were obliged, to our eternal disgrace, to call in rasberry brandy as an auxiliary.

You would have died to see the men; they look just like so many bears in their open carrioles,[2] all wrapped in furs from head to foot; you see nothing of the human form appear, but the tip of a nose.

They have intire coats of beaver skin exactly like Friday's in Robinson Crusoe, and casques[3] on their heads like the old knights errant in romance; you never saw such tremendous figures; but without this kind of cloathing it would be impossible to stir out at present.

1 Adapted from a passage in Pope, 'Two Chorus's to the Tragedy of Brutus' (1717), about the Muses going into exile from ancient Greece to distant Britain, whereupon the island will:

See arts her savage sons controul,
And Athens *rising near the pole!*

2 A kind of sleigh, usually for one person.
3 Helmets.

The ladies are equally covered up, tho' in a less unbecoming style; they have long cloth cloaks with loose hoods, like those worn by the market-women in the north of England. I have one in scarlet, the hood lined with sable, the prettiest ever seen here, in which I assure you I look amazingly handsome; the men think so, and call me the *Little red riding-hood*; a name which becomes me as well as the hood.

The Canadian ladies wear these cloaks in India silk in summer, which, fluttering in the wind, look really graceful on a fine woman.

Besides our riding-hoods, when we go out, we have a large buffaloe's skin under our feet, which turns up, and wraps round us almost to our shoulders; so that, upon the whole, we are pretty well guarded from the weather as well as the men.

Our covered carrioles too have not only canvas windows (we dare not have glass, because we often overturn), but cloth curtains to draw all around us; the extreme swiftness of these carriages also, which dart along like lightening, helps to keep one warm, by promoting the circulation of the blood.

I pity the Fitz;[4] no tiger was ever so hard-hearted as I am this weather: the little god[5] has taken his flight, like the swallows. I say nothing, but cruelty is no virtue in Canada; at least at this season.

I suppose Pygmalion's statue was some frozen Canadian gentlewoman, and a sudden warm day thawed her.[6] I love to expound ancient fables, and I think no exposition can be more natural than this.

Would you know what makes me chatter so this morning? Papa has made me take some excellent liqueur; 'tis the mode here; all the Canadian ladies take a little, which makes them so coquet and agreable. Certainly brandy makes a woman talk like an angel. Adieu!

Yours,

A. Fermor

4 Captain J. Fitzgerald, Arabella's suitor in Canada.
5 Cupid.
6 In Greek mythology Pygmalion was a sculptor who made a statue of such beauty that he fell in love with it. The goddess Aphrodite took pity on his plight and brought the statue to life.

LETTER 80

To Miss Rivers, Clarges Street
[From Arabella Fermor]

Silleri, Feb. 25

Those who have heard no more of a Canadian winter than what regards the intenseness of its cold, must suppose it a very joyless season: 'tis, I assure you, quite otherwise; there are indeed some days here of the severity of which those who were never out of England can form no conception; but those days seldom exceed a dozen in a whole winter; nor do they come in succession, but at intermediate periods, as the winds set in from the North-West; which, coming some hundred leagues, from frozen lakes and rivers, over woods and mountains covered with snow, would be insupportable, were it not for the furs with which the country abounds, in such variety and plenty as to be within the reach of all its inhabitants.

Thus defended, the British belles set the winter of Canada at defiance; and the season of which you seem to entertain such terrible ideas, is that of the utmost chearfulness and festivity.

But what particularly pleases me is, there is no place where women are of such importance:[1] not one of the sex, who has the least share of attractions, is without a levee[2] of beaux interceding for the honor of attending her on some party, of which every day produces three or four.

I am just returned from one of the most agreable jaunts imagination can paint, to the island of Orleans, by the falls of Montmorenci; the latter is almost nine miles distant, across the great bason of Quebec; but as we are obliged to reach it in winter by the waving line, our direct road being intercepted by the inequalities of the ice, it is now perhaps a third more. You will possibly suppose a ride of this kind must want one of the greatest essentials to entertainment, that of variety, and imagine it only one dull whirl over an unvaried plain of snow; on the contrary, my dear, we pass hills and mountains of ice in the trifling space of these few miles. The bason of Quebec is formed by the conflux of the rivers St Charles and Montmorenci with the great river St Lawrence, the rapidity of whose flood-tide, as these rivers are gradually seized by the frost, breaks up the ice, and drives it back in heaps, till it forms ridges of transparent rock to an height that is astonishing, and of a strength which bids defiance to the utmost rage of the most furiously rushing tide.

This circumstance makes this little journey more pleasing than you can possibly conceive: the serene blue sky above, the dazzling brightness of the sun, and the colors from the refraction of its rays on the transparent part of these ridges of ice, the winding course these oblige you to make, the sudden disappearing of a train of fifteen or twenty carrioles, as these ridges intervene, which again discover themselves on your rising to the top of the frozen mount, the tremendous appearance both of the ascent and descent, which however are not attended with the least danger; all together give a grandeur and variety to the scene, which almost rise to enchantment.

Your dull foggy climate affords nothing that can give you the least idea of our frost pieces in Canada; nor can you form any notion of our amusements, of the agreableness of a covered carriole, with a sprightly fellow, rendered more sprightly by the keen air and romantic scene about him; to say nothing of the fair lady at his side.

Even an overturning has nothing alarming in it; you are laid gently down on a soft bed of snow, without the least danger of any kind; and an accident of this sort only gives a pretty fellow occasion to vary the style of his civilities, and shew a greater degree of attention.

But it is almost time to come to Montmorenci; to avoid, however, fatiguing you or myself, I shall refer the rest of our tour to another letter, which will probably accompany this: my meaning is, that two moderate letters are vastly better than one long one; in which sentiment I know you agree with.

Yours,

A. Fermor

1 In Letter 6 Brooke had Ed. Rivers say almost the same thing of the women he encounters among the French farmers: they play a civilizing role and 'Their conversation is lively and amusing, all the little knowledge of Canada is confined to the [female] sex. . . .'

2 An assembly of visitors, especially but not necessarily in the morning.

LETTER 123

To the Earl of ———
[From Captain Wm. Fermor[1]]

Silleri, April 14

England, however populous, is undoubtedly, my Lord, too small to afford very large supplies of people to her colonies: and her people are also too useful, and of too much value, to be suffered to emigrate, if they can be prevented, whilst there is sufficient employment for them at home.

It is not only our interest to have colonies; they are not only necessary to our commerce, and our greatest and surest source of wealth, but our very being as a powerful commercial nation depends on them: it is therefore an object of all others most worthy our attention, that they should be as flourishing and populous as possible.[2]

It is however equally our interest to support them at as little expence of our own inhabitants as possible: I therefore look on the acquisition of such a number of subjects as we found in Canada, to be a much superior advantage to that of gaining ten times the immense tract of land ceded to us, if uncultivated and destitute of inhabitants.

But it is not only contrary to our interest to spare many of our own people as settlers in America; it must also be considered, that, if we could spare them, the English are the worst settlers on new lands in the universe.

Their attachment to their native country, especially amongst the lower ranks of people, is so very strong, that few of the honest and industrious can be prevailed on to leave it; those therefore who go, are generally the dissolute and the idle, who are of no use any where.

The English are also, though industrious, active, and enterprizing, ill fitted to bear the hardships, and submit to the wants, which inevitably attend an infant settlement even on the most fruitful lands.

The Germans, on the contrary, with the same useful qualities, have a patience, a perseverance, and abstinence, which peculiarly fit them for the cultivation of new countries; too great encouragement therefore cannot be given to them to settle in our colonies: they make better settlers than our own people; and at the same time their numbers are an acquisition of real strength where they fix, without weakening the mother country.

It is long since the populousness of Europe has been the cause of her sending out colonies: a better policy prevails; mankind are enlightened; we are now convinced, both by reason and experience, that no industrious people can be too populous.

The northern swarms[3] were compelled to leave their respective countries, not because those countries were unable to support them, but because they were too idle to cultivate the ground: they were a ferocious, ignorant, barbarous people, averse to

1 Arabella's father. A Polonius-like character, he writes letters full of pompous statements and conventional wisdom. In Letter 135 Fermor says: 'People who have no ideas out of the common road are, I believe, generally the greatest talkers.'

2 Fermor's colonial attitude is expressed even more emphatically in Letter 133: 'Every advantage you give the North American trade centers at last in the mother, they are the bees, who roam abroad for that honey which enriches the paternal hive.'

3 Fermor here apparently refers to the medieval migration of barbarians out of northern Europe.

labor, attached to war, and, like our American savages, believing every employment not relative to this favorite object, beneath the dignity of man.

Their emigrations therefore were less owing to their populousness, than to their want of industry, and barbarous contempt of agriculture and every useful art.

It is with pain I am compelled to say, the late spirit of encouraging the monopoly of farms, which, from a narrow, short-sighted policy, prevails amongst our landed men at home, and the alarming growth of celibacy amongst the peasantry, which is its necessary consequence, to say nothing of the same ruinous increase of celibacy in higher ranks, threatens us with such a decrease of population, as will probably equal that caused by the ravages of those scourges of heaven, the sword, the famine, and the pestilence.[4]

If this selfish policy continues to extend itself, we shall in a few years be so far from being able to send emigrants to America, that we shall be reduced to solicit their return, and that of the posterity, to prevent England's becoming in its turn an uncultivated desert.

But to return to Canada; this large acquisition of people is an invaluable treasure, if managed, as I doubt not it will be, to the best advantage; if they are won by the gentle arts of persuasion, and the gradual progress of knowledge, to adopt so much of our manners as tends to make them happier in themselves, and more useful members of the society to which they belong: if with our language, which they should by every means be induced to learn, they acquire the mild genius of our religion and laws, and that spirit of industry, enterprize, and commerce, to which we owe all our greatness.

* * *

Your Lordship enquires into the nature of this climate in respect to health. The air being uncommonly pure and serene, it is favorable to life beyond any I ever knew: the people live generally to a very advanced age; and are remarkably free from diseases of every kind, except consumptions, to which the younger part of the inhabitants are a good deal subject.

It is however a circumstance one cannot help observing, that they begin to look old much sooner than the people in Europe; on which my daughter observes, that it is not very pleasant for women to reside in a country where people have a short youth, and a long old age.

The diseases of cold countries are in general owing to want of perspiration; for which reason exercise, and even dissipation are here the best medicines.

The Indians therefore shewed their good sense in advising the French, on their first arrival, to use dancing, mirth, chearfulness, and content, as the best remedies against the inconveniences of the climate.

I have already swelled this letter to such a length, that I must postpone to another time my account of the peculiar natural productions of Canada; only observing, that one would imagine heaven intended a social intercourse between the most distant

4 For much of the previous century, holdings of farmland in Britain had been becoming more and more concentrated among relatively few large landholders. The notion that the consequent displacement of farm families would result in a decline in fertility seems to have been a common—if unwarranted—fear of the time.

nations, by giving them productions of the earth so very different each from the other, and each more than sufficient for itself, that the exchange might be the means of spreading the bond of society and brotherhood over the whole globe.

In my opinion, the man who conveys, and causes to grow in any country, a grain, a fruit, or even a flower, it never possessed before, deserves more praise than a thousand heroes: he is a benefactor, he is in some degree a creator.

I have the honor to be,

My Lord,

Your Lordship's, &c.

William Fermor

LETTER 127

To John Temple, ESQ; Pall Mall
[From Arabella Fermor]

Silleri, April 18

* * *

Cruel creature! why did you give me the idea of flowers? I now envy your foggy climate: the earth with you at this moment covered with a thousand lovely children of the spring; with us, it is an universal plain of snow.

Our beaux are terribly at a loss for similies: you have lilies of the valley for comparisons; we nothing but what with the idea of whiteness gives that of coldness too.

This is all the quarrel I have with Canada: the summer is delicious, the winter pleasant with all its severities; but alas! the smiling spring is not here; we pass from winter to summer in an instant, and lose the sprightly season of the Loves.

A letter from the God of my idolatry[1]—I must answer it instantly.

Adieu! Yours, &c.

A. Fermor

1 Captain Fitzgerald.

LETTER 131

To the Earl of ———
[From Wm. Fermor]

Silleri, April 20, Evening

We are returned, my Lord, from having seen an object as beautiful and magnificent in itself, as pleasing from the idea it gives of renewing once more our intercourse with Europe.

Before I saw the breaking up of the vast body of ice, which forms what is here called *the bridge,* from Quebec to Point Levi, I imagined there could be nothing in it worth attention; that the ice would pass away, or dissolve gradually, day after day, as the influence of the sun, and warmth of the air and earth increased; and that we should see the river open, without having observed by what degrees it became so.

But I found the *great river*, as the savages with much propriety call it, maintain its dignity in this instance as in all others, and assert its superiority over those petty streams which we honor with the names of rivers in England. Sublimity is the characteristic of this western world; the loftiness of the mountains, the grandeur of the lakes and rivers, the majesty of the rocks shaded with a picturesque variety of beautiful trees and shrubs, and crowned with the noblest of the offspring of the forest, which form the banks of the latter, are as much beyond the power of fancy as that of description: a landscape-painter might here expand his imagination, and find ideas which he will seek in vain in our comparatively little world.

The object of which I am speaking has all the American magnificence.

The ice before the town, or, to speak in the Canadian stile, *the bridge*, being of a thickness not less than five feet, a league in length, and more than a mile broad, resists for a long time the rapid tide that attempts to force it from the banks.

We are prepared by many circumstances to expect something extraordinary in this event, if I may so call it: every increase of heat in the weather for near a month before the ice leaves the banks; every warm day gives you terror for those you see venturing to pass it in carrioles; yet one frosty night makes it again so strong, that even the ladies, and the timid amongst them, still venture themselves over in parties of pleasure; though greatly alarmed at their return, if a few hours of uncommon warmth intervene.

But, during the last fortnight, the alarm grows indeed a very serious one: the eye can distinguish, even at a considerable distance, that the ice is softened and detached from the banks; and you dread every step being death to those who have still the temerity to pass it, which they will continue always to do till one or more pay their rashness with their lives.

From the time the ice is no longer a bridge on which you see crowds driving with such vivacity on business or pleasure, every one is looking eagerly for its breaking away, to remove the bar to the continually wished and expected event, of the arrival of ships from that world from whence we have seemed so long in a manner excluded.

The hour is come; I have been with a crowd of both sexes, and all ranks, hailing the propitious moment: our situation, on the top of Cape Diamond, gave us a prospect some leagues above and below the town; above Cape Diamond the river was open, it was so below Point Levi, the rapidity of the current having forced a passage for the water under the transparent bridge, which for more than a league continued firm.

We stood waiting with all the eagerness of expectation; the tide came rushing with an amazing impetuosity; the bridge seemed to shake, yet resisted the force of the waters; the tide recoiled, it made a pause, it stood still, it returned with redoubled fury, the immense mass of ice gave way.

A vast plain appeared in motion; it advanced with solemn and majestic pace: the points of land on the banks of the river for a few moments stopped its progress; but the immense weight of so prodigious a body, carried along by a rapid current, bore down all opposition with a force irresistible.

There is no describing how beautiful the opening river appears, every moment gaining on the sight, till, in a time less than can possibly be imagined, the ice passing Point Levi, is hid in one moment by the projecting land, and all is once more a clear plain before you; giving at once the pleasing, but unconnected, ideas of that direct intercourse with Europe from which we have been so many months excluded, and of the earth's again opening her fertile bosom, to feast our eyes and imagination with her various verdant and flowery productions.

I am afraid I have conveyed a very inadequate idea of the scene which has just passed before me; it however struck me so strongly, that it was impossible for me not to attempt it.

If my painting has the least resemblance to the original, your Lordship will agree with me, that the very vicissitudes of season here partake of the sublimity which so strongly characterizes the country.

The changes of season in England, being slow and gradual, are but faintly felt; but being here sudden, instant, violent, afford to the mind, with the lively pleasure arising from meer change, the very high additional one of its being accompanied with grandeur. I have the honor to be,

My Lord,

Your Lordship's, &c.

William Fermor

LETTER 169

To Captain Fermor, at Silleri
[From Ed. Rivers[1]]

Aug. 6

I have been taking an exact survey of the house and estate with my mother, in order to determine on some future plan of life.

'Tis inconceivable what I felt on returning to a place so dear to me, and which I had not seen for many years; I ran hastily from one room to another; I traversed the garden with inexpressible eagerness: my eye devoured every object; there was not a tree, not a bush, which did not revive some pleasing, some soft idea.

I felt, to borrow a very pathetic expression of Thompson's,

'A thousand little tendernesses throb',[2]

on revisiting those dear scenes of infant happiness; which were increased by having with me that estimable, that affectionate mother, to whose indulgence all my happiness had been owing.

* * *

The situation of the house is enchanting; and with all my passion for the savage luxuriance of America, I begin to find my taste return for the more mild and regular charms of my native country.

1 After his return to England.
2 Actually 'Ten thousand little tendernesses throb': James Thomson, *Agamemnon. A Tragedy* (1738), I, iii, 8.

We have no Chaudieres, no Montmorencis, none of those magnificent scenes on which the Canadians have a right to pride themselves; but we excel them in the lovely, the smiling: in enameled meadows, in waving corn-fields, in gardens the boast of Europe; in every elegant art which adorns and softens human life; in all the riches and beauty which cultivation can give.

I begin to think I may be blest in the possession of my Emily, without betraying her into a state of want; we may, I begin to flatter myself, live with decency, in retirement; and, in my opinion, there are a thousand charms in retirement with those we love.

Upon the whole, I believe we shall be able to live, taking the word live in the sense of lovers, not of the *beau monde*, who will never allow a little country squire of four hundred pounds a year to live.[3]

Time may do more for us; at least, I am of an age and temper to encourage hope.

All here are perfectly yours.

Adieu! my dear friend,
Your affectionate

Ed. Rivers

1769

3 As in many works of the period that deal with marriage among the landed gentry on fixed incomes, the question of money plays an important role in the question of matrimony. The opposition in this passage between fashionable society (the *beau monde*) and a simple country life that embodies the pastoral ideal of moderation occurs several times in the book. Compare Letter 177: 'Upon the whole, I believe, the most agreable, as well as most free of all situations, to be that of a little country gentleman, who lives upon his income, and knows enough of the world not to envy his richer neighbours.' In her conclusion, however, Brooke places Ed. Rivers and his new wife beyond all financial constraints by having Emily turn out to be a lost heir.

Samuel Hearne

1745–1792

Exploration Narratives

A desire to observe the environment closely, to map physical and relational space, to document the details of one's milieu, and to discover the source of events has been evident in Canadian writing across historical eras and literary movements. This habit of mind may have arisen out of a need to make the new country visible: it has manifested itself as an imperative to record the objective details of experience and has shaped the early non-fiction of what became English Canada.

The narratives of exploration that have come down to us were a particularly important form of this early communication. The English-language explorers, land surveyors, and traders who, after Britain took over France's North American colonies in the mid-eighteenth century, arrived as representatives of the Empire and as agents of commercial institutions such as the fur-trading Hudson's Bay and North West Companies, came seeking information about the Canadian seacoasts and about the remoter parts of Canada. Their records are not just useful sources of information; they are documents that helped form British understanding of the new territories that had been acquired. Reworked from hasty field notes into finished and shapely stories, they found a ready market among a British public for whom tales of endurance and discovery were compelling reading. The establishing of trade and the opening up of the land often became secondary in their focus on individual experience: they recorded the personal suffering and danger that seemed to European readers to epitomize exploration of a northern land such as Canada. These were narratives of survival that affirmed the ability of British men, often accompanied by their helpful French-Canadian or Métis guides and assisted by the Native peoples they encountered, to overcome extreme conditions in distant outposts.

The fact that these tales of exploration were, when published, intended for a European audience played a role in determining what these accounts described and how they were told. While close attention to detail and a desire to provide detached observation and useful scientific knowledge about the flora and fauna remained an important feature of these texts, they also employ narrative tension to hold the reader's attention.

As Germaine Warkentin observes, in her preface to *Canadian Exploration Literature*, these stories are best understood as '"incremental" texts' because they passed through 'several stages of composition of which the daily log is only the first': some had 'additions by fellow explorers'; most were 'revised by other hands before appearing as a grand quarto volume of "travels" to ornament a gentleman's library'.

Samuel Hearne

The variety of goals that sent these early wanderers out into the wilderness is eloquently attested to in the 'Orders and Instructions' given to Samuel Hearne by the Hudson's Bay Company in 1769. Instructed to explore 'the Northern Indians Country, &c.', Hearne was told to locate the Indian guide Matonabbee and, with him, to seek out 'a river represented by the Indians to abound with copper ore, animals of the furr kind, &c., and which is said to be so far to the Northward, that in the middle of the Summer the Sun does not set. . . . And if the said river be likely to be of any utility, take possession of it on behalf of the Hudson's Bay Company.' If this were not enough, a subsequent letter of instruction enjoins him also to undertake a 'quest of a North West Passage, Copper Mines, or any other thing that may be serviceable to the British Nation in general, or the Hudson's Bay Company in particular'.

Hearne, a Londoner, had already served in the Royal Navy for nearly ten years before joining the Hudson's Bay Company in 1766 at the age of twenty-one. After sailing for a time in Hudson Bay, he demonstrated his ability to travel on foot by making an overland trip along the west coast of the Bay from Fort Prince of Wales (Churchill, Man.) to York Factory and back. The series of three journeys that Hearne eventually made in fulfillment of his 1769 commission took him into difficult territory. A line in the introduction to his journals gives a sense of how little was known of the area he entered: 'I drew a Map on a large skin of parchment . . . but left the interior parts blank, to be filled up during my Journey.' In 1771–2 he arrived at the Coppermine River; following it to its mouth, recording his travels as he went, he became the first European to reach the Arctic Ocean by travelling over land.

In 1774 Hearne founded Cumberland House, the Company's first inland post; the next year he was made governor of Fort Prince of Wales. In 1782 he made a controversial surrender to a French expedition led by the Comte de Lapérouse. Lapérouse destroyed the fort but returned Hearne's journals to him after extracting a promise that Hearne would have them published. When the fort was rebuilt in 1783, Hearne returned as governor, remaining until 1787. He then retired to London, where he spent the rest of his life working on a final version of his journals, *A Journey from Prince of Wales's Fort in Hudson's Bay, to the northern ocean, undertaken by order of the Hudson's Bay Company, for the discovery of copper mines, a north west passage, &c. in the years 1769, 1770, 1771, & 1772.* Not published until three years after his death, this understated chronicle of stoic endeavour has become one of the classic exploration narratives. Its author's scrupulous concern for accuracy can be seen in the careful descriptions of the animals and plants of the North, which show Hearne as an excellent natural historian with exceptional powers of memory and observation. Hearne was also the first explorer known to have lived alone with the Natives, travelling with them in nomadic fashion and, like them, depending on the land for his sustenance. Although not free from cultural bias, his accounts avoided the earlier stereotypes that idealized North American Aboriginals or treated them as barbarous savages. Because they depict Native peoples more dispassionately than did earlier travellers, they have been of value to later ethnographers.

From *A Journey from Prince of Wales's Fort in Hudson's Bay to the Northern Ocean*

[Between 6 November and 11 December 1769 Samuel Hearne made an abortive journey from Fort Prince of Wales through the Barren Lands in search of copper and the Coppermine River. Hardships were increased by the perfidy of his first Native guide, Chawchinahaw. In February 1770 he set out on a second attempt to find the Coppermine with a new guide, Conne-e-queese, who led him on a slow, uncertain trek during which Hearne became assimilated into the migratory life of the Natives.]

June 5th–23rd 1770

The snow was by this time so soft as to render walking in snow-shoes very laborious; and though the ground was bare in many places, yet at times, and in particular places, the snow-drifts were so deep, that we could not possibly do without them. By the sixth, however, the thaws were so general, and the snows so much melted, that as our snow-shoes were attended with more trouble than service, we all consented to throw them away. Till the tenth, our sledges proved serviceable, particularly in crossing lakes and ponds on the ice; but that mode of travelling now growing dangerous on account of the great thaws, we determined to throw away our sledges, and every one to take a load on his back.

This I found to be much harder work than the winter carriage, as my part of the luggage consisted of the following articles, viz. the quadrant[1] and its stand, a trunk containing books, papers, &c., a land-compass, and a large bag containing all my wearing apparel; also a hatchet, knives, files, &c. beside several small articles, intended for presents to the natives. The aukwardness of my load, added to its great weight, which was upward of sixty pounds, and the excessive heat of the weather, rendered walking the most laborious task I had ever encountered; and what considerably increased the hardship, was the badness of the road, and the coarseness of our lodging, being, on account of the want of proper tents, exposed to the utmost severity of the

1 An instrument used in navigation for measuring angles and taking bearings.

weather. The tent we had with us was not only too large, and unfit for barren ground service, where no poles were to be got, but we had been obliged to cut it up for shoes, and each person carried his own share. Indeed my guide behaved both negligently and ungenerously on this occasion; as he never made me, or my Southern Indians,[2] acquainted with the nature of pitching tents on the barren ground; which had he done, we could easily have procured a set of poles before we left the woods. He took care, however, to procure a set for himself and his wife; and when the tent was divided, though he made shift to get a piece large enough to serve him for a complete little tent, he never asked me or my Southern Indians to put our heads into it.

Beside the inconvenience of being exposed to the open air, night and day, in all weathers, we experienced real distress from the want of victuals. When provisions were procured, it often happened that we could not make a fire, so that we were obliged to eat the meat quite raw; which at first, in the article of fish particularly, was as little relished by my Southern companions as myself.

Notwithstanding these accumulated and complicated hardships, we continued in perfect health and good spirits; and my guide, though a perfect niggard of his provisions, especially in times of scarcity, gave us the strongest assurance of soon arriving at a plentiful country, which would not only afford us a certain supply of provisions, but where we should meet with other Indians, who probably would be willing to carry part of our luggage. This news naturally gave us great consolation; for at that time the weight of our constant loads was so great, that when Providence threw any thing in our way,[3] we could not carry above two days provisions with us, which indeed was the chief reason of our being so frequently in want.

From the twentieth to the twenty-third we walked every day near twenty miles, without any other subsistence than a pipe of tobacco, and a drink of water when we pleased: even partridges and gulls, which some time before were in great plenty, and easily procured, were now so scarce and shy, that we could rarely get one; and as to geese, ducks, &c. they had all flown to the Northward to breed and molt.

Early in the morning of the twenty-third, we set out as usual, but had not walked above seven or eight miles before we saw three musk-oxen grazing by the side of a small lake. The Indians immediately went in pursuit of them; and as some of them were expert hunters, they soon killed the whole of them. This was no doubt very fortunate; but, to our great mortification, before we could get one of them skinned, such a fall of rain came on, as to put it quite out of our power to make a fire; which, even in the finest weather, could only be made of moss, as we were near an hundred miles from any woods. This was poor comfort for people who had not broke their fast for four or five days. Necessity, however, has no law; and having been before initiated into the method of eating raw meat, we were the better prepared for this repast: but this was by no means so well relished, either by me or the Southern Indians, as either raw venison or raw fish had been: for the flesh of the musk-ox is not only coarse and tough, but smells and tastes so strong of musk as to make it very disagreeable when raw, though it is tolerable eating when properly cooked. The weather continued so remarkably bad,

2 The Cree or Chipewyan.
3 That is, when heaven provided game.

accompanied with constant heavy rain, snow, and sleet, and our necessities were so great by the time the weather permitted us to make a fire, that we had nearly eat to the amount of one buffalo quite raw.

Notwithstanding I mustered up all my philosophy on this occasion, yet I must confess that my spirits began to fail me. Indeed our other misfortunes were greatly aggravated by the inclemency of the weather, which was not only cold, but so very wet that for near three days and nights I had not one dry thread about me. When the fine weather returned, we made a fire, though it was only moss, as I have already observed; and having got my cloaths dry, all things seemed likely to go on in the old channel, though that was indifferent enough; but I endeavoured, like a sailor after a storm, to forget past misfortunes.

None of our natural wants, if we except thirst, are so distressing, or hard to endure, as hunger; and in wandering situations, like that which I now experienced, the hardship is greatly aggravated by the uncertainty with respect to its duration, and the means most proper to be used to remove it, as well as by the labour and fatigue we must necessarily undergo for that purpose, and the disappointments which too frequently frustrate our best concerted plans and most strenuous exertions: it not only enfeebles the body, but depresses the spirits, in spite of every effort to prevent it. Besides, for want of action, the stomach so far loses its digestive powers, that after long fasting it resumes its office with pain and reluctance. During this journey I have too frequently experienced the dreadful effects of this calamity, and more than once been reduced to so low a state by hunger and fatigue, that when Providence threw any thing in my way, my stomach has scarcely been able to retain more than two or three ounces, without producing the most oppressive pain. Another disagreeable circumstance of long fasting is, the extreme difficulty and pain attending the natural evacuations for the first time; and which is so dreadful, that of it none but those who have experienced can have an adequate idea.

To record in detail each day's fare since the commencement of this journey, would be little more than a dull repetition of the same occurrences. A sufficient idea of it may be given in a few words, by observing that it may justly be said to have been either all feasting, or all famine: sometimes we had too much, seldom just enough, frequently too little, and often none at all. It will be only necessary to say that we have fasted many times two whole days and nights; twice upwards of three days; and once, while at the She-than-nee,[4] near seven days, during which we tasted not a mouthful of any thing, except a few cranberries, water, scraps of old leather, and burnt bones. On those pressing occasions I have frequently seen the Indians examine their wardrobe, which consisted chiefly of skin-clothing, and consider what part could best be spared; sometimes a piece of an old, half-rotten deer skin, and at others a pair of old shoes, were sacrificed to alleviate extreme hunger. The relation of such uncommon hardships may perhaps gain little credit in Europe; while those who are conversant with the history of Hudson's Bay, and who are thoroughly acquainted with the distress which the natives of the country about it frequently endure, may consider them as no more than the common occurrences of an Indian life. . . .

4 A lake on the Seal River, not far from Fort Prince of Wales.

[Hearne and Conne-e-queese eventually lost their way. His quadrant broken, Hearne turned back, arriving at the fort in November after nearly nine months of fruitless wandering—though on the last leg of this journey he met Matonabbee, the knowledgeable guide he had been searching for all along. Soon after his return, in December 1770, with Matonabbee and a company of Chipewyans, Hearne set out on his third and longest journey. Under Matonabbee's leadership they drew near to the Coppermine River over six months later.]

May 31st 1771

Though it was so late when we left the women, we walked about ten miles that night before we stopped. In our way we saw many deer; several of which the Indians killed. To talk of travelling and killing deer in the middle of the night, may at first view have the appearance of romance; but our wonder will speedily abate, when it is considered that we were then to the Northward of 64° of North latitude, and that, in consequence of it, though the Sun did not remain the whole night above the horizon, yet the time it remained below it was so short, and its depression even at midnight so small at this season of the year, that the light, in clear weather, was quite sufficient for the purpose both of walking, and hunting any kind of game.

It should have been observed, that during our stay at Clowey[5] a great number of Indians entered into a combination of those of my party to accompany us to the Copper-mine River; and with no other intent than to murder the Esquimaux, who are understood by the Copper Indians[6] to frequent that river in considerable number. This scheme, notwithstanding the trouble and fatigue, as well as danger, with which it must be obviously attended, was nevertheless so universally approved by those people, that for some time almost every man who joined us proposed to be of the party. Accordingly, each volunteer, as well as those who were properly of my party, prepared a target, or shield, before we left the woods of Clowey. Those targets were composed of thin boards, about three quarters of an inch thick, two feet broad, and three feet long; and were intended to ward off the arrows of the Esquimaux. Notwithstanding these preparations, when we came to leave the women and children, as has been already mentioned, only sixty volunteers would go with us; the rest, who were nearly as many more, though they had all prepared targets, reflecting that they had a great distance to walk, and that no advantage could be expected from the expedition, very prudently begged to be excused, saying, that they could not be spared for so long a time from the maintenance of their wives and families; and particularly, as they did not see any then in our company, who seemed willing to encumber themselves with such a charge. This seemed to be a mere evasion, for I am clearly of opinion that poverty on one side, and avarice on the other, were the only impediments to their joining our party; had they possessed as many European goods to squander away among their countrymen as Matonabbee and those of my party did, in all probability many might have been found who would have been glad to have accompanied us.

5 A small lake east of Great Slave Lake.

6 Also known as the Yellowknives; like the Chipewyan, they were an Athapaskan band. Formerly widespread and powerful, they had been driven north and west at the beginning of the eighteenth century, when the Hudson's Bay Company's practice of supplying guns to the Chipewyan upset the historic balance among the bands.

When I was acquainted with the intentions of my companions, and saw the war-like preparations that [they] were carrying on, I endeavoured as much as possible to persuade them from putting their inhuman design into execution; but so far were my intreaties from having the wished-for effect, that it was concluded I was actuated by cowardice; and they told me, with great marks of derision, that I was afraid of the Esquimaux. As I knew my personal safety depended in a great measure on the favourable opinion they entertained of me in this respect, I was obliged to change my tone, and replied, that I did not care if they rendered the name and race of the Esquimaux extinct; adding at the same time, that though I was no enemy to the Esquimaux, and did not see the necessity of attacking them without cause, yet if I should find it necessary to do it, for the protection of any one of my company, my own safety out of the question, so far from being afraid of a poor defenceless Esquimaux, whom I despised more than feared, nothing should be wanting on my part to protect all who were with me. This declaration was received with great satisfaction; and I never afterwards ventured to interfere with any of their war-plans. Indeed, when I came to consider seriously, I saw evidently that it was the highest folly for an individual like me, and in my situation, to attempt to turn the current of a national prejudice which had subsisted between those two nations from the earliest periods, or at least as long as they had been acquainted with the existence of each other.

* * *

[In July 1771 Hearne and his company at last 'arrived at that long wished-for spot, the Coppermine River', which turned out to be a much less impressive body of water than reports had led Hearne to expect. He began to map the river, though he quickly realized that it was not navigable.]

July 15th–17th 1771

Early in the morning of the fifteenth, we set out, when I immediately began my survey, which I continued about ten miles down the river, till heavy rain coming on we were obliged to put up; and the place where we lay that night was the end, or edge of the woods, the whole space between it and the sea being entirely barren hills and wide open marshes. In the course of this day's survey, I found the river as full of shoals as the part which I had seen before; and in many places it was so greatly diminished in its width, that in our way we passed by two more capital falls.

Early in the morning of the sixteenth, the weather being fine and pleasant, I again proceeded with my survey, and continued it for ten miles farther down the river; but still found it the same as before, being every where full of falls and shoals. At this time (it being about noon) the three men who had been sent as spies met us on their return, and informed my companions that five tents of Esquimaux were on the west side of the river. The situation, they said, was very convenient for surprising them; and, according to their account, I judged it to be about twelve miles from the place we met the spies. When the Indians received this intelligence, no farther attendance or attention was paid to my survey, but their whole thoughts were immediately engaged in planning the best method of attack, and how they might steal on the poor Esquimaux the ensuing night, and kill them all while asleep. To accomplish this bloody design more effectually, the Indians thought it necessary to cross the river as soon as possible; and, by the account of the spies, it appeared that no part was more convenient for the purpose than that where we had met them, it being there very smooth, and at a considerable distance from any fall. Accordingly, after the Indians had put all their guns, spears, targets, &c. in good order, we crossed the river, which took up some time.

When we arrived on the West side of the river, each painted the front of his target or shield; some with the figure of the Sun, others with that of the Moon, several with different kinds of birds and beasts of prey, and many with the images of imaginary beings, which, according to their silly notions, are the inhabitants of the different elements, Earth, Sea, Air, &c.

On enquiring the reason of their doing so, I learned that each man painted his shield with the image of that being on which he relied most for success in the intended engagement. Some were contented with a single representation; while others, doubtful, as I suppose, of the quality and power of any single being, had their shields covered to the very margin with a group of hieroglyphics quite unintelligible to every one except the painter. Indeed, from the hurry in which this business was necessarily done, the want of every colour but red and black, and the deficiency of skill in the artist, most of those paintings had more the appearance of a number of accidental blotches, than 'of any thing that is on the earth, or in the water under the earth';[7] and though some few of them conveyed a tolerable idea of the thing intended, yet even these were many degrees worse than our country sign-paintings in England.

When this piece of superstition was completed, we began to advance toward the Esquimaux tents; but were very careful to avoid crossing any hills, or talking loud, for fear of being seen or overheard by the inhabitants; by which means the distance was not only much greater than it otherwise would have been, but, for the sake of keeping in the lowest grounds, we were obliged to walk through entire swamps of still marly clay, sometimes up to the knees. Our course, however, on this occasion, though very serpentine, was not altogether so remote from the river as entirely to exclude me from view of it the whole way: on the contrary, several times (according to the situation of the ground) we advanced so near it, as to give me an opportunity of convincing myself that it was as unnavigable as it was in those parts which I had surveyed before, and which entirely corresponded with the accounts given of it by the spies.

It is perhaps worth remarking, that my crew, though an undisciplined rabble, and by no means accustomed to war or command, seemingly acted on this horrid occasion with the utmost uniformity of sentiment. There was not among them the least altercation or separate opinion; all were united in the general cause, and as ready to follow where Matonabbee led, as he appeared to be ready to lead, according to the advice of an old Copper Indian, who had joined us on our first arrival at the river where this bloody business was first proposed.

7 A loose paraphrase of Revelation 5: 13: 'And every creature which is in heaven, and on the earth, and under the earth, and such as are in the sea . . .'

Never was reciprocity of interest more generally regarded among a number of people, than it was on the present occasion by my crew, for not one was a moment in want of any thing that another could spare; and if ever the spirit of disinterested friendship expanded the heart of a Northern Indian, it was here exhibited in the most extensive meaning of the word. Property of every kind that could be of general use now ceased to be private, and every one who had any thing which came under that description, seemed proud of an opportunity of giving it, or lending it to those who had none, or were most in want of it.

The number of my crew was so much greater than that which five tents could contain, and the warlike manner in which they were equipped so greatly superior to what could be expected of the poor Esquimaux, that no less than a total massacre of every one of them was likely to be the case, unless Providence should work a miracle for their deliverance.

The land was so situated that we walked under cover of the rocks and hills till we were within two hundred yards of the tents. There we lay in ambush for some time, watching the motions of the Esquimaux; and here the Indians would have advised me to stay till the fight was over, but to this I could by no means consent; for I considered that when the Esquimaux came to be surprised, they would try every way to escape, and if they found me alone, not knowing me from an enemy, they would probably proceed to violence against me when no person was near to assist. For this reason I determined to accompany them, telling them at the same time, that I would not have any hand in the murder they were about to commit, unless I found it necessary for my own safety. The Indians were not displeased at this proposal; one of them immediately fixed me a spear, and another lent me a broad bayonet for my protection, but at that time I could not be provided with a target, nor did I want to be encumbered with such an unnecessary piece of lumber.

While we lay in ambush, the Indians performed the last ceremonies which were thought necessary before the engagement. These chiefly consisted in painting their faces; some all black, some all red, and others with a mixture of the two; and to prevent their hair from blowing into their eyes, it was either tied before and behind, and on both sides, or else cut short all round. The next thing they considered was to make themselves as light as possible for running; which they did, by pulling off their stockings, and either cutting off the sleeves of their jackets, or rolling them up close to their arm-pits; and though the muskettoes at that time were so numerous as to surpass all credibility, yet some of the Indians actually pulled off their jackets and entered the lists quite naked, except their breech-cloths and shoes. Fearing I might have occasion to run with the rest, I thought it also advisable to pull off my stockings and cap, and to tie my hair as close up as possible.

By the time the Indians had made themselves thus completely frightful, it was near one o'clock in the morning of the seventeenth; when finding all the Esquimaux quiet in their tents, they rushed forth from their ambuscade, and fell on the poor unsuspecting creatures, unperceived till close at the very eves of their tents, when they soon began the bloody massacre, while I stood neuter in the rear.

In a few seconds the horrible scene commenced; it was shocking beyond description; the poor unhappy victims were surprised in the midst of their sleep, and had neither time nor power to make any resistance; men, women, and children, in all upward of twenty, ran out of their tents stark naked, and endeavoured to make their escape; but the Indians having possession of all the land-side, to no place could they fly for shelter. One alternative only remained, that of jumping into the river; but, as none of them attempted it, they all fell a sacrifice to Indian barbarity!

The shrieks and groans of the poor expiring wretches were truly dreadful; and my horror was much increased at seeing a young girl, seemingly about eighteen years of age, killed so near me, that when the first spear was stuck into her side she fell down at my feet, and twisted round my legs, so that it was with difficulty that I could disengage myself from her dying grasps. As two Indian men pursued this unfortunate victim, I solicited very hard for her life; but the murderers made no reply till they had stuck both their spears through her body, and transfixed her to the ground. They then looked me sternly in the face, and began to ridicule me, by asking if I wanted an Esquimaux wife; and paid not the smallest regard to the shrieks and agony of the poor wretch, who was twining round their spears like an eel! Indeed, after receiving much abusive language from them on the occasion, I was at length obliged to desire that they would be more expeditious in dispatching their victim out of her misery, otherwise I should be obliged, out of pity, to assist in the friendly office of putting an end to the existence of a fellow-creature who was so cruelly wounded. On this request being made, one of the Indians hastily drew his spear from the place where it was first lodged, and pierced it through her breast near the heart. The love of life, however, even in this most miserable state, was so predominant, that though this might justly be called the most merciful act that could be done for the poor creature, it seemed to be unwelcome, for though much exhausted by pain and loss of blood, she made several effort to ward off the friendly blow. My situation and the terror of my mind at beholding this butchery, cannot easily be conceived, much less described; though I summed up all the fortitude I was master of on the occasion, it was with difficulty that I could refrain from tears; and I am confident that my features must have feelingly expressed how sincerely I was affected at the barbarous scene I then witnessed; even at this hour I cannot reflect on the transactions of that horrid day without shedding tears.

[Hearne reached the mouth of the Coppermine and found that the 'mine' he had heard about was a disappointment. His commission fulfilled, he turned back. During his final trek, the most difficult of all, several of the Natives accompanying him died of sickness and starvation. Hearne did not arrive back at Fort Prince of Wales until a year and a half after he had left it. His account of his explorations concludes with these words: 'Though my discoveries are not likely to prove of any material advantage to the Nation at large, or indeed to the Hudson's Bay Company, yet I have the pleasure to think that I have fully complied with the orders of my Masters, and that it has put a final end to all disputes concerning a North West Passage through Hudson's Bay.']

1795

David Thompson

1770–1857

David Thompson was recruited from a London charity school at fourteen to become an apprentice clerk with the Hudson's Bay Company. Although he later wrote that when he arrived at Fort Prince of Wales (Churchill, Man.) in 1784, 'I bid a long and sad farewell to my . . . country, an exile for ever', Thompson seems to have been eager to learn what he could of the company's operations. Confined by a broken leg at nineteen, he spent almost a year at Cumberland House studying mathematics, astronomy, and field surveying, and made himself one of the best cartographers of his time. In twenty-eight years of exploring the West he managed to survey and map nearly two million square miles with such accuracy that maps at the beginning of this century were still based on his work. The explorer J.B. Tyrrell, who oversaw the first publication of Thompson's narrative, called him 'the greatest practical land geographer that the world had produced'.

In 1797 Thompson left the employ of the Hudson's Bay Company and went to the rival North West Company as a surveyor and mapmaker, instructed to determine the position of company posts in relation to the recently established boundary at the forty-ninth parallel. Thompson travelled widely in the West and Northwest in the years that followed. He married Charlotte Small, the daughter of an English fur trader and a Native mother. In 1815 Thompson and his wife retired to Williamstown, Upper Canada; however, he did not cease working. He served as astronomer and surveyor to the British Boundary Commission, establishing the United States–Canada boundary for Ontario and Quebec, and revised the maps he made on his trips of Western exploration. In 1846 he began to write a narrative account of his travels based on journals that he had begun in 1789 (they eventually ran to thirty-nine volumes). He laboured on this project for the next five years, but blindness brought it to a halt before it was completed. *David Thompson's Narrative of his Explorations in Western North America 1784–1812*, edited by J.B. Tyrrell, was published in 1916.

When he first arrived at Fort Prince of Wales, Thompson served under Hearne and disliked the older man, both for his supposed cowardice in surrendering the fort to the French and for being a free-thinker and follower of Voltaire. He may, however, have known Hearne's journals in manuscript; certainly in his narrative Thompson reveals the same strengths as the earlier writer-explorer. He was a keen observer and diligent recorder who provided accounts that are both factual and anecdotal; and he expressed himself in an unaffected style that gives his writing authority and immediacy. In particular, like Hearne, he was able to learn the languages of the Native peoples, and to understand and be accepted by those he visited. Beginning with the stories he gathered after travelling, at the age of seventeen, to the foothills of the Rockies to winter over with the Peigans in 1787–8 and to learn their language, through his later setting down of what he learned during the time he spent with the Nahathaways (he lived with them for three extended periods between 1792 and 1806), his journals are among the most valuable sources for the depiction of eighteenth-century Canada and its peoples.

All Thompson's activities were governed by an intensely inquiring mind. He was never intimidated by harsh conditions in his determined effort to study and understand his environment, as may be seen in his description of crossing the Rockies by way of the Athabasca Pass:

The view now before us was an ascent of deep snow. . . . It was to me a most exhilarating sight, but to my uneducated men a dreadful sight. They had no scientific object in view, their feelings were of the place they were. . . . Many reflections came on my mind; a new world was in a manner before me.

From *Narrative of His Explorations in Western North America, 1784–1812*

CHAPTER IV
NAHATHAWAY INDIANS

* * *

Of all the several distinct Tribes of Natives on the east side of the mountains, the Nahathaway Indians appear to deserve the most consideration; under different names the great families of this race occupy a great extent of country, and however separated and unknown to each other, they have the same opinions on religion, on morals, and their customs and manners differ very little. They are the only Natives that have some remains of ancient times from tradition. In the following account I have carefully avoided as their national opinions all they have learned from white men, and my knowledge was collected from old men, whom with my own age, extend backwards to upwards of one hundred years ago, and I must remark that, what[ever] other people may write as the creed of these natives, I have always found it very difficult to learn their real opinion on what may be termed religious subjects. Asking them questions on this head, is to no purpose, they will give the answer best adapted to avoid other questions, and please the enquirer. My knowledge has been gained when living and travelling with them and in times of distress and danger hearing their prayers to invisible powers, and their view of a future state of themselves and others, and like most mankind, those in youth and in the prime of life think only of the present but declining manhood, and escapes from danger turn their thoughts on futurity.

After a weary day's march we sat by a log fire, the bright Moon, with thousands of sparkling stars passing before us, we could not help enquiring who lived in those bright mansions; for I frequently conversed with them as one of themselves; the brilliancy of the planets always attracted their attention, and when their nature was explained to them they concluded them to be the abodes of the spirits of those that had led a good life.

A Missionary has never been among them, and my knowledge of their language has not enabled me to do more than teach the unity of God and a future state of rewards and punishments; hell fire they do not believe, for they do not think it possible that any thing can resist the continued action of fire: It is doubtful if their language in its present simple state can clearly express the doctrines of Christianity in their full force. They believe in the self existence of the Keeche Keeche Manito[1] (the Great, Great Spirit) they appear to derive their belief from tradition, and [believe] that the visible world, with all its inhabitants must have been made by some powerful being: but have not the same idea of his constant omnipresence, omniscience and omnipotence that we have, but [think] that he is so when he pleases, he is the master of life, and all things are at his disposal; he is always kind to the human race, and hates to see the

1 Now usually spelled 'Manitou'.

blood of mankind on the ground, and sends heavy rain to wash it away. He leaves the human race to their own conduct, but has placed all other living creatures under the care of Manitos (or inferior Angels) all of whom are responsible to Him; but all this belief is obscure and confused, especially on the Manitos, the guardians and guides of every genus of Birds and Beasts; each Manito has a separate command and care, as one has the Bison, another the Deer; and thus the whole animal creation is divided amongst them. On this account the Indians, as much as possible, neither say, nor do anything to offend them, and the religious hunter, at the death of each animal, says, or does, something, as thanks to the Manito of the species for being permitted to kill it. At the death of a Moose Deer, the hunter in a low voice cries 'wut, wut, wut'; cuts a narrow stripe of skin from off the throat, and hangs it up to the Manito. The bones of the head of a Bear are thrown into the water, and thus of other animals; if this acknowledgment was not made the Manito would drive away the animals from the hunter, although the Indians often doubt their power or existence yet like other invisible beings they are more feared than loved. They believe in ghosts but as very rarely seen, and those only of wicked men, or women; when this belief takes place, their opinion is, that the spirit of the wicked person being in a miserable state comes back to the body and round where he used to hunt; to get rid of such a hateful visitor, they burn the body to ashes and the ghost then no longer haunts them. The dark Pine Forests have spirits, but there is only one of them which they dread, it is the Pah kok, a tall hateful spirit, he frequents the depths of the Forest; his howlings are heard in the storm, he delights to add to its terrors, it is a misfortune to hear him, something ill will happen to the person, but when he approaches a Tent and howls, he announces the death of one of the inmates; of all beings he is the most hateful and the most dreaded. The Sun and Moon are accounted Divinities and though they do not worship them, [they] always speak of them with great reverence. They appear to think [of] the Stars only as a great number of luminous points perhaps also divinities, and mention them with respect; they have names for the brightest stars, as Sirius, Orion and others, and by them learn the change of the seasons, as the rising of Orion for winter, and the setting of the Pleiades for summer. The Earth is also a divinity, and is alive, but [they] cannot define what kind of life it is, but say, if it was not alive it could not give and continue life to other things and to animated creatures.

The Forests, the ledges and hills of Rock, the Lakes and Rivers have all something of the Manito about them, especially the Falls in the Rivers, and those to which the fish come to spawn. The Indians when the season is over, frequently place their spears at the Manito stone and the Fall, as an offering to the Spirit of the Fall, for the fish they have caught. These stones are rare, and sought after by the native to place at the edge of a water fall; they are the shape of a Cobler's lap stone, but much larger, and polished by the wash of the water. The 'Metchee Manito', or Evil Spirit, they believe to be evil, delighting in making men miserable, and bringing misfortune and sickness on them, and if he had the power would wholly destroy them; he is not the tempter, his whole power is for mischief to, and harrassing of, them, to avert all which they use many ceremonies, and other sacrifices, which consists of such things as they can spare, and sometimes a dog is painted and killed; whatever is given to him is laid on the ground, frequently at the foot of a pine tree. They believe in the immortality of the soul, and that death is only a change of existence which takes place directly after death. The good find themselves in a happy country, where they rejoin their friends and relations, the Sun is always bright, and the animals plenty; and most of them carry this belief so far, that they believe whatever creatures the great Spirit has made must continue to exist somewhere, and under some form; But this fine belief is dark and uncertain; when danger was certain, and it was doubtful if we saw the day, or if we saw it, whether we should live through it, and a future state appeared close to them, their minds wavered, they wished to believe what they felt to be uncertain, all that I could do was to show the immortality of the soul, as necessary to reward of the good and punishment of the wicked but all this was the talk of man with man. It wanted the sure and sacred promise of the Heavenly Redeemer of mankind, who brought life and immortality to light.[2]

There is an important being, with whom the Natives appear better acquainted with than the other, whom they call 'Weesarkejauk' (the Flatterer) he is the hero of all their stories always promising them some good, or inciting them to some pleasure, and always deceiving them. They have some tradition of the Deluge, as may be seen from the following account related by the old men. After the Great Spirit made mankind, and all the animals, he told Weesarkejauk to take care of them and teach them how to live, and not to eat of bad roots; that would hurt and kill them; but he did not mind the Great Spirit; became careless and incited them to pleasure, mankind and the animals all did as they pleased, quarelled and shed much blood, with which the Great Spirit was displeased; he threatened Weesarkejauk that if he did not keep the ground clean he would take everything from him and make him miserable, but he did not believe the Great Spirit and in a short time became more careless; and the quarrels of Men, and the animals made the ground red with blood, and so far from taking care of them he incited them to do and live badly; this made the Great Spirit very angry and he told Weesarkejauk that he would take every thing from him, and wash the ground clean; but still he did not believe; until the Rivers and Lakes rose very high and over flowed the ground for it was always raining; and the Keeche Gahme (the Sea) came on the land, and every man and animal were drowned, except one Otter, one Beaver and one Musk Rat. Weesarkejauk tried to stop the sea, but it was too strong for him, and he sat on the water crying for his loss, the Otter, the Beaver and the Musk Rat rested their heads on one of his thighs.

When the rain ceased and the sea went away, he took courage, but did not dare to speak to the Great Spirit. After musing a long time upon his sad condition he thought if he could get a bit of the old ground he could make a little island of it, for he has the power of extending, but not creating anything; and as he had not the power of diving under the water, and did not know the depth to the old ground he was at a loss what to do. Some say the Great Spirit took pity on him, and gave him the power to renovate everything, provided he made use of the old materials, all of which lay buried under water to an unknown depth. In this sad state, as he sat floating on the water he told the

2 Because they have had the Christian revelation available to them, Thompson sees Europeans as having religious advantage over Native peoples.

three animals that they must starve unless he could get a bit of the old ground from under the water of which he would make a fine Island for them, then addressing himself to the Otter, and praising him for his courage, strength and activity and promising him plenty of fish to eat, he persuaded the Otter to dive, and bring up a bit of earth; the Otter came up without having reached the ground: by praises, he got the Otter to make two more attempts, but without success, and [he] was so much exhausted he could do no more. Weesarkejauk called him a coward of a weak heart, and [said] that the Beaver would put him to shame: then, speaking to the Beaver, praised his strength and wisdom and promised to make him a good house for winter, and telling him to dive straight down, the Beaver made two attempts without success, and came up so tired that Weesarkejauk had to let him repose a long time, then promising him a wife if he brought up a bit of earth, told him to try a third time; to obtain a wife, he boldly went down and staid so long, that he came up almost lifeless. Weesarkejauk was now very sad, for what the active Otter and strong Beaver could not do, he had little hopes the Musk Rat could do; but this was his only resource: He now praised the musk rat and promised him plenty of roots to eat, with rushes and earth to make himself a house; the Otter and the Beaver he said were fools, and lost themselves, and he would find the ground, if he went straight down. Thus encouraged he dived, and came up, but brought nothing; after reposing, he went down a second time, and staid a long time, on coming up Weesarkejauk examined his fore paws and found they had the smell of earth, and showing this to the Musk Rat, promised to make him a Wife, who should give him a great many children, and become more numerous than any other animal, and telling him to have a strong heart; and go direct down, the Musk Rat went down the third time and staid so long that Weesarkejauk feared he was drowned. At length seeing some bubbles come up, he put down his long arm and brought up the Musk Rat, almost dead, but to his great joy with a piece of earth between his forepaws and his breast, this he seized, and in a short time extended it to a little island, on which they all reposed. Some say Weesarkejauk procured a bit of wood, from which he made the Trees, and from bones, he made the animals; but the greater number deny this, and say, the Great Spirit made the rivers take the water to the Keeche gahma of bad water (the salt sea) and then renovated Mankind, the Animals, and the Trees; in proof of which, the Great spirit deprived him of all authority over Mankind and the animals, and he has since had only the power to flatter and deceive. It has been already noticed that this visionary being is the hero of many stories, which the women relate to amuse away the evenings. They are all founded upon the tricks he plays upon, and the mischief he leads the animals into, by flattering and deceiving them, especially the Wolf and the Fox. But the recital of the best of these stories would be tameness itself to the splendid Language and gorgeous scenery of the tales of the oriental nations.[3]

The Nahathaway Indians have also another tradition relative to the Deluge to which no fable is attached. In the latter end of May 1806, at the Rocky Mountain House,[4] (where I passed the summer) the Rain continued the very unusual space of full three weeks, the Brooks and the River became swollen, and could not be forded, each

3 Thompson has earlier mentioned his nostalgic fondness for *The Arabian Nights*.

4 A Hudson's Bay fort on the North Saskatchewan River.

stream became a torrent, and [there was] much water on the ground: A band of these Indians were at the house, waiting [for] the Rain to cease and the streams to lower before they could proceed to hunting; all was anxiety, they smoked and made speeches to the Great Spirit for the Rain to cease, and at length became alarmed at the quantity of water on the ground; at length the rain ceased, I was standing at the door watching the breaking up of the clouds, when of a sudden the Indians gave a loud shout, and called out 'Oh, there is the mark of life, we shall yet live.' On looking to the eastward there was one of the widest and most splendid Rainbows I ever beheld; and joy was now in every face.

The name of the Rainbow is Peeshim Cappeah (Sun lines). I had now been twenty two years among them, and never before heard the name of the mark of life given to the rainbow (Peemah tisoo nan oo Chegun) nor have I ever heard it since; upon enquiring of the old Men why they kept this name secret from me, they gave me the usual reply, You white men always laugh and treat with contempt what we have heard and learned from our fathers, and why should we expose ourselves to be laughed at; I replied I have never done so, our books also call the Rainbow the mark of life[5]. . . .

5 Thompson refers to the promise God makes Noah in Genesis 9, after the flood: 'And I will establish my covenant with you; neither shall all flesh be cut off any more by the waters of a flood; neither shall there any more be a flood to destroy the earth. . . . I do set my bow in the cloud, and it shall be for a token of a covenant between me and the earth. And it shall come to pass, when I bring a cloud over the earth, that the bow shall be seen in the cloud.'

CHAPTER VI
LIFE AMONG THE NAHATHAWAYS

* * *

It may now [be time to] say something of myself, and of the character of the Natives and the French Canadians entertained of me, they were almost my only companions. My instruments for practical astronomy were a brass Sextant of ten inches radius, an achromatic Telescope[1] of high power for observing the Satellites of Jupiter and other phenomena, one of the same construction for common use, Parallel glasses and quicksilver horizon for double Altitudes; Compass, Thermometer, and other requisite instruments, which I was in the constant practice of using in clear weather for observations on the Sun, Moon, Planets and Stars to determine the positions of the Rivers, Lakes, Mountains and other parts of the country I surveyed from Hudson Bay to the Pacific Ocean. Both Canadians and Indians often inquired of me why I observed the Sun, and sometimes the Moon, in the daytime, and passed whole nights with my instruments looking at the Moon and Stars. I told them it was to determine the distance and

1 An achromatic lens is one that does not introduce colour by breaking light into its constituent parts. In taking readings with his sextant, Thompson needed an artificial horizon since he could not, as mariners could, always see the true horizon; for this purpose mercury ('quicksilver') was carried in a flat rectangular tray, shielded from the wind by glass plates that had to have truly parallel faces so as not to introduce any distortion in the light passing through them (hence 'parallel glasses'). Position could then be calculated by taking the angle of an astronomical body, and of its reflection, in the horizontal surface of the mercury pool at rest (a 'double altitude').

direction from the place I observed to other places. Neither the Canadians nor the Indians believed me; for both argued that if what I said was truth, I ought to look to the ground and over it and not to the Stars. Their opinions were that I was looking into futurity and seeing everybody and what they were doing [and that I knew] how to raise the wind, but did not believe I could calm it. This they argued from seeing me obliged to wait the calming of the wind on the great Lakes, to which the Indians added that I knew where the Deer were, and other superstitious opinions.

During my life I have always been careful not to pretend to any knowledge of futurity, and [said] that I knew nothing beyond the present hour. Neither argument nor ridicule had any effect and I had to leave them to their own opinions, and yet inadvertingly on my part several things happened to confirm their opinions. One fine evening in February two Indians came to the house to trade. The Moon rose bright and clear with the planet Jupiter a few degrees on its east side and the Canadians as usual predicted that Indians would come to trade in the direction of this star. To show them the folly of such predictions I told them the same bright star, the next night, would be as far from the Moon on its west side. This of course took place from the Moon's motion in her orbit and is the common occurence of almost every month, and yet all parties were persuaded I had done it by some occult power to falsify the predictions of the Canadians. Mankind are fond of the marvelous; it seems to heighten their character by relating they have seen such things.

I had always admired the tact of the Indian in being able to guide himself through the darkest pine forests to exactly the place he intended to go; his keen, constant attentions on everything: the removal of the smallest stone, the bent or broken twig, a slight mark on the ground, all spoke plain language to him. I was anxious to acquire this knowledge, and often being in company with them, sometimes for several months, I paid attention to what they pointed out to me, and became almost equal to some of them, which became of great use to me. The North West Company of Furr Traders, from their Depot in Lake Superior sent off Brigades of Canoes loaded with about three Tons weight of Merchandise, Provisions and Baggage. Those for the most distant trading Posts are sent off first, with an allowance of two days' time between each Brigade to prevent incumbrances on the Carrying Places. I was in my first year in the third Brigade of six Canoes each and having nothing to do but sketch off my survey and make Observations. I was noticing how far we gained or lost ground on the Brigade before us by the fires they made, and other marks, as we were equally manned with five men to each canoe. In order to prevent the winter coming on us, before we reached our distant winter quarters, the Men had to work very hard from daylight to sunset, or later, and at night slept on the ground, constantly worried by Musketoes, and had no time to look about them. I found we gained very little on them. At the end of fifteen days we had to arrive at lake Winnipeg (that is the Sea Lake from its size) and for more than two days it had been blowing northwest gale, which did not allow the Brigade before us to proceed; and I told the Guide that early the next morning we should see them. These Guides have charge of conducting the march and are all proud of coming up to the canoes ahead of them, and by dawn of day we entered the Lake now calm, and as the day came on us saw the Brigade that were before us only one Mile ahead of us. The Guide and the men shouted with joy, and when we came up to them told them of my wonderful predictions, and that I had pointed out every place they had slept at, and all by looking at the Stars. One party seemed delighted in being credulous, the other in exageration; such are ignorant men, who never give themselves a moment's reflection.

* * *

This section of the Stony Region is called the Musk Rat Country and contains an area of about 22,360 square miles, of which full two fifths of this surface is Rivers and Lakes, having phenomena distinct from the dry, elevated, distant, interior countries. The Natives are Nahathaway Indians, whose fathers from time, beyond any tradition, have hunted in these Lands. In conversing with them on their origin they appear never to have turned their minds to this subject; and [think] that mankind and the animals are in a constant state of succession; and the time of their great grandfathers is the extent of their actual knowledge of times past. Their tradition of the Deluge and of the Rainbow I have already mentioned; yet their stories all refer to times when Men were much taller and stronger than at present, the animals more numerous, and many could converse with mankind, particularly, the Bear, Beaver, Lynx and Fox. Writers on the North American Indians always write as comparing them with themselves, who are all men of education, and of course [the Indians] lose by comparison. This is not fair. Let them be compared with those who are uneducated in Europe; yet even in this comparison the Indian has the disadvantage in not having the light of Christianity. Of course his moral character has not the firmness of Christian morality, but in practice he is fully equal to those of his class in Europe; living without law, they are a law to themselves. The Indian is said to be a creature of apathy. When he appears to be so he is in an assumed character to conceal what is passing in his mind, as he has nothing of the almost infinite diversity of things which interest and amuse the civilised man. His passions, desires and affections are strong, however appeared subdued, and engage the whole man. The law of retaliation, which is fully allowed, makes the life of man respected; and in general he abhors the shedding of blood, and should sad necessity compel him to it, which is sometimes the case, he is held to be an unfortunate man. But he who has committed wilful murder is held in abhorrence, as one with whom the life of no person is in safety, and possessed with an evil spirit.

When Hudson Bay was discovered, and the first trading settlement made, the Natives were far more numerous than at present. In the year 1782 the small pox from Canada extended to them and more than one half of them died; since which, although they had no enemies [and] their country [is] very healthy, yet their numbers increase very slowly. The Musk Rat country, of which I have given the area, may have ninety-two families, each of seven souls, giving to each family an area of two-hundred-and-forty-eight square miles of hunting grounds; or thirty-five square miles to each soul—a very thin population. A recent writer (Ballantyne)[2] talks of myriads of wild animals.

2 The Scottish writer R.M. Ballantyne (1825–94), who was employed by the Hudson's Bay Company from 1841 to 1847, began publishing his stories of life among Company fur traders around the time Thompson was writing his memoirs.

Such writers talk at random; they have never counted nor calculated. The animals are by no means numerous, and only in sufficient numbers to give a tolerable subsistence to the Natives, who are too often obliged to live on very little food and sometimes all but perish with hunger. Very few Beaver are to be found, the Bears are not many, and all the furr-bearing animals an Indian can kill can scarcely furnish himself and family with the bare necessaries of life.

A strange Idea prevails among these Natives, and also of all the Indians to the Rocky Mountains, though unknown to each other, that when they were numerous, before they were destroyed by the Small Pox, all the animals of every species were also very numerous and more so in comparison of the number of Natives than at present; and this was confirmed to me by old Scotchmen in the service of the Hudson's Bay Company, and by the Canadians from Canada. The knowledge of the latter extended over all the interior countries, yet no disorder was known among the animals; the fact was certain, and nothing they knew of could account for it. It might justly be supposed the destruction of Mankind would allow the animals to increase, even to become formidable to the few Natives who survived, but neither the Bison, the Deer, nor the carnivorous animals increased, and as I have already remarked, are no more than sufficient for the subsistence of the Natives and Traders. The trading Houses over the whole country are situated on the banks of lakes of at least twenty miles in length by two or three miles in width . . . as it is only large and deep Lakes that have Fish sufficient to maintain the Trader and his Men, for the Indians at best can only afford a Deer now and then.

* * *

Formerly the Beavers were very numerous. The many Lakes and Rivers gave them ample space and the poor Indian had then only a pointed stick shaped and hardened in the fire, a stone Hatchet, Spear and Arrowheads of the same. Thus armed he was weak against the sagacious Beaver who, on the banks of a Lake, made itself a house of a foot thick or more, composed of earth and small flat stones, crossed and bound together with pieces of wood, upon which no impression could be made but by fire. But when the arrival of the White People had changed all their weapons from stone to iron and steel, and added the fatal Gun, every animal fell before the Indian. The Bear was no longer dreaded, and the Beaver became a desirable animal for food and clothing and the furr a valuable article of trade; and as the Beaver is a stationary animal, it could be attacked at any convenient time in all seasons, and thus their numbers soon became reduced. The old Indians, when speaking of their ancestors, wonder how they could live, as the Beaver was wiser and the Bear stronger than them, and confess that if they were deprived of the Gun they could not live by the Bow and Arrow and must soon perish.

The Beaver skin is the standard by which other Furrs are traded; and London prices have very little influence on this value of barter, which is more a matter of expedience and convenience to the Trader and the Native than of real value. The only

Bears of this country are the small black Bear, with a chance Yellow Bear;[3] this latter has a fine furr and trades for three Beavers in barter when full grown. The Black Bear is common, and according to size passes for one or two Beavers. The young are often tamed by the Natives and are harmless and playful until near full grown, when they become troublesome and are killed or sent into the woods. While they can procure roots and berries they look for nothing else; but in the Spring, when they leave their winter dens, they can get neither the one nor the other, prowl about, and go to the Rapids where the Carp are spawning. Here Bruin lives in plenty; but not content with what it can eat, amuses itself with tossing ashore ten times more than it can devour, each stroke of its forepaw sending a fish eight or ten yards according to its size. The fish thus thrown ashore attract the Eagle and the Raven. The sight of these birds flying about leads the Indian to the place and Bruin loses his life and his skin. The meat of the Bear feeding on the roots and berries becomes very fat and good, and in this condition it enters its den for the winter, at the end of which the meat is still good, and has some fat; but [at] the very first meal of fish the taste of the meat is changed for the worse, and soon becomes disagreeable. When a Mahmees Dog in the winter season has discovered a den and the Natives go to kill the Bear, on uncovering the top of the den Bruin is found roused out of its dormant state and sitting ready to defend itself. The eldest man now makes a speech to it, reproaching the Bear and all its race with being the old enemies of Man, killing the children and women when it was large and strong, but now, since the Manito has made him small and weak to what he was before, he has all the will, though not the power, to be as bad as ever; that he is treacherous and cannot be trusted; that although he has sense he makes bad use of it and must therefore be killed. Parts of the speech have many repetitions to impress its truth on the Bear, who all the time is grinning and growling, willing to fight, but more willing to escape, until the axe descends on its head, or [it] is shot—the latter more frequently, as the den is often under the roots of fallen trees and protected by the branches of the roots.

When a Bear thus killed was hauled out of its den I enquired of the Indian who made the speech whether he really thought the Bear understood him. He replied, 'How can you doubt it? Did you not see how ashamed I made him, and how he held down his head?' 'He might well hold down his head when you were flourishing a heavy axe over it, with which you killed him.' On this animal they have several superstitions, and he acts a prominent part in many of their tales.

* * *

What is called Mirage is common on all these Lakes, but frequently [is] simply an elevation of the woods and shores that bound horizon; yet at times draws attention to the change of scenery it exhibits, and on these Lakes has often kept me watching it for many minutes; and [I] would have stayed longer if the cold had permitted. The first and most changeable Mirage is seen in the latter part of February and the month of March, the weather clear, the wind calm, or light; the Thermometer from ten above to

3 Actually a colour phase of the black bear.

twelve degrees below zero, the time about ten in the morning. On one occasion, going to an Isle where I had two traps for Foxes, when about one mile distant the ice between me and the Isle appeared of a concave form, which, if I entered, I should slide into its hollow; [and although I was] sensible of the illusion, it had the power to perplex me. I found my snow shoes on a level and advanced slowly, as afraid to slide into it; in about ten minutes this mirage ceased, the ice became [distinct] and showed a level surface, and with confidence I walked to my traps, in one of which I found a red Fox. This sort of Mirage is not frequent. That most common elevates and depresses objects, and sometimes makes them appear to change places.

In the latter end of February at the Reed Lake, at its west end, a Mirage took place in one of its boldest forms. About three miles from me was the extreme shore of the Bay; the Lake was near three miles in width, in which was a steep Isle of rock and another of tall Pines; on the other side a bold Point of steep rock. The Mirage began slowly to elevate all objects, then gently to lower them, until the Isles and the Point appeared like black spots on the ice, and no higher than its surface. The above bold Bay Shore was a dark black curved line on the ice. In the time of three minutes they all arose to their former height and became elevated to twice their height. Beyond the Bay the rising grounds, distant eight miles, with all their woods appeared, and remained somewhat steady for a few minutes; the Isles and Point again disappeared. The Bay Shore with the distant Forests came rolling forward with an undulating motion, as if in a dance; the distant Forests became so near to me I could see their branches, then with the same motion retired to half distance. The Bay shore could not be distinguished; it was blended with the distant land, thus advancing and retiring with different elevations for about fifteen minutes when the distant Forests vanished, the Isles took their place, and the Lake shores their form. The wild scenery was a powerful illusion, too fleeting and changeful for any pencil.

This was one of the clearest and most distinct Mirages I had ever seen. There can be no doubt it is the effect of a cause which, perhaps, was waves of the atmosphere loaded with vapours, though not perceptible to the eye, between the beholder and the objects on which the mirage acts, with the Sun in a certain position. When the objects were seen on the ridge of the wave, it gave them their elevation; when in the hollow of the wave, their greatest depression; and viewed obliquely to the direction of the wave, the objects appeared to change places. There may be a better theory to account for the Mirage.

While the Mirage is in full action, the scenery is so clear and vivid, the illusion so strong, as to perplex the Hunter and the Traveller. It appears more like the power of magic than the play of nature. When enquiring of the Natives what they thought of it, they said it was Manito Korso—the work of a Manito—and with this argument they account for everything that is uncommon.

Although the climate and country of which I am writing is far better than that of Hudson's Bay, yet the climate is severe in Winter, the Thermometer often from thirty to forty degrees below Zero. The month of December is the coldest. The long absence of the Sun gives full effect to the action of the cold; the Snow increases in depth—it may be said to fall as dry as dust; the ice rapidly increases in thickness and the steady cold of the rest of winter adds but little to that of the end of the month. But its contraction by intense cold causes the ice to rend in many places with a loud rumbling noise, and through these rents water is often thrown out and flows over part of the ice, making bad walking. This month has very variable weather; sometimes a calm of several days, then Gales of wind with light snow, which from its lightness is driven about like dust. This dull month of long nights we wish to pass away. The country affords no tallow for candles nor fish oil for lamps; the light of the fire is what we have to work and read by. Christmas when it comes finds us glad to see it and pass; we have nothing to welcome it with.

In one of the calms of this month Tapahpahtum, a good hunter, came to us for some provisions and fish hooks. He said his three wives and his children had had very little to eat for nearly a whole Moon, adding, 'You may be sure that we suffer hunger when I come to beg fish, and get hooks for my women to angle with.' He took away about thirty pounds of fish, which he had to carry about twenty miles to his tent. I felt for him, for nothing but sad necessity can compel a Nahathaway hunter to carry away fish, and angle for them; this is too mean for a hunter. Meat he carries with pleasure, but fish is degradation. The calm still continued, and two days after Tapahpahtum came in the evening. He looked somewhat wild; he was a powerful man of strong passions. As usual I gave him a bit of Tobacco. He sat down and smoked, inhaling the smoke as if he would have drawn the tobacco through the pipe stem; then saying, 'Now I have smoked, I may speak. I do not come to you for fish. I hope never to disgrace myself again. I now come for a wind which you must give me.' In the mood he was in, to argue with him was of no use, and I said, 'Why did you not bring one of your women with you? She would have taken some fish to the tent.' 'My women are too weak. They snare a hare, or two every day, barely enough to keep them alive. I am come for a wind which you must give me.' 'You know as well as I do that the Great Spirit alone is master of the Winds; you must apply to him and not to me.' 'Ah, that is always your way of talking to us. When you will not hear us, then you talk to us of the Great Spirit. I want a Wind. I must have it. Now think on it and dream how I am to get it.' I lent him an old Bison Robe to sleep on, which was all we could spare. The next day was calm. He sat on the floor in a despondent mood, at times smoking his pipe, and saying to me, 'Be kind to me, be kind to me, give me a Wind that we may live.' I told him the Good Spirit alone could cause the wind to blow. And my French Canadians were as foolish as the poor Indian, saying to one another, 'It would be a good thing, and well done, if he got a wind. We should get meat to eat.'

The night was very fine and clear. I passed most of it observing the Moon and Stars as usual. The small meteors were very numerous, which indicated a Gale of Wind. The morning rose fine, and before the appearance of the Sun, tho' calm with us, the tops of the tall Pines were waving, all foretelling a heavy gale, which usually follows a long calm. All this was plain to everyone. Very early Tapahpahtum said, 'Be kind and give me a strong wind.' Vexed with him, I told him to go and take care that the trees did not fall upon him. He shouted, 'I have got it', sprang from the floor, snatched his gun, whipt on his Snow Shoes, and dashed away at five miles an hour. The gale from North East came on as usual with snow and high drift and lasted three days. For the two first days we could not visit the nets, which sometimes happens; the third day the drift ceased, but the nets had been too long in the water without being washed, and we had to take them up. On this gale of wind, a common occurence, I learnt my men were more strangely foolish than the Indians. Something better than two months after this gale I sent three of the men with letters to another trading house and to bring some articles I wanted. Here these men related how I had raised a storm of wind for the Indian, but had made it so strong that for two days they got no fish from the nets, adding they thought I would take better care another time. In these distant solitudes, Men's minds seem to partake of the wildness of the country they live in. . . .

Wiskahoo was naturally a cheerful, good-natured, careless man, but hard times had changed him. He was a good Beaver worker and trapper, but an indifferent Moose Hunter, [though] now and then [he] killed one by chance. He had been twice so reduced by hunger as to be twice on the point of eating one of his children to save the others, when he was fortunately found and relieved by the other Natives. These sufferings had at times unhinged his mind, and made him dread being alone. He had for about a month been working Beaver and had now joined Tapahpahtum, and their Tents were together. He came to trade, and brought some meat the other had sent. It is usual when the Natives come to trade to give them a pint of grog, a liquor which I always used very sparingly. It was a bad custom, but could not be broken off. Wikahoo, as soon as he got, and while drinking of it, used to say in a thoughtful mood, 'Nee weet to go' 'I must be a Man eater.' This word seemed to imply, 'I am possessed of an evil spirit to eat human flesh', 'Wee tee go'[4] is the evil Spirit that devours humankind. When he had said this a few times, one of the Men used to tie him slightly and he soon became quiet. These sad thoughts at times came upon him from the dreadful distress he had suffered; and at times took him in his tent, when he always allowed himself to be tied during this sad mood, which did not last long.

Three years afterwards this sad mood came upon him so often that the Natives got alarmed. They shot him and burnt his body to ashes to prevent his ghost remaining in this world.

[1846–51], 1916

4 Also spelled 'Windigo': a cannibalistic monster, formerly a man. Thompson's is one of the earliest records of this Native myth, which is thought to have functioned both as a prohibition of cannibalism and as a warning against the abuses of power—especially among shamans and other powerful leaders who needed to remember not to use their strength to consume the essence of their companions.

John Franklin

1786–1847

Dr John Richardson

1787–1865

The Northwest Passage and the Search for Franklin

For more than three hundred years Europeans searched for a Northwest Passage, a water route passing through Arctic sea lanes that would make possible travel to Asia and the Indies by way of North America. The most famous attempt to find this passage, the legendary Franklin expedition of 1845, was also the most ill-fated. After John Franklin and his crew disappeared, along with his two ships, the *Terror* and the *Erebus*, a search, begun in 1847, found a series of tantalizing clues—first, a few graves, then a cairn of discarded tins, stories among the Inuit, and a message left behind—but they did not discover the final fate of the expedition until 1859. During the intervening twelve years, some thirty expeditions went out to look for the missing ships and men—in the process, contributing substantially to our knowledge of the Arctic—turning the search for Franklin into one of the most famous quests of the nineteenth century, one that acquired mythic dimensions and inspired a popular ballad.

The *Terror* and the *Erebus* are mentioned at the beginning of Joseph Conrad's *Heart of Darkness*, and the search for Franklin is alluded to in Thoreau's *Walden*; however, the longest-lasting impressions of Franklin and his lost crew have been left on Canadian culture. In *Strange Things: The Malevolent North in Canadian Literature* (1995), Margaret Atwood surveyed some of the responses of Canada's writers—from E.J. Pratt (who considered, but did not pursue, an epic poem on the subject), through Gwendolyn MacEwen and Al Purdy, to Mordecai Richler and Rudy Wiebe. Atwood, who herself made the expedition's fate a central metaphor in her 1991 story 'The Age of Lead' (reprinted in this anthology), concludes her survey by reproducing the song called 'Northwest Passage'—by the Canadian singer-songwriter Stan Rogers—which has for its chorus, 'Ah, for just one time, I would take the Northwest Passage / To find the hand of Franklin reaching for the Beaufort Sea / Tracing one warm line through a land so wild and savage / And make a Northwest Passage to the sea.'

John Franklin

Born in Lincolnshire, England, John Franklin became the epitome of the nineteenth-century scientific adventurer. He joined the Royal Navy at the age of fourteen and saw action for the first time the following year. Two years after that he survived a shipwreck, and he later took part in the Battle of Trafalgar in 1805 and in the War of 1812. He rose through the ranks to become a lieutenant and retired on half-pay after the Napoleonic Wars ended. A few years later he returned to service to join the Navy's search for the Northwest Passage. (The quest for the passage had not been actively pursued for some time. The decision to take it up again seems to have been stimulated by the need to employ the men and ships left idle after the defeat of Napoleon.)

After travelling as second in command on an abortive venture in 1818, Franklin was asked, in 1819, to lead the first of what eventually became three Arctic expeditions under his command. The 1819 expedition was a near disaster, costing the lives of some ten men (most of them voyageurs and Natives who joined him after he reached North America). Despite—or because of—his difficulties, the book he published a year after his return, his *Narrative of a Journey to the Shores of the Polar Sea in the Years 1819, 20, 21 and 22*, was immensely popular and secured him an enduring reputation as a man of heroic stature. It was mostly based on Franklin's own journals, but it also incorporated excerpts from those of the three men who accompanied him. As well as being a chronicle of suffering and epic endurance, the book's extensive appendices on the flora and fauna of the area and on the crew's scientific observations on the aurora and the actions of the compass near the pole showed that Franklin took a deep scientific interest in his voyage. He was elected a fellow of the Royal Society soon after his return.

He exercised more caution on his next expedition, undertaken in 1825, and succeeded in mapping and gathering new information about the Arctic before turning back in 1827. He was knighted in 1829, and, after retiring once more from naval service, he was appointed lieutenant-governor of Van Diemen's Land (now Tasmania), a post he held from 1837 to 1843. In 1845, when he was 59 years old, Franklin, believing that developments in technology would help him overcome difficulties previously encountered, offered to lead another expedition into the North. He assumed the command of the *Erebus* and the *Terror*, which were sailing vessels, outfitted them with a propeller and steam engines, and clad their prows with sheets of iron to help them push their way through the ice. (John Ross, whom Franklin knew, had previously experimented with a steam engine in his Arctic exploration of 1829 but had been caught in an ice pack where he had remained for an unprecedented four years before being rescued.) Franklin's were massive steam engines, originally designed for railway locomotives, but they did not prevent him from becoming similarly icebound.

By 1867, Franklin's searchers were able to reconstruct the details of his fate: after he was trapped by ice, he had waited through the two following summers for a thaw. Franklin died in June 1847, not long after his supplies ran out and his next in command, Capt. Francis Crozier, led the starving crew off the ships to attempt an overland trek back to civilization. They made it as far as Victory Point (where they left a brief record of events) but perished shortly after pushing on from there.

Neither the remains of the ships themselves nor the grave of Franklin has ever been found. The reasons for the lost expedition's failure continue to intrigue investigators. In the 1980s, a group of anthropologists found the bodies of three of Franklin's sailors buried in the frozen tundra and discovered that the men had suffered from severe lead poisoning. The food Franklin had taken along had included 8,000 tins sealed with lead; and the lead, had apparently contaminated the contents—leading scientists to suspect that lead toxicity, which leaves individuals confused and debilitated, contributed to the failure of the expedition.

Dr John Richardson

John Richardson, who took part in and contributed sections to Franklin's accounts of his first and second Arctic journeys, was born in Dumfries, Scotland. He studied medicine at the University of Edinburgh before becoming a surgeon in the Royal Navy. A naturalist as well as a physician, he, along with the midshipmen George Back and Robert Hood, was appointed by the Lords Commissioners of the Admiralty to join Franklin's first expedition. He returned to the Arctic with Franklin in 1825 but did not join the expedition of 1845. (He was knighted for his services to the state the year after it departed.) He did, however, decide to return to the Arctic in 1848 to join the search for Franklin. He published a record of this unsuccessful trip and went on to write other books about his adventures and explorations. The most important of Richardson's later works is *The Polar Regions* (1861), in which, as well as discussing the Canadian North in detail, he summarized what had been learned of Franklin and his men. Observing that Franklin's expedition had come within miles of reaching the known waters to the west, he wrote that they had 'forged the last link of the North-West Passage with their lives'.

Stories of Northern Exploration

The excerpt reprinted here appears near the end of Franklin's first book, an account of an overland journey to the Coppermine River (some fifty years after Hearne first traversed the area) and Coronation Gulf, then eastward to Point Turnagain (Kent Peninsula) and back by the Hood River. Although Franklin derived great satisfaction in being the first European to map the area he passed through, as well as in naming its various features after friends and famous Englishmen, what most strikes readers are the grave hardships and constant suffering caused by the extremes of the cold and by the fact that food was in such short supply. These journals show the travellers preoccupied with the simple necessities for bare survival—not only food but, in land without trees, enough wood for a fire. Members of the expedition were sometimes driven to eat whatever they could find—even parts of their own garments—and to burn pieces of their shelters for warmth.

These tales of sheer endurance (Dr Richardson praises Robert Hood for 'the patience and fortitude with which he sustained . . . unparalleled bodily sufferings'), especially in extremes of climate, became a popular genre in their day: prompted by the example of Franklin's narrative, a number of Arctic and Polar adventurers set out to prove their own mettle and to return, after enduring comparable adversity, to write their own bestselling accounts. And just as the popularity of American westerns gave rise to the American myth of the Old West, so these books played a powerful role in shaping the expectations of, and even a myth of, the North and in that way played a significant role in forming the Canadian identity.

From *Narrative of a Journey to the Shores of the Polar Sea in the Years 1819, 20, 21 and 22*

[On his 1819 expedition to determine the exact position of the mouth of the Coppermine River and to map the shore of the Polar Sea to the east, Franklin was accompanied by three other officers, George Back, Robert Hood, and Dr John Richardson, along with two sailors, John Hepburn and Samuel Wilkes, and four Orkney boatmen. On 30 August 1819, the party arrived at York Factory, on the west coast of Hudson Bay (south of where Churchill, Manitoba, now stands). From there they began an overland journey north, following a chain of Hudson's Bay posts, to Lake Athabaska. On 29 July 1820, they arrived at the most northerly post of the North West Company, Fort Providence, at the western end of Great Slave Lake. Joined by a party that included Willard Wentzel (a trader at Fort Providence), Native guides, voyageurs, interpreters, and three women accompanying their husbands (and their three children), they now formed a group of thirty-one and made slow progress north, stopping in August 1820 at Winter Lake to construct a winter base camp, which they dubbed Fort Enterprise. They explored the area around their camp and made contact with a small band of Copper Indians; their leader, Akaitcho, assisted and advised Franklin.

Because they were beginning to run low on supplies, George Back set off with a small group on a winter journey to the outposts at Forts Providence, Resolution, and Chipewyan, before returning with supplies to the main party. His account of that trek concludes: 'on the 17th [of March 1821], at an early hour, we arrived at Fort Enterprise, having travelled about eighteen miles a-day. I had the pleasure of meeting my friends all in good health, after an absence of nearly five months, during which time I had travelled one thousand one hundred and four miles, on snow shoes, and had no other covering at night, in the woods, than a blanket and deer-skin, with the thermometer frequently at –40° and once at –57°; and sometimes passing two and three days without tasting food.'

In June 1821, the expedition travelled on to Point Lake and then, using two birchbark canoes, began their descent to the coast of the Arctic Ocean. On 14 July 1821, Dr Richardson climbed a hill at the mouth of the Coppermine River to become the fourth European to view the Arctic Ocean from the mainland of North America. The next day they met Inuit for the first time. Franklin recorded that nearby: 'Several human skulls which bore the marks of violence, and many bones were strewed about the ground. . . . [A]s the spot exactly answers the description given by Mr Hearne, of the place where the Chipewyans who accompanied him perpetrated the dreadful massacre on the Esquimaux, we had no doubt of this being the place. . . . We have, therefore, preserved the appellation of Bloody Fall, which he bestowed upon it.' On 18 August, they reached what became the most easterly point in their travels, a place on the Arctic coast that Franklin dubbed Point Turnagain. Inferring from the presence of whales that open sea lay ahead, he concluded, 'Our researches, as far as they have gone, seem to favour the opinion of those who contend for the practicability of a North-West Passage.' The extract that follows tells of their arduous return to Fort Enterprise across the Barren Grounds.]

CHAPTER XI

About noon Samandrè coming up, informed us that Crédit and Vaillant[1] could advance no further. Some willows being discovered in a valley near to us, I proposed to halt the party there, while Dr Richardson went back to visit them. I hoped too, that when the sufferers received the information of a fire being kindled at so short a distance, they would be cheered, and use their utmost efforts to reach it, but this proved a vain hope. The Doctor found Vaillant about a mile and a half in the rear, much exhausted with cold and fatigue. Having encouraged him to advance to the fire, after repeated solicitations he made the attempt, but fell down amongst the deep snow at every step. Leaving him in this situation, the Doctor went about half a mile farther back, to the spot where Crédit was said to have halted, and the track being nearly obliterated by the snow drift, it became unsafe for him to go further. Returning he passed Vaillant, who having moved only a few yards in his absence had fallen down, was unable to rise, and could scarcely answer his questions. Being unable to afford him any effectual assistance, he hastened on to inform us of his situation. . . . Mr Hood and Dr Richardson proposed to remain behind, with a single attendant, at the first place where sufficient wood and *tripe de roche*[2] should be found for ten days consumption;

1 François Samandrè, Crédit (the name given to Mathew Pelonquin), and Registe Vaillant, along with Joseph Peltier and Joseph Benoit (mentioned later in this extract), were among the 'Canadians' (i.e. voyageurs) who joined Franklin's expedition after its arrival in the North. (Samandrè, Pelonquin, and Peltier all died while with the expedition.)

2 Franklin has earlier explained *tripe de roche*: 'In the afternoon we got into a more hilly country, where the ground was strewed with large stones. The surface of these was covered with lichens of the genus gyrophora, which the Canadians term *tripe de roche*.' Also known as rock tripe, this lichen can be found on rocks in the northern parts of the United States and extends into the Far North. It forms broad, flat, leathery brown, greyish-black, or blackish expansions several inches wide. Its nutritional value is slight, and it is eaten only in cases of extreme need. Not long after the members of the expedition begin to make it a staple, Franklin comments on the difficulty they have digesting the plant: 'this unpalatable weed was now quite nauseous to the whole party, and in several it produced bowel complaints. Mr Hood was the greatest sufferer from this cause.'

and that I should proceed as expeditiously as possible with the men to the house, and thence send them immediate relief. . . .

At length we reached Fort Enterprise, and to our infinite disappointment and grief found it a perfectly desolate habitation. There was no deposit of provision, no trace of the Indians, no letter from Mr Wentzel to point out where the Indians might be found. It would be miserable for me to describe our sensations after entering the miserable abode, and discovering how we had been neglected: the whole party shed tears, not so much for our own fate, as for that of our friends in the rear, whose lives depended entirely on our sending immediate relief from this place. . . .

We now looked round for the means of subsistence, and were gratified to find several deer skins, which had been thrown away during our former residence. The bones were gathered from the heap of ashes, these with the skins, and the addition of *tripe de roche*, we considered would support us tolerably well for a time. . . . When I arose the following morning, my body and limbs were so swollen that I was unable to walk more than a few yards. Adam was in a still worse condition, being absolutely incapable of rising without assistance. My other companions fortunately experienced this inconvenience in a less degree, and went to collect bones, and some *Tripe de roche* which supplied us with two meals. The bones were quite acrid, and the soup extracted from them excoriated the mouth if taken alone, but it was somewhat milder when boiled with *tripe de roche*, and we even thought the mixture palatable, with the addition of salt, of which a cask had been fortunately left here in the spring. . . .

In making arrangements for our departure, Adam disclosed to me, for the first time, that he was affected with œdematous swellings[3] in some parts of the body, to such a degree as to preclude the slightest attempt at marching. . . . It now became necessary to abandon the original intention of proceeding with the whole party towards Fort Providence, and Peltier and Samandrè having volunteered to remain with Adam, I determined on setting out with Benoit and Augustus, intending to send them relief by the first party of Indians we should meet. My clothes were so much torn, as to be quite inadequate to screen me from the wind, and Peltier and Samandrè fearing that I might suffer on the journey in consequence, kindly exchanged with me parts of their dress, desiring me to send them skins in return by the Indians. Having patched up three pair of snow-shoes, and singed a considerable quantity of skin for the journey, we started on the morning of the 20th. Previous to my departure, I packed up the journals of the officers, the charts, and some other documents, together with a letter addressed to the Under-Secretary of State, detailing the occurrences of the Expedition up to this period, which package was given to Peltier and Samandrè, with direction that it should be brought away by the Indians who might come to them. I also instructed them to forward succour immediately on its arrival to our companions in the rear, which they solemnly promised to do, and I left a letter for my friends, Richardson and Hood, to be sent at the same time. I thought it necessary to admonish Peltier, Samandrè, and Adam, to eat two meals every day, in order to keep up their

3 Jean-Baptiste Adam travelled with the group as an interpreter; 'oedematous': resulting from oedema (now usually spelled 'edema'), i.e. swollen because of an accumulation of subdermal fluids—here as a result of prolonged exposure to severe cold.

strength, which they promised me they would do. No language that I can use could adequately describe the parting scene. I shall only say there was far more calmness and resignation for the Divine will evinced by every one than could have been expected. We were all cheered by the hope that the Indians would be found by the one party, and relief sent to the other. Those who remained entreated us to make all the haste we could, and expressed their hope of seeing the Indians in ten or twelve days.

At first starting we were so feeble as scarcely to be able to move forwards, and the descent of the bank of the river through the deep snow was a severe labour. When we came upon the ice, where the snow was less deep, we got on better, but after walking six hours we had only gained four miles, and were then compelled by fatigue to encamp on the borders of Round-Rock Lake. Augustus[4] tried for fish here, but without success, so that our fare was skin and tea. Composing ourselves to rest, we lay close to each other for warmth. We found the night bitterly cold, and the wind pierced through our famished frames.

The next morning was mild and pleasant for travelling, and we set out after breakfast. We had not, however, gone many yards before I had the misfortune to break my snow-shoes by falling between two rocks. This accident prevented me from keeping pace with Benoit and Augustus, and in the attempt I became quite exhausted. Being convinced that their being delayed on my account might prove of fatal consequence to the rest, I resolved on returning to the house, and letting them proceed alone in search of the Indians. I therefore halted them only whilst I wrote a note to Mr Back, stating the reason of my return, and requesting he would send meat from Rein-Deer Lake by these men, if St Germain should kill any animals there. If Benoit should miss Mr Back, I directed him to proceed to Fort Providence, and furnished him with a letter to the gentlemen in charge of it, requesting immediate supplies might be sent to us.

On my arrival at the house, I found Samandrè very dispirited, and too weak, as he said, to render any assistance to Peltier; upon whom the whole labour of getting wood and collecting the means of subsistence would have devolved. Conscious, too, that his strength would have been unequal to these tasks, they had determined upon taking only one meal each day; under these circumstances I considered my return as particularly fortunate, as I hoped to stimulate Samandrè to exertion, and at any rate I could contribute some help to Peltier. I undertook the office of cooking, and insisted they should eat twice a-day whenever food could be procured, but as I was too weak to pound the bones, Peltier agreed to do that in addition to his more fatiguing task of getting wood. We had a violent snow storm all the next day, and this gloomy weather contributed to the depression of spirits under which Adam and Samandrè were labouring. Neither of them would quit their beds, and they scarcely ceased from shedding tears all day; in vain did Peltier and myself endeavour to cheer them. We had even to use much entreaty before we prevailed upon them to take the meals we had prepared. Our situation was indeed distressing, but in comparison with that of our friends in the rear, we considered it happy. Their condition gave us unceasing solicitude, and was the principal subject of our conversation.

4 The name by which the expedition referred to Tattannoeuck, an Inuit guide who had joined the party.

Though the weather was stormy on the 26th, Samandrè assisted me to gather *tripe de roche*. Adam, who was very ill, and could not now be prevailed upon to eat this weed, subsisted principally on bones, though he also partook of the soup. The *tripe de roche* had hitherto afforded us our chief support, and we naturally felt great uneasiness at the prospect of being deprived of it, by its being so frozen as to render it impossible for us to gather it.

We perceived our strength decline every day, and every exertion began to be irksome; when we were once seated the greatest effort was necessary in order to rise, and we had frequently to lift each other from our seats; but even in this pitiable condition we conversed cheerfully, being sanguine as to the speedy arrival of the Indians. We calculated indeed that if they should be near the situation where they had remained last winter, our men would have reached them by this day. Having expended all the wood which we could procure from our present dwelling, without endangering its falling, Peltier began this day to pull down the partitions of the adjoining houses. Though these were only distant about twenty yards, yet the increase of labour in carrying the wood fatigued him so much, that by the evening he was exhausted. On the next day his weakness was such, especially in the arms, of which he chiefly complained, that he with difficulty lifted the hatchet: still he persevered, Samandrè and I assisting him in bringing in the wood, but our united strength could only collect sufficient to replenish the fire four times in the course of the day. As the insides of our mouths had become sore from eating the bone-soup, we relinquished the use of it, and now boiled our skin, which mode of dressing we found more palatable than frying it, as we had hitherto done.

On the 29th, Peltier felt his pains more severe, and could only cut a few pieces of wood. Samandrè, who was still almost as weak, relieved him a little time, and I assisted them in carrying in the wood. We endeavoured to pick some *tripe de roche*, but in vain, as it was entirely frozen. In turning up the snow, in searching for bones, I found several pieces of bark, which proved a valuable acquisition, as we were almost destitute of dry wood proper for kindling the fire. We saw a herd of rein-deer sporting on the river, about half a mile from the house; they remained there a considerable time, but none of the party felt themselves sufficiently strong to go after them, nor was there one of us who could have fired a gun without resting it.

Whilst we were seated round the fire this evening, discoursing about the anticipated relief, the conversation was suddenly interrupted by Peltier's exclaiming with joy, '*Ah! le monde!*' imagining that he heard the Indians in the other room; immediately afterwards, to his bitter disappointment, Dr Richardson and Hepburn entered, each carrying his bundle. Peltier, however, soon recovered himself enough to express his joy at their safe arrival, and his regret that their companions were not with them. When I saw them alone my own mind was instantly filled with apprehensions respecting my friend Hood, and our other companions, which were immediately confirmed by the Doctor's melancholy communication, that Mr Hood and Michel[5] were dead. Perrault and Fontano had neither reached the tent, nor been heard of by them. This intelligence

5 Michel Teroahauté, an Iroquois voyageur. Vincenza Antonio Fontano was an Italian national who, after serving in North America with a British regiment, remained and became a voyageur.

produced a melancholy despondency in the minds of my party, and on that account the particulars were deferred until another opportunity. We were all shocked at beholding the emaciated countenances of the Doctor and Hepburn, as they strongly evidenced their extremely debilitated state. The alteration in our appearance was equally distressing to them, for since the swellings had subsided we were little more than skin and bone. The Doctor particularly remarked the sepulchral tone of our voices, which he requested us to make more cheerful if possible, unconscious that his own partook of the same key.

Hepburn having shot a partridge, which was brought to the house, the Doctor tore out the feathers, and having held it to the fire a few minutes, divided it into seven portions. Each piece was ravenously devoured by my companions, as it was the first morsel of flesh any of us had tasted for thirty-one days, unless indeed the small gristly particles which we found occasionally adhering to the pounded bones may be termed flesh. Our spirits were revived by this small supply, and the Doctor endeavoured to raise them still higher by the prospect of Hepburn's being able to kill a deer next day, as they had seen, and even fired at, several near the house. He endeavoured, too, to rouse us to some attention to the comfort of our apartment, and particularly to roll up, in the day, our blankets which (expressly for the convenience of Adam and Samandrè,) we had been in the habit of leaving by the fire where we lay on them. The Doctor having brought his prayer-book and testament, some prayers and psalms, and portions of scripture, appropriate to our situation, were read, and we retired to bed.

Next morning the Doctor and Hepburn went out early in search of deer; but, though they saw several herds and fired some shots, they were not so fortunate as to kill any, being too weak to hold their guns steadily. The cold compelled the former to return soon, but Hepburn persisted until late in the evening.

My occupation was to search for skins under the snow, it being now our object immediately to get all that we could, but I had not strength to drag in more than two of those which were within twenty yards of the house until the Doctor came and assisted me. We made up our stock to twenty-six, but several of them were putrid, and scarcely eatable, even by men suffering the extremity of famine. Peltier and Samandrè continued very weak and dispirited, and they were unable to cut fire-wood. Hepburn had in consequence that laborious task to perform after he came back. The Doctor having scarified the swelled parts of Adam's body, a large quantity of water flowed out, and he obtained some ease, but still kept his bed.

After our usual supper of singed skin and bone soup, Dr Richardson acquainted me with the afflicting circumstances attending the death of Mr Hood and Michel, and detailed the occurrences subsequent to my departure from them, which I shall give from his journal, in his own words; but, I must here be permitted to express the heartfelt sorrow with which I was overwhelmed at the loss of so many companions; especially for that of my friend Mr Hood, to whose zealous and able co-operation I had been indebted for so much invaluable assistance during the Expedition, whilst the excellent qualities of his heart engaged my warmest regard. His scientific observations, together with his maps and drawings, evince a variety of talent, which, had his life been spared, must have rendered him a distinguished ornament to his profession, and which will cause his death to be felt as a loss to the service.

DR RICHARDSON'S NARRATIVE

After Captain Franklin had bidden us farewell we remained seated by the fire-side as long as the willows, the men had cut for us before they departed, lasted. We had no *tripe de roche* that day, but drank an infusion of the country tea-plant,[6] which was grateful from its warmth, although it afforded no sustenance. We then retired to bed, where we remained all the next day, as the weather was stormy, and the snow-drift so heavy, as to destroy every prospect of success in our endeavours to light a fire with the green and frozen willows, which were our only fuel. Through the extreme kindness and forethought of a lady, the party, previous to leaving London, had been furnished with a small collection of religious books, of which we still retained two or three of the most portable, and they proved of incalculable benefit to us. We read portions of them to each other as we lay in bed, in addition to the morning and evening service, and found that they inspired us on each perusal with so strong a sense of the omnipresence of a beneficent God, that our situation, even in these wilds, appeared no longer destitute; and we conversed, not only with calmness, but with cheerfulness, detailing with unrestrained confidence the past events of our lives, and dwelling with hope on our future prospects. Had my poor friend been spared to revisit his native land, I should look back to this period with unalloyed delight.

On the morning of the 29th, the weather, although still cold, was clear, and I went out in quest of *tripe de roche*, leaving Hepburn to cut willows for a fire, and Mr Hood in bed. I had no success, as yesterday's snow-drift was so frozen on the surface of the rocks that I could not collect any of the weed; but, on my return to the tent, I found that Michel, the Iroquois, had come with a note from Mr Franklin, which stated, that this man, and Jean Baptiste Belanger being unable to proceed, were about to return to us, and that a mile beyond our present encampment there was a clump of pine trees, to which he recommended us to remove the tent. Michel informed us that he quitted Mr Franklin's party yesterday morning, but, that having missed his way, he had passed the night on the snow a mile or two to the northward of us. Belanger, he said, being impatient, had left the fire about two hours earlier, and, as he had not arrived, he supposed he had gone astray. It will be seen in the sequel, that we had more than sufficient reason to doubt the truth of this story.

Michel now produced a hare and a partridge which he had killed in the morning. This unexpected supply of provision was received by us with a deep sense of gratitude to the Almighty for his goodness, and we looked upon Michel as the instrument he had chosen to preserve all our lives. He complained of cold, and Mr Hood offered to share his buffalo robe with him at night: I gave him one of two shirts which I wore, whilst Hepburn, in the warmth of his heart, exclaimed, 'How I shall love this man if I find that he does not tell lies like the others.' Our meals being finished, we arranged that the greatest part of the things should be carried to the pines the next day; and, after reading the evening service, retired to bed full of hope.

6 Richardson probably refers to what Franklin elsewhere identifies as Labrador tea, a northern rhododendron that, in Arctic areas, grows as a dwarf, low and close to the ground. Its leaves, when crushed and brewed, produce an aromatic herbal tea, rich in vitamin C.

Early in the morning Hepburn, Michel, and myself, carried the ammunition, and most of the other heavy articles to the pines. Michel was our guide, and it did not occur to us at the time that his conducting us perfectly straight was incompatible with his story of having gone astray on his way to us. He now informed us that he had, on his way to the tent, left on the hill above the pines a gun and forty-eight balls, which Perrault had given to him when with the rest of Mr Franklin's party, he took leave of him. It will be seen, on a reference to Mr Franklin's journal, that Perrault carried his gun and ammunition with him when they parted from Michel and Belanger. After we had made a fire, and drank a little of the country tea, Hepburn and I returned to the tent, where we arrived in the evening, much exhausted with our journey. Michel preferred sleeping where he was, and requested us to leave him the hatchet, which we did, after he had promised to come early in the morning to assist us in carrying the tent and bedding. Mr Hood remained in bed all day. Seeing nothing of Belanger to-day, we gave him up for lost.

On the 11th, after waiting until late in the morning for Michel, who did not come, Hepburn and I loaded ourselves with the bedding, and, accompanied by Mr Hood, set out for the pines. Mr Hood was much affected with dimness of sight, giddiness, and other symptoms of extreme debility, which caused us to move very slow, and to make frequent halts. On arriving at the pines, we were much alarmed to find that Michel was absent. We feared that he had lost his way in coming to us in the morning, although it was not easy to conjecture how that could have happened, as our footsteps of yesterday were very distinct. Hepburn went back for the tent, and returned with it after dusk, completely worn out with the fatigue of the day. Michel too arrived at the same time, and relieved our anxiety on his account. He reported that he had been in chase of some deer which passed near his sleeping place in the morning, and although he did not come up with them, yet that he found a wolf which had been killed by the stroke of a deer's horn, and had brought a part of it. We implicitly believed this story then, but afterwards became convinced from circumstances, the detail of which may be spared, that it must have been a portion of the body of Belanger or Perrault. A question of moment here presents itself; namely, whether he actually murdered these men, or either of them, or whether he found the bodies on the snow. Captain Franklin, who is the best able to judge of this matter, from knowing their situation when he parted from them, suggested the former idea, and that both Belanger and Perrault had been sacrificed. When Perrault turned back, Captain Franklin watched him until he reached a small group of willows, which was immediately adjoining to the fire, and concealed it from view, and at this time the smoke of fresh fuel was distinctly visible. Captain Franklin conjectures, that Michel having already destroyed Belanger, completed his crime by Perrault's death, in order to screen himself from detection. Although this opinion is founded only on circumstances, and is unsupported by direct evidence, it has been judged proper to mention it, especially as the subsequent conduct of the man shewed that he was capable of committing such a deed. The circumstances are very strong. It is not easy to assign any other adequate motive for his concealing from us that Perrault had turned back, and his request overnight that we should leave him the hatchet; and his cumbering himself with it when he went out in the morning, unlike a hunter who makes use only of his knife when he kills a deer, seem to indicate that he took it for the purpose of cutting up something that he knew to be frozen. These opinions, however, are the result of subsequent consideration. We passed this night in the open air.

On the following morning the tent was pitched, and Michel went out early, refused my offer to accompany him, and remained out the whole day. He would not sleep in the tent at night, but chose to lie at the fire-side.

On the 13th there was a heavy gale of wind, and we passed the day by the fire. Next day, about two, p.m., the gale abating, Michel set out as he said to hunt, but returned unexpectedly in a very short time. This conduct surprised us, and his contradictory and evasory answers to our questions excited some suspicions, but they did not turn towards the truth.

October 15th.—In the course of this day Michel expressed much regret that he had stayed behind Mr Franklin's party, and declared that he would set out for the house at once if he knew the way. We endeavoured to soothe him, and to raise his hopes of the Indians speedily coming to our relief, but without success. He refused to assist us in cutting wood, but about noon, after much solicitation, he set out to hunt. Hepburn gathered a kettle of *tripe de roche*, but froze his fingers. Both Hepburn and I fatigued ourselves much to-day in pursuing a flock of partridges from one part to another of the group of willows, in which the hut was situated, but we were too weak to be able to approach them with sufficient caution. In the evening Michel returned, having met with no success.

Next day he refused either to hunt or cut wood, spoke in a very surly manner, and threatened to leave us. Under these circumstances, Mr Hood and I deemed it better to promise if he would hunt diligently for four days, that then we would give Hepburn a letter for Mr Franklin, a compass, inform him what course to pursue, and let them proceed together to the fort. The non-arrival of the Indians to our relief, now led us to fear that some accident had happened to Mr Franklin, and we placed no confidence in the exertions of the Canadians that accompanied him, but we had the fullest confidence in Hepburn's returning the moment he could obtain assistance.

On the 17th I went to conduct Michel to where Vaillant's blanket was left, and after walking about three miles, pointed out the hills to him at a distance, and returned to the hut, having gathered a bagful of *tripe de roche* on the way. It was easier to gather this weed on a march than at the tent, for the exercise of walking produced a glow of heat, which enabled us to withstand for a time the cold to which we were exposed in scraping the frozen surface of the rocks. On the contrary, when we left the fire, to collect it in the neighbourhood of the hut, we became chilled at once, and were obliged to return very quickly.

Michel proposed to remain out all night, and to hunt next day on his way back. He returned in the afternoon of the 18th, having found the blanket, together with a bag containing two pistols, and some other things which had been left beside it. We had some *tripe de roche* in the evening, but Mr Hood, from the constant griping[7] it produced, was unable to eat more than one or two spoonfuls. He was now so weak as

7 Sharp pains in the bowels.

to be scarcely able to sit up at the fire-side, and complained that the least breeze of wind seemed to blow through his frame. He also suffered much from cold during the night. We lay close to each other, but the heat of the body was no longer sufficient to thaw the frozen rime formed by our breaths on the blankets that covered him.

At this period we avoided as much as possible conversing upon the hopelessness of our situation, and generally endeavoured to lead the conversation towards our future prospects in life. The fact is, that with the decay of our strength, our minds decayed, and we were no longer able to bear the contemplation of the horrors that surrounded us. Each of us, if I may be allowed to judge from my own case, excused himself from so doing by a desire of not shocking the feelings of the others, for we were sensible of one another's weakness of intellect though blind to our own. Yet we were calm and resigned to our fate, not a murmur escaped us, and we were punctual and fervent in our addresses to the Supreme Being.

On the 19th Michel refused to hunt, or even to assist in carrying a log of wood to the fire, which was too heavy for Hepburn's strength and mine. Mr Hood endeavoured to point out to him the necessity and duty of exertion, and the cruelty of his quitting us without leaving something for our support; but the discourse far from producing any beneficial effect, seemed only to excite his anger, and amongst other expressions, he made use of the following remarkable one: 'It is no use hunting, there are no animals, you had better kill and eat me.' At length, however, he went out, but returned very soon, with a report that he had seen three deer, which he was unable to follow from having wet his foot in a small stream of water thinly covered with ice, and being consequently obliged to come to the fire. The day was rather mild and Hepburn and I gathered a large kettleful of *tripe de roche*; Michel slept in the tent this night.

Sunday, October 20.—In the morning we again urged Michel to go a hunting that he might if possible leave us some provision, to-morrow being the day appointed for his quitting us; but he shewed great unwillingness to go out, and lingered about the fire, under the pretence of cleaning his gun. After we had read the morning service I went about noon to gather some *tripe de roche*, leaving Mr Hood sitting before the tent at the fire-side, arguing with Michel; Hepburn was employed cutting down a tree at a short distance from the tent, being desirous of accumulating a quantity of fire wood before he left us. A short time after I went out I heard the report of a gun, and about ten minutes afterwards Hepburn called to me in a voice of great alarm, to come directly. When I arrived, I found poor Hood lying lifeless at the fire-side, a ball having apparently entered his forehead. I was at first horror-struck with the idea, that in a fit of despondency he had hurried himself into the presence of his Almighty Judge, by an act of his own hand; but the conduct of Michel soon gave rise to other thoughts, and excited suspicions which were confirmed, when upon examining the body, I discovered that the shot had entered the back part of the head, and passed out at the forehead, and that the muzzle of the gun had been applied so close as to set fire to the night-cap behind. The gun, which was of the longest kind supplied to the Indians, could not have been placed in a position to inflict such a wound, except by a second person. Upon inquiring of Michel how it happened, he replied, that Mr Hood had sent him into the tent for the short gun, and that during his absence the long gun had gone off, he did not know whether by accident or not. He held the short gun in his hand at the time he was speaking to me. Hepburn afterwards informed me that previous to the report of the gun Mr Hood and Michel were speaking to each other in an elevated angry tone; that Mr Hood being seated at the fire-side, was hid from him by intervening willows, but that on hearing the report he looked up, and saw Michel rising up from before the tent-door, or just behind where Mr Hood was seated, and then going into the tent. Thinking that the gun had been discharged for the purpose of cleaning it, he did not go to the fire at first; and when Michel called to him that Mr Hood was dead, a considerable time had elapsed. Although I dare not openly to evince any suspicion that I thought Michel guilty of the deed, yet he repeatedly protested that he was incapable of committing such an act, kept constantly on his guard, and carefully avoided leaving Hepburn and me together. He was evidently afraid of permitting us to converse in private, and whenever Hepburn spoke, he inquired if he accused him of the murder. It is to be remarked, that he understood English very imperfectly, yet sufficiently to render it unsafe for us to speak on the subject in his presence. We removed the body into a clump of willows behind the tent, and, returning to the fire, read the funeral service in addition to the evening prayers. The loss of a young officer, of such distinguished and varied talents and application, may be felt and duly appreciated by the eminent characters under whose command he had served; but the calmness with which he contemplated the probable termination of a life of uncommon promise; and the patience and fortitude with which he sustained, I may venture to say, unparalleled bodily sufferings, can only be known to the companions of his distresses. Owing to the effect that the *tripe de roche* invariably had, when he ventured to taste it, he undoubtedly suffered more than any of the survivors of the party. *Bickersteth's Scripture Help* was lying open beside the body, as if it had fallen from his hand, and it is probable that he was reading it at the instant of his death. We passed the night in the tent together without rest, every one being on his guard. Next day, having determined on going to the Fort, we began to patch and prepare our clothes for the journey. We singed the hair off a part of the buffalo robe that belonged to Mr Hood, and boiled and ate it. Michel tried to persuade me to go to the woods on the Copper-Mine River, and hunt for deer instead of going to the Fort. In the afternoon a flock of partridges coming near the tent, he killed several which he shared with us.

Thick snowy weather and a head wind prevented us from starting the following day, but on the morning of the 23d we set out, carrying with us the remainder of the singed robe. Hepburn and Michel had each a gun, and I carried a small pistol, which Hepburn had loaded for me. In the course of the march Michel alarmed us much by his gestures and conduct, was constantly muttering to himself, expressed an unwillingness to go to the Fort, and tried to persuade me to go to the southward to the woods, where he said he could maintain himself all the winter by killing deer. In consequence of this behaviour, and the expression of his countenance, I requested him to leave us and to go to the southward by himself. This proposal increased his ill-nature, he threw out some obscure hints of freeing himself from all restraint on the morrow; and I overheard him muttering threats against Hepburn, whom he openly accused of having told stories against him. He also, for the first time, assumed such a tone of superiority in addressing me, as evinced that he considered us to be completely in his power, and he gave vent to several expressions of hatred towards the white people, or as he termed us in the idiom of the voyagers, the French, some of whom, he said, had killed and eaten his uncle and two of his relations. In short, taking every circumstance of his conduct into consideration, I came to the conclusion, that he would attempt to destroy us on the first opportunity that offered, and that he had hitherto abstained from doing so from his ignorance of the way to the Fort, but that he would never suffer us to go thither in company with him. In the course of the day he had several times remarked that we were pursuing the same course that Mr Franklin was doing when he left him, and that by keeping towards the setting sun he could find his way himself. Hepburn and I were not in a condition to resist even an open attack, nor could we by any device escape from him. Our united strength was far inferior to his, and, beside his gun, he was armed with two pistols, an Indian bayonet, and a knife. In the afternoon, coming to a rock on which there was some *tripe de roche*, he halted, and said he would gather it whilst we went on, and that he would soon overtake us. Hepburn and I were now left together for the first time since Mr Hood's death, and he acquainted me with several material circumstances, which he had observed of Michel's behaviour, and which confirmed me in the opinion that there was no safety for us except in his death, and he offered to be the instrument of it. I determined, however, as I was thoroughly convinced of the necessity of such a dreadful act, to take the whole responsibility upon myself; and immediately upon Michel's coming up, I put an end to his life by shooting him through the head with a pistol. Had my own life alone been threatened, I would not have purchased it by such a measure; but I considered myself as intrusted also with the protection of Hepburn's, a man, who, by his humane attentions and devotedness, had so endeared himself to me, that I felt more anxiety for his safety than for my own. Michel had gathered no *tripe de roche*, and it was evident to us that he had halted for the purpose of putting his gun in order, with the intention of attacking us, perhaps, whilst we were in the act of encamping.

I have dwelt in the preceding part of the narrative upon many circumstances of Michel's conduct, not for the purpose of aggravating his crime, but to put the reader in possession of the reasons that influenced me in depriving a fellow-creature of life. Up to the period of his return to the tent, his conduct had been good and respectful to the officers, and in a conversation between Captain Franklin, Mr Hood, and myself, at Obstruction Rapid, it had been proposed to give him a reward upon our arrival at a post. His principles, however, unsupported by a belief in the divine truths of Christianity, were unable to withstand the pressure of severe distress. His countrymen, the Iroquois, are generally Christians, but he was totally uninstructed and ignorant of the duties inculcated by Christianity; and from his long residence in the Indian country, seems to have imbibed, or retained, the rules of conduct which the southern Indians prescribe to themselves. . . .

On the 26th, the weather being clear and extremely cold, we resumed our march, which was very painful from the depth of the snow, particularly on the margins of the small lakes that lay in our route. We frequently sunk under the load of our blankets, and were obliged to assist each other in getting up. After walking about three miles and a half, however, we were cheered by the sight of a large herd of rein-deer, and Hepburn went in pursuit of them; but his hand being unsteady through weakness he missed. He was so exhausted by this fruitless attempt that we were obliged to encamp upon the spot, although it was a very unfavourable one.

Next day we had fine and clear, but cold, weather. We set out early, and, in crossing a hill, found a considerable quantity of *tripe de roche.* About noon we fell upon Little Marten Lake, having walked about two miles. The sight of a place that we knew inspired us with fresh vigour, and there being comparatively little snow on the ice, we advanced at a pace to which we had lately been unaccustomed. In the afternoon we crossed a recent track of a wolverine, which, from a parallel mark in the snow, appeared to have been dragging something. Hepburn traced it, and upon the borders of the lake found the spine of a deer, that it had dropped. It was clean picked, and, at least, one season old; but we extracted the spinal marrow from it, which, even in its frozen state, was so acrid as to excoriate the lips. We encamped within sight of the Dog-rib Rock, and from the coldness of the night and the want of fuel, rested very ill.

On the 28th we rose at day-break, but from the want of the small fire, that we usually made in the mornings to warm our fingers, a very long time was spent in making up our bundles. This task fell to Hepburn's share, as I suffered so much from the cold as to be unable to take my hands out of my mittens. We kept a straight course for the Dog-rib Rock, but, owing to the depth of the snow in the valleys we had to cross, did not reach it until late in the afternoon. We would have encamped, but did not like to pass a second night without fire; and though scarcely able to drag our limbs after us, we pushed on to a clump of pines, about a mile to the southward of the rock, and arrived at them in the dusk of the evening. During the last few hundred yards of our march, our track lay over some large stones, amongst which I fell down upwards of twenty times, and became at length so exhausted that I was unable to stand. If Hepburn had not exerted himself far beyond his strength, and speedily made the encampment and kindled a fire, I must have perished on the spot. This night we had plenty of dry wood.

On the 29th we had clear and fine weather. We set out at sunrise, and hurried on in our anxiety to reach the house, but our progress was much impeded by the great depth of the snow in the valleys. Although every spot of ground over which we travelled to-day, had been repeatedly trodden by us, yet we got bewildered in a small lake. We took it for Marten Lake, which was three times its size, and fancied that we saw the rapid and the grounds about the fort, although they were still far distant. Our disappointment when this illusion was dispelled, by our reaching the end of the lake, so operated on our feeble minds as to exhaust our strength, and we decided upon encamping; but upon ascending a small eminence to look for a clump of wood, we caught a glimpse of the Big-Stone, a well known rock upon the summit of a hill opposite to the Fort, and determined upon proceeding. In the evening we saw several large herds of rein-deer, but Hepburn, who used to be considered a good marksman, was now unable to hold the gun straight, and although he got near them all his efforts proved fruitless. In passing through a small clump of pines we saw a flock of partridges, and he succeeded in killing one after firing several shots. We came in sight of the fort at dusk, and it is impossible to describe our sensations, when on attaining the eminence that overlooks it, we beheld the smoke issuing from one of the chimneys. From not having met with any footsteps in the snow, as we drew nigh our once cheerful residence, we had been agitated by many melancholy forebodings. Upon entering the now desolate building, we had the satisfaction of embracing Captain Franklin, but no words can convey an idea of the filth and wretchedness that met our eyes on looking around. Our own misery had stolen upon us by degrees, and we were accustomed to the contemplation of each other's emaciated figures, but the ghastly countenances, dilated eye-balls, and sepulchral voices of Mr Franklin and those with him were more than we could at first bear.

Conclusion of Dr Richardson's Narrative.

The morning of the 31st was very cold, the wind being strong from the north. Hepburn went again in quest of deer, and the Doctor endeavoured to kill some partridges: both were unsuccessful. A large herd of deer passed close to the house, the Doctor fired once at them, but was unable to pursue them. Adam was easier this day, and left his bed. Peltier and Samandrè were much weaker, and could not assist in the labours of the day. Both complained of soreness in the throat, and Samandrè suffered much from cramps in his fingers. The Doctor and Hepburn began this day to cut the wood, and also brought it to the house. Being too weak to aid in these laborious tasks, I was employed in searching for bones, and cooking, and attending to our more weakly companions.

In the evening Peltier, complaining much of cold, requested of me a portion of a blanket to repair his shirt and drawers. The mending of these articles occupied him and Samandrè until past one a.m., and their spirits were so much revived by the employment, that they conversed even cheerfully the whole time. Adam sat up with them. The Doctor, Hepburn, and myself, went to bed. We were afterwards agreeably surprised to see Peltier and Samandrè carry three or four logs of wood across the room to replenish the fire, which induced us to hope they still possessed more strength than we had supposed.

November 1.—This day was fine and mild. Hepburn went hunting, but was as usual unsuccessful. As his strength was rapidly declining, we advised him to desist from the pursuit of deer; and only to go out for a short time, and endeavour to kill a few partridges for Peltier and Samandrè. The Doctor obtained a little *tripe de roche*, but Peltier could not eat any of it, and Samandrè only a few spoonfuls, owing to the soreness of their throats. In the afternoon Peltier was so much exhausted, that he sat up with difficulty, and looked piteously; at length he slided from his stool upon his bed, as we supposed to sleep, and in this composed state he remained upwards of two hours, without our apprehending any danger. We were then alarmed by hearing a rattling in his throat, and on the Doctor's examining him, he was found to be speechless. He died in the course of the night. Samandrè sat up the greater part of the day, and even assisted in pounding some bones; but on witnessing the melancholy state of Peltier, he became very low, and began to complain of cold and stiffness of the joints. Being unable to keep up a sufficient fire to warm him, we laid him down and covered him with several blankets. He did not, however, appear to get better, and I deeply lament to add he also died before daylight. We removed the bodies of the deceased into the opposite part of the house, but our united strength was inadequate to the task of interring them, or even carrying them down to the river.

It may be worthy of remark that poor Peltier, from the time of Benoit's departure, had fixed on the first of November as the time when he should cease to expect any relief from the Indians, and had repeatedly said that if they did not arrive by that day, he should not survive.

Peltier had endeared himself to each of us by his cheerfulness, his unceasing activity, and affectionate care and attentions, ever since our arrival at this place. He had nursed Adam with the tenderest solicitude the whole time. Poor Samandrè was willing to have taken his share in the labours of the party, had he not been wholly incapacitated by his weakness and low spirits. The severe shock occasioned by the sudden dissolution of our two companions rendered us very melancholy. Adam became low and despondent, a change which we lamented the more, as we had perceived he had been gaining strength and spirits for the two preceding days. I was particularly distressed by the thought that the labour of collecting wood must now devolve upon Dr Richardson and Hepburn, and that my debility would disable me from affording them any material assistance; indeed both of them most kindly urged me not to make the attempt. They were occupied the whole of the next day in tearing down the logs of which the store-house was built, but the mud plastered between them was so hard frozen that the labour of separation exceeded their strength, and they were completely exhausted by bringing in wood sufficient for less than twelve hours' consumption.

I found it necessary in their absence, to remain constantly near Adam, and to converse with him, in order to prevent his reflecting on our condition, and to keep up his spirits as far as possible. I also lay by his side at night.

On the 3d the weather was very cold, though the atmosphere was cloudy. This morning Hepburn was affected with swelling in his limbs, his strength as well as that of the Doctor, was rapidly declining; they continued, however, to be full of hope. Their utmost exertions could only supply wood, to renew the fire thrice, and on making it up the last time we went to bed. Adam was in rather better spirits, but he could not bear to be left alone. Our stock of bones was exhausted by a small quantity of soup we made this evening. The toil of separating the hair from the skins, which in fact were our chief support, had now become so wearisome as to prevent us from eating as much as we should otherwise have done.

November 4.—Calm and comparatively mild weather. The Doctor and Hepburn, exclusive of their usual occupation, gathered some *tripe de roche*. I went a few yards from the house in search of bones, and returned quite fatigued, having found but three. The Doctor again made incisions in Adam's leg, which discharged a considerable quantity of water, and gave him great relief. We read prayers and a portion of the New Testament in the morning and evening, as had been our practice since Dr Richardson's arrival; and I may remark that the performance of these duties always afforded us the greatest consolation, serving to reanimate our hope in the mercy of the Omnipotent, who alone could save and deliver us.

On the 5th the breezes were light, with dark cloudy weather, and some snow. The Doctor and Hepburn were getting much weaker, and the limbs of the latter were now greatly swelled. They came into the house frequently in the course of the day to rest themselves, and when once seated, were unable to rise without the help of one another, or of a stick. Adam was for the most part in the same low state as yesterday, but sometimes he surprised us by getting up and walking with an appearance of increased strength. His looks were now wild and ghastly, and his conversation was often incoherent.

The next day was fine, but very cold. The swellings in Adam's limbs having subsided, he was free from pain, and arose this morning in much better spirits, and spoke of cleaning his gun ready for shooting partridges, or any animals that might appear near the house, but his tone entirely changed before the day was half over; he became again dejected, and could scarcely be prevailed upon to eat. The Doctor and Hepburn were almost exhausted. The cutting of one log of wood occupied the latter half an hour; and the other took as much time to drag it into the house, though the distance did not exceed thirty yards. I endeavoured to help the Doctor, but my assistance was very trifling. Yet it was evident that, in a day or two, if their strength should continue to decline at the same rate, I should be the strongest of the party.

I may here remark that owing to our loss of flesh, the hardness of the floor, from which we were only protected by a blanket, produced soreness over the body, and especially those parts on which the weight rested in lying, yet to turn ourselves for relief was a matter of toil and difficulty. However, during this period, and indeed all along after the acute pains of hunger, which lasted but three or four days, had subsided, we generally enjoyed the comfort of a few hours' sleep. The dreams which for the most part, but not always accompanied it, were usually (though not invariably,) of a pleasant character, being very often about the enjoyments of feasting. In the day-time we fell into the practice of conversing on common and light subjects, although we sometimes discussed with seriousness and earnestness topics connected with religion. We generally avoided speaking directly of our present sufferings, or even of the prospect of relief. I observed, that in proportion as our strength decayed, our minds exhibited symptoms of weakness, evinced by a kind of unreasonable pettishness with each other. Each of us thought the other weaker in intellect than himself, and more in need of advice and assistance. So trifling a circumstance as a change of place, recommended by one as being warmer and more comfortable, and refused by the other from a dread of motion, frequently called forth fretful expressions which were no sooner uttered than atoned for, to be repeated perhaps in the course of a few minutes. The same thing often occurred when we endeavoured to assist each other in carrying wood to the fire; none of us were willing to receive assistance, although the task was disproportioned to our strength. On one of these occasions Hepburn was so convinced of this waywardness that he exclaimed, 'Dear me, if we are spared to return to England, I wonder if we shall recover our understandings.'

November 7.—Adam had passed a restless night, being disquieted by gloomy apprehensions of approaching death, which we tried in vain to dispel. He was so low in the morning as to be scarcely able to speak. I remained in bed by his side to cheer him as much as possible. The Doctor and Hepburn went to cut wood. They had hardly begun their labour, when they were amazed at hearing the report of a musket. They could scarcely believe that there was really any one near, until they heard a shout, and immediately espied three Indians close to the house. Adam and I heard the latter noise, and I was fearful that a part of the house had fallen upon one of my companions, a disaster which had in fact been thought not unlikely. My alarm was only momentary; Dr Richardson came in to communicate the joyful intelligence that relief had arrived. He and myself immediately addressed thanksgiving to the throne of mercy for this deliverance, but poor Adam was in so low a state that he could scarcely comprehend the information. When the Indians entered, he attempted to rise but sank down again. But for this seasonable interposition of Providence, his existence must have terminated in a few hours, and that of the rest probably in not many days.

The Indians had left Akaitcho's encampment on the 5th November, having been sent by Mr Back with all possible expedition, after he had arrived at their tents. They brought but a small supply of provision that they might travel quickly. It consisted of dried deer's meat, some fat, and a few tongues. Dr Richardson, Hepburn, and I, eagerly devoured the food, which they imprudently presented to us, in too great abundance, and in consequence we suffered dreadfully from indigestion, and had no rest the whole night. Adam being unable to feed himself, was more judiciously treated by them, and suffered less; his spirits revived hourly. The circumstance of our eating more food than was proper in our present condition, was another striking proof of the debility of our minds. We were perfectly aware of the danger, and Dr Richardson repeatedly cautioned us to be moderate; but he was himself unable to practise the caution he so judiciously recommended.

[After wintering over at Fort Resolution, the party set off at the end of May 1822 and reached York Factory that July. Franklin's narrative ends: 'And thus terminated our long, fatiguing, and disastrous travels in North America, having journeyed by water and by land (including our navigation of the Polar Sea) five thousand five hundred and fifty miles.']

1823

Anna Brownell Jameson

1794–1860

Travel Writing

Travel writing, a very old form, became increasingly popular and important after the Renaissance voyages of discovery. In the nineteenth century, readers came to look to it for an account of the individual's subjective experience of a distant milieu. British travellers went out from the centre of the Empire to experience Africa, Asia, the Americas, and then came home to publish accounts that spoke to those in their own country, not from the perspective of explorers who faced the unknown nor that of emigrants trying to establish new homes, but rather as representatives of their culture who could serve as temporary windows from which their compatriots could view the world abroad. In contrast to the reports of explorers that were initially prepared for the organizations that had sponsored their efforts, these narratives, conceived of as for a general readership, were not characterized by the same degree of accuracy and non-narrative detail; in place of novel landscapes and geographies, they focused on contrasting societies and cultures, often comparing the alien landscapes to the familiar homeland of the traveller and her readers. Although risk-taking was sometimes an aspect of travel books and the encounter with the sublime was characteristic of this genre, they were usually more quietly adventuresome than were exploration or even pioneer narratives.

Sometimes the excursions they described were made within western Europe, where their *raison d'être* was exposing the traveller, and thus the reader, to the broadening experience of more 'sophisticated' cultures. But in the nineteenth century, stories of visits to non-European environments grew increasingly popular, and for their readers the interest often lay in the tension between their confirmation of the traveller's and the reader's expectations and the discovery that some things are not as anticipated. Among these nineteenth-century travel narratives, Anna Jameson's *Winter Studies and Summer Rambles in Canada* (London, 1838) is the best-known book about Canada. It was successful in its own day and has remained in print (if often in abridged form) ever since its original publication.

Anna Brownell Jameson

Born in Dublin, Anna Brownell Murphy was a traveller from the time she was four. By age nine, she had moved with her parents—but without her older sisters—three times across England. Her family was finally reunited in London, where her father Denis Brownell Murphy became a court painter of miniatures. A precocious child—Murphy read all of Shakespeare's plays between the ages of seven and ten—she became a governess for the Marquis of Winchester in 1810. In her mid-teens, she met Robert Jameson, a lawyer and friend of Montagu, Coleridge, and Lamb. She consented to an engagement but, though they shared interests in art and literature, both were strong-willed and seemed to have been temperamentally unsuited to one another. Calling off their engagement, she chose instead to travel as governess with the Rowles family on their tour of Italy in 1821. Returning a year later, she took another position as governess for Mr Littleton (later Lord Hatherton), and lived with that family, with whom she remained friends, in Staffordshire for three years. In 1825, she finally did consent to marry Robert Jameson, and shortly after, she published, with Robert's encouragement, her first major work, *A Lady's Diary* (1826; subsequently retitled *The Diary of an Ennuyée*). This well-received anonymous and sentimental account of travels in Italy received some notoriety when public knowledge of its little-disguised authorship revealed it to be highly fictionalized and less autobiographical than it had appeared. Following its success, she became part of a group of writers whose work was regularly published in recently established magazines such as *Blackwoods*. These new periodicals catered to women eager to acquire knowledge and culture, and Jameson's writing was valued for the way it dealt with the rights of women, emphasized the need for female education, and generally reflected attitudes aligned with the proto-feminism that developed in England in the years that followed the publication of Mary Wollstonecraft's *Vindication of the Rights of Women* (1792).

Although the Jamesons lived together in London for a few years, in 1829 Robert left for a post as a judge in Dominica while Anna went to the Continent with her father and his patron, Sir Gerard Noel. Nor did she join her husband when, after a brief return to London, he became, in 1833, attorney-general of Upper Canada. Anna continued to travel, particularly in Germany where she met Robert Noel and his cousin Lady Byron, both of whom became close friends. Through Noel, Jameson also became acquainted with the Goethe family. Summoned back to England to attend to her father's illness, she returned in 1834 to live in Germany for another two years. During this period she wrote five more books, four of which were about women: *Memoirs of the Lovers of the Poets* (1829), *Memoirs of the Celebrated Female Sovereigns* (1831), *Memoirs of the Beauties of the Court of Charles II* (1831), and *Characteristics of Woman* (1832). The last of these, a series of psychological studies of the female characters in Shakespeare's dramas (subsequently retitled *Shakespeare's Heroines*), is the book for which she became best known. She also completed a second travel diary, *Visits and Sketches at Home and Abroad* (1834).

After a summer in England, Jameson decided to join her husband in Canada in an attempt to resume their marriage. Arriving in the winter of 1836, she remained in Canada through the summer of 1837 and, after reaching an agreement with Robert for a formal separation and the settlement of an allowance, she left for New York for six months, before returning to England and then to Germany and Paris. After her father's death in 1842, she stayed in England to arrange quarters for her mother and unmarried sisters, whom she had already been supporting for a number of years. During this period she visited Scotland before returning to Germany and Italy. On her way to Italy, she met Robert and Elizabeth Browning in Paris and aided them in their flight to Florence. (They remained close friends until her death.) When Robert Jameson died in 1854, Anna discovered that, counter to their agreement, he had willed his estate to others, and she was left with no source of income. She began to give lectures that focused on women's issues and that resulted in two books, *Sisters of Charity* and *The Communion of Labour*. As her health failed, her friends put together an annuity to supplement her income. She died in 1860 after a brief illness.

Winter Studies and Summer Rambles in Canada

While her stay in Canada was brief, it did provide Jameson with the opportunity to write *Winter Studies and Summer Rambles in Canada*. Her unhappiness—since both the attempted reconciliation with her husband was left unsuccessful and she deeply regretted having left behind the culture and civilization of Europe—may have influenced her perceptions; her first entry in *Winter Studies and Summer Rambles*, for 20 Dec. 1836, records her disillusionment on arriving at her new home:

> *What Toronto may be in summer, I cannot tell; they say it is a pretty place. At present its appearance to me, a stranger, is most strangely mean and melancholy. A little ill-built town on low land, at the bottom of a frozen bay, with one very ugly church, without tower or steeple; some government offices, built of staring red brick, in the most tasteless, vulgar style imaginable; three feet of snow all around; and the grey, sullen, wintry lake, and the dark gloom of the pine forest bounding the prospects; such seems Toronto to me now. I did not expect much; but for this I was not prepared.*

Determined to provide a written record of her Canadian experience, she set about acquainting herself with Toronto society. In the 'Winter Studies' portion of her book she sets down her observations, intermixed with reflections on literature and life, and quotations from works of German literature that she was then reading. 'I know no better way of coming at the truth', she wrote, 'than by observing and recording faithfully the impressions made by objects and characters on my own mind—or, rather, the impress they receive from my own mind.' She took particular interest in the condition of women in the province, observing, 'I have not often in my life met with contented and cheerful-minded women, but I never met with so many repining and discontented women as in Canada,' though she also believed that 'really accomplished women, accustomed to what is called the best society, have more resources here, and manage better. . . .'

Deciding that she wanted to see more of Upper Canada, in June 1837 Mrs Jameson embarked—over her husband's objections and in an age when a woman travelling without friends or escort was extremely unusual, especially in such primitive conditions—on the journey that was to provide materials for the 'summer rambles' section of her account.

To undertake such a journey alone is rash perhaps—yet alone it must be achieved, I find, or not at all; I shall have neither companion nor manservant, nor femme de chambre, *nor even a 'little foot-page', to give notice of my fate, should I be swamped in a bog, or eaten up by a bear, or scalped, or disposed of in some strange way; but shall I leave this fine country without seeing anything of its great characteristic features?*

The trip included visits to Niagara Falls (with which she expressed disappointment), Hamilton, London, and Port Talbot, and she eventually made her way through Detroit and as far north as what she called her 'Ultima Thule', Sault Ste Marie. Her curiosity about North American Native peoples led her to call on Henry Schoolcraft (whose extensive collection of Aboriginal lore later furnished material for Longfellow's *Hiawatha*) and to attend a Native conclave at Manitoulin Island. In the more distant parts of her trip, Mrs Jameson travelled with only a few other passengers in small boats rowed by voyageurs, and she was the first European woman to pass through the rapids at the Sault. When she returned to Toronto in August, she recorded that 'the people here are in great enthusiasm about me and stare at me as if I had done some most wonderful thing; the most astonished of all is Mr Jameson.'

Mrs Jameson returned to England in 1838, and the publication of *Winter Sketches and Summer Rambles* in that year proved timely, for many of her countrymen were especially interested in observations of Canada made on the eve of the 1837 Rebellion. (Her drawings for *Winter Sketches and Summer Rambles*, which had been omitted by its publisher, were eventually published on their own in 1958 as *Early Canadian Sketches*.) She herself realized that her regrets about leaving behind an established career in England gave a negative cast to her perceptions of Upper Canada, but the scope and acuity of her observations are, especially given the brevity of her visit, admirable. Particularly penetrating are her insights into the difficulties of forming a new society in Canada, which anticipate those of Susanna Moodie and of many later writers.

From *Winter Studies and Summer Rambles in Canada*

January 16.

Some philosopher has said or written, that our good and bad qualities, our virtues and our vices, depend more on the influence of climate, than the pride of civilised humanity would be willing to allow; and this is a truth or truism, which for my own part I cannot gainsay—yet which I do not much like to believe. Whatever may be the climate in which the human being is born or reared, can he not always by moral strength raise himself above its degrading, or benumbing, or exciting influence? and yet more, rather than less, easily, when, at a mature age and with habits formed, he is subjected accidentally to such influences? Is there most wisdom, in such a case, in passively assimilating ourselves, our habits, and our feelings, to external circumstances, or resisting and combating them, rather to defend the integrity of our own individual being, than with the hope of changing or controlling the physical or social influence around us?

How I might have settled this question with myself, long ago, when in possession of the health and energy and trusting spirit of my young years, I know—but now it is too late. I could almost wish myself a dormouse, or a she-bear, to sleep away the rest of this cold, cold winter, and wake only with the first green leaves, the first warm breath of the summer wind. I shiver through the day and through the night; and, like poor Harry Gill, 'my teeth they chatter, chatter still;'[1] and then at intervals I am burned up with a dry hot fever: this is what my maid, a good little Oxfordshire girl, calls the *hager* (the ague,) more properly the lake fever, or cold fever. From the particular situation of Toronto, the disorder is very prevalent here in the spring: being a stranger, and not yet *acclimatée,* it has attacked me thus unseasonably. Bark is the general and unfailing remedy.

The cold is at this time so intense, that the ink freezes while I write, and my fingers stiffen round the pen; a glass of water by my bed-side, within a few feet of the hearth, (heaped with logs of oak and maple kept burning all night long,) is a solid mass of ice in the morning. God help the poor emigrants who are yet unprepared against the rigour of the season!—yet this is nothing to the climate of the lower province, where, as we hear, the thermometer has been thirty degrees below zero. I lose all heart to write home, or to register a reflection or a feeling;—thought stagnates in my head as the ink in my pen—and this will never do!—I *must* rouse myself to occupation; and if I cannot find it without, I must create it from within. There are yet four months of winter and leisure to be disposed of. How?—I know not; but they *must* be employed, not wholly lost.

* * *

Toronto, February 7.

Mr B. gave me a seat in his sleigh, and after a rapid and very pleasant journey, during which I gained a good deal of information, we reached Toronto yesterday morning.

The road was the same as before, with one deviation however—it was found expedient to cross Burlington Bay on the ice, about seven miles over, the lake beneath being twenty, and five-and-twenty fathoms in depth. It was ten o'clock at night, and the only light was that reflected from the snow. The beaten track, from which it is not safe to deviate, was very narrow, and a man, in the worst, if not the last stage of intoxication, noisy and brutally reckless, was driving before us in a sleigh. All this, with the novelty of the situation, the tremendous cracking of the ice at every instant, gave me a sense of apprehension just sufficient to be exciting, rather than very unpleasant, though I will confess to a feeling of relief when we were once more on the solid earth.

1 Wordsworth's poem 'Goody Blake and Harry Gill: A True Story' (1798) recounts the legend of a man who beats a poor woman for gathering firewood from his hedge, and is thereafter cursed with feeling cold for the rest of his life. The poem opens: 'Oh! what's the matter? What's the matter? / What is't that ails young Harry Gill? / That evermore his teeth they chatter, / Chatter, chatter, chatter still.'

B. is said to be a hard, active, clever, practical man. I liked him, and thought him intelligent and good-natured: we had much talk. Leaving his servant to drive, he would jump down, stand poised upon one of runners, and, thus gliding smoothly along, we conversed.

It is a remarkable fact, with which you are probably acquainted, that when one growth of timber is cleared from the land, another of quite a different species springs up spontaneously in its place. Thus, the oak or the beech succeeds to the pine, and the pine to the oak or maple. This is not accounted for, at least I have found no one yet who can give me a reason for it. We passed by a forest lately consumed by fire, and I asked why, in clearing the woods, they did not leave groups of the finest trees, or even single trees, here and there, to embellish the country? But it seems that this is impossible—for the trees thus left standing, when deprived of the shelter and society to which they have been accustomed, uniformly perish—which, for mine own poor part, I thought very natural.

A Canadian settler *hates* a tree, regards it as his natural enemy, as something to be destroyed, eradicated, annihilated by all and any means. The idea of useful or ornamental is seldom associated here even with the most magnificent timber trees, such as among the Druids had been consecrated, and among the Greeks would have sheltered oracles and votive temples. The beautiful faith which assigned to every tree of the forest its guardian nymph, to every leafy grove its tutelary divinity, would find no votaries here. Alas! for the Dryads and Hamadryads of Canada![2]

There are two principal methods of killing trees in this country, besides the quick, unfailing destruction of the axe; the first by setting fire to them, which sometimes leaves the root uninjured to rot gradually and unseen, or be grubbed up at leisure, or, more generally, there remains a visible fragment of a charred and blackened stump, deformed and painful to look upon: the other method is slower, but even more effectual; a deep gash is cut through the bark into the stem, quite round the bole of the tree. This prevents the circulation of the vital juices, and by degrees the trees droops and dies. This is technically called *ringing* timber. Is not this like the two ways in which a woman's heart may be killed in this world of ours—by passion and by sorrow? But better far the swift fiery death than this 'ringing', as they call it!

* * *

February 17.

'There is no *society* in Toronto,' is what I hear repeated all around me—even by those who compose the only society we have. 'But', you will say, 'what could be expected in a remote town, which forty years ago was an uninhabited swamp, and twenty years ago only began to exist?' I really do not know what I expected, but I will tell you what I did *not* expect. I did not expect to find here in this capital of a new country, with the boundless forest within half a mile of us on almost every side,—concentrated as it were the worst evils of our old and most artificial social system at home, with none of its *agrémens*, and none of its advantages. Toronto is like a fourth or fifth rate provincial

2 Wood nymphs.

town, with the pretensions of a capital city. We have here a petty colonial oligarchy, a self-constituted aristocracy, based upon nothing real, nor even upon anything imaginary; and we have all the mutual jealousy and fear, and petty gossip, and mutual meddling and mean rivalship, which are common in a small society of which the members are well known to each other, a society composed, like all societies, of many heterogeneous particles; but as these circulate within very confined limits, there is no getting out of the way of what one most dislikes: we must necessarily hear, see, and passively endure much that annoys and disgusts any one accustomed to the independence of a large and liberal society, or the ease of continental life. It is curious enough to see how quickly a new fashion, or a new folly, is imported from the old country, and with what difficulty and delay a new idea finds its way into the heads of the people, or a new book into their hands. Yet, in the midst of all this, I cannot but see that good spirits and corrective principles are at work; that progress is making: though the march of intellect be not here in double quick time, as in Europe, it does not absolutely sand stock-still.

There reigns here a hateful factious spirit in political matters, but for the present no public or patriotic feeling, no recognition of general or generous principles of policy: as yet I have met with none of these. Canada is a colony, not a *country*; it is not yet identified with the dearest affections and associations, remembrances, and hopes of its inhabitants: it is to them an adopted, not a real mother. Their love, their pride, are not for poor Canada, but for high and happy England; but a few more generations must change all this.

We have here Tories, Whigs, and Radicals, so called; but these words do not signify exactly what we mean by the same designations at home.

You must recollect that the first settlers in Upper Canada were those who were obliged to fly from the United States during the revolutionary war, in consequence of their attachment to the British government, and the soldiers and non-commissioned officers who had fought during the war. These were recompensed for their losses, sufferings, and services, by grants of land in Upper Canada. Thus the very first elements out of which our social system was framed, were repugnance and contempt for the new institutions of the United States, and a dislike to the people of that country,—a very natural result of foregone causes; and thus it has happened that the slightest tinge of democratic, or even liberal principles in politics, was for a long time a sufficient impeachment of the loyalty, a stain upon the personal character, of those who held them. The Tories have therefore been hitherto the influential party; in their hands we find the government patronage, the principal offices, the sales and grants of land, for a long series of years.

Another party, professing the same boundless loyalty to the mother country, and the same dislike for the principles and institutions of their Yankee neighbours, may be called the Whigs of Upper Canada; these look with jealousy and scorn on the power and prejudices of the Tory families, and insist on the necessity of many reforms in the colonial government. Many of these are young men of talent, and professional men, who find themselves shut out from what they regard as their fair proportion of social consideration and influence, such as, in a small society like this, their superior education and character ought to command for them.

Another set are the Radicals, whom I generally hear mentioned as 'those scoundrels', or 'those rascals', or with some epithet expressive of the utmost contempt and disgust. They are those who wish to see this country erected into a republic, like the United States. A few among them are men of talent and education, but at present they are neither influential nor formidable.

There is among all parties a general tone of complaint and discontent—a mutual distrust—a languor and supineness—the causes of which I cannot as yet understand. Even those who are enthusiastically British in heart and feeling, who sincerely believe that it is the true interest of the colony to remain under the control of the mother country, are as discontented as the rest: they bitterly denounce the ignorance of the colonial officials at home, with regard to the true interests of the country: they ascribe the want of capital for improvement on a large scale to no mistrust in the resources of the country, but to a want of confidence in the measures of the government, and the security of property.

In order to understand something of the feelings which prevail here, you must bear in mind the distinction between the two provinces of Upper and Lower Canada. The project of uniting them once more into one legislature, with a central metropolis, is most violently opposed by those whose personal interests and convenience would suffer materially by a change in the seat of government. I have heard some persons go so far as to declare, that if the union of the two provinces were to be established by law, it were sufficient to absolve a man from his allegiance. On the other hand, the measure has powerful advocates in both provinces. It seems, on looking over the map of this vast and magnificent country, and reading its whole history, that the political division into five provinces,[3] each with its independent governor and legislature, its separate correspondence with the Colonial-office, its local laws, and local taxation, must certainly add to the amount of colonial patronage, and perhaps render more secure the subjection of the whole to the British crown; but may it not also have perpetuated local distinctions and jealousies—kept alive divided interests, narrowed the resources, and prevented the improvement of the country on a large and general scale?

But I had better stop here, ere I get beyond my depth. I am not one of those who opine sagely, that women have nothing to do with politics. On the contrary; but I do seriously think that no one, be it man or woman, ought to talk, much less write, on what they do not understand. Not but that I have my own ideas on these matters, though we were never able to make out, either to my own satisfaction or to yours, whether I am Whig or Tory or Radical. In politics I acknowledge but two parties,—those who hope and those who fear. In morals, but two parties—those who lie and those who speak the truth: and all the world I divide into those who love, and those who hate. This comprehensive arrangement saves me a vast deal of trouble, and answers all my own purposes to admiration.

* * *

3 Viz. Upper Canada, Lower Canada, Nova Scotia, New Brunswick, and Prince Edward's Island. [Jameson's note]

February 18.

* * *

Here, as everywhere else, I find the women of the better class lamenting over the want of all society, except of the lowest grade in manners and morals. For those who have recently emigrated, and are settled more in the interior, there is absolutely no social intercourse whatever; it is quite out of the question. They seem to me perishing of ennui, or from the want of sympathy which they cannot obtain, and, what is worse, which they cannot feel: for being in general unfitted for out-door occupations, unable to comprehend or enter into the interests around them, and all their earliest prejudices and ideas of the fitness of things continually outraged in a manner exceedingly unpleasant, they may be said to live in a perpetual state of inward passive discord and fretful endurance—

> 'All too timid and reserved
> For onset, for resistance too inert—
> Too weak for suffering, and for hope too tame.'[4]

A gentleman well known to me by name, who was not a resident of London, but passing through it on his way from a far western settlement up by Lake Huron, was one of my morning visitors. He had been settled in the bush for five years, had a beautiful farm, well cleared, well stocked. He was pleased with his prospects, his existence, his occupations: all he wanted was a wife, and on this subject he poured forth a most eloquent appeal.

'Where', said he, 'shall I find such a wife as I could, with a safe conscience, bring into these wilds, to share a settler's fate, a settler's home? You, who know your own sex so well, point me out such a one, or tell me at least where to seek her. I am perishing and deteriorating, head and heart, for want of a companion—a wife, in short. I am becoming as rude and coarse as my own labourers, and as hard as my own axe. If I wait five years longer, no woman will be able to endure such a fellow as I shall be by that time—no woman, I mean, whom I could marry—for in this lies my utter unreasonableness. Habituated to seek in woman those graces and refinements which I have always associated with her idea, I must have them here in the forest, or dispense with all female society whatever. With some one to sympathise with me—to talk to—to embellish the home I return to at night—such a life as I now lead, with all the cares and frivolities of a too artificial society cast behind us, security and plenty all around us, and nothing but hope before us, a life of "cheerful yesterdays and confident to-morrows"[5]—were it not delicious? I want for myself nothing more, nothing better; but—perhaps it is a weakness, an inconsistency!—I could not love a woman who was inferior to all my preconceived notions of feminine elegance and refinement—inferior to my own mother and sisters. You know I was in England two years ago;—well, I have

4 'Despondency', from Wordsworth's *The Excursion* (1814).

5 Also from *The Excursion*; a peasant seen by the poet is idealized as 'A Man . . . of cheerful yesterday / And confident to-morrows' (VII. 557–8).

a vision of a beautiful creature, with the figure of a sylph and the head of a sibyl, bending over her harp, and singing "*A te, O cara*";[6] and when I am logging in the woods with my men, I catch myself meditating on that vision, and humming *A te, O cara*, which somehow or other runs strangely in my head. Now, what is to be done? What could I do with that fair vision here? Without coxcombry may I not say, that I need not entirely despair of winning the affections of an amiable, elegant woman, and might even persuade her to confront, for my sake, worse than all this? For what will not your sex do and dare for the sake of us men creatures, savages that we are? But even for that reason shall I take advantage of such sentiments? You know what this life is—this isolated life in the bush—and so do I; but by what words could I make it comprehensible to a fine lady? Certainly I might draw such a picture of it as should delight by its novelty and romance, and deceive even while it does not deviate from the truth. A cottage in the wild woods—solitude and love—the world forgetting, by the world forgot—the deer come skipping by—the red Indian brings game, and lays it at her feet—how pretty and how romantic! And for the first few months, perhaps the first year, all goes well; but how goes it the next, and the next? I have observed with regard to the women who come out, that they do well enough the first year, and some even the second; but the third is generally fatal: and the worst with you women—or the best shall I not say?—is, that you cannot, and do not, forget domestic ties left behind. We men go out upon our land, or to the chase, and the women, poor souls, sit, and sew, and *think*. You have seen Mrs A. and Mrs B., who came out here, as I well remember, full of health and bloom—what are they now? premature old women, sickly, careworn, without nerve or cheerfulness:—and as for C, who brought his wife to his place by Lake Simcoe only three years ago, I hear the poor fellow must sell all off, or see his wife perish before his eyes. Would you have me risk the alternative? Or perhaps you will say, marry one of the women of the country—one of the daughters *of the bush*. No, I cannot; I must have something different. I may not have been particularly fortunate, but the women I have seen are in general coarse and narrow-minded, with no education whatever, or with an education which apes all I most dislike, and omits all I could admire in the fashionable education of the old country. What could I do with such women? In the former I might find an upper servant, but no companion—in the other, neither companionship nor help!'

To this discontented and fastidious gentleman I ventured to recommend two or three very amiable girls I had known at Toronto and Niagara; and I told him, too, that among the beautiful and spirited girls of New England he might also find what would answer his purpose. But with regard to Englishwomen of that grade in station and education, and personal attraction, which would content him, I could not well speak; not because I knew of none who united grace of person and lively talents with capabilities of strong affection, ay, and sufficient energy of character to meet trials and endure privations; but in women, as now educated, there is a strength of local habits and attachments, a want of cheerful self-dependence, a cherished physical delicacy, a weakness of temperament,—deemed, and falsely deemed, in deference to the pride of

6 The Italian song she sings begins, 'To you, O love'.

man, essential to feminine grace and refinement,—altogether unfitting them for a life which were otherwise delightful:—the active out-of-door life in which she must share and sympathise, and the in-door occupations which in England are considered servile; for a woman who cannot perform for herself and others all household offices, has no business here. But when I hear some men declare that they cannot endure to see women eat, and others speak of brilliant health and strength in young girls as being rude and vulgar, with various notions of the same kind too grossly absurd and perverted even for ridicule, I cannot wonder at any nonsensical affectations I meet with in my own sex; nor do otherwise than pity the mistakes and deficiencies of those who are sagely brought up with the one end and aim—to get married. As you always used to say, 'Let there be a demand for a better article, and a better article will be supplied.'

* * *

1838

Thomas Chandler Haliburton

1796–1865

Early Humour

The kind of comic writing that emerged in nineteenth-century North America drew on British traditions—especially the humorous sketches and biting satire of the eighteenth century—while at the same time responding to the colonial and wilderness experience that produced an interest in the tall tale, a fascination with the way formal language breaks down and reconstitutes itself in new societies, and concerns about the social and cultural changes being brought about by a new location. As can be seen in Thomas Chandler Haliburton's clockmaker sketches, this meeting of the Old World with the New could produce a humour pulled between two poles: a half-ironic longing for the values, customs, and sophistication of the Empire joined with an admiration for the new freedoms that crossed class boundaries and challenged status quo. With his irreverent tone and his use for comic effect of broad dialect, of folk and oral traditions, and of the eccentric character type known in America as 'an original', Haliburton became one of the key figures in the emergence of the new North American literary humour, influencing, among others, Mark Twain (who called Haliburton 'the father of American humor').

Addressing readers who were first of all the colonists themselves, rather than a distant audience 'back home', Haliburton employed this new humour in its satiric mode, using it for social commentary. In contrast to the gentler comedy favoured by some American contemporaries such as Washington Irving, who celebrated more than criticized his new postcolonial society and its values, Haliburton attacked the complacent acceptance of things as they were. At the same time, he didn't, in the fashion of many satirists, look back to a past era whose values had been better. In contrast to the more conservative satire of *The Mephibosheth Stepsure Letters* (originally published serially in

1821–2), created by his fellow Nova Scotian Dr Thomas McCulloch, Haliburton's sketches were aimed at encouraging the advancement of his colonial society. While Haliburton's humour did set the old and the new in opposition, he was willing to affirm what he saw as admirable in the new ways and, as he continued his dramatizations of the rough, even uncultured, aspects of the emerging North American code embodied by his American salesman Sam Slick, he increasingly found things worth valuing.

Satire has been a more important form in Canada than in the United States. From earlier Canadian writers like Haliburton, McCulloch, and Stephen Leacock, through later fiction writers and poets like W.O. Mitchell, Mordecai Richler, Robert Kroetsch, Jack Hodgins, Aritha van Herk, and Lorna Crozier and, more recently, in the edgy TV and pop culture satirists and comedians for which Canada has become well known, Canadian humorists have developed a reputation for an iconoclastic ability to look sidelong at things and see them fresh: as perennial outsiders, they call attention to what society at large has too often been willing to ignore.

Thomas Chandler Haliburton

Born in Windsor, NS, of old Loyalist stock, Haliburton grew up in a colony that seemed to him a well-established society on the eve of its industrial age. He was eager to participate in Nova Scotia's future development and in righting its social inequities: his education at King's College in Windsor, the accepted preparation for a young Anglican Tory professional, was a means of readying himself for his place in society, and after establishing a successful law practice in Annapolis Royal, he became a member of the legislative assembly, where he argued for various social and governmental reforms that were intended to maintain the strong colonial relationship with England. He lacked political effectiveness, however: a man of blunt and undiplomatic manners, he alienated the Tories, by supporting reforms, and the reformers, by arguing for close ties to the Empire. In 1829 he accepted a propitious call to the bench, taking the judgeship in the Court of Common Pleas that had recently been vacated after his father's death. In 1841 Haliburton became chief justice of the Supreme Court of Nova Scotia, a position he held until his retirement in 1856. As he grew older, Haliburton was attracted to Britain, and he moved there after his retirement. In England he took up politics once more, becoming a Conservative MP at the end of his life, often arguing in the British Parliament against the reforms he had supported as a young man.

Haliburton's first two books—*A General Description of Nova Scotia* (1823) and *An Historical and Statistical Account of Nova Scotia* (1829)—are not works of humour, but they do show his deep knowledge of, and wide-ranging interest in, the colony. By becoming a circuit judge Haliburton was able to learn still more of the particulars of daily life as he travelled widely through Nova Scotia—good preparation for his creation of Sam Slick, another circuit rider. Indeed, it was in his first years as a judge, when he was disenchanted with politics and convinced that the only changes of real importance would come through a transformation in the character of his countrymen (who struck him as apathetic) that Haliburton hit on the idea of writing satirical sketches that would hold up a mirror to Nova Scotians and goad them into action. To this end he created two principal characters, using their dialogues to debate his chief ideas. One of these was Sam Slick from Slickville, an American clock salesman who, though a trickster who could not be trusted, exemplified the new unrestrained individual and the virtues of 'Industry, Enterprise, Economy', qualities associated with, in Slick's phrase, the 'Go ahead' of American society. Haliburton's counterbalancing character was the Squire, a representative of the old traditions of the British hierarchy—and of Haliburton's own Tory colonial ideals. Through their biting discussions about the somnambulant colonial society of Nova Scotia, their creator sought to awaken his readers to the charged political climate that followed the American and French Revolutions, to shake his fellow colonials from the stupor induced by their lack of enfranchisement and freedom, and to make them conscious of a middle way that blended the opposing values of revolution and empire by marrying energy and assertiveness with moral behaviour. These sketches unite Burkeian Tory principles such as stability, respect for law, and fair-mindedness, with an appreciation of the attributes Haliburton most admired in New Englanders, their outspoken self-confidence, adaptability, and work ethic.

The Clockmaker sketches began to appear in 1835 in *The Nova Scotian*, a newspaper edited by Joseph Howe, a friend and a reformer with whom Haliburton had once been politically allied. In 1836 Howe gathered thirty-three of the sketches and published *The Clockmaker; or, The Sayings and Doings of Samuel Slick, of Slickville*, the first of what eventually became eleven volumes chronicling Slick. Their success was such that in 1858 Haliburton became the first colonial to be given an honorary degree for literary merit by Oxford University. Within fifty years of the Yankee clock pedlar's first appearance there were more than a hundred editions of these books, and Haliburton was being read not only in Canada, England, and the United States but, in translation, in France and Germany, making him the first Canadian author to gain an international readership.

As the years passed, Haliburton's humour became less satiric and the clockmaker less morally complex. By the time Haliburton published his last set of sketches, *The Old Judge; or, Life in a Colony* (1849), a book notable for its observations of society, Sam Slick had disappeared altogether, and the presentation of Nova Scotian life had become a sympathetic one.

The Trotting Horse

I was always well mounted. I am fond of a horse, and always piqued[1] myself on having the fastest trotter in the Province. I have made no great progress in the world. I feel doubly, therefore, the pleasure of not being surpassed on the road. I never feel so well or so cheerful as on horseback, for there is something exhilarating in quick motion; and, old as I am, I feel a pleasure in making any person whom I meet on the way put his horse to the full gallop, to keep pace with my trotter. Poor Ethiope! You recollect him, how he was wont to lay back his ears on his arched neck, and push away from all competition. He is done, poor fellow! The spavin[2] spoiled his speed, and he now roams at large upon 'my farm at Truro'. Mohawk never failed me till this summer.

I pride myself (you may laugh at such childish weaknesses in a man of my age), but still I pride myself in taking the conceit out of coxcombs I meet on the road, and on the ease with which I can leave a fool behind, whose nonsense disturbs my solitary musings.

On my last journey to Fort Lawrence, as the beautiful view of Colchester had just opened upon me, and as I was contemplating its richness and exquisite scenery, a tall thin man, with hollow cheeks and bright twinkling black eyes, on a good bay horse, somewhat out of condition, overtook me; and drawing up, said, 'I say, stranger, I guess you started early this morning, didn't you?' 'I did sir,' I replied. 'You did not come from Halifax, I presume, sir, did you?' in a dialect too rich to be mistaken as genu*ine* Yankee. 'And which way may you be travelling?' asked my inquisitive companion. 'To Fort Lawrence.' 'Ah!' said he, 'so am I, it is *in my circuit*.'[3] The word *circuit* sounded so professional, I looked again at him to ascertain whether I had ever seen him before,

1 Prided.
2 A bony tumour on a horse's leg, which causes inflammation and pain.
3 The regular journey through an area made by certain itinerant professionals such as preachers and judges.

or whether I had met with one of those nameless but innumerable limbs of the law who now flourish in every district of the Province. There was a keenness about his eye, and an acuteness of expression, much in favour of the law; but the dress, and general bearing of the man, made against the supposition. His was not the coat of a man who can afford to wear an old coat, nor was it one of 'Tempest and More's' that distinguish country lawyers from country boobies. His clothes were well made, and of good materials, but looked as if their owner had shrunk a little since they were made for him; they hung somewhat loose on him. A large brooch, and some superfluous seals and gold keys, which ornamented his outward man, looked 'New England' like. A visit to the States had, perhaps, I thought, turned this Colchester beau into a Yankee fop. Of what consequence was it to me who he was—in either case I had nothing to do with him, and I desired neither his acquaintance nor his company—still I could not but ask myself who can this man be? 'I am not aware', said I, 'that there is a court sitting at this time at Cumberland?' 'Nor am I,' said my friend. What then could he have to do with the circuit? It occurred to me he must be a Methodist preacher. I looked again, but his appearance again puzzled me. His attire might do—the colour might be suitable—the broad brim not out of place; but there was a want of that staidness of look, that seriousness of countenance, that expression, in short, so characteristic of the clergy.

I could not account for my idle curiosity—a curiosity which, in him, I had the moment before viewed both with suspicion and disgust; but so it was—I felt a desire to know who he could be who was neither lawyer nor preacher, and yet talked of his *circuit* with the gravity of both. How ridiculous, I thought to myself, is this; I will leave him. Turning towards him, I said, I feared I should be late for breakfast, and must, therefore, bid him good morning. Mohawk felt the pressure of my knees, and away we went at a slapping pace. I congratulated myself on conquering my own curiosity, and on avoiding that of my travelling companion. This, I said to myself, this is the value of a good horse; I patted his neck—I felt proud of him. Presently I heard the steps of the unknown's horse—the clatter increased. Ah, my friend, thought I, it won't do; you should be well mounted if you desire my company; I pushed Mohawk faster, faster, faster—to his best. He outdid himself; he had never trotted so handsomely—so easily—so well.

'I guess that is a pretty considerable smart horse,' said the stranger as he came beside me, and apparently reined in, to prevent his horse passing me. 'There is not, I reckon, so spry a one on *my circuit*.'

Circuit, or no circuit, one thing was settled in my mind; he was a Yankee, and a very impertinent Yankee too. I felt humbled, my pride was hurt, and Mohawk was beaten. To continue this trotting contest was humiliating; I yielded, therefore, before the victory was palpable, and pulled up.

'Yes,' continued he, 'a horse of pretty considerable good action, and a pretty fair trotter, too, I guess.' Pride must have a fall—I confess mine was prostrate in the dust. These words cut me to the heart. What! is it come to this, poor Mohawk, that you, the admiration of all but the envious, the great Mohawk, the standard by which all other horses are measured—trots next to Mohawk, only yields to Mohawk, looks like

Mohawk—that you are, after all, only a counterfeit, and pronounced by a straggling Yankee to be merely a 'pretty fair trotter'!

'If he was trained, I guess that he might be made to do a little more. Excuse me, but if you divide your weight between the knee and the stirrup, rather most on the knee, and rise forward on the saddle, so as to leave a little daylight between you and it, I hope I may never ride *this circuit again*, if you don't get a mile more an hour out of him.'

What! not enough, I mentally groaned, to have my horse beaten, but I must be told that I don't know how to ride him; and that, too, by a Yankee. Aye, there's the rub—a Yankee what? Perhaps a half-bred puppy, half yankee, half blue-nose.[4] As there is no escape, I'll try to make out my riding master. '*Your circuit*', said I, my looks expressing all the surprise they were capable of—'your circuit, pray what may that be?' 'Oh,' said he, 'the eastern circuit—I am on the eastern circuit, sir.' 'I have heard,' said I, feeling that I now had a lawyer to deal with, 'that there is a great deal of business on this circuit—pray, are there many cases of importance?' 'There is a pretty fair business to be done, at least there has been,' said he, 'but the cases are of no great value—we don't make much out of them. We get them up very easy, but they don't bring much profit.' What a beast, thought I, is this; and what a curse to a country, to have such an unfeeling pettifogging rascal practising in it—a horse jockey,[5] too, what a finished character! I'll try him on that branch of his business.

'That is a superior animal you are mounted on,' said I. 'I seldom meet one that can keep pace with mine.' 'Yes,' said he coolly, 'a considerable fair traveller, and most particular good bottom.'[6] I hesitated: this man who talks with such unblushing effrontery of getting up cases, and making profit out of them, cannot be offended at the question—yes, I will put it to him. 'Do you feel an inclination to part with him?' 'I never part with a horse, sir, that suits me,' said he. 'I am fond of a horse—I don't like to ride in the dust after every one I meet, and I allow no man to pass me but when I choose.' Is it possible, I thought, that he can know me? that he has heard of my foible, and is quizzing[7] me, or have I this feeling in common with him? 'But', continued I, 'you might supply yourself again.' 'Not on *this circuit*, I guess,' said he, 'nor yet in Campbell's circuit.' 'Campbell's circuit—pray, sir, what is that?' 'That', said he, 'is the western—and Lampton rides the shore circuit; and as for the people on the shore, they know so little of horses that Lampton tells me a man from Aylesford once sold a hornless ox there, whose tail he had cut and nicked, for a horse of the Goliath breed.' 'I should think', said I, 'that Mr Lampton must have no lack of cases among such enlightened clients.' 'Clients, sir!' said my friend, 'Mr Lampton is not a lawyer.' 'I beg pardon, I though you said he rode the *circuit*.' 'We call it a circuit,' said the stranger, who seemed by no means flattered by the mistake. 'We divide the Province, as in the Almanack, into circuits, in each of which we separately carry on our business of manufacturing and selling clocks. There are few, I guess,' said the Clockmaker, 'who go upon

4 A Nova Scotian is 'known throughout America as Mr Blue Nose, a sobriquet acquired from a superior potato of that name' (Haliburton's Preface to The Old Judge).

5 Horse trader.

6 Physical endurance; strength.

7 Mocking.

tick[8] as much as we do, who have so little use for lawyers. If attornies could wind a *man up again*, after he has been fairly *run down*, I guess they'd be a pretty harmless sort of folks.'

This explanation restored my good humour, and as I could not quit my companion, and he did not feel disposed to leave, I made up my mind to travel with him to Fort Lawrence, the limit of *his circuit.*

8 To be 'on tick' has two idiomatic meaings, both available here: 'punctually' and 'on credit'.

The Clockmaker

I had heard of Yankee clock pedlars, tin pedlars, and bible pedlars, especially of him who sold Polyglot Bibles[1] (*all in English*) to the amount of sixteen thousand pounds. The house of every substantial farmer had three substantial ornaments, a wooden clock, a tin reflector, and a Polyglot Bible. How is it that an American can sell his wares, at whatever price he pleases, where a blue-nose would fail to make a sale at all? I will inquire of the Clockmaker the secret of his success.

'What a pity it is, Mr *Slick*,' (for such was his name), 'what a pity it is', said I, 'that you, who are so successful in teaching these people the value of *clocks*, could not also teach them the value of *time*.' 'I guess', said he, 'they have got that ring to grow on their horns yet,[2] which every four-year-old has in our country. We reckon hours and minutes to be dollars and cents. They do nothin in these parts but eat, drink, smoke, sleep, ride about, lounge at taverns, make speeches at temperance meetings, and talk about "*House of Assembly*". If a man don't hoe his corn, and he don't get a crop, he says it is all owin to the Bank; and if he runs into debt and is sued, why he says lawyers are a cuss to the country. They are a most idle set of folks, I tell *you*.'

'But how is it', said I, 'that you manage to sell such an immense number of clocks (which certainly cannot be called necessary articles) among a people with whom there seems to be so great a scarcity of money?'

Mr Slick paused, as if considering the propriety of answering the question, and looking me in the face, said, in a confidential tone, 'Why I don't care if I do tell you, for the market is glutted, and I shall quit this circuit. It is done by a knowledge of *soft sawder* and *human natur*. But here is Deacon Flint's,' said he. 'I have but one clock left, and I guess I will sell it to him.'

At the gate of a most comfortable-looking farmhouse stood Deacon Flint, a respectable old man, who had understood the value of time better than most of his neighbours, if one might judge from the appearance of everything about him. After the usual salutation, an invitation to 'alight' was accepted by Mr Slick, who said he wished to take leave of Mrs Flint before he left Colchester.

1 Bibles published in several Biblical languages as well as in modern translation; used to settle textual disputes; 'tin reflector': a reflector placed behind a candle to allow it to serve as a lamp.

2 Cattle and oxen grow rings on their horns as they mature.

We had hardly entered the house before the Clockmaker pointed to the view from the window, and addressing himself to me, said, 'If I was to tell them in Connecticut there was such a farm as this away down east here in Nova Scotia, they wouldn't believe me—why there ain't such a location in all New England. The deacon has a hundred acres of dyke.'[3] 'Seventy,' said the Deacon, 'only seventy.' 'Well, seventy; but then there is your fine deep bottom. Why I could run a ramrod into it.' 'Interval, we call it,' said the Deacon, who, though evidently pleased at this eulogium,[4] seemed to wish the experiment of the ramrod to be tried in the right place. 'Well, interval if you please (though Professor Eleazer Cumstick, in his work on Ohio, calls them bottoms) is just as good as dyke. Then there is that water privilege,[5] worth 3,000 or 4,000 dollars, twice as good as what Governor Cass paid 15,000 dollars for.[6] I wonder, Deacon, you don't put up a carding mill[7] on it: the same works would carry a turning lathe, a shingle machine, a circular saw, grind bark, and—' 'Too old,' said the Deacon, 'too old for all those speculations.' 'Old,' repeated the Clockmaker, 'not you; why you are worth half a dozen of the young men we see now-a-days; you are young enough to have—' Here he said something in a lower tone of voice, which I did not distinctly hear; but whatever it was, the Deacon was pleased. He smiled, and said he did not think of such things now.

'But your beasts, dear me, your beasts must be put in and have a feed,' saying which he went out to order them to be taken to the stable.

As the old gentleman closed the door after him, Mr Slick drew near to me, and said in an undertone, 'Now that is what I call "*soft sawder*". An Englishman would pass that man as a sheep passes a hog in a pastur, without lookin at him. Or,' said he, looking rather archly, 'if he was mounted on a pretty smart horse, I guess he'd trot away, *if he could.* Now I find—' Here his lecture on '*soft sawder*' was cut short by the entrance of Mrs Flint. 'Jist come to say goodbye, Mrs Flint.' 'What, have you sold all your clocks?' 'Yes, and very low, too, for money is scarce, and I wished to close the consarn.[8] No, I am wrong in saying all, for I have jist one left. Neighbour Steel's wife asked to have the refusal of it, but I guess I won't sell it. I had but two of them, this one and the feller of it that I sold Governor Lincoln.[9] General Green, the Secretary of State for Maine, said he'd give me 50 dollars for this here one—it has composition wheels and patent axles, it is a beautiful article—a real first chop[10]—no mistake. Genuine superfine. But I guess I'll take it back; and beside, Squire Hawk might think kinder harder that I didn't give him the offer.' 'Dear me,' said Mrs Flint, 'I should like to see it. Where is it?' 'It is in a chist of mine over the way, at Tom Tape's store. I guess he can ship it on to Eastport.' 'That's a good man,' said Mrs Flint, 'jist let's look at it.'

3 Land built up to hold water back; a 'bottom' or an 'interval' is low-lying land, usually along a river.
4 Formal expression of praise.
5 Right to use water, especially running water to turn machinery.
6 A governor of the territory of Michigan who paid $12,000 for 500 acres at the mouth of the Detroit River; though the sum was deemed exorbitant at the time, the property made the governor's personal fortune.
7 Mill for combing and cleansing raw wool.
8 Concern.
9 Fourth governor of Maine, 1827–9.
10 First-rate article.

Mr Slick, willing to oblige, yielded to these entreaties, and soon produced the clock—a gawdy, highly varnished, trumpery looking affair. He placed it on the chimney-piece, where its beauties were pointed out and duly appreciated by Mrs Flint, whose admiration was about ending in a proposal, when Mr Flint returned from giving his directions about the care of the horses. The Deacon praised the clock. He too thought it a handsome one; but the Deacon was a prudent man, he had a watch—he was sorry, but he had no occasion for a clock. 'I guess you're in the wrong furrow this time, Deacon, it an't for sale,' said Mr Slick. 'And if it was, I reckon neighbour Steel's wife would have it, for she gives me no peace about it.' Mrs Flint said that Mr Steel had enough to do, poor man, to pay his interest, without buying clocks for his wife. 'It's no consarn of mine,' said Mr Slick, 'so long as he pays me what he has to do. But I guess I don't want to sell it, and besides it comes too high; that clock can't be made at Rhode Island under 40 dollars. Why it an't possible,' said the Clockmaker, in apparent surprise, looking at his watch, 'why as I'm alive, it is 4 o'clock, and if I hav'nt been two blessed hours here—how on airth shall I reach River Philip tonight? I'll tell you what, Mrs Flint, I'll leave the clock in your care till I return on my way to the States—I'll set it a goin, and put it to the right time.'

As soon as this operation was performed, he delivered the key to the Deacon with a sort of serio-comic injunction to wind up the clock every Saturday night, which Mrs Flint said she would take care should be done, and promised to remind her husband of it in case he should chance to forget it.

'That,' said the Clockmaker, as soon as we were mounted, 'that I call "*human natur*"! Now that clock is sold for 40 dollars—it cost me jist 6 dollars and 50 cents. Mrs Flint will never let Mrs Steel have the refusal—nor will the Deacon larn, until I call for the clock, that having once indulged in the use of a superfluity, how difficult it is to give it up. We can do without any article of luxury we have never had, but when once obtained, it isn't "*in human natur*" to surrender it voluntarily. Of fifteen thousand sold by myself and partners in this Province, twelve thousand were left in this manner, and only ten clocks were ever returned—when we called for them, they invariably bought them. We trust to "*soft sawder*" to get them into the house, and to "human natur" that they never come out of it.

1836

Catharine Parr Traill

1802–1899

Pioneer Memoirs

Pioneer memoirs are a non-fiction genre that enjoyed some popularity in the nineteenth and early twentieth centuries. A form that sometimes lacks dramatic shape, the account of a pioneer is usually a story of hardship and struggle against nature. Its appeal is its realistic representation of an experience that is often shared by its readers, either first-hand or in family memory. Unlike the explorers' stories of extreme privation in what seemed to Europeans a virtually uninhabitable landscape, and in contrast to the traveller's tale of romantic and exotic trips, the pioneer memoir tends to be a narrative of the ordinary marked by long years of repetitious combat against the environment—an enemy that can also be a friend and resource. It is the story of human spirit exposed to Job-like trials by nature and climate. The tendency in recent years to refer to these memoirs as 'settlement narratives' emphasizes the way these individual accounts have come to be seen as representative of a collective experience in the development of a nation. Their later fictional equivalent in Canada is the pioneer novel, a form made popular by several early twentieth-century prairie authors, including Martha Ostenso (in *Wild Geese*, 1925), Robert Stead (see especially *Grain*, 1926), and Frederick Philip Grove in his several accounts of the life of Manitoba farmers (such as *Fruits of the Earth*, 1933).

Catharine Parr Traill

Catharine Strickland was born in London into a large and literary family. Writing as Catharine Parr Traill she became one of three siblings to provide accounts of pioneer experience in nineteenth-century Canada. Her brother Samuel Strickland was the author of *Twenty-seven Years in Canada West* (1853), while her younger sister, Susanna Moodie, became famous as the author of *Roughing It in the Bush* (1852). It was through Susanna and her new husband, Lieut. John Moodie, that Catharine first met Lieut. Thomas Traill, a half-pay officer. The Traills were married in 1832, and both they and the Moodies emigrated to Upper Canada in that year, departing within a week of one another. The Traills settled in Douro Township (near Peterborough), at Rice Lake; their farm was next to that of Samuel Strickland, who had preceded them in 1825.

By the time she came to Canada, Catharine Traill had already written children's stories as well as a book on her future homeland—*The Young Emigrants; or, Pictures of Canada* (1826), based on the experiences of family friends and on information from travel books. Four years after her arrival she published *The Backwoods of Canada* (1836), a work drawing on letters she had written home. It was undertaken, as she later said, 'with the view of preparing females of my class . . . for the changes that awaited them in the life of a Canadian emigrant's wife'. In 1852 she published a children's book about her adopted country, *Canadian Crusoes*, which remains interesting both for its idealized treatment of the union in Canada of English and French, Scots and Indians, and also because Crusoe, like Noah, has been an emblematic figure in Canadian writing: the individual who carries with him and re-creates the civilization from which he has been separated. In 1854 Traill published *The Female Emigrant's Guide* (reprinted as *The Canadian Settler's Guide*), a work that continues the project begun in *The Backwoods of Canada* of conveying to emigrating gentlewomen the knowledge Traill won through hard experience. Already interested in nature, she displayed considerable talents as a naturalist once in Canada, collecting and cataloguing the plant life she found around her. Her chapter on flowers in *The Backwoods of Canada* and in such later studies as *Canadian Wild Flowers* (1869) and

Studies of Plant Life in Canada (1885) are botanical landmarks. Traill, whose life spanned the nineteenth century, continued to write even into her nineties: *Pearls and Pebbles; or, Notes of an Old Naturalist* was published when she was ninety-two.

The Backwoods of Canada is often contrasted with Susanna Moodie's *Roughing It in the Bush.* Though Traill, like her younger sister, does tell of many hardships, her overall outlook is much more optimistic. Indeed, she so buoyed the despairing Susanna's spirits that Moodie writes midway through *Roughing It*: 'My conversation with her [Catharine] had quite altered the aspect of the country, and predisposed me to view things in the most favourable light.' Traill saw the pleasanter traits of nature as expressing God's benevolence, and she believed that in adversity the individual's duty to self and to God lay in strong-willed determination: 'In cases of emergency, it is folly to fold one's hands and sit down to bewail in abject terror: it is better to be up and doing' (*The Female Emigrant's Guide*). Hers was clearly an attitude valuable to new pioneers; lacking it, they tended, as she observed, to 'blame the Colony for the failure of the individual'. In *The Diviners* (1974) Margaret Laurence has her central character enter into imaginary dialogues with Catharine Traill, even to the point of invoking her: 'Saint Catharine: Where are you now that we need you?'

From *The Backwoods of Canada*

LETTER IX

Lake House
April 18, 1833

But it is time that I should give you some account of our log-house, into which we moved a few days before Christmas. Many unlooked-for delays having hindered its completion before that time, I began to think it would never be habitable.

The first misfortune that happened was the loss of a fine yoke of oxen that were purchased to draw in the house-logs, that is, the logs for raising the walls of the house. Not regarding the bush as pleasant as their former master's cleared pastures, or perhaps foreseeing some hard work to come, early one morning they took into their heads to ford the lake at the head of the rapids, and march off, leaving no trace of their route excepting their footing at the water's edge. After many days spent in vain search for them, the work was at a stand, and for one month they were gone, and we began to give up all expectation of hearing any news of them. At last we learned they were some twenty miles off, in a distant township, having made their way through bush and swamp, creek and lake, back to their former owner, with an instinct that supplied to them the want of roads and compass.

Oxen have been known to traverse a tract of wild country to a distance of thirty or forty miles going in a direct line for their former haunts by unknown paths, where memory could not avail them. In the dog we consider it is scent as well as memory that guides him to his far-off home;—but how is this conduct of the oxen to be accounted for? They returned home through the mazes of interminable forests, where man, with all his reason and knowledge, would have been bewildered and lost.

It was the latter end of October before even the walls of our house were up. To effect this we called 'a bee'.[1] Sixteen of our neighbours cheerfully obeyed our summons;

1 Any gathering for communal work.

and though the day was far from favourable, so faithfully did our hive perform their tasks, that by night the outer walls were raised.

The work went merrily on with the help of plenty of Canadian nectar (whiskey), the honey that our *bees* are solaced with. Some huge joints of salt pork, a peck of potatoes, with a rice-pudding, and a loaf as big as an enormous Cheshire cheese, formed the feast that was to regale them during the raising. This was spread out in the shanty,[2] in a *very rural style*. In short, we laughed, and called it a *pic-nic in the backwoods*; and rude as was the fare, I can assure you, great was the satisfaction expressed by all the guests of every degree, our 'bee' being considered as very well conducted. In spite of the difference of rank among those that assisted at the bee, the greatest possible harmony prevailed, and the party separated well pleased with the day's work and entertainment.

The following day I went to survey the newly-raised edifice, but was sorely puzzled, as it presented very little appearance of a house. It was merely an oblong square of logs raised one above the other, with open spaces between every row of logs. The spaces for the doors and windows were not then chopped out, and the rafters were not up. In short, it looked a very queer sort of a place, and I returned home a little disappointed, and wondering that my husband should be so well pleased with the progress that had been made. A day or two after this I again visited it. The *sleepers*[3] were laid to support the floors, and the places for the doors and windows cut out of the solid timbers, so that it had not quite so much the look of a bird-cage as before.

After the roof was shingled, we were again at a stand, as no boards could be procured nearer than Peterborough, a long day's journey through horrible roads. At that time no saw-mill was in progress; now there is a fine one building within a little distance of us. Our flooring-boards were all to be sawn by hand, and it was some time before any one could be found to perform this necessary work, and that at high wages—six-and-sixpence per day. Well, the boards were at length down, but of course of unseasoned timber: this was unavoidable; so as they could not be planed we were obliged to put up with their rough unsightly appearance, for no better were to be had. I began to recall to mind the observation of the old gentleman with whom we travelled from Cobourg to Rice Lake.[4] We console ourselves with the prospect that by next summer the boards will all be seasoned, and then the house is to be turned topsy-turvy, by having the floors all relaid, jointed, and smoothed.

The next misfortune that happened, was, that the mixture of clay and lime that was to plaster the inside and outside of the house between the chinks of the logs was one night frozen to stone. Just as the work was about half completed, the frost suddenly setting in, put a stop to our proceeding for some time, as the frozen plaster

2 Used here in its French-Canadian sense: 'workshop'.

3 Supporting beams.

4 '"If you go into the backwoods your house must necessarily be a log-house," said an elderly gentleman, who had been a settler many years in the country, "for you will most probably be out of the way of a saw-mill, and you will find so much to do, and so many obstacles to encounter, for the first two or three years, that you will hardly have opportunity for carrying these improvements into effect.

'"There is an old saying," he added: . . . "'first creep and then go.' Matters are not carried on quite so easily here as at home. . . . At the end of ten or fifteen years you may begin to talk of these pretty improvements and elegancies and you will then be able to see a little what you are about. . . ."' (Letter V)

yielded neither to fire nor to hot water, the latter freezing before it had any effect on the mass, and rather making bad worse. Then the workman that was hewing the inside walls to make them smooth, wounded himself with the broad axe, and was unable to resume his work for some time.

I state these things merely to show the difficulties that attend us in the fulfilment of our plans, and this accounts in a great measure for the humble dwellings that settlers of the most respectable description are obliged to content themselves with at first coming to this country,—not, you may be assured, from inclination, but necessity: I could give you such narratives of this kind as would astonish you. After all, it serves to make us more satisfied than we should be on casting our eyes around to see few better off than we are, and many not half so comfortable, yet of equal, and, in some instances, superior pretensions as to station and fortune.

Every man in this country is his own glazier; this you will laugh at: but if he does not wish to see and feel the discomfort of broken panes, he must learn to put them in his windows with his own hands. Workmen are not easily to be had in the backwoods when you want them, and it would be preposterous to hire a man at high wages to make two days' journey to and from the nearest town to mend your windows. Boxes of glass of several different sizes are to be bought at a very cheap rate in the stores. My husband amused himself by glazing the windows of the house preparatory to their being fixed in.[5]

To understand the use of carpenter's tools, I assure you, is not despicable or useless kind of knowledge here. I would strongly recommend all young men coming to Canada to acquire a little acquaintance with this valuable art, as they will often be put to great inconvenience for the want of it.

I was once much amused with hearing the remarks made by a very fine lady, the reluctant sharer of her husband's emigration, on seeing the son of a naval officer of some rank in the service busily employed in making an axe-handle out of a piece of rock-elm.

'I wonder that you allow George to degrade himself so,' she said, addressing his father.

The captain looked up with surprise. 'Degrade himself? In what manner, madam? My boy neither swears, drinks whiskey, steals, nor tells lies.'

'But you allow him to perform tasks of the most menial kind. What is he now better than a hedge carpenter;[6] and I suppose you allow him to chop, too?'

'Most assuredly I do. That pile of logs in the cart there was all cut by him after he had left study yesterday,' was the reply.

'I would see my boys dead before they should use an axe like common labourers.'

'Idleness is the root of all evil,' said the captain. 'How much worse might my son be employed if he were running wild about the street with bad companions.'

'You will allow this is not a country for gentlemen or ladies to live in,' said the lady.

'It is the country for gentlemen that will not work and cannot live without, to starve in,' replied the captain bluntly; 'and for that reason I make my boys early accustom themselves to be usefully and actively employed.'

5 That is, he placed the glass in the window frames before putting the frames in place.
6 Fence repairer.

'My boys shall never work like common mechanics,'[7] said the lady, indignantly.

'Then, madam, they will be good for nothing as settlers; and it is a pity you dragged them across the Atlantic.'

'We were forced to come. We could not live as we had been used to do at home, or I never would have come to this horrid country.'

'Having come hither you would be wise to conform to circumstances. Canada is not the place for idle folks to retrench a lost fortune in. In some parts of the country you will find most articles of provision as dear as in London, clothing much dearer, and not so good, and a bad market to choose in.'

'I should like to know, then, who Canada is good for?' said she, angrily.

'It is a good country for the honest, industrious artisan. It is a fine country for the poor labourer, who, after a few years of hard toil, can sit down in his own log-house, and look abroad on his own land, and see his children well settled in life as independent freeholders.[8] It is a grand country for the rich speculator, who can afford to lay out a large sum in purchasing land in eligible situations; for if he have any judgment, he will make a hundred per cent as interest for his money after waiting a few years. But it is a hard country for the poor gentleman, whose habits have rendered him unfit for manual labour. He brings with him a mind unfitted to his situation; and even if necessity compels him to exertion, his labour is of little value. He has a hard struggle to live. The certain expenses of wages and living are great, and he is obliged to endure many privations if he would keep within compass, and be free of debt. If he have a large family, and brings them up wisely, so as to adapt themselves early to a settler's life, why he does well for them, and soon feels the benefit on his own land; but if he is idle himself, his wife extravagant and discontented, and the children taught to despise labour, why, madam, they will soon be brought down to ruin. In short, the country is a good country for those to whom it is adapted; but if people will not conform to the doctrine of necessity and expediency, they have no business in it. It is plain Canada is not adapted to every class of people.'

'It was never adapted for me or my family,' said the lady, disdainfully.

'Very true,' was the laconic reply; and so ended the dialogue.

But while I have been recounting these remarks, I have wandered far from my original subject, and left my poor log-house quite in an unfinished state. At last I was told it was in a habitable condition, and I was soon engaged in all the bustle and fatigue attendant on removing our household goods. We received all the assistance we required from ———, who is ever ready and willing to help us. He laughed and called it a '*moving* bee'; I said it was a 'fixing bee'; and my husband said it was a 'settling bee'; I know we were unsettled enough till it was over. What a din of desolation is a small house, or any house under such circumstances. The idea of chaos[9] must have been taken from a removal or a setting to rights, for I suppose the ancients had their *flitting*,[10] as the Scotch call it, as well as the moderns.

7 Manual labourers.
8 Those that own land without restrictions on its sale or use.
9 That is, the ancient idea that chaos preceded and furnished the materials for the creation of the world.
10 Moving from place to place.

Various were the valuable articles of crockery-ware that perished in their short but rough journey through the woods. Peace to their manes.[11] I had a good helper in my Irish maid, who soon roused up famous fires, and set the house in order.

We have not got quite comfortably settled, and I shall give you a description of our little dwelling. What is finished is only a part of the original plan; the rest must be added next spring, or fall, as circumstances may suit.

A nice small sitting-room with a store closet, a kitchen, pantry, and bed-chamber form the ground floor; there is a good upper floor that will make three sleeping-rooms.

'What a nut-shell!' I think I hear you exclaim. So it is at present; but we purpose adding a handsome frame front as soon as we can get boards from the mill, which will give us another parlour, long hall, and good spare bed-room. The windows and glass door of our present sitting-room command pleasant lake-views to the west and south. When the house is completed, we shall have a verandah in front; and at the south side, which forms an agreeable addition in the summer, being used as a sort of outer room, in which we can dine, and have the advantage of cool air, protected from the glare of the sunbeams. The Canadians call these verandahs 'stoups'. Few houses, either log or frame, are without them. The pillars look extremely pretty, wreathed with the luxuriant hop-vine, mixed with the scarlet creeper and 'morning glory', the American name for the most splendid of major convolvuluses. These stoups are really a considerable ornament, as they conceal in a great measure the rough logs, and break the barnlike form of the building.

Our parlour is warmed by a handsome Franklin stove with brass galley, and fender. Our furniture consists of a brass-railed sofa, which serves upon occasion for a bed, Canadian painted chairs, a stained pine table, green and white curtains, and a handsome Indian mat that covers the floor. One side of the room is filled up with our books. Some large maps and a few good prints nearly conceal the rough wall, and form the decoration of our little dwelling. Our bed-chamber is furnished with equal simplicity. We do not, however, lack comfort in our humble home; and though it is not exactly such as we could wish, it is as good as, under existing circumstances, we could have.

* * *

11 Spirits (Latin: the deified souls of departed ancestors).

LETTER X

Lake House
May the 9th, 1833

* * *

Though the Canadian winter has its disadvantages, it also has its charms. After a day or two of heavy snow the sky brightens, and the air becomes exquisitely clear and free from vapour; the smoke ascends in tall spiral columns till it is lost: seen against the saffron-tinted sky of an evening, or early of a clear morning, when the hoar-frost sparkles on the trees, the effect is singularly beautiful.

I enjoy a walk in the woods of a bright winter-day, when not a cloud, or the faint shadow of a cloud, obscures the soft azure of the heavens above; when but for the silver covering of the earth I might look upwards to the cloudless sky and say, 'It is June, sweet June.' The evergreens, as the pines, cedars, hemlock, and balsam firs, are bending their pendent branches, loaded with snow, which the least motion scatters in a mimic shower around, but so light and dry is it that it is shaken off without the slightest inconvenience.

The tops of the stumps look quite pretty, with their turbans of snow; a blackened pine-stump, with its white cap and mantle, will often startle you into the belief that some one is approaching you thus fancifully attired. As to ghosts or spirits they appear totally banished from Canada. This is too matter-of-fact country for such supernaturals to visit. Here there are no historical associations, no legendary tales of those that came before us. Fancy would starve for lack of marvellous food to keep her alive in the backwoods. We have neither fay nor fairy, ghost nor bogle,[1] satyr nor wood-nymph; our very forests disdain to shelter dryad or hamadryad. No naiad haunts the rushy margin of our lakes, or hallows with her presence our forest-rills. No Druid claims our oaks; and instead of poring with mysterious awe among our curious limestone rocks, that are often singularly grouped together, we refer them to the geologist to exercise his skill in accounting for their appearance: instead of investing them with the solemn characters of ancient temples or heathen altars, we look upon them with the curious eye of natural philosophy alone.

Even the Irish and Highlanders of the humblest class seem to lay aside their ancient superstitions on becoming denizens of the woods of Canada. I heard a friend exclaim, when speaking of the want of interest this country possessed, 'It is the most unpoetical of all lands; there is no scope for imagination; here all is new—the very soil seems newly formed; there is no hoary ancient grandeur in these woods; no recollections of former deeds connected with the country. The only beings in which I take any interest are the Indians, and they want the warlike character and intelligence that I had pictured to myself they would possess.'

This was the lamentation of a poet. Now, the class of people to whom this country is so admirably adapted are formed of the unlettered and industrious labourers and artisans. They feel no regret that the land they labour on has not been celebrated by the pen of the historian or the lay of the poet. The earth yields her increase to them as freely as if it had been enriched by the blood of heroes. They would not spare the ancient oak from feelings of veneration, nor look upon it with regard for any thing but its use as timber. They have no time, even if they possessed the taste, to gaze abroad on the beauties of Nature, but their ignorance is bliss.

After all, these are imaginary evils, and can hardly be considered just causes for dislike to the country. They would excite little sympathy among every-day men and women, though doubtless they would have their weight with the more refined and intellectual members of society, who naturally would regret that taste, learning, and genius should be thrown out of its proper sphere.

1 Goblin; 'dryad' and 'hamadryad': wood nymphs; 'naiad': water nymph; 'Druid': primitive Celtic priest.

For myself, though I can easily enter into the feelings of the poet and the enthusiastic lover of the wild and the wonderful of historic lore, I can yet make myself very happy and contented in this country. If its volume of history is yet a blank, that of Nature is open, and eloquently marked by the finger of God; and from its pages I can extract a thousand sources of amusement and interest whenever I take my walks in the forest or by the borders of the lakes.

1836

Susanna Moodie

1803–1885

Susanna Moodie, like her older sister Catharine Parr Traill, began her literary career early, publishing her first novel by the time she was nineteen. She continued writing and published a collection of her poetry in 1831, the year she married John Dunbar Moodie, a retired army officer from the Orkneys. The couple immigrated to Canada in 1832, settling near Cobourg. After two difficult years they relocated to Douro Township to be closer to Susanna's brother Samuel Strickland and her sister Catharine. Farming was still so difficult, however, that only when Dunbar Moodie was recalled to active service because of the Rebellion of 1837 did the family gain some measure of financial security. When, in 1839, Mr Moodie was appointed sheriff of Victoria District (later Hastings County), it was with relief that the couple moved to Belleville, abandoning forever their attempts at managing a bush farm.

Once Mrs Moodie left rural life behind, she was able to return to her faltering literary career. Between 1829 and 1851 she contributed seventy-five poems and twenty pieces of prose to various magazines, including *The Canadian Literary Magazine, The North American Review*, and *The Literary Garland.* She integrated several of her published sketches into a larger narrative recounting her years of struggle as a farm wife, entitling it *Roughing It in the Bush; or, Forest Life in Canada*; it appeared in 1852. In Moodie's lifetime, this book was republished in several editions, the contents of which varied somewhat; in some later versions whole chapters were deleted. (In 1988, the Centre for Editing Early Canadian Texts brought out a scholarly edition of *Roughing It in the Bush.*) A sequel, *Life in the Clearings versus the Bush*, appeared in 1853. There Moodie explained that while *Roughing It* was intended 'to point out the error of gentlemen bringing delicate women and helpless children to toil in woods', she nevertheless affirmed 'the REAL benefits to be derived from a judicious choice of settlement in this great and rising country'. Moodie wrote very rapidly in the years that followed, turning out several novels and helping to fill the pages of *The Literary Garland* and other magazines. Most of what she wrote is little read today except *Roughing It*, to which is sometimes added *Life in the Clearings* and the introduction of her novel *Mark Hurdlestone* for its account of literary activity in Canada in 1853. Her letters and those of her husband have been preserved and published: Susanna's correspondence to friends and literary acquaintances was gathered as *Letters of a Lifetime* (1985), and the letters that she and her husband exchanged during their periods of separation (their existence was not known until 1987) were collected as *Letters of Love and Duty* (1993). These two volumes add considerable depth to our knowledge of Moodie and her social milieu.

Roughing It in the Bush, originally published in London, was not immediately popular in Canada, where it was not published until 1871. In a preface to that edition the author expressed her hard-won affection for her adopted country. Perhaps because of those comments, or because the events were now sufficiently distant, the book gained its Canadian readership at last. It has maintained one since, even though Moodie's real purpose in writing was to warn unwary immigrants about the deceptive appearances they would find in Canada. In fact, Moodie has become an archetype of the modern settler for modern Canadians—so much so that Margaret Atwood responded to her Canadian chronicles with a collection of poems, *The Journals of Susanna Moodie* (1970), which in its own way has become as much of a classic as *Roughing It*.

Moodie's book is made up of a series of anecdotes that reveal its author as a practised storyteller with a remarkable ability to convey the variety of characters she met in the bush by using their colourful, idiomatic speech in lively dialogue. As a whole, *Roughing It* takes the form of a complaint: a speech in Chapter 19 by an acquaintance seems almost to capture its essence: 'Bah!—The only consolation one feels for such annoyances is to complain. Oh, the woods!—the cursed woods!—how I wish I were out of them.' In her afterword to the *Journals* Atwood sees Moodie as 'divided down the middle'—an emblem of the 'violent duality' of Canada itself. Indeed, what most engages the modern reader is that, although Moodie reveals herself as melancholy, inflexible, and proud to the point of condescension, she still continues to struggle against the perpetual defeat of her hopes, all the while giving vent to a confused mixture of feelings. Combining in her narrative the perspective of the time of the events described with the 'reconciled' viewpoint of the older woman recalling those events, she shows us her exhilaration in small victories, a degree of pleasure in enduring painful experiences, and even the tearful sadness she felt at leaving the scene of her hardships. It is in watching Moodie make her choice and achieve—if almost despite herself—her reconciliation with the land that the greatest attraction of her story lies.

From *Roughing It in the Bush*

INTRODUCTION TO THE THIRD EDITION

In most instances, emigration is a matter of necessity, not of choice; and this is more especially true of the emigration of persons of respectable connections, or of any station or position in the world. Few educated persons, accustomed to the refinements and luxuries of European society, ever willingly relinquish those advantages, and place themselves beyond the protective influence of the wise and revered institutions of their native land, without the pressure of some urgent cause. Emigration may, indeed, generally be regarded as an act of severe duty, performed at the expense of personal enjoyment, and accompanied by the sacrifice of those local attachments which stamp the scenes amid which our childhood grew, in imperishable characters, upon the heart. Nor is it until adversity has pressed sorely upon the proud and wounded spirit of the well-educated sons and daughters of old but impoverished families, that they gird up the loins of the mind, and arm themselves with fortitude to meet and are the heart-breaking conflict.

The ordinary motive for the emigration of such persons may be summed up in a few brief words;—the emigrant's hope of bettering his condition, and of escaping from the vulgar sarcasms too often hurled at the less wealthy by the purse-proud, commonplace people of the world. But there is a higher motive still, which has its origin in that love of independence which springs up spontaneously in the breasts of the high-souled children of a glorious land. They cannot labour in a menial capacity in the country where they were born and educated to command. They can trace no difference between themselves and the more fortunate individuals of a race whose blood warms their veins, and whose name they bear. The want of wealth alone places an impassable barrier between them and the more favoured offspring of the same parent stock; and they go forth to make for themselves a new name and to find another country, to forget the past and to live in the future, to exult in the prospect of their children being free and the land of their adoption great.

The choice of the country to which they devote their talents and energies depends less upon their pecuniary means than upon the fancy of the emigrant or the popularity of a name. From the year 1826 to 1829, Australia and the Swan River were all the rage. No other portions of the habitable globe were deemed worthy of notice. These were the *El Dorados*[1] and land of Goshen to which all respectable emigrants eagerly flocked. Disappointment, as a matter of course, followed their high-raised expectations. Many of the most sanguine of these adventurers returned to their native shores in a worse condition than when they left them. In 1830, the great tide of emigration flowed westward. Canada became the great land-mark for the rich in hope and poor in purse. Public newspapers and private letters teemed with the unheard-of advantages to be derived from a settlement in this highly-favoured region.

Its salubrious climate, its fertile soil, commercial advantages, great water privileges, its proximity to the mother country, and last, not least, its almost total exemption from taxation—that bugbear which keeps honest John Bull in a state of constant ferment—were the theme of every tongue, and lauded beyond all praise. The general interest, once excited, was industriously kept alive by pamphlets, published by interested parties, which prominently set forth all the *good* to be derived from a settlement in the Backwoods of Canada; while they carefully concealed the toil and hardship to be endured in order to secure these advantages. They told of lands yielding forty bushels to the acre, but they said nothing of the years when these lands, with the most careful cultivation, would barely return fifteen; when rust and smut, engendered by the vicinity of damp over-hanging woods, would blast the fruits of the poor emigrant's labour, and almost deprive him of bread. They talked of log houses to be raised in a single day, by the generous exertions of friends and neighbours, but they never ventured upon a picture of the disgusting scenes of riot and low debauchery exhibited during the raising, or upon a description of the dwellings when raised—dens of dirt and misery, which would, in many instances, be shamed by an English pig-sty. The necessaries of life were described as inestimably cheap; but they forgot to add that in remote bush settlements, often twenty miles from a market town, and some of them even that distance from the nearest dwelling, the necessaries of life which would be deemed indispensable to the European, could not be procured at all, or, if obtained, could only

1 A fabled city of gold sought by early Spanish explorers of the New World. In the Book of Exodus, Goshen was the fertile land alloted the Israelites in Egypt, in which there was light during the plague of darkness; hence, a land of light and plenty.

be so by sending a man and team through a blazed forest road,—a process far too expensive for frequent repetition.

Oh, ye dealers in wild lands—ye speculators in the folly and credulity of your fellow-men—what a mass of misery, and of misrepresentation productive of that misery, have ye not to answer for! You had your acres to sell, and what to you were the worn-down frames and broken hearts of the infatuated purchasers? The public believed the plausible statements you made with such earnestness, and men of all grades rushed to hear your hired orators declaim upon the blessings to be obtained by the clearers of the wilderness.

Men who had been hopeless of supporting their families in comfort and independence at home, thought that they had only to come out to Canada to make their fortunes; almost even to realize the story told in the nursery, of the sheep and oxen that ran about the streets, ready roasted, and with knives and forks upon their backs. They were made to believe that if it did not actually rain gold, that precious metal could be obtained, as is now stated of California and Australia, by stooping to pick it up.

The infection became general. A Canada mania pervaded the middle ranks of British society; thousands and tens of thousands, for the space of three or four years, landed upon these shores. A large majority of the higher class were officers of the army and navy, with their families—a class perfectly unfitted by their previous habits and education for contending with the stern realities of emigrant life. The hand that has long held the sword, and been accustomed to receive implicit obedience from those under its control, is seldom adapted to wield the spade and guide the plough, or try its strength against the stubborn trees of the forest. Nor will such persons submit cheerfully to the saucy familiarity of servants, who, republicans in spirit, think themselves as good as their employers. Too many of these brave and honourable men were easy dupes to the designing land-speculators. Not having counted the cost, but only looked upon the bright side of the picture held up to their admiring gaze, they fell easily into the snares of their artful seducers.

To prove their zeal as colonists, they were induced to purchase large tracts of wild land in remote and unfavourable situations. This, while it impoverished and often proved the ruin of the unfortunate immigrant, possessed a double advantage to the seller. He obtained an exorbitant price for the land which he actually sold, while the residence of a respectable settler upon the spot greatly enhanced the value and price of all other lands in the neighbourhood.

It is not by such instruments as those I have just mentioned, that Providence works when it would reclaim the waste places of the earth, and make them subservient to the wants and happiness of its creatures. The Great Father of the souls and bodies of men knows the arm which wholesome labour from infancy has made strong, the nerves which have become iron by patient endurance, by exposure to weather, coarse fare, and rude shelter; and he chooses such, to send forth into the forest to hew out the rough paths for the advance of civilisation. These men become wealthy and prosperous, and form the bones and sinews of a great and rising country. Their labour is wealth, not exhaustion; its produce independence and content, not home-sickness and despair. What the Backwoods of Canada are to the industrious and ever-to-be-honoured sons of honest poverty, and what they are to the refined and accomplished gentleman, these simple sketches will endeavour to portray. They are drawn principally from my own experience, during a sojourn of nineteen years in the colony.

In order to diversify my subject, and make it as amusing as possible, I have between the sketches introduced a few small poems, all written during my residence in Canada, and descriptive of the country.

In this pleasing task I have been assisted by my husband, J.W. Dunbar Moodie, author of 'Ten Years in South Africa'.[2]

BELLEVILLE, UPPER CANADA

1854

2 Pubished in 1835, the story of Dunbar Moodie's years (1819–29) with his brother at his farm near Sellendam, South Africa.

I. A VISIT TO GROSSE ISLE

* * *

As the sun rose above the horizon, all these matter-of-fact circumstances were gradually forgotten and merged in the surpassing grandeur of the scene that rose majestically before me. The previous day had been dark and stormy; and a heavy fog had concealed the mountain chain, which forms the stupendous background to this sublime view, entirely from our sight. As the clouds rolled away from their grey, bald brows, and cast into denser shadow the vast forest belt that girdled them round, they loomed out like mighty giants—Titans of the earth, in all their rugged and awful beauty—a thrill of wonder and delight pervaded my mind. The spectacle floated dimly on my sight—my eyes were blinded with tears—blinded with the excess of beauty. I turned to the right and to the left, I looked up and down the glorious river; never had I beheld so many striking objects blended into one mighty whole! Nature had lavished all her noblest features in producing that enchanting scene.

The rocky isle in front, with its neat farm-houses at the eastern point, and its high bluff at the western extremity, crowned with the telegraph—the middle space occupied by tents and sheds for the cholera patients, and its wooded shores dotted over with motley groups—added greatly to the picturesque effect of the land scene. Then the broad glittering river, covered with boats darting to and fro, conveying passengers from twenty-five vessels, of various size and tonnage, which rode at anchor, with their flags flying from the mast-head, gave an air of life and interest to the whole. Turning to the south side of the St Lawrence, I was not less struck with its low fertile shores, white houses, and neat churches, whose slender spires and bright tin roofs shone like silver as they caught the first rays of the sun. As far as the eye could reach, a line of white buildings extended along the bank; their background formed by the purple hue of the dense, interminable forest. It was a scene unlike any I had ever beheld, and to which Britain contains no parallel. Mackenzie, an old Scotch dragoon, who was one of our passengers, when he rose in the morning and saw the parish of St Thomas for the first time, exclaimed: 'Weel, it beats a'! Can thae white clouts[1] be a' houses? They look like claes hung out to drie!' There was some truth in this odd comparison, and for some minutes I could scarcely convince myself that the white patches scattered so thickly over the opposite shore could be the dwellings of a busy, lively population.

'What sublime views of the north side of the river those *habitans* of St Thomas must enjoy,' thought I. Perhaps familiarity with the scene has rendered them indifferent to its astonishing beauty.

Eastward, the view down the St Lawrence towards the Gulf is the finest of all, scarcely surpassed by anything in the world. Your eye follows the long range of lofty mountains until their blue summits are blended and lost in the blue of the sky. Some of these, partially cleared round the base, are sprinkled over with neat cottages, and the green slopes that spread around them are covered with flocks and herds. The surface of the splendid river is diversified with islands of every size and shape, some in wood, others partially cleared, and adorned with orchards and white farm-houses. As the early sun streamed upon the most prominent of these, leaving the others in deep shade, the effect was strangely novel and imposing. In more remote regions, where the forest has never yet echoed to the woodman's axe, or received the impress of civilisation, the first approach to the shore inspires a melancholy awe which becomes painful in its intensity.

Land of vast hills, and mighty streams,
The lofty sun that o'er thee beams
On fairer clime sheds not his ray,
When basking in the noon of day
Thy waters dance in silver light,
And o'er them frowning, dark as night,
Thy shadowy forests, soaring high,
Stretch forth beyond the aching eye,
And blend in distance with the sky.

And silence—awful silence broods
Profoundly o'er these solitudes;
Not but the lapsing of the floods
Breaks the deep stillness of the woods;
A sense of desolation reigns
O'er these unpeopled forest plains
Where sounds of life ne'er wake a tone
Of cheerful praise round Nature's throne,
Man finds himself with God—alone.

My daydreams were dispelled by the return of the boat, which brought my husband and the captain from the island.

1 Cloths; 'claes', clothes.

'No bread,' said the latter, shaking his head; 'you must be content to starve a little longer. Provision-ship not in till four o'clock.' My husband smiled at the look of blank disappointment with which I received these unwelcome tidings. 'Never mind, I have news which will comfort you. The officer who commands the station sent a note to me by an orderly, inviting us to spend the afternoon with him. He promises to show us everything worthy of notice on the island. Captain ——— claims acquaintance with me; but I have not the least recollection of him. Would you like to go?'

'Oh, by all means. I long to see the lovely island. It looks a perfect paradise at this distance.'

The rough sailor-captain screwed his mouth on one side, and gave me one of his comical looks; but he said nothing until he assisted in placing me and the baby in the boat.

'Don't be too sanguine, Mrs Moodie; many things look well at a distance which are bad enough when near.'

I scarcely regarded the old sailor's warning, so eager was I to go on shore—to put my foot upon the soil of the new world for the first time. I was in no humour to listen to any depreciation of what seemed so beautiful.

It was four o'clock when we landed on the rocks, which the rays of an intensely scorching sun had rendered so hot that I could scarcely place my foot upon them. How the people without shoes bore it I cannot imagine. Never shall I forget the extraordinary spectacle that met our sight the moment we passed the low range of bushes which formed a screen in front of the river. A crowd of many hundred Irish emigrants had been landed during the present and former day and all this motley crew—men, women, and children, who were not confined by sickness to the sheds (which greatly resembled cattle-pens)—were employed in washing clothes or spreading them out on the rocks and bushes to dry.

The men and boys were *in* the water, while the women, with their scanty garments tucked above their knees, were tramping their bedding in tubs or in holes in the rocks, which the retiring tide had left half full of water. Those who did not possess washing tubs, pails, or iron pots, or could not obtain access to a hole in the rocks, were running to and fro, screaming and scolding in no measured terms. The confusion of Babel was among them. All talkers and no hearers—each shouting and yelling in his or her uncouth dialect, and all accompanying their vociferations with violent and extraordinary gestures, quite incomprehensible to the uninitiated. We were literally stunned by the strife of tongues. I shrank, with feelings almost akin to fear, from the hard-featured, sun-burnt harpies as they elbowed rudely past me.

I had heard and read much of savages, and have since seen, during my long residence in the bush, somewhat uncivilised life; but the Indian is one of Nature's gentlemen—he never says or does a rude or vulgar thing. The vicious, uneducated barbarians, who form the surplus of overpopulous European countries, are far behind the wild man in delicacy of feeling or natural courtesy. The people who covered the island appeared perfectly destitute of shame, or even a sense of common decency. Many were almost naked, still more but partially clothed. We turned in disgust from the revolting scene, but were unable to leave the spot until the captain had satisfied a noisy group of his own people, who were demanding a supply of stores.

And here I must observe that our passengers, who were chiefly honest Scotch labourers and mechanics from the vicinity of Edinburgh, and who while on board ship had conducted themselves with the greatest propriety, and appeared the most quiet, orderly set of people in the world, no sooner set foot upon the island than they became infected by the same spirit of insubordination and misrule, and were just as insolent and noisy as the rest.

While our captain was vainly endeavouring to satisfy the unreasonable demands of his rebellious people, Moodie had discovered a woodland path that led to the back of the island. Sheltered by some hazel-bushes from the intense heat of the sun, we sat down by the cool, gushing river, out of sight, but, alas! not out of hearing of the noisy, riotous crowd. Could we have shut out the profane sounds which came to us on every breeze, how deeply should we have enjoyed an hour amid the tranquil beauties of that retired and lovely spot!

* * *

[*Leaving Montreal, the Moodies travelled by steamboat to Cobourg, Upper Canada (Ontario), near Peterborough. There they purchased a farm that had been lost by a bankrupt Loyalist identified as 'Old Joe R——' (called Uncle Joe in the next chapter). Though the purchase was concluded in the September following the Moodies' arrival, they were prevented from occupying their new home immediately by an agreement allowing Joe and his family to remain in the house (while his mother lived in a nearby shanty) until 'the commencement of sleighing'. Until then the Moodies were to live in an adjoining farm in 'a small dilapidated log tenement', which they rented from an especially untrustworthy Loyalist known as Old Satan.*]

VIII. UNCLE JOE AND HIS FAMILY

Ay, your rogue is a laughing rogue, and not a whit the less dangerous for the smile on his lip, which comes not from an honest heart, which reflects the light of the soul through the eye. All is hollow and dark within; and the contortion of the lip, like the prehistoric glow upon decayed timber, only serves to point out the rottenness within.

Uncle Joe! I see him now before me, with his jolly red face, twinkling black eyes, and rubicund nose. No thin, weasel-faced Yankee was he, looking as if he had lived upon 'cute[1] ideas and speculations all his life; yet Yankee he was by birth, ay, and in mind, too; for a more knowing fellow at a bargain never crossed the lakes to abuse British institutions and locate himself comfortably among the despised Britishers. But, then,

1 Acute, cunning.

he had such a good-natured, fat face, such a mischievous, mirth-loving smile, and such a merry, roguish expression in those small, jet-black, glittering eyes, that you suffered yourself to be taken in by him, without offering the least resistance to his impositions.

Uncle Joe's father had been a New England loyalist, and his doubtful attachment to the British government had been repaid by a grant of land in the township of H——. He was the first settler in that township, and chose his location in a remote spot, for the sake of a beautiful natural spring, which bubbled up in a small stone basin in the green bank at the back of the house.

'Father might have had the pick of the township,' quoth Uncle Joe; 'but the old coon preferred that sup of good water to the site of a town. Well, I guess it's seldom I trouble the spring; and whenever I step that way to water the horses, I think what a tarnation fool the old one was, to throw away such a chance of making his fortune for such cold lap.'[2]

'Your father was a temperance man?'[3]

'Temperance!—He had been fond enough of the whiskey bottle in his day. He drank up a good farm in the United States, and then he thought he could not do better than turn loyal, and get one here for nothing. He did not care a cent, not he, for the King of England. He thought himself as good, anyhow. But he found that he would have to work hard here to scratch along, and he was mightily plagued with the rheumatics, and some old woman told him that good spring water was the best cure for that; so he chose this poor, light, stony land on account of the spring, and took to hard work and drinking cold water in his old age.'

'How did the change agree with him?'

'I guess better than could have been expected. He planted that fine orchard, and cleared his hundred acres, and we got along slick enough as long as the old fellow lived.'

'And what happened after his death, that obliged you to part with your land?'

'Bad times—bad crops,' said Uncle Joe, lifting his shoulders. 'I had not my father's way of scraping money together. I made some deuced clever speculations, but they all failed. I married young, and got a large family; and the women critters ran up heavy bills at the stores, and the crops did not yield enough to pay them; and from bad we got to worse, and Mr C—— put in an execution,[4] and seized upon the whole concern. He sold it to your man for double what it cost him; and you got all that my father toiled for during the last twenty years of his life for less than half the cash he laid out upon clearing it.'

'And had the whiskey nothing to do with this change?' said I, looking him in the face suspiciously.

'Not a bit! When a man gets into difficulties, it is the only thing to keep him from sinking outright. When your husband has had as many troubles as I have had, he will know how to value the whiskey bottle.'

2 Weak drink.

3 A man advocating abstinence from liquor, or one who has sworn to abstain.

4 The seizure of goods under law in default of payment.

This conversation was interrupted by a queer-looking urchin of five years old, dressed in a long-tailed coat and trowsers, popping his black shock head in at the door, and calling out,

'Uncle Joe!—You're wanted to hum.'[5]

'Is that your nephew?'

'No! I guess 'tis my woman's eldest son,' said Uncle Joe, rising, 'but they call me Uncle Joe. 'Tis a spry chap that—as cunning as a fox. I tell you what it is—he will make a smart man. Go home, Ammon, and tell your ma that I am coming.'

'I won't,' said the boy; 'you may go hum and tell her yourself. She has wanted wood cut this hour, and you'll catch it!'

Away ran the dutiful son, but not before he had applied his forefinger significantly to the side of his nose, and, with a knowing wink, pointed in the direction of home.

Uncle Joe obeyed the signal, drily remarking that he could not leave the barn door without the old hen clucking him back.

At this period we were still living in Old Satan's log house, and anxiously looking out for the first snow to put us in possession of the good substantial log dwelling occupied by Uncle Joe and his family, which consisted of a brown brood of seven girls, and the highly prized boy who rejoiced in the extraordinary name of Ammon.

Strange names are to be found in this free country. What think you, gentle reader, of *Solomon Sly*, *Reynard Fox*, and *Hiram Dolittle*; all veritable names, and belonging to substantial yeomen? After Ammon and Ichabod,[6] I should not be at all surprised to meet with Judas Iscariot, Pilate, and Herod. And then the female appellations! But the subject is a delicate one, and I will forbear to touch upon it. I have enjoyed many a hearty laugh over the strange affectations which people designate here *very handsome names.* I prefer the old homely Jewish names, such as that which it pleased my godfather and godmothers to bestow upon me, to one of those high-sounding christianities, the Minervas, Cinderellas, and Almerias of Canada. The love of singular names is here carried to a marvellous extent. It is only yesterday that, in passing through one busy village, I stopped in astonishment before a tombstone headed thus:—'Sacred to the memory of *Silence* Sharman, the beloved wife of Asa Sharman.' Was the woman deaf and dumb, or did her friends hope by bestowing upon her such an impossible name to still the voice of Nature, and check, by an admonitory appellative, the active spirit that lives in the tongue of woman? Truly, Asa Sharman, if thy wife was silent by name as well as by nature, thou wert a fortunate man!

But to return to Uncle Joe. He made many fair promises of leaving the residence we had bought, the moment he had sold his crops and could remove his family. We could see no interest which could be served by his deceiving us, and therefore we believed him, striving to make ourselves as comfortable as we could in the meantime in our present wretched abode. But matters are never so bad but that they may be worse.

5 At home.

6 Ammon is the name of a Biblical land inhabited by a warlike people with whom the Israelites came into conflict. Ichabod can be found in 1 Samuel 4: 21: 'She named the child Ichabod, meaning "The glory has departed from Israel, for the ark of God had been captured."' Moodie's point is that names from the Old Testament are being used without consideration of their negative connotations, as foolish in its way as would be using those of New Testament villains such as Judas, Pilate, and Herod.

One day when we were at dinner, a waggon drove up to the door, and Mr ——— alighted, accompanied by a fine-looking, middle-aged man, who proved to be Captain S——, who had just arrived from Demerara[7] with his wife and family. Mr ———, who had purchased the farm of Old Satan, had brought Captain S—— over to inspect the land, as he wished to buy a farm, and settle in that neighbourhood. With some difficulty, I contrived to accommodate the visitors with seats, and provide them with a tolerable dinner. Fortunately, Moodie had brought in a brace of fine fat partridges that morning; these the servant transferred to a pot of boiling water, in which she immersed them for the space of a minute—a novel but very expeditious way of removing the feathers, which then come off at the least touch. In less than ten minutes they were stuffed, trussed, and in the bake-kettle; and before the gentlemen returned from walking over the farm, the dinner was on the table.

To our utter consternation, Captain S—— agreed to purchase, and asked if we could give him possession in a week!

'Good heavens!' cried I, glancing reproachfully at Mr ———, who was discussing[8] his partridge with stoical indifference. 'What will become of us? Where are we to go?'

'Oh, make yourself easy; I will force that old witch, Joe's mother, to clear out.'

'But 'tis impossible to stow ourselves into that pig-sty.'

'It will only be for a week or two, at farthest. This October; Joe will be sure to be off the first of sleighing.'

'But if she refuses to give up the place?'

'Oh, leave her to me. I'll talk her over,' said the knowing land speculator. 'Let it come to the worst,' he said, turning to my husband, 'she will go out for the sake of a few dollars. By-the-by, she refused to bar the dower[9] when I bought the place; we must cajole her out of that. It is a fine afternoon; suppose we walk over the hill, and try our luck with the old nigger?'

I felt so anxious about the result of the negotiation, that, throwing my cloak over my shoulders, and tying on my bonnet without assistance of a glass, I took my husband's arm, and we walked forth.

It was a bright, clear afternoon, the first week in October, and the fading woods, not yet denuded of their gorgeous foliage, glowed in a mellow, golden light. A soft, purple haze rested on the bold outline of the Haldimand hills, and in the rugged beauty of the wild landscape I soon forgot the purport of our visit to the old woman's log hut.

On reaching the ridge of the hill, the lovely valley in which our future home lay smiled peacefully upon us from amidst its fruitful orchards, still loaded with their rich, ripe fruit.

'What a pretty place it is!' thought I, for the first time feeling something like a local interest in the spot springing up in my heart. 'How I wish those odious people would give us possession of the home which for some time has been our own!'

7 British Guiana.

8 Consuming (humorous).

9 Void her right to legal tenancy. Joe had inherited the land from his father, but his mother had use of it during her lifetime.

The log hut that we were approaching, and in which the old woman, H——, resided, by herself—having quarrelled years ago with her son's wife—was of the smallest dimensions, only containing one room, which served the old dame for kitchen, and bed-room, and all. The open door, and a few glazed panes, supplied it with light and air; while a huge hearth, on which crackled two enormous logs—which are technically termed a front and a back stick—took up nearly half the domicile; and the old woman's bed, which was covered with an unexceptionably clean patched quilt, nearly the other half, leaving just room for a small home-made deal[10] table, of the rudest workmanship, two basswood-bottomed chairs, stained red, one of which was a rocking-chair, appropriated solely to the old woman's use, and a spinning-wheel. Amidst this muddle of things—for, small as was the quantum of furniture, it was all crowded into such a tiny space that you had to squeeze your way through it in the best manner you could—we found the old woman, with a red cotton handkerchief tied over her grey locks, hood-fashion, shelling white bush-beans into a wooden bowl. Without rising from her seat, she pointed to the only remaining chair. 'I guess, miss, you can sit there; and if the others can't stand, they can make a seat of my bed.

The gentlemen assured her that they were not tired, and could dispense with seats. Mr ——— then went up to the old woman, and proffering his hand, asked after her health in his blandest manner.

'I'm none the better for seeing you, or the like of you,' was the ungracious reply. 'You have cheated my poor boy out of his good farm; and I hope it may prove a bad bargain to you and yours.'

'Mrs H——,' returned the land speculator, nothing ruffled by her unceremonious greeting, 'I could not help your son giving way to drink, and getting into my debt. If people will be so imprudent, they cannot be so stupid as to imagine that others can suffer for their folly.'

'*Suffer!*' repeated the old woman, flashing her small, keen black eyes upon him with a glance of withering scorn. 'You suffer! I wonder what the widows and orphans you have cheated would say to that! My son was a poor, silly fool to be sucked in by the like of you. For a debt of eight hundred dollars—the goods never cost you four hundred—you take from us our good farm; and these, I s'pose,' pointing to my husband and me, 'are the folk you sold it to. Pray, miss,' turning quickly to me, 'what might your man give for the place?'

'Three hundred pounds in cash.'

'Poor sufferer!' again sneered the hag. 'Four hundred dollars is a very *small* profit in as many weeks. Well, I guess, you beat the Yankees hollow. And pray, what brought you here to-day, scenting about you like a carrion-crow? We have no more land for you to seize from us.'

Moodie now stepped forward, and briefly explained our situation, offering the old woman anything in reason to give up the cottage and reside with her son until he removed from the premises; which, he added, must be in a very short time.

10 Pine wood.

The old dame regarded him with a sarcastic smile. 'I guess, Joe will take his own time. The house is not built which is to receive him; and he is not a man to turn his back upon a warm hearth to camp in the wilderness. You were *green* when you bought a farm of that man, without getting along with it the right of possession.'[11]

'But, Mrs H——, your son promised to go out the first of sleighing.'

'Wheugh!' said the old woman. 'Would you have a man give away his hat and leave his own head bare? It's neither the first snow nor the last frost that will turn Joe out of his comfortable home. I tell you that he will stay here, if it is only to plague you.'

Threats and remonstrances were alike useless, the old woman remained inexorable; and we were just turning to leave the house, when the cunning old fox exclaimed, 'And now, what will you give me to leave my place?'

'Twelve dollars, if you give us possession next Monday,' said my husband.

'Twelve dollars! I guess you won't get me out for that.'

'The rent would not be worth more than a dollar a month,' said Mr ———, pointing with his cane to the dilapidated walls. 'Mr Moodie has offered you a year's rent for the place.'

'It may not be worth a cent,' returned the woman, 'for it will give everybody the rheumatism that stays a week in it—but it is worth that to me, and more nor[12] double that just now to him. But I will not be hard with him,' continued she, rocking herself to and fro. 'Say twenty dollars, and I will turn out on Monday.'

'I dare say you will,' said Mr ———, 'and who do you think would be fool enough to give you such an exorbitant sum for a ruined old shed like this?'

'Mind your own business, and make your own bargains,' returned the old woman, tartly. 'The devil himself could not deal with you, for I guess he would have the worst of it. What do you say sir?' and she fixed her keen eyes upon my husband, as if she would read his thought. 'Will you agree to my price?'

'It is a very high one, Mrs H——; but as I cannot help myself, and you take advantage of that, I suppose I must give it.'

''Tis a bargain,' cried the old crone, holding out her hard, bony hand. 'Come, cash down!'

'Not until you give me possession on Monday next; or you might serve me as your son has done.'

'Ha!' said the old woman, laughing and rubbing her hands together; 'you begin to see daylight, do you? In a few months, with the help of him', pointing to Mr ———, 'you will be able to go alone; but have a care of your teacher, for it's no good that you will learn from him. But will you really stand to your word, mister?' she added, in a coaxing tone, 'if I go out on Monday?'

'To be sure I will; I never break my word.'

'Well, I guess you are not so clever as our people, for they only keep it as long as it suits them. You have an honest look; I will trust you; but I will not trust him,' nodding to Mr ———, 'he can buy and sell his word as fast as a horse can trot. So on Monday I will turn out my traps. I have lived here six-and-thirty years; 'tis a pretty place, and it

11 Right of occupancy as distinguished from ownership.

12 Than.

vexes me to leave it,' continued the poor creature, as a touch of natural feeling softened and agitated her world-hardened heart. 'There is not an acre in cultivation but I helped to clear it, nor a tree in yonder orchard but I held it while my poor man, who is dead and gone, planted it; and I have watched the trees bud from year to year, until their boughs over-shadowed the hut, where all my children, but Joe, were born. Yes, I came here young, and in my prime; and must leave it in age and poverty. My children and husband are dead, and their bones rest beneath the turf in the burying-ground on the side of the hill. Of all that once gathered about my knees, Joe and his young ones alone remain. And it is hard, very hard, that I must leave their graves to be turned by the plough of a stranger.'

I felt for the desolate old creature—the tears rushed to my eyes; but there was no moisture in hers. No rain from the heart could filter through that iron soil.

'Be assured, Mrs H——,' said Moodie, 'that the dead will be held sacred; the place will never be disturbed by me.'

'Perhaps not; but it is not long that you will remain here. I have seen a good deal in my time; but I never saw a gentleman from the old country make a good Canadian farmer. The work is rough and hard, and they get out of humour with it, and leave it to their hired helps, and then all goes wrong. They are cheated on all sides, and in despair take to the whiskey bottle, and that fixes them. I tell you what it is, mister—I give you just three years to spend your money and ruin yourself; and then you will become a confirmed drunkard, like the rest.'

The first part of her prophecy was only too true. Thank God! the last has never been fulfilled, and never can be.

Perceiving that the old woman was not a little elated with her bargain, Mr ——— urged upon her the propriety of barring the dower. At first, she was outrageous, and very abusive, and rejected all his proposals with contempt; vowing that she would meet him in a certain place below, before she would sign away her right to the property.

'Listen to reason, Mrs H——,' said the land speculator. 'If you will sign the papers before the proper authorities, the next time that your son drives you to C——, I will give you a silk gown.'

'Pshaw! Buy a shroud for yourself; you will need it before I want a silk gown,' was the ungracious reply.

'Consider, woman; a black silk of the best quality.'

'To mourn in for my sins, or for the loss of the farm?'

'Twelve yards,' continued Mr ———, without noticing her rejoinder, 'at a dollar a yard. Think what a nice church-going gown it will make.'

'To the devil with you! I never go to church.'

'I thought as much,' said Mr ———, winking to us. 'Well, my dear madam, what will satisfy you?'

'I'll do it for twenty dollars,' returned the old woman, rocking herself to and fro in her chair; her eyes twinkling, and her hands moving convulsively, as if she already grasped the money so dear to her soul.

'Agreed,' said the land speculator. 'When will you be in town?'

'On Tuesday, if I be alive. But, remember, I'll not sign till I have my hand on the money.'

'Never fear,' said Mr ———, as we quitted the house; then, turning to me, he added, with a peculiar smile, 'That's a devilish smart woman. She would have made a clever lawyer.'

Monday came, and with it all the bustle of moving, and, as is generally the case on such occasions, it turned out a very wet day. I left Old Satan's hut without regret, glad, at any rate, to be in a place of my own, however humble. Our new habitation, though small, had a decided advantage over the one we were leaving. It stood on a gentle slope; and a narrow but lovely stream, full of speckled trout, ran murmuring under the little window; the house, also, was surrounded by fine fruit trees.

I know not how it was, but the sound of that tinkling brook, for ever rolling by, filled my heart with a strange melancholy, which for many nights deprived me of rest. I loved it, too. The voice of waters, in the stillness of night, always had an extraordinary effect upon my mind. Their ceaseless motion and perpetual sound convey to me the idea of life—eternal life; and looking upon them, glancing and flashing on, now in sunshine, now in shade, now hoarsely chiding with the opposing rock, now leaping triumphantly over it,—creates within me a feeling of mysterious awe of which I never could wholly divest myself.

A portion of my own spirit seemed to pass into that little stream. In its deep wailings and fretful sighs, I fancied myself lamenting for the land I had left for ever; and its restless and impetuous rushings against the stones which choked its passage, were mournful types of my own mental struggles against the strange destiny which hemmed me in. Through the day the stream still moaned and travelled on,—but, engaged in my novel and distasteful occupations, I heard it not; but whenever my winged thoughts flew homeward, then the voice of the brook spoke deeply and sadly to my heart, and my tears flowed unchecked to its plaintive and harmonious music.

In a few hours I had my new abode more comfortably arranged than the old one, although its dimensions were much smaller. The location was beautiful, and I was greatly consoled by this circumstance. The aspect of Nature ever did, and I hope ever will, continue—

> 'To shoot marvellous strength into my heart'.[13]

As long as we remain true to Divine Mother, so long will she remain faithful to her suffering children.

At that period my love for Canada was a feeling very nearly allied to that which the condemned criminal entertains for his cell—his only hope of escape being through the portals of the grave.

The fall rains had commenced. In a few days the cold wintry showers swept all the gorgeous crimson from the trees, and a bleak and desolate waste presented itself to the shuddering spectator. But, in spite of wind and rain, my little tenement was never free

13 Moodie is recasting a passage from Coleridge's verse-drama 'The Death of Wallenstein', in which the title character longs for the sight of the planet Jupiter: 'If I but saw him, 'twould be well with me. / He, is the star of my nativity, / And often marvellously hath his aspect / Shot strength into my heart' (V. i. 33–6).

from the intrusion of Uncle Joe's wife and children. Their house stood about a stone's-throw from the hut we occupied, in the same meadow, and they seemed to look upon it still as their own, although we had literally paid for it twice over. Fine strapping girls they were, from five years old to fourteen, but rude and unnurtured as so many bears. They would come in without the least ceremony, and, young as they were, ask me a thousand impertinent questions; and when I civilly requested them to leave the room, they would range themselves upon the door-step, watching my motions, with their black eyes gleaming upon me through their tangled, uncombed locks. Their company was a great annoyance, for it obliged me to put a painful restraint upon the thoughtfulness in which it was so delightful to me to indulge. Their visits were not visits of love, but of mere idle curiosity, not unmingled with malicious hatred.

The simplicity, the fond, confiding faith of childhood is unknown in Canada. There are no children here. The boy is a miniature man—knowing, keen, and wide awake; as able to drive a bargain and take an advantage of his juvenile companion as the grown-up, world-hardened man. The girl, a gossipping flirt, full of vanity and affectation, with a premature love of finery, and an acute perception of the advantages to be derived from wealth, and from keeping up a certain appearance in the world.

The flowers, the green grass, the glorious sunshine, the birds of the air, and the young lambs gambolling down the verdant slopes, which fill the heart of the British child with a fond ecstacy, bathing the young spirit in Elysium, would float unnoticed before the vision of a Canadian child; while the sight of a dollar, or a new dress, or a gay bonnet, would swell its proud bosom with self-importance and delight. The glorious blush of modest diffidence, the tear of gentle sympathy, are so rare on the cheek, or in the eye of the young, that their appearance creates a feeling of surprise. Such perfect self-reliance in beings so new to the world is painful to a thinking mind. It betrays a great want of sensibility and mental culture, and a melancholy knowledge of the arts of life.

For a week I was alone, my good Scotch girl having left me to visit her father. Some small baby-articles were needed to be washed, and after making a great preparation, I determined to try my unskilled hand upon the operation. The fact is, I knew nothing about the task I had imposed upon myself, and in a few minutes rubbed the skin off my wrists without getting the clothes clean.

The door was open, as it generally was, even during the coldest winter days, in order to let in more light, and let out the smoke, which otherwise would have enveloped us like a cloud. I was so busy that I did not perceive that I was watched by the cold, heavy, dark eyes of Mrs Joe, who, with a sneering laugh, exclaimed,

'Well, thank God! I am glad to see you brought to work at last. I hope you may have to work as hard as I have. I don't see, not I, why you, who are no better than me, should sit still all day, like a lady!'

'Mrs H——,' said I, not a little annoyed at her presence, 'what concern is it of yours whether I work or sit still? I never interfere with you. If you took it into your head to lie in bed all day, I should never trouble myself about it.'

'Ah, I guess you don't look upon us as fellow-critters, you are so proud and grand. I s'pose you Britishers are not made of flesh and blood, like us. You don't choose to sit down at meat with your helps. Now, I calculate, we think them a great deal better nor you.'

'Of course,' said I, 'they are more suited to you than we are; they are uneducated, and so are you. This is no fault in either; but it might teach you to pay a little more respect to those who are possessed of superior advantages. But, Mrs H——, my helps, as you call them, are civil and obliging, and never make unprovoked and malicious speeches. If they could so far forget themselves, I should order them to leave the house.'

'Oh, I see what you are up to,' replied the insolent dame; 'you mean to say that if I were your help, you would turn me out of your house; but I'm a free-born American, and I won't go at your bidding. Don't think I come here out of regard to you. No, I hate you all; and I rejoice to see you at the wash-tub, and I wish that you may be brought down upon your knees to scrub the floors.'

This speech caused a smile, and yet I felt hurt and astonished that a woman whom I had never done anything to offend should be so gratuitously spiteful.

In the evening she sent two of her brood over to borrow my 'long iron', as she called an Italian iron.[14] I was just getting my baby to sleep, sitting upon a low stool by the fire. I pointed to the iron upon the shelf, and told the girl to take it. She did so, but stood beside me, holding it carelessly in her hand, and staring at the baby, who had just sunk to sleep upon my lap.

The next moment the heavy iron fell from her relaxed grasp, giving me a severe blow upon my knee and foot; and glanced so near the child's head that it drew from me a cry of terror.

'I guess that was nigh braining the child,' quoth Miss Amanda, with the greatest coolness, and without making the least apology. Master Ammon burst into a loud laugh. 'If it had, Mandy, I guess we'd have cotched it.' Provoked at their insolence, I told them to leave the house. The tears were in my eyes, for I felt certain that had they injured the child, it would not have caused them the least regret.

The next day, as we were standing at the door, my husband was greatly amused by seeing fat Uncle Joe chasing the rebellious Ammon over the meadow in front of the house. Joe was out of breath, panting and puffing like a small steam-engine, and his face flushed to deep red with excitement and passion.

'You ——— young scoundrel!' he cried, half choked with fury, 'if I catch up to you, I'll take the skin off you!'

'You ——— old scoundrel, you may have my skin if you can get at me,' retorted the precocious child, as he jumped up upon the top of the high fence, and doubled his fist in a menacing manner at his father.

'That boy is growing too bad,' said Uncle Joe, coming up to us out of breath, the perspiration streaming down his face. 'It is time to break him in, or he'll get the master of us all.'

'You should have begun that before,' said Moodie. 'He seems a hopeful pupil.'

14 An iron of a special shape for pressing clothes. In Chapter 5, 'Our First Settlement, & the Borrowing System', Moodie describes how this woman perpetually borrowed items: 'Day after day I was tormented by this importunate creature; she borrowed of me tea, sugar, candles, starch, blueing, irons, pots, bowls—in short, every article in common domestic use—while it was with utmost difficulty we could get them returned. . . . This method of living upon their neighbours is a most convenient one to unprincipled people.'

'Oh, as to that, a little swearing is manly,' returned the father; 'I swear myself, I know, and as the old cock crows, so crows the young one. It is not his swearing that I care a pin for, but he will not do a thing I tell him to.'

'Swearing is a dreadful vice,' said I, 'and, wicked as it is in the mouth of a grown-up person, it is perfectly shocking in a child; it painfully tells he has been brought up without the fear of God.'

'Pooh! pooh! that's all cant; there is no harm in a few oaths, and I cannot drive oxen and horses without swearing. I dare say that you can swear, too, when you are riled, but you are too cunning to let us hear you.'

I could not help laughing outright at this supposition, but replied very quietly, 'Those who practise such iniquities never take any pains to conceal them. The concealment would infer a feeling of shame; and when people are conscious of their guilt, they are in the road to improvement.' The man walked whistling away, and the wicked child returned unpunished to his home.

The next minute the old woman came in. 'I guess you can give me a piece of silk for a hood,' said she, 'the weather is growing considerable cold.'

'Surely it cannot well be colder than it is at present,' said I, giving her the rocking-chair by the fire.

'Wait a while; you know nothing of a Canadian winter. This is only November; after the Christmas thaw, you'll know something about cold. It is seven-and-thirty years ago since I and my man left the U-ni-ted States. It was called the year of the great winter. I tell you, woman, that the snow lay deep on the earth, that it blocked up all the roads, and we could drive a sleigh whither we pleased, right over the snake fences.[15] All the cleared land was one wide white level plain; it was a year of scarcity, and we were half starved; but the severe cold was far worse nor the want of provisions. A long and bitter journey we had of it; but I was young then, and pretty well used to trouble and fatigue; my man stuck to the British government. More fool he! I was an American born, and my heart was with the true cause. But his father was English, and, says he, "I'll live and die under their flag." So he dragged me from my comfortable fireside to seek a home in the far Canadian wilderness. Trouble! I guess you think you have your troubles; but what are they to mine?' She paused, took a pinch of snuff, offered me the box, sighed painfully, pushed the red handkerchief from her high, narrow, wrinkled brow, and continued:—'Joe was a baby then, and I had another helpless critter in my lap—an adopted child. My sister had died from it, and I was nursing it at the same breast with my boy. Well, we had to perform a journey of four hundred miles in an ox-cart, which carried, besides me and the children, all our household stuff. Our way lay chiefly through the forest, and we made but slow progress. Oh! what a bitter cold night it was when we reached the swampy woods where the city of Rochester now stands. The oxen were covered with icicles, and their breath sent up clouds of steam. "Nathan," says I to my man, "you must stop and kindle a fire; I am dead with cold, and I fear the babes will be frozen." We began looking about for a good spot to camp in, when I spied a light through the trees. It was a lone shanty, occupied by two French

15 Zigzag fences made of split rails.

lumberers. The men were kind; they rubbed our frozen limbs with snow, and shared with us their supper and buffalo skins. On that very spot where we camped that night, where we heard nothing but the wind soughing amongst the trees, and the rushing of the river, now stands the great city of Rochester. I went there two years ago, to the funeral of a brother. It seemed to me like a dream. Where we foddered our beasts by the shanty fire, now stands the largest hotel in the city; and my husband left this fine growing country to starve here.'

I was so much interested in the old woman's narrative—for she was really possessed of no ordinary capacity, and, though rude and uneducated, might have been a very superior person under different circumstances—that I rummaged among my stores, and soon found a piece of black silk, which I gave her for the hood she required.

The old woman examined it carefully over, smiled to herself, but, like all her people, was too proud to return a word of thanks. One gift to the family always involved another.

'Have you any cotton-batting, or black sewing-silk, to give me, to quilt it with?'

'No.'

'Humph!' returned the old dame, in a tone which seemed to contradict my assertion. She then settled herself in her chair, and, after shaking her foot a while, and fixing her piercing eyes upon me for some minutes, she commenced the following list of interrogatories:—

'Is your father alive?'

'No; he died many years ago, when I was a young girl.'

'Is your mother alive?'

'Yes.'

'What is her name?' I satisfied her on this point.

'Did she ever marry again?'

'She might have done so, but she loved her husband too well, and preferred living single.'

'Humph! We have no such notions here. What was your father?'

'A gentleman, who lived upon his own estate.'

'Did he die rich?'

'He lost the greater part of his property from being surety for another.'[16]

'That's a foolish business. My man burnt his fingers with that. And what brought you out to this poor country—you, who are no more fit for it than I am to be a fine lady?'

'The promise of a large grant of land, and the false statements we heard regarding it.'

'Do you like the country?'

'No; and I fear I never shall.'

'I thought not; for the drop is always on your cheek, the children tell me; and those young ones have keen eyes. Now, take my advice: return while your money lasts; the longer you remain in Canada the less you will like it; and when your money is all spent, you will be like a bird in a cage; you may beat your wings against the bars, but

16 Guaranteeing a loan by becoming responsible for the debt.

you can't get out.' There was a long pause. I hoped that my guest had sufficiently gratified her curiosity, when she again commenced:—

'How do you get your money? Do you draw it from the old country, or have you it with you in cash?'

Provoked by her pertinacity, and seeing no end to her cross-questioning, I replied very impatiently, 'Mrs H——, is it the custom in your country to catechize strangers whenever you meet with them?'

'What do you mean?' said she, colouring, I believe, for the first time in her life.

'I mean', quoth I, 'an evil habit of asking impertinent questions.'

The old woman got up, and left the house without speaking another word.

[*During the winter of 1883 the Moodies finally moved into their new house. When spring came they brought in a man and his wife to help work the farm in return for a share of the produce. These people unfortunately proved to be untrustworthy. With them, Mrs Moodie writes, 'commenced that long series of losses and troubles to which their conduct formed the prelude'.*]

XI. BRIAN, THE STILL-HUNTER

O'er memory's glass I see his shadow flit,
Though he was gathered to the silent dust
Long years ago. A strange and wayward man,
That shunn'd companionship, and lived apart;
The leafy covert of the dark brown woods,
The gleamy lakes, hid in their gloomy depths,
Whose still, deep waters never knew the stroke
Of cleaving oar, or echoed to the sound
Of social life, contained for him the sum
Of human happiness. With dog and gun
Day after day he track'd the nimble deer
Through all the tangled mazes of the forest.

It was early day. I was alone in the old shanty, preparing breakfast, and now and then stirring the cradle with my foot, when a tall, thin, middle-aged man walked into the house, followed by two large, strong dogs.

Placing the rifle he had carried on his shoulder in a corner of the room, he advanced to the hearth, and, without speaking, or seemingly looking at me, lighted his pipe, and commenced smoking. The dogs, after growling and snapping at the cat, who had not given the strangers a very courteous reception, sat down on the hearthstone on either side of their taciturn master, eyeing him from time to time, as if long habit had made them understand all his motions. There was a great contrast between the dogs. The one was a brindled bull dog of the largest size, the most formidable and powerful brute; the other a stag hound, tawny, deep-chested, and strong-limbed. I regarded the man and his hairy companions with silent curiosity.

He was between forty and fifty years of age; his head, nearly bald, was studded at the sides with strong, coarse, black curling hair. His features were high, his compexion brightly dark, and his eyes, in size, shape, and colour, greatly resembling the eyes of a hawk. The face itself was sorrowful and taciturn; and his thin, compressed lips looked as if they were not much accustomed to smile, or often to unclose to hold social communion with any one. He stood at the side of the huge hearth, silently smoking, his eyes bent on the fire, and now and then he patted the heads of his dogs, reproving their exuberant expressions of attachment with—'Down, Music, down, Chance!'

'A cold, clear morning,' said I, in order to attract his attention and draw him into conversation.

A nod, without raising his head, or withdrawing his eyes from the fire, was his only answer; and, turning from my unsociable guest, I took up the baby, who just then awoke, sat down on a low stool by the table, and began feeding her. During this operation, I once or twice caught the stranger's hawk-eye fixed upon me and the child, but word spoke he none; and presently, after whistling to his dogs, he resumed his gun, and strode out.

When Moodie and Monaghan[1] came in to breakfast, I told them what a strange visitor I had had; and Moodie laughed at my vain attempt to induce him to talk.

'He is a strange being,' I said; 'I must find out who and what he is.'

In the afternoon an old soldier, called Layton, who had served during the American war, and got a grant of land about a mile in the rear of our location, came in to trade for a cow. Now, this Layton was a perfect ruffian; a man whom no one liked, and whom all feared. He was a deep drinker, a great swearer, in short, a perfect reprobate; who never cultivated his land, but went jobbing about from farm to farm, trading horses and cattle, and cheating in a pettifogging way. Uncle Joe had employed him to sell Moodie a young heifer, and he had brought her over for him to look at. When he came in to be paid, I described the stranger of the morning; and as I knew that he was familiar with every one in the neighbourhood, I asked if he knew him.

'No one should know him better than myself,' he said, ''tis old Brian B——, the still-hunter,[2] and a near neighbour of your'n. A sour, morose, queer chap he is, and as mad as a March hare! He's from Lancashire, in England, and came to this country some twenty years ago, with his wife, who was a pretty young lass in those days, and slim enough then, though she's so awfully fleshy now. He had lots of money, too, and he bought four hundred acres of land, just at the corner of the concession line,[3] where it meets the main road. And excellent land it is; and a better farmer, while he stuck to his business, never went into the bush, for it was all bush here then. He was a dashing, handsome fellow, too, and did not hoard the money either; he loved his pipe and his pot too well; and at last he left off farming, and gave himself to them altogether. Many a jolly booze he and I have had, I can tell you. Brian was an awful passionate man, and, when

1 The Moodies' new hired man.
2 One who hunts game on foot or in a quiet or stealthy manner.
3 Rural road separating concessions (grants of land).

the liquor was in, and the wit was out, as savage and as quarrelsome as a bear. At such times there was no one but Ned Layton dared go near him. We once had a pitched battle, in which I was conqueror, and ever arter he yielded a sort of sulky obedience to all I said to him. Arter being on the spree for a week or two, he would take fits of remorse, and return home to his wife; would fall down at her knees, and ask her forgiveness, and cry like a child. At other times he would hide himself up in the woods, and steal home at night, and get what he wanted out of the pantry, without speaking a word to any one. He went on with these pranks for some years, till he took a fit of the blue devils.

'"Come away, Ned, to the ——— lake, with me," said he; "I am weary of my life, and I want a change."

'"Shall we take the fishing-tackle?" says I. "The black bass are in prime season, and F—— will lend us the old canoe. He's got some capital rum up from Kingston. We'll fish all day, and have a spree at night."

'"It's not to fish I'm going," says he.

'"To shoot, then? I've bought Rockwood's new rifle."

'"It's neither to fish nor to shoot, Ned; it's a new game I'm going to try; so come along."

'Well, to the ——— lake we went. The day was very hot, and our path lay through the woods, and over those scorching plains, for eight long miles. I thought I should have dropped by the way; but during our long walk my companion never opened his lips. He strode on before me, at a half-run, never once turning his head.

'"The man must be a devil!" says I, "and accustomed to a warmer place, or he must feel this. Hollo, Brian! Stop there! Do you mean to kill me?"

'"Take it easy," says he; "you'll see another day arter this—I've business on hand and cannot wait."

'Well, on we went, at the same awful rate, and it was midday when we got to the little tavern on the lake shore, kept by one F——, who had a boat for the convenience of strangers who came to visit the place. Here we got our dinner, and a glass of rum to wash it down. But Brian was moody, and to all my jokes he only returned a sort of grunt; and while I was talking with F——, he steps out, and a few minutes arter we saw him crossing the lake in the old canoe.

'"What's the matter with Brian?" says F——; "all does not seem right with him, Ned. You had better take the boat and look arter him."

'"Pooh!" says I; "he's often so, and grows so glum now-a-days that I will cut his acquaintance altogether if he does not improve."

'"He drinks awful hard," says F——; "maybe he's got a fit of the delirium-tremulous. There is no telling what he may be up to at this minute."

'My mind misgave me too, so I e'en takes the oars, and pushes out, right upon Brian's tracks; and by the Lord Harry! if I did not find him, upon my landing on the opposite shore, lying wallowing in his blood, with his throat cut. "Is that you, Brian?" says I, giving him a kick with my foot, to see if he was alive or dead. "What upon earth tempted you to play me and F—— such a dirty, mean trick, as to go and stick yourself like a pig, bringing such a discredit upon the house?—and you so far from home and those who should nurse you."

'I was so mad with him, that (saving your presence, ma'am) I swore awfully, and called him names that would be ondacent to repeat here; but he only answered with groans and a horrid gurgling in his throat. "It's a choking you are," said I; "but you shan't have your own way and die so easily either, if I can punish you by keeping you alive." So I just turned him upon his stomach, with his head down the steep bank; but he still kept choking and growing black in the face.'

Layton then detailed some particulars of his surgical practice which it is not necessary to repeat. He continued—

'I bound up his throat with my handkerchief, and took him neck and heels, and threw him into the bottom of the boat. Presently he came to himself a little, and sat up in the boat; and—would you believe it?—made several attempts to throw himself into the water. "This will not do," says I; "you've done mischief enough already by cutting your weasand![4] If you dare to try that again, I will kill you with the oar." I held it up to threaten him; he was scared, and lay down as quiet as a lamb. I put my foot upon his breast. "Lie still, now! or you'll catch it." He looked piteously at me; he could not speak, but his eyes seemed to say, "Have pity on me, Ned; don't kill me."

'Yes, ma'am, this man, who had just cut his throat, and twice arter that had tried to drown himself, was afraid that I should knock him on the head and kill him. Ha! ha! I never shall forget the work that F—— and I had with him arter I got him up to the house.

'The doctor came and sewed up his throat; and his wife—poor crittur!—came to nurse him. Bad as he was, she was mortal fond of him! He lay there, sick and unable to leave his bed, for three months, and did nothing but pray to God to forgive him, for he thought the devil would surely have him for cutting his own throat; and when he got about again, which is now twelve years ago, he left off drinking entirely, and wanders about the woods with his dogs, hunting. He seldom speaks to any one, and his wife's brother carries on the farm for the family. He is so shy of strangers that 'tis a wonder he came in here. The old wives are afraid of him; but you need not heed him—his troubles are to himself, he harms no one.'

Layton departed, and left me brooding over the sad tale which he had told in such an absurd and jesting manner. It was evident from the account he had given of Brian's attempt at suicide, that the hapless hunter was not wholly answerable for his conduct—that he was a harmless maniac.

The next morning, at the very same hour, Brian again made his appearance; but instead of the rifle across his shoulder, a large stone jar occupied the place, suspended by a stout leather thong. Without saying a word, but with a truly benevolent smile that flitted slowly over his stern features, and lighted them up like a sunbeam breaking from beneath a stormy cloud, he advanced to the table, and unslinging the jar, set it down before me, and in a low and gruff, but by no means an unfriendly, voice, said, 'Milk, for the child,' and vanished.

'How good it was of him! How kind!' I exclaimed, as I poured the precious gift of four quarts of pure new milk out into a deep pan. I had not asked him—had never said

4 Windpipe or throat.

that the poor weanling wanted milk. It was the courtesy of a gentleman—of a man of benevolence and refinement.

For weeks did my strange, silent friend steal in, take up the empty jar, and supply its place with another replenished with milk. The baby knew his step, and would hold out her hands to him and cry, 'Milk!' and Brian would stoop down and kiss her, and his two great dogs lick her face.

'Have you any children, Mr B——?'

'Yes, five; but none like this.'

'My little girl is greatly indebted to you for your kindness.'

'She's welcome, or she would not get it. You are strangers; but I like you all. You look kind, and I would like to know more about you.'

Moodie shook hands with the old hunter, and assured him that we should always be glad to see him. After this invitation, Brian became a frequent guest. He would sit and listen with delight to Moodie while he described to him elephant-hunting at the Cape;[5] grasping his rifle in a determined manner, and whistling an encouraging air to his dogs. I asked him one evening what made him so fond of hunting.

''Tis the excitement,' he said; 'it drowns thought, and I love to be alone. I am sorry for the creatures, too, for they are free and happy; yet I am led by an instinct I cannot restrain to kill them. Sometimes the sight of their dying agonies recalls painful feelings; and then I lay aside the gun, and do not hunt for days. But 'tis fine to be alone with God in the great woods—to watch the sunbeams stealing through the thick branches, the blue sky breaking in upon you in patches, and to know that all is bright and shiny above you, in spite of the gloom that surrounds you.'

After a long pause, he continued, with much solemn feeling in his look and tone—

'I lived a life of folly for years, for I was respectably born and educated, and had seen something of the world, perhaps more than was good, before I left home for the woods; and from the teaching I had received from kind relatives and parents I should have known how to have conducted myself better. But, madam, if we associate long with the depraved and ignorant, we learn to become even worse than they. I felt deeply my degradation—felt that I had become the slave to low vice, and in order to emancipate myself from the hateful tyranny of evil passions, I did a very rash and foolish thing. I need not mention the manner in which I transgressed God's holy laws; all the neighbours know it, and must have told you long ago. I could have borne reproof, but they turned my sorrow into indecent jests, and, unable to bear their coarse ridicule, I made companions of my dogs and gun, and went forth into the wilderness. Hunting became a habit. I could no longer live without it, and it supplies the stimulant which I lost when I renounced the cursed whiskey-bottle.

'I remember the first hunting excursion I took alone in the forest. How sad and gloomy I felt! I thought that there was no creature in the world so miserable as myself. I was tired and hungry, and I sat down upon a fallen tree to rest. All was still as death around me, and I was fast sinking to sleep, when my attention was aroused by a long, wild cry. My dog, for I had not Chance then, and he's no hunter, pricked up his ears,

5 Cape of Good Hope, South Africa.

but instead of answering with a bark of defiance, he crouched down, trembling, at my feet. "What does this mean?" I cried, and I cocked my rifle and sprang upon the log. The sound came nearer upon the wind. It was like the deep baying of a pack of hounds in full cry. Presently a noble deer rushed past me, and fast upon his trail—I see them now, like so many black devils—swept by a pack of ten or fifteen large, fierce wolves, with fiery eyes and bristling hair, and paws that seemed hardly to touch the ground in their eager haste. I thought not of danger, for, with their prey in view, I was safe; but I felt every nerve within me tremble for the fate of the poor deer. The wolves gained upon him at every bound. A close thicket intercepted his path, and, rendered desperate, he turned at bay. His nostrils were dilated, and his eyes seemed to send forth long streams of light. It was wonderful to witness the courage of the beast. How bravely he repelled the attacks of his deadly enemies, how gallantly he tossed them to the right and left, and spurned them from beneath his hoofs; yet all his struggles were useless, and he was quickly overcome and torn to pieces by his ravenous foes. At that moment he seemed more fortunate even than myself, for I could not see in what manner he had deserved his fate. All his speed and energy, his courage and fortitude, had been exerted in vain. I had tried to destroy myself; but he, with every effort vigorously made for self-preservation, was doomed to meet the fate he dreaded! Is God just to his creatures?'

With this sentence on his lips, he started abruptly from his seat and left the house.

One day he found me painting some wild flowers, and was greatly interested in watching the progress I made in the group. Late in the afternoon of the following day he brought me a large bunch of splendid spring flowers.

'Draw these,' said he; 'I have been all the way to the ——— lake plains to find them for you.'

Little Katie, grasping them one by one, with infantile joy, kissed every lovely blossom.

'These are God's pictures,' said the hunter, 'and the child, who is all nature, understands them in a minute. Is it not strange that these beautiful things are hid away in the wilderness, where no eyes but the birds of the air, and the wild beasts of the wood, and the insects that live upon them, ever see them? Does God provide, for the pleasure of such creatures, these flowers? Is His benevolence gratified by the admiration of animals whom we have been taught to consider as having neither thought nor reflection? When I am alone in the forest, these thoughts puzzle me.'

Knowing that to argue with Brain was only to call into action the slumbering fires of his fatal malady, I turned the conversation by asking him why he called his favourite dog Chance?

'I found him', said he, 'forty miles back in the bush. He was a mere skeleton. At first I took him for a wolf, but the shape of his head undeceived me. I opened my wallet,[6] and called him to me. He came slowly, stopping and wagging his tail at every step, and looking me wistfully in the face. I offered him a bit of dried venison, and he soon became friendly, and followed me home, and has never left me since. I called him Chance, after the manner I happened with him; and I would not part with him for twenty dollars.'

6 Knapsack.

Alas, for poor Chance! he had, unknown to his master, contracted a private liking for fresh mutton, and one night he killed no less than eight sheep that belonged to Mr D——, on the front road; the culprit, who had been long suspected, was caught in the very act, and this *mischance* cost him his life. Brian was sad and gloomy for many weeks after his favourite's death.

'I would have restored the sheep fourfold', he said, 'if he would but have spared the life of my dog.'

* * *

XXIII. THE FIRE

Now, Fortune, do thy worst! For many years,
Thou, with relentless and unsparing hand,
Hast sternly pour'd on our devoted heads
The poison'd phials of they fiercest wrath.

The early part of the winter of 1837, a year never to be forgotten in the annals of Canadian history, was very severe. During the month of February, the thermometer often ranged from eighteen to twenty-seven degrees below zero. Speaking of the coldness of one particular day, a genuine brother Jonathan[1] remarked, with charming simplicity, that it was thirty degrees below zero that morning, and it would have been much colder if the thermometer had been longer.

The morning of the seventh was so intensely cold that everything liquid froze in the house. The wood that had been drawn for the fire was green, and it ignited too slowly to satisfy the shivering impatience of women and children; I vented mine inaudibly grumbling over the wretched fire, at which I in vain endeavoured to thaw frozen bread, and to dress crying children.

It so happened that an old friend, the maiden lady before alluded to,[2] had been staying with us for a few days. She had left us for a visit to my sister, and as some relatives of hers were about to return to Britain, by the way of New York, and had offered to convey letters to friends at home, I had been busy all the day before preparing a packet for England.

It was my intention to walk to my sister's with this packet, directly after the important affair of breakfast had been discussed; but the extreme cold of the morning had occasioned such delay, that it was late before breakfast-things were cleared away.

After dressing, I found the air so keen that I could not venture out without some risk to my nose, and my husband kindly volunteered to go in my stead.

1 Typical Yankee.
2 In the chapter that precedes this one, Moodie writes: 'I was surprised by a visit from an old maiden lady, a friend of mine from C——. She had walked up with a Mr. Crowe, from Peterborough, a young, brisk-looking farmer, in breeches and top-boots, just out from the old country, who, naturally enough thought he would like to roost among the woods.'

I had hired a young Irish girl the day before. Her friends were only just located in our vicinity, and she had never seen a stove until she came to our house. After Moodie left, I suffered the fire to die away in the Franklin stove in the parlour, and went into the kitchen to prepare bread for the oven.

The girl, who was a good-natured creature, had heard me complain bitterly of the cold, and the impossibility of getting the green wood to burn, and she thought that she would see if she could not make a good fire for me and the children, against[3] my work was done. Without saying one word about her intention, she slipped out through a door that opened from the parlour into the garden, ran round to the woodyard, filled her lap with cedar chips, and, not knowing the nature of the stove, filled it entirely with the light wood.

Before I had the least idea of my danger, I was aroused from the completion of my task by the crackling and roaring of a large fire, and a suffocating smell of burning soot. I looked up at the kitchen cooking-stove. All was right there. I knew I had left no fire in the parlour stove; but not being able to account for the smoke and smell of burning, I opened the door, and, to my dismay, found the stove red-hot, from the front plate to the topmost pipe that let out the smoke through the roof.

My first impulse was to plunge a blanket, snatched from the servant's bed, which stood in the kitchen, into cold water. This I thrust into the stove, and upon it I threw water, until all was cool below. I then ran up to the loft, and, by exhausting all the water in the house, even to that contained in the boilers upon the fire, contrived to cool down the pipes which passed through the loft. I then sent the girl out of doors to look at the roof, which, as a very deep fall of snow had taken place the day before, I hoped would be completely covered, and safe from all danger of fire.

She quickly returned, stamping, and tearing her hair, and making a variety of uncouth outcries, from which I gathered that the roof was in flames.

This was terrible news, with my husband absent, no man in the house, and a mile and a quarter from any other habitation. I ran out to ascertain the extent of the misfortune, and found a large fire burning in the roof between the two stove-pipes. The heat of the fires had melted off all the snow, and a spark from the burning pipe had already ignited the shingles. A ladder, which for several months had stood against the house, had been moved two days before to the barn, which was at the top of the hill near the road; there was no reaching the fire through that source. I got out the dining-table, and tried to throw water upon the roof by standing on a chair placed upon it, but I only expended the little water that remained in the boiler, without reaching the fire. The girl still continued weeping and lamenting.

'You must go for help,' I said. 'Run as fast as you can to my sister's, and fetch your master.'

'And lave you, ma'arm, and the childher alone wid the burnin' house?'

'Yes, yes! Don't stay one moment.'

'I have no shoes, ma'arm, and the snow is so deep.'

'Put on your master's boots; make haste, or we shall be lost before help comes.'

3 Until.

The girl put on the boots and started, shrieking 'Fire!' the whole way. This was utterly useless, and only impeded her progress by exhausting her strength. After she had vanished from the head of the clearing into the wood, and I was left quite alone, with the house burning over my head, I paused one moment to reflect what had best be done.

The house was built of cedar logs; in all probability it would be consumed before any help could arrive. There was a brisk breeze blowing up from the frozen lake, and the thermometer stood at eighteen degrees below zero. We were placed between the two extremes of heat and cold, and there was as much danger to be apprehended from the one as the other. In the bewilderment of the moment, the direful extent of the calamity never struck me; we wanted but this to put the finishing stroke to our misfortunes, to be thrown naked, houseless, and penniless, upon the world. '*What shall I save first?*' was the thought just then uppermost in my mind. Bedding and clothing appeared the most essentially necessary, and, without another moment's pause, I set to work with a right good will to drag all that I could from my burning home.

While little Agnes, Dunbar, and baby Donald filled the air with their cries, Katie, as if fully conscious of the importance of exertion, assisted me in carrying out sheets and blankets, and dragging trunks and boxes some way up the hill, to be out of the way of the burning brands when the roof should fall in.

How many anxious looks I gave to the head of the clearing as the fire increased, and large pieces of burning pine began to fall through the boarded ceiling about the lower rooms where we were at work. The children I had kept under a large dresser in the kitchen, but it now appeared absolutely necessary to remove them to a place of safety. To expose the young, tender things to the direct cold, was almost as bad as leaving them to the mercy of the fire. At last I hit upon a plan to keep them from freezing. I emptied all the clothes out of a large, deep chest of drawers, and dragged the empty drawers up the hill; these I lined with blankets, and placed a child in each drawer, covering it well over with the bedding, giving to little Agnes the charge of the baby to hold between her knees, and keep well covered until help should arrive. Ah, how long it seemed coming!

The roof was now burning like a brush-heap, and, unconsciously, the child and I were working under a shelf upon which were deposited several pounds of gunpowder, which had been procured for blasting a well, as all our water had to be brought uphill from the lake. This gunpowder was in a stone jar, secured by a paper stopper; the shelf upon which it stood was on fire, but it was utterly forgotten by me at the time, and even afterwards, when my husband was working on the burning loft over it.

I found that I should not be able to take many more trips for goods. As I passed out of the parlour for the last time, Katie looked up at her father's flute, which was suspended upon two brackets, and said,

'Oh, dear mamma! do save papa's flute; he will be so sorry to lose it.'

God bless the dear child for the thought! the flute was saved; and, as I succeeded in dragging out a heavy chest of clothes, and looked up once more despairingly to the road, I saw a man running at full speed. It was my husband. Help was at hand, and my heart uttered a deep thanksgiving as another and another figure came upon the scene.

I had not felt the intense cold, although without cap, or bonnet, or shawl; with my hands bare and exposed to the bitter, biting air. The intense excitement, the anxiety to save all I could, had so totally diverted my thoughts from myself, that I had felt nothing of the danger to which I had been exposed; but now that help was near, my knees trembled under me, I felt giddy and faint, and dark shadows seemed dancing before my eyes.

The moment my husband and brother-in-law entered the house, the latter exclaimed,

'Moodie, the house is gone; save what you can of your winter stores and furniture.'

Moodie thought differently. Prompt and energetic in danger, and possessing admirable presence of mind and coolness when others yield to agitation and despair, he sprang upon the burning loft and called for water. Alas, there was none!

'Snow, snow; hand me pailfuls of snow!'

Oh! it was bitter work filling those pails with frozen snow; but Mr T—— and I worked at it as fast as we were able.

The violence of the fire was greatly checked by covering the boards of the loft with this snow. More help had now arrived. Young B—— and S—— had brought the ladder down with them from the barn, and were already cutting away the burning roof, and flinging the flaming brands into the deep snow.

'Mrs Moodie, have you any pickled meat?'

'We have just killed one of our cows and salted it for winter stores.'

'Well, then, fling the beef into the snow, and let us have the brine.'

This was an admirable plan. Wherever the brine wetted the shingles, the fire turned from it, and concentrated into one spot.

But I had not time to watch the brave workers on the roof. I was fast yielding to the effects of over excitement and fatigue, when my brother's team dashed down the clearing, bringing my excellent old friend, Miss B——, and the servant-girl.

My brother sprang out, carried me back into the house, and wrapped me up in one of the large blankets scattered about. In a few minutes I was seated with the dear children in the sleigh, and on the way to a place of warmth and safety.

Katie alone suffered from the intense cold. The dear little creature's feet were severely frozen, but were fortunately restored by her uncle discovering the fact before she approached the fire, and rubbing them well with snow.

In the meanwhile, the friends we had left so actively employed at the house, succeeded in getting the fire under before it had destroyed the walls. The only accident that occurred was to a poor dog that Moodie had called Snarleyowe. He was struck by a burning brand thrown from the house, and crept under the barn and died.

Beyond the damage done to the building, the loss of our potatoes and two sacks of flour, we had escaped in a manner almost miraculous. This fact shows how much can be done by persons working in union, without bustle and confusion, or running in each other's way. Here were six men, who, without the aid of water, succeeded in saving a building, which, at first sight, almost all of them had deemed past hope. In after-years, when entirely burnt out in a disastrous fire that consumed almost all we were worth in the world, some four hundred persons were present, with a fire-engine to second their endeavours, yet all was lost. Every person seemed in the way; and though the fire was discovered immediately after it took place, nothing was done beyond saving some of the furniture.

* * *

[*After the fire, circumstances improved for the Moodies, so much so that Mrs Moodie writes of that time: 'We were always cheerful, and sometimes contented and happy.' The Rebellion of 1837 brought this period to a sudden close, and in 1839, the Moodies departed from the bush to begin their 'life in the clearings'. In the final chapter, Mrs Moodie bids a somewhat sentimental 'Adieu to the Woods,' but concludes her book with two paragraphs of stern warning.*]

XXV. ADIEU TO THE WOODS

* * *

Reader! it is not my intention to trouble you with the sequel of our history. I have given you a faithful picture of a life in the backwoods of Canada, and I leave you to draw from it your own conclusions. To the poor, industrious working man it presents many advantages; to the poor gentleman, none! The former works hard, puts up with coarse, scanty fare, and submits, with good grace, to hardships that would kill a domesticated animal at home. Thus he becomes independent, inasmuch as the land that he has cleared finds him in the common necessaries of life; but it seldom, if ever, in remote situations, accomplishes more than this. The gentleman can neither work so hard, live so coarsely, nor endure so many privations as his poorer but more fortunate neighbour. Unaccustomed to manual labour, his services in the field are not of a nature to secure for him a profitable return. The task is new to him, he knows not how to perform it well; and, conscious of his deficiency, he expends his little means in hiring labour, which his bush-farm can never repay. Difficulties increase, debts grow upon him, he struggles in vain to extricate himself, and finally sees his family sink into hopeless ruin.

If these sketches should prove the means of deterring one family from sinking their property, and shipwrecking all their hopes, by going to reside in the backwoods of Canada, I shall consider myself amply repaid for revealing the secrets of the prison-house, and feel that I have not toiled and suffered in the wilderness in vain.

1852

Charles Sangster

1822–1893

Early Canadian Poetry

Even before the nation came into being in 1867, many living in Canada felt it was important to keep poetry alive in the colonies as a way of giving cultural values to the incipient nation. The first Canadian poets were United Empire Loyalists who made their way across the border as a result of the American Revolution and who used their verse to defend the King and to protest what they viewed as America's folly. Perhaps the best known of these Loyalist poets were Joseph Stansbury and Jonathan Odell. The latter, who accused the Americans of having 'broken the most sacred ties', tells how:

When civil madness first from man to man
In these devoted climes like wildfire ran,
There were who gave the moderating hint,
In conversation some, and some in print;
Wisely they spake—and what was their
reward?—
The tar, the rail, the prison, and the cord!

The descendents of such Loyalists, and the generation of British and American immigrants who came after them, may have been less interested in politics and more interested in the space they found themselves inhabiting, but their conservative nature, suggested by the desire to be numbered among those who gave 'the moderating hint', meant that they continued to take British writers as their models, filling inherited poetic forms with new content and employing old conventions to describe new situations. In 1825, for example, Oliver Goldsmith, the Canadian grand-nephew and namesake of the famous British writer of the eighteenth century, closely imitated his great-uncle's long pastoral poem, *The Deserted Village*, to create a response, *The Rising Village*, that argued that the emergence of Canadian agrarian society would recompense Britain for its loss of village society. Although the closeness of ties to Britain have grown less essential, the long poem form that *The Rising Village* and many other early works of Canadian poetry employed—along with the positive value placed on agrarian and small town life—have remained important to Canadian writing.

As Canada approached nationhood, a desire for a 'native' poetry written first of all for a Canadian audience began to manifest itself. A year after immigrating from Ireland in 1857, Thomas D'Arcy McGee, later one of the Fathers of Confederation, expressed concerns about this absence; to address this need he wrote his own book of poems, *Canadian Ballads and Occasional Verses* (1858). Edward Hartley Dewart, concerned that Canada's status as a colony left its writers neither part of the mainstream of British literature nor able to develop an independent voice in the way American authors had, put together, in 1864, the first significant anthology of Canadian poems. In his introductory essay to that volume he argued against the indifference to Canadian subject matter he felt resulted from a colonial mentality that respected only the products and associations of the mother country.

The most famous of the poets featured in Dewart's volume and the first Canadian poet to achieve recognition in Canada in his lifetime was Charles Sangster; Dewart said he occupied 'first place' among his peers. Called in his own time 'Canada's national bard' and the 'first important national poet', Sangster became, by virtue of two books published in his thirties, the unofficial poet laureate of his day. Choosing to work in the tradition of the English Romantic poets, Sangster's poetry was important for the way it attempted to respond to his immediate milieu rather than remaining in the more formalized neo-classic mode of his predecessors. However, though Sangster attempted to depict a Canadian landscape in his 1856 poem

'The St Lawrence and the Saguenay', a work indebted to Wordsworth's late sonnet sequence 'The River Duddon', Sir Daniel Wilson argued, in what has become an important commentary, that the poem was not true to its Canadian environment and that it failed to utilize a native idiom:

Were we to transport the scene to the firth of Clyde, or any other islanded home river, and change only a single term; that of the Red Man *for the* old Pict. . . . *there is nothing in the description that would betray its new-world parentage. At best it is no true Indian, but only the white man dressed in his attire; strip him of his paint and feathers, and it is our old-world familiar acquaintance. . . . However much taste and refinement may be displayed in such echoes of the old thought and fancy of Europe, the path to success lies not in this direction for the poet of the new world.* [Wilson, *The Canadian Journal of Industry, Science, and Art* (January 1858)]

Wilson's argument, one that has, in some form, been reiterated many times since, may have had an effect on Sangster. The poems in his 1860 sequence 'Sonnets Written in the Orillia Woods' suffer much less from these defects: they begin to evoke the Canadian experience without imposing artificial poetics.

Charles Sangster

Sangster was born at the Navy Yard in Kingston, Upper Canada, in 1822; his father died while he was still an infant. At fifteen he went to work full-time at Fort Henry, where he was employed to make cartridges. After two years there his job changed to one in which, as he later said, he was 'ranked as a messenger, received the pay of a labourer, and did the duty of a clerk'. Of the loss of schooling, which might have given him better preparation for a career as a poet, he wrote:

like many leading Canadians, [I am] a self-made man. . . . I have not the advantages of a classical education. All that I possess mentally has been acquired by careful reading of the best authors (chiefly Fiction), properly directed thought, and a tolerable share of industry. . . . Even as a boy my ear seems to have been tuned to the harmony of sounds. I would have read more in my younger days, but books were not to be had—the Bible, and the 'Citizen of the World' in two volumes, constituted my library for many years. That I have read the former attentively is apparent from my poems.

Having begun to write poems for newspapers and magazines such as *The Literary Garland* and *The Anglo-American Review*, Sangster quit Fort Henry in 1849 to become the editor of the Courier at Amherstburg. Unfortunately the paper collapsed when its publisher died, and in 1850 he took more menial employment with the Kingston *British Whig*, remaining there for the next fourteen years. Despite the arduousness of his tasks, he managed to write the poems collected in *The St Lawrence and the Saguenay and Other Poems* (1856) and *Hesperus, and Other Poems, and Lyrics* (1860).

The presence of love poetry in these collections coincided with Sangster's two marriages—the first to Mary Kilborne, whose death eighteen months later greatly saddened the poet; the second to Henrietta Meagher. In 1864 Sangster became a reporter for the Kingston *Daily News*. In 1868 he joined the newly formed federal post office in Ottawa as a clerk, and in 1882 he was honoured with a charter membership in the Royal Society of Canada. A breakdown forced his retirement in 1886. He had hoped to ready two more volumes of his poetry for publication but was unable to do so. (These were later edited by Frank Tierney and published in the 1970s.)

From *The St. Lawrence and the Saguenay*[1]

* * *

The bark leaps love-fraught from the land; the sea
Lies calm before us. Many an isle is there,[2]
Clad with soft verdure; many a stately tree
Uplifts its leafy branches through the air;
The amorous current bathes the islets fair,
As we skip, youth-like, o'er the limpid waves;
White cloudlets speck the golden atmosphere,
Through which the passionate sun looks down, and graves
His image on the pearls that boil from the deep caves,

And bathe the vessel's prow. Isle after isle
Is passed, as we glide tortuously through
The opening vistas, that uprise and smile
Upon us from the ever-changing view.
Here nature, lavish of her wealth, did strew
Her flocks of panting islets on the breast
Of the admiring River, where they grew,
Like shapes of Beauty, formed to give a zest
To the charmed mind, like waking Visions of the Blest.

The silver-sinewed arms of the proud Lake
Love-wild, embrace each islet tenderly,
The zephyrs kiss the flowers when they wake
At morn, flushed with a rare simplicity;
See how they bloom around yon birchen tree,
And smile along the bank, by the sandy shore,
In lovely groups—a fair community!
The embossed rocks glitter like golden ore,
And here, the o'erarching trees form a fantastic bower.

Red walls of granite rise on either hand,
Rugged and smooth; a proud young eagle soars
Above the stately evergreens, that stand
Like watchful sentinels on these God-built towers;
And near yon beds of many-colored flowers
Browse two majestic deer, and at their side
A spotted fawn all innocently cowers;
In the rank brushwood it attempts to hide,
While the strong-antlered stag steps forth with lordly stride,

1 Stanzas 3 to 11.
2 The setting of this first section is the Thousand Islands.

And slakes his thirst, undaunted, at the stream.
Isles of o'erwhelming beauty! surely here
the wild enthusiast might live, and dream
His life away. No Nymphic trains appear,
To charm the pale Ideal Worshipper
Of Beauty; nor Neriads[3] from the deeps below;
Nor hideous Gnomes, to fill the breast with fear:
But crystal streams through endless landscapes flow,
And o'er the clustering Isles the softest breezes blow.

LYRIC TO THE ISLES

Here the Spirit of Beauty keepeth
Jubilee for evermore;
Here the Voice of Gladness leapeth,
Echoing from shore to shore.
O'er the hidden watery valley,
O'er each buried wood and glade,
Dances our delighted galley,
Through the sunlight and the shade—
Dances o'er the granite cells,
Where the Soul of Beauty dwells:

Here the flowers are ever springing,
While the summer breezes blow;
Here the Hours are ever clinging,
Loitering before they go;
Playing round each beauteous islet,
Loath to leave the sunny shore,
Where, upon her couch of violet,
Beauty sits for evermore—
Sits and smiles by day and night,
Hand in hand with pure Delight.

Here the Spirit of Beauty dwelleth
In each palpitating tree,
In each amber wave that welleth
From its home, beneath the sea;
In the moss upon the granite,
In each calm, secluded bay,
With the zephyr trains that fan it

3 Water nymphs.

With their sweet breaths all the day—
On the waters, on the shore,
Beauty dwelleth evermore!

Yes, here the Genius[4] of Beauty truly dwells.
I worship Truth and Beauty in my soul.
The pure prismatic globule that upwells
From the blue deep; the psalmy waves that roll
Before the hurricane; the outspread scroll
Of heaven, with its written tomes of stars;
The dew-drop on the leaf: These I extol,
And all alike—each one a Spirit-Mars,
Guarding my Victor-Soul above Earth's prison bars.

There was a stately Maiden once, who made
These Isles her home. Oft has her lightsome skiff
Toyed with the waters; and the velvet glade,
The shadowy woodland, and the granite cliff,
Joyed at her footsteps. Here the Brigand Chief,
Her Father, lived, an outlaw. Her soul's pride
Was ministering to his wants. In brief,
The wildest midnight she would cross the tide,
Full of a daughter's love, to hasten to his side.

Queen of the Isles! she well deserved the name:
In look, in action, in repose a Queen!
Some Poet-Muse may yet hand down to fame
Her woman's courage, and her classic mien;
Some Painter's skill immortalize the scene,
And blend with it that Maiden's history;
Some Sculptor's hand from the rough marble glean
An eloquent Thought, whose truthfulness shall be
The expounder of her worth and moral dignity.

On, through the lovely Archipelago,
Glides the swift bark. Soft summer matins ring
From every isle. The wild fowl come and go,
Regardless of our presence. On the wing,
And perched upon the boughs, the gay birds sing

4 Guardian spirit.

Their loves: This is their summer paradise;
From morn till night their joyous caroling
Delights the ear, and through the lucent skies
Ascends the choral hymn in softest symphonies.

* * *

1856

From *Sonnets Written in the Orillia Woods*

IV

The birds are singing merrily, and here
A squirrel claims the lordship of the woods,
And scolds me for intruding. At my feet
The tireless ants all silently proclaim
The dignity of labour. In my ear
The bee hums drowsily; from sweet to sweet
Careering, like a lover weak in aim.
I hear faint music in the solitudes;
A dreamlike melody that whispers peace
Imbues the calmy forest, and sweet rills
Of pensive feeling murmur through my brain,
Like ripplings of pure water down the hills
That slumber in the moonlight. Cease, oh, cease!
Some day my weary heart will coin these into pain.

VII

Our life is like a forest, where the sun
Glints down upon us through the throbbing leaves;
The full light rarely finds us. One by one,
Deep rooted in our souls, there springeth up
Dark groves of human passion, rich in gloom,
At first no bigger than an acorn-cup.
Hope threads the tangled labyrinth, but grieves
Till all our sins have rotted in their tomb,
And made the rich loam of each yearning heart
To bring forth fruits and flowers to new life.
We feel the dew from heaven, and there start

From some deep fountain little rills whose strife
Is drowned in music. Thus in light and shade
We live, and move, and die, through all this earthly glade.

XIII

I've almost grown a portion of this place;
I seem familiar with each mossy stone;
Even the nimble chipmunk passes on,
And looks, but never scolds me. Birds have flown
And almost touched my hand; and I can trace
The wild bees to their hives. I've never known
So sweet a pause from labour. But the tone
Of a past sorrow, like a mournful rill
Threading the heart of some melodious hill,
Or the complainings of the whippoorwill,
Passes through every thought, and hope, and aim.
It has its uses; for it cools the flame
Of ardent love that burns my being up—
Love, life's celestial pearl, diffused through all its cup.

1860

Isabella Valancy Crawford

1850–1887

Born in Dublin, Ireland, Isabella Valancy Crawford emigrated with her family to North America, settling in Canada West, in 1858, in the town of Paisley (near the Bruce Peninsula). Her father was the first doctor there, but his practice was never profitable, and the family's fortunes worsened when, as treasurer of the township, he was convicted of misappropriation of funds. To escape the cloud of public scandal, the Crawford family retreated to the Kingston area in 1862, then to Lakefield (where they lived for a time with Robert Strickland, nephew of Susanna Moodie and Catharine Parr Traill), and eventually to Peterborough around 1870. This series of moves only exacerbated the family's impoverishment.

Dr Crawford died in Peterborough in 1875. Nine of Crawford's eleven siblings had already died in childhood, possibly because of a congenital heart condition that may have been aggravated by malnutrition. Crawford's lone remaining sister died in 1876 as a young woman, either 'from consumption' or of heart failure. (Not surprisingly, mortality is a recurring concern in Crawford's poetry.) With her only surviving brother gone north to seek his own livelihood, Crawford was left to care for her mother.

Crawford had been educated at home by her parents, who instructed her in Latin and French as well as in English. Her rich imagination was shaped by the classics—Horace and Dante were said to be her favourite poets—and by contemporary English and French literature. Her poetry has affinities with Tennyson and with the Pre-Raphaelites, but Crawford brought to that British tradition a Canadian background that not only served as a source for her depictions of landscape and milieu but also provided her with imagery and mythology drawn from the Native people.

A poet whose work stands out against much of the more conventional poetry of her time, Crawford so imbues nature with life in her poems that her settings become animistic, and her images (as in 'Said the Canoe') have a quality so sensual that critics have sometimes offered Freudian interpretations. She shows remarkable control over a wide range of forms, including long narrative poems (such as her famous 'Malcolm's Katie'), song-like lyrics, poems in dialect, and dramatic monologues. Her vision is repeatedly one of a world of forces in opposition, sometimes universalized to a cosmic struggle between darkness and light, hope and despair.

Having formed an early ambition to write, Crawford moved with her mother to Toronto around 1876 to be close to newspapers and publishers. Because she hoped to succeed as a commercial writer, much of what she published was in newspapers and periodicals. She discovered that poems earned her little: the collection *'Old Spookses' Pass', 'Malcolm's Katie' and Other Poems* (1884), which she issued at her own expense, sold few copies, despite receiving good reviews in Canada and Britain. It was her fiction that provided her with just enough to live on. In 1873 she won a prize for one of her short stories ($500, of which she unfortunately received only $100), and she later saw the serialization of at least two novels in Toronto papers: one in the *Evening Globe* in 1885–6 and another in a journal called the *Fireside Weekly*. Only a single chapter of the Globe novel survives; the other novel has been entirely lost.

Crawford died of heart failure at the age of thirty-six having gained neither the financial success or the readership she longed for; however, her work began to receive critical recognition following the publication of *The Collected Poems of Isabella Valancy Crawford*, edited by John Garvin in 1905. Her reputation was further enhanced later in the century when Dorothy Livesay and James Reaney became interested in her poetry, and in 1972, her collected poems were reprinted with a new introduction by Reaney. Around that time, Livesay's work on Crawford's unpublished manuscripts led to the recovery (from an incomplete and fragmented state) of the long poem now known as *Hugh and Ion*. Livesay published a version of the poem, with commentary, in *Canadian Literature* in 1973 (her proposed title was *The Hunters Twain*); that was followed by a more satisfactory if speculative reconstruction of the poem by Glen Clever, published as a chapbook in 1977. (That edition is the one followed in the selection from *Hugh and Ion* that appears here.) By adding to Crawford's oeuvre a previously unknown major poem, *Hugh and Ion* has played a significant role in the revaluation of Crawford's work.

Although the increased interest in Crawford also led to the publication of *Selected Stories of Isabella Valancy Crawford* (1975) and *Fairy Tales of Isabella Valancy Crawford* (1977), Crawford's literary reputation today continues to be based primarily on her poetry.

Hugh and Ion

The opening of this poem, which tells of a young man rejected by the woman he loves, suggests that it will be a witty and urbane story of courtship. But Crawford quickly moves the poem in other directions. A daring step beyond her earlier lyrics, *Hugh and Ion* uses even its courtship scene to invite questions about the nature—and desirability—of love and about the lover's free will. In subsequent sections, the poem becomes by turns an investigation of the psychology of the spurned lover; a satirical critique of the suffering and evils of the city and its 'busy marts'; a quasi-allegorical dramatization of the soul struggling to save the body; and a Wordsworthian vision of redemption in nature. The continuation of the poem (not reprinted here) goes still further—into an allegorical passage in which the lover, now divided in two, enters into a dialogue with himself. One speaker, called Hugh, optimistically affirms his faith in God and holds out hope for a better future; the other, Ion, responds with a dark vision of a meaningless universe.

The ideas raised in this debate between Hugh and Ion—and in the larger poem—show Crawford aware of and entering into the important philosophical discussions taking place in her own time. Ion offers a view of life as inherently tragic, in which human beings go on struggling to survive only because they live in delusion and are fuelled by unwarranted hope. To counter this, Hugh responds:

Shame, Ion, shame! You of the feeble folk
Who bend their own weak knees and
wav'ring spines
To God, and chitter-chatter of despair
Of ruins and of chaos—nor have sheer
strength
To clamber up God's breast, and look abroad
From thence across the universe. And see
All His broad purpose.

This debate ends with Ion asking Hugh for some proof of his hopeful view, and Hugh responding with a further affirmation of faith ('seek my God, and you shall find His Hope'). In the last lines that we have of the poem, Hugh finds himself alone, confronting 'Deep dawns of newer darkness'—which seem to be at war with the intermittent light created by flashes of lightning. The poem, never completed by Crawford, breaks off in mid-sentence. Had Crawford concluded this ambitious work, it is not apparent whether she would have opted for an optimistic resolution or a tragic one—and her failure to finish the poem could suggest her own indecision.

The recovery of *Hugh and Ion* has provided an important addition to Crawford's body of work, not only because of its engagement with philosophical issues: the poem is filled with powerful turns of language that go beyond anything found in the work published in Crawford's lifetime; and it is enlivened by an unusual fluidity of allusion and of imagery—in which flowers, gardens, and serpents; blindness; hunting; and the 'clay' of human flesh reappear in changed contexts and associations that demand their meaning be reassessed as the poem progresses—which suggests the influence of the French *symbolistes.* Even in its partial form, *Hugh and Ion* stands as a further affirmation of Northrop Frye's observation that Crawford had 'the most remarkable mythopoeic imagination in Canadian poetry'.

Esther[1]

Unheard of others, voices called all night:—
The babble of young voices, the strong cries
Of men and women mourned amid the palms,
And gathered in mine ear, as winds that blow
About the earth and, gathering in some cave,
Give ghostly utterance of ghostly things—
'Esther, the Queen, arise and move the King
To sheathe the sword that lies upon the throats
Of thine own people!'

1 The Biblical Book of Esther explains how the Persian king chooses the Jewish maiden Esther to be his queen. When Esther's uncle, Mordecai, angers the king's vizier, the latter decides to take revenge by slaughtering all of Persia's Jews. Mordecai asks Esther to intercede with the king, even though for Esther to enter the throne room without being summoned is a breach of protocol that, if it meets with the king's disfavour, will result in her execution.

When the sun sprang up
His tresses were as blood that stained the courts
And beat upon the walls, and sent its tide
To bathe my naked feet when I thrust back
The golden tissue of the door to catch
Some sweetness of the morn upon my brow;
And lo! my God, a sweetness filled my soul
That came not from the morning but from Thee!

The winds that stirred the foldings of my robe
Were children's fingers—ghostly, clinging clasps
That said, 'O Esther, plead before the King!'
Ah me! how often when a little maid,
Playing amid the fountains and the flowers
Of mine own people, have such dimpled hands
Caught at my flying robe in mimic fright,
And great round eyes buried themselves therein;
But then the voices laughed, 'O Esther, stay
That wicked brother, for he chases us,
And pelts with blushing roses.' Now I hear,
'O Esther, stay the King, he slaughters us!'

Alas my courage is so weak a blade
It trembles at a breath. God, temper it to strength!
I perish if I go uncalled before the King.
Yea! let him smite me down a sacrifice
For Israel! Perchance that, dying thus, my blood
May creep about his heart and soften it
To those for whom I die. O God, when Thou
Didst veil Thy handmaid's soul in this fair flesh
'Twas for some strait sore as the present need!

What is it that glimmers ready by my couch?
The symbol of my state, the crown the King
Hath set upon my brows. On, crown, and deck
My triumph or my death! O robes of state,
Ye jewelled splendours, how ye mock this flesh
That quivers with monitions of that hour
When this night's moon shall peer above the palms
And find no life in Esther but that cold, cold life,
Blazing from diamond crown and golden robe,
Mocks of her life's brief sun and briefer state.

But still will Esther go. Jehovah calls!
And if I die—Hark! as I go by court
And golden pillar, sweet, shrill voices cry,
Unheard of others, 'Esther, stay the King!'
O yea, my lambs of Israel! how your hands
Cling to my robes and pluck me to the King!
God, lift his sceptre up before my face!
But if I die—I die!

[*c.* 1874], 1905

Canada to England

Gone are the days, old Warrior of the Seas,
When thine armed head, bent low to catch my voice,
Caught but the plaintive sighings of my woods,
And the wild roar of rock-dividing streams,
And the loud bellow of my cataracts,
Bridged with the seven splendours of the bow.
When Nature was a Samson yet unshorn,[1]
Filling the land with solitary might,
Or as the Angel of the Apocalypse,
One foot upon the primeval bowered land
One foot upon the white mane of the sea,[2]
My voice but faintly swelled the ebb and flow
Of the wild tides and storms that beat upon
Thy rocky girdle,—loud shrieking from the Ind[3]
Ambrosial-breathing furies; from the north
Thundering with Arctic bellows, groans of seas
Rising from tombs of ice disrupted by
The magic kisses of the wide-eyed sun.

The times have won a change. Nature no more
Lords it alone and binds the lonely land
A serf to tongueless solitudes; but Nature's self
Is led, glad captive, in light fetters rich
As music-sounding silver can adorn;
And man has forged them, and our silent God

1 That is, Samson before losing his innate strength when his hair—which, as a sign of his dedication to God, he must not cut—is cut by the Philistine Delilah.

2 An image from the Book of Revelation 10: 5–10.

3 India (poetic). The 'furies' (Maenads)—ecstatic followers of Dionysus—are said to have followed him to India and back.

Behind His flaming worlds smiles on the deed.
'Man hath dominion'—words of primal might;[4]
'Man hath dominion'—thus the words of God.

If destiny is writ on night's dusk scroll,
Then youngest stars are dropping from the hand
Of the Creator, sowing on the sky
My name in seeds of light. Ages will watch
Those seeds expand to suns, such as the tree
Bears on its boughs, which grows in Paradise.[5]

How sounds my voice, my warrior kinsman, now?
Sounds it not like to thine in lusty youth—
A word-possessing shout of busy men,
Veined with the clang of trumpets and the noise
Of those who make them ready for the strife,
And in the making ready bruise its head?
Sounds it not like to thine—the whispering vine,
The robe of summer rustling thro' the fields,
The lowing of the cattle in the meads,
The sound of Commerce, and the music-set,
Flame-brightened step of Art in stately halls,—
All the infinity of notes which chord
The diapason[6] of a Nation's voice?

My infants' tongues lisp word for word with thine;
We worship, wed, and die, and God is named
That way ye name Him,—strong bond between
Two mighty lands when as one mingled cry,
As of one voice, Jehovah turns to hear.
The bonds between us are no subtle links
Of subtle minds binding in close embrace,
Half-struggling for release, two alien lands,
But God's own seal of kindred, which to burst
Were but to dash His benediction from
Our brows. 'Who loveth not his kin,
Whose face and voice are his, how shall he love
God whom he hath not seen?'[7]

[*c.* 1874], 1905

4 An allusion to the naming of 'the Dominion of Canada', which is based on Psalm 72: 8: 'He shall have dominion also from sea to sea, and from the river unto the ends of the earth' (Psalm 72: 8).
5 That is, the Tree of Knowledge, which in the Book of Genesis, is found in the Garden of Eden.
6 The entire musical range of an instrument or voice.
7 A paraphrase of 1 John 4: 20: 'If a man say, I love God, and hateth his brother, he is a liar: for he that loveth not his brother whom he hath seen, how can he love God whom he hath not seen?'

Said the Canoe

My masters twain made me a bed
Of pine-boughs resinous, and cedar;
Of moss, a soft and gentle breeder
Of dreams of rest; and me they spread
With furry skins and, laughing, said:
'Now she shall lay her polished sides
As queens do rest, or dainty brides,
Our slender lady of the tides!'

My masters twain their camp-soul[1] lit;
Streamed incense from the hissing cones;
Large crimson flashes grew and whirled;
Thin golden nerves of sly light curled
Round the dun camp; and rose faint zones,
Half way about each grim bole knit,
Like a shy child that would bedeck
With its soft clasp a Brave's red neck,
Yet sees the rough shield on his breast,
The awful plumes shake on his crest,
And, fearful, drops his timid face,
Nor dares complete the sweet embrace.

Into the hollow hearts of brakes—
Yet warm from sides of does and stags
Passed to the crisp, dark river-flags—
Sinuous, red as copper-snakes,
Sharp-headed serpents, made of light,
Glided and hid themselves in night.

My masters twain the slaughtered deer
Hung on forked boughs with thongs of leather:
Bound were his stiff, slim feet together,
His eyes like dead stars cold and drear.
The wandering firelight drew near
And laid its wide palm, red and anxious,
On the sharp splendour of his branches,
On the white foam grown hard and sere
    On flank and shoulder.
Death—hard as breast of granite boulder—
    Under his lashes
Peered thro' his eyes at his life's grey ashes.

1 i.e. the campfire.

My masters twain sang songs that wove—
As they burnished hunting-blade and rifle—
A golden thread with a cobweb trifle,
Loud of the chase and low of love:

'O Love! art thou a silver fish,
Shy of the line and shy of gaffing,
Which we do follow, fierce, yet laughing,
Casting at thee the light-winged wish?
And at the last shall we bring thee up
From the crystal darkness, under the cup
　Of lily folden
　On broad leaves golden?

'O Love! art thou a silver deer
With feet as swift as wing of swallow,
While we with rushing arrows follow?
And at the last shall we draw near
And o'er thy velvet neck cast thongs
Woven of roses, stars and songs—
　New chains all moulden
　Of rare gems olden?'

They hung the slaughtered fish like swords
　On saplings slender; like scimitars,
　Bright, and ruddied from new-dead wars,
Blazed in the light the scaly hordes.

They piled up boughs beneath the trees,
　Of cedar web and green fir tassel.
　Low did the pointed pine tops rustle,
The camp-fire blushed to the tender breeze.

The hounds laid dewlaps on the ground
　With needles of pine, sweet, soft and rusty,
　Dreamed of the dead stag stout and lusty;
A bat by the red flames wove its round.

The darkness built its wigwam walls
　Close round the camp, and at its curtain
　Pressed shapes, thin, woven and uncertain
As white locks of tall waterfalls.

1884, 1905

From *Hugh and Ion*

I

She had the full, fell frankness of her kind
Nor made a rose-ball of the saucy 'No'
She flung across her tea-cup at his heart.
She had within the strong stone of her soul
A little feeble seed of womanhood,
That stirr'd, and pitied when the blow went home.
'Now, now,' she said, 'for comfort here's a tale.
For some fell tyrant's freak,[1] once was a man
Condemned to crucifixion. In deep dark
They laid his long, strong limbs upon a cross
And bound his great thews to it with thin cords
Then said, "lie there, thou valiant fool, and die."
And so he lay, and wither'd inch by inch,
In the dense dark—nor mov'd a finger-tip
To test the ropes that bound him. Came a day,
The Sultan miss'd his beauty and his sword,
And said "If still he live, why, bring him forth."
Then the grim gaoler flash'd a torch on him
And seeing he still liv'd, cried "Up, and come—
The Sultan needs thee." As the light stream'd wide
He saw his cross—a shadow built of wings
Of moth and butterfly, and wither'd limbs
Of feeble rose-vines—and about him blaz'd
The long, free halls that once had own'd him lord
And nought had held him to his deadly cross,
And Liberty had waited for one leap
Of his into wide arms—a Sultan's jest,
With death its grim wit-sparkle. Come, my friend
Leap from thy phantom little cross of love,
Burst on the world unshackl'd by thy dreams—
My "no" the torch to light thy freedom up.
Love is the deep dense darkness of the soul
Beaten by arms that passionately grope
And catch the void. Away with Love, away!'

'And give us up Barabbas,'[2] said the man
Looking to where the other lover lean'd

1 A capricious urge or notion.

2 The notorious prisoner chosen by the people to be released by Pontius Pilate at Passover instead of Jesus (Matt. 27: 16). Crawford identifies him as a robber (an identification found only in one of the Gospels), which allows her to make him an embodiment of the contemporary capitalistic society that is robbing the poor.

A portly shoulder by a distant door
And cup in hand, laid all the little light
Of dull and dreamy eyes—not on his love
But on the phantom of the dead day's 'deal'
On stocks and margins, 'long' and 'short', and all
The licens'd weapons of the world's wild war
Against large Plenty, where, all pitiful,
She holds to Want the wealth of weighty sheaves.

She laugh'd—the light, shrill laughter of her kind,
The fell frank music of a hard, high soul,
That knows not Love, lie, tenderness, nor shame.
'Barabbas was a robber. Lack-a-day!
We of the golden tissues floating far
And sandals jewel-lac'd—we need our thieves
Our Benedict[3] Barabbas who can steal
With such bland gestures, and wise brows bent down
In plans financial, that the feeble folk
Stand all at gaze in envy and delight
Yes—even while he plucks the crusts from lips
Blue with their torture for it. Away with Love
Dark God of voids. And if his frame be knit
Of any tissue tougher than a dream
Crucify him—pierce him to death with doubt,
Loose us Barabbas—we of the Jewell'd coifs!'
She sleek'd the pansy darkness of her robe
With the pale pearl of a rose-lin'd palm
And drove the rubied arrow through the dusk
And stormy purple of the raven braid
That built its blackness over falcon eyes
Hooded by lashes like the fall of night[4]
Over sharp, shining waters. Then she smote
Him in the heart with that keen, kindly smile
(Sharp *coup de grace* for many a sturdy stag)
Of wider wisdom—and she knew he knew
Her soul was blind, and could not look on Love.
'Blind, blind so safe,' she answer'd to the scorn
That slowly rose against her in his gaze.
'If there be pits, I pass them on a hair
If there be heights, they breed no whirling brain;

3 Blessed. Barabbas here is compared to businessmen whom the poor foolishly admire even while being plundered by them.

4 In the sport of falconry, the falcon is kept hooded until the falconer sends it to pursue its prey. This metaphor, developed in the lines that follow, is later associated with traditional depictions of the god of love as blindfolded.

If Love bask like a serpent by my feet
If Love lie like a lion in my way
If Love lure like a lily to dark deeps
I see him not—so blind and blessèd pass!'

'So creeps the slow-worm,[5] blind and blessed thing
Not knowing heights nor depths, nor if it cling
To the peak'd mountain lording all the land;
Or to the leaf that rolls along the mire
In Autumn's blast. But you, fierce falcon soul
You pluck the jewell'd hood across keen eyes
And dash bold wings against the face of God
Who loos'd you to the air—and cry "Blind, blind!
Blame not the blind!" And when you plunge your beak
In some strong quarry breasting up the sky
You cry for pardon with that lying plaint
"Blind, blind, blame not the blind!" O wing'd keen curse
Blind by strong willing that you will not see!'

She drew the golden glamour of a rose
Across her eyes. 'Hooded with joys and blind
To dreams and ghosts and phantoms of delight,
Where is this Love? God! if he have his birth
As love—but watch him as he walks the world
And see him at the end, stretch'd stark, and chang'd
To Hate, and dead, with cold veins virus fill'd.
These wedded lovers—like twin seraphs[6] clasp'd
Within the arms of a meek, bright moon
Whose light is honey dripping from clear cusps
Eternity is theirs—until Time rounds
Some twenty fiery pathways round the world
Lo, then the man—why, watch him stand at gaze
At ev'ry budding girl that matches May,
His wife the pale, wan priestess at a shrine
Whose star has faded to a ball of dust,
Dead in dark space! O if Love be born
Strangle the imp while yet the dimples stray
Across full baby cheeks—before he change
To virile Hate—or to languid Loathing
Or merge his modern monogamic mind

5 Or 'blindworm': a legless lizard (long thought to be a snake), once commonly found in pastures, under stones or logs.

6 Seraphim, a class of angels. The presumed derivation of the word from a Hebrew root meaning 'to burn' led to the view that the seraphim are specially distinguished by their fervent love.

For patriarchal mood plus many wives.'[7]
She laugh'd, and he that lov'd her sigh'd and went.

II

Without the West drew flaming gates across
The grey, gaunt distance of the wintry street
Low down were welded fast against the sky
Dull, purple bars that held the first, fine snow.
Lower, the old unutterable pray'r
That glows in golden script behind the day
Stretch'd its still strength about the dark'ning world
And as a cobweb delicately spun
Bare black thin boughs hung orb'd against the sky
And in their subtle lacings seem'd to cling
Arachne-like, the round, full Evening Star.
Dark on near hills the primal forest heav'd
Its haughty heart against the City's claws
That lengthen'd towards its ramparts day by day;
Dark on near sands the tideless waters stood
Meek with dun mist—moaning against wan wharves
Dying to dumbness as the fierce young frost
Gaz'd on the shudd'ring world, ere serpent-wise
He coil'd chill crystal folds about its breast.
On such an eve despair seems no strange growth,
But a chief vein that feeds the chilling heart,
With pausing billows stiff'ning as they burst
And Hope an alien flame fall'n from the wick
Of a cold lamp that chills the failing hand.
Dust, sharp as spear points in the rising frost
Whirl'd in keen simoons,[8] and, sullen orbs
The base stars of the city lamps, leap'd up.

III

Where's speech in auguish? O she never throve
On the high swell of Sorrow's bursting heart.
Two groans are hers that give themselves to speech
'God, God!' with this she wails Him up before[9]

7 That is, or replace modern standards of monogamy with those of the Biblical patriarchs, who made plural marriages.
8 Sandstorms.
9 That is, Sorrow (personified) has only two words in her vocabulary. The first of these summons God before a tribunal presided over by a personified Desolation.

Her Bar of Desolation—then, 'Why? Why?'
Spurts through her hollowed graves and empty shrines
For who will fling the iron doors apart
Where naked Sorrow sits, and free her shriek
To beat in strength against the granite world?
One caught the mutter of his cag'd despair[10]
And passing, struck a light, lascivious palm
Upon his arm, and serpent-like her glance
Curv'd at him over plump and ruddy cheeks
For she no draggled weed, but tense and hale
Strong Flower of Vice, and foliag'd soberly
In rich demureness of all sombre hues
A fine aesthetic motion of the mind
To suit her colours to the tow'ring walls
Of churches, churches pressing on her path,
And the grave grey-beards tott'ring in her wake.
Behind the springing of her sudden look
She solv'd swift problems on the problem, man;
So laugh'd and pass'd, and, looking at the gates
He stood by, mutter'd, 'Aye—he freezes now
Before some sudden frost in woman's shape,
Or in some blast that burst some shard apart
And let the half-blown, half-seen bud he lov'd
Swing all its stinging poison on the air.
Lord, what an interchange of wonderment
There is when man finds ev'ry woman foul
And woman weeds her dream away, and through
Clear spaces sees the strong, smooth tiger, Man.
Tush! let him be—he's in the wonder-throe'—
And the sharp dust caught, and veil'd her, and she pass'd.

IV

The bitter eve grew vocal as he went.
The infant city nursing on the breast
Of unhewn woods found virile voice to shout
The cry of eighteen hundred years ago.
The church tow'rs roar'd it on their ev'ning chime
'Loose us Barabbas!—he will rear us high;
Will lay his gold upon our organ pipes;
Will beat his stolen silver in our bells;

10 A prostitute, hearing him and seeing his distraught state, places a hand upon his shoulder.

And stain our windows with the blood he robs
From the free Helot's[11] heart. O Christ, O Christ!
Thy robe is sordid and Thy palms are hard
Hang on Thy cross! Loose us Barabbas, yes!
And while Christ hangs, the thief shall build to Him.'

'Loose us Barabbas!' all the busy marts
Buzzed with the cry, 'for none but robber thews
Can wrestle with fierce Fortune, now-a-days.'
Vice rear'd its supple, serpent-head and hiss'd
'Loose us Barabbas—let our fellow free.'

Want, lean, lank giant, honest hunger-blind
Stood groaning 'tween the cries, and questioning
Might not Barabbas be a newer Christ?
With newer gospel fitter for the time?'

V

With the illimitable wilderness around
From the close city hives rang up the groan
'So little space!—we starve—we faint, we die!'
Lord! Lord! to see the gaping city sewer
Beaded with haggard heads—and hungry eyes
Peering above the heaving of the drains
And hear the harsh, unreasonable cry
'We starve, we starve!' While half a world lay fresh
And teeming, out beyond the city gates!
Alas, for him who feels a Samson soul
Within the sinews of a medium mind
And lays weak willing hands on lion jaws
And clasps strong columns in a flaccid arm.[12]
One such there was—the Samson in him grew
At sight of pillars bearing wrongs aloft
On firm, flint shoulders, and of lions crouch'd
To guard grim evils tott'ring on their staves,
By the fierce, tender wonder of his mind
That what man calls 'a man', should choose to pave

11 Slave's. When capitalized, as here, it may be specific to its original meaning: a Spartan who was neither a slave nor a free citizen.

12 In the Book of Judges, Samson, at the height of his powers, encounters and destroys a young lion. Later, once deprived of his strength, he is captured by the Philistines, who make the mistake of letting his hair regrow; when they bring him to a great party, he finds his strength restored and pulls down the pillars supporting the house, killing his captors and himself.

The city kennels with his juiceless bones,
To lick the city dust with siccous[13] tongue,
To raven at its flesh marts with fierce eyes,
And feel the iron soles of rushing feet
Crush his lean breast, trample his puny babes
And bring the dark divorce of hunger pangs
Between all life and him—while prairie breasts
Mounded, all teeming with the milk of life,
And forests shouted to his leaden ears
Of food and shelter. He who pities man
Has keener sword pricks on his tender breast
Than the gaunt bosom of the victim bears
Aye, though the sword is hilt deep in his heart
And he who sees the mountain reel and fall
Had more of death than him that falls with it.
For Hugh, the giant in him hurl'd the clay
He groan'd in, blindly up against the rocks,
And flung it on the levell'd spears, and thrust
It close against the furnaces, and play'd
A thousand antics with the shade of earth
It scorn'd, and lov'd and loath'd; and the poor ghost
Of flesh and blood lay at the strong soul's feet
Trembling to dust, and smitten with despair.
Then, almost free, the soul had clearer light
And lifting high the pale clay on its breast
Mourn'd the young fury of its holy rage
And on its necessary brother blew
The strong breath of its mouth, and sought to slip
The vital fetter in its place again.[14]

'Up, up, thou weakling! Wouldst thou lay thy palms
Against a stubborn world, to hurl it fair
Into a truer orbit—up, up and forge
Strong sinews for the deed: I, fed of God,
Grow lusty—feed thy fainting flesh beside
His lowlier fountains running for thy lips—
Weld strength with strength, so let us face the world.
I err'd in hate of thee—arise—forgive!'

So spake his Soul, and pluck'd him from the town
With its young walls and venerable sins,

13 Dry; 'raven': ravage or plunder.

14 That is, Hugh has abused himself to the point of death, but his soul, on the verge of departing, breathes life back into his body. The body is here described not only as the soul's 'necessary brother' but also as its 'vital fetter' in the sense that it holds the soul bound to earthly existence.

The smell of primal woods upon its air
The groans of Ancient Famine in its slums.

VI

There came an April day all tremulous
And shaking like a shining reed between
Two soft winds blowing at it with purs'd lips
That drove its polish'd stem now into shade
Now into sunshine. Then there came a night
That bore between its dark still palms a cloud
An alabaster box that held the balm
Bright, in the sunset, as a yellow gourd—
She bore it to the peak of midnight—there
With thunder claps she burst its darken'd sides
And through warm blackness fell the bless'd spring balm
Of rain upon the world. All through the night
Life loos'd the awful fountain of his heart,
And earth grew tremulous with pulsing seeds
And leaping stems, and juices rushing up
From her wide veins along the barren woods.
And all the budding boughs in that short night,
Did dimple with small leaves a dew drop large.

[By 1883], 1977

Charles G.D. Roberts

1860–1943

Charles G.D. Roberts, his cousin Bliss Carman, Archibald Lampman, and Duncan Campbell Scott are central to the group of writers referred to as the 'Poets of the Confederation': their prominence between 1867 and World War I, their concern with nationalism, and their interrelated lives make them truly members of a school of poetry. The oldest and the first to publish (*Orion and Other Poems*, 1880), Roberts seemed to his fellow poets their founding father. A famous essay by Lampman suggests his importance:

It was almost ten years ago, and I was very young, an undergraduate at college. One May evening somebody lent me Orion and Other Poems, *then recently published. Like most of the young fellows about me I had been under the depressing conviction that we were situated hopelessly on the outskirts of civilization, where no art and no literature could be, and it was useless to expect that anything great could be done by any of our companions, still more useless to expect that we could do it ourselves. I sat up all night reading and re-reading Orion in a state of the wildest excitement and when I went to bed I could not sleep. It seemed to me a wonderful thing that such work could be done by a Canadian, by a young man, one of ourselves.* ('Two Canadian Poets: A Lecture', 1891)

Roberts' youth, the resource out of which much of his best poetry is constructed, combined many of the common elements of Confederation life: an English and Loyalist background, a rural boyhood in close contact with the wilderness, and a broad classical education received at home. When Roberts was fourteen, his father, an Anglican clergyman, accepted a new post at Fredericton, moving the boy away from the Tantramar region of New Brunswick, where he had spent his childhood and which he loved, into a larger world. At Fredericton Collegiate School, he expanded his classical education to include recent British poets; later, at the University of New Brunswick, he added philosophy and political economy to his studies. While completing his degree he began writing poetry. By the time he was twenty-three Roberts had not only married and been head of two schools, but had published three books of verse. The first of these, *Orion*, received international praise, and Matthew Arnold among others saw it as distinctively Canadian; at home, however, it was criticized as being too regional. Roberts took this criticism to heart and by 1886 was calling for a more national approach in the writing of Canadian poetry: 'We must forget to ask of a work whether it is Nova Scotian or British Columbian, of Ontario, or of New Brunswick, until we have inquired if it be broadly and truly Canadian.' This changed attitude was partly due to his having come in contact with the Canada First Movement, a loose union of people who were intent on developing national pride by celebrating Anglo-Canadian history, encouraging Canadian arts, and strengthening Canada politically.

In 1883 Roberts became literary editor of *The Week*, a Toronto periodical founded by Goldwin Smith (who was active in the Canada First Movement). During his brief association with *The Week* Roberts used it as a forum to encourage young writers, and he himself became more involved with the literary community. In 1885 he returned to teaching, accepting a post at King's College, Windsor, NS, and during his ten years there he wrote prolifically. Shortly after he left teaching in 1895, he also left his wife, family, and then Canada, becoming an expatriate for many years. He worked as an editor and wrote numerous books, including collections of highly popular animal stories, historical romances, works of non-fiction, and further collections of verse. He lived in New York until 1907 and in London from 1912 to 1925, when he returned to Canada for a triumphant and extended lecture tour. He became active in the Canadian literary scene once more and settled permanently in Toronto. He was knighted in 1935 and died eight years later at the age of eighty-three.

Like many of his contemporaries, Roberts was marked by contradictions. A man of letters, at various times in his life he earned most of his income through commercial writing; a nationalist who wrote patriotic verse and a history of Canada, he lived in exile for an extended period. Though he preached the primacy of nation over region, his best poems—like the sonnet sequence in *Songs of the Common Day* (1893)—are early ones that portray nature in New Brunswick from season to season. And though he owes a considerable debt to the pre-Raphaelite tradition and to Transcendentalism, a surprisingly modern vision pervades other early poems, such as 'The Tantramar Revisited', in which man's belief in permanence is seen as an illusion in a world dominated by 'chance and change'. (In 'A Note on Modernism', which first appeared in *Open House*, 1931, a collection of his essays, Roberts recognizes the transitional role that he and the other Confederate poets played in breaking the ground in Canada for the modernist movement.)

This vision of continual flux that informed his poetry until his death is also central in the animal stories to which Roberts turned once he began to support himself through his writing. Collected in *The Kindred of the Wild* (1902) and many other books, these stories, told from the animals' point of view, express a Darwinian vision. As seen in 'In the Deep of the Grass', every creature lives in danger from what one story calls 'all the foraging world', and survival is often a matter of luck as much as of fitness. Confirming that human beings were part of this vision, the massive savagery of the First World War, which Roberts responded to in 'Going

Over (The Somme, 1917)', moved him to expand his understanding of Darwinian existence. Eventually he found harmony within the chaos of existence: in 'As Down the Woodland Ways' death is 'but a travail-pang of life, / Destruction but a name'.

Tantramar Revisited[1]

Summers and summers have come, and gone with the flight of the swallow;
Sunshine and thunder have been, storm, and winter, and frost;
Many and many a sorrow has all but died from remembrance,
Many a dream of joy fall'n in the shadow of pain.
Hands of chance and change have marred, or moulded, or broken,
Busy with spirit or flesh, all I most have adored;
Even the bosom of Earth is strewn with heavier shadows,—
Only in these green hills, aslant to the sea, no change!
Here where the road that has climbed from the inland valleys and woodlands,
Dips from the hill-tops down, straight to the base of the hills,—
Here, from my vantage-ground, I can see the scattering houses,
Stained with time, set warm in orchards, meadows, and wheat,
Dotting the broad bright slopes outspread to southward and eastward,
Wind-swept all day long, blown by the south-east wind.

Skirting the sunbright uplands stretches a riband[2] of meadow,
Shorn of the labouring grass, bulwarked well from the sea,
Fenced on its seaward border with long clay dikes from the turbid
Surge and flow of the tides vexing the Westmoreland shores.
Yonder, toward the left, lie broad the Westmoreland marshes,—
Miles on miles they extend, level, and grassy, and dim,
Clear from the long red sweep of flats to the sky in the distance,
Save for the outlying heights, green-rampired[3] Cumberland Point;
Miles on miles outrolled, and the river-channels divide them,—
Miles on miles of green, barred by the hurtling gusts.

Miles on miles beyond the tawny bay is Minudie.
There are the low blue hills; villages gleam at their feet.
Nearer a white sail shines across the water, and nearer
Still are the slim, grey masts of fishing boats dry on the flats.
Ah, how well I remember those wide red flats, above tide-mark

1 The Tantramar is a tidal river that empties into the Cumberland Basin of the Bay of Fundy. The region includes the village of Westcock in Westmoreland County, NB, and the fertile farmlands, tidal flats, and marshes that slope down to the river. Cumberland Point, now called Dorchester, is a village west of Westcock; Minudie is a village that lies across the bay in Nova Scotia.

2 Ribbon.

3 Barricaded. 'Green-rampired' refers to the natural fortification of the sloping land.

Pale with scurf[4] of the salt, seamed and baked in the sun!
Well I remember the piles of blocks and ropes, and the net-reels
Wound with the beaded nets, dripping and dark from the sea!
Now at this season the nets are unwound; they hang from the rafters
Over the fresh-stowed hay in upland barns, and the wind
Blows all day through the chinks, with the streaks of sunlight, and sways them
Softly at will; or they lie heaped in the gloom of a loft.

Now at this season the reels are empty and idle; I see them
Over the lines of the dikes, over the gossiping grass.
Now at this season they swing in the long strong wind, thro' the lonesome
Golden afternoon, shunned by the foraging gulls.
Near about sunset the crane will journey homeward above them;
Round them, under the moon, all the calm night long,
Winnowing soft grey wings of marsh-owls wander and wander,
Now to the broad, lit marsh, now to the dusk of the dike.
Soon, thro' their dew-wet frames, in the live keen freshness of morning,
Out of the teeth of the dawn blows back the awakening wind.
Then, as the blue day mounts, and the low-shot shafts of the sunlight
Glance from the tide to the shore, gossamers jewelled with dew
Sparkle and wave, where late sea-spoiling fathoms of drift-net
Myriad-meshed, uploomed sombrely over the land.

Well I remember it all. The salt, raw scent of the margin;
While, with men at the windlass, groaned each reel, and the net,
Surging in ponderous lengths, uprose and coiled in its station;
Then each man to his home,—well I remember it all!

Yet, as I sit and watch, this present peace of the landscape,—
Stranded boats, these reels empty and idle, the hush,
One grey hawk slow-wheeling above yon cluster of haystacks,—
More than the old-time stir this stillness welcomes me home.
Ah, the old-time stir, how once it stung me with rapture,—
Old-time sweetness, the winds freighted with honey and salt!
Yet will I stay my steps and not go down to the marshland,—
Muse and recall far off, rather remember than see,—
Lest on too close sight I miss the darling illusion,
Spy at their task even here the hands of chance and change.

1886

4 Scaly flakes.

In an Old Barn

Tons upon tons the brown-green fragrant hay
O'erbrims the mows[1] beyond the time-warped eaves,
Up to the rafters where the spider weaves,
Though few flies wander his secluded way.
Through a high chink one lonely golden ray,
Wherein the dust is dancing, slants unstirred.
In the dry hush some rustlings light are heard,
Of winter-hidden mice at furtive play.

Far down, the cattle in their shadowed stalls,
Nose-deep in clover fodder's meadowy scent,
Forget the snows that whelm their pasture streams,
The frost that bites the world beyond their walls.
Warm housed, they dream of summer, well content
In day-long contemplation of their dreams.

1893

1 Haylofts.

The Flight of the Geese

I hear the low wind wash the softening snow,
The low tide loiter down the shore. The night,
Full filled with April forecast, hath no light.
The salt wave on the sedge-flat[1] pulses slow.
Through the hid furrows lisp in murmurous flow
The thaw's shy ministers; and hark! The height
Of heaven grows weird[2] and loud with unseen flight
Of strong hosts prophesying as they go!

High through the drenched and hollow night their wings
Beat northward hard on Winter's trail. The sound
Of their confused and solemn voices, borne
Athwart the dark to their long Arctic morn,
Comes with a sanction and an awe profound,
A boding of unknown, foreshadowed things.

1893

1 A flat terrain covered with rushes or rough grasses.
2 Mysterious.

The Skater

My glad feet shod with the glittering steel
I was the god of the wingèd heel.

The hills in the far white sky were lost;
The world lay still in the wide white frost;

And the woods hung hushed in their long white dream
By the ghostly, glimmering, ice-blue stream.

Here was a pathway, smooth like glass,
Where I and the wandering wind might pass

To the far-off palaces, drifted deep,
Where Winter's retinue rests in sleep.

I followed the lure, I fled like a bird,
Till the startled hollows awoke and heard

A spinning whisper, a sibilant twang,
As the stroke of the steel on the tense ice rang;

And the wandering wind was left behind
As faster, faster I followed my mind;

Till the blood sang high in my eager brain,
And the joy of my flight was almost pain.

Then I stayed the rush of my eager speed
And silently went as a drifting seed,—

Slowly, furtively, till my eyes
Grew big with the awe of a dim surmise,

And the hair of my neck began to creep
At hearing the wilderness talk in sleep.

Shapes in the fir-gloom drifted near.
In the deep of my heart I heard my fear.

And I turned and fled, like a soul pursued,
From the white, inviolate solitude.

1901

Going Over[1]

(The Somme, 1917)

A girl's voice in the night troubled my heart
Across the roar of the guns, the crash of the shells,
Low and soft as a sigh, clearly I heard it.

Where was the broken parapet, crumbling about me?
Where my shadowy comrades, crouching expectant?
A girl's voice in the dark troubled my heart.

A dream was the ooze of the trench, the wet clay slipping.
A dream the sudden out-flare of the wide-flung Verys.[2]
I saw but a garden of lilacs, a-flower in the dusk.

What was the sergeant saying?—I passed it along.—
Did *I* pass it along? I was breathing the breath of the lilacs.
For a girl's voice in the night troubled my heart.

Over! How the mud sucks! Vomits red the barrage.
But I am far off in the hush of a garden of lilacs.
For a girl's voice in the night troubled my heart.
Tender and soft as a sigh, clearly I heard it.

1919

1 This poem takes place during World War I among soldiers stationed on the Allied front at the Somme River, in the aftermath, or 'Second Phase', of the Battle of the Somme. The original battle, waged for five months in 1916, is remembered as the most disastrous and futile battle of the war, and as perhaps the bloodiest single battle in history. (The combined German and Allied losses in the 1916 battle are estimated at nearly 1.3 million, of which almost 25,000 were Canadians and Newfoundlanders.) The fighting at the Somme was characteristic of World War I trench warfare, in which men huddled for weeks and months at a time at the front of the action in fortified trenches strung with barbed wire, trenches that were often filled with water and mud. They left these positions to charge out periodically, often under heavy gunfire from machine-gun emplacements or barrages of heavier artillery, in an attempt to gain a few additional yards of territory. The men in such charges were said to be 'going over the top' as they left the relative safety of the trenches, in that they stepped up onto the top, or parapet, of the trench as they charged out into the open. Roberts was well informed about these events: in England when the war broke out, he lied about his age and enlisted as a private. He was subsequently made a major and attached to the Canadian War Records Office in London. In that capacity he visited the Western Front in December 1916 and saw the Allied and German lines entrenched at the Somme not long after winter had brought an end to the first round of fighting there. He was subsequently commissioned to write the story of Canadian involvement in the Battle of the Somme when he was asked to complete the third volume of Lord Beaverbrook's war history, *Canada in Flanders.*

2 Verys Lights were red flares.

As Down the Woodland Ways

As down the woodland ways I went
With every wind asleep
I felt the surge of endless life
About my footsteps creep.

I felt the urge of quickening mould
That had been once a flower
Mount with the sap to bloom again
At its appointed hour.

I saw gray stumps go crumbling down
In sodden, grim decay,
To soar in pillared green again
On some remoter day.

I saw crushed beetles, mangled grubs,
All crawling, perished things,
Whirl up in air, an ecstasy
Of many-coloured wings.

Through weed and world, through worm and star,
The sequence ran the same:—
Death but the travail-pang of life,
Destruction but a name.

1937

In the Deep of the Grass

Misty gray green, washed with tints of the palest violet, spotted with red clover-blooms, white oxeyes, and hot orange Canada lilies, the deep-grassed levels basked under the July sun. A drowsy hum of bees and flies seemed to distil, with warm aromatic scents, from the sun-steeped blooms and grass-tops. The broad, blooming, tranquil expanse, shimmering and softly radiant in the heat, seemed the very epitome of summer. Now and again a small cloud-shadow sailed across it. Now and again a little wind, swooping down upon it gently, bent the grass-tops all one way, and spread a sudden silvery pallor. Save for the droning bees and flies there seemed to be but one live creature astir between the grass and the blue. A solitary marsh-hawk, far over by the rail fence, was winnowing slowly, slowly hither and thither, lazily hunting.

All this was in the world above the grass-tops. But below the grass-tops was a very different world—a dense, tangled world of dim green shade, shot with piercing shafts of sun, and populous with small, furtive life. Here, among the brown and white roots, the crowded green stems and the mottled stalks, the little earth kindreds went busily about their affairs and their desires, giving scant thought to the aerial world above them. All that made life significant to them was here in the warm, green gloom; and when anything chanced to part the grass to its depths they would scurry away in unanimous indignation.

On a small stone, over which the green closed so thickly that, when he chanced to look upward, he caught but the scantiest shreds of sky, sat a half-grown field-mouse, washing his whiskers with his dainty claws. His tiny, bead-like eyes kept ceaseless watch, peering through the shadowy tangle for whatever might come near in the shape of foe or prey. Presently two or three stems above his head were beaten down, and a big green grass-hopper, alighting clumsily from one of his blind leaps, fell sprawling on the stone. Before he could struggle to his long legs and climb back to the safer region of the grass-tops, the little mouse was upon him. Sharp, white teeth pierced his green mail, his legs kicked convulsively twice or thrice, and the faint iridescence faded out of his big, blank, foolish eyes. The mouse made his meal with relish, daintily discarding the dry legs and wing-cases. Then, amid the green débris scattered upon the stone, he sat up, and once more went through his fastidious toilet.

But life for the little mouse in his grass-world was not quite all watching and hunting. When his toilet was complete, and he had amiably let a large black cricket crawl by unmolested, he suddenly began to whirl round and round on the stone, chasing his own tail. As he was amusing himself with this foolish play, another mouse, about the same size as himself, and probably of the same litter, jumped upon the stone, and knocked him off. He promptly retorted in kind; and for several minutes, as if the game were a well-understood one, the two kept it up, squeaking soft merriment, and apparently forgetful of all peril. The grass-tops above this play rocked and rustled in a way that would certainly have attracted attention had there been any eyes to see. But the marsh-hawk was still hunting lazily at the other side of the field, and no tragedy followed the childishness.

Both seemed to tire of the sport at the same instant; for suddenly they stopped, and hurried away through the grass on opposite sides of the stone, as if remembered business had just called to them. Whatever the business was, the first mouse seemed to forget it very speedily, for in half a minute he was back upon the stone again, combing his fine whiskers and scratching his ears. This done to his satisfaction, he dropped like a flash from his seat, and disappeared into a small hollow beneath it. As he did so, a hairy black spider darted out, and ran among the roots.

A minute or two after the disappearance of the mouse, a creature came along which appeared gigantic in the diminutive world of the grass folk. It was nearly three feet long, and of the thickness of a man's finger. Of a steely gray black, striped and reticulated in a mysterious pattern with a clear whitish yellow, it was an ominous shape indeed, as it glided smoothly and swiftly, in graceful curves, through the close green tangle. The cool shadows and thin lights touched it flickeringly as it went, and never a grass-top stirred to mark its sinister approach. Without a sound of warning it came straight up to the stone, and darted its narrow cruel head into the hole.

There was a sharp squeak, and instantly the narrow head came out again, ejected by the force of the mouse's agonized spring. But the snake's teeth were fastened in the little animal's neck. The doom of the green world had come upon him while he slept.

But doomed though he was, the mouse was game. He knew there was no poison in those fangs that gripped him, and he struggled desperately to break free. His powerful hind legs kicked the ground with a force which the snake, hampered at first by the fact of its length being partly trailed out through the tangle, was unable to quite control. With unerring instinct—though this was the first snake he had ever encountered—the mouse strove to reach its enemy's back and sever the bone with the fine chisels of his teeth. But it was just this that the snake was watchful to prevent. Three times in his convulsive leaps the mouse succeeded in touching the snake's body—but with his feet only, never once with those destructive little teeth. The snake held him inexorably, with a steady, elastic pressure which yielded just so far, and never quite far enough. And in a minute or two the mouse's brave struggles grew more feeble.

All this, however—the lashing and the wriggling and the jumping—had not gone on without much disturbance to the grass-tops. Timothy head and clover-bloom, oxeye and feathery plume-grass, they had bowed and swayed and shivered till the commotion, very conspicuous to one looking down upon the tranquil, flowery sea of green, caught the attention of the marsh-hawk, which at that moment chanced to be perching on a high fence stake. The lean-headed, fierce-eyed, trim-feathered bird shot from his perch, and sailed on long wings over the grass to see what was happening. As the swift shadow hovered over the grass-tops, the snake looked up. Well he understood the significance of that sudden shade. Jerking back his fangs with difficulty from the mouse's neck, he started to glide off under the thickest matting of the roots. But lightning quick though he was, he was not quite quick enough. Just as his narrow head darted under the roots, the hawk, with wings held straight up and talons reaching down, dropped upon him, and clutched the middle of his back in a grip of steel. The next moment he was jerked into the air, writhing and coiling, and striking in vain frenzy at his captor's mail of hard feathers. The hawk flew off with him over the sea of green to the top of the fence stake, there to devour him at leisure. The mouse, sore wounded but not past recovery, dragged himself back to the hollow under the stone. And over the stone the grass-tops, once more still, hummed with flies, and breathed warm perfumes in the distilling heat.

1904

Sara Jeannette Duncan

1861–1922

Before settling on the form of her name by which she is now remembered, the woman who became Canada's first modernist writer was born Sarah Janet Duncan in Brantford, Canada West. She used several versions of her name and some pseudonyms: after she married, the author's name on most of her books was Mrs Everard Cotes—though she continued to be identified parenthetically on the title pages as Sara Jeannette Duncan.

Almost as various as her pen-names were the roles Duncan played and the voices she made use of in her writing. Trained to be a school teacher, she established herself in her twenties as a breezy, colloquial journalist, and her first books—light fiction made up of loosely linked sketches—are written in a casual journalistic style. She soon abandoned the masculine pseudonym 'Garth' that she had found necessary in order to be taken seriously in the journalistic world of her day, and she adopted instead the role of a late nineteenth-century 'American girl'—an emancipated, brash, slangy young woman, the ambiguous union of innocence and immodesty portrayed by Henry James in *Daisy Miller* (1878)—and she often played this persona off against British national stereotypes, as in *A Social Departure: How Orthodocia and I Went Round the World by Ourselves* (1890), *An American Girl in London* (1891), and *A Voyage of Consolation* (1898). A restless traveller, Duncan chronicled her visit to New Orleans in 1884, where she met the flamboyant American poet Joaquin Miller. (With Miller, along with other 'Bohemians', she travelled to Florida in a whimsical search for the Fountain of Youth.) She also described her brief sojourn in British Honduras, and her world tour with fellow Canadian journalist Lily Lewis, a trip that took them through western Canada on the recently completed Canadian Pacific Railway—they daringly rode on the cowcatcher fastened to the front of the train through the Rockies—as well as to Japan and India.

After failing to secure a staff position at the Toronto *Globe* in 1885 (she later complained about the conservatism of Canadian journalism with regard to its employment of women), Duncan accepted a job at the Washington *Post.* The following year, however, she was hired by the *Globe* after all and, placed in charge of the 'Woman's World' section, she became the first woman to hold a full-time position in Canadian journalism. Always interested in politics, she moved, in 1888, to the Montreal *Star* to become its parliamentary correspondent.

Between 1886 and 1888 Duncan also contributed columns and book reviews to Goldwin Smith's important Canadian journal of ideas, *The Week*; in them she struck a more elevated and intellectual (and sometimes more rhetorical) tone than in her other journalism. Interested in literary fiction and the arts, she found *The Week* gave her an opportunity to discuss questions of Canadian culture and to stress the need for Canada to move beyond colonial self-definition:

> *In our character as colonists we find the root of all our sins of omission in letters. . . . Our enforced political humility is the distinguishing characteristic of every phase of our national life. We are ignored, and we ignore ourselves. . . . So long as Canada remains in political obscurity, content to thrive only at the roots, so long will the leaves and blossoms of art and literature be scanty and stunted products of our national energy. . . . A national literature cannot be looked for as an outcome of anything less than a complete national existence.* (1886)

She was nevertheless convinced that 'national literature cannot be wholly evoked from within', and she took a lively interest in the novelists then emerging in America, particularly James and W.D. Howells (whom she met in Washington), and in the controversies that arose from Howells' advocacy of realism.

In 1890, Duncan married Everard Cotes, a museum official she had met during her earlier trip to Calcutta; in 1891, she moved to India. Though she later wearied of it, her new home seems at first to have both engaged and energized her, and she began to write serious fiction. In *The Simple Adventures of a Memsahib* (1893), she tells of a young English woman's difficult entry into the somewhat cloistered world of the Anglo-Indian community. *A Daughter of To-Day* (1894) is an account of a nonconformist woman who leaves America for a career as an expatriate artist and writer in Europe but eventually commits suicide over her lack of success. *His Honour, and a Lady* (1896), an acutely observed portrait of Anglo-Indian politics, shows Duncan's continued interest in women who play untraditional roles.

In 1901 Duncan published *On the Other Side of the Latch*, an affecting memoir that describes her summer convalescence from tuberculosis, which had probably been brought on by conditions in India. Her only short fiction, the highly-polished novellas and the short stories collected in *The Pool in the Desert* (1903), which treat in a Jamesian manner the emotions suppressed beneath the formal surfaces of the highly mannered Anglo-Indian community, were written around this time. Their subtle psychological nuances of situation outweigh external events, as these stories carefully filter the narrative through the consciousness of one highly subjective character.

Although initially attracted to its exoticism, Duncan came to feel that India was, as she wrote in a letter, 'too far out upon the periphery of the Empire'. She increasingly made use of her earnings as a writer to get away, making return visits to Canada and living for extended periods in London, England, where her health seemed better. In the first decade of the twentieth century she published the two books that deal extensively with Canada: *The Imperialist* (1904; an extract from that novel has been chosen to represent Duncan here) and *Cousin Cinderella: A Canadian Girl in London* (1908).

Duncan's later career, which was increasingly spent in England, saw the publication of *Set in Authority* (1906), a second examination of political themes and of the relationship of colony and empire, this time using an Anglo-Indian context; a Kensington memoir, *Two in a Flat* (1908); several more novels, most of which rework the 'international theme' that preoccupied James; and popular plays. By the time she died in England in 1922, she had written twenty books, in addition to numerous plays and a great quantity of journalism.

The Imperialist

Now regarded as Duncan's masterpiece, *The Imperialist* was not well received at the time of its publication. The coolness of its initial reception in England seems to have stemmed from a lack of interest in Canada among British readers of the time; the lukewarm and sometimes hostile response from several Canadian reviewers appears to have been based on a feeling that a woman could not be a shrewd enough political observer to carry off this kind of novel—especially one about the issue of 'Imperial Federation', a highly controversial issue at the turn of the twentieth century. Nonetheless, her precise descriptive power did receive praise—as in a review published in *Saturday Night*, which lauded the novel for its 'photographic . . . fidelity to local conditions' as well as for its 'subtle humour and literary finish'.

Despite the high quality of several of her books of fiction, Duncan's reputation today rests chiefly on *The Imperialist*, which, after it was brought back into print in 1961, found a place in the Canadian canon. In a 1905 letter to Lord Lansdowne, then governor general of Canada, Duncan wrote: 'It seemed to me that among the assumptions and disputes over here [she was writing from England] as to what the "colonial view" really is, it might be worth while to present the situation as it appears to the average Canadian of the average small town, inarticulate except at election times.'

Her complexly ironic tale is set in the town of Elgin, Ontario, easily recognized as a fictional version of Brantford, and it focuses on the Scottish Canadian family of the Murchisons. ('No one could say the Murchisons were demonstrative.') In it, *balance* is both a theme and a technique, and the way the second and third chapters, reprinted here, are counterpoised—so that the public world of Mr

Murchison, dominated by commerce, religion, and politics, is set against the domestic world of Mrs Murchison, the demands of family, and the home—suggests the artful design of this novel. Its plot revolves around Lorne Murchison, a young man who romanticizes England and all its values, and the balancing figure of his perspicacious (and un-domestic) older sister Advena. As their town becomes involved in an election in which the central debate is over the strengthening of Canada's ties to the British Empire, Lorne campaigns for office as an enthusiastic supporter of Canada's becoming more closely tied to the Empire. This was not an anti-national concept at the time; he speaks for those who saw Canada as having an important role in the future of the British Empire. (Lorne tells his auditors in his climactic election speech: 'the centre of the Empire must shift—and where, if not to Canada?' And he later stresses the importance of resisting American dominance of the Canadian economy.) Against this ambition, however, the novel suggests that bringing together the values of the Old World and the New may be the best course. It also reminds us of the distance that Elgin (and Canada) actually lies from the centres of power. As with Leacock's depiction of Mariposa in the later *Sunshine Sketches of a Small Town,* much of the humour in the novel stems from Duncan's sharp eye for the exact nuance of manners combined with an ability to skewer a small town's tendency to take itself too seriously.

From *The Imperialist*

CHAPTER II

'We've seen changes, Mr Murchison. Aye. We've seen changes.'

Dr Drummond and Mr Murchison stood together in the store door, over which the sign, 'John Murchison: Hardware', had explained thirty years of varying commercial fortune. They had pretty well begun life together in Elgin. John Murchison was one of those who had listened to Mr Drummond's trial sermon, and had given his vote to 'call' him to the charge. Since then there had been few Sundays when, morning and evening, Mr Murchison had not been in his place at the top of his pew, where his dignified and intelligent head appeared with the isolated significance of a strong individuality. People looked twice at John Murchison in a crowd; so did his own children at home. Hearing some discussion of the selection of a Premier, Alec, looking earnestly at him once said, 'Why don't they tell Father to be it?' The young minister looked twice at him that morning of the trial sermon, and asked afterward who he was. A Scotchman, Mr Drummond was told, not very long from the old country, who had bought the Playfair business on Main Street, and settled in the 'Plummer Place', which already had a quarter of a century's standing in the annals of the town. The Playfair business was a respectable business to buy; the Plummer Place, though it stood in an unfashionable outskirt, was a respectable place to settle in; and the minister, in casting his lot in Elgin, envisaged John Murchison as part of it, thought of him confidently as a 'dependence',[1] saw him among the future elders and office-bearers of the congregation, a man who would be punctual with his pew-rent, sage in his judgments, and whose views upon church attendance would be extended to his family.

So the two came, contemporaries, to add their labour and their lives to the building of this little outpost of Empire. It was the frankest transfer, without thought of return;

1 A person or thing on which one relies or may rely; the object of one's trust.

they were there to spend and be spent within the circumference of the spot they had chosen, with no ambition beyond. In the course of nature, even their bones and their memories would enter into the fabric. The new country filled their eyes; the new town was their opportunity, its destiny their fate. They were altogether occupied with its affairs, and the affairs of the growing Dominion, yet obscure in the heart of each of them ran the undercurrent of the old allegiance. They had gone the length of their tether, but the tether was always there. Thus, before a congregation that always stood in the early days, had the minister every Sunday morning for thirty years besought the Almighty, with ardour and humility, on behalf of the Royal Family. It came in the long prayer, about the middle. Not in the perfunctory words of a ritual, but in the language of his choice, which varied according to what he believed to be the spiritual needs of the reigning House, and was at one period, touching certain of its members, though respectful, extremely candid.[2] The General Assembly of the Church of Scotland, 'now in session', also—was it ever forgotten once? And even the Prime Minister, 'and those who sit in council with him', with just a hint of extra commendation if it happened to be Mr Gladstone.[3] The minister of Knox Church, Elgin, Ontario, Canada, kept his eye on them all. Remote as he was, and concerned with affairs of which they could know little, his sphere of duty could never revolve too far westward to embrace them, nor could his influence, under any circumstances, cease to be at their disposal. It was noted by some that after Mr Drummond had got his 'D.D.'[4] from an American University he also prayed occasionally for the President of the neighbouring Republic; but this was rebutted by others, who pointed out that it happened only on the occurrence of assassinations, and held it reasonable enough. The cavillers mostly belonged to the congregation of St Andrew's, 'Established'[5]—a glum, old-fashioned lot indeed, who now and then dropped in of a Sunday evening to hear Mr Drummond preach. (There wasn't much to be said for the preaching at St Andrew's.) The Established folk went on calling the minister of Knox Church 'Mr' Drummond long after he was 'Doctor' to his own congregation, on account of what they chose to consider the dubious source of the dignity; but the Knox Church people had their own theory to explain this hypercriticism, and would promptly turn the conversation to the merits of the sermon.

2 In Duncan's serialized version of *The Imperialist*, published in England in 1903 (in *The Queen: The Lady's Newspaper*), the phrase 'touching the Heir Apparent'—deleted in the book's subsequent publication—made it clear that this was a reference to the Prince of Wales, who had ascended to the throne in 1901, and whose social life had given much scandal. (The specific incident referred to may be a libel case about cheating at cards, in which he had to appear in 1891.) In the following chapter, there is an allusion to the young Prince's celebrated visit to Canada in 1860, when he was just eighteen. (It included a stopover in Brantford.)

3 Liberal prime minister of England during the periods 1868–74, 1880–5, 1886, and 1892–4.

4 Doctor of Divinity. (Since Dr Drummond receives the degree from an American university after his ministry has begun, it is presumably an honorary one.) The 'occurrence of assassinations' alludes to the assassinations of the US presidents James Garfield in 1881 and William McKinley in 1901.

5 Because the church of the 'cavillers' is named after St Andrew (the patron saint of Scotland), it is clear that the competition here is not between Dr Drummond's Presbyterian faith and the Anglican Church of Canada—which is what would ordinary be meant in Canada when someone spoke of the 'Established' church, i.e. that recognized as the national church or religion. (The Anglican church is instead referred to, later in this chapter, as Episcopalian, its usual designation in the US, where no church is 'Established'). Duncan's joke here is that Elgin is so Scottish that 'Established' is understood in this context as referring to the Established Church of Scotland—as opposed to Dr Drummond's own Presbyterian congregation, which is associated with one of the strains of Presbyterianism that had dissociated itself from the Established Presbyterian faith.

Twenty-five years it was, in point, this Monday morning when the Doctor—not being Established we need not hesitate, besides by this time nobody did—stood with Mr Murchison in the store door and talked about having seen changes. He had preached his anniversary sermon the night before to a full church, when, laying his hand upon his people's heart, he had himself to repress tears. He was aware of another strand completed in their mutual bond: the sermon had been a moral, an emotional, and an oratorical success; and in the expansion of the following morning Dr Drummond had remembered that he had promised his housekeeper a new gas cooking-range, and that it was high time he should drop into Murchison's to inquire about it. Mrs Forsyth had mentioned at breakfast that they had ranges with exactly the improvement she wanted at Thompson's, but the minister was deaf to the hint. Thompson was a Congregationalist,[6] and, improvement or no improvement, it wasn't likely that Dr Drummond was going 'outside the congregation' for anything he required. It would have been on a par with a wandering tendency in his flock, upon which he systematically frowned. He was as great an autocrat in this as the rector of any country parish in England undermined by Dissent;[7] but his sense of obligation worked unfailingly both ways.

John Murchison had not said much about the sermon; it wasn't his way, and Dr Drummond knew it. 'You gave us a good sermon last night, Doctor;' not much more than that, 'and I noticed the Milburns there; we don't often get Episcopalians;' and again, 'The Wilcoxes'—Thomas Wilcox, wholesale grocer, was the chief prop of St Andrew's—'were sitting just in front of us. We overtook them going home, and Wilcox explained how much they liked the music. "Glad to see you," I said. "Glad to see you for any reason,"' Mr Murchison's eye twinkled. 'But they had a great deal to say about "the music."' It was not an effusive form of felicitation; the minister would have liked it less if it had been, felt less justified, perhaps, in remembering about the range on that particular morning. As it was, he was able to take it with perfect dignity and good humour, and to enjoy the point against the Wilcoxes with that laugh of his that did everybody good to hear; so hearty it was, so rich in the grain of the voice, so full of the zest and flavour of the joke. The range had been selected, and their talk of changes had begun with it, Mr Murchison pointing out the new idea in the boiler, and Dr Drummond remembering his first kitchen stove that burned wood and stood on its four legs, with nothing behind but the stove pipe, and if you wanted a boiler you took off the front lids and put it on, and how remarkable even that had seemed to his eyes, fresh from the conservative kitchen notions of the old country. He had come, unhappily, a widower to the domestic improvements on the other side of the Atlantic. 'Often I used to think', he said to Mr Murchison, 'if my poor wife could have seen that stove how delighted she would have been! But I doubt this would have been too much for her altogether!'

6 Another Protestant denomination. (The Congregationalists, Presbyterians, and Methodists were later united, in 1925, to form the United Church of Canada.)

7 Duncan here continues her joke about the Scottishness of Elgin and its treating Presbyterianism as the Established religion. Dr Drummond views Protestant faiths other than Presbyterianism in the way Anglican rectors in England would view Dissenting faiths (those Protestant faiths, including Presbyterianism, that broke away from both Roman Catholicism and the Established faith of the Church of England).

'That stove!' answered Mr Murchison. 'Well I remember it. I sold it myself to your predecessor, Mr Wishart, for thirty dollars—the last purchase he ever made, poor man. It was great business for me—I had only two others in the store like it. One of them old Milburn bought—the father of this man, d'ye mind him?—the other stayed by me a matter of seven years. I carried a light stock in those days.'

It was no longer a light stock. The two men involuntarily glanced round them for the satisfaction of the contrast Murchison evoked, though neither of them, from motives of vague delicacy, felt inclined to dwell upon it. John Murchison had the shyness of an artist in his commercial success, and the minister possibly felt that his relation toward the prosperity of a member had in some degree the embarrassment of a tax-gatherer's. The stock was indeed heavy now. You had to go upstairs to see the ranges, where they stood in rows, and every one of them bore somewhere upon it, in raised black letters, John Murchison's name. Through the windows came the iterating ring on the iron from the foundry in Chestnut Street which fed the shop, with an overflow that found its way from one end of the country to the other. Finicking visitors to Elgin found this wearing, but to John Murchison it was the music that honours the conqueror of circumstances. The ground floor was given up to the small wares of the business, chiefly imported; two or three young men, steady and knowledgeable-looking, moved about in their shirt sleeves among shelves and packing cases. One of them was our friend Alec; our other friend Oliver[8] looked after the books at the foundry. Their father did everything deliberately; but presently, in his own good time, his commercial letter paper would be headed, with regard to these two, 'John Murchison and Sons'. It had long announced that the business was 'Wholesale and Retail'.

Dr Drummond and Mr Murchison, considering the changes in Elgin from the store door, did it at their leisure, the merchant with his thumbs thrust comfortably in the armholes of his waist-coat, the minister, with that familiar trick of his, balancing on one foot and suddenly throwing his slight weight forward on the other. 'A bundle of nerves' people called the Doctor: to stand still would have been a penance to him; even as he swayed backward and forward in talking his hand must be busy at the seals on his watch chain and his shrewd glance travelling over a dozen things you would never dream so clever a man would take notice of. It was a prospect of moderate commercial activity they looked out upon, a street of mellow shop-fronts, on both sides, of varying height and importance, wearing that air of marking a period, a definite stop in growth, that so often co-exists with quite a reasonable degree of activity and independence in colonial towns. One could almost say, standing there in the door at

8 Alec and Oliver are two of John Murchison's sons. In Chapter One the narrator explains: 'We must take this matter of names seriously; the Murchisons always did,' and explains that the full names given the boys are Alexander Mackenzie Murchison and Oliver Mowat Murchison because 'neither an Alexander Mackenzie nor an Oliver Mowat could very well grow up into anything but a sound Liberal in that part of the world without feeling himself an unendurable paradox.' (Mackenzie was the Liberal prime minister of Canada, 1873–8; Mowat, the Liberal premier of Ontario, 1872–96.) The narrator also informs us of the source of Lorne Murchison's name, which was given him 'at the period of a naïve fashion of christening the young sons of Canada in the name of her Governor-General' (i.e. Sir John Campbell, Marquis of Lorne, Governor-General of Canada 1878–83). In contrast, the two oldest children, the daughters Advenna and Abigail, are named for their grandmothers; and the youngest child, also a daughter, is named Stella because Mrs Murchison 'was thankful to have a girl at last whom she could name without regard to her own relations or anybody else's.'

Murchison's, where the line of legitimate enterprise had been over-passed and where its intention had been none too sanguine—on the one hand in the faded and pretentious red brick building with the false third story, occupied by Cleary, which must have been let at a loss to dry-goods or anything else; on the other hand in the solid 'Gregory block', opposite the market, where rents were as certain as the dividends of the Bank of British North America.

Main Street expressed the idea that, for the purpose of growing and doing business, it had always found the days long enough. Drays[9] passed through it to the Grand Trunk station, but they passed one at a time; a certain number of people went up and down about their affairs, but they were never in a hurry; a street car jogged by every ten minutes or so, but nobody ran after it. There was a decent procedure; and it was felt that Bofield—he was dry-goods, too—in putting in an elevator was just a little unnecessarily in advance of the times. Bofield had only two stories, like everybody else, and a very easy staircase, up which people often declared they preferred to walk rather than wait in the elevator for a young man to finish serving and work it. These, of course, were the sophisticated people of Elgin; country folk, on a market day, would wait a quarter of an hour for the young man, and think nothing of it; and I imagine Bofield found his account in the elevator, though he did complain sometimes that such persons went up and down on frivolous pretexts or to amuse the baby. As a matter of fact, Elgin had begun as the centre of 'trading' for the farmers of Fox County, and had soon over-supplied that limit in demand; so that when other interests added themselves to the activity of the town there was still plenty of room for the business they brought. Main Street was really, therefore, not a fair index; nobody in Elgin would have admitted it. Its appearance and demeanour would never have suggested that it was now the chief artery of a thriving manufacturing town, with a collegiate institute, eleven churches, two newspapers, and an asylum for the deaf and dumb, to say nothing of a fire department unsurpassed for organization and achievement in the Province of Ontario. Only at twelve noon it might be partly realized, when the prolonged 'toots' of seven factory whistles at once let off, so to speak, the hour. Elgin liked the demonstration; it was held to be cheerful and unmistakable, and indication of 'go-ahead' proclivities which spoke for itself. It occurred while yet Dr Drummond and Mr Murchison stood together in the store door.

'I must be getting on,' said the minister, looking at his watch. 'And what news have you of Lorne?'

'Well, he seems to have got through all right.'

'What—you've heard already, then?'

'He telegraphed from Toronto on Saturday night.' Mr Murchison stroked his chin, the better to retain his satisfaction. 'Waste of money—the post would have brought it this morning—but it pleased his mother. Yes, he's through his Law Schools examination, and at the top, too, as far as I can make out.'

'Dear me, and you never mentioned it!' Dr Drummond spoke with the resigned impatience of a familiar grievance. It was certainly a trying characteristic of John

9 Low carts without sides, used for hauling.

Murchison that he never cared about communicating anything that might seem to ask for congratulation. 'Well, well! I'm very glad to hear it.'

'It slipped my mind,' said Mr Murchison. 'Yes, he's full-fledged "barrister and solicitor" now; he can plead your case or draw you up a deed with the best of them. Lorne's made a fair record, so far. We've no reason to be ashamed of him.'

'That you have not.' Personal sentiments between these two Scotchmen were rather indicated than indulged. 'He's going in with Fulke and Warner, I suppose—you've got that fixed up?'

'Pretty well. Old man Warner was in this morning to talk it over. He says they look to Lorne to bring them in touch with the new generation. It's a pity he lost that son of his.'

'Oh, a great pity. But since they had to go outside the firm they couldn't have done better; they couldn't have done better. I hope Lorne will bring them a bit of Knox Church business too; there's no reason why Bob Mackintosh should have it all. They'll be glad to see him back at the Hampden Debating Society. He's a great light there, is Lorne; and the Young Liberals, I hear, are wanting him for chairman this year.'

'There's some talk of it. But time enough—time enough for that! He'll do first-rate if he gets the law to practise, let alone the making of it.'

'Maybe so; he's young yet. Well, good-morning to you. I'll just step over the way to the *Express* office and get a proof out of them of that sermon of mine. I noticed their reporter fellow—what's his name?—Rawlins with his pencil out last night, and I've no faith in Rawlins.'

'Better cast an eye over it,' responded Mr Murchison, cordially, and stood for a moment or two longer in the door watching the crisp, significant little figure of the minister as he stepped briskly over the crossing to the newspaper office. There Dr Drummond sat down, before he explained his errand, and wrote a paragraph.

'We are pleased to learn', it ran, 'that Mr Lorne Murchison, eldest son of Mr John Murchison, of this town, has passed at the capital of the Province his final examination in Law, distinguishing himself by coming out at the top of the list. It will be remembered that Mr Murchison, upon entering the Law Schools, also carried off a valuable scholarship. We are glad to be able to announce that Mr Murchison, junior, will embark upon his profession in his native town, where he will enter the well-known firm of Fulke and Warner.'

The editor, Mr Horace Williams, had gone to dinner, and Rawlins was out, so Dr Drummond had to leave it with the press foreman. Mr Williams read it appreciatively on his return, and sent it down with the following addition—

'This is doing it as well as it can be done. Elgin congratulates Mr L. Murchison upon having produced these results, and herself upon having produced Mr L. Murchison.'

CHAPTER III

From the day she stepped into it Mrs Murchison knew that the Plummer Place was going to be the bane of her existence. This may have been partly because Mr Murchison had bought it, since a circumstance welded like that into one's life is very apt to assume the character of a bane, unless one's temperament leads one to philosophy, which

Mrs Murchison's didn't. But there were other reasons more difficult to traverse: it was plainly true that the place did require a tremendous amount of 'looking after', as such things were measured in Elgin, far more looking after than the Murchison's could afford to give it. They could never have afforded, in the beginning, to possess it, had it not been sold, under mortgage, at a dramatic sacrifice. The house was a dignified old affair, built of wood and painted white, with wide green verandahs compassing the four sides of it, as they often did in days when the builder had only to turn his hand to the forest. It stood on the very edge of the town; wheatfields in the summer billowed up to its fences, and cornstacks in the autumn camped around it like a besieging army. The plank sidewalk finished there; after that you took the road, or, if you were so inclined, the river, into which you could throw a stone from the orchard of the Plummer Place. The house stood roomily and shadily in ornamental grounds, with a lawn in front of it and a shrubbery at each side, an orchard behind, and a vegetable garden, the whole intersected by winding gravel walks, of which Mrs Murchison was wont to say that a man might do nothing but weed them and have his hands full. In the middle of the lawn was a fountain, an empty basin with a plaster Triton,[1] most difficult to keep looking respectable and pathetic in his frayed air of exile from some garden of Italy sloping to the sea. There was also a barn with stabling, a loft, and big carriage doors opening on a lane to the street. The originating Plummer, Mrs Murchison often said, must have been a person of large ideas, and she hoped he had the money to live up to them. The Murchisons at one time kept a cow in the barn, till a succession of 'girls' left on account of the milking, and the lane was useful as an approach to the back yard by the teams that brought the cordwood in the winter. It was trying enough for a person with the instinct of order to find herself surrounded by out-of-door circumstances which she simply could not control, but Mrs Murchison often declared that she could put up with the grounds if it had stopped there. It did not stop there. Though I was compelled to introduce Mrs Murchison in the kitchen, she had a drawing-room in which she might have received the Lieutenant Governor, with French windows and a cut-glass chandelier, and a library with an Italian marble mantelpiece. She had an ice-house and wine cellar, and a string of bells in the kitchen that connected with every room in the house; it was a negligible misfortune that not one of them was in order. She had far too much, as she declared, for any one pair of hands and a growing family, and if the ceiling was not dropping in the drawing-room, the cornice was cracked in the library, or the gas was leaking in the dining-room, or the verandah wanted re-flooring if any one coming to the house was not to put his foot through it; and as to the barn, if it was dropping to pieces it would just have to drop. The barn was definitely outside the radius of possible amelioration—it passed gradually, visibly, into decrepitude, and Mrs Murchison often wished she could afford to pull it down.

It may be realized that in spite of its air of being impossible to 'overtake'—I must, in this connection, continue to quote its mistress—there was an attractiveness about the dwelling of the Murchisons, the attractiveness of the large ideas upon which it had been built and designed, no doubt by one of those gentlefolk of reduced income who

1 A god of the sea, having the head and trunk of a man and the tail of a fish.

wander out to the colonies with a nebulous view to economy and occupation, to perish of the readjustment. The case of such persons, when they arrive, is at once felt to be pathetic; there is a tacit local understanding that they have made a mistake. They may be entitled to respect, but nothing can save them from the isolation of their difference and their misapprehension. It was like that with the house. The house was admired—without enthusiasm—but it was not copied. It was felt to be outside the general need, misjudged, adventitious; and it wore its superiority in the popular view like a folly. It was in Elgin, but not of it; it represented a different tradition; and Elgin made the same allowance for its bedroom bells and its old-fashioned dignities as was conceded to its original master's habit of a six o'clock dinner, with wine.

The architectural expression of the town was on a different scale, beginning with 'frame', rising through the semi-detached, culminating expensively in Mansard roofs, cupolas and modern conveniences, and blossoming, in extreme instances, into Moorish fretwork and silk portières for interior decoration.[2] The Murchison house gained by force of contrast: one felt, stepping into it, under influences of less expediency and more dignity, wider scope and more leisured intention; its shabby spaces had a redundancy the pleasanter and its yellow plaster cornices a charm the greater for the numerous close-set examples of contemporary taste in red brick which made, surrounded by geranium beds, so creditable an appearance in the West Ward. John Murchison in taking possession of the house had felt in it these satisfactions, had been definitely penetrated and soothed by them, the more perhaps because he brought to them a capacity for feeling the worthier things of life which circumstances had not previously developed. He seized the place with a sense of opportunity leaping sharp and conscious out of early years in the grey 'wynds'[3] of a northern Scottish town; and its personality sustained him, very privately but none the less effectively, through the worry and expense of it for years. He would take his pipe and walk silently for long together about the untidy shrubberies in the evening for the acute pleasure of seeing the big horse-chestnuts in flower; and he never opened the hall door without a feeling of gratification in its weight as it swung under his hand. In so far as he could, he supplemented the idiosyncrasies he found. The drawing-room walls, though mostly bare in their old-fashioned French paper—lavender and gilt, a grape-vine pattern—held a few good engravings; the library was reduced to contain a single bookcase, but it was filled with English classics. John Murchison had been made a careful man, not by nature, by the discipline of circumstances; but he would buy books. He bought them between long periods of abstinence, during which he would scout the expenditure of an unnecessary dollar, coming home with a parcel under his arm for which he vouchsafed no explanation, and which would disclose itself to be Lockhart, or Sterne, or Borrow, or Defoe. Mrs Murchison kept a discouraging eye upon such purchases; and when her husband brought home Chambers' *Dictionary of English Literature*, after shortly and definitely repulsing her demand that he should get himself a new winter

2 The Murchison home, which combines a variety of decorative motifs, is a monument of Victorian architectural whimsy: Mansard roofs form an additional upper story by being pitched sharply vertical, then topped with a nearly horizontal peak; cupolas are small domed structures surmounting a roof; fretwork is an ornamental design of repeated, interlaced, and symmetrical figures, and Moorish fretwork a particularly ornate form of this; portieres are ornamental curtains hung across doorways.

3 Sidestreets (Scottish).

overcoat, she declared that it was beyond all endurance. Mrs Murchison was surrounded, indeed, by more of 'that sort of thing' than she could find use or excuse for; since, though books made but a sporadic appearance, current literature, daily, weekly, and monthly, was perpetually under her feet. The Toronto paper came as a matter of course, as the London daily takes its morning flight into the provinces, the local organ as simply indispensable, the Westminster as the corollary of church membership and for Sunday reading. These were constant, but there were also mutables—*Once a Week, Good Words for the Young, Blackwood's* and *The Cornhill*,[4] they used to be; years of back numbers Mrs Murchison had packed away in the attic, where Advena on rainy days came into the inheritance of them, and made an early acquaintance of fiction in *Ready Money Mortiboy* and *Verner's Pride*, while Lorne, flat on his stomach beside her, had glorious hours on *The Back of the North Wind.* Their father considered such publications and their successors essential, like tobacco and tea. He was also an easy prey to the subscription agent, for works published in parts and paid for in instalments, a custom which Mrs Murchison regarded with abhorrence. So much so that when John put his name down for *Masterpieces of the World's Art* which was to cost twenty dollars by the time it was complete, he thought it advisable to let the numbers accumulate at the store.

Whatever the place represented to their parents, it was pure joy to the young Murchisons. It offered a margin and a mystery to life. They saw it far larger than it was; they invested it, arguing purely by its difference from other habitations, with a romantic past. 'I guess when the Prince of Wales came to Elgin, mother, he stayed here,' Lorne remarked, as a little boy. Secretly he and Advena took up boards in more than one unused room, and rapped on more than one thick wall to find a hollow chamber; the house revealed so much that was interesting, it was apparent to the meanest understanding that it must hide even more. It was never half lighted, and there was a passage in which fear dwelt—wild were the gallopades from attic to cellar in the early nightfall, when every young Murchison tore after every other, possessed, like cats, by a demoniac ecstasy of the gloaming. And the garden, with the autumn moon coming over the apple trees and the neglected asparagus thick for ambush, and a casual untrimmed boy or two with the delicious recommendation of being utterly without credentials, to join in the rout and be trusted to make for the back fence without further hint at the voice of Mrs Murchison—these were joys of the very fibre, things to push ideas and envisage life with an attraction that made it worth while to grow up.

And they had all achieved it—all six. They had grown up sturdily, emerging into sobriety and decorum by much the same degrees as the old house, under John Murchison's improving fortunes, grew cared for and presentable. The new roof went on, slate replacing shingles, the year Abby put her hair up; the bathroom was contemporary with Oliver's leaving school; the electric light was actually turned on for the first time in honour of Lorne's return from Toronto, a barrister and solicitor; several rooms had been done up for Abby's wedding. Abby had married, early and satisfactorily, Dr Harry Johnson, who had placidly settled down to await the gradual succession of his

4 Victorian weeklies, which serialized literary fiction but also contained works of popular fiction such as those mentioned later in this sentence, the romances *Ready Money Mortiboy* and *Verner's Pride* and the children's novel *The Back of the North Wind* by George Macdonald.

father's practice; 'Dr Harry and Dr Henry' they were called. Dr Harry lived next door to Dr Henry, and had a good deal of the old man's popular manner. It was an unacknowledged partnership, which often provided two opinions for the same price; the town prophesied well of it. That left only five at home, but they always had Abby over in the West Ward, where Abby's housekeeping made an interest and Abby's baby a point of pilgrimage. These considerations almost consoled Mrs Murchison, declaring, as she did, that all of them might have gone but Abby, who alone knew how to be 'any comfort or any dependence' in the house; who could be left with a day's preserving; and I tell you that to be left by Mrs Murchison with a day's preserving, be it cherries or strawberries, damsons or pears, was a mark of confidence not easy to obtain. Advena never had it; Advena, indeed, might have married and removed no prop of the family economy. Mrs Murchison would have been 'sorry for the man'—she maintained a candour toward and about those belonging to her that permitted no illusions—but she would have stood cheerfully out of the way on her own account. When you have seen your daughter reach and pass the age of twenty-five without having learned properly to make her own bed, you know, without being told, that she will never be fit for the management of a house—don't you? Very well then. And for ever and for ever, no matter what there was to do, with a book in her hand—Mrs Murchison would put an emphasis on the 'book' which scarcely concealed a contempt for such absorption. And if, at the end of your patience, you told her for any sake to put it down and attend to matters, obeying in a kind of dream that generally drove you to take the thing out of her hands and do it yourself, rather than jump out of your skin watching her.

Sincerely Mrs Murchison would have been sorry for the man if he had arrived, but he had not arrived. Advena justified her existence by taking the university course for women at Toronto, and afterward teaching the English branches to the junior forms in the Collegiate Institute, which placed her arbitrarily outside the sphere of domestic criticism. Mrs Murchison was thankful to have her there—outside—where little more could reasonably be expected of her than that she should be down in time for breakfast. It is so irritating to be justified in expecting more than seems likely to come. Mrs Murchison's ideas circulated strictly in the orbit of equity and reason; she expected nothing from anybody that she did not expect from herself; indeed, she would spare others in far larger proportion. But the sense of obligation which led her to offer herself up to the last volt of her energy made her miserable when she considered that she was not fairly done by in return. Pressed down and running over were the services she offered to the general good, and it was on the ground of the merest justice that she required from her daughters 'some sort of interest' in domestic affairs. From her eldest she got no sort of interest, and it was like the removal of a grievance form the hearth when Advena took up employment which ranged her definitely beyond the necessity of being of any earthly use in the house. Advena's occupation to some extent absorbed her shortcomings, which was much better than having to attribute them to her being naturally 'through-other', or naturally clever, according to the bias of the moment. Mrs Murchison no longer excused or complained of her daughter; but she still pitied the man.

'The boys', of course, were too young to think of matrimony. They were still the boys, the Murchison boys; they would be the boys at forty if they remained under their father's roof. In the mother country, men in short jackets and round collars emerge from the preparatory schools; in the daughter lands boys in tail coats conduct serious affairs. Alec and Oliver, in the business, were frivolous enough as to the feminine interest. For all Dr Drummond's expressed and widely-known views upon the subject, it was a common thing for one or both of these young men to stray from the family pew on Sunday evenings to the services of other communions, thereafter to walk home in the dusk under the maples with some attractive young person, and be sedately invited to finish the evening on her father's verandah. Neither of them was guiltless of silk ties knitted or handkerchiefs initialled by certain fingers; without repeating scandal, one might say by various fingers. For while the ultimate import of these matters was not denied in Elgin, there was a general feeling against giving too much meaning to them, probably originating in a reluctance among heads of families to add to their responsibilities. These early spring indications were belittled and laughed at; so much so that the young people themselves hardly took them seriously, but regarded them as a form of amusement almost conventional. Nothing would have surprised or embarrassed them more than to learn that their predilections had an imperative corollary, that anything should, of necessity, 'come of it'. Something, of course, occasionally did come of it; and, usually after years of 'attention', a young man of Elgin found himself mated to a young woman, but never under circumstances that could be called precipitate or rash. The cautious blood and far sight of the early settlers, who had much to reckon with, were still preponderant social characteristics of the town they cleared the site for. Meanwhile, however, flowers were gathered, and all sorts of evanescent idylls came and went in the relations of young men and maidens. Alec and Oliver Murchison were already in the full tide of them.

From this point of view they did not know what to make of Lorne. It was not as if their brother were in any way ill calculated to attract that interest which gave to youthful existence in Elgin almost the only flavour that it had. Looks are looks, and Lorne had plenty of them; taller by an inch than Alec, broader by two than Oliver, with a fine square head and blue eyes in it, and features which conveyed purpose and humour, lighted by a certain simplicity of soul that pleased even when it was not understood. 'Open', people said he was, and 'frank'—so he was, frank and open, with horizons and intentions; you could see them in his face. Perhaps it was more conscious of them than he was. Ambition, definitely shining goals, adorn the perspectives of young men in new countries less often than is commonly supposed. Lorne meant to be a good lawyer, squarely proposed to himself that the country should hold no better; and as to more selective usefulness, he hoped to do a little stumping for the right side when Frank Jennings ran for the Ontario House in the fall. It wouldn't be his first electioneering: from the day he became chairman of the Young Liberals the party had an eye on him, and when occasion arose, winter or summer, by bobsleigh or buggy, weatherbeaten local bosses would convey him to country schoolhouses for miles about to keep a district sound on railway policy, or education, or tariff reform. He came home smiling with the triumphs of these occasions, and offered them, with the slow, good-humoured, capable drawl that inspired such confidence in him, to his family at breakfast, who said 'Great!' or 'Good for you, Lorne!' John Murchison oftenest said nothing, but would glance significantly at his wife, frowning and pursing his lips when she, who had most spirit of them all, would exclaim, 'You'll be Premier yet, Lorne!'

It was no part of the Murchison policy to draw against future balances: they might believe everything, they would express nothing; and I doubt whether Lorne himself had any map of the country he meant to travel over in that vague future, already defining in local approbation, and law business coming freely in with a special eye on the junior partner. But the tract was there, sub-conscious, plain in the wider glance, the alerter manner; plain even in the grasp and stride which marked him in a crowd; plain, too, in the preoccupation with other issues, were it only turning over a leader in the morning's *Dominion*, that carried him along indifferent to the allurements I have described. The family had a bond of union in their respect for Lorne, and this absence of nugatory inclinations in him was among its elements. Even Stella, who, being just fourteen, was the natural mouthpiece of family sentiment, would declare that Lorne had something better to do than go hanging about after girls, and for her part she thought all the more of him for it.

1904

E. Pauline Johnson

1861–1913

Emily Pauline Johnson was born in 'Chiefswood', a mansion built on the Six Nations Reserve in the Grand River valley near Brantford, Ont., by her Mohawk father (Chief George Henry Martin Johnson) for his English bride, Emily Susanna Howells. Johnson's early learning was derived from stories told by her grandfather, John Smoke Johnson, and from her governesses. Although her formal education was limited—she spent two years at a school on the reserve and two more at Central Collegiate in Brantford (1875–7)—her mother introduced her to the work of Longfellow, Byron, Shakespeare, and Emerson. Johnson also read the important poets and prose writers of her own day. At school, she pursued her interest in the performing arts, and learned the rhetorical skills that would be the cornerstone of her career.

After her return to Chiefswood, Johnson began to write poetry. In 1886 she adopted the Mohawk name 'Tekahionwake' (or 'Double Wampum'), and she published her first poem that year, after reading it at the unveiling of the Joseph Brant statue in Brantford's Victoria Park. In 1892, her reading of 'A Cry from an Indian Wife' at the Young Liberals' Club in Toronto was so well received that it launched her career as a poet-performer. She toured as the 'Mohawk Princess', emphasizing her ability to move between the two cultures by wearing a buckskin costume when reading Indian poems and then changing into evening dress for the remainder of her performance. She performed with the comedian and musician Owen Smiley (until 1897) and with Walter McRaye (after 1901). In 1909 she retired to Vancouver.

Johnson's reputation as a poet was established when two of her poems were included in the anthology *Songs of the Great Dominion* (London, 1889). By the time her first collection of poetry, *The White Wampum*, was published in Britain in 1895 she was a popular performer both there and in North America. This collection and her next, *Canadian Born* (1903), increased the interest in her performances. Her last collection, *Flint and Feather* (1912), published just before her death, is drawn principally from the two previous volumes.

A tension in Johnson's work, a product of her mixed traditions, is evident in such poems as 'A Cry from an Indian Wife'. Although she makes use of her Mohawk heritage for both content and perspective, the poem (which conveys an Indian wife's thoughts on the North-West rebellion of 1869–70 led by Louis Riel) also draws heavily on Johnson's knowledge of the tradition and conventions of English verse. The speaker's hesitations, for instance, are more reminiscent of a Shakespeare soliloquy than of the oral tradition of Johnson's Mohawk ancestors. This combination was the key to Johnson's appeal to her white audiences: this 'Mohawk Princess' communicated the unfamiliar in a way wholly familiar to them. In 'Silhouette', for example—part of the Smiley-Johnson performance routine called 'There and Back'—Johnson uses the familiar ballad form to paint a picture of a noble and endangered way of life and to make it readily accessible to her audience. No wonder she was so well received in England in 1894 and again in 1906, or that her first book was published by the distinguished British house of Bodley Head.

After 1904 Johnson began to concentrate on writing prose, and she completed three collections of short fiction: *Legends of Vancouver* (1911); and *The Shagganappi* and *The Moccasin Maker*, both of which were published posthumously in 1913. Perhaps the most interesting manifestation of Johnson's complex relationships with the First Nations communities may be seen in *Legends of Vancouver*. Prior to writing this book she had spent her career generalizing about Aboriginal groups; mixing the myths and customs of a number of peoples; and expressing this mélange in a language alien to its subject matter. For the stories in *Legends of Vancouver*, she uses a form closer to that of oral narrative and more suited to its Native content. The tales in this volume are told by an elder to a Westernized listener, the pattern of Johnson's own experience. She first heard most of these narratives, which she describes as legends previously 'unknown to . . . Pale-faces', from the Squamish Chief Joe Capilano. The oral quality of Capilano's narration is retained in such stories as 'The Lost Island', a tale explaining earlier Squamish power and providing for the possibility of its return.

A Cry from an Indian Wife

My Forest Brave, my Red-skin love, farewell;
We may not meet to-morrow; who can tell
What mighty ills befall our little band,
Or what you'll suffer from the white man's hand?
Here is your knife! I thought 'twas sheathed for aye.
No roaming bison calls for it to-day;
No hide of prairie cattle will it maim;
The plains are bare, it seeks a nobler game:
'Twill drink the life-blood of a soldier host.
Go; rise and strike, no matter what the cost.
Yet stay. Revolt not at the Union Jack,
Nor raise Thy hand against this stripling pack
Of white-faced warriors, marching West to quell
Our fallen tribe that rises to rebel.
They all are young and beautiful and good;
Curse to the war that drinks their harmless blood.
Curse to the fate that brought them from the East

To be our chiefs—to make our nation least
That breathes the air of this vast continent.
Still their new rule and council is well meant.
They but forget we Indians owned the land
From ocean unto ocean; that they stand
Upon a soil that centuries agone
Was our sole kingdom and our right alone.
They never think how they would feel to-day,
If some great nation came from far away,
Wresting their country from their hapless braves,
Giving what they gave us—but wars and graves.
Then go and strike for liberty and life,
And bring back honour to your Indian wife.
Your wife? Ah, what of that, who cares for me?
Who pities my poor love and agony?
What white-robed priest prays for your safety here,
As prayer is said for every volunteer
That swells the ranks that Canada sends out?
Who prays for vict'ry for the Indian scout?
Who prays for our poor nation lying low?
None—therefore take your tomahawk and go.
My heart may break and burn into its core,
But I am strong to bid you go to war.
Yet stay, my heart is not the only one
That grieves the loss of husband and of son;
Think of the mothers o'er the inland seas;
Think of the pale-faced maiden on her knees;
One pleads her God to guard some sweet-faced child
That marches on toward the North-West wild.
The other prays to shield her love from harm,
To strengthen his young, proud uplifted arm.
Ah, how her white face quivers thus to think,
Your tomahawk his life's best blood will drink.
She never thinks of my wild aching breast,
Nor prays for your dark face and eagle crest
Endangered by a thousand rifle balls,
My heart the target if my warrior falls.
O! coward self I hesitate no more;
Go forth, and win the glories of the war.
Go forth, nor bend to greed of white men's hands,
By right, by birth we Indians own these lands,
Though starved, crushed, plundered, lies our nation low . . .
Perhaps the white man's god has willed it so.

1895

The Flight of the Crows

The autumn afternoon is dying o'er
The quiet western valley where I lie
Beneath the maples on the river shore,
Where tinted leaves, blue waters and fair sky
Environ all; and far above some birds are flying by

To seek their evening haven in the breast
And calm embrace of silence, while they sing
Te Deums to the night, invoking rest
For busy chirping voice and tired wing—
And in the hush of sleeping trees their sleeping cradles swing.

In forest arms the night will soonest creep,
Where sombre pines a lullaby intone,
Where Nature's children curl themselves to sleep,
And all is still at last, save where alone
A band of black, belated crows arrive from lands unknown.

Strange sojourn has been theirs since waking day,
Strange sights and cities in their wanderings blend
With fields of yellow maize, and leagues away
With rivers where their sweeping waters wend
Past velvet banks to rocky shores, in cañons bold to end.

O'er what vast lakes that stretch superbly dead,
Till lashed to life by storm-clouds, have they flown?
In what wild lands, in laggard flight have led
Their aërial career unseen, unknown,
'Till now with twilight come their cries in lonely monotone?

The flapping of their pinions in the air
Dies in the hush of distance, while they light
Within the fir tops, weirdly black and bare,
That stand with giant strength and peerless height,
To shelter fairy, bird and beast throughout the closing night.

Strange black and princely pirates of the skies,
Would that your wind-tossed travels I could know!
Would that my soul could see, and, seeing, rise
To unrestricted life where ebb and flow
Of Nature's pulse would constitute a wider life below!

Could I but live just here in Freedom's arms,
A kingly life without a sovereign's care!
Vain dreams! Day hides with closing wings her charms,
And all is cradled in repose, save where
Yon band of black, belated crows still frets the evening air.

1895

The Song My Paddle Sings

West wind, blow from your prairie nest,
Blow from the mountains, blow from the west
The sail is idle, the sailor too;
O! wind of the west, we wait for you.
Blow, blow!
I have wooed you so,
But never a favour you bestow.
You rock your cradle the hills between,
But scorn to notice my white lateen.[1]

I stow the sail, unship the mast:
I wooed you long but my wooing's past;
My paddle will lull you into rest.
O! drowsy wind of the drowsy west,
Sleep, sleep,
By your mountain steep,
Or down where the prairie grasses sweep!
Now fold in slumber your laggard wings,
For soft is the song my paddle sings.

August is laughing across the sky,
Laughing while paddle, canoe and I,
Drift, drift,
Where the hills uplift
On either side of the current swift.

The river rolls in its rocky bed;
My paddle is plying its way ahead;
Dip, dip,
While the waters flip
In foam as over their breast we slip.

1 A small triangular sail.

And oh, the river runs swifter now;
The eddies circle about my bow.
Swirl, swirl!
How the ripples curl
In many a dangerous pool awhirl!

And forward far the rapids roar,
Fretting their margin for evermore.
Dash, dash,
With a mighty crash,
They seethe, and boil, and bound, and splash.

Be strong, O paddle! be brave, canoe!
The reckless waves you must plunge into.
Reel, reel.
On your trembling keel,
But never a fear my craft will feel.

We've raced the rapid, we're far ahead!
The river slips through its silent bed.
Sway, sway,
As the bubbles spray
And fall in tinkling tunes away.

And up on the hills against the sky,
A fir tree rocking its lullaby,
Swings, swings,
Its emerald wings,
Swelling the song that my paddle sings.

[1891–2], 1895

His Majesty the West Wind

Once in a fit of mental aberration
I wrote some stanzas to the western wind,
A very stupid, maudlin invocation
That into ears of audiences I've dinned.

A song about a sail, canoe and paddle
Recited by a sailor flannel dressed,
And when they heard it, people would skedaddle,
Particularly those who had been west.

For they alas had knowledge I was missing
To write of something I had never known,
That I had never experienced the driving
Of western winds across a prairie blown.

I never thought when grinding out those stanzas
I'd have to swallow specks of prairie dust,
That I'd deny my old extravaganzas
And wish His Majesty distinctly—cussed!

1894, 1990[1]

1 Johnson wrote this ironic commentary on her immensely popular performance piece 'The Song My Paddle Sings' in August 1894 when a late summer tour with Smiley took her, for the first time, to the Canadian prairies; she published it in the Toronto *Globe* that December. Many of Johnson's fans were offended by this poem's descent from the high rhetoric to which they were accustomed to 'slang'; this controversy prompted a debate over Johnson's merits as a poet in the letters column of *The Week.* Johnson never republished this poem, and it was not reprinted anywhere until it appeared in *The Beaver* (Dec. 1986/Jan. 1987); its appearance in the 1990 *Anthology of Canadian Literature in English* marked its first book publication.

Silhouette

The sky-line melts from russet into blue,
Unbroken the horizon, saving where
A wreath of smoke curls up the far, thin air,
And points the distant lodges of the Sioux.

Etched where the lands and cloudlands touch and die
A solitary Indian tepee stands,
The only habitation of these lands,
That roll their magnitude from sky to sky.

The tent poles lift and loom in thin relief,
The upward floating smoke ascends between,
And near the open doorway, gaunt and lean,
And shadow-like, there stands an Indian Chief.

With eyes that lost their lustre long ago,
With visage fixed and stern as fate's decree,
He looks towards the empty west, to see
The never-coming herd of buffalo.

Only the bones that bleach upon the plains,
Only the fleshless skeletons that lie
In ghastly nakedness and silence, cry
Out mutely that naught else to him remains.

1903

'Through Time and Bitter Distance'[1]

Unknown to you, I walk the cheerless shore.
   The cutting blast, the hurl of biting brine
May freeze, and still, and bind the waves at war,
   Ere you will ever know, O! Heart of mine,
That I have sought, reflected in the blue
   Of these sea depths, some shadow of your eyes;
Have hoped the laughing waves would sing of you,
   But this is all my starving sight descries—

I

Far out at sea a sail
      Bends to the freshening breeze,
Yields to the rising gale
      That sweeps the seas;

II

Yields, as a bird wind-tossed,
      To saltish waves that fling
Their spray, whose rime and frost
      Like crystals cling

III

To canvas, mast and spar,
      Till, gleaming like a gem,
She sinks beyond the far
      Horizon's hem.

1 For this title the author is indebted to Mr Charles G.D. Roberts. It occurs in his sonnet, 'Rain' [Johnson's note]. The longer passage from which this line comes reads: 'Ah God, if love had power / to voice its utmost yearning, even tho' / Thro' time and bitter distance, not in vain, / Surely Her heart would hear me at this hour.'

IV
Lost to my longing sight,
  And nothing left to me
Save an oncoming night,—
  An empty sea.

1903

The Lost Island

'Yes,' said my old tillicum,[1] 'we Indians have lost many things. We have lost our lands, our forests, our game, our fish; we have lost our ancient religion, our ancient dress; some of the younger people have even lost their fathers' language and the legends and traditions of their ancestors. We cannot call those old things back to us; they will never come again. We may travel many days up the mountain-trail, and look in the silent places for them. They are not there. We may paddle many moons on the sea, but our canoes will never enter the channel that leads to the yesterdays of the Indian people. These things are lost, just like "The Island of the North Arm". They may be somewhere near by, but no one can ever find them.'

'But there are many islands up the North Arm,' I asserted.

'Not the island we Indian people have sought for many tens of summers,' he replied sorrowfully.

'Was it ever there?' I questioned.

'Yes, it was there,' he said. 'My grandsires and my great-grandsires saw it; but that was long ago. My father never saw it, though he spent many days in many years searching, always searching for it. I am an old man myself, and I have never seen it, though from my youth, I, too, have searched. Sometimes in the stillness of the nights I have paddled up in my canoe.' Then, lowering his voice: 'Twice I have seen its shadow: high rocky shores, reaching as high as the tree-tops on the mainland, then tall pines and firs on its summit like a king's crown. As I paddled up the Arm one summer night, long ago, the shadow of these rocks and firs fell across my canoe, across my face, and across the waters beyond. I turned rapidly to look. There was no island there, nothing but a wide stretch of waters on both sides of me, and the moon almost directly overhead. Don't say it was the shore that shadowed me,' he hastened, catching my thought. 'The moon was above me; my canoe scarce made a shadow on the still waters. No, it was not the shore.'

'Why do you search for it?' I lamented, thinking of the old dreams in my own life whose realization I have never attained.

'There is something on that island that I want. I shall look for it until I die, for it is there,' he affirmed.

There was a long silence between us after that. I had learned to love silences when with my old tillicum, for they always led to a legend. After a time he began voluntarily:

1 Friend (from Chinook Jargon, a trade language of the Pacific Northwest).

'It was more than one hundred years ago. This great city of Vancouver was but the dream of the Sagalie Tyee [God] at that time. The dream had not yet come to the white man; only one great Indian medicine-man knew that some day a great camp for Pale-faces would lie between False Creek and the Inlet. This dream haunted him; it came to him night and day—when he was amid his people laughing and feasting, or when he was alone in the forest chanting his strange songs, beating his hollow drum, or shaking his wooden witch-rattle to gain more power to cure the sick and the dying of his tribe. For years this dream followed him. He grew to be an old, old man, yet always he could hear voices, strong and loud, as when they first spoke to him in his youth, and they would say: "Between the two narrow strips of salt water the white men will camp, many hundreds of them, many thousands of them. The Indians will learn their ways, will live as they do, will become as they are. There will be no more great war-dances, no more fights with other powerful tribes; it will be as if the Indians had lost all bravery, all courage, all confidence." He hated the voices, he hated the dream; but all his power, all his big medicine, could not drive them away. He was the strongest man on all the North Pacific Coast. He was mighty and very tall, and his muscles were as those of Leloo, the timber-wolf, when he is strongest to kill his prey. He could go for many days without food; he could fight the largest mountain-lion; he could overthrow the fiercest grizzly bear; he could paddle against the wildest winds and ride the highest waves. He could meet his enemies and kill whole tribes single-handed. His strength, his courage, his power, his bravery, were those of a giant. He knew no fear; nothing in the sea, or in the forest, nothing in the earth or the sky, could conquer him. He was fearless, fearless. Only this haunting dream of the coming white man's camp he could not drive away; it was the only thing in life he had tried to kill and failed. It drove him from the feasting, drove him from the pleasant lodges, the fires, the dancing, the story-telling of his people in their camp by the water's edge, where the salmon thronged and the deer came down to drink of the mountain-streams. He left the Indian village, chanting his wild songs as he went. Up through the mighty forests he climbed, through the trailless deep mosses and matted vines, up to the summit of what the white men call Grouse Mountain. For many days he camped there. He ate no food, he drank no water, but sat and sang his medicine-songs through the dark hours and through the day. Before him—far beneath his feet—lay the narrow strip of land between the two salt waters. Then the Sagalie Tyee gave him the power to see far into the future. He looked across a hundred years, just as he looked across what you call the Inlet, and he saw mighty lodges built close together, hundreds and thousands of them—lodges of stone and wood, and long straight trails to divide them. He saw these trails thronging with Pale-faces; he heard the sound of the white man's paddle-dip on the waters, for it is not silent like the Indian's; he saw the white man's trading posts, saw the fishing-nets, heard his speech. Then the vision faded as gradually as it came. The narrow strip of land was his own forest once more.

'"I am old," he called, in his sorrow and his trouble for his people. "I am old, O Sagalie Tyee! Soon I shall die and go to the Happy Hunting Grounds of my fathers. Let not my strength die with me. Keep living for all time my courage, my bravery, my fearlessness. Keep them for my people that they may be strong enough to endure the white man's rule. Keep my strength living for them; hide it so that the Pale-face may never find or see it."

'Then he came down from the summit of Grouse Mountain. Still chanting his medicine-songs, he entered his canoe and paddled through the colours of the setting sun far up the North Arm. When night fell he came to an island with misty shores of great grey rock; on its summit tall pines and firs encircled like a king's crown. As he neared it he felt all his strength, his courage, his fearlessness, leaving him; he could see these things drift from him on to the island. They were as the clouds that rest on the mountains, grey-white and half transparent. Weak as a woman, he paddled back to the Indian village; he told them to go and search for "The Island", where they would find all his courage, his fearlessness and his strength, living, living for ever. He slept then, but—in the morning he did not wake. Since then our young men and our old have searched for "The Island." It is there somewhere, up some lost channel, but we cannot find it. When we do, we will get back all the courage and bravery we had before the white man came, for the great medicine-man said those things never die—they live for one's children and grandchildren.'

His voice ceased. My whole heart went out to him in his longing for the lost island. I thought of all the splendid courage I knew him to possess, so made answer: 'But you say that the shadow of this island has fallen upon you; is it not so, tillicum?'

'Yes,' he said half mournfully. 'But only the shadow.'

1911, 1920, 1961

Archibald Lampman

1861–1899

Archibald Lampman—like Charles G.D. Roberts—was born into a Loyalist Anglican family. Although he grew up on the edge of the wilderness, his education and career carried him into the increasingly urban world of the emerging Canadian nation. Born in Morpeth, a village in Canada West on Lake Erie, Lampman spent his childhood in the Rice Lake district, first at Gore's Landing—where he met the Strickland sisters, Susanna Moodie and Catharine Parr Traill—and then, after a brief time in Cobourg, where his clergyman father had taken a new parish, as a boarder at Trinity College School in Port Hope. He next went to Trinity College, Toronto, on a scholarship, but his pursuit of the less academic side of undergraduate life cost him a first-class degree, and an academic career. After realizing that he disliked teaching high school, he settled into a permanent position in the civil service, working as a clerk in the Post Office Department. In 1887 Lampman married Maud Playter, against his family's wishes; the union was apparently unhappy for both partners. However, he found kinship with a group of people, members of the Ottawa Literary and Scientific Society, who shared his national and intellectual interests; among them were two other poets and civil servants, Wilfred Campbell and Duncan Campbell Scott.

Scott and Lampman became close friends, for they shared a love of the wilderness, joining in many canoeing expeditions while they discussed their real work, the writing of poetry. As a naturalist poet Lampman learned to employ vivid yet simple images and diction, to build poems out of the sounds, the motion, and even the colours of the wilderness. A poet in the Romantic tradition, Lampman saw himself as being a manifestation of Keats, even saying, 'I have an idea that he has found a sort of faint reincarnation in me'; however, his importance lies in his attempts to capture a uniquely Canadian landscape, for he believed that 'climate and scenic conditions have much to do with the molding of national character'. Like other Romantics, Lampman feared that the city was a threat to nature, yet because he considered Canada to be 'still in the house-building, land-breaking stage', he believed that the growth and materialism of the new Confederation were necessary in order for future generations to have the leisure to create a balanced culture.

Lampman's writing was well received in his time, appearing in various journals in Canada and the United States. In spite of this popularity, he had to publish his first volume of poetry, *Among the Millet* (Ottawa, 1888), at his own expense. Though he was unable to interest anyone in a book of sonnets, Lampman found an American publisher who accepted a volume of nature lyrics, *Lyrics of the Earth* (Boston, 1895). Around this time his health began to deteriorate rapidly, owing in part to the lingering effects of rheumatic fever contracted in childhood and to the depression he suffered following the deaths of his son (1894) and his father (1897). He died of heart disease at thirty-seven, before a third volume, *Alcyone*, reached the printing stage. (Shortly after Lampman's death, D.C. Scott ordered a printing of twelve copies.) As Lampman's literary executor, Scott published a memorial collection of his friend's poems in 1900. In 1943 Scott and E.K. Brown discovered 'At the Long Sault' in manuscript and published it in a new edition of Lampman's poems. Among other unpublished poems Lampman left behind when he died were a group of love poems inspired by his close friendship with Katherine Waddell, a fellow civil servant. Suppressed by Scott—except for six sonnets that appeared in *At the Long Sault and Other New Poems* (1943)—they were finally published in *Lampman's Kate* (1975), edited by Margaret Coulby Whitridge.

Roberts and Lampman present an informative contrast. Where Roberts found change at the heart of things, Lampman saw change as existing only in the superficialities of appearance, and he sought instead the vision (he often called it a dream) of the true and unchanging reality that lies beneath the surface. His poetry, which records those moments of intense experience with nature that offer glimpses of eternal truth, may therefore be said to look back to the English Romantics in a way that Robert's poetry does not—but its expression is so effective that Lampman is now generally thought of as the best of the Confederation poets. His description of how Emerson responded to the 'cosmic sympathy' of the universe might well be applied to himself: 'He is drawn to nature because in the energy of his own soul he is aware of a kinship to the forces of nature, and feels with an elemental joy as if it were a part of himself the eternal movement of life' ('At the Mermaid Inn', 22 April 1893). Although nature played a large role in Lampman's writing, his poetry also looks at the urban landscape, as in 'The Railway Station'. Its disturbing urban images, such as the fiery engine and the dazed crowds, grow apocalyptic in the later dream-like poem 'The City of the End of Things', in which the individual is endangered by a city that, with its increasing mechanical and industrialized invention, has become a version of Pandemonium, a nightmare of a dehumanized, eternal city.

The Railway Station

The darkness brings no quiet here, the light
    No waking: ever on my blinded brain
    The flare of lights, the rush, and cry, and strain,
The engines' scream, the hiss and thunder smite:

I see the hurrying crowds, the clasp, the flight,
   Faces that touch, eyes that are dim with pain:
   I see the hoarse wheels turn, and the great train
Move labouring out into the bourneless night.

So many souls within its dim recesses,
   So many bright, so many mournful eyes:
Mine eyes that watch grow fixed with dreams and guesses;
   What threads of life, what hidden histories,
What sweet or passionate dreams and dark distresses,
What unknown thoughts, what various agonies!

1888

Heat

From plains that reel to southward, dim,
   The road runs by me white and bare;
Up the steep hill it seems to swim
   Beyond, and melt into the glare.
Upward half-way, or it may be
   Nearer the summit, slowly steals
A hay-cart, moving dustily
   With idly clacking wheels.

By his cart's side the wagoner
   Is slouching slowly at his ease,
Half-hidden in the windless blur
   Of white dust puffing to his knees.
This wagon on the height above,
   From sky to sky on either hand,
Is the sole thing that seems to move
   In all the heat-held land.

Beyond me in the fields the sun
   Soaks in the grass and hath his will;
I count the marguerites[1] one by one;
   Even the buttercups are still.
On the brook yonder not a breath
   Disturbs the spider or the midge.
The water-bugs draw close beneath
   The cool gloom of the bridge.

1 Daisies.

Where the far elm-tree shadows flood
Dark patches in the burning grass,
The cows, each with her peaceful cud,
Lie waiting for the heat to pass.
From somewhere on the slope near by
Into the pale depth of the noon
A wandering thrush slides leisurely
His thin revolving tune.

In intervals of dreams I hear
The cricket from the droughty ground;
The grasshoppers spin into mine ear
A small innumerable sound.
I lift mine eyes sometimes to gaze:
The burning sky-line blinds my sight:
The woods far off are blue with haze:
The hills are drenched in light.

And yet to me not this or that
Is always sharp or always sweet;
In the sloped shadow of my hat
I lean at rest, and drain the heat;
Nay more, I think some blessèd power
Hath brought me wandering idly here:
In the full furnace of this hour
My thoughts grow keen and clear.

1888

The Frogs

I

Breathers of wisdom won without a quest,
Quaint uncouth dreamers, voices high and strange;
Flutists of lands where beauty hath no change,
And wintry grief is a forgotten guest,
Sweet murmurers of everlasting rest,
For whom glad days have ever yet to run,
And moments are as aeons, and the sun
But ever sunken half-way toward the west.

Often to me who heard you in your day,
With close rapt ears, it could not choose but seem
That earth, our mother, searching in what way
Men's hearts might know her spirit's inmost dream;
Ever at rest beneath life's change and stir,
Made you her soul, and bade you pipe for her.

II

In those mute days when spring was in her glee,
And hope was strong, we knew not why or how,
And earth, the mother, dreamed with brooding brow,
Musing on life, and what the hours might be,
When love should ripen to maternity
Then like high flutes in silvery interchange
Ye piped with voices still and sweet and strange,
And ever as ye piped, on every tree
The great buds swelled; among the pensive woods
The spirits of first flowers awoke and flung
From buried faces the close-fitting hoods,
And listened to your piping till they fell,
The frail spring-beauty[1] with her perfumed bell,
The wind-flower, and the spotted adder-tongue.

III

All the day long, wherever pools might be
Among the golden meadows, where the air
Stood in a dream, as it were moorèd there
For ever in a noon-tide reverie,
Or where the birds made riot of their glee
In the still woods, and the hot sun shone down,
Crossed with warm lucent shadows on the brown
Leaf-paven pools, that bubbled dreamily,

Or far away in whispering river meads[2]
And watery marshes where the brooding noon,
Full with the wonder of its own sweet boon,

1 A common spring wildflower (*Claytonia virginica*) having small white or pinkish flowers; 'windflower': an anemone, a flower of the buttercup family; 'adder-tongue': a spring flower with mottled leaves, also known as the dogtooth violet or trout lily.

2 Meadows.

Nestled and slept among the noiseless reeds,
Ye sat and murmured, motionless as they,
With eyes that dreamed beyond the night and day.

IV

And when day passed and over heaven's height,
Thin with the many stars and cool with dew,
The fingers of the deep hours slowly drew
The wonder of the every-healing night,
No grief or loneliness or rapt delight
Or weight of silence ever brought to you
Slumber or rest; only your voices grew
More high and solemn; slowly with hushed flight

Ye saw the echoing hours go by, long-drawn,
Nor ever stirred, watching with fathomless eyes,
And with your countless clear antiphonies
Filling the earth and heaven, even till dawn,
Last-risen, found you with its first pale gleam,
Still with soft throats unaltered in your dream.

V

And slowly as we heard you, day by day,
The stillness of enchanted reveries
Bound brain and spirit and half-closed eyes,
In some divine sweet wonder-dream astray;
To us no sorrow or upreared dismay
Nor any discord came, but evermore
The voices of mankind, the outer roar,
Grew strange and murmurous, faint and far away.

Morning and noon and midnight exquisitely,
Rapt with your voices, this alone we knew,
Cities might change and fall, and men might die,
Secure were we, content to dream with you
That change and pain are shadows faint and fleet,
And dreams are real, and life is only sweet.

1888

The City of the End of Things

Beside the pounding cataracts
Of midnight streams unknown to us
'Tis builded in the leafless tracts
And valleys huge of Tartarus.[1]
Lurid and lofty and vast it seems;
It hath no rounded name that rings,
But I have heard it called in dreams
The City of the End of Things.

Its roofs and iron towers have grown
None knoweth how high within the night,
But in its murky streets far down
A flaming terrible and bright
Shakes all the stalking shadows there,
Across the walls, across the floors,
And shifts upon the upper air
From out a thousand furnace doors;
And all the while an awful sound
Keeps roaring on continually,
And crashes in the ceaseless round
Of a gigantic harmony.
Through its grim depths re-echoing
And all its weary height of walls,
With measured roar and iron ring,
The inhuman music lifts and falls.
Where no thing rests and no man is,
And only fire and night hold sway;
The beat, the thunder and the hiss
Cease not, and change not, night nor day.

And moving at unheard commands,
The abysses and vast fires between,
Flit figures that with clanking hands
Obey a hideous routine;
They are not flesh, they are not bone,
They see not with the human eye,
And from their iron lips is blown
A dreadful and monotonous cry;
And whoso of our mortal race
Should find that city unaware,

1 Infernal abyss below Hades, where Zeus threw the rebel Titans.

Lean Death would smite him face to face,
And blanch him with its venomed air:
Or caught by the terrific spell,
Each thread of memory snapt and cut,
His soul would shrivel and its shell
Go rattling like an empty nut.

It was not always so, but once,
In days that no man thinks upon,
Fair voices echoed from its stones,
The light above it leaped and shone:
Once there were multitudes of men,
That built that city in their pride,
Until its might was made, and then
They withered age by age and died.
But now of that prodigious race,
Three only in an iron tower,
Set like carved idols face to face,
Remain the masters of its power;
And at the city gate a fourth,
Gigantic and with dreadful eyes,
Sits looking toward the lightless north,
Beyond the reach of memories;
Fast rooted to the lurid floor,
A bulk that never moves a jot,
In his pale body dwells no more,
Or mind or soul,—an idiot!
But sometime in the end those three
Shall perish and their hands be still,
And with the master's touch shall flee
Their incommunicable skill.
A stillness absolute as death
Along the slacking wheels shall lie,
And, flagging at a single breath,
The fires shall moulder out and die.
The roar shall vanish at its height,
And over that tremendous town
The silence of eternal night
Shall gather close and settle down.
All its grim grandeur, tower and hall,
Shall be abandoned utterly,
And into rust and dust shall fall
From century to century;
Nor ever living thing shall grow,

Nor trunk of tree, nor blade of grass;
No drop shall fall, no wind shall blow,
Nor sound of any foot shall pass:
Alone of its accursèd state,
One thing the hand of Time shall spare,
For the grim Idiot at the gate
Is deathless and eternal there.

1895

A Summer Dream[1]

One in a dream, between two troubled slips
Of sleep, I saw you in your brightest guise.
Methought you stood, but tears were in your eyes,
Softer than rain or any dew that drips.
On my cold hand you laid your finger tips
And I, touched by a sudden sweet surprise,
Caught you in both mine arms with sobs and sighs
And kissed your brow, beloved, and your lips.

And you—ah yes! even you, upon my breast
Leaned for a moment, with cheeks wet and wan,
Then smiled and vanished; but for many hours
I wandered in a speechless dream, caressed
By winds from such a magic summer dream
As never wantoned over earthly flowers.

[1896], 1975

1 One of the poems addressed to Katherine Waddell that remained in manuscript until 1975.

Voices of Earth

We have not heard the music of the spheres,[1]
The song of star to star, but there are sounds
More deep than human joy and human tears,
That Nature uses in her common rounds;
The fall of streams, the cry of winds that strain

1 Cosmic harmonies, supposed to be produced by the movement of heavenly bodies.

The oak, the roaring of the sea's surge, might
Of thunder breaking afar off, or rain
That falls by minutes in the summer night.
These are the voices of earth's secret soul,
Uttering the mystery from which she came.
To him who hears them grief beyond control,
Or joy inscrutable without a name,
Wakes in his heart thoughts bedded there, impearled,
Before the birth and making of the world.

1899

Winter Evening

To-night the very horses springing by
Toss gold from whitened nostrils. In a dream
The streets that narrow to the westward gleam
Like rows of golden palaces; and high
From all the crowded chimneys tower and die
A thousand aureoles. Down in the west
The brimming plains beneath the sunset rest,
One burning sea of gold. Soon, soon shall fly
The glorious vision, and the hours shall feel
A mightier master; soon from height to height,
With silence and the sharp unpitying stars,
Stern creeping frosts, and winds that touch like steel,
Out of the depth beyond the eastern bars,
Glittering and still shall come the awful night.

1899

To a Millionaire

The world in gloom and splendor passes by,
And thou in the midst of it with brows that gleam,
A creature of that old distorted dream
That makes the sound of life an evil cry.
Good men perform just deeds, and brave men die,
And win not honor such as gold can give,
While the vain multitudes plo on, and live,

And serve the curse that pins them down: But I
Think only of the unnumbered broken hearts,
The hunger and the mortal strife for bread,
Old age and youth alike mistaught, misfed,
By want and rags and homelessness made vile,
The griefs and hates, and all the meaner parts
That balance thy one grim misgotten pile.

1900

At the Long Sault: May, 1660[1]

Under the day-long sun there is life and mirth
  In the working earth,
And the wonderful moon shines bright
  Through the soft spring night,
The innocent flowers in the limitless woods are springing
  Far and away
  With the sound and the perfume of May,
And ever up from the south the happy birds are winging,
  The waters glitter and leap and play
  While the gray hawk soars.

But far in an open glade of the forest set
  Where the rapid plunges and roars,
Is a ruined fort with a name that men forget,—
  A shelterless pen
  With its broken palisade,
  Behind it, musket in hand,
  Beyond message or aid
  In this savage heart of the wild,
  Mere youngsters, grown in a moment to men,
  Grim and alert and arrayed,
  The comrades of Daulac stand.
  Ever before them, night and day,
  The rush and skulk and cry
  Of foes, not men but devils, panting for prey;
  Behind them the sleepless dream

1 On 1 May 1660 Adam Dollard des Ormeaux (sometimes called Daulac), with 16 companions and 44 Hurons and Algonquins, laid an ambush for some Iroquois at an abandoned fort on the Ottawa River. The Iroquois were joined by a reinforcement of 500, but it took them ten days to vanquish the Frenchmen and their allies. Until fairly recently this event was considered to have saved the colony of Montreal from Iroquois attack, and the Frenchmen were considered martyrs for the faith.

Of the little frail-walled town,[2] far away by the plunging stream.
Of maiden and matron and child,
With ruin and murder impending, and none but they
To beat back the gathering horror
Deal death while they may,
And then die.

Day and night they have watched while the little plain
Grew dark with the rush of the foe, but their host
Broke ever and melted away, with no boast
But to number their slain;
And now as the days renew
Hunger and thirst and care
Were they never so stout, so true,
Press at their hearts; but none
Falters or shrinks or utters a coward word,
Though each setting sun
Brings from the pitiless wild new hands to the Iroquois horde,
And only to them despair.

Silent, white-faced, again and again
Charged and hemmed round by furious hands,
Each for a moment faces them all and stands
In his little desperate ring; like a tired bull moose
Whom scores of sleepless wolves, a ravening pack,
Have chased all night, all day
Through the snow-laden woods, like famine let loose;
And he turns at last in his track
Against a wall of rock and stands at bay;
Round him with terrible sinews and teeth of steel
They charge and recharge; but with many a furious plunge and wheel,
Hither and thither over the trampled snow,
He tosses them bleeding and torn;
Till, driven, and ever to and fro
Harried, wounded, and weary grown,
His mighty strength gives way
And all together they fasten upon him and drag him down.

So Daulac turned him anew
With a ringing cry to his men
In the little raging forest glen,
And his terrible sword in the twilight whistled and slew.

2 Montreal.

And all his comrades stood
With their backs to the pales,[3] and fought
Till their strength was done;
The thews that were only mortal flagged and broke
Each struck his last wild stroke,
And they fell one by one,
And the world that had seemed so good
Passed like a dream and was naught.

And then the great night came
With the triumph-songs of the foe and the flame
Of the camp-fires.
Out of the dark the soft wind woke,
The song of the rapid rose alway
And came to the spot where the comrades lay,
Beyond help or care,
With none but the red men round them
To gnash their teeth and stare.

All night by the foot of the mountain
The little town lieth at rest,
The sentries are peacefully pacing;
And neither from East not from West
Is there rumor of death or of danger;
None dreameth tonight in his bed
That ruin was near and the heroes
That met it and stemmed it are dead.

But afar in the ring of the forest,
Where the air is so tender with May
And the waters are wild in the moonlight
They lie in their silence of clay.

The numberless stars out of heaven
Look down with a pitiful glance;
And the lilies asleep in the forest
Are closed like the lilies of France.[4]

[1899], 1943

3 Row of spiked wooden poles, here the walls of the fort.

4 That is, the fleur-de-lis, the emblematic flower of France, often appearing as a heraldic emblem on the shields of warriors.

Duncan Campbell Scott

1862–1947

The writing of Duncan Campbell Scott, like that of other Confederate poets, developed out of a profound response to the Canadian landscape and its people, influenced by mid-nineteenth-century British and American thought. Born in Ottawa and raised in villages in Ontario and Quebec, where his father served as a Methodist minister, Scott became interested as a boy in the life and customs of Aboriginal peoples, frontier lumbermen, and French-Canadian *habitants*—all of whom became important subjects in his writing.

Unlike Charles G.D. Roberts and Archibald Lampman, however, Scott was unable to attend university for financial reasons. In 1879, after an interview with the prime minister, Sir John A. Macdonald, he accepted a clerkship at $1.50 a day in the Department of Indian Affairs, where he remained for over fifty years, eventually assuming that department's highest permanent office. He began to write in the mid-1880s, after meeting Lampman, another civil servant. As Roberts had earlier inspired Lampman, so Lampman supplied Scott with the confidence he needed. Within the next few years Scott's stories and poems began to appear in periodicals. He published his first book of poetry, *The Magic House and Other Poems*, in 1893, and in 1896, his first volume of short stories, *In the Village of Viger*. In 1892 Scott and Lampman joined another civil servant, Wilfred Campbell, in writing 'At the Mermaid Inn', for the Toronto *Globe*, a column in which they commented on the Canadian cultural milieu and developed their own literary theories. Scott also continued his interest in wilderness life, taking long recreational canoe trips with Lampman, as well as making an increasing number of professional expeditions to visit Native bands.

In his second book of verse, *Labour and the Angel* (1898), Scott began to move away from the shadowy, lush poetry of his earlier volume and introduce the first of a number of poems on First Nations subjects for which he became well known. In this book Scott's depiction of large conflicts between contrasting forces—producing a dialectic that recurs throughout his work—emerges. For him the natural struggle often resolves itself in moments of beauty and serenity that are, like those in 'The Height of Land', 'deeper than peace'. As well as continuing to write poetry and prose throughout his lifetime, Scott edited several volumes of Lampman's verse after his friend died in 1899. Among Scott's other books are *New World Lyrics* (1905); *Lundy's Land and Other Poems* (1916); *Beauty and Life* (1921); *The Poems of Duncan Campbell Scott* (1926); *The Green Cloister and Other Poems* (1935); and the short story collection, *The Witching of Elspie* (1923).

While Scott continued to work within the more conservative traditions of Confederation poetry, he helped to open the doors of what had become a staid literary establishment to the postwar writers, many of whom were proponents of modernism. In a 1922 speech he gave as president of the Royal Society he condemned the static condition of Canadian writing and recommended new voices:

> *It is the mission of new theories in the arts, and particularly of new theories that come to us illustrated by practice, to re-examine the grounds of our preferences, and to retest our accepted dogmas. . . . We require more rage of our poets. We should like them to put to the proof that saying of William Blake: 'The tigers of wrath are wiser than the horses of instruction.'*

Scott's request for poetic rage may derive from his own strong sense of man in confrontation with a violent universe. His answer to that violence was, when the struggle was a losing one, an affirmation of death as a part of life. In 'At the Cedars' the lumberman Isaàc Dufour, swept along by forces beyond his control, keeps his balance and sings; when neither his skill nor his nonchalance can continue to protect him, he makes a gesture of graceful acceptance: 'And when he was there /

In the air, / Kissed his hand / To the land.' Scott saw this calm way of meeting death as heroism whether it took place in war, as in 'The Battle of Lundy's Lane', or in extraordinary conditions of peace, as in 'The Forsaken'.

Although the heroic Chipewyan woman in 'The Forsaken' follows a similar pattern to that found in non-Native poems—she stays alive when she must by bravely fishing with her own flesh, but later she accepts her inevitable death unflinchingly, as she meets the 'silence deeper than silence'—the way we read this and other of Scott's poems about Natives has changed. It is not just that many readers now have some difficulty accepting depictions of Natives that come to us through the eyes and voice of a non-Aboriginal but also that we view Scott himself differently from the way readers once did. In contrast to readers who simply saw him as writing sympathetically about Native peoples (in poems such as 'The Onondaga Madonna') based on his extensive contact with them, we find it hard today to ignore the fact that the same people about whom he seems objective or idealizing in his poems are those who in real life were adversely affected by Scott's role in Indian Affairs.

The isolation of the individual apparent in several of his poems is often a feature of Scott's fiction as well, as may be seen in the story printed here. In 'Labrie's Wife', which borrows the form of many exploration narratives—a Hudson's Bay journal—the first-person narrator's inability to respond to people not only cuts him off from society but leads him into foolish self-deception.

At the Cedars

You had two girls—Baptiste—
One is Virginie—
Hold hard—Baptiste!
Listen to me.

The whole drive was jammed
In that bend at the Cedars,
The rapids were dammed
With the logs tight rammed
And crammed; you might know
The Devil had clinched them below.

We worked three days—not a budge,
'She's as tight as a wedge, on the ledge,'
Says our foreman;
'Mon Dieu! boys, look here,
We must get this thing clear.'
He cursed at the men
And we went for it then;
With our cant-dogs[1] arow,
We just gave he-yo-ho;
When she gave a big shove
From above.

1 Hooked tools that bite into logs.

The gang yelled and tore
For the shore,
The logs gave a grind
Like a wolf's jaws behind,
And as quick as a flash,
With a shove and a crash,
They were down in a mash,
But I and ten more,
All but Isaàc Dufour,
Were ashore.

He leaped on a log in the front of the rush,
And shot out from the bind
While the jam roared behind;
As he floated along
He balanced his pole
And tossed us a song.
But just as we cheered,
Up darted a log from the bottom,
Leaped thirty feet square and fair,
And came down on his own.

He went up like a block
With the shock,
And when he was there
In the air,
Kissed his hand
To the land;
When he dropped
My heart stopped,
For the first logs had caught him
And crushed him;
When he rose in his place
There was blood on his face.

There were some girls, Baptiste,
Picking berries on the hillside,
Where the river curls, Baptiste,
You know—on the still side
One was down by the water,
She saw Isaàc
Fall back.

She did not scream, Baptiste,
She launched her canoe;
It did seem, Baptiste,
That she wanted to die too,
For before you could think
The birch cracked like a shell
In that rush of hell,
And I saw them both sink—

Baptiste!—
He had two girls,
One is Virginie,
What God calls the other
Is not known to me.

1893

The Onondaga[1] Madonna

She stands full-throated and with careless pose,
This woman of a weird and waning race,
The tragic savage lurking in her face,
Where all her pagan passion burns and glows;
Her blood is mingled with her ancient foes,
And thrills with war and wildness in her veins;
Her rebel lips are dabbled with the stains
Of feuds and forays and her father's woes.

And closer is the shawl about her breast,
The latest promise of her nation's doom,
Paler than she her baby clings and lies,
The primal warrior gleaming from his eyes;
He sulks, and burdened with his infant gloom,
He draws his heavy brows and will not rest.

1898

1 An Iroquois tribe.

Night Hymns on Lake Nipigon

Here in the midnight, where the dark mainland and island
Shadows mingle in shadow deeper, profounder,
Sing we the hymns of the churches, while the dead water
 Whispers before us.

Thunder is travelling slow on the path of the lightning;
One after one the stars and the beaming planets
Look serene in the lake from the edge of the storm-cloud,
 Then have they vanished.

While our canoe, that floats dumb in the bursting thunder,
Gathers her voice in the quiet and thrills and whispers,
Presses her prow in the star-gleam, and all her ripple
 Lapses in blackness.

Sing we the sacred ancient hymns of the churches,
Chanted first in old-world nooks of the desert,
While in the wild, pellucid Nipigon reaches
 Hunted the savage.

Now have the ages met in the Northern midnight,
And on the lonely, loon-haunted Nipigon reaches
Rises the hymn of triumph and courage and comfort,
 Adeste Fideles.

Tones that were fashioned when the faith brooded in darkness,
Joined with sonorous vowels in the noble Latin,
Now are married with the long-drawn Ojibwa,
 Uncouth and mournful.

Soft with the silver drip of the regular paddles
Falling in rhythm, timed with the liquid, plangent
Sounds from the blades where the whirlpools break and are carried
 Down into darkness;

Each long cadence, flying like a dove from her shelter
Deep in the shadow, wheels for a throbbing moment,
Poises in utterance, returning in circles of silver
 To nest in the silence.

All wild nature stirs with the infinite, tender
Plaint of a bygone age whose soul is eternal,
Bound in the lonely phrases that thrill and falter
    Back into quiet.

Back they falter as the deep storm overtakes them,
Whelms them in splendid hollows of booming thunder,
Wraps them in rain, that, sweeping, breaks and onrushes
    Ringing like cymbals.

1905

The Forsaken

I

Once in the winter
Out on a lake
In the heart of the north-land,
Far from the Fort
And far from the hunters,
A Chippewa woman
With her sick baby,
Crouched in the last hours
Of a great storm.
Frozen and hungry,
She fished through the ice
With a line of the twisted
Bark of the cedar,
And a rabbit-bone hook
Polished and barbed;
Fished with the bare hook
All through the day,
Fished and caught nothing;
While the young chieftain
Tugged at her breasts,
Or slept in the lacings
Of the warm *tikanagan.*[1]

1 Moss-filled cradle board.

All the lake-surface
Streamed with the hissing
Of millions of iceflakes,
Hurled by the wind;
Behind her the round
Of a lonely island
Roared like a fire
With the voice of the storm
In the deeps of the cedars.
Valiant, unshaken,
She took of her own flesh,
Baited the fish-hook,
Drew in a grey-trout,
Drew in his fellows,
Heaped them beside her,
Dead in the snow.
Valiant, unshaken,
She faced the long distance,
Wolf-haunted and lonely,
Sure of her goal
And the life of her dear one;
Tramped for two days,
On the third in the morning,
Saw the strong bulk
Of the Fort by the river,
Saw the wood-smoke
Hang soft in the spruces,
Heard the keen yelp
Of the ravenous huskies
Fighting for whitefish:
Then she had rest.

II

Years and years after,
When she was old and withered,
When her son was an old man
And his children filled with vigour,
They came in their northern tour on the verge of winter,
To an island in a lonely lake.

There one night they camped, and on the morrow
Gathered their kettles and birch-bark[1]
Their rabbit-skin robes and their mink-traps,
Launched their canoes and slunk away through the islands,
Left her alone forever,
Without a word of farewell,
Because she was old and useless,
Like a paddle broken and warped,
Or a pole that was splintered.
Then, without a sigh,
Valiant, unshaken,
She smoothed her dark locks under her kerchief,
Composed her shawl in state,
Then folded her hands ridged with sinews and corded with veins,
Folded them across her breasts spent with the nourishing of children,
Gazed at the sky past the tops of the cedars,
Saw two spangled nights arise out of the twilight,
Saw two days go by filled with the tranquil sunshine,
Saw, without pain, or dread, or even a moment of longing:
Then on the third great night there came thronging and thronging
Millions of snowflakes out of a windless cloud;
They covered her close with a beautiful crystal shroud,
Covered her deep and silent.
But in the frost of the dawn,
Up from the life below,
Rose a column of breath
Through a tiny cleft in the snow,
Fragile, delicately drawn,
Wavering with its own weakness,
In the wilderness a sign of the spirit,
Persisting still in the sight of the sun
Till day was done.
Then all light was gathered up by the hand of God and hid in His breast,
Then there was born a silence deeper than silence,
Then she had rest.

1905

1 Waterproof birch-bark bowls or buckets.

The Battle of Lundy's Lane[1]

(Rufus Gale speaks—1852)

Yes,—In the Lincoln Militia,—in the war of eighteen-twelve;
Many's the day I've had since then to dig and delve—
But those are the years I remember as the brightest years of all,
When we left the plow in the furrow to follow the bugle's call.
Why, even our son Abner wanted to fight with the men!
'Don't you go, d'ye hear, sir!'—I was angry with him then.
'Stay with your mother!' I said, and he looked so old and grim—
He was just sixteen that April—I couldn't believe it was him;
But I didn't think—I was off—and we met the foe again,
Five thousand strong and ready, at the hill by Lundy's Lane.
There as the night came on we fought them from six to nine,
Whenever they broke our line we broke their line,
They took our guns and we won them again, and around the levels
Where the hill sloped up—with the Eighty-ninth,—we fought like devils
Around the flags; and on they came and we drove them back,
Until with its very fierceness the fight grew slack.
It was then about nine and dark as a miser's pocket,
When up came Hercules Scott's[2] brigade swift as a rocket,
And charged,—and the flashes sprang in the dark like a lion's eyes;
The night was full of fire—groans, and cheers, and cries;
Then through the sound and the fury another sound broke in—
The roar of a great old duck-gun shattered the rest of the din;
It took two minutes to charge it and another to set it free.
Every time I heard it an angel spoke to me;
Yes, the minute I heard it I felt the strangest tide
Flow in my veins like lightning, as if, there, by my side,
Was the very spirit of Valour. But 'twas dark—you couldn't see—
And the one who was firing the duck-gun fell against me
And slid down to the clover, and lay there still;
Something went through me—piercing—with a strange, swift thrill;
The noise fell away into silence, and I heard as clear as thunder
The long, slow roar of Niagara: O the wonder

1 In June 1812, at the height of the Napoleonic Wars, the US declared war on Britain and attacked the only British possession on the continent—Canada. Lundy's Lane, near Niagara Falls, was the site of one of the bitterest encounters of the War of 1812 (24–5 July 1814), fought between US troops and British regulars, including the Royal Scots and the 8th, 41st, and 89th regiments on foot, aided by Canadian militia. Both sides suffered heavy losses, and the battle was inconclusive, although the Americans were forced to withdraw to Fort Erie. The War itself ended in a stalemate, with all conquered territories restored to their pre-war owners under conditions set out in the Treaty of Ghent (signed 24 Dec. 1814); nevertheless, for Canadians it helped develop a sense of identity and community, as Scott's poem illustrates.

2 Presumably Winfield Scott (1786–1866), the American brigadier general who was severely wounded during the Battle of Lundy's Lane. His heroic performance made him a national hero in the US.

Of that deep sound. But again the battle broke
And the foe, driven before us desperately—stroke upon stroke,
Left the field to his master, and sullenly down the road
Sounded the boom of his guns, trailing the heavy load
Of his wounded men and his shattered flags, sullen and slow,
Setting fire in his rage to Bridgewater mills, and the glow
Flared in the distant forest. We rested as we could,
And for a while I slept in the dark of a maple wood:
But when the clouds in the east were red all over,
I came back there to the place we made the stand in the clover;
For my heart was heavy then with a strange, deep pain,
As I thought of the glorious fight, and again and again
I remembered the valiant spirit and the piercing thrill;
But I knew it all when I reached the top of the hill,—
For there, there with the blood on his dear, brave head,
There on the hill in the clover lay our Abner—dead!—
No—thank you—no, I don't need it; I'm solid as granite rock,
But every time that I tell it I feel the old, cold shock,
I'm eighty-one my next birthday—do you breed such fellows now?
There he lay with the dawn cooling his broad fair brow,
That was no dawn for him; and there was the old duck-gun
That many and many's the time,—just for the fun,
We together, alone, would take to the hickory rise,
And bring home more wild pigeons than ever you saw with your eyes.
Up with Hercules Scott's brigade, just as it came on night—
He was the angel beside me in the thickest of the fight—
Wrote a note to his mother—He said, 'I've got to go;
Mother, what would home be under the heel of the foe!'
Oh! she never slept a wink, she would rise and walk the floor;
She'd say this over and over, 'I knew it all before!'
I'd try to speak of the glory to give her a little joy.
'What is the glory to me when I want my boy, my boy!'
She'd say, and she'd wring her hands; her hair grew white as snow—
And I'd argue with her up and down, to and fro,
Of how she had mothered a hero, and his was a glorious fate,
Better than years of grubbing to gather an estate.
Sometimes I'd put it this way: 'If God was to say to me now
"Take him back as he once was helping you with the plow,"
I'd say, "No, God, thank You kindly; 'twas You that he obeyed;
You told him to fight and he fought, and he wasn't afraid;
You wanted to prove him in battle, You sent him to Lundy's Lane,
'Tis well!"' But she only would answer over and over again,
'Give me back my Abner—give me back my son!'
It was so all through the winter until the spring had begun,

And the crocus was up in the dooryard, and the drift by the fence was thinned,
And the sap drip-dropped from the branches wounded by the wind,
And the whole earth smelled like a flower,—then she came to me one night—
'Rufus!' she said, with a sob in her throat,—'Rufus, you're right.'
I hadn't cried till then, not a tear—but then I was torn in two—
There, it's all right—my eyes don't see as they used to do!
But O the joy of that battle—it was worth the whole of life,
You felt immortal in action with the rapture of the strife,
There in the dark by the river, with the flashes of fire before,
Running and crashing along, there in the dark, and the roar
Of the guns, and the shrilling cheers, and the knowledge that filled your heart
That there was a victory making and you must do your part,
But—there's his grave in the orchard where the headstone glimmers white:
We could see it, we thought, from our window even on the darkest night;
It is set there for a sign that what one lad could do
Would be done by a hundred hundred lads whose hearts were stout and true.
And when in the time of trial you hear the recreant say,
Shooting his coward lips at us, 'You shall have had your day:
For all your state and glory shall pass like a cloudy wrack,[3]
And here some other flag shall fly where flew the Union Jack,'—
Why tell him a hundred thousand men would spring from these sleepy farms,
To tie that flag in its ancient place with the sinews of their arms;
And if they doubt you and put you to scorn, why you can make it plain,
With the tale of the gallant Lincoln men and the fight at Lundy's Lane.

1916

3 A mass of high, fast-moving clouds.

The Height of Land[1]

Here is the height of land:
The watershed on either hand
Goes down to Hudson Bay
Or Lake Superior;
The stars are up, and far away
The wind sounds in the wood, wearier
Than the long Ojibwa cadence

1 Here, the Arctic watershed; north of that point all rivers flow into the Arctic Ocean.

In which Potàn the Wise[2]
Declares the ills of life
And Chees-que-ne-ne makes a mournful sound
Of acquiescence. The fires burn low
With just sufficient glow
To light the flakes of ash that play
At being moths, and flutter away
To fall in the dark and die as ashes:
Here there is peace in the lofty air,
And Something comes by flashes
Deeper than peace;—
The spruces have retired a little space
And left a field of sky in violet shadow
With stars like marigolds in a water-meadow.

Now the Indian guides are dead asleep;
There is no sound unless the soul can hear
The gathering of the waters in their sources.
We have come up through the spreading lakes
From level to level,—
Pitching our tents sometimes over a revel
Of roses that nodded all night,
Dreaming within our dreams,
To wake at dawn and find that they were captured
With no dew on their leaves;
Sometimes mid sheaves
Of bracken and dwarf-cornel,[3] and again
On a wide blueberry plain
Brushed with the shimmer of a bluebird's wing;
A rocky islet followed
With one lone poplar and a single nest
Of white-throat-sparrows that took no rest
But sang in dreams or woke to sing,—
To the last portage and the height of land—:
Upon one hand
The lonely north enlaced with lakes and streams,
And the enormous targe[4] of Hudson Bay,
Glimmering all night
In the cold arctic light;

2 The name of the one of the two Indian guides who led the speaker into the wilderness in Scott's poem 'Spring on Mattagami'; Cheese-que-ne-ne, or Jeesekeewinini, is a shaman who is able to summon supernatural powers or beings.

3 Cornel: one of a group of trees or shrubs similar to the dogwood and the cherry.

4 Shield.

On the other hand
The crowded southern land
With all the welter of the lives of men.
But here is peace, and again
That Something comes by flashes
Deeper than peace,—a spell
Golden and inappelable[5]
That gives the inarticulate part
Of our strange being one moment of release
That seems more native than the touch of time,
And we must answer in chime;
Though yet no man may tell
The secret of that spell
Golden and inappellable.

Now are there sounds walking in the wood,
And all the spruces shiver and tremble,
And the stars move a little in their courses.
The ancient disturber of solitude
Breathes a pervasive sigh,
And the soul seems to hear
The gathering of the waters at their sources;
Then quiet ensues and pure starlight and dark;
The region-spirit murmurs in meditation,
The heart replies in exaltation
And echoes faintly like an inland shell
Ghost tremors of the spell;
Thought reawakens and is linked again
With all the welter of the lives of men.
Here on the uplands where the air is clear
We think of life as of a stormy scene,—
Of tempest, of revolt and desperate shock;
And here, where we can think, on the bright uplands
Where the air is clear, we deeply brood on life
Until the tempest parts, and it appears
As simple as to the shepherd seems his flock:
A Something to be guided by ideals—
That in themselves are simple and serene—
Of noble deed to foster noble thought,
And noble thought to image noble deed,
Till deed and thought shall interpenetrate,

5 From which there can be no appeal.

Making life lovelier, till we come to doubt
Whether the perfect beauty that escapes
Is beauty of deed or thought or some high thing
Mingled of both, a greater boon than either:
Thus we have seen in the retreating tempest
The victor-sunlight merge with the ruined rain,
And from the rain and sunlight spring the rainbow.

The ancient disturber of solitude
Stirs his ancestral potion in the gloom,
And the dark wood
Is stifled with the pungent fume
Of charred earth burnt to the bone
That takes the place of air.
Then sudden I remember when and where,—
The last weird lakelet foul with weedy growths
And slimy viscid things the spirit loathes,
Skin of vile water over viler mud
Where the paddle stirred unutterable stenches,
And the canoes seemed heavy with fear,
Not to be urged toward the fatal shore
Where a bush fire, smouldering, with sudden roar
Leaped on a cedar and smothered it with light
And terror. It had left the portage-height
A tangle of slanted spruces burned to the roots,
Covered still with patches of bright fire
Smoking with incense of the fragrant resin
That even then began to thin and lessen
Into the gloom and glimmer of ruin.

'Tis overpast.[6] How strange the stars have grown;
The presage of extinction glows on their crests
And they are beautied with impermanence;
They shall be after the race of men
And mourn for them who snared their fiery pinions,
Entangled in the meshes of bright words.

A lemming stirs the fern and in the mosses
Eft-minded things feel the air change, and dawn
Tolls out from the dark belfries of the spruces.
How often in the autumn of the world
Shall the crystal shrine of dawning be rebuilt

6 Over, ended.

With deeper meaning! Shall the poet then,
Wrapped in his mantle on the height of land,
Brood on the welter of the lives of men
And dream of his ideal hope and promise
In the blush sunrise? Shall he base his flight
Upon a more compelling law than Love
As Life's atonement; shall the vision
Of noble deed and noble thought immingled
Seem as uncouth to him as the pictograph
Scratched on the cave side by the cave-dweller
To us of the Christ-time? Shall he stand
With deeper joy, with more complex emotion,
In closer commune with divinity,
With the deep fathomed, with the firmament charted,
With life as simple as a sheep-boy's song,
What lies beyond a romaunt[7] that was read
Once on a morn of storm and laid aside
Memorious with strange immortal memories?
Or shall he see the sunrise as I see it
In shoals of misty fire the deluge-light
Dashes upon and whelms with purer radiance,
And feel the lulled earth, older in pulse and motion,
Turn the rich lands and the inundant[8] oceans
To the flushed colour, and hear as now I hear
The thrill of life beat up the planet's margin
And break in the clear susurrus[9] of deep joy
That echoes and reëchoes in my being?
O Life is intuition the measure of knowledge
And do I stand with heart entranced and burning
At the zenith of our wisdom when I feel
The long light flow, the long wind pause, the deep
Influx of spirit, of which no man may tell
The Secret, golden and inappellable?

1916

7 Romantic tale or poem.
8 Flooding.
9 Whispering.

To a Canadian Aviator Who Died for His Country in France

Tossed like a falcon from the hunter's wrist,
A sweeping plunge, a sudden shattering noise,
And thou hast dared, with a long spiral twist,
The elastic stairway to the rising sun.
Peril below thee and above, peril
Within thy car;[1] but peril cannot daunt
Thy peerless heart: gathering wing and poise,
Thy plane transfigured, and thy motor-chant
Subduèd to a whisper—then silence,—
And thou art but a disembodied venture
In the void.

But Death, who has learned to fly,
Still matchless when his work is to be done,
Met thee between the armies and the sun;
Thy speck of shadow faltered in the sky;
Then thy dead engine and thy broken wings
Drooped through the arc and passed in fire,
A wreath of smoke—a breathless exhalation.
But ere that came a vision sealed thine eyes,
Lulling thy senses with oblivion;
And from its sliding station in the skies
Thy dauntless soul upward in circles soared
To the sublime and purest radiance whence it sprang.

In all their eyries,[2] eagles shall mourn thy fate,
And leaving on the lonely crags and scaurs
Their unprotected young, shall congregate
High in the tenuous heaven and anger the sun
With screams, and with a wild audacity
Dare all the battle danger of thy flight;
Till weary with combat one shall desert the light,
Fall like a bolt of thunder and check his fall
On the high ledge, smoky with mist and cloud,
Where his neglected eaglets shriek aloud,
And drawing the film across his sovereign sight
Shall dream of thy swift soul immortal
Mounting in circles, faithful beyond death.

1917[3]

1 Cockpit.
2 Nests.
3 Published in a chapbook, *'To the Canadian Mothers' and Three Other Poems*, in support of the Prisoners of War Fund.

Labrie's Wife

Being an excerpt from the manuscript journal of Archibald Muir, Clerk of The Honourable The Hudson's Bay Company at Nipigon House in the year of our Lord, 1815.

May Twenty-second, 1815

Today something happened which is bound to be of consequence in this outlandish place, and that I will set down here and make of record. Alec, who is getting more gumption now, although as unsteady in all his performances as he was ever, returned from his trip to the Flat Rock, and arrived safe with his two canoes and Ogemah-ga-bow, little Needic and his two sons. It appears that they had, by reason of the rough weather, to lay by at Dry Beaver Islands and had like to have starved if the wind had not gone down, for these fools of Indians will never learn not to devour half their rations in the first day out from the Post. They came in looking like wasps, their belts girt so tightly about their middles.

I could tell the moment I clapped eyes upon Alec that he had some bee in his bonnet, for he can no more control his countenance than an otter can help fishing. His face was all of a jump, and he spoke as if he had no spittle under his tongue. I have a plan to let the youngster speak when he is ready, and by this means I have the enjoyment of witnessing him cast about to get me to question him and assist him out with his story. When we were having a bit of dinner he fairly simmered, but he did not boil until I lit my pipe. Then he could stand my coolness no longer.

'We're to have opposition!' he blurted out. I did not want to show any astonishment, but I nearly dropped my pipe, such a matter never having been thought of in Nipigon before. 'You see,' he went on, 'I determined when I was at that part of the lake to go over to Keg Island and see if the cache was all right, and on St Paul's Island, when we went ashore to roast some fish, we found two canoes loaded, and a Frenchman and three Indians.

'He asked me if I was with the English, and I lied to him straight enough, and said No! I was trading alone. Then he wanted to know where our Post was, and I said it was beyond the large island to the west. He said his name was Labrie, and that he was for the North West Company, and was sent in opposition to the English on the lake. So I decided to camp where I was, and not to go to Keg Island, but to come on here. I told him to keep due west, and not to land until he struck the big island, which was Caribboo Island, and not for any reason to camp on a little flat island half way there, which was full of snakes.'

The youngster was mighty proud of himself at outwitting the Frenchman, but to take down his pride a bit, I provoked him by saying, 'Well, poor Donald used to call you a clavering[1] idiot, but if he had lived to this day he'd have had to invent a new kind of word for you. If your Labrie is anything of a trader he watched you away in the morning, and he will treat us in good Hudson's Bay Company rum when we first meet, having visited your little flat island full of snakes.' Off went Alec trying to bite

1 Babbling.

his beard, aping Donald's manner, poor lad; but he had yet a beard no longer than a pinfeather.

May Twenty-third, 1815

I was up before sun this day, as I had a restless night, thinking what I should do now we were to have opposition on the lake, a thing new to me who have scant experience. I determined to be smooth with them and observe them closely, and spoil them if I might with a fair face, and in all events to fight them with what weapons they may choose. I had wakened from a light doze with a sudden thought that I should posses myself of the point of land below the Post where I have always said the buildings should have been placed, which commands and oversees our present position. If it were seized by these pirates of Frenchmen, what then would become of our trade? They would eat it like a bear eats honey-comb. Alec could not see that, and provoked me with much grumbling that it was a useless work and a weary waste of muscle. It is curious how block-headed he is about all matters connected with trade; he has some acuteness belike but of what sort God alone knows. In the end I was mightily satisfied to see a stout staff with the ensign flying, and a small boat-landing, with one of the boats moored. We had the work done before midday, and for the rest of the time I had pleasure in looking down at the point which had an inhabited and secure look, under the Hudson's Bay Company's flag. If the Frenchmen have any idea of the shore about here there will be some *sacré*ing[2] when they find the point taken up, for northwards there is no place for a foothold, and only in a cove, half a mile to the south, can they find level land enough for building upon. So when our Indians come down, and they should be here in a matter of four weeks, they are bound to reach the Post first, and I can keep my eye upon the rascals, who would, if they could, trade with the newcomers and forget old kindnesses and obligations.

May Twenty-fourth, 1815

Ogemah-ga-bow came up to say that one of Needic's boys had died last night, having over-eaten himself after his fast on the Dry Beaver Islands. Rain today.

May Twenty-sixth, 1815

Sundown yesterday on my bench before the door, whereby Needic had made a smudge[3] to keep off the flies, which are now very bad, when I saw a canoe that was none of ours land at the point, and a man step out onto the new boat-landing. He looked all about him as if he was making an inventory of the place, and then he came slowly up the hill. He was a stout-shouldered, low-set fellow, with a black beard and small, bad eyes. Said I to myself as I saw him approach, 'There is something mainly dishonest in your make-up, my man, and whatever one may have to do to keep trade from you it won't be very savoury in the doing if your methods are to be used.'

'My name's Labrie,' he said, running a hand through his hair.

2 That is, cursing, swearing. 'Sacré' (literally 'holy') is a common French expletive.
3 A fire with a dense smoke, used to repel insects.

I got upon my legs and said politely, 'I heard of your being in the Lake from my man. Will you be seated?'

He said, 'No' and looked over his shoulders at the Point.

'You have the Point under your flag,' he remarked.

'Aye,' I said, as dry as I could.

'The work has marks of newness.'

'You are right, it was only finished yesterday.'

The blood came into his face in an ugly way.

'Well, there can be no great objection to my trading a little.'

'Not there,' said I bluntly. 'Under my company's flag what we take we claim and keep.'

He breathed rather heavily, but held his tongue, and was going to walk away.

'Hold on,' said I, 'strangers are not treated so here, you must have a dram.'

I called Alec, who brought the rum and the glasses. We drank health courteously, then were ready to cut one another's throats.

'Did you ever taste better than that?' said I.

'I have as good,' said he, 'though it is the best, I can match it.'

'Match it!' said I in a tone of surprise, winking at Alec, who flew as red as a bubble jock.[4] We parted then but just as he was getting away he said over his shoulder, 'Your man there has a damned queer idea of direction.'

May Twenty-seventh, 1815

Sent Needic and his live boy and Ogemah-ga-bow's brother to Poplar Lodge, to have news of the hunters. The Osnaburgh packs from the north should now be two weeks out, unless the ice is later this year than last. Tomorrow I will put Alec and Ogemah-ga-bow to work clearing out the storehouse and setting things to rights. I am much exercised in mind over my responsibilities. It was bad enough last year, but now I have the whole management, and this opposition to contend with upon the back of it. I begin to be worn with it, what with loss of sleep at night, and thinking about nought else in the day. No sign of Labrie or any of his party.

May Thirtieth, 1815

This morning Labrie came up to borrow an adze, which I lent to him without any question. He seemed to want to be civil enough. When I asked him, however, if Madame Labrie had arrived, he seemed quite put about and mumbled something in his beard, which sounded nearly like 'What affair is that of yours?' I paid no attention to him, not wishing to quarrel yet awhile, and without any further parley off he went with the adze, which I am fortunate if I ever see again.

Heat intense today, bring on a great storm of thunder and much rain. Had a great debate with Alec, when we were indoors, as to when the Osnaburgh packs will be in. I calculated in three weeks, as the water is like to be high, they will take the route through Mud Lakes to Negodina, as I wrote Godfrey. The old route to Wabinosh

4 A male turkey (Scottish); usually 'bubbly jock'.

should take them much longer and, what with broken water and two desperate, long carries, there is a great risk of loss by that way. Alec thinks they will be down sooner. There is no doubt they have had a fine winter and if the pack can be safely landed it will be a great matter, and no doubt I shall hear good of it from the partners.

May Thirty-first, 1815

This morning when I was cleaning my pistols I heard a clear sound of laughter. Now laughter is an uncommon thing in this country, visiting us very infrequently. To be sure the Indians laugh, but that to me always has an unmeaning sound, and sometimes a bestial. Moreover, this laugher was different in kind, and one must have listened to it however absorbed he might have been. It was high-pitched and very clear and had something merry and withal innocent about it. It was contagious also and the mere sound of it made my very muscles twitch. There was no one visible, but after I had gazed awhile I saw Alec come up the steps from the warehouse. Not to appear interested before the lad I went back to my work. After a little he came in. I noticed his face was flushed and his manner excited. I paid no attention to him until he had knocked a dish off the table. It broke in three pieces. I was angry with him, good crockery not being by any means very plentiful in this country.

'Good God, man!' I cried. 'If you're in such a state that you cannot avoid breaking the dishes, will you lie upon your bed for a while.' He glared at me terribly, but had not a word to say. Then I kept quiet for as much as a quarter of an hour, and I could see it was fretting him; he fidgeted about greatly. Then he got up and went to the door.

'It seems to me you take mighty small interest in things.'

I said never a word.

'Are you deaf this morning?'

I made no sound. He made no move for a minute, then he said, just as he was going out of the door, in an exasperated way, 'That was Labrie's wife.'

I could have laughed to myself, but when I had thought upon it for a time I began to perceive something bitter in his tone, and I reflected that of late I had treated him much as poor Donald used unthinkingly to treat me, and that he must be occupying my old position of complaint, and my heart was softened a bit, and I resolved to be more kind to him in the future, who is in much a good boy and canny in a sort about many things.

June First, 1815

I saw Labrie's wife for the first time this morning. An uncommon looking wench, with black hair and eyes and a mouthful of white teeth. I discussed her thoroughly with Alec, who sticks up for it that she is a handsome one. So she is, after her manner, though that I do not acknowledge to Alec. She looked me all over as if I were for sale, and when I coolly turned my back on her, that she might have a good look at that, she went off in a mighty huff.

Alec reports that there are two other women in Labrie's party, rather old and haggish. I have not clapped eyes upon them, not having visited the Cove. Although she went off in a huff, the young wench is a merry one, and it amuses her to hear Alec so aboundingly polite to her with his 'Madame Labrie'. 'Madame Labrie' this and 'Madame Labrie' that, whereupon she giggles or breaks out into wild laughter.

June Third, 1815

Needic back from Poplar Lodge, where everything is all right. Had an amusing conversation with the lad Alec anent[5] Labrie's wife. The hussy comes about the house constantly, even when we are not here.

'Now what is she after?' said I.

'You have no understanding of women,' he replied. 'Of course she will come back when you treat her in that way.'

'Now in what way?' said I. 'Never do I look at her or pass the time of day with her.

'That is it,' he retorts. 'You are fairly insulting her, and she comes back.'

'Do you try and be sweet to her and mayhap she would stay away.'

'It is different with me,' he says, biting his whiskers and shrugging up his shoulders, just as the wench does herself. He has taken on a sort of mincing, balancing, half-Frenchified accent, and shrugs his shoulders.

'Are you afraid she would fall into love weez you, Alec?' I remarked, trying hard to imitate the accent.

'It is not me she will be in love with.'

'No, who then? Needic?'

'Needic!' he cried, going off with a great French shrug.

June Fourth, 1815

No word from Godfrey about the packs. I am getting a trifle anxious. Alec says there are more guns than yardsticks in Labrie's quarters, and makes out they are on for a fight. Labrie's wife came up at noon and made us an omelette with gull's eggs and fresh onion-tops. She is a clever wench and sat looking at me as I devoured it. I talked a bit to her. After she left, Alec sat frowning.

'You were very free with her.'

'I merely spoke to her, but then she made a good omelette.'

'You said too much to her. You nearly told her we expected the packs at Negodina by the Mud Lake route this year instead of Wabinosh.'

'Well, and if I did?'

'It is all she wanted to know.'

'Well, you seem to be always ready to stand up for the spy, if she be one,' said I, turning the French accent upon him. This made him wroth, as it always does.

'You never seem to understand that a woman's not like a man. The best of them you have to watch, and more particularly when one of them is in love with you.'

'That does not apply here,' I said, 'unless you have her assurances yourself.'

'I would not make love to a married woman,' he said hotly.

'That's why you guard yourself so carefully, is it? You are mighty pious. It is a pity you are not like me. Now for me Mr Labrie's wife has no attraction whatever, commandments or no commandments.'

5 About, concerning (chiefly Scottish).

This set him off again.

'Be careful you, Archibald Muir, that is what I have to say to you.'

We could hear the lady herself laughing down at the landing, and it sounded so innocent that I could not refrain from smiling at the boy.

June Fifth, 1815

We had a scene last night with Labrie's wife, for which Alec has to be thanked, and in which I think he had a small revenge for my baiting of him. I will set down the occurrence here although it be against myself, and our national instrument. She had been hardly before the house, and it was in the dusk of the evening, when she asked me to play upon the pipes.

'Will you play upon the bag-pipes, Mr Muir?' she said in a very civil voice. 'I have never heard the bag-pipes.'

Now I am always at pains to oblige a lady, if it be possible, so I went in and got the pipes, hearing Alec urge me also, so I had two willing to be pleased.

Well, scarcely had I begun to get the skin filled with wind when Labrie's wife began to laugh. Now I am willing to admit that the foreword to a performance on the pipes may be dispiriting, but I charge that what follows after when the instrument is well controlled, and when the melody pours forth in full cry, would serve to obliterate a greatly more dispiriting prelude. But in this case I did not get beyond that stage, for Labrie's wife laughed with so little judgement that I was put about. I saw something in Alec's face which led me to think that the whole matter was preconceived by him, and with that I laid down my pipes on the bench beside me. Not another note would I play. I am not much versed in women's ways, and what Labrie's wife did puzzled me. But of that I shall give Alec's explanation. At first she kept on laughing, and then she stopped suddenly and came forward looking sober enough, but with the wrinkles of the laugher not yet gone out of her face. There she stood about four feet from me with a bit of her dress in her hand, as I have seen school girls stand abashed having been found at fault.

'You are angry because I laughed?' she said.

I did not answer.

Then she came close to me and made as if to put her hands upon my shoulders, and when I looked straight upon her eyes she dropped her hands, made a sound in her throat, and turned and went away.

Then young Alec began to strut about like a bantam cock.

'I have to thank you for that performance,' I said.

'Why would you prevent a woman from laughing?' says he, in a rage. 'Don't you know enough of women to let them laugh and let them talk?'

'I can lay no claim to such knowledge as yourself.' said I, in a mighty sneering voice. 'In truth I know naught about them.'

'You have proved that this night,' retorted Alec.

'Expound that, you young oracle,' said I.

'Expound? You have sent her away with a sore heart, and she was minded to be playful with you, and that cuts sore on a heart such as hers. Don't you see it, man?' he cried, sort of dashing his hands down.

'I see nothing of the sort. She was angry simply because I wouldn't speak back to her.'

'You might have spoken to her or not spoken, and she would never have minded if you hadn't looked at her in the way you did.'

I saw it was no use my trying to fathom the young donkey, so I would speak no more to him.

June Sixth, 1815

Labrie's wife was up last night but I would not go out to see her, being tired of the body and her endless chatter. Alec and she talked for an hour; the boy would be contented to go on vapouring forever, I believe. I pretended to be busy with my papers, and in the end she went away. She came to the window just before she went, and I heard her fingers on the sash, but I did not look up, and I heard her low gurgling laugh as she ran away from Alec, who would go down to the landing with her.

He is as polite to her and as formal as if he were living by a code of court etiquette. I twitted him with that.

'Well,' he says, mighty stiff, and pulling a solemn face, 'she is a woman, and she is another man's wife.'

'That last is her great virtue,' said I, with a tone of sarcasm, at which he looked scornful and exceeding pious.

June Seventh, 1815

Good news yesterday. Toma came in with a message from Godfrey. The Osnaburgh packs are safe at Cache point on the Mud Lake route. The water is high and they have not had a mishap. In three days they should reach Negodina at the end of the lake. It is, as I have always said, a route more clean and handy than the Wabinosh route, and it will be adopted now from this out.

Woke up with a mighty sore head this morning and had words with Alec. It is inconceivable how domineering that lad has become.

'You were drinking with Madame Labrie last night,' he said.

'And my lord is jealous,' I replied, sneering at him.

'Ye have made a fool of yourself. What did you tell her?'

'Nothing that I rightly remember. Since when were you ordained my catechist?'

'Now I have told you many times', he said in a parsoning way, 'that you did not understand the nature of women, and that you would let slip something that Labrie wanted to know. Now you have done so, I believe, between a glass too much of whisky and a pretty woman.'

'Do you call yon a pretty woman?' I said, mocking his accent.

'I pity you!' he said, with great contempt.

He went away swinging his shoulders, much more the master than the man.

To set down the truth, although it be against myself, Labrie's wife came up in the evening of yesterday. I was more decent with the bitch, having had good news, and I treated her to some whisky, and drank with her. Alec was off watching Toma, as he thought Labrie might try to get hold of him. I do not just remember when she went away. God forgive me, I do not rightly remember anything about it.

Hardly had Alec dismissed himself when he came back very greatly excited, but in anger this time.

'They have gone,' said he.

'Who?' said I, not thinking for a moment.

'Who! My God! Who? Why Labrie.'

'Well what of that?' I said. 'It is a good riddance of a vile lot of thieves out of God's country.'

'That is all you see to it?' he said.

'Well, what more?' I replied.

'I seem to see that last night you told Madame Labrie the packs were coming by the Mud Lake route to Negodina, and that they have gone to stop them. I have my doubt they will not barter with them. I seem to see that they will capture the furs and that by no very gentle means.'

'You have said it before,' I cried out, wroth with him and with myself. 'So yon slut is what I have always supposed her to be.'

A dark look came into his face. 'Choose your words!' he cried, taking a step towards me.

'I'll neither pick nor choose my words,' I said. 'What do you call her then that would take our hospitality and then do us wrong?'

'Madaline would do no such thing,' he cried, strutting about in a way that looked comical to me. I laughed at him.

'Madaline! Madaline! We shall see what Madaline will have done when we lose our furs. Why, man, you said out of your own mouth that she had done it.'

'You lie,' he cried, but it was here not impudence, so I paid no attention to him.

After some parley and conversation, I sent him with three canoes and all the able men, except Needic, to Negodina to see what had fallen out. He is to send me back a letter, as soon as he can, with the word. I am here now quite alone, and in mind very much put about. I have been striving to recall what passed between Labrie's wife and myself, but without any clear recollection. Ah, those women! I well remember my father used to say, 'At the bottom of every trouble, there you will find a woman,' and my mother used to retort, 'And likewise at the bottom of every happiness.' Whereupon he would kiss her.

June Tenth, 1815

Last night—waiting for word from Alec. This morning I went down to Labrie's camp with Needic. They had left two tents and some rubbish, and a little green box marked 'M.L.'. Turning the lot over I found two empty kegs marked 'H.B. Co.', once full of rum, which they had stolen from the cache on Keg Island. So we heaped all together and set fire to it. It burned merrily, and they are at least by that much poorer.

June Eleventh, 1815

I am in great spirits today. Last night I was awakened by Needic, who had his boy with him. Everything had reached Negodina safely, and there was no sign anywhere of Labrie's party. They will push on at once.

June Twelfth, 1815

This morning Labrie came back. Needic came up and told me, so about noon I took my pistols and went down with him to the cove. They had one tent up and the women were making the fire. The men went off and none of them would speak to us. I stood smiling in a taunting way, and just as I was about to leave, Labrie's wife came over to me. I perceived she had her arm wound in a cloth.

'Well, Madame Labrie, how did you hurt your arm?'

'Why do you call me Madame Labrie?'

'One must call you something. My boy, Alec, calls you Madaline.'

Her face grew a darker red.

'You have been away for a while?'

'Yes,' she said, 'we were at Wabinosh, and I see you burned my box when I was gone.

'Were you ever in love?' she asked suddenly.

'Never,' said I, 'praise be to God.'

'When you are I pray heaven you may be tortured in it.'

'I am thankful of your good wishes.'

'The other night you told me your packs were coming by Negodina. You understand? It was Labrie who shot me through the arm. He wanted to kill me for taking them to Wabinosh, but the others would not let him.'

'The low rascal,' I said, 'to shoot a woman.'

'And *you* have nothing to say about *me?*' She looked at me curiously, and put an odd emphasis on the *you* and the *me.*

'It is fortunate you made a mistake.'

'A mistake!' she said. 'Your boy Alec is twice the man you are.'

The hussy said that with a fluff of pride.

'Goodbye,' said I from my canoe.

'Is that all, Archibald Muir, is that all?'

'Goodbye,' said I, 'and I hope your husband won't shoot at you again.'

I looked back when we had gone a bit, and she still stood there. She did not make any sign towards me, though I waved to her in courtesy. Then she covered up her face in her hands.

No word of Godfrey and Alec. I sent Needic to Labrie's wife with two gold guineas for the box I had burned, probably the only gold she ever clapped her eyes on, as it is unknown in this trade almost.

June Thirteenth, 1815

The packs came in yesterday evening. Godfrey and the men all well. I mixed a keg of spirits for them and they made a hideous night of it. Too busy to write much now, but can do nothing more tonight. Looking back in the store ledgers I can see no such winter's catch. Great good luck. Labrie's party still hanging around. Alec went down as soon as he got back, and stayed longer than he ought, so I berated him soundly. Tonight at supper he said:

'Labrie shot her through the arm because she had taken them to Wabinosh and had misled them.'

I paid no attention to him. By and by he said:

'You will be glad to know that she says you told her nothing about the packs.'

'Did she?' said I, puzzled, as she had told me the contrary.

'I don't believe her,' he added.

'You're complimentary to the ladies,' I remarked.

'Here is something she asked me to give you.'

It was the money I had sent her for that box of hers I burnt.

June Fourteenth, 1815

Busy all day between the storehouse and the fur press. Half the Indians are drunk yet. Alec says Labrie and his party have gone. May the devil's luck go with them. I thought Alec looked a trifle white in the face, and as if he was impatient to make me talk, but I had no time to be spending with him.

A wonderfully warm day, and the flies very bad, enough to madden one. Have pressed all the packs and now everything is in order for a move. What a grand night for the partners it will be when they see our canoes full of the finest come to land at Fort William. It should be of profit to me, and I expect to come back here or go somewhere a factor,[6] if I comprehend the rules properly. About an hour ago I had just finished writing the last words when Alec's shadow came over the window. He seemed to stand there over long, and I was just on the point of crying out to him when he moved off. In a moment he came in to me. I did not look up from my writing when he flung a scrap of paper down before me.

'There!' he said, in an odd voice. 'I found it under the sash. It fell face down, so I saw printing on the back, I thought it was but a scrap torn off a fur bill.

'Read it,' said he.

I turned it over and observed that there were some words in writing on the other side. I made them out to be: 'Why do you call me Labrie's wife? She is my aunt. Do you think I would marry an ugly fellow like Labrie? They brought me up here to help their plans. We shall see. If you want to know my name it's Madaline Lesage. I learned to write from the Sister St Theresa at Wikwemikong. Is it not pretty? M.L.'

Then I recalled how she had come to the window, one night not very long ago, when, I opine, she had left the paper there.

'Well!' I said coolly, 'and what is it now that you have to say about Madaline Lesage?'

His face had a tortured look upon it. He tried to speak. 'She was—she was the bravest, the dearest'—he stopped there and hung down his head. 'Oh, my God, you cannot understand. You can never understand!'

He moved away and stood by the door. I thought upon what he had said. No, I did not understand. Then I tried once more to go on with my page. But I was detained by the sound which is as uncommon as that of laughter in these outlandish parts. The sound of sobbing. Just for a moment it brought back to me the sound of my sister's voice as she sobbed for her lover when they brought him back dead and

6 An agent or trader; a rank higher than that of clerk.

dripping out of the sea. I had a vision of it as if it were snapped upon my eye in a flash of lightning, she leaning her forehead upon her wrists against the wall. I looked up at Alec and there he was leaning at the door-post, his shoulders all moving with his sobs. I understood in a flash. I pray God to forgive me for the sin of blindness, and for always being so dead to others in my own affairs. I went towards him knowing that I could not give him any comfort. So he went out from the house and walked alone through the gloaming.[7] I perceived that a change had come over him. I had always considered him a bit of a boy to be ordered about, but there was a man walking away from me, resolute in his steps, big in his bulk, and weighed down as if he was carrying a load, bearing it as if he was proud of it, with energy and trust in himself.

1923

7 Twilight.

J.G. Sime

1868–1958

The realization among the current generation of literary scholars that many women writers deserving of serious attention had been forgotten has brought new attention to female poets, novelists, and short story writers who were dropped from—or who had never made it into—the literary canon. One Canadian writer being revalued is Jessie Georgina Sime. Born in Edinburgh, Scotland, Sime was the only child of Jessie Wilson and James Sime—themselves writers and educators who moved in literary circles. She grew up in London, England, and in Chiswick (then a suburb of London), and became acquainted through her parents with such notable writers and thinkers as Thomas Hardy, George Bernard Shaw, and William Morris. Through her employment as secretary to Dr Freeland Barbour (an eminent gynecologist closely associated with the University of Edinburgh), she met and worked for William James, the father of American psychology. She assisted her father as reader for Macmillan Press, which had been founded by her mother's friend, Daniel Macmillan; she worked as a journalist in London; and she was an editor and writer in London and Edinburgh. Thus from an early age she was made generally aware of literary and social issues, especially those relevant to socialism and reform politics.

She attended Queen's College in London, an institution founded in the mid-nineteenth century to promote the education of women. At seventeen she travelled to Berlin for a year to study singing. After she returned, she became still more engaged in the intellectual ferment of the time, especially in the debate over the 'New Woman'. Following her father's death in 1895 she returned to Edinburgh—but, after the changes in women's roles she had seen in London and Berlin, it struck her as puritanical and unreceptive. During this period she became involved both professionally and personally with a young Canadian physician who was two years her senior. Completing his degree at the University of Edinburgh in 1898, he remained for two further years of postgraduate study before returning to his wife in Montreal and her life of privileged social status. Sime stayed on in Scotland until her mother's death in 1907, and then moved to Montreal to renew her relationship with the doctor and to work as his secretary. It has been suggested that Sime's portrayals of 'irregular unions' (the title of one of the stories in *Sister Woman*) were reflections on her own situation.

Even before she arrived, Canada was a place that was known to Sime. Her maternal uncle, Daniel Wilson—a professor and the chancellor of the University of Toronto—had previously told her about the country that she now made her home and that provided the subject matter of her fiction for the next three decades. In addition to taking up a professional life as a business woman, which included serving as vice president of the Quebec branch of the Canadian Women's Press Club, Sime, after coming to Canada, became a well-known and effective lecturer on women, women's writing, and the literary depiction of women. As well, she was the president and founding member of the Montreal chapter of the international literary organization PEN and the president of the Montreal branch of the new Canadian Author's Association.

Although Sime wrote on a variety of topics in journalism, sketches, and short stories, her subject matter often focused on the social, economic, and emotional impact on women of the changes in modern life and culture. Her interest in women's roles is evident in the three early works she published between 1913 and 1917. In the years immediately following the war, British librarian Frank Carr Nicholson, a friend and long-time correspondent, acted on her behalf as literary agent and editor: he found her a supportive publisher in England, Grant Richards, who brought out her first two books with serious literary aspirations: *Sister Woman* (1919; reprinted in 1992) and *Our Little Life: A Novel of Today* (1921; reprinted in 1994).

These are books that, breaking with the idealistic portrayals of the pre-war era, offer pictures of women not yet seen. Sime's characters vary in class and economic security but, like Bertha Martin, the protagonist of 'Munitions!', they all face the problems encountered by women at the beginning of the twentieth century—and they are frequently shown facing these new complexities without support. Women in *Our Little Life* and *Sister Woman* often lose their companions and must live alone, even have and raise their children on their own. Sime describes, from a woman's perspective, the way the lives of working-class women had been altered by the move into the city from small towns and farms; the particular problems immigrants had to deal with; and the way issues around national identity affected newcomers.

In a framing prologue and epilogue to *Sister Woman*, Sime made clear her desire to use her fiction to try to change the world. In the first of these two self-reflexive sketches, a man wants to discuss 'The Woman's Question' with the dramatized author, who responds by saying: 'The woman's and the man's. It's the same thing. There's no difference.' And when he challenges her to 'state your grievance,' she seats herself at her typewriter. The book that follows is her response. In the epilogue, the book having now been written, the man distresses the author by asking her if that is 'all you have to say'. The conclusion of the sketch is a protest and a commitment to go on writing, and it forms the book's final words:

> *'Why, I'm not even started yet,' I said. . . .*
>
> *I've got reams and reams and reams to say. . . . Let me tell you what we women want is simple—but the world isn't simple. Don't you see,' I said, 'you've got to start the world again if—We can't fight the world the way it is. You—you've got to . . .'*
>
> *. . . I ran my fingers over the typewriter keys—and felt them lovingly.*

A pioneer in Canadian realist and urban modernist fiction, Sime met with a range of critical reception: some readers were shocked by her subject matter and her focus on what seemed to them women's trivialities; others praised her for her spare style and her close and frank attention to the details of everyday life. She continued to publish throughout her long lifetime, although her emphasis shifted, with the times, from her earlier urban realism to a focus on the interior life of the mind.

Sime's later books include a critical study, *Thomas Hardy of the Wessex Novels: An Essay and a Biographical Note* (1928), and an autobiographical sketch, *In a Canadian Shack* (1937), as well as additional works of fiction. With Nicholson she co-authored *A Tale of Two Worlds* (1953), a consideration of German life after World War II.

Munitions!

Bertha Martin sat in the street car in the early morning going to her work. Her work was munitions. She had been at it exactly five weeks.

She sat squeezed up into a corner, just holding on to her seat and no more, and all round her were women and girls also working at munitions—loud, noisy, for ever talking—extraordinarily happy. They sat there filling the car with their two compact rows, pressed together, almost in one another's laps, joking, chewing tobacco—flinging the chewed stuff about.

It wasn't in the least that they were what is technically known as 'bad women'. Oh no—no! If you thought that, you would mistake them utterly. They were decent women, good, self-respecting girls, for the most part 'straight girls'—with a black sheep here and there, to be sure, but where aren't there black sheep here and there? And the reason they made a row and shrieked with laughter and cracked an unseemly jest or two was simply that they were turned loose. They had spent their lives caged, most of them, in shop or house, and now they were drunk with the open air and the greater freedom and the sudden liberty to do as they liked and damn whoever stopped them.

Bertha Martin looked round at her companions. She saw the all sorts that make the world. Here and there was a pretty, young, flushed face, talking—talking—trying to express something it felt inside and couldn't get out. And here and there Bertha Martin saw an older face, a face with a knowledge of the world in it and that something that comes into a woman's eyes if certain things happen to her, and never goes out of them again. And then Bertha Martin saw quite elderly women, or so they seemed to her—women of forty or so, decent bodies, working for someone besides themselves—they had it written on their faces; and she saw old women—old as working women go—fifty and more, sitting there with their long working lives behind them and their short ones in front. And now and then some woman would draw her snuff-box from her shirt-waist and it would pass up and down the line and they would all take great pinches of the brown, pungent powder and stuff it up their noses—and laugh and laugh. . . . Bertha Martin looked round the car and she couldn't believe it was she who was sitting in it.

It was the very early spring. The white March sunshine came streaming into the car, and when Bertha, squeezed sideways in her corner, looked through the window, she saw the melting snow everywhere—piles and piles of it uncleared because the men whose job it was to clear it were at the war. She saw walls of snow by the sides of the streets—they went stretching out into infinity. And the car went swinging and lurching between them, out through the city and into the country where the factory was.

There were puddles and little lakes of water everywhere; winter was melting away before the birth of another spring.

Bertha looked. She looked up into the clear—into the crystal clearness of the morning sky. It was the time of the spring skies of Canada—wonderful, delicate, diaphanous skies that come every spring to the Northern Land—skies the colour of bluebells and primroses—transparent, translucent, marvellously beautiful. Bertha looked up into the haze of colour—and she smiled. And then she wondered why she smiled.

It was the very early springtime.

Just five weeks before and Bertha had been a well-trained servant in a well-kept, intensely self-respecting house—a house where no footfall was heard on the soft, long-piled rugs; where the lights were shaded and the curtains were all drawn at night; where the mistress lay late in bed and 'ordered' things; where life was put to bed every night with hot bottles to its feet; where no one ever spoke of anything that mattered; where meals were paramount. There had Bertha Martin lived five long, comfortable years.

She had gone about her business capably. She had worn her uniform like any soldier—a white frock in the mornings and a cap upon her head, and her hair had been orderly, her apron accurately tied. She had been clean. There were no spring skies in sight—or else she had not looked to see them. She had got up—not too unreasonably early—had had her early morning cup of tea with the other servants, had set the dining-room breakfast, waited on it—quiet—respectful—as self-respecting as the house. And in the afternoons there she had been in her neat black gown with her cap and apron immaculate—her hair still orderly and unobtrusive—everything about her, inside and out, still self-respecting and respectful. She had 'waited on table', cleaned silver, served tea, carried things everlastingly in and out, set them on tables, taken them off again, washed them, put them away, taken them out again, reset tables with them—it was a circular game with never any end to it. And she had done it well. 'Martin is an excellent servant,' she had heard the lady of the house say once. 'I can trust her thoroughly.'

One afternoon in the week she went out. At a certain hour she left the house; at another certain hour she came back again. If she was half-an-hour late she was liable to be questioned: 'Why?' And when she had given her explanation then she would hear the inevitable 'Don't let it occur again.' And Sunday—every other Sunday—there was the half day, also at certain hours. Of course—how otherwise could a well-run house *be* well run? And down in the kitchen the maids would dispute as to whether you got out half-an-hour sooner last time and so must go half-an-hour later this—they would quarrel and squabble over the silliest little things. Their horizon was so infinitesimally small, and they were so much too comfortable—they ate so much too much and they did so far too little—what could they do but squabble? They were never all on speaking-terms at one time together. Either the old cook was taking the housemaid's part or she and the housemaid were at daggers drawn; and they all said the same things over and over and over again—to desperation.

Bertha Martin looked up at the exquisite sky—and she smiled. The sun came streaming in, and the girls and women talked and jabbered and snuffed and chewed their tobacco and spat it out. And sometimes when the car conductor put his head in at the door they greeted him with a storm of chaff—a hail of witticisms—a tornado of personalities. And the little French-Canadian, overpowered by numbers, would never even try to break a lance with them. He would smile and shrug and put his hand up to his ears and run the door back between himself and them. And the women would laugh and clap their hands and stamp with their feet and call things to him—shout. . . .

Bertha turned to the girl next her—nearly atop of her—and looked her over. She was a fragile-looking, indoors creature—saleslady was written all over her—with soft rings of fair curled hair on her temples, and a weak, smiling mouth, and little useless feet in her cheap, high-heeled pumps. She was looking intently at a great strap of a girl opposite, with a great mouth on her, out of which was reeling a broad story.

'My, ain't she the girl!' said Bertha's little neighbour; and with the woman's inevitable gesture, she put her two hands up to her hair behind, and felt, and took a hairpin out here and there and put it in again.

She turned to Bertha.

'Say, ain't she the girl alright? Did you hear?'

Bertha nodded.

The little indoors thing turned and glanced at Bertha—took her in from head to foot with one feminine look.

'You gittin' on?' she said.

'Fine!' said Bertha.

The eyes of the women met. They smiled at one another. Fellow-workers—out in the world together. That's what their eyes said: Free! And then the little creature turned away from Bertha—bent forward eagerly. Another of the stories was coming streaming out.

'Ssh! . . . ssh!' cried some of the older women. But their voices were drowned in the sea of laughter as the climax took possession of the car. The women rocked and swayed—they clutched each other—they shrieked.

'Where's the harm?' the big strap cried.

Five weeks ago and Bertha had never heard a joke like that. Five weeks ago she would hardly have taken in the utter meaning of that climax. Now! Something in her ticked—something went beating. She smiled—not at the indecency, not at the humour. What Bertha smiled at was the sense of liberty it gave her. She could hear stories if she liked. She could *act* stories if she liked. She was earning money—good money—she was capable and strong. Yes, she was strong, not fragile like the little thing beside her, but a big, strong girl—twenty-four—a woman grown—alive.

It seemed a long, dim time ago when all of them sat round that kitchen table to their stated meals at stated hours. Good, ample, comfortable meals. Plenty of time to eat them. No trouble getting them—that was the cook's affair—just far too much to eat and too much time to eat it in. Nothing to think about. Inertia. A comfortable place. What an age ago it seemed! And yet she had expected to spend her life like that—till she married someone! She never would have thought of 'giving in her notice' if it hadn't been for Nellie Ford. How well Bertha remembered it—that Sunday she met Nellie—a Nellie flushed, with shining eyes.

'I'm leaving,' Nellie had said to her. 'I'm leaving—for the factory!'

And Bertha had stopped, bereft of words.

'*The factory* . . . !' she had said. That day the factory had sounded like the bottomless pit. 'The factory . . . !'

'Come on,' Nellie had said, 'come on—it's fine out there. You make good money. Give in your notice—it's the life.'

And Bertha had listened helplessly, feeling the ground slipping.

'But, Nellie——' she kept saying.

'It's the life,' Nellie had kept reiterating; 'it's the life, I tell you. Come on, Bert, *sure* it's the life. Come on—it's great out there. We'll room together if you'll come.'

Then Nellie had told her hurriedly, brokenly, as they walked along that Sunday afternoon, all that she knew about the factory. What Agnes Dewie, that was maid to Lady Something once—what she said. 'It was great!' That's what *she* said. 'Liberty,' said Agnes Dewie, 'a room you paid for, good money, disrespect to everything, nothing above you—freedom. . . .'

Nellie had panted this out to Bertha. 'Come on, come *on*, Bert,' she had said; 'it's time we lived.'

And slowly the infection had seized on Bertha. The fever touched her blood—ran through it. Her mental temperature flew up. She was a big girl, a slow-grower, young for her years, with a girl's feelings in her woman's body. But Nellie Ford had touched the spring of life in her. After that Sunday when Bertha looked round the quiet, self-respecting house—she hated it. She hated the softness of it—the quietness—hated the very comfort. What did all these things matter? Nellie Ford had said: 'It's time we *lived*. . . .'

Bertha gazed upward through the window of the car—twisted and turned so that she could look right into the morning blue. The car was clear of city life. It sped along a country road. Fields were on either side, and only now and then a solitary house. Great trees stretched out bare branches.

Then in that far-off life came the giving in of the notice. Bertha remembered the old cook's sour face—that old sour face past every hope of life and living. Could one grow to look like that? Can such things be? 'You'll live to rue the day, my lady!' said the cook. And Bertha remembered how the lady at the head of things had said: 'Do you realise that you'll *regret* leaving a good place like this?' And then, more acidly: 'I wouldn't have believed it of you, Martin.' And as she turned to go: 'If you choose to reconsider——'

Regret! Reconsider! Never again would she hear bells and have to answer them. Never again would someone say to her: 'Take tea into the library, Martin.' Never again need she say: 'Yes, ma'am.' Think of it! Bertha smiled. The sun came streaming in on her—she smiled.

Liberty! Liberty to work the whole day long—ten hours at five and twenty cents an hour—in noise and grime and wet. Damp floors to walk on. Noise—distracting noise all round one. No room to turn or breathe. No time to stop. And then at lunch-time no ample comfortable meal—some little hurried hunch of something you brought with you. Hard work. Long hours. Discomfort. Strain. That was about the sum of it, of all that she had gained . . . but then, the sense of freedom! The joy of being done with cap and apron. The feeling that you could draw your breath—speak as you liked—wear overalls like men—curse if you wanted to.

Oh, the relief of it! The going home at night, dead-tired, to where you had your room. Your own! The poor, ill-cooked suppers—what a taste to them! The deep, dreamless sleep. And Sunday—if you ever got a Sunday off—when you could lie abed, no one to hunt you up, no one to call you names and quarrel with you. Just Nellie there.

What did it matter if you had no time to stop or think or be? What did anything matter if life went pulsing through you amidst dirt and noise and grime? The old life—that treading round with brush and dust-pan—that making yourself noiseless with a duster: 'Martin, see you dust well *beneath* the bed.' 'Yes, ma'am.' And now the factory! A new life with other women working round you—bare-armed—grimy—roughened—unrestrained. What a change! What a sense of broadening out! What . . . !

Bertha Martin smiled. She smiled so that a woman opposite smiled back at her; and then she realised that she was smiling. She felt life streaming to her very finger-tips. She felt the spring pass through her being—insistent and creative. She felt her blood speak to her—say things it never said when she was walking softly in the well-ordered house she helped to keep for five long, comfortable years. 'Selfish to leave me.' That was what the lady of the house had said to her. 'Selfish—you're all selfish. You think of nothing but yourselves.'

Well—why not? What if that were true? Let it go anyway. That half-dead life was there behind . . . and Bertha Martin looked out at the present. The car went scudding in the country road. There was the Factory—the Factory, with its coarse, strong, beckoning life—its noise—its dirt—its men.

Its men! And suddenly into Bertha Martin's cheek a wave of colour surged. Yesterday—was it yesterday?—that man had caught her strong, round arm as she was passing him—and held it.

Her breath came short. She felt a throbbing. She stopped smiling—and her eyes grew large.

It was the very early spring.

Then suddenly the flock of women rose—felt in the bosoms of their shirt-waists for their cigarettes and matches—surged to the door—talking—laughing—pushing one another—the older ones expostulating.

And, massed together in the slushy road, they stood, lighting up, passing their matches round—happy—noisy—fluttered—not knowing what to do with all the life that kept on surging up and breaking in them—waves of it—wave on wave. Willingly would they have fought their way to the Munitions Factory. If they had known the *Carmagnole* they would have danced it in the melting snow. . . .

It was the spring.

1919

Stephen Leacock

1869–1944

Stephen Leacock once explained his having left England at six in this way: 'My parents migrated to Canada in 1876, and I decided to go with them.' We recognize in this line the ironic and often self-mocking quality that characterizes much of Leacock's best writing—the sense of deflation that comes when individuals try to assert more control over their fate than they can ever really have. Perhaps it was Leacock's early years that led him to regard the world as an unreliable place: after coming to Canada he grew up on a farm (near Lake Simcoe, Ont.) that, as a result of his father's mismanagement, teetered continually on the edge of financial collapse. Although Leacock's mother provided the family with stability, she may also have sharpened his sense of the absurd as she engaged in her constant struggle to instill into eleven children the manners of a distant British aristocracy. The Leacock family's insecure life never reached the point of complete disaster only because occasional assistance from England kept the family afloat, even allowing Stephen to attend Upper Canada College, in Toronto, as a boarder.

As an adult, Leacock lived two lives: he was an academic first and only later a humorist. He began his teaching career at Upper Canada College while completing a BA at the University of Toronto. He later left UCC to pursue graduate work at the University of Chicago, where he studied economics under Thorstein Veblen. His Ph.D. completed, he joined the Department of Economics and Political Science at McGill University in 1903. He gained distinction as an engaging classroom lecturer, and his first book, *Elements of Political Science* (1906), which earned him a reputation for clarity of thought and vigour of expression, soon became a standard text. In 1907, at the request of the governor general, Leacock undertook a year-long tour of the British Empire to speak on Imperial unity; and upon his return he was placed in charge of his department.

Leacock began his second career in 1910 when—against the advice of a friend who thought he would harm his scholarly reputation—he collected the occasional pieces of humour he had written for magazines and published them at his own expense as *Literary Lapses*. An immediate success, the collection was reprinted in England and America, as well as in Canada. Leacock quickly followed it with *Nonsense Novels* (1911), a book that gave the world his famous description of the young man who 'flung himself upon his horse and rode madly off in all directions'. His third book of humour, *Sunshine Sketches of a Little Town*, was published in 1912, after appearing as a series in the Montreal *Star*.

Sunshine Sketches was based on Leacock's experiences in Orillia, near which, in 1908, he had bought a farm for his annual summer holidays. His friend B.K. Sandwell later observed of the book that 'It was the only really large-scale commission ever received [by Leacock] for a fictional job to be done for a purely Canadian audience. . . . he had a wealth of material not too suitable for his American buyers.' Leacock's decision to write this book for a Canadian readership was probably the reason the book achieved neither the international popularity nor the commercial success of his others, although it is now generally regarded as his best as well as his most unified work. It remains in print, and in 1996 a critical edition appeared. In 1914 Leacock made use, in a similar fashion, of events and scenes drawn from Montreal life for *Arcadian Adventures with the Idle Rich*, a companion volume to *Sunshine Sketches*—but he transposed the setting of that work to an American city.

For the rest of his career Leacock worked at an intense pace, averaging a book of humour a year, as well as writing biographies, social commentary, and popular histories. The quality of his humorous writing suffered as a result of this industry, which was fuelled by a strong desire for money and prestige. In 1921 he was instrumental in organizing the Canadian Authors' Association as a means of working out a satisfactory agreement on Canadian copyright. After his enforced retirement from McGill at the age of sixty-five, Leacock, already a popular public speaker, embarked on a lecture tour of western Canada that led to *My Discovery of the West* (1937), for which he won a Governor General's Award.

Despite its satire and comedy, *Sunshine Sketches* is Leacock's adaptation of the 'regional idyll' that was the dominant literary form in Canada between 1900 and 1920. Although many Orillia citizens were angered by Leacock's failure to disguise the identities of the people on whom he modelled his characters, there is an evident fondness in the book for its fictional town of 'Mariposa'—an affection most evident in the nostalgic sketch that closes the work, 'L'Envoi: The Train to Mariposa'. There Leacock writes of how we all dream of returning to that 'little Town in the Sunshine that once we knew':

Look from the window as you go. The city is far behind now and right and left of you there are trim farms with elms and maples near them and with tall windmills beside the old barns that you can still see in the gathering dusk. There is a dull red light from the windows of the farmstead. It must be comfortable there after the roar and clatter of the city, and only think of the still quiet of it. . . .

What? It feels nervous and strange to be coming here again after all these years? It must indeed. No, don't bother to look at the reflection of your face in the window-pane shadowed by the night outside. Nobody could tell you now after all these years. Your face has changed in these long years of money-getting in the city. Perhaps if you had come back now and again, just at odd times, it wouldn't have been so.

The Marine Excursion of the Knights of Pythias

Half-past six on a July morning? The *Mariposa Belle* is at the wharf, decked in flags, with steam up ready to start.

Excursion day!

Half-past six on a July morning, and Lake Wissanotti lying in the sun as calm as glass. The opal colours of the morning light are shot from the surface of the water.

Out on the lake the last thin threads of the mist are clearing away like flecks of cotton wool.

The long call of the loon echoes over the lake. The air is cool and fresh. There is in it all the new life of the land of the silent pine and the moving waters. Lake Wissanotti in the morning sunlight! Don't talk to me of the Italian lakes, on the Tyrol or the Swiss Alps. Take them away. Move them somewhere else. I don't want them.

Excursion Day, at half-past six of a summer morning! With the boat all decked in flags and all the people in Mariposa on the wharf, and the band in peaked caps with big cornets tied to their bodies ready to play at any minute! I say! Don't tell me about the Carnival of Venice and the Delhi Durbar.[1] Don't! I wouldn't look at them. I'd shut my eyes! For light and colour give me every time an excursion out of Mariposa down the lake to the Indian's Island out of sight in the morning mist. Talk of your Papal

1 During the period of the British Empire in India, a durbar was a state reception given for a British sovereign. The Coronation Durbar at Delhi for King Edward VII, which lasted from 31 December 1902 to 7 January 1903, was a highly elaborate spectacle that attracted international attention.

Zouaves[2] and your Buckingham Palace Guard! I want to see the Mariposa band in uniform and the Mariposa Knights of Pythias with their aprons and their insignia and their picnic baskets and their five-cent cigars!

Half-past six in the morning, and all the crowd on the wharf and the boat due to leave in half an hour. Notice it!—in half an hour. Already she's whistled twice (at six, and at six fifteen), and at any minute now, Christie Johnson will step into the pilot house and pull the string for the warning whistle that the boat will leave in half an hour. So keep ready. Don't think of running back to Smith's Hotel for the sandwiches. Don't be fool enough to try to go up to the Greek Store, next to Netley's, and buy fruit. You'll be left behind for sure if you do. Never mind the sandwiches and the fruit! Anyway, here comes Mr Smith himself with a huge basket of provender that would feed a factory. There must be sandwiches in that. I think I can hear them clinking. And behind Mr Smith is the German waiter from the caff[3] with another basket—undubitably lager beer; and behind him, the bartender of the hotel, carrying nothing, as far as one can see. But of course if you know Mariposa you will understand that why he looks so nonchalant and empty-handed is because he has two bottles of rye whisky under his linen duster.[4] You know, I think, the peculiar walk of a man with two bottles of whisky in the inside pockets of a linen coat. In Mariposa, you see, to bring beer to an excursion is quite in keeping with public opinion. But, whisky—well, one has to be a little careful.

Do I say that Mr Smith is here? Why, everybody's here. There's Hussell, the editor of the *Newspacket*, wearing a blue ribbon on his coat, for the Mariposa Knights of Pythias are, by their constitution, dedicated to temperance; and there's Henry Mullins, the manager of the Exchange Bank, also a Knight of Pythias, with a small flask of Pogram's Special in his hip pocket as a sort of amendment to the constitution. And there's Dean Drone, the Chaplain of the Order, with a fishing-rod (you never saw such green bass as lie among the rocks at Indian's Island), and with a trolling line in case of maskinonge,[5] and a landing-net in case of pickerel, and with his eldest daughter, Lilian Drone, in case of young men. There never was such a fisherman as the Rev. Rupert Drone.

Perhaps I ought to explain that when I speak of the excursion as being of the Knights of Pythias, the thing must not be understood in any narrow sense. In Mariposa practically everybody belongs to the Knights of Pythias just as they do to everything else. That's the great thing about the town and that's what makes it so different from the city. Everybody is in everything.

2 A troop of soldiers (eventually including more than 500 Canadian volunteers—who became the first substantial body of troops from Canada to take part in an overseas campaign), formed in 1860 to protect the Vatican. Their colourful uniforms of baggy trousers, braided jacket, and tasselled fez were patterned after the North African-inspired uniforms of the French Zouaves, who had a romantic reputation as dashing daredevils.

3 In 'The Hostelry of Mr Smith', the first of Leacock's *Sunshine Sketches*, Josh Smith, the proprietor of the local hotel, has—in order to persuade the town to support the renewal of his liquor licence—opened the Ladies' and Gents' Café. (Once his licence is renewed, he fires his French chef and gets rid of all of its distinctive flourishes.) Mr Smith explains that he has patterned it after 'a real French Caff' with a 'Rat's Cooler' (his misunderstanding of rathskeller): these mistakes made by Mariposans in pronunciation (as in 'Gothey' for Goethe later in this story) are a source of humour for Leacock throughout *Sunshine Sketches.*

4 A loose full-length coat.

5 Pike.

You should see them on the seventeenth of March, for example, when everybody wears a green ribbon and they're all laughing and glad—you know what the Celtic nature is—and talking about Home Rule.[6]

On St Andrew's Day every man in town wears a thistle and shakes hands with everybody else, and you see the fine old Scotch honesty beaming out of their eyes.

And on St George's Day!—well, there's no heartiness like the good old English spirit, after all; why shouldn't a man feel glad that he's an Englishman?

Then on the Fourth of July there are stars and stripes flying over half the stores in town, and suddenly all the men are seen to smoke cigars, and to know all about Roosevelt and Bryan and the Philippine Islands.[7] Then you learn for the first time that Jeff Thorpe's people came from Massachusetts and that his uncle fought at Bunker Hill[8] (anyway Jefferson will swear it was in Dakota all right enough); and you find that George Duff has a married sister in Rochester and that her husband is all right; in fact, George was down there as recently as eight years ago. Oh, it's the most American town imaginable is Mariposa—on the fourth of July.

But wait, just wait, if you feel anxious about the solidity of the British connexion, till the twelfth of the month,[9] when everybody is wearing an orange streamer in his coat and the Orangemen (every man in town) walk in the big procession. Allegiance! Well, perhaps you remember the address they gave to the Prince of Wales[10] on the platform of the Mariposa station as he went through on his tour to the west. I think that pretty well settled that question.

So you will easily understand that of course everybody belongs to the Knights of Pythias and the Masons and Oddfellows, just as they all belong to the Snow Shoe Club and the Girls' Friendly Society.

And meanwhile the whistle of the steamer has blown again for a quarter to seven—loud and long this time, for anyone not here now is late for certain, unless he should happen to come down in the last fifteen minutes.

What a crowd upon the wharf and how they pile onto the steamer! It's a wonder that the boat can hold them all. But that's just the marvellous thing about the *Mariposa Belle*.

I don't know—I have never known—where the steamers like the *Mariposa Belle* come from. Whether they are built by Harland and Wolff of Belfast, or whether, on

6 Home Rule for Ireland (that is, Irish independence from British rule) was a popular cause among Irish Catholics and those sympathetic to them, and was therefore promoted when St Patrick's Day was celebrated.

7 During the Spanish-American War (1898) Theodore Roosevelt led the First US Volunteer Calvary (the 'Rough Riders') in a famous charge up San Juan Hill in Cuba. (Roosevelt subsequently became the vice president and then president of the US in 1901, following the assassination of William McKinley.) One outcome of the US victory in that war was the annexation of Philippines from Spain. Although this development stirred anti-imperialist debate in the US, pro-imperialists carried the tide of opinion. One of the strongest of the pro-imperialist speeches was made by William Jennings Bryan, who, in his 'White Man's Burden' oration on the fourth of July in 1906, argued that the US was performing the same noble service in governing the Philippines that England was performing by ruling over the people of India.

8 A famous battle (in Boston) of the American Revolutionary War.

9 July twelfth is the date of the annual Orange parade. This affirmation of Irish Protestantism is, of course, entirely contrary to the affirmation of Irish Catholicism shown by Mariposa's residents on St Patrick's Day.

10 The narrator here is apparently referring to the 1860 visit of Albert Edward, Prince of Wales, to Upper and Lower Canada, rather than to the visit of George Prince of Wales to Quebec in 1908—though the former is not likely to actually be in the living memory of those addressed.

the other hand, they are not built by Harland and Wolff of Belfast, is more than one would like to say offhand.

The *Mariposa Belle* always seems to me to have some of those strange properties that distinguish Mariposa itself. I mean, her size seems to vary so. If you see her there in the winter, frozen in the ice beside the wharf with a snowdrift against the windows of the pilot house, she looks a pathetic little thing the size of a butternut. But in the summer time, especially after you've *been* in Mariposa for a month or two, and have paddled alongside of her in a canoe, she gets larger and taller, and with a great sweep of black sides, till you see no difference between the *Mariposa Belle* and the *Lusitania.*[11] Each one is a big steamer and that's all you can say.

Nor do her measurements help you much. She draws about eighteen inches forward, and more than that—at least half an inch more, astern, and when she's loaded down with an excursion crowd she draws a good two inches more. And above the water—why, look at all the decks on her! There's the deck you walk onto, from the wharf, all shut in, with windows along it, and the after cabin with the long table, and above that the deck with all the chairs piled upon it, and the deck in front where the band stand round in a circle, and the pilot house is higher than that, and above the pilot house is the board with the gold name and the flag pole and the steel ropes and the flags; and fixed in somewhere on the different levels is the lunch counter where they sell the sandwiches, and the engine room, and down below the deck level, beneath the water line, is the place where the crew sleep. What with steps and stairs and passages and piles of cordwood for the engine—oh, no, I guess Harland and Wolff didn't build her. They couldn't have.

Yet even with a huge boat like the *Mariposa Belle*, it would be impossible for her to carry all of the crowd that you see in the boat and on the wharf. In reality, the crowd is made up of two classes—all of the people in Mariposa who are going on the excursion and all those who are not. Some come for the one reason and some for the other.

The two tellers of the Exchange Bank are both there standing side by side. But one of them—the one with the cameo pin and the long face like a horse—is going, and the other—with the other cameo pin and the face like another horse—is not. In the same way, Hussell of the *Newspacket* is going, but his brother, beside him, isn't. Lilian Drone is going, but her sister can't; and so on all through the crowd.

And to think that things should look like that on the morning of a steamboat accident.

How strange life is!

To think of all these people so eager and anxious to catch the steamer, and some of them running to catch it, and so fearful that they might miss it—the morning of a steamboat accident. And the captain blowing his whistle, and warning them so severely that he would leave them behind—leave them out of the accident! And everybody crowding so eagerly to be in the accident.

Perhaps life is like that all through.

11 When it was launched in June 1906, RMS *Lusitania* took the title of largest liner afloat.

Strangest of all to think, in a case like this, of the people who were left behind, or in some way or other prevented from going, and always afterwards told of how they had escaped being on board of the *Mariposa Belle* that day!

Some of the instances were certainly extraordinary.

Nivens, the lawyer, escaped from being there merely by the fact that he was away in the city.

Towers, the tailor, only escaped owing to the fact that, not intending to go on the excursion he had stayed in bed till eight o'clock and so had not gone. He narrated afterwards that waking up that morning at half-past five, he had thought of the excursion and for some unaccountable reason had felt glad that he was not going.

The case of Yodel, the auctioneer, was even more inscrutable. He had been to the Oddfellows' excursion on the train the week before and to the Conservative picnic the week before that, and had decided not to go on this trip. In fact, he had not the least intention of going. He narrated afterwards how the night before someone had stopped him on the corner of Nippewa and Tecumseh Streets (he indicated the very spot) and asked: 'Are you going to take in the excursion tomorrow?' and he had said, just as simply as he was talking when narrating it: 'No.' And ten minutes after that, at the corner of Dalhousie and Brock Street (he offered to lead a party of verification to the precise place) somebody else had stopped him and asked: 'Well, are you going on the steamer trip tomorrow?' Again he had answered: 'No,' apparently almost in the same tone as before.

He said afterwards that when he heard the rumour of the accident it seemed like the finger of Providence, and he fell on his knees in thankfulness.

There was the similar case of Morison (I mean the one in Glover's hardware store that married one of the Thompsons). He said afterwards that he had read so much in the papers about accidents lately—mining accidents, and aeroplanes and gasoline—that he had grown nervous. The night before his wife had asked him at supper: 'Are you going on the excursion?' He had answered: 'No, I don't think I feel like it,' and had added: 'Perhaps your mother might like to go.' And the next evening just at dusk, when the news ran through the town, he said the first thought that flashed through his head was: 'Mrs Thompson's on that boat.'

He told this right as I say it—without the least doubt or confusion. He never for a moment imagined she was on the *Lusitania* or the *Olympic* or any other boat. He knew she was on this one. He said you could have knocked him down where he stood. But no one had. Not even when he got halfway down—on his knees, and it would have been easier still to knock him down or kick him. People do miss a lot of chances.

Still, as I say, neither Yodel nor Morison nor anyone thought about there being an accident until just after sundown when they—

Well, have you ever heard the long booming whistle of a steamboat two miles out on the lake in the dusk, and while you listen and count and wonder, seen the crimson rockets going up against the sky and then heard the fire bell ringing right there beside you in the town, and seen the people running to the town wharf?

That's what the people of Mariposa saw and felt that summer evening as they watched the Mackinaw lifeboat go plunging out into the lake with seven sweeps to a side and the foam clear to the gunwale with the lifting stroke of fourteen men!

But, dear me, I am afraid that this is no way to tell a story. I suppose the true art would have been to have said nothing about the accident till it happened. But when you write about Mariposa, or hear of it, if you know the place, it's all so vivid and real, that a thing like the contrast between the excursion crowd in the morning and the scene at night leaps into your mind and you must think of it.

But never mind about the accident—let us turn back again to the morning.

The boat was due to leave at seven. There was no doubt about the hour—not only seven, but seven sharp. The notice in the *Newspacket* said: 'The boat will leave sharp at seven'; and the advertising posters on the telegraph poles on Missinaba Street that began, 'Ho, for Indian's Island!' ended up with the words: 'Boat leaves at seven sharp.' There was a big notice on the wharf that said: 'Boat leaves sharp on time.'

So at seven, right on the hour, the whistle blew loud and long, and then at seven-fifteen three short peremptory blasts, and at seven-thirty one quick angry call—just one—and very soon after that they cast off the last of the ropes and the *Mariposa Belle* sailed off in her cloud of flags, and the band of the Knights of Pythias, timing it to a nicety, broke into the 'Maple Leaf for Ever!'

I suppose that all excursions when they start are much the same. Anyway, on the *Mariposa Belle* everybody went running up and down all over the boat with deck chairs and camp stools and baskets, and found places, splendid places to sit, and then got scared that there might be better ones and chased off again. People hunted for places out of the sun and when they got them swore that they weren't going to freeze to please anybody; and the people in sun said that they hadn't paid fifty cents to get roasted. Others said that they hadn't paid fifty cents to get covered with cinders, and there were still others who hadn't paid fifty cents to get shaken to death with the propeller.

Still, it was all right presently. The people seemed to get sorted out into the places on the boat where they belonged. The women, the older ones, all gravitated into the cabin on the lower deck and by getting round the table with needlework, and with all the windows shut, they soon had it, as they said themselves, just like being at home.

All the young boys and the toughs and the men in the band got down on the lower deck forward, where the boat was dirtiest and where the anchor was and the coils of rope.

And upstairs on the after deck there were Lilian Drone and Miss Lawson, the high-school teacher, with a book of German poetry—Gothey I think it was—and the bank teller and the young men.

In the centre, standing beside the rail, were Dean Drone and Dr Gallagher, looking through binocular glasses at the shore.

Up in front on the little deck forward of the pilot house was a group of the older men, Mullins and Duff and Mr Smith in a deck chair, and beside him Mr Golgotha Gingham, the undertaker of Mariposa, on a stool. It was part of Mr Gingham's principles to take in an outing of this sort, a business matter, more or less—for you never know what may happen at these water parties. At any rate, he was there in a neat suit of black, not, of course, his heavier or professional suit, but a soft clinging effect as of burnt paper that combined gaiety and decorum to a nicety.

'Yes,' said Mr Gingham, waving his black glove in a general way towards the shore, 'I know the lake well, very well. I've been pretty much all over it in my time.'

'Canoeing?' asked somebody.

'No,' said Mr Gingham, 'not in a canoe.' There seemed a peculiar and quiet meaning in his tone.

'Sailing, I suppose,' said somebody else.

'No,' said Mr Gingham. 'I don't understand it.'

'I never knowed that you went onto the water at all, Gol,' said Mr Smith, breaking in.

'Ah, not now,' explained Mr Gingham; 'it was years ago, the first summer I came to Mariposa. I was on the water practically all day. Nothing like it to give a man an appetite and keep him shape.'

'Was you camping?' asked Mr Smith.

'We camped at night,' assented the undertaker, 'but we put in practically the whole day on the water. You see, we were after a party that had come up here from the city on his vacation and gone out in a sailing canoe. We were dragging. We were up every morning at sunrise, lit a fire on the beach and cooked breakfast, and then we'd light our pipes and be off with the net for a whole day. It's great life,' concluded Mr Gingham wistfully.

'Did you get him?' asked two or three together.

There was a pause before Mr Gingham answered.

'We did,' he said '—down in the reeds past Horseshoe Point. But it was no use. He turned blue on me right away.'

After which Mr Gingham fell into such a deep reverie that the boat had steamed another half-mile down the lake before anybody broke the silence again. Talk of this sort—and after all what more suitable for a day on the water?—beguiled the way.

Down the lake, mile by mile over the calm water, steamed the *Mariposa Belle.* They passed Poplar Point where the high sand-banks are with all the swallows' nests in them, and Dean Drone and Dr Gallagher looked at them alternately through the binocular glasses, and it was wonderful how plainly one could see the swallows and the banks and the shrubs—just as plainly as with the naked eye.

And a little farther down they passed the Shingle Beach, and Dr Gallagher, who knew Canadian history, said to Dean Drone that it was strange to think that Champlain had landed there with his French explorers three hundred years ago; and Dean Drone, who didn't know Canadian history, said it was stranger still to think that the hand of the Almighty had piled up the hills and rocks long before that; and Dr Gallagher said it was wonderful how the French had found their way through such a pathless wilderness; and Dean Drone said that it was wonderful also to think that the Almighty had placed even the smallest shrub in its appointed place. Dr Gallagher said it filled him with admiration. Dean Drone said it filled him with awe. Dr Gallagher said he'd been full of it every since he was a boy and Dean Drone said so had he.

Then a little further, as the *Mariposa Belle* steamed on down the lake, they passed the Old Indian Portage where the great grey rocks are; and Dr Gallagher drew Dean Drone's attention to the place where the narrow canoe track wound up from the shore to the woods, and Dean Drone said he could see it perfectly well without the glasses.

Dr Gallagher said that it was just here that a party of five hundred French had made their way with all their baggage and accoutrements across the rocks of the divide and down to the Great Bay. And Dean Drone said that it reminded him of Xenophon leading his ten thousand Greeks over the hill passes of Armenia down to the sea. Dr Gallagher said that he had often wished he could have seen and spoken to Champlain, and Dean Drone said how much he regretted to have never known Xenophon.

And then after that they fell to talking of relics and traces of the past, and Dr Gallagher said that if Dean Drone would come round to his house some night he would show him some Indian arrow heads that he had dug up in his garden. And Dean Drone said that if Dr Gallagher would come round to the rectory any afternoon he would show him a map of Xerxes' invasion of Greece. Only he must come some time between the Infant Class and the Mothers' Auxiliary.

So presently they both knew that they were blocked out of one another's houses for some time to come, and Dr Gallagher walked forward and told Mr Smith, who had never studied Greek, about Champlain crossing the rock divide.

Mr Smith turned his head and looked at the divide for half a second and then said he had crossed a worse one up north back of the Wahnipitae and that the flies were Hades—and then went on playing freezeout poker with the two juniors in Duff's bank.

So Dr Gallagher realized that that's always the way when you try to tell people things, and that as far as gratitude and appreciation goes one might as well never read books or travel anywhere or do anything.

In fact, it was at this very moment that he made up his mind to give the arrows to the Mariposa Mechanics' Institute—they afterwards became, as you know, the Gallagher Collection. But, for the time being, the doctor was sick of them and wandered off around the boat and watched Henry Mullins showing George Duff how to make a John Collins[12] without lemons, and finally went and sat down among the Mariposa band and wished that he hadn't come.

So the boat steamed on and the sun rose higher and higher, and the freshness of the morning changed into the full glare of noon, and pretty soon the *Mariposa Belle* had floated out onto the lake again and they went on to where the lake began to narrow in at its foot, just where the Indian's Island is—all grass and tress and with a log wharf running into the water. Below it the Lower Ossawippi runs out of the lake, and quite near are the rapids, and you can see down among the trees the red brick of the power house and hear the roar of the leaping water.

The Indian's Island itself is all covered with trees and tangled vines, and the water about it is so still that it's all reflected double and looks the same either way up. Then

12 A John Collins is a mixed drink made with sweet gin, lemon juice, and sugar.

when the steamer's whistle blows as it comes into the wharf, you hear it echo among the trees of the island, and reverberate back from the shores of the lake.

The scene is all so quiet and still and unbroken, that Miss Cleghorn[13]—the sallow girl in the telephone exchange, that I spoke of—said she'd like to be buried there. But all the people were so busy getting their baskets and gathering up their things that no one had time to attend to it.

I mustn't even try to describe the landing and the boat crunching against the wooden wharf and all the people running to the same side of the deck and Christie Johnson calling out to the crowd to keep to the starboard and nobody being able to find it. Everyone who has been on a Mariposa excursion knows all about that.

Nor can I describe the day itself and the picnic under the trees. There were speeches afterwards, and Judge Pepperleigh gave such offence by bringing in Conservative politics that a man called Patriotus Canadiensis wrote and asked for some of the invaluable space of the *Mariposa Times-Herald* and exposed it.

I should say that there were races too, on the grass on the open side of the island, graded mostly according to ages—races for boys under thirteen and girls over nineteen and all that sort of thing. Sports are generally conducted on that plan in Mariposa. It is realized that a woman of sixty has an unfair advantage over a mere child.

Dean Drone managed the races and decided the ages and gave out the prizes; the Wesleyan minister helped, and he and the young student, who was relieving in the Presbyterian Church, held the string at the winning point.

They had to get mostly clergymen for the races because all the men had wandered off, somehow, to where they were drinking lager beer out of two kegs stuck on pine logs among the trees.

But if you've ever been on a Mariposa excursion you know all about these details anyway.

So the day wore on and presently the sun came through the trees on a slant and the steamer whistle blew with a great puff of white steam and all the people came straggling down to the wharf and pretty soon the *Mariposa Belle* had floated out onto the lake again and headed for the town, twenty miles away.

I suppose you have often noticed the contrast there is between an excursion on its way out in the morning and what it looks like on the way home.

In the morning everybody is so restless and animated and moves to and from all over the boat and asks questions. But coming home, as the afternoon gets later and later and the sun sinks beyond the hills, all the people seem to get so still and quiet and drowsy.

13 Miss Cleghorn is mentioned in the preceding sketch, 'The Speculations of Jefferson Thorpe', where she serves as a foil for Myra Thorpe, with whom she works in the Telephone Exchange: 'Myra had golden hair and a Greek face. . . . As you saw her swinging up the street to the Telephone Exchange . . . there was style written all over her—the kind of thing that Mariposa recognized and did homage to. . . . [Y]ou could understand why it was that the commercial travellers would stand round the Exchange calling up all sorts of impossible villages, and waiting about so pleasant and genial!—it made one realize how naturally good-tempered men are. And then when Myra would go off duty and Miss Cleghorn, who was sallow, would come on, the commercial men would be off again like autumn leaves.'

So it was with the people on the *Mariposa Belle.* They sat there on the benches and the deck chairs in little clusters, and listened to the regular beat of the propeller and almost dozed off asleep as they sat. Then when the sun set and the dusk drew on, it grew almost dark on the deck and so still that you could hardly tell there was anyone aboard.

And if you had looked at the steamer from the shore or from one of the islands, you'd have seen the row of lights from the cabin windows shining on the water and the red glare of the burning hemlock from the funnel, and you'd have heard the soft thud of the propeller miles away over the lake.

Now and then, too, you could have heard them singing on the steamer—the voices of the girls and the men blended into unison by the distance, rising and falling in long-drawn melody: '*O—Can-a-da—O—Can-a-da*'.

You may talk as you will about the intoning choirs of your European cathedrals, but the sound of '*O—Can-a-da*', borne across the waters of a silent lake at evening is good enough for those of us who know Mariposa.

I think that it was just as they were singing like this: '*O—Can-a-da*', that word went round that the boat was sinking.

If you have ever been in any sudden emergency on the water, you will understand the strange psychology of it—the way in which what is happening seems to become known all in a moment without a word being said. The news is transmitted from one to the other by some mysterious process.

At any rate, on the *Mariposa Belle* first one and then the other heard that the steamer was sinking. As far as I could ever learn the first of it was that George Duff, the bank manager, came very quietly to Dr Gallagher and asked him if he thought that the boat was sinking. The doctor said no, that he had thought so earlier in the day but that he didn't now think that she was.

After that Duff, according to his own account, had said to Macartney, the lawyer, that the boat was sinking, and Macartney said that he doubted it very much.

Then somebody came to Judge Pepperleigh and woke him up and said that there was six inches of water in the steamer and that she was sinking. And Pepperleigh said it was perfect scandal and passed the news on to his wife and she said that they had no business to allow it and that if the steamer sank that was the last excursion she'd go on.

So the news went all round the boat and everywhere the people gathered in groups and talked about it in the angry and excited way that people have when a steamer is sinking on one of the lakes like Lake Wissanotti.

Dean Drone, of course, and some others were quieter about it, and said that one must make allowances and that naturally there were two sides to everything. But most of them wouldn't listen to reason at all. I think, perhaps, that some of them were frightened. You see the last time but one that the steamer had sunk, there had been a man drowned and it made them nervous.

What? Hadn't I explained about the depth of Lake Wissanotti? I had taken it for granted that you knew; and in any case parts of it are deep enough, though I don't suppose in this stretch of it from the big reed beds up to within a mile of the town wharf, you could find six feet of water in it if you tried. Oh, pshaw! I was not talking about a steamer sinking in the ocean and carrying down its screaming crowds of people into the hideous depths of green water. Oh, dear me, no! That kind of thing never happens on Lake Wissanotti.

But what does happen is that the *Mariposa Belle* sinks every now and then, and sticks there on the bottom till they get things straightened up.

On the lakes round Mariposa, if a person arrives late anywhere and explains that the steamer sank, everybody understands the situation.

You see when Harland and Wolff built the *Mariposa Belle*, they left some cracks in between the timbers that you fill up with cotton waste every Sunday. If this is not attended to, the boat sinks. In fact, it is part of the law of the province that all the steamers like the *Mariposa Belle* must be properly corked[14]—I think that is the word—every season. There are inspectors who visit all the hotels in the province to see that it is done.

So you can imagine now that I've explained it a little straighter, the indignation of the people when they knew that the boat had come uncorked and that they might be stuck out there on a shoal or a mud-bank half the night.

I don't say either that there wasn't any danger; anyway, it doesn't feel very safe when you realize that the boat is settling down with every hundred yards that she goes, and you look over the side and see only the black water in the gathering night.

Safe! I'm not sure now that I come to think of it that it isn't worse than sinking in the Atlantic. After all, in the Atlantic there is wireless telegraphy, and a lot of trained sailors and stewards. But out on Lake Wissanotti—far out, so that you can only just see the lights of the town away off to the south—when the propeller comes to a stop—and you and hear the hiss of steam as they start to rake out the engine fires to prevent explosion—and when you turn from the red glare that comes from the furnace doors as they open them, to the black dark that is gathering over the lake—and there's a night wind beginning to run among the rushes—and you see the men going forward to the roof of the pilot house to send up the rockets to rouse the town—safe? Safe yourself, if you like; as for me, let me once get back to Mariposa again, under the night shadow of the maple trees, and this shall be the last, last time I'll go on Lake Wissanotti.

Safe! Oh, yes! Isn't it strange how safe other people's adventures seem after they happen? But you'd have been scared, too, if you'd been there just before the steamer sank, and seen them bringing up all the women on to the top deck.

I don't see how some of the people took it so calmly; how Mr Smith, for instance, could have gone on smoking and telling how he'd had a steamer 'sink on him' on Lake Nipissing and a still bigger one, a side-wheeler, sink on him in Lake Abbitibbi.

Then, quite suddenly, with a quiver, down she went. You could feel the boat sink, sink—down, down—would it never get to the bottom? The water came flush up to the lower deck, and then—thank heaven—the sinking stopped and there was the *Mariposa Belle* safe and tight on a reed bank.

14 A malapropism for 'caulked'; also slang for very drunk.

Really, it made one positively laugh! It seemed so queer and, anyway, if a man has a sort of natural courage, danger makes him laugh. Danger? pshaw! fiddlesticks! everybody scouted the idea. Why, it is just the little things like this that give zest to a day on the water.

Within half a minute they were all running round looking for sandwiches and cracking jokes and talking of making coffee over the remains of the engine fires.

I don't need to tell at length how it all happened after that.

I suppose the people on the *Mariposa Belle* would have had to settle down there all night or till help came from the town, but some of the men who had gone forward and were peering out into the dark said that it couldn't be more than a mile across the water to Miller's Point. You could almost see it over there to the left—some of them, I think, said 'off on the port bow', because you know when you get mixed up in these marine disasters, you soon catch the atmosphere of the thing.

So pretty soon they had the davits swung out over the side and were lowering the old lifeboat from the top deck into the water.

There were men leaning out over the rail of the *Mariposa Belle* with lanterns that threw the light as they let her down, and the glare fell on the water and the reeds. But when they got the boat lowered, it looked such a frail, clumsy thing as one saw it from the rail above, that the cry was raised: 'Women and children first!' For what was the sense, if it should turn out that the boat wouldn't even hold women and children, of trying to jam a lot of heavy men into it?

So they put in mostly women and children and the boat pushed out into the darkness so freighted down it would hardly float.

In the bow of it was the Presbyterian student who was relieving the minister, and he called out that they were in the hands of Providence. But he was crouched and ready to spring out of them at the first moment.

So the boat went and was lost in the darkness except for the lantern in the bow that you could see bobbing on the water. Then presently it came back and they sent another load, till pretty soon the decks began to thin out and everybody got impatient to be gone.

It was about the time that the third boat-load put off that Mr Smith took a bet with Mullins for twenty-five dollars, that he'd be home in Mariposa before the people in the boats had walked round the shore.

No one knew just what he meant, but pretty soon they saw Mr Smith disappear down below the lowest part of the steamer with a mallet in one hand and a big bundle of marline in the other.

They might have wondered more about it, but it was just at this time that they heard the shouts from the rescue boat—the big Mackinaw lifeboat—that had put out from the town with fourteen men at the sweeps when they saw the first rockets go up.

I suppose there is always something inspiring about a rescue at sea, or on the water.

After all, the bravery of the lifeboat man is the true bravery—expended to save life, not to destroy it.

Certainly they told for months after of how the rescue boat came out to the *Mariposa Belle.*

I suppose that when they put her in the water the lifeboat touched it for the first time since the old Macdonald Government placed her on Lake Wissanotti.

Anyway, the water poured in at every seam. But not for a moment—even with two miles of water between them and the steamer—did the rowers pause for that.

By the time they were halfway there the water was almost up to the thwarts, but they drove her on. Panting and exhausted (for mind you, if you haven't been in a fool boat like that for years, rowing takes it out of you), the rowers stuck to their task. They threw the ballast over and chucked into the water the heavy cork jackets and lifebelts that encumbered their movements. There was no thought of turning back. They were nearer to the steamer than the shore.

'Hang to it, boys,' called the crowd from the steamer's deck, and hang they did.

They were almost exhausted when they got them; men leaning from the steamer threw them ropes and one by one every man was hauled aboard just as the lifeboat sank under their feet.

Saved! by heaven, saved by one of the smartest pieces of rescue work ever seen on the lake.

There's no use describing it; you need to see rescue work of this kind by lifeboats to understand it.

Nor were the lifeboat crew the only ones that distinguished themselves.

Boat after boat and canoe after canoe had put out from Mariposa to the help of the steamer. They got them all.

Pupkin, the other bank teller with a face like a horse, who hadn't gone on the excursion—as soon as he knew that the boat was signalling for help and that Miss Lawson was sending up rockets—rushed for a row boat, grabbed an oar (two would have hampered him)—and paddled madly out into the lake. He struck right out into the dark with the crazy skiff almost sinking beneath his feet. But they got him. They rescued him. They watched him, almost dead with exhaustion, make his way to the steamer, where he was hauled up with ropes. Saved! Saved!

They might have gone on that way half the night, picking up the rescuers, only, at the very moment when the tenth load of people left for the shore—just as suddenly and saucily as you please, up came the *Mariposa Belle* from the mud bottom and floated.

Floated?

Why, of course she did. If you take a hundred and fifty people off a steamer that has sunk, and if you get a man as shrewd as Mr Smith to plug the timber seams with mallet and marline, and if you turn ten bandsmen of the Mariposa band onto your hand pump on the bow of the lower decks—float? why, what else can she do?

Then, if you stuff in hemlock into the embers of the fire that you were raking out, till it hums and crackles under the boiler, it won't be long before you hear the propeller thud—thudding at the stern again, and before the long roar of the steam whistle echoes over to the town.

And so the *Mariposa Belle*, with all steam up again and with the long train of sparks careering from the funnel, is heading for the town.

But no Christie Johnson at the wheel in the pilot house this time.

'Smith! Get Smith!' is the cry.

Can he take her in? Well, now! Ask a man who has had steamers sink on him in half the lakes from Temiscaming to the Bay, if he can take her in? Ask a man who has run a York boat down the rapids of the Moose when the ice is moving, if he can grip the steering wheel of the *Mariposa Belle*? So there she steams safe and sound to the town wharf!

Look at the lights and the crowds! If only the federal census taker could count us now! Hear them calling and shouting back and forward from the deck to the shore! Listen! There is the rattle of the shore ropes as they get them ready, and there's the Mariposa band—actually forming in a circle on the upper deck just as she docks, and the leader with his baton—one—two—ready now—

'O CAN-A-DA!'

1912

Emily Carr

1871–1945

Emily Carr, born a Canadian the year British Columbia joined Canada, was raised in Victoria, BC, by English parents who died when she was in her teens. Although she began to produce drawings and watercolours early, she did not begin formal art training until 1891, at the California School of Design in San Francisco. She returned to British Columbia in 1893, where she taught children's art classes until she had saved the money to study in London, England. Accompanied by her sister, Carr remained in England from 1899 to 1904: she at first lived in London, then moved to the countryside to recover from a physical and emotional breakdown. On her trips home to Canada and then after she returned to Canada to live, Carr became interested in the totems she saw on the west coast of BC, first in Ucluelet and, in 1912, on a six-week trip through the Skeena River regions and the Queen Charlotte Islands. Concerned with the way in which totemic art was being left to decay without any visual record, she sketched and painted Haida and Tlingit subjects, including houses and villages as well as totem poles. Although her early paintings were in watercolour, she spent an extended time abroad in 1910 studying post-impressionist painting techniques, and when she returned, her documentary watercolours gave way to bolder, more emotive oil paintings. Although Carr maintained that she was an accurate recorder of the totems, the artist in her increasingly shaped what she saw in terms of her individual aesthetic.

In 1913, Carr had an exhibition in Victoria of over 200 of her images. She also petitioned the British Colombia government to buy her paintings and drawings as a record of the culture they portrayed and to fund her ongoing project. That request was turned down and, finding herself needing to earn a living, she built a boarding house that she named the 'House of All Sorts' and abandoned her art for the next fifteen years.

The turning point in Carr's career came in 1927 when the National Gallery of Canada organized an exhibit of Native and Modern West Coast Art. Carr's work, largely unknown outside BC, was made central to the exhibition. When Carr travelled to Ottawa for the opening of the show, she met several Group of Seven painters, including Lawren Harris, with whom she developed a long correspondence. The encouragement of these established and respected artists renewed her enthusiasm for her own work. Returning to Victoria, she began to rework some earlier efforts, to paint from photographs she had taken, and to make long sketching trips through the woods. West Coast forests and other natural subjects began to replace Native themes in her work.

After 1927 Carr's work began to receive more and more critical attention and acclaim, though a full appreciation of her artistic achievement continues to grow. Her later paintings, moving from the vivid to the visionary, transcend her subject matter.

Carr took a creative writing course in 1926, and in 1927 she began to keep a journal in which she recorded ideas for later artwork. In 1937 she suffered the first of several serious heart attacks; with the decline in her health, she increasingly turned her creative focus to writing—though she never entirely gave up her visual art. In 1940 some of her stories were broadcast on the CBC, and in 1941 she published her first book, *Klee Wyck*, a series of sketches based on her visits to West Coast Native villages, for which she received a Governor General's award. In the autobiographical *Book of Small* (1942), Carr remembers her family, narrating the account from the child's point of view. She died shortly after the publication of *The House of All Sorts* (1944), in which she described her life as a landlady and dog breeder. Several more works of her prose—*Growing Pains* (1946); *The Heart of a Peacock* (1953); *Pause* (1953); and *Hundreds and Thousands: The Journals of an Artist* (1965)—were published posthumously.

'Kitwancool', a good example of Carr's prose, takes its name from a village Carr visited in 1928, an inland community in the Queen Charlottes considered unfriendly to Europeans. Straightforward in its telling, this tale shows us how Carr perceived Haida life and the relationship of white and Native cultures. Although like Carr's totem paintings it may sacrifice some accuracy for the sake of aesthetic patterning, it depicts much of interest about village and family life, including its hierarchy and gender roles. Most of all, perhaps, it suggests something about the life the artist must lead to find her subjects.

Kitwancool

When the Indians told me about the Kitwancool totem poles, I said:

'How can I get to Kitwancool?'

'Dunno,' the Indians replied.

White men told me about the Kitwancool poles too, but when I told them I wanted to go there, they advised me—'Keep out.' But the thought of those old Kitwancool poles pulled at me. I was at Kitwangak, twenty or so miles from Kitwancool.

Then a halfbreed at Kitwangak said to me, 'The young son of the Kitwancool Chief is going in tomorrow with a load of lumber. I asked if he would take you; he will.'

'How can I get out again?'

'The boy is coming back to Kitwangak after two days.'

The Chief's son Aleck was shy, but he spoke good English. He said I was to be at the Hudson's Bay store at eight the next morning.

I bought enough food and mosquito oil to last me two days; then I sat in front of the Hudson's Bay store from eight to eleven o'clock, waiting. I saw Aleck drive past to load his lumber. The wagon had four wheels and a long pole. He tied the lumber to the pole and a sack of oats to the lumber; I was to sit on the oats. Rigged up in front somehow was a place for the driver—no real seat, just a couple of coal-oil boxes bound to some boards. Three men sat on the two boxes. The road was terrible. When we bumped, the man on the down side of the boxes fell off.

A sturdy old man trudged behind the wagon. Sometimes he rode a bit on the end of the long pole, which tossed him up and down like a see-saw. The old man carried a gun and walked most of the way.

The noon sun burnt fiercely on our heads. The oat-sack gave no support to my back, and my feet dangled. I had to clutch the corner of the oat-sack with one hand to keep from falling off—with the other I held my small griffon dog. Every minute I though we would be pitched off the pole. You could seldom see the old man because of clouds of yellow dust rolling behind the wagon. The scrub growth at the road-side smelt red hot.

The scraggy ponies dragged their feet heavily; sweat cut rivers through the dust that was caked on their sides.

One of the three men on the front seat of the wagon seemed to be a hero. The other men questioned him all the way, though generally Indians do not talk as they travel. When one of the men fell off the seat he ran round the wagon to the high side and jumped up again and all the while he did not stop asking the hero questions. There were so many holes in the road and the men fell off so often that they were always changing places, like birds on a roost in cold weather.

Suddenly we gave such an enormous bump that we all fell off together, and the horses stopped. When the wheels were not rattling any more we could hear water running. The old man came out of the clouds of dust behind us and said there was a stream close by.

We threw ourselves onto our stomachs, put our lips to the water and drank like horses. The Indians took the bits out of their horses' mouths and gave them food. Then the men crawled under the wagon to eat their lunch in its shade; I sat by the shadiest wheel. It was splendid to put my legs straight out and have the earth support them and the wheel support my back. The old man went to sleep.

After he woke and after the horses had pulled the wagon out of the big hole, we rumbled on again.

When the sun began to go down we were in woods, and the clouds of mosquitoes were as thick as the clouds of dust, but more painful. We let them eat us because, after bumping for seven hours, we were too tired to fight.

At last we came to a great dip where the road wound around the edge of a ravine shaped like an oblong bowl. There were trees growing in this earth bowl. It seemed to be bottomless. We were level with the tree-tops as we looked down. The road was narrow—its edges broken.

I was afraid and said, 'I want to walk.'

Aleck waved his hand across the ravine. 'Kitwancool,' he said and I saw some grey roofs on the far side of the hollow. After we had circled the ravine and climbed the road on the other side we would be there, unless we were lying dead in that deep bowl.

I said again, 'I want to walk.'

'Village dogs will kill you and the little dog,' said Aleck. But I did walk around the bend and up the hill, until the village was near. Then I rode into Kitwancool on the oat-sack.

The dogs rushed out in a pack. The village people came out too. They made a fuss over the hero-man, clustering about him and jabbering. They paid no more attention to me than to the oat-sack. All of them went into the nearest house taking Aleck, the hero, the old man, and the other man with them, and shut the door.

I wanted to cry, sticking alone up there on top of the oats and lumber, the sagging horses in front and the yapping dogs all round, nobody to ask about anything and very tired. Aleck had told me I could sleep on the verandah of his father's house, because I only had a cot and a tent-fly[1] with me, and bears came into the village often at night. But how did I know which was his father's house? The dogs would tear me if I got down and there was no one to ask, anyway.

Suddenly something at the other end of the village attracted the dogs. The pack tore off and the dust hid me from them.

Aleck came out of the house and said, 'We are going to have dinner in this house now.' Then he went in again and shut the door.

The wagon was standing in the new part of the village. Below us, on the right, I could see a row of old houses. They were dim, for the light was going, but above them, black and clear against the sky stood the old totem poles of Kitwancool. I jumped down from the wagon and came to them. That part of the village was quite dead. Between the river and the poles was a flat of green grass. Above, stood the houses, grey and broken. They were in a long, wavering row, with wide, windowless fronts. The totem poles stood before them there on the top of a little bank above the green flat. There were a few poles down on the flat too, and some graves that had fences round them and roofs over the tops.

When it was almost dark I went back to the wagon.

The house of Aleck's father was the last one at the other end of the new village. It was one great room like a hall and was built of new logs. It had seven windows and two doors; all the windows were propped open with blue castor-oil bottles.

I was surprised to find that the old man who had trudged behind our wagon was Chief Douse—Aleck's father.

Mrs Douse was more important than Mr Douse; she was chieftainess in her own right, and had great dignity. Neither of them spoke to me that night. Aleck showed me where to put my bed on the verandah and I hung the fly over it. I ate a dry scrap of food and turned into my blankets. I had no netting, and the mosquitoes tormented me.

1 The part of a tent that covers the opening; when used alone, it functions as an awning or wind break.

My heart said into the thick dark, 'Why did I come?'
And the dark answered, 'You know.'

In the morning the hero-man came to me and said, 'My mother-in-law wishes to speak with you. She does not know English words so she will talk through my tongue.'

I stood before the tall, cold woman. She folded her arms across her body and her eyes searched my face. They were as expressive as if she were saying the words herself instead of using the hero's tongue.

'My mother-in-law wishes to know why you have come to our village.'

'I want to make some pictures of the totem poles.'

'What do you want our totem poles for?'

'Because they are beautiful. They are getting old now, and your people make very few new ones. The young people do not value the poles as the old ones did. By and by there will be no more poles. I want to make pictures of them, so that your young people as well as the white people will see how fine your totem poles used to be.'

Mrs Douse listened when the young man told her this. Her eyes raked my face to see if I was talking 'straight'. Then she waved her hand towards the village.

'Go along', she said through the interpreter, 'and I shall see.' She was neither friendly nor angry. Perhaps I was going to be turned out of this place that had been so difficult to get into.

The air was hot and heavy. I turned towards the old village with the pup Ginger Pop at my heels. Suddenly there was a roar of yelpings, and I saw my little dog putting half a dozen big ones to rout down the village street. Their tails were flat, their tongues lolled and they yelped. The Douses all rushed out of their house to see what the noise was about, and we laughed together so hard that the strain, which before had been between us, broke.

The sun enriched the poles grandly. They were carved elaborately and with great sincerity. Several times the figure of a woman that held a child was represented. The babies had faces like wise little old men. The mothers expressed all womanhood—the big wooden hands holding the child were so full of tenderness they had to be distorted enormously in order to contain it all. Womanhood was strong in Kitwancool. Perhaps, after all, Mrs Douse might let me stay.

I sat in front of a totem mother and began to draw—so full of her strange, wild beauty that I did not notice the storm that was coming, till the totem poles went black, flashed vividly white, and then went black again. Bang upon bang, came the claps of thunder. The hills on one side tossed it to the hills on the other; sheets of rain washed over me. I was beside a grave down on the green flat; some of the pickets of its fence were gone, so I crawled through on to the grave with Ginger Pop in my arms to shelter under its roof. Stinging nettles grew on top of the grave with mosquitoes hiding under their leaves. While I was beating down the nettles with my easel, it struck the head of a big wooden bear squatted on the grave. He startled me. He was painted red. As I sat down upon him my foot hit something that made a hollow rattling noise. It was a shaman's rattle. This then must be a shaman's, a medicine-man's, grave, and this the rattle he had used to scare away evil spirits. Shamen worked black magic. His body lay here just a few feet below me in the earth. At the thought I made a dash for the broken community house on the bank above. All the Indian horses had got there first and taken for their shelter the only corner of the house that had any roof over it.

I put my stool near the wall and sat upon it. The water ran down the wall in rivers. The dog shivered under my coat—both of us were wet to the skin. My sketch sack was so full of water that when I emptied it on to the ground it made the pool we sat in bigger.

After two hours the rain stopped suddenly. The horses held their bones stiff and quivered their skins. It made the rain fly out of their coats and splash me. One by one they trooped out through a hole in the wall. When their hooves struck the baseboard there was a sodden thud. Ginger Pop shook himself too, but I could only drip. Water poured from the eyes of the totems and from the tips of their carved noses. New little rivers trickled across the green flat. The big river was whipped to froth. A blur like boiling mist hung over it.

When I got back to the new village I found my bed and things in a corner of the Douses' great room. The hero told me, 'My mother-in-law says you may live in her house. Here is a rocking-chair for you.'

Mrs Douse acknowledged my gratitude stolidly. I gave Mr Douse a dollar and asked if I might have a big fire to dry my things and make tea. There were two stoves—the one at their end of the room was alight. Soon, mine too was roaring and it was cosy. When the Indians accepted me as one of themselves, I was very grateful.

The people who lived in that big room of the Douses were two married daughters, their husbands and children, the son Aleck, and an orphan girl called Lizzie. The old couple came and went continually, but they ate and slept in a shanty at the back of the new house. This little place had been made round them. The floor was of earth and the walls were of cedar. The fire on the ground sent its smoke through a smoke-hole in the roof. Dried salmon hung on racks. The old people's mattress was on the floor. The place was full of the themselves—they had breathed themselves into it as a bird, with its head under its wing, breathes itself into its own cosiness. The Douses were glad for their children to have the big fine house and be modern but this was the right sort of place for themselves.

Life in the big house was most interesting. A baby swung in its cradle from the rafters; everyone tossed the cradle as he passed and the baby cooed and gurgled. There was a crippled child of six—pinched and white under her brown skin; she sat in a chair all day. And there was Orphan Lizzie who would slip out into the wet bushes and come back with a wild strawberry or a flower in her grubby little hand, and kneeling by the sick child's chair, would open her fingers suddenly on the surprise.

There was no rush, no scolding, no roughness in this household. When anyone was sleepy he slept; when they were hungry they ate; if they were sorry they cried, and if they were glad they sang. They enjoyed Ginger Pop's fiery temper, the tilt of his nose, and particularly the way he kept the house free of Indian dogs. It was Ginger who bridged the gap between their language and mine with laughter. Ginger's snore was the only sound in that great room at night. Indians sleep quietly.

Orphan Lizzie was shy as a rabbit but completely unselfconscious. It was she who set the food on the big table and cleared away the dishes. There did not seem to be any particular meal-times. Lizzie always took a long lick at the top of the jam-tin as she passed it.

The first morning I woke at the Douses', I went very early to wash myself in the creek below the house. I was kneeling on the stones brushing my teeth. It was very cold. Suddenly I looked up—Lizzie was close by me watching. When I looked up, she darted away like a fawn, leaving her water pails behind. Later, Mrs Douse came to my corner of the house, carrying a tin basin; behind her was Lizzie with a tiny glass cream pitcher full of water, and behind Lizzie was the hero.

'My mother-in-law says the river is too cold for you to wash in. Here is water and a basin for you.'

Everyone watched my washing next morning. The washing of my ears interested them most.

One day after work I found the Douse family all sitting round on the floor. In the centre of the group was Lizzie. She was beating something in a pail, beating it with her hands; her arms were blobbed with pink froth to the elbows. Everyone stuck his hand into Lizzie's pail and hooked out some of the froth in the crook of his fingers, then took long delicious licks. They invited me to lick too. It was 'soperlallie', or soap berry. It grows in the woods; when you beat the berry it froths up and has a queer bitter taste. The Indians love it.

For two days from dawn till dark I worked down in the old part of the village. On the third day Aleck was to take me back to Kitwangak. But that night it started to rain. It rained for three days and three nights without stopping; the road was impossible. I had only provisioned for two days, had been here five, and had given all the best bits from my box to the sick child. All the food I had left for the last three days was hard tack and raisins. I drank hot water, and rocked my hunger to the tune of the rain beating on the window. Ginger Pop munched hard tack unconcerned—amusing everybody.

The Indians would have shared the loaf and jam-tin with me, but I did not tell them that I had no food. The thought of Lizzie's tongue licking the jam-tin stopped me.

When it rained, the Indians drowsed like flies, heavy as the day itself.

On the sixth day of my stay in Kitwancool the sun shone again, but we had to wait a bit for the puddles to drain.

I straightened out my obligations and said goodbye to Mr and Mrs Douse. The light wagon that was taking me out seemed luxurious after the thing I had come in on. I climbed up beside Aleck. He gathered his reins and 'giddapped'.

Mrs Douse, followed by her husband, came out of the house and waved a halt. She spoke to Aleck.

'My mother wants to see your pictures.'

'But I showed her every one before they were packed.'

At the time I had thought her stolidly indifferent.

'My mother wishes to see the pictures again.'

I clambered over the back of the wagon, unpacked the wet canvases and opened the sketchbooks. She went through them all. The two best poles in the village belonged to Mrs Douse. She argued and discussed with her husband. I told Aleck to ask if his mother would like to have me give her pictures of her poles. If so, I would send them through the Hudson's Bay store at Kitwangak. Mrs Douse's neck loosened. Her head nodded violently and I saw her smile for the first time.

Repacking, I climbed over the back of the seat to Aleck.

'Giddap!'

The reins flapped: we were off. The dust was laid; everything was keen and fresh; indeed the appetites of the mosquitoes were very keen.

When I got back to Kitwangak the Mounted Police came to see me.

'You have been in to Kitwancool?'

'Yes.'

'How did the Indians treat you?'

'Splendidly.'

'Learned their lesson, eh?' said the man. 'We have had no end of trouble with those people—chased missionaries out and drove surveyors off with axes—simply won't have whites in their village. I would never have advised anyone going in—particularly a woman. No, I would certainly have said, "Keep out".'

'Then I am glad I did not ask for your advice,' I said. 'Perhaps it is because I am a woman that they were so good to me.'

'One of the men who went in on the wagon with you was straight from jail, a fierce, troublesome customer.'

Now I knew who the hero was.

1941

L.M. Montgomery

1874–1942

Lucy Maud Montgomery, now known worldwide as the author of *Anne of Green Gables* (1908), was a fifth-generation Prince Edward Islander. Her childhood resembled that of several of her heroines, most particularly Emily (whose life is chronicled in a series of books beginning with *Emily of New Moon*, 1923). Her mother died when Montgomery was two, and her father left her behind with her maternal grandparents when he moved to Saskatchewan shortly after (he remarried and began a new family). Her grandparents were harsh and critical of the child, causing her to turn inward at a young age and to begin to write stories. Educated at Prince of Wales College, Charlottetown, and at Dalhousie University, Montgomery taught school in PEI and worked briefly for the Halifax *Daily Echo* (1901–2) before returning home to care for her grandmother.

Montgomery began publishing poems and stories while still a teenager, but she had difficulty getting her first novel, *Anne of Green Gables*, into print. However, once she did find a publisher (L.C. Page, an American company), her story of a spirited and imaginative orphan's passage from childhood into adolescence was an immediate success: within five months it went through six printings, selling 19,000 copies and eliciting praise from Mark Twain, among others. It has now been translated into at least fifteen languages, and its heroine, Anne Shirley, is a cult hero in Japan. Its seven sequels include *Anne of Avonlea* (1909), *Anne of the Island* (1915), and *Anne of Ingleside* (1939).

After the death of her grandmother in 1911, Montgomery married the Rev. Ewan Macdonald and moved to Leaksdale, Ontario. She continued to pursue her writing career while taking care of a young family and performing the duties of a minister's wife.

The Emily series, which followed *Emily of New Moon* with *Emily Climbs* (1925) and *Emily's Quest* (1927), brought Montgomery continued popularity and recognition, as did later books for young readers such as *Pat of Silver Bush* (1933) and *Jane of Lantern Hill* (1937). *The Story Girl* (1911), from which the story reprinted in this anthology comes, is one of Montgomery's several collections of short stories. (One of these—*Further Chronicles of Avonlea*, 1920—became the occasion of a nine-year legal battle with her first publisher, which Montgomery ultimately won.) She wrote two novels for adults: *The Blue Castle* (1926) and *A Tangled Web* (1931), which were less successful, and also produced a volume of poetry, *The Watchman and Other Poems* (1916). Among her many posthumously published works are *The Road to Yesterday* (1974), *The Doctor's Sweetheart: and Other Stories* (1979), *The Alpine Path: The Story of My Career* (1974)—a collection of autobiographical magazine articles—and four volumes of selections from her journals. These published journals have been much admired and have deepened our understanding of Montgomery by showing the shadows (including her growing restiveness because her 'publishers keep me at this sort of stuff because it sells. . . . they claim that the public, having become used to this from my pen, would not tolerate a change' [26 Dec. 1918] and, especially in her later years, her husband's declining mental health) that sometimes hung over the woman whose pastoral landscapes hold few hints of darkness.

Like later writers such as Hugh MacLennan, Montgomery is important in part because she wrote about a particular place within the Canadian landscape, giving Canadians vivid depictions of places and individuals in their world at a time when such representations were not yet common. While the nostalgic quality of her rural idylls may make them seem backward looking, Montgomery created within the body of her work a picture of modern girlhood that is itself as important as any one of her books. Anne, Emily, Pat, Jane, and the Story Girl captured the imagination of twentieth-century readers (not just those who were adolescent and female) in much the same way Mark Twain's earlier depictions of Tom Sawyer and Huckleberry Finn—also the subject of several sequels—provided an image of boyhood in a changing United States. Just as endangered American definitions of masculinity and nationhood are played out in Huck's innocence of social restraint and his restless boundary crossing in the face of the impending loss of the frontier—and the imaginative freedom it symbolized—so in Montgomery's young women readers found individuals similarly testing the restraints of conformity and discovering new outlets at a time of changing social structures. Because the emerging society will force Montgomery's girls to grow up with the knowledge that they will no longer be insulated from the world, they must find a way to exist *within* social constraints without compromising their values and intelligence; and they must learn to become self-sufficient. If for Huck and the American male he spoke to, the world is free yet somehow diminishing, for Montgomery's newly modern girls, the world is restraining yet expanding, and the women who read her fiction knew their horizons were broadening.

The Story Girl

The Story Girl is a good example of the way Montgomery's work functions in a sphere that goes beyond fiction for young readers. It captures a timeless world in PEI, as well as showing us the development of a new kind of woman—the Story Girl, who shakes hands 'with an air of frank comradeship, which was very different from the shy, feminine advances' of other girls. The framing device of this collection of stories—the trip of two brothers, Beverley and Felix, to their father's old home on PEI (with 'the glamour of old family traditions and tales . . . lending its magic to all sights and sounds around us') and their adventures with a group of children, including the coquettish Felicity and her opposite number, the master storyteller known to the neighbourhood as the Story Girl (she is another of Montgomery's orphaned girls)—creates a container for remembered tales that show the character of the early days of Prince Edward Island. Of the Story Girl herself, the young boy who narrates the frame tells us:

Never had we heard a voice like hers. Never, in all my life since, have I heard such a voice. I cannot describe it. I might say it was clear; I might say it was sweet; I might say it was vibrant and far-reaching and bell-like; all this would be true, but would give you no real idea of the peculiar quality which made the Story Girl's voice what it was.

If voices had colour, hers would have been like a rainbow. It made words live. Whatever she said became a breathing entity, not a mere verbal statement or utterance.

In 'How Betty Sherman Won a Husband', the Story Girl tells an old curmudgeon (and the other children, who have reluctantly come along) a story about one of his ancestors. In *The Alpine Path* Montgomery explains that the tale is based on the experiences of her own great-grandmother, Betsy Penman. The horse and cutter Donald takes in the Story Girl's narrative were much less romantic in real life: a 'half-broken steer, hitched to a rude, old wood-sled'. And Montgomery adds: 'If Betsy were alive today, I have no doubt, she would be an ardent suffragette. The most advanced feminist could hardly spurn old conventions more effectually than she did when she proposed to David.'

How Betty Sherman Won a Husband

The rest of us did not share the Story Girl's enthusiasm regarding our call on Mr Campbell. We secretly dreaded it. If, as was said, he detested children, who knew what sort of a reception we might meet?

Mr Campbell was a rich, retired farmer, who took life easily. He had visited New York and Boston, Toronto and Montreal; he had even been as far as the Pacific coast.

Therefore he was regarded in Carlisle as a much travelled man; and he was known to be 'well read' and intelligent. But it was also known that Mr Campbell was not always in a good humour. If he liked you there was nothing he would not do for you; if he disliked you—well, you were not left in ignorance of it. In short, we had the impression that Mr Campbell resembled the famous little girl with the curl in the middle of her forehead. 'When he was good, he was very, very good, and when he was bad he was horrid.' What if this were one of his horrid days?

'He can't *do* anything to us, you know,' said the Story Girl. 'He may be rude, but that won't hurt any one but himself.'

'Hard words break no bones,' observed Felix philosophically.

'But they hurt your feelings. *I* am afraid of Mr Campbell,' said Cecily candidly.

'Perhaps we'd better give up and go home,' suggested Dan.

'You can go home if you like,' said the Story Girl scornfully. 'But *I* am going to see Mr Campbell. I know I can manage him. But if I have to go alone, and he gives me anything, I'll keep it all for my own collection, mind you.'

That settled it. We were not going to let the Story Girl get ahead of us in the matter of collecting.

Mr Campbell's housekeeper ushered us into his parlour and left us. Presently Mr Campbell himself was standing in the doorway, looking us over. We took heart of grace. It seemed to be one of his good days, for there was a quizzical smile on his broad, clean-shaven, strongly-featured face. Mr Campbell was a tall man, with a massive head, well thatched with thick, black hair, gray-streaked. He had big, black eyes, with many wrinkles around them, and a thin, firm, long-lipped mouth. We thought him handsome, for an old man.

His gaze wandered over us with uncomplimentary indifference until it fell on the Story Girl, leaning back in an armchair. She looked like a slender red lily in the unstudied grace of her attitude. A spark flashed into Mr Campbell's black eyes.

'Is this a Sunday School deputation?' he inquired rather ironically.

'No. We have come to ask a favour of you,' said the Story Girl.

The magic of her voice worked its will on Mr Campbell, as on all others. He came in, sat down, hooked his thumb into his vest pocket, and smiled at her.

'What is it?' he asked.

'We are collecting for our school library, and we have called to ask you for a contribution,' she replied.

'Why should *I* contribute to your school library?' demanded Mr Campbell.

This was a poser for us. Why should he, indeed? But the Story Girl was quite equal to it. Leaning forward, and throwing an indescribable witchery into tone and eyes and smile, she said,

'Because a lady asks you.'

Mr Campbell chuckled.

'The best of all reasons,' he said. 'But see here, my dear young lady, I'm an old miser and curmudgeon, as you may have heard. I *hate* to part with my money, even for a good reason. And I *never* part with any of it, unless I am to receive some benefit from the expenditure. Now, what earthly good could I get from your three by six school library? None whatever. But I shall make you a fair offer. I have heard from my housekeeper's urchin of a son that you are a 'master hand' to tell stories. Tell me one, here and now. I shall pay you in proportion to the entertainment you afford me. Come now, and do your prettiest.'

There was a fine mockery in his tone that put the Story Girl on her mettle instantly. She sprang to her feet, an amazing change coming over her. Her eyes flashed and burned; crimson spots glowed in her cheeks.

'I shall tell you the story of the Sherman girls, and how Betty Sherman won a husband,' she said.

We gasped. Was the Story Girl crazy? Or had she forgotten that Betty Sherman was Mr Campbell's own great-grandmother, and that her method of winning a husband was not exactly in accordance with maidenly traditions.

But Mr Campbell chuckled again.

'An excellent test,' he said. 'If you can amuse *me* with that story you must be a wonder. I've heard it so often that it has no more interest for me than the alphabet.'

'One cold winter day, eighty years ago,' began the Story Girl without further parley, 'Donald Fraser was sitting by the window of his new house, playing his fiddle for company, and looking out over the white, frozen bay before his door. It was bitter, bitter cold, and a storm was brewing. But, storm, or no storm, Donald meant to go over the bay that evening to see Nancy Sherman. He was thinking of her as he played "Annie Laurie", for Nancy was more beautiful than the lady of the song. "Her face, it is the fairest that e'er the sun shone on," hummed Donald—and oh, he thought so, too! He did not know whether Nancy cared for him or not. He had many rivals. But he knew that if she would not come to be the mistress of his new house no one else ever should. So he sat there that afternoon and dreamed of her, as he played sweet old songs and rollicking jigs on his fiddle.

'While he was playing a sleigh drove up to the door, and Neil Campbell came in. Donald was not overly glad to see him, for he suspected where he was going. Neil Campbell, who was Highland Scotch and lived down at Berwick, was courting Nancy Sherman, too; and, what was far worse, Nancy's father favoured him, because he was a richer man than Donald Fraser. But Donald was not going to show all he thought—Scotch people never do—and he pretended to be very glad to see Neil, and made him heartily welcome.

'Neil sat down by the roaring fire, looking quite well satisfied with himself. It was ten miles from Berwick to the bay shore, and a call at a half way house[1] was just the thing. Then Donald brought out the whisky. They always did that eighty years ago, you know. If you were a woman, you could give your visitors a dish of tea; but if you were a man and did not offer them a "taste" of whisky, you were thought either very mean or very ignorant.

'"You look cold," said Donald, in his great, hearty voice. "Sit nearer the fire, man, and put a bit of warmth in your veins. It's bitter cold the day. And now tell me the Berwick news. Has Jean McLean made up with her man yet? And is it true that Sandy

1 A house situated midway between the beginning and the end of a journey; a convenient stopping point.

McQuarrie is to marry Kate Ferguson? 'Twill be a match now! Sure, with her red hair, Sandy will not be like to lose his bride past finding."

'Neil had plenty of news to tell. And the more whisky he drank the more he told. He didn't notice Donald was not taking much. Neil talked on and on, and of course he soon began to tell things it would have been much wiser not to tell. Finally he told Donald that he was going over the bay to ask Nancy Sherman that very night to marry him. And if she would have him, then Donald and all the folks should see a wedding that *was* a wedding.

'Oh, wasn't Donald taken aback! This was more than he had expected. Neil hadn't been courting Nancy very long, and Donald never dreamed he would propose to her *quite* so soon.

'At first Donald didn't know what to do. He felt sure deep down in his heart, that Nancy liked *him.* She was very shy and modest, but you know a girl can let a man see she likes him without going out of her way. But Donald knew that if Neil proposed first he would have the best chance. Neil was rich and the Shermans were poor, and old Elias Sherman would have the most to say in the matter. If he told Nancy she must take Neil Campbell she would never dream of disobeying him. Old Elias Sherman was a man who had to be obeyed. But if Nancy had only promised some one else first her father would not make her break her word.

'Wasn't it a hard plight for poor Donald? But he was a Scotchman, you know, and it's pretty hard to stick a Scotchman long. Presently a twinkle came into his eyes, for he remembered that all was fair in love and war. So he said to Neil, oh, so persuasively,

'"Have some more, man, have some more. 'Twill keep the heart in you in the teeth of that wind. Help yourself. There's plenty more where that came from."

'Neil didn't want *much* persuasion. He took some more, and said slyly,

'"Is it going over the bay the night that yourself will be doing?"

'Donald shook his head.

'"I had thought of it," he owned, "but it looks a wee like a storm, and my sleigh is at the blacksmith's to be shod. If I went it must be on Black Dan's back, and he likes a canter over the ice in a snow-storm as little as I. His own fireside is the best place for a man to-night, Campbell. Have another taste, man, have another taste."

'Neil went on "tasting", and that sly Donald sat there with a sober face, but laughing eyes, and coaxed him on. At last Neil's head fell forward on his breast, and he was sound asleep. Donald got up, put on his overcoat and cap, and went to the door.

'"May your sleep be long and sweet, man," he said, laughing softly, "and as for the waking, 'twill be betwixt you and me."

'With that he untied Neil's horse, climbed into Neil's sleigh, and tucked Neil's buffalo robe about him.

'"Now, Bess, old girl, do your bonniest," he said. "There's more than you know hangs on your speed. If the Campbell wakes too soon Black Dan could show you a pair of clean heels for all your good start. On, my girl."

'Brown Bess went over the ice like a deer, and Donald kept thinking of what he should say to Nancy—and more still of what she would say to him. *Suppose* he was mistaken. *Suppose* she said "no"!

'"Neil will have the laugh on me then. Sure he's sleeping well. And the snow is coming soon. There'll be a bonny swirl on the bay ere long. I hope no harm will come to the lad if he starts to cross. When he wakes up he'll be in such a fine Highland temper that he'll never stop to think of danger. Well, Bess, old girl, here we are. Now, Donald Fraser, pluck up heart and play the man. Never flinch because a slip of a lass looks scornful at you out of the bonniest dark-blue eyes on earth."

'But in spite of his bold words Donald's heart was thumping as he drove into the Sherman yard. Nancy was there, milking a cow by the stable door, but she stood up when she saw Donald coming. Oh, she was very beautiful! Her hair was like a skein of golden silk, and her eyes were as blue as the gulf water when the sun breaks out after a storm. Donald felt more nervous than ever. But he knew he must make the most of his chance. He might not see Nancy alone again before Neil came. He caught her hand and stammered out,

'"Nan, lass, I love you. You may think 'tis a hasty wooing, but that's a story I can tell you later maybe. I know well I'm not worthy of you, but if true love could make a man worthy there'd be none before me. Will you have me, Nan?"

'Nancy didn't *say* she would have him. She just *looked* it, and Donald kissed her right there in the snow.

'The next morning the storm was over. Donald knew Neil must be soon on his track. He did not want to make the Sherman house the scene of a quarrel, so he resolved to get away before the Campbell came. He persuaded Nancy to go with him to visit some friends in another settlement. As he brought Neil's sleigh up to the door he saw a black speck far out on the bay and laughed.

'"Black Dan goes well, but he'll not be quick enough," he said.

'Half an hour later Neil Campbell rushed into the Sherman kitchen and oh, how angry he was! There was nobody there but Betty Sherman, and Betty was not afraid of him. She was never afraid of anybody. She was very handsome, with hair as brown as October nuts and black eyes and crimson cheeks; and she had always been in love with Neil Campbell herself.

'"Good morning, Mr Campbell," she said, with a toss of her head. "It's early abroad you are. And on Black Dan, no less! Was I mistaken in thinking that Donald Fraser said once that his favourite horse should never be backed by any man but him? But doubtless a fair exchange is no robbery, and Brown Bess is a good mare in her way."

'"Where is Donald Fraser?" said Neil, shaking his fist. "It's him I'm seeking, and it's him I will be finding. Where is he, Betty Sherman?"

'"Donald Fraser is far enough away by this time," mocked Betty. "He is a prudent fellow, and has some quickness of wit under that sandy thatch of his. He came here last night at sunset, with a horse and sleigh not his own, or lately gotten, and he asked Nan in the stable yard to marry him. Did a man ask *me* to marry him at the cow's side, with a milking pail in my hand, it's a cold answer he'd get for his pains. But Nan thought differently, and they sat late together last night, and 'twas a bonny story Nan wakened me to hear when she came to bed—the story of a braw[2] lover who let his secret out

2 Brave, splendid, worthy (Scottish).

when the whisky was above the wit, and then fell asleep while his rival was away to woo and win his lass. Did you ever hear a like story, Mr Campbell?"

'"Oh, yes," said Neil fiercely. "It is laughing at me over the country side and telling that story that Donald Fraser will be doing, is it? But when I meet him it is not laughing he will be doing. Oh, no. There will be another story to tell!"

'"Now, don't meddle with the man," cried Betty. "What a state to be in because one good-looking lass likes sandy hair and gray eyes better than Highland black and blue! You have not the spirit of a wren, Neil Campbell. Were I you, I would show Donald Fraser that I could woo and win a lass as speedily as any Lowlander of them all; that I would! There's many a girl would gladly say 'yes' for your asking. And here stands one! Why not marry *me*, Neil Campbell? Folks say I'm as bonny as Nan—and I could love you as well as Nan loves her Donald—ay, and ten times better!"

'What do you suppose the Campbell did? Why, just the thing he ought to have done. He took Betty at her word on the spot; and there was a double wedding soon after. And it is said that Neil and Betty were the happiest couple in the world—happier even than Donald and Nancy. So all was well because it ended well!'

The Story Girl curtsied until her silken skirts swept the floor. Then she flung herself in her chair and looked at Mr Campbell, flushed, triumphant, daring.

The story was old to us. It had once been published in a Charlottetown paper, and we had read in Aunt Olivia's scrapbook, where the Story Girl had learned it. But we had listened entranced. I have written down the bare words of the story, as she told it; but I can never reproduce the charm and colour and spirit she infused into it. It *lived* for us. Donald and Neil, Nancy and Betty, were there in that room with us. We saw the flashes of expression on their faces, we heard their voices, angry or tender, mocking or merry, in Lowland and Highland accent. We realized all the mingled coquetry and feeling and defiance and archness in Betty Sherman's daring speech. We had even forgotten all about Mr Campbell.

That gentlemen, in silence, took out his wallet, extracted a note therefrom, and handed it gravely to the Story Girl.

'There are five dollars for you,' he said, 'and your story was well worth it. You *are* a wonder. Some day you will make the world realize it. I've been about a bit, and heard some good things, but I've never enjoyed anything more than that threadbare old story I heard in my cradle. And now, will you do me a favour?'

'Of course,' said the delighted Story Girl.

'Recite the multiplication table for me,' said Mr Campbell.

We stared. Well might Mr Campbell be called eccentric. What on earth did he want the multiplication table recited for? Even the Story Girl was surprised. But she began promptly, with twice one and went through it to twelve times twelve. She repeated it simply, but her voice changed from one tone to another as each in succession grew tired. We had never dreamed that there was so much in the multiplication table. As she announced it, the fact that three times three was nine was exquisitely ridiculous, five times six almost brought tears to our eyes, eight times seven was the most tragic and frightful thing ever heard of, and twelve times twelve rang like a trumpet call to victory.

Mr Campbell nodded his satisfaction.

'I thought you could do it,' he said. 'The other day I found this statement in a book. "Her voice would have made the multiplication table charming!" I thought of it when I heard yours. I didn't believe it before, but I do now.'

Then he let us go.

'You see,' said the Story Girl as we went home, 'you need never be afraid of people.'

'But we are not all Story Girls,' said Cecily.

That night we heard Felicity talking to Cecily in their room.

'Mr Campbell never noticed one of us except the Story Girl,' she said, 'but if *I* had put on *my* best dress as she did maybe she wouldn't have taken all the attention.'

'Could you ever do what Betty Sherman did, do you suppose?' asked Cecily absently.

'No; but I believe the Story Girl could,' answered Felicity rather snappishly.

1911

Frederick Philip Grove

1879–1948

Frederick Philip Grove was a writer devoted not only to the idea of literary realism—that is, to the depiction of fictional characters, events, and milieus in such an unidealized way as to convince the reader that the narrative was based in real life and was objective and accurate—but to applying such 'realism' to the presentation of his own life story. His two apparently autobiographical books, *A Search for America* (1927) and *In Search of Myself* (1946; it received the Governor General's Award for non-fiction) were regarded as generally accurate accounts when they were published. They are now, however, recognized as more fiction than fact.

According to *In Search of Myself*, Grove was born in 1871 in Russia of mixed Swedish, Scottish, and English descent, and was educated in Paris, Munich, and Rome. The son of a wealthy Swedish landowner, he came to North America in 1891, and, after working for some months as a waiter in Toronto, began an odyssey that carried him across the North American continent in a twenty-year search for an identity and a true home. In *A Search for America* he describes how, drawn by the American myth of equal opportunity, his search became a quest for an idealized 'America' as defined by Lincoln and Thoreau, which paradoxically leads him in the end to choose Canada, finding it the place in North America where the positive values of an agrarian order still endured, as opposed to the 'graft . . . cruelty . . . failure' that, by the beginning of the twentieth century, seemed to him to have corrupted a once noble American way of living.

Grove's 'realist' presentation of himself as a simple man who, through difficult experience, comes to find a simple and healthful rural life, one where hard work and moral integrity are their own reward, was in sharp contrast to the more romantic existence we now know that he himself led as a young man. In 1973 Douglas O. Spettigue's biography, *F.P.G.: The European Years*, revealed the background of the man who had transformed himself into Frederick Philip Grove. Spettigue discovered that his name before he came to North America was Felix Paul Greve, and that he had been born—eight years later than 'Grove'—in Radomno, a German town on the Russian border. Greve was raised in Hamburg and educated in the famous Gymnasium Johanneum, and attended universities in Bonn and Munich—where he studied classical philology and archaeology and was part of several of the literary circles that blossomed in early twentieth-century Germany. Though his literary interests brought him a marginal living translating English and French texts into German, he was an unprincipled young man who deceitfully borrowed large sums from friends (one such incident led to his serving a year in prison for fraud) and who double-sold at least one of his translations to an unsuspecting publisher. During this period he formed a triangular relationship with Else and August Endell in which the three lived together in Switzerland, France, and Berlin.

While in Europe he published two poetic works—*Wanderungen* (1902), a book of poems, and, in the same year, *Helena and Damon*, a verse drama—and two novels, *Fanny Essler* (1905) and *Mauremeister Ihles Haus* (1906). When, in 1909, Greve's financial practices appeared to be catching up with him again, he faked a suicide, adopted a new name, and fled to the United States, where Else followed him a year later. He seems to have lived with her for a while on a farm in Kentucky, before leaving her in 1911 and emerging in Manitoba, as Grove, in 1912. Else, for her part, made her way to New York, married again, and became a well-known participant in the avant-garde Dada movement, which celebrated artistic nonsense.

Grove chose a very different life from the one Else found. In Manitoba he became a teacher; married a fellow teacher, Catherine Wiens, in 1914; and attended the University of Manitoba part-time, graduating in 1922 with a BA in French and German. As early as 1914 he had become part of the German-Canadian community, publishing an essay in the German-language newspaper *Der Nordwesten.* Although he never entirely lost his European identity or his connections to its culture (he and André Gide conducted a long correspondence), the Canadian perception was not that his was the writing of an immigrant, but that of a pioneer. His early non-fiction accounts of his life in Manitoba—*Over Prairie Trails* (1922) and *The Turn of the Year* (1923)—and his four prairie novels—*Settlers of the Marsh* (1925), *Our Daily Bread* (1928), *Yoke of Life* (1930), and *Fruits of the Earth* (1933)—show us why his commitment to a realistic, unsentimental treatment of prairie life and his deliberate use of language that doesn't strive for literary elegance made Grove one of the founders of prairie realism, a mode of writing that exerted a powerful influence on twentieth-century Canadian fiction.

As with early realists in Europe and America, the frankness of his fiction got him into trouble with the moral arbiters of his time: in particular, *Settlers of the Marsh* was condemned as pornographic. The part of the novel considered most offensive—a striking passage about a prairie wife who deliberately induces abortions by engaging in punishing work—now seems to readers simply one of the many instances in which Grove was responding compassionately and sensitively to the suffering and deprivation that was endured by women on lonely northern farms.

In his depiction of pioneer men Grove was more ambivalent. He showed that in the monumental task of clearing the land there lay the possibility of acts of noble stoicism and even grandeur, and that the common materials of daily rural life could therefore be given epic sweep, even take on mythic dimensions. But he also depicted the ways in which the sense of a heroic contest with the environment could lead men to great folly and the loss of an inner life.

Grove and his wife had one daughter, Phyllis May, who died of appendicitis in 1927, shortly before she was twelve. Two years later, Grove quit teaching and moved to Ontario to become a full-time writer. The Groves settled first in Ottawa, where he founded the short-lived Ariston Press and where their son Leonard was born, and then on a farm north of Simcoe. Although he never gained the financial security he sought, Grove continued to write and publish until he died.

All of Grove's prairie writing deals in some ways with change—whether the changing aspects of the natural cycle or the tremendous social and technological transformations that were affecting the fabric of life around him. In *Two Generations* (1939) and *The Master of the Mill* (1944), the two novels set in Ontario after he moved there, the difficult demands of pioneer life are absent as a subject, but the way technological change and new economic structures disrupt the family and produce social conflicts becomes even more important. In particular, *The Master of the Mill* offers a trenchant critique of monopoly capitalism.

Grove's last novel, *Consider Her Ways*, is a social satire in the form of an allegory about ants: published in 1947, the year before his death, it marked a departure from his realistic mode. His other writing includes a selection of short stories edited by Desmond Pacey, *Tales from the Margin* (1971), and a collection of his speeches, *It Needs to be Said* (1929). In those, Grove emphasizes his commitment to an objective realism in opposition to romance, and explains his tragic view of life: 'It remains my impression—as, American authors excepted, it is the universal verdict of mankind—that all of us who conceive a great aim must necessarily fail and fall short of achieving it.' The last of the pieces collected there, 'Nationhood', was a speech Grove gave to more than twenty Canadian Clubs while travelling across Canada; in it he argued that Canada was achieving real nationhood at last, that it had to resist the influence of the US, and that there was a distinctive Canadian character, which could best be seen among 'plain, rough people of the prairies'.

The sketch that follows is one of the seven that make up *Over Prairie Trails*. Each tells the story of one of Grove's weekend trips from the school where he taught to the house where his wife and daughter waited. In the author's preface, Grove wrote:

> *I procured a buggy and horse and went 'home' on Fridays, after school was over, to return to my town on Sunday evening—covering thus, while the season was clement and allowed straight cross-country driving, coming and going, a distance of sixty-eight miles. Beginning with the second week of January this distance was raised to ninety miles because . . . the straight cross-country roads became impassable through snow.*
>
> *These drives, the fastest of which was made in somewhat over four hours and the longest of which took me nearly eleven . . . soon became what made my life worth living. . . .*
>
> *I made thirty-six of these trips: seventy-two drives in all. I think I could still rehearse every smallest incident of every single one of them. With all their weirdness, with all their sometimes dangerous adventure—most of them were made at night, and with hardly ever any regard being paid to the weather or to the state of the roads—they stand out in the vast array of memorable trifles that constitute the story of my life as among the most memorable ones. Seven drives seem, as it were, lifted above the mass of others as worthy to be described in some detail.*

'Snow' is an account of the most difficult of these trips, a heroic contest against a hostile climate; it is an excellent example of Grove's careful detailing of the northern Manitoba milieu, while using his close observations to suggest larger ideas.

Snow[1]

The blizzard started on Wednesday morning. It was that rather common, truly western combination of a heavy snowstorm with a blinding northern gale—such as piles the snow in hills and mountains and makes walking next to impossible.

I cannot exactly say that I viewed it with unmingled joy. There were special reasons for that. It was the second week in January; when I had left 'home' the Sunday before, I had been feeling rather bad; so my wife would worry a good deal, especially

1 'Snow', the fourth sketch in *Over Prairie Trails*, is entirely different from the Grove short story of the same title.

if I did not come at all. I knew there was such a thing as its becoming quite impossible to make the drive. I had been lost in a blizzard once or twice before in my lifetime. And yet, so long as there was the least chance that horse-power and human will-power combined might pull me through at all, I was determined to make or anyway to try it.

At noon I heard the first dismal warning. For some reason or other I had to go down into the basement of the school. The janitor, a highly efficient but exceedingly bad-humoured cockney, who was dissatisfied with all things Canadian because 'in the old country we do things differently'—whose sharp tongue was feared by many, and who once remarked to a lady teacher in the most casual way, 'If you *was* a lidy, I'd wipe my boot on you!'—this selfsame janitor, standing by the furnace, turned slowly around, showed his pale and hollow-eyed face, and smiled a withering and commiserating smile. 'Ye won't go north this week,' he remarked—not without sympathy, for somehow he had taken a liking to me, which even prompted him off and on to favour me with caustic expressions of what he thought of the school board and the leading citizens of the town. I, of course, never encouraged him in his communicativeness which seemed to be just what he would expect, and no rebuff ever goaded him into the slightest show of resentment. 'We'll see,' I said briefly. 'Well, Sir,' he repeated apodeictically,[2] 'ye won't.' I smiled and went out.

But in my classroom I looked from the window across the street. Not even in broad daylight could you see the opposite houses or trees. And I knew that, once a storm like that sets in, it is apt to continue for days at a stretch. It was one of those orgies in which Titan Wind indulges ever so often on our western prairies. I certainly needed something to encourage me, and so, before leaving the building, I went upstairs to the third story and looked through a window which faced north. But, though I was now above the drifting layer, I could not see very far here either; the snowflakes were small and like little round granules, hitting the panes of the windows with little sounds of 'ping-ping'; and they came, driven by a relentless gale, in such numbers that they blotted out whatever was more than two or three hundred yards away.

The inhabitant of the middle latitudes of this continent has no data to picture to himself what a snowstorm in the north may be. To him snow is something benign that comes soft-footedly over night, and on the most silent wings like an owl, something that suggests the sleep of Nature rather than its battles. The further south you go, the more, of course, snow loses of its aggressive character.

At the dinner table in the hotel I heard a few more disheartening words. But after four I defiantly got my tarpaulin out and carried it to the stable. If I had to run the risk of getting lost, at least I was going to prepare for it. I had once stayed out, snowbound, for a day and a half, nearly without food and altogether without shelter; and I was not going to get thus caught again. I also carefully overhauled my cutter.[3] Not a bolt but I tested it with a wrench; and before the stores were closed, I bought myself enough canned goods to feed me for a week should through any untoward accident the need arise. I always carried a little alcohol stove, and with my tarpaulin I could convert

2 As if based on incontrovertible evidence.
3 A light horse-drawn sleigh.

my cutter within three minutes into a windproof tent. Cramped quarters, to be sure, but better than being given over to the wind at thirty below!

More than any remark on the part of friends or acquaintances one fact depressed me when I went home. There was not a team in town which had come in from the country. The streets were deserted: the stores were empty. The north wind and the snow had the town to themselves.

On Thursday the weather was unchanged. On the way to the school I had to scale a snowdrift thrown up to a height of nearly six feet, and, though it was beginning to harden, from its own weight and the pressure of the wind, I still broke in at every step and found the task tiring in the extreme. I did my work, of course, as if nothing oppressed me, but in my heart I was beginning to face the possibility that, even if I tried, I might fail to reach my goal. The day passed by. At noon the school-children, the teachers, and a few people hurrying to the post-office for the mail lent a fleeting appearance of life to the street. It nearly cheered me; but soon after four the whole town again took on that deserted look which reminded me of an abandoned mining camp. The lights in the store windows had something artificial about them, as if they were merely painted on the canvas-wings of a stage-setting. Not a team came in all day.

On Friday morning the same. Burroughs[4] would have said that the weather had gone into a rut. Still the wind whistled and howled through the bleak, dark, hollow dawn; the snow kept coming down and piling up, as if it could not be any otherwise. And as if to give notice of its intentions, the drift had completely closed up my front door. I fought my way to the school and thought things over. My wife and I had agreed, if ever the weather should be so bad that there was danger in going at night, I was to wait till Saturday morning and go by daylight. Neither one of us ever mentioned the possibility of giving the attempt up altogether. My wife probably understood that I would not bind myself by any such promise. Now even on this Friday I should have liked to go by night, if for no other reason, then for the experience's sake; but I reflected that I might get lost and not reach home at all. The horses knew the road—so long as there was any road; but there was none now. I felt it would not be fair to wife and child. So, reluctantly and with much hesitation, but definitely at last, I made up my mind that I was going to wait till morning. My cutter was ready—I had seen to that on Wednesday. As soon as the storm had set in, I had instinctively started to work in order to frustrate its designs.

At noon I met in front of the post-office a charming lady who with her husband and a young Anglican curate constituted about the only circle of real friends I had in town. 'Why!' I exclaimed, 'what takes you out into this storm, Mrs ______?' 'The desire', she gasped against the wind and yet in her inimitable way, as if she were asking a favour, 'to have you come to our house for tea, my friend. You surely are not going this week?' 'I am going to go to-morrow morning at seven,' I said. 'But I shall be delighted to have tea with you and Mr ______.' I read her at a glance. She knew that in not going out at night I should suffer—she wished to help me over the evening, so I should not feel too much thwarted, too helpless, and too lonesome. She smiled.

4 John Burroughs (1837–1921), a popular and prolific American nature writer to whom Grove alludes several times in *Over Prairie Trails*.

'You really want to go? But I must not keep you. At six, if you please.' And we went our ways without a salute, for none was possible at this gale-swept corner.

After four o'clock I took word to the stable to have my horses fed and harnessed by seven in the morning. The hostler[5] had a tale to tell. 'You going out north?' he enquired although he knew perfectly well I was. 'Of course,' I replied. 'Well,' he went on, 'a man came in from ten miles out; he was half dead; come, look at his horses! He says, in places the snow is over the telephone posts.' 'I'll try it anyway,' I said. 'Just have the team ready. I know what I can ask my horses to do. If it cannot be done, I shall turn back, that is all.'

When I stepped outside again, the wind seemed bent upon shaking the strongest faith. I went home to my house across the bridge and dressed. As soon as I was ready, I allowed myself to be swept past stable, past hotel and post-office till I reached the side street which led to the house where I was to be the guest.

How sheltered, homelike, and protected everything looked inside. The hostess, as usual, was radiantly amiable. The host settled back after supper to talk old country. The Channel Islands, the French Coast, Kent and London—those were from common knowledge our most frequently recurring topics. Both host and hostess, that was easy to see, were bent upon beguiling the hours of their rather dark-humoured guest. But the howling gale outside was stronger than their good intentions. It was not very long before the conversation got around—reverted, so it seemed—to stories of storms, or being lost, of nearly freezing. The boys were sitting with wide eager eyes, afraid they might be sent to bed before the feast of yarns was over. I told one or two of my most thrilling escapes, the host contributed a few more, and even the hostess had had an experience, driving on top of a railroad track for several miles, I believe, with a train, snowbound, behind her. I leaned over. 'Mrs ______,' I said, 'do not try to dissuade me. I am sorry to say it, but it is useless. I am bound to go.' 'Well,' she said, 'I wish you would not.' 'Thanks,' I replied and looked at my watch. It was two o'clock. 'There is only one thing wrong with coming to have tea in this home,' I continued and smiled; 'it is so hard to say good-bye.'

I carefully lighted my lantern and got into my wraps. The wind was howling dismally outside. For a moment we stood in the hall, shaking hands and paying the usual compliments; then one of the boys opened the door for me; and in stepping out I had one of the greatest surprises. Not far from the western edge of the world there stood the setting half-moon in a cloudless sky; myriads of stars were dusted over the vast, dark blue expanse, twinkling and blazing at their liveliest. And though the wind still whistled and shrieked and rattled, no snow came down, and not much seemed to drift. I pointed to the sky, smiled, nodded, and closed the door. As far as the drifting of the snow went, I was mistaken, as I found out when I turned to the north, into the less sheltered street, past the post-office, hotel, and stable. In front of a store I stopped to read a thermometer which I had found halfways reliable the year before. It read minus thirty-two degrees. . . .[6]

5 Stableman.

6 The ellipsis mark is frequently used by Grove to punctuate these sketches. There are no editorial deletions.

It was still dark, of course, when I left the house on Saturday morning to be on my way. Also, it was cold, bitterly cold, but there was very little wind. In crossing the bridge which was swept nearly clean of snow I noticed a small, but somehow ominous-looking drift at the southern end. It had such a disturbed, lashed-up appearance. The snow was still loose, yet packed just hard enough to have a certain degree of toughness. You could no longer swing your foot through it: had you run into it at any great speed, you would have fallen; but as yet it was not hard enough to carry you. I knew that kind of a drift; it is treacherous. On a later drive one just like it, only built on a vastly larger scale, was to lead to the first of a series of little accidents which finally shattered my nerve. That was the only time that my temerity failed me. I shall tell you about that drive later on.[7]

At the stable I went about my preparations in a leisurely way. I knew that a supreme test was ahead of myself and the horses, and I meant to have daylight for tackling it. Once more I went over the most important bolts; once more I felt and pulled at every strap in the harness. I had a Clark footwarmer[8] and made sure that it functioned properly. I pulled the flaps of my military fur cap down over neck, ears, and cheeks. I tucked a pillow under the sweater over my chest and made sure that my leggings clasped my furlined moccasins well. Then, to prevent my coat from opening even under the stress of motion, just before I got into the cutter, I tied a rope around my waist.

The hostler brought the horses into the shed. They pawed the floor and snorted with impatience. While I rolled my robes about my legs and drew the canvas curtain over the front part of the box, I weighed Dan with my eyes. I had no fear for Peter, but Dan would have to show to-day that he deserved the way I had fed and nursed him. Like a chain, the strength of which is measured by the strength of its weakest link, my team was measured by Dan's pulling power and endurance. But he looked good to me as he danced across the pole and threw his head, biting back at Peter who was teasing him.

The hostler was morose and in a biting mood. Every motion of his seemed to say, 'What is the use of all this? No teamster would go out on a long drive in this weather, till the snow has settled down; and here a schoolmaster wants to try it.'

At last he pushed the slide doors aside, and we swung out. I held the horses tight and drove them into that little drift at the bridge to slow them down right from the start.

The dawn was white, but with a strictly localised angry glow where the sun was still hidden below the horizon. In a very few minutes he would be up, and I counted on making that first mile just before he appeared.

This mile is a wide, well levelled road, but ever so often, at intervals of maybe fifty to sixty yards, steep and long promontories of snow had been flung across—some of them five to six feet high. They started at the edge of the field to the left where a rank growth of shrubby weeds gave shelter for the snow to pile in. Their base, alongside the fence, was broad, and they tapered across the road, with a perfectly flat top, and with concave sides of a most delicate, smooth, and finished looking curve, till at last they ran out into a sharp point, mostly beyond the road on the field to the right.

7 In the seventh and concluding sketch, 'Skies and Scares', Grove tells this story of how 'the cumulative effect of three mishaps, one following the other,' combined with 'the aspect of the skies' and 'broke my nerve that night'.

8 A kind of metal box containing coal.

The wind plays strange pranks with snow; snow is the most plastic medium it has to mould into images and symbols of its moods. Here one of these promontories would slope down, and the very next one would slope upward as it advanced across the open space. In every case there had been two walls, as it were, of furious blow, and between the two a lane of comparative calm, caused by the shelter of a clump of brush or weeds, in which the snow had taken refuge from the wind's rough and savage play. Between these capes of snow there was an occasional bare patch of clean swept ground. Altogether there was an impression of barren, wild, bitter-cold windiness about the aspect that did not fail to awe my mind; it looked inhospitable, merciless, and cruelly playful.

As yet the horses seemed to take only delight in dashing through the drifts, so that the powdery crystals flew aloft and dusted me all over. I peered across the field to the left, and a curious sight struck me. There was apparently no steady wind at all, but here and there, and every now and then a little swirl of snow would rise and fall again. Every one of them looked for all the world like a rabbit reconnoitring in deep grass. It jumps up on its hindlegs, while running, peers out, and settles down again. It was as if the snow meant to have a look at me, the interloper at such an early morning hour. The snow was so utterly dry that it obeyed the lightest breath; and whatever there was of motion in the air, could not amount to more than a cat's-paw's sudden reach.

At the exact moment when the snow where it stood up highest became suffused with a rose-red tint from the rising sun, I arrived at the turn to the correction line.[9] Had I been a novice at the work I was engaged in, the sight that met my eye might well have daunted me. Such drifts as I saw here should be broken by drivers who have short hauls to make before the long distance traveller attempts them. From the fence on the north side of the road a smoothly curved expanse covered the whole of the road allowance and gently sloped down into the field at my left. Its north edge stood like a cliff, the exact height of the fence, four feet I should say. In the centre it rose to probably six feet and then fell very gradually, whaleback fashion, to the south. Not one of the fence posts to the left was visible. The slow emergence of the tops of these fence posts became during the following week, when I drove out here daily, a measure for me of the settling down of the drift. I believe I can say from my observations that if no new snow falls or drifts in, and if no very considerable evaporation takes place, a newly piled snowdrift, undisturbed except by wind-pressure, will finally settle down to about from one-third to one-half of its original height, according to the pressure of the wind that was behind the snow when it first was thrown down. After it has, in this contracting process, reached two-thirds of its first height, it can usually be relied upon to carry horse and man.

The surface of this drift, which covered a ditch besides the grade and its grassy flanks, showed that curious appearance that we also find in the glaciated surfaces of granite rock and which, in them, geologists call exfoliation. In the case of rock it is the consequence of extreme changes in temperature. The surface sheet in expanding under sudden heat detaches itself in large, leaflike layers. In front of my wife's cottage up

9 A correction made along the longitudinal line of a survey to compensate for the curvature of the earth. On the Prairies, roads are generally laid out along survey lines; north-south roads, therefore, turn east-west for a short distance along the correction line.

north there lay an exfoliated rock in which I watched the process for a number of years. In snow, of course, the origin of this appearance is entirely different; snow is laid down in layers by the waves in the wind. 'Adfoliation' would be a more nearly correct appellation of the process. But from the analogy of the appearance I shall retain the more common word and call it exfoliation. Layers upon layers of paperlike sheets are superimposed upon each other, their edges often 'cropping out' on sloping surfaces; and since these edges, according to the curvatures of the surfaces, run in wavy lines, the total aspect is very often that of 'moire' silk.

I knew the road as well as I had ever known a road. In summer there was a grassy expanse some thirty feet wide to the north; then followed the grade, flanked to the south by a ditch; and the tangle of weeds and small brush beyond reached right up to the other fence. I had to stay on or rather above the grade; so I stood up and selected the exact spot where to tackle it. Later, I knew, this drift would be harmless enough; there was sufficient local traffic here to establish a well-packed trail. At present, however, it still seemed a formidable task for a team that was to pull me over thirty-three miles or more. Besides it was a first test for my horses; I did not know yet how they would behave in snow.

But we went at it. For a moment things happened too fast for me to watch details. The horses plunged wildly and reared on their hind feet in a panic, straining against each other, pulling apart, going down underneath the pole, trying to turn and retrace their steps. And meanwhile the cutter went sharply up at first, as if on the crest of a wave, then toppled over into a hole made by Dan, and altogether behaved like a boat tossed on a stormy sea. Then order returned into the chaos. I had the lines short, wrapped doubled and treble around my wrists; my feet stood braced in the corner of the box, knees touching the dashboard; my robes slipped down. I spoke to the horses in a soft, quiet, purring voice; and at last I pulled in. Peter hated to stand. I held him. Then I looked back. This first wild plunge had taken us a matter of two hundred yards into the drift. Peter pulled and champed at the bit; the horses were sinking nearly out of sight. But I knew that many and many a time in the future I should have to go through just this and that from the beginning I must train the horses to tackle it right. So, in spite of my aching wrists I kept them standing till I thought that they were fully breathed. Then I relaxed my pull the slightest bit and clicked my tongue. 'Good,' I thought, 'they are pulling together!' And I managed to hold them in line. They reared and plunged again like drowning things in their last agony, but they no longer clashed against nor pulled away from each other. I measured the distance with my eye. Another two hundred yards or thereabout, and I pulled them in again. Thus we stopped altogether four times. The horses were steaming when we got through this drift which was exactly half a mile long; my cutter was packed level full with slabs and clods of snow; and I was pretty well exhausted myself.

'If there is very much of this', I thought for the moment, 'I may not be able to make it.' But then I knew that a north-south road will drift in badly only under exceptional circumstances. It is the east-west grades that are most apt to give trouble. Not that I minded my part of it, but I did not mean to kill my horses. I had sized them up in their behaviour towards snow. Peter, as I had expected, was excitable. It was hard to recognize in him just now, as he walked quietly along, the uproar of playing muscle and rearing limbs that he had been when we first struck the snow. That was well and good for a short, supreme effort; but not even for Peter would it do in the long, endless drifts which I had to expect. Dan was quieter, but he did not have Peter's staying power; in fact, he was not really a horse for the road. Strange, in spite of his usual keenness on the level road, he seemed to show more snow sense in the drift. This was to be amply confirmed in the future. Whenever an accident happened, it was Peter's fault. As you will see if you read on, Dan once lay quiet when Peter stood right on top of him.

On this road north I found the same 'promontories' that had been such a feature of the first one, flung across from the northwest to the southeast. Since the clumps of shrubs to the left were larger here, and more numerous, too, the drifts occasionally also were larger and higher; but not one of them was such that the horses could not clear it with one or two leaps. The sun was climbing, the air was winter-clear and still. None of the farms which I passed showed the slightest sign of life. I had wrapped up again and sat in comparative comfort and at ease, enjoying the clear sparkle and glitter of the virgin snow. It was not till considerably later that the real significance of the landscape dawned upon my consciousness. Still there was even now in my thoughts a speculative undertone. Subconsciously I wondered what might be ahead of me.

We made Bell's corner[10] in good time. The mile to the west proved easy. There were drifts, it is true, and the going was heavy, but at no place did the snow for any length of time reach higher than the horses' hocks. We turned to the north again, and here, for a while, the road was very good indeed; the underbrush to the left, on those expanses of wild land, had fettered, as it were, the feet of the wind. The snow was held everywhere, and very little of it had drifted. Only one spot I remember where a clump of Russian willow close to the trail had offered shelter enough to allow the wind in the narrow roadgap to a depth of maybe eight or nine feet; but here it was easy to go around to the west. Without any further incident we reached the point where the useless, supernumerary fence post had caught my eye on my first trip out. I had made nearly eight miles now.

But right here I was to get my first inkling of sights that might shatter my nerve. You may remember that a grove of tall poplars ran to the east, skirted along its southern edge by a road and a long line of telephone posts. Now here, in this shelter of the poplars, the snow from the more or less level and unsheltered spaces to the northwest had piled in indeed. It sloped up to the east; and never shall I forget what I beheld.

The first of the posts stood a foot in snow; at the second one the drift reached six or seven feet up; the next one looked only half as long as the first one, and you might have imagined, standing as it did on a sloping hillside, that it had intentionally been made so much shorter than the others; but at the bottom of the visible part the wind, in sweeping around the pole, had scooped out a funnel-shaped crater which seemed to open into the very earth like a sinkhole. The next pole stood like a giant buried up to this chest and looked singularly helpless and footbound; and the last one I saw showed

10 The corner of a farm that served Grove as a landmark, signalling the completion of the first leg of his journey, a distance of about six miles from town. Later in this sketch he mentions other landmarks by which he judges his progress, such as the 'hovel', 'half way farms', and the 'White Range Line House'.

just its crossbar with three glassy, green insulators above the mountain of snow. The whole surface of this gigantic drift showed again that 'exfoliated' appearance which I have described. Strange to say, this very exfoliation gave it something of a quite peculiarly desolate aspect. It looked so harsh, so millennial-old, so antediluvian and pre-adamic! I still remember with particular distinctness the slight dizziness that overcame me, the sinking feeling in my heart, the awe, and the foreboding that I had challenged a force in Nature which might defy all tireless effort and the most fearless heart.

So the hostler had not been fibbing after all!

But not for a moment did I think of turning back. I am fatalistic in temperament. What is to be, is to be, that is not my outlook.[11] If at last we should get bound up in a drift, well and good, I should then see what the next move would have to be. While the wind blows, snow drifts; while my horses could walk and I was not disabled, my road led north, not south. Like the snow I obeyed the laws of my nature. So far the road was good, and we swung along.

Somewhere around here a field presented a curious view. Its crop had not been harvested; it still stood in stooks.[12] But from my side I saw nothing of the sheaves—it seemed to be flax, for here and there a flag of loose heads showed at the top. The snow had been blown up from all directions, so it looked, by the counter-currents that set up in the lee of every obstacle. These mounds presented one and all the appearance of cones or pyramids of butter patted into shape by upward strokes made with a spoon. There were the sharp ridges, irregular and erratic, and there were the hollows running up their flanks—exactly as such a cone of butter will show them. And the whole field was dotted with them, as if there were so many fresh graves.

I made the twelve-mile bridge—passing through the cottonwood gate—reached the 'hovel', and dropped into the wilderness again. Here the bigger trees stood strangely bare. Winter reveals the bark and the 'habit'[13] of trees. All ornaments and unessentials have been dropped. The naked skeletons show. I remember how I was more than ever struck by that dappled appearance of the bark of the balm:[14] an olive-green, yellowish hue, ridged and spotted with the black of ancient, overgrown leaf-scars; there was actually something gay about it; these poplars are certainly beautiful winter trees. The aspens were different. Although their stems stood white on white in the snow, that greenish tinge in their white gave them a curious look. From the picture that I carry about in my memory of this morning I cannot help the impression that they looked as if their white were not natural at all; they looked whitewashed! I have often since confirmed this impression when there was snow on the ground.

In the copses of saplings the zigzagging of the boles from twig to twig showed very distinctly, more so, I believe, than to me it had ever done before. How slender and straight they look in their summer garb—now they were stripped, and bone and sinew appeared.

11 The sense of this passage seems to call for this sentence to conclude with the words, '. . . that is my outlook', but Grove's original manuscript does not support an emendation.
12 Sheaves.
13 In botany, the characteristic growth and appearance of a plant.
14 Balsam poplar.

We came to the 'half way farms', and the marsh lay ahead. I watered the horses, and I do not know what made me rest them for a little while, but I did. On the yard of the farm where I had turned in there was not a soul to be seen. Barns and stables were closed—and I noticed that the back door of the dwelling was buried tight by the snow. No doubt everybody preferred the neighbourhood of the fire to the cold outside. While stopping, I faced for the first time the sun. He was high in the sky by now—it was half-past ten—and it suddenly came home to me that there was something relentless, inexorable, cruel, yes, something of a sneer in the pitiless way in which he looked down on the infertile waste around. Unaccountably two Greek words formed on my lips: Homer's Pontos atrygetos—the barren sea.[15] Half an hour later I was to realize the significance of it.

I turned back to the road and north again. For another half mile the fields continued on either side; but somehow they seemed to take on a sinister look. There was more snow on them than I had found on the level land further south; the snow lay more smoothly, again under those 'exfoliated' surface sheets which here, too, gave it an inhuman, primeval look; in the higher sun the vast expanse looked, I suppose, more blindingly white; and nowhere did buildings or thickets seem to emerge. Yet, so long as the grade continued, the going was fair enough.

Then I came to the corner which marked half the distance, and there I stopped. Right in front, where the trail had been and where a ditch had divided off the marsh, a fortress of snow lay now: a seemingly impregnable bulwark, six or seven feet high, with rounded top, fitting descriptions which I had read of the underground bombproofs around Belgian strongholds—those forts which were hammered to pieces by the Germans in their first, heartbreaking forward surge in 1914. There was not a wrinkle in this inverted bowl. There it lay, smooth and slick—curled up in security, as it were, some twenty, thirty feet across; and behind it others, and more of them to the right and to the left. This had been a stretch, covered with brush and bush, willow and poplar thickets; but my eye saw nothing except a mammiferous[16] waste, cruelly white, glittering in the heatless, chuckling sun, and scoffing at me, the intruder. I stood up again and peered out. To the east it seemed as if these buttes of snow were a trifle lower; but maybe the ground underneath also sloped down. I wished I had travelled here more often by daytime, so I might know. As it was, there was nothing to it; I had to tackle the task. And we plunged in.

I had learned something from my first experience in the drift one mile north of town, and I kept my horses well under control. Still, it was a wild enough dash. Peter had lost his footing two or three times and worked himself into a mild panic. But Dan—I could not help admiring the way in which, buried over his back in snow, he would slowly and deliberately rear on his hindfeet and take his bound. For fully five minutes I never saw anything of the horses except their heads. I inferred their motions from the dusting snowcloud that rose above their bodies and settled on myself. And then somehow we emerged. We reached a stretch of ground where the snow was just high enough to cover the hocks of the horses. It was a hollow scooped out by some freak

15 A common Homeric formula in *The Odyssey*.

16 Breast-like.

of the wind. I pulled in, and the horses stood panting. Peter no longer showed any desire to fret and to jump. Both horses apparently felt the wisdom of sparing their strength. They were all white with the frost of their sweat and the spray of the snow. . . .

While I gave them their time, I looked around, and here a lesson came home to me. In the hollow where we stood, the snow did not lie smoothly. A huge obstacle to the northwest, probably a buried clump of brush, had made the wind turn back upon itself, first downward, then, at the bottom of the pit, in a direction opposite to that of the main current above, and finally slantways upward again to the summit of the obstacle, where it rejoined the parent blow. The floor of the hollow was cleanly scooped out and chiselled in low ridges; and these ridges came from the southeast, running their points to the northwest. I learned to look out for this sign, and I verily believe that, had I not learned that lesson right now, I should never have reached the creek which was still four or five miles distant.

The huge mound in the lee of which I was stopping was a matter of two hundred yards away; nearer to it the snow was considerably deeper; and since it presented an appearance very characteristic of Prairie bush-drifts, I shall describe it in some detail. Apparently the winds had first bent over all the stems of the clump; for whenever I saw one of them from the north, it showed a smooth, clean upward sweep. On the south side the snow first fell in a sheer cliff; then there was a hollow which was partly filled by a talus-shaped[17] drift thrown in by the counter currents from the southern pit in which we were stopping; the sides of this talus again showed the marks that reminded of those left by the spoon when butter is roughly stroked into the shape of a pyramid. The interesting parts of the structure consisted in the beetling brow of the cliff and the roof of the cavity underneath. The brow had a honey-combed appearance; the snow had been laid down in layers of varying density (I shall discuss this more fully in the next chapter when we are going to look in on the snow while it is actually at work[18]); and the counter currents that here swept upward in a slanting direction had bitten out the softer layers, leaving a fine network of little ridges which reminded strangely of the delicate fretwork-tracery in wind-sculptured rock—as I had seen it in the Black Hills in South Dakota. This piece of work of the wind is exceedingly short-lived in snow, and it must not be confounded with the honeycombed appearance of those faces of snow cliffs which are 'rotting' by reason of their exposure to the heat of the noonday sun. These latter are coarse, often dirty, and nearly always have something bristling about them which is entirely absent in the sculptures of the wind. The under side of the roof in the cavity looked very much as a very stiff or viscid treacle would look when spread over a meshy surface, as, for instance, over a closely woven netting of wire. The stems and the branches of the bush took the place of the wire, and in their meshes the snow had been pressed through by its own weight, but held together by its curious ductility or tensile strength of which I was to find further evidence soon enough. It thus formed innumerable, blunted little stalactites, but without the corresponding stalagmites which you find in limestone caves or on the north side of buildings when the

17 Like a sloping wall in a fortification, wider at its base than at its top.

18 In the fifth sketch, 'Wind and Waves', Grove describes his return trip to school, taken the next day during a blowing snowstorm—the experience of which he details with the scientific detachment of a naturalist.

snow from the roof thaws and forms icicles and slender cones of ice growing up to meet them from the ground where the trickling drops fall and freeze again.

By the help of these various tokens I had picked my next resting place before we started up again. It was on this second dash that I understood why those Homeric words had come to my lips a while ago. This was indeed like nothing so much as like being out on rough waters and in a troubled sea, with nothing to brace the storm with but a wind-tossed nutshell of a one-man sailing craft. I knew that experience for having outridden many a gale in the mouth of the mighty St Lawrence River. When the snow reached its extreme depth, it gave you the feeling which a drowning man may have when fighting his desperate fight with the salty waves. But more impressive than that was the frequent outer resemblance. The waves of the ocean rise up and reach out and batter against rocks and battlements of the shore, retreating again and ever returning to the assault, covering the obstacles thrown in the way of their progress with thin sheets of licking tongues at least. And if such a high crest wave had suddenly been frozen into solidity, its outline would have mimicked to perfection many a one of the snow shapes that I saw around.

Once the horses had really learned to pull exactly together—and they learned it thoroughly here—our progress was not too bad. Of course, it was not like going on a grade, be it ever so badly drifted in. Here the ground underneath, too, was uneven and overgrown with a veritable entanglement of brush in which often the horses' feet would get caught. As for the road, there was none left, nothing that even by the boldest stretch of imagination could have been considered even as the slightest indication of one. And worst of all, I knew positively that there would be no trail at any time during the winter. I was well aware of the fact that, after it once snowed up, nobody ever crossed this waste between the 'half-way farms' and the 'White Range Line House'. This morning it took me two and a half solid hours to make four miles.

But the ordeal had its reward. Here where the fact that there was snow on the ground, and plenty of it, did no longer need to be sunk into my brain—as soon as it has lost its value as a piece of news and a lesson, I began to enjoy it just as the hunter in India will enjoy the battle of wits when he is pitted against a yellow-black tiger. I began to catch on to the ways of this snow; I began, as it were, to study the mentality of my enemy. Though I never kill, I am after all something of a sportsman. And still another thing gave me back that mental equilibrium which you need in order to see things and to reason calmly about them. Every dash of two hundred yards or so brought me that much near to my goal. Up to the 'half-way farms' I had, as it were, been working uphill: there was more ahead than behind. This was now reversed: there was more behind than ahead, and as yet I did not worry about the return trip.

Now I have already said that snow is the only really plastic element in which the wind can carve the vagaries of its mood and leave a record of at least some permanency. The surface of the sea is a wonderful book to be read with a lightning-quick eye; I do not know anything better to do as a cure for ragged nerves—provided you are a good sailor. But the forms are too fleeting, they change too quickly—so quickly, indeed, that I have never succeeded in so fixing their record upon my memory as to be able to develop one form from the other in descriptive notes. It is that very fact, I believe, upon which hinges the curative value of the sight: you are so completely absorbed by the moment, and all other things fall away. Many and many a day have I lain on my deck chair on board a liner and watched the play of the waves; but the pleasure, which was very great indeed, was momentary; and sometimes, when in an unsympathetic mood, I have since impatiently wondered in what that fascination may have consisted. It was different here. Snow is very nearly as yielding as water and, once it fully responds in its surface to the carving of forces of the wind, it stays—as if frozen into the glittering marble image of its motion. I know few things that are as truly fascinating as the sculptures of the wind in snow; for here you have time and opportunity a-plenty to probe not only into the what, but also into the why. Maybe that one day I shall write down a fuller account of my observations. In this report I shall have to restrict myself to a few indications, for this is not the record of the whims of the wind, but merely the narrative of my drives.

In places, for instance, the rounded, 'bomb-proof'[19] aspect of the expanses would be changed into the distinct contour of gigantic waves with a very fine, very sharp crest-line. The upsweep from the northwest would be ever so slightly convex, and the downward sweep into the trough was always very distinctly concave. This was not the ripple which we find in beach sand. That ripple was there, too, and in places it covered the wide backs of these huge waves all over; but never was it found on the concave side. Occasionally, but rarely, one of these great waves would resemble a large breaker with a curly crest. Here the onward sweep from the northwest had built the snow out, beyond the supporting base, into a thick overhanging ledge which here and there had sagged; but by virtue of that tensile strength and cohesion in snow which I have mentioned already, it still held together and now looked convoluted and ruffled in the most deceiving way. I believe I actually listened for the muffled roar which the breaker makes when its subaqueous part begins to sweep the upward sloping beach. To make this illusion complete, or to break it by the very absurdity and exaggeration of a comparison drawn out too far—I do not know which—there would, every now and then, from the crest of one of these waves, jut out something which closely resembled the wide back of a large fish diving down into the concave side towards the trough. This looked very much like porpoises or dolphins jumping in a heaving sea; only that in my memory picture the real dolphins always jump in the opposite direction, against the run of the waves, bridging the trough.

In other places a fine, exceedingly delicate crest-line would spring up from the high point of some buried obstacle and sweep along in the most graceful curve as far as the eye would carry. I particularly remember one of them, and I could discover no earthy reason for the curvature in it.

Again there would be a triangular—or should I say 'tetrahedral'?—up-sweep from the direction of the wind, ending in a sharp, perfectly plane down-sweep on the south side; and the point of this three-sided but oblique pyramid would hang over like the flap of a tam. There was something of the consistency of very thick cloth about this overhanging flap.

Or an up-slope from the north would end in a long, nearly perpendicular cliffline facing south. And the talus formation which I have mentioned would be perfectly

19 Bomb-shelter.

smooth; but it did not reach quite to the top of the cliff, maybe to within a foot of it. The up-sloping layer from the north would hang out again, with an even brow; but between this smooth cornice and the upper edge of the talus the snow looked as if it had been squeezed out by tremendous pressure from above, like an exceedingly viscid liquid—cooling glue, for instance, which is being squeezed out from between the core and the veneer in a veneering press.

Once I passed close to and south of, two thickets which were completely buried by the snow. Between them a ditch had been scooped out in a very curious fashion. It resembled exactly a winding river bed with its water drained off; it was two or three feet deep, and wherever it turned, its banks were undermined on the 'throw'[20] side by the 'wash' of the furious blow. The analogy between the work of the wind and the work of flowing water constantly obtrudes, especially where this work is one of 'erosion'.

But as flowing water will swing up and down in the most surprising forms where the bed of the river is rough with rocks and throws it into choppy waves which do not seem to move, so the snow was thrown up into the most curious forms where the frozen swamp ground underneath had bubbled, as it were, into phantastic shapes. I remember several places where a perfect circle was formed by a sharp crestline that bounded an hemispherical, crater-like hollow. When steam bubbles up through thick porridge, in its leisurely and impeded way, and the bubble bursts with a clucking sound, then for a moment a crater is formed just like these circular holes; only here in the snow they were on a much larger scale, of course, some of them six to ten feet in diameter.

And again the snow was thrown up into a bulwark, twenty and more feet high, with that always repeating cliff-face to the south, resembling a miniature Gibraltar, with many smaller ones of most curiously similar form on its back: bulwarks upon bulwarks, all lowering to the south. In these the aggressive nature of storm-flung snow was most apparent. They were formidable structures; formidable and intimidating, more through the suggestiveness of their shape than through mere size.

I came to places where the wind had had its moments of frolicsome humour, where it had made grim fun of its own massive and cumbersome and yet so pliable and elastic majesty. It has turned around and around, running with breathless speed, with its tongue lolling out, as it were, and probably yapping and snapping in mocking mimicry of a pup trying to catch its tail; and it had scooped out a spiral trough with overhanging rim. I felt sorry that I had not been there to watch it, because after all, what I saw, was only the dead record of something that had been very much alive and vociferatingly noisy. And in another place it had reared and raised its head like a boa constrictor, ready to strike at its prey; up to the flashing, forked tongue it was there. But one spot I remember, where it looked exactly as if quite consciously it had attempted the outright ludicrous: it had thrown up the snow into the semblance of some formidable animal—more like a gorilla than anything else it looked, a gorilla that stands on its four hands and raises every hair on its back and snarls in order to frighten that which it is afraid of itself—a leopard maybe.

And then I reached the 'White Range Line House'. Curiously enough, there it stood, sheltered by its majestic bluff to the north, as peaceful looking as if there were

20 In geology, a displacement of a bed or strata.

no such thing as that record, which I had crossed, of the uproar and fury of one of the forces of Nature engaged in an orgy. And it looked so empty, too, and so deserted, with never a wisp of smoke curling from its flue-pipe, that for a moment I was tempted to turn in and see whether maybe the lonely dweller was ill. But then I felt as if I could not be burdened with any stranger's worries that day.

The effective shelter of the poplar forest along the creek made itself felt. The last mile to the northeast was peaceful driving. I felt quite cheered, though I walked the horses over the whole of the mile since both began to show signs of wear. The last four miles had been a test to try any living creature's mettle. To me it had been one of the culminating points in that glorious winter, but the horses had lacked the mental stimulus, and even I felt rather exhausted.

On the bridge I stopped, threw the blankets over the horses, and fed. Somehow this seemed to be the best place to do it. There was no snow to speak of, and I did not know yet what might follow. The horses were drooping, and I gave them an additional ten minutes' rest. Then I slowly made ready. I did not really expect serious trouble.

We turned at a walk, and the chasm of the bush road opened up. Instantly I pulled the horses in. What I saw, baffled me for a moment so completely that I just sat there and gasped. There was no road. The trees to both sides were not so overly high, but the snow had piled in level with their tops; the drift looked like a gigantic barricade. It was that fleeting sight of the telephone posts over again, though on a slightly smaller scale; but this time it was in front. Slowly I started to whistle and then looked around. I remembered now. There was newly cut-out road running north past the school which lay embedded in the bush. It had offered a lane to the wind; and the wind, going there, in cramped space, at a doubly furious stride, had picked up and carried along all the loose snow from the grassy glades in its path. The road ended abruptly just north of the drift, where the east-west grade sprang up. When the wind had reached this end of the lane, where the bush ran at right angles to its direction, it had found itself in something like a blind alley, and, sweeping upward, to clear the obstacle, it had dropped every bit of its load into the shelter of the brush, gradually, in the course of three long days, building up a ridge that buried underbrush and trees. I might have known it, of course. I knew enough about snow; all the conditions for an exceptionally large drift were provided for here. But it had not occurred to me, especially after I had found the northern fringe of the marsh so well sheltered. Here I felt for a moment as if all the snow of the universe had piled in. As I said, I was so completely baffled that I could have turned the horses then and there.

But after a minute or two my eyes began to cast about. I turned to the south, right into the dense underbrush and towards the creek which here swept south in a long, flat curve. Peter was always intolerant of anything that moved underfoot. He started to bolt when the dry and hard-frozen stems snapped and broke with reports resembling pistol shots. But since Dan kept quiet, I held Peter well in hand. I went along the drift for maybe three to four hundred yards, reconnoitring. Then the trees began to stand too dense for me to proceed without endangering my cutter. Just beyond I saw the big trough of the creek bed, and though I could not make out how conditions were at its bottom, the drift continued on its southern bank, and in any case it was impossible to cross the hollow. So I turned; I had made up my mind to try the drift.

About a hundred and fifty yards from the point where I had turned off the road there was something like a fold in the flank of the drift. At its foot I stopped. For a moment I tried to explain that fold to myself. This is what I arrived at. North of the drift, just about where the new cut-out joined the east-west grade, there was a small clearing caused by a bush fire which a few years ago had penetrated thus far into this otherwise virgin corner of the forest. Unfortunately it stood so full of charred stumps that it was impossible to get through there. But the main currents of the wind would have free play in this opening, and I knew that, when the blizzard began, it had been blowing from a more northerly quarter than later on, when it veered to the northwest. And though the snow came careering along the lane of the cut-out, that is, from due north, its 'throw' and therefore, the direction of the drift would be determined by the direction of the wind that took charge of it on this clearing. Probably, then, a first, provisional drift whose long axis lay nearly in a north-south line, had been piled up by the first, northerly gale. Later a second larger drift had been superimposed upon it at an angle, with its main axis running from the northwest to the southeast. The fold marked the point where the first, smaller drift still emerged from the second larger one. This reasoning was confirmed by a study of the clearing itself which I came to make two or three weeks after.

Before I called on the horses to give me their very last ounce of strength, I got out of my cutter once more and made sure that my lines were still sound. I trusted my ability to guide the horses even in this crucial test, but I dreaded nothing so much as that the lines might break; and I wanted to guard against any accident. I should mention that, of course, the top of my cutter was down, that the traces of the harness were new, and that the cutter itself during its previous trials had shown an exceptional stability. Once more I thus rested my horses for five minutes; and they seemed to realize what was coming. Their heads were up, their ears were cocked. When I got back into my cutter, I carefully brushed the snow from moccasins and trousers, laid the robe around my feet, adjusted my knees against the dashboard, and tied two big loops into the lines to hold them by.

Then I clicked my tongue. The horses bounded upward in unison. For a moment it looked as if they intended to work through, instead of over, the drift. A wild shower of angular snow-slabs swept in upon me. The cutter reared up and plunged and reared again—and then the view cleared. The snow proved harder than I had anticipated—which bespoke the fury of the blow that had piled it. It did not carry the horses, but neither—once we had reached a height of five or six feet—did they sink beyond their bellies and out of sight. I had no eye for anything except them. What lay to right or left, seemed not to concern me. I watched them work. They went in bounds, working beautifully together. Rhythmically they reared, and rhythmically they plunged. I had dropped back to the seat, holding them with a firm hand, feet braced against the dashboard; and whenever they got ready to rear, I called to them in a low and quiet voice, 'Peter—Dan—now!' And their muscles played with the effort of desperation. It probably did not take more than five minutes, maybe considerably less, before we had reached the top, but to me it seemed like hours of nearly fruitless endeavour. I did not realize at first that we were high. I shall never forget the weird kind of astonishment when the fact came home to me that what snapped and crackled in the snow under the horses' hoofs, were the tops of trees. Nor shall the feeling of estrangement, as it were—as if I were not myself, but looking on from the outside at the adventure of somebody who yet was I—the feeling of other-worldliness, if you will pardon the word, ever fade from my memory—a feeling of having been carried beyond my depth where I could not swim—which came over me when with two quick glances to right and left I took in the fact that there were no longer any trees to either side, that I was above that forest world which had so often engulfed me.

Then I drew my lines in. The horses fought against it, did not want to stand. But I had to find my way, and while they were going, I could not take my eyes from them. It took a supreme effort on my part to make them obey. At last they stood, but I had to hold them with all my strength, and with not a second's respite. Now that I was on top of the drift, the problem of how to get down loomed larger than that of getting up had seemed before. I knew I did not have half a minute in which to decide upon my course; for it became increasingly difficult to hold the horses back, and they were fast sinking away.

During this short breathing spell I took in the situation. We had come up in a northeast direction, slanting along the slope. Once on top, I had instinctively turned to the north. Here the drift was about twenty feet wide, perfectly level and with an exfoliated surface layer. To the east the drift fell steeply, with a clean, smooth cliff-line marking off the beginning of the descent; this line seemed particularly disconcerting, for it betrayed the concave curvature of the down-sweep. A few yards to the north I saw below, at the foot of the cliff, the old logging-trail, and I noticed that the snow on it lay as it had fallen, smooth and sheer, without a ripple of a drift. It looked like mockery. And yet that was where I had to get down.

The next few minutes are rather a maze in my memory. But two pictures were photographed with great distinctness. The one is of the moment when we went over the edge. For a second Peter reared up, pawing the air with his forefeet; Dan tried to back away from the empty fall. I had at this excruciating point no purchase whatever on the lines. Then apparently Peter sat or fell down, I do not know which, on his haunches and began to slide. The cutter lurched to the left as if it were going to spill all it held. Dan was knocked off his hind feet by the drawbar—and we plunged. . . . We came to with a terrific jolt that sent me in a heap against the dash board. One jump, and I stood on the ground. The cutter—and this is the second picture which is etched clearly on the plate of my memory—stood on its pole, leaning at an angle of forty-five degrees against the drift. The horses were as stunned. 'Dan, Peter!' I shouted, and they struggled to their feet. They were badly winded, but otherwise everything seemed all right. I looked wistfully back and up at the gully which we had torn into the flank of the drift.

I should gladly have breathed the horses again, but they were hot, the air was at zero or colder, the rays of the sun had begun to slant. I walked for a while alongside the team. They were drooping sadly. Then I got in again, driving them slowly till we came to the crossing of the ditch. I had no eye for the grade ahead. On the bush road the going was good—now and then a small drift, but nothing alarming anywhere. The anti-climax had set in. Again the speckled trunks of the balm poplars struck my eye, now interspersed with the scarlet stems of the red osier dogwood. But they failed to cheer me—they were mere facts, unable to stir moods. . . .

I began to think. A few weeks ago I had met that American settler with the French sounding name who lived alongside the angling dam further north. We had talked snow, and he had said, 'Oh, up here it never is bad except along this grade',—we were stopping on the last east-west grade, the one I was coming to—'there you cannot get through. You'd kill your horses. Level with the treetops.' Well, I had had just that a little while ago—I could not afford any more of it. So I made up my mind to try a new trail, across a section which was fenced. It meant getting out of my robes twice more, to open the gates, but I preferred that to another tree-high drift. To spare my horses was now my only consideration. I should not have liked to take the new trail by night, for fear of missing the gates; but that objection did not hold just now. Horses and I were pretty well spent. So, instead of forking off the main trail to the north we went straight ahead.

In due time I came to the bridge which I had to cross in order to get up on the dam. Here I saw—in an absent-minded, half unconscious, and uninterested way—one more structure built by architect wind. The deep master ditch from the north emptied here, to the left of the bridge, into the grade ditch which ran east and west. And at the corner the snow had very nearly bridged it—so nearly that you could easily have stepped across the remaining gap. But below it was hollow—nothing supported the bridge—it was a mere arch, with a vault underneath that looked temptingly sheltered and rosy to wearied eyes.

The dam was bare, and I had to pull off to the east, on to the swampy plain. I gave my horses the lines, and slowly, slowly they took me home! Even had I not always lost interest here, to-day I should have leaned back and rested. Although the horses had done all the actual work, the strain of it had been largely on me. It was the after-effect that set in now.

I thought of my wife, and how she would have felt had she been able to follow the scenes in some magical mirror through every single vicissitude of my drive. And once more I saw with the eye of recent memory the horses in that long, endless plunge through the corner of the marsh. Once more I felt my muscles a-quiver with the strain of that last wild struggle over that last, inhuman drift. And slowly I made up my mind that the next time, the very next day, on my return trip, I was going to add another eleven miles to my already long drive and to take a different road. I knew the trail over which I had been coming so far was closed for the rest of the winter—there was no traffic there—no trail would be kept open. That other road of which I was thinking and which lay further west was the main cordwood trail to the towns in the south. It was out of my way, to be sure, but I felt convinced that I could spare my horses and even save time by making the detour.

Being on the east side of the dam, I could not see school or cottage till I turned up on the correction line. But when at last I saw it, I felt somewhat as I had felt coming home from my first big trip overseas. It seemed a lifetime since I had started out. I seemed to be a different man.

Here, in the timber land, the snow had not drifted to any extent. There were signs of the gale, but its record was written in fallen tree trunks, broken branches, a litter of twigs—not in drifts of snow. My wife would not surmise what I had gone through.

She came out with a smile on her face when I pulled in on the yard. It was characteristic of her that she did not ask why I came so late; she accepted the fact as something for which there were no doubt compelling reasons. 'I was giving our girl a bath,' she said; 'she cannot come.' And then she looked wistfully at my face and at the horses. Silently I slipped the harness off their backs. I used to let them have their freedom for a while on reaching home. And never yet but Peter at least had had a kick and a caper and a roll before they sought their mangers. To-day they stood for a moment knock-kneed, without moving, then shook themselves in a weak, half-hearted way and went with drooping heads and weary limbs straight to the stable.

'You had a hard trip?' asked my wife; and I replied with as much cheer as I could muster, 'I have seen sights to-day that I did not expect to see before my dying day.' And taking her arm, I looked at the westering sun and turned towards the house.

1922

E.J. Pratt

1882–1964

The publication in 1923 of Pratt's *Newfoundland Verse* marked a turning-point in Canadian literary history, introducing into Canadian writing an imagism that would evolve into the Canadian modernist movement. Pratt himself, however, was never a member of any school or movement but a poet who went his own way: his work was strongly imagistic but also narrative, a work that fused, in dramatic situations, individuals, their sense of place, and the elements with which they were often in conflict. (See, for example, 'Silences'.) Unlike most of his contemporaries, Pratt worked extensively in longer poetic forms. Indeed, the magnitude of Pratt's long poems has sometimes overshadowed his shorter lyrics, though they remain important in their own right. The density and complex dramatic construction of 'Come Away, Death', for example, make it one of the most memorable poems in our literature.

E.J. Pratt—'Ned' as he was called by his many friends, who remembered his personal warmth and conviviality with affection—was born in 1882 in Western Bay, Nfld. Growing up on the Newfoundland coast gave him an intense feeling for the sea, especially as a place where the individual is tested by nature. As a young man Pratt prepared himself to follow his father into the Methodist ministry and, after his education at St John's Methodist College, he served as both a student-minister and a teacher in several small Newfoundland communities. In 1907 he came to Canada to continue his education, enrolling in Victoria College, University of Toronto, where he studied theology, philosophy, and psychology. Although taking his Bachelor of Divinity and being ordained in 1913, he remained at the university, becoming a demonstrator for the Department of Psychology and completing a Ph.D. thesis on the eschatology of St Paul. In 1919 Pelham Edgar, the chairman of the Department of English and a staunch supporter of Canadian poetry, provided Pratt with an alternative to a religious career by making him an associate professor of English at Victoria, largely on the strength of his promise as a poet. Pratt remained there until he retired in 1953.

Pratt's choice not to enter the ministry, apparently the result of a crisis of faith not uncommon in the late Victorian era, was specifically rooted in his childhood encounters with the tragedies of Newfoundland seafaring life. As he later wrote, he was puzzled by 'the ironic enigma of Nature in relation to the Christian view of the world'. Struggling with traditional perceptions of God and human existence, he turned toward Darwinian ideas that came in his poetry to express what Sandra Djwa has called an 'evolutionary vision'. The philosophical position in this poetry is not, however, entirely clear: it variously commends humanism, stoic heroism, and aspects of Christianity. Perhaps the closest Pratt came to synthesizing his beliefs was in a radio broadcast about the self-sacrificing heroism shown in the sea-rescue that was the subject of *The Roosevelt and the Antinoe* (1930): 'Science in league with good will; individual courage and humanity behind the machine. It's that sort of thing that's the hope of the world.'

Newfoundland Verse was followed by *The Witches' Brew* (1925), a comic saga about the intoxication of the ocean's creatures that demonstrates the exuberant humour often found in Pratt's writing. The next year Pratt published *Titans*, a volume made up of two long poems, 'The Cachalot', about a hunt for a great whale, and 'The Great Feud', a fable of prehistoric war among the animals. Especially striking among Pratt's long poems is his 1935 *The Titanic*, with its journalistic style, dramatic dialogue, and fragmented form. It is an example of the way Pratt used historical details in most of his poetry (he was a painstaking researcher) and of what Dorothy Livesay has called a new kind of poetry, one that is 'neither epic nor narrative, but documentary'. This documentary quality in Pratt's poetry, also visible in the Second World War poems *Dunkirk* (1941) and *Behind the Log* (1947), derives not only from subject matter but also from its specialized language, filled with technical names, precise bits of knowledge, and arcane facts.

Pratt turned to Canadian history to create two national epics—extended considerations of crucial episodes in the nation's development: *Brébeuf and His Brethren* (1940), the story of seventeenth-century Jesuit missionaries to the Hurons, and *Towards the Last Spike* (1952), about the building of the CPR. (Both won Governor General's Awards.) To Northrop Frye, who edited Pratt's *Collected Poems* (1958), Pratt took on the role of epic bard in Canada—a 'poet of an oral and pre-literate society', transforming the history and, in *Towards the Last Spike*, the scientific knowledge of a culture into a heroic and mythic whole (*The Bush Garden*). Pratt's continuing importance for Canadian literature is signalled by the University of Toronto Pratt project: his complete poems and two volumes of his collected prose—*E.J. Pratt on His Life and Poetry* (1983) and *Pursuits Amateur and Academic* (1995)—have appeared: the plan is for all of Pratt's writing to be available in print and on a website.

Towards the Last Spike

Pratt's choice of subject was a considered one: the building of the Canadian Pacific Railroad was viewed both in its own day and in Pratt's as a crucial act of bringing the new Dominion of Canada into existence by giving that nation the sea-to-sea span its national motto promised. The sense that the unification of the provinces into a single nation had become necessary following the end of the American Civil War—if British North America was not to be taken over by the US—along with the developing demographics of Canada, with the bulk of its population stretched along the northern border of the United States, created an enduring sense that Canadian union depended on drawing the country together with an east–west transportation system that did not necessitate crossing into the US at any point. Thus the successful completion of the Canadian Pacific Railroad—symbolized by the driving of the last spike—meant much more than the conquest of the wilderness by commercial interests: it came to be understood as a heroic struggle for national and cultural independence and autonomy.

In 'The Truant', Pratt showed himself impressed by the immense technological and scientific abilities that his age has achieved. In *Towards the Last Spike* he carried that sense of the new age still further: the hero of his epic is the whole community of engineers, builders, and politicians who, by joining together, achieve what seems almost impossible. Perhaps because the rhetoric of the Second World War was still lingering when Pratt composed the poem, their struggle to succeed is frequently cast in martial terms, but this lexicon also suggests that the building of the railroad is what, in Canada, took the place of a revolutionary war—a long battle fought both against a landscape that resists with all the energy of a prehistoric monster and against the competition of the American entrepreneurial railroads, which had more funds at their disposal and much easier terrain to cross. That Canada's railroad depended on a mix of government and private participation, that Pratt's epic hero is a community of individuals rather than a single man, that the main quality of epic heroism in *Towards the Last Spike* is endurance and faith in the future, and that the final victory is celebrated modestly made this poem one that spoke out of and to Canada at mid-twentieth century.

The poem as reprinted here has been abridged. Pratt saw the struggle to build the CPR as one that had to be fought politically as well as physically; in *Towards the Last Spike* he sets two combats in balanced counterpoint, the one led by William Van Horne against the resistant landscape made possible by the other, led by Sir John A. Macdonald, who must engage in heroic debates and endure grave conflicts in the Canadian Parliament to maintain support for the venture. Although the political passages retain considerable interest, for contemporary readers the sections detailing the opening of the railway—through the north, across the prairies, and in the difficult passage across the Rockies—hold a greater attraction. Pratt supplied subheads and brief synopses at key moments in the poem, and these have been retained, giving readers a sense of what has been elided.

The Shark

He seemed to know the harbour,
So leisurely he swam;
His fin,
Like a piece of sheet-iron,
Three-cornered,
And with knife-edge,
Stirred not a bubble
As it moved
With its base-line on the water.

His body was tubular
And tapered
And smoke-blue,
And as he passed the wharf
He turned,
And snapped at a flat-fish
That was dead and floating.
And I saw the flash of a white throat,
And a double row of white teeth,
And eyes of metallic grey,
Hard and narrow and slit.

Then out of the harbour,
With that three-cornered fin
Shearing without a bubble the water
Lithely,
Leisurely,
He swam—
That strange fish,
Tubular, tapered, smoke-blue,
Part vulture, part wolf,
Part neither—for his blood was cold.

1923

Newfoundland

Here the tides flow,
And here they ebb;
Not with that dull, unsinewed tread of waters
Held under bonds to move
Around unpeopled shores—
Moon-driven through a timeless circuit
Of invasion and retreat;
But with a lusty stroke of life
Pounding at stubborn gates,
That they might run
Within the sluices of men's hearts,
Leap under throb of pulse and nerve,
And teach the sea's strong voice
To learn the harmonies of new floods,
The peal of cataract,
And the soft wash of currents
Against resilient banks,
Or the broken rhythms from old chords
Along dark passages
That once were pathways of authentic fires.

Red is the sea-kelp on the beach,
Red as the heart's blood,
Nor is there power in tide or sun
To bleach its stain.
It lies there piled thick
Above the gulch-line.

It is rooted in the joints of rocks,
It is tangled around a spar,
It covers a broken rudder,
It is red as the heart's blood,
And salt as tears.

Here the winds blow,
And here they die,
Not with that wild, exotic rage
That vainly sweeps untrodden shores,
But with familiar breath
Holding a partnership with life,
Resonant with the hopes of spring,
Pungent with the airs of harvest.
They call with the silver fifes of the sea,
They breathe with the lungs of men,
They are one with the tides of the sea,
They are one with the tides of the heart,
They blow with the rising octaves of dawn,
They die with the largo[1] of dusk,
Their hands are full to the overflow,
In their right is the bread of life,
In their left are the waters of death.

Scattered on boom
And rudder and weed
Are tangles of shells;
Some with backs of crusted bronze,
And faces of porcelain blue,
Some crushed by the beach stones
To chips of jade;
And some are spiral-cleft
Spreading their tracery on the sand
In the rich veining of an agate's heart;
And others remain unscarred,
To babble of the passing of the winds.

Here the crags
Meet with winds and tides—
Not with that blind interchange
Of blow for blow
That spills the thunder of insentient seas;

1 A musical passage in a slow, dignified style.

But with the mind that reads assault
In crouch and leap and the quick stealth,
Stiffening the muscles of the waves.
Here they flank the harbours,
Keeping watch
On thresholds, altars and the fires of home,
Or, like mastiffs,
Over-zealous,
Guard too well.

Tide and wind and crag,
Sea-weed and sea-shell
And broken rudder—
And the story is told
Of human veins and pulses,
Of eternal pathways of fire,
Of dreams that survive the night,
Of doors held ajar in storms.

1923

Silences

There is no silence upon the earth or under the earth like the
silence under the sea;
No cries announcing birth,
No sounds declaring death.
There is silence when the milt is laid on the spawn in the
weeds and fungus of the rock-clefts;
And silence in the growth and struggle for life.
The bonitoes pounce upon the mackerel,
And are themselves caught by the barracudas,
The sharks kill the barracudas
And the great molluscs rend the sharks,
And all noiselessly—
Though swift be the action and final the conflict,
The drama is silent.

There is no fury upon the earth like the fury under the sea.
For growl and cough and snarl are the tokens of spendthrifts
who know not the ultimate economy of rage.

Moreover, the pace of the blood is too fast.
But under the waves the blood is sluggard and has the same temperature as that of the sea.

There is something pre-reptilian about a silent kill.

Two men may end their hostilities just with their battle-cries,
'The devil take you,' says one.
'I'll see you in hell first,' says the other.
And these introductory salutes followed by a hail of gutturals and sibilants are often the beginning of friendship, for who would not prefer to be lustily damned than to be half-heartedly blessed?
No one need fear oaths that are properly enunciated, for they belong to the inheritance of just men made perfect, and, for all we know, of such may be the Kingdom of Heaven.
But let silent hate be put away for it feeds upon the heart of the hater.
Today I watched two pairs of eyes. One pair was black and the other grey. And while the owners thereof, for the space of five seconds, walked past each other, the grey snapped at the black and the black riddled the grey.
One looked to say—'The cat,'
And the other—'The cur.'
But no words were spoken;
Not so much as a hiss or a murmur came through the perfect enamel of the teeth; not so much as a gesture of enmity.
If the right upper lip curled over the canine, it went unnoticed.
The lashes veiled the eyes not for an instant in the passing.
And as between the two in respect to candour of intention or eternity of wish, there was no choice, for the stare was mutual and absolute.
A word would have dulled the exquisite edge of the feeling.
An oath would have flawed the crystallization of the hate.
For only such culture could grow in a climate of silence—
Away back before emergence of fur or feather, back to the unvocal sea and down deep where the darkness spills its wash on the threshold of light, where the lids never close upon the eyes, where the inhabitants slay in silence and are as silently slain.

1937

Come Away, Death[1]

Willy-nilly, he comes or goes, with the clown's logic,
Comic in epitaph, tragic in epithalamium.[2]
And unseduced by any mused rhyme.
However blow the winds over the pollen,
Whatever the course of the garden variables,
He remains the constant,
Ever flowering from the poppy seeds.

There was a time he came in formal dress,
Announced by Silence tapping at the panels
In deep apology.
A touch of chivalry in his approach,
He offered sacramental wine,
And with acanthus[3] leaf
And petals of the hyacinth
He took the fever from the temples
And closed the eyelids,
Then led the way to his cool longitudes
In the dignity of the candles.

His mediaeval grace is gone—
Gone with the flame of the capitals[4]
And the leisured turn of the thumb
Leafing the manuscripts,
Gone with the marbles
And the Venetian mosaics,

1 In Shakespeare's *Twelfth Night* a clown sings an 'old and plain' song that begins:

Come away, come away, death
And in sad cypress let me be laid
Fly away, fly away, breath,
I am slain by a fair cruel maid
My shroud of white, stuck all with yew,
Oh, prepare it!
My part of death, no one so true
Did share it!

Sandra Djwa (in *The E.J. Pratt Symposium*, 1977) has pointed out that in the opening of Pratt's poem there is a further echo of one of Shakespeare's clowns: 'If a man . . . drown himself, it is, will he, nill he, he goes' (the gravedigger in *Hamlet*, V. i. 16–17).

2 A formal poem on the occasion of a wedding.

3 A herb once in wide use for its supposed mollifying properties. Hyacinth petals were associated with the ancient festival honouring the mythic youth Hyacinthus, who was turned into a hyacinth after his death at the hands of Apollo; the festival began with funeral offerings and lamentations but ended with songs of joy for his achievement of immortality.

4 That is, the illustrated letters that begin passages in illuminated medieval manuscripts; but with a possible pun on capital cities.

With the bend of the knee
Before the rose-strewn feet of the Virgin.
The *paternosters* of his priests,
Committing clay to clay,
Have rattled in their throats
Under the gride[5] of his traction tread.

One night we heard his footfall—one September night—
In the outskirts of a village near the sea.
There was a moment when the storm
Delayed its fist, when the surf fell
Like velvet on the rocks—a moment only;
The strangest lull we ever knew!
A sudden truce among the oaks
Released their fratricidal arms;
The poplars straightened to attention
As the winds stopped to listen
To the sound of a motor drone—
And then the drone was still.[6]
We heard the tick-tock on the shelf,
And the leak of valves in our hearts.
A calm condensed and lidded
As at the core of a cyclone ended breathing.
This was the monologue of Silence
Grave and unequivocal.

What followed was a bolt
Outside the range and target of the thunder,
And human speech curved back upon itself
Through Druid runways[7] and the Piltdown scarps,
Beyond the stammers of the Java caves,
To find its origins in hieroglyphs
On mouths and eyes and cheeks
Etched by a foreign stylus never used
On the outmoded page of the Apocalypse.[8]

1943

5 Grating sound; perhaps also with its alternate meaning of a spasm of pain. The whole line refers to the introduction of tanks in modern warfare.

6 The reference here is to the German bombs that fell during the Battle of Britain in 1940. (Pratt's poem was first published in April 1941.) After the planes passed over, there was a moment of silence before the explosion of the bombs.

7 The paths that form a part of primitive religious monuments such as those at Avebury and Stonehenge, which were formerly believed to be the work of the Druids (early Celtic priests). 'Piltdown', 'Java': when Pratt wrote the poem, Piltdown man and Java man were believed to be among the most primitive ancestors of modern man (the fossil evidence for Piltdown man was subsequently discovered to be fraudulent).

8 Another name for Revelation, the last book of the Bible, which predicts the events leading up to the end of the world, including Armageddon—the final battle between good and evil.

The Truant[1]

'What have you there?' the great Panjandrum[2] said
To the Master of the Revels[3] who had led
A bucking truant with a stiff backbone
Close to the foot of the Almighty's throne.

'Right Reverend, most adored,
And forcibly acknowledged Lord
By the keen logic of your two-edged sword!
This creature has presumed to classify
Himself—a biped, rational, six feet high
And two feet wide; weighs fourteen stone;
Is guilty of a multitude of sins.
He has abjured his choric origins,
And like an undomesticated slattern,
Walks with tangential step unknown
Within the weave of the atomic pattern.
He has developed concepts, grins
Obscenely at your Royal bulletins,
Possesses what he calls a will
Which challenges your power to kill.'

'What is his pedigree?'

'The base is guaranteed, your Majesty—
Calcium, carbon, phosphorus, vapour
And other fundamentals spun
From the umbilicus[4] of the sun,
And yet he says he will not caper
Around your throne, nor toe the rules
For the ballet of the fiery molecules.'

'His concepts and denials—scrap them, burn them—
To the chemists with them promptly.'

1 For the intellectual debate that provides the context for this poem, see Djwa, *E.J. Pratt: The Evolutionary Vision* (1974), pp. 114–20. Of this poem Pratt himself wrote to Desmond Pacey: 'My own profession of faith was expressed in "The Truant", a comparatively late poem. . . . It is an indictment of absolute power without recognition of moral ends.'

2 A pompous and pretentious official; here, God, not as traditionally conceived but as a deity embodying mechanistic theories of the universe as a set of explicable scientific principles.

3 Formerly, a person appointed to organize merrymaking; here a satanic figure.

4 Core (literally, 'navel').

'Sire,
The stuff is not amenable to fire.
Nothing but their own kind can overturn them.
The chemists have sent back the same old story—
"With our extreme gelatinous apology,
We beg to inform your Imperial Majesty,
Unto whom be dominion and power and glory,
There still remains that strange precipitate
Which has the quality to resist
Our oldest and most trusted catalyst.
It is a substance we cannot cremate
By temperatures known to our Laboratory." '

And the great Panjandrum's face grew dark—
'I'll put those chemists to their annual purge,
And I myself shall be the thaumaturge[5]
To find the nature of this fellow's spark.
Come, bring him nearer by yon halter rope:
I'll analyse him with the cosmoscope.'

Pulled forward with his neck awry,
The little fellow six feet short,
Aware he was about to die,
Committed grave contempt of court
By answering with a flinchless stare
The Awful Presence seated there.

The ALL HIGH swore until his face was black.
He called him a coprophagite.[6]
A genus *homo*, egomaniac,
Third cousin to the family of worms,
A sporozoan[7] from the ooze of night,
Spawn of a spavined troglodyte:
He swore by all the catalogue of terms
Known since the slang of carboniferous[8] Time.
He said that he could trace him back
To pollywogs and earwigs in the slime.
And in his shrillest tenor he began
Reciting his indictment of the man,
Until he closed upon this capital crime—

5 Miracle worker.
6 Feces eater.
7 A parasitic protozoan, a primitive form of life; 'spavined': lame; 'troglodyte': prehistoric cave dweller.
8 The Carboniferous period, in the latter part of the Paleozoic era, began about 345 million years ago.

'You are accused of singing out of key,
(A foul unmitigated dissonance)
Of shuffling in the measures of the dance,
Then walking out with that defiant, free
Toss of your head, banging the doors,
Leaving a stench upon the jacinth[9] floors.
You have fallen like a curse
On the mechanics of my Universe.

'Herewith I measure out your penalty—
Hearken while you hear, look while you see:
I send you now upon your homeward route
Where you shall find
Humiliation for your pride of mind.
I shall make deaf the ear, and dim the eye,
Put palsy in your touch, make mute
Your speech, intoxicate your cells and dry
Your blood and marrow, shoot
Arthritic needles through your cartilage,
And having parched you with old age,
I'll pass you wormwise through the mire;
And when your rebel will
Is mouldered, all desire
Shrivelled, all your concepts broken,
Backward in dust I'll blow you till
You join my spiral festival of fire.[10]
Go, Master of the Revels—I have spoken.'

And the little genus *homo*, six feet high,
Standing erect, countered with this reply—
'You dumb insouciant invertebrate,
You rule a lower than a feudal state—
A realm of flunkey decimals that run,
Return; return and run; again return,
Each group around its little sun,
And every sun a satellite.
There they go by day and night,
Nothing to do but run and burn,

9 A reddish-orange gem.

10 An allusion to Dante's *Divina Commedia*. That long poem is divided into three sections laying out the medieval cosmology: in the first part (the 'Inferno'), Dante makes a spiralling descent into the ever narrowing depths of Hell; in the second part (the 'Purgatorio') he makes a mirroring ascent—alluded to by Pratt in the phrase 'spiral stairs' at l. 138—through Purgatory; finally, in the section called 'Paradiso', he passes into the celestial realm and climbs ever higher, coming, in the final lines, to the pinnacle of Heaven where God resides (thus moving, as in Pratt's l. 139, 'from nadir depth to zenith height').

Taking turn and turn about,
Light-year in and light-year out,
Dancing, dancing in quadrillions,[11]
Never leaving their pavilions.

'Your astronomical conceit
Of bulk and power is anserine.[12]
Your ignorance so thick,
You did not know your own arithmetic.
We flung the graphs about your flying feet;
We measured your diameter—
Merely a line
Of zeros prefaced by an integer.
Before we came
You had no name.
You did not know direction or your pace;
We taught you all you ever knew
Of motion, time and space.
We healed you of your vertigo
And put you in our kindergarten show,
Perambulated you through prisms, drew
Your mileage through the Milky Way,
Lassoed your comets when they ran astray,
Yoked Leo, Taurus, and your team of Bears
To pull our kiddy cars of inverse squares.[13]

'Boast not about your harmony,
Your perfect curves, your rings
Of *pure and endless light*[14]—'Twas we
Who pinned upon your seraphim their wings,
And when your brassy heavens rang
With joy that morning while the planets sang
Their choruses of archangelic lore,
'Twas we who ordered the notes upon their score
Out of our winds and strings.
Yes! all your shapely forms
Are ours—parabolas of silver light,
Those blueprints of your spiral stairs
From nadir depth to zenith height,

11 10^{15}; with a pun on 'quadrille', a square dance for four couples.
12 Goose-like, foolish.
13 The inverse-square law is that principle in physics for calculating such things as the intensity of light over distance. (Any point source that spreads its influence equally in all directions without a limit to its range will obey the inverse square law; i.e., light decreases as the inverse square of the distance travelled.)
14 An allusion to the opening lines of 'The World' by the seventeenth-century mystical poet Henry Vaughan: 'I saw Eternity the other night / Like a great Ring of pure and endless light.'

Coronas, rainbows after storms,
Auroras on your eastern tapestries
And constellations over western seas.

'And when, one day, grown conscious of your age,
While pondering an eolith,[15]
We turned a human page
And blotted out a cosmic myth
With all its baby symbols to explain
The sunlight in Apollo's eyes,[16]
Our rising pulses and the birth of pain,
Fear, and that fern-and-fungus breath
Stalking our nostrils to our cave of death—
That day we learned how to anatomize
Your body, calibrate your size
And set a mirror up before your face
To show you what you really were—a rain
Of dull Lucretian atoms[17] crowding space,
A series of concentric waves which any fool
Might make by dropping stones within a pool,
Or an exploding bomb forever in flight[18]
Bursting like hell through Chaos and Old Night.

'You oldest of the hierarchs
Composed of electronic sparks,
We grant you speed,
We grant you power, and fire
That ends in ash, but we concede
To you no pain nor joy nor love nor hate,
No final tableau of desire,
No causes won or lost, no free
Adventure at the outposts—only
The degradation of your energy[19]
When at some late
Slow number of your dance your sergeant-major Fate

15 Stone-Age artifact.

16 Apollo, especially under his epithet Phoebus ('The Bright One'), was identified as the god of the sun by early writers.

17 Lucretius (96?–55 BC) was a Roman poet and philosopher and one of the early atomists; he believed that the universe was made of primordial 'seeds' of infinitesimal size dropping through a void.

18 The concept of the universe as beginning with an explosion from a single point and continuing to expand as matter moves away from this point was first formulated in the 1920s and became a well-established scientific theory during the 1930s. 'Chaos and Old Night': In Milton's *Paradise Lost* the fallen angels give 'A shout that tore Hell's Concave, and beyond / Frighted the Reign of *Chaos* and Old Night' (I. 542–3). 'Old night' or 'eldest night', the outer limit of the universe in Milton's cosmology, was the eternal uncreated aspect of God out of which God derived Chaos, undifferentiated inchoate matter; God then produced Creation from Chaos.

19 A reference to the concept of entropy, the idea—implicit in the second law of thermodynamics—that the universe is running down because of a continuing loss of available energy.

Will catch you blind and groping and will send
You reeling on that long and lonely
Lockstep of your wave-lengths towards your end.

'We who have met
With stubborn calm the dawn's hot fusillades;
Who have seen the forehead sweat
Under the tug of pulleys on the joints,
Under the liquidating tally[20]
Of the cat-and-truncheon[21] bastinades;
Who have taught our souls to rally
To mountain horns and the sea's rockets
When the needle ran demented through the points;
We who have learned to clench
Our fists and raise our lightless sockets
To morning skies after the midnight raids,
Yet cocked our ears to bugles on the barricades,
And in cathedral rubble found a way to quench
A dying thirst within a Galilean[22] valley—
No! by the Rood, we will not join in your ballet.'

1943

20 Record or score, but with a possible pun on the original meaning of 'tally', a notched stick, because 'bastinade' is a beating with a stick.
21 Whip (cat-o'-nine-tails) and club.
22 Of Galilee, the area, in northern Palestine, associated with Jesus' ministry; 'Rood': the cross.

Towards the Last Spike

It was the same world then as now—the same,
Except for little differences of speed
And power, and means to treat myopia
To show an axe-blade infinitely sharp
Splitting things infinitely small, or else
Provide the telescopic sight to roam
Through curved dominions never found in fables.
The same, but for new particles[1] of speech—
Those algebraic substitutes for nouns
That sky cartographers would hang like signboards
Along the trespass of our thoughts to stop
The stutters of our tongues with their equations.

1 Here, referring to the new discoveries of particle physics, but punning on the fact that 'particle' is a term from grammar for minor parts of speech or common prefixes.

As now, so then, blood kept its ancient colour,
And smoothly, roughly, paced its banks; in calm
Preserving them, in riot rupturing them.
Wounds needed bandages and stomachs food:
The hands outstretched had joined the lips in prayer—
'Give us our daily bread, give us our pay.'
The past flushed in the present and tomorrow
Would dawn upon today; only the rate
To sensitize or numb a nerve would change;
Only the quickening of a measuring skill
To gauge the onset of a birth or death
With the precision of micrometers.
Men spoke of acres then and miles and masses,
Velocity and steam, cables that moored
Not ships but continents, world granaries,
The east-west cousinship, a nation's rise,
Hail of identity, a world expanding,
If not the universe: the feel of it
Was in the air—'Union required the Line.'[2]
The theme was current at the banquet tables,
And arguments profane and sacred rent
God-fearing families into partisans.
Pulpit, platform and floor were sounding-boards;
Cushions beneath the pounding fists assumed
The hues of western sunsets; nostrils sniffed
The prairie tang; the tongue rolled over texts:
Even St Paul was being invoked to wring
The neck of Thomas in this war of faith
With unbelief.[3] Was ever an adventure
Without its cost? Analogies were found
On every page of history or science.
A nation, like the world, could not stand still.
What was the use of records but to break them?
The tougher armour followed the new shell;
The newer shell the armour; lighthouse rockets
Sprinkled their stars over the wake of wrecks.
Were not the engineers at work to close
The lag between the pressures and the valves?

2 When British Columbia was admitted into Confederation in 1871 it was with the promise that a railway would be built within ten years to connect that province with eastern Canada. Sir John A. Macdonald and his Conservative party argued in Parliament that Canada's hold on the West and Northwest depended on the fulfillment of that promise, and that an all-Canadian route was essential to future national unity.

3 St Paul preached a doctrine of faith. The unbelievers are like the apostle Thomas who, before acknowledging the resurrected Christ, required physical proof (hence 'doubting Thomas'). Pratt is playfully alluding to the fact that men who built the CPR gained their railroad experience revitalizing the St Paul and Pacific Railway (see p. 289, note 8).

The same world then as now thirsting for power
To crack those records open, extra pounds
upon the inches, extra miles per hour.
The mildewed static schedules which before
Had like asbestos been immune to wood
Now curled and blackened in the furnace coal.
This power lay in the custody of men
From down-and-outers needing roofs, whose hands
Were moulded by their fists, whose skins could feel
At home incorporate with dolomite.[4]
To men who with the marshal instincts in them,
Deriving their authority from wallets,
Directed their battalions from the trestles.

THE GATHERING

('Oats—a grain which in England is generally given to horses,
but in Scotland supports the people.'
—Dr Samuel Johnson.

'True, but where will you find such horses, where such men?'
—Lord Elibank's reply as recorded by Sir Walter Scott.)

Oatmeal was in their blood and in their names.
Thrift was the title of their catechism.
It governed all things but their mess of porridge
Which, when it struck the hydrochloric acid
With treacle and skim-milk, became a mash.
Entering the duodenum, it broke up
Into amino acids: then the liver
Took on its natural job as carpenter:
Foreheads grew into cliffs, jaws into juts.
The meal, so changed, engaged the follicles:
Eyebrows came out as gorse, the beards as thistles,
And the chest-hair the fell[5] of Grampian rams.
It stretched and vulcanized the human span:
Nonagenarians worked and thrived upon it.
Out of such chemistry run through by genes,
The food released its fearsome racial products:—
The power to strike a bargain like a foe,
To win an argument upon a burr,

4 An important mineral in building, found in much limestone and some marble.
5 Fleece; the Grampians are the principal mountains of Scotland.

Invest the language with a Bannockburn,[6]
Culloden or the warnings of Lochiel,
Weave loyalties and rivalries in tartans,
Present for the amazement of the world
Kilts and the civilized barbaric Fling,
And pipes which, when they acted on the mash,
Fermented lullabies to *Scots wha hae.*[7]

Their names were like a battle-muster—Angus[8]
(He of the Shops) and Fleming (of the Transit),
Hector (of the *Kicking Horse*), Dawson,
'Cromarty' Ross, and Beatty (Ulster Scot),
Bruce, Allan, Galt and Douglas, and the 'twa'—
Stephen (Craigellachie) and Smith (Strathcona)—
Who would one day climb from their Gaelic hide-outs,
Take off their plaids and wrap them round the mountains.
And then the everlasting tread of the Macs,
Vanguard, centre and rear, their roving eyes
On summits, rivers, contracts, beaver, ledgers;

6 The English were beaten back by the Scots at the Battle of Bannockburn in 1314. In 1746 the forces of Bonnie Prince Charlie were defeated at Culloden, a celebrated battle that marked the breakup of the Highland Clans. Donald Cameron of Lochiel was a famous Highland chieftain allied with Charles Stuart; in 'Lochiel's Warning' (1802) the poet Thomas Campbell tells of a wizard appearing to Lochiel and forecasting the coming defeat.

7 A reference to 'Robert Bruce's March to Bannockburn' by Robert Burns (1759–96), a warlike patriotic song beginning, 'Scots wha hae wi' Wallace bled, / Scots, wham Bruce has aften led, / Welcome to your gory bed / Or to Victorie!'

8 Richard B. Angus (1821–1922) became general manager in 1879 of the St Paul and Pacific Railway following its purchase in 1877 by Donald Smith, George Stephen, Jim Hill, John S. Kennedy, Duncan McIntyre, and Norman Kittson; in 1880 Angus became part of the syndicate—with Smith, Stephen, McIntyre, and Henry Beatty—that was formed for the construction of the Canadian Pacific Railway. He later established shops in Montreal for the building of railway equipment. Sandford Fleming (1827–1915) was appointed engineer-in-chief for the CPR in 1871 and made the original surveys through the mountain ranges that presented the greatest obstacle between east and west. (A transit is a surveyor's instrument.) James Hector (1834–1907), geologist, discovered the Kicking Horse Pass through the Rocky Mountains, the pass eventually chosen over the more northerly Yellowhead Pass favoured by Fleming. Simon James Dawson (1820–1902), a civil engineer, first opened communications with the Red River country by means of the 'Dawson Route', and therefore was an important forerunner of the railway builders. James Ross (1848–1913), born in Cromarty, Scotland, took charge of the CPR west of Winnipeg in 1883. Randolph Bruce (1863–1942) was an engineer on surveys investigating alternate passes through the Rockies in 1891. Sir Hugh Allan (1810–82), one of the original projectors of the CPR, was given the initial contract for its construction in 1872; subsequent revelations of financial improprieties resulted in the fall of the Macdonald government and the loss of the contract. Alexander Galt (1817–93), one of the chief architects of the British North America Act, was an early railroad builder in Canada, associated with the Grand Trunk Railway. Sir James Douglas (1803–77) was the first governor of British Columbia (1858–64). George Stephen (1829–1921) was president of the syndicate formed to build the CPR and one of its two most important members along with Donald Smith (1820–1914), later Baron Strathcona. It was Smith who drove the last spike in 1885, symbolizing the completion of the laying of tracks. In 1884 Stephen, who had gone to England to raise funds to keep the railway solvent in a period of financial crisis, sent a famous cable to Smith with the message 'Stand Fast. Craigellachie'—the defiant war cry of the Clan Grant, which refers to a sentinel rock in the Scottish countryside familiar to both men. All of the men named in these lines came from Scotland except for Galt, who was born in England but was the son of the Scottish novelist John Galt.

Their ears cocked to the skirl of Sir John A.,
The general of the patronymic march.[9]

(Sir John revolving round the Terms of Union with British Columbia. Time, late at night.)

Insomnia had ripped the bed-sheets from him
Night after night. How long was this to last?
Confederation had not played this kind
Of trickery on him. That was rough indeed,
So gravelled,[10] that a man might call for rest
And take it for a life accomplishment.
It was his laurel though some of the leaves
Had dried. But this would be a longer tug
Of war which needed for his team thick wrists
And calloused fingers, heavy heels to dig
Into the earth and hold—men with bull's beef
Upon their ribs. Had he himself the wind,
The anchor-waist to peg at the rope's end?
'Twas bad enough to have these questions hit
The waking mind: 'twas much worse when he dozed;
For goblins had a way of pinching him,
Slapping a nightmare on to dwindling snoozes.
They put him and his team into a tug
More real than life. He heard a judge call out—
'Teams settle on the rope and take the strain!'
And with the coaches' *heave*, the running welts
Reddened his palms, and then the gruelling *backlock*
Inscribed its indentations on his shoulders.
This kind of burn he knew he had to stand;
It was the game's routine; the other fire
Was what he feared the most for it could bake him—
That white dividing rag tied to the rope
Above the centre pole had with each heave
Wavered with chances equal. With the backlock,
Despite the legs of Tupper[11] and Cartier,
The western anchor dragged; the other side
Remorselessly was gaining, holding, gaining.
No sleep could stand this strain and, with the nightmare
Delivered of its colt, Macdonald woke.

9 That is, many of those involved in the railroad had the patronymic prefix 'Mac' on their names, chief among them Sir John A. Macdonald.

10 Perplexed.

11 Charles Tupper (1812–1915) and George Etienne Cartier (1811–73) were Macdonald's staunchest allies in Parliament during the 1871 debate with Alexander Mackenzie's Liberals over the proposed transcontinental railway. Tupper later served as Macdonald's minister of railways and canals (1879–84).

Tired with the midnight toss, lock-jawed with yawns,
He left the bed and, shuffling to the window,
He opened it. The air would cool him off
And soothe his shoulder burns. He felt his ribs:
Strange, nothing broken—how those crazy drowses
Had made the fictions tangle with the facts!
He must unscramble them with steady hands.
Those Ranges pirouetting in his dreams
Had their own knack of standing still in light,
Revealing peaks whose known triangulation
Had to be read in prose severity.
Seizing a telescope, he swept the skies,
The north-south drift, a self-illumined chart.
Under Polaris was the Arctic Sea
And the sub-Arctic gates well stocked with names:
Hudson, Davis, Baffin, Frobisher;[12]
And in his own day Franklin, Ross and Parry
Of the Canadian Archipelago;
Kellett, McClure, McClintock, of *The Search*.
Those straits and bays had long been kicked by keels,
And flags had fluttered on the Capes that fired
His youth, making familiar the unknown.
What though the odds were nine to one against,
And the Dead March was undertoning trumpets,
There was enough of strychnine[13] in the names
To make him flip a penny for the risk,
Though he had palmed the coin reflectively
Before he threw and watched it come down *heads*.
That stellar path looked too much like a road map
Upon his wall—the roads all led to market—
The north-south route. He lit a candle, held
It to a second map full of blank spaces
And arrows pointing west. Disturbed, he turned
The lens up to the zenith, followed the course
Tracked by a cloud of stars that would not keep
Their posts—Capella,[14] Perseus, were reeling;

12 That is, these early explorers gave their names to Hudson Bay, Davis Strait, Baffin Bay, and Frobisher Bay. John Ross accompanied by Edward Parry in 1818, and Parry in 1819, made voyages that added vastly to knowledge about the region, as did John Franklin's expeditions into the Arctic archipelago between 1819 and 1825. After Franklin departed on a third voyage in 1845, from which he never returned, a reward was offered for information about his fate, and a famous search was mounted that lasted from 1847 until 1859; Henry Kellett, Robert McClure, and Leopold McClintock were among those who took part. For details see the headnote to Franklin, pp. 50.

13 Although highly toxic, strychnine was formerly used for its properties as a stimulant.

14 Brightest star in the constellation Auriga, which is one of the prominent constellations of the northern celestial hemisphere, with Perseus, Cassiopeia (a queen seated on a throne), Aries (the ram), and Cygnus (the swan).

Low in the north-west, Cassiopeia
Was qualmish, leaning on her starboard arm-rest,
And Aries was chasing, butting Cygnus,
Just diving. Doubts and hopes struck at each other.
Why did those constellations look so much
Like blizzards? And what lay beyond the blizzards?

'Twas chilly at the window. He returned
To bed and savoured soporific terms:
Superior, the *Red River*, *Selkirk*, *Prairie*,
Port Moody and *Pacific*. Chewing them,
He spat out *Rocky* grit before he swallowed.
Selkirk![15] This had the sweetest taste. Ten years
Before, the Highland crofters had subscribed
Their names in a memorial[16] for the Rails.
Sir John reviewed the story of the struggle,
That four months' journey from their native land—
The Atlantic through the Straits to Hudson Bay,
Then the Hayes River to Lake Winnipeg
Up to the Forks of the Assiniboine.
He could make use of that—just what he needed,
A Western version of the Arctic daring,
Romance and realism, double dose.
How long ago? Why, this is '71.
Those fellows came the time Napoleon
Was on the steppes.[17] For sixty years they fought
The seasons, 'hoppers, drought, hail, wind and snow;
Survived the massacre at Seven Oaks,
The 'Pemmican War' and the Red River floods.
They wanted now the Road—those pioneers
Who lived by spades instead of beaver traps.
Most excellent word that, pioneers! Sir John
Snuggled himself into his sheets, rolling
The word around his tongue, a theme for song,
Or for a peroration to a speech.

15 The town founded by the Red River settlers. The lines that follow recapitulate the progress of these distressed Highlanders who came to Canada under the leadership of Lord Selkirk (1771–1820) as they journeyed to the Red River to found a settlement there, on land granted to Selkirk by the Hudson's Bay Company; crucial events in the history of the Settlement are mentioned in lines 186–99. The massacre at Seven Oaks took place in 1816 when the governor of the colony and twenty of his men were killed by Métis; this hostility had been prompted by the North West Company, which found that the location of the Red River Settlement cut off its vital supply of pemmican (preserved buffalo meat); the union in 1821 of the rival Hudson's Bay Company with the North West Company ended that conflict, but flooding in 1826 (and again in 1852) brought new hardship to the Selkirk settlers.

16 Petition.

17 Napoleon invaded Russia in 1812 (the year the Red River Settlement was founded), although he never actually reached the steppes, southeast of Moscow.

THE HANGOVER AT DAWN

He knew the points that had their own appeal.
These did not bother him: the patriot touch,
The Flag, the magnetism of explorers,
The national unity. These could burn up
The phlegm in most of the provincial throats.
But there was one tale central to his plan
(The focus of his headache at this moment),
Which would demand the limit of his art—
The ballad of his courtship in the West:
Better reveal it soon without reserve.

THE LADY OF BRITISH COLUMBIA

Port Moody and Pacific! He had pledged
His word the Line should run from sea to sea.
'From sea to sea', a hallowed phrase.[18] Music
Was in that text if the right key were struck,
And he must strike it first, for, as he fingered
The clauses of the pledge, rough notes were rasping—
'No Road, No Union', and the converse true.
East-west against the north-south run of trade,
For California like a sailor-lover
Was wooing over-time. He knew the ports.
His speech was as persuasive as his arms,
As sinuous as Spanish arias—
Tamales, Cazadero, Mendocino,
Curling their baritones around the Lady.
Then Santa Rosa, Santa Monica,[19]
Held absolution in their syllables.
But when he saw her stock of British temper
Starch at ironic sainthood in the whispers—
'Rio de nuestra señora de Buena guia',[20]
He had the tact to gutturalize the liquids,[21]

18 'Hallowed' because its original source is Psalm 72: 8: 'He shall have dominion also from sea to sea'; the phrase (in Latin, 'a mari usque ad mari') was adopted as Canada's national motto in 1866, when 'dominion' was chosen to designate Canada.

19 The Bay of Tamoles (or Tamales) and the other places named here are in California, chiefly northern California. The temptation of linking a north-south rail line to California with its seaports was very real, and Pratt seems to be specifically alluding to the California coastal rail line that ran north from Sausalito to Cazadero, beginning in 1875, and eventually on to Mendocino.

20 'River of Our Lady of Safe Conduct' [Pratt's note].

21 Pratt is playing here with the sense of 'liquids' in the linguistic sense, i.e. the sounds of the *r* and the *l* in the Spanish place names, which the personified California is gutturalizing to make them sound more familiar to English Canadian ears, and the fact that these names are associated with coastal ports and therefore with literal liquids.

Steeping the tunes to drinking songs, then take
Her on a holiday where she could watch
A roving sea-born Californian pound
A downy chest and swear by San Diego.

Sir John, wise to the tricks, was studying hard,
A fresh proposal for a marriage contract.[22]
He knew a game was in the ceremony.
That southern fellow had a healthy bronze
Complexion, had a vast estate, was slick
Of manner. In his ardour he could tether
Sea-roses to the blossoms of his orchards,
And for his confidence he had the prime
Advantage of his rival—*he was there.*

THE LONG-DISTANCE PROPOSAL

A game it was, and the Pacific lass
Had poker wisdom on her face. Her name
Was rich in values—*British*; this alone
Could raise Macdonald's temperature: so could
Columbia[23] with a different kind of fever,
And in between the two, *Victoria.*
So the *Pacific* with its wash of letters
Could push the Fahrenheit another notch.
She watched for bluff on those Disraeli features,[24]
Impassive but for arrowy chipmunk eyes,
Engaged in fathoming a contract time.
With such a dowry she could well afford
To take the risk of tightening the terms—
'Begin the Road in two years, end in ten'[25]—
Sir John, a moment letting down his guard,
Frowned at the Rocky skyline, but agreed.

22 Pratt's image of British Columbia as a prospective bride has its source in popular journalism of the period; for example, on 2 January 1871 the British Colonist wrote: 'Clad in bridal attire, she is about to unite her destinies with a country which is prepared to do much for her.'

23 A name used to personify the United States.

24 Benjamin Disraeli (1804–88) was prime minister of England in 1868 (and again in 1874–80). Both Macdonald and Disraeli were thought of as being physically unattractive, with prominent noses.

25 The first clause of the agreement negotiated with British Columbia in 1870 read: 'The Government of the Dominion undertake to secure the commencement simultaneously, within two years from the date of the union, of the construction of a railway, from the Pacific towards the Rocky Mountains, and from such point as may be selected, east of the Rocky Mountains towards the Pacific, to connect the seaboard of British Columbia with the railway system of Canada, and further, to secure the completion of such railway within ten years from the date of such union.'

(The Terms ratified by Parliament, British Columbia enters Confederation July, 1871, Sandford Fleming being appointed engineer-in-chief of the proposed Railway, Walter Moberly[26] *to cooperate with him in the location of routes. 'Of course, I don't know how many millions you have, but it is going to cost you money to get through those canyons.'—Moberly to Macdonald.)*

THE PACIFIC SCANDAL[27]

(Huntingdon's charges of political corruption based on correspondence and telegrams rifled from the offices of the solicitor of Sir Hugh Allan, Head of the Canada Pacific Company; Sir John's defence; and the appearance of the Honourable Edward Blake[28] *who rises to reply to Sir John at 2 a.m.)*

* * *

(The Charter granted to The Canadian Pacific Railway, February 17, 1881, with George Stephen as first President . . . One William Cornelius Van Horne[29] *arrives in Winnipeg, December 31, 1881, and there late at night, forty below zero, gives vent to a soliloquy.)*

Stephen had laid his raw hands on Van Horne,
Pulled him across the border, sent him up
To get the feel of northern temperatures.
He knew through Hill[30] the story of his life
And found him made to order. Nothing less
Than geologic space his field of work,
He had in Illinois explored the creeks
And valleys, brooded on the rocks and quarries.
Using slate fragments, he became a draughtsman,
Bringing to life a landscape or a cloud,
Turning a tree into a beard, a cliff
Into a jaw, a creek into a mouth

26 (1852–1915); Moberly had had extensive experience in railway construction prior to taking charge of the difficult Rocky Mountain and British Columbia surveys in 1871.

27 Name given the general charges of bribery, corruption, and underhand dealing that were brought by Liberal MP L.S. Huntingdon in 1872 against Macdonald and Hugh Allan. The charges, based on correspondence and papers stolen from Allan's office, suggested that Allan had paid Macdonald and Cartier for railway contracts. Subsequent investigation showed that at the very least the prime minister had acted unwisely in accepting substantial campaign contributions from Allan. On 3 November 1873 Macdonald defended himself in Parliament in a famous speech that lasted five hours.

28 Although Alexander Mackenzie was the formally chosen leader of the Liberals, Blake (1833–1912)—famous for his intellectual capacity and for his long and meticulously argued orations—was regarded as the party's real leader. He responded to Macdonald's speech for about half an hour immediately after it was over, and then for a further four hours the next day. The Macdonald government fell on 5 November 1873.

29 (1843–1915); Van Horne, an American, became general manager of the CPR in 1881.

30 James Hill (1838–1916), the Canadian-born American investor who was responsible for the formation of the Canadian group (which included George Stephen) that purchased the St Paul and Pacific Railway in 1877, recommended Van Horne to Stephen as 'a man of great mental and physical power to carry this line through'.

With banks for lips. He loved to work on shadows.
Just now the man was forcing the boy's stature,
The while the youth tickled the man within.
Companioned by the shade of Agassiz,[31]
He would come home, his pockets stuffed with fossils—
Crinoids and fish-teeth—and his tongue jabbering
Of the earth's crust before the birth of life,
Prophetic of the days when he would dig
Into Laurentian rock. The morse-key tick
And tape were things mesmeric—space and time
Had found a junction. Electricity
And rock, one novel to the coiling hand,
The other frozen in the lap of age,
Were playthings for the boy, work for the man.
As man he was the State's first operator;[32]
As boy he played a trick upon his boss
Who, cramped with current, fired him on the instant;
As man at school, escaping Latin grammar,
He tore the fly-leaf from the text to draw
The contour of a hill; as boy he sketched
The principal, gave him flapdoodle ears,
Bristled his hair, turned eyebrows into quills,
His whiskers into flying buttresses,
His eye-tusks into rusted railroad spikes,
And made a truss between his nose and chin.
Expelled again, he went back to the keys,
To bush and rock and found companionship
With quarry-men, stokers and station-masters,
Switchmen and locomotive engineers.

Now he was transferred to Winnipeg.
Of all the places in an unknown land
Chosen by Stephen for Van Horne, this was
The pivot on which he could turn his mind.
Here he could clap the future on the shoulder
And order Fate about as his lieutenant,
For he would take no nonsense from a thing
Called Destiny—the stars had to be with him.
He spent the first night in soliloquy,

31 Jean-Louis Agassiz (1807–73) was a Swiss-American naturalist who greatly added to the knowledge of North American zoology and geology; 'Crinoids': small plantlike sea animals ('crinoid' means 'lily-shaped').

32 Van Horne became a telegraph operator on the Illinois Central Railway when he was fourteen, thereby beginning a lifelong association with railroads; however, he lost that first job because he set up a ground plate that would give a mild shock to anyone who stepped on it.

Like Sir John A. but with a difference.
Sir John wanted to sleep but couldn't do it:
Van Horne could sleep but never wanted to.
It was a waste of time, his bed a place
Only to think or dream with eyes awake.
Opening a jack-knife, he went to the window,
Scraped off the frost. Great treks ran through his mind,
East-west. Two centuries and a half gone by,
One trek had started from the Zuyder Zee
To the new Amsterdam.[33] 'Twas smooth by now,
Too smooth. His line of grandsires and their cousins
Had built a city from Manhattan dirt.
Another trek to Illinois; it too
Was smooth, but this new one it was his job
To lead, then build a highway which men claimed
Could not be built. Statesmen and engineers
Had blown their faces blue with their denials:
The men who thought so were asylum cases
Whose monomanias harmless up to now
Had not swept into cells. His bearded chin
Pressed to the pane, his eyes roved through the west.
He saw the illusion at its worst—the frost,
The steel precision of the studded heavens,
Relentless mirror of a covered earth.
His breath froze on the scrape: he cut again
And glanced at the direction west-by-south.
That westward trek was the American,
Union-Pacific—easy so he thought,
Their forty million stacked against his four.
Lonely and desolate this. He stocked his mind
With items of his task: the simplest first,
Though hard enough, the Prairies, then the Shore
North of the Lake—a quantity half-guessed.
Mackenzie like a balky horse had shied
And stopped at this. Van Horne knew well the reason,
But it was vital for the all-land route.
He peered through at the South. Down there Jim Hill
Was whipping up his horses on a road[34]
Already paved. The stations offered rest
With food and warmth, and their well-rounded names
Were tossed like apples to the public taste.

33 The former name for New York City; i.e., from an area in the Netherlands to a city in North America named after one in the Netherlands.
34 The St Paul and Pacific Railway.

He made a mental note of his three items.
He underlined the Prairies, double-lined
The Shore and triple-lined *Beyond the Prairies*,
Began counting the Ranges—first the Rockies;
The Kicking Horse ran through them, this he knew;
The Selkirks? Not so sure. Some years before
Had Moberly and Perry[35] tagged a route
Across the lariat loop of the Columbia.
Now Rogers was traversing it on foot,
Reading an aneroid and compass, chewing
Sea-biscuit and tobacco. Would the steel
Follow this trail? Van Horne looked farther west.
There was the Gold Range, there the Coastal Mountains.
He stopped, putting a period to the note,
As rivers troubled nocturnes in his ears.
His plans must not seep into introspection—
Call it a night, for morning was at hand,
And every hour of daylight was for work.

* * *

NUMBER ONE

Oak Lake to Calgary. Van Horne took off
His coat. The North must wait, for that would mean
His shirt as well. First and immediate
This prairie pledge—five hundred miles,[36] and it
Was winter. Failure of this trial promise
Would mean—no, it must not be there for meaning.
An order from him carried no repeal:
It was as final as an execution.
A cable started rolling mills in Europe:
A tap of Morse sent hundreds to the bush,
Where axes swung on spruce and the saws sang,
Changing the timber into pyramids
Of poles and sleepers. Clicks, despatches, words,
Like lanterns in a night conductor's hands,

35 Albert Perry accompanied Moberly on his 1866 search for a pass through the Selkirk Mountains. Though the quest was unsuccessful then, and also when Moberly returned in 1871–2, Major A.B. Rogers later found in Moberly's journal a description of a valley that was partially investigated by Perry in 1866. Acting on that lead, Rogers eventually found the pass (named after him) that would take the CPR from the Kicking Horse Pass in the Rockies through the Selkirks. The Columbia River system forms a large, elliptical loop in the Selkirks, with Rogers Pass lying in the middle. An aneroid barometer measures elevation.

36 When Van Horne became manager of the CPR he promised the directors that he would lay 500 miles of track in the 1882 season.

Signalled the wheels: a nod put Shaughnessy[37]
In Montreal: supplies moved on the minute.
Thousands of men and mules and horses slipped
Into their togs and harness night and day.
The grass that fed the buffalo was turned over,
The black alluvial mould laid bare, the bed
Levelled and scraped. As individuals
The men lost their identity; as groups,
As gangs, they massed, divided, subdivided,
Like numerals only—sub-contractors, gangs
Of engineers, and shovel gangs for bridges,
Culverts, gangs of mechanics stringing wires,
Loading, unloading and reloading gangs,
Gangs for the fish-plates[38] and the spiking gangs,
Putting a silver polish on the nails.
But neither men nor horses ganged like mules:
Wiser than both they learned to unionize.
Some instinct in their racial nether regions
Had taught them how to sniff the five-hour stretch
Down to the fine arithmetic of seconds.
They tired out their rivals and they knew it.
They'd stand for overwork, not overtime.
Faster than workmen could fling down their shovels,
They could unhinge their joints, unhitch their tendons;
Jumping the foreman's call, they brayed 'Unhook'
With a defiant, corporate instancy.
The promise which looked first without redemption
Was being redeemed. From three to seven miles
A day the parallels were being laid,
Though Eastern throats were hoarse with the old question—
Where are the settlements? And whence the gift
Of tongues which could pronounce place-names that purred
Like cats in relaxation after kittens?
Was it a part of the same pledge to turn
A shack into a bank for notes renewed;
To call a site a city when men saw
Only a water-tank? This was an act
Of faith indeed—substance of things unseen—
Which would convert preachers to miracles,
Lure teachers into lean-to's for their classes.
And yet it happened that while labourers

37 Thomas Shaughnessy (1853–1933), known for his organizing ability, joined the CPR in 1882 as its purchasing agent.
38 Connecting metal plates, bolted alongside two rails where they meet to make them stable.

Were swearing at their blisters in the evening
And straightening out their spinal kinks at dawn,
The tracks joined up Oak Lake to Calgary.

NUMBER TWO

On the North Shore a reptile[39] lay asleep—
A hybrid that the myths might have conceived,
But not delivered, as progenitor
Of crawling, gliding things upon the earth.
She lay snug in the folds of a huge boa
Whose tail had covered Labrador and swished
Atlantic tides, whose body coiled itself
Around the Hudson Bay, then curled up north
Through Manitoba and Saskatchewan
To Great Slave Lake. In continental reach
The neck went past the Great Bear Lake until
Its head was hidden in the Arctic Seas.
This folded reptile was asleep or dead:
So motionless, she seemed stone dead—just seemed:
She was too old for death, too old for life,[40]
For as if jealous of all living forms
She had lain there before bivalves began
To catacomb their shells on western mountains.
Somewhere within this life-death zone she sprawled,
Torpid upon a rock-and-mineral mattress.
Ice-ages had passed by and over her,
But these, for all their motion, had but sheared
Her spotty carboniferous hair or made
Her ridges stand out like the spikes of molochs.[41]
Her back grown stronger every million years,
She had shed water by the longer rivers
To Hudson Bay and by the shorter streams
To the great basins to the south, had filled
Them up, would keep them filled until the end
Of Time.

39 Pratt uses two images of reptiles as personifications of the Laurentian Shield. The first, a sleeping reptile, is a female lizard that corresponds to the area of the shield along the North Shore of Lake Superior; it lies 'snug' against a larger reptile, a huge boa constrictor that represents the full extent of the Laurentian Shield itself.

40 Because the Shield is composed of rock from the Precambrian period, dating mostly from before the advent of recorded life on earth.

41 Spiny-backed lizard of Australia, said to be the most grotesque of living reptiles; also the name of one of Satan's company in John Milton's *Paradise Lost*.

Was this the thing Van Horne set out
To conquer? When Superior lay there
With its inviting levels? Blake, Mackenzie,
Offered this water like a postulate.
'Why those twelve thousand men sent to the North?
Nonsense and waste with utter bankruptcy.'
And the Laurentian monster at the first
Was undisturbed, presenting but her bulk
To the invasion. All she had to do
Was lie there neither yielding nor resisting.
Top-heavy with accumulated power
And overgrown survival without function,
She changed her spots as though brute rudiments
Of feeling foreign to her native hour
Surprised her with a sense of violation
From an existence other than her own—
Or why take notice of this unknown breed,
This horde of bipeds that could toil like ants,
Could wake her up and keep her irritated?
They tickled her with shovels, dug pickaxes,
Into her scales and got under her skin,
And potted holes in her with drills and filled
Them up with what looked like find grains of sand,
Black sand. It wasn't noise that bothered her,
For thunder she was used to from her cradle—
The head-push and nose-blowing of the ice,
The height and pressure of its body: these
Like winds native to clime and habitat
Had served only to lull her drowsing coils.
It was not size or numbers that concerned her.
It was their foreign build, their gait of movement.
They did not crawl—nor were they born with wings.
They stood upright and walked, shouted and sang;
They needed air—that much was true—their mouths
Were open but the tongue was alien.
The sounds were not the voice of winds and waters,
Nor that of any beasts upon the earth.
She took them first with lethargy, suffered
The rubbing of her back—those little jabs
Of steel were like the burrowing of ticks
In an elk's hide needing an antler point,
Or else left in a numb monotony.
These she could stand but when the breed
Advanced west on her higher vertebrae,

Kicking most insolently at her ribs,
Pouring black powder in her cavities,
And making not the clouds but her insides
The home of fire and thunder, then she gave
Them trial of her strength: the trestles tottered;
Abutments, bridges broke; her rivers flooded:
She summoned snow and ice, and then fell back
On the last weapon in her armoury—
The first and last—her passive corporal bulk,
To stay or wreck the schedule of Van Horne.

NUMBER THREE

The big one was the mountains—seas indeed!
With crests whiter than foam: they poured like seas,
Fluting the green banks of the pines and spruces.
An eagle-flight above they hid themselves
In clouds. They carried space upon their ledges.
Could these be overridden frontally,
Or like typhoons outsmarted on the flanks?
And what were on the flanks? The troughs and canyons,
Passes more dangerous to the navigator
Than to Magellan when he tried to read
The barbarous language of his Strait by calling
For echoes from the rocky hieroglyphs
Playing their pranks of hide-and-seek in fog:
As stubborn too as the old North-West Passage,
More difficult, for ice-packs could break up;
And as for bergs, what polar architect
Could stretch his compass points to draught such peaks
As kept on rising there beyond the foothills?
And should the bastions of the Rockies yield
To this new human and unnatural foe,
Would not the Selkirks stand? This was a range
That looked like some strange dread outside a door
Which gave its name but would not show its features,
Leaving them to the mind to guess at. This
Meant tunnels—would there be no end to boring?
There must be some day. Fleming and his men
Had nosed their paths like hounds; but paths and trails,
Measured in every inch by chain and transit,
Looked easy and seductive on a chart.
The rivers out there did not flow: they tumbled.

The cataracts were fed by glaciers;
Eddies were thought as whirlpools in the Gorges,
And gradients had paws that tore up tracks.

Terror and beauty like twin signal flags
Flew on the peaks for men to keep their distance.
The two combined as in a storm at sea—
'Stay on the shore and take your fill of breathing,
But come not to the decks and climb the rigging.'
The Ranges could put cramps in hands and feet
Merely by the suggestion of the venture.
They needed miles to render up their beauty,
As if the gods in high aesthetic moments,
Resenting the profanity of touch,
Chiselled this sculpture for the eye alone.

(Van Horne in momentary meditation at the Foothills.)

His name was now a legend. The North Shore,
Though not yet conquered, yet had proved that he
Could straighten crooked roads by pulling at them,
Shear down a hill and drain a bog or fill
A valley overnight. Fast as a bobcat,
He'd climb and run across the shakiest trestle
Or, with a locomotive short of coal,
He could supply the head of steam himself.
He breakfasted on bridges, lunched on ties;
Drinking from gallon pails, he dined on moose.
He could tire out the lumberjacks; beat hell
From workers but no more than from himself.
Only the devil or Paul Bunyan shared
With him the secret of perpetual motion,
And when he moved among his men they looked
For shoulder sprouts upon the Flying Dutchman.[42]

But would his legend crack upon the mountains?
There must be no retreat: his bugles knew
Only one call—the summons to advance
Against two fortresses: the mind, the rock.
To prove the first defence was vulnerable,
To tap the treasury at home and then

42 The ghostly captain of a legendary ship doomed to sail the seas forever.

Untie the purse-strings of the Londoners,
As hard to loosen as salt-water knots—
That job was Stephen's, Smith's, Tupper's, Macdonald's.
He knew its weight: had heard, as well as they,
Blake pumping at his pulmonary bellows,
And if the speeches made the House shock-proof
Before they ended, they could still peal forth
From print more durable than spoken tones.
Blake had returned to the attack and given
Sir John the ague with another phrase
As round and as melodious as the first:
'The Country's wealth, its millions after millions
Squandered—LOST IN THE GORGES OF THE FRASER':[43]
A beautiful but ruinous piece of music
That could only be drowned with drums and fifes.
Tupper, fighting with fists and nails and toes,
Had taken the word *scandal* which had cut
His master's ballots, and had turned the edge
With his word *slander*, but Blake's *sea*, how turn
That edge? Now this last devastating phrase!
But let Sir John and Stephen answer this
Their way. Van Horne must answer it in his.

INTERNECINE STRIFE

The men were fighting foes which had themselves
Waged elemental civil wars and still
Were hammering one another at this moment.
The peaks and ranges flung from ocean beds
Had wakened up one geologic morning
To find their scalps raked off, their lips punched in,
The colour of their skins charged with new dyes.
Some of them did not wake or but half-woke;
Prone or recumbent with the eerie shapes
Of creatures that would follow them. Weather
Had acted on their spines and frozen them
To stegosaurs[44] or, taking longer cycles,
Divining human features, had blown back
Their hair and, pressing on their cheeks and temples,
Bestowed on them the gravity of mummies.

43 On 15–16 April 1880 Blake delivered his long speech opposing construction west of the Rockies, concluding in part: 'All that we can raise by taxes or loans, all that we can beg or borrow, is to be sunk in the gorges of the Fraser. . . . do not by your present action based on airy dreams and vain imaginings risk the ruin of your country.'
44 Dinosaurs with a double row of upright bony plates along their backs.

But there was life and power which belied
The tombs. Guerrilla evergreens were climbing
In military order: at the base
The *ponderosa* pine; the fir backed up
The spruce; and it the Stoney Indian lodge-poles;[45]
And these the white-barks; then, deciduous,
The outpost suicidal Lyell larches[46]
Aiming at summits, digging scraggy roots
Around the boulders in the thinning soil,
Till they were stopped dead at the timber limit—
Rock *versus* forest with the rock prevailing.
Or with the summer warmth it was the ice,
In treaty with the rock to hold a line
As stubborn as a Balkan boundary,
That left its caves to score the Douglases,[47]
And smother them with half a mile of dirt,
And making snow-sheds, covering the camps,
Futile as parasols in polar storms.
One enemy alone had battled rock
And triumphed: searching levels like lost broods,
Keen on their ocean scent, the rivers cut
The quartzite, licked the slate and softened it,
Till mud solidified was mud again,
And then, digesting it like earthworms, squirmed
Along the furrows with one steering urge—
To navigate the mountains in due time
Back to their home in worm-casts on the tides.

Into this scrimmage came the fighting men,
And all but rivers were their enemies.
Whether alive or dead the bush resisted:
Alive, it must be slain with axe and saw,
If dead, it was in tangle at their feet.
The ice could hit men as it hit the spruces.
Even the rivers had betraying tricks,
Watched like professed allies across a border.
They smiled from fertile plains and easy runs
Of valley gradients: their eyes got narrow,
Full of suspicion at the gorges where
They leaped and put the rickets in the trestles.

45 The lodge-pole pine, characterized by slim, straight trunks; 'white-barks': the white-bark pine.
46 Or subalpine larch, which thrives at the timberline. The larch is the only tree with needlelike leaves that sheds them; hence it is deciduous.
47 Douglas firs, but with an echo of ancient Scottish battles, in which the Douglases were often prominent.

Though natively in conflict with the rock,
Both leagued against invasion. At Hell's Gate[48]
A mountain laboured and brought forth a bull
Which, stranded in mid-stream, was fighting back
The river, and the fight turned on the men,
Demanding from this route their bread and steel.
And there below the Gate was the Black Canyon
With twenty-miles-an-hour burst of speed.

(Onderdonk[49] builds the 'skuzzy' to force the passage.)

'Twas more than navigation: only eagles
Might follow up this run; the spawning salmon
Gulled by the mill-race had returned to rot
Their upturned bellies in the canyon eddies.
Two engines at the stern, a forrard[50] winch,
Steam-powered, failed to stem the cataract.
The last resource was shoulders, arms and hands.
Fifteen men at the capstan,[51] creaking hawsers,
Two hundred Chinese tugging at shore ropes
To keep her bow-on from the broadside drift,
The *Skuzzy* under steam and muscle took
The shoals and rapids, and warped through the Gate,
Until she reached the navigable water—
The adventure was not sailing: it was climbing.

As hard a challenge were the precipices
Worn water-smooth and sheer a thousand feet.
Surveyors from the edges looked for footholds,
But, finding none, they tried marine manoeuvres.
Out of a hundred men they drafted sailors
Whose toes as supple as their fingers knew
The wash of reeling decks, whose knees were hardened
Through tying gaskets[52] at the royal yards:
They lowered them with knotted ropes and drew them
Along the face until the lines were strung
Between the juts. Barefooted, dynamite

48 The most treacherous section of the Fraser canyon.

49 Andrew Onderdonk (1848–1905) supervised the building of the BC section of the CPR; 'skuzzy': a small, sturdy steamboat that Onderdonk had built when he became unhappy with the cost of hauling freight ('bread and steel') over the wagon road. Few believed that the boat would be able to navigate the treacherous rapids.

50 Forward.

51 Vertical revolving barrel onto which the cables ('hawsers') were wound; it was turned by men walking around it, pushing on horizontal levers. This was used to supplement the steam-driven forward winch.

52 A small rope that secures a furled sail to its supporting yard-arm.

Strapped to their waists, the sappers[53] followed, treading
The spider films and chipping holes for blasts,
Until the cliffs delivered up their features
Under the civil discipline of roads.

RING, RING THE BELLS

Ring, ring the bells, but not the engine bells:
Today only the ritual of the steeple
Chanted to the dull tempo of the toll.
Sorrow is stalking through the camps, speaking
A common mother-tongue. 'Twill leave tomorrow
To turn that language on a Blackfoot tepee,
Then take its leisurely Pacific time
To tap its fingers on a coolie's door.
Ring, ring the bells but not the engine bells:
Today only that universal toll,
For granite, mixing dust with human lime,
Had so compounded bodies into boulders
As to untype the blood, and, then, the Fraser,
Catching the fragments from the dynamite,
Had bleached all birthmarks from her swirling dead.

Tomorrow and the engine bells again!

* * *

DYNAMITE ON THE NORTH SHORE

The lizard was in sanguinary mood.
She had been waked again: she felt her sleep
Had lasted a few seconds of her time.
The insects had come back—the ants, if ants
They were—dragging *those* trees, *those* logs athwart
Her levels, driving in *those* spikes; and how
The long grey snakes unknown within her region
Wormed from the east, unstriped, sunning themselves
Uncoiled upon the logs and then moved on,
Growing each day, ever keeping abreast!
She watched them, waiting for a bloody moment,
Until the borers halted at a spot,
The most invulnerable of her whole column,

53 Men who dig tunnels or trenches for blasting to undermine the mountain walls; 'films': filaments, fine threads, i.e., the men climbing down the rock walls on ropes are like spiders walking along their webs.

Drove in that iron, wrenched it in the holes,
Hitting, digging, twisting. Why that spot?
Not this the former itch. That sharp proboscis
Was out for more than self-sufficing blood
About the cuticle:[54] 'twas out for business
In the deep layers and the arteries.
And this consistent punching at her belly
With fire and thunder slapped her like an insult,
As with the blasts the caches of her broods
Broke—nickel, copper, silver and fool's gold,
Burst from their immemorial dormitories
To sprawl indecent in the light of day.
Another warning—this time different.

Westward above her webs she had a trap—
A thing called muskeg, easy on the eyes
Stung with the dust of gravel. Cotton grass,
Its white spires blending with the orchids,
Peeked through green table-cloths of sphagnum moss.
Carnivorous bladder-wort studded the acres,
Passing the water-fleas through their digestion.
Sweet-gale and sundew[55] edged the dwarf black spruce;
And herds of cariboo had left their hoof-marks,
Betraying visual solidity,
But like the thousands of the pitcher plants,
Their downward-pointing hairs alluring insects,
Deceptive—and the men were moving west!
Now was her time. She took three engines, sank them
With seven tracks down through the hidden lake
To the rock bed, then over them she spread
A counterpane of leather-leaf[56] and slime.
A warning, that was all for now. 'Twas sleep
She wanted, sleep, for drowsing was her pastime
And waiting through eternities of seasons.
As for intruders bred for skeletons—
Some day perhaps when ice began to move,
Or some convulsion ran fires through her tombs,
She might stir in her sleep and far below
The reach of steel and blast of dynamite,

54 Here, the epidermis, i.e., the surface.

55 A shrub and a flower that, like the other plants mentioned in this passage, attests to the bog-like quality of the apparently solid muskeg. The sundew, like the bladder-wort and the pitcher plant, is carnivorous, trapping and consuming insects in its sticky leaves.

56 A low evergreen shrub, so called because of the texture of its leaves.

She'd claim their bones as her possessive right
And wrap them cold in her pre-Cambrian folds.

* * *

BACK TO THE MOUNTAINS

As grim an enemy as rock was time.
The little men from five-to-six feet high,
From three-to-four score years in lease of breath,
Were flung in double-front[57] against them both
In years a billion strong; so long was it
Since brachiopods[58] in mollusc habitats
Were clamping shells on weed in ocean mud.
Now only yesterday had Fleming's men,
Searching for toeholds on the sides of cliffs,
Five thousand feet above sea-level, set
A tripod's leg upon a trilobite.[59]
And age meant pressure, density. Sullen
With aeons, mountains would not stand aside;
Just block the path—morose but without anger,
No feeling in the menace of their frowns,
Immobile for they had no need of motion;
Their veins possessed no blood—they carried quartzite.
Frontal assault! To go through them direct
Seemed just as inconceivable as ride
Over their peaks. But go through them the men
Were ordered and their weapons were their hands
And backs, pickaxes, shovels, hammers, drills
And dynamite—against the rock and time;
For here the labour must be counted up
In months subject to clauses of a contract
Distinguished from the mortgage-run an age
Conceded to the trickle of the rain
In building river-homes. The men bored in,
The mesozoic rock arguing the inches.

This was a kind of surgery unknown
To mountains or the mothers of the myths.
These had a chloroform in leisured time,
Squeezing a swollen handful of light-seconds,

57 That is, they were like soldiers engaged in battles on two fronts.

58 A bivalve mollusc that Darwin singled out as an example of a life-form that had not changed much from a remote geological epoch.

59 Fossil marine arthropods from the Paleozoic era (600 million to 230 million years ago).

When water like a wriggling casuist[60]
Had probed and found the areas for incision.
Now time was rushing labour—inches grew
To feet, to yards: the drills—the single jacks,
The double jacks—drove in and down; the holes
Gave way to excavations, these to tunnels,
Till men sodden with mud and roof-drip steamed
From sunlight through the tar-black to the sunlight.

* * *

(The last gap in the mountains—between the Selkirks and Savona's Ferry—is closed.)

The Road itself was like a stream that men
Had coaxed and teased or bullied out of Nature.
As if watching for weak spots in her codes,
It sought for levels like the watercourses.
It sinuously took the bends, rejoiced
In plains and easy grades, found gaps, poured through them,
But hating steep descents avoided them.
Unlike the rivers which in full rebellion
Against the canyons' hydrophobic slaver[61]
Went to the limit of their argument:
Unlike again, the stream of steel had found
A way to climb, became a mountaineer.
From the Alberta plains it reached the Summit,
And where it could not climb, it cut and curved,
Till from the Rockies to the Coastal Range
It had accomplished what the Rivers had,
Making a hundred clean Caesarian cuts,
And bringing to delivery in their time
Their smoky, lusty-screaming locomotives.

THE SPIKE

Silver or gold? Van Horne had rumbled '*Iron*'.
No flags or bands announced this ceremony,
No Morse in circulation through the world,
And though the vital words like Eagle Pass,

60 Here, one who specializes in quibbling, convoluted arguments.
61 That is, the canyons' walls seem to drool as would a rabid dog.

Craigellachie,[62] were trembling in their belfries,
No hands were at the ropes. The air was taut
With silences as rigid as the spruces
Forming the background in November mist.
More casual than camera-wise, the men
Could have been properties upon a stage,[63]
Except for road maps furrowing their faces.

Rogers, his both feet planted on a tie,
Stood motionless as ballast. In the rear,
Covering the scene with spirit-level eyes,
Predestination on his chin, was Fleming.[64]
The only one groomed for the ritual
From smooth silk hat and well-cut square-rig beard
Down through his Caledonian[65] longitude,
He was outstaturing others by a foot,
And upright as the mainmast of a brig.
Beside him, barely reaching to his waist,
A water-boy had wormed his way in front
To touch this last rail with his foot, his face
Upturned to see the cheek-bone crags of Rogers.
The other side of Fleming, hands in pockets,
Eyes leaden-lidded under square-crowned hat,
And puncheon-bellied[66] under overcoat,
Unsmiling at the focused lens—Van Horne.
Whatever ecstasy played round that rail
Did not leap to his face. Five years had passed,
Less than five years—so well within the pledge.

The job was done. Was this the slouch of rest?
Not to the men he drove through walls of granite.
The embers from the past were in his soul,
Banked for the moment at the rail and smoking,
Just waiting for the future to be blown.

62 The driving of the last spike signifying the completion of the CPR (which was deliberately done without the elaborate ritual that marked the completion of the Union Pacific in the States) took place in the Eagle Pass; the place was called Craigellachie because of the name's significance for Smith and Stephen (see p. 289, conclusion of note 8).
63 The lines that follow are based on the famous photograph of the driving of the last spike.
64 That is, Fleming's square-cut beard made him look like the typical Scots-Calvinist that he was. (Calvinists believe in the doctrine of predestination, i.e. that one was born already destined for Heaven or Hell.)
65 Scottish (poetic).
66 Pot-bellied (a puncheon is a large cask of liquor).

At last the spike and Donald with the hammer!
His hair like frozen moss from Labrador
Poked out under his hat, ran down his face
To merge with streaks of rust in a white cloud.
What made him fumble the first stroke?[67] Not age:
The snow belied his middle sixties. Was
It lapse of caution or his sense of thrift,
That elemental stuff which through his life
Never pockmarked his daring but had made
The man the canniest trader of his time,
Who never missed a rat-count,[68] never failed
To gauge the size and texture of a pelt?
Now here he was caught by the camera,
Back bent, head bowed, and staring at a sledge,
Outwitted by an idiotic nail.
Though from the crowd no laughter, yet the spike
With its slewed[69] neck was grinning up at Smith.
Wrenched out, it was replaced. This time the hammer
Gave a first tap as with apology,
Another one, another, till the spike
Was safely stationed in the tie and then
The Scot, invoking his ancestral clan,
Using the hammer like a battle-axe,
His eyes bloodshot with memories of Flodden,[70]
Descended on it, rammed it to its home.

The stroke released a trigger for a burst
Of sound that stretched the gamut of the air.
The shouts of engineers and dynamiters,
Of locomotive-workers and explorers,
Flanking the rails, were but a tuning-up
For a massed continental chorus. Led
By Moberly (of the Eagles and *this* Pass)
And Rogers (of *his own*), followed by Wilson,[71]

67 Smith bent the first spike and had to drive a second.

68 That is, who never miscounted muskrat pelts.

69 Twisted.

70 A Scottish battle against the English in 1513, of which John Hill Burton writes, in his *History of Scotland*: 'From other battles Scotland has suffered more unhappy political results, but this was the most disastrous of all in immediate loss. As a calamity rather than a disgrace, it has ever been spoken of with a mournful pride for the unavailing devotedness which it called out.'

71 All the men named in this passage were present at the driving of the last spike: Tom Wilson had served as Rogers' guide in the Kicking Horse surveys; John Egan was general superintendent of the CPR western division under Van Horne; Henry J. Cambie was a government engineer who supervised a difficult section of the road in the Fraser Canyon; Marcus Smith took over the BC surveys in 1873; George Harris was a Boston financier and company director; John H. McTavish was the CPR land commissioner.

And Ross (charged with the Rocky Mountain Section),
By Egan (general of the Western Lines),
Cambie and Marcus Smith, Harris of Boston,
The roar was deepened by the bass of Fleming,
And heightened by the laryngeal fifes
Of Dug McKenzie and John H. McTavish.
It ended when Van Horne spat out some phlegm
To ratify the tumult with 'Well Done'[72]
Tied in a knot of monosyllables.

Merely the tuning up! For on the morrow
The last blow on the spike would stir the mould
Under the drumming of the prairie wheels,
And make the whistles from the steam out-crow
The Fraser. Like a gavel it would close
Debate, making Macdonald's 'sea to sea'
Pour through two oceanic megaphones—
Three thousand miles of *Hail* from port to port;
And somewhere in the middle of the line
Of steel, even the lizard heard the stroke.
The breed had triumphed after all. To drown
The traffic chorus, she must blend the sound
With those inaugural, narcotic notes
Of storm and thunder which would send her back
Deeper than ever in Laurentian sleep.

1952

72 Van Horne's famous speech at the driving of the last spike was brief and to the point: 'All I can say is that the work has been done well in every way.'

Marjorie Pickthall

1883–1922

Born in Middlesex, England, Marjorie Lowry Christie Pickthall immigrated with her parents to Toronto in 1889. She attended Saint Mildred's Girls' School and the Bishop Strachan School for Girls, selling her first story, 'Two Ears', to the Toronto *Globe* in 1898. After her mother's death in 1910 (an event that upset her greatly), she became an assistant librarian at Victoria College. In 1912 she returned to England to live with relatives, in an attempt to improve her failing health. There she contributed to the war effort as much as her health permitted, working as an ambulance driver, farm labourer, and assistant librarian in a meteorological office. She returned briefly to Toronto in 1919 before moving to Victoria and then to Vancouver, where she died of complications following heart surgery.

Although Pickthall had turned more towards prose at the time of her death (she was working on a novel, *The Beaten Man*), she was known primarily in Canada as a poet. Only two collections of poetry, however, were published during her lifetime: *The Drift of Pinions* (1913) and *The Lamp of Poor Souls* (1916; rpr. 1972). The others were published posthumously: *Mary Tired* (a Christmas remembrance; 1922), *The Woodcarver's Wife and Other Poems* (a one-act verse drama; 1922), *Two Poems* ('Vision' and 'Ebb Tide'; 1923), *Little Songs* (1925), and *The Naiad and Five Other Poems* (1931). *The Complete Poems of Marjorie Pickthall* (1925), collected by her father, Arthur C. Pickthall, saw a series of editions.

A prolific writer, Pickthall worked in a variety of forms and published her work in well-known magazines, both in North America and in England. Twenty-four of her many short stories were collected in *Angels' Shoes* (1922). As well, she wrote three juvenile novels—*Dick's Desertion: A Boy's Adventures in Canadian Forests* (1905), *The Straight Road* (1906), and *Billy's Hero; or, The Valley of Gold* (1908)—and two adult novels, *Little Hearts* (1915) and *The Bridge: A Story of the Great Lakes* (1921). *The Bridge* appeared both in *Everybody's* (New York) and *Sphere* (London, England); the juvenile novels were published serially in *East and West*, a paper sponsored by the Presbyterian Church.

In her day, Pickthall received both popular and critical acclaim, earning great praise from such influential critics as Archibald MacMechan, Andrew Macphail, and Lorne Pierce (who wrote her biography in 1925). The Montreal Branch of the Canadian Authors' Association noted at the time of her death that 'her place is secure, not only as the first poet of Canada, but one of the first poets of the English language' (23 April). Condemned, however, in the 1940s by E.K. Brown, and then in the 1950s by Desmond Pacey, her poetry fell out of fashion at a time when literary tastes favoured irony over reverie, and a realistic vision over a stylized romantic one.

Ironically, Pickthall's early success may have contributed to her decline in popularity. She received public recognition even before the publication of her first collection of poetry by winning the Christmas poetry competition sponsored by the *The Mail and Empire* in 1900, and because of her many smaller publications in prominent magazines across North America. The poems of her first volume were collected at the suggestion of Sir Andrew Macphail, which guaranteed its success; the first edition of 1000 copies sold out in ten days. Because of the early praise she received she was never pushed to develop beyond the lyric conventions she inherited from the English Romantic poets and from the Confederation poets, her literary forebears in Canada. It is unfortunate that her career was cut short by her untimely death, because there is evidence in her poetry to suggest that she was beginning to question her use of these conventions. As Diana Relke points out, Pickthall, as a female poet, had difficulty locating herself in a lyric tradition that deals with the relationship between man and nature (*Canadian Literature*, 1987). Her discomfort is evident in 'The Sleep-

Seekers', for example, where the poetic voice, striving to identify itself in terms of 'there/here' and 'you/we', finally affirms a dream world lying beyond life and nature.

Much of Pickthall's poetry deals with this mystical and imaginative space, characterized by the colour silver and accessible only through a kind of artistic reverie. This poetic dream world provided Pickthall with a refuge—in her early work, from the painful memory of her mother's death, and in later work, from a modern war-stricken world. In 'Made in His Image', she expresses some of her concerns about a God who may be all-powerful, even all-knowing, but ultimately unfeeling. This troubled tone in her work led a contemporary essayist, John Daniel Logan, to describe her as not 'a natural, happy poet of Nature' but as a 'wistful, sorrowing poet of the Spirit' torn between a naturally 'pagan' spirit and a learned Christian 'asceticism' that did not wholly satisfy her (*Marjorie Pickthall: Her Poetic Genius and Art*, 1922).

The speaker's discomfort with her subject is echoed in the halting repetitions and alliterations of 'Made in His Image'. Unlike the flowing internal rhymes of 'The Sleep-Seekers', which inspired Archibald MacMehan to mourn the loss of 'the truest, sweetest singing voice ever heard in Canada', the play with rhythm and repetition in such poems as 'Made in His Image' and 'The Bird in the Room' demonstrates the range and variety of Pickthall's skill.

'The Third Generation,' a good example of a Gothic form popular throughout the twentieth century—the ironic ghost story—suggests the guilt European settlers felt about their effect on the First Nations. It also serves as a prose continuation of Pickthall's concerns with the spirit, with sorrow, and with death.

The Sleep-Seekers

Lift thou the latch whereon the wild rose clings,
Touch the green door to which the briar has grown.
If you seek sleep, she dwells not with these things,—
The prisoned wood, the voiceless reed, the stone.
But where the day yields to one star alone,
Softly Sleep cometh on her brown owl-wings,
Sliding above the marshes silently
To the dim beach between the black pines and the sea.

There; or in one leaf-shaken loveliness
Of birchen light and shadow, deep she dwells,
Where the song-sparrow and the thrush are heard,
And once a wandering flute-voiced mocking-bird,
Where, when the year was young,
Grew sweet faint bloodroot, and the adder-tongue
Lifting aloft her spire of golden bells.

Here shall we lift our lodge against the rain,
Walling it deep
With tamarac branches and the balsam fir,
Sweet even as sleep,
And aspen boughs continually astir

To make a silver-gleaming,—
Here shall we lift our lodge and find again
A little space for dreaming.

1925

The Bird in the Room

Last autumn when they aired the house
A bird got in, and died in this room.
Here it fluttered
Close to the shuttered
Window, and beat in the airless gloom,
No space for its wing, no drop for its mouth,—
A swallow, flying south.

And the velvet-creeping unsleeping mouse
Trampled that swiftness where it fell
On the dusty border
Pattern'd in order
With a citron flower and a golden shell,—
But it might not fly and it might not drink,
On the carpet's sunless brink.

A thought of you beat into my mind,
Empty and shuttered, dark, and spread
With dusty sheeting
To hide the beating
Tread of the hours. But the thought was dead
When I opened the door of that room, to find
If the Spring
Had left me anything—

1936

Made in His Image

Between the archangels and the old eclipse
Of glory on perfect glory, does He feel
A vision, thin as frost at midnight, steal

And lay a nameless shadow on His lips?
Does He, Who gave the power, endure the pain?—
Look down the hollow'd universe, and see
His works, His worlds, choiring Him endlessly,—
His worlds, His works, all made, and made in vain?
Then does He bid all heaven beneath His hand,
In blossom of worship, flame on flame of praise,
And taste their thunders, and grow sick, and gaze
At some gray silence that He had not planned,
And shiver among His stars, and nurse each spark
That wards Him from the uncreated dark?

1936

The Third Generation[1]

No shanty fires shall cheer them,
No comrades march beside,
But the northern lights shall beckon
And the wandering winds shall guide.
They shall cross the silent waters
By a trail that is wild and far,
To the place of the lonely lodges
Under a lonely star.
—*La Longue Traverse.*

'Bob, is this Lake Lemaire?'

Bob Lemaire, leaning against a wind-twisted tamarack on the ridge above the portage, looked long and very long at the desolate country spread out beneath them. Then he looked at a map, drawn on parchment in faded ink, which he had just unfolded from a waterproof case. 'I can't identify it,' he confessed at last, 'but I think—'

'If you say another word', groaned Barrett, 'about the reliability of your grandfather, I—I'll heave rocks at you.' Lemaire smiled slowly, and the smile transfigured his lean, serious face; he folded the map and replaced it in the little case. 'Well,' he answered, comfortingly, 'we can't mistake P'tite Babiche, anyway, when we come to it.'

'If the thing exists . . . Oh, I know your grandfather said he found it, and stuck it on his map. But no one else has ever found it since.'

'No one else', said Lemaire, quietly, 'has been so far west from the Gran' Babiche.'

1 An allusion to a passage in the Bible about 'visiting the iniquity of the fathers upon the children, and upon the children's children, unto the third and to the fourth generation (Exodus 34: 7).

He looked again at the land, one of the most desolate in the world, across which they must go. Lake, rapid, river; rock, scrub, pine, and caribou moss—here the world held only these things, repeated to infinity. But as Lemaire's grave eyes rested on them, those eyes showed nothing but stillness and a strange content. And Barrett, who had been watching his friend and not the new chain of lakes ahead, cried suddenly, 'Bob, I believe you like it!'

'Yes, I like it—if like is the word.'

'O gosh! And you never saw it till five years ago?'

'No.'

'And your father never saw it at all?'

'No. He married young, you know, and had no money. He worked in an office all his life. My mother said he used to talk in his sleep of—all this—which he had never seen. And when I saw it, it just seemed to—come natural.' He smiled again. 'We've three—four—more portages', he went on, 'before we camp.'

'And it's along of having Forbes Lemaire for a grandfather,' groaned Barrett, as he limped after Lemaire's light stride, down the rocky slope to the little beach where they had left their canoe.

They launched the canoe, thigh deep in the rush of the ice-clear water, and put out into yet another of that endless chain of unknown and uncharted lakes whose course they were following. Only one map in the world showed these lakes, those low iron hills, that swamp—the map made by Bob Lemaire's grandfather fifty years before; as far as was known, only one white man before themselves had ever tried the journey from the Gran' Babiche due west to the P'tite Babiche, that mythical river; and that had been Forbes Lemaire. As Barrett said, it was a tour personally conducted by the ghost of a grandfather.

Another wet portage—tripping and sliding under a low cliff among fallen shale and willow bushes—another lake, as wide, as lonely, as the former one. So for three hours. And then the afternoon shut down in drive on drive of damp gray mist; and they edged the canoe inshore, and beached it at last upon a dun ridge of sand, the shadows of dwarfed bullpines promising firing.

Too tired to speak, they made their camp, deftly, as long practice had taught them. Tinned beef, flapjacks and coffee had power, however, to change the very aspect of the weather. And Barrett, smoking the pipe of repletion, under a wisp of tent, had time to admire the Japanese effect of the writhed pines in the fog, to hear a sort of wild music in the voices of rain and water, and to meditate on the chances of an ouananiche for the morning's meal.

The shadows of the fog were changing to the shadows of night, and the silent Lemaire rose and flung wood on the fire. It sent out a warm glow; and as if it had been a signal, a living shadow crept from the shadow of the rocks, and very timidly approached the light.

Both men rose with an exclamation; for they had not seen a human being for nearly a month. Barrett said, 'An Indian,' and sank back on his blanket, leaving Lemaire to ask questions. Lemaire went round the fire, and stooped over the queer huddled shadow on the ground.

'Well?' Barrett called after him at last.

'A Montagnais,' Lemaire answered after a pause, some trouble in his voice. 'About the oldest old Indian I've ever seen; they aren't long-lived. . . . He seems a bit wrong in the head. He doesn't seem to know his name or where he comes from. But—he says he's going to a big encampment many days' journey west. He says he's been following us. He says he's a friend of mine.'

'Is he?'

'I never saw him before. . . . That's all I can get out of him. He's probably been cast off by his tribe. Why? Oh, too old to be useful.'

'Cruel brutes.'

'Not so cruel as some white men,' said Lemaire, half to himself. He had come back to the firelight, and was rummaging among their stores, none too plentiful. He returned to the old Indian, carrying food; and presently Barrett heard snapping sounds, as of a hungry dog feeding. Lemaire came again to his nook under the tent; and Barrett smoked out his pipe in silence. Then, as he knocked the ashes, fizzling, into a little pool of rain, he said gently, 'Bob, what makes you so uncommonly good to the Indians?'

Quiet Lemaire did not attempt to evade the direct question. But a rather shy flush rose to his dark, lean cheeks as he said diffidently, 'I suppose—because I feel my family—any one of my name—owes 'em something.'

'The grandfather again, eh?'

'Yes. . . . Men had no souls in those days, Barrett. I think the tremendous loneliness—the newness—the lack of responsibility—something killed their souls. . . . Wait.'

Leaning forward, he flung more wood on the fire. And the red light flickered on his strong and gentle face. He glanced at his friend, and went on abruptly. 'I've my grandfather's maps and journals, you know—what my father called the shameful records of his fame. He was absolutely explicit in 'em. I never saw them in father's lifetime, but he left them to me, saying I could read them or not, as I liked. I was very proud of them. I read them. And upon my word—though from them I got the hints that may lead us to the rediscovery of the Lost Babiche—I'm almost sorry I did. It leaves a bad taste in the mind, if you know what I mean, to think that one's father's father was such a heroic scoundrel.'

'A bad record, Bobby?'

'Bad even for those days. Listen to me. While he was on this very expedition we're on now, he was taken sick. He was very sick, and going to be worse. He knew what it was. He was near the big summer camp of a tribe of Indians that had been very kind to him, coast Indians, come inland for the caribou hunting; he went to them. He was sick, and they took him in, and nursed him. And all the time he knew what it was he had. It was the smallpox.

'You know what La Picotte is in the wilds. They've a song about it still, down along the Lamennais. . . . For of all that tribe, only one family, they say, escaped. All the others died; they died as if the Angel of Destruction had come among them with his sword—they died like flies, they died in heaps. And over the bones of the dead the tepees stood for years, ragged, blowing in the winds. And then the skins rotted, and the bare poles stood, gleaming white, over the rotting bones that covered an acre of ground, they say. No one ever went to that place any more. It was cursed . . . because of my grandfather.'

'Monsieur Forbes made his get-away?'

'Yes, or I shouldn't be telling you about it.' Lemaire summoned a smile, but his eyes were sombre. 'And so I guess—that's one reason why. One among many.'

'You're a likeable old freak,' murmured Barrett affectionately, 'but—*you* ain't responsible you know!'

'As I look at it, we're all responsible.'

'Well—anyway, I wouldn't give that old scarecrow too much of our grubstake, old man. We've none too much, if the Babiche doesn't turn up according to schedule.'

'Probably we won't see any more of him. He'll be gone by the morning.'

He was gone with the morning. But as day followed weary day, and there was still no sign of the lakes narrowing to the long-sought river, Barrett was increasingly conscious that the old man was close upon their trail. Sometimes, in the brief radiance of the September dawns, he would see, far and far behind on the wrinkled silver water, a warped canoe paddling feebly. They always hauled away, by miles, from that decrepit canoe. But always, some time in the dark hours, it crept up again. Sometimes, he would see, in the sunset, a wavering thread of smoke arising from the site of their last-camp-but-one. It irritated him at last; the thought of that ragged, cranky canoe, paddled by the ragged, dirty, old imbecile, forever following them—creeping, creeping, under the great gaunt stars, creeping, creeping, under the flying dawns, the stormy moons; when he found Lemaire leaving little scraps of precious tobacco, a pinch of flour in a screw of paper, or a fresh-caught fish beside the trodden ashes of their cooking-place, he exploded.

'I can't help it,' Lemaire apologized, 'I *know* I'm all kinds of a fool, Barrett. But the poor old wretch is nearly blind—from long-ago smallpox, I should think. He can't catch things for himself much.'

Barrett, aware that wisdom was on his side, yet felt sorry for his explosion. He said nothing more. Soon he forgot the matter, having much else to think about.

For the Lost Babiche, the once-discovered river, did not 'turn up according to schedule.'

The chain of lakes they had been following turned due south. They left them, and, after a terrible portage, launched the canoe in a stream that ran west. Here their progress was very slow, for there were rapids, and consequent portages, every mile or so. This stream, instead of feeding another lake, died out in impassable quaking mosses. They saw a range of low hills some four or five miles ahead; so again they left the canoe and struck out for them on foot, half-wading, half-walking. It was exhausting work. At last they climbed the barren spurs and saw beyond, under a flaring sunset, a world of interlacing waterways, unvisited and unknown, that seemed then as if they smoked under the vast clouds and spirals of wildfowl settling homeward to the reeds. The two men watched that wonderful sight in silence.

At last, 'They're gathering to go south,' said Lemaire briefly. And Barrett answered, 'D'you know what date it is? It's the day on which we said we'd turn back if we hadn't found the Lost Babiche. It's the fifteenth of September.'

'Well . . . are we going back?'

'Not till we've found our river,' cried Barrett, with half a laugh and half a curse. They gripped hands, smiling rather grimly. They made a miserable, fireless camp, and went back the next day, carrying canoe and supplies, in four toilsome trips, across the hills; repacking and relaunching the second day on a new lake, where in all probability no white man—but one—had ever before dipped paddle.

They had been in the wilderness so long that they had fallen into the habit of carrying on conversations as if the lapse of two or three days had been as many minutes. Barrett knew to what Lemaire referred when he said abruptly, 'After all, it isn't as if you were ignorant of the risks.'

'I guess I know just as much about them as you,' said Barrett, cheerily. 'We're taking chances on the grub, aren't we? If we find the Lost Babiche before the game moves, we'll be alright, though our own supplies won't take us there. Once there, Bob, we're pretty sure to find friendly Indians when we link up with the Silver Fork—which we do seventy miles down the P'tite Babiche if your grandpa's map's correct. Well there are a good many 'if's' in the programme, but don't you worry. We'll get through or out, somehow. There's always fish. I've a feeling that this country *can't* go back on a Lemaire!'

They went on to a pleasant camp that night on a sandy islet overgrown with dwarf willow, and a wild-duck supper. The current of these new lakes went west with such increasing strength that Lemaire thought they were feeling the 'pull' of some big river into which the system drained; and if so, it could be no river but the lost Babiche. They slept, all a-tingle with the fever of discovery and re-made maps in their dreams.

Behind them many miles, a wandering smoke arose from the ashes of their last camp. The old Indian, about whom they had almost forgotten, had gained on them while they packed their supplies over the hills. Now he was close upon them again.

The life of that old savage seemed thin and wavering as the smoke of the fire he made. All night he sat in the ashes, motionless as a stone. Only once, just before the fierce dawn, he rose to his feet with an inarticulate cry, stirred to some instinctive excitement. For in a moment the vast, chill dusk was filled with a musical thrill, a tremendous clamour and rush of life, as thousand by thousand after their kinds, teal and widgeon, mallard and sheldrake, lifted from the reeds and fled before the coming cold. As the old man dimly watched, two delicate things fell and touched his face; one was a feather, the second was a flake of snow.

In those few delicate flakes, Lemaire and Barrett seemed to feel for the first time the ever-present hostility of nature; with such a brief, exquisite touch were they first made aware of the powers against which they strove. The new waterways seemed to stretch interminably. Each time they cleared one of the deep-cut channels which linked lake with lake as regularly as a thread links beads, they looked ahead with the same question. Each time they saw the same expanse of gray water, low islets, barren shores; the country passed them changing and unchanging as a dream. They seemed to be moving in a dream, conscious of nothing but the pressure of the current on their paddles.

Then came the mist.

It shut them into a circle ten feet wide, a pearl-white prison. Outside the circle were shadows, wandering voices, trees as men walking. For two days they felt their way westward through this fog; two nights they shivered over a damp-wood fire, hearing nothing but water beading and dripping everywhere with a sound of grief. It strangely broke Lemaire's steel nerve. On the second night he said, restlessly, 'We must turn back to-morrow.'

'Bob!'

He flung out a tanned hand passionately. 'I know. . . . But can't you feel it? Things have turned against us. These things.' He pointed at the veiled sky, the milky water. 'I daren't go on. If we don't find the river to-morrow, we'll go back. And then . . . the land will have done for me what it never did for my grandfather.'

'What, Bob, old fellow?'

'Beaten me,' said Lemaire, and rolled into his blankets without another word.

He woke next morning with the touch of clear sunlight on his eyelids. He leaped to his feet silently, without waking Barrett, and as he did so, ice broke and tinkled like glass where the edge of the blankets had lain in a little pool of moisture. The last of the fog was draining in golden smoke from the low, dark hills. He strode to the edge of the water, and stopped, shaking suddenly as if he were cold. Then he went to Barrett, and stooped over him.

'Hullo, Bob, is it morning?' Then, as he saw Lemaire's face, 'My God, what is it?'

Twice Lemaire tried to speak. Then he pointed eastward to three high rocky islands which lay across the water, exactly spaced, like the ruined spans of a great bridge which once had stretched from shore to shore.

'Barrett,' he said huskily, 'We entered the Lost Babiche yesterday in the fog, and never knew. Those islands are ten miles down the river on Forbes Lemaire's map.'

They faced each other in silence, too much moved to speak. Their hands met in a long grip. Then Barrett said suddenly, 'Anything else.'

'Yes. It's freezing hard.'

'But . . . we've won, Bob, we've won!'

'Not yet,' said the man whose fathers had been bred in the wilderness, and wed to it. 'Not yet. It's still against us.'

But there was no talk now of turning back.

The Lost Babiche—lost no more—was a noble river; a gray and ice-clear stream winding in generous curves between high cliffs of slate-coloured rock. These cliffs were much cut into ravines and gullies, where grew timber of fine size for that country. But as their tense excitement lessened a little, they were struck by the absence of all life; even in the deep rock-shadows they saw no fish. Of human life there was not a sign; though in Forbes Lemaire's days the country had supported many Indians. And now—'Not a soul but ourselves,' said Barrett, in an awed voice; 'not a living soul . . .'

Yes. One soul yet living. Far behind them, in the staggering old canoe, the old Indian paddled valiantly on their trail. But he had forgotten them now, as they had long forgotten him. He stopped no more for the offal of their camps. A stronger instinct even than that of hunger was drawing him on the way they also went; down the Lost Babiche. Had they looked, they would not have seen him. And soon, between him and them, the clouds which had been gathering all day dropped a curtain of fine snow.

The first sting of the tiny balled flakes on his knuckles was to Lemaire like the thunder of guns, the opening of a battle.

He had no need to speak to Barrett. They bent over the paddles and the canoe surged forward. It was a race; a race between the early winter and themselves. If the cold weather set in so soon, if they found no Indians on the little-known Silver Fork—there were a dozen 'ifs' in their minds as, mile after mile, they fled down the P'tite Babiche. Even as they fled from the winter, so that other white man long ago had fled from the sickness; seen those stark bluffs unrolling; viewed perhaps those very trees.

They made a record distance that day. 'We're winning, Bob, we're winning,' said Barrett over the fire that night. Lemaire had not the heart to contradict him; but Lemaire's instincts, inherited from generations, told him that the wilderness was still mysteriously their enemy. He sat smoking, silent, hearing nothing but the faint, innumerable hiss of the snowflakes falling into the flames.

The snow was thickening in the morning, and by noon a bitter wind arose, blowing in their faces and against the stream. Soon the canoe was smack-smack-smacking on the waves, and the snow was driving almost level. The continual pressure of wind and snow drugged their senses. They never heard the voice of the rapids until, rounding an abrupt bend, the ravelled water seemed to leap at them from under the very bow of the canoe.

There was only one thing to be done, and—'Let her go!' yelled Lemaire, crouching tense as a spring above the steering paddle.

Now for the trained eye, the strong hand—the eye to see the momentary chance, the hand to obey without a falter.

Now for the sleeping instincts of a brain inherited from far generations of wanderers and voyageurs. Flash on flash of leaping water, the drive of spray and snow, the canoe staggering and checking like a thing hurt, but always recovering.

Barrett, in the bows, paddled blindly. His life lay in Bob Lemaire's hands, and he was content to leave it there during those roaring moments. But those hands failed—by an inch.

They were in smooth water. Barrett would have paused to take a breath, but Lemaire's voice barked at him from the stern. He obeyed. The canoe drove forward again—forward in great leaps, towards the point of a small island ahead, dimly seen through the snow—something was wrong, though, thought Barrett, grunting; he could get no 'beef' on the thing—it dragged; you'd have thought Bob was paddling against him. Then, suddenly, he understood. He called up the last of his strength, drove the paddle in, once, twice—again—heard a shout, flung himself overside into water waist-deep, and just as the canoe was sinking under them, he and Lamaire caught it and ran it ashore. Then, dripping, they looked each other in the face, and each seemed to see the face of disaster.

'It was a rock,' said Lemaire at last, very quietly, 'a few inches below the surface. It has almost cut the canoe in two.'

'What's to be done?'

'Find shelter, I suppose.'

They were very quiet about it. There was no shelter on their islet but a few rocks and a dead spruce in the middle. Here they set up their tent as a wind-break. It was bitterly cold; the island was sheathed in white ice, for the spray from the rough water froze now as it fell; everything in the canoe was wet; they were wet to their waists. They tried to induce the dead tree to burn, but the wood was so rotted with wet it only smouldered and went out. They had a little cooking lamp and a few squares of compressed fuel for it; they lighted this, and Lemaire made tea with numbed hands. It renewed the life in them, but could not dry them. They huddled against the little lamp in silence, waiting—waiting.

After some time Lemaire heard a curious sound from Barrett; his teeth were chattering. Lemaire saw that his face had taken a waxy white hue. He spoke to him, and Barrett looked up, but his eyes were dim and glazed. 'It'll be all right,' he said, thickly, 'we'll get through, somehow. I've a feeling that this country can't go back on a Lemaire.'

They were the first symptoms of collapse. Lemaire groaned. He got to his feet, and staggered across the slippery rocks. He shook his fist in the implacable face of the desolation. He shouted, foolish rage and defiance, caught back at his sanity; shouted again. . . . This time he thought he heard a faint cry in the snow. It whipped him back to self-control. He splashed out into the curdling shallows, shouting desperately.

Out of the gray drive of snow loomed the ghost of a canoe; paddled, as it seemed, by a ghost. It was the old Indian, whom Lemaire had long forgotten; the weather had not hindered him, the rapids had not wrecked him. At Lemaire's cry he raised his head, and the canoe put inshore, waveringly. Lemaire splashed to meet it, met the incurious gaze of the half-blind old eyes under the scarred lids, and read into the wrinkled, foul old face, a sort of animal kindness.

Five minutes later he was desperately trying to rouse Barrett. Barrett looked at him at last, and Lemaire saw that the brief delirium was past. 'What is it, Bob?' he asked, weakly. And Lemaire broke into a torrent of words.

'The old Indian—the old Indian you said was a hoodoo—don't you remember? He's here. He has caught us up, God knows how. He says his canoe'll hold three. He says that a very little way on there's a big camp, and that he'll take us there—in a very little while. He says his tribe is always kind to strangers, to white men. . . . I can't make out all he says, he's queer in his head. But he's dead sure of the encampment. He says it's always there . . .'

Still talking eagerly, Lemaire snatched together a few things, got an arm round Barrett, lifted him up to his feet, got him reeling to the canoe, laid him in the bottom, and helped the old Indian push off. There was no second paddle. There was no need of it. The current took them at once.

The cold was increasing, as the wind died and the snow thinned. Lemaire ceased to be conscious of the passing of time, but within himself the stubborn life burned; he was strongly curious to know the end, to discover what it was the wilderness had in store for him after five years, to read the riddle of that relationship with himself which had called him from the cities to this.

He was aware, at last, of a vast, golden light. The clouds were parting behind the snow, and the sunset was gleaming through. It turned the snow into a mist of rose and molten gold. The old Indian feebly turned the canoe. It crept toward the shore.

'The lodges of my people,' muttered the old Indian. He stood erect, and pointed with his bleached paddle. 'They are very many—a very strong tribe.'

Lemaire also looked, and saw.

Silently, the canoe took the half-frozen sand. Silently, very slowly, Lemaire stepped out. The old Indian waited for him. It seemed that the whole world was waiting for him.

He, like a man in a dream, moved slowly into the midst of a level stretch of sand, and stood there. All about him, covering the whole level, were the ridgepoles of wigwams, but the coverings had long fallen away and rotted, and the sunset glowed through the gaunt poles. Lemaire stretched out his hand, and touched the nearest; they fell into dust and rot. . . . Under his feet he crushed the bones of the dead—the dead, who had died fifty years before, and had waited for him here ever since, under the blown sand and the ground willows. . . . 'They've a song about it, down along the Lamennais. For of all that tribe, only one family, they say, escaped. All the others died . . . they died like flies, they died in heaps. And over the bones of the dead the tepees stood for years. . . . No one ever went to that place any more. It was cursed . . . because of my grandfather.'

He went back to the canoe. Whining like an old animal, the old Indian was busied above Barrett. 'The lodges of my people,' he muttered, 'a very strong tribe, and kind to the white men.'

Very gently, Lemaire put aside the blind old hands that touched Barrett's unconscious face. 'Don't wake him,' he said.

1922

Ethel Wilson

1888–1980

Ethel Davis Bryant Wilson, a daughter of a Methodist missionary, was born in South Africa and raised in England until her parents' death in 1898. At the age of ten she went to live in Vancouver with relatives who sent her to schools there and in Britain. She taught school until 1920, when she married a Vancouver physician, Dr Wallace Wilson. The two lived in various countries before returning home to Vancouver and the province they loved.

After Wilson's first short story was published in England in 1937, her wartime work—the editing of a Red Cross magazine—curtailed her serious writing for almost ten years. In 1947 Wilson, nearing sixty, published her first novel, *Hetty Dorval.* Over the next fourteen years she produced three more novels: *The Innocent Traveller* (1949), *Swamp Angel* (1954), and *Love and Salt Water* (1956). Her shorter fiction includes the two novellas, published together in *The Equations of Love* (1952), and *Mrs Golightly and Other Stories* (1961), which draws together her previously published short stories. A number of previously unpublished stories appeared in a posthumous volume, *Ethel Wilson: Stories, Essays and Letters* (1987), edited by David Stouck.

Wilson's elegant, balanced style, with its seemingly artless surfaces, belies the complex structures of her narratives. Her stories—simple tales of slightly absurd characters who live in a dream-like world—achieve their effect through the imposition of a comic, even biting, vision upon what is otherwise a meticulously realistic presentation. This yoking of literary modes allows her to examine two important topics in twentieth-century Canadian literature: the universe as a tricky, unreliable place, and society as an increasingly dehumanized milieu. 'The Window' deals with both of these themes. Hugo McPherson has observed that 'its title image, the window framing by day the empty scene and mirroring by night the sterile life of the protagonist, is central not only to her but to much Canadian fiction.'

The Window

The great big window must have been at least twenty-five feet wide and ten feet high. It was constructed in sections divided by segments of something that did not interfere with the view; in fact the eye by-passed these divisions and looked only at the entrancing scenes beyond. The window, together with a glass door at the western end, composed a bland shallow curve and formed the entire transparent north-west (but chiefly north) wall of Mr Willy's living-room.

Upon his arrival from England Mr Willy had surveyed the various prospects of living in the quickly growing city of Vancouver with the selective and discarding characteristics which had enabled him to make a fortune and retire all of a sudden from business and his country in his advanced middle age. He settled immediately upon the very house. It was a small old house overlooking the sea between Spanish Banks and English Bay. He knocked out the north wall and made the window. There was nothing particular to commend the house except that it faced immediately on the sea-shore and the view. Mr Willy had left his wife and her three sisters to play bridge together until death should overtake them in England. He now paced from end to end of his living-room, that is to say from east to west, with his hands in his pockets, admiring the northern view. Sometimes he stood with his hands behind him looking through the great glass window, seeing the wrinkled or placid sea and the ships almost at his feet and beyond the sea the mountains, and seeing sometimes his emancipation. His emancipation drove him into a dream, and sea sky mountains swam before him, vanished, and he saw with immense release his wife in still another more repulsive hat. He did not know, nor would have cared, that much discussion went on in her world, chiefly in the afternoons, and that he was there alleged to have deserted her. So he had, after providing well for her physical needs which were all the needs of which she was capable. Mrs Willy went on saying '. . . and he would come home my dear and never speak a word I can't tell you my dear how *frightful* it was night after night I might say for *years* I simply can't tell you . . .' No, she could not tell but she did, by day and night. Here he was at peace, seeing out of the window the crimped and wrinkled sea and the ships which passed and passed each other, the seabirds and the dream-inducing sky.

At the extreme left curve of the window an island appeared to slope into the sea. Behind this island and to the north, the mountains rose very high. In the summer time the mountains were soft, deceptive in their innocency, full of crags and crevasses and arêtes and danger. In the winter they lay magnificent, white and much higher, it seemed, than in the summer time. They tossed, static, in almost visible motion against the sky, inhabited only by eagles and—so a man had told Mr Willy, but he didn't believe the man—by mountain sheep and some cougars, bears, wild cats and, certainly, on the lower slopes, deer, and now a ski camp far out of sight. Mr Willy looked at the mountains and regretted his past youth and his present wealth. How could he endure to be old and rich and able only to look at these mountains which in his youth he had not known and did not climb. Nothing, now, no remnant of his youth would come and enable him to climb these mountains. This he found hard to believe, as old people do. He was shocked at the newly realized decline of his physical powers which had proved good enough on the whole for his years of success, and by the fact that now he had, at last, time and could not swim (heart), climb mountains (heart and legs), row a boat in a rough enticing sea (call that old age). These things have happened to other people, thought Mr Willy, but not to us, now, who have been so young, and yet it will happen to those who now are young.

Immediately across the water were less spectacular mountains, pleasant slopes which in winter time were covered with invisible skiers. Up the dark mountain at night sprang the lights of the ski-lift, and ceased. The shores of these mountains were strung with lights, littered with lights, spangled with lights, necklaces, bracelets, constellations, far more beautiful as seen through this window across the dark water than if Mr Willy had driven his car across the Lions' Gate Bridge and westwards among those constellations which would have disclosed only a shopping centre, people walking the streets, street lights, innumerable cars and car lights like anywhere else and, up the slopes, peoples' houses. Then, looking back to the south across the dark water towards his own home and the great lighted window which he would not have been able to distinguish so far away, Mr Willy would have seen lights again, a carpet of glitter thrown over the slopes of the city.

Fly from one shore to the other, fly and fly back again, fly to a continent or to an island, but you are no better off than if you stayed all day at your own window (and such a window), thought Mr Willy pacing back and forth, then into the kitchen to put the kettle on for a cup of tea which he will drink beside the window, back for a glass of whisky, returning in time to see a cormorant flying level with the water, not an inch too high not an inch too low, flying out of sight. See the small ducks lying on the water, one behind the other, like beads on a string. In the mornings Mr Willy drove into town to see his investment broker and perhaps to the bank or round the park. He lunched, but not at a club. He then drove home. On certain days a woman called Mrs Ogden came in to 'do' for him. This was his daily life, very simple, and a routine was formed whose pattern could at last be discerned by an interested observer outside the window.

One night Mr Willy beheld a vast glow arise behind the mountains. The Arctic world was obviously on fire—but no, the glow was not fire glow, flame glow. The great invasion of colour that spread up and up the sky was not red, was not rose, but of a synthetic cyclamen colour. This cyclamen glow remained steady from mountain to zenith and caused Mr Willy, who had never seen the Northern Lights, to believe that these were not Northern Lights but that something had occurred for which one must be prepared. After about an hour, flanges of green as of putrefaction, and a melodious yellow arose and spread. An hour later the Northern Lights faded, leaving Mr Willy small and alone.

Sometimes as, sitting beside the window, he drank his tea, Mr Willy thought that nevertheless it is given to few people to be as happy (or contented, he would say), as he was, at his age, too. In his life of decisions, men, pressures, more men, antagonisms, fusions, fissions and Mrs Willy, in his life of hard success, that is, he had sometimes looked forward but so vaguely and rarely to a time when he would not only put this life down; he would leave it. Now he had left it and here he was by his window. As time went on, though, he had to make an effort to summon this happiness, for it seemed to elude him. Sometimes a thought or a shape (was it?), gray, like wood ash that falls in pieces when it is touched, seemed to be behind his chair, and this shape teased him and communicated to him that he had left humanity behind, that a man needs humanity and that if he ceases to be in touch with man and is not in touch with God, he does not matter. 'You do not matter any more', said the spectre like wood ash before it fell to pieces, 'because you are no longer in touch with any one and so you do not exist. You are in a vacuum and so you are nothing.' Then Mr Willy, at first uneasy, became satisfied again for a time after being made uneasy by the spectre. A storm would get up and the wind, howling well, would lash the windows sometimes carrying the salt spray from a very high tide which it flung against the great panes of glass. That was a satisfaction to Mr Willy and within him something stirred and rose and met the storm and effaced the spectre and other phantoms which were really vague regrets. But the worst that happened against the window was that from time to time a little bird, sometimes but not often a seabird, flung itself like a stone against the strong glass of the window and fell, killed by the passion of its flight. This grieved Mr Willy, and he could not sit unmoved when the bird flew at the clear glass and was met by death. When this happened, he arose from his chair, opened the glass door at the far end of the window, descended three or four steps and sought in the grasses for the body of the bird. But the bird was dead, or it was dying, its small bones were smashed, its head was broken, its beak split, it was killed by the rapture of its flight. Only once Mr Willy found the bird a little stunned and picked it up. He cupped the bird's body in his hands and carried it into the house.

Looking up through the grasses at the edge of the rough terrace that descended to the beach, a man watched him return into the house, carrying the bird. Still looking obliquely through the grasses the man watched Mr Willy enter the room and vanish from view. Then Mr Willy came again to the door, pushed it open, and released the bird which flew away, who knows where. He closed the door, locked it, and sat down on the chair facing east beside the window and began to read his newspaper. Looking over his paper he saw, to the east, the city of Vancouver deployed over rising ground with low roofs and high buildings and at the apex the tall Electric Building which at night shone like a broad shaft of golden light.

This time, as evening drew on, the man outside went away because he had other business.

Mr Willy's investment broker was named Gerald Wardho. After a time he said to Mr Willy in a friendly but respectful way, 'Will you have lunch with me at the Club tomorrow?' and Mr Willy said he would. Some time later Gerald Wardho said, 'Would you like me put you up at the Club?'

Mr Willy considered a little the life which he had left and did not want to re-enter and also the fact that he had only last year resigned his membership in three clubs, so he said, 'That's very good of you, Wardho, but I think no. I'm enjoying things as they are. It's a novelty, living in a vacuum . . . I like it, for a time anyway.'

'Yes, but,' said Gerald Wardho, 'you'd be some time on the waiting list. It wouldn't hurt—'

'No,' said Mr Willy, 'no.'

Mr Willy had, Wardho thought, a distinguished appearance or perhaps it was an affable accustomed air, and so he had. When Mrs Wardho said to her husband, 'Gerry, there's not an extra man in this town and I need a man for Saturday,' Gerald Wardho said, 'I know a man. There's Willy.'

Mrs Wardho said doubtfully, 'Willy? Willy who? Who's Willy?'

Her husband said, 'He's fine, he's okay, I'll ask Willy.'

'How old is he?'

'About a hundred . . . but he's okay.'

'Oh-h-h,' said Mrs Wardho, 'isn't there anyone anywhere unattached young any more? Does he play bridge?'

'I'll invite him, I'll find out,' said her husband, and Mr Willy said he'd like to come to dinner.

'Do you care for a game of bridge, Mr Willy?' asked Gerald Wardho.

'I'm afraid not,' said Mr Willy kindly but firmly. He played a good game of bridge but had no intention of entering servitude again just yet, losing his freedom, and being enrolled as what is called a fourth. Perhaps later; not yet. 'If you're having bridge I'll come another time. Very kind of you, Wardho.'

'No no no,' said Gerald Wardho, 'there'll only be maybe a table of bridge for anyone who wants to play. My wife would be disappointed.'

'Well thank you very much. Black tie?'

'Yes. Black tie,' said Gerald Wardho.

And so, whether he would or no, Mr Willy found himself invited to the kind of evening parties to which he had been accustomed and which he had left behind, given by people younger and more animated than himself, and he realized that he was on his way to becoming old odd man out. There was a good deal of wood ash at these parties—that is, behind him the spectre arose, falling to pieces when he looked at it, and said 'So this is what you came to find out on this coast, so far from home, is it, or is there something else. What else is there?' The spectre was not always present at these parties but sometimes awaited him at home and said these things.

One night Mr Willy came home from an evening spent at Gerald Wardho's brother-in-law's house, a very fine house indeed. He had left lights burning and begun to turn out the lights before he went upstairs. He went into the living-room and before turning out the last light gave a glance at the window which had in the course of the evening behaved in its accustomed manner. During the day the view through the window was clear or cloudy, according to the weather or the light or absence of light in the sky; but there it was—the view—never quite the same though, and that is owing to the character of oceans or of any water, great or small, and of light. Both water and light have so great an effect on land observed on any scene, rural, urban or wilderness, that one begins to think that life, that a scene, is an illusion produced by influences such as water and light. At all events, by day the window held this fine view as in a frame, and the view was enhanced by ships at sea of all kinds, but never was the sea crowded, and by birds, clouds, and even aeroplanes in the sky—no people to spoil this fine view. But as evening approached, and moonless night, all the view (illusion again) vanished slowly. The window, which was not illusion, only the purveyor of illusion, did not vanish, but became a mirror which reflected against the blackness every detail of the shallow living-room. Through this clear reflection of the whole room, distant lights from across the water intruded, and so chains of light were thrown across the reflected mantel-piece, or a picture, or a human face, enhancing it. When Mr Willy had left his house to dine at Gerald Wardho's brother-in-law's house the view through the window was placidly clear, but when he returned at 11:30 the window was dark and the room was reflected from floor to ceiling against the blackness. Mr Willy saw himself entering the room like a stranger, looking at first debonair with such a gleaming shirt front and then—as he approached himself—a little shabby, his hair perhaps. He advanced to the window and stood looking at himself with the room in all its detail behind him.

Mr Willy was too often alone, and spent far too much time in that space which lies between the last page of the paper or the turning-off of the radio in surfeit, and sleep. Now as he stood at the end of the evening and the beginning of the night, looking at himself and the room behind him, he admitted that the arid feeling which he had so often experienced lately was probably what is called loneliness. And yet he did not want another woman in his life. It was a long time since he had seen a woman whom he wanted to take home or even to see again. Too much smiling. Men were all right, you talked to them about the market, the emergence of the Liberal Party, the impossibility of arriving anywhere with those people while that fellow was in office, nuclear war (instant hell opened deep in everyone's mind and closed again), South Africa where Mr Willy was born, the Argentine where Mr Wardho's brother-in-law had spent many years—and then everyone went home.

Mr Willy, as the months passed by, was dismayed to find that he had entered an area of depression unknown before, like a tundra, and he was a little frightened of this tundra. Returning from the dinner party he did not at once turn out the single last light and go upstairs. He sat down on a chair beside the window and at last bowed his head upon his hands. As he sat there, bowed, his thoughts went very stiffly (for they had not had much exercise in that direction throughout his life), to some area that was not tundra but that area where there might be some meaning in creation which Mr Willy supposed must be the place where some people seemed to find a God, and perhaps a personal God at that. Such theories, or ideas, or passions had never been of interest to him, and if he had thought of such theories, or ideas, or passions he would have dismissed them as invalid and having no bearing on life as it is lived, especially when one is too busy. He had formed the general opinion that people who hold such beliefs were either slaves to an inherited convention, hypocrites, or nit-wits. He regarded such people without interest, or at least he thought them negligible as he returned to the exacting life in hand. On the whole, though, he did not like them. It is not easy to say why Mr Willy thought these people were hypocrites or nit-wits because some of them, not all, had a strong religious faith, and why he was not a hypocrite or nit-wit because he had not a strong religious faith; but there it was.

As he sat on and on looking down at the carpet with his head in his hands he did not think of these people, but he underwent a strong shock of recognition. He found himself looking this way and that way out of his aridity for some explanation or belief beyond the non-explanation and non-belief that had always been sufficient and had always been his, but in doing this he came up against a high and solid almost visible wall of concrete or granite, set up between him and a religious belief. This wall had, he thought, been built by him through the period of his long life, or perhaps he was congenitally unable to have a belief; in that case it was no fault of his and there was no religious belief possible to him. As he sat there he came to have the conviction that the absence of a belief which extended beyond the visible world had something to do with his malaise; yet the malaise might possibly be cirrhosis of the liver or a sort of delayed male menopause. He recognized calmly that death was as inevitable as tomorrow morning or even tonight and he had a rational absence of fear of death. Nevertheless his death (he knew) had begun, and had begun—what with his awareness of age and this malaise of his—to assume a certainty that it had not had before. His death did not trouble him as much as the increasing tastelessness of living in this tundra of mind into which a belief did not enter.

The man outside the window had crept up through the grasses and was now watching Mr Willy from a point rather behind him. He was a morose man and strong. He had served two terms for robbery with violence. When he worked, he worked up the coast. Then he came to town and if he did not get into trouble it was through no fault of his own. Last summer he had lain there and, rolling over, had looked up through the grasses and into—only just into—the room where this guy was who seemed to live alone. He seemed to be a rich guy because he wore good clothes and hadn't he got this great big window and—later, he discovered—a high-price car. He had lain in the grasses and because his thoughts always turned that way, he tried to figger out how he could get in there. Money was the only thing that was any good to him and maybe the old guy didn't keep money or even carry it but he likely did. The man thought quite a bit about Mr Willy and then went up the coast and when he came down again he remembered the great big window and one or two nights he went around and about the place and figgered how he'd work it. The doors was all locked, even that glass door. That was easy enough to break but he guessed he'd go in without warning when the old guy was there so's he'd have a better chance of getting something off of him as well. Anyways he wouldn't break in, not that night, but if nothing else offered he'd do it some time soon.

Suddenly Mr Willy got up, turned the light out, and went upstairs to bed. That was Wednesday.

On Sunday he had his first small party. It seemed inevitable if only for politeness. Later he would have a dinner party if he still felt sociable and inclined. He invited the Wardhos and their in-laws and some other couples. A Mrs Lessways asked if she might bring her aunt and he said yes. Mrs Wardho said might she bring her niece who was arriving on Saturday to meet her fiancé who was due next week from Hong Kong, and the Wardhos were going to give the two young people a quiet wedding, and Mr Willy said 'Please do.' Another couple asked if they could bring another couple.

Mr Willy, surveying his table, thought that Mrs Ogden had done well. 'Oh I'm so glad you think so,' said Mrs Ogden, pleased. People began to arrive. 'Oh!' they exclaimed without fail, as they arrived, 'what a beautiful view!' Mrs Lessways' aunt who had blue hair fell delightedly into the room, turning this way and that way, acknowledging smiles and tripping to the window. 'Oh,' she cried turning to Mr Willy in a fascinating manner, 'isn't that just lovely! Edna says you're quite a recluse! I'm sure I don't blame you! Don't you think that's the loveliest view Edna . . . oh how d'you do how d'you do, isn't that the loveliest view? . . .' Having paid her tribute to the view she turned away from the window and did not see it again. The Aunt twirled a little bag covered with iridescent beads on her wrist. 'Oh!' and 'Oh!' she exclaimed, turning, 'Mr dear how *lovely* to see you! I didn't even know you were back! Did you have a good time?' She reminded Mr Willy uneasily of his wife. Mr and Mrs Wardho arrived accompanied by their niece Sylvia.

A golden girl, thought Mr Willy taking her hand, but her young face surrounded by sunny curls was stern. She stood, looking from one to another, not speaking, for people spoke busily to each other and the young girl stood apart, smiling only when need be and wishing that she had not had to come to the party. She drifted to the window and seemed (and was) forgotten. She looked at the view as at something seen for the first and last time. She inscribed those notable hills on her mind because had she not arrived only yesterday? And in two days Ian would be here and she would not see them again.

A freighter very low laden emerged from behind a forest and moved slowly into the scene. So low it was that it lay like an elegant black line upon the water with great bulkheads below. Like an iceberg, thought Sylvia, and her mind moved along with the freighter bound for foreign parts. Someone spoke to her and she turned. 'Oh thank you!' she said for her cup of tea.

Mr Willy opened the glass door and took with him some of the men who had expressed a desire to see how far his property ran. 'You see, just a few feet, no 'distance,' he said.

After a while day receded and night came imperceptibly on. There was not any violence of reflected sunset tonight and mist settled down on the view with only distant dim lights aligning the north shore. Sylvia, stopping to respond to ones and twos, went to the back of the shallow room and sat down behind the out-jut of the fireplace where a wood fire was burning. Her mind was on two levels. One was all Ian and the week coming, and one—no thicker than a crust on the surface—was this party and all these people talking, the Aunt talking so busily that one might think there was a race on, or news to tell. Sylvia, sitting in the shadow of the corner and thinking about her approaching lover, lost herself in this reverie, and her lips, which had been so stern, opened slightly in a tender smile. Mr Willy who was serving drinks from the dining-room where Mrs Ogden had left things ready, came upon her and, struck by her beauty, saw a different sunny girl. She looked up at him. She took her drink from him with a soft and tender smile that was grateful and happy and was only partly for him. He left her, with a feeling of beauty seen.

Sylvia held her glass and looked towards the window. She saw, to her surprise, so quickly had black night come, that the end of the room which had been a view was now a large black mirror which reflected the glowing fire, the few lights, and the people unaware of the view, its departure, and its replacement by their own reflections behaving to each other like people at a party. Sylvia watched Mr Willy who moved amongst them, taking a glass and bringing a glass. He was removed from the necessities, now, of conversation, and looked very sad. Why does he look sad, she wondered and was young enough to think, he shouldn't look sad, he is well off. She took time off to like Mr Willy and to feel sorry that he seemed melancholy.

People began to look at their watches and say good-bye. The Aunt redoubled her vivacity. The women all thanked Mr Willy for his tea party and for the beautiful beautiful view. They gave glances at the window but there was no view.

When all his guests had gone, Mr Willy, who was an orderly man, began to collect glasses and take them into the kitchen. In an armchair lay the bag covered with iridescent beads belonging to the Aunt. Mr Willy picked it up and put it on a table, seeing the blue hair of the Aunt. He would sit down and smoke for awhile. But he found that when, lately, he sat down in the evening beside the window and fixed his eyes upon the golden shaft of the Electric Building, in spite of his intention of reading or smoking, his thoughts turned towards this subject of belief which now teased him, eluded, yet compelled him. He was brought up, every time, against the great stone wall, how high, how wide he knew, but not how thick. If he could, in some way, break through the wall which bounded the area of his aridity and his comprehension, he knew without question that there was a light (not darkness) beyond, and that this light could in some way come through to him and alleviate the sterility and lead him, lead him. If there was some way, even some conventional way—although he did not care for convention—he would take it in order to break the wall down and reach the light so that it would enter his life; but he did not know the way. So fixed did Mr Willy become in contemplation that he looked as though he were graven in stone.

Throughout the darkened latter part of the tea party, the man outside had lain or crouched near the window. From the sands, earlier, he had seen Mr Willy open the glass door and go outside, followed by two or three men. They looked down talking, and soon went inside again together. The door was closed. From anything the watcher knew, it was not likely that the old guy would turn and lock the door when he took the other guys in. He'd just close it, see.

As night came on the man watched the increased animation of the guests preparing for departure. Like departing birds they moved here and there in the room before taking flight. The man was impatient but patient because when five were left, then three, then no one but the old guy who lived in the house, he knew his time was near.

(How gay and how meaningless the scene had been, of these well-dressed persons talking and talking, like some kind of a show where nothing happened—or so it might seem, on the stage of the lighted room from the pit of the dark shore.)

The watcher saw the old guy pick up glasses and take them away. Then he came back into the room and looked around. He took something out of a chair and put it on a table. He stood still for a bit, and then he found some kind of a paper and sat down in the chair facing eastward. But the paper dropped in his hand and then it dropped to the floor as the old guy bent his head and then he put his elbows on his knees and rested his head in his hands as if he was thinking, or had some kind of headache.

The watcher, with a sort of joy and a feeling of confidence that the moment had come, moved strongly and quietly to the glass door. He turned the handle expertly, slid inside, and slowly closed the door so that no draught should warn his victim. He moved cat-like to the back of Mr Willy's chair and quickly raised his arm. At the selfsame moment that he raised his arm with a short blunt weapon in his hand, he was aware of the swift movement of another person in the room. The man stopped still, his arm remained high, every fear was aroused. He turned instantly and saw a scene clearly enacted beside him in the dark mirror of the window. At the moment and shock of turning, he drew a sharp intake of breath and it was this that Mr Willy heard and that caused him to look up and around and see in the dark mirror the intruder, the danger, and the victim who was himself. At that still moment, the telephone rang shrilly, twice as loud in that still moment, on a small table near him.

It was not the movement of that figure in the dark mirror, it was not the bell ringing close at hand and insistently. It was an irrational and stupid fear lest his action, reproduced visibly beside him in the mirror, was being faithfully registered in some impossible way that filled the intruder with fright. The telephone ringing shrilly, Mr Willy now facing him, the play enacted beside him, and this irrational momentary fear caused him to turn and bound towards the door, to escape into the dark, banging the glass door with a clash behind him. When he got well away from the place he was angry—everything was always against him, he never had no luck, and if he hadn'ta lost his head it was a cinch he coulda done it easy.

'Damn you!' shouted Mr Willy in a rage, with his hand on the telephone, 'you might have broken it! Yes?' he said into the telephone, moderating the anger that possessed him and continuing within himself a conversation that said It was eighteen inches away, I was within a minute of it and I didn't know, it's no use telephoning the police but I'd better do that, it was just above me and I'd have died not knowing. 'Yes? Yes?' he said impatiently, trembling a little.

'Oh,' said a surprised voice, 'It is Mr Willy, isn't it? Just for a minute it didn't sound like you Mr Willy that was the *loveliest* party and what a lovely view and I'm sorry to be such a nuisance I kept on ringing and ringing because I though you couldn't have gone out so soon' (tinkle tinkle) 'and you couldn't have gone to bed so soon but I do believe I must have left my little bead bag it's not the *value* but . . .' Mr Willy found himself shaking more violently now, not only with death averted and the rage of the slammed door but with the powerful thoughts that had usurped him and were interrupted by the dangerous moment which was now receding, and the tinkling voice on the telephone.

'I have it here. I'll bring it tomorrow,' he said shortly. He hung up the telephone and at the other end the Aunt turned and exclaimed, 'Well if he isn't the rudest man I never was treated like that in my whole life d'you know what he . . .'

Mr Willy was in a state of abstraction.

He went to the glass door and examined it. It was intact. He turned the key and drew the shutter down. Then he went back to the telephone in this state of abstraction. Death or near-death was still very close, though receding. It seemed to him at that moment that a crack had been coming in the great wall that shut him off from the light but perhaps he was wrong. He dialled the police, perfunctorily not urgently. He knew that before him lay the hardest work of his life—in his life out of the country. He must in some way and very soon break the great wall that shut him off from whatever light there might be. Not for fear of death oh God not for fear of death but for fear of something else.

1961

F.R. Scott

1899–1985

Francis Reginald Scott was a second-generation Canadian poet, the son of Frederick George Scott (1861–1944), one of the less prominent Confederation poets. Born in Quebec City, where his father was rector of St Matthew's Church, Frank Scott received a traditional Anglican upbringing. After attending the private High School of Quebec and then his father's *alma mater*, Bishop's College, he won a Rhodes Scholarship to Oxford University in 1920 and read history at Magdalen College. As Scott once said, 'I spent three blissful years at Oxford soaking up everything I could learn about the past and paying very little attention to the present.' On his return to Canada in 1923 he taught for a brief period at Lower Canada College before enrolling in law at McGill University. He was called to the bar in 1927 and was made a professor in the Faculty of Law in 1928: he served as its dean from 1961 to 1964 and retired in 1968.

His father's own writing and literary concerns nurtured Scott's interest in poetry, both as a reader and a writer, but before 1925 this interest progressed little beyond reading the Georgian poets and writing sonnets. At McGill he was befriended by A.J.M. Smith, who introduced him to the new American poets, including Pound and Eliot. Together Scott and Smith founded the *McGill Fortnightly Review* (1925–7), for which they wrote so prolifically that it became necessary for them to invent pseudonyms.

The modernist poets changed Scott's conception of poetry, and the social decay of the Depression altered his ideas about politics and economics. He rejected not only the romantic poetry of his father's generation ('Amid the crash of systems, was Romantic poetry to survive?' he wrote in *The Canadian Forum* in 1931) but its capitalism as well. He became a social reformer and a socialist, an authority on constitutional law, and a defender of civil liberties and social justice. He assisted in the formation of the Co-operative Commonwealth Federation

(CCF, the forerunner of the NDP), of which he was national chairman from 1942 to 1950. In the 1950s he fought three celebrated court cases in Quebec: against Premier Duplessis' padlock law, against the censorship of Lawrence's *Lady Chatterley's Lover*, and Roncarelli v. Duplessis, a famous civil-liberties case. In the 1960s he was a member of the Royal Commission on Bilingualism and Biculturalism. A sampler of his political writings, *A New Endeavour: Selected Political Essays, Letters, and Addresses* (1986), has been compiled by Michiel Horn.

Scott's poetry reflected his social consciousness. As early as 1928 he joined other writers in helping to found the *Canadian Mercury*, a literary magazine that gave voice to three members of the 'Montreal Group', Leo Kennedy, A.M. Klein, and Scott himself. With Smith, Scott edited an anthology of this 'new' poetry, *New Provinces* (1936), which served as a public announcement that Canadian poetry was indeed changing. Over the years Scott continued to be interested in helping to provide a public outlet for new voices, often by his support of literary magazines. He helped to found *Preview* in 1942, which, like the *Canadian Mercury* and the *McGill Fortnightly Review* before it, gave a new generation of writers a public forum. Then in 1956 he became one of the founding editors of *Tamarack Review*, which for more than a quarter of a century was the leading literary journal in Canada. His commitment to a fully bicultural Canada is reflected in his continuing interest in French Canadian culture and in his activities as a translator. His *St-Denys Garneau and Anne Hébert* (1962) helped make two important Francophone writers more visible in English Canada; in 1977 his *Poems of French Canada* won a Canada Council Translation Prize.

Scott's poems were collected in *Overture* (1945), *Events and Signals* (1954), *The Eye of the Needle: Satires, Sorties, Sundries* (1957), *Signature* (1964), and *The Dance Is One* (1973). His *Selected Poems* appeared in 1966, and his *Collected Poems*, which won a Governor General's Award, was published in 1981. With Smith, Scott compiled a popular anthology, *The Blasted Pine: An Anthology of Satire, Invective and Disrespectful Verse; Chiefly by Canadian Writers* (1957).

Scott's poetry has sometimes been divided into 'public' and 'private' poems. But even the public satire of a poem like 'The Canadian Authors Meet' is not without a personal voice. Whether he is treating a political subject such as Mackenzie King's role as prime minister or responding to the developments of technology (in 'Trans Canada') or recording his plunge into the elemental world of nature in 'Lakeshore', his is a comprehensive poetry that can unite the mythic nature of the land with the reality of personal experience and that can scrutinize the trivialities of a self-indulgent society while also seeing with the eye of a visionary.

A.J.M. Smith's poem commemorating his friend's seventieth birthday, 'To Frank Scott, Esq.', brings together the threefold career of the lawyer, the poet, and the politician. It begins:

Poet and Man of Law—O brave anomaly!—
dove wise and serpent-tongued for Song
  or Plea—
a parti-coloured animal, committed,
  parti-pris
but not a party man, a Man, and free.

The Canadian Authors[1] Meet

Expansive puppets percolate self-unction
Beneath a portrait of the Prince of Wales.
Miss Crotchet's muse has somehow failed to function,
Yet she's a poetess. Beaming, she sails

1 The Canadian Authors' Association, founded in 1921, appeared to Scott a self-congratulatory and self-indulgent group that was mostly a refuge for poetasters and that celebrated safely established poets while ignoring modern innovators. He wrote this poem after attending a meeting of the CAA in the spring of 1925.

From group to chattering group, with such a dear
Victorian saintliness, as is her fashion,
Greeting the other unknowns with a cheer—
Virgins of sixty who still write of passion.

The air is heavy with Canadian topics,
And Carman, Lampman, Roberts, Campbell, Scott,
Are measured for their faith and philanthropics,
Their zeal for God and King, their earnest thought.

The cakes are sweet, but sweeter is the feeling
That one is mixing with the *literati*;
It warms the old, and melts the most congealing.
Really, it is a most delightful party.

Shall we go round the mulberry bush, or shall
We gather at the river, or shall we
Appoint a Poet Laureate this fall,[2]
Or shall we have another cup of tea?

O Canada, O Canada, Oh can
A day go by without new authors springing
To paint the native maple, and to plan
More ways to set the selfsame welkin[3] ringing?

1927,[4] 1945

2 At the meeting Scott attended the appointment of a Canadian poet laureate was discussed.
3 Sky (poetic archaism).
4 When first published in the *McGill Fortnightly Review* (27 April 1927), this poem concluded with an additional stanza:

Far in a corner sits (though none would know it)
The very picture of disconsolation,
A rather lewd and most ungodly poet
Writing these verses, for his soul's salvation.

Trans Canada

Pulled from our ruts by the made-to-order gale
We sprang upward into a wider prairie
And dropped Regina below like a pile of bones.[1]

1 Early settlers' name for Regina.

Sky tumbled upon us in waterfalls,
But we were smarter than a Skeena salmon
And shot our silver body over the lip of air
To rest in a pool of space
On the top storey of our adventure.

A solar peace
And a six-way choice.[2]

Clouds, now, are the solid substance,
A floor of wool roughed by the wind
Standing in waves that halt in their fall.
A still of troughs.

The plane, our planet,
Travels on roads that are not seen or laid
But sound in instruments on pilots' ears,
While underneath
The sure wings
Are the everlasting arms of science.

Man, the lofty worm, tunnels his latest clay,
And bores his new career.

This frontier, too, is ours.
This everywhere whose life can only be led
At the pace of a rocket
Is common to man and man,
And every country below is an I land.

The sun sets on its top shelf,
And stars seem farther from our nearer grasp.

I have sat by night beside a cold lake
And touched things smoother than moonlight on still water,
But the moon on this cloud sea is not human,
And here is no shore, no intimacy,
Only the start of space, the road to suns.

1945

2 In that 'up and down' have been added to the usual four points of the compass.

Lakeshore

The lake is sharp along the shore
Trimming the bevelled edge of land
To level curves; the fretted sands
Go slanting down through liquid air
Till stones below shift here and there
Floating upon their broken sky
All netted by the prism wave
And rippled where the currents are.

I stare through windows at this cave
Where fish, like planes, slow-motioned, fly.
Poised in a still of gravity
The narrow minnow, flicking fin,
Hangs in a paler, ochre sun,
His doorways open everywhere.

And I am a tall frond that waves
Its head below its rooted feet
Seeking the light that draws it down
To forest floors beyond its reach
Vivid with gloom and eerie dreams.

The water's deepest colonnades
Contract the blood, and to this home
That stirs the dark amphibian
With me the naked swimmers come
Drawn to their prehistoric womb.

They too are liquid as they fall
Like tumbled water loosed above
Until they lie, diagonal,
Within the cool and sheltered grove
Stroked by the fingertips of love.

Silent, our sport is drowned in fact
Too virginal for speech or sound
And each is personal and laned
Along his private aqueduct.

Too soon the tether of the lungs
Is taut and straining, and we rise
Upon our undeveloped wings

Toward the prison of our ground
A secret anguish in our thighs
And mermaids in our memories.

This is our talent, to have grown
Upright in posture, false-erect,
A landed gentry, circumspect,
Tied to a horizontal soil
The floor and ceiling of the soul;
Striving, with cold and fishy care
To make an ocean of the air.

Sometimes, upon a crowded street,
I feel the sudden rain come down
And in the old, magnetic sound
I hear the opening of a gate
That loosens all the seven seas.
Watching the whole creation drown
I muse, alone, on Ararat.[1]

1954

1 The mountain on which Noah is said to have landed after the flood.

Poetry

Nothing can take its place. If I write 'ostrich'
Those who have never seen the bird see it
With its head in the sand and its plumes fluffed with the wind
Like Mackenzie King talking on Freedom of Trade.[1]

And if I write 'holocaust', and 'nightingales',
I startle the insurance agents and the virgins
Who belong, by this alchemy, in the same category,
Since both are very worried about their premiums.

A rose and a rose are two roses; a rose is a rose is a rose.[2]
Sometimes I have walked down a street marked No Outlet

1 In the late 1930s King supported closer economic ties with the US as a way of distancing Canada from Britain. In the period after the end of World War II, King abandoned free trade talks with the US, increasingly fearful of American domination of the Canadian economy. For details on King as a political leader and Scott's opinion of him, see the following poem and its notes.

2 This alludes to a line from Gertrude Stein's poem 'Sacred Emily' (1913)—'Rose is a rose is a rose is a rose'—that came to exemplify her particular brand of difficult modern writing.

Only to find that what was blocking my path
Was a railroad track roaring away to the west.

So I know it will survive. Not even the decline of reading
And the substitution of advertising for genuine pornography
Can crush the uprush of the mushrooming verb
Or drown the overtone of the noun on its own.

1954

W.L.M.K.[1]

How shall we speak of Canada,
Mackenzie King dead?
The Mother's boy in the lonely room
With his dog, his medium and his ruins?[2]

He blunted us.

We had no shape
Because he never took sides,
And no sides
Because he never allowed them to take shape.

He skilfully avoided what was wrong
Without saying what was right,
And never let his on the one hand
Know what his on the other hand was doing.

The height of his ambition
Was to pile a Parliamentary Committee on a Royal Commission,
To have 'conscription if necessary
But not necessarily conscription',

1 William Lyon Mackenzie King (1874–1950) became the leader of the Liberal party in 1919 and served as prime minister of Canada for twenty-two years (non-consecutively) between 1921 and 1948. His administration was characterized by caution and compromise (his critics found him weak and evasive). In the 1942 debate about whether or not the Liberals would abandon their previous anti-conscription stand (English Canadians believed they should; French Canadians strongly opposed conscription), King famously declared, 'Not necessarily conscription, but conscription if necessary.' He kept detailed diaries, which revealed, after his death, that he doted on his pet dog and that he had occasionally invited mediums to his home to hold seances, believing that he could communicate with departed spirits—especially that of his mother, to whom he had always been deeply devoted.

2 King lived on a lavish family estate, Kingsmere, to which he added false 'ruins' to make it look more like an English estate of significant antiquity.

To let Parliament decide—
Later.

Postpone, postpone, abstain.

Only one thread was certain:
After World War I
Business as usual,
After World War II
Orderly decontrol.
Always he led us back to where we were before.

He seemed to be in the centre
Because we had no centre,
No vision
To pierce the smoke-screen of his politics.

Truly he will be remembered
Wherever men honour ingenuity,
Ambiguity, inactivity, and political longevity.

Let us raise up a temple
To the cult of mediocrity,
Do nothing by halves
Which can be done by quarters.

1957

All the Spikes But the Last[1]

Where are the coolies in your poem, Ned?
Where are the thousands from China who swung
their picks with bare hands at forty below?

Between the first and the million other spikes
they drove, and the dressed-up act of
Donald Smith,[2] who has sung their story?

1 A response to E.J. ('Ned') Pratt's poem, *Towards the last Spike* (see p. 286–313). Some 6,000 Chinese labourers, imported because of their willingness to accept low wages, endured brutal conditions while playing a vital role in the completion of the CPR in British Columbia.
2 Donald Smith (1820–1913) was recognized for his role in the building of the CPR by being chosen to drive the last spike in 1884, a ritual he performed in frock-coat and high hat.

Did they fare so well in the land they helped to
unite? Did they get one of the 25,000,000 CPR acres?

Is all Canada has to say to them written in the Chinese
Immigration Act?[3]

1957

3 The Chinese Immigration Act, more commonly known as the Chinese Exclusion Act, was passed in 1923. A late outgrowth of continued reaction against this imported labour, it virtually prohibited further entry into Canada by Chinese. The act was repealed in 1947.

Harry Robinson

1900–1990

One of the important tellers of Native tales and experiences in twentieth-century Canada was Harry Robinson, who, late in his long life, said that he could tell stories 'twenty-one hours or more . . . because this is my job. I'm a storyteller.' His stories have been important for younger First Nations writers such as Thomas King, who described his first encounter with Robinson's tales thus:

I couldn't believe the power and the skill with which Robinson could work up a story—in English: they weren't translated, they were simply transcribed—and how well he understood the power of the oral voice in a written piece. . . . It was inspirational. . . . *I remember sitting in my office, just sort of sweating, reading this stuff: it was so* good.

Born in Oyama, near Kelowna, BC, in the Okanagan Valley, Robinson grew up in the Similkameen Valley near Keremeos. An Okanagan, he was a member of the Lower Similkameen Band of the Interior Salish people. Because he received only five months of formal schooling, he didn't learn to read and write until he was twenty-two. He spent most of his early life in an orally based culture, learning many of his stories from his grandmother and other elders in the community. Until 1971 he worked as a rancher; after the death of his wife, he retired to a small bungalow on a friend's ranch.

As a storyteller in an age of electronic media, Robinson considered himself among the last of a dying breed: he therefore retold the stories he had heard as a boy, not only for their own value, but also as a way of keeping alive both the tales themselves and also the tradition of storytelling. At first he told his stories in his native Okanagan; however, he found, as he grew older, that even Okanagan listeners could not always understand the language, so he began to tell his stories in English.

Robinson's tales have been compiled in two volumes by the ethnologist Wendy Wickwire, who first met Robinson in 1977. Becoming a friend, she recorded and transcribed more than a hundred stories during twelve years of interviews. The first of these two volumes, *Write It on Your Heart: The Epic World of an Okanagan Storyteller* (1989), was published shortly before his death. A second volume, *Nature Power: In the Spirit of an Okanagan Storyteller*, appeared three years later. In the introduction to the 1989 collection Wickwire describes how she would visit the 'quiet setting beside the Similkameen River in British Columbia's southern interior, [where] in a neat and simple house without television, radio or newspapers, Harry lives with an unbroken contact to a deep past'.

Robinson divided his stories into two kinds: *chap-TEEK-whl* and *shmee-MA-ee* (these are Wickwire's phonetic spellings). *Chap-TEEK-whl* stories explain the nature of the world and its creation, often featuring animal-creators and animal-people who existed in a timeless period before the Okanagan people became fully human. Shmee-MA-ee stories, of which 'Captive in an English Circus' is a good example, deal with human beings and take place within time.

Publication of oral stories, especially those that also involve translation, can distort the style if not the content of the narratives. Moving to print loses the nuances of speech when transcribers reshape tales to the conventions of print culture—for example, regularizing syntax, or eliminating the repetition that is present in and important to all spoken communication. Wickwire, sensing that the oral stories she was hearing were 'really performed events', worked with Robinson to avoid these losses as much as possible. Robinson told his stories in English, not in Okanagan, and he taught Wickwire about the oral structure of his narratives. Wickwire's transcriptions retain much of the oral nature of the stories through the use of line breaks that show the rhythm of Robinson's speech, including his pauses and repetitions: the result is that 'Captive of an English Circus' feels more like speech than writing.

In reading such transcriptions we should nevertheless remember that, in contrast to the fixed nature of written texts, oral narratives are protean. Though many of Robinson's stories have their origins at least as far back as the 1840s (the period of his grandmother's girlhood), they have not remained unaffected by Robinson's own experiences or by the conditions of their telling. One reason oral stories continually change shape is that their tellers form each rendition to suit their audience. Robinson told his stories to Wickwire, who was a friend but also a woman of European descent, with the knowledge that they would later be read by an audience comprised mostly of non-Okanagans—factors that would have influenced what he told and his way of telling it.

Captive in an English Circus

A man from the Similkameen Valley goes to prison in New Westminster for killing a man. One night he is secretly abducted and taken on a long journey.

This is about George Jim.
He belongs to Ashnola Band, George Jim.
Those days, I had it written down—1886.
No, I mean 1887.
That's one year I'm out there.
That's supposed to be in the 1886
instead of 1887.
That time, 1886,
the people, Indians from Penticton,
all the Okanagan Indians,
they were some from Similkameen,
and they all move to where Oroville is now

in the month of August,
about the last week in the month of August.
And they all get together in Oroville.
And that's when the salmon coming up.
The salmon comes up, you know, from way down.
They come up on the Columbia River
and they come up on the Okanogan, some.
And some of them go up, they split up there.
Some of them go up the Columbia River.
But some of them, they coming up on the Okanogan River.
They had a good place for catching them there in Oroville.
Kind of shallow.
Only a small river.

So the people moved over there.
They stay there.
Put in a camp.
There is no town there yet.
There was some white people,
they got two or three houses there.
Not many.
Then they get the salmon.
They get the salmon for,
could be about a week or ten days.
Then the salmon keep going and go by.
They come to Osoyoos Lake
and they follow Osoyoos Lake
and then they come to Okanogan River again
and they keep going to Okanagan Falls.
They can never go any farther than Okanagan Falls.
There's a dam there.
That's as far as the salmon can go.

These Indian, when they run out of salmon,
they know the salmon, they go by.
So they move.
Follow the salmon.
Then they come to Okanagan Falls.
Then the salmon, they can't go no more.
They were there.
They can get salmon.
Some of them died in the water
and get bad, you know, get spoiled.
Then they quit.

When they get together at Falls,
there's a lot of Indians and they put in a camp.
Some of them, they play stickgame.
They kind of celebrate.
But still some of them get the salmon
at night or the daytime.
And some of them get whiskey from someplace,
from Penticton, I guess, or somewhere.
And they drink.

And this time,
that Jim,
supposed to be a big man, stout man.
And he's a funny looking man.
He's got short legs,
but he's pretty wide in the shoulders.
And he's got big hips.
Kinda tough-looking man.
And he was.
He's a strong man.

Then there was a white man
that lived there at Okanagan Falls.
And he's got an Indian woman from Penticton.
And they got some children,
maybe one or two.
And this white man, his name, Shattleworth.

A lot of people drinking, you know.
And then George Jim, and Shattleworth, and some others,
they drinking at night,
and then they fighting.
But this time, that Shattleworth,
he got beat badly by George Jim.
George Jim, he beat him almost till death.
Then, some of the boys, they stopped him and grab him.
Because he's strong, it takes a few men to hold him.
Then they take the man who's wounded.
They take him to the camp.
They laid him in the camp.
He's hurt very bad.
He's got a broken ribs
and he was hurt in the head, you know.
Quite a few cuts.

With a club, you know, he hit him in the head with a club
    and then he cut the skin, you know, by the club.
Not knife, but the club.
Then he kicked him in the ribs
    and his ribs were broken inside.
And then some of that bone,
    they must have gone to the lungs.
Could be.

He thought,
    I hurt him badly
        and I might as well kill him.

So, who's going to stop him?
He's a strong man.
He went to the teepee.
Bunch of women in there,
    maybe two or three old men
        and maybe five women, old women.

So, he come there and he says,
    'How's that Shattleworth?
    I'm going to kill him if he's alive yet.'
And these people told him,
    'He's dead.
    He died.
    Already died.'

And they covered him with a white blanket.
He lay on the bed
    and they cover him, all his head.
And he looked like he was dead all right
    because he was covered with a white cloth.
They tell him,
    'You better stay away.
    He died.
    He dead already.'

All right, he go away.

But he didn't die, that Shattleworth.
After that he was living for about seven or eight months.
But he died just from getting beat
    because the way I see, maybe the ribs they were broken
        and maybe some, they go to the lungs.

But if not go to the lungs,
the ribs they be heal up.
He wouldn't die.
But this one here, it's bad.
Maybe it goes in the lung,
the bone, the broken rib.

But anyway, George got away.
And then they report that to the policeman
because this Shattleworth, he's a white man
and he's got an Indian wife.
And it was reported to the police.
But the police, they couldn't get him.
Kinda scared of him because Jim,
he's got a revolver on his hip all the time,
and yet he's a strong man.
And the policeman, they kinda scared of him.
They just let him go.
They look for a chance to sneak to him and then get him.

So Jim, he stay away for quite a while,
for almost one year.
About eleven months after he did that,
that was next August and somebody, they cheat him.
Then they got him.
And he been around to Ashnola and down to Chopaka.
But he always keep away from the policeman.
They go over there and look for him,
but they're scared of him.
They always around there but nobody get him.
He hide in the daytime in the hillside.
At night he goes to the Indian camp
and sometimes he didn't.

Then, there was one boy, eleven years old.
And he make a lunch,
a big lunch for Jim.
Then he told that boy,
he told an old man,
'You take that boy
and show him the place
where he can leave that lunch for Jim.
And tell him what he's going to do.
And tell him what's he's got to say if somebody met him.'

That old man used to take the lunch,
but he a little afraid
maybe the policeman or some man
might think the old man
must have take a lunch to that wanted man.
But if the boy,
he give him a gun, you know,
a 22-gun, you know,
to shoot the grouse.
And he tell him,
'If somebody come and met you,
if they ask you what you're doing here,
you tell 'em,
"I'm hunting, hunting for grouse,
willow grouse, or rabbit, or something like that." '

Then, he's got bags on his shoulders.
'When I get a grouse I can put it in there.'
But that's where he had the lunch.
And he showed him where he can take the lunch
and where he can leave it.
There was a big stone
and there was kind of hollow underneath the stone.
That was kind of a shade.
In the daytime he could put the lunch there.

But this man is up on the hill.
He could be watching him.
When it gets dark,
this man will come down and take the lunch
and go up the hill again.
That's Jim.
So the old man, he show the boy
and tell all about what to do and what to say.
And he can take the lunch every once in awhile,
every two days,
because they make a big lunch at a time.

But not long after that,
that was in the month of August, could be,
because they say that choke cherries were ripe.
They don't know if it was August or September those days.
Now I can figure myself.

When they say it's choke cherries time,
choke cherries, they ripe,
choke cherries they ripe in the month of August.
I know that.
That could be August.
Then he was there for quite a while.

And the road gang, they building a road.
And they call it McCurdy place.
And after that, they call it,
I forget the new man that lived there.
Anyway, McCurdy place,
that's the first man that lived there.
McCurdy for about a mile
and the river it's curved like that.
Kind of bent.
And that's where they camp, the road gang,
they had a camp there.
Those days wherever they can build a road,
if it's far away from town,
they can move camp.
They got to have a camp there.
But nowadays, the workers,
they can go from town.
It don't matter how far.
They don't put no camp.
But those days they got a camp.
They use horses, you know,
scraper and plough to make a grade.
And they had a camp there,
the road gang, the bunch of them.
And they had a cookhouse and a cook.
Bunch of men workers.
And there was a trail,
but they widen out that trail to be a wagon road.
That was in 1887 then.
That's a long time ago.
No highway those days.

So the road gang was there.
and one of these boys, like the boss,
maybe, the foreman, you know,
he has to ride the horse.

No car those days,
no motorcycle,
no bicycle,
no nothing.
Only saddle horse.
You know that.

Then these men
they go to Fairview.
That's a town, you know.
Mine town.
Their head boss is there.
Government.

All right.
They went over there to see him
and come back.
So he went over there
and then in the afternoon, he come back from Fairview.
He went over there in the morning.
In the afternoon he come back from there.

And this George Jim,
he took a horse and ride him around by Nighthawk.
Then he must have gone by Oroville or somewhere.
But he come back
and he come back where that Osoyoos Road is now.

You remember when we come up there?
And I showed you, 'Here is the old road'?
But now the highway is above the old road.

So Jim, he come on that road.
And the other one,
that man who goes to Fairview,
he takes the trail like from Fairview.
And they met at the top, just above Spotted Lake.

When we were at Spotted Lake
and you took pictures, I and him?
And I told you, the old road, it's higher up there?
Yeah, that's where they meet,
this man from Fairview.
He go by Spotted Lake.

And Jim was coming on the road
and they met there.
Then, because Jim, he's a 'wanted man',
it was written in the government office,
his name and how he look like and all that.
And all the white people knew that
even if they never seen him before.
But as soon as they see him,
they can tell that was the 'wanted man'.

So this man, one of the government men,
the one that goes to Fairview,
soon as he met him,
he knew he was the one.
There was a reward, you know,
because whoever catch him is going to get paid.
Then he said to George,
they go together and they talk
and they make a good friend to one another,
and they are good friend
and it's getting late in the afternoon.
Finally they rode together
and they're getting close to the camp.
Then, it's just about supper-time then.
And this white man, he tell Jim,
'You better come with me to the camp.
Then you can eat there.
Eat supper.
Now, it's just about supper-time.'
He tell him,
'I am one of the bosses in that camp,
so you come with me
and you stay there
and after supper you can go.'
And Jim, he says,
'No, I better keep going.
I can stop someplace in some of them Indians.'
'Oh no. You better come.
You eat here. You'll be all right.'

But you know, he figure,
when he get there,
he figure he can tell the other boys right away
and that was their judge to catch him.

So anyway,
George, he must have been hungry or something
because he stop there
and he went with that man.
And he tie up his horse.
Then, I think this white man,
the one that's with him,
he must have tell the other ones right away.
And then he didn't know.

And then,
one of the working man,
big man, strong man,
he take the apron and he put it here.
He's not a waiter.
He's not a cook.
He's one of the ploughmen.
But he puts the apron on so he looks like a waiter, cook.
Long table
and he takes the grub
and he move over there
and he goes back and gets some more.

And Jim was sitting there
and he wanted to sit on the other side against the tent wall.
But they tell him
'You can sit here.
Already the boys are over there.'

He didn't like to sit there because it's open.

So this waiter goes by him
on his back two, three times.
And then I guess these other boys,
nobody know,
they might get a club and then they hide it.
When the waiter gets over the other end of the table
and he give him that club.
Then he come back.
That was the fourth time or the fifth time
when he go by George's back.

Then this time when he go by there,
and George was watching all the time.

He always watching.
But finally he quieted down
  and he eat.
And he's got a revolver on his hip, you know.

And when this waiter go by him,
  down it went on the back of his head
    and George just drop!
And he knocked out
  and drop off the chair.
And all the men are just on him, you know.
Bunch of men, three or four men,
  they just right on him.
And they get the rope
  and they tie his arms
    and they tie his feet.
Before he come to, he's already tied up.
He can't do nothing.
They take his gun away from him.

Then they sent one of the boys to Fairview for the policeman
  after supper, after six o'clock.
Then, whoever they went from there to Fairview,
  that's about ten or fifteen miles,
    they get there and tell the police
      and then the policemen come.
When the policemen gets there
  and they handcuff him,
    put the handcuffs on him.
Then, nothing he can do after they got the handcuffs.
They take the ropes off his feet
  and then they tell him,
    'Get on your horse.'
And these policemen,
  they come on horses,
    the two of them.
Then they lead him
  and they tie his feet with a rope under the belly
    so he could never jump off.
They got handcuffs, iron handcuffs.
He can't get away.
So they lead him to Fairview
  and then they put him in jail.

Because the one, he beat Shattleworth.
He did.
After the six or seven months after he was beat,
    he died.
He's a murderer anyway.

So, they held him in that jail for a while
    and they had a trial there once or twice.
Then they take him to Penticton.
There was another courthouse there.
Just small.
They held him there awhile
    and then they took him to Kamloops.
There must have been a little court in Vernon those days.
But Kamloops.
Then they had him there for a while
    and then they got a sentence seven years.
Only seven years.
Take him to Westminster.
And the railroad drives into Westminster in 1886.
And they already had a railroad right in Vancouver.

And Mr. Jim,
    they sent him from Kamloops on the railroad to Westminster.
And then they had him in that penitentiary.
And he was in there three years.
Supposed to be seven years and then he'll come out.
That's his sentence.
Seven years.

He was in jail three years
    and one night towards morning,
        about two o'clock in the morning then
            because all the cells, you know,
                whoever's in the cell, maybe one or two,
                    the policeman lock 'em.
Then, in the morning they could open 'em.
Unlock 'em.
But Jim was locked.
All alone in one cell.
But towards morning,
    about two o'clock in the morning,
        somebody open that.

They got a key,
    open the door,
        and they come in.
There's three of them—policemen.
They got the clothes, uniform—guards.
Those days, the policemen,
    they haven't got no uniform.
But the guards, they got some kind of a uniform.

So, the three of them come in.
And Jim, he wake up.
Still in bed.
And told him,
    'Jim, you get up and put your clothes on.
    We come and get you.'

I'm not sure if it was three.
I think it's only two.
But the driver, that makes three.
They got a driver on the buggy out there.
But these two,
    they're both guards,
        go in and tell Jim,
            'You dress up and we come and get you.
            There's a buggy outside with a driver.
            You get on the buggy
            and we all get on and we go to Vancouver.
        Early in the morning,
            the train is going to leave Vancouver.
        We got to go on the train.
        We move you.
        There was one jail a long long way from here.
        We move you.
        You're going to be over at that jail.
        Long ways from here.
        You leave this place.'

Well what can he say,
    because this is the policeman, guard, you know.
He has to do whatever they tell him.
All right, he dress up and he went out.
There was a buggy there
    and he get on the buggy
        and they all get on the buggy
            and they go to Vancouver early in the morning.

At that time they got a different time.
Now, they leave there eight o'clock in the evening from Vancouver.
But at that time it might have been in the morning.
Might be four o'clock in the morning
    or something like that.

Anyway,
    early in the morning they get on the train
        and they went.
And they going all day and all night
    and all day and all night again.
And Mr. Jim, he thinks,
    By God, that was a long way.
    Where did they take me?
    I wonder where they take me.

They take him into where they eat, you know,
    on the train.
And he got a chance to ask the waiter.
I guess the policemen who look after him, they went back,
    and just only himself.
And he asked the waiter,
    and the waiter told him,
        'They take you to Halifax.
        Then there, you're going to take the boat
            from Halifax to England.'

So he find that out,
    but what has he got to say?
So anyway, they get him to Halifax.
Then they told him,
    'We're going to be here for a while.
    We're waiting for the boat.'
Because those days
    it takes the boat a month to go over the sea to England.
One month.
But now it's only about four days.
So they wait there about four or five days.
Then the boat came.
Then they put him in the boat,
    the whole bunch.
These two, they always along with him,
    the same man.

So, he mention that.
He see one Indian in England
    and he told him,
        this Indian from Enderby,
            not Indian altogether,
                he's a half-breed,
                    but he speak in Okanagan.
So, he says in his stories that he went on the water.
He could see the mountains, the ground,
    for one week and no more.
Two weeks,
    never see nothing but water.
Then he see again a little ridge.
Little ground.
One week and then they landed.
Then from there
    they took him on the buggy
        or on the train or something for quite a ways.

Then they leave him there.
But not in jail no more.
They give him a good house,
    a good big house,
        big room,
            good bed.
They feed him good
    and then they kept him.
They watch him all the time.
But once in awhile they took him
    and put him on the train
        and they went away.
They stay away for two or three months
    and then come back.
That was his home place.
In two months or more,
    they come back to England
        and they stay there for two or three weeks,
            maybe one month,
                then they took him to another direction.
That's in European somewhere.

They took him everywhere for show.
Whenever they get somewhere
    and there's be a big forum
        and table or something.

Then they tell him to get up there
  and walk around there.
Then, the people in the big room,
  big house chock full of people,
    and he watching them.
And these people, they pay.
Pay money to see that Indian.
There is no Indian in Europe at that time.
Only him.

So the white people, they make money out of him.
And he was there four years.

And this man from Enderby,
  he's a half-breed.
His name, Charlie.
Charlie Harvie, his name.
He talks in Okanagan.
He's half-breed.
And he don't say,
  but I think myself he must be in the army,
    that Charlie,
      because he went and he get to England.
Then he come back from England
  and he came home to Enderby.
And when he got home,
  he said when he was in England,
    he said, there's a big bunch of boys,
      all young boys just like he was,
        just like his age.
Bunch of them and they were there.

So one of these boys told him,
  asked him where he come from.
And he said he came from the Okanagan, British Columbia.
Okanagan.
Then, he told him,
  'There was a man not far from here,
    he is supposed to come from Okanagan, British Columbia.
  He is supposed to speak in your language.
  Maybe we should take you over there
    and then you can see that man.'

Then, he said,
  'No, I don't like to go because',
  (see, he's got a boss, he must be an army man),
  'My boss they may not like it that way.'
So, the other boss says,
  'Your boss, he's not going to know that.
  We take you over there.
  We're not going to tell your boss.
  You're going to see that man.'

All right.
So they went.
The boys took him over there.
Then they get to that place
  and they go in to where that Jim was.
That's his house.
Then the boys told him,
  'This man, he speak in your language.'
Then the both of them started to speak in Okanagan.

Not only one.
He went over there two or three times
  to see him and visit him
    for quite a while.

And Jim,
  he told him all about what they have done
    and so on.
And then they took him from Westminster
  and they took him on the train a long ways
    and they put him on the boat for one month.
Then they had him there.
  'Then they take me out from here a long ways.
  I don't know which way,
    but they take me out a long ways.
  Whenever I stop, a lot of people get in there.
  Then they make me walk around on the boards.
  High.
  Then I walk around and all the people look at me.
  Then I go.
  We go to another place.
  Then we go to another place.
  A lot of places.

In one month or two months
we come back.
And this is my home place.'

But he says,
'Charlie, when you get back to British Columbia,
you can go from Enderby to Ashnola.'
Right in Ashnola he's got aunt and he's got uncle.
And he said to Charlie,
'You could tell my uncle and my aunt
to make a business,
to see if they can come and get me.
They got a lot of money.
They got a lot of cattle.
They got enough money.
They should come and get me.
In another way they can talk to the Indian agent.
And then the Indian agent can contact to Ottawa,
to the Indian Affairs.
Then, whoever they is coming to get me,
their fare can be paid that way.
But maybe they'll have a little money with them anyway.
But my people, they're well-off.
They should do that and come and get me.'

So Charlie, he said,
'I will when I get home.'

And about a year after that,
Charlie came back.
Come back to Enderby.
He stay there almost one year after that and he come back.
And then he ride on the saddle horse all the way to Ashnola.
Then he see that John, his name was,
and Mary.
They are cousins.
That's Jim's aunt, that Mary,
and his uncle, John.
He told them all about it
to contact the Indian agent and to Ottawa
and all that.
And he said,
'If you want me, I can be with you,'
because he can speak in English, you know.

But these Indians, they couldn't understand.
They don't know.
In another way, they don't like it.

They say,
 'He should not pay for our fare
  because that's a lot of money.'
They figure they could pay for their own fare
 but it takes a lot of money
And they could never understand about the contact
 so they could get paid their fare from the Indian affairs.
Charlie told them,
 but they couldn't understand.
Charlie, he was waiting around,
 and he said,
  'I go home, but if you need me, I come back and help you,
   or else I can go with you for interpreter over there
    to get that man back.'

But they just dismissed.
No more.
They never get him.

But, before they find out he was alive yet
 at the time when they took Jim from Westminster,
  take him away,
   then they rode from the jail to John.
He was a chief, you know.
And they told John that
 'Jim was in jail here
  but he died and we bury him.'

But he not die.
They lie.
They take him away.

So they think, his people,
 they just got to know he died and that's all.
But they decided they should come and get the body.
Take it out and bring him home.
So they did.
They come, that John and Mary and some others.
They got an interpreter, you know,
 who can speak in English.

Then they come on horseback with the packhorses to Hope.
Then they talk to the people in Hope
  and they tell them,
    'You can't leave your horses here.
    There's no feed for the horses.
    You have to go to Chilliwack
      and then you can put your horses in there with the Indians.
    There's all kinds of feed there for horses.
    And then you can take the boat from Chilliwack to Westminster.'

So, they did.
They did get to Westminster
  and then they go to the jail office
    and they tell 'em,
      'We're coming to get George Jim.
      He's already buried here.'
So, they said,
  'Yeah, we talk to one another.
  We'll see.
  Just wait awhile, a couple of days.'

Then, they talk to one another
  and I guess they find out what to say about him.
Then they say,
  'All right, we know,
  This is the one right there in the graveyard.
  We can dig him.
  We dig him out and we clean 'em and we change the coffin.
  Then you guys can take him on the boat as far as Chilliwack
    and then you could put him on the packhorse.'

Well, it's in a box
  because they could pack the horse on each side of something.
Then they could put the box crossways
  all the ways from Chilliwack to Ashnola.
Then they did that
  and they take him out and clean him
    and put medicine on him
      so he wouldn't be smell.
Change the coffin and seal it
  and told them not to open it.
    'Don't open it
      because we give him medicine.

But in the box he's not cold.
They might be kinda smell,
by the time you get it over there,
not to open 'em.'

All right, they bring 'em
and they never open 'em.
But when they get him to Ashnola,
then, whoever they were there,
and they tell 'em,
'We should open 'em.
We should make sure if that was him.'
Well, these other people said,
'If he's going to be smelly, that don't matter.
Open 'em.
We want to see.'
So, they break it open and they looked at 'em.
'That's not Jim. That was a Chinaman.'
Kinda stout Chinaman.
He must have been in jail.

They can't take him back, so they bury him there.
They were around there for a while
and they thought maybe they make a mistake over there.
'We better go again to get Jim.
They might mistake.
Maybe Jim is still there.'

They went again
and they get there
and they told 'em,
'This is not Jim you give us.
This is a Chinaman.'
'By gosh, that's too bad.
We made a mistake.
We know that.
We find that out,
but you fellas are gone.
George is there.
Now that you've come back,
we can take him out and clean him
and you can take him away.
Take him home.'

They do the same thing.
Dug him out, clean him, put medicine on him
    and changed the box, and tell him not to open it.

So, they bring him,
    and that was the second time.
From Westminster to Chilliwack.
Then, they packed him from Chilliwack to Ashnola.
When they got there,
    whoever they were home tell 'em,
        'We got to open 'em, see,
            to make sure if it was Jim.
        Maybe another Chinaman.'

Anyhow, they open 'em.
They looked at him
    and he was a negro boy.
A small man too.

Well, they bury him there.
But there's no use to go back and get George.

And George is not dead.
They take him away.

Then later on, a few years after that,
    and Charlie Harvie come back from England.
Then he ride over there and he tell them about it.

Long time, quite a few years after that,
    and then they find out
        George Jim, he's not dead.
He's alive yet, but he's in England.

So, that's the end of that story.

1989

A.J.M. Smith

1902–1980

Poet, anthologist, critic, teacher, and one of the founders of the modernist literary movement in Canada, Arthur James Marshall Smith had a profound effect on modern Canadian poetry, beginning in his student days and carrying on through a long career. Born in Montreal, he entered McGill in 1921, completing an undergraduate degree in science before taking an MA in literature. While at McGill he began two literary publications: the *Literary Supplement of the McGill Daily* (1924–5), which lasted less than a year, and then, with F.R. Scott, the *McGill Fortnightly Review* (1925–7), which published the poetry of the nascent 'Montreal group' (F.R. Scott, Leo Kennedy, and Smith himself, among others), along with Smith's early critical statements about the need for a modernist poetry in Canada.

In 1927 Smith married and left Montreal for Edinburgh, where he began a Ph.D. in English on seventeenth-century poetry. While in Scotland, his brief but influential critical article, 'Wanted—Canadian Criticism', appeared in the *Canadian Forum* (April 1928). In it he called for a modern criticism that would guide Canadian writers into twentieth century aesthetics and away from the moral patriotism and subservience to commerce that he saw seducing contemporary writers. He thought that Canadian critics had so far been misguided because they used moral rather than artistic criteria and supported writers who used clichéd themes and trite Canadian images. He argued that Canada's adolescence was now over and that the 'adult' writing to come would be realistic; would be able to utilize irony, cynicism, and liberalism without stigma; and would be conscious not so much of its position in space as of its location in time. This article was his formal declaration of a split between those who supported modernist sensibilities and those who adhered to nationalistic goals in order to support Canadian literature. Around this time he also contributed poems to the *Canadian Mercury* (1928–9), which in its brief lifetime continued the policies that had guided the *McGill Fortnightly*.

In 1929 he returned briefly to Montreal. Unable to find a university teaching position in Canada during the Depression, he took several temporary ones in the United States. He completed his doctorate in 1931 and in 1938 was appointed to the faculty of Michigan State University in East Lansing. That became his permanent home, though he retuned to Canada to spend his summers at a family cottage in Quebec. When he retired in 1972, he stayed on at Michigan State as writer-in-residence.

Despite his American residence, his deep interest in, and editorial involvement with, Canadian literature continued. In the thirties Smith and Scott compiled *New Provinces* (1936); containing work by four members of the now-dispersed 'Montreal group' (Kennedy, A.M. Klein, Scott, and Smith), and by E.J. Pratt and Robert Finch of Toronto, it was presented as an anthology of 'new' Canadian poets intended to define Canadian modernist poetry. Its publication was clouded, however, by the rejection of Smith's deliberately provocative preface by Hugh Eayrs, the publisher of Macmillan, and by Finch and Pratt. They objected to the way Smith characterized romantic poetry of feeling as inferior to an impersonal one of intellect, knowing that this preference would be understood as an attack on earlier Canadian poets and would convey an implicit suggestion that worthwhile Canadian poetry began with the New Provinces writers. Scott replaced it with a less-controversial preface. Smith's objectionable one was finally published in 1965, in the journal *Canadian Literature*, as 'A Rejected Preface'.

Although Raymond Knister, Dorothy Livesay, and W.W.E. Ross were writing imagist and modernist poetry before the Montreal group, it was Smith who—responding to his reading of Yeats, to the Imagist movement defined by Pound, and to Eliot's *Waste Land*—attempted, in a series of critical pronouncements, to establish the poetic principles of Canadian modernism. Writing in 1926, he described the job of the early modernists such as Yeats as having been 'to overthrow an effete and decadent diction and to bring the subject matter of poetry out of the library and the afternoon-tea salon into the open air, dealing in the language of present-day speech with subjects of living interest'; Smith believed that the undertaking of his own generation of modernists was 'a turning back to the Seventeenth Century, a renewed interest in the poems of John Donne, an attempt to recapture and exploit in a new way the poetics of the Metaphysical poets'—and that by incorporating into that endeavour 'various psychological theories of the subconscious', this type of modernism would be able to 'forge . . . what is almost a new form of expression—a form which has found so far its culmination in the prose of James Joyce and the poetry of T.S. Eliot'. These new modernists were writers, he observed, who 'turned aside from the world, concerned themselves with abstruse questions of technique', and emphasized 'the importance of form'.

In the 1940s, Smith sought to apply his formalist principles to national literature by making a controversial distinction, in his 1943 preface to *The Book of Canadian Poetry*, between 'cosmopolitan' and 'native' verse. For Smith the 'cosmopolitan' poet responded to what Canadian life 'had in common with life everywhere', while the 'native' poet 'concentrated on what was individual and unique in Canadian life'. Historically Smith saw the 'native' poet as having sought to 'come to terms with an environment that is only now ceasing to be colonial', while the 'cosmopolitan' writer 'from the very beginning has made a heroic effort to transcend colonialism by entering into the universal, civilizing culture of ideas'. For Smith colonialism, which he equated with parochialism, was a threat to Canadian writing, while cosmopolitanism admitted Canadian writers to the world of international modernism.

This preface to the 1943 anthology began a dispute between Smith and another group of writers whose work often appeared in the literary magazine *First Statement*, edited by John Sutherland. In his preface to *Other Canadians: Anthology of the New Poetry in Canada; 1940–1946* (1947), Sutherland defended the 'hardfisted' proletarian writers who valued not the civilized poetry of 'cosmopolitanism' but a more local verse that was 'racy and vigorous', 'healthy and masculine'—exemplified by poets like Irving Layton, Louis Dudek, and Raymond Souster. These, he argued, were poets who wrote a different sort of native poetry from that which Smith disliked, one not focused on the physical world but on the people within it, a poetry 'of the common man'. The debate between Smith and Sutherland came to be viewed as a debate between two schools of Canadian modernist poetry, the writers associated with *First Statement* and those with *Preview*, a Montreal literary magazine that was publishing the work of Scott, Klein, and P.K. Page, and it reflected a growing division in modernism itself—between those who valued an elegant, spare verse and those who rejected the refined diction and form associated with Eliot's form of modernism. (What was often ignored was the fact that both groups had turned away from the nature-based poetry of earlier Canadian writing.)

The debate was not merely about aesthetics. In the 1940s modernism was being increasingly criticized as an anti-national approach to writing at a time when national literature and identity were becoming important goals again. In the same year as Smith's advocacy of cosmopolitan poetry, E.K. Brown argued, in his influential book *On Canadian Poetry*, that Canadian literature had always been colonial because it had looked first to Britain for its models and then to the United States rather than developing an independent literature that confidently drew on its own traditions and reflected back its own experiences and places.

Smith's influence on Canadian writing went beyond his role as spokesperson for modernism. As an anthologist, he helped shape the Canadian literary canon. The collections of poetry and prose he compiled include *The Oxford Book of Canadian Verse* (1960), *Modern Canadian Verse* (1967); *The Blasted Pine: An Anthology of Satire, Invective and Disrespectful Verse; Chiefly by Canadian Writers* (edited with F.R. Scott, 1957); as well as two anthologies of critical essays, *Masks of Fiction* (1961) and *Masks of Poetry* (1962). His own criticism was collected in *Towards a View of Canadian Poetry:*

Selected Critical Essays 1928–1971 (1973) and *On Poetry and Poets* (1977).

Although Smith published his own poems over the years—mostly in periodicals such as the *Canadian Forum*—he long refrained from collecting them in book form. His first volume of poems, *News of the Phoenix*, which won a Governor General's Award, did not appear until 1943. There followed *A Sort of Ecstasy* (1954), *Collected Poems* (1963), *Poems: New and Collected* (1967), and *The Classic Shade: Selected Poems* (1978).

All of Smith's poetry is characterized by an assured command of form that controls his intricate allusions; by a style that can incorporate, within a single poem, a convoluted syntax derived from seventeenth-century poetry ('How all men wrongly death to dignify / Conspire. I tell') and the wry humour and colloquial speech rhythms of the jazz world ('a worth / Beyond all highfalutin' woes or shows'). A severe critic of his own efforts, and a constant reviser, Smith believed that a poem should be 'a highly organized, complex, and unified re-creation of experience in which the maximum use of meaning and suggestion in the sounds of words has been achieved with the minimum essential outlay of words. A poem is not the description of an experience, it is itself an experience, and it awakens in the mind of the alert and receptive reader a new experience analogous to the one in the mind of the poet ultimately responsible for the creation of the poem' ('The Refining Fire: The Meaning and Use of Poetry', 1954).

The Lonely Land[1]

Cedar and jagged fir
uplift sharp barbs
against the gray
and cloud-piled sky;
and in the bay
blown spume and windrift
and thin, bitter spray
snap
at the whirling sky;
and the pine trees
lean one way.

A wild duck calls
to her mate,
and the ragged
and passionate tones
stagger and fall,
and recover,
and stagger and fall,
on these stones—
are lost
in the lapping of water
on smooth, flat stones.

1 Originally subtitled 'Group of Seven' (in the *McGill Fortnightly Review*, 1926), this poem was revised for two other periodical publications, in 1927 and again in 1929.

This is a beauty
of dissonance,
this resonance
of stony strand,
this smoky cry
curled over a black pine
like a broken
and wind-battered branch
when the wind
bends the tops of the pines
and curdles the sky
from the north.

This is the beauty
of strength
broken by strength
and still strong.

1926; 1936

Far West

Among the cigarettes and the peppermint creams
Came the flowers of fingers, luxurious and bland,
Incredibly blossoming in the little breast.
And in the Far West
The tremendous cowboys in goatskin pants
Shot up the town of her ignorant wish.

In the gun flash she saw the long light shake
Across the lake,[1] repeating that poem
At Finsbury Park.
But the echo was drowned in the roll of the trams—
Anyway, who would have heard? Not a soul.
Not one noble and toxic like Buffalo Bill.

1 An allusion to Tennyson's 'The Princess', iv, Introductory Song:

The splendour falls on castle walls
And snowy summits old in story:
The long light shakes across the lakes,
And the wild cataract leaps in glory.
Blow, bugle, blow, set the wild echoes flying,
Blow, bugle; answer, echoes, dying, dying, dying.

'Finsbury Park' is an area in northwest London. The movie theatre in the poem is apparently located there.

In the holy name *bang! bang!* the flowers came
With the marvellous touch of fingers
Gentler than the fuzzy goats
Moving up and down up and down as if in ecstasy
As the cowboys rode their skintight stallions
Over the barbarous hills of California.

1943

Sea Cliff

Wave on wave
and green on rock
and white between
the splash and black
the crash and hiss
of the feathery fall,
the snap and shock
of the water wall
and the wall of rock:

after—
after the ebb-flow,
wet rock,
high—
high over the slapping green,
water sliding away
and the rock abiding,
new rock riding
out of the spray.

1943

The Wisdom of Old Jelly Roll[1]

How all men wrongly death to dignify
Conspire, I tell. Parson, poetaster, pimp,
Each acts or acquiesces. They prettify,
Dress up, deodorize, embellish, primp,

1 Ferdinand Joseph La Menthe ('Jelly Roll') Morton (1885–1941), American jazz pianist and composer.

And make a show of Nothing. Ah, but met-
aphysics laughs; she touches, tastes, and smells
—Hence knows—the diamond holes that make a net.
Silence resettled testifies to bells.
'Nothing' depends on 'Thing', which is or was:
So death makes life or makes life's worth, a worth
Beyond all highfalutin' woes or shows
To publish and confess, 'Cry at the birth,
Rejoice at the death,' old Jelly Roll said,
Being on whiskey, ragtime, chicken, and the scriptures fed.

1962

Morley Callaghan

1903–1990

Morley Callaghan's short stories, like Ethel Wilson's, seem straightforward in their presentation, yet each narrative is actually a carefully planned structure in which a character faces a crisis that will determine the course of his life. The crossroads in Callaghan's stories do not merely serve a melodramatic purpose; they have a didactic function. A committed Catholic, Callaghan saw himself as a writer who, in giving 'a shape and form to human experience', had to 'become a moralist'.

Born and educated in Toronto, Callaghan took a general BA in 1925 from St Michael's College, University of Toronto, and completed law school in 1928. While a student he spent his summers working as a cub reporter for the Toronto *Daily Star*. It was there, in 1923, that he met Ernest Hemingway. Callaghan, having already begun to compose fiction, showed the American writer his stories. Hemingway, who left for France shortly after, passed them on to some of the editors of Paris literary magazines and presses. As a result, Callaghan's first published story, 'A Girl with Ambition', made its appearance in Paris in 1926, in the important modernist literary magazine *This Quarter*. (His work was later published in other distinguished European literary magazines of the time, *transition* and Ezra Pound's *Exile*.) Callaghan was also successful when he submitted his fiction to American magazines, publishing, from 1928 on, in such journals as *Atlantic Monthly, Scribner's Magazine, Harper's Bazaar*, and *The New Yorker*. F. Scott Fitzgerald, after reading some of Callaghan's stories, recommended him to his editor at Scribner's, Maxwell Perkins, who oversaw the publication of Callaghan's first novel, *Strange Fugitive* (1928), and his first collection of stories, *A Native Argosy* (1929).

During this period Callaghan lived and worked as a journalist in Toronto and Montreal. In 1929 he and his wife travelled to Paris, where he met writers in the expatriate community. (Many years later he wrote a memoir of his visit, *That Summer in Paris*, 1963, the best-known episode of which describes his victory in a boxing match with Hemingway; Fitzgerald was the time-keeper.) Returning to North America later in the year, the Callaghans settled in Toronto.

In the thirties, Callaghan wrote prolifically, completing six novels and placing sixty-five stories in high-paying American magazines. In addition to a large number of stories, he published seven volumes of fiction in eight years: *It's Never Over* (1930), *No Man's Meat* (1931), *A Broken Journey* (1932), *Such Is My Beloved* (1934), *They Shall Inherit the Earth* (1935), *Now That April's Here and Other Stories* (1936), and *More Joy in Heaven* (1937). In 1938, however, Callaghan entered a decade he described as a 'period of spiritual dryness' during which he produced little new fiction. During that time he worked as a journalist, a script-writer, and even as a moderator and panellist on CBC radio. In 1948 he returned to fiction; among his later works are *The Loved and the Lost* (1951), *Morley Callaghan's Stories* (1959), and *A Passion in Rome* (1961). His last two novels, *A Fine and Private Place* (1975), and *A Wild Old Man on the Road* (1988), contain loosely autobiographical portraits. In 1985, Callaghan's son, the poet, short story writer, and editor Barry Callaghan, brought together a number of his father's previously uncollected stories as *The Lost and Found Stories of Morley Callaghan.*

Though Callaghan received early international recognition, praise in Canada was not always forthcoming. It was not until the fifties that he received a Governor General's award (1951); this was followed by the Lorne Pierce Medal in 1960 and, in 1970, by the Molson Prize and the Royal Bank Award. Callaghan had been criticized at home by both academics and newspaper reviewers for universalizing his characters and settings, a strategy they saw his having developed in order to gain an international market at the denial of his own Canadian identity. (In *On Canadian Poetry*, E.K. Brown used him as his representative of the Canadian colonial mentality.) However, one could argue that Callaghan's tendency to blur or make transparent particular features is not limited to Canadian locales: as the American critic Edmund Wilson, who was a long-time admirer, pointed out, Callaghan was more abstract than writers like Fitzgerald and Hemingway — removing even his own presence from his writing: 'Callaghan is so much interested in moral character as exhibited in other people's behavior that, unlike his two exhibitionistic friends, he never shows himself at all.' In choosing to obscure both himself and his environment, Callaghan took the option that A.J.M. Smith had seen as the choice of modernist 'cosmopolitan' writers. That has, however, turned out to run counter to the choice made by most twentieth-century Canadian writers, who have more often been concerned with the need to portray Canadian locales in order to establish a Canadian identity.

Callaghan's tendency to generalize is consistent with his interest in 'timeless' issues. His fiction is concerned with the universal problem of mankind's imperfect condition. While early in his career he thought of social realism and Marxism as possible responses to man's difficulties, from the mid-thirties he found his solution in Christian humanism. Following his meetings in 1933 with the French philosopher Jacques Maritain, Callaghan developed the view that in an increasingly oppressive society, the individual needs to control not so much his physical destiny as his personal salvation. This position resulted, in Callaghan's fiction, in a preoccupation with a particular kind of 'criminality' that sets itself in opposition to moral codes and social laws: his hero is often a criminal saint, a social martyr of individual conscience.

Nowhere is the extremity of the individual's situation more evident than in Callaghan's short stories, where the conflict is internalized inside a single character, one who often must choose between personal relationships and his desire to be part of an impersonal society. The merits of Callaghan's novels have sometimes been debated, but the quality of his best stories has always been evident. They are crystallizations of man's sense of loss, of his longing for Edens that are no longer attainable. In the short stories especially, Callaghan's laconic style suggests objectivity, an unemotional mirroring of life. At the same time, beneath this surface detachment, a homiletic voice sounds a warning against a dehumanized world and a law that has largely forgotten the personal dimensions of morality.

Watching and Waiting

Whenever Thomas Hilliard, the lawyer, watched his young wife dancing with men of her own age, he was very sad, for she seemed to glow with a laughter and elation that didn't touch her life with him at all. He was jealous, he knew; but his jealousy at that time made him feel humble. It gave him the fumbling tenderness of a young boy. But as time passed and he saw that his humility only added to her feeling of security, he grew sullen and furtive and began to spy on her.

At times he realized that he was making her life wretched, and in his great shame he struggled hard against the distrust of her that was breaking the peace of his soul. In his longing to be alone with her, so that he would be free to offer her whatever goodness there was in him, he insisted that they move out to the country and renovate the old farmhouse on the lake where he had been born. There they lived like two scared prisoners in the house that was screened from the lane by three old oak trees. He went into the city only three days a week and his business was soon ruined by such neglect.

One evening Thomas Hilliard was putting his bag in the car, getting ready to return to the city. He was in a hurry, for the sky was darkening; the wind had broken the surface of the lake into choppy little waves with whitecaps, and soon it would rain. A gust of wind slammed an open window. Above the noise of the water on the beach, he heard his wife's voice calling, rising eagerly as it went farther away from the house.

She was calling, 'Just a minute, Joe,' and she was running down to the gate by the lane, with the wind blowing her short fair hair back from her head as she ran.

At the gate a young man was getting out of a car, waving his hand to her like an old friend, and calling: 'Did you want to speak to me, Mrs Hilliard?'

'I wanted to ask you to do something for me,' she said.

The young man, laughing, lifted a large green bass from a pail in the back of his car, and he said: 'I caught it not more than half an hour ago. Will you take it, Mrs Hilliard?'

'Isn't it a beauty!' she said, holding it out at arm's length on the stick he had thrust through the jaws. 'You shouldn't be giving such a beauty away.' And she laughed, a free careless laugh that was carried up to the house on the wind.

For a while there was nothing Thomas Hilliard could hear but the murmur of his wife's voice mixed with the murmur of the young man's voice; but the way the laughter had poured out of her, and the look of pleasure on the young man's face, made him tense with resentment. He began to feel sure he had been actually thinking of that one man for months without ever naming him, that he had even been wondering about him while he was packing his bag and thinking of the drive into the city. Why was the young man so friendly that first time he had stopped them, on the main street of the town, when they were doing their weekend shopping, to explain that his name was Joe Whaley and he was their neighbour? That was something he had been wondering about for a long time. And every afternoon when Joe Whaley was off shore in his motorboat, he used to stand up and wave to them, the length of his lean young body outlined against the sky. It was as though all these things had been laid aside in Thomas Hilliard's head, to be given a sudden meaning now in the eager laughter of his wife, in her voice calling, and the pleasure on the young man's face.

He became so excited that he started to run down to the gate; and as he ran, his face was full of yearning and despair. They watched him coming, looking at each other doubtfully. When his wife saw how old and broken he looked, she suddenly dropped the fish in the dust of the road.

'Hey, there! Wait a minute,' he was calling to the young man, who had turned away awkwardly.

'Did you want to speak to me, Mr Hilliard?' Joe Whaley said.

'Is there something you want?' Hilliard asked.

'I just stopped a moment to give you people the fish.'

'I'd like to know, that's all,' Hilliard said, and he smiled foolishly.

The young man, who was astonished, mumbled some kind of an apology and got into his car. He drove up the lane with the engine racing, and the strong wind from the lake whirling the dust in a cloud across the fields.

Speaking quietly, as if nothing had happened to surprise her, Mrs Hilliard began, 'Did you think there was something the matter, Tom?' But then her voice broke, and she cried out: 'Why did you come running down here like that?'

'I heard the way you laughed,' he said.

'What was the matter with the way I laughed?'

'Don't you see how it would strike me? I haven't heard you laugh like that for such a long time.'

'I was only asking him if he'd be passing by the station tonight. I was going to ask him if he'd bring my mother here, if she was on the right train.'

'I don't believe that. You're making up a story,' he shouted.

It was the first time he had openly accused her of deceit; and when she tried to smile at him, her eyes were full of terror. It was as though she knew she was helpless at last, and she said slowly: 'I don't know why you keep staring at me. You're frightening me. I can't bear the way you watch me. It's been going on for such a long time. I've got to speak to someone—can't you see? It's dreadfully lonely here.'

She was staring out over the choppy wind-swept water: she turned and looked up with a child's wonder at the great oak trees that shut the house off from the road. 'I can't stand it any longer,' she said, her voice soft and broken. 'I've been a good wife. I had such an admiration for you when we started. There was nothing I wouldn't have trusted you with. And now—I don't know what's happened to us.' This was the first time she had ever tried to tell him of her hidden desolation; but all he could see was that her smile as she pleaded with him was pathetically false.

'You're lying. You're scared of what might happen,' he shouted.

'I've known how you've been watching me, and I've kept asking myself what the both of us have been waiting for,' she said. As the wind, driving through the leaves of the trees, rattled a window on the side of the house, and the last of the light faded from the lake, she cried out: 'What are we waiting for, day after day?'

'I'm not waiting any more,' he shouted. 'I'm going. You don't need to worry about me watching you any more. I'll not come back this time.' He felt crazy as he started to run over to the car.

Running after him, she cried out: 'I've kept hoping something would happen to make it different, something that would save us. I've prayed for it at night, just wanting you to be like you were three years ago.'

But he had started the car, and it came at her so suddenly that she had to jump out of the way. When the car lurched up the lane, he heard her cry out, but the words were blown away on the wind. He looked back, and saw her standing stiff by the gate, with both hands up to her head.

He drove up to the highway, swinging the car around so wildly at the turn by the grocery-store that the proprietor shouted at him. He began to like the way the car dipped at high speed down the deep valleys, and rose and fell with him always rigid and unthinking. When he reached the top of the highest hill in the country, the first of the rain whipped across his face, slashing and cutting at him in the way they slap the face of a fighter who has been beaten and is coming out of a stupor. His arms were trembling so he stopped the car; and there he sat for a long time, looking out over the hills in the night rain, at the low country whose roll and rise could be followed by the line of lights curving around the lake through the desolation of the wooded valleys and the rain-swept fields of this country of his boyhood, a gleaming line of light leading back to the farm and his wife.

There was a flash of lightning, and the fields and pasture-land gleamed for a moment in the dark. Then he seemed to hear her voice crying out above the wind: 'I've been waiting for so long!' And he muttered: 'How lost and frightened she'll be alone there on a night like this.' He knew then that he could go no farther. With his heart full of yearning for the tenderness he knew she had offered to him, he kept repeating: 'I can't leave her. I can't ever leave her. I'll go back and ask her to forgive me.'

So he sighed and was ashamed; and he drove back slowly along the way he had come, making up in his head fine little speeches that would make his wife laugh and forgive him.

But when he had turned off the highway and was going down the lane that led to the house, he suddenly thought it could do no harm if he stopped the car before it was heard, and went up to the house quietly to make sure no one else was there.

Such a notion made him feel terribly ashamed. As the car rocked in the ruts and puddles of the dirt road, and the headlights gleamed on the wet leaves from overhanging branches, he was filled with a profound sadness, as if he knew instinctively that no matter how he struggled, he would not be able to stop himself from sneaking up to the house like a spy. Stopping the car, he sat staring at the shuttered windows through which the light hardly filtered, mumbling: 'I've got a heart like a snake's nest. I've come back to ask her to forgive me.' Yet as he watched the strips of light on the shutters, he found himself thinking it could do no harm to make sure she was alone, that this would be the last time he would ever spy on her.

As he got out of the car, he stood a while in the road, getting soaking wet, assuring himself he had no will to be evil. And then as he started to drag his feet through the puddles, he knew he was helpless against his hunger to justify his lack of faith in her.

Swinging open the gate and crossing the grass underneath the oak tree, he stopped softly on the veranda and turned the door-knob slowly. When he found that the door was locked, his heart began to beat unevenly, and he went to pound the door with his fist. Then he grew very cunning. Jumping down to the grass, he went cautiously around to the side of the house, pressed his head against the shutters and listened. The rain streamed down his face and ran into his open mouth.

He heard the sound of his wife's voice, and though he could not make out the words, he knew she was talking earnestly to someone. Her voice seemed to be breaking; she seemed to be sobbing, pleading that she be comforted. His heart began to beat so loud he was sure they would be able to hear it. He grabbed at the shutter and tried to pry it open with his hand, but his fingers grew numb, and the back of his hand began to bleed. Stepping back from the house, he looked around wildly for some heavy stick or piece of iron. He remembered where there was an old horseshoe imbedded in the mud by the gate, and running there, he got down on his knees and scraped with his fingers, and he grinned in delight when he tugged the old horseshoe out of the mud.

But when he had inserted the iron prongs of the shoe between the shutters, and had started to use his weight, he realized that his wife was no longer talking. She was coming over to the window. He heard her gasp and utter a little cry. He heard her running from the room.

Full of despair, as though he were being cheated of the discovery he had been patiently seeking for years, he stepped back from the house, trembling with eagerness. The light in the room where he had loosened the shutter was suddenly turned out. He turned and ran back up the lane to the car, and got his flashlight.

This time he went round to the other side of the house, listening for the smallest sounds which might tell him where they were hiding, but it was hard to hear anything above the noise of the wind in the trees and the roll of the waves on the shore. At the kitchen window at the back of the house he pulled at the shutter. He heard them running out of the room.

The longing to look upon the face of the one who was with his wife became so great that he could hardly think of his wife at all. 'They probably went upstairs to the bedroom. That's where they'll be. I think I heard them going up the stairs.' He went over to the garage and brought out the ladder they had used to paint the house, and put it up against the bedroom window and started to climb on the slippery rungs with the flashlight clutched in his hand, eager for the joy that would be his if he could see without being seen.

The voices he heard as he lay against the ladder were broken with fright; he began to feel all the terror that grew in them as they ran from room to room and whispered and listened and hid in the darkness and longed to cry out.

But they must have heard some noise he made at the window, for before he was ready to use the flashlight, they ran from the room; they hurried downstairs in a way that showed they no longer cared what noise they made, they fled as though they intended to keep on going out of the front door and up the lane.

If he had taken the time to climb down the ladder, they might have succeeded; but instead of doing that, he wrapped his arms and legs around the wet rails and slid to the ground; he got over to the oak tree, and was hidden, his flashlight pointed at the door, before they came out.

As they came running from the house, he kept hidden and flashed the light on them, catching his wife in the strong beam of light, and making her stop dead and scream. She was carrying the rifle he used for hunting in the fall.

With a crazy joy he stepped out and swung the light on the other one; it was his wife's mother, stooped in horror. They were both held in the glare of the light, blinking and cringing in terror, while he tried to remember that the mother was to come to the house. And then his wife shrieked and pointed the gun into the darkness at the end of the beam of light, and fired; and he called out helplessly: 'Marion—'

But it was hurting him on his breast. The light dropped from his hand as he sank to the ground and began to cough.

Then his wife snatched up the light and let it shine on his face: 'Oh, Tom, Tom! Look what I've done,' she moaned.

The mother was still on her knees, stiff with fright.

His hand held against his breast was wet with warm blood; and as his head sank back on the grass he called out jerkily to the mother: 'Go on—hurry! Get someone—for Marion. I'm dying. I want to tell them how it happened.'

The mother, shrieking, hobbled over to the lane, and her cries for help were carried away on the wind.

With his weeping wife huddled over him, he lay dying in the rain. But when he groped with his hand and touched her head, his soul was suddenly overwhelmed by an agony of remorse for his lack of faith in her: in these few moments he longed to be able to show her all the comforting tenderness she had missed in the last three years. 'Forgive me,' he whispered. 'It was my fault—if only you could forgive me.' He wanted to soothe the fright out of her before the others came running up from the lane.

1959

Earle Birney

1904–1995

Born in Alberta, Alfred Earle Birney was raised there and in rural British Columbia, on small frontier farms and in the developing town of Banff. As a boy and young man Birney worked to help support his family and to earn enough money to attend university. The jobs he held—'chain-and-rod man with a Waterton survey party, pick-and-shovel and sledge-hammer man on a road crew, mountain guide, fossil hunter, axeman and oiler in a mosquito-control project', as well as suburban newspaper editor—influenced his poetry. In 1926 he graduated with a first-class honours BA in English literature from the University of British Columbia. He took a Ph.D. (1936) in Old and Middle English at the University of Toronto, writing a dissertation on Chaucer's irony, while he held temporary positions at UBC and the University of California and studied at the University of London. In the year he completed his degree, he accepted a teaching post at University College, Toronto, and remained there until he joined the army as a personnel officer in 1942. Invalided out of the war in 1945, Birney worked briefly for the CBC in Montreal before accepting a professorship in medieval literature at UBC. After his retirement in 1965, he was writer-in-residence at the Universities of Toronto (1965–7), Waterloo (1967–8), and Western Ontario (1981–2), as well as Regents Professor at the University of California. In 1987 he suffered a catastrophic heart attack from which he never recovered.

Birney received wide recognition: he won Governor General's Awards for poetry in 1942 and 1945; the Leacock Medal for Humour, for his novel *Turvey*, in 1949; the Lorne Pierce Medal for Literature from the Royal Society of Canada; and the Canada Council Medal 'for outstanding achievement' in 1968.

An extensive traveller, he gave readings of his work throughout the world under Canada Council grants and fellowships. Geographical location even became the organizing principle of his *Collected Poems* (1975). Believing that geography links man to his history, Birney took pains in his poetry to mark, document, and define the significance of being in a particular place at a specific time.

No mere observer, Birney was a maker of new pathways in Canadian writing. Although he deprecates his role as innovator, he was the first writer in Canada to emphasize a metrics based on normal speech rhythms rather than artificial cadences; his 'doodles' (Birney's description of his visual poems) coincided with the beginnings of concrete poetry, and his need to write down 'the particular sound of my own voice' resulted in the first sound poems in Canada. Birney also helped to provide Canadian writers with new outlets for publication, both as literary editor of the *Canadian Forum* (1936–40) and as editor of the *Canadian Poetry Magazine* (1946–8). He further contributed to Canadian writing by organizing one of the first creative-writing courses in Canada (at the University of Toronto in 1941) and the first department of creative writing (at the University of British Columbia in 1963). Out of this teaching experience came *The Creative Writer* (1966) and a book in which he discusses the composition of his own poems, *The Cow Jumped Over the Moon* (1972).

Around the time Birney began to edit and to teach creative writing, he also made a serious commitment to his own poetry. His first book, *David and Other Poems*, was published in 1942, and his second, *Now Is Time*, in 1945. He published some fifteen volumes of verse, as well as two novels, *Turvey* and *Down the Long Table* (1955). He also wrote widely on poetry and poetics; some of his essays are collected in *Spreading Time: Remarks on Canadian Writing and Writers 1904–1949* (1980).

Birney's poetry reflects a range of interests, from political beliefs (in the thirties and early forties he was an active Trotskyite) to Anglo-Saxon poetics; but despite the seriousness of many of his poems, they are rarely without a sense of playfulness. Always a public poet, Birney reacted both to A.J.M. Smith's notion of 'cosmopolitanism' and to the more radical theories of the leftist poets of the forties in setting out his ideas for a Canadian poetics:

> *A revolutionary approach to the world today is somehow associated with a revolt against syntax and the beauties of lucidity. In all this what is lost sight of is that the true cosmopolite in poetry, the great world figure, always had his roots deep in the peculiar soil of his own country, and made himself international because he spoke from his own nation even when he spoke for and to the world. . . . The most cosmopolitan service a Canadian poet can do is to make himself . . . a clear and memorable and passionate interpreter of Canadians themselves, in the language of Canada. . . .* ('Has Poetry a Future in Canada?', 1946)

Vancouver Lights

About me the night   moonless   wimples the mountains
wraps ocean   land   air   and mounting
sucks at the stars   The city   throbbing below
webs the sable peninsula   The golden
strands overleap the seajet[1]   by bridge and buoy
vault the shears of the inlet   climb the woods
toward me   falter   and halt   Across to the firefly
haze of a ship on the gulf's erased horizon
roll the lambent spokes of a lighthouse

Through the feckless years we have come to the time
when to look on this quilt of lamps is a troubling delight
Welling from Europe's bog   through Africa flowing
and Asia   drowning the lonely lumes[2] on the oceans
tiding up over Halifax   now to this winking
outpost comes flooding the primal ink[3]

On this mountain's brutish forehead with terror of space
I stir   of the changeless night and the stark ranges
of nothing   pulsing down from beyond and between
the fragile planets   We are a spark beleaguered
by darkness   this twinkle we make in a corner of emptiness
how shall we utter our fear that the black Experimentress[4]
will never in the range of her microscope find it?   Our Phoebus

1 Black sea.
2 Lights.
3 In this stanza Birney describes the progress of the Axis powers in the Second World War, which had caused 'the blackouts spreading from Europe through North Africa, over to Halifax, and [was] now threatening the lights of Vancouver' (Birney, *The Cow Jumped Over the Moon*, hereafter abbreviated as *CJOM*).
4 Night, and the larger concept of the cosmic void, are personified as a black woman, a Nubian, whose experiment is the universe. Our sun, Phoebus, is only a small star or bubble to her; the nebulae or galaxies are but a necklace she has casually chosen to wear. This myth of a female progenitor of the universe recalls the Orphic legend of creation.

himself is a bubble that dries on Her slide   while the Nubian
wears for an evening's whim a necklace of nebulae

Yet we must speak   we the unique glowworms
Out of the waters and rocks of our little world
we conjured these flames   hooped these sparks
by our will   From blankness and cold we fashioned stars
to our size   and signalled Aldebaran[5]
This must we say   whoever may be to hear us
if murk devour   and none weave again in gossamer:

These rays were ours
we made and unmade them   Not the shudder of continents
doused us   the moon's passion   nor crash of comets
In the fathomless heat of our dwarfdom   our dream's combustion
we contrived the power   the blast that snuffed us
No one bound Prometheus   Himself he chained
and consumed his own bright liver[6]   O stranger
Plutonian   descendant   or beast in the stretching night—
there was light

1942, rev. 1966[7]

5 One of the twenty brightest stars in the sky, Aldebaran is used for navigation.
6 When Prometheus stole divine fire for mankind, Zeus punished him by having him chained to a rock where a vulture perpetually devoured his liver. 'Plutonian': (i) pertaining to the god of the dead; (ii) of the planet Pluto.
7 Birney revised many of his poems for *Selected Poems* (1966), mostly by replacing traditional punctuation with spaces.

Anglosaxon Street[1]

Dawn drizzle ended   dampness steams from
blotching brick and   blank plasterwaste
Faded housepatterns   hoary and finicky
unfold stuttering   stick like a phonograph

Here is a ghetto   gotten for goyim
O with care denuded   of nigger and kike
No coonsmell rankles   reeks only cellarrot
Ottar[2] of carexhaust   catcorpse and cookinggrease

1 This poem utilizes conventions of Old English, or Anglo-Saxon, poetry, including a caesura that breaks each line in two; single and double alliteration connecting the two halves; accented speech rhythms; kennings (metaphoric compounds substituted for ordinary words—e.g. 'learninghall' for school and 'whistleblow' for the end of the workday); and litotes (ironic understatement by negation—'not humbly' for proudly).
2 Attar: fragrant essence, usually rose-like.

Imperial hearts heave in this haven
Cracks across windows are welded with slogans
There'll Always Be An England enhances geraniums
and V's for Victory vanquish the housefly

Ho! with climbing sun march the bleached beldames
festooned with shopping bags farded[3] flatarched
bigthewed Saxonwives stepping over buttrivers
waddling back wienerladen to suckle smallfry

Hoy! with sunslope shrieking over hydrants
flood from learninghall the lean fingerlings
Nordic nobblecheeked[4] not all clean of nose
leaping Commandowise into leprous lanes

What! after whistleblow! spewed from wheelboat
after daylight doughtiness dire handplay
in sewertrench or sandpit come Saxonthegns[5]
Junebrown Jutekings jawslack for meat

Sit after supper on smeared doorsteps
not humbly swearing hatedeeds on Huns[6]
profiteers politicians pacifists Jews

Then by twobit magic to muse in movie
unlock picturehoard or lope to alehall
soaking bleakly in beer skittleless

Home again to hotbox and humid husbandhood
in slumbertrough adding sleepily to Anglekin
Alongside in lanenooks carling[7] and leman
caterwaul and clip[8] careless of Saxonry
with moonglow and haste and a higher heartbeat

Slumbers now slumtrack unstinks cooling
waiting brief for milkmaid mornstar and worldrise

TORONTO 1942

rev. 1966

3 Rouged.
4 Pimpled. Compare Chaucer's description of the Summoner, who could not find an ointment to cure him of the 'knobbes sittynge on his cheeks' ('General Prologue' to *The Canterbury Tales*, I. 633).
5 Freemen who provided military services for the Saxon lords; 'Jute kings' refers to the Jutes, the German tribe which, invading England in the fifth century, spearheaded the Anglo-Saxon conquest.
6 The savage Asiatic people who invaded Europe in the fourth century; also a modern term of contempt for Germans.
7 Churl, young man; leman: lover.
8 Embrace.

The Ebb Begins from Dream

The stars like stranded starfish pale and die
and tinted sands of dawning dry
The ebb begins from dream   leaving a border
of morning papers on the porches

From crusted reefs of homes   from unkempt shores
the workers slip reluctant   half-asleep
lapse back into the city's deep
The waves of factory hands and heads   of salesman
eyes and waiting waitress faces
slide soughing out from night's brief crannies
suck back along the strand of streets
rattling pebbled smalltalk

O then the curves and curls
of girl stenographers
the loops and purls[1]
of children foaming in the ooze
that by the ceaseless moon of living moves
through heaving flats of habit down the day

And late   from tortuous coves   remoter bays
there sets the sinuous undertow
of brokers   and the rolling politicians flow
to welter in the one pelagic[2] motion

Housewives   beached like crabs in staling pools
crisscross   are swashed in search of food
down to the midtown breakers' booming

At last with turning earth   relentless moon
slow but flooding comes the swell once more
with gurge[3] and laughter's plash and murmur
back to the fraying rocks   far-freighted now
with briny flotsam of each morning vow
a wrack of deeds that dulls with neaping[4]
dead thoughts that float again to sea
salt evening weeds that lie

1 Murmuring ripples.
2 Of the open sea.
3 Whirlpool.
4 The coming of neap tide (here synonymous with ebbing).

and rot between the cracks of life
and hopes that waterlogged will never link
with land   but will be borne until they sink

Now tide is full and sighing creeps
into the clean sought coigns[5] of sleep
And yet in sleep begins to stir
to mutter in the dark its yearning
and to the round possessive mother turning
dreams of vaster wellings
makes the last cliff totter
cradles all the globe in swaying water

The ebb begins from dream. . . .

TORONTO 1945/EAGLECLIFF 1947

rev. 1966

5 Corners.

Pacific Door[1]

Through or over the deathless feud
of the cobra sea and the mongoose wind
you must fare to reach us
Through hiss and throttle come
by a limbo of motion humbled
under cliffs of cloud
and over the shark's blue home
Across the undulations of this slate
long pain and sweating courage chalked
such names as glimmer yet
Drake's crewmen scribbled here their paradise

1 In early maps and explorers' accounts, the Strait of Anian was the name given to the body of water that, by connecting Frobisher's Strait with the Pacific, was supposed to provide the much-sought-for Northwest Passage. The explorers mentioned in this poem were all interested in dangerous, often deadly, explorations to prove or disprove the existence of this 'Pacific door'. Birney's *The Strait of Anian: Selected Poems* (1948), which contains 'Pacific Door', begins with an epigraph concerning Sir Francis Drake (1540–90): . . . *Sir Francis himselfe (as I haue heard) was of very good will to have sailed still more Northward hoping to find passage through the narrow sea Anian . . . and so from thence to haue taken his course Northeast, and so to retourne . . . into England, but his Mariners finding the coast of Noua Albion to be very cold, had no good will to sayle any further Northward . . .* —Thos. Blundeville, . . . *Of Sir Francis Drake His First Voyage into the Indies* (1594).

and dying Bering[2] lost in fog
turned north to mark us off from Asia still
Here cool Cook traced in sudden blood his final bay
and scurvied traders trailed the wakes of yesterday
until the otter rocks were bare
and all the tribal feathers plucked
Here Spaniards and Vancouver's boatmen scrawled
the problem that is ours and yours
that there is no clear Strait of Anian
to lead us easy back to Europe
that men are isled in ocean or in ice
and only joined by long endeavour to be joined
Come then on the waves of desire that well forever
and think no more than you must
of the simple unhuman truth of this emptiness
that down deep below the lowest pulsing of primal cell
tar-dark and still
lie the bleak and forever capacious tombs of the sea

LOWRY'S 'ERIDANUS', DOLLARTON 1947

1948

2 Vitas Jonassen Bering (1680–1741), Danish-born explorer for Russia, discovered Bering Strait and Alaska; he lost his life on this voyage when his ship was wrecked. James Cook (1728–79), master in the British Navy, in 1778 explored the northwest Pacific coast as far as Bering Strait and was killed the next year by native inhabitants of a Hawaiian beach. Spanish explorer Juan Perez sailed with his men in 1774 to take possession of Russian trading posts in the North Pacific; they were the first Europeans to sight the coast of British Columbia. Captain George Vancouver (1757–98) commanded a British expedition to the west coast to take over the Nootka Sound territory from Spanish officers, as provided for in the Nootka Convention.

Bushed

He invented a rainbow but lightning struck it
shattered it into the lake-lap of a mountain
so big his mind slowed when he looked at it

Yet he built a shack on the shore
learned to roast porcupine belly and
wore the quills on his hatband

At first he was out with the dawn
whether it yellowed bright as wood-columbine
or was only a fuzzed moth in a flannel of storm

But he found the mountain was clearly alive
sent messages whizzing down every hot morning
boomed proclamations at noon and spread out
a white guard of goat
before falling asleep on its feet at sundown

When he tried his eyes on the lake   ospreys
would fall like valkyries
choosing the cut-throat[1]
He took then to waiting
till the night smoke rose from the boil of the sunset

But the moon carved unknown totems
out of the lakeshore
owls in the beardusky woods derided him
moosehorned cedars circled his swamps and tossed
their antlers up to the stars
then he knew   though the mountain slept   the winds
were shaping its peak to an arrowhead
poised

And now he could only
bar himself in and wait
for the great flint to come singing into his heart

WRECK BEACH 1951

1952

1 Cut-throat: (i) BC trout that osprey prey upon; (ii) the slain upon the field of battle who are gathered up by the Valkyries, the spirit-guides to the afterlife (Valkyries take the form of both women and birds of prey).

Can. Lit.

(or *them able leave her ever*[1])

since we'd always sky about
when we had eagles they flew out
leaving no shadow bigger than wren's
to trouble even our broodiest hens

1 Word play on 'The Maple Leaf Forever'.

too busy bridging loneliness
to be alone
we hacked in railway ties
what Emily[2] etched in bone

we French&English never lost
our civil war
endure it still
a bloody civil bore

the wounded sirened off
no Whitman wanted
it's only by our lack of ghosts
we're haunted

SPANISH BANKS, VANCOUVER 1947/1966

1962, rev. 1966

2 Emily Dickinson.

El Greco: *Espolio*[1]

The carpenter is intent on the pressure of his hand

on the awl   and the trick of pinpointing his strength
through the awl to the wood   which is tough
He has no effort to spare for despoilings
or to worry if he'll be cut in on the dice
His skill is vital to the scene   and the safety of the state
Anyone can perform the indignities   It's his hard arms
and craft that hold the eyes of the convict's women
There is the problem of getting the holes exact
(in the middle of this elbowing crowd)
and deep enough to hold the spikes
after they've sunk through those bared feet
and inadequate wrists he knows are waiting behind him

1 'Espolio [is] an imagining of the scene when Christ waited on the Hill of Calvary before his execution. Meantime he endured the Espolio or "spoliation" (latin *expolio*, that is "despoiling"), a tearing away of his clothes by greedy spectators who would then gamble for the strips. In [El Greco's] painting, there is a prominent figure in the right foreground, in workmen's clothes, whom I take to be the carpenter; he is busy putting holes in the cross' *(CJOM)*.

He doesn't sense perhaps that one of the hands
is held in a curious gesture over him—
giving or asking forgiveness?—
but he'd scarcely take time to be puzzled by poses
Criminals come in all sorts
as anyone knows who makes crosses
are as mad or sane as those who decide on their killings
Our one at least has been quiet so far
though they say he talked himself into this trouble
a carpenter's son who got notions of preaching
Well here's a carpenter's son who'll have carpenter sons
God willing and build what's wanted
temples or tables mangers or crosses
and shape them decently
working alone in that firm and profound abstraction
which blots out the bawling of rag-snatchers
To construct with hands knee-weight braced thigh
keeps the back turned from death

But it's too late now for the other carpenter's boy
to return to this peace before the nails are hammered

POINT GREY 1960

1962, rev. 1966

Hugh MacLennan

1907–1990

Although John Hugh MacLennan was the first writer to utilize the novel for a serious and extensive delineation of Canadian identity, he was raised in a milieu in which 'Canada' was a rather distant concept. Born in Glace Bay, a Cape Breton mining town where his father was a physician, he grew up in a Nova Scotia that acknowledged its relationship to Britain proudly and to New England grudgingly but looked upon its place in the dominion as at best an uneasy alliance.

MacLennan received much of his education in Halifax, where he moved with his family in 1915. He studied classics at Dalhousie (BA, 1929) and continued his studies at Oxford as a Rhodes Scholar, before going on to Princeton for his Ph.D. His doctoral thesis, *Oxyrhynchus* (1935; published in 1968), was a study of the decline of a Roman town in Egypt after the Roman Empire withdrew from the area; it has been pointed out that the topic of that dissertation—the fate of a colony once the influence of the mother country is cut off—foreshadows the concerns of his fiction. After he completed his degree, MacLennan accepted a job teaching Latin and history at Lower Canada College,

Montreal. The move to Quebec was, he said, like a move into Canada: 'I emigrated and put down my roots in the continent and learnt to think in continental terms.' He taught at the college until 1945 and then left teaching for a time to work as a full-time writer. After six years, he returned to the classroom, taking a part-time position at McGill. He became a full-time professor of English there in 1964 and professor emeritus in 1979, continuing to teach one course. He made his home in Montreal and North Hatley, Que.

While he was at Oxford, MacLennan wrote poetry, and at Princeton he completed a novel imitative of Hemingway (it was never published) and began another, British in style. His wife Dorothy Duncan—an American whom he married in 1936—suggested that he would be more successful if he made Canada the centre of his fiction. Thereafter, beginning with *Barometer Rising* in 1941, MacLennan dealt explicitly with a specific aspect of Canada's culture in each of his novels, utilizing a form that married fiction and essay. In 1960, in an essay called 'Literature in a New Country', MacLennan argued that 'literature, unlike science, is an activity neither importable nor exportable. It must grow out of society itself. . . . [L]iterature is not an international activity in any sense, and though new visions and new techniques can flow across international borders, the substance of any living literature must come out of the society to which the writer belongs.'

Barometer Rising provides an extraordinarily detailed placement of its protagonist within a recognizable Canadian landscape, while examining the development, as a product of World War I, of a Canadian sensibility distinct from either a colonial or a regional one. *Two Solitudes* (1945) caught the public imagination with its exploration of the gulf that existed between the French and English cultures in Quebec; its title (taken from one of the letters of the German poet Rilke) has since become a catchphrase to describe Canada's divided condition. (MacLennan rexamined, in *Return of the Sphinx*, 1967, the nature of Canada's double identity and its impact on the nation as a whole.) His Scottish Calvinist background led MacLennan to investigate the negative effects of Puritanism in *The Precipice* (1948), which also looks at the relationship between English Canada and the United States, and in *Each Man's Son* (1951), which portrays the disintegration of a family in a Cape Breton mining town, precipitated by the conflicts between contemporary society and an older way of life. *The Watch That Ends the Night* (1959) is an examination of the social and political effects of the Depression on a generation of Canadians; it is also MacLennan's most personal novel, drawing on his experiences with Dorothy, whose lifelong battle with heart disease ended with her death in 1957.

After abandoning the novel for some years, MacLennan returned with a venture into science fiction, *Voices of Time* (1980), a story of how, after a nuclear holocaust, a new Canada must rebuild itself from the fragments of the old.

MacLennan received virtually every important literary award in Canada. In addition to the three Governor General's Awards he was given for his novels, he received two for collections of his essays: *Cross Country* (1949) and *Thirty and Three* (1954). His other non-fiction includes *Scotchman's Return and Other Essays* (1960), *Seven Rivers of Canada* (1961), and *The Other Side of Hugh MacLennan: Selected Essays Old and New* (1978), edited by Elspeth Cameron. As well, *Hugh MacLennan's Best* (1991), edited by Douglas Gibson, draws together a potpourri of the work: essays, journalism, poetry, and excerpts from all of his novels.

MacLennan's interest in history and society gives his fiction a vitality that is not dependent on plot or form—which are often the least interesting aspects of his work. At his best he builds relationships between ideas, constructing in the sum of the work an imaginative synthesis of national identity. His recurring premise—that we construct our future in the present by looking into our past—is not simply a product of his training as a classicist: it is central to many Canadian novels written since World War II. Like Callaghan, MacLennan is a moralist who writes about a fallen world, one in which, according to the central character of *Return of the Sphinx*, men are made desperate by the loss of philosophy and religion and 'crack up—and don't know they have'. Unlike Callaghan, however, MacLennan asserts that society is to be rebuilt, not abandoned by the moral individual. For him destruction and construction, disbelief and faith, are cyclical aspects of man's history and his nature.

Barometer Rising

The opposition of contraries, central to much of his thinking, led MacLennan toward the creation of a Canadian legend or mythology in which thesis and antithesis are resolved into a synthesis that will eventually spawn its own opposition. *Barometer Rising* was his first attempt to depict this pattern. Set in Halifax, one of the first British strongholds in Canada and a key naval base for the British Empire, it recasts the actions of contemporary Canadians in terms reminiscent of Homer's epics, particularly *The Odyssey*. Out of the terrible loss suffered by Haligonians as a result of the disastrous munitions explosion in the Halifax Harbour on 6 December 1917, MacLennan builds a myth of a new people who rise Phoenix-like from the ashes of colonial identity that has bound them to form a new nation free to choose its actions and its loyalties. The opening section of that novel, printed here, stands as an overture, mapping the Odysseus-like return of a hero on a quest for justice, a hero returning from a monstrous war to a home that must itself be liberated if it is to survive.

From *Barometer Rising*

SUNDAY, DEC. 2, 1917.[1]

four o'clock

He had been walking around Halifax all day, as though by moving through familiar streets he could test whether he belonged here and had at last reached home. In the west the winter sky was brilliant and clouds massing under the sun were taking on colour, but smoke hung low in the streets, the cold air holding it down. He glanced through the dirty window of a cheap restaurant, saw the interior was empty and went in through the double doors. There was a counter and a man in a soiled apron behind it, a few tables and chairs, and a smell of mustard. He sat on one of the warped stools at the counter and ordered bovril[2] and a ham sandwich.

'You English?' the man behind the counter said.

'No. I used to live around here.'

'Funny, I thought you were an English fella. You been over there, though?'

'I just got back.'

He glanced restlessly over his shoulder before he let his muscles relax, but there was no need for caution in a restaurant like this. No one he had ever known in Halifax would be seen in the place.

'You been away long?' the restaurant man said. He poured steaming water over the glutinous bovril essence after he had ladled it into a thick mug.

'Quite a while.'

The man set the drink on the counter and began cutting slices from a loaf of brown bread.

'Guess you been in the war, too,' he said. 'I was in it myself for a while but I didn't get very far. I got to Quebec. My wife thinks that's funny. She says, when you got in

1 MacLennan's brief foreword to the novel concludes: 'Eight days are involved in the story: Sunday, December second, to Monday, December tenth, in 1917.'

2 A commercial brand of beef bouillon.

the army you started moving backwards before you even began.' He pulled a thin slice of boiled ham loose from a pile on a plate and slapped it on the bread.

'What was your outfit?' he said.

The customer stared at the counter without answering and the restaurant man shifted his feet uneasily.

'I was only asking. Hell, it's no skin off my ass.'

'Never mind. I was with a lot of outfits, and I didn't sail from here in the first place.'

'Mustard?' When he received no answer the man passed the sandwich over the counter. 'A lot goes on in town these days. You'd be surprised.'

The sandwich was eaten in a fierce silence, then he swallowed the bovril in one passage of the cup to his mouth. He drew a deep breath and asked for more, and while the restaurant man was supplying it he asked casually, 'Are you still in with the army around here?'

'No. They let me out on account of varicose veins. That's why I only got to Quebec.'

A tram rumbled around the corner in the gathering shadows of the street and its flanges screamed on the uneven rails. The young man jerked nervously at the sudden noise and cleared his throat. All his muscles had tightened involuntarily, giving him a rigid appearance like an animal bunched for a spring. He remained taut and this physical tenseness invested his words with a dramatic value he did not intend.

'There's a chap I knew overseas,' he said. 'I was wondering if you'd ever heard of him. Alec MacKenzie . . . Big Alec, we called him.'

'I knew a man called Alec MacKenzie once, but he was a little fella.'

'Do you know Colonel Wain?'

The man shoved the second cup of bovril closer to his customer. 'How would a guy like me be knowing colonels?'

'I didn't mean was he a friend of yours. I meant, did you ever hear of him?'

'There's one Colonel Wain here in Halifax.' He glanced at the younger man's thin and shabby overcoat. 'But you wouldn't be meaning him, either. He's pretty rich, they say.'

'So?' He picked up the mug and drained it slowly, then stood straight and looked at himself in the mirror behind the counter. The war had made as big a change in him as it seemed to have made in Halifax. His shoulders were wide, he was just under six feet tall, but his appearance was of run-down ill health, and he knew he looked much older than when he had left three years ago. Although he was barely twenty-eight, deep lines ran in parentheses around his mouth, and there was a nervous tic in his left cheek and a permanent tension in the expression of his eyes. His nails were broken and dirty, he carried himself without confidence, and it seemed an effort for him to be still for more than a moment at a time. In England he would have been labelled a gentleman who had lost caste.

He buttoned his coat and laid some coins on the counter. He turned to leave and then turned back. 'This Colonel Wain . . . is he in town now?' he said.

'I saw his picture in the *Chronicle* last week some time,' the restaurant man said. 'I guess he must be.'

When he left the café he turned toward George Street and slowly began the climb toward Citadel Hill. When he reached the last intersection he continued across the pavement, then upward along a wavering footpath through the unkempt grasses which rustled over the slope of the hill. He pulled himself up slowly, with a jerky nervousness that indicated he was not yet accustomed to his limping left leg, which seemed more to follow his body than propel it forward. At the top of the hill he stopped on a narrow footpath that outlined the rim of the star-shaped moat which defended the half-hidden buildings of the central garrison. An armed soldier stood guard over an open drawbridge giving access to the military enclosure. Over it all rose a flagpole and signal masts.

He turned about and surveyed the town. A thin breeze was dragging in from the sea; it was a soundless breath on the cheek, but it made him feel entirely solitary. Though it was early December, the winter snow had not yet fallen and the thin soil had frozen onto the rocks, the trees were bare and the grass was like straw, and the land itself had given up most of its colour.

The details of Halifax were dim in the fading light but the contours were clear and he had forgotten how good they were. The Great Glacier had once packed, scraped, and riven this whole land; it had gouged out the harbour and left as a legacy three drumlins . . . the hill on which he stood and two islands in the harbour itself. Halifax covers the whole of an oval peninsula, and the Citadel is about in the centre of it. He could look south to the open Atlantic and see where the park at the end of the town thrusts its nose directly into the outer harbour. At the park the water divides, spreading around the town on either side; to the west the inlet is called the Northwest Arm, to the east it is called the Stream, and it is here that the docks and ocean terminals are built. The Stream bends with the swell of Halifax peninsula and runs inland a distance of four miles from the park to a deep strait at the northern end of town called the Narrows. This strait opens directly into Bedford Basin, a lake-like expanse which bulges around the back of the town to the north.

He followed the footpath and looked for familiar landmarks, walking around the moat until he had boxed the compass.[3] From here even a landsman could see why the harbour had for a century and a half been a link in the chain of British sea power. It is barricaded against Atlantic groundswells by McNab's Island at the mouth of the outer harbour, and by the smaller bowl of George's Island at the entrance to the Stream. It was defended now against enemy battle squadrons by forts set on rocky promontories running over the horizon into the sea. It was fenced off from prowling submarines by a steel net hung on pontoons from McNab's to the mainland. This harbour is the reason for the town's existence; it is all that matters in Halifax, for the place periodically sleeps between great wars. There had been a good many years since Napoleon, but now it was awake again.

The forests to the far west and north were nothing but shadows under the sky at this time of day. Above the horizon rim the remaining light was a turmoil of rose and saffron and pallid green, the colours of blood and flowers and the sheen of sunlight on summer grass. As his eyes shifted from the dull floor of the distant sea to this shredding

3 That is, moved to all four points of the compass.

blaze of glory crowning the continent, he felt an unexpected wave of exultation mount in his mind. Merely to have been born on the western side of the ocean gave a man something for which the traditions of the Old World could never compensate. This western land was his own country. He had forgotten how it was, but now he was back, and to be able to remain was worth risking everything.

After sunset the hilltop grew colder. The colours died quickly and as the landscape faded into darkness the street lights of the city came on. They made bluish pools at intervals along the narrow thoroughfares that fanned away from the roots of the hill, and all the way down to the waterfront the life of Halifax began to reveal itself in flashes. Barrington, Granville, and Hollis Streets, running north and south, were visible only at the intersections where the inclines plunging from the hill to the waterfront crossed them, and at these corners pedestrians could be seen moving back and forth, merged in irregular streams.

Children were playing a game with a whole block of a George Street slum for their playground. They darted in and out of his vision as they pursued each other in and out of doorways and back and forth across the street. Here and there in the withered grass along the slope of the Citadel the forms of men and girls lay huddled, scarcely moving; they clung together on the frozen ground in spite of the cold, sailors with only a night on shore and local girls with no better place to be.

Halifax seemed to have acquired a meaning since he had left it in 1914. Quietly, almost imperceptibly, everything had become harnessed to the war. Long ribbons of light crossed on the surface of the water from the new oil refinery on the far shore of the Stream, and they all found their focus in himself. Occasionally they were broken, as undiscernible craft moved through the harbour, and he suddenly realized that this familiar inlet had become one of the most vital stretches of water in the world. It still gleamed faintly in the dusk as its surface retained a residual glow of daylight. Ferryboats glided like beetles across it, fanning ruffled water in their wake. A freighter drifted inland with a motion so slight he had to watch a full minute before it was perceptible. Its only identification was riding lights; no one but the port authorities knew its home port or its destination. While he watched, its anchor ran out with a muted clatter to the bottom and its bow swung to the north.

Then the Stream became static. The smoke of Halifax lay like clouds about a mountain; the spire of St Mary's Cathedral cut George's Island in two; the only moving object was the beam of the lighthouse on McNab's, circling like a turning eye out to sea, along the coast and into the harbour again.

He descended the hill slowly, easing his left leg carefully along the dirt path. Down on the street the contours of Halifax were lost in the immediate reality of grim red brick and smoky stone. In the easy days before the war he had winced at the architecture, but it no longer bothered him. Halifax was obviously more than its buildings. Its functional aspect was magnificent, its solid docks piled with freight to the edge of deep water, Bedford Basin thronged with ships from all over the world, the grimy old naval and military buildings crowded once more with alert young men. However much he loathed the cause of this change, he found the throbbing life of the city at once a stimulation and a relief.

For twelve hours he had been back, and so far he had been recognized by no one. He stopped in the shadow of a doorway and the muscles of his face tightened again as his mind returned to its endless calculations. Big Alec MacKenzie had returned from France—and so had Wain. The colonel had probably been back for more than a year. The problem was to find MacKenzie before he himself was discovered by Wain. If only he could get to Big Alec first. . . . He began to smile to himself.

When he reached Barrington Street and the shops he found himself in a moving crowd. Girls with English faces brushed by him in twos and threes, sailors from a British cruiser rolled as though the pavement were a ship's deck. Although most of them were walking the main street because they had no better place to go—soldiers, dockworkers in flat cloth caps, civilians—they did not appear aimless. Even their idleness seemed to have a purpose, as though it were also part of the war.

By the time he had walked to the South End where the crowds were thinner, he realized that underneath all this war-begotten activity Halifax remained much the same. It had always looked an old town. It had a genius for looking old and for acting as though nothing could possibly happen to surprise it. Battalions passed through from the West, cargoes multiplied, convoys left every week and new ships took over their anchorages; yet underneath all this the old habits survived and the inhabitants did not alter. All of them still went to church regularly; he had watched them this morning. And he was certain they still drank tea with all their meals. The field-gun used in the past as a curfew for the garrison was fired from the Citadel every noon and at nine-thirty each night, and the townspeople took out their watches automatically twice a day to check the time. The Citadel itself flew the Union Jack in all weathers and was rightly considered a symbol and bastion of the British Empire.

Grinding on the cobblestones behind a pair of plunging Clydesdales came one of Halifax's most typical vehicles, a low-swung dray with a high driver's box, known as a sloven.[4] This one was piled high with bags of feed and it almost knocked him down as the driver brought it around to level ground. He cursed as he jumped clear of the horses and the driver spat and flourished his whip, and the lash flicked in a quick, cracking arc over the sidewalk. The sloven moved north onto Barrington Street as the horses were pulled in to a walk. Traffic slowed down behind it, a few horns sounded and the column stopped behind a stationary tram.

His leg pained after the sudden pull on his muscles and he walked more slowly until the soreness abated. Images flashed through his mind and out again . . . shell-shock simultaneous with a smashed thigh and no time to be frightened by either; the flash of destruction out of the dark; who knew until it was experienced how intense the molten whiteness could be at the heart of an exploding chemical? . . . Naked when they picked him up, unconscious . . . and afterwards memory gone and no identity disk to help the base hospital.

The English doctor had done a fine job in mending his thigh and a better one in saving his reason. This, at least, had been no accident; more than twenty centuries of medical history had been behind that doctor. Even though his world was composed

4 A long, low wagon drawn by horses (here by the powerful workhorses known as Clydesdales).

now of nothing but chance, it was unreasonable to believe that a series of accidents should ultimately matter. One chance must lead to another with no binding link but a peculiar tenacity which made him determined to preserve himself for a future which gave no promise of being superior to the past. It was his future, and that was all he could say of it. At the moment it was all he had.

A motor horn sounded and he leaped convulsively again. Every time a sudden noise struck his ears his jangled nerves set his limbs jumping and trembling in automatic convulsions which made him loathe his own body for being so helpless. He stopped and leaned against a lamppost until the trembling stopped. Like a fish on the end of a hook, he thought, squirming and fighting for no privilege except the opportunity to repeat the same performance later.

People moved past him in both directions, laughing, talking, indifferent. Were they too stupid to care what was happening to the world, or did they enjoy the prospect of a society in process of murdering itself? Did he care himself, for that matter; weren't any emotions he had left reduced to the simple desire for an acknowledged right to exist here in the place he knew as home? He had long ago given up the attempt to discover a social or spiritual reason which might justify what had happened to himself and millions of others during the past three years. If he could no longer be useful in the hell of Europe, then he must find a way to stay in Canada where he had been born.

He took his bearings when the trembling in his limbs subsided and was astonished to see how far south he had walked. Had the years in London made him lose all perspective of distance? He walked slowly to the next corner and knew he had reached his objective. But now he was here he felt nervous and unreasonably disappointed. He surveyed the cross-street to his right as though he were searching casually for his bearings, but he knew every inch of it and every doorway as far up the hill as he could see.

It seemed to have lost all its graciousness, and yet nothing was actually changed. Then he realized that he had been remembering it as it was in summer with the horse chestnuts and elms and limes towering their shade over the roofs, with the doorways secluded under vine-covered porches, with everything so quiet that it always seemed to be Sunday afternoon. Actually there was little difference; winter had always made it look bare, stripped as ruthlessly as the rest of Halifax. There was no town anywhere that changed in appearance so quickly when the foliage went.

He fumbled for a cigarette and lit it slowly, looking carefully in all directions as though he were deciding which way to shield himself from the wind. Then he began the steep ascent of the hill, his movements furtive and his hat pulled low over his left eye. He stopped at the crest and stood panting, hardly believing that after so much time he was really here, that the red house opposite had stayed just as he remembered it, that the trees still crowded its windows and the high wooden fence shut the garden away from the eyes of passersby.

At least the war had not dulled his trained appreciation of good architecture. Among the many nondescript Victorian houses of Halifax, this one stood out as a masterpiece. It was neither gracious nor beautiful, in a way it was almost forbidding, but it so typified the history and character of its town that it belonged exactly as it was: solid British colonial with a fanlight[5] over the door, about six feet of lawn separating it from the sidewalk, four thick walls and no ells or additions, high ceilings and high windows, and shutters on the inside where they could be useful if not decorative. It had stood just as it was for over a hundred years; it looked permanent enough to last forever.

To cross the street and knock on the door, to take a chance on the right person[6] opening it would be so easy. Just a few movements and it would be done, and then whatever else he might feel, this loneliness which welled inside like a salt spring would disappear. Spasmodically he clasped one hand with the other and squeezed it hard, then turned back down the hill and followed it to Barrington Street.

There was nothing more he could do today. Sunday was the worst possible time to hunt for Alec MacKenzie or anyone else too poor to own a telephone. He walked north to the junction of Spring Garden Road and waited for a tram. Evening service was under way in St Matthew's Church and the sound of a hymn penetrated its closed Gothic doors. 'O God of Bethel by whose hand thy people still are fed . . . Who, through this weary pilgrimage, Hast all our fathers led. . . .'

The girls went by in twos and threes, sailors rolled past, evening loafers lounged against the stone wall of the military cemetery opposite, a soldier picked up a girl in front of the iron gate of the Crimean monument.[7] 'God of our fathers, be the God of their succeeding race.' With a muffled sigh the congregation sat down.

A tram ground around the corner and stopped, heading north. Fifteen minutes later when he left it he could hear a low, vibrant, moaning sound that permeated everything, beating in over the housetops from the sea. For a second he was puzzled; it sounded like an animal at some distance, moaning with pain. Then he realized that the air was salty and moist and the odour of fishmeal was in his nostrils. The wind had changed and now it was bringing in the fog. Pavements were growing damp and bells and groaning buoys at the harbour-mouth were busy. When he reached his room in the cheap sailor's lodging he had rented that morning he lay down, and the sounds of the harbour seemed to be in the walls.

1941

5 A semicircular window about the front door.

6 The house is that of Colonel Wain. The 'right person' to open its door would be his daughter Penelope, with whom Neil Macrae, the (so far) unnamed protagonist, is in love. Neil has returned to Halifax hoping to find Alec Mackenzie, who can help clear him from a false charge of insubordination in wartime conditions, laid by Colonel Wain.

7 A monument to Canadian soldiers who fell fighting on the side of the British in the Crimean War (with Russia, 1853–6).

Sinclair Ross

1908–1996

The youngest of three children, James Sinclair Ross was born on his parents' homestead near Prince Albert, Sask. While Ross was a small child his father suffered a severe injury when he was thrown from a horse. The permanent personality change this caused resulted in a breakup of the family, and from the age of seven Ross lived alone with his mother. They moved from place to place, with her working as a housekeeper on farms in the area, until the need for a stable income led Ross to leave school after grade eleven. At sixteen he took a job with the Union Bank of Canada (later part of the Royal Bank) and, except for four years' service in the Royal Canadian Ordinance Corps during the Second World War, spent his life working in banks, first in three small Saskatchewan towns (between 1924 and 1933), then in Winnipeg (1933–42) and Montreal (1946–68). He lived with his mother until his wartime service, and supported her until her death in 1957. After retiring in 1968, he lived for three years in Greece and then a decade in Spain before returning to Canada in 1981. Suffering from Parkinson's disease, he spent his last years in Vancouver.

Ross's experience in banking would have provided him ample opportunity to learn about the aspirations and disappointments of those around him. As a witness to the difficulties of farm life on the Prairies, and especially to the economic failures caused by the Depression and the disastrous weather of the thirties, he created stories (published between 1934 and 1952, chiefly in *Queen's Quarterly*) and a first novel, *As for Me and My House* (1941), that captured the sense of oppression and desolation felt by a whole generation. Written in a style that does not call attention to itself, this fiction is both more crafted and more colloquial than that of the Prairie realists, like Grove, who preceded him. In the introduction to a collection of Ross's short stories, *The Lamp at Noon and Other Stories* (1968), Margaret Laurence observed: 'Ross's style is always beautifully matched to his material—spare, lean, honest, no gimmicks, and yet in its very simplicity setting up continuing echoes in the mind.'

The struggle and alienation depicted in this fiction is not limited to agrarian life: in *As for Me and My House*, the narrator, Mrs Bentley, describes the gulf that separates her from her husband, a minister in the small town of Horizon, and from the town's other residents. This novel, like Ross's short stories, carries an intense emotional impact. It did not, however, find a readership when it was originally published (it appeared only in the US) in the early years of World War II. It was rediscovered in 1957 when it was (with works by Grove, Leacock, and Callaghan) one of the first four books selected by Malcolm Ross for reprint in his New Canadian Library series. Following this republication, the novel came to be recognized as a classic of Canadian literature and a touchstone of Western fiction.

As with other classics, the way *As for Me and My House* has been understood changed over time. Originally seen primarily as a fictional journal that revealed the hidden depths in the lives of a quiet couple or as a narrative that recorded hardship and celebrated endurance, it later came to be read as a story told by a complexly unreliable narrator who reveals more than she knows. It has also been viewed as a window into Ross's own complex psyche.

Laurence is one of many writers who said that Ross gave impetus to her own writing. The poet Lorna Crozier has described *As for Me and My House* as her most important influence, adding: 'It was the first book I read that was set in the landscape where I grew up. It made me realize that someone from my area could actually be a writer and, in some ways, it gave me the courage to try.' In 1996 Crozier paid tribute to the novel by creating *A Saving Grace: The Collected Poems of Mrs Bentley*, a series of poems that she imagines Ross's protagonist having written.

Ross did not publish a second novel until *The Well* (1958), the story of a troubled city boy who finds redemption by returning to rural Saskatchewan. His third novel, *Whir of Gold* (1970), brings a character that first appeared in one of his early stories to Montreal and shows the difficulties he encounters in an urban world. In his last novel, *Sawbones Memorial* (1974), Ross returned to the milieu of a small Western town and to the period of his own Prairie experiences—but now with 'a little humour in the face of the inscrutable'. In its interweaving of dialogue with monologues and its complex use of multiple points of view *Sawbones Memorial* is Ross's most experimental novel. In 1982 the short fiction that remained uncollected and two newer stories were published as *The Race and Other Stories.*

None of Ross's later fiction ever quite matched the achievement of his early writing, with its powerful delineations of individuals working out private destinies within a profoundly shaping landscape. In these moving accounts, such as 'The Runaway', each individual clings to a faint but abiding hope; Margaret Laurence described it as a 'desperate persistence':

The real wonder is that so many of these men and women continue somehow—stumbling, perhaps, but still going on. Hope never quite vanishes. In counterpoint to desolation runs the theme of renewal. Tomorrow it may rain. The next spring will ultimately come.

In *As for Me and My Body: A Memoir of Sinclair Ross,* the Canadian fiction writer Keath Fraser tells of visiting Ross in his last years, many of which were spent in a nursing home. Near the end of his life Ross revealed to Fraser that he had been a closeted homosexual. His need to conceal his sexual identity in an era of intense homophobia may be one of the reasons Ross—one of the most solitary figures in Canadian writing—found himself drawn to portraits not only of the loneliness of the human soul but also of its capacity to carry on.

The Runaway

You would have thought that old Luke Taylor was a regular and welcome visitor, the friendly, unconcerned way he rode over that afternoon, leading two of his best Black Diamond mares.

'Four-year-olds,' he said with a neighbourly smile. 'None better in my stable. But I'm running short of stall room—six more foals last spring—so I thought if you were interested we might work out a trade in steers.'

My father was interested. We were putting a load of early alfalfa in the loft, and he went on pitching a minute, aloof, indifferent, but between forkfuls he glanced down stealthily at the Diamonds, and at each glance I could see his suspicion and resistance ebb.

For more than twenty years old Luke had owned a stableful of Diamonds. They were his special pride, his passion. He bred them like a man dedicated to an ideal, culling and matching tirelessly. A horse was a credit to the Black Diamond Farm, a justification of the name, or it disappeared. There were broad-rumped, shaggy-footed work horses, slim-legged runners, serviceable in-betweens like the team he had with him now, suitable for saddle or wagon—at a pinch, even for a few days on the plough—but all, whatever their breed, possessed a flawless beauty, a radiance of pride and spirit, that quickened the pulse and brought a spark of wonder to the dullest eye.

When they passed you turned from what you were doing and stood motionless, transfixed. When you met them on the road you instinctively gave them the right of way. And it didn't wear off. The hundredth time was no different from the first.

'None better in my stable,' old Luke repeated, and for once it was easy to believe him. Black coats shining in the sun like polished metal; long, rippling manes; imperious heads—the mares were superb, and they knew it. First, in a fine display of temperament, rearing rebelliously, they pretended astonishment and indignation: a barn with peeling paint and a sway-backed roof—it wasn't their due, they wouldn't submit to it! A moment later, all coy conciliation, they minced forward daintily for a nibble of our alfalfa.

I knew that since it was old Luke making the offer there must be a trick in it, that the bland voice and shifty smile must conceal some sly design, but far from trying to warn my father I held my breath, and hoped he would be weak and take them.

He was weak. A frown of annoyance at being interrupted in his work, a few critical preliminaries, looking at their teeth, feeling their knees, then a dubious, 'I've seen worse, but right now I've no real need of them. What would you be wanting in the way of trade?'

Old Luke was reasonable. He began with seven steers, and after a brief argument settled for four. 'Since we're old neighbours', he agreed, 'and I'm running short of stall room.'

I saddled my pony Gopher and helped him home with the steers. He was talkative and friendly on the way, and when the pasture gate was safely closed he invited me into the house for a glass of lemonade. I made my excuses, of course—a barrel of lemonade, and he would still have been the man who foreclosed on a quarter-section of our land in a dry year, who up and down the countryside was as notorious for his shady deals as he was famous for his Diamonds; but cantering home I found myself relenting a little, deciding that maybe he had some good points after all.

I had wavered, it was true, before. Riding past the Taylor place it had always been a point of honour with me to keep my eyes fixed straight ahead, disdainfully, yet somehow the details of the barnyard and the aspect of the buildings had become as familiar to me as our own. My scorn had never been quite innocent of envy. The handsome greystone house might be the abode of guile, but I knew from one of the boys at school, whose parents sometimes visited the Taylors, that it contained a bathroom with hot and cold running water, just like the ones in town, and a mechanical piano that you played with pedals instead of your fingers. The big red hip-roofed barn might have been built with what my mother called 'his ill-gotten gains', but in its stalls there were never fewer than twenty-four Black Diamonds. So I had my lapses. Sometimes I wished for a miracle harvest which would enable us to buy old Taylor out. Sometimes I went so far as to speculate on reconciliation and partnership.

Today, though, I wasn't just coveting the bathroom and piano. I was taking a critical look at ourselves, wondering whether our attitude towards Luke wasn't uncharitably severe, whether some of the stories told about him mightn't have been exaggerated. This time, in any case, he had been more than fair. Ten steers instead of four, and the trade would still have been in our favour.

My father had been similarly impressed. 'Luke must be getting close to seventy,' he met my mother's anger at the supper-table, 'and for all you know he's starting to repent. If he wants to turn honest and God-fearing at last it's for us to help him, not to keep raking up his past.'

'Old Luke turn God-fearing!' my mother cried bitterly. 'That's something I'll believe when I see him trying to mend a little of the harm he's done. And you of all people to be taken in again! For a team of fancy horses!'

'But you can trust him where the Diamonds are concerned. They're his whole life. You'll find nothing in his stable but the best.'

'That's what I mean—those there's something wrong with he trades off for good fat steers.'

'Come out and look at them,' my father persisted. 'See for yourself.'

'I don't need to see. I know. If Luke got rid of them he had his reasons. They're spavined,[1] or roarers, or old.'

'Four-year-olds, and I checked them—teeth, feet—'

'But there are things you can't check. All the years we've known him has he once done what was right or decent? Do you know a man for twenty miles who'd trust him? Didn't he get your own land away from you for half what it was worth?' And she went on, shrill and exasperated, to pour out instance upon instance of his dishonesty and greed, everything from foreclosures on mortgages and bribes at tax and auction sales to the poker games in which, every fall for years, he had been fleecing his harvest-hands right after paying them.

Now, though, it all fell a little flat. I sat bored and restless, wondering when she would be done, and with a mild, appeasing gesture my father said, 'A lot of it's talk. For once let's give him the benefit of the doubt. We owe it to him till we're sure. It's only Christian charity.'

For a moment my mother struggled to control her anger. Then, her voice withering, she said, 'He's a sneak thief, one of the meanest, but with such fools for neighbours, just waiting to be taken in, I don't know that I can blame him.'

'We'll see,' my father answered. 'I'm going to town with them tomorrow, to see what they can do. Why don't you come along?'

My mother sat up straight and scornful. 'I'd walk first barefoot, and be less ashamed.'

The next day, however, she changed her mind. She even primped and curled a little, and found a brighter ribbon for her hat. My father, too, made his preparations. He washed the democrat,[2] greased the axles, carefully cleaned and polished his two best sets of harness, and finally, after dinner, changed into his Sunday suit and a clean white shirt. His hands shook as he dressed. He called me in twice to crawl under the bed for a cuff button, and my mother had to help him with his tie.

At the last minute it was decided that I should stay home and hoe potatoes. For a while I sulked indignantly, but watching their departure I understood why they didn't want me with them. My father, driving up to the door with a reckless flourish of the

1 Suffering from a disorder of the hock, often leading to lameness; 'roarer': a horse that makes a loud noise in breathing as a symptom of disease of the larynx.

2 Light wagon seating two or more people, usually drawn by two horses.

whip, was so jaunty and important, and above the pebbly whirl of wheels as the Diamonds plunged away there was such a girlish peal of laughter from my mother! They were young again. My father had a team of Diamonds, and my mother had something that his envious passion for them had taken from her twenty years ago. Walking over to the potato patch I realized that they couldn't possibly have taken me with them. Today's events, properly understood, were all before my time.

It was shortly after one o'clock when they set out. The round trip to town, travelling light, was about five hours with an ordinary team, and I expected, therefore, that with the Diamonds they would easily be back in good time for supper. But I had bedded down the stable, taken my own supper cold from the pantry and begun to fear there must have been a runaway or accident, when at last they arrived.

It was a return as dejected and shamefaced as the departure had been dashing and high-spirited. No whirl of wheels, no peal of laughter, no snorts or capers from the Diamonds. For a minute or two, peering through the dusk, I thought that my father must have made another trade. Then I ran out to meet them, and my shout of welcome sagged to silence and bewilderment. It was a strange team of nondescript bays hitched to the democrat. The Diamonds were jogging along ignominiously behind.

'Did you think we were never coming?' my mother greeted me, the false brightness of her voice worse than the defeat of my father's rounded shoulders. 'Run along and help your father with the horses. I'll have a good supper ready in no time.'

My father's face, drawn and grey in the late twilight, restrained my curiosity as we unhitched. It wasn't till we had finished at the stable and were on our way to the house that he explained. 'They're balky—you know what that means. Not worth their keep. Trust old Luke—I might have known he'd put it over me.'

It was a bitter word. I swallowed hard and asked hopefully, 'Both of them?'

'Both of them. Right in Main Street, wouldn't take a step. Just as we were ready to start for home. Two hours—the whole town watching. I even took the whip to them, but with balky horses nothing helps. The longer they stand the worse they get. I had to unhitch at last, and hire a team from the livery stable.'

Nothing more was said, by either him or my mother, but not much imagination was needed to reconstruct the scene. His pride as he spanked[3] up Main Street, the same pride I had witnessed earlier that day, the same youth and showmanship; and then the sudden collapse of it all, the unbearable moment of humiliation when the Diamonds, instead of springing away with flying manes and foaming mouths, striking sparks of envy and wonder from the heart of every beholder, simply stood there, chewed their bits and trembled.

For my mother, too, it had been a memorably cruel experience. Doubly cruel, for in addition to her embarrassment—and perched up on the democrat seat with the crowd around her, a town-shy woman, sensitive to her rough hands and plain clothes, she must have suffered acutely—in addition to that there was the burden of concealing it from my father, suppressing criticism and anger, pretending not to have noticed that he had made a fool of himself. For of the two she was in many ways the stronger,

3 Moved briskly.

the more responsible, and she must have known instantly, even as they sat there in the democrat, that the Diamonds were a crisis in his life, and that to bring him safely through there was urgent need of all her skill and sympathy.

Even so, he came through badly. For it wasn't just four good steers against two balky Diamonds. It wasn't just a matter of someone getting the better of him. It was that after all these years old Taylor should still be practising fraud and trickery, still getting away with it, still prospering.

According to his lights my father was a good man, and his bewilderment was in proportion to his integrity. For years he had been weakened and confused by a conflict, on the one hand resentment at what Luke had done and got away with, on the other sincere convictions imposing patience and restraint; but through it all he had been sustained by the belief that scores were being kept, and that he would live to see a Day of Reckoning. Now, though, he wasn't sure. You could see in his glance and frown that he was beginning to wonder which he really was: the upright, God-fearing man that he had always believed himself to be, or a simple, credulous dupe. There was the encounter with the Taylors at church, for instance, just a Sunday or two after his trip to town with the Diamonds. It wasn't an accidental or inevitable encounter. After the service they deliberately came over and spoke to us. There were a few polite remarks; then old Luke, screwing up his little eyes and leering, enquired about the Diamonds. He understood we had been having trouble with them, and hoped that they were doing better now. 'They're touchy and high-strung, you know,' he said blandly. 'You can't treat them just like ordinary horses.'

My father turned without a word and walked over to the democrat. 'He's an old man,' he said quietly as we drove off. 'It's for the Lord to judge, not me.' But his expression belied the charity of his words. His mouth was hard with the suspicion that the Lord saw nothing in his behaviour to condemn.

We drove a while in silence. Then I suggested, 'He traded them off on you—why don't you try it now on someone else?'

'Two wrongs never make a right,' my mother reproved me quickly. 'Besides, they're good mares, and we'll get good colts out of them. They may even turn out all right themselves, if your father separates them, and gives them a spell of good hard work. Touchy and high-strung is right. What they need is to be brought down a peg or two.'

How could she? My father glanced at her sidewise without answering, and I saw the reproach in his eyes. Had she no feelings, then, at all? Did she not know that it was only as a team, flashing along in unison, striking sparks, taking corners on two wheels, that they were Diamonds? That separated, their identities lost among old Bill and Ned and Bessie, they would be clods, nonentities? And watching the lines around his mouth grow firm I knew that he would never consent to such a degradation. They would always be a team of Diamonds. Their foam-flecked, sun-sparked loveliness might disappoint his vanity, might elude his efforts to exploit it, but it would live on, in stall and pasture, finally in memory, resplendent and inviolate.

His vanity, though, died hard. 'Balky horses', he remarked casually a few days later, 'are just scared horses. Nerves—a fright, maybe, when they were colts. Treat them right and they should get over it. Keep cool, I mean, and help them through their bad spells.'

Of course he was wrong. He should have known what every horseman knows, that a balky horse is never cured. If you're unscrupulous, you'll trade it off or sell it. If you're honest, you'll shoot it. Promptly, humanely, before it exasperates you to moments of rage and viciousness from which your self-respect will never quite recover. For weeks and months on end it will be a model horse, intelligent, co-operative, and then one fine day, when you're least expecting trouble, it will be a balky one again. You'll waste time and patience on it. You'll try persuasion first, then shouts and curses. You'll go back to persuasion, then degrade yourself to blows. And at last, weary and ashamed, you'll let the traces down and lead it to its stall.

But to renounce the Diamonds, now that he actually owned them, wasn't easy. He was a simple, devout man, but not by any means an other-worldly one, and all these years, struggling along in the shadow of Luke's prosperity, he had suffered, discipline himself as he would, the pangs of envy and frustration. Three hundred acres against two thousand, weather-beaten old buildings against the big stone house and hip-roofed barn, plodding work-horses against the handsome, show-off Diamonds—comparisons and a sense of failure had been inevitable.

From the beginning it was the Diamonds that had hurt him most. If Luke had indulged himself in anything else, tractors or pedigreed bulls, it would have been comparatively easy. But a horseman more passionate and discerning than my father never lived. In ordinary circumstances, being genuine, he would probably have found satisfaction in ordinary horses, like the ones he owned—humble, worthy creatures, their only fault a lack of grace and fire—but there was a splendour about the Diamonds, a poise, a dramatic loftiness, that left in its wake a blight of shabbiness and discontent. Arching their necks like emperor horses, flinging their heads up, pealing trumpet neighs—how could my father *help* wanting them? How could he turn to his own dull, patient brutes and feel anything but shame?

Yet he had never tried to acquire Black Diamonds or their equals for himself. At least one team would have been possible. He was a poor farmer, but he managed other things. In part, no doubt, it was because of his faith, his childlike sincerity. He prayed for deliverance from the vanities of the world because he wanted deliverance, and while unable to control his desire for the Diamonds, he could at least resist the temptation to possess them. But if it was in part because he struggled against the vanities of the world, it was also in part because he yielded to the vanity within himself. For one team would have been to reveal his desire, his ambition. One team would have been to set himself up for public comparison, two Black Diamonds against twenty-four.

But all that was forgotten now, lost in the excitement of actual possession. 'Nothing but nerves,' he kept saying, 'scared when they were little. I'd be balky too, if old Luke had ever had the handling of me.'

Give him his due, he worked intelligently. He took them out, for instance, when he wasn't pressed for time. He kept to quiet side-roads, where he wasn't likely to be watched or flustered. Usually he had me go along on Gopher, because it was their nature to resent another horse in front of them, and if I rode ahead they invariably responded with a competitive burst of speed. In the main things went well. So well that as the summer wore on he gradually became a little careless, and absently, as it were, began to leave the unfrequented side-roads for the highway. At that, the highway was safe enough so long as they kept going. They never stopped of their own accord. There was no danger except when it came time to start them.

Mindful of this, my father always left the front gate open. His route was always a non-stop square, cross-road to cross-road, with right angle turns that could be taken at a trot. He never went so far that it was necessary to rest the Diamonds. When he met a neighbour, he resisted the temptation to discuss crops and weather, and sailed past grandly with a nod or wave.

There was one hazard, however, that he overlooked. A gust of wind took his hat one day, and impulsively, before he could think of the possible consequences, or notice old Taylor approaching from the opposite direction on horseback, he reined in the Diamonds to a standstill.

And after weeks without a single lapse, that had to be the moment for them to balk again. Was it the arrival of Taylor, I have often wondered, something about his smell or voice, that revived colthood memories? Or was it my father's anger that flared at the sight of him, and ran out through his fingers and along the reins like an electric current, communicating to them his own tensions, his conflicting impulses of hatred and forbearance? No matter—they balked, and as if to enjoy my father's mortification, old Luke too reined in and sat watching. 'Quite a man with horses,' he laughed across at me. 'One of the finest teams for miles and just look at the state he's got them in. Better see what you can do, son, before he ruins them completely.' And then, squinting over his shoulder as he rode off, he added. 'I'll tell you how to get a balky horse going. It's easy—just build a little fire under him.'

'I wouldn't put it past him at that,' my father muttered, as he climbed down and started to unhitch. 'Being what he is, the idea of fire comes natural.'

But for the time being that was all. Harvest was on us, and for the next two months the Diamonds pawed their stall. It wasn't till November, after threshing was finished and the grain hauled, that my father was free to hitch them up again. And by that time, eager as colts after their long idleness, they were in no mood for balking. Instead, they seemed ashamed of their past, and to want nothing more than to live it down, to establish themselves as dependable members of our little farmyard community. 'All they needed was the right care,' my father said complacently one day. 'They're not mean or stubborn horses by nature. It's as I've always said—something must have happened when they were colts.'

And for a week or two he was young again. Young, light-hearted, confident. Confident in the Diamonds, confident in the rightness of the world. Old Luke had traded off balky horses on him, but now, in the service of an upright man, they were already willing, loyal ones. It showed you. Plant potatoes eyes down, and up they come the right way. They were such fine, mettled horses, such a credit to creation. Watching and working with them it was impossible to doubt that at the heart of things there was wisdom, goodness and a plan. They were an affirmation, a mighty Yea. They made the world right, and old Taylor unimportant.

With it all, though, my father was a practical man, and soon he decided that the Diamonds must be put to work. There had been enough driving round the country in the democrat. It was time they got used to pulling loads and spending an entire day in harness.

Care and patience were still necessary, and as a cautious beginning he hitched them up one afternoon and went for straw. (We used straw in considerable quantities for bedding down the stable, and not having loft room for it, brought it in, a rackful at a time, from the field, every week or ten days.) It was a short haul, and a light load. The day, moreover, was cold and windy, and it was to be expected that after standing while we built the load they would be impatient for their stall. As usual I rode Gopher, and set off for home a minute or two ahead of them.

But it was one of their bad days. I looked back after a short distance, and they hadn't moved. My father was up on the load, clicking them forward vainly.

We both tried to be nonchalant. My father climbed down and lit his pipe, threw on another forkful of straw as if he hadn't noticed anything. I led Gopher close to the Diamonds so that they could sniff at one another, then mounted him and started home a second time.

But to no avail. My father picked up the reins again; they only mouthed their bits and trembled. He tried to lead them forward; they only braced themselves, cowering against each other as if in fear of a blow.

'Let's unhitch,' I said uneasily. 'It's nearly dark, and we're only wasting time.' But ignoring me, he turned his back and lit his pipe again.

I knew there was trouble brewing. I knew from the way he was standing that the contagion had spread, that his real nature, too, was paralyzed and darkened.

'Let's unhitch,' I repeated. 'They're only getting worse. First thing they'll be as bad as when you started.'

'They're that already,' he replied, hunching his shoulders and scowling at the Diamonds. 'Unhitching's getting us nowhere. It's only giving in. I think I'll take old Luke's advice, and see what a fire will do.'

I began to protest, but he assured me that it would be a small fire. 'Not enough to burn them—just so they'll feel the heat coming up around their legs. I've heard of it before. They'll take a jump ahead, and then keep going.'

It sounded sensible enough. There was something about his voice and shoulders that forbade further protest, anyway. Without looking round again he tossed a small forkful of straw under the Diamonds, then bent cautiously to light it.

I closed my eyes a moment. When I opened them he had straightened and stepped back, and there on the ground between the Diamonds' feet, like something living that he had slipped out of his coat, was a small yellow flame, flickering up nervously against the dusk.

For a second or two, feeling its way slowly round the straw, it remained no larger than a man's outspread hand. Then, with a spurt of sparks and smoke, it shot up right to the Diamonds' bellies.

They gave a frightened snort, lunged ahead a few feet, stopped short again. The fire now, burning briskly, was directly beneath the load of straw, and even as I shouted to warn my father a tongue of flame licked up the front of the rack, and the next instant, sudden as a fan being flicked open, burst into a crackling blaze.

The Diamonds shook their heads and pawed a moment, then in terror of the flames and my father's shouts, set off across the field at a thundering, break-neck gallop. I followed on Gopher, flogging him with the ends of the reins, but straining his utmost he couldn't overtake or pass them. A trail of smoke and sparks was blowing back, and as we galloped along he kept shaking his head and coughing. Through my half-closed eyes I could see the wagon lurching dangerously over the frozen ruts of the rough wagon-trail we were following, and it flashed across my mind that if the rack upset we would ride right into it. But still I kept on lashing Gopher, pounding him with my heels. The gate was open, and there were oatstacks beside the stable. If I didn't get ahead and turn them, they would set the buildings on fire.

They turned, though, of their own accord. About a quarter of a mile from where we started the road forked, one branch turning into the barnyard, the other circling out to the highway. Riding close behind, my head lowered against the smoke and sparks, I didn't realize, till the wagon took the little ditch onto the highway at a sickening lurch, that the Diamonds were going home. Not to their new home, where they belonged now, but to old Luke Taylor's place.

I lashed and pommelled Gopher even harder, but still we couldn't gain. The highway stretched out straight and smooth, and the Diamonds were going home. Terror in their hearts, hitched to a load of fire. Through the clatter of wheels their hoof-beats sounded sharp and rhythmic like an urgent drum. Telephone poles leaped up startled and pale as we tore along, and an instant later flicked out again into the dark. Once I caught a glimpse of a horse and buggy down in the ditch, the horse rearing and white-eyed, the man leaning back on the reins with all his strength. Once it was a frantic cow, struggling to escape through the barbed-wire fence that ran alongside the road. Gopher, meanwhile, was gaining, and presently the hot smoke in our faces was a cold blast of wind. Then I could see the Diamonds, the flying manes, the sheen of the flames on their glossy hides. Then we were riding neck and neck with them.

It was a good ride. The sparks flew and the hooves thundered, and all the way I knew that for months to come the telling of it would be listened to. A good ride, but a fatal finish. The Taylor gate was open, and still galloping hard the Diamonds made a sharp swerve off the road and through it. There was a faint, splintering sound as the hind hub caught one of the posts; the next instant, only twenty or thirty feet in front of the big hip-roofed barn, wagon and rack turned over.

It was a well-built, solid load of straw, scarcely half burned away, and what was left spilled out across the yard in loose, tumbling masses that blazed up fiercely as if drenched with gasoline. I was sick with fright by this time, scarcely able to control Gopher, but even as I turned him through the gate, jerking and sawing at his bit, yelling at the top of my voice for old Taylor, I realized the danger. The loft door, where they had been putting in feed, was standing wide open. Sparks and bits of burning straw were already shooting up towards it in a steady stream.

I knew the door had to be closed, that there wasn't a second to lose, but as I jumped down from Gopher Mrs Taylor ran out of the house and began shouting at me to get back on my horse and go for Luke. He and his man had been away all afternoon to town. By this time, though, they should be nearly home again, and while I went to meet them she would telephone the neighbours.

There wasn't time to go for Luke, and I had sense enough to turn my back on her, but the Diamonds now, still hitched to the overturned wagon, were kicking and snorting wildly about the barnyard, and for two or three minutes, until the whiffle-tree[4] snapped and they plunged off free into the darkness, I could only stand petrified and watch them. Gopher too was excited. Getting him quietened and tied meant another delay. Then I had to make my way into the barn, completely strange to me, and grope along through the darkness in search of a stairway leading to the loft.

The flames were ahead of me. Already they were licking across the littered, clear space round the door, and up the hay that was stacked and mounded to within a few feet of the roof. I watched helplessly for a minute, then sprang down the stairs again. Mrs Taylor had come as far as the door, and was still shouting at me to go for Luke. I knew that the barn was lost, but responding to the urgency in her voice, I ran across the yard and untied Gopher. I had mounted, and was two or three hundred yards down the road to meet Luke, before I came abruptly to my senses and realized that there were horses in the barn.

By the time I had Gopher tied again the loft door was a bright rectangle of flame, and when I reached the barn the air was already dense with smoke. Shrill neighs greeted me, but for a moment I could see nothing. Then there was a sudden blaze at the far end of the feed-ally, and an instant later the out-thrust nose and flattened ears of one of the Diamonds were silhouetted against the glow.

I ran forward and squeezed in past its heels, then untied the halter-shank, but when I tried to lead it out it trembled and crushed its body tight against the side of the stall. I climbed into the manger, struck it hard across the nose; it only stamped and tossed its head. Then I tried the next stall, then the next and the next. Each time I met the same fear-crazed resistance. One of the Diamonds lashed out with its heels. Another caught me such a blow with a swing of its head that I leaned half-stunned for a minute against the manger. Another, its eyes rolling white and glassy, slashed with its teeth as I turned, and ripped my smock from shoulder to shoulder.

Meanwhile the smoke was thickening, biting at my throat and eyes like acid, and suddenly panic-stricken, racked by a violent fit of coughing, I stumbled out dizzily to safety.

The cold wind revived me. The sight of the leaping flames cleared my eyes of smoke and sting.

I stood rooted a minute, staring. The roof by this time had burned through in several places, and huge spouts of flame and smoke were shooting up high against the darkness, spark-streaked and swift, as if blown out by a giant forge. Then I was roused by the sound of galloping hooves and the rattle of wheels, and a minute or two later the neighbours began to arrive. They came in buggies and wagons and on horseback. All at once the yard was alive with them, shouting advice and warnings to one another,

4 Crossbar pivoted in the middle to which the harness traces of a horse are attached and which is in turn attached to a wagon.

running about aimlessly. A few entered the barn, only to stagger out again retching and coughing. My father was among them, and in his relief at finding me unhurt he clutched the collar of my smock and shook me till fire and men and horses were all spinning. Then old Luke arrived, and agile as a boy he leapt down from his wagon and started across the yard towards the barn. Three or four of the neighbours closed in to intercept him, but swerving sharply, then doubling back, he sprang away from them and through the door.

The same moment that he disappeared the floor of the loft collapsed. It was as if when running through the door he had sprung a trap, the way the great, billowy masses of burning hay plunged down behind him. There were tons and tons of it. The air caught it as it fell, and it blazed up throbbing like a furnace. We put our hands to our faces before the heat, and fell back across the yard.

A cry came from Mrs Taylor that was sucked up quickly into the soft, roaring silence of the flames. One of the neighbours helped her into the house. The rest of us stood watching. It was terrible and long because we didn't know whether it had already happened, whether it was happening now, or whether it was still to happen. At last my father slipped away, and presently returned leading our own team of Diamonds. They stood quiet and spent, their heads nearly to the ground, while we righted the wagon and tied up the broken whiffle-tree. Afraid they might balk again, I mounted Gopher as usual and rode through the gate ahead of them, but at the first click of the reins they trotted off obediently. Obediently and dully, like a team of reliable old ploughhorses. Riding along beside them, listening to the soft creak and jingle of the harness, I had the feeling that we, too, had lost our Diamonds.

It was nearly nine o'clock when we reached home, but my mother was still waiting supper. 'It's as I've always said,' she kept repeating, filling our plates and taking them away untouched. '*Though the mills of God grind slowly, yet they grind exceeding small.*[5] His own balky Diamonds, and look what they carried home to him.' She hadn't been there to see it—that was why she could say such things. 'You sow the wind and you reap the whirlwind.[6] Better for him today if he had debts and half-a-section like the rest of us.'

But my father sat staring before him as though he hadn't heard her. There was a troubled, old look in his eyes, and I knew that for him it was not so simple as that to rule off a man's account and show it balanced. Leave Luke out of it now—say that so far as he was concerned the scores were settled—but what about the Diamonds? What kind of reckoning was it that exacted life and innocence for an old man's petty greed? Why, if it was retribution, had it struck so clumsily?

'All of them,' he said at last, 'all of them but the team he was driving and my own two no-good balky ones. Prettiest horses a man ever set eyes on. It wasn't coming to them.'

'But you'll raise colts,' my mother said quickly, pouring him a fresh cup of coffee, 'and there'll be nothing wrong with them. Five or six years—why, you'll have a stableful.'

5 The lines are those of the seventeenth-century German epigrammatist Friedrich von Logau (1604–55). The full translation is: 'Though the mills of God grind slowly, yet they grind exceeding small; / Though with patience He stands waiting, with exactness grinds He all.'

6 A paraphrase of Hosea 8: 7: 'For they have sown the wind, and they shall reap the whirlwind.'

He sipped his coffee in silence a moment and then repeated softly, 'Prettiest horses a man ever set eyes on. No matter what you say, it wasn't coming to them.' But my mother's words had caught. Even as he spoke his face was brightening, and it was plain that he too, now, was thinking of the colts.

1935, 1968

A.M. Klein

1909–1972

Abraham Moses Klein was born in Ratno, Ukraine, one of twin sons (his brother died in his first year). In 1910 his family, seeking freedom from persecution, moved to Montreal, settling in the Jewish ghetto of that city.

Klein received an orthodox upbringing, supplementing his lessons in Montreal's English Protestant schools with instruction in Hebrew, and in the Torah (the five books of scripture attributed to Moses) and the Talmud (commentaries on the Torah). A natural scholar from his early days, Klein steeped himself in the Talmudic tradition of textual study and learned commentary, and also became fluent in five languages (English, Yiddish, Hebrew, French, and Latin). He graduated from McGill University in 1930, then took a law degree at the University of Montreal. He was called to the bar in 1933 and in 1939 established his own firm.

Klein began his studies at McGill in 1926, the last year of publication of the *McGill Fortnightly Review*. Although his only submission to the journal was not accepted, he was deeply affected by the poetic fervour he found among the *Fortnightly* group, which included Leon Edel, Leo Kennedy, F.R. Scott, and A.J.M. Smith. When the *Canadian Mercury* (1928–9) was created to take the *Fortnightly*'s place, Klein was one of the first contributors. Within twelve months he had published thirty poems in periodicals ranging from the *Canadian Mercury* and the *Canadian Forum* through the *Menorah Journal* to the prestigious *Poetry* (Chicago). Seven years later, when *New Provinces* (1936) belatedly affirmed the existence of modern poetry in Canada, Klein was one of the six poets represented in that volume.

In the decade that followed, Klein, while continuing to practise law and write poetry, became increasingly active in the Jewish community, especially in the Zionist movement. From 1936 to 1937 he edited the *Canadian Zionist*, and in 1939 he became the editor of the *Canadian Jewish Chronicle*, a position he held for the next fifteen years. In 1948, combining his Zionism with political activism, Klein unsuccessfully campaigned as a CCF candidate for civic office.

Klein's poetry passed through two major stages. The first comprises the poems published between 1929 and 1944—most of which were collected in *Hath Not a Jew . . .* (1940) and *Poems* (1944). These draw heavily on his Jewish background and are written in a style that owes something to Biblical rhetoric on the one hand and to such varied English influences as the Renaissance poets and T.S. Eliot on the other. In 1944 Klein also published the *Hitleriad*, a satire on Nazism, written in a form and style derived from Alexander Pope. The growing anti-Semitism of the era must have been extremely painful for a man who has been described as 'easily bruised', and his poetry often reflects his struggle to understand a world that permits evil and injustice. Even when the poems depict a grim existence, however, their irony and humour save them from being despairing. What Irving Layton wrote of the sequence of Psalms that opens *Poems* might be said about much of Klein's work up to this time:

they wonderfully express the Jew's attitude towards his God, an attitude which is a rich and puzzling alloy of self-abasement and pride, of humility and defiance; it is one of accepting the heavenly scourge while establishing at the same time his human dignity by questioning its necessity or its timing.

The second stage of Klein's poetry coincided with the emergence in the forties of the new and vigorous poetry in Montreal that was associated with the journals *Preview* and *First Statement*. These literary magazines received contributions from a number of younger poets with whom Klein was in contact—including P.K. Page, Patrick Anderson, Layton, and Louis Dudek—and the influence of these poets and an appointment from 1945 to 1947 as visiting lecturer in English at McGill University encouraged Klein to experiment with a more broadly based poetry and a somewhat simpler style. A collection of this new poetry, *The Rocking Chair and Other Poems* (1948), won a Governor General's Award.

For the poems in *The Rocking Chair* Klein turned mostly to the milieu of French Quebec for inspiration. He explained in a letter to the American poet Karl Shapiro: 'Two books I wrote, both stemming out of my ancestral traditions; both praised ancient virtues; when I looked around for those virtues in the here and now, I found them in Quebec. . . . here was a minority, like my own, which led a compact life; continued, unlike my own, an ancient tradition, preserved inherited values, felt that it "belonged".'

After *The Rocking Chair*, Klein devoted most of his creative energies to a study of Joyce's *Ulysses*, a book that had long preoccupied him, and to writing a novel that showed Joyce's influence, *The Second Scroll*. The first three chapters of his Joyce study, appearing in journals between 1949 and 1951, are detailed and insightful critiques of the textual complexities of Joyce's elaborate, mythic fiction. They, along with Klein's other critical pieces, are reprinted in *Literary Essays and Reviews* (1987).

In its own way Klein's novel, published in 1951, is, like *Ulysses*, a radical departure from the conventions of storytelling. The tale of a young Jew in quest of his heroic and mysterious uncle, *The Second Scroll* combines traditional narrative with poetry, essay, and even drama, and casts the whole into a complicated structure based on the Torah and its Talmudic commentaries.

Around 1954 Klein suffered a breakdown from which he never fully recovered. He retired from active life and gave up his writing, leaving his work on Joyce unfinished. In 1957 he was awarded the Lorne Pierce Medal by the Royal Society of Canada. Two years after his death Miriam Waddington edited *The Collected Poems of A.M. Klein* (1974), a volume that brought together his four books of poetry as well as previously uncollected poems from periodicals and *The Second Scroll*.

Since Klein's day a substantial contribution to the writing of poetry and fiction in Canada has been made by Jewish writers as diverse as Irving Layton, Leonard Cohen, Eli Mandel, Mordecai Richler, Miriam Waddington, Adele Wiseman, Matt Cohen, Joe Rosenblatt, Norman Levine, Marian Engel, and Anne Michaels. Klein, the first of this distinguished company, prepared the way for the rest. Indeed, as the critic Ludwig Lewisohn suggested in his foreword to Klein's first book, *Hath Not a Jew*, Klein is 'the first contributor of authentic Jewish poetry to the English language'. Lewisohn adds that by not trying to disguise his Jewishness as earlier Jewish writers in English had done, Klein also became 'the first Jew to contribute authentic poetry to the literatures of English speech'.

A uniform edition of The Collected Works of A.M. Klein, published by the University of Toronto Press, includes *Beyond Sambation: Selected Essays and Editorials 1928–1955* (1982), *The Short Stories of A.M. Klein* (1983), *Literary Essays and Reviews* (1987), *The Complete Poems* (1990), *Notebooks: Selections from the A.M. Klein Papers* (1994), *Selected Poems* (1997), and a new scholarly edition of *The Second Scroll* (2000). Within the pages of those volumes, the reader can discover how well Klein fulfilled the task he set himself in one of his earliest lyrics: 'I will disguise the drab in mystery, / . . . I will contrive to fill days with strange words.'

Reb Levi Yitschok[1] Talks to God

Reb Levi Yitschok, crony of the Lord,
Familiar of heaven, broods these days.
His heart erupts in sighs. He will have a word
At last, with Him of the mysterious ways.

He will go to the synagogue of Berditchev,[2]
And there sieve out his plaints in a dolorous sieve.

Rebono shel Olam[3]—he begins—
Who helps you count our little sins?
Whosoever it be, saving your grace,
I would declare before his face,
He knows no ethics,
No, nor arithmetics.

For if from punishments we judge the sins,
Thy midget Hebrews, even when they snore,
Are most malefic djinns,[4]
And wicked to the core of their heart's core;
Not so didst thou consider them,
Thy favourite sons of yore.

How long wilt thou ordain it, Lord, how long
Will Satan fill his mickle-mouth[5] with mirth,

1 Reb (or Rabbi) Levi Yitschok (d. 1809) was one of the early followers of the Baal Shem Tov, the founder of Chassidic Judaism in the eighteenth century (see p. 412, note 2). Chassidism was a populist movement that to some extent replaced the Messianic preoccupations of earlier Judaism, shifting away from an emphasis on some future deliverer to an ecstatic affirmation of the here and now achieved through a knowledge of an immanent God expressed in his visible creation. Among the Chassidic rabbis Levi Yitschok was especially noted for his intimate and direct address to God (as opposed to the traditional Judaic manner of reverential and indirect address), and for the fact that he would even call God to account and demand of him an explanation for the suffering of the Jews. G.K. Fischer (in *In Search of Jerusalem*, 1975) suggests that Klein may have been partly inspired by the traditional Yiddish folksong 'Levi Yitschok's Kaddish', which begins:

> *Good morning, Lord of the Universe!*
> *I, Levi Yitschok, son of Sarah, of Berditchev,*
> *Have come to you in a law-suit*
> *On behalf of your people Israel.*
> *What have you against your people Israel?*
> *And why do you oppress*
> *Your people Israel?*

For more information about the influences of Chassidism on the poetry of Klein, see also the essays by Phyllis Gotlieb and Fischer in *The A.M. Klein Symposium* (1975).

2 Town in Ukraine of which Levi Yitschok was rabbi.
3 'Master of the universe' (Hebrew).
4 Or 'jinn': here, evil spirits.
5 Large mouth (archaic).

Beholding him free, the knave who earned the thong,[6]
And Israel made the buttocks of the earth?

The moon grinned from the window-pane; a cat
Standing upon a gable, humped and spat;
Somewhere a loud mouse nibbled at a board,
A spider wove a niche in the House of the Lord.

Reb Levi Yitschok talking to himself,
Addressed his infant arguments to God:
Why hast thou scattered him like biblic dust,
To make a union with unhallowed sod,
Building him temples underneath a mound,
Compatriot of the worm in rain-soaked ground?

The lion of Judah![7] no such parable
Is on my lips; no lion, nor lion's whelp,
But a poor bag'o'bones goat[8] which seeks thy help,
A scrawny goat, its rebel horns both broken,
Its beard uncouthly plucked, its tongue so dumbly lolling
Even its melancholy ma-a- remains unspoken.

The candles flicker,
And peeping through the windows, the winds snicker.
The mice digest some holy rune,
And gossip of the cheeses of the moon. . . .

Where is the trumpeted Messiah? Where
The wine long-soured into vinegar?
Have cobwebs stifled his mighty shofar?[9] Have
Chilblains weakened his ass's one good hoof?[10]

So all night long Reb Levi Yitschok talked,
Preparing words on which the Lord might brood.
How long did even angels guard a feud?

6 Whip, lash.
7 Judah is the ancestor of one of the twelve tribes of Israel; in Genesis 49: 9 Jacob, Judah's father, prophesies power for him, saying: 'Judah is a lion's whelp.'
8 Recalling the scapegoat (Leviticus 16: 8); in general, that which suffers for the sins of others.
9 A horn made of ram's horn, the shofar is sounded on ceremonial occasions; traditionally, when the Messiah finally comes he will be 'trumpeted' by a great shofar, the sounding of which will also denote the final defeat of Satan.
10 Traditionally the Messiah will first manifest himself riding on an ass. That his ass is lame seems to be Reb Levi's own ironic jest.

When would malign Satanas[11] be unfrocked?
Why were the tortured by their echoes mocked?
Who put Death in his ever-ravenous mood?
Good men groaned: Hunger; bad men belched of food;
Wherefore? And why? Reb Levi Yitschok talked . . .
Vociferous was he in his monologue.
He raged, he wept. He suddenly went mild
Begging the Lord to lead him through the fog;
Reb Levi Yitschok, an ever-querulous child,
Sitting on God's knees in the synagogue,
Unanswered even when the sunrise smiled.

1940

11 Satan.

Heirloom

My father bequeathed me no wide estates;
No keys and ledgers were my heritage;
Only some holy books with *yahrzeit*[1] dates
Writ mournfully upon a blank front page—

Books of the Baal Shem Tov,[2] and of his wonders;
Pamphlets upon the devil and his crew;
Prayers against road demons, witches, thunders;
And sundry other tomes for a good Jew.

Beautiful: though no pictures on them,[3] save
The scorpion crawling on a printed track;
The Virgin floating on a scriptural wave,
Square letters twinkling in the Zodiac.

The snuff left on this page, now brown and old,
The tallow stains of midnight liturgy—
These are my coat of arms, and these unfold
My noble lineage, my proud ancestry!

1 'Literally anniversary. It is customary to inscribe the date of the passing of an ancestor on the flyleaf of some sacred book. Special prayers are said on that anniversary date' [Klein's note; the notes by Klein to this poem, and to 'Autobiographical', are from a 1945 letter to A.J.M. Smith, reprinted in *The A.M. Klein Symposium*].

2 'Literally, the Master of the Good Name—a saintly rabbi of the eighteenth century, founder of the movement known as Chassidism; he placed good works above scholarship. He was a simple good man, a St Francis of Assisi, without birds or flowers' [Klein].

3 'Hebrew prayer books are never illustrated. The only drawings that appear in the liturgy are the signs of the Zodiac illustrating the prayers for rain and fertility' [Klein].

And my tears, too, have stained this heirloomed ground,
When reading in these treatises some weird
Miracle, I turned a leaf and found
A white hair fallen from my father's beard.

1940

Psalm XXXVI: A Psalm Touching Genealogy

Not sole was I born, but entire genesis:
For to the fathers that begot me, this
Body is residence. Corpuscular,
They dwell in my veins, they eavesdrop at my ear,
They circle, as with Torahs, round my skull,
In exit and in entrance all day pull
The latches of my heart, descend, and rise—
And there look generations through my eyes.

1944

The Rocking Chair

It seconds the crickets of the province. Heard
in the clean lamplit farmhouses of Quebec,—
wooden,—it is no less a national bird;
and rivals, in its cage, the mere stuttering clock.
To its time, the evenings are rolled away;
and in its peace the pensive mother knits
contentment to be worn by her family,
grown-up, but still cradled by the chair in which she sits.

It is also the old man's pet, pair to his pipe,
the two aids of his arithmetic and plans,
plans rocking and puffing into market-shape;
and it is the toddler's game and dangerous dance.
Moved to the verandah, on summer Sundays, it is,
among the hanging plants, the girls, the boy-friends,
sabbatical and clumsy, like the white haloes
dangling above the blue serge suits of the young men.

It has a personality of its own;
is a character (like that old drunk Lacoste,
exhaling amber,[1] and toppling on his pins);
it is alive; individual; and no less
an identity than those about it. And
it is tradition. Centuries have been flicked
from its arcs, alternately flicked and pinned.
It rolls with the gait of St Malo.[2] It is act

and symbol, symbol of this static folk
which moves in segments, and returns to base,—
a sunken pendulum; *invoke, revoke*;
loosed yon, leashed hither, motion on no space.
O, like some Anjou ballad, all refrain,[3]
which turns about its longing, and seems to move
to make a pleasure out of repeated pain,
its music moves, as if always back to a first love.

1948

1 Perfume (perhaps from having drunk bay rum or cologne).
2 With the walk of sailors. (St Malo is a town on the coast of France.)
3 Anjou is a former province of western France. What Klein seems to have in mind is the repetitive quality of those French-Canadian songs that had their roots in medieval France. About these, Edith Fowke quotes an early traveller in Canada: '[the song] seems endless. After each short line comes the refrain, and the story twines itself along like a slender creeping plant' (*The Penguin Book of Canadian Folk Songs*, 1973).

Political Meeting

for Camillien Houde[1]

On the school platform, draping the folding seats,
they wait the chairman's praise and glass of water.
Upon the wall the agonized Y[2] initials their faith.

Here all are laic;[3] the skirted brothers have gone.
Still, their equivocal absence is felt, like a breeze
that gives curtains the sounds of surplices.

1 (1889–1958), mayor of Montreal almost continuously from 1928 to 1954; also MLA for Quebec in the 1920s, later elected MP in 1949. During the Second World War, Houde was interned because of his stand against conscription: he advised French Canadians to resist serving in what he viewed as an English cause.
2 The crucifix.
3 Of the laity; not priestly.

The hall is yellow with light, and jocular;
suddenly some one lets loose upon the air
the ritual bird which the crowd in snares of singing

catches and plucks, throat, wings, and little limbs.
Fall the feathers of sound, like *alouette's*.[4]
The chairman, now, is charming, full of asides and wit,

building his orators, and chipping off
the heckling gargoyles popping in the hall.
(Outside, in the dark, the street is body-tall,

flowered with faces intent on the scarecrow thing
that shouts to thousands the echoing
of their own wishes.) The Orator has risen!

Worshipped and loved, their favourite visitor,
a country uncle with sunflower seeds in his pockets,
full of wonderful moods, tricks, imitative talk,

he is their idol: like themselves, not handsome,
not snobbish, not of the *Grande Allée! Un homme!*[5]
Intimate, informal, he makes bear's compliments

to the ladies; is gallant; and grins;
goes for the balloon, his opposition, with pins;
jokes also on himself, speaks of himself

in the third person, slings slang, and winks with folklore;
and knows now that he has them, kith and kin.
Calmly, therefore, he begins to speak of war,

praises the virtue of being *Canadien*,
of being at peace, of faith, of family,
and suddenly his other voice: *Where are your sons?*[6]

He is tearful, choking tears; but not he
would blame the clever English; in their place
he'd do the same; maybe.

4 Banquets and social gatherings in Quebec traditionally opened or closed with the singing of the folk song '*Alouette*'. Klein's lines here play with the fact that in the refrain ('*je t'y plumerai*'), the singers promise to pluck the skylark's head, beak, nose, eyes, wings, feet, etc.

5 That is, a man of the people, not from an aristocratic neighbourhood.

6 A rallying cry among Québécois in their opposition to conscription.

Where *are* your sons?
The whole street wears one face,
shadowed and grim; and in the darkness rises
the body-odour of race.

1948

Portrait of the Poet as Landscape

I

Not an editorial-writer, bereaved with bartlett,[1]
mourns him, the shelved Lycidas.[2]
No actress squeezes a glycerine tear for him.
The radio broadcast lets his passing pass.
And with the police, no record. Nobody, it appears,
either under his real name or his alias,
missed him enough to report.

It is possible that he is dead, and not discovered.
It is possible that he can be found some place
in a narrow closet, like the corpse in a detective story,
standing, his eyes staring, and ready to fall on his face.
It is also possible that he is alive
and amnesiac, or mad, or in retired disgrace,
or beyond recognition lost in love.

We are sure only that from our real society
he has disappeared; he simply does not count,
except in the pullulation[3] of vital statistics—
somebody's vote, perhaps, an anonymous taunt
of the Gallup poll, a dot in a government table—
but not felt, and certainly far from eminent—
in a shouting mob, somebody's sigh.

O, he who unrolled our culture from his scroll—
the prince's quote, the rostrum-rounding roar—
who under one name made articulate

1 Bartlett's *Familiar Quotations.*
2 *Lycidas* (1637) is Milton's pastoral elegy mourning the death by drowning of the young poet Edward King.
3 Rapid breeding; teeming.

heaven, and under another the seven-circled air,[4]
is, if he is at all, a number, an x,
a Mr Smith in a hotel register,—
incognito, lost, lacunal.[5]

II

The truth is he's not dead, but only ignored—
like the mirroring lenses forgotten on a brow
that shine with the guilt of their unnoticed world.
The truth is he lives among neighbours, who, though they will allow
him a passable fellow, think him eccentric, not solid,
a type that one can forgive, and for that matter, forgo.

Himself he has his moods, just like a poet.
Sometimes, depressed to nadir, he will think all lost,
will see himself as throwback, relict,[6] freak,
his mother's miscarriage, his great-grandfather's ghost,
and he will curse his quintuplet senses, and their tutors
in whom he put, as he should not have put, his trust.

Then he will remember his travels over that body—
the torso verb, the beautiful face of the noun,
and all those shaped and warm auxiliaries!
A first love it was, the recognition of his own.
Dear limbs adverbial, complexion of adjective,
dimple and dip of conjugation!

And then remember how this made a change in him
affecting for always the glow and growth of his being;
how suddenly was aware of the air, like shaken tinfoil,[7]
of the patents of nature, the shock of belated seeing,
the lonelinesses peering from the eyes of crowds;
the integers of thought; the cube-roots of feeling.

Thus, zoomed to zenith, sometimes he hopes again,
and sees himself as a character, with a rehearsed role:

4 According to early pre-Copernican versions of the universe, the earth was surrounded by seven concentric spheres (the sun, the moon, and the five known planets).

5 That is, of a lacuna or empty space.

6 An organism from a previous age surviving in a changed environment.

7 An echo of the opening lines of Gerard Manley Hopkins' 'God's Grandeur': 'The world is charged with the grandeur of God. / It will flame out, like shining from shook foil.'

the Count of Monte Cristo,[8] come for his revenges;
the unsuspected heir, with papers; the risen soul;
or the chloroformed prince awaking from his flowers;
or—deflated again—the convict on parole.

III

He is alone; yet not completely alone.
Pins on a map of a colour similar to his,
each city has one, sometimes more than one;
here, caretakers of art, in colleges;
in offices, there, with arm-bands, and green-shaded;
and there, pounding their catalogued beats in libraries,—

everywhere menial, a shadow's shadow.
And always for their egos—their outmoded art.
Thus, having lost the bevel[9] in the ear,
they know neither up nor down, mistake the part
for the whole, curl themselves in a comma,
talk technics, make a colon their eyes. They distort—

such is the pain of their frustration—truth
to something convolute and cerebral.
How they do fear the slap of the flat of the platitude!
Now Pavlov's victims, their mouths water at bell,
the platter empty.
                    See they set twenty-one jewels
into their watches; the time they do not tell!

Some, patagonian[10] in their own esteem,
and longing for the multiplying word,
join party and wear pins, now have a message,
an ear, and the convention-hall's regard.
Upon the knees of ventriloquists, they own,
of their dandled[11] brightness, only the paint and board.

And some go mystical, and some go mad.
One stares at a mirror all day long, as if

8 In the novel *The Count of Monte Cristo* (1844–5), by Alexandre Dumas *père*, an innocent man, imprisoned on trumped-up charges, escapes to the Island of Monte Cristo, where he finds fabulous riches. He returns to Paris a powerful man and, under various guises, takes revenge on those responsible for his ill treatment.

9 A tool for ascertaining angles.

10 Gigantic. Klein is referring to old travellers' tales about a mythical race of giant Natives in South America.

11 Moved lightly up and down on the knee.

to recognize himself; another courts
angels,—for here he does not fear rebuff;
and a third, alone, and sick with sex, and rapt,
doodles him symbols convex and concave.

O schizoid solitudes! O purities
curdling upon themselves! Who live for themselves,
or for each other, but for nobody else;
desire affection, private and public loves;
are friendly, and then quarrel and surmise
the secret perversions of each other's lives.

IV

He suspects that something has happened, a law
been passed, a nightmare ordered. Set apart,
he finds himself, with special haircut and dress,
as on a reservation. Introvert.
He does not understand this; sad conjecture
muscles and palls thrombotic on his heart.

He thinks an imposter, having studied his personal biography,
his gestures, his moods, now has come forward to pose
in the shivering vacuums his absence leaves.
Wigged with his laurel, that other, and faked with his face,
he pats the heads of his children, pecks his wife,
and is at home, and slippered, in his house.

So he guesses at the impertinent silhouette
that talks to his phone-piece and slits open his mail.
Is it the local tycoon who for a hobby
plays poet, he so epical in steel?
The orator, making a pause? Or is that man
he who blows his flash of brass in the jittering hall?

Or is he cuckolded by the troubadour
rich and successful out of celluloid?
Or by the don who unrhymes atoms? Or
the chemist death built up? Pride, lost impostor'd pride,
it is another, another, whoever he is,
who rides where he should ride.

V

Fame, the adrenalin: to be talked about;
to be a verb; to be introduced as *The*:
to smile with endorsement from slick paper; make
caprices anecdotal; to nod to the world; to see
one's name like a song upon the marquees played;
to be forgotten with embarrassment; to be—
to be.

It has its attractions, but is not the thing;
nor is it the ape mimesis[12] who speaks from the tree
ancestral; nor the merkin joy[13] . . .
Rather it is stark infelicity
which stirs him from his sleep, undressed, asleep
to walk upon roofs and window-sills and defy
the gape of gravity.

VI

Therefore he seeds illusions. Look, he is
the nth Adam taking a green inventory
in world but scarcely uttered, naming, praising,
the flowering fiats in the meadow, the
syllabled fur, stars aspirate, the pollen
whose sweet collision sounds eternally.
For to praise

the world—he, solitary man—is breath
to him. Until it has been praised, that part
has not been. Item by exciting item—
air to his lungs, and pressured blood to his heart.—
they are pulsated, and breathed, until they map,
not the world's, but his own body's chart!

And now in imagination he has climbed
another planet, the better to look
with single camera view upon this earth—
its total scope, and each afflated[14] tick,

12 Imitation; perhaps in reference to the Aristotelian concept of poetry as an imitation of an action.
13 A deceptive joy; 'merkin': a wig for the female pubic area.
14 Breathed upon, inspired.

its talk, its trick, its tracklessness—and this,
this, he would like to write down in a book!

To find a new function for the *déclassé* craft
archaic like the fletcher's;[15] to make a new thing;
to say the word that will become sixth sense;
perhaps by necessity and indirection bring
new forms to life, anonymously, new creeds—
O, somehow pay back the daily larcenies of the lung!

These are not mean ambitions. It is already something
merely to entertain them. Meanwhile, he
makes of his status as zero a rich garland,
a halo of his anonymity,
and lives alone, and in his secret shines
like phosphorus. At the bottom of the sea.

1948

15 Arrow maker's.

Autobiographical[1]

Out of the ghetto streets where a Jewboy
Dreamed pavement into pleasant Bible-land,
Out of the Yiddish slums where childhood met
The friendly beard, the loutish Sabbath-goy,[2]
Or followed, proud, the Torah-escorting band,[3]
Out of the jargoning city I regret,
Rise memories, like sparrows rising from
The gutter-scattered oats,
Like sadness sweet of synagogal hum,
Like Hebrew violins
Sobbing delight upon their Eastern notes.

1 This poem first appeared in *The Canadian Forum* in 1943; it later became one of the 'glosses' in *The Second Scroll*.

2 'A Gentile employed by Jews to kindle their fires on the Sabbath, such labour being prohibited on that day to the children of Israel. Goy = Gentile' [Klein].

3 'The Torah is the scroll of the Law, written on parchment. When such a scroll is donated to a synagogue by a rich knave who seeks with his piety to atone for the wretchedness of his soul, the said scroll is customarily carried from the home of the donor through the streets leading to the synagogue, the whole to the accompaniment of music, to wit, a couple of violins and a flute' [Klein].

Again they ring their little bells, those doors[4]
Deemed by the tender-year'd, magnificent:
Old Ashkenazi's[5] cellar, sharp with spice;
The widows' double-parloured candy-stores
And nuggets sweet bought for one sweaty cent;
The warm fresh-smelling bakery, its pies,
Its cakes, its navel'd bellies of black bread;
The lintels candy-poled
Of barber-shop, bright-bottled, green, blue, red;
And fruit-stall piled, exotic,
And the big synagogue door, with letters of gold.

Again my kindergarten home is full—
Saturday night—with kin and compatriot:
My brothers playing Russian card-games; my
Mirroring sisters looking beautiful,
Humming the evening's imminent fox-trot;
My uncle Mayer, of blessed memory,
Still murmuring Maariv,[6] counting holy words;
And the two strangers, come
Fiery from Volhynia's[7] murderous hordes—
The cards and humming stop.
And I too swear revenge for that pogrom.

Occasions dear: the four-legged aleph[8] named
And angel pennies dropping on my book;[9]
The rabbi patting a coming scholar-head;
My mother, blessing candles, Sabbath-flamed,
Queenly in her Warsovian perruque;[10]
My father pickabacking me to bed
To tell tall tales about the Baal Shem Tov[11]—
Letting me curl his beard.
Oh memory of unsurpassing love,
Love leading a brave child
Through childhood's ogred corridors, unfear'd!

4 'The impression of my childhood days is that the only people who kept groceries were widows, who always had little bells over their doors, so that they might hear the entering customer, even from the remoteness of the back kitchen, the emporium usually being located in the front double-parlor' [Klein].

5 Jews of central European descent, as opposed to Sephardic Jews (from Spain and Portugal); also a surname.

6 Evening prayer (Hebrew).

7 Province in northwestern Ukraine; the site of pogroms against the Jews.

8 'The first letter of the Hebrew alphabet, cf. Alpha. Called "running" because written with four legs . . .' [Klein].

9 'If I knew my lesson well, my father would, unseen, drop a penny on my book, and then proclaim it the reward of angels for good study' [Klein].

10 'Jewesses (married and pious) wear perruques. The custom has died out in America; but not for my mother' [Klein]. A perruque (also spelled 'peruke') is a wig. 'Warsovian': in the style of Warsaw.

11 See p. 412, note 2.

The week in the country at my brother's—(May
He own fat cattle in the fields of heaven!)
Its picking of strawberries from grassy ditch,
Its odour of dogrose and of yellowing hay—
Dusty, adventurous, sunny days, all seven!—
Still follow me, still warm me, still are rich
With the cow-tinkling peace of pastureland.
The meadow'd memory
Is sodded with its clover, and is spanned
By that same pillow'd sky
A boy on his back one day watched enviously.

And paved again the street: the shouting boys,
Oblivious of mothers on the stoops,
Playing the robust robbers and police,
The corncob battle—all high-spirited noise
Competitive among the lot-drawn groups.
Another day, of shaken apple trees
In the rich suburbs, and a furious dog,
And guilty boys in flight;
Hazelnut games,[12] and games in the synagogue—
The burrs, the Haman rattle,[13]
The Torah dance on Simchas-Torah night.[14]

Immortal days of the picture calendar
Dear to me always with the virgin joy
Of the first flowering of senses five,
Discovering birds, or textures, or a star,
Or tastes sweet, sour, acid, those that cloy;
And perfumes. Never was I more alive.
All days thereafter are a dying off,
A wandering away
From home and the familiar. The years doff
Their innocence.
No other day is ever like that day.

12 *Nisslach*, or 'Nuts', a game played during Passover. In one version, players tossed handfuls of hazelnuts at a small hole dug in the ground, guessing in advance whether the number to drop in would be odd or even.

13 'The Ninth of Ab (a month in the Jewish calendar) commemorates the destruction of the Temple. It is a day of mourning and fasting. It is customary on that day for youngsters to gather burrs and thistles, bring them to the synagogue, and throw them—not always with impunity—into the beards of the mourning elders—so as to give a touch or realism to their historic weeping. For the kids, this is a lot of fun' [Klein]. 'Haman rattle': 'Haman is the villain of the Book of Esther. On Purim, which is the festival commemorating its events, the Book of Esther is read in the synagogue. Every time the name of Haman is uttered by the reader of the scroll, the youngsters, armed with rattles, make a furious noise, so as to drown out those unspeakable syllables' [Klein].

14 Festival celebrating God's giving his law to Moses; it is marked by the carrying of the parchment scrolls containing the Law seven (or more) times around the synagogue in a dancing procession.

I am no old man fatuously intent
On memoirs, but in memory I seek
The strength and vividness of nonage days,
Not tranquil recollection of event.[15]
It is a fabled city that I seek;
It stands in Space's vapours and Time's haze;
Thence comes my sadness in remembered joy
Constrictive of the throat;
Thence do I hear, as heard by a Jewboy,
The Hebrew violins,
Delighting in the sobbed Oriental note.

1951

15 Arguing that his own 'nonage' (youth) remains vivid, Klein here rejects Wordsworth's famous formula about poetry being an expression of 'emotion recollected in tranquility'.

Dorothy Livesay

1909–1996

Winnipeg was a focal point for Dorothy Livesay. There her parents, both newspaper reporters, met; there she was born; and there she returned often throughout her life. Livesay grew up in a household in which her mother, Florence Randal Livesay, wrote her own poetry and translated Ukrainian poems and novels, while her iconoclast father, John F.B. Livesay, pursued his interest in politics and economics. In *A Winnipeg Childhood* (1973), a series of stories based on her early childhood, Livesay describes this home life, against a background of the First World War and the Winnipeg General Strike of 1919.

When Livesay's father organized the Canadian Press and became its first manager, the family moved to Toronto. There John Livesay encouraged his daughter to read great books, especially those written by women, and also to attend lectures and listen to speakers—including advocates of women's and worker's rights. At the same time, Florence Livesay's acquaintance with both new and established Canadian writers brought her daughter into contact not only with the Victorian sensibilities that still dominated Canada's literature but also with the new movements that were developing.

In this politicized and literary atmosphere, Livesay herself began to write. When she was just thirteen her first published poem appeared in the Vancouver *Province*, and in her second year at Trinity College, University of Toronto, Livesay, still in her teens, not only won the Jardine Memorial Prize for her poem 'City Wife' but had her first book, *Green Pitcher* (1928), published. After a year of graduate work at the Sorbonne, in Paris, she returned to Canada in 1932 and published her second book, *Signposts*. In these early books Livesay established herself as a member of the imagist movement in Canada. Like her fellow imagists Raymond Knister and W.W.E. Ross, she sought simplicity of form and the direct impact of the image to express unromanticized observations about everyday life.

Livesay divided her writing into four categories: *agit-prop, documentary, lyric,* and *confessional.* The latter two divisions include the writing of both her very early career before the Depression and her 'second season'—work done after her middle age. 'Agit-prop' is a term that arose in the Communist party during the thirties to describe writing, usually drama, in which political techniques of agitation (oral persuasion) and propaganda (written proselytizing) are united in simple pieces for working-class audiences. In the thirties Livesay wrote a number of agit-prop plays as part of her activities in Communist and proletarian artist groups. At the same time she earned a living as a social worker in Montreal and in Englewood, New Jersey. In the reminiscences, essays, letters, and poems gathered in *Right Hand, Left Hand* (1977) she provided an account of this period.

Out of her experiences in the Depression, Livesay fashioned 'Day and Night', a poem that expresses the concerns of the agit-prop plays while working primarily as a 'documentary'. In applying this term to poetry Livesay was describing what she considered a particularly Canadian genre,

> *in which historical or other 'found' material is incorporated into a writer's own thoughts, in order to create a dialectic between the objective facts and the subjective feeling of the poet. The effect is often ironic; it is always intensely personal.*

Livesay saw most of her longer poems—those collected in *The Documentaries* (1968)—working in this tradition, which descends from Crawford, Lampman, and D.C. Scott, and includes later poets such as Pratt and Birney.

In 1936 Livesay moved west, settling in Vancouver. Remaining politically active (especially as a member of the CCF), she and her future husband, Duncan Macnair, organized a writers' group that originally served as a conduit for stories and articles for the Toronto-based *New Frontier* (1936–7). She herself became a contributor to this periodical, which stood politically between the radically Communist *Masses* (1932–4), which she had earlier helped to found, and the more moderate *Canadian Forum.* During this period she also began to teach creative writing. As a result of her suggestion that a poetry magazine be started on the West Coast to complement Pratt's *Canadian Poetry Magazine* in the east, Alan Crawley founded *Contemporary Verse* (1941–53). In 1975 Livesay established the Winnipeg-based journal *CV/II* (the title of which is a tribute to Crawley's magazine).

The poetry Livesay wrote in the 1940s and early 1950s often lacked the assured voice that her earlier political militancy had given her. Nevertheless, it was during this period that she received two Governor General's Awards—one for *Day and Night* (1944), a collection of poems actually written in the mid-thirties, and one for *Poems for People* (1947). In 1958 Livesay returned to school to prepare herself for a teaching career. While at the University of London, she learned of her husband's death. In 1960, with her children grown, she took a job in what is now Zambia, teaching for UNESCO. The three years she spent there revitalized her poetry. After her return she published *The Unquiet Bed* (1967), which drew new attention to her work—partly because of the frank sensuality of some of the poems. That was followed by several books of new poetry, including *Plainsongs* (1969), *The Woman I Am* (1977), *Phases of Love* (1983), and *Feeling the Worlds* (1984), as well as her *Collected Poems: The Two Seasons* (1972) and *The Self-Completing Tree: Selected Poems* (1986). *Archive for Our Times: The Previously Uncollected and Unpublished Poems of Dorothy Livesay* (1998), edited by Dean J. Irvine, was published posthumously. Livesay created a body of poetry that is frequently epigrammatic yet also personal—even confessional—*and* socially engaged. In poems like 'Day and Night', which assimilates the rhythms of the factory work-song and of popular music, she celebrated the flux of life by adapting form to suit her content.

Livesay's prose works include *The Husband: A Novella* (1990)—a story of a woman's search for personal and artistic fulfillment and the strains it puts on her marriage—and *Journey With My Selves: A Memoir, 1909–1963* (1991). Her autobiographical story collection *A Winnipeg Childhood* was reprinted in an expanded version as *Beginnings* in 1988.

Green Rain

I remember long veils of green rain
Feathered like the shawl of my grandmother—
Green from the half-green of the spring trees
Waving in the valley.

I remember the road
Like the one which leads to my grandmother's house,
A warm house, with green carpets,
Geraniums, a trilling canary
And shining horse-hair chairs;
And the silence, full of the rain's falling
Was like my grandmother's parlour
Alive with herself and her voice, rising and falling—
Rain and wind intermingled.

I remember on that day
I was thinking only of my love
And of my love's house.
But now I remember the day
As I remember my grandmother.
I remember the rain as the feathery fringe of her shawl.

1932

The Difference

Your way of loving is too slow for me.
For you, I think, must know a tree by heart
Four seasons through, and note each single leaf
With microscopic glance before it falls—
And after watching soberly the turn
Of autumn into winter and the slow
Awakening again, the rise of sap—
Then only will you cry: 'I love this tree!'

As if the beauty of the thing could be
Made lovelier or marred by any mood
Of wind, or by the sun's caprice; as if
All beauty had not sprung up with the seed—
With such slow ways you find no time to love
A falling flame, a flower's brevity.

1932

Day and Night[1]

1

Dawn, red and angry, whistles loud and sends
A geysered shaft of steam searching the air.
Scream after scream announces that the churn
Of life must move, the giant arm command.
Men in a stream, a moving human belt
Move into sockets, every one a bolt.
The fun begins, a humming, whirring drum—
Men do a dance in time to the machines.

2

One step forward
Two steps back
Shove the lever,
Push it back

While Arnot[2] whirls
A roundabout
And Geoghan shuffles
Bolts about.

One step forward
Hear it crack
Smashing rhythm—
Two steps back

Your heart-beat pounds
Against your throat
The roaring voices
Drown your shout

Across the way
A writhing whack

1 In her 1968 'Commentary on "Day and Night"' Livesay wrote: 'This documentary is dominated by themes of struggle: class against class, race against race. The sound of Negro spirituals mingled in my mind with Cole Porter's "Night and Day" and Lenin's words (I quote from memory): "To go two steps forward we may have to take one step back." That phrase captured my imagination for it seemed to me that the capitalist system was putting that concept in reverse.'

2 'Arnot' and 'Geoghan' are names Livesay gives to two workers.

Sets you spinning
Two steps back—

One step forward
Two steps back.

3

Day and night are rising and falling
Night and day shift gears and slip rattling
Down the runway, shot into storerooms
Where only arms and a note-book remember
The record of evil, the sum of commitments.
We move as through sleep's revolving memories
Piling up hatred, stealing the remnants,
Doors forever folding before us—
And where is the recompense, on what agenda
Will you set love down? Who knows of peace?

Day and night
Night and day
Light rips into ribbons
What we say.

I called to love
Deep in dream:
Be with me in the daylight
As in gloom.

Be with me in the pounding
In the knives against my back
Set your voice resounding
Above the steel's whip crack.

High and sweet
Sweet and high
Hold, hold up the sunlight
In the sky!

Day and night
Night and day
Tear up all the silence
Find the words I could not say . . .

4

We were stoking coal in the furnaces; red hot
They gleamed, burning our skins away, his and mine.
We were working together, night and day, and knew
Each other's stroke; and without words, exchanged
An understanding about kids at home,
The landlord's jaw, wage-cuts and overtime.
We were like buddies, see? Until they said
That nigger is too smart the way he smiles
And sauces back the foreman; he might say
Too much one day, to others changing shifts.
Therefore they cut him down, who flowered at night
And raised me up, day hanging over night—
So furnaces could still consume our withered skin.

Shadrach, Meshach and Abednego[3]
Turn in the furnace, whirling slow.
    Lord, I'm burnin' in the fire
    Lord, I'm steppin' on the coals
    Lord, I'm blacker than my brother
    Blow your breath down here.

    Boss, I'm smothered in the darkness
    Boss, I'm shrivellin' in the flames
    Boss, I'm blacker than my brother
    Blow your breath down here.
Shadrach, Meshach and Abednego
Burn in the furnace, whirling slow.

5

Up in the roller room, men swing steel
Swing it, zoom; and cut it, crash.
Up in the dark the welder's torch
Makes sparks fly light lightning reel.

Now I remember storm on a field
The trees bow tense before the blow
Even the jittering sparrows' talk
Ripples into the still tree shield.

3 In Daniel 3, Shadrach, Meshack, and Abednego, sent by Daniel to help rule Babylon, were condemned by its king, Nebuchadnezzar, to the 'fiery furnace' for failing to worship his golden idol. These men were saved by God and emerged from the fire unharmed. The poem here echoes a popular gospel song of the period.

We are in storm that has no cease
No lull before, no after time
When green with rain the grasses grow
And air is sweet with fresh increase.

We bear the burden home to bed
The furnace glows within our hearts:
Our bodies hammered through the night
Are welded into bitter bread.

Bitter, yes:
But listen, friend:
We are mightier
In the end.

We have ears
Alert to seize
A weakness
In the foreman's ease

We have eyes
To look across
The bosses' profit
At our loss.

Are you waiting?
Wait with us
After evening
There's a hush—

Use it not
For love's slow count:
Add up hate
And let it mount

Until the lifeline
Of your hand
Is calloused with
A fiery brand!

Add up hunger,
Labour's ache
These are figures
That will make

The page grow crazy
Wheels go still,
Silence sprawling
On the till—

Add your hunger,
Brawn and bones,
Take your earnings:
Bread, not stones!

6

Into thy maw I commend my body[4]
But the soul shines without
A child's hands as a leaf are tender
And draw the poison out.

Green of new leaf shall deck my spirit
Laughter's roots will spread:
Though I am overalled and silent
Boss, I'm far from dead!

One step forward
Two steps back
Will soon be over:
Hear it crack!

The wheels may whirr
A roundabout
And neighbour's shuffle
Drown your shout

The wheel must limp
Till it hangs still
And crumpled men
Pour down the hill.

Day and night
Night and day
Till life is turned
The other way!

1944

4 Compare Luke 23: 46: 'Father, into thy hand I commit my spirit'—Jesus' final words on the cross.

Bartok[1] and the Geranium

She lifts her green umbrellas
Towards the pane
Seeking her fill of sunlight
Or of rain;
Whatever falls
She has no commentary
Accepts, extends,
Blows out her furbelows,[2]
Her bustling boughs;

And all the while he whirls
Explodes in space,
Never content with this small room:
Not even can he be
Confined to sky
But must speed high and higher still
From galaxy to galaxy,
Wrench from the stars their momentary notes
Steal music from the moon.

She's daylight
He is dark
She's heaven-held breath
He storms and crackles
Spits with hell's own spark.

Yet in this room, this moment now
These together breathe and be:
She, essence of serenity,
He in a mad intensity
Soars beyond sight
Then hurls, lost Lucifer,
From heaven's height.

And when he's done, he's out:
She leans a lip against the glass
And preens herself in light.

1955

1 Béla Bartók (1881–1945), Hungarian composer who profoundly influenced modern music by his departure from the traditional diatonic scale; his compositions are noted for their emotional intensity.
2 Flounces; used figuratively here to suggest that the petals are like the ornamental pleats on the hem of a gown or petticoat.

The Three Emilys[1]

These women crying in my head
Walk alone, uncomforted:
The Emilys, these three
Cry to be set free—
And others whom I will not name
Each different, each the same.

Yet they had liberty!
Their kingdom was the sky:
They batted clouds with easy hand,
Found a mountain for their stand;
From wandering lonely they could catch
The inner magic of a heath—
A lake their palette, any tree
Their brush could be.

And still they cry to me
As in reproach—
I, born to hear their inner storm
Of separate man in woman's form,
I yet possess another kingdom, barred
To them, these three, this Emily.
I move as mother in a frame,
My arteries
Flow the immemorial way
Towards the child, the man;
And only for a brief span
Am I an Emily on mountain snows
And one of these.

And so the whole that I possess
Is still much less—
They move triumphant through my head:
I am the one
Uncomforted.

1953

1 Emily Brontë (1818–78), the British writer best known for her novel *Wuthering Heights* (1847); Emily Dickinson (1830–86), the nineteenth-century American poet; and Emily Carr, the Canadian painter and writer (see the headnote and selection in this volume): all three remained unmarried and childless.

The Secret Doctrine of Women

I

The solution is always at hand:
lurking unsuspected just around
the corner; on the wave-torn shore
or vivid on a path in springing woods;
in the gnarled patience of that oak—look there!
or deep in a crowd at traffic halt
once face alight
one woman's hair

2

In a dream I heard the familiar words:
Knock, and it shall be opened unto you;
Seek, and ye shall find.
All day I hugged that message
close to my heart—
all month I remembered it—
all year I groped
aching for that truth, as yet unlocked
searching far and wide
and all the while you bided there
close by
offering yourself, your love.
As at a stroke of lightning I awoke
and found you at my side
and saw revealed
the secret doctrine we must share—
share and divide

3

A private eye, only the sun
sees us
stretched on the shore
your torso gleaming against rock
I on sand alongside
soaking up the whiteness of your skin
marble flow of flesh

whose veins
explore with rock
the pathway to the sea.

4

I am amazed at me
so joined
my blood racing and pounding
beside yours
my mind hooded within your head
the pressure of our fingers locked
as ankle is to foot
knee to thigh
heart to lung—

5

The solution
opens up like morning
seizes us every day
with a new song:
you are the watcher in my brain
who tells me how to dream

6

Beside you without needing any dream
here on the boundary of land, sea, sky
I am a more living, pulsing, breathing one
than on that first blind naked thrust—
my journey into the world's light.

7

The secret doctrine of women
despair and creation

1983

The Artefacts: West Coast

In the middle of the night
I hear this old house breathing
a steady sigh
when oak trees and rock shadows
assemble silence
under a high
white moon

I hear the old house turn
in its sleep
shifting the weight of long dead footsteps
from one wall to another
echoing the children's voices
shrilly calling
from one room to the next
repeating those whispers in the master bedroom
a cry, a long sigh of breath
from one body to another
when the holy ghost takes over

In the middle of the night
I wake
and hear time speaking

First it was forest; rock;
hidden ups and downs
a hill where oaks and pines
struggled
and if a stranger climbed
the topmost pine
he'd see the ocean flattening the mountains
the forest, serried—
below, only the sculpted bays
native encampments
ceremonial lodges, totem poles
and winter dances
the Raven overall
giver-of-light, supervising
and the white whale imminent
evil lurking

to be appeased with ritual
long hair dancing
feathered masks

But history begins
the woman said
when you are thirty
that tomtom, time
begins to beat
to beat for you

And in this city on the brink
of forest—sea—
history delights that Queen Victoria
made marriage with the totem wilderness
the cedar silences
the raven's wing

Now ravens build here still
seagulls spiral
the happy children in these attics
breathe and cry
unwittingly
the names of history
tumble from their lips:
Nootka[1]   Nanaimo
Masset   Ucluelet
The map leaps up
here did I live
was born and reared
here died

So also said Chief Maquinna[2]   Jewitt   Emily Carr

The map leaps up
from namelessness
to history

1 Historic fur-trading centre and former summer village of the Mowach'ath group of the Nuu-chah-nulth (or Nootka) First Nation; 'Nanaimo': city on the east coast of Vancouver Island, originally inhabited by the Central Coast Salish; 'Masset': village on Graham Island, the largest of the Queen Charlotte Islands, the traditional home of the Haida; 'Ucluelet': village on the west coast of Vancouver Island, originally home to the Nuu-chah-nulth.

2 Ranking leader of the Mowach'ath during the early years of European contact, when Nootka Sound became an important fur-trading centre; John Jewitt (1783–1821), armourer aboard the American fur-trading ship Boston, whose life was spared by Maquinna when the boat was destroyed by the Mowach'ath in Nootka Sound, 22 March 1803.

each place made ceremonial
when named
and its name
peopled!
events shouted!

here the waters divided
here the whale bellowed

In the middle of the night
the house heaves, unmoored
launched on a vast sea.

1986

Sheila Watson

1909–1998

Born Sheila Martin Doherty in New Westminster, BC, Watson grew up on the grounds of the mental hospital there (her father, a physician, was its superintendent). Initially educated at home, she entered convent school when she was ten. She enrolled at the University of British Columbia in 1927, taking a BA, a teaching certificate, and an MA there. Between 1933 and 1951 she taught in the British Columbia school system for extended periods. In the 1930s she wrote, but did not publish, a novel based on her experiences as a teacher in a remote community in the Cariboo region. In 1941 she married the poet Wilfred Watson, and in 1946 began further graduate studies at the University of Toronto.

In 1948 Watson returned to BC, where she wrote a series of four delicate fables that resembled contemporary short stories of manners except for one striking feature—their principal characters have names from Greek mythology. The effect of this technique is to overlay the personal experiences at the core of these stories with the qualities of a mythic cycle. (These tales were later collected in a single volume as *Four Stories*, 1979.) It was after moving to Calgary and Edmonton with her husband in the early 1950s that she wrote *The Double Hook*, which also grew out of her experiences in the Cariboo. Because of its innovative style and form she had difficulty finding a publisher for the book, which did not appear until 1959. In the interim she spent a year in Paris, and then returned to graduate study at the University of Toronto in 1956, working under Marshall McLuhan on a thesis about the English novelist and painter Wyndham Lewis. A teaching fellow at Toronto for her last two years there, in 1961 she joined the English department at the University of Alberta, while continuing work on her thesis. She completed her Ph.D. in 1965 and—except for a return to Toronto in 1968–9 with Wilfred to assist McLuhan in his courses during an illness—she taught at Alberta until she retired in 1975 as full professor.

Her active involvement in the literary community in Edmonton led her to help found and co-edit, with her husband among others, the little magazine *White Pelican* (1971–5), which novelist Henry Kreisel described as a 'unique journal that is in one way a cooperative enterprise, yet bears everywhere the imprint of her personality'. A 1975 special issue of *Open Letter* brought together all her published writing (other than *The Double Hook*), which consisted of the four stories, a brief commentary on her novel, and literary essays on Wyndham Lewis, Gertrude Stein, Jonathan Swift, and Michael Ondaatje. It also contains a reproduction of the first page of the manuscript of *The Double Hook*, which shows how Watson's revisions worked to make the novel more elliptical.

In 1980, shortly after moving to Vancouver with her husband, Watson published a fifth story in a small circulation edition, a fragment of narrative more akin to *The Double Hook* than to her previous short fiction: 'And the Four Animals' (the title is a Biblical allusion). As in *The Double Hook*, Coyote is present as Trickster, representing the destruction and regeneration that maintain the eternal cycle of life and death. All of her stories were published together in 1984 as *Five Stories*. In 1992, she published *Deep Hollow Creek*, the novel she had originally written in the 1930s and had previously withheld from publication. More clearly based on her personal experiences in the community of Dog Creek (it tells of a schoolteacher who comes to the Cariboo 'to find a life for herself'), it shows Watson working within the conventions of modernism. She once explained to a class that she had to learn how to 'get the narrator out' of that apprenticeship novel before she could write *The Double Hook*.

Near the end of her life Watson passed on an extensive collection of papers, correspondence, journals, and unpublished manuscripts to her literary executor, Fred Flahiff. Flahiff is currently readying her journals for publication and is working on a biography of this figure who, in her lifetime, remained intensely private.

The Double Hook

Appearing in 1959, *The Double Hook* is a remarkable work within the Canadian literary canon. A small book—128 pages in its first edition—it had a tremendous impact on Canadian writing. bp Nichol said it was his encounter with *The Double Hook* that first made him want to be a writer, and its influence may be seen in Robert Kroetsch's Out West triptych, Mordecai Richler's *St. Urbain's Horseman*, Margaret Atwood's *The Robber Bride*, and Michael Ondaatje's *In the Skin of a Lion*.

The Double Hook has variously been viewed as an exemplar of late modernism's arrival in Canada, as an innovative work of magic realism, and as the first postmodern Canadian novel. However one describes it, it marked the appearance in Canada of a work of fiction in which form, style, and idea took precedence over character and event. And while it owed a debt to the mythic modernists such as T.S. Eliot and James Joyce, Sheila Watson's novel was a different kind of mythic work, one in which myths were not just subtexts giving heightened meaning to an account of twentieth-century life but themselves a significant part of the narrative: the story cannot be read without taking them into account.

The novel's particular innovation lies in the way a wide range of sources—the North American Coyote-Trickster figure, Biblical figures and images, and the anguished family dynamics of Greek tragedy—are brought together to form a complexly intertextual labyrinth that draws the reader further and further into the world of the novel. *The Double Hook* also provided a solution to what seemed to many the impasse faced by Canadian writers at the middle of the twentieth century: how to break out of the constraints of regionalism without becoming (like Morley Callaghan) simply part of an International Modernist movement. Watson escaped this dilemma by focusing on a definite region while giving it a symbolic and allegorical cast, transforming it into a landscape of the imagination. In one of her very rare public statements, she observed:

I began the writing of The Double Hook . . . *in answer to a challenge that you could not write about particular places in Canada: that what you'd end up with was a regional novel of some kind. It was at the time, I suppose, when people were thinking that if you wrote a novel it had to be, in some mysterious way, international. It had to be about what I would call something else. And so I thought . . . how are you international if you're not international? If you're very provincial, very local, and very much part of your own milieu.*

I wanted to do something too about the West, which wasn't a Western; and about Indians which wasn't about . . . Indians. . . . And there was something I wanted to say: about how people are driven . . . in one of two ways, either towards violence or towards insensibility.

Readers who come to Watson's *The Double Hook* for the first time may find it difficult going if they look for the conventional rewards of narrative. A poetic novel, it is structured around images, tableaus, and resonating echoes more than around plot and character. Because it follows the logic of music as much as that of story, it needs to be listened to as well as read.

Like Eliot's *Waste Land*, *The Double Hook* opens in a period of dryness—not only a literal dryness caused by a lack of rainfall but also a spiritual dryness in a tiny community that has fallen into disunity and from which God appears to be absent. And yet, in contrast to Eliot's poem, there is no fisher king to 'shore up' the fragments of a destroyed postwar culture. This arid landscape is inhabited instead by a kind of fisher queen, one who seems to fragment rather than reconstruct—Mrs Potter, a matriarch who dies at her son's hand in the opening section but continues haunting the local streams and pools. Where the mythic fisher king's fishing was usually in service of his kingdom, Mrs Potter's presence there seems threatening to her small society.

The Double Hook also differs from *The Waste Land* in that there *is* a god of a sort present: Coyote, under whose eye the characters exist and the action takes place. A Native Trickster figure, Coyote represents an ethical vision different from the one Watson grew up with: his is a world in which the dialectic of good and evil is replaced by opposing forces in balance. This way of seeing the world is symbolized by the 'double hook' of the novel's title, and, in a work that sets tragedy against redemption and renewal, its doubleness of vision is made plain in a passage near the end:

It seems a strange sort of thing . . . to light another fire on the top of what fire has destroyed. The curious thing about fire . . . is you need it and you fear it at once. Every time a shoe has to be shaped, or the curve of a bit altered, or a belly filled, someone lights a fire. In winter we cry out for the sun, but half the time it's too hot, the butter melts, the cream sours, the earth crumbles and rises in the dust.

This doubleness is also suggested in a passage that was extracted from the novel by the publisher (it describes Kip) and used as the novel's epigraph:

He doesn't know you can't catch the glory on a hook and hold on to it. That when you fish for the glory you catch the darkness too. That if you hook twice the glory you hook twice the fear.

The selection that follows is Part One of the five-part novel: proportionately it represents about a third of the entire work.

From *The Double Hook*

In the folds of the hills

under Coyote's eye

lived

the old lady, mother of William
of James and of Greta

lived James and Greta
lived William and Ara his wife
lived the Widow Wagner
the Widow's girl Lenchen
the Widow's boy
lived Felix Prosper and Angel
lived Theophil
and Kip

until one morning in July

Greta was at the stove. Turning hotcakes. Reaching for the coffee beans. Grinding away James's voice.

James was at the top of the stairs. His hand half-raised. His voice in the rafters.

James walking away. The old lady falling. There under the jaw of the roof. In the vault of the bed loft. Into the shadow of death. Pushed by James's will. By James's hand. By James's words: This is my day. You'll not fish today.

2

Still the old lady fished. If the reeds had dried up and the banks folded and crumbled down she would have fished still. If God had come into the valley, come holding out the long finger of salvation, moaning in the darkness, thundering down the gap at the lake head, skimming across the water, drying up the blue signature like blotting-paper, asking where, asking why, defying an answer, she would have thrown her line against the rebuke; she would have caught a piece of mud and looked it over; she would have drawn a line with the barb when the fire of righteousness baked the bottom.

3

Ara saw her fishing along the creek. Fishing shamelessly with bait. Fishing without a glance towards her daughter-in-law, who was hanging washing on the bushes near the rail fence.

I might as well be dead for all of her, Ara said. Passing her own son's house and never offering a fry even today when he's off and gone with the post.

The old lady fished on with a concentrated ferocity as if she were fishing for something she'd never found.

Ara hung William's drawers on a rail. She had covered the bushes with towels.

Then she looked out from under her shag of bangs at the old lady's back.

It's not for fish she fishes, Ara thought. There's only three of them. They can't eat all the fish she'd catch.

William would try to explain but he couldn't. He only felt, but he always felt he knew. He could give half a dozen reasons for anything. When a woman on his route flagged him down with a coat and asked him to bring back a spool of thread from the town below, he'd explain that thread has a hundred uses. When it comes down to it, he'd say, there's no telling what thread is for. I knew a woman once, he'd say, who used it to sew up her man after he was throwed on a barbed-wire fence.

Ara could hear the cow mumbling dry grass by the bushes. There was no other sound.

The old lady was rounding the bend of the creek. She was throwing her line into a rock pool. She was fishing upstream to the source. That way she'd come to the bones of the hills and the flats between where the herd cows ranged. They'd turn their tails to her and stretch their hides tight. They'd turn their living flesh from her as she'd turned hers from others.

The water was running low in the creek. Except in the pools, it would be hardly up to the ankle. Yet as she watched the old lady, Ara felt death leaking through from the centre of the earth. Death rising to the knee. Death rising to the loin.

She raised her chin to unseat the thought. No such thing could happen. The water was drying away. It lay only in the deep pools.

Ara wasn't sure where water started.

William wouldn't hesitate: It comes gurgling up from inside the hill over beyond the lake. There's water over and it falls down. There's water under and it rushes up. The trouble with water is it never rushes at the right time. The creeks dry up and the grass with them. There are men, he'd say, have seen their whole place fade like a cheap shirt. And there's no way a man can fold it up and bring it in out of the sun. You can save a cabbage plant or a tomato plant with tents of paper if you've got the paper, but there's no human being living can tent a field and pasture.

I've seen cows, he'd say, with lard running off them into the ground. The most unaccountable thing, he'd say, is the way the sun falls. I've seen a great cow, he'd say, throw no more shadow for its calf than a lean rabbit.

Ara looked over the fence. There was no one on the road. It lay white across the burnt grass.

Coyote made the land his pastime. He stretched out his paw. He breathed on the grass. His spittle eyed it with prickly pear.

Ara went into the house. She filled the basin at the pump in the kitchen and cooled her feet in the water.

We've never had a pump in our house all the years we've lived here, she'd heard Greta say. Someday, she'd say, you'll lift the handle and stand waiting till eternity. James brings water in barrels from the spring. The thing about a barrel is you take it where you take it. There's something fixed about a pump, fixed and uncertain.

Ara went to the door. She threw the water from the basin into the dust. She watched the water roll in balls on the ground. Roll and divide and spin.

The old lady had disappeared.

Ara put on a straw hat. She tied it with a bootlace under the chin. She wiped the top of the table with her apron which she threw behind a pile of papers in the corner.

She went to the fence and leaned against the rails.

If a man lost the road in the land round William Potter's, he couldn't find his way by keeping to the creek bottom for the creek flowed this way and that at the land's whim. The earth fell away in hills and clefts as if it had been dropped carelessly wrinkled on the bare floor of the world.

Even God's eye could not spy out the men lost here already, Ara thought. He had looked mercifully on the people of Nineveh though they did not know their right hand and their left.[1] But there were not enough people here to attract his attention. The cattle were scrub cattle. The men lay like sift in the cracks of the earth.

Standing against the rails of the fence, she looked out over the yellow grass. The empty road leading from James's gate went on from William's past the streaked hills, past the Wagners', down over the culvert, past Felix Prosper's.

4

Felix saw the old lady. She was fishing in his pool where the water lay brown on the black rocks, where the fish lay still under the fallen log. Fishing far from her own place. Throwing her line into his best pool.

He thought: I'll chase her out.

1 Nineveh, the ancient capital of Assyria, on the eastern bank of the River Tigris, was the most powerful city in the world until captured by the Babylonians and Medes in 612 BCE. Watson's allusion is to the Book of Jonah, which describes how Jonah flees his commission from God to preach to the people of Nineveh. As punishment for this disobedience, Jonah is thrown overboard from his ship and swallowed by 'a great fish', remaining alive in its belly for three days until released again by God. He grudgingly accepts a second call to preach to Nineveh; but when the city repents and is spared by God, he is, oddly enough, displeased. God teaches him a lesson by having a gourd vine grow up and whither overnight, telling him: 'Thou hast had pity on the gourd, for the which thou hast not laboured, neither madest it grow; which came up in a night, and perished in a night. And should not I spare Nineveh, that great city, wherein are more than sixscore thousand person that cannot discern between their right hand and their left hand; and also much cattle?' (Jonah 4: 10–11)

But he sat, tipped back in his rocking-chair, his belly bulging his bibbed overalls, while the old lady fished, while the thistles thrust his potato plants aside and the potatoes baked in the shallow soil.

When at last he went down to the creek the old lady had gone. And he thought: Someday I'll put a catcher on the fence and catch her for once and all.

Then he fished himself, letting his line fall from an old spool, his hook catch in the leaves. Fished with his chin rolled over the bib of his overalls, while his fiddle lay against his rocker and the potatoes baked in the vertical glory of the July sun.

Fished and came from the creek. Pulled the fish out of his pocket. Slit them from tail to chin. Sloshed them in the hand basin. Dropped them into bacon fat until the edges browned. Cooked them to a curl while the dogs sniffed. Cooked them in peace alone with his dogs.

Angel had gone. She had walked across the yard like a mink trailing her young behind her. She had climbed the high seat of Theophil's wagon. Now she lived with Theophil at the bend of the road near the old quarry.

He lifted the brown edge of the fish and took out the bones. The terrier sat under the shadow of his belly. The hounds stood, dewlaps trembling, their paws shoved over the sill. Felix fed the terrier where it sat. The hounds waited, their lips wet, their eyes quick with longing.

When Felix had finished, he rolled out of his chair and gathered up a pan of scraps from the trestle on which the buckets rest. The hounds backed away from the door, jostling shoulder to shoulder, tail bisecting tail. He gave them scraps.

If they walked out of his gate like Angel, he would not ask if they had hay to lie on. His own barn was often empty.

He went back to the table and gathered up the bones that lay around his plate. He stood with a fish spine in his hand. Flesh mountainous contemplating. Saint Felix with a death's head meditating.

At last he threw the bones into the stove. The heat from the stove, the heat crept in from the day outside, anointed his face. Blest, he sat down again in the rocker, and the boards creaked and groaned as he fiddled.

The old lady did not come back to disturb his peace. But somewhere below the house a coyote barked, and the hounds raised their heads, gathered their limbs and sprang into the brush. The terrier sat in Felix's shadow, its ear turned to the voice of Felix's fiddle.

But the hounds heard Coyote's song fretting the gap between the red boulders:

In my mouth is the east wind.[2]
Those who cling to the rocks I will
bring down
I will set my paw on the eagle's nest.

2 All of Coyote's songs have Biblical echoes. Throughout the Old Testament the east wind is particularly associated with drought and destruction, as in Ezekiel 17: 10: 'Yea, behold, being planted, shall it prosper? Shall it not utterly wither, when the east wind toucheth it? It shall wither in the furrows where it grew.' See also Jonah 4: 8.

The hounds came back, yellow forms in the yellow sunlight. Creeping round the barn. Flattening themselves to rest.

Felix put down his fiddle and slept.

5

The Widow's boy saw the old lady.

The old lady from above is fishing down in our pool, he said, coming into the Widow's kitchen. I'm going down to scare her out.

The Widow's eyes closed.

Dear God, she said, what does she want? So old, so wicked, fishing the fish of others. Slipping her line under our fence before my boy can get the fish on his hook.

The Widow's daughter Lenchen sat behind the table. Her yellow hair pulled straight above her eyes like a ragged cap. Her hands in the pockets of her denim jeans. Her heavy heeled boots beating impatience into the boards of the floor.

At the far end of the table the Widow was straining milk into shallow pans. The boy sat down and rested his elbows on the other end of the table.

Where's she fishing? the girl asked.

Down at the grass pool, the boy said.

It's enough to turn a person mad, the girl said, to have an old woman sneaking up and down the creek day in and day out. I can't stand it any longer. It's just what I was telling Ma. I've got to get away, right away from here. It's time I learned something else, anyway. I've learned all there is to learn here. I know everything there is to know. I know even as much as you and James Potter.

How do you know what James Potter knows? The boy asked.

The Widow went on with her work.

All you'd learn in town, she said, is men. And you'd be lucky if they didn't learn you first. The things they know would be the death of me for you to know. They'd teach you things it isn't easy to forget.

She put the milk-pail down on the floor beside her, but she kept her eyelids folded over her eyes.

It's easier to remember than to forget, she said.

These are things too real for a person to forget, the boy thought. There are things so real that a person has to see them. A person can't keep her eyes glazed over like a dead bird's forever. What will Ma do, the boy thought.

You've got to take me, the girl said to the boy.

Why don't you just go? he said.

You've been out with the men on the beef drive, she said. You know what it's like down there. I've had enough of round this place, but I don't know where to go.

Place is the word, said the boy. I only know a place where men drink beer, he said. A bunch of men and an old parrot.

He got up and went to the window.

I'm going down to put a fence right across the creek, he said, so James Potter's mother can't go up and down here any more.

6

He went out of the kitchen into the sun. Outside the world floated like a mote in a straight shaft of glory. A horse coming round the corner of the barn shone copper against the hewn logs, Kip riding black on its reflected brightness.

The boy raised his hand.

Kip rode his horse forward to a stop. He rested his hands on the pommel of his saddle and shook his feet free of the wooden stirrups to ease his legs.

There's nothing doing round here, said the boy, unless you've come to trade that bag of bones you're riding for another.

Some day, Kip said. Some day.

Where are you going? the boy asked.

On the road, Kip said. Riding. Just riding. Just coming and going. Where's the girl?

I don't know, said the boy.

I got a message for her, Kip said.

She's in the house, the boy said. Give her the message yourself. I'm not having anything to do with that sort of thing, one way or another.

He went over to the barn and picked up a roll of wire. Then he put it down and looked at Kip.

Kip's face was turned towards the house.

What in hell are you doing? said the boy.

Looking, said Kip.

Get out of here, the boy said. Wherever you are there's trouble. If a man is breaking a horse when you come round it hangs itself on the halter, or throws itself, or gets out and back on the range. Take your message back where it came from.

A'right, said Kip. A'right.

He shoved his feet into his stirrups and gathered up his lines.

The girl don't need no telling, he said.

He bent down over the saddle. His face hung close to the boy's.

When a stallion's broke down your fence, he said, there's nothing you can do except put the fence back up again.

He swung his horse around away from the boy, but he kept his face turned over his shoulder.

Wipe off that look, the boy said.

Then he called after Kip: James Potter's mother is fishing in our creek. It's her I'm going to fence out.

7

As Kip moved off, the boy noticed the light again. Caught in the hide of the beast which picked its way along, its eyes on the dust of the road.

He stood thinking of the light he'd known. Of pitch fires lit on the hills. Of leaning out of the black wind into the light of a small flame. Stood thinking how a horse can stand in sunlight and know nothing but the saddle and the sting of sweat on hide and the salt line forming under the saddle's edge. Stood thinking of sweat and heat and the pain of living, the pain of fire in the middle of a haystack. Stood thinking of light burning free on the hills and flashing like the glory against the hides of things.

All along the fence the road had been cut by the wheels of William Potter's truck. Cut to plague the feet of beasts. To plague the very wheels which cut it. The whole road cut when a day's wait would have let the mud bake flat. Cut anyway, William said, by the feet of the beasts themselves, moving singly or in herds, by the old moose, his face above man-level, and the herds moving, moving.

The boy wrestled with the roll of wire, which curled in on itself seeking the bend into which it had been twisted. The sun beat down on him as it beat down on Kip's horse.

I'm afraid, thought the boy, and even the light won't tell me what to do.

He thought of the posts he would have to drive. He wondered: Is it Lenchen I'm afraid of. Or Ma. Or Kip. Is it the old lady fishing in the creek. Or is it seeing light the way I've never noticed before.

He gathered up the wire and went down to the creek. He looked through the stems of the cottonwood trees, but the old lady had gone. The water caught the light and drew it into itself. Dragonflies floated over the surface as if the water had not been stirred since the beginning of time. But the grass by the pool was bent.

I knew it was the old lady, the boy said. Shadows don't bend grass. I know a shadow from an old woman.

Above on the hills
Coyote's voice rose among the rocks:
In my mouth is forgetting
In my darkness is rest.

8

From the kitchen window the Widow looked out to the hills.

Dear God, she said, the country. Nothing but dust. Nothing but old women fishing. What can a person do? Wagner and me were cousins. I came, and what I could I brought. I've things for starting a girl. Things belonging in my family for years. Things laid by. The spoons. The sheets. The bedcover I crocheted with my own hands. The shame. A fat pig of a girl, Almighty Father. Who would want such a girl?

I could tell you, the girl said.

You can tell me nothing, the Widow said. Go. Go. I hear nothing. I see nothing. Men don't ask for what they've already taken.

She went to the bottom of the stairs.

You want to go, she said. Go. Don't keep asking. Go.

9

Lenchen watched her mother walk away. She kept pulling the tongue of her belt until the belt bit into her flesh.

James had not come as he promised. She had not seen him for days. Except from the crest of the hill. She had seen him below at work in the arms of the hills near his own house. Going from house to barn. Sometimes alone. Sometimes with Greta. She could not imagine the life he lived when the door closed behind him.

She remembered him on his knees in the corral. Holding a heifer down. The sweat beading the hairs of his chest where his shirt divided. She smelt smoke, and flesh seared with the branding-iron. She saw him on his knees with a bull calf under him, the gelding knife bright in his hand.

She heard his voice again: This is no place for her. And Heinrich's voice: She's been at it from a kid, like me. You've just not noticed before. She's been round here always, like the rest of us.

She remembered James's face above his plaid shirt, and how she'd slipped down from the fence where she'd been sitting with Kip and had begun roping one of their own calves so that James could see what he'd noticed for the first time.

10

If Lenchen had been looking down from the hill just then, she would have seen James saddling his horse. He was alone.

Greta was in the kitchen talking to Angel Prosper. William had stopped his truck at Theophil's that morning and asked Angel to go up the creek to give Greta a hand.

She's getting played out doing for Ma, he said. She thinks nobody cares. When you go, tell her I stopped and asked.

And on Theophil's doorstep before the work was done he'd paid Angel her day's wages.

Greta was polishing a lamp globe.

I've seen Ma standing with the lamp by the fence, she said. Holding it up in broad daylight. I've seen her standing looking for something even the birds couldn't see. Something hid from every living thing. I've seen her defying. I've seen her take her hat off in the sun at noon, baring her head and asking for the sun to strike her. Holding the lamp and looking where there's nothing to be found. Nothing but dust. No person's got a right to keep looking. To keep looking and blackening lamp globes for others to clean.

Angel sat back on her heels. She had been moving, half squatting, to scrub the floor. The water from her brush made a pool on the boards.

You mean you're not going to let her do it any more, Angel said. One person's got as much right as another. Maybe she don't ask you to clean those globes. There's things people want to see. There's things too, she said as she leant on the brush in the wall shadow below the window light, there's things get lost.

For nothing I'd smash it, Greta said. A person could stand so much. A person could stand to see her fish if they had to depend on her doing it to eat. But I can tell you we've not eaten fish of hers in this house. Ask anybody what she did with her fish. Ask them. Not me. I don't know anything.

Why didn't you take your own lamp and go looking for something? Angel said. You've never all your life burned anything but a little oil to finish doing in the house.

What are you saying? Greta asked. You don't even know. You don't know a thing. You don't know what a person knows. You don't know what a person feels. You've burned and spilled enough oil to light up the whole country, she said. It's easy enough to see if you make a bonfire and walk around in the light of it.

Angel scrubbed the last boards, and threw the water into the roots of the honeysuckle which grew over the porch.

They need all the water they can get, Angel said.

Then she saw Ara passing by in the road. She saw her loosening the bootlace and taking off her hat to shove back her damp hair. She thought: William Potter got an ugly one. Then she shook the last drop out of the pan and went back into the house.

Do you want me to clean up the stairs? she asked Greta.

No, Greta said. I don't like people looking round. I won't have people walking up and down in my house.

II

Ara hadn't intended to come to her mother-in-law's. She had wanted to get away from the house. From the sound of the cow's breath in the dry grass. From the smell of empty buckets and dust heavy with sage. She had thought of going up the hill into the clump of jack pines to smell the smell of pine needles. She had walked up the hill, stopping now and then to knock off a prickly pear which clung to her sneakers. But when she reached the shoulder, instead of turning away from the valley, she had cut down through the sand and dust and patches of scorched grass to the road which led to her mother-in-law's.

If she had gone up to the old lookout she might have seen something to think about as William saw things when he was coming and going with the post. She might have seen a porcupine rattling over the rock on business which had nothing to do with her; or a grouse rising and knotting itself to a branch, settling fork-angled so that the tree seemed to put out a branch, before her eyes.

Roads went from this to that. But the hill led up to the pines and on to the rock rise which flattened out and fell off to nowhere on the other side.

Yet she had cut down from the hill because she had to talk. She had to talk to some living person. She had to tell someone what she felt about the old lady and the water.

It couldn't rise, William would say. Not in summer. Why, the wonder is there's any water at all. I've known the creeks fall so low, he'd say, that the fish were gasping in the shallowness. The day will come, he'd say, when the land will swallow the last drop. The creek'll be dry as a parched mouth. The earth, he'd say, won't have enough spit left to smack its lips.

It couldn't rise, William would say; but she'd felt it rise.

There was no use telling Greta. Greta wouldn't listen. She could hear Greta's voice rattling like the rattle of dry cowhide: All these years we've never had a wipe-up linoleum. But I like boards better. You know when the floor's splintering away. You know when the rats have gnawed it. I don't like a linoleum. It's smooth like ice, but you can't tell when it's been eat away beneath.

She would tell James, Ara thought. He could do what he liked. She'd be free of the thought.

There were more
than sixscore thousand persons
in Nineveh;
but here were only
herself and William
Greta and James
Lenchen
the boy her brother
the Widow
Prosper, Angel and Theophil
the old lady, lost like Jonah perhaps
in the cleft belly of the rock[3]
the water washing over her.

She didn't think of Kip at all until she saw him leaning over the pommel of his saddle talking to James.

12

James was standing by the barn. Kip's hands rested on the pommel. His face was bent down over his horse's neck towards James.

James, William said, there was no accounting for. He had gamebird ways. He was like a gay cock on the outside in his plaid shirt and studded belt. Myself, William said, I never needed more than a razor-strop to hitch up my jeans. Yet inside, he said, there's something's cooked James's fibre. He's more than likely white and dry and crumbling like breast of pheasant.

Ara heard Kip's voice.

She's fishing down to Wagner's, he said. How're you going to go now? The boy Wagner's there too, he said.

3 Compare Micah 1: 4: 'And the mountains shall be molten under him, and the valleys shall be cleft, as wax before the fire, and as the waters that are poured down a steep place.'

James's back was towards her. She saw him take a step forward. Kip pulled himself up and sat loosely against the cantle.

Ara had stopped at the corner of the barn. James's horse, saddled, waited on the lines. Ara saw it there. She felt the weight of nickel plate pulling its head to the earth.

She untied the bootlace again and hat in hand went towards James as if she had just come.

Didn't you hear the gate? she said.

James started round.

Overhead the sky was tight as rawhide. About them the bars of the earth darkened. The flat ribs of the hills.

Beyond James over the slant of the ground Ara saw the path down to the creek. The path worn deep by horses' feet. And higher up on the far side she saw the old lady, the branches wrapped like weeds above her head, dropping her line into the stream.

She saw and motioned with her hand.

Kip's eyes looked steadily before him.

Your old lady's down to Wagner's he said to James.

She's here, Ara said.

James turned on his heel. But when he turned, he saw nothing but the water-hole and the creek and the tangle of branches which grew along it.

Ara went down the path, stepping over the dried hoof-marks down to the creek's edge. She, too, saw nothing now except a dark ripple and the padded imprint of a coyote's foot at the far edge of the moving water.

She looked up the creek. She saw the twisted feet of the cottonwoods shoved naked into the stone bottom where the water moved, and the matted branches of the stunted willow. She saw the shallow water plocking over the roots of the cottonwood, transfiguring bark and stone.

She bent towards the water. Her fingers divided it. A stone breathed in her hand. Then life drained to its centre.

And in a loud voice
Coyote cried:
Kip, my servant Kip.[4]

Startled by the thunder, Ara dropped the stone into the water.

James was staring down the road. The hills were touched with light, but darkness had begun to close in.

She's going to break, James said. There's nothing else for it. You'd better go in, Ara. Greta'll make you welcome until it's over.

He spoke for the first time.

Kip's face was turned to the sky. To the light stampeded together and bawling before the massed darkness. The white bulls of the sky shoulder to shoulder.

4 There are a number of instances of crying out in a loud voice in the Bible that are echoed here (including Jesus' dying words on the cross). See particularly, Revelation 10: 1ff: 'And I saw another mighty angel come down from heaven . . . And [he] cried with a loud voice, as when a lion roareth: and when he had cried, seven thunders uttered their voices.'

He had risen in his stirrups until the leathers were pulled taut. His had reaching to pull down the glory.

Ara looked up too. For a minute she saw the light. Then only the raw skin of the sky drawn over them like a sack.

Then the rain swung into the mouth of the valley like a web. Strand added to strand. The sky, Ara thought, filled with adder tongues. With lariats. With bull-whips.

She reached the porch before the first lash hit the far side of the house. She looked back at Kip and at James. James had taken shelter in the doorway of the barn. Kip's knees had relaxed. He was sitting in the saddle.

13

Greta and Angel had been drinking tea at the table by the kitchen window. There were two cups on the table and a teapot. But Greta was standing by the stove when the door opened. Standing with her fingers on the lid of the metal water tank so that she looked across the stove at Ara.

The rain drove you in to see us, she said, Sit down. Make yourself at home.

Angel said nothing. She sat tracing the grain of the scrubbed table top with her nail.

I was walking across the hill, Ara said, and I dropped in to ask after Ma. I thought I saw her this morning down by our place, but she didn't stop.

The room was dark. Greta made no movement in the corner.

You almost need a lamp, Ara said. Did Ma come in? She's too old to be out in this. It comes on sudden in the summer.

She's not been out, Greta said.

She must be sleeping, Angel said. Not a single board has creaked.

She's been sleeping, Greta said.

You've been seeing things, Ara, Greta said. Like everyone else round here. You've been looking into other people's affairs. Noticing this. Remarking that. Seeing too much. Hearing too much.

Who's had the trouble of her? Greta asked. Who's cooked and care for her? I'm not complaining. It's my place here, and I know my place. If I'd married a man and gone off, there's no telling what might have happened. He might be riding round the country in a truck. Stopping and talking to women in the road. He might be leaning over the counter buying thread for somebody. He might be playing the fiddle while the pains was on me. He might be meeting the Widow's girl down in the creek bottom. He might be laying her down in the leaves.

Ara had been looking at Greta.

You've no right to speak that way of the girl, Ara said. You don't know.

You don't know what I know, Greta said.

Angel got up and reached for the lamp.

Leave it down, Greta said. I light the lamps in this house now.

14

The storm which drove Ara into Greta's kitchen woke Felix Prosper. He sat up in his chair. The hounds cowered down, their dewlaps pressed to the earth.

Who's shouting on Kip? Felix asked. What's Kip doing here?

Recalled as if urgently from sleep he looked around for the cause. The heat was still heavy in the air. Felix noticed the darkening of the sky and heard above the beginning of the storm.

Thunder. It meant nothing to him.

Rain. He picked up the fiddle and took it into the house. Then he came back for an armful of wood.

The hounds had slunk off somewhere. Like old women to a feather-bed. He'd seen Angel light a lamp against the storm. Not a wax candle to the Virgin, but the light she'd said her father kept burning against the mist that brought death.

A candle. He had no need for one.

He lit a fire in the stove. He poured water on the grounds in the granite pot. Ground a few fresh beans and added them to the brew. Sat on a backless wooden chair. Splay-legged. His mind floating in content of being. His lips drinking the cup already.

The cup which Angel had put into his hand, her bitter going, he'd left untouched. Left standing. A something set down. No constraint to make him drink. No struggle against the drinking. No let-it-pass. No it-is-done.[5] Simply redeemed. Claiming before death a share of his inheritance.

The cup for which he reached was not the hard ironware lined with the etch of tea and coffee. It was the knobbed glass moulded to the size of his content. Pleasure in the light of it. The knowing how much to drink. How much drunk. The rough knobbed heat of it.

Above him the blow and the answer. The rain pounding the tar-paper roof. The memory of the time Angel had seen the bear at the fish camp. Seen the bear rising on its haunches. Prostrating itself before the unsacked winds. Rising as if to strike. Bowing to the spirits let out of the sack, Angel thought, by the meddler Coyote. The bear advancing. Mowing. Scraping. Genuflecting. Angel furious with fear beating wildly. Her hunting-knife pounding the old billycan.

He chuckled, remembering the noise and the white face of Angel when he picked up the bear in its devotions. Picked up paper blown off the fish-shack roof.

The remembrance of event and the slash of rain merged. Time annihilated in the concurrence. The present contracted into the sweet hot cup he fondled. Vast fingers circling it.

Then he heard dogs bark somewhere in the direction of the barn, as if they'd found a rat in the manger and raftered it. He looked round for the terrier and wondered at her going. She would not run with the hounds or rub hides for manger berth.

5 Allusions to Jesus' final hours in the garden of Gethsemane ('And he went a little farther, and fell on his face, and prayed, saying, O my Father, if it be possible, let this cup pass from me: nevertheless not as I will, but as thou wilt' [Matt. 26: 39]) and at the moment of his death ('When Jesus therefore had received the vinegar, he said, It is finished: and he bowed his head, and gave up the ghost' [John 19: 30]).

She was equal to a rat her own size. Would tackle one. Like the one he'd poked down. Poked at. For the thing crouching, its tail hanging there above his head, had sprung. Had jumped to the pole seeking it. Had run from pole to arm, its teeth sinking in his neck crevice, its claws clutching mad with dread. He had shaken it off, uncertain in its rage, and her teeth had closed on its throat. White foam on the brown swirl of it. The old lady fishing in the brown water for fish she'd never eat. The old lady year after year.

He heard a bark. And then the soft shuffling thud of unshod horse feet and the clink of bit chains. He heard the step boards creak. He sat, his face pendulous above his horizontal bib, his knees wide, his belly resting between his thighs.

The door opened.

Felix did not move. His bare feet pressed the boards. His hand still held the cup. For a moment he thought it was Angel come out of some storm of her own.

It was the Widow's daughter, Lenchen.

15

The girl stood, the door open behind her. Stood resting on her heels as he'd seen Angel stand when she was heavy with young.

You'd best put your mare in, he said. The stall's empty. You're welcome until it's over.

She turned and went out. Shaking her hair back from her eyes. Walking in her heeled boots as a man might walk. Rolling. Lurching. As if legs had taken shape from the beast clamped between them. Beast turned to muscle twist. Beast answering movement of shank and thigh.

Walked in jerky defiance, Felix thought. Like a colt too quickly broken.

She's been rid on the curb,[6] Felix thought. And felt the prick of steel.

He'd never broken Angel. He'd never tried to. He'd lived with her as he'd lived in his father's cabin. By chance. By necessity. By indifference. He'd thought of nothing but the drift of sunlight, the fin-flick of trout, the mournful brisk music made sweet by repetition.

Angel had borne his children. She'd hoed his potatoes. One day she'd walked out of his gate and Theophil had taken her away in his wagon. Theophil had lived by himself without wife or children. Now Felix lived by himself. Things came. Things went. A colt was dropped in the pasture. A hen's nest was robbed. A vine grew or it was blown down.

He reached for his fiddle and began to play.

The girl came back and sat on the bench beside the stove. The water was dripping from her hair. Her shirt was rumpled and caught to her skin. She said nothing at all.

In the sky above evil had gathered strength. It took body writhing and twisting under the high arch. Lenchen could hear the breath of it in the pause. The swift indrawing.

6 That is, ridden by someone constantly holding back on the curb, which is a chain or strap passed under a horse's lower jaw in conjunction with the bit to make it easier for a rider to restrain the horse. Too much use of a curb is a bad way to 'break' or train a colt for riding.

The silence of the contracting muscle. The head drop for the wild plunge and hoof beat of it.

She leant forward a little.

I wanted Angel, she said. But she's not at Theophil's.

16

In Greta's kitchen Angel had set down the lamp.

Ara thought: Why is James so long coming.

I suppose William's gone for the post, Greta said. I'm waiting for the catalogue. There are things one needs from time to time. There are things people think other people have no need of. There are things that other people think people need that no one needs at all.

She turned to Angel.

Take her, she said. I don't want her. I don't want you coming Ara. I don't want anything from William. My post I'll come for myself. James'll come for it. I don't want my things pried over and then brought along here. The government pays William to carry our things as far as your post office. No farther. The government pays you to hand me my things out of the sack. I'll come along and get my catalogue myself. I don't want anyone coming here disturbing James and me. There's been more than I could stand. More than anyone could be held responsible for standing. I've been waiting all my life. A person waits and waits. You've got your own house, Ara. You don't have to see lamps in the night and hear feet walking on the stairs and have people coming in on you when they should be in their beds. I want this house to myself. Every living being has a right to something.

17

James had turned into the barn. Kip had gone off.

He might have climbed down from his horse, James thought, and set himself on the bottom rung of the ladder leading to the loft. Looking wise. Knowing too much. Like the old lady. Like Greta. Like Angel sitting now in the kitchen. Waiting to catch you in the pits and snares of silence. Mist rising from the land and pressing in. Twigs cracking like bone. The loose boulder and the downdrop. The fear of dying somewhere alone, caught against a tree or knocked over in an inch of water.

All around the hollow where he'd taken the girl there was nothing but the stems of trees so close packed that a man had to kick loose of the stirrups and leave his legs flat and push forward on his horse's shoulders to get through them. So still you could hear the frost working in the bark. No other sound except the shift of a horse's hip and the clink of bit on teeth grazing the short grass. But when he'd looked up he'd seen Kip standing in the pines.

He went to the door of the barn and looked out through the rain to the house. Since the fury of the morning he'd not been able to act. He'd thrown fear as a horse balks. Then he'd frozen on the trail. He was afraid. He was afraid what Greta might do.

She had said nothing. She'd not even looked at the door slammed shut. She'd set his breakfast in front of him and had sat herself down in their mother's chair. While, however his mother lay, he knew, her eyes were looking down where the boards had been laid apart.

This is the way they'd lived. Suspended in silence. When they spoke they spoke of hammers and buckles, of water for washing, of rotted posts, of ringbone and distemper.

The whole world's got distemper, he wanted to shout. You and me and the old lady. The ground's rotten with it.

They'd lived waiting. Waiting to come together at the same lake as dogs creep out of the night to the same fire. Moving their lips when they moved at all as hunters talk smelling the deer. Edged close wiping plates and forks while the old lady sat in her corner. Moved their lips saying: She'll live forever. And when they'd raised their eyes their mother was watching as a deer watches.

Now Greta'd sat in the old lady's chair. Eyes everywhere. In the cottonwoods the eyes of foolhens. Rats' eyes on the barn rafters. Steers herded together. Eyes multiplied. Eyes. Eyes and padded feet. Coyote moving in rank-smelling.

Nothing had changed. The old lady was there in every fold of the country. Seen by Kip. Seen by Ara.

He had to speak. He had to say to Greta: I'm through. I'll take the girl, and we'll go away out of the creek and you can stop here or go to William. Or I'll bring her to wait on you as you waited on Ma. Or I'll bring her and you can do as you like.

He could hear the chair grating back on the boards. He could hear her voice dry in his ear: I've waited to be mistress in my house. I never expected anything.

He could hear Greta listening at doors. He could see her counting the extra wash. Refusing to eat at table. He felt on his shoulder a weight of clay sheets. He smelt the stench of Coyote's bedhole.

His horse waited, water dripping from its sides. He stood with his foot on the doorframe. Then went out into the yard. Unsaddled the horse. And turned it into the pasture.

18

As James opened the house door the Widow's boy swung into the yard. Water was running from the scoop of his hat brim. His moosehide jacket was heavy with rain.

In the sky above darkness had overlaid light. But the boy knew as well as he knew anything that until the hills fell on him or the ground sucked him in the light would come again. He had tried to hold darkness to him, but it grew thin and formless and took shape as something else. He could keep his eyes shut after the night, but it would be light he knew. Light would be flaming off the bay mare's coat. Light would be kindling on the fish in the dark pools.

He had met Kip on the road.

You and your messages, he said. The girl's gone. I've come to speak myself at this end of the creek. If there's anything any man wants from us, let him come asking on his own feet at our door.

He untied the knot in his reins and threw his leg over the horn. As he came down his feet slipped in the mud of the dooryard.

He can't have her here, he thought. The old lady's out, but Greta's not been off in months.

James opened the door again. This time to look out.

You'd best put your beast in, he said. The far stall's empty.

The boy walked towards the steps.

I'm not stopping, he said.

You'd best come in, James said, till it blows over.

What I've come about won't blow over, said the boy.

Then you'd best go away with it, James said.

The boy saw the door closing. He jumped the steps and caught at the handle, pulling the door open into the wind.

Behind the metal tank Greta stood fingering the knob. Angel sat at the table. And Ara, in the darkness of the room, her eyes wide under her shaggy bangs.

Ara! The boy laughed.

Ara laughed too.

What's so funny, she said.

By God, Ara, the boy said, when I saw you glaring from under that forelock—

You thought, said Greta, coming round the tank and reaching to pull the kettle over the flame—you thought that James had rounded up the herd. An animal can hide in a herd.

Angel stood. She picked up the teapot.

Let it down, Greta said. In this house if tea's offered—

I'm clearing away, Angel said.

I'm come to tell you, the boy said turning to James.

What won't blow will keep, James said. Set down.

I'm come to tell you, the boy said.

He hesitated. He felt the women about him leaning against his silence.

His voice dropped. He turned to James.

I came to tell you, he said, that your Ma's out in the storm. Before it broke she was down to our place fishing in our pool.

Not at your place, Ara said. Up beyond us. Up the elbow-joint towards the hills. Up to the source.

Greta looked at James. Then she turned to the others.

I ask you, she said, if knowing Ma was out in this I'd not look for her? Do you think James would stand there letting her come to harm? I told you she didn't go out.

But it's easy enough to find out if Ma's here, Ara said. All we've got to do is call her. All we've got to do is look. I've not been up in your house, Greta. It's not my place to go.

I've not been up myself lately, Greta said. The thing about stairs is that they separate you from things.

If your Ma is still sleeping this late in the day, Angel said, she's sleeping quieter than most living things. There's no living being don't turn and creak the bed a little.

How could we both have seen her? Ara asked. How would we have seen her at both our places? She wasn't fishing downstream. She was fishing up, and I saw her ahead of me and moving on. Greta just doesn't know, she said. Go back down to your own creek, James. I saw her there too. There by the cottonwoods when Kip was telling you—

Oh Kip, said James. It's always Kip, Kip, Kip.

Get out, he said, turning to Angel. Go home. The rain's stopped. Is this the first time it has rained? Is this the first time that no one knows where Ma is? She'll come back. She always comes back.

A person has to go out to come back, Greta said.

She walked across the kitchen and stood by James.

Go home, Ara, she said.

Go home, she said to the boy. Ma's my business and James's business. Who's had the care of her all these years that you bother yourself about her now? What makes you choose today to bother?

It was Ma herself, Ara said.

James moved away from Greta.

She'll be back, James said.

He opened the door as if to look out.

Kip was standing on the doorstep, peering into the darkness of the room. Light flowed round him from outside. The sun was shining again low in the sky. The mist rose in wisps from the mud of the dooryard and steamed off two horses standing there.

If you want to go down to Wagner's now, Kip said, I saw your old lady climb down through the split rock with Coyote, her fishes stiff in her hand.

He smiled.

The boy's here, he said. There's nothing stopping you. I just came to tell you, he said.

Greta looked at James.

I knew what you wanted, she said.

She went to the foot of the stairs and turned to Kip.

You didn't see her, she said. You couldn't. I tell you she's here.

Get out, she said. Go way. This is my house. Now Ma's lying dead in her bed I give the orders here. When a person's dead in a house there should be a little peace.

She pointed to the door. But when the others went out James did not move.

1959

Irving Layton

b. 1912

Irving Layton has become one of Canada's best-known poets, not only because of his sizeable body of writing, which includes a number of exceptional poems, but also because of a reputation—extending well beyond his reading audience—for controversy, for obstreperous antagonism to those who fail to agree with him, and for having kept himself in the public eye. He was often at the centre of bitter feuds and, in prefaces to many of his early books of poetry, he attacked English professors, critics and reviewers, and even his fellow poets for effete elitism; at the same time he scorned the general public for their insensitivity and lack of concern for matters of art and intellect. Although sympathetic to Marxism as a young man, he later became a staunch anti-Communist who supported the US involvement in Vietnam at a time when such a stand made one a pariah in most intellectual circles. Moreover, throughout his poetry he chronicled his sexual adventures and offered his opinions in language sufficiently frank and bawdy to offend some readers and lose him his first connection with a commercial press in Canada.

Layton acknowledged that he sometimes deliberately assumed 'the role of public exhibitionist'. Indeed, perhaps more than any other poet in Canada he played the part of the artist as it was defined in the early days of the modernist movement: the gadfly and rebel, outraging the middle class and challenging the assumptions of an anaesthetized Philistine society. He seems, at that same time, to have been a battler by instinct. 'I would not have had it any other way,' he wrote in the preface to *Engagements: The Prose of Irving Layton* (1972). 'I owe them [his many conflicts] some of the most delicious moments of my life.'

Layton was more complex, however, than his public roles suggest. For example, despite his oft-expressed scorn for academics, he took a master's degree and devoted almost as much of his career to teaching as to writing. As a young man he worked patiently with new immigrants to help them master English, and he also taught in a parochial school in Montreal; later he taught at Sir George Williams (now Concordia) University and at York University and spent a year as writer-in-residence at the University of Toronto. Similarly, despite his disparaging remarks about his rivals in poetry, he was extremely solicitous towards beginning writers and often took time to introduce both them and his creative-writing students to an understanding and appreciation of the fellow poets he publicly criticized. Indeed, despite what sometimes came across as a generalized contempt for mankind, Layton was always generous with his time and energy, answering correspondence from readers he had never met, conversing patiently after his public readings, or working with the students in his classes.

Born in Romania to Jewish parents (he later changed his family name, Lazarovitch), Irving Layton came to Montreal with his family when he was an infant. He has written of how his developmental years made him 'suspicious of both literature and reality':

Let me explain. My father was an ineffectual visionary; he saw God's footprint in a cloud and lived only for his books and meditations. A small bedroom in a slum tenement which in the torrid days steamed and blistered and sweated, he converted into a tabernacle for the Lord of Israel; and here, like the patriarch Abraham, he received his messengers. Since there was nothing angelic about me or his other children, he no more noticed us than if we had been flies on a wall. Had my mother been as otherworldly as he was, we should have starved. Luckily for us, she was not; she was tougher than nails, shrewd and indomitable. Moreover, she had a gift for cadenced vituperation; to which, doubtless, I owe my impeccable ear for rhythm. With parents so poorly matched and dissimilar, small wonder my entelechy [realization of potential] was given a terrible squint from the outset. I am not at ease in the world (what poet ever is?); but neither am I fully at ease in the world of the imagination. I require some third realm, as yet undiscovered, in which to live. My dis-ease has spurred me on to bridge the two with the stilts of poetry, or to create inside me an ironic balance of tensions. (Foreword, *A Red Carpet for the Sun, 1959*)

Like A.M. Klein before him and Mordecai Richler after him, Layton attended Baron Byng High School, working at a variety of jobs to earn the monthly fee of $1.50. There he first discovered his love of poetry, but—because of an argument with one of his teachers when he fell behind in payment of his fee—he was expelled in his last year. He prepared himself for his exams anyway and, after passing them, plunged into what may have been the most important phase of his education, an extended period of reading and self-instruction, supplemented by debates in the evenings at Horn's Cafeteria (a gathering place during the Depression for many of Montreal's radicals and disaffected intellectuals). Eventually he returned to school, completing a B.Sc. in agricultural science at Macdonald College in 1939. (Of this Layton has remarked, 'you can see the agricultural images in my poems. I worked on farms for three or four summers, something significant for an urban Jew.') After a period of wartime military service, Layton continued his education, completing an MA in political science at McGill in 1945. The subtitle of his thesis on British labourite Harold Laski—'The Paradoxes of a Liberal Marxist'—further testifies to Layton's 'ironic balance of tensions'.

The postwar forties was a period of intense activity for Layton, a period characterized by 'exciting personalities, living poetry twenty-four hours a day, thinking, talking, analyzing, arguing, reading and above all writing'. At McGill he met Louis Dudek (both of them published poems in the *McGill Daily*) and heard about John Sutherland's newly established mimeographed magazine *First Statement* (1942–5). Layton sent Sutherland some poems and later, with Dudek, joined him in editing the often controversial little magazine. Together the three of them set out to establish a new poetry movement in Canada, one that would challenge the 'cosmopolitan' writers who had grouped themselves around Patrick Anderson's rival magazine *Preview* (1942–5), with a less abstract and more earthy poetry. In 'Montreal Poets of the Forties' (*Canadian Literature*, No. 14) Wynn Francis describes how the rivalry, though sometimes acrimonious, stimulated the more established poets of *Preview*, while making the younger ones at *First Statement* work harder. 'Not that we wanted to be like them,' she quotes Layton as saying, 'but we wanted to be as good as they were in our way.'

In 1945 the *First Statement* group launched a series of printed chapbooks with a collection of Layton's poems, *Here and Now*, later following this with Layton's second book, *Now Is the Place* (1948). When the group around Sutherland eventually broke up, Layton and Dudek joined Raymond Souster to found Contact Press, a co-operative venture in which the editors and several younger writers funded the publication of their own books. As well as *Cerberus* (1952), an anthology of the work of all three editors, Contact Press published a number of Layton's most important books of poetry, including *The Black Huntsman* (1951), *Love the Conqueror Worm* (1952), *The Long Pea-Shooter* (1954), *The Cold Green Element* (1955), and *The Bull-Calf and Other Poems* (1956). Though these books were not much noticed in Canada, Layton caught the attention of American poets and editors. Robert Creeley praised Layton's poetry in the first issue of the *Black Mountain Review* and published Layton's *In the Midst of My Fever* (1954) with his Divers Press; the American small-press editor Jonathan Williams brought out Layton's first substantial volume of selected poems, *The Improved Binoculars* (1956), and a collection of new poems, *A Laughter in the Mind* (1958). Even though the Ryerson Press reneged on its agreement to distribute *The Improved Binoculars* in Canada, this book gained Layton his first sustained readership in Canada, partly as a result of a preface by William Carlos Williams in which, after avowing his admiration for the younger poet, Williams concluded: 'In short, I believe this poet to be capable, to be capable of anything. . . . There will, if I am not mistaken, be a battle: Layton against the rest of the world.'

Soon after this, Layton was approached by McClelland and Stewart, who agreed to publish a compilation of the poems Layton valued most from his previous books. Entitled *A Red Carpet for the Sun*, this collection won the Governor General's Award for Poetry in 1959. With a commercial publisher supporting him, and an audience established in Canada at last, Layton began to publish frequently; for the next twenty years he brought out one or two works each year. He has published more than forty books of poetry, including the 589-page *Collected Poems of Irving Layton* (1971); two collections of prose; a memoir of his formative years, *Waiting for the Messiah* (1985); and several volumes of correspondence, including *Wild Gooseberries: The Selected Letters of Irving Layton* (1989), edited by Francis Mansbridge, and *Irving Layton and Robert Creeley: The Complete Correspondence, 1953–1978* (1990), edited by Ekbert Faas and Sabrina Reed.

From his first poems to his most recent ones, two aspects of Layton's personality dominated: his exuberance and his drive to enlighten his readers. Deeply influenced by Nietzsche, Layton declared that the 'poet has a public function as a prophet'. His poems have frequently drawn their vitality from the depiction of animals, especially animal victims: in suffering and death, these animals express his concern over human failures and reflect man's own mortality while at the same time testifying to his violation of nature.

If man is a threatening predator, he in turn lives in a predatory world. 'The Cold Green Element' gives one of the fullest accounts of Layton's vision: the universe is seen variously here: as an indifferent sea in which we swim or drown; or, in the image of the robin devouring the worm, as actively hostile, a consumer of life. But the poem suggests that worm-like humanity need not go meekly to his annihilation. Instead—recalling Isaàc Dufours in Duncan Campbell Scott's poem 'At the Cedars'—an individual should acclaim his brief moment with celebration and like a poet become one with 'the worm / who sang for an hour in the throat of a robin'.

The Birth of Tragedy[1]

And me happiest when I compose poems.
        Love, power, the huzza of battle
        are something, are much;
yet a poem includes them like a pool
        water and reflection.
In me, nature's divided things—
        tree, mould on tree—
        have their fruition;
I am their core. Let them swap,
bandy, like a flame swerve
I am their mouth; as a mouth I serve.

1 A reference to *The Birth of Tragedy out of the Spirit of Music* (1872), a work by the German philosopher Friedrich Nietzsche (1844–1900). In that book—ostensibly an attempt to explain the origins of Greek tragedy—Nietzsche discusses classical Greek culture as a union of two religious systems: the first based on the worship of the immortal gods of Olympus (such as Apollo), the second celebrating a dying god in rituals for Dionysus, the god of fertility and wine. From this observation Nietzsche generalizes two responses to the universe: 'Apollonian', which seeks the ideal world and believes in order and restraint, and 'Dionysiac', which confronts the chaos that actually underlies the appearance of order. Identifying Apollonian with 'dream' and Dionysiac with 'vision', he sees the power of Greek tragic playwrights deriving from their ability to unite Apollonian form and Dionysiac content.

And I observe how the sensual moths
big with odour and sunshine
dart into the perilous shrubbery;
or drop their visiting shadows
upon the garden I one year made
of flowering stone to be a footstool
for the perfect gods:
who, friends to the ascending orders,
sustain all passionate meditations
and call down pardons
for the insurgent blood.

A quiet madman, never far from tears,
I lie like a slain thing
under the green air the trees
inhabit, or rest upon a chair
towards which the inflammable air
tumbles on many robins' wings;
noting how seasonably
leaf and blossom uncurl
and living things arrange their death,
while someone from afar off
blows birthday candles for the world.

1954

The Cold Green Element

At the end of the garden walk
the wind and its satellite wait for me;
their meaning I will not know
until I go there,
but the black-hatted undertaker

who, passing, saw my heart beating in the grass,
is also going there. Hi, I tell him,
a great squall in the Pacific blew a dead poet
out of the water,
who now hangs from the city's gates.

Crowds depart daily to see it, and return
with grimaces and incomprehension;

if its limbs twitched in the air
they would sit at its feet
peeling their oranges.

And turning over I embrace like a lover
the trunk of a tree, one of those
for whom the lightning was too much
and grew a brilliant
hunchback with a crown of leaves.

The ailments escaped from the labels
of medicine bottles are all fled to the wind;
I've seen myself lately in the eyes
of old women,
spent streams mourning my manhood,

in whose old pupils the sun became
a bloodsmear on broad catalpa[1] leaves
and hanging from ancient twigs,
my murdered selves
sparked the air like the muted collisions

of fruit. A black dog howls down my blood,
a black dog with yellow eyes;
he too by someone's inadvertence
saw the bloodsmear
on the broad catalpa leaves.

But the furies clear a path for me to the worm
who sang for an hour in the throat of a robin,
and misled by the cries of young boys
I am again
a breathless swimmer in that cold green element.

1955

1 Tree with large heart-shaped leaves.

The Fertile Muck

There are brightest apples on those trees
but until I, fabulist, have spoken
they do not know their significance

or what other legends are hung like garlands
on their black boughs twisting
like a rumour. The wind's noise is empty.

Nor are the winged insects better off
though they wear my crafty eyes
wherever they alight. Stay here, my love;
you will see how delicately they deposit
me on the leaves of elms
or fold me in the orient dust of summer.

And if in August joiners and bricklayers
are thick as flies around us
building expensive bungalows for those
who do not need them, unless they release
me roaring from their moth-proofed cupboards
their buyers will have no joy, no ease.

I could extend their rooms for them without cost
and give them crazy sundials
to tell the time with, but I have noticed
how my irregular footprint horrifies them
evenings and Sunday afternoons:
they spray for hours to erase its shadow.

How to dominate reality? Love is one way;
imagination another. Sit here
beside me, sweet; take my hard hand in yours.
We'll mark the butterflies disappearing over the hedge
with tiny wristwatches on their wings:
our fingers touching the earth, like two Buddhas.

1956

Whatever Else Poetry Is Freedom

Whatever else poetry is freedom.
Forget the rhetoric, the trick of lying
All poets pick up sooner or later. From the river,
Rising like the thin voice of grey castratos[1]—the mist;

1 Historically, males castrated before puberty to retain a soprano or alto singing voice into adulthood.

Poplars and pines grow straight but oaks are gnarled;
Old codgers must speak of death, boys break windows;
Women lie honestly by their men at last.

And I who gave my Kate a blackened eye[2]
Did to its vivid changing colours
Make up an incredible musical scale;
And now I balance on wooden stilts and dance
And thereby sing to the loftiest casements.
See how with polish I bow from the waist.
Space for these stilts! More space or I fail!

And a crown I say for my buffoon's head.
Yet no more fool am I than King Canute,[3]
Lord of our tribe, who scanned and scorned;
Who half-deceived, believed; and, poet, missed
The first white waves come nuzzling at his feet;
Then damned the courtiers and the foolish trial
With a most bewildering and unkingly jest.

It was the mist. It lies inside one like a destiny.
A real Jonah it lies rotting like a lung.
And I know myself undone who am a clown
And wear a wreath of mist for a crown;
Mist with the scent of dead apples,
Mist swirling from black oily waters at evening,
Mist from the fraternal graves of cemeteries.

It shall drive me to beg my food and at last
Hurl me broken I know and prostrate on the road;
Like a huge toad I saw, entire but dead,
That Time mordantly had blacked; O pressed
To the moist earth it pled for entry.
I shall be I say that stiff toad for sick with mist
And crazed I smell the odour of mortality.

And Time flames like a paraffin stove
And what it burns are the minutes I live.

2 Apparently a reference to Shakespeare's *The Taming of the Shrew*, though Kate, the Shrew, is not actually struck in the play. (She strikes Petruchio, who threatens to hit her back.)

3 Eleventh-century king of England who is said to have placed his throne on the shore and commanded the tide not to rise. In some versions, when the tide rolled over him anyway, he explained that he had done this to rebuke his courtiers, who thought or acted as if he had God-like powers.

At certain middays I have watched the cars
Bring me from afar their windshield suns;
What lay to my hand were blue fenders,
The suns extinguished, the drivers wearing sunglasses.
And it made me think I had touched a hearse.

So whatever else poetry is freedom. Let
Far off the impatient cadences reveal
A padding for my breathless stilts. Swivel,
O hero, in the fleshy groves, skin and glycerine,
And sing of lust, the sun's accompanying shadow
Like a vampire's wing, the stillness in dead feet—
Your stave[3] brings resurrection, O aggrievèd king.

1958

3 Rod, lance; but also with the punning meaning of 'stanza'.

Keine Lazarovitch 1870–1959

When I saw my mother's head on the cold pillow,
Her white waterfalling hair in the cheeks' hollows,
I thought, quietly circling my grief, of how
She had loved God but cursed extravagantly his creatures.

For her final mouth was not water but a curse,
A small black hole, a black rent in the universe,
Which damned the green earth, stars and trees in its stillness
And the inescapable lousiness of growing old.

And I record she was comfortless, vituperative,
Ignorant, glad, and much else besides; I believe
She endlessly praised her black eyebrows, their thick weave,
Till plagiarizing Death leaned down and took them for his mould.

And spoiled a dignity I shall not again find,
And the fury of her stubborn limited mind;
Now none will shake her amber beads and call God blind,
Or wear them upon a breast so radiantly.

O fierce she was, mean and unaccommodating;
But I think now of the toss of her gold earrings,
Their proud carnal assertion, and her youngest sings
While all the rivers of her red veins move into the sea.

1961

Butterfly on Rock

The large yellow wings, black-fringed,
were motionless

They say the soul of a dead person
will settle like that on the still face

But I thought: the rock has borne this;
this butterfly is the rock's grace,
its most obstinate and secret desire
to be a thing alive made manifest

Forgot were the two shattered porcupines
I had seen die in the bleak forest.
Pain is unreal; death, an illusion:
There is no death in all the land,
I heard my voice cry;
And brought my hand down on the butterfly
And felt the rock move beneath my hand.

1963

A Tall Man Executes a Jig

I

So the man spread his blanket on the field
And watched the shafts of light between the tufts
And felt the sun push the grass towards him;
The noise he heard was that of whizzing flies,
The whistlings of some small imprudent birds,

And the ambiguous rumbles of cars
That made him look up at the sky, aware
Of the gnats that tilted against the wind
And in the sunlight turned to jigging motes.
Fruitflies he'd call them except there was no fruit
About, spoiling to hatch these glitterings,
These nervous dots for which the mind supplied
The closing sentences from Thucydides,[1]
Or from Euclid having a savage nightmare.

II

Jig, jig, jig, jig. Like miniscule black links
Of a chain played with by some playful
Unapparent hand or the palpitant
Summer haze bored with the hour's stillness.
He felt the sting and tingle afterwards
Of those leaving their orthodox unrest,
Leaving their undulant excitation
To drop upon his sleeveless arm. The grass,
Even the wildflowers became black hairs
And himself a maddened speck among them.
Still the assaults of the small flies made him
Glad at last, until he saw purest joy
In their frantic jiggings under a hair,
So changed from those in the unrestraining air.

III

He stood up and felt himself enormous.
Felt as might Donatello[2] over stone,
Or Plato, or as a man who has held
A loved and lovely woman in his arms
And feels his forehead touch the emptied sky
Where all antinomies[3] flood into light.
Yet jig jig jig, the haloing black jots
Meshed with the wheeling fire of the sun:

1 The conclusion to *The Peloponnesian War* by the Greek historian Thucydides (*c.* 470–*c.* 400 BC) is missing. The poet here connects the gnats with the ellipses used in texts to indicate incompleteness, while in the line that follows they become like the points that are the smallest defining element in Euclid's geometry.

2 Name taken by Donato di Niccolò (*c.* 1386–1466), considered to be the father of Renaissance sculpture because he was the first to portray the human figure in realistic and dynamic terms.

3 Paradoxes, especially contradictions in law.

Motion without meaning, disquietude
Without sense or purpose, ephemerids[4]
That mottled the resting summer air till
Gusts swept them from his sight like wisps of smoke.
Yet they returned, bringing a bee who, seeing
But a tall man, left him for a marigold.

IV

He doffed his aureole of gnats and moved
Out of the field as the sun sank down,
A dying god upon the blood-red hills.
Ambition, pride, the ecstasy of sex,
And all circumstance of delight and grief,
That blood upon the mountain's side, that flood
Washed into a clear incredible pool
Below the ruddied peaks that pierced the sun.
He stood still and waited. If ever
The hour of revelation was come
It was now, here on the transfigured steep.
The sky darkened. Some birds chirped. Nothing else.
He thought the dying god had gone to sleep:
An Indian fakir on his mat of nails.

V

And on the summit of the asphalt road
Which stretched towards the fiery town, the man
Saw one hill raised like a hairy arm, dark
With pines and cedars against the stricken sun
—The arm of Moses or of Joshua.[5]
He dropped his head and let fall the halo
Of mountains, purpling and silent as time,
To see temptation coiled before his feet:
A violated grass snake that lugged
Its intestine like a small red valise.
A cold-eyed skinflint it now was, and not
The manifest of that joyful wisdom,

4 Small insects that live only a day in their adult form.

5 A reference to Exodus 10: 22: 'And Moses stretched forth his hand toward heaven; and there was a thick darkness in all the land of Egypt'; and to Joshua 10: 12, in which Joshua commands the sun to stand still (glossed by later commentators as also being a command for darkness).

The mirth and arrogant green flame of life;
Or earth's vivid tongue that flicked in praise of earth.

VI

And the man wept because pity was useless.
'Your jig's up; the flies come like kites,' he said
And watched the grass snake crawl towards the hedge,
Convulsing and dragging into the dark
The satchel filled with curses for the earth,
For the odours of warm sedge, and the sun,
A blood-red organ in the dying sky.
Backwards it fell into a grassy ditch
Exposing its underside, white as milk,
And mocked by wisps of hay between its jaws;
And then it stiffened to its final length.
But though it opened its thin mouth to scream
A last silent scream that shook the black sky,
Adamant and fierce, the tall man did not curse.

VII

Beside the rigid snake the man stretched out
In fellowship of death; he lay silent
And stiff in the heavy grass with eyes shut,
Inhaling the moist odours of the night
Through which his mind tunnelled with flicking tongue
Backwards to caves, mounds, and sunken ledges
And desolate cliffs where come only kites,
And where of perished badgers and racoons
The claws alone remain, gripping the earth.
Meanwhile the green snake crept upon the sky,
Huge, his mailed coat glittering with stars that made
The night bright, and blowing thin wreaths of cloud
Athwart the moon; and as the weary man
Stood up, coiled above his head, transforming all.

1963

Robertson Davies

1913–1995

Novelist, playwright, actor, belletrist, storyteller, columnist, editor, publisher, historian, and the first master of Massey College at University of Toronto, a cosmopolitan, a connoisseur, and a lover of all the arts, Robertson Davies grew up in small-town Ontario—Thamesville, Renfrew, and Kingston.

In all three of these towns his father was owner-editor of the local newspaper. Davies began his own career in journalism early—at Upper Canada College, Toronto, where he was the student editor of the school newspaper. While at UCC he also developed an interest in theatre, which continued in his undergraduate years at Queen's University, Kingston, and then at Balliol College, Oxford. After receiving a B.Litt. from Oxford University in 1938, he remained in England and joined the Old Vic Theatre Company, working with Tyrone Guthrie. (Guthrie later became the first artistic director of the Stratford Festival in Ontario—about which Davies wrote three books.) In 1940, after two years with the Old Vic playing minor roles and also working as a writer and a teacher of drama history, Davies married Brenda Matthews, one of the stage managers for the company, and returned to Canada.

Davies spent two years as literary editor of *Saturday Night* before joining the Peterborough *Examiner* as its editor in 1942. He became publisher and editor of the newspaper in 1946 when his father transferred its ownership to his three sons. A column he created for the *Examiner*, in which he disguised his own identity under the cheerful but crustily eccentric persona of Samuel Marchbanks, may be said to have been the beginning of Davies' career as creative writer. Behind this mask he pontificated humorously on a wide variety of topics. Four collections of these columns were eventually published, including *The Diary of Samuel Marchbanks* (1947), *The Table Talk of Samuel Marchbanks* (1949), and—long after the column had ended—*Samuel Marchbanks' Almanack* (1967). A final reprise of Marchbanks' writing appeared in 1985 as *The Papers of Samuel Marchbanks*; this volume reprints most of the previous pieces as a 'scholarly' edition, accompanied by an introduction and historical notes prepared by Marchbanks' old friend and look-alike, Robertson Davies.

In addition to writing a column and running the *Examiner*, Davies began, in the late 1940s, to establish himself as a playwright. He first wrote one-act plays, the best known of which is *Overlaid* (1948), and then full-length dramas such as *Fortune, My Foe* (1948), *At My Heart's Core* (1950)—in which Susanna Moodie and Catharine Parr Traill are characters—and *Question Time* (1975), as well as the libretto for the 1999 opera *The Golden Ass*.

Although by the end of the 1940s Davies had established himself as an important Canadian playwright, he was disappointed by failure on the New York stage. In the fifties he therefore also began to publish fiction. His first three novels—*Tempest-Tost* (1951), *Leaven of Malice* (1954), and *A Mixture of Frailties* (1958)—known as the Salterton trilogy, after the fictional town in which they are set (a thinly disguised Kingston), are satirical comedies of manners that mock the mores of provincial Ontario communities, suggesting that narrow conventionality stifles the human spirit and restricts the creation of art.

During this period, Davies also continued as a journalist. With the Marchbanks series completed, he resumed the post of literary editor of *Saturday Night* (1953–9), writing on books in each issue. After he left that post, he wrote a weekly column called 'A Writer's Diary' for the Toronto *Star* (1959–63). His literary journalism from the fifties is gathered in *A Voice from the Attic* (1960), a book of observations on literary works both trivial and grand that pleads generally for more responsiveness from what Davies calls 'the clerisy' (intelligent and informed readers who are not primarily academics). Davies' career as a newspaper editor ended in 1963, although he remained connected to the *Examiner* until it was sold in 1968.

Four volumes of Davies' later essays have also been published: *The Enthusiasms of Robertson Davies* (1979) and *The Well-Tempered Critic* (1981)—both of these edited by Judith Skelton Grant, who has also edited a selection of his letters, *For Your Eyes Alone* (1999)—as well as *The Merry Heart* (1996) and *Happy Alchemy* (1997), which were published posthumously. An interesting volume of speeches from the sixties and seventies, *One Half of Robertson Davies* (1977), provides additional perspective on his public role.

In 1963, Davies was appointed the master of Massey College, the University of Toronto's new college of graduate studies, to which he sought to impart the flavour of the 1930s Oxford he had known. To say that he delighted in his role would be an understatement. He engaged fully in the official social life of the college, even entertaining students, faculty, and guests with stories he wrote for special occasions in his aim to instill a sense of new-made traditions. The ghost stories he wrote for and read aloud at the Gaudy Night celebration each Christmas are collected as *High Spirits* (1982).

In the seventies Davies published a second set of connected novels, called the Deptford trilogy after the small town from which its principal characters come. Generally regarded as his most important work and as one of the major achievements in Canadian fiction, *Fifth Business* (1970), *The Manticore* (1972, which won a Governor General's Award), and *World of Wonders* (1975) were for Davies a move from manners to myth, and from the omniscient author to first-person narration. With its schoolteacher-narrator, Dunstan Ramsay, obsessed by a desire to understand the nature of sainthood in all its darkness as well as its light, *Fifth Business* also announced the religious dimension that runs through Davies' later novels. By making extensive use of the concepts of the Swiss psychoanalyst Carl Jung and his ideas about archetypal figures and the collective unconscious—as well as showing the influence of Northrop Frye, whose *Anatomy of Criticism* (1957) had immense impact on a generation of Canadian writers; of Goethe; and of *The Golden Bough*—this trilogy provides a complex examination of the interplay of myth and reality as it affected the psychological development of the individual. As one of the characters in *The Manticore* suggests, an understanding of myth allows one to detect the unifying patterns under the mass of apparently unrelated detail and gives heightened meaning to life. Yet that novel also warns its readers against the modernist habit of searching for hidden explanations that turn life into a detective story with a neat solution.

In 1981 (the year Davies retired as master of Massey), his seventh novel, *The Rebel Angels*, appeared. This was the first book in his Cornish trilogy, named for Francis Cornish, whose story is told in the second volume of the trilogy, *What's Bred in the Bone* (1985), by the angel of biography. *The Rebel Angels* opens after Cornish's death and deals with the inheritance of his estate; the third volume, *The Lyre of Orpheus* (1988), asks how the foundation set up with Cornish's wealth shall best spend its money: by funding the writing of Cornish's biography or by providing funds for a new work of art. Focusing respectively on the university, painting, and opera, Davies' third trilogy deals with Canada's cultural maturation and treats large questions about the development of artistic and intellectual traditions. The possibilities of the supernatural that were encountered as myth in the Deptford trilogy become part of the plot in the Cornish novels, which features, as well as the angels in the second volume, a commentary from the ghost of the Romantic composer E.T.A. Hoffman in the third.

Davies' last two novels, *Murther and Walking Spirits* (1991) and *The Cunning Man* (1994), appear to be the first volumes of what would have been yet another trilogy. These last books explore the roots of contemporary Canada. *Murther and Walking Spirits*, which is narrated by a ghost, tells the story of a recently dead man who begins to understand himself by looking back on scenes from the lives of ancestors who immigrated to Canada. *The Cunning Man* focuses on a physician who treats not only the body but also the soul and who wants to hold on to some of the discarded wisdom of an earlier age. It contains a brief reappearance by Ramsay, the narrator of *Fifth Business* who spent his career investigating 'the borderland between history and myth'.

With his great beard, his charmingly gruff and awe-inspiring presence, his courtly manners and general formal elegance, Davies sometimes seemed like the last Victorian. This stereotype isn't entirely distorting: his Victorian persona may have been the elaborate role of a man who loved playing a part, but an attraction to Victorian qualities was in keeping with the works he created and with the way he aimed them all at the clerisy, a continuation of that literate general readership that existed before the modern era broke culture into high and low. With such a readership in mind, he created novels that combined the strong narrative appeal of Charles Dickens' tales with an unabashed interest in ideas in the tradition of Thomas Love Peacock.

To be called a Victorian would probably not have seemed an insult to the man who, in his later fiction, investigated such questions as the need for preserving the best of the old ways of medical knowledge, or of asking why art has to be 'timely' and if a forger creating a new painting in the style of an old master hasn't added to the world's store of great art. Yet for all his nineteenth-century affinities, Davies' fictional investigations of myth, history, and morality bear a distinctively contemporary stamp. He was one of the shapers of a Canadian fictional tradition that continues to be visible in such wonderfully magical tales as Ann-Marie MacDonald's novel *Fall on Your Knees* (1996). A man of immense imagination and creative energy and an extraordinarily varied and productive career, Davies seems to have been informed and sustained by a spirit like that described—in the third volume of the Deptford trilogy—by the magician Magnus Eisengrim:

It's just the way things strike me after the life I've lived, which looks pretty much like a World of Wonders when I spread it out before me, as I've been doing. Everything has its astonishing wondrous aspect, if you bring a mind to it that's really your own.

World of Wonders

World of Wonders tells for the first time in the Deptford trilogy the full story of Magnus Eisengrim, the character who remains Davies' most striking creation. More precisely, we learn how Paul Dempster, the child who was victimized into birth in *Fifth Business*, was transformed into Eisengrim, a renowned performer whose life is filled with people of culture and refinement. In the selection that follows, Paul/Magnus recounts, for the benefit of filmmakers with whom he's now working, how the first World of Wonders he encountered was a carnival by that name—Wanless's World of Wonders. A ten-year-old tormented by the fact that his beloved mother is chained inside her house because of her apparent madness (in *Fifth Business* Ramsay thinks she is saint-like rather than mad) and made miserable by his minister father, whose views are so harsh that he sees it a religious duty to beat his son, Paul had sought a moment's escape by going to the town's annual fair without his father's permission. After viewing its agricultural and domestic parts, he then moved on to the calliope (merry-go-round), and thence to the carnival—in his father's eyes a place of wretched sin and degradation.

Ironically his father is proved right when Paul is sodomized and abducted by Willard—the magician in the carnival. By the time the woman known as Gus, the American manager of the carnival, learns of the boy's presence, he has been held captive without food or water for several days. Fearing that the Canadian authorities will close down her organization if she releases the boy, she cares for him and reluctantly agrees to let him to join the show. In 'A Bottle in the Smoke', Part I of *World of Wonders*, from which this selection is drawn, Paul recounts how he becomes useful when he learns to operate a trick that Willard wants to use in his act, and he describes more generally his life in the carnival.

Davies is clearly working in the tradition of Dickens here, both in his telling of a Dickensian story of a mistreated and isolated child and in his fondness for a colourful narrative filled with vivid details. Unlike Dickens, however, Davies is much less judgmental about the morality of his story, even suggesting later in the novel that Paul, though warped by his experiences, has become through them 'like a bottle in the smoke'. The phrase is drawn from

Psalm 119: a 'bottle' in this context is a goatskin that has been scraped, tanned, and hung over a fire to be smoked into a hardness that will allow it to be used as a container for wines. Thus Davies suggests that the fire and smoke experienced in life are what produce creative genius and provide the ability to break out of the everyday for someone like Eisengrim.

Listening to Paul's account, Ramsay describes Paul's relationship with Willard as the story of a 'man who is in search of his soul, and who must struggle with a monster to secure it'. The novel shows, throughout, Davies' characteristic fondness for archetypal, mythic, and folkloric patterns. Paul in Abdullah is said to resemble Jonah 'in the belly of the great fish'—thereby readying us for the idea that he will eventually emerge from the belly of the beast to achieve his destiny. His experiences in the carnival also recall the archetypal pattern of Dante's descent into Hell (and out the other side, to journey on to Paradise), a pattern already apparent in *The Manticore.* We can also see resemblances to the story of Pinocchio, the puppet who gets caught up in a show run by an ogre and who has to spend time in the belly of a giant fish before attaining his goal of becoming a true human being at last.

From *World of Wonders*

FROM 'A BOTTLE IN THE SMOKE'

That was how I became the soul of Abdullah, and entered into a long servitude to the craft and art of magic.

We began at once. Gus bustled away on some of the endless business she always had in hand, but Charlie remained, and he and Willard began to uncover something at the very back of the car—the only object in it which the handlers had not unloaded for Monday's fair—which was under several tarpaulins. Whatever it was, this was the prison in which I had spent my wretched, starving hours.

When it was pulled forward and the wraps thrown aside, it was revealed as, I think still, the most hideous and offensive object I have ever seen in my life. You gentlemen know how particular I have always been about the accoutrements of my show. I have spent a great deal of money, which foolish people have thought unnecessary, on the beauty and workmanship of everything I have exhibited. In this I have been like Robert-Houdin,[1] who also thought that the best was none too good for himself and his audiences. Perhaps some of my fastidiousness began with my hatred of the beastly figure that was called Abdullah.

It was a crude effigy of a Chinese, sitting on top of a chest, with his legs crossed. To begin with, the name was crassly wrong. Why call a Chinese figure Abdullah? But everything about it was equally inartistic and inept. Its robes were of frowsy sateen; its head was vulgarly moulded in papier mâché with an ugly face, sharply slanted eyes, dangling moustaches, and yellow fangs which hung down over the lower lip. The thing was, in itself, reason for a sharp protest from the Chinese Ambassador, if there had been one. It summed up in itself all that spirit combined of jocosity and hatred with which ignorant people approach whatever is foreign and strange.

1 The famous French conjurer and magician (1805–71). The first to use electromagnetism for his effects, Houdin was celebrated for his optical illusions and mechanical devices and for attributing 'magic' to natural instead of supernatural means. His book *Secrets of Prestidigitation and Magic* (1868) inspired many later magicians, including Harry Houdini, who took his stage-name as a tribute to the elder magician.

The chest on which this monster sat was in the same mode of workmanship. It was lacquered with somebody's stupid notion of a dragon, half hideous and half cute, in gaudy red on a black background. A lot of cheap gold paint had been splashed about.

Neither Willard nor Charlie explained to me what this thing was, or what relationship I was expected to bear to it. However, I was used to being ignored and rather liked it; being noticed had, in my experience, usually meant trouble. All they told me was that I was to sit in this thing and make it work, and my lesson began as soon as Abdullah was unveiled.

Once again, but this time in daylight and with some knowledge of what I was doing, I crawled into the chest at the back of the figure, and thence upward, rather like an old-fashioned chimney-sweep climbing a chimney, into the body, where there was a tiny ledge on which I could sit and allow my feet to hang down. But that was not the whole of my duty. When I was in place, Willard opened various doors in the front of the chest, then turned the whole figure around on the wheels which supported the chest, and opened a door in the back. These doors revealed to the spectators an impressive array of wheels, cogs, springs, and other mechanical devices, and when Willard touched a lever they moved convincingly. But the secret of these mechanisms was that they were shams, displayed in front of polished steel mirrors, so that they seemed to fill the whole of the chest under the figure of Abdullah, but really left room for a small person to conceal himself when necessary. And that time came after Willard had closed the doors in the chest, and pulled aside Abdullah's robes to show some mechanism, and nothing else, in the figure itself. When that was happening, I had to let myself down into the secret open space in the chest and keep out of the way. Once Abdullah's mechanical innards had been displayed I crept back up into the figure, thrust aside the fake mechanism, which folded out of the way, and prepared to make Abdullah do his work.

Willard and Charlie both treated me as if I were very stupid, which God knows I was not. However, I thought it best not to be too clever in the beginning. This was intuition; I did not figure it out consciously. They showed me a pack of cards, and painstakingly taught me the suits and the values. What Abdullah had to do was to play cards, on a very simple principle, with anybody who would volunteer from an audience to try their luck with him. This spectator—the Rube, as Willard called him—shuffled and cut a deck which lay on a little tray across Abdullah's knees. Then the Rube drew a card and laid it face down on the tray. At this point Willard pulled a lever on the side of Abdullah's chest, which set up a mechanical sound in the depths of the figure, which in fact I, the concealed boy, set going by pumping a pedal with my left foot. While this was going on it was my job to discover what card the Rube had drawn—which was easy, because he had put it face downward on a ground-glass screen, and I could fairly easily make it out—and to select a higher card from a rack concealed inside Abdullah ready to my hand. Having chosen my card, I set Abdullah's left arm in motion, slipping my own arm into the light framework in its sleeve; at the far end of this framework was a device into which I inserted the card that was to confound the Rube. I then made Abdullah's right arm move slowly to the deck of cards on the tray, and cut them; this was possible because the fingers had a pincers device in them which could be worked from inside the arm by squeezing a handle. When

Abdullah had cut the cards his left hand moved to the deck and took a card from the top. But in fact he did nothing of the sort, because his sleeve fell forward for a moment and concealed what was really happening; it was at this instant I pushed the little slide which shot the card I had chosen from the rack into Abdullah's fingers, and it seemed to the spectators that this was the card he picked up from the deck. The Rube was then invited to turn up his card—a five, let us say; then a spectator was asked to turn up Abdullah's card. A seven in the same suit! Consternation of the Rube! Applause of the audience! Great acclaim for Willard, who had never touched a card at any time and had merely pulled the lever which set in motion Abdullah, the Card-Playing Automaton, and Scientific Marvel of the Age.

* * *

Charlie had his way, and I was soon on the show. Charlie was right; Abdullah pulled them in because people cannot resist automata. There is something in humanity that is repelled and entranced by a machine that seems to have more than human powers. People love to frighten themselves. Look at the fuss nowadays about computers; however deft they may be they can't do anything that a man isn't doing, through them; but you hear people giving themselves delicious shivers about a computer-dominated world. I've often thought of working up an illusion, using a computer, but it would be prohibitively expensive, and I can do anything the public would find amusing better and cheaper with clockwork and bits of string. But if I invented a computer-illusion I would take care to dress the computer up to look like a living creature of some sort—a Moon Man or a Venusian—because the public cannot resist clever dollies. Abdullah was a clever dolly of a simple kind, and the Rubes couldn't get enough of him.

That was where Gus had to use her showman's discretion. Charlie and Willard would have put Abdullah in a separate tent to milk him for twenty shows a day, but Gus knew that would exhaust his appeal. Used sparingly, Abdullah was good for years, and Gus took the long view. It appeared, too, that I was an improvement on the dwarf, who had become unreliable through some personal defect—booze, I would guess—and was apt to make a mess of the illusion, or give way to a fit of temperament and deal a low card when he should have dealt a high one. Willard had had no luck with Abdullah; he had bought the thing, and hired the dwarf, but the dwarf was so unreliable it was risky to put the automaton on the show, and then the dwarf had disappeared. It had been months since Abdullah was in commission, and so far as the show was concerned it was a new attraction.

I was anxious to succeed as Abdullah, though I had no particular expectation of gaining anything thereby. I had no notion of the world, and for quite a long time I did not understand how powerful I was, or that I might profit by it. Nor did anyone in the World of Wonders seek to enlighten me. So far as I can recall my feelings during those first few months, they were restricted to a desire to do the best I could, lest I should be sent back to my father and inevitable punishment. To begin with, I liked being the hidden agent who helped in the great game of hoodwinking Rubes, and I was happiest when I was out of sight, in the smelly bowels of Abdullah.

When I was in the open air I was Cass Fletcher. I always hated the name, but Willard liked it because he had invented it in one of his very few flights of fancy. Willard had no imagination, to speak of. I learned as time went on that he had learned his conjuring skill from an old performer, and had never expanded it or altered it by a jot. He had as little curiosity as any man I have ever known. But when we were riding on the train, in my very first week, he found that I must have a name, because the other performers, riding in the car reserved for the World of Wonders, were surprised to see a small boy in their midst, for whom no credentials were offered. Who was I?

When the question was put directly to him by the wife of Joe Dark the Knife Thrower, Willard hesitated a moment, looked out of the window and said: 'Oh, this is young Cass, a kind of relative of mine; Cass Fletcher.' Then he went off into one of his very rare fits of laughter.

As soon as he could catch Charlie, who wandered up and down the car as it travelled through the flatlands of Western Ontario, and gossiped with everybody, Willard told him his great joke. 'Em Dark wanted to know the kid's name, see, and I was thinking who the hell is he, when I looked outa the window at one of these barns with a big sign saying FLETCHER'S CASTORIA,[2] CHILDREN CRY FOR IT; and quick as a wink I says Cass Fletcher, that's his name. Pretty smart way to name a kid, eh?' I was offended at being named from a sign on a barn, but I was not consulted, and a general impression spread that I was Willard's nephew.

At least, that was the story that was agreed on. As time went on I heard whispers between Molza the Fire Eater and Sonny Sonnenfels the Strong Man that Willard was something they called an arse-bandit—an expression I did not understand—and that the kid was probably more to him than just a nephew and the gaff for Abdullah.

Gaff. That was a word I had to learn at once, in all its refinements. The gaff was the element of deception in an exhibition, and though all the Talent would have admitted you couldn't manage without it, there was a moral stigma attaching to it. Sonnenfels was not gaffed at all; he really was a strong man who picked up big bar-bells and tore up telephone books with his hands and lifted anybody who would volunteer to sit in a chair, which Sonny then heaved aloft with one hand. There are tricks to being a strong man, but no gaff; anybody was welcome to heft the bar-bells if they wanted to. Frank Molza the Fire Eater and Sword Swallower was partly gaffed, because his swords weren't as sharp as he pretended, and eating fire is a complicated chemical trick which usually proves bad for the health. But Professor Spencer, who had been born without arms—really he had two pathetic little flippers but he did not show them—was wholly free of gaff; he wrote with his feet, on a blackboard and, if you wanted to pay twenty-five cents, in an elegant script on twelve visiting cards, where your name would be handsomely displayed. Joe Dark and his wife Emily were not gaffed at all; Joe threw knives at Emily with such accuracy that he outlined her form on the soft board against which she stood; it was skill, and the only skill poor Joe possessed, for he was certainly the dullest man in the World of Wonders. Nor could you say that there was any gaff about Heinie Bayer and his educated monkey Rango; it was

2 A popular prune-flavoured laxative of the time; its advertising slogan was 'Children cry for Fletcher's Castoria.'

an honest monkey, as monkeys go, and its tricks were on the level. The Midget Juggler, Piccino Zovene, was honest as a juggler, but as crooked as a corkscrew in any human dealings; he wasn't much of a juggler, and might have been improved by a little gaff.

Gaff may have been said to begin with Zitta the Jungle Queen, whose snakes were kept quiet by various means, especially her sluggish old cobra who was over-fed and drugged. Snakes don't live long in the sort of life Zitta gave them; they can't stand constant mauling and dragging about; she was always wiring a supplier in Texas for new rattlers. I judged that a snake lived about a month to six weeks when once Zitta had got hold of it; they were nasty things, and I never felt much sympathy for them. Zitta was a nasty thing, too, but she was too stupid to give her nastiness serious play. Andro the Hermaphrodite was all gaff. He was a man, of a kind, and besottedly in love with himself. The left side of his body was supposed to be the female half, and he spent a lot of time on it with depilatories and skin creams; when he attached a pretty good left breast to it, and combed out the long, curly hair he allowed to grow on one side of his head, he was an interesting sight. His right side he exercised strenuously, so that he had big leg and arm muscles which he touched up with some fancy shadowing. I never became used to finding him using the men's bucket in the donniker—which was the word used on the show for the primitive sanitary conveniences in the small back dressing tent. He was a show-off; in show business you get used to vanity, but Andro was a very special case.

Of course Abdullah was one hundred per cent gaff. I don't think anybody would have cared greatly, if they had not been stirred up to it by the one very remarkable Talent I haven't yet mentioned. She was Happy Hannah the Fat Lady.

A Fat Lady, or a Fat Man, is almost a necessity for a show like Wanless's. Just as the public is fascinated by automata, it is unappeasable in its demand for fat people. A Human Skeleton is hardly worth having if he can't do something else—grow hair to his feet, or eat glass or otherwise distinguish himself. But a Fat Lady merely has to be fat. Happy Hannah weighed 487 pounds; all she needed to do was to show herself sitting in a large chair, and her living was assured. But that wasn't her style at all; she was an interferer, a tireless asserter of opinions, and—worst of all—a determined Moral Influence. It was this quality in her which made it a matter of interest whether she was gaffed or not.

Willard was her enemy, and Willard said she was gaffed. For one thing, she wore a wig, a very youthful chestnut affair, curly and flirtatious; a kiss-curl coiled like a watchspring in front of each rosy ear. The rosy effect was gaffed, too, for Hannah was thickly made up. But these things were simple showmanship. Willard's insistence that the Fat Lady was gaffed rose from an occupational disability of Fat Ladies; this is copious sweating, which results, in a person whose bodily creases may be twelve inches deep, in troublesome chafing. Three or four times a day Hannah had to retire to the women's part of the dressing tent, and there Gus stripped her down and powdered her in these difficult areas with cornstarch. Very early in my experience on the show I peeped through a gap in the lacing of the canvas partition that divided the men's dressing-room from the women's, and was much amazed by what I saw; Hannah, who looked fairly jolly sitting on her platform, in a suit of pink cotton rompers, was a sorry mass of blubber when she was bent forward, her hands on the back of a chair; she had collops of fat on her flanks, like the wicked man in the Book of Job;[3] her monstrous abdomen hung almost to her knees, the smart wig concealed an iron-grey crewcut, and her breasts hung like great half-filled wallets[4] of suet far down on her belly. I have seen nothing like her since, except for an effigy of Smet Smet, the Hippopotamus Goddess, in an exhibition of African art Liesl made me attend a few years ago. The gaffing consisted of two large bath-towels, which were rolled and tucked under her breasts, giving them what was, in comparison with the reality, a buxom contour. These towels were great matters of contention between Hannah and Willard, for she insisted that they were sanitary necessities, and he said they were gross impostures on the public. He cared nothing about gaffing; it was Hannah who made it a moral issue and drew a sharp line between gaffed Talent, like Abdullah, and honest Talent, like Fat Ladies.

They wrangled about it a good deal. Hannah was voluble and she had a quality of shrewishness that came strangely from one whose professional personality depended on an impression of sunny good nature. She would nag about it for half an hour at a stretch, as we travelled on the train, until at last the usually taciturn Willard would say, in a low, ugly voice: 'Listen, Miz Hannah, you shut your goddam trap or next time we got a big crowd I'm gonna tell 'em about those gaffed tits of yours. See? Now shut up, I tell ya!'

He would never have done it, of course. It would have been unforgivable professional conduct, and even Charlie would not have been able to keep Gus from throwing him off the show. But the menace in his voice would silence Hannah for a few hours.

I was entranced by the World of Wonders during those early weeks and I had plenty of time to study it, for it was part of the agreement under which I lived that I must never be seen during working hours, except when real necessity demanded a quick journey to the donniker, between tricks. I often ate in the seclusion of Abdullah. The hours of the show were from eleven in the morning until eleven at night, and so I ate as big a breakfast as I could get, and depended on a hot dog or something of the sort being brought to me at noon and toward evening. Willard was supposed to attend to it, but he often forgot, and it was good-hearted Emily Dark who saw that I did not starve. Willard never ate much, and like so many people he could not believe that anyone wanted more than himself. There was an agreement of some sort between Willard and Gus as to what my status was; I know he got extra money for me, but I never saw any of it; I know Gus made him promise he would look after me and treat me well, but I don't think he had any idea what such words meant, and from time to time Gus would give him a dressing down about the condition I was in; for years I never had any clothes except those Gus bought me, stopping the money out of Willard's pay, but Gus had no idea of how to dress a child, and always bought everything too big, so that I would have lots of room to grow into it. Not that I needed many clothes; inside Abdullah I wore nothing but cotton shorts. I see now that it was a miserable life, and

3 In the Book of Job, Eliphaz the Temanite declares that the 'wicked man' 'covereth his face with his fatness, and maketh collops of fat on his flanks' (15: 27). 'Collops' are folds of flesh.

4 Pouches or bags for holding provisions, especially when travelling.

it is a wonder it didn't kill me; but at the time I accepted it as children must accept the world made for them by their guardians.

At the beginning I was beglamoured by the show, and peeped at it out of Abdullah's bosom with unresting excitement. There was one full show an hour, and the whole of it was known as a trick. The trick began outside the tent on a platform beside the ticket-seller's box, and this part of it was called the bally. Not ballyhoo, which was an expression I never heard in the carnival world in my time. Gus usually sold the tickets, though there was someone to spell her when she had other business to attend to. Charlie was the outside talker, not a barker, which is another expression I did not hear until a movie or a play made it popular. He roared through a megaphone to tell the crowd about what was to be seen inside the tent. Charlie was a flashy dresser and handsome in a flashy way, and he did his job well, most of the time.

High outside the tent hung the banners, which were the big painted signs advertising the Talent; each performer had to pay for his own banner, though Gus ordered them from the artist and assured that there would be a pleasing similarity of style. As well as the banners, some of the Talent had to appear on the bally, and this boring job usually fell to the lesser artistes; Molza ate a little fire, Sonny heaved a few weights, the Professor would lie on his back and write 'Pumpkin Centre, Agricultural Capital of Pumpkin County' on a huge piece of paper with his feet, and this piece of paper was thrown into the crowd, for whoever could grab it; Zovene the Midget Juggler did a few stunts, and now and then if business was slow Zitta would take out a few snakes, and the Darks would have to show themselves. But the essence of the bally was to create an appetite for what was inside the tent, not to give away entertainment, and Charlie pushed the purchase of tickets as hard as he could.

After Abdullah was put on the show, which was as soon as we could get a fine banner sent up from New York, Willard did not have to take a turn on the bally.

The bally and the sale of tickets took about twenty minutes, after which a lesser outside talker than Charlie did what he could to collect a crowd, and Charlie hurried inside, carrying a little cane he used as a pointer. Once in the tent he took on another role, which was called the lecturer, because everything in the World of Wonders was supposed to be improving and educational; Charlie's style underwent a change, too, for outside he was a great joker, whereas inside he was professorial, as he understood the word.

I was much impressed by the fact that almost all the Talent spoke two versions of English—whatever was most comfortable when they were off duty, and a gaudy, begemmed, and gilded rhetoric when they were before the public. Charlie was a master of the impressive introduction when he presented the Talent to an audience.

As spectators bought their tickets they were permitted into the tent, where they walked around and stared until the show began. Sometimes they asked questions, especially of Happy Hannah. 'You will assuredly hear everything in due season,' she would reply. The show was not supposed to begin without Charlie. When he pranced into the tent—he had an exaggeratedly youthful, high-stepping gait—he would summon the crowd around him and begin by introducing Sonny, *the Strongest Man you have ever seen, ladies and gentlemen, and the best-natured giant in the known world.* Poor old Sonny wasn't allowed to speak, because he had a strong German accent, and

Germans were not popular characters in rural Canada in the late summer of 1918. Sonny was not allowed to linger over his demonstration, either, because Charlie was hustling the crowd toward Molza the Human Salamander, who thrust a lighted torch into his mouth, and then blew out a jet of flame which ignited a piece of newspaper Charlie held in his hand; Molza then swallowed swords until he had four of them stuck in his gullet. When I came to know him I got him to show me how to do it, and I can still swallow a paper-knife, or anything not too sharp. But swallowing swords and eating fire are hard ways to get a living, and dangerous after a few years. Then Professor Spencer wrote with his feet, having first demonstrated with some soap and a safety-razor with no blade in it how he shaved himself every day; the Professor would write the name of anybody who wished it; with his right foot he would write from left to right, and at the same time, underneath it and with his left foot, he would write the name from right to left. He wrote with great speed in a beautiful hand—or foot, I should say. It was quite a showy act, but the Professor never had his full due, I thought, because people were rather embarrassed by him. Then the Darks did their knife-throwing act.

It was a very good act, and if only Joe had possessed some instinct of showmanship it would have been much better. But Joe was a very simple soul, a decent, honest fellow who ought to have been a workman of some sort. His talent for throwing knives was one of those freakish things that are sometimes found in people who are otherwise utterly unremarkable. His wife, Emily, was ambitious for him; she wanted him to be a veterinary, and when we were on the train she kept him pegging away at a correspondence course which would, when it was completed, bring him a diploma from some cut-rate college deep in the States. But it was obvious to everybody but Emily that it would never be completed, because Joe couldn't get anything into his head from a printed page. He could throw knives, and that was that. They both wore tacky home-made costumes, which bunched unbecomingly in the wrong places, and Emily stood in front of a pine board while Joe outlined her pleasant figure in knives. Nice people: minor Talent.

By this time the audience had climbed the ladder of marvels to Rango the Missing Link, exhibited by Heinie Bayer. Rango was an orang-outang, who could walk a tightrope carrying a parasol; at the mid-point, he would suddenly swing downward, clinging to the rope with his toes, and reflectively eat a banana; then he would whirl upright, throw away the skin, and complete his journey. After that he sat at a table, and rang a bell, and Heinie, dressed as a clown waiter, served him a meal, which Rango ate with affected elegance, until he was displeased with a badly prepared dish, and pelted Heinie with food. Rango was surefire. Everybody loved him, and I was of their number until I tried to make friends with him and Rango spat some chewed-up nuts in my face. It was part of Heinie's deal with the management that Rango had to share a berth with him in our Pullman; although he was house-trained he was a nuisance because he was a bad sleeper, and likely to stick his hand into your berth in the night an pinch you—a very mean, twisting pinch. It was uncanny to poke your head out of your berth and see Rango swinging along the car, holding on to the tops of the green curtains, as if they were part of his native jungle.

After Rango came Zitta the Jungle Queen. Snake acts are all the same. She pulled the snakes around her neck, wound them around her arms, and as a topper she knelt down and charmed her cobra *by no other power than that of the unaided human eye, with which she exerts hypnotic dominance over this most dreaded of jungle monsters*, as Charlie said, and ended by kissing it on its ugly snout.

This was good showmanship. First the funny side of nature, then the ominous side of nature. The trick, I learned, was that Zitta leaned down to the cobra from above its head; cobras cannot strike upwards. It was a thrill, and Zitta had to know her business. As I grew older and more cynical I sometimes wondered what it would be like if Zitta exercised her hypnotic powers on Rango, and kissed him, for a change. I don't think Rango was a lady's man.

This left only Willard, Andro the Hermaphrodite, and Happy Hannah to complete the show; Zovene the Midget Juggler was only useful to get the audience out of the tent. On the basis of public attraction it was acknowledged that Willard must have the place of honour once Abdullah was on display. Charlie was in favour of giving Andro the place just before Abdullah but Happy Hannah would have none of it. She was clamorous. If a natural, educational wonder like herself, without any gaff about her, didn't take precedence over a gaffed monsterosity she was prepared to leave carnival life and despair of the human race. She made herself so unpleasant that she won the argument; Andro became very shrewish when he was under attack, but he lacked Hannah's large, embracing, Biblical flow of condemnation. When he had said that Hannah was a fat, loud-mouthed old bitch his store of abuse was exhausted; but she sailed into him with all guns firing.

'Don't think I hold it against you personally, Andro. No, I know you for what you are. I know the rock from whence ye are hewn[5]—that no-good bunch o'Boston Greek fish-peddlers and small-time thieves; and I likewise know the hole of the Pit whence ye are digged—offering yourself to stand bare-naked in front of artists, some of 'em women, at fifty cents an hour. So I know it isn't really you that's speaking against me; it's the spirit of an unclean devil inside of you,[6] crying with a loud voice; and I rebuke it just as our dear Lord did; I'm sitting right here, crying, "Hold thy peace and come out of him!" '

This was Hannah's strength. All her immense bulk was crammed with Bible knowledge and quotations and it oozed out of her like currant-juice oozing out of a jelly-bag. She offered herself to the public as a biblical marvel, a sort of she-Leviathan.[7] She would not allow Charlie to speak for her. As soon as he had given her a lead—*And now, ladies and gentlemen, I present Happy Hannah, four hundred and eighty-seven pounds of good*

5 An allusion to Isaiah 51: 1: 'Hearken to me, ye that follow after righteousness, ye that seek the LORD: look unto the rock whence ye are hewn, and to the hole of the pit whence ye are digged.'

6 An allusion to Luke 4: 33: 'And in the synagogue there was a man, which had a spirit of an unclean devil, and cried out with a loud voice, Saying, Let us alone; what have we to do with thee, thou Jesus of Nazareth? art thou come to destroy us? I know thee who thou art; the Holy One of God. And Jesus rebuked him, saying, Hold thy peace, and come out of him. And when the devil had thrown him in the midst, he came out of him, and hurt him not.'

7 A Biblical sea-monster. See Isaiah 27: 1: 'In that day the LORD with his sore and great and strong sword shall punish leviathan the piercing serpent, even leviathan that crooked serpent; and he shall slay the dragon that is in the sea.'

humour and chuckles—she would burst in, 'Yes friends, and I'm the living proof of how fat a person can get and still bear it gladly in the Lord's name. I hope every person here knows his Bible and if they do, they know the comforting message of Proverbs eleven, twenty-five: *The liberal soul shall be made fat.* Yes friends, I am here not as a curiosity and certainly not as a monsterosity but to attest in my daily life and my public career to the Lord's abounding grace. I don't hafta be here; many offers from missionary societies and the biggest evangelists have been turned down in order that I may get around this whole continent and talk to the biggest possible audience of the real people, God's own folks, and attest to the Faith. Portraits of me as you see me now, each one individually autographed by my own hand, may be purchased at twenty-five cents apiece, and for another mere quarter I will include a priceless treasure, this copy of the New Testament which fits in the pocket and in which each and every word uttered by our Lord Jesus Christ during his earthly ministry is printed in RED. No Testament sold except with a portrait. Don't miss this great offer which is made by me at a financial sacrifice in order that the Lord's will may be done more abundantly here in Pumpkin Centre. Don't hang back folks; grab what I'm giving you; I been made fat and when you possess this portrait of me as you see me now and this New Testament you'll hafta admit that I'm certainly the Liberal Soul. Come on, now, who's gonna be the first?"

Hannah was able to hawk her pictures and her Testaments because of an arrangement written into every artiste's contract that they should be allowed to sell something at every show. They made their offer, or Charlie made it for them, as the crowd was about to move on to the next Wonder. The price was always twenty-five cents. Sonny had a book on body-building; Molza had only a picture of himself with his throat full of swords—a very slow item in terms of sales; Professor Spencer offered his personally written visiting cards, which were a nuisance because they took quite a while to prepare; Em Dark sold throwing knives Joe made in his spare time out of small files—a throwing knife has no edge, only a point; Heinie sold pictures of Rango; Zitta offered belts and bracelets which she made out of the skins of the snakes she had mauled to death—though Charlie didn't put it quite like that; Andro was another seller of pictures; Willard sold a pamphlet called *Secrets of Gamblers Revealed*, which was offered by Charlie as an infallible protection against dishonest card-players you might meet on trains; a lot of people bought them who didn't look like travellers, and I judged they wanted to know the secrets of gamblers for some purpose of their own. I read it several times, and it was a stupefyingly uncommunicative little book, written at least thirty years before 1918. The agreement was that each Wonder offered his picture or whatever it might be after he had been exhibited, and that when the show had been completed, except for the Midget Juggler, Charlie would invite the audience once again not to leave without one of *these valuable mementoes of a unique and unforgettable personal experience and educational benefit.*

From being an extremely innocent little boy it did not take me long to become a very knowing little boy. I picked up a great deal as we travelled from village to village on the train, for our Pullman[8] was an educational benefit and certainly, for me, an

8 A railway car with berths for sleeping in.

unforgettable personal experience. I had an upper berth at the very end of the car, at some distance from Willard, whose importance in the show secured him a lower in the area where the shock of the frequent shuntings and accordion-like contractions of the train were least felt. I came to know who had bottles of liquor, and also who was generous with it and who kept it for his own use. I knew that neither Joe nor Em Dark drank, because it would have been ruinous indulgence for a knife-thrower. The Darks, however, were young and vigorous, and sometimes the noises from their berth were enough to raise comment from the other Talent. I remember one night when Heinie, who shared his bottle with Rango, put Rango up to opening the curtains of the Darks' upper; Em screamed, and Joe grabbed Rango and threw him down into the aisle so hard that Rango screamed; Heinie offered to fight Joe, and Joe, stark naked and very angry, chased Heinie back to his berth and pummelled him. It took a full hour to soothe Rango; Heinie assured us that Rango was used to love and could not bear rough usage; Rango had to have at least two strong swigs of straight rye before he could sleep. But in the rough-and-tumble I had had a good look at Em Dark naked, and it was very different from Happy Hannah, I can assure you. All sorts of things that I had never heard of began, within a month, to whirl and surge and combine in my mind.

A weekly event of some significance in our Pullman was Hannah's Saturday-night bath. She lived in continual hope of managing it without attracting attention, but that was ridiculous. First Gus would bustle down the aisle with a large tarpaulin and an armful of towels. Then Hannah, in an orange mobcap[9] and a red dressing-gown, would lurch and stumble down the car; she was too big to fall into anybody's berth, but she sometimes came near to dragging down the green curtains when we were going around a bend. We all knew what happened in the Ladies' Retiring Room; Gus spread the tarpaulin, Hannah stood on it hanging onto the wash-basin, and Gus swabbed her down with a large sponge. It was for this service of Christian charity that she was called Elephant Gus when she was out of earshot. Drying Hannah took a long time, because there were large portions of her that she could not reach herself, and Gus used to towel her down, making a hissing noise between her teeth, like a groom.

Sometimes Charlie and Heinie and Willard would be sitting up having a game of poker, and while the bath was in progress they would sing a hymn, 'Wash me and I shall be whiter than snow'. If they were high they had another version—

Wash me in the water
  That you washed the baby in,
And I shall be whiter
  Than the whitewash on the wall.

This infuriated Hannah, and on her return trip she would favour them with a few Biblical admonitions; she had a good deal to say about lasciviousness, lusts, excess of wine, revellings, banquetings, games of hazard, and abominable idolatries, out of First

9 A large, soft, frilly cap covering all of the hair, worn indoors by women in the eighteenth and early nineteenth centuries.

Peter.[10] But she hocussed the text. There is no mention of 'games of hazard' or gambling anywhere in the Bible. She put that in for her own particular satisfaction. I knew it, and I soon recognized Hannah as my first hypocrite. A boy's first recognition of hypocrisy is, or ought to be, more significant than the onset of puberty. By the time Gus had stowed her into her special lower, which was supported from beneath with a few fence-posts, she was so refreshed by anger that she fell asleep at once, and snored so that she could be heard above the noise of the train.

Very soon I became aware that the World of Wonders which had been a revelation to me, and I suppose to countless other country village people, was a weary bore to the Talent. This is the gnawing canker of carnival life: it is monstrously boring.

Consider. We did ten complete shows a day; we had an hour off for midday food and another hour between six and seven; otherwise it was unremitting. We played an average of five days a week, which means fifty shows. We began our season as early as we could, but nothing much was stirring in the outdoor carnival line till mid-May, and after that we traipsed across country playing anywhere and everywhere—I soon stopped trying to know the name of the towns, and called them all Pumpkin Centre, like Willard—until late October. That makes something over a thousand shows. No wonder the Talent was bored. No wonder Charlie's talks began to sound as if he was thinking about something else.

The only person who wasn't bored was Professor Spencer. He was a decent man, and couldn't give way to boredom, because his affliction meant perpetual improvisation in the details of his life. For instance, he had to get somebody to help him in the donniker, which most of us were ready to do, but wouldn't have done if he had not always been cheerful and fresh. He offered to teach me some lessons, because he said it was a shame for a boy to leave school as early as I had done. So he taught me writing, and arithmetic, and an astonishing amount of geography. He was the one man on the show who had to know where we were, what the population of the town was, the name of the mayor, and other things that he wrote on his blackboard as part of his show. He was a good friend to me, was Professor Spencer. Indeed, it was he who persuaded Willard to teach me magic.

Willard had not been interested in doing that, or indeed anything, for me. I was necessary, but I was a nuisance. I have never met anyone in my life who was so bleakly and unconsciously selfish as Willard, and for one whose life has been spent in the theatre and carnival world that is a strong statement. But Professor Spencer nagged him into it—you could not shame or bully or cajole Willard into anything, but he was open to nagging—and he began to show me a few things with cards and coins. As my years with the World of Wonders wore on, I think what he taught me saved my reason. Certainly it is at the root of anything I can do now.

Whoever taught Willard did it very well. He never gave names to the things he taught me, and I am sure he didn't know them. But since that time I have found that

10 See 1 Peter 4: 1–3: 'Forasmuch then as Christ hath suffered for us in the flesh, arm yourselves likewise with the same mind: for he that hath suffered in the flesh hath ceased from sin; That he no longer should live the rest of his time in the flesh to the lusts of men, but to the will of God. For the time past of our life may suffice us to have wrought the will of the Gentiles, when we walked in lasciviousness, lusts, excess of wine, revellings, banquetings, and abominable idolatries.'

he taught me all there is to know about shuffling, forcing, and passing cards, and palming, ruffling, changing, and bridging, and the wonders of the *biseauté*[11] pack, which is really the only trick pack worth having. With coins he taught me all the basic work of palming and passing, the French drop, *La Pincette, La Coulée,* and all the other really good ones. His ideal among magicians was Nelson Downs, whose great act, The Miser's Dream, he had seen at the Palace Theatre, New York, which was the paradise of his limited imagination. Indeed, it was a very much debased version of The Miser's Dream that he had been doing when I first saw him. He now did little conjuring in the World of Wonders, because of the ease of managing Abdullah.

Inside Abdullah I was busy for perhaps five minutes in every hour. My movement was greatly restricted; I could not make a noise. What was I to do? I practised my magic, and for hours on end I palmed coins and developed my hands in the dark, and that is how I gained the technique which has earned me the compliment of this film you gentlemen are making. I recommend the method to young magicians; get yourself into a close-fitting prison for ten hours a day, and do nothing but manipulate cards and coins; keep that up for a few years and, unless you are constitutionally incapable, like poor Ramsay here, you should develop some adroitness, and you will at least have no chance to acquire the principal fault of the bad magician, which is looking at your hands as you work. That was how I avoided boredom: constant practice, and entranced observation, through Abdullah's bosom, of the public and the Talent of the World of Wonders.

Boredom is rich soil for every kind of rancour and ugliness. In my first months on the show this attached almost entirely to the fortunes of the War. I knew nothing about the War, although as a schoolchild I had been urged to bring all my family's peachstones to school, where they were collected for some warlike purpose. Knowing boys said that a terrible poison gas was made from them. Every morning in prayers our teacher mentioned the Allied Forces, and especially the Canadian. Once again knowing boys said you could always tell where her brother Jim was by the prayer, which was likely to contain a special reference to 'our boys at the Front', and later, 'our boys in the rest camps', and later still, 'our boys in the hospitals'. The War hung over my life like the clouds in the sky, and I heeded it as little. Once I saw Ramsay in the street, in what I later realized was the uniform of a recruit, but at the time I couldn't understand why he was wearing such queer clothes. I saw men in the streets with black bands on their arms, and asked my father why they wore them, but I can't remember what he answered.

In the World of Wonders the War seemed likely at times to tear the show to pieces. The only music on the fairgrounds where we appeared came from the merry-go-round; tunes were fed into its calliope by the agency of large steel discs, perforated with rectangular holes; they worked on the same principle as the roll of a player-piano, but were much more durable, and rotated instead of uncoiling. Most of the music was of the variety we associate with merry-go-rounds. Who wrote it? Italians, I suspect, for it always had a gentle, quaintly melodious quality, except for one new tune which Steve,

11 Forcing and the other manoeuvres named here are sleight-of-hand moves done with cards; they can be found described in standard texts on magic. Similarly palming, the French drop, and the like are basic sleight-of-hand moves with coins. A biseauté pack is a deck of marked cards. The Miser's Dream is a set piece of stage magic in which coins are produced, through sleight of hand, from the ears, nose, etc., of a volunteer brought on stage.

who ran the machine, had bought to give the show a modern air. It was the American war song—by that noisy fellow Cohan, was it?—called 'Over There!'. It was less than warlike on a calliope, played at merry-go-round tempo, but everybody recognized it, and now and then some Canadian wag would sing loudly, to the final phrase—

And we won't be over
Till it's over
Over there!

If Hannah heard this, she became furious, for she was an inflamed American patriot and the War, for her, had begun when the Americans entered it in 1917. The Darks were Canadians, and not as tactful as Canadians usually are when dealing with their American cousins. I remember Em Dark, who was a most unlikely person to tell a joke, saying one midday, in September of 1918, when the Talent was in the dressing tent, eating its hasty picnic: 'I heard a good one yesterday. This fellow says, Say, why are the American troops called Doughboys? And the other fellow says, Gee, I dunno; why? And the first fellow says, It's because they were needed in 1914 but they didn't rise till 1917. Do you get it? Needed, you, see, like kneading bread, and—' But Em wasn't able to continue with her explanation of the joke because Hannah threw a sandwich at her and told her to knead that, and she was sick and tired of ingratitude from the folks in a little, two-bit backwoods country where they still had to pay taxes to the English King, and hadn't Em heard about the Argonne and the American blood that was being shed there by the bucketful, and how did Em think they would make the Hun say Uncle anyways with a lot of fat-headed Englishmen and Frenchmen messing it all up, and what they needed over there was American efficiency and American spunk?

Em didn't have a chance to reply, because Hannah was immediately in trouble with Sonnenfels and Heinie Bayer, who smouldered under a conviction that Germany was hideously wronged and that everybody was piling on the Fatherland without any cause at all, and though they were just as good Americans as anybody they were damn well sick of it and hoped the German troops would show Pershing[12] something new about efficiency. Charlie tried to quiet them down by saying that everybody knew the War was a put-up job and nobody was getting anything out of it but the Big Interests. This was a mistake, because Sonny and Heinie turned on him and told him that they knew why he was so glad to be in Canada, and if they were younger men they'd be in the scrap and they weren't going to say which side they'd be on, neither, but if they met anything like Charlie on the battlefield they'd just put a chain on him and show him off beside Rango.

The battle went on for weeks, during which Joe Dark suffered the humiliation of having Em tell everybody that he wasn't in the Canadian Army because he had flat feet, and Hannah replying that you didn't need feet to fly a plane, but you sure needed brains. The only reasonable voice was that of Professor Spencer, who was a great reader of the papers, and an independent thinker; he was all for an immediate armistice and a peace conference. But as nobody wanted to listen to him, he lectured me, instead, so

12 John J. Pershing (1860–1948), the US general who commanded the US Expeditionary Force in the First World War.

that I still have a very confused idea of the causes of that War, and the way it was fought. Hannah got a Stars and Stripes from somewhere, and stuck it up on her little platform. She said it made her feel good just to have it there.

It all came about because of boredom. Boredom and stupidity and patriotism, especially when combined, are three of the greatest evils of the world we live in. But a worse and more lasting source of trouble was the final show in each village, which was called the Last Trick.

It was agreed that the Last Trick ought to be livelier than the other nine shows of the day. The fair was at its end, the serious matters like the judging of animals and fancy-work had been completed, and most of the old folks had gone home, leaving young men and their girls, and the village cutups on the fairground. It was then that the true, age-old Spirit of Carnival descended on Wanless's World of Wonders, but of course it didn't affect everybody in the same way. Outside, the calliope was playing its favourite tune, 'The Poor Butterfly Waltz'; supposedly unknown to Gus, the man who ran the cat-rack had slipped in the gaff, so that the eager suitor who was trying to win a Kewpie Doll for the girl of his heart by throwing baseballs found that the stuffed pussy-cats wouldn't be knocked down. It was a sleazier, crookeder fair altogether than the one the local Fair Board had planned, but there was always a young crowd that liked it that way.

On the bally, Charlie allowed his wit a freer play. As Zovene juggled with his spangled Indian clubs, Charlie would say, in a pretended undertone which carried well beyond his audience: 'Pretty good, eh? He isn't big, but he's good. Anyways, how big would you be if you'd been strained through a silk handkerchief?' The young bloods would guffaw at this, and their girls would clamour to have it explained to them. And when Zitta showed her snakes, she would drag the old cobra suggestively between her legs and up her front, while Charlie whispered, 'Boys-oh-boys, who wouldn't be a snake?'

Inside the tent Charlie urged the young men to model themselves on Sonnenfels, so that all the girls would be after them, and they'd be up to the job. And when he came to Andro he would ogle his hearers and say, 'He's the only guy in the world who's glad to wake up in the morning and find he's beside himself.' He particularly delighted in tormenting Hannah. She did her own talking, but as she shrieked her devotion to the Lord Jesus, Charlie would lean down low, and say, in a carrying whisper, 'She hasn't seen her ace o' spades in twenty years.' The burst of laughter made Hannah furious, though she never caught what was said. She knew, however, that it was something dirty. However often she complained to Gus, and however often Gus harangued Charlie, the Spirit of Carnival was always too much for him. Nor was Gus whole-hearted in her complaints; what pleased the crowd was what Gus liked.

Hannah attempted to fight fire with fire. She often made it known, in the Pullman, that in her opinion these modern kids weren't bad kids, and if you gave them a chance they didn't want this Sex and all like that. Sure, they wanted fun, and she knew how to give 'em fun. She was just as fond of fun as anybody, but she didn't see the fun in all this Smut and Filth. So she gave 'em fun.

'Lots o'fun in your Bible, boys and girls,' she would shout. 'Didn't you know that? Didya think the Good Book was all serious? You just haven't read it with the Liberal

Heart, that's all. Come on now! Come on now, all of you! Who can tell me why you wouldn't dare to take a drink outa the first river in Eden? Come on, I bet ya know. Sure ya know. You're just too shy to say. Why wouldn't ya take a drink outa the first river in Eden?—Because it was Pison, that's why! If you don't believe me, look in Genesis two, eleven.' Then she would go off into a burst of wheezing laughter.

Or she would point—and with an arm like hers, pointing was no trifling effort—at Zovene, shouting: 'You call him small? Say, he's a regular Goliath compared with the shortest man in the Bible. Who was he? Come on, who was he?—He was Bildad the Shu-hite, Job two, eleven. See, the Liberal Heart can even get a laugh outa one of Job's Comforters. I betcha never thought of that, eh?' And again, one of her terrible bursts of laughter.

Hannah understood nothing of the art of the comedian. It is dangerous to laugh at your own jokes, but if you must, it is a great mistake to laugh first. Fat people, when laughing, are awesome sights, enough to strike gravity into the onlooker. But Hannah was a whole World of Wonders in herself when she laughed. She forced her laughter, for after all, when you have told people for weeks that the only man in the Bible with no parents was Joshua, the son of Nun, the joke loses some of its savour. So she pushed laughter out of herself in wheezing, whooping cries, and her face became unpleasantly marbled with dabs of a darker red under the rouge she wore. Her collops wobbled uncontrollably, her vast belly heaved and trembled as she sucked her breath, and sometimes she attempted to slap her thigh, producing a wet splat of sound. Fat Ladies ought not to tell jokes; their mirth is of the flesh, not of the mind. Fat Ladies ought not to laugh; a chuckle is all they can manage without putting a dangerous strain on their breathing and circulatory system. But Hannah would not listen to reason. She was determined to drive Smut back into its loathsome den with assaults of Clean Fun, and if she damaged herself in the battle, her wounds would be honourable.

Sometimes she had an encouraging measure of success. Quite often there would be in the crowd some young man who was of a serious, religious turn of mind, and usually he was accompanied by a girl who had preacher's daughter written all over her. They had been embarrassed by Charlie's jokes when they understood them. They had been even more embarrassed when Rango, at a secret signal from Heinie, left his pretended restaurant table and urinated in a corner, while Heinie pantomimed a waiter's dismay. But with that camaraderie which exists among religious people just as it does among tinhorns[13] and crooks, they recognized Hannah as a benign influence, and laughed with her, and urged her on to greater flights. She gave them her best. 'What eight fellas in the Bible milked a bear? You know! You musta read it a dozen times. D'ya give it up? Well, listen carefully: Huz, Buz, Kemuel, Chesed, Hazo, Pildash, Jidlaph, and Bethuel—*these eight did Milcah bear to Nahor, Abraham's brother*. Didya never think of it that way? Eh? Didn't ya? Well, it's in Genesis twenty-two.'

When one of these obviously sanctified couples appeared, it was Hannah's pleasure to single them out and hold them up to the rest of the crowd as great cutups. 'Oh, I see ya,' she would shout; 'it's the garden of Eden all over again; the trouble isn't with

13 Someone pretending to have money, influence, or ability; a fraud.

the apple in the tree, it's with that pair on the ground.' And she would point at them, and they would blush and laugh and be grateful to be given a reputation for wickedness without having to do anything to acquire it.

All of this cost Hannah dearly. After a big Saturday night, when she had exhausted her store of Bible riddles, she was almost too used up for her ritual bath. But she had worked herself up into a shocking sweat, and sometimes the smell of wet cornstarch from her sopping body spread a smell like a gigantic nursery pudding through the whole of the tent, and bathed she had to be, or there would be trouble with chafing.

Her performance on these occasions made Willard deeply, cruelly angry. He would stand beside Abdullah and I could hear him swearing, repetitively but with growing menace, as she carried on. The worst of it was, if she secured any sort of success, she was not willing to stop; even when the crowd had passed on to see Abdullah, she would continue, at somewhat lesser pitch, with a few lingerers, who hoped for more Bible fun. In the Last Trick it was Willard's custom to have three people cut the cards for the automaton, instead of the usual one, and he wanted the undivided attention of the crowd. He hated Hannah, and from my advantageous peephole I was not long in coming to the conclusion that Hannah hated him.

There were plenty of places in southern Ontario at that time where religious young people were numerous, and in these communities Hannah did not scruple to give a short speech in which she looked forward to seeing them next year, and implored them to join her in a parting hymn. 'God be with you till we meet again,' she would strike up, in her thin, piercing voice, like a violin string played unskilfully and without a vibrato, and there were always those who, from religious zeal or just because they liked to sing, would join her. Nor was one verse enough. Charlie would strike in, as boldly as he could: *And now, ladies and gentlemen, our Master Marvel of the World of Wonders—Willard the Wizard and his Card-Playing Automaton, Abdullah, as soon to be exhibited on the stage of the Palace Theatre, New York*—but Hannah would simply put on more steam, and slow down, and nearly everybody in the tent would be wailing—

God be with you till we meet again!
Keep love's banner floating o'er you,
Smite death's threatening wave before you:
God be with you till we meet again!

And then the whole dismal chorus. It was a hymn of hate, and Willard met it with such hate as I have rarely seen.

As for me, I was only a child, and my experience of hatred was slight, but so far as I could, and with what intensity of spirit I could muster, I hated them both. Hate and bitterness were becoming the elements in which I lived.

1975

W.O. Mitchell

1914–1998

Basing his novels, stories, and plays on his own experience of life in rural Saskatchewan, William Ormond Mitchell became one of Canada's most popular authors. A major novelist, a writer of a popular series for Canadian radio and television, an accomplished playwright, and a famous raconteur, Mitchell was an all-round performer who, as a self-described 'folksy old Foothills fart', travelled the lecture circuit like a Canadian Mark Twain. (A collection of his performance pieces appeared in 1997 as *An Evening with W.O. Mitchell.*) In the tradition of Twain (for whom he had a high regard) and of Haliburton and Leacock, he cast his highly crafted narratives as popular tales in order to 'hit a serious balance' between art and entertainment.

Born in Weyburn, Sask., Mitchell contracted tuberculosis as a boy and for health reasons spent four of his teenage years in the United States (first in California, then Florida), returning to Canada each summer. In 1931 he enrolled in the University of Manitoba, leaving before he completed the degree to travel and work in western Canada and the northwestern US. During the thirties he picked up a number of odd jobs, chiefly in sales, though he also did a bit of acting. In 1941 he completed his BA at the University of Alberta, earning a teaching certificate the following year. While a student at Alberta, he began writing *Who Has Seen the Wind* in a creative-writing course taught by Professor F.M. Salter. (Salter's influence on two generations of western writers has been significant: his students also included Sheila Watson and Rudy Wiebe.) Impressed with his potential, Salter took Mitchell under his wing—tutoring him on the writer's craft, working with him on drafts, and ultimately shepherding his first stories (they were actually fragments from what became *Who Has Seen the Wind*) into the *Atlantic Monthly*, at that time, the leading magazine for serious fiction in North America. Edward Weeks, the editor of the *Atlantic*, impressed with how the first of these stories, 'The Owl and the Bens', captured 'the raw authentic vigor of Canada', showed it to Wallace Stegner, himself an outstanding western novelist, who expressed great admiration.

With his success in publishing his stories in magazines such as *Atlantic* and the old *Maclean's*, Mitchell realized that he could support himself from his fiction and, in 1944, quit teaching to write full-time, publishing *Who Has Seen the Wind* in 1947. In contrast with the serious and often tragic quality of earlier Canadian fiction associated with the prairies—in which the landscape always seems to threaten its inhabitants—Mitchell's novel combined good-natured humour with a Wordsworthian vision of a nature that enlightens and heals. It has since become, along with *Anne of Green Gables*, one of the bestselling Canadian novels of all time.

In 1948 Mitchell moved to Toronto to serve as the fiction editor at *Maclean's*. During his years in Toronto he became intensely involved with the popular media, and, drawing on the gentle rural comedy and colourful characterization that he had mastered in *Who Has Seen the Wind*, he created 'Jake and the Kid' in 1949, a radio series that eventually ran for 320 episodes. After it ended in 1957, a television production of 'Jake and the Kid' ran in 1961. A collection of *Jake and the Kid* stories published that year won the Stephen Leacock Medal for Humour.

Mitchell returned to Alberta in 1951, where he remained except for intervals of teaching creative writing outside the province. He was writer-in-residence at various universities, including Calgary, Alberta, York, Toronto, and Windsor, and he regularly taught creative writing at the Banff School of Fine Arts, serving as the director of the writing program from 1983 to 1985. At Banff he would encourage beginning writers to write down any narrative, especially any memories of the past, that occurred to them, telling them not to try to shape stories out of the material until later: he called that technique 'freefall', and sometimes jokingly referred to it as 'Mitchell's messy method'.

Mitchell's sense that something like 'freefall' was needed as a way to unblock a novelist's creativity may have reflected his own difficulty in following up on his success with *Who Has Seen the Wind.* His second novel, *The Kite,* did not appear until 1962; his third, *The Vanishing Point,* not until 1973. That third novel was a revision of an unpublished work he had long struggled with—*The Alien,* parts of which had been serialized in *Maclean's* in 1953 and 1954. It was only in his later years that Mitchell began to publish new fiction regularly. *How I Spent My Summer Holidays* (1981) is a coming-of-age story about a twelve-year-old boy in 1920s Saskatchewan: though it revisits the theme of lost innocence central to *Who Has Seen The Wind,* the nostalgic and humorous reminiscences characteristic of the earlier work give way to darker, occasionally violent, overtones. The four novels that followed, *Since Daisy Creek* (1984), *Ladybug, Ladybug . . .* (1988), *For Art's Sake* (1992), and *Roses Are Difficult Here* (1990), all revolve around older characters (three of them university professors) coming to terms with their aging. In *Since Daisy Creek* and *Roses Are Difficult Here* characters from Mitchell's earlier fiction return, confirming the reader's sense that his literary universe is an imagined continuum, an autonomous prairie world of the mind that stretches from the 1930s to the 1990s. Mitchell also published a second collection of his Jake and the Kid stories, *According to Jake and the Kid* (1989): in 1990 a taped version of Mitchell reading seven of these stories was released.

Mitchell had a substantial career as a playwright ranging from his many radio dramas to several plays produced on stage in his later years. *Dramatic W.O. Mitchell* (1982) draws together five of these, including *The Black Bonspiel of Wullie MacCrimmon,* a radio drama that was originally produced in 1951 and that Mitchell later rewrote and published as a novella in 1993.

Underlying everything Mitchell wrote, there is a prairie sense of man and nature at odds in a constantly shifting balance. But if Mitchell's fiction does portray a struggle to endure, that struggle is tempered by the comic vision of a man who believed that 'there are no total victories; there are no total defeats. You end up accepting that life involves dilemma, contradiction, and no absolutes or simplicities'. Resolution therefore gives way to cyclic renewal; finality is replaced by fleeting victories that must be won repeatedly. Mitchell's sense of a cycle that brings both loss and gain, a 'next-year' outlook that is endemic to prairie life, led him to treat life as a serious comedy in which ironic amusement is necessary if one is to stay sane. His ideal qualities may be those he saw in Jake, the creative liar: 'He's graceful, and he's got a sense of climax, and he's got a sense of humour, and he's got a sense of illusion.'

The way Mitchell constructed narratives out of episodic personal recollections coupled with his comic sense of a cyclic pattern gave all his fiction the diffuse structure of oral narrative. Indeed, his stories bring together the qualities of the folk tale and of that kind of local gossip that seems to need retelling because of its deeper truths. Later writers such as Robert Kroetsch, Jack Hodgins, and Thomas Wharton have followed Mitchell's lead, creating similarly artful narratives that draw energy from this oral and tall-tale quality of western story-telling.

Who Has Seen the Wind

Mitchell's novel opens with one of the great descriptions of prairie landscape: 'Here was the least common denominator of nature, the skeleton requirements simply, of land and sky—Saskatchewan prairie.' Yet *Who Has Seen the Wind* does not prove to be a story about the determining quality of environment: it describes instead the young Brian O'Connal's struggle to understand the metaphysical dimensions of this world, and it shows how the various individuals he encounters help him think through his questions about life.

The novel takes its title from a Christina Rossetti poem that suggests we know God indirectly, through his effects in the visible world ('Who has seen the wind? / Neither you nor I: / But when the trees bow down their heads / The wind is passing by')—and it shows Brian responding intensely and intuitively to the nature he finds whenever he enters the 'sudden emptiness' of the prairie stretching out like an ocean on all sides of his little town. As well, the dwellers out on that prairie have an intense effect on him. These include a family of outsiders, known as the Bens, and 'Saint Sammy', who has lost all that he once had and has taken shelter in a large crate. The Old Ben, the head of his clan, is a man who brews and sells illegal liquor, the kind of rogue that Mitchell loved to portray—a 'drunken, irresponsible and utterly mindless' individual who is 'always at odds with some law or convention': in one of the most comic scenes in the novel his still, hidden in the basement of the church, explodes, causing him to be briefly jailed. But it is his son, the Young Ben, who is of especial importance to the story: no less imprisoned by being forced to go to school, he proves to be a conduit for Brian's sense of nature as a redemptive and even visionary agent.

Unlike the Bens, who have always lived outside society, Saint Sammy moved out onto the 'bald prairie' when he could no longer sustain his place within the social order. Transformed from an ordinary member of the farm community into a madman tending a herd of cows and untamed horses with Biblical names, collecting labels and match boxes, and ranting in a high rhetoric drawn from the Old Testament prophets, the Book of Job, the Gospels, and the Book of Revelation, Sammy allows Mitchell to suggest that insanity is the individual's final refuge when life's travails become too overwhelming: 'Yearsa gittin' rusted out an saw flied out an' cutwormed out an' hoppered out an' hailed out an' droughted out an' rusted out an' smutted out; he up an' got good an' goddam tired out. Crazier'n a cut calf.'

However, even though—or perhaps because—Sammy is 'either childlike, senile, or gently insane', he is able to protect himself and his horses from the acquisitiveness of the comic villain of the novel, Bent Candy. Sammy's prophecies of God's vengeance seem fulfilled in the windstorm that flattens Candy's barn and reawakens in Candy a belief in a Providence that protects and punishes.

Saint Sammy's first appearance in print preceded the publication of *Who Has Seen the Wind.* It came in a story called 'Saint Sammy', which appeared in the *Atlantic Monthly* in 1945. In a letter to the managing editor of the magazine, Mitchell explained something of his intentions:

I have made liberal use of religious symbolism in the prairie descriptions before and after the Lord's coming. . . . My aim has been to create in the reader the same feeling of incongruity he would feel in talking with an actual dementia praecox case, hence . . . the pun on hail, the deliberate unseating of dignity from time to time.

Not all of my characters are odd . . . but the nature of 'Who Has Seen the Wind' had dictated these particular people. It is a story of the influence on a boy of the prairie and his search for God. The Young Ben is used as a foil for him, and his acquaintance with Saint Sammy comes at a time when his conception of God is much that of Sammy's. (Quoted in Barbara and Ormand Mitchell, *W.O.: The Life of W.O. Mitchell*)

The text that follows is based on the 1991 edition of *Who Has Seen the Wind,* which reprints the original 1947 Canadian version of the novel (adding to it illustrations later made by the prairie artist William Kurelek). The first American edition of the novel (which appeared a few months before the Canadian edition) was shortened in a way that toned down Mitchell's vigorous portrayals of prairie characters. Until the Canadian edition was brought back into print in 1991, this shorter American edition had been used for all subsequent Canadian reprints.

From *Who Has Seen the Wind*

Saint Sammy

Saint Sammy, Jehovah's Hired Man, lifted the sacking from the front of his piano box and looked out over the prairie sweeping to the horizon's bare finality.

Today was the fifth day.

The first day after Bent Candy's visit had not been the day; the Lord had been busy; for one thing he had been lightening and darkening His earth by slipping the melting edges of slow clouds over the prairie.

The second day after Mr Candy's visit had not been the day. Saint Sammy had known that as he walked to the corner of the poplar pole corral, one shoulder high, walking as though he had a spring under one heel. Far to the West, he decided, the Lord was occupied with a honing wind and a black dust-storm that needed His attention.

The third day after Bent Candy's visit had not been the day. That day there had been no frightened feeling in the pit of Sammy's stomach. So the third day had not been the day.

Nor was the fourth day. That day had been the Lord's hail day. He had been mixing up a batch of hail. Hail to the Lord that was mixing hail! Hail to the bunging brown grasshopper that leaped! Hail to his bulging shanks! Hail to Saint Sammy too!

Today, the fifth day, was the day. As he watched Habbakuk and Haggar cropping the grass by the empty wagon box and the others, Hannah, Naomi, Ruth, Hosea, Joel, Malachi, and the two colts, Corinthians One and Two, in the far corner of the pasture, Saint Sammy knew that today was the Lord's day to punish Bent Candy. The Lord wasn't letting him get any Clydes![1]

Bent Candy, the caterpillar man,[2] had added another five sections to his holdings that year; he had put all his land into flax, and with his usual luck had managed to have a moderate amount of rain fall on his crops. Some of it was burned, but most of it would still return him enough to show a profit, small though it was. He was called the Flax King now.

As Sammy walked over the prairie toward the Lord's corner of the pasture he was aware of a rising wind in the grasses; the stitching ring of crickets was in his ears like the pulsing of his own blood. He heard a meadow lark sing. A gopher squeaked.

Whatever the Lord did to Bent Candy, it would serve him right; he ought to have known better than to fool around with the Lord and Saint Sammy. Going to church and passing the collection plate were not going to help him now; it hadn't helped the Pharisees.[3] After the Lord had smited him for coveting the Clydes, Bent Candy wouldn't be called the Flax King any longer.

Time and again since Candy had first made an offer for the horses Sammy had been visited by the voice of the Lord, reminding him always of the day ten years ago.

1 Clydesdales, a breed of large, powerful draft horses.

2 So called because of his Caterpillar tractor. A section is one square mile (640 acres) of agricultural land.

3 Members of a Jewish sect who, in the New Testament period, emphasized strict observance of religious laws; because of their treatment in the Gospels, they have come to be synonymous with religious hypocrisy.

That had been the bad hail year, when Sammy had stood on the edge of his ruined crop, looking at the countless broken wheat heads lying down their stalks.

As he had stared, the wind turning upon itself had built up a black body from the top soil, had come whirling toward him in a smoking funnel that snatched up tumbleweeds, lifting them and rolling them over in its heart. The voice of the Lord had spoken to him.

'Sammy, Sammy, ontuh your fifty-bushed crop have I sent hail stones the size a baseballs. The year before did I send the cutworm which creepeth an' before that the rust which rusteth an' the saw-fly which saweth.

'Be you not downcast, fer I have prepared a place fer you. Take with you Miriam and Immaculate Holstein and also them Clydes. Go you to Magnus Petersen, who is even now pumping full his stock trought. He will give ontuh you his south eighty fer pasture, and there will you live to the end of your days when I shall take you up in the twinkling of an eye.

'But I say ontuh you, Sammy, I say this—don't ever sell them Clydes, fer without them ye shall not enter. I will take them up with you when I shall fill the air with Cherubim an' Serubim from here to the correction line.[4]

'Even as I did ontuh Elijah an' Elisha an' John, will I speak ontuh you just liken now. So git, Sammy—git to Magnus Petersen before he's finished of pumping full that stock trought an' shall commence to stook the oats which I have made ready for him.

'There will you find the box off of Miss Henchbaw's piannah, which Magnus will give ontuh you together with his stone boat[5] fer hawlin' it.

'Hail, Saint Sammy!' the Lord had said. 'Hail, Jehovah's Hired Man!

'Mr Candy must not get the Clydes!'

And today was the Lord's smiting day, decided Sammy as he walked over the prairie to the Lord's corner. It was a perfect smiting day.

Ahead of Saint Sammy the sun had haloed the soft heads of foxtails bending in the rising wind; it glistened from the amber wings of a red-bodied dragon-fly hovering; it gleamed from the shrunken surface of the slough. High in the sky a goshawk hung, over the prairie flat as the palm of a suppliant hand, inscrutable and unsmiling, patched dark with summer fallow, strung long with the black crosses of telephone poles marching to the prairie's rim.

The vengeance of the Lord upon Bent Candy would be awful. Mr Candy would wish he'd never tried to get Saint Sammy's horses; he'd wish he had never ordered them off the Petersen pasture. The vengeance of the Lord would be enough to give a badger the heartburn.

Saint Sammy thought of the day that Bent Candy had called on him. He had climbed under the barbed wire and had said, 'I come to see was you gonna sell them there Clydes.'

4 A correction made along the longitudinal line of a survey to compensate for the curvature of the earth. On the prairies, because north-south roads and boundary lines are generally laid out along survey lines, they periodically turn east-west along the correction line. 'Serubim' is a malapropism for 'seraphim', the highest order of angels.

5 A flat-bottomed sled used for removing stones from fields.

'Over the breadth a the earth there ain't no horses like mine!' Saint Sammy cried, 'an' the voice a the Lord come ontuh me sayin', "Sammy, Sammy, don't you sell them there Clydes." An' moreover I say ontuh you, I ain't!'

'Like I thought. Figgered to give you one more chance. You ain't takin' it. Got a week to git off of here.'

Saint Sammy's mouth made a little round hole in his grey beard, and as he looked into Bent Candy's expressionless red face under white hair, the wildness of panic came to his eyes. 'All a this here land was give ontuh me an' the Herb thereoff fer me an' my critters! Magnus Petersen he—'

'Sold her.'

'But—the Lord, He wouldn't—'

'No blaspheemy. Sell er git off. My land now. Them horses ain't no good to anybody—way they are. You ain't broke 'em. You don't work 'em. Sell er git off!'

'But—Magnus—he wouldn't—'

'He did.'

'From here to the ridge there ain't no pasture fer—the Lord hath mighty lightnin', Bent Candy.'

'Mebee He has.'

'An' He moves in—'

'Sell er git off!'

'The Lord hit a man I knew an' it come to pass between the well an' the back stoop an' the Lord's lightnin' burnt every stitch of clothin' from off of him an' left him standin' bare-naked with a bucket of water in each hand—once.'

'I got no time to listen—'

'An' his wife she arose an' she went fer tuh emp'y the slop pail an' she was sore afraid when she saw him there an' she yelled an' he come to with a great start an' spilt the water from them red-hot buckets over him an' got scalded nigh ontuh death.'

'You got a week.'

'The Lord will—'

'Sell er git off!'

After Mr Candy had gone, Saint Sammy had been afraid. He had gone into his piano box and lain there. He plunged his hand deep into the raw sheep's wool and binder twine bits to bring out the tin box with its broken glass and pebbles and twigs and empty match boxes and labels. He had counted them as he always counted when troubled. Count your labels, count them one by one.

It did not help. He put the red and blue underwear labels back, and for a long time he watched the wedge face of a field mouse sitting just outside the piano box opening.

When the fence post shadows lay long over the prairie and the whole pasture was transfigured with the dying light of day, he went out to milk Miriam and turn the calf loose on Immaculate. Then he started across the prairie to Bent Candy's. He found him in the act of rolling gasoline barrels off his truck, that stood by the barn. It was a new barn, hip-roofed and painted red, a thing of beauty and pride. One looked at the flawless red siding and felt as a child must feel in gazing upon a new, red wagon. The metal runner and pulleys on the broad door were hardly rusted yet, since Candy had built the barn only that spring. It was the barn that was to become the home of Saint Sammy's Clydes, a barn built by a man who did his farming by tractor, and who, although he had no use for horses, had been obsessed for years by a desire to possess Sammy's.

He turned upon Saint Sammy. 'Whatta you want?'

'I come to see would you—ain't there any way me an' my critters could dwell on—'

'Jist sell me them ten head a horses—stay as long as you please.'

'But—the Lord He won't take me up in the twink—'

'You got a week.'

'The Lord might knock yer flax flatter'n a platter a—'

'You heard me.'

Saint Sammy's long arm came slowly up, and the finger pointed at Bent Candy, trembled. 'The glory of the Lord come out a the East an' His voice was the wind a-comin' over the prairie's far rim!'

On Mr Candy's red face there was a look of discomfort; in the district, he enjoyed the reputation of a religious man; he was serving his fifteenth year as Baptist deacon. 'Now—don't you go startin' none a that—'

'An' the voice a the Lord come ontuh me, sayin', "I kin do the drouthin' out an' the hailin' out an' the hopperin' out an' the blowin' out till Bent Candy gits good an' tired out! She shall come to pass—" '

Mr Candy reached behind himself and knocked with his knuckles against the manure fork handle leaning against his new barn. He *was* a religious man, and years of prairie farming had deepened in him faith in a fate as effective as that of Greek drama. There had been a mental struggle through the years since he had first seen and wanted the Clydes. Before he could go to Magnus Petersen and secretly buy the land, it had been necessary for him to want the horses badly.

' "—sorra an' sighin' shall come to Bent Candy, for he hath played the sinner in the sight a the Lord, an' it shall come tuh pass the horned owl mourneth an' the kiy-oot howleth!" ' Saint Sammy's arm had come down.

For a long time after Sammy had left, Bent Candy stood by his shining barn. Then as he walked back to his house he looked up to the evening sky where high clouds still caught the lingering light of day and held it unexpected there. His Baptist conscience told him that the Clydes were horses after all. A killdeer sadly called. The church, thought Bent Candy, could use new pews.

Coin clear, the sun had sunk to leave an orange stain behind on clouds above the prairie's western line.

And now, thought Saint Sammy, waiting in the Lord's corner of the pasture, the fifth day was the day. He said it aloud to the weasel a short distance away with his slant head bolt upright in Presbyterian propriety, his toy ears round.

The rising wind tossed the prairie grasses now, stirring Saint Sammy's long and tangled beard, lifting the grey hair that hung to his shoulders. A butterfly came pelting by to pause on one of the dusty leaves laddering up a goldenrod's stem, its wings closed up like hands held palms together; it untouched itself to go winking and blinking, now here, now there, echoing itself over the empty, wind-stirred prairie.

And off toward the town a small boy's figure could be seen, leaning into the strengthening wind, as it walked toward Saint Sammy's. Brian wished that he had not decided to call on Sammy; he would have turned back now in the face of the threatening windstorm, but he was closer to the Petersen pasture than he was to the town. So while Saint Sammy waited for the Lord to button up the top button of His work smock, give a hitch to His Boss of the Road pants, and call for a whirlwind, Brian walked on, the grasses all around him, tossing like demented souls, their sibilance lost in the voice of the strengthening wind.

Brian reached the Lord's corner of the pasture just as Sammy shaded his eyes with his hand and looked out over the prairie:

'An' the Heavens will be opened up!' Saint Sammy cried, 'just south a the correction line! Sorrah an' sighin' shall come to Bent Candy today!'

'It's going to storm, Sammy!' shouted Brian.

Sammy plucked the yellow head from a flower at his feet, crushed it, and stared down at the threads of gum stringing from the ball of his thumb. 'The vengeance of the Lord shall be tenfold on Bent Candy—an' it shall be somethin' fearful!'

Calm and peace were in Sammy now; the terror had left him as he watched the far cloud hung low on the horizon, perceptibly spreading its darkness up the sky. 'The Lord is on His way! He shall smite Bent hip an' thigh an' shin, an' there shall be none to comfort him!'

A tumble-weed went bounding past the boy and the old man, caught itself against the strands of the fence, then, released, went rolling on its way. An unnatural dusk that had grown over the whole prairie made Brian strain his eyes to see through the spread darkness of dust licked up by the wind in its course across the land. His ears were filled with the sound of the wind, singing fierce and lost and lonely, rising and rising again, shearing high and higher still, singing vibrance in a void, forever and forever wild.

As far as the two could see, the grasses lay flat to the prairie earth, like ears laid along a jack rabbit's back. They could feel the wind solid against their chests, solid as the push of a hand. It had plastered Sammy's beard around his cheek. Brian felt it sting his face with dust and snatch at his very breath. He was filled again with that ringing awareness of himself that he had experienced so often before.

He looked at Saint Sammy and say that the old man had his head cocked on one side in a listening attitude. From the darkness all around, scarcely distinguishable from the throating wind, the voice of the Lord came to Saint Sammy.

'Sammy, Sammy, this is her, and I say ontuh you she is a dandy! Moreover I have tried her out! I have blew over Tourigny's henhouse; I have uprooted Dan Tate's windbreak, tooken the back door off of the schoolhouse, turned over the girls' toilet, three racks, six grain wagons; I have blew down the power line in four places; I have wrecked the sails on Magnus Petersen's windmill!

'In two hours did I cook her up; in two hours will I cook her down! An' when she hath died down, go you ontuh Bent Candy's where he languishes an' you shall hear the gnashing of teeth which are Bent Candy's an' he shall be confounded! Thus seth the Lord God of Hosts, enter intuh thy pianah box an' hide for the fear a the Lord! Take the Kid with you!

'Count yer labels, Sammy, count them one by one!'

'C'mon!' cried Sammy to Brian, and as the boy stared questioningly up to him, 'He's invited you in! C'mon!' He took Brian by the shoulder and led him toward the piano box.

In the dark depths of Sammy's house, they crouched, and Sammy did the Lord's bidding, going over his collected underwear labels by the light of the flickering lantern.

In town, a bounding garbage can, flung by the wind, clanged against the bars of the town hall basement window plastered with papers and tumble-weed. For the first time in his jail term the Ben was still, standing in the centre of his cell, his wild eyes up to the swirling darkness outside.

By her open window on the second floor of the O'Connal house, Brian's grandmother sat quite still in her rocker, her hands black with blown dust driven into the room between frantic curtains. Maggie O'Connal entered, struggled with the window, then turned anxiously to her mother.

Mrs Abercrombie and Mr Powelly, their planning of the Auxiliary garden party interrupted, stared at each other from uncomfortable throne chairs; they felt the large frame house around them shake like a spaniel after a swim. Over the sound of the wind came a rending crash; the house jumped.

'Let us pray!'

'What!'

'Let us pray!' Mr Powelly called again.

'Oh.'

The two got down on their knees with elbows on the rich velvet of Renaissance chairs.

The light of Sammy's lantern had become weak, and outside, the light of day had become strong again. Saint Sammy lifted the sacking.

The wind was discreet in the grass; Brian saw that just the loose blow dirt piled slightly higher, sharply rippled as the sand of a creek bed engraved by the water's current, showed that the Lord's wind had passed. Silence lay over everything, Brian and Sammy stood just outside the piano box. A gopher squeaked hesitantly. A suave-winged hawk slipped his shadow over the prairie's face, and a jack rabbit, startled, ears erect, went off past the fence in an exuberant bounce.

With his right shoulder high and his walk punctuated as though he had a spring under one heel, his arm swinging wide, Saint Sammy started off over the pasture. Brian, drawn, followed. The prairie grass clung at their pant legs; looping grasshoppers sprang sailing ahead of them and disappeared to lift again in brief, arcing flight. Here and there the yellow petals of black-eyed susans hung about their chocolate domes.

They crossed the road before Bent Candy's farm.

Mr Candy stood where his new, red barn had been.

Sammy and Brian halted; they stared at the utter, kindling ruin of what had once been a barn. No stick stood. In the strewn wreckage not even the foundation outline was discernible. The result was what might have been expected if the barn had been put through a threshing machine and exhaled through the blower. Certainly the Lord's vengeance had been enough to give a gopher heartburn.

There was awe in the old and quavering voice of Saint Sammy as it lifted in the hush of Bent Candy's farmyard.

'The Lord hath blew! He hath blew down the new an' shinin' barn of the fundamental Baptist that hath sinned in His sight! Like He said, "Sorra an' sighin' hath cometh to Bent Candy!" '

Candy turned to Saint Sammy; he looked into the old man's eyes, water-blue, mildly wild with a fey look which said that he was either childlike, senile, or gently insane. He looked at the squeezed intensity of Sammy's face, and he thought of the spreading fields of flax he had planted, even now thirsting for moisture; he thought of the years of drouth and rust and hail and the many wheat plagues which had touched him only lightly.

He said:

'You kin stay.'

Brian watched Saint Sammy lift his arms wide.

'I looked an' I beheld! The Heavens was opened up, an' there was a whirlwind a-comin' outa the East, liftin' like a trumpet a-spinnin' on her end, an' there was fire inside a her, an' light like a sunset was all around about her! Plumb outa the midst a her come the voice a the Lord, sayin', "Sammy, Sammy, git up from offa thy knees fer I am gonna speak ontuh you! The prairie shall be glad, an' she shall blossom like the rose! Yay, she shall blossom abundantly! The eyes a the blind shall see, an' the ears a the deef shall hear! The lame is gonna leap like the jack rabbit, an' the water shall spout ontuh the prairie, an' the sloughs shall be full—plumb full!" '

Saint Sammy's arms came down.

'Amen,' said Mr Candy.

1947

P.K. Page
b. 1916

Patricia Kathleen Page calls herself a traveller without a map. Certainly journeys have played an important role in her life and work. Born in England and raised in a military family in Calgary, Winnipeg, and Saint John, NB, she moved in the 1940s to Montreal, and then, after a year in Victoria, to Ottawa in 1946, where she worked as a scriptwriter for the National Film Board. There she met NFB head W. Arthur Irwin, whom she later married. When Irwin entered the Department of External Affairs, his diplomatic career took the two of them abroad in the early fifties to Australia, Brazil, and Mexico. It was not until 1964 that they returned to Canada and settled in Victoria, BC.

Although P.K. Page began to write in her teens, her work did not receive public recognition until Alan Crawley published her poetry, beginning with the first issue of his *Contemporary Verse* (1941–52). When Page moved to Montreal she began an association with the group of writers around Patrick Anderson's *Preview* (1942–5). In 1944 her work appeared in *Unit of Five*, an anthology that, like the earlier *New Provinces*, showcased the artistic and philosophical positions of a small group of poets then emerging in Canada. In 1947 these and other like-minded poets were among those included in *Other Canadians*, a large anthology compiled by John Sutherland as a riposte to the first edition of A.J.M. Smith's *Book of Canadian Poetry* (1943)—which itself contained poems by Page. The first two of Page's own collections of poetry also appeared during this period—*As Ten, as Twenty* (1946) and *The Metal and the Flower* (1954), which won a Governor General's Award.

Page continued to produce poetry during her three years in Australia. However, after moving to Latin America she found that art forms new to her—drawing and painting—became her chief creative outlets. Her 1987 book *Brazilian Journal*, a work based on her letters and journal entries from 1957–9, records the way in which, as she was learning to become a visual artist, her ability to write poetry temporarily left her.

Since returning to Canada, Page has worked as both a writer and—under the name P.K. Irwin—as a visual artist. Her books of poetry and short fiction include *Cry Ararat: Poems New and Selected* (1967); *The Sun and the Moon and Other Fictions* (1973); *Poems Selected and New* (1974); *Evening Dance of the Grey Flies* (1981), which contains both poems and the short story 'Unless the Eye Catch Fire . . .'; *The Glass Air* (1985), a collection of selected and new poems that also includes two essays and nine drawings; *Hologram* (1994); *The Hidden Room* (1997; 2 vols.), which draws together almost all of her published poetry along with new work; and the chapbook *Alphabetical* (1998), which features interconnected poems on each letter of the alphabet.

In addition to her poetry and short stories, Page has also written books for children, including *The Travelling Musicians of Bremen* (1992), an adaptation of the Grimm fairy tale, as well as *A Flask of Sea Water* (1989) and *The Goat that Flew* (1993).

Not only has Page's writing spanned a long period but it also reflects the wide range of artists, thinkers, and writers to whom she has responded. (She describes these associations and influences as 'affinities'.) In her 1997 poem 'Kaleidoscope', Page describes the 'trick with mirrors' that makes the 'slender tube' of the title such a fascinating toy—and ends by calling it 'the perfect, all-inclusive metaphor'. In fact, the kaleidoscope is a particularly useful metaphor for Page's poetry. Just as the mirrored planes in this toy turn the objects one sees through it into dazzling designs by reduplicating aspects of the original image, so Page assimilates into new patterns the ideas she responds to in order to create her own new and unique—if ever-changing—vision. While she was in Mexico, she read widely in works of spiritual and philosophical investigation, including Zen philosophy, the psychology of Carl Jung, the Christian mysticism of St John of the Cross, the mystical philosophy of G.I. Gurdjieff, and the Sufi thought of the Afghan writer Idries Shah. With the help of friends such as the Mexican surrealist painter Leonora Carrington, Maurice Nicol (a follower of Gurdjieff), and the Tasmanian writer Stella Kent she came to understand that she was on a journey into the self and that, by taking cues from her dreams and giving them formal expression in art, she could find a way of moving beyond the illusory world of everyday reality. The recurring images in Page's writing, such as the circles and spirals that also dominate her visual art, speak not only to her interest in Jung, Plato, and Sufi philosophy but also to the designs she finds in the writing of W.B. Yeats, Stephen Spender, Rainer Maria Rilke, and Federico Garcia Lorca.

In *Hologram,* Page carries this process of drawing on the inheritance of others to its logical poetic end by employing a form that creates poems by responding to the poems of others—the early Renaissance Spanish *glosa,* which can be seen in 'The Gold Sun' and 'Poor Bird'. The *glosa* is a formal homage that begins with a *cabeza* ('head') consisting of a four-line stanza taken from a poem by another poet, followed by four ten-line stanzas, each of which must contain a line from the *cabeza.*

In an interview that appeared in a special issue of *The Malahat Review* devoted to her work, Page explained why she called her collection *Hologram* and why the idea of the hologram has become important to her:

David Bohm was . . . one of the world's most respected quantum physicists. Karl Pribram is a neurophysiologist of great standing. And both of them arrived at their conclusions about the hologram independently. . . . Bohm became convinced of the universe's holographic nature after years of dissatisfaction with standard theory's inability to explain various neurophysiological puzzles. And these two men, working from different fields, came to the idea that the brain and the universe are both holograms. This is a very startling idea, when you consider that the quintessential feature of a hologram is the illusion that things are located where they are not. *It could mean that our world and everything in it are projections from a level of reality so beyond our own it is literally both space and time—and everything, from snowflakes, to maple trees, to falling stars and spinning electrons, is only ghostly images.*

For Page the four primary approaches to perceiving such a totality are science, philosophy, religion, and art: each can move us towards insight, or more specifically to an epiphany—a vision of the central point that mediates between these four, the numinous force that each is striving to understand.

The story selected here, 'Unless the Eye Catch Fire . . .', seems at one level to be an ecological warning, and a story about the end of the world. But it can also be read as Page's fable of how epiphany takes place, an allegorical parable about the metaphysical world's irruption into the physical.

It is the sense that such a world lies beneath this one that has served Page as a source of consolation and creativity:

I seem to be attempting to copy exactly something which exists in a dimension where worldly senses are inadequate. As if a thing only felt had to be extracted from invisibility and transposed into a seen thing, a heard thing. The struggle is to fit the 'made' to the 'sensed' in such a way that the whole can occupy a world larger than the one I normally inhabit. (*Canadian Literature* 46, 1970)

But if Page is preoccupied with apocalypse in its literal sense more than in its acquired meaning—that is, in the lifting of the veil that covers what we normally cannot see—she has never given her readers a poetry that is vague or abstract. Her writing is filled with highly charged imagery that triggers the sensorium, integrating the mystical and worldly dimensions so effectively that mystery becomes a necessary part of, and arises out of, each individual's sensory experience. Page achieves this integration chiefly by means of visual cues—references to eyes and seeing, to space and shape, and to colour—but she can also make images dissolve into one another in a way that unbalances the reader's concept of the nature of reality.

Stories of Snow

Those in the vegetable rain retain
an area behind their sprouting eyes
held soft and rounded with the dream of snow
precious and reminiscent as those globes —
souvenir of some never-nether land —
which hold their snow-storms circular, complete,
high in a tall and teakwood cabinet.

In countries where the leaves are large as hands
where flowers protrude their fleshy chins
and call their colours,
an imaginary snow-storm sometimes falls
among the lilies.
And in the early morning one will waken
to think the glowing linen of his pillow
a northern drift, will find himself mistaken
and lie back weeping.
And there the story shifts from head to head,
of how in Holland, from their feather beds
hunters arise and part the flakes and go
forth to the frozen lakes in search of swans —
the snow-light falling white along their guns,
their breath in plumes.
While tethered in the wind like sleeping gulls
ice-boats wait the raising of their wings
to skim the electric ice at such a speed
they leap jet strips of naked water,
and how these flying, sailing hunters feel
air in their mouths as terrible as ether.
And on the story runs that even drinks
in that white landscape dare to be no colour;
how flasked and water clear, the liquor slips
silver against the hunters' moving hips.
And of the swan in death these dreamers tell
of its last flight and how it falls, a plummet,
pierced by the freezing bullet
and how three feathers, loosened by the shot,
descend like snow upon it.
While hunters plunge their fingers in its down
deep as a drift, and dive their hands
up to the neck of the wrist
in that warm metamorphosis of snow

as gentle as the sort that woodsmen know
who, lost in the white circle, fall at last
and dream their way to death.

And stories of this kind are often told
in countries where great flowers bar the roads
with reds and blues which seal the route to snow—
as if, in telling, raconteurs unlock
the colour with its complement and go
through to the area behind the eyes
where silent, unrefractive whiteness lies.

1946

Photos of a Salt Mine

How innocent their lives look,
how like a child's
dream of caves and winter, both combined;
the steep descent to whiteness
and the stope[1]
with its striated walls
their folds all leaning as if pointing to
the greater whiteness still,
that great white bank
with its decisive front,
that seam upon a slope,
salt's lovely ice.

And wonderful underfoot the snow of salt
the fine
particles a broom could sweep,
one thinks
muckers might make angels in its drifts
as children do in snow,
lovers in sheets,
lie down and leave imprinted where they lay
a feathered creature holier than they.

1 An excavation in the form of steps made as ore is mined from vertical or steeply inclined veins.

And in the outworked stopes
with lamps and ropes
up miniature matterhorns
the miners climb
probe with their lights
the ancient folds of rock—
syncline[2] and anticline—
and scoop from darkness an Aladdin's cave:
rubies and opals glitter from its walls.

But hoses douse the brilliance of these jewels,
melt fire to brine.
Salt's bitter water trickles thin and forms,
slow fathoms down,
a lake within a cave,
lacquered with jet—
white's opposite.
There grey on black the boating miners float
to mend the stays and struts of that old stope
and deeply underground
their words resound,
are multiplied by echo, swell and grow
and make a climate of a miner's voice.

So all the photographs like children's wishes
are filled with caves or winter,
innocence
has acted as a filter,
selected only beauty from the mine.
Except in the last picture,
it is shot
from an acute high angle. In a pit
figures the size of pins are strangely lit
and might be dancing but you know they're not.
Like Dante's vision of the nether hell[3]
men struggle with the bright cold fires of salt,
locked in the black inferno of the rock:
the filter here, not innocence but guilt.

1954

2 Low, troughlike fold in stratified rock, the opposite of 'anticline': fold with strata sloping downwards on both sides away from a common crest.

3 In *The Inferno*, which forms the first part of Dante's fourteenth-century poem *The Divine Comedy*, hell is divided into three parts. The lowest part contains both fire and ice.

Cry Ararat![1]

I

In the dream the mountain near
but without sound.
A dream through binoculars
seen sharp and clear:
the leaves moving, turning
in a far wind
no ear can hear.

First soft in the distance,
blue in blue air
then sharpening, quickening
taking on green.
Swiftly the fingers
seek accurate focus
(the bird
has vanished so often
before the sharp lens
could deliver it)
then as if from the sea
the mountain appears
emerging new-washed
growing maples and firs.
The faraway, here.

Do not reach to touch it
nor labour to hear.
Return to your hand
the sense of the hand;
return to your ear
the sense of the ear.
Remember the statue,
that space in the air
which with nothing to hold
what the minute is giving
is through each point
where its marble touches air.

1 Mountain range on which Noah's ark landed. As the flood waters began to recede, Noah—believing that God would once again provide a fertile earth—sent out the dove which, on its second excursion, returned bearing an olive branch.

Then will each leaf and flower
each bird and animal
become as perfect as
the thing its name evoked
when busy as a child
the world stopped at the Word
and Flowers more real than flowers
grew vivid and immense;
and Birds more beautiful
and Leaves more intricate
flew, blew and quilted all
the quick landscape.

So flies and blows the dream
embracing like a sea
all that in it swims
when dreaming, you desire
and ask for nothing more
than stillness to receive
the I-am animal,
the We-are leaf and flower,
the distant mountain near.

II

So flies and blows the dream that haunts us when we wake
to the unreality of bright day:
the far thing almost sensed by the still skin
and then the focus lost, the mountain gone.
This is the loss that haunts our daylight hours
leaving us parched at nightfall
blowing like last year's leaves
sibilant on blossoming trees
and thirsty for the dream of the mountain
more real than any event:
more real than strangers passing on the street
in a city's architecture white as bone
or the immediate companion.

But sometimes there is one
raw with the dream of flying:
'I, a bird,
landed that very instant

and complete—
as if I had drawn a circle in my flight
and filled its shape—
find air a perfect fit.
But this my grief,
that with the next tentative lift
of my indescribable wings
the ceiling looms
heavy as a tomb.

'Must my most exquisite and private dream
remain unleavened?
Must this flipped and spinning coin that sun
could gild and make miraculous become
so swiftly pitiful?
The vision of the flight it imitates
burns brightly in my head as if a star
rushed down to touch me where I stub against
what must forever be my underground.'

III

These are the dreams that haunt us,
these the fears.
Will the grey weather wake us,
toss us twice in the terrible night to tell us
the flight is cancelled
and the mountain lost?

O, then cry Ararat!

The dove believed
in her sweet wings and in the rising peak
with such a washed and easy innocence
that she found rest on land for the sole of her foot
and, silver, circled back,
a green twig in her beak.

The leaves that make the tree by day,
the green twig the dove saw fit
to lift across a world of water
break in a wave about our feet.
The bird in the thicket with his whistle

the crystal lizard in the grass
the star and shell
tassel and bell
of wild flowers blowing where we pass,
this flora-fauna flotsam, pick and touch,
requires the focus of the total I.

A single leaf can block a mountainside;
all Ararat be conjured by a leaf.

1967

Arras[1]

Consider a new habit—classical,
and trees espaliered[2] on the wall like candelabra.
How still upon that lawn our sandalled feet.

But a peacock rattling his rattan tail and screaming
has found a point of entry. Through whose eye
did it insinuate in furled disguise
to shake its jewels and silk upon that grass?

The peaches hang like lanterns. No one joins
those figures on the arras.
                                        Who am I
or who am I become that walking here
I am observer, other, Gemini,
starred for a green garden of cinema?

I ask, what did they deal me in this pack?
The cards, all suits, are royal when I look.
My fingers slipping on a monarch's face
twitch and grow slack.
I want a hand to clutch, a heart to crack.

No one is moving now, the stillness is
infinite. If I should make a break. . . .
take to my springy heels. . . . ? But nothing moves.
The spinning world is stuck upon its poles,

1 Wall hanging, particularly a tapestry.
2 That is, with trees' branches trained to grow flat against a wall, supported on a lattice or framework of stakes.

the stillness points a bone[3] at me. I fear
the future on this arras.
I confess:

It was my eye.
Voluptuous it came.
Its head the ferrule[4] and its lovely tail
folded so sweetly; it was strangely slim
to fit the retina. And then it shook
and was a peacock—living patina,
eye-bright, maculate!
Does no one care?

I thought their hands might hold me if I spoke.
I dreamed the bite of fingers in my flesh,
their poke smashed by an image, but they stand
as if within a treacle,[5] motionless,
folding slow eyes on nothing. While they stare
another line has trolled the encircling air,
another bird assumes its furled disguise.

1967

3 'Aboriginal projective magic. A prepared human or kangaroo bone is pointed by a sorcerer at an intended victim (who may be miles away) to bring about his death' (from Page's glossary of Australian terms in *Cry Ararat!*).
4 Metal cap used to reinforce or secure the end of a pole or handle—here belonging to an umbrella.
5 Molasses or sweet syrup; used here as that which entraps the insects it attracts.

The Gold Sun

Trace the gold sun about the whitened sky
Without evasion by a single metaphor.
Look at it in its essential barrenness
And say this, this is the centre that I seek.

—Wallace Stevens, 'Credences of Summer'

Sky whitened by a snow on which no swan
is visible, and no least feather falling
could possibly or impossibly be seen,
sky whitened like the blank page of a book,
no letters forming into words unless
written in paleness—a pallidity
faint as the little rising moons on nails—

and so, forgettable and so, forgot.
Blue eyes dark as lapis lazuli[1]
trace the gold sun about the whitened sky.

You'll see the thing itself no matter what.
Though it may blind you, what else will suffice?
To smoke a glass or use a periscope
will give you other than the very thing,
or more, or elements too various.
So let the fabulous photographer
catch Phaeton[2] in his lens and think he is
the thing itself, not knowing all the else
he is become. But you will see it clear
without evasion by a single metaphor.

How strip the sun of all comparisons?
That spinning coin—moving, yet at rest
in its outflinging course across the great
parabola of space—is Phoebus,[3]
sovereign: heroic principle,
the heat and light of us. And gold—no less
a metaphor than sun—is not the least
less multiple and married. Therefore how
rid the gold sun of all its otherness?
Look at it in its essential barrenness.

Make a prime number of it, pure, and know
it indivisible and hold it so
in the white sky behind your lapis eyes.
Push aside everything that isn't sun
the way a sculptor works his stone,
the way a mystic masters the mystique
of making more by focusing on one
until at length, all images are gone
except the sun, the thing itself, deific,
and say this, this is the centre that I seek.

1994

1 An intensely blue rock, often with light streaks, used in jewellery and, before 1828, in the preparation of the pigment ultramarine.

2 In Greek mythology, Phaeton was the son of Helios the sun god, who brought each day into existence when he rode his solar chariot across the sky. When Phaeton rashly attempted to drive his father's chariot one day, he could not control the horses. Because the chariot was plunging dangerously close to the earth, Zeus killed Phaeton with a thunderbolt to save the world from destruction.

3 An epithet of the Greek god Apollo, used when he is identified with the sun.

Poor Bird

. . . looking for something, something, something.
Poor bird, he is obsessed!
The millions of grains are black, white, tan, and gray,
mixed with quartz grains, rose and amethyst.

—Elizabeth Bishop, 'Sandpiper'

From birth, from the first astonishing moment
when he pecked his way out of the shell, pure fluff,
he was looking for something—warmth, food, love
or light, or darkness—we are all the same stuff,
all have the same needs: to be one of the flock
or to stand apart, a singular fledgling.
So the search began—the endless search
that leads him onward—a vocation
year in, year out, morning to evening
looking for something, something, something.

Nothing will stop him. Although distracted
By nest-building, eggs, high winds, high tides
and too short a lifespan for him to plan
an intelligent search—still, on he goes
with his delicate legs and spillikin[1] feet
and the wish to know what he's almost guessed.
Can't leave it alone, that stretch of sand.
Thinks himself Seurat[2] (pointilliste)
Or a molecular physicist.
Poor bird, he is obsessed!

And just because he has not yet found
what he doesn't know he is searching for
is not a sign he's off the track.
His track is the sedge, the sand, the suck
of the undertow, the line of shells.
Nor would he have it another way.
And yet—the nag—is there something else?
Something more, perhaps, or something less.
And though he examine them, day after day
the millions of grains are black, white, tan and gray.

1 That is, thin, straw-like. 'Spillikins', or 'jackstraws', is a game played with a heap of small, thin rods of wood, bone, or plastic (called 'spillikins'), in which players try to remove one at a time without disturbing the others.
2 Georges Pierre Seurat (1859–91), French painter chiefly associated with pointillism, a painting technique that uses dots of various pure colours, rather than unbroken fields of blended colours to suggest shapes.

But occasionally, when he least expects it,
in the glass of a wave a painted fish
like a work of art across his sight
reminds him of something he doesn't know
that he has been seeking his whole long life—
something that may not even exist!
Poor bird, indeed! Poor dazed creature!
Yet when his eye is sharp and sideways seeing
oh, *then* the quotidian unexceptional sand is
mixed with quartz grains, rose and amethyst.

1994

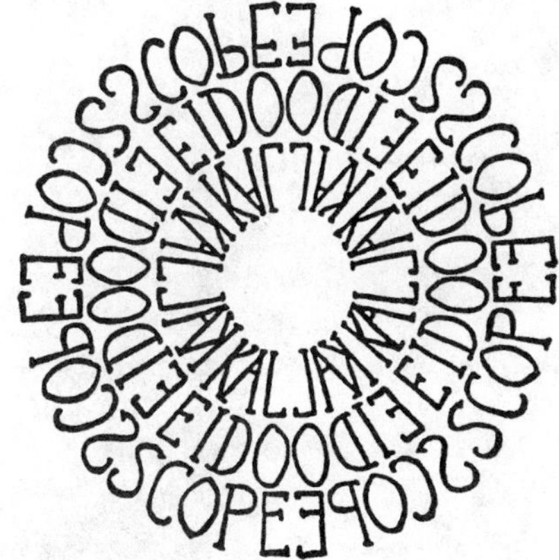

I. A Little Fantasy

> *I send you a very well-constructed Kaleidoscope, a recently invented Toy.*
>
> —John Murray to Byron, 1818[1]

So—Murray to Byron in Italy
when B. was falling in love again. In love.
Teresa this time. Guiccioli.
What a gift
to view her through that tube!
Her palms, sand dollars—
pale, symmetrical—

1 John Murray was Alfred Lord Byron's publisher and correspondent. He published the early cantos of *Don Juan,* Byron's epic satire about a legendary Spanish nobleman famous for his dissolute lifestyle and his many seductions of women; Byron's last major work, it was left unfinished at its death, in spite of Murray's letters asking Byron to send him more sections of the poem. In 1818 Byron was living in Italy; in 1821 the Contessa Teresa Guiccioli (*c.* 1800–73) left her husband to become Byron's last lover.

changed with his breathing
into petalled stars.
Four hearts her mouth, then eight,
a single flower
become a bunch
to kiss and kiss and kiss
and kiss a fourth time.
What a field of mouths!
Her navel—curling, complex—
shells and pearls
quadrupling for him
and her soft hair—ah,
the flat, sweet plait of it
beneath the glass—
a private hair brooch[2]
such as ladies wear
pinned to their *peau de soie.*

Byron is breathing heavily
the tube—a lover's perfect toy—
weighting his palm.
'Quite a celestial kaleidoscope.'
But Murray demands more cantos.
(Damn the man!)
Oh, multiple Terese,
'*Don Juan*' calls.

II. A Little Reality

My eye falls headlong
down this slender tube,
its eyebeam glued
to shift and flux and flow.
(Mirrors. A trick with mirrors.)
I cannot
budge from this cylinder.
An octagonal rose
holds me as though I were its stem.

2 A brooch that carries 'hair art', usually hair plaited in an abstract pattern or hair braided around an armature in a shape such as a flower. These brooches, along with hair bracelets and rings, were often a form of mourning jewellery, preserving the hair of a departed loved one—and often combining hair from more than one person. '*Peau de soie*' is smooth, finely ribbed, but dull-finished silk fabric.

We move
interdependent
paired in serious play
that is not play.
Part of the art
of dance.

Gwendolyn,
your garden of square roots[3]
grows in this circle:
from my pots and pans—
a silver chaparral of leaves and flowers—
the tap's drip dew
upon them—diamonds, stars;
the yellow plastic
of my liquid soap—
a quatrefoil of buttercups—
unfolds
in four-leaf clovers on a field of gold.

Nothing is what it seems.
Through this glass eye
each single thing is other—
all-ways joined
to every other thing.
Familiar here is foreign
fresh and fair
as never-seen-before.
And this kaleidoscope uniting all,
this tube, this conduit optical,
this lens
is magic. Through it—see
(who dares?)
the perfect, all-inclusive metaphor.

1997

3 'The Garden of Square Roots: An Autobiography' is a 1968 poem by Gwendolyn MacEwen (see page 851). It reads in part:

this city i live in i built with bones
. . . .
for i was the i interior
. . . .
and all my gardens grew backwards
and all the roots were finally square
and Ah! the flowers grew there like algebra

Unless the Eye Catch Fire

Unless the eye catch fire
The God will not be seen . . .

—Theodore Roszak, *Where the Wasteland Ends*

Wednesday, September 17. The day began normally enough. The quail cockaded[1] as antique foot soldiers, arrived while I was having my breakfast. The males black-faced, white-necklaced, cinnamon-crowned, with short, sharp, dark plumes. Square bibs, Payne's grey;[2] belly and sides with a pattern of small stitches. Reassuring, the flock of them. They tell me the macadamization[3] of the world is not complete.

A sudden alarm, and as if they had one brain among them, they were gone in a rush—a sideways ascending Niagara—shutting out the light, obscuring the sky and exposing a rectangle of lawn, unexpectedly emerald. How bright the berries on the cotoneaster. Random leaves on the cherry twirled like gold spinners. The garden was high-keyed, vivid, locked in aspic.

Without warning, and as if I were looking down the tube of a kaleidoscope, the merest shake occurred—moiréed[4] the garden—rectified itself. Or, more precisely, as if a range-finder through which I had been sighting found of itself a more accurate focus. Sharpened, in fact, to an excoriating exactness.

And then the colours changed. Shifted to a higher octave—a *bright spectrum.* Each colour with its own *light,* its own *shape.* The leaves of the trees, the berries, the grasses—as if shedding successive films—disclosed layer after layer of hidden perfections. And upon these rapidly changing surfaces the 'range-finder'—to really play hob with metaphor!—sharpened its small invisible blades.

I don't know how to describe the intensity and speed of focus of this gratuitous zoom lens through which I stared, or the swift and dizzying adjustments within me. I became a 'sleeping top', perfectly centred, perfectly sighted. The colours vibrated beyond the visible range of the spectrum. Yet I saw them. With some matching eye. Whole galaxies of them, blazing and glowing, flowing in rivulets, gushing in fountains—volatile, mercurial, and making lacklustre and off-key the colours of the rainbow.

I had no time or inclination to wonder, intellectualize. My mind seemed astonishingly clear and quite still. Like a crystal. A burning glass.

And then the range-finder sharpened once again. To alter space.

The lawn, the bushes, the trees—still super-brilliant—were no longer *there. There,* in fact, had ceased to exist. They were now, of all places in the world, *here.* Right in the centre of my being. Occupying an immense inner space. Part of me. Mine. Except the

1 That is, with its distinctive plume of feathers standing up from its crown. A cockade is a rosette or knot of ribbons worn in a hat as a badge of office.

2 A very dark blue-grey.

3 That is, the process of paving the world. Macadam is broken stone used for building roads, usually combined with tar or asphalt.

4 That is, gave the garden a luminous, rippled appearance like that of moiré silk, which has a pattern of lustrous, irregular wavy lines that seem to shimmer.

whole idea of ownership was beside the point. As true to say I was theirs as they mine. I and they were here; they and I, there. (*There, here* . . . odd . . . but for an irrelevant, inconsequential 't' which comes and goes, the words are the same.)

As suddenly as the world had altered, it returned to normal. I looked at my watch. A ridiculous mechanical habit. As I had no idea when the experience began it was impossible to know how long it had lasted. What had seemed eternity couldn't have been more than a minute or so. My coffee was still steaming in its mug.

The garden, through the window, was as it had always been. Yet not as it had always been. Less. Like listening to mono after hearing stereo. But with a far greater loss of dimension. A grievous loss.

I rubbed my eyes. Wondered, not without alarm, if this was the onset of some disease of the retina—glaucoma or some cellular change in the eye itself—superlatively packaged, fatally sweet as the marzipan cherry I ate as a child and *knew* was poison.

If it *is* a disease, the symptoms will recur. It will happen again.

Tuesday, September 23. It has happened again.

Tonight, taking Dexter for his late walk, I looked up at the crocheted tangle of boughs against the sky. Dark silhouettes against the lesser dark, but beating now with an extraordinary black brilliance. The golden glints in obsidian or the lurking embers in black opals are the nearest I can come to describing them. But it's a false description, emphasizing as it does the wrong end of the scale. This was a *dark spectrum.* As if the starry heavens were translated into densities of black—black Mars, black Saturn, black Jupiter; or a master jeweller had crossed his jewels with jet and set them to burn and wink in the branches and twigs of oaks whose leaves shone luminous—a leafy Milky Way—fired by black chlorophyll.

Dexter stopped as dead as I. Transfixed. His thick honey-coloured coat and amber eyes, glowing with their own intense brightness, suggested yet another spectrum. A *spectrum of light.* He was a constellated dog, shining, supra-real, against the foothills and mountain ranges of midnight.

I am reminded now, as I write, of a collection of lepidoptera in Brazil—one entire wall covered with butterflies, creatures of daylight—enormous or tiny—blue, orange, black. Strong-coloured. And on the opposite wall their antiselves—pale night flyers spanning such a range of silver and white and lightest snuff-colour that once one entered their spectral scale there was no end to the subleties and delicate nuances. But I didn't think like this then. All thought, all comparisons were prevented by the startling infinities of darkness and light.

Then, as before, the additional shake occurred and the two spectrums moved swiftly from without to within. As if two equal and complementary circles centred inside me—or I in them. How explain that I not only *saw* but actually *was* the two spectrums? (I underline a simple, but in this case exactly appropriate, anagram.)

Then the range-finder lost its focus and the world, once again, was back to normal. Dexter, a pale, blurred blob, bounded about within the field of my peripheral vision, going on with his doggy interests just as if a moment before he had not been frozen in his tracks, a dog entranced.

I am no longer concerned about my eyesight. Wonder only if we are both mad, Dexter and I? Angelically mad, sharing hallucinations of epiphany. *Folie à deux*?

Friday, October 3. It's hard to account for my secrecy, for I *have* been secretive. As if the cat had my tongue. It's not that I don't long to talk about the colours but I can't risk the wrong response—(as Gaby once said of a companion after a faultless performance of *Giselle*: 'If she had criticized the least detail of it, I'd have hit her!').

Once or twice I've gone so far as to say, 'I had the most extraordinary experience the other day . . .' hoping to find some look or phrase, some answering, 'So did I.' None has been forthcoming.

I can't forget the beauty. Can't get it out of my head. Startling, unearthly, indescribable. Infuriatingly indescribable. A glimpse of—somewhere else. Somewhere alive, miraculous, newly made yet timeless. And more important still—significant, luminous, with a meaning of which I was part. Except that I—the I who is writing this—did not exist: was flooded out, dissolved in that immensity where subject and object are one.

I have to make a deliberate effort now not to live my life in terms of it; not to sit, immobilized, awaiting the shake that heralds a new world. Awaiting the transfiguration.

Luckily the necessities of life keep me busy. But upstream of my actions, behind a kind of plate glass, some part of me waits, listens, maintains a total attention.

Tuesday, October 7. Things are moving very fast.

Some nights ago my eye was caught by a news item. 'Trucker Blames Colours', went the headline. Reading on: 'R.T. Ballantyne, driver for Island Trucks, failed to stop on a red light at the intersection of Fernhill and Spender. Questioned by traffic police, Ballantyne replied: "I didn't see it, that's all. There was this shake, then all these colours suddenly in the trees. Real bright ones I'd never seen before. I guess they must have blinded me." A breathalyzer test proved negative.' Full stop.

I had an overpowering desire to talk to R.T. Ballantyne. Even looked him up in the telephone book. Not listed. I debated reaching him through Island Trucks in the morning.

Hoping for some mention of the story, I switched on the local radio station, caught the announcer mid-sentence:

'. . . to come to the studio and talk to us. So far no one has been able to describe just what the "new" colours are, but perhaps Ruby Howard can. Ruby, you say you actually *saw* "new" colours?'

What might have been a flat, rather ordinary female voice was sharpened by wonder. 'I was out in the garden, putting it to bed, you might say, getting it ready for winter. The hydrangeas are dried out—you know the way they go. Soft beiges and greys. And I was thinking maybe I should cut them back, when there was this—shake, like—and there they were shining. Pink. And blue. But not like they are in life. Different. Brighter. With little lights, like . . .'

The announcer's voice cut in, 'You say "not like they are in life". D'you think this wasn't life? I mean, do you think maybe you were dreaming?'

'Oh, no,' answered my good Mrs Howard, positive, clear, totally unrattled. 'Oh, no, I wasn't *dreaming*. Not *dreaming*— . . . Why—*this* is more like dreaming.' She was quiet a moment and then, in a matter-of-fact voice, 'I can't expect you to believe it,' she said. 'Why should you? I wouldn't believe it myself if I hadn't seen it.' Her voice expressed a kind of compassion as if she was really sorry for the announcer.

I picked up the telephone book for a second time, looked up the number of the station. I had decided to tell Mrs Howard what I had seen. I dialled, got a busy signal, depressed the bar and waited, cradle in hand. I dialled again. And again.

Later. J. just phoned. Curious how she and I play the same game over and over.
J: Were you watching Channel 8?
ME: No, I . . .
J: An interview. With a lunatic. One who sees colours and flashing lights.
ME: Tell me about it.
J: He was a logger—a high-rigger—not that that has anything to do with it. He's retired now and lives in an apartment and has a window-box with geraniums. This morning the flowers were like neon, he said, flashing and shining . . . *Honestly!*
ME: Perhaps he saw something you can't . . .
J: (*Amused*) I might have known you'd take his side. Seriously, what *could* he have seen?
ME: Flashing and shining—as he said.
J: But they couldn't. Not geraniums. And you know it as well as I do. *Honestly*, Babe . . . (She is the only person left who calls me the name my mother called me.) Why are you always so perverse?

I felt faithless. I put down the receiver, as if I had not borne witness to my God.

October 22. Floods of letters to the papers. Endless interviews on radio and TV. Pros, cons, inevitable spoofs.

One develops an eye for authenticity. It's as easy to spot as sunlight. However they may vary in detail, true accounts of the colours have an unmistakable common factor—a common factor as difficult to convey as sweetness to those who know only salt. True accounts are inarticulate, diffuse, unlikely—impossible.

It's recently crossed my mind that there may be some relationship between having seen the colours and their actual manifestation—something as improbable as *the more one sees them the more they are able to be seen.* Perhaps they are always there in some normally invisible part of the electro-magnetic spectrum and only become visible to certain people at certain times. A combination of circumstances or some subtle refinement in the organ of sight. And then—from quantity to quality perhaps, like water to ice—a whole community changes, is able to see, catches fire.

For example, it was seven days between the first time I saw the colours and the second. During that time there were no reports to the media. But once the reports began, the time between lessened appreciably *for me.* Not proof, of course, but worth noting. And I can't help wondering why some people see the colours and others don't. Do some of us have extra vision? Are some so conditioned that they're virtually blind to what's there before their very noses? Is it a question of more, or less?

Reports come in from father and farther afield; from all walks of life. I think now there is no portion of the inhabited globe without 'shake freaks' and no acceptable reason for the sightings. Often, only one member of a family will testify to the heightened vision. In my own small circle, I am the only witness—or so I think. I feel curiously hypocritical as I listen to my friends denouncing the 'shakers'. Drugs, they say. Irrational—possibly dangerous. Although no sinister incidents have occurred yet—just some mild shake-baiting here and there—one is uneasily reminded of Salem.

Scientists pronounce us hallucinated or mistaken, pointing out that so far there is no hard evidence, no objective proof. That means, I suppose, no photographs, no spectroscopic measurement—if such is possible. Interestingly, seismographs show very minor earthquake tremors—showers of them, like shooting stars in August.[5] Pundits claim 'shake fever'—as it has come to be called—is a variant on flying saucer fever and that it will subside in its own time. Beneficent physiologists suggest we are suffering (why is it *always* suffering, never enjoying?) a distorted form of *ocular spectrum* or after-image. (An after-image of what?) Psychologists disagree among themselves. All in all, it is not surprising that some of us prefer to keep our experiences to ourselves.

January 9. Something new has occurred. Something impossible. Disturbing. So disturbing, in fact, that according to rumour it is already being taken with the utmost seriousness at the highest levels. TV, press and radio—with good reason—talk of little else.

What seemingly began as a mild winter has assumed sinister overtones. Farmers in southern Alberta are claiming the earth is unnaturally hot to the touch. Golfers at Harrison[6] complain that the soles of their feet burn. Here on the coast, we notice it less. Benign winters are our speciality.

Already we don't lack for explanations as to why the earth could not be hotter than usual, nor why it is naturally 'un-naturally' hot. Vague notes of reassurance creep into the speeches of public men. They may be unable to explain the issue, but they can no longer ignore it.

To confuse matters further, reports on temperatures seem curiously inconsistent. What information we get comes mainly from self-appointed 'earth touchers'. And now that the least thing can fire an argument, their conflicting readings lead often enough to inflammatory debate.

For myself, I can detect no change at all in my own garden.

Thursday . . .? There is no longer any doubt. The temperature of the earth's surface *is* increasing.

It is unnerving, horrible, to go out and feel the ground like some great beast, warm, beneath one's feet. As if another presence—vast, invisible—attends one. Dexter, too, is perplexed. He barks at the earth with the same indignation and, I suppose, fear, with which he barks at the first rumblings of earthquake.

Air temperatures, curiously, don't increase proportionately—or so we're told. It doesn't make sense, but at the moment nothing makes sense. Countless explanations

5 That is, during the Perseids meteor shower, visible every August.

6 Harrison Hot Springs, a resort village, with a golf course, on Harrison Lake, northeast of Chilliwack, BC.

have been offered. Elaborate explanations. None adequate. The fact that the air temperature remains temperate despite the higher ground heat must, I think, be helping to keep panic down. Even so, these are times of great tension.

Hard to understand these two unexplained—unrelated?—phenomena: the first capable of dividing families; the second menacing us all. We are like animals trapped in a burning building.

Later. J. just phoned. Terrified. Why don't I move in with her, she urges. After all she has the space and we have known each other forty years. (Hard to believe when I don't feel even forty!) She can't bear it—the loneliness.

Poor J. Always so protected, insulated by her money. And her charm. What one didn't provide, the other did . . . diversions, services, attention.

What do I think is responsible for the heat, she asks. But it turns out she means who. Her personal theory is that the 'shake-freaks' are causing it—involuntarily, perhaps, but the two are surely linked.

'How could they possibly cause it?' I enquire. 'By what reach of the imagination . . . ?'

'Search *me*!' she protests. 'How on earth should *I* know?' And the sound of the dated slang makes me really laugh.

But suddenly she is close to tears. 'How can you *laugh*?' she calls. 'This is nightmare. Nightmare!'

Dear J. I wish I could help but the only comfort I could offer would terrify her still more.

September. Summer calmed us down. If the earth was hot, well, summers *are* hot. And we were simply having an abnormally hot one.

Now that it is fall—the season of cool nights, light frosts—and the earth like a feverish child remains worryingly hot, won't cool down, apprehension mounts.

At last we are given official readings. For months the authorities have assured us with irrefutable logic that the temperature of the earth could not be increasing. Now, without any apparent period of indecision of confusion, they are warning us with equal conviction and accurate statistical documentation that it has, in fact, increased. Something anyone with a pocket-handkerchief of lawn has known for some time.

Weather stations, science faculties, astronomical observatories all over the world are measuring and reporting. Intricate computerized tables are quoted. Special departments of Government have been set up. We speak now of a new Triassic Age[7]—the Neo-Triassic—and of the accelerated melting of the ice caps. But we are elaborately assured that this could not, repeat not, occur in our lifetime.

Interpreters and analysts flourish. The media are filled with theories and explanations. The increased temperature has been attributed to impersonal agencies such as bacteria from outer space; a thinning of the earth's atmosphere; a build-up of carbon-dioxide in the air; some axial irregularity; a change in the earth's core (geologists are

7 The Triassic Age, from about 65 million to 2 million years ago, seems in North America to have been a period of unusually warm, perhaps even tropical, temperatures. Volcanoes spewed out lava flows, and forests and lush vegetation grew in many places where it does not today.

reported to have begun test borings). No theory is too far-fetched to have its supporters. And because man likes a scapegoat, blame has been laid upon NASA, atomic physicists, politicians, the occupants of flying saucers, and finally upon mankind at large—improvident, greedy mankind—whose polluted, strike-ridden world is endangered now by the fabled flames of hell.

Yet, astonishingly, life goes on. The Pollack baby was born last week. I received the news as if it were a death. Nothing has brought the irony of our situation home to me so poignantly. And when I saw the perfect little creature in its mother's arms, the look of adoration on her face, I found myself saying the things one always says to a new mother—exactly as if the world had not changed. Exactly as if our radio was not informing us that Nostradamus,[8] the Bible, and Jeane Dixon have all foreseen our plight. A new paperback, *Let Edgar Cayce Tell You Why*, sold out in a matter of days. Attendance at churches has doubled. Cults proliferate. Yet even in this atmosphere, we, the 'shake freaks', are considered lunatic fringe. Odd men out. In certain quarters I believe we are seriously held responsible for the escalating heat, so J. is not alone. There have now been one or two nasty incidents. It is not surprising that even the most vocal among us have grown less willing to talk. I am glad to have kept silent. As a woman living alone, the less I draw attention to myself the better.

But, at the same time, we have suddenly all become neighbours. Total strangers greet each other on the street. And the almost invisible couple behind the high hedge appears every time I pass with Dexter—wanting to talk. Desperately wanting to talk.

For our lives are greatly altered by this overhanging sense of doom. It is already hard to buy certain commodities. Dairy products are in very short supply. On the other hand, the market is flooded with citrus fruits. We are threatened with severe shortages for the future. The authorities are resisting rationing but it will have to come, if only to prevent artificial shortages resulting from hoarding.

Luckily the colours are an almost daily event. I see them now, as it were, with my entire being. It is as if all my cells respond to their brilliance and become light too. At such times I feel I might shine in the dark.

No idea of the date. It is evening and I am tired but I am so far behind in my notes I want to get something down. Events have moved too fast for me.

Gardens, parks—every tillable inch of soil—have been appropriated for food crops. As an able, if aging body, with an acre of land and some knowledge of gardening, I have been made responsible for soybeans—small trifoliate plants rich with the promise of protein. Neat rows of them cover what were once my vegetable garden, flower beds, lawn.

Young men from the Department of Agriculture came last month, bulldozed, cultivated, planted. Efficient, noisy desecrators of my twenty years of landscaping. Dexter

8 Michel de Nostredame (1503–66), French physician and astrologer who produced two collections of cryptic and apocalyptic predictions in rhymed quatrains (1555; 1558); Jeane Dixon (1918–97), popular American psychic and astrologer who became associated with predicting the death of US president John F. Kennedy; Edgar Cayce (1877–1945), the so-called 'sleeping prophet', who either fell asleep or entered a trance state during which he discussed cures or exhibited knowledge of which he claimed to have no awareness when awake. In one of these sessions he 'revealed' the fate of the legendary continent Atlantis.

barked at them from the moment they appeared and I admit I would have shared his indignation had the water shortage not already created its own desolation.

As a Government gardener I'm a member of a new privileged class. I have watering and driving permits and coupons for gasoline and boots—an indication of what is to come. So far there has been no clothes rationing.

Daily instructions—when to water and how much, details of mulching, spraying—reach me from the Government radio station to which I tune first thing in the morning. It also provides temperature readings, weather forecasts and the latest news releases on emergency measures, curfews, rationing, insulation. From the way things are going I think it will soon be our only station. I doubt that newspapers will be able to print much longer. In any event, I have already given them up. At first it was interesting to see how quickly drugs, pollution, education, women's lib., all became bygone issues; and, initially, I was fascinated to see how we rationalized. Then I became bored. Then disheartened. Now I am too busy.

Evening. A call came from J. Will I come for Christmas?

Christmas! Extraordinary thought. Like a word from another language learned in my youth, now forgotten.

'I've still got some Heidseck. We can get tight.'

The word takes me back to my teens. 'Like old times . . .'

'Yes.' She is eager. I hate to let her down. 'J., I can't. How could I get to you?'

'In your *car*, silly. *You* still have gas. You're the only one of us who has.' Do I detect a slight hint of accusation, as if I had acquired it illegally?

'But J., it's only for emergencies.'

'My God, Babe, d'you think *this* isn't an emergency?'

'J. dear . . .'

'*Please*, Babe,' she pleads. 'I'm so afraid. Of the looters. The eeriness. You must be afraid too. *Please!*'

I should have said, yes, that of course I was afraid. It's only natural to be afraid. Or, unable to say that, I should have made the soothing noises a mother makes to her child. Instead, 'There's no reason to be afraid, J.,' I said. It must have sounded insufferably pompous.

'No reason!' She was exasperated with me. 'I'd have thought there was every reason.'

She will phone again. In the night perhaps when she can't sleep. Poor J. She feels so alone. She *is* so alone. And so idle. I don't suppose it's occurred to her yet that telephones will soon go. That a whole way of life is vanishing completely.

It's different for me. I have the soybeans which keep me busy all the daylight hours. And Dexter. And above all I have the colours and with them the knowledge that there are others, other people, whose sensibilities I share. We are as invisibly, inviolably related to one another as the components of a molecule. I say 'we'. Perhaps I should speak only for myself, yet I feel as sure of these others as if they had spoken. Like the quail, we share one brain—no, I think it is one heart—between us. How do I know this? How *do* I know? I know by knowing. We are less alarmed by the increasing heat than those who have not seen the colours. I can't explain why. But seeing the colours seems to change one—just as certain diagnostic procedures cure the complaint they are attempting to diagnose.

In all honesty I admit to having had moments when this sense of community was not enough, when I have had a great longing for my own kind—for so have I come to think of these others—in the way one has a great longing for someone one loves. Their presence in the world is not enough. One must see them. Touch them. Speak with them.

But lately that longing has lessened. All longing, in fact. And fear. Even my once great dread that I might cease to see the colours has vanished. It is as if through seeing them I have learned to see them. Have learned to be ready to see—passive; not striving to see—active. It keeps me very wide awake. Transparent even. Still.

The colours come daily now. Dizzying. Transforming. Life-giving. My sometimes back-breaking toil in the garden is lightened, made full of wonder, by the incredible colours shooting in the manner of children's sparklers from the plants themselves and from my own work-worn hands. I hadn't realized that I too am part of this vibrating luminescence.

Later. I have no idea how long it is since I abandoned these notes. Without seasons to measure its passing, without normal activities—preparations for festivals, occasional outings—time feels longer, shorter or—more curious still—simultaneous, undifferentiated. Future and past fused in the present. Linearity broken.

I had intended to write regularly, but the soybeans keep me busy pretty well all day and by evening I'm usually ready for bed. I'm sorry however to have missed recording the day-by-day changes. They were more or less minor at first. But once the heat began its deadly escalation, the world as we have known it—'our world'—had you been able to put it alongside 'this world'—would have seemed almost entirely different.

No one, I think, could have foreseen the speed with which everything has broken down. For instance, the elaborate plans made to maintain transportation became useless in a matter of months. Private traffic was first curtailed, then forbidden. If a man from another planet had looked in on us, he would have been astonished to see us trapped who were apparently free.

The big changes only really began after the first panic evacuations from the cities. Insulated by concrete, sewer pipes and underground parkades, high density areas responded slowly to the increasing temperatures. But once the heat penetrated their insulations, Gehennas[9] were created overnight and whole populations fled in hysterical exodus, jamming highways in their futile attempts to escape.

Prior to this the Government had not publicly acknowledged a crisis situation. They had taken certain precautions, brought in temporary measures to ease shortages and dealt with new developments on an *ad hoc* basis. Endeavoured to play it cool. Or so it seemed. Now they levelled with us. It was obvious that they must have been planning for months, only awaiting the right psychological moment to take everything

9 Places of fiery suffering, hells. This New Testament word comes from Hebrew *ge' hinnom*, literally 'valley of Hinnom', a place near Jerusalem where worshippers of foreign gods supposedly sacrificed children by burning; later this place was used continuously to burn refuse, hence the imagery of a burning pit where the damned were forever consumed.

over. That moment had clearly come. What we had previously thought of as a free world ended. We could no longer eat, drink, move without permits or coupons. This was full-scale emergency.

Yet nothing proceeds logically. Plans are made only to be remade to accommodate new and totally unexpected developments. The heat, unpatterned as disseminated sclerosis,[10] attacks first here, then there. Areas of high temperature suddenly and inexplicably cool off—or vice versa. Agronomists are doing everything possible to keep crops coming—taking advantage of hot-house conditions to force two crops where one had grown before—frantically playing a kind of agriculture roulette, gambling on the length of time a specific region might continue to grow temperate-zone produce.

Mails have long since stopped. And newspapers. And telephones. As a member of a new privileged class, I have been equipped with a two-way radio and a permit to drive on Government business. Schools have of course closed. An attempt was made for a time to provide lessons on TV. Thankfully the looting and rioting seem over. Those desperate gangs of angry citizens who for some time made life additionally difficult, have now disappeared. We seem at last to understand that we are all in this together.

Life is very simple without electricity. I get up with the light and go to bed as darkness falls. My food supply is still substantial and because of the soybean crop I am all right for water. Dexter has adapted well to his new life. He is outdoors less than he used to be and has switched to a mainly vegetable diet without too much difficulty.

Evening. This morning a new order over the radio. All of us with special driving privileges were asked to report to our zone garage to have our tires treated with heat-resistant plastic.

I had not been into town for months. I felt rather as one does on returning home from hospital—that the world is unexpectedly large, with voluminous airy spaces. This was exaggerated perhaps by the fact that our whole zone had been given over to soybeans. Everywhere the same rows of green plants—small pods already formed—march across gardens and boulevards. I was glad to see the climate prove so favourable. But there was little else to make me rejoice as I drove through ominously deserted streets, paint blistering and peeling on fences and houses, while overhead a haze of dust, now always with us, created a green sun.

The prolonged heat has made bleak the little park opposite the garage. A rocky little park, once all mosses and rhododendrons, it is bare now, and brown. I was seeing the day as everyone saw it. Untransmuted.

As I stepped out of my car to speak to the attendant I cursed that I had not brought my insulators. The burning tarmac made me shift rapidly from foot to foot. Anyone from another planet would have wondered at this extraordinary quirk of earthlings. But my feet were forgotten as my eyes alighted a second time on the park across the way. I had never before seen so dazzling and variegated a display of colours. How could there be such prismed brilliance in the range of greys and browns? It was as if

10 That is, like the intermittent pattern occurring in some cases of multiple sclerosis, in which the illness flares up in one area of the body and then goes into remission before showing up in a new location.

the perceiving organ—wherever it is—sensitized by earlier experience, was now correctly tuned for this further perception.

The process was as before: the merest shake and the whole park was 'rainbow, rainbow, rainbow'. A further shake brought the park from *there* to *here.* Interior. But this time the interior space had increased. Doubled. By a kind of instant knowledge that rid me of all doubt, I knew that the garage attendant was seeing it too. *We saw the colours.*

Then, with that slight shift of focus, as if a gelatinous film had moved briefly across my sight, everything slipped back.

I really looked at the attendant for the first time. He was a skinny young man standing up naked inside a pair of loose striped overalls cut off at the knee, *Sidney* embroidered in red over his left breast pocket. He was blond, small-boned, with nothing about him to stick in the memory except his clear eyes which at that moment bore an expression of total comprehension.

'You . . .' we began together and laughed.

'Have you seen them before?' I asked. But it was rather as one would say 'how do you do'—not so much a question as a salutation.

We looked at each other for a long time, as if committing each other to memory.

'Do you know anyone else?' I said.

'One or two. Three, actually. Do you?

I shook my head. 'You are the first. Is it . . . is it . . . always like that?'

'You mean . . . ?' he gestured towards his heart.

I nodded.

'Yes,' he said. 'Yes, it is.'

There didn't seem anything more to talk about. Your right hand hasn't much to say to your left, or one eye to the other. There was comfort in the experience, if comfort is the word, which it isn't. More as if an old faculty had been extended. Or a new one activated.

Sidney put my car on the hoist and sprayed its tires.

Some time later. I have not seen Sidney again. Two weeks ago when I went back he was not there and as of yesterday, cars have become obsolete. Not that we will use that word publicly. The official word is *suspended.*

Strange to be idle after months of hard labour. A lull only before the boys from the Department of Agriculture come back to prepare the land again. I am pleased that the soybeans are harvested, that I was able to nurse them along to maturity despite the scorching sun, the intermittent plagues and the problems with water. Often the pressure was too low to turn the sprinklers and I would stand, hour after hour, hose in hand, trying to get the most use from the tiny trickle spilling from the nozzle.

Sometimes my heart turns over as I look through the kitchen window and see the plants shrivelled and grotesque, the baked earth scored by a web of fine cracks like the glaze on a plate subjected to too high an oven. Then it comes to me in a flash that of course, the beans are gone, the harvest is over.

The world is uncannily quiet. I don't think anyone had any idea of how much noise even distant traffic made until we were without it. It is rare indeed for vehicles other than Government mini-cars to be seen on the streets. And there are fewer and fewer pedestrians. Those who do venture out move on their thick insulators with the slow gait of rocking-horses. Surreal and alien, they heighten rather than lessen one's sense of isolation. For one *is* isolated. We have grown used to the sight of helicopters like large dragon-flies hovering overhead—addressing us through their PA systems, dropping supplies—welcome but impersonal.

Dexter is my only physical contact. He is delighted to have me inside again. The heat is too great for him in the garden and as, officially, he no longer exists, we only go out under cover of dark.

The order to destroy pets, when it came, indicated more clearly than anything that had gone before, that the Government had abandoned hope. In an animal-loving culture, only direct necessity could validate such an order. It fell upon us like a heavy pall.

When the Government truck stopped by for Dexter, I reported him dead. Now that the welfare of so many depends upon our co-operation with authority, law-breaking is a serious offence. But I am not uneasy about breaking this law. As long as he remains healthy and happy, Dexter and I will share our dwindling provisions.

No need to be an ecologist or dependent on non-existent media to know all life is dying and the very atmosphere of our planet is changing radically. Already no birds sing in the hideous hot dawns as the sun, rising through a haze of dust, sheds its curious bronze-green light on a brown world. The trees that once gave us shade stand leafless now in an infernal winter. Yet as if in the masts and riggings of ships, St Elmo's fire[11] flickers and shines in their high branches, and bioplasmic pyrotechnics light the dying soybeans. I am reminded of how the ghostly form of a limb remains attached to the body from which it has been amputated. And I can't help thinking of all the people who don't see the colours, the practical earth-touchers with only their blunt senses to inform them. I wonder about J. and if, since we last talked, she has perhaps been able to see the colours too. But I think not. After so many years of friendship, surely I would be able to sense her, had she broken through.

Evening. . . ? The heat has increased greatly in the last few weeks—in a quantum leap. This has resulted immediately in two things: a steady rising of the sea level throughout the world—with panic reactions and mild flooding in coastal areas; and, at last, a noticeably higher air temperature. It is causing great physical discomfort.

It was against this probability that the authorities provided us with insulator spray. Like giant cans of pressurized shaving cream. I have shut all rooms but the kitchen and by concentrating my insulating zeal on this one small area, we have managed to keep fairly cool. The word is relative, of course. The radio has stopped giving temperature readings and I have no thermometer. I have filled all cracks and crannies with the foaming plastic, even applied a layer to the exterior wall. There are no baths, of course, and no cold drinks. On the other hand I've abandoned clothes and given Dexter a shave and a haircut. Myself as well. We are a fine pair. Hairless and naked.

11 A phenomenon in which a luminous electrical discharge appears as a ball of fire on a ship during a storm.

When the world state of emergency was declared we didn't need to be told that science had given up. The official line had been that the process would reverse itself as inexplicably as it had begun. The official policy—to hold out as long as possible. With this in mind, task forces worked day and night on survival strategy. On the municipal level, which is all I really knew about, everything that could be centralized was. Telephone exchanges, hydro plants, radio stations became centres around which vital activities took place. Research teams investigated the effects of heat on water mains, sewer pipes, electrical wiring; work crews were employed to prevent, protect, or even destroy incipient causes of fires, flood, and asphyxiation.

For some time now the city has been zoned. In each zone a large building has been selected, stocked with food, medical supplies, and insulating materials. We have been provided with zone maps and an instruction sheet telling us to stay where we are until ordered to move to what is euphemistically called our 'home'. When ordered, we are to load our cars with whatever we still have of provisions and medicines and drive off *at once.* Helicopters have already dropped kits with enough gasoline for the trip and a small packet, somewhat surprisingly labelled 'emergency rations', which contains one cyanide capsule—grim reminder that all may not go as the planners plan. We have been asked to mark out maps, in advance, with the shortest route from our house to our 'home', so that in a crisis we will know what we are doing. These instructions are repeated *ad nauseam* over the radio, along with hearty assurances that everything is under control and that there is no cause for alarm. The Government station is now all that remains of our multimedia. When it is not broadcasting instructions, its mainly pre-recorded tapes sound inanely complacent and repetitive. Evacuation Day, as we have been told again and again, will be announced by whistle blast. Anyone who runs out of food before that or who is in need of medical aid is to use the special gas ration and go 'home' at once.

As a long-time preserver of fruits and vegetables, I hope to hold out until E. Day. When that time comes it will be a sign that broadcasts are no longer possible, that contact can no longer be maintained between the various areas of the community, that the process will not reverse itself in time and that, in fact, our world is well on the way to becoming—oh, wonder of the modern kitchen—a self-cleaning oven.

Spring, Summer, Winter, Fall. What season is it after all? I sense the hours by some inner clock. I have applied so many layers of insulating spray that almost no heat comes through from outside. But we have to have air and the small window I have left exposed acts like a furnace. Yet through it I see the dazzling colours; sense my fellow-men.

Noon. The sun is hidden directly overhead. The world is topaz. I see it through the minute eye of my window. I, the perceiving organ that peers through the house's only aperture. We are one, the house and I—parts of some vibrating sensitive organism in which Dexter plays his differentiated but integral role. The light enters us, dissolves us. We are the golden motes in the jewel.

Midnight. The sun is directly below. Beneath the burning soles of my arching feet it shines, a globe on fire. Its rays penetrate the earth. Upward beaming, they support and sustain us. We are held aloft, a perfectly balanced ball in the jet of a golden fountain. Light, dancing, infinitely upheld.

Who knows how much later. I have just 'buried' Dexter.

This morning I realized this hot little cell was no longer a possible place for a dog.

I had saved one can of dog food against this day. As I opened it Dexter's eyes swivelled in the direction of so unexpected and delicious a smell. He struggled to his feet, joyous, animated. The old Dexter. I was almost persuaded to delay, to wait and see if the heat subsided. What if tomorrow we awakened to rain? But something in me, stronger than this wavering self, carried on with its purpose.

He sat up, begging, expectant.

I slipped the meat out of the can.

'You're going to have a really good dinner,' I said, but as my voice was unsteady, I stopped.

I scooped a generous portion of the meat into his dish and placed it on the floor. He was excited, and as always when excited about food, he was curiously ceremonial, unhurried—approaching his dish and backing away from it, only to approach it again at a slightly different angle. As if the exact position was of the greatest importance. It was one of his most amusing and endearing characteristics. I let him eat his meal in his own leisurely and appreciative manner and then, as I have done so many times before, I fed him his final *bonne bouche* by hand. The cyanide pill, provided by a beneficent Government for me, went down in a gulp.

I hadn't expected it to be so sudden. Life and death so close. His small frame convulsed violently, then collapsed. Simultaneously, as if synchronized, the familiar 'shake' occurred in my vision. Dexter glowed brightly, whitely, like phosphorus. In that dazzling, light-filled moment he was no longer a small dead dog lying there. I could have thought him a lion, my sense of scale had so altered. His beautiful body blinded me with its fires.

With the second 'shake' his consciousness must have entered mine for I felt a surge in my heart as if his loyalty and love had flooded it. And like a kind of ground bass, I was aware of scents and sounds I had not known before. Then a great peace filled me—an immense space, light and sweet—and I realized that this was death. Dexter's death.

But how describe what is beyond description?

As the fires emanating from his slight frame died down, glowed weakly, residually, I put on my insulators and carried his body into the now fever-hot garden. I laid him on what had been at one time an azalea bed. I was unable to dig a grave in the baked earth or to cover him with leaves. But there are no predators now to pick the flesh from his bones. Only the heat which will, in time, desiccate it.

I returned to the house, opening the door as little as possible to prevent the barbs and briars of burning air from entering with me. I sealed the door from inside with foam sealer.

The smell of the canned dog food permeated the kitchen. It rang in my nostrils. Olfactory chimes, lingering, delicious. I was intensely aware of Dexter. Dexter immanent. I contained him as simply as a dish contains water. But the simile is not exact.

For I missed his physical presence. One relies on the physical more than I had known. My hands sought palpable contact. The flesh forgets slowly.

Idly, abstractedly, I turned on the radio. I seldom do now as the batteries are low and they are my last. Also, there is little incentive. Broadcasts are intermittent and I've heard the old tapes over and over.

But the Government station was on the air. I tuned with extreme care and placed my ear close to the speaker. A voice, faint, broken by static, sounded like that of the Prime Minister.

'. . . all human beings can do, your Government has done for you.' (Surely not a political speech *now*?) 'But we have failed. Failed to hold back the heat. Failed to protect ourselves against it; to protect you against it. It is with profound grief that I send this farewell message to you all.' I realized that this, too, had been pre-recorded, reserved for the final broadcast. 'Even now, let us not give up hope . . .'

And then, blasting through the speech, monstrously loud in the stone-silent world, the screech of the whistle summoning us 'home'. I could no longer hear the PM's words.

I began automatically, obediently, to collect my few remaining foodstuffs, reaching for a can of raspberries, the last of the crop to have grown in my garden when dawns were dewy and cool and noon sun fell upon us like golden pollen. My hand stopped in mid-air.

I would not go 'home'.

The whistle shrilled for a very long time. A curious great steam-driven cry—man's last. Weird that our final utterance should be this anguished inhuman wail.

The end. Now that it is virtually too late, I regret not having kept a daily record. Now that the part of me that writes has become nearly absorbed, I feel obliged to do the best I can.

I am down to the last of my food and water. Have lived on little for some days—weeks, perhaps. How can one measure passing time? Eternal time grows like a tree, its roots in my heart. If I lie on my back I see winds moving in its high branches and a chorus of birds is singing in its leaves. The song is sweeter than any music I have ever heard.

My kitchen is as strange as I am myself. Its walls bulge with many layers of spray. It is without geometry. Like the inside of an eccentric Styrofoam coconut. Yet, with some inner eye, I see its intricate mathematical structure. It is as ordered and no more random than an atom.

My face is unrecognizable in the mirror. Wisps of short damp hair. Enormous eyes. I swim in their irises. Could I drown in the pits of their pupils?

Through my tiny window when I raise the blind, a dead world shines. Sometimes dust storms fill the air with myriad particles burning bright and white as the lion body of Dexter. Sometimes great clouds swirl, like those from which saints receive revelations.

The colours are almost constant now. There are times when, light-headed, I dance a dizzying dance, feel part of that whirling incandescent matter—what I might once have called inorganic matter!

On still days the blameless air, bright as a glistening wing, hangs over us, hangs its extraordinary beneficence over us.

We are together now, united, indissoluble. Bonded.

Because there is no expectation, there is no frustration.

Because there is nothing we can have, there is nothing we can want.

We are hungry of course. Have cramps and weakness. But they are as if in *another body*. Our body is inviolate. Inviolable.

We share one heart.

We are one with the starry heavens and our bodies are stars.

Inner and outer are the same. A continuum. The water in the locks is level. We move to a higher water. A high sea.

A ship could pass through.

1981

Margaret Avison

b. 1918

Margaret Avison was born in Galt, Ont., and grew up in Calgary, Alta. She studied English literature at Victoria College, University of Toronto, where she earned her BA in 1940, a year after her first published poem, 'Gatineau', appeared in the *Canadian Forum*. In 1951, while working as a librarian at the University of Toronto, she published *A History of Ontario*, a high-school text. After attending the University of Chicago (1956–7) and earning a Guggenheim Fellowship, Avison returned, in 1963, to the University of Toronto as a graduate student. After spending two years as a lecturer at the university's Scarborough Campus (1967–8), she began work as a social worker for the Presbyterian Mission in Toronto, where she remained for five years before spending a brief period as writer-in-residence at the University of Western Ontario (1972–3). From 1978 to 1986 she worked as a secretary with the Mustard Seed Mission in Toronto. Meanwhile, she has written book reviews, translated poems, and worked steadily at her own poetry, producing a small corpus of excellence.

Avison's poems began to appear in the thirties. She was long diffident about collecting them for book publication, even though the clusters of poems collected in anthologies such as A.J.M. Smith's *Book of Canadian Poetry* in 1943 established her as an outstanding poet. It was not until 1960 that, encouraged by her friends, she published her first book, *Winter Sun* (it won a Governor General's Award). Two years later the American literary magazine *Origin* featured her poetry, printing thirteen poems and a letter she had written to its editor, Cid Corman, expressing her thoughts on the writing of poetry.

In 1963 Avison's life changed dramatically when she actively embraced Christianity and committed herself to a life of contemplation and service (an account of this conversion can be found in *A Kind of Perseverance*, 1993, a record of Avison's Pascal Lectures on Christianity and the University given at the University of Waterloo). The poetry that followed reflects this event clearly, but the seeds of her religious concerns may be seen in some of her earlier works, which depict a fallen world where spacious, open landscapes and awesome skies (like those she experienced growing up on the prairies) are lost to a darker world of urban decay and atrophy. These earlier poems struggle with the question of a creator who seems omnipotent but absent or unresponding; after her conversion there is a reassessment of the distance between man and God and an attempt to show the effects of a closer relationship between the two.

In 1966 Avison produced *The Dumfounding*, a volume of less introspective and somewhat more accessible poems. Her third collection, *Sunblue*, which appeared in 1978, shows more clearly the effects of her Christianity. That book was followed by *No Time* (1989), which earned her a second Governor General's Award. In 1991 she finally permitted her *Selected Poems* to be brought together: it includes some new and some previously uncollected work as well as her adaptations of Ilona Duczynska's literal translations of poems by two Hungarian poets. Avison has since published *Not Yet, but Still* (1997) and *Concrete and Wild Carrot* (2002).

Avison's earlier poems—much like those of T.S. Eliot and Wallace Stevens—depend upon a wide knowledge of history and poetic tradition, of contemporary events and universal myths. A.J.M. Smith described her diction in this period as 'erudite, complex, archaic, simple, modern—an amalgam of the scientific and philosophical with the familiar and the new, a high style and low, pillaged and put to work'. This kind of poetry is dense and challenging, full of both difficulties and rewards. Witty and complex, it can juxtapose the painter's rules of vanishing-point perspective with our view of the world as we move through it; or it can turn the sonnet into a weapon against all sonnets.

In the poems written after Avison turned away from the difficult modernist mode of her early poetry, the contemplative life she has chosen often imbues her poems with a tension that replaces the intricacies of her earlier, more philosophical verse: under the surfaces of her later poems the reader may sense a struggle between the natural ego of a writer and the self-effacement demanded by a religious life. Still, as in her early work, the act of seeing is not passive: an 'optic heart' must continue to labour intellectually and spiritually to retain its passionate Christian perspective. Indeed, the act of seeing becomes even more important in the later poetry because her work increasingly locates itself within the visionary tradition, often recalling the religious voice of such poets as George Herbert, Thomas Traherne, Emily Dickinson, and Gerard Manley Hopkins. Like many drawn to mystical ways of knowing, Avison longs to articulate that which can not be named, to speak what she calls the 'one word / we know no way to now' ('asap; etc.').

Neverness

OR, THE ONE SHIP BEACHED
ON ONE FAR DISTANT SHORE

Old Adam, with his fist-full of plump earth,
His sunbright gaze on his eternal hill
Is not historical:
His tale is never done
For us who know a world no longer bathed
In harsh splendor of economy.
We millions hold old Adam in our thoughts
A pivot for the future-past, a core
Of the one dream that never goads to action
But stains our entrails with nostalgia
And wrings the sweat of death in ancient eyes.

The one-celled plant is not historical.
Leeuwenhoek[1] peered through his magic window
And in a puddle glimpsed the tiny grain
Of firmament that was before the Adam.

I'd like to pull that squinting Dutchman's sleeve
And ask what were his thoughts, lying at night,
And smelling the sad spring, and thinking out
Across the fullness of night air, smelling
The dark canal, and dusty oat-bag, cheese,
And wet straw-splintered wood, and rust-seamed leather
And pearly grass and silent deeps of sky
Honey-combed with its million years' of light
And prune-sweet earth
Honey-combed with the silent worms of dark.
Old Leeuwenhoek must have had ribby thoughts
To hoop the hollow pounding of his heart
Those nights of spring in 1600-odd.
It would be done if he could tell it us.

The tissue of our metaphysic cells
No magic window yet has dared reveal.
Our bleared world welters on
Far past the one-cell Instant. Points are spread
And privacy is unadmitted prison.

Why, now I know the lust of omnipresence!
You thousands merging lost,
        I call to you
Down the stone corridors that wall me in.

I am inside these days, snug in a job
In one of many varnished offices
Bleak with the wash of daylight
And us, the human pencils wearing blunt.
Soon I'll be out with you,
Another in the lonely unshut world
Where sun blinks hard on yellow brick and glazed,
On ads in sticky posterpaint
        And fuzzy
            At midday intersections.

1 Anton van Leeuwenhoek (1632–1723), Dutch naturalist, was an important pioneer in microscopy.

The milk is washed down corded throats at noon
Along a thousand counters, and the hands
That count the nickel from a greasy palm
Have never felt an udder.
        The windy dark
That thrums high among towers and nightspun branches
Whirs through our temples with a dry confusion.
We sprawl abandoned into disbelief
And feel the pivot-picture of old Adam
On the first hill that ever was, alone,
And see the hard earth seeded with sharp snow
And dream that history is done.

*

And if that be the dream that whortles[2] out
Into unending night
Then must the pivot Adam be denied
And the whole cycle ravelled and flung loose.
Is this the Epoch[3] when the age-old Serpent
Must writhe and loosen, slacking out
To a new pool of Time's eternal sun?
O Adam, will your single outline blur
At this long last when slow mist wells
Fuming from all the valleys of the earth?
Or will our unfixed vision rather blind
Through agony to the last gelid stare
And none be left to witness the blank mist?

1943

2 Here, 'hurtles'.
3 That is, Armageddon, as described in Revelation; 'Serpent': Satan, see Revelation 12ff.

The Butterfly

An uproar,
a spruce-green sky, bound in iron,
the murky sea running a sulphur scum:
I saw a butterfly suddenly;
it clung between the ribs of the storm, wavering
and flung against the battering bone-wind.

I remember it, glued to the grit of that rain-strewn beach
that glowered around it, swallowed its startled design
in the larger iridescence of unstrung dark.

That wild, sour air, the miles of crouching forest, those wings,
when all-enveloping air is a
thin glass globe, swirling with storm,
tempt one to the abyss.

The butterfly's meaning, even though smashed.
Imprisoned in endless cycle? No. The meaning!
Can't we stab that one angle
into the curve of space that sweeps beyond
our farthest knowing, out into light's
place of invisibility?

1943; rev. 1989[1]

1 'This is a revision, because I have learned that "moth" and "butterfly" are not interchangeable terms (as I had written them in ignorance in the earlier version), and because the "angle" seems indicated in Rom. 8: 21 and Eph. 1: 10'. [Avison's note] The first verse Avison cites in this note says that 'the creature itself also shall be delivered from the bondage of corruption into the glorious liberty of the children of God'; the second, that God has promised that 'in the dispensation of the fulness of times he might gather together in one all things in Christ, both which are in heaven, and which are on earth'. Avison's revision of the original poem goes beyond correcting the 'moth' of the first version: she also dropped the lines that ended the original second stanza, which said that the elements of the situation 'tempt us to stare, and seize analogies. / The Voice that stilled the sea of Galilee / overtoned by the new peace, the fierce subhuman peace / of such an east sky, blanched like Eternity' (a reference to Christ calming the storm in the boat with his disciples in Mark 4: 36–41).

Perspective

A sport,[1] an adventitious sprout
These eyeballs, that have somehow slipped
The mesh of generations since Mantegna?[2]

Yet I declare, your seeing is diseased
That cripples space. The fear has eaten back
Through sockets to the caverns of the brain
And made of it a sifty habitation.

1 A mutation, used later in the poem in the more familiar sense of the word.
2 Andrea Mantegna (1431–1506), Italian painter and engraver famous for his use of perspective of great depth.

We stand beholding the one plain
And in your face I see the chastening
Of its small tapering design
That brings up *punkt.*[3]
(The Infinite, you say,
Is an unthinkable—and pointless too—
Extension of that *punkt.*)

But do you miss the impact of that fierce
Raw boulder five miles off? You are not pierced
By that great spear of grass on the horizon?
You are not smitten with the shock
Of that great thundering sky?

Your law of optics is a quarrel
Of chickenfeet on paper. Does a train
Run pigeon-toed?

I took a train from here to Ottawa
On tracks that did not meet. We swelled and roared
Mile upon mightier mile, and when we clanged
Into the vasty station we were indeed
Brave company for giants.

Keep your eyes though,
You, and not I, will travel safer back
To Union station.

Your fear has me infected, and my eyes
That were my sport so long, will soon be apt
Like yours to press out dwindling vistas from
The massive flux massive Mantegna knew
And all its sturdy everlasting foregrounds.

1948[4]

3 Point; the vanishing point in perspective.
4 This poem and the two preceding poems received their first book publication in *The Book of Canadian Poetry,* edited by A.J.M. Smith: 'Neverness' and 'The Butterfly' in the first edition (1943), and 'Perspective' in the second edition (1948).

Snow

Nobody stuffs the world in at your eyes.
The optic heart must venture: a jail-break
And re-creation. Sedges and wild rice
Chase rivery pewter. The astonished cinders quake
With rhizomes.[1] All ways through the electric air
Trundle candy-bright disks; they are desolate
Toys if the soul's gates seal, and cannot bear,
Must shudder under, creation's unseen freight.
But soft, there is snow's legend: colour of mourning
Along the yellow Yangtze[2] where the wheel
Spins an indifferent stasis that's death's warning.
Asters of tumbled quietness reveal
Their petals. Suffering this starry blur
The rest may ring your change,[3] sad listener.

1960

1 Rootlike stems running along or under the ground, from which roots, stalks, and leaves grow.
2 River in China, the longest in Asia.
3 Change ringing is the ringing of church bells in all the permutations of a given pattern; thus, to ring changes is to play with permutations.

Butterfly Bones; or Sonnet Against Sonnets

The cyanide jar seals life, as sonnets move
towards final stiffness. Cased in a white glare
these specimens stare for peering boys, to prove
strange certainties. Plane dogsled and safari
assure continuing range. The sweep-net skill,
the patience, learning, leave all living stranger.
Insect—or poem—waits for the fix, the frill
precision can effect, brilliant with danger.
What law and wonder the museum spectres
bespeak is cryptic for the shivery wings,
the world cut-diamond-eyed, those eyes' reflectors,
or herbal grass, sunned motes, fierce listening.
Might sheened and rigid trophies strike men blind
like Adam's lexicon locked in the mind?

1960

Light (I)

The stuff of flesh and bone
is given, *datum.* Down
the stick-men, plastiscene-
people, clay-lump children, are strewn,
each casting shadow in the eye of day.

Then—listen!—I see
breath of delighting rise from
those stones the sun touches
and hear a snarl of breath
as a mouth sucks air. And with
shivery sighings—see: they stir
and turn and move, and power
to build, to undermine, is theirs,
is ours.

The stuff, the breath, the power to move even thumbs
and with them, things: *data.* What is
the harpsweep on the heart for?
What does the constructed power
of speculation reach for?
Each of us casts a shadow in the bewildering day,
an own-shaped shadow only.

The light has looked on Light.

He from elsewhere
speaks; he breathes impasse-
crumpled hope even
in us:
that near.

1978

A Thief in the Night

A thief? There's nothing here!
dust-balls, mouse-seed,
mud-crumbs, even

motes a sunstreak would discover.
These the break-and-enter
artist sweeps clean, invading
space as its window-polishing
architect—surprising!

Yet thief indeed where are
harpsichord, china cabinet,
hifidelity speakers, humidifier,
orangerie, wine pantry, who knows
what all. But the
break-and-enter man
was after none of that
so so much more a threat—
surprising!

(A royal progress would have been a figure
more fitting,
if someone other than the
'thief' were designator.)

1991

asap; etc.

Acronyms, alas,
become words-without-etymology;
components crumble blind;
the agglomerating initials find
themselves picked up by ear without apology
by those too used to symbols without mass.

Are moon and foreheads, and this opening rose
(massively present), nonetheless
the cryptic relics of one word
we know no way to now? have heard
of only in distress
from some original who chose

to spot particulars as part
of utterance, acronymic,
not conceived as final? Sense

and sound of the immense?
fully articulate in a tongue untaught?

Well, that's a place to start.

1997

Music Was in the Wind

It was Orpheus[1] all along!
He carried Eurydice down, down
into the earth
in his arms, going himself with her
since this was the only way
out of her mortal maze now.
All he had then he risked
except a love strong and steady enough
never to share her
relief in this fine-sifted silence, nor
her torn
loyalties to this private place
and to the devastated but remembered
home where she was known.

First it had to be down.
He was no
stoic, no ascetic, moved to
goodness without experience
of all our billion moments. Did he
hear what the shepherds overheard?
sweet singing in the choir?

He carried her he loved
the whole way down.

The strange travail home
up into light
emptied his arms. He

1 The figure from Greek myth who could entrance wild beasts with the beauty of his singing and lyre playing. After the death of his wife Eurydice, he descended into the underworld and secured her release from the dead; he lost her, however, when he failed to obey the condition that he not look back at her until they had returned to the world of the living.

took her by the hand, and she was walking.
And on the way they would be
sometimes sensitive to a loss as she
lived it out in a familiar
and yet an altered world,
remembering a morning, in a song,
going about the city in the streets,
yet even then
knowing him once again beyond our wall:
'Arise, and come. . . .'[2]

1997

2 The phrasing of this closing passage recalls several Biblical passages, many of them injunctions by Jesus. Compare Acts 9: 11: 'And the Lord said unto him, Arise, and go into the street which is called Straight'. An association of Orpheus with Jesus is a traditional one, based on an analogy between the first part of Orpheus' story, his descent into the underworld to rescue a departed soul and the extra-Biblical tradition of the Harrowing of Hell, which holds that, during his three days in the grave, Jesus descended into hell to rescue the virtuous souls there.

In Season and Out of Season

Today the blueness burns
inbetween new greens and space's
soundless blackness.
Yet we even now
discern more, cry:
No, lovely as May is
we would hear more.

Moses, you are the voice
the Voice spoke with.[1]
Centuries have not, will not,
still that, therefore. The marvel
of the pitched cradle of reeds, the appeal
to a ruler-murderer's daughter's[2]
mothering heart, the barter
of true for foster care that became both;

1 That is, Moses, as God's prophet, gave human voice to God's divine voice, particularly when he brought the Ten Commandments down from Mount Sinai. The whole of this poem is structured around allusions to the story of Moses, as found in the Books of Exodus, Leviticus, Numbers, and Deuteronomy.
2 The opening of Exodus describes how the Egyptian Pharaoh, concerned that the Israelites were becoming too numerous, ordered that all newborn boys be put to death. To save her son, Moses' mother puts him into a basket made of reeds and sealed with pitch, setting it afloat on the river. It is found by the Pharaoh's daughter, who takes Moses as her adopted son.

your growing,
that unexceptional miracle
of years: it all made way for
what? One small pure drop—
anticipation? hope?—hung on life's
strange leaf-edge; trembling in the light
for years, for all your years indeed,
for 'By faith Moses . . .'.[3] It is said.

Exult in warmth and depth
of branches here? Yes, and yet Antarctica
in this same season,
snarls, pounces, gnaws—even while
today the earth
rejoices in deliverance in this zone.

Moses, your early privilege turned
when you saw abuse into
an alienating cause? What burned
was not the authorities' heartless
indignation, not
the mute slaves', not
even your own
violent indignation, in the end.
Bare-soled on desert sand
you bowed,
and bartered with your seclusion for
your people's whole concern,
the Other's deep concern,
finally given to both.[4]

For many days
here, a sagging cloud and stiff
dark mat of branch and twig,
clacking, entombed us all. Now that winter's over

3 An allusion to a brief retelling of Moses' story in Christian terms in Hebrews 11: 23–5: 'By faith Moses, when he was born, was hid three months of his parents, because they saw he was a proper child; and they were not afraid of the king's commandment. By faith Moses, when he was come to years, refused to be called the son of Pharaoh's daughter; Choosing rather to suffer affliction with the people of God, than to enjoy the pleasures of sin for a season.'

4 When Moses came to manhood, he grew angry when he saw an Egyptian overseer beating an Israelite and killed the Egyptian. Though he attempted to conceal his deed, he found that it was known by the other Israelites and soon after by the Pharaoh. He fled into the wilderness, and once there realized that his true identity was that of 'an alien residing in a foreign land'. God appears to him in the form of a burning bush—commanding him to remove his sandals because he is on holy ground—and gives him the commission to lead his people out of bondage and across the desert wilderness towards the Promised Land.

the trees and shrubs are thimbleberried with
chestnut flowers, with deep-breathed lilacs.

Moses, how does your solitary death[5]—
and you went up the lonely crags
as bidden—
follow? Did the Voice
seek silence then? from faith
were you led . . . further?
It may be heaven is the
light that . . . conceals?

Your longing then was
not so much to
realize the Land for you were
sure about the Land
long since by faith,
but to be brought
where the celestial Other would
be known in fullness
however dark?

He saw the Lord. He, Moses, was seen
transfigured too, in mountain light,[6] when
much was made plain by once
caring enough to pray to be
blotted out.
(For he had stood among his
fractious protesting people; he
recognized too his own
moment of failure to
stand with the Voice, heeding instead
an unholy flare of
exasperated nature.[7] Once. Enough.)

5 The story of Moses' death is told in Deuteronomy 34: 'Then Moses went up from the plains of Moab to Mount Nebo, to the top of Pisgah, which is opposite Jericho, and the LORD showed him the whole land. . . . The LORD said to him, "This is the land of which I swore to Abraham, to Isaac, and to Jacob, saying, 'I will give it to your descendants'; I have let you see it with your eyes, but you shall not cross over there." '

6 According to Exodus 34: 29, when 'Moses came down from Mount Sinai . . . Moses did not know that the skin of his face shone because he had been talking with God.' Avison's allusion here also recalls the event in the Gospels known as the Transfiguration. (See Mark 9: 2ff, which describes how Jesus ascends a mountain with Peter, James, and John, and 'his clothes became dazzling white . . . And there appeared . . . Elijah with Moses.')

7 Moses is not permitted to enter the Promised Land because of an event described in Numbers 20: 2–13: impatient with the unruly temper of the people he leads, he rashly strikes a rock to make it yield water.

Not in season, in the revolving
solar system, in which we turn
changeably, always.
Not without the appalling
lightless depth. Not but as a way station
perhaps is the
unimaginable light where
all maybe is plain.

1997

Cycle of Community

Mid-morning paraffin film over the
dayshine has
incidentally opened the ear
to little clanks and whirrs
out there, the hum
of a world going on,
untroubled by the silent witness, sky.
We here are silent. Yet being
drawn into, with, each
creature, each machine-work
thump, each step, faraway bark,
buzz, whine, rustle, etc.
goes to give our city
a voice, dampered by distance;
serves, through outer
windless openness of skywash, to
open a bud of tremulous hearing.

Full day will blare away
later. Then—
walk (an even pace) where cars, trucks, a
cement-mixer, teenagers out of school,
and a tied puppy keening
outside the grocer's,
provide a mix the studios would
take pride in.
Go steadily for your sake and
the others' on the sidewalk
burrowing by. And keep your face

like anyone's, in
pedestrious preoccupation—
although
you'll have to part your lips
a little, to play in.
First, test the pitch of the
prevailing din
(humming), then (still with no
perceptible opening of the mouth)
intone on the same tone-level
with all the enveloping street-sound.
Louder. As loudly as you can!
Nobody hears a thing,
                    even yourself!
Otherwise surely someone would
give that quick glance of
furtive avoidance that flicks
some flushed and angrily
gesturing man you may
hear shouting along
anywhere about town. He chooses
to stray apart from the
condemnable crazy world.

Surprisingly, evening, after the hours
of sharp light, closes in
overcast. Our thunderous busynesses
shift into calmer surge and flow.
Before dark (sky and windows
contemplating emptiness) we half-
hear the foghorn and remember
the lake, and night.

2002

Al Purdy

1918–2000

In the opening lines of 'The Country North of Belleville' Al Purdy maps out the home territory where he grew up and where he spent most of his life: it is a 'Bush land scrub land' near the eastern end of Lake Ontario, a landscape that can both give a man 'some sense of what beauty / is' yet it is also 'the country of our defeat'. And though he calls it a region 'where the young / leave quickly', Purdy himself spent most of his life in this contradictory landscape, making it the subject of his most powerful poetry.

Descended from what he described as 'degenerate Loyalist stock' and born in Wooler, Ont.—a small town, a little west of Belleville, that he called 'mythological because the same village could not now be found'—Alfred Wellington Purdy (before settling on 'Al Purdy' he signed his poems 'Alfred W. Purdy' and 'A.W. Purdy') attended school in Trenton until he dropped out at sixteen. He held a number of casual jobs in the Trenton-Belleville area before deciding, in 1936, to travel west, first hitch-hiking and then riding the rails. After working his way across Canada and then working in Vancouver, he returned to Ontario in time for the beginning of the Second World War and his enlistment in the Royal Canadian Air Force (he remained in the Air Force until 1945). Around this time, he met Eurithe Parkhurst, the woman who became his wife of fifty-nine years—and who makes many appearances in his poems as his straight man. After the war was over, the Purdys moved back to Ontario for a few years, then returned to the West Coast until the late 1950s. Thereafter they settled in Ameliasburg, where Purdy built his own home on Roblin Lake. Though they frequently travelled away from that home base—Purdy's journeys to the Cariboo country of BC, to Baffin Island, to Hiroshima, and throughout Latin America served to reinvigorate his poetry and to provide further occasions for his reflections on the relationship of the individual to place—Roblin Lake remained from that time the centre of his psychic universe. Even after he retired to Sidney, BC, he spent part or all of his summers there.

His attachment to place as a source of identity and self-worth can be seen in 'A Handful of Earth', with its desire to articulate the 'true language' that 'speaks from inside / the land itself', and in a late poem like 'Say the Names', in which the place names of Canada themselves become a lyric and moving tribute to the landscape they have denominated. As Michael Ondaatje wrote in his foreword to Purdy's final book:

Cashel and Ameliasburg and Elzevir and Weslemkoon are names we can now put on a literary map alongside the Mississippi and the Strand. For a person of my generation, Al Purdy's poems mapped and named the landscape of Ontario.

Having begun to write poetry in his teens, Purdy paid to have his amateurish first book, *The Enchanted Echo*, published in 1944 (only a few copies still exist to record the fact that his poems once contained lines like 'Now oft, anon, as in a dream, / Oe'r sculptured heights ascending'). In the 1950s Purdy produced three more collections of largely derivative work, patterned on traditional models, including the work of Rudyard Kipling and of Confederation poets Roberts and Carman. He credits two influences with bringing about his maturation into a real poet. One of these was the Vancouver bookseller Steve McIntyre who, around this time, told him that he couldn't pretend to be a serious writer without having first steeped himself in the great works of the literary tradition: as a result Purdy became an omnivorous reader and one of the great autodidacts, eventually turning himself into a remarkably erudite man. The other and balancing influence was the friendship he formed with the Maritime poet Milton Acorn, whose use of a vigorous and highly vernacular voice and humble subject matter earned him the title of 'the People's Poet' and whose example showed Purdy that knowing the poetic tradition and techniques didn't mean having to write imitations of poems long out of date.

The result was that, with the publication of *Poems for All the Annettes* (1962), Purdy made a remarkable breakthrough. As Dennis Lee has observed: 'the mature Purdy simply vaults free of three decades of dead-end and marking time, in a riot of exuberant, full-throated energy'. Purdy continued to develop this newly found power in *The Cariboo Horses* (1965), which earned him his first Governor General's Award. In 1968 *Poems for All the Annettes* was reissued in an expanded edition: in it Purdy collected and revised the earlier poetry he wished to preserve.

Though he became a prolific poet—by the mid-eighties he estimated that he had written over a thousand poems and published more than seven hundred of them—Purdy was also a stern judge of his own work. In his first *Collected Poems*, which appeared in 1986, he retained only two hundred and fifty of these. (That book also received a Governor General's Award.) Near the end of his life Purdy co-edited, with Sam Solecki, *Beyond Remembering*, an expanded and updated version of the collected poems: it was published posthumously in 2000.

Purdy's success in the 1960s and 1970s introduced into Canada a loose, colloquial style that influenced many of the poets who came after him, including Bronwen Wallace and Lorna Crozier. In his distinctive voice—relaxed in tone, conversational, unaffected, sometimes gruff, and often joking—he wrote of the jobs he took in his early years, of the landscape of home, and of the people he met in his own region of Canada and when travelling. His subject was often his own always slightly awkward progress through the world, and the 'I' who dominates these poems is half autobiographical and half a fictional character that Purdy created to respond to his moment in time.

Purdy never stopped maturing as a writer: some of his best work can be found in the five books published in the last years of his nearly sixty-year career: *The Stone Bird* (1981), *Piling Blood* (1984), *A Woman on the Shore* (1990), *Naked with Summer in Your Mouth* (1994), and *To Paris Never Again* (1997). In these later poems he began to risk a serious tone, speaking in a less ironic and a more intense and reflective manner.

Because time is no less important than place in Purdy's poetry, the connections made in these poems are often temporal ones: they move from present to past and back again, seeking lost continuities. This tendency is apparent in 'A Handful of Earth', in which the poet urges René Lévesque to 'Go back a little' to consider the shared history of the French and English communities in Canada. In poems such as 'Elegy for a Grandfather' and 'Roblin Mills (2)', he struggles to understand the vanished era he glimpsed in his childhood. The origins of family and place became the subject of a book-length verse cycle, *In Search of Owen Roblin* (1974), in which Purdy assembled much of his poetry on the Loyalist heritage and history of rural Ontario.

In some poems the time span is much longer than just the history of a family or community, for Purdy—like Pratt and many other modern Canadian writers—found the sources of the present in the vestiges of a primitive era, a remote past that still lives and gives meaning to such poems as 'On the Flood Plain' and 'Lament for the Dorsets'. In the latter, Purdy shows the continuing life of a work of art while at the same time revealing how that work contains its own history, stretching back to the earliest human moments. In these investigations of time and place, the most striking feature may be the sense Purdy's poetry conveys of a mind in motion, a mind synthesizing its environment and looking for connections and meaning—even (as in 'Trees at the Arctic Circle') a mind still engaged in composing the poem that we are now reading.

In addition to producing a voluminous body of poetry Purdy wrote a large number of prose pieces—book reviews, critical essays, anecdotes, and vignettes: a representative selection of these is gathered in *Starting from Ameliasburg* (1995). Near the end of his career Purdy wrote a novel, *A Splinter in the Heart* (1990)—an account of how a boy's life is shaken by the 1918 explosion of the British Chemical plant in Trenton, Ont.—and published a memoir, *Reaching for the Beaufort Sea* (1993). Several volumes of his correspondence have also been published, including *Margaret Laurence—Al Purdy: A Friendship in Letters* (1993).

The Country North of Belleville

Bush land scrub land—
    Cashel Township and Wollaston
Elzevir Mclure and Dungannon
green lands of Weslemkoon Lake
where a man might have some
    opinion of what beauty
is and none deny him
        for miles—

Yet this is the country of defeat
where Sisyphus[1] rolls a big stone
year after year up the ancient hills
picnicking glaciers have left strewn
with centuries' rubble
        backbreaking days
        in the sun and rain
when realization seeps slow in the mind
without grandeur or self-deception in
        noble struggle
of being a fool—

A country of quiescence and still distance
a lean land
    not like the fat south
with inches of black soil on
    earth's round belly—
And where the farms are
    it's as if a man stuck
both thumbs in the stony earth and pulled

        it apart
        to make room
enough between the trees
for a wife
    and maybe some cows and
    room for some
of the more easily kept illusions—
And where the farms have gone back
to forest

1 As a punishment for his misdeeds, Sisyphus was condemned to Hades, where his task was to roll a large boulder to the top of a hill, at which point it rolled back down. In *Le Mythe de Sisyphe* (1942) Albert Camus depicts him as a symbol of existentialist man.

are only soft outlines
shadowy differences—

Old fences drift vaguely among the trees
a pile of moss-covered stones
gathered for some ghost purpose
has lost meaning under the meaningless sky
—they are like cities under water
and the undulating green waves of time
are laid on them—

This is the country of our defeat
and yet
during the fall plowing a man
might stop and stand in a brown valley of the furrows
and shade his eyes to watch for the same
red patch mixed with gold
that appears on the same
spot in the hills
year after year
and grow old
plowing and plowing a ten-acre field until
the convolutions run parallel with his own brain—

And this is a country where the young
leave quickly
unwilling to know what their fathers know
or think the words their mothers do not say—

Herschel Monteagle and Faraday
lakeland rockland and hill country
a little adjacent to where the world is
a little north of where the cities are and
sometime
we may go back there
to the country of our defeat
Wollaston Elzevir and Dungannon
and Weslemkoon lake land
where the high townships of Cashel
McClure and Marmora once were—
But it's been a long time since
and we must enquire the way
of strangers—

1965, rev. 1972

Trees at the Arctic Circle

(Salix cordifolia—Ground Willow)

They are 18 inches long
or even less
crawling under rocks
grovelling among the lichens
bending and curling to escape
making themselves small
finding new ways to hide
Coward trees
I am angry to see them
like this
not proud of what they are
bowing to weather instead
careful of themselves
worried about the sky
afraid of exposing their limbs
like a Victorian married couple

I call to mind great Douglas firs
I see tall maples waving green
and oaks like gods in autumn gold
the whole horizon jungle dark
and I crouched under that continual night
But these
even the dwarf shrubs of Ontario
mock them
Coward trees

And yet—and yet—
their seed pods glow
like delicate grey earrings
their leaves are veined and intricate
like tiny parkas
They have about three months
to make sure the species does not die
and that's how they spend their time
unbothered by any human opinion
just digging in here and now
sending their roots down down down
And you know it occurs to me
                    about 2 feet under

those roots must touch permafrost
ice that remains ice forever
and they use it for their nourishment
they use death to remain alive

I see that I've been carried away
in my scorn of the dwarf trees
most foolish in my judgments
To take away the dignity
                    of any living thing
even tho it cannot understand
                    the scornful words
is to make life itself trivial
and yourself the Pontifex Maximus[1]
                    of nullity
I have been stupid in a poem
I will not alter the poem
but let the stupidity remain permanent
as the trees are
in a poem
the dwarf trees of Baffin Island

PANGNIRTUNG

1967

1 The chief priest in ancient Rome; in later use, the Pope.

Wilderness Gothic

Across Roblin Lake, two shores away,
they are sheathing the church spire
with new metal. Someone hangs in the sky
over there from a piece of rope,
hammering and fitting God's belly-scratcher,
working his way up along the spire
until there's nothing left to nail on—

Perhaps the workman's faith reaches beyond:
touches intangibles, wrestles with Jacob,[1]
replacing rotten timber with pine thews,
pounds hard in the blue cave of the sky,
contends heroically with difficult problems of
gravity, sky navigation and mythopoeia,
his volunteer time and labour donated to God,
minus sick benefits of course on a non-union job—

Fields around are yellowing into harvest,
nestling and fingerling are sky and water borne,
death is yodelling quiet in green woodlots,
and bodies of three young birds have disappeared
in the sub-surface of the new county highway—

That picture is incomplete, part left out
that might alter the whole Dürer[2] landscape:
gothic ancestors peer from medieval sky,
dour faces trapped in photograph albums escaping
to clop down iron roads with matched greys:
work-sodden wives groping inside their flesh
for what keeps moving and changing and flashing
beyond and past the long frozen Victorian day.
A sign of fire and brimstone? A two-headed calf
born in the barn last night? A sharp female agony?
An age and a faith moving into transition,
the dinner cold and new-baked bread a failure,
deep woods shiver and water drops hang pendant,
double yolked eggs and the house creaks a little—

1 Jacob wrestled with God, or with an angel, until he was given a blessing; see Genesis 32: 24–9. In this line 'with' should probably be understood in the sense of 'alongside'.

2 Albrecht Dürer (1471–1528), painter and engraver, the greatest artist of the northern Renaissance; caught up in a period of intense change, and influential in bringing Italian Renaissance styles into Germany, Dürer also maintained some of the dominant Gothic style of earlier German art.

Something is about to happen. Leaves are still.
Two shores away, a man hammering in the sky.
Perhaps he will fall.

1968

Lament for the Dorsets

(Eskimos extinct in the 14th century AD)[1]

Animal bones and some mossy tent rings
scrapers and spearheads   carved ivory swans
all that remains of the Dorset giants
who drove the Vikings back to their long ships
talked to spirits of earth and water
—a picture of terrifying old men
so large they broke the backs of bears
so small they lurk behind bone rafters
in the brain of modern hunters
among good thoughts and warm things
and come out at night
to spit on the stars

The big men with clever fingers
who had no dogs and hauled their sleds
over the frozen northern oceans
awkward giants
                        killers of seal
they couldn't compete with little men
who came from the west with dogs
Or else in a warm climatic cycle
the seals went back to cold waters
and the puzzled Dorsets scratched their heads
with hairy thumbs around 1350 AD
—couldn't figure it out
went around saying to each other
plaintively
            'What's wrong? What happened?
            Where are the seals gone!'
And died

1 The date of the mysterious disappearance of the Dorset, who were probably absorbed or expelled by the Thule Inuit, is now placed at around AD 1000, during a gradual warming period that began around then. To preserve good relations with the spirits of the animals they hunted, Dorset craftsmen carved finely detailed miniature replicas.

Twentieth-century people
apartment dwellers
executives of neon death
warmakers with things that explode
—they have never imagined us in their future
how could we imagine them in the past
squatting among the moving glaciers
six hundred years ago
with glowing lamps?
As remote or nearly
as the trilobites[2] and swamps
when coal became
or the last great reptile hissed
at a mammal the size of a mouse
that squeaked and fled

Did they ever realize at all
what was happening to them?
Some old hunter with one lame leg
a bear had chewed
sitting in a caribou-skin tent
—the last Dorset?
Let's say his name was Kudluk
and watch him sitting there
carving 2-inch ivory swans
for a dead grand-daughter
taking them out of his mind
the places in his mind
where pictures are
He selects a sharp stone tool
to gouge a parallel pattern of lines
on both sides of the swan
holding it with his left hand
bearing down and transmitting
his body's weight
from brain to arm and right hand
and one of his thoughts
turns to ivory
The carving is laid aside
in beginning darkness
at the end of hunger
and after a while wind

2 Fossil marine arthropods from the Paleozoic era (600 million to 230 million years ago).

blows down the tent and snow
begins to cover him

After 600 years
the ivory thought
is still warm

1968

Roblin's Mills (2)[1]

The wheels stopped
and the murmur of voices
behind the flume's tremble
stopped
          and the wind-high ships
that sailed from Rednersville[2]
to the sunrise ports of Europe
are delayed somewhere
in a toddling breeze
The black millpond
turns an unreflecting eye
to look inward
like an idiot child
locked in the basement
when strangers come
whizzing past on the highway
above the dark green valley
a hundred yards below
The mill space is empty
even stones are gone
where hands were shaken
and walls enclosed laughter
saved up and brought here
from the hot fields
where all stories
are rolled into one

1 Originally published as 'Roblin's Mills: Circa 1842'. Purdy later retitled this poem 'Roblin's Mills (2)' to distinguish it from an earlier poem entitled 'Roblin's Mills'. Purdy also used 'Roblin's Mills (2)' as the conclusion of his long poem *In Search of Owen Roblin* (1974).

2 Town on the Bay of Quinte, not far from Roblin Mills.

And white dust floating
above the watery mumble
and bright human sounds
to shimmer among the pollen
where bees dance now
Of all these things
no outline remains
no shadow on the soft air
no bent place in the heat glimmer
where the heavy walls pressed
And some of those who vanished
lost children of the time
kept after school
left alone in a graveyard
who may not change
or ever grow six inches
in one hot summer
or turn where the great herons
graze the sky's low silver
—stand between the hours
in a rotting village
near the weed-grown eye
that looks into itself
deep in the black crystal
that holds and contains
the substance of shadows
manner and custom
          of the inarticulate
departures and morning rumours
gestures and almost touchings
announcements and arrivals
gossip of someone's marriage
when a girl or tired farm woman
whose body suddenly blushes
beneath a faded house dress
with white expressionless face
turns to her awkward husband
to remind him of something else
The black millpond
                              holds them
movings and reachings and fragments
the gear and tackle of living
under the water eye

all things laid aside
discarded
forgotten
but they had their being once
and left a place to stand on

1968, rev. 1972

A Handful of Earth

to René Lévesque[1]

Proposal:
let us join Quebec
if Quebec won't join us
I don't mind in the least
being governed from Quebec City
by Canadiens instead of Canadians
in fact the fleur-de-lis
and maple leaf
are only symbols
and our true language
speaks from inside
the land itself

Listen:
you can hear soft wind blowing
among tall fir trees on Vancouver Island
it is the same wind we knew
whispering along Côte des Neiges
on the island of Montreal
when we were lovers and had no money
Once flying in a little Cessna 180
above that great spine of mountains
where a continent attempts the sky
I wondered who owns this land
and knew that no one does
for we are tenants only

Go back a little:
to hip-roofed houses on the Isle d'Orléans
and scattered along the road to Chicoutimi

1 Founder of the separatist Parti Québécois, Lévesque (1922–87) led his party to power in Quebec in 1976. (He remained premier until 1985 and would be responsible for the first referendum on sovereignty-association, in 1980.)

the remaining few log houses in Ontario
sod huts of sunlit prairie places
dissolved in rain long since
the stones we laid atop of one another
a few of which still stand
those origins
in which children were born
in which we loved and hated
in which we built a place to stand on
and now must tear it down?
—and here I ask all the oldest questions
of myself
the reasons for being alive
the way to spend this gift and thank the giver
but there is no way

I think of the small dapper man
chain-smoking at PQ headquarters
Lévesque
on Avenue Christophe Colomb in Montreal
where we drank coffee together six years past
I say to him now: my place is here
whether Côte des Neiges Avenue Christophe Colomb
Yonge Street Toronto Halifax or Vancouver
this place is where I stand
where all my mistakes were made
when I grew awkwardly and knew what I was
and that is Canadian or Canadien
it doesn't matter which to me

Sod huts break the prairie skyline
then melt in rain
the hip-roofed houses of New France as well
but French no longer
nor are we any longer English
—limestone houses
lean-tos and sheds our fathers built
in which our mothers died
before the forests tumbled down
ghost habitations
only this handful of earth
for a time at least
I have no other place to go

1977, rev. 1978

Elegy for a Grandfather [1986]

Well, he died I guess. They said he did.
His wide whalebone hips will make a prehistoric barrow
men of the future may find or maybe not:
where this man's relatives ducked their heads
in real and pretended sorrow
for the dearly beloved gone thank Christ to God,
after a bad century, a tough big-bellied Pharaoh,
with a deck of cards in his pocket and a Presbyterian grin—

Maybe he did die, but the boy didn't understand it;
the man knows now and the scandal never grows old
of a happy lumberjack who lived on rotten whiskey,
and died of sin and Quaker oats age 90 or so.
But all he was was too much for any man to be,
a life so full he couldn't include one more thing,
nor tell the same story twice if he'd wanted to,
and didn't and didn't—

Just the same he's dead. A sticky religious voice
folded his century sideways to get it out of sight,
and lowered him into the ground like someone still alive
who had to be handled very carefully,
even after death he made people nervous:
and earth takes him as it takes more beautiful things:
populations of whole countries,
museums and works of art,
and women with such a glow
it makes their background vanish
                    they vanish too,
and Lesbos' singer[1] in her sunny islands
stopped when the sun went down—

No, my grandfather was decidedly unbeautiful,
260 pounds of scarred slag,
barnraiser and backwoods farmer:
become an old man in a one-room apartment
over a drygoods store,
become anonymous as a dead animal
whose chemicals may not be reconstituted.

1 Lesbos, an island in the northeastern Aegean Sea, was the home of the ancient Greek poet Sappho. Only fragments remain of her passionate writing, which has been called the greatest lyric poetry of ancient Greece.

There is little doubt that I am the sole
repository of his remains: which consist of
these flashing pictures in my mind,
which I can't bequeath to anyone,
which stop here: juice and flavour
of the old ones, whose blood runs thin
in us: mustard, cayenne, ammonia,
brimstone (trace only above his grave)
—a dying soup-stained giant
I will never let go of—not yet.
He scared hell out of me sometimes,
but sometimes I caught myself, fascinated,
overhearing him curse God in my own arteries:
even after death I would never dare
admit to loving him, which he'd despise,
and his ghost haunt the poem forever
(which is an exaggeration of course,
but he liked those)—

1956; rev. 1986

The Dead Poet

I was altered in the placenta
by the dead brother before me
who built a place in the womb
knowing I was coming:
he wrote words on the walls of flesh
painting a woman inside a woman
whispering a faint lullaby
that sings in my blind heart still

The others were lumberjacks
backwoods wrestlers and farmers
their women were meek and mild
nothing of them survives
but an image inside an image
of a cookstove and the kettle boiling
—how else explain myself to myself
where does the song come from?

Now on my wanderings:
at the Alhambra's lyric dazzle

where the Moors built stone poems[1]
a wan white face peering out
—and the shadow in Plato's cave[2]
remembers the small dead one
—at Samarkand[3] in pale blue light
the words came slowly from him
—I recall the music of blood
on the Street of the Silversmiths[4]

Sleep softly spirit of earth
as the days and nights join hands
when everything becomes one thing
wait softly brother
but do not expect it to happen
that great whoop announcing resurrection
expect only a small whisper
of birds nesting and green things growing
and a brief saying of them
and know where the words came from

1986

1 The Alhambra is a fortified palace near Granada, Spain. Built between 1248 and 1354, it was the last stronghold of the Muslim kings of Granada and is an outstanding example of highly ornate Moorish architecture.
2 In Plato's *Republic*, Socrates tells the parable of the cave, in which our inability to see anything but the passing illusion of real life, rather than its essences (which Plato believed existed elsewhere, beyond normal sensory experience), is compared to the condition of humans doomed to sit in a cave with a fire behind them, able to see only the shadows the fire cast on the wall in front of them, not the actual objects between them and the fire.
3 A city in eastern Uzbekistan; one of the oldest cities in Asia, founded in the third or fourth millennium BCE, and a prosperous centre of the silk trade in the middle ages.
4 An ancient area in Delhi, India.

For Steve McIntyre
(1912–1984)

He said I was ignorant
and didn't mince words about it
my deficiency was GREAT BOOKS
—so I read Proust Woolf Cervantes
Dostoyevsky Joyce the works
and they were just as boring
as I'd always suspected
—but one night just before sleep
words were suddenly shining in the dark
like false teeth in a glass of water

like the laughter of Australopithecus
mocking other beasts surrounding his tree
like *Thalassa* for Xenophon and the Greeks
like Joshua's trumpet at Jericho
like sunlight under the bedsheets
with her arms around my neck
And I climbed down from the tree
instructed Darwin's non-evoluted
critters to get lost
delighted in the Black Sea with Xenophon
and the Greek Ten Thousand
and stole the wavetips' green diamonds
for my ballpoint—
All because of Steve McIntyre
a dead man who hears nothing
not *Thalassa* nor Joshua's trumpet
not Australopithecus inventing laughter
nor the tenderness I softly withdraw
from my breast in the form of
words that say *Goodbye*
beyond his hearing—
a man was puzzled in his mind
trying to figure it out?
—a woman half lost in a trance,
getting used to another self.

What could it have been?—not booze,
sex, mundane reward for virtue;
and maybe different for everyone,
the mystery that makes us human,
whatever 'human' is—
then blue aftermath and depression,
ever oncoming whips of trivia
to settle ourselves in dullness.
Coming alive at the womb's doorway,
we inherited everything—sun, moon,
all: and resent knowing more than we know,
the dictatorship of the senses enough,
the stone ship we ride on enough
for now—: then the rare arrival
of something entirely beyond us,
beyond this repeated daily dying,
the singing moment—

1986

Red Leaves

—all over the earth
little fires starting up
especially in Canada
some yellow leaves too
buttercup and dandelion yellow
dancing across the hillside
I say to my wife
'What's the yellowest thing there is?
'School buses'
a thousand school buses are double-
parked on 401 all at once

I suppose this is the one thing
your average level-headed Martian
or Venusian could not imagine
about Earth:
                    red leaves
and the way humans attach emotion
to one little patch of ground
and continually go back there
in the autumn of our lives
to deal with some of the questions
that have troubled us
on our leapfrog trip thru the Universe
for which there are really no answers
except at this tranquil season
of falling leaves
watching them a kind of jubilation
sometimes mistaken for sadness

1990

On the Flood Plain

Midnight:
it's freezing on the lake
and wind whips ice eastward
but most of the water remains open
—and stars visit earth

tumbled about like floating candles
on the black tumulus[1]
then wind extinguishes the silver fire
but more flash down
and even those reflections reflect
on the sides of waves
even the stars' reflections reflect stars

Ice:
far older than earth
primordial as the Big Bang
—cold unmeasured by Celsius and Fahrenheit
quarrelling about it on a Jurassic shingle[2]
—before Pangaea and Gondwanaland
arrive here in the 20th century
born like a baby
under the flashlight beam
Bend down and examine the monster
and freeze for your pains
—tiny oblong crystals
seem to come from nowhere
little transparent piano keys
that go tinkle tinkle tinkle
while the wind screams
—and you feel like some shivering hey
presto god grumbling at his fucked-up weather
hurry indoors hurry indoors to heaven

People have told us we built too near the lake
'The flood plain is dangerous' they said
and no doubt they know more about it than we do
—but here wind pressed down on new-formed ice
trembles it like some just-invented musical instrument
and that shrieking obbligato to winter
sounds like the tension in a stretched worm
when the robin has it hauled halfway out of the lawn
I stand outside
between house and outhouse
feeling my body stiffen in fossilized rigor mortis
and listening

1 An ancient burial mound or barrow.

2 That is, a stretch of gravelled beach from the Jurassic period (the second period of the Mesozoic Era, 65 million to 230 million years ago). 'Pangaea' is the name given, in theories of continental drift, to a vast 'supercontinent', comprising all the continental crust of the earth, postulated to have existed in late Palaeozoic and Mesozoic times before it broke up into two smaller but still immense landmasses, Laurasia and Gondwanaland.

thinking
this is the reason we built on the flood plain
damn right
the seriousness of things beyond your understanding

Whatever I have not discovered and enjoyed
is still waiting for me
and there will be time
but now are these floating stars on the freezing lake
and music fills the darkness
holds me there listening
—it's a matter of separating these instants from others
that have no significance
so that they keep reflecting each other
a way to live and contain eternity
in which the moment is altered and expanded
my consciousness hung like a great silver metronome
suspended between stars
on the dark lake
and time pours itself into my cupped hands shimmering

1990

Grosse Isle

Look, stranger, at this island now
The leaping light for your delight discovers

—W.H. Auden

Look stranger
a diseased whale in the St Lawrence
this other island than Auden's
dull grey when the weather is dull grey
and an east wind brings rain
this Appalachian outcrop
a stone ship foundered in the river estuary
now in the care and keeping of Parks Canada
—a silence here like no mainland silence
at Cholera Bay where the dead bodies
awaited high tide and the rough kindness
of waves sweeping them into the dark—

Look stranger
at this other island
weedgrown graves in the three cemeteries
be careful your clothes don't get hooked
by wild raspberry canes and avoid the poison ivy
—here children went mad with cholera fever
and raging with thirst they ran into the river
their parents following a little way
before they died themselves
—and don't stumble over the rusted tricycle
somehow overlooked at the last big cleanup
or perhaps left where it is for the tourists?

Look stranger
where the sea wind sweeps westward
down the estuary
this way the other strangers came
potato-famine Irish and Scotch crofters
refugees from the Highland clearances
and sailing ships waited here
to remove their corpses
and four million immigrants passed through
—now there's talk of a Health Spa and Casino
we could situate our billboard
right under the granite cross by the river:
UNLIMITED INVESTMENT OPPORTUNITIES

Look stranger
see your own face reflected in the river
stumble up from the stinking hold
blinded by sunlight and into the leaky dinghy
only half-hearing the sailors taunting you
'Shanty Irish! Shanty Irish!'
gulp the freshening wind and pinch yourself
trying to understand if the world is a real place
stumble again and fall when you reach the shore
and bless this poisoned earth
but stranger no longer
for this is home

1994

Say the Names

—say the names say the names
and listen to yourself
an echo in the mountains
Tulameen   Tulameen
say them like your soul
was listening and overhearing
and you dreamed you dreamed
you were a river
and you were a river
Tulameen   Tulameen
—not the flat borrowed imitations
of foreign names
not Brighton Windsor Trenton
but names that ride the wind
Spillimacheen and Nahanni
Kleena Kleene and Horsefly
Illecillewaet and Whachamacallit
Lillooet and Kluane
Head-Smashed-In Buffalo Jump
and the whole sky falling
when the buffalo went down
Similkameen and Nahanni
say them say them remember
if ever you wander elsewhere
'the North as a deed and forever'
Kleena Kleen   Nahanni
Osoyoos and Similkameen
say the names
as if they were your soul
lost among the mountains
a soul you mislaid
and found again rejoicing
Tulameen   Tulameen
till the heart stops beating

say the names

1999

Mavis Gallant

b. 1922

Mavis Gallant, born Mavis de Trafford Young in Montreal, entered, at the age of four, a strict French-Catholic boarding school where, as a Protestant child of Scottish heritage, she was something of an anomaly. Perhaps that experience is responsible for a sense of being an outsider that has been part of her life and a continuing theme of her stories. In any case, her father's early death and her peripatetic education (she attended over seventeen schools in Canada and the United States) prepared her for an independent and, by choice, solitary existence. After high school she worked briefly for the National Film Board and then became a reporter for the Montreal *Standard*. Gallant had begun to write fiction during these years but was disinclined to submit her work for publication. Two of her stories—'Good Morning and Goodbye' and 'Three Brick Walls'—were published as early as 1944 in the Montreal little magazine *Preview* (because a friend forwarded them to its editor, Patrick Anderson), but she did not send out her manuscripts herself until after she had decided, in 1950, to quit reporting and become a full-time writer.

At twenty-eight, after a brief marriage, Gallant left Canada for Europe, settling eventually in Paris. Before leaving she had submitted her first story to *The New Yorker*, which returned it, saying that it was too Canadian for American readers, but asking to see more of her work. *The New Yorker* did publish her second submission in 1951; since then most of her stories—even her 'Canadian' ones—have appeared first in that magazine.

Over the years Gallant has become famous for her highly polished, urbane short stories and novellas. They have been collected in *The Other Paris* (1956); *My Heart Is Broken* (1964); *The Pegnitz Junction* (1973), linked stories about the sources of German fascism; *The End of the World and Other Stories* (1974), selected by Robert Weaver; and *From the Fifteenth District* (1979). In 1981 her stories about Canadians were gathered in a volume called *Home Truths*, which won a Governor General's Award. (The story reprinted here was published in that volume after first appearing in *The New Yorker* in 1976.) In the eighties Gallant published two more books of short stories, *Overhead in a Balloon: Stories of Paris* (1985) and *In Transit* (1988), which contains previously uncollected stories from the fifties and sixties. Her most recent collections are *Across the Bridge* (1993) and *The Moslem Wife and Other Stories* (1994), a selection of her stories made by Mordecai Richler, who also added an afterword. In 1996 *The Selected Stories* was published: a massive 900-page volume, containing over fifty stories, it includes everything Gallant herself wished to preserve from the 1930s through the 1990s and is a clear record of the accomplishment of one of the finest short-story writers in the English language today. Robert Fulford describes her achievement thus: 'One begins comparing her best moments to those of major figures in literary history. Names like Henry James, Chekhov, and George Eliot dance across the mind.'

Although she clearly prefers the short story to the novel (she describes writing the story as 'like being on tip-toe the whole time. . . . It's very tense'), Gallant has also published two novels, *Green Water, Green Sky* (1959) and *A Fairly Good Time* (1970). Like her stories, these focus on the interior dramas of their characters. Her play, *What Is to Be Done?* (1984), was produced at the Tarragon Theatre, Toronto, in 1982, during a return to Canada as writer-in-residence at the University of Toronto, and was later made into a TV film.

Gallant occasionally has written non-fiction as well, reporting and reviewing from her position as an observer of France. Her views on French life can be found in such pieces as 'The Events in May: A Paris Notebook', a first-hand account of the 1968 Paris student riots, and her long introduction to *The Affair of Gabrielle Russier* (1971), a book about a complex French legal scandal involving a teacher and her student. These two pieces as well as many of her essays and reviews are collected in *Paris Notebooks* (1986).

Bilingual from childhood, Gallant has immersed herself in French culture and life for over thirty years but writes only in English, believing that 'one needs a strong, complete language . . . to anchor one's understanding.' She has always been concerned with the individual's experience of an unfamiliar culture, and while her stories capture the universal sense of alienation that has dominated modern society, she has a special feel for exiled people like the remittance man Frank Cairns in 'Varieties of Exile', who struggle to hang onto threads of their former cultures. They are cut off not simply from their physical homeland but also from other people. They stand apart, unable to make contact, unable to join those around them, the psychic distance intensified by the loss of traditional codes. As in the fiction of Henry James, the truncated form of communication that remains takes place in the twilight of an obsolescent world.

Gallant's method of portraying characters obliquely, often by focusing on specific social customs and on unconscious behaviour, recalls Proust as well as James. In a dialogue filled with nuances, little is said directly and communication is an elaborate, unspoken ritual—but what *is* said is of great importance. Gallant's detached characters, unable to make outspoken judgments, recall the reticent figures so often found in stories by Sinclair Ross, Alice Munro, and Margaret Atwood. They share the malady that Northrop Frye called 'strangled articulation': burdened by history yet isolated by it, they find society moving away from the familiar patterns that both bind and reassure them.

The selection reprinted here is from the Linnet Muir cycle, a series of stories that are perhaps the most autobiographical of her works. While Gallant's familiar themes of exile and alienation are highlighted in the character of Frank Cairns, the expatriate Brit unable to fit into the Canadian social, cultural, and political milieu, and more generally by the flood of refugees and displaced persons that World War II has produced, we realize that Linnet, the narrator and protagonist who has returned to the city where she was born and raised, is also struggling to find and understand her place in 1940s Montreal. This is partly true because, as was the case for Gallant herself, who had difficulty being accepted as a woman who was also a reporter, Linnet is unsure of how she fits into the gendered wartime society and its roles.

Despite Gallant's own long exile, she frequently returns to Canada and has retained a cultural identity with her homeland, which in turn has bestowed honours upon her. She was made a Companion of the Order of Canada in 1993 and awarded an honorary doctorate by the University of Toronto in 1994. In 2002 she was given a lifetime achievement award at the Blue Metropolis International Literary Festival in Montreal.

Varieties of Exile

In the third summer of the war I began to meet refugees. There were large numbers of them in Montreal—to me a source of infinite wonder. I could not get enough of them. They came straight out of the twilit Socialist-literary landscape of my reading and my desires. I saw them as prophets of a promised social order that was to consist of justice, equality, art, personal relations, courage, generosity. Each of them—Belgian, French, Catholic German, Socialist German, Jewish German, Czech—was a book I tried to read from start to finish. My dictionaries were films, poems, novels, Lenin, Freud. That the refugees tended to hate one another seemed no more than a deplorable accident.

Nationalist pigheadedness, that chronic, wasting, and apparently incurable disease, was known to me only on Canadian terms and I did not always recognize its symptoms. Anything I could not decipher I turned into fiction, which was my way of untangling knots. At the office where I worked I now spent my lunch hour writing stories about people in exile. I tried to see Montreal as an Austrian might see it and to feel whatever he felt. I was entirely at home with foreigners, which is not surprising—the home was all in my head. They were the only people I had met until now who believed, as I did, that our victory would prove to be a tidal wave nothing could stop. What I did not know was how many of them hoped and expected their neighbours to be washed away too.

I was nineteen and for the third time in a year engaged to be married. What I craved at this point was not love, or romance, or a life added to mine, but conversation, which was harder to find. I knew by now that a man in love does not necessarily have anything interesting to say: If he has, he keeps it for other men. Men in Canada did not talk much to women and hardly at all to young ones. The impetus of love—of infatuation, rather—brought on a kind of conversation I saw no reason to pursue. A remand such as 'I can't live without you' made the speaker sound not only half-witted to me but almost truly, literally, insane. There is a girl in a Stefan Zweig[1] novel who says to her lover, 'Is that all?' I had pondered this carefully many years before, for I supposed it had something unexpected to do with sex. Now I gave it another meaning, which was that where women were concerned men were satisfied with next to nothing. If every woman was a situation, she was somehow always the same situation, and what was expected from the woman—the situation—was so limited it was insulting. I had a large opinion of what I could do and provide, yet it came down to 'Is that all? Is that all you expect?' Being promised to one person after another was turning into a perpetual state of hesitation and refusal: I was not used to hesitating over anything and so I supposed I must be wrong. The men in my office had warned me of the dangers of turning into a married woman; if this caution affected me it was only because it coincided with a misgiving of my own. My private name for married women was Red Queens. They looked to me like the Red Queen in *Through the Looking-Glass*,[2] chasing after other people and minding their business for them. To get out of the heat that summer I had taken a room outside Montreal in an area called simply 'the Lakeshore'. In those days the Lakeshore was a string of verdant towns with next to no traffic. Dandelions grew in the pavement cracks. The streets were thickly shaded. A fragrance I have never forgotten of mown grass and leaf smoke drifted from yard to yard. As I walked to my commuters' train early in the morning I saw kids still in their pajamas digging holes in the lawns and Red

1 Zweig (1881–1942) was a cosmopolitan Austrian Jewish poet, essayist, and novelist who advocated the idea of a united Europe under one government. His works were immensely popular throughout Europe in the 1930s, but when the Nazi party took control he went into exile in 1934, eventually committing suicide.

2 When Alice passes through the mirror in *Through the Looking-Glass* (Lewis Carroll's 1872 sequel to *Alice in Wonderland*), she finds herself in a world in which the pieces of the chess set have come alive. Seeing the Red Queen, she begins moving toward her, but the Red Queen vanishes. She is told by a rose to go the other way instead and—this being a looking-glass world—when she does so she finds herself now facing the Red Queen. In the world Alice has come to, hills can become valleys, straight can become curvy, and progress can be made only by going in the opposite direction. When the Red Queen begins to run and Alice runs after her, neither makes any progress; the Red Queen explains: '*here*, you see, it takes all the running *you* can do to keep in the same place'.

Queen wives wearing housecoats. They stuck their heads out of screen doors and yelled instructions—to husbands, to children, to dogs, to postmen, to a neighbour's child. How could I be sure I wouldn't sound that way—so shrill, so discontented? As for a family, the promise of children all stamped with the same face, cast in the same genetic mould, seemed a cruel waste of possibilities. I would never have voiced this to anyone, for it would have been thought unnatural, even monstrous. When I was very young, under seven, my plan for the future had been to live in every country of the world and have a child in each. I had confided it: with adult adroitness my listener led me on. How many children? Oh, one to a country. And what would you do with them? Travel in trains. How would they go to school? I hate schools. How will they learn to read and write, then? They'll know already. What would you live on? It will all be free. That's not very sensible, is it? Why not? As a result of this idyll, of my divulgence of it, I was kept under watch for a time and my pocket money taken away lest I save it up and sail to a tropical island (where because of the Swiss Family Robinson I proposed to begin) long before the onset of puberty. I think no one realized I had not even a nebulous idea of how children sprang to life. I merely knew two persons were required for a ritual I believed had to continue for nine months, and which I imagined in the nature of a long card game with mysterious rules. When I was finally 'told'—accurately, as it turned out—I was offended at being asked to believe something so unreasonable, which could not be true because I had never come across it in books. This trust in the printed word seems all the more remarkable when I remember that I thought children's books were written by other children. Probably at nineteen I was still dim about relevant dates, plain facts, brass tacks, consistent reasoning. Perhaps I was still hoping for magic card games to short-circuit every sort of common sense—common sense is only an admission we don't know much. I know that I wanted to marry this third man but that I didn't want to be anybody's Red Queen.

The commuters on the Montreal train never spoke much to each other. The mystifying and meaningless 'Hot enough for you?' was about the extent of it. If I noticed one man more than the anonymous others it was only because he looked so hopelessly English, so unable or unwilling to concede to anything, even the climate. Once, walking a few steps behind him, I saw him turn into the drive of a stone house, one of the few old French-Canadian houses in that particular town. The choice of houses seemed to me peculiarly English too—though not, of course, what French Canadians call 'English', for that includes plain Canadians, Irish, Swedes, anything you like not natively French. I looked again at the house and at the straight back going along the drive. His wife was on her knees holding a pair of edging shears. He stopped to greet her. She glanced up and said something in a carrying British voice so wild and miserable, so resentful, so intensely disagreeable that it could not have been the tag end of a morning quarrel; no, it was the thunderclap of some new engagement. After a second he went on up the walk, and in another I was out of earshot. I was persuaded that he had seen me; I don't know why. I also thought it must have been humiliating for him to have had a witness.

Which of us spoke first? It could not have been him and it most certainly could not have been me. There must have been a collision, for there we are, speaking, on a station platform. It is early morning, already hot. I see once again, without surprise, that he is not dressed for the climate.

He said he had often wondered what I was reading. I said I was reading 'all the Russians'. He said I really ought to read Arthur Waley.[3] I had never heard of Arthur Waley. Similar signalling takes place between galaxies rushing apart in the outer heavens. He said he would bring me a book by Arthur Waley the next day.

'Please don't. I'm careless with books. Look at the shape this one's in.' It was the truth. 'All the Russians' were being published in a uniform edition with flag-red covers, on greyish paper, with microscopic print. The words were jammed together; you could not have put a pin between the lines. It was one of those cheap editions I think we were supposed to be sending the troops in order to cheer them up. Left in the grass beside a tennis court *The Possessed*[4] now curved like a shell. A white streak ran down the middle of the shell. The rest of the cover had turned pink. That was nothing, he said. All I needed to do was dampen the cover with a sponge and put a weight on the book. *The Wallet of Kai Lung*[5] had been to Ceylon with him and had survived. Whatever bait 'Ceylon' may have been caught nothing. Army? Civil Service? I did not take it up. Anyway I thought I could guess.

'You'd better not bring a book for nothing. I don't always take this train.'

He had probably noticed me every morning. The mixture of reserve and obstinacy that next crossed his face I see still. He smiled, oh, not too much: I'd have turned my back on a grin. He said, 'I forgot to . . . Frank Cairns.'

'Muir, Linnet Muir.' Reluctantly.

The thing is, I knew all about him. He was, one, married and, two, too old. But there was also three: Frank Cairns was stamped, labelled, ticketed by his tie (club? regiment? school?); by his voice, manner, haircut, suit; by the impression he gave of being stranded in a jungle, waiting for a rescue party—from England, of course. He belonged to a species of British immigrant known as remittance men. Their obsolescence began on 3 September 1939 and by 8 May 1945 they were extinct. I knew about them from having had one in the family. Frank Cairns worked in a brokerage house—he told me later—but he probably did not need a job, at least not for a living. It must have been a way of ordering time, a flight from idleness, perhaps a means of getting out of the house.

The institution of the remittance man was British, its genesis a chemical structure of family pride, class insanity, and imperial holdings that seemed impervious to fission but in the end turned out to be more fragile than anyone thought. Like all superfluous and marginal persons, remittance men were characters in a plot. The plot began with a fixed scene, an immutable first chapter, which described a powerful father's taking umbrage at his son's misconduct and ordering him out of the country. The pound

3 (1889–1966); poet, translator, and scholar, Waley introduced Chinese and Japanese literature and culture to a broad twentieth-century public through his English translations of East Asian classics.

4 Fyodor Dostoevsky's novel (1871–2), which contains negative portraits of radical political movements in Russia, including Nihilism, Anarchism, and Socialism.

5 Like *Kai Lung's Golden Hours*, mentioned subsequently, a pseudo-Oriental tale (published in 1900) by Ernest Bramah. Bramah's Kai Lung stories are written in an ornate, whimsical manner and have no authentic Chinese background.

was then one to five dollars, and there were vast British territories everywhere you looked. Hordes of young men who had somehow offended their parents were shipped out, golden deportees, to Canada, South Africa, New Zealand, Singapore. They were reluctant pioneers, totally lacking any sense of adventure or desire to see that particular world. An income—the remittance—was provided on a standing banker's order, with one string attached: 'Keep out of England'. For the second chapter the plot allowed a choice of six crimes as reasons for banishment: Conflict over the choice of a profession—the son wants to be a tap-dancer. Gambling and debts—he has been barred from Monte Carlo. Dud cheques—'I won't press a charge, sir, but see that the young rascal is kept out of harm's way.' Marriage with a girl from the wrong walk of life—'Young man, you have made your bed!' Fathering an illegitimate child: '. . . and broken your mother's heart'. Homosexuality, if discovered: too grave for even a lecture—it was a criminal offence.

This is the plot of the romance: this is what everyone repeated and what the remittance man believed of himself. Obviously, it is a load of codswallop. A man legally of age could marry the tattooed woman in a circus, be arrested for cheque-bouncing or for soliciting boys in Green Park, be obliged to recognize his by-blow and even to wed its mother, become a ponce or a professional wrestler, and still remain where he was born. All he needed to do was eschew the remittance and tell his papa to go to hell. Even at nineteen the plot was a story I wouldn't buy. The truth came down to something just as dramatic but boring to tell: a classic struggle for dominance with two protagonists—strong father, pliant son. It was also a male battle. No son was ever sent into exile by his mother, and no one has ever heard of a remittance *woman*. Yet daughters got into scrapes nearly as often as their brothers. Having no idea what money was, they ran up debts easily. Sometimes, out of ignorance of another sort, they dared to dispose of their own virginity, thus wrecking their value on the marriage market and becoming family charges for life. Accoucheurs[6] had to be bribed to perform abortions; or else the daughters were dispatched to Austria and Switzerland to have babies they would never hear of again. A daughter's disgrace was long, expensive, and hard to conceal, yet no one dreamed of sending her thousands of miles away and forever: on the contrary, she became her father's unpaid servant, social secretary, dog walker, companion, sick nurse. Holding on to a daughter, dismissing a son were relatively easy: it depended on having tamely delinquent children, or a thunderous personality no child would dare to challenge, and on the weapon of money—bait or weapon, as you like.

Banished young, as a rule, the remittance man (the RM, in my private vocabulary) drifted for the rest of his life, never quite sounding or looking like anyone around him, seldom raising a family or pursuing an occupation (so much for the 'choice of profession' legend)—remote, dreamy, bored. Those who never married often became low-key drunks. The remittance was usually ample without being handsome, but enough to keep one from doing a hand's turn; in any case few remittance men were fit to do much of anything, being well schooled but half educated, in that specifically English way, as well as markedly unaggressive and totally uncompetitive, which would have meant early

6 Midwives (French).

death in the New World for anyone without an income. They were like children waiting for the school vacation so that they could go home, except that at home nobody wanted them: the nursery had been turned into a billiards room and Nanny dismissed. They were parted from mothers they rarely mentioned, whom in some way they blended with a Rupert Brooke[7] memory of England, of the mother country, of the Old Country as everyone at home grew old. Often as not the payoff, the keep-away blackmail funds, came out of the mother's marriage settlement—out of the capital her own father had agreed to settle upon her unborn children during the wear and tear of Edwardian engagement negotiations. The son disgraced would never see more than a fixed income from this; he was cut off from a share of inheritance by his contract of exile. There were cases where the remittance ended abruptly with the mother's death, but that was considered a bad arrangement. Usually the allowance continued for the exile's lifetime and stopped when he died. No provision was made for his dependants, if he had them, and because of his own subject attitude to money he was unlikely to have made any himself. The income reverted to his sisters and brothers, to an estate, to a cat-and-dog hospital—whatever his father had decreed on some black angry day long before.

Whatever these sons had done their punishment was surely a cruel and singular one, invented for naughty children by a cosmic headmaster taking over for God: they were obliged to live over and over until they died the first separation from home, and the incomparable trauma of rejection. Yes, they were like children, perpetually on their way to a harsh school; they were eight years of age and sent 'home' from India to childhoods of secret grieving among strangers. And this wound, this amputation, they would mercilessly inflict on their own children when the time came—on sons always, on daughters sometimes—persuaded that early heartbreak was right because it was British, hampered only by the financial limit set for banishment: it costs money to get rid of your young.

And how they admired their fathers, those helpless sons! They spoke of them with so much admiration, with such a depth of awe: only in memory can such voices still exist, the calm English voice on a summer night—a Canadian night so alien to the speaker—insisting, with sudden firmness, with a pause between words. 'My . . . father . . . once . . . said . . . to . . . me . . .' and here would follow something utterly trivial, some advice about choosing a motorcar or training a dog. To the Canadian grandchildren the unknown grandfather was seven foot tall with a beard like George V, while the grandmother came through weepy and prissy and not very interesting. It was the father's Father, never met, never heard, who made Heaven and Earth and Eve and Adam. The father in Canada seemed no more than an apostle transmitting a paternal message from the Father in England—the Father of us all. It was, however, rare for a remittance man to marry, rarer still to have any children; how could he become a father when he had never stopped being a son?

If the scattered freemasonry of offspring the remittance man left behind, all adult to elderly now, had anything in common it must have been their degree of incompetence.

7 (1887–1915); English poet famous for his wartime poetry and his idealized patriotism, Brooke came to be remembered as an emblem of the flower of young British manhood lost in World War I.

They were raised to behave well in situations that might never occur, trained to become genteel poor on continents where even the concept of genteel poverty has never existed. They were brought up with plenty of books and music and private lessons, a nurse sometimes, in a household where certain small luxuries were deemed essential—a way of life that, in North America at least, was supposed to be built on a sunken concrete base of money; otherwise you were British con men, a breed of gypsy, and a bad example.

Now, your remittance man was apt to find this assumption quite funny. The one place he would never take seriously was the place he was in. The identification of prominent local families with the name of a product, a commodity, would be his running joke: 'The Allseeds are sugar, the Bilges are coal, the Cumquats are cough medicine, the Doldrums are coffins, the Earwigs are saucepans, the Fustians are timber, the Grindstones are beer.' But his young, once they came up against it, were bound to observe that their concrete base was the dandelion fluff of a banker's order, their commodity nothing but 'life in England before 1914', which was not negotiable. Also, the constant, nagging 'What does your father really do?' could amount to persecution.

'Mr Bainwood wants to know what you do.'

'Damned inquisitive of him.'

Silence. Signs of annoyance. Laughter sometimes. Or something silly: 'What do *you* do when you aren't asking questions?'

No remittance man's child that I know of ever attended a university, though care was taken over the choice of schools. There they would be, at eighteen and nineteen, the boys wearing raincoats in the coldest weather, the girls with their hair ribbons and hand-knits and their innocently irritating English voices, well read, musical, versed in history, probably because they had been taught that the past is better than now, and somewhere else better than here. They must have been the only English-Canadian children to speak French casually, as a matter of course. Untidy, unpunctual, imperially tactless, they drifted into work that had to be 'interesting', 'creative', never demeaning, and where—unless they'd had the advantage of a rough time and enough nous[8] to draw a line against the past—they seldom lasted. There was one in every public-relations firm, one to a radio station, two to a publisher—forgetting appointments, losing contracts, jamming typewriters, sabotaging telephones, apologizing in accents it would have taken elocution lessons to change, so strong had been paternal pressure against the hard Canadian 'r', not to mention other vocables:

'A-t-e is *et* darling, not *ate.*'

'I can't say *et.* Only farmers say it.'

'Perhaps here, but you won't always be here.'

Of course the children were guilt-drenched, wondering which of the six traditional crimes they ought to pin on their father, what his secret was, what his past included, why he had been made an outcast. The answer was quite often 'Nothing, no reason,' but it meant too much to be unravelled and knit up. The saddest were those unwise enough to look into the families who had caused so much inherited

8 Common sense (chiefly British informal).

woe. For the family was often as not smaller potatoes than the children had thought, and their father's romantic crime had been just the inability to sit for an examination, to stay at university, to handle an allowance, to gain a toehold in any profession, or even to decide what he wanted to do—an ineptitude so maddening to live with that the Father preferred to shell out forever rather than watch his heir fall apart before his eyes. The male line, then, was a ghost story. A mother's vitality would be needed to create ectoplasm, to make the ghost offspring visible. Unfortunately the exiles were apt to marry absentminded women whose skirts are covered with dog hairs—the drooping, bewildered British-Canadian mouse, who counts on tea leaves to tell her 'what will happen when Edward goes'. None of us is ever saved entirely, but even an erratic and alarming maternal vitality could turn out to be better than none.

Frank Cairns was childless, which I thought wise of him. He had been to Ceylon, gone back to England with a stiff case of homesickness disguised as malaria, married, and been shipped smartly out again, this time to Montreal. He was a neat, I think rather a small, man, with a straight part in his hair and a quick, brisk walk. He noticed I was engaged. I did not reply. I told him I had been in New York, had come back about a year ago, and missed 'different things'. He seemed to approve. 'You can't make a move here,' he said more than once. I was not sure what he meant. If he had been only the person I have described I'd have started taking an earlier train to be rid of him. But Frank Cairns was something new, unique of his kind, and almost as good as a refugee, for he was a Socialist. At least he said he was. He said he had never voted anywhere but that if he ever in the future happened to be in England when there was an election he would certainly vote Labour. His Socialism did not fit anything else about him, and seemed to depend for its life on the memory of talks he'd once had with a friend whom he described as brilliant, philosophical, farseeing, and just. I thought, Like Christ, but did not know Frank Cairns well enough to say so. The non-believer I had become was sometimes dogged by the child whose nightly request had been 'Gentle Jesus, meek and mild, look upon a little child,' and I sometimes got into ferocious arguments with her, as well as with other people. I was too curious about Frank Cairns to wish to quarrel over religion—at any rate not at the beginning. He talked about his friend without seeming able to share him. He never mentioned his name. I had to fill in the blank part of this conversation without help; I made the friend a high-ranking civil servant in Ceylon, older than anyone—which might have meant forty-two—an intellectual revolutionary who could work the future out on paper, like arithmetic.

Wherever his opinions came from, Frank Cairns was the first person ever to talk to me about the English poor. They seemed to be a race, different in kind from other English. He showed me old copies of *Picture Post* he must have saved up from the Depression. In our hot summer train, where everyone was starched and ironed and washed and fed, we considered slum doorways and the faces of women at the breaking point. They looked like Lenin's 'remnants of nations' except that there were too many of them for a remnant. I thought of my mother and her long preoccupation with the fate of the Scottsboro Boys.[9] My mother had read and mooned and fretted about the Scottsboro case, while I tried to turn her attention to something urgent, such as that my school uniform was now torn in three places. It is quite possible that my mother had seldom seen a black except on railway trains. (If I say 'black' it is only because it is expected. It was a rude and offensive term in my childhood and I would not have been allowed to use it. 'Black' was the sort of thing South Africans said.) Had Frank Cairns actually seen those *Picture Post* faces, I wondered. His home, his England, was every other remittance man's—the one I called 'Christopher-Robin-land' and had sworn to keep away from. He hated Churchill, I remember, but I was used to hearing that. No man who remembered the Dardanelles[10] really trusted him. Younger men (I am speaking of the handful I knew who had any opinions at all) were not usually irritated by his rhetoric until they got into uniform.

Once in a book I lent him he found a scrap of paper on which I had written the title of a story I was writing, 'The Socialist RM', and some scrawls in, luckily, a private shorthand of mine. A perilous moment: 'remittance man' was a term of abuse all over the Commonwealth and Empire.

'What is it?' he asked. 'Resident Magistrate?'

'It might be Royal Marine. Royal Mail. I honestly don't remember. I can't read my own writing sometimes.' The last sentence was true.

His Socialism was unlike a Czech's or a German's; though he believed that one should fight hard for social change, there was a hopelessness about it, an almost moral belief that improving their material circumstances would get the downtrodden nowhere. At the same time, he thought the poor *were* happy, that they had some strange secret of happiness—the way people often think all Italians are happy because they have large families. I wondered if he really believed that a man with no prospects and no teeth in his head was spiritually better off than Frank Cairns and why, in that case, Frank Cairns did not let him alone with his underfed children and his native good nature. This was a British left-wing paradox I was often to encounter later on. What it seemed to amount to was leaving people more or less as they were, though he did speak about basic principles and the spread of education. It sounded dull. I was Russian-minded; I read Russian books, listened to Russian music. After Russia came Germany and Central Europe—that was where the real mystery and political

9 The nine black youths who were indicted in 1931 at Scottsboro, Alabama, on charges of raping two white women. Despite the paucity of evidence against the young men, all nine were found guilty by an all-white jury. The decision sparked outrage outside the southern US, particularly among Northern liberal and radical groups, who championed and sometimes exploited the cause of the Scottsboro Boys. (The US Supreme Court twice reversed guilty decisions on procedural grounds, but retrials of the youths resulted in reconvictions. In response to persistent pressure from citizens' groups, charges against five of the youths were dropped in 1937, while two of the youths were paroled in 1944 and another in 1951. The remaining Scottsboro boy, Haywood Patterson, escaped prison in 1948 and was later convicted of manslaughter in a separate incident.)

10 As the first lord of the admiralty, William Churchill championed the 1915 campaign for the Dardanelles, a narrow strip of water that divided European from Asiatic Turkey. The campaign, thought to be critical to the Allies in World War I, ended with a difficult Allied retreat and became emblematic of strategic bungling and lost opportunities. Churchill lost his admiralty post and his political power as a result.

excitement lay. His Webbs[11] and his Fabians were plodding and grey. I saw the men with thick moustaches, wearing heavy boots, sharing lumpy meals with moral women. In the books he brought me I continued to find his absent friend. He produced Housman and Hardy (I could not read either), Siegfried Sassoon and Edmund Blunden, H.G. Wells and Bernard Shaw. The friend was probably a Scot—Frank Cairns admired them. The Scots of Canada, to me, stood for all that was narrow, grasping, at a standstill. How I distrusted those granite bankers who thought it was sinful to smoke! I was wrong, he told me. The true Scots were full of poetry and political passion. I said, 'Are you sure?' and turned his friend into a native of Aberdeen and a graduate from Edinburgh. I also began a new notebook: 'Scottish Labour Party. Keir Hardie.[12] Others'. This was better than the Webbs but still not as good as Rosa Luxemburg.

It was Frank Cairns who said to me 'Life has no point,' without emphasis, in response to some ignorant assumption of mine. This was his true voice. I recall the sidelong glance, the lizard's eye that some men develop as they grow old or when they have too much to hide. I was no good with ages. I cannot place him even today. Early thirties, probably. What else did he tell me? That 'Scotch' was the proper term and 'Scots' an example of a genteelism overtaking the original. That unless the English surmounted their class obsessions with speech and accent Britain would not survive in the world after the war. His remedy (or his friend's) was having everyone go to the same schools. He surprised me even more by saying, 'I would never live in England, not as it is now.'

'Where, then?'

'Nowhere. I don't know.'

'What about Russia? They all go to the same schools.'

'Good Lord,' said Frank Cairns.

He was inhabited by a familiar who spoke through him, provided him with jolting outbursts but not a whole thought. Perhaps that silent coming and going was the way people stayed in each other's lives when they were apart. What Frank Cairns was to me was a curio cabinet. I took everything out of the cabinet, piece by piece, examined the objects, set them down. Such situations, riddled with ambiguity, I would blunder about with for a long time until I learned to be careful.

The husband of the woman from whom I rented my summer room played golf every weekend. On one of those August nights when no one can sleep and the sky is nearly

11 Beatrice (1858–1943) and Sidney (1859–1947) Webb, English socialists and economists who helped establish the London School of Economics (1895) and were prominent members of the Fabian Society, an organization of British socialists favouring the gradual rather than revolutionary achievement of socialism. (Shaw was also a member.) Much of the point of the list of authors that follows is that while the literary works that we have seen Linnet reading are by Continental European and non-European writers and all have a strong philosophical character, Cairns prefers writers like Housman, Hardy, Edmund Blunden (a lesser-known English poet, whose poetry speaks of his love for the English countryside), and others, all of whom are strongly identified with the United Kingdom and who created works that are descriptions of English life.

12 (1856–1915); Scottish labour activist, lay minister, temperance leader, supporter of women's suffrage, and eventually Labour politician. Rosa Luxemburg (1871–1919), a Polish-born German revolutionary leader, co-founder of the revolutionary group known as the Spartacus League (1916) and the German Communist party (1918), gained considerable international attention through her fiery manner, stirring platform rhetoric, and rabble-rousing approach—not least because she was a charismatic woman espousing a radical left political agenda.

bright enough to read by, I took to the back yard and found him trying to cool off with a glass of beer. He remembered he had offered to give me golf lessons. I did not wish to learn, but did not say so. His wife spoke up from a deck chair: 'You've never offered to teach me, I notice.' She then compounded the error by telling me everyone was talking about me and the married man on the train. The next day I took the Käthe Kollwitz[13] prints down from the walls of my room and moved back to Montreal without an explanation. Frank Cairns and I met once more that summer to return some books. That was all. When he called me at my office late in November, I said, '*Who?*'

He came into the coffee shop at Windsor Station, where I was waiting. He was in uniform. I had not noticed he was good-looking before. It was not something I noticed in men. He was a first lieutenant. I disapproved: 'Couldn't they make you a private?'

'Too old,' he said. 'As it is I am too old for my rank.' I thought he just meant he might be promoted faster because of that.

'You don't look old.' I at once regretted this personal remark, the first he had heard from me. Indeed, he had shed most of his adult life. He must have seemed as young as this when he started out to Ceylon. The uniform was his visa to England; no one could shut him away now. His face was radiant, open: he was halfway there. This glimpse of a purpose astonished me; why should a uniform make the change he'd been unable to make alone? He was not the first soldier I saw transfigured but he was the first to affect me.

He kept smiling and staring at me. I hoped he was not going to make a personal remark in exchange for mine. He said, 'That tam makes you look, I don't know. Canadian. I've always thought of you as English. I still think England is where you might be happy.'

'I'm happy here. You said you'd never live there.'

'It would be a good place for you,' he said. 'Well, well, we shall see.'

He would see nothing. My evolution was like freaky weather then: a few months, a few weeks even, were the equivalent of long second thoughts later on. I was in a completely other climate. I no longer missed New York and 'different things'. I had become patriotic. Canadian patriotism is always anti-American in part, and feeds upon anecdotes. American tourists were beginning to arrive in Montreal looking for anything expensive or hard to find in the United States; when they could not buy rationed food such as meat and butter, or unrationed things such as nylon stockings (because they did not exist), they complained of ingratitude. This was because Canada was thought to be a recipient of American charity and on the other end of Lend-Lease.[14] Canadians were, and are, enormously touchy. Great umbrage had been taken over a story that was going around in the States about Americans who had been soaked for black-market butter in Montreal; when they got back across the border they opened the package and found the butter stamped 'Gift of the American People'. This fable persisted through-

13 (1867–1945); German graphic artist and sculptor, as well as a socialist, Kollwitz's stark and powerful images reflect her compassion for the poor.

14 Lend-lease was an arrangement for the transfer of war supplies, including food, machinery, and services, to nations whose defence was considered vital to the defence of the United States in World War II. In effect Lend-Lease allowed the executive branch of the American government to enter the war indirectly, circumventing the desire of its citizenry and the Congress for continued US neutrality. Many Americans resented the cost of Lend-Lease and believed Allied and Commonwealth countries were benefiting at the expense of the US taxpayer.

out the war and turned up in print. An American friend saw it in, I think, Westbrook Pegler's column and wrote asking me if it was true. I composed a letter I meant to send to the *New York Times*, demolishing the butter story. I kept rewriting and reshaping it, trying to achieve a balance between crippling irony and a calm review of events. I never posted it, finally, because my grandmother appeared to me in a dream and said that only fools wrote to newspapers.

Our coffee was tepid, the saucers slopped. He complained, and the waitress asked if we knew there was a war on. 'Christ, what a bloody awful country this is,' he said.

I wanted to say, Then why are you with a Canadian regiment? I provided my own answer: They pay more than the Brits. We were actually quarrelling in my head, and on such a mean level. I began to tear up a paper napkin and to cry.

'I have missed you,' he remarked, but quite happily; you could tell the need for missing was over. I had scarcely thought of him at all. I kept taking more and more napkins out of the container on the table and blotting my face and tearing the paper up. He must be the only man I ever cried about in a public place. I hardly knew him. He was not embarrassed, as a Canadian would have been, but looked all the happier. The glances we got from other tables were full of understanding. Everything gave the wrong impression—his uniform, my engagement ring, my tears. I told him I was going to be married.

'Nonsense,' he said.

'I'm serious.'

'You seem awfully young.'

'I'll soon be twenty.' A slip. I had told him I was older. It amazed me to remember how young I had been only the summer before. 'But I won't actually be a married woman,' I said, 'because I hate everything about them. Another thing I won't be and that's the sensitive housewife—the one who listens to Brahms while she does the ironing and reads all the new books still in their jackets.'

'No, don't be a sensitive housewife,' he said.

He gave me *The Wallet of Kai Lung* and *Kai Lung's Golden Hours*, which had been in Ceylon with him and had survived.

Did we write to each other? That's what I can't remember. I was careless then; I kept moving on. Also I really did, that time, get married. My husband was posted three days afterward to an American base in the Aleutian Islands—I have forgotten why. Eight months later he returned for a brief embarkation leave and then went overseas. I had dreaded coming in to my office after my wedding for fear the men I worked with would tease me. But the mixture of war and separation recalled old stories of their own experiences, in the First World War. Also I had been transformed into someone with a French surname, which gave them pause.

'Does he—uh—speak any French?'

'Not a word. He's from the West.' Ah. 'But he ought to. His father is French.' Oh.

I had disappeared for no more than four days, but I was Mrs Something now, not young Linnet. They spoke about me as 'she', and not 'Linnet' or 'the kid'. I wondered what they saw when they looked at me. In every head bent over a desk or a drawing board there was an opinion about women; expressed, it sounded either prurient or coarse, but I still cannot believe that is all there was to it. I know I shocked them profoundly once by saying that a wartime ditty popular with the troops, 'Rock me to sleep, Sergeant-Major, tuck me in my little bed', was innocently homosexual. That I could have such a turn of thought, that I could use such an expression, that I even knew it existed seemed scandalous to them. 'You read too damned much,' I was told. Oddly enough, they had never minded my hearing any of the several versions of the song, some of which were unspeakable; all they objected to was my unfeminine remark. When I married they gave me a suitcase, and when I left for good they bought me a Victory Bond. I had scrupulously noted every detail of the office, and the building it was in, yet only a few months later I would walk by it without remembering I had ever been inside, and it occurs to me only now that I never saw any of them again.

I was still a minor, but emancipated by marriage. I did not need to ask parental consent for anything or worry about being brought down on the wing. I realized how anxious I had been once the need for that particular anxiety was over. A friend in New York married to a psychiatrist had sent me a letter saying I had her permission to marry. She did not describe herself as a relative or state anything untrue—she just addressed herself to whom it may concern, said that as far as *she* was concerned I could get married, and signed. She did not tell her husband, in case he tried to put things right out of principle, and I mentioned to no one that the letter was legal taradiddle and carried about as much weight as a library card. I mention this to show what essential paperwork sometimes amounts to. My husband, aged twenty-four, had become my legal guardian under Quebec's preposterous Napoleonic law, but he never knew that. When he went overseas he asked me not to join any political party, which I hadn't thought of doing, and not to enlist in the Army or the Air Force. The second he vanished I tried to join the Wrens,[15] which had not been on the list only because it slipped his mind. Joining one of the services had never been among my plans and projects—it was he who accidentally put the idea in my head. I now decided I would turn up overseas, having made it there on my own, but I got no further than the enlistment requirements, which included '. . . of the white race only.' This barrier turned out to be true of nearly all the navies of the Commonwealth countries. I supposed everyone must have wanted it that way, for I never heard it questioned. I was only beginning to hear the first rumblings of hypocrisy on our side—the right side; the wrong side seemed to be guilty of every sin humanly possible except simulation of virtue. I put the blame for the racial barrier on Churchill, who certainly *knew*, and had known since the First World War; I believed that Roosevelt, Stalin, Chiang Kai-shek, and de Gaulle did not know, and that should it ever come to their attention they would be as shocked as I was.

Instead of enlisting I passed the St John Ambulance first-aid certificate, which made me a useful person in case of total war. The Killed-Wounded-Missing columns of the afternoon paper were now my daily reading. It became a habit so steadfast that I would automatically look for victims even after the war ended. The summer of the

15 The Women's Royal Canadian Naval Service, whose members served at Royal Canadian Navy establishments in North American and in the UK, participating in a wide range of support trades, including clerical and signals work.

Scottish Labour Party, Keir Hardie, and Others fell behind, as well as a younger, discarded Linnet. I lighted ferocious autos-da-fé.[16] Nothing could live except present time. In the ever-new present I read one day that Major Francis Cairns had died of wounds in Italy. Who remembers now the shock of the known name? It was like a flat white light. One felt apart from everyone, isolated. The field of vision drew in. Then, before one could lose consciousness, vision expanded, light and shadow moved, voices pierced through. One's heart, which had stopped, beat hard enough to make a room shudder. All this would occupy about a second. The next second was inhabited by disbelief. I saw him in uniform, so happy, halfway there, and myself making a spectacle of us tearing a paper napkin. I was happy for him that he would never need to return to the commuting train and the loneliness and be forced to relive his own past. I wanted to write a casual letter saying so. One's impulse was always to write to the dead. Nobody knew I knew him, and in Canada it was not done to speak of the missing. I forgot him. He went under. I was doing a new sort of work and sharing a house with another girl whose husband was also overseas. Montreal had become a completely other city. I was no longer attracted to refugees. They were going through a process called 'integrating'. Some changed their names. Others applied for citizenship. A refugee eating cornflakes was of no further interest. The house I now lived in contained a fireplace, in which I burned all my stories about Czech and German anti-Fascists. In the picnic hamper I used for storing journals and notebooks I found a manila envelope marked 'Lakeshore'. It contained several versions of 'The Socialist RM' and a few other things that sounded as if they were translated from the Russian by Constance Garnett.[17] I also found a brief novel I had no memory of having written, about a Scot from Aberdeen, a left-wing civil servant in Ceylon—a man from somewhere, living elsewhere, confident that another world was entirely possible, since he had got it all down. It had a shape, density, voice, but I destroyed it too. I never felt guilt about forgetting the dead or the living, but I minded about that one manuscript for a time. All this business of putting my life through a sieve and then discarding it was another variety of exile; I knew that even then, but it seemed quite right and perfectly natural.

1981

16 The term applied to the burning of heretics by the Spanish Inquisition. (Its literal meaning is 'acts of faith', that is, acts of pious sacrifice.)

17 (1861–1946); the English translator famous for having made the literary works of the great Russian writers such as Dostoyevsky, Tolstoy, and Chekhov available to an English-speaking audience. (It is her translation of *The Possessed* that Linnet would have been reading.)

Margaret Laurence

1926–1987

Born Jean Margaret Wemys in Neepawa, Man., Margaret Laurence transformed the small prairie town in which she grew up into Manawaka, the backdrop for a series of five interrelated works of fiction that begins with *The Stone Angel* (1964) and concludes with *The Diviners* (1974). Laurence's early years in Neepawa—in which she struggled to reconcile several deaths in her family (including her mother's when she was four and her father's when she was nine) with the powerful vision of a just God that was handed down from her Scots-Presbyterian grandparents—colour all her Manawaka fiction, especially the highly autobiographical Vanessa MacLeod stories, collected in *A Bird in the House* (1970). Like Vanessa, the adolescent Laurence felt herself trapped in her grandfather's house, until a Manitoba scholarship awarded in 1943 allowed her to attend United College in Winnipeg and to begin an independent life.

In 1947, after graduating from United College, Laurence began working as a reporter for the Winnipeg *Citizen.* That same year she married Jack Laurence and moved with him to England. In the following year they moved to Africa, where he, a civil engineer, worked as a dam builder for the British Overseas Development Service, first in the British Protectorate of Somaliland (now Somalia) and then in the Gold Coast (now Ghana). In Africa, Laurence began her career as a writer, first with *A Tree for Poverty* (1954), a translation and recasting of Somali poetry and tales, and then with a series of stories about the Africans she saw caught in a transitional moment between the old tribal world and the modern one. These stories, set in the Gold Coast, began to appear in periodicals in 1954 and were collected in *The Tomorrow-Tamer* (1963). Three other books grew out of Laurence's African years: *This Side Jordan* (1960), a novel that deals with Ghana's struggle for independence; *The Prophet's Camel Bell* (1963), an account of two years spent in Somaliland, prepared from the journal she kept while there; and *Long Drums and Cannons* (1968), a critical study of the English-language writers emerging in Nigeria. Although *This Side Jordan* remains an apprentice novel, Laurence's African short stories are among her best work, and her experience of the various African struggles for freedom and nationhood sharpened her sense of Canada as a new country still coming to terms with its own colonial influence.

Laurence seems to have valued the perspective gained through expatriation. Although she and her husband returned to Canada in 1957, settling in Vancouver, five years after their return they separated, and she moved to England. It was there that she wrote the first three Manawaka novels—*The Stone Angel, A Jest of God* (1966), and *The Fire-Dwellers* (1969). In 1969 Laurence began returning to Canada, spending summers at a cottage on the Otonabee River, near Peterborough, Ont., and winters in England. During this period she also served as writer-in-residence at the University of Toronto, Trent University, and the University of Western Ontario; and she was named a Companion of the Order of Canada. She moved back to Canada permanently in 1974, settling in Lakefield, Ont. In the same year she published *The Diviners,* her most ambitious work of fiction, which draws together characters and themes from the four other Manawaka novels and, by its use of reciprocal parallels with *The Stone Angel,* provides a formal close to the sequence. *Like A Jest of God, The Diviners* won a Governor General's Award.

Following *The Diviners* Laurence published only children's stories and short non-fiction pieces. *Heart of a Stranger* (1976) is a selection of her essays and magazine articles from the previous twelve years. Throughout the eighties she was active in organizations that promoted such causes as nuclear disarmament, energy conservation, environmental protection, and various social issues. From 1981 through 1983 she was chancellor of Trent University. After being diagnosed with terminal cancer, Laurence died by her own hand in 1987. In 1989, her daughter Jocelyn brought to final form *Dance on the Earth*, the collection of memoirs Laurence had begun to gather together in 1985. In addition to these memoirs, several selections of her letters, including *A Very Large Soul: Selected Letters from Margaret Laurence to Canadian Writers* (1995), edited by J.A. Wainwright, and *Selected Letters of Margaret Laurence and Adele Wiseman* (1997), edited by John Lennox, give insight into Laurence's development as a writer.

From her early African writing through the later novels, and even in one of her books for children, *Jason's Quest* (1970), Laurence repeatedly chronicled a search for autonomy and an accompanying joy. To find independence and happiness the individual must come to see the bondage both society and oneself have created, as ninety-year-old Hagar Shipley at last realizes in the moving close to *The Stone Angel*:

> *This knowing comes upon me so forcefully, so shatteringly, and with such bitterness as I have never felt before. I must always, always, have wanted that—simply to rejoice. How is it I never could?... Every good joy I might have held, in my man or any child of mine or even the plain light of morning, of walking the earth, all were forced to a standstill by some brake of proper appearances—oh, proper to whom? When did I ever speak the heart's truth?*
>
> *Pride was my wilderness, and the demon that led me there was fear. I was alone, never anything else, and never free, for I carried my chains within me, and they spread out from me and shackled all I touched.*

Even though Hagar and the women of her era seem unable to experience fully freedom and joy, each of the protagonists who follow Hagar come closer to grasping that ideal—and, as we discover in *The Diviners*, Hagar's struggle (her name is the same as that of Abraham's bondswoman in the Bible) has served to free Morag (whose name is the Scottish equivalent of Sarah, Abraham's wife).

The way in which Hagar's experiences eventually touch and help Morag suggests the importance of *inheritance* in Laurence's work. Inheritance—which becomes not only genetic makeup, but also the unobserved but profoundly shaping influences of culture, society, and environment—is a prominent theme in all her Manawaka fiction. While our inheritance is often the restraint against which we must struggle, it is also our chief source of strength, the thing that allows us to survive in a world characterized by bewildering uncertainty.

Laurence herself has left us an inheritance: her fiction brings the life and landscape of Canada into the reader's imagination and gives expression to the complexity of our cultural heritage. No one response accounts for the way readers look at her and her work. For some, she speaks as a regionalist, telling us about prairie life and history; for others, it is her voice as a woman, recording the progress of women's place in Canadian society, that makes her work important; and for many, her stories are those of a child of immigrants, struggling with a tradition partly frozen in time and partly being created. Perhaps it is the breadth of her appeal that helps us understand why we want to designate such writing as universal rather than local.

To Set Our House in Order

When the baby was almost ready to be born, something went wrong and my mother had to go into hospital two weeks before the expected time. I was wakened by her crying in the night, and then I heard my father's footsteps as he went downstairs to phone. I stood in the doorway of my room, shivering and listening, wanting to go to my mother but afraid to go lest there be some sight there more terrifying than I could bear.

'Hello—Paul?' my father said, and I knew he was talking to Dr Cates. 'It's Beth. The waters have broken, and the fetal position doesn't seem quite—well, I'm only thinking of what happened the last time, and another like that would be—I wish she were a little huskier, damn it—she's so—no, don't worry, I'm quite all right. Yes, I think that would be the best thing. Okay, make it as soon as you can, will you?'

He came back upstairs, looking bony and dishevelled in his pyjamas, and running his fingers through his sand-coloured hair. At the top of the stairs, he came face to face with Grandmother MacLeod, who was standing there in her quilted black satin dressing gown, her slight figure held straight and poised, as though she were unaware that her hair was bound grotesquely like white-feathered wings in the snare of her coarse night-time hairnet.

'What is it, Ewen?'

'It's all right, Mother. Beth's having—a little trouble. I'm going to take her into the hospital. You go back to bed.'

'I told you,' Grandmother MacLeod said in her clear voice, never loud, but distinct and ringing like the tap of a sterling teaspoon on a crystal goblet, 'I did tell you, Ewen, did I not, that you should have got a girl in to help her with the housework? She would have rested more.'

'I couldn't afford to get anyone in,' my father said. 'If you thought she should've rested more, why didn't you ever—oh God, I'm out of my mind tonight—just go back to bed, Mother, please. I must get back to Beth.'

When my father went down to the front door to let Dr Cates in, my need overcame my fear and I slipped into my parents' room. My mother's black hair, so neatly pinned up during the day, was startlingly spread across the white pillowcase. I stared at her, not speaking, and then she smiled and I rushed from the doorway and buried my head upon her.

'It's all right, honey,' she said. 'Listen, Vanessa, the baby's just going to come a little early, that's all. You'll be all right. Grandmother MacLeod will be here.'

'How can she get the meals?' I wailed, fixing on the first thing that came to mind. 'She never cooks. She doesn't know how.'

'Yes, she does,' my mother said. 'She can cook as well as anyone when she has to. She's just never had to very much, that's all. Don't worry—she'll keep everything in order, and then some.'

My father and Dr Cates came in, and I had to go, without ever saying anything I had wanted to say. I went back to my own room and lay with the shadows all around me. I listened to the night murmurings that always went on in that house, sounds which never had a source, rafters and beams contracting in the dry air, perhaps, or mice in the walls, or a sparrow that had flown into the attic through the broken skylight there. After a while, although I would not have believed it possible, I slept.

The next morning I questioned my father. I believed him to be not only the best doctor in Manawaka, but also the best doctor in the whole of Manitoba, if not in the entire world, and the fact that he was not the one who was looking after my mother seemed to have something sinister about it.

'But it's always done that way, Vanessa,' he explained. 'Doctors never attend members of their own family. It's because they care so much about them, you see, and—'

'And what?' I insisted, alarmed at the way he had broken off. But my father did not reply. He stood there, and then he put on that difficult smile with which adults seek to conceal pain from children. I felt terrified, and ran to him, and he held me tightly.

'She's going to be fine,' he said. 'Honestly she is. Nessa, don't cry—'

Grandmother MacLeod appeared beside us, steel-spined despite her apparent fragility. She was wearing a purple silk dress and her ivory pendant. She looked as though she were all ready to go out for afternoon tea.

'Ewen, you're only encouraging the child to give way,' she said. 'Vanessa, big girls of ten don't make such a fuss about things. Come and get your breakfast. Now, Ewen, you're not to worry. I'll see to everything.'

Summer holidays were not quite over, but I did not feel like going out to play with any of the kids. I was very superstitious, and I had the feeling that if I left the house, even for a few hours, some disaster would overtake my mother. I did not, of course, mention this feeling to Grandmother MacLeod, for she did not believe in the existence of fear, or if she did, she never let on. I spent the morning morbidly, in seeking hidden places in the house. There were many of these—odd-shaped nooks under the stairs, small and loosely nailed-up doors at the back of clothes closets, leading to dusty tunnels and forgotten recesses in the heart of the house where the only things actually to be seen were drab oil paintings stacked upon the rafters, and trunks full of outmoded clothing and old photograph albums. But the unseen presences in these secret places I knew to be those of every person, young or old, who had ever belonged to the house and had died, including Uncle Roderick who got killed on the Somme,[1] and the baby who would have been my sister if only she had managed to come to life. Grandfather MacLeod, who had died a year after I was born, was present in the house in more tangible form. At the top of the main stairs hung the mammoth picture of a darkly uniformed man riding upon a horse whose prancing stance and dilated nostrils suggested that the battle was not yet over, that it might indeed continue until Judgment Day. The stern man was actually the Duke of Wellington, but at the time I believed him to be my grandfather MacLeod, still keeping an eye on things.

We had moved in with Grandmother MacLeod when the Depression got bad and she could no longer afford a housekeeper, but the MacLeod house never seemed like home to me. Its dark red brick was grown over at the front with Virginia creeper that turned crimson in the fall, until you could hardly tell brick from leaves. It boasted a small tower in which Grandmother MacLeod kept a weedy collection of anaemic ferns. The verandah was embellished with a profusion of wrought-iron scrolls, and the circular rose-window upstairs contained glass of many colours which permitted an outlooking eye to see the world as a place of absolute sapphire or emerald, or if one wished to look with a jaundiced eye, a hateful yellow. In Grandmother MacLeod's opinion, their features gave the house style.

1 One of the most costly campaigns of the First World War. The British offensive at the Somme, which began in July 1915, was joined by the 4th Canadian Division in September; despite severe losses on both sides, the results were indecisive.

Inside a multitude of doors led to rooms where my presence, if not actually forbidden, was not encouraged. One was Grandmother MacLeod's bedroom, with its stale and old-smelling air, the dim reek of medicines and lavender sachets. Here resided her monogrammed dresser silver, brush and mirror, nail-buffer and button hook and scissors, none of which must even be fingered by me now, for she meant to leave them to me in her will and intended to hand them over in the same flawless and unused condition in which they had always been kept. Here, too, were the silver-framed photographs of Uncle Roderick—as a child, as a boy, as a man in his Army uniform. The massive walnut spool bed had obviously been designed for queens or giants, and my tiny grandmother used to lie within it all day when she had a migraine, contriving somehow to look like a giant queen.

The living room was another alien territory where I had to tread warily, for many valuable objects sat just-so on tables and mantelpiece, and dirt must not be tracked in upon the blue Chinese carpet with its birds in eternal motionless flight and its water-lily buds caught forever just before the point of opening. My mother was always nervous when I was in this room.

'Vanessa, honey,' she would say, half apologetically, 'why don't you go and play in the den, or upstairs?'

'Can't you leave her, Beth?' my father would say. 'She's not doing any harm.'

'I'm only thinking of the rug,' my mother would say, glancing at Grandmother MacLeod, 'and yesterday she nearly knocked the Dresden shepherdess off the mantel. I mean, she can't help it, Ewen, she has to run around—'

'Goddamn it, I know she can't help it,' my father would growl, glaring at the smirking face of the Dresden shepherdess.

'I see no need to blaspheme, Ewen,' Grandmother MacLeod would say quietly, and then my father would say he was sorry, and I would leave.

The day my mother went to the hospital, Grandmother MacLeod called me at lunch-time, and when I appeared, smudged with dust from the attic, she looked at me distastefully as though I had been a cockroach that had just crawled impertinently out of the woodwork.

'For mercy's sake, Vanessa, what have you been doing with yourself? Run and get washed this minute. Here, not that way—you use the back stairs, young lady. Get along now. Oh—your father phoned.'

I swung around. 'What did he say? How is she? Is the baby born?'

'Curiosity killed a cat,' Grandmother MacLeod said, frowning. 'I cannot understand Beth and Ewen telling you all these things, at your age. What sort of vulgar person you'll grow up to be, I dare not think. No, it's not born yet. Your mother's just the same. No change.'

I looked at my grandmother, not wanting to appeal to her, but unable to stop myself. 'Will she—will she be all right?'

Grandmother MacLeod straightened her already-straight back. 'If I said definitely yes, Vanessa, that would be a lie, and the MacLeods do not tell lies, as I have tried to impress upon you before. What happens is God's will. The Lord giveth, and the Lord taketh away.'

Appalled, I turned away so she would not see my face and my eyes. Surprisingly, I heard her sigh and felt her papery white and perfectly manicured hand upon my shoulder.

'When your Uncle Roderick got killed,' she said, 'I thought I would die. But I didn't die, Vanessa.'

At lunch, she chatted animatedly, and I realised she was trying to cheer me in the only way she knew.

'When I married your Grandfather MacLeod,' she related, 'he said to me, "Eleanor, don't think because we're going to the prairies that I expect you to live roughly. You're used to a proper house, and you shall have one." He was as good as his word. Before we'd been in Manawaka three years, he'd had this place built. He earned a good deal of money in his time, your grandfather. He soon had more patients than either of the other doctors. We ordered our dinner service and all our silver from Birks' in Toronto. We had resident help in those days, of course, and never had less than twelve guests for dinner parties. When I had a tea, it would always be twenty or thirty. Never any less than half a dozen different kinds of cake were ever served in this house. Well, no one seems to bother much these days. Too lazy, I suppose.'

'Too broke,' I suggested. 'That's what Dad says.'

'I can't bear slang,' Grandmother MacLeod said. 'If you mean hard up, why don't you say so? It's mainly a question of management, anyway. My accounts were always in good order, and so was my house. No unexpected expenses that couldn't be met, no fruit cellar running out of preserves before the winter was over. Do you know what my father used to say to me when I was a girl?'

'No,' I said. 'What?'

"God loves Order,' Grandmother MacLeod replied with emphasis. 'You remember that, Vanessa. God loves Order—he wants each one of us to set our house in order. I've never forgotten those words of my father's. I was a MacInnes before I got married. The MacInnes is a very ancient clan, the lairds of Morven and constables of the Castle of Kinlochaline. Did you finish that book I gave you?'

'Yes,' I said. Then, feeling some additional comment to be called for, 'It was a swell book, Grandmother.'

This was somewhat short of the truth. I had been hoping for her cairngorm[2] brooch on my tenth birthday, and had received instead the plaid-bound volume entitled *The Clans and Tartans of Scotland*.[3] Most of it was too boring to read, but I had looked up the motto of my own family and those of some of my friends' families. *Be then a wall of brass. Learn to suffer. Consider the end. Go carefully.* I had not found any of these slogans reassuring. What with Mavis Duncan learning to suffer, and Laura Kennedy considering the end, and Patsy Drummond going carefully, and I spending my time in being a wall of brass, it did not seem to me that any of us were going to lead very interesting lives. I did not say this to Grandmother MacLeod.

2 Also called 'Scotch topaz'; a semi-precious stone frequently worn as part of the Highland Scots costume.

3 Vanessa would have discovered in Robert Bain's *The Clans and Tartans of Scotland* (1938, and many subsequent editions; the mottoes were added later) that the MacInneses were 'a Celtic clan of ancient origin', their earliest-known territory that of Morven. Bain says that they 'remained in possession of Morven, and as late as 1645 it appears that a MacInnes was in command of the Castle of Kinlochaline when it was besieged and burnt. . . .'

'The MacInnes motto is *Pleasure Arises from Work,*' I said.

'Yes,' she agreed proudly. 'And an excellent motto it is, too. One to bear in mind.'

She rose from the table, rearranging on her bosom the looped ivory beads that held the pendant on which a fullblown ivory rose was stiffly carved.

'I hope Ewen will be pleased,' she said.

'What at?'

'Didn't I tell you?' Grandmother MacLeod said. 'I hired a girl this morning, for the housework. She's to start tomorrow.'

When my father got home that evening, Grandmother MacLeod told him her good news. He ran one hand distractedly across his forehead.

'I'm sorry, Mother, but you'll just have to unhire her. I can't possibly pay anyone.'

'It seems distinctly odd', Grandmother MacLeod snapped, 'that you can afford to eat chicken four times a week.'

'Those chickens', my father said in an exasperated voice, 'are how people are paying their bills. The same with the eggs and the milk. That scrawny turkey that arrived yesterday was for Logan MacCardney's appendix, if you must know. We probably eat better than any family in Manawaka, except Niall Cameron's. People can't entirely dispense with doctors or undertakers. That doesn't mean to say I've got any cash. Look, Mother, I don't know what's happening with Beth. Paul thinks he may have to do a Caesarean. Can't we leave all this? Just leave the house alone. Don't touch it. What does it matter?'

'I have never lived in a messy house, Ewen,' Grandmother MacLeod said, 'and I don't intend to begin now.'

'Oh Lord,' my father said. 'Well, I'll phone Edna, I guess, and see if she can give us a hand, although God knows she's got enough, with the Connor house and her parents to look after.'

'I don't fancy having Edna Connor in to help,' Grandmother MacLeod objected.

'Why not?' my father shouted. 'She's Beth's sister, isn't she?'

'She speaks in such a slangy way,' Grandmother MacLeod said. 'I have never believed she was a good influence on Vanessa. And there is no need for you to raise your voice to me, Ewen, if you please.'

I could barely control my rage. I thought my father would surely rise to Aunt Edna's defence. But he did not.

'It'll be all right,' he soothed her. 'She'd only be here for part of the day, Mother. You could stay in your room.'

Aunt Edna strode in the next morning. The sight of her bobbed black hair and her grin made me feel better at once. She hauled out the carpet sweeper and the weighted polisher and got to work. I dusted while she polished and swept, and we got through the living room and the front hall in next to no time.

'Where's her royal highness, kiddo?' she enquired.

'In her room,' I said. 'She's reading the catalogue from Robinson & Cleaver.'

'Good Glory, not again?' Aunt Edna cried. 'The last time she ordered three linen tea-cloths and two dozen serviettes. It came to fourteen dollars. Your mother was absolutely frantic. I guess I shouldn't be saying this.'

'I knew anyway,' I assured her. 'She was at the lace handkerchiefs section when I took up her coffee.'

'Let's hope she stays there. Heaven forbid she should get onto the banqueting cloths. Well, at least she believes the Irish are good for two things—manual labour and linen-making. She's never forgotten Father used to be a blacksmith, before he got the hardware store. Can you beat it? I wish it didn't bother Beth.'

'Does it?' I asked, and immediately realised this was the wrong move, for Aunt Edna was suddenly scrutinizing me.

'We're making you grow up before your time,' she said. 'Don't pay any attention to me, Nessa. I must've got up on the wrong side of the bed this morning.'

But I was unwilling to leave the subject.

'All the same,' I said thoughtfully, 'Grandmother MacLeod's family were the lairds of Morven and the constables of the Castle of Kinlochaline. I bet you didn't know that.'

Aunt Edna snorted. 'Castle, my foot. She was born in Ontario, just like your Grandfather Connor, and her father was a horse doctor. Come on, kiddo, we'd better shut up and get down to business here.'

We worked in silence for a while.

'Aunt Edna—' I said at last, 'what about Mother? Why won't they let me go and see her?'

'Kids aren't allowed to visit maternity patients. It's tough for you, I know that. Look, Nessa, don't worry. If it doesn't start tonight, they're going to do the operation. She's getting the best of care.'

I stood there, holding the feather duster like a dead bird in my hands. I was not aware that I was going to speak until the words came out.

'I'm scared,' I said.

Aunt Edna put her arms around me, and her face looked all at once stricken and empty of defences.

'Oh, honey, I'm scared, too,' she said.

It was this way that Grandmother MacLeod found us when she came stepping lightly down into the front hall with the order in her hand for two dozen lace-bordered handkerchiefs of pure Irish linen.

I could not sleep that night, and when I went downstairs, I found my father in the den. I sat down on the hassock beside his chair, and he told me about the operation my mother was to have the next morning. He kept on saying it was not serious nowadays.

'But you're worried,' I put in, as though seeking to explain why I was.

'I should at least have been able to keep from burdening you with it,' he said in a distant voice, as though to himself. 'If only the baby hadn't got itself twisted around—'

'Will it be born dead, like the little girl?'

'I don't know,' my father said. 'I hope not.'

'She'd be disappointed, wouldn't she, if it was?' I said bleakly, wondering why I was not enough for her.

'Yes, she would,' my father replied. 'She won't be able to have any more, after this. It's partly on your account that she wants this one, Nessa. She doesn't want you to grow up without a brother or sister.'

'As far as I'm concerned, she didn't need to bother,' I retorted angrily.

My father laughed. 'Well, let's talk about something else, and then maybe you'll be able to sleep. How did you and Grandmother make out today?'

'Oh, fine, I guess. What was Grandfather MacLeod like, Dad?'

'What did she tell you about him?'

'She said he made a lot of money in his time.'

'Well, he wasn't any millionaire,' my father said, 'but I suppose he did quite well. That's not what I associate with him, though.'

He reached across to the bookshelf, took out a small leather-bound volume and opened it. On the pages were mysterious marks, like doodling, only much neater and more patterned.

'What is it?' I asked.

'Greek,' my father explained. 'This is a play called *Antigone*. See, here's the title in English. There's a whole stack of them on the shelves there. *Oedipus Rex. Electra. Medea.* They belonged to your Grandfather MacLeod. He used to read them often.'

'Why?' I enquired, unable to understand why anyone would pore over those undecipherable signs.

'He was interested in them,' my father said. 'He must have been a lonely man, although it never struck me that way at the time. Sometimes a thing only hits you a long time afterwards.'

'Why would he be lonely?' I wanted to know.

'He was the only person in Manawaka who could read these plays in the original Greek,' my father said. 'I don't suppose many people, if anyone, had even read them in English translations. Maybe he would have liked to be a classical scholar—I don't know. But his father was a doctor, so that's what he was. Maybe he would have liked to talk to somebody about these plays. They must have meant a lot to him.'

It seemed to me that my father was talking oddly. There was a sadness in his voice that I had never heard before, and I longed to say something that would make him feel better, but I could not, because I did not know what was the matter.

'Can you read this kind of writing?' I asked hesitantly.

My father shook his head. 'Nope. I was never very intellectual, I guess. Rod was always brighter than I, in school, but even he wasn't interested in learning Greek. Perhaps he would've been later, if he'd lived. As a kid, all I ever wanted to do was go into the merchant marine.'

'Why didn't you, then?'

'Oh well,' my father said offhandedly, 'a kid who'd never seen the sea wouldn't have made much of a sailor. I might have turned out to be the seasick type.'

I had lost interest now that he was speaking once more like himself.

'Grandmother MacLeod was pretty cross today about the girl,' I remarked.

'I know,' my father nodded. 'Well, we must be as nice as we can to her, Nessa, and after a while she'll be all right.'

Suddenly I did not care what I said.

'Why can't she be nice to us for a change?' I burst out. 'We're always the ones who have to be nice to her.'

My father put his hand down and slowly tilted my head until I was forced to look at him.

'Vanessa,' he said, 'she's had troubles in her life which you really don't know much about. That's why she gets migraine sometimes and has to go to bed. It's not easy for her these days, either—the house is still the same, so she thinks other things should be, too. It hurts her when she finds they aren't.'

'I don't see—' I began.

'Listen,' my father said, 'you know we were talking about what people are interested in, like Grandfather MacLeod being interested in Greek plays? Well, your grandmother was interested in being a lady, Nessa, and for a long time it seemed to her that she was one.'

I thought of the Castle of Kinlochaline, and of horse doctors in Ontario.

'I didn't know—' I stammered.

'That's usually the trouble with most of us,' my father said. 'You go on up to bed now. I'll phone tomorrow from the hospital as soon as the operation's over.'

I did sleep at last, and in my dreams I could hear the caught sparrow fluttering in the attic, and the sound of my mother crying, and the voices of the dead children.

My father did not phone until afternoon. Grandmother MacLeod said I was being silly, for you could hear the phone ringing all over the house, but nevertheless I refused to move out of the den. I had never before examined my father's books, but now, at a loss for something to do, I took them out one by one and read snatches here and there. After I had been doing this for several hours, it dawned on me that most of the books were of the same kind. I looked again at the titles.

Seven-League Boots. Arabia Deserta. The Seven Pillars of Wisdom. Travels in Tibet. Count Lucknor the Sea Devil.[4] And a hundred more. On a shelf by themselves were copies of the *National Geographic* magazine, which I looked at often enough, but never before with the puzzling compulsion which I felt now, as though I were on the verge of some discovery, something which I had to find out and yet did not want to know. I riffled through the picture-filled pages. Hibiscus and wild orchids grew in a soft-petalled confusion. The Himalayas stood lofty as gods, with the morning sun on their peaks of snow. Leopards snarled from the vined depths of a thousand jungles. Schooners buffeted their white sails like the wings of giant angels against the great sea winds.

'What on earth are you doing?' Grandmother MacLeod enquired waspishly, from the doorway. 'You've got everything scattered all over the place. Pick it all up this minute, Vanessa, do you hear?'

So I picked up the books and magazines, and put them all neatly away, as I had been told to do.

4 Five classic works of travel literature, published between the two world wars, by Richard Halliburton, C.M. Doughty, T.E. Lawrence, H. Harrier, and Lowell Thomas respectively.

When the telephone finally rang, I was afraid to answer it. At last I picked it up. My father sounded faraway, and the relief in his voice made it unsteady.

'It's okay, honey. Everything's fine. The boy was born alive and kicking after all. Your mother's pretty weak, but she's going to be all right.'

I could hardly believe it. I did not want to talk to anyone. I wanted to be by myself, to assimilate the presence of my brother, towards whom, without ever having seen him yet, I felt such tenderness and such resentment.

That evening, Grandmother MacLeod approached my father, who, still dazed with the unexpected gift of neither life now being threatened, at first did not take her seriously when she asked what they planned to call the child.

'Oh, I don't know. Hank, maybe, or Joe. Fauntleroy, perhaps.'

She ignored his levity.

'Ewen,' she said, 'I wish you would call him Roderick.'

My father's face changed. 'I'd rather not.'

'I think you should,' Grandmother MacLeod insisted, very quietly, but in a voice as pointed and precise as her silver nail-scissors.

'Don't you think Beth ought to decide?' my father asked.

'Beth will agree if you do.'

My father did not bother to deny something that even I knew to be true. He did not say anything. Then Grandmother MacLeod's voice, astonishingly, faltered a little.

'It would mean a great deal to me,' she said.

I remembered what she had told me—*When your Uncle Roderick got killed, I thought I would die. But I didn't die.* All at once, her feeling for that unknown dead man became a reality for me. And yet I held it against her, as well, for I could see that it had enabled her to win now.

'All right,' my father said tiredly. 'We'll call him Roderick.'

Then, alarmingly, he threw back his head and laughed.

'Roderick Dhu!' he cried. 'That's what you'll call him, isn't it? Black Roderick. Like before. Don't you remember? As though he were a character out of Sir Walter Scott, instead of an ordinary kid who—'

He broke off, and looked at her with a kind of desolation in his face.

'God, I'm sorry, Mother,' he said. 'I had no right to say that.'

Grandmother MacLeod did not flinch, or tremble, or indicate that she felt anything at all.

'I accept your apology, Ewen,' she said.

My mother had to stay in bed for several weeks after she arrived home. The baby's cot was kept in my parents' room, and I could go in and look at the small creature who lay there with his tightly closed fists and his feathery black hair. Aunt Edna came in to help each morning, and when she had finished the housework, she would have coffee with my mother. They kept the door closed, but this did not prevent me from eavesdropping, for there was an air register in the floor of the spare room, which was linked somehow with the register in my parents' room. If you put your ear to the iron grille, it was almost like a radio.

'Did you mind very much, Beth?' Aunt Edna was saying.

'Oh, it's not the name I mind,' my mother replied. 'It's just the fact that Ewen felt he had to. You know that Rod had only had the sight of one eye, didn't you?'

'Sure, I knew. So what?'

'There was only a year and a half between Ewen and Rod,' my mother said, 'so they often went around together when they were youngsters. It was Ewen's air-rifle that did it.'

'Oh Lord,' Aunt Edna said heavily. 'I suppose she always blamed him?'

'No, I don't think it was so much that, really. It was how he felt himself. I think he even used to wonder sometimes if—but people shouldn't let themselves think like that, or they'd go crazy. Accidents do happen, after all. When the war came, Ewen joined up first. Rod should never have been in the Army at all, but he couldn't wait to get in. He must have lied about his eyesight. It wasn't so very noticeable unless you looked at him closely, and I don't suppose the medicals were very thorough in those days. He got in as a gunner, and Ewen applied to have him in the same company. He thought he might be able to watch out for him, I guess, Rod being—at a disadvantage. They were both only kids. Ewen was nineteen and Rod was eighteen when they went to France. And then the Somme. I don't know, Edna, I think Ewen felt that if Rod had had proper sight, or if he hadn't been in the same outfit and had been sent somewhere else—you know how people always think these things afterwards, not that it's ever a bit of use. Ewen wasn't there when Rod got hit. They'd lost each other somehow, and Ewen was looking for him, not bothering about anything else, you know, just frantically looking. Then he stumbled across him quite by chance. Rod was still alive, but—'

'Stop it, Beth,' Aunt Edna said. 'You're only upsetting yourself.'

'Ewen never spoke of it to me,' my mother went on, 'until once his mother showed me the letter he'd written to her at the time. It was a peculiar letter, almost formal, saying how gallantly Rod had died, and all that. I guess I shouldn't have, but I told him she'd shown it to me. He was very angry that she had. And then, as though for some reason he were terribly ashamed, he said—*I had to write something to her, but men don't really die like that, Beth. It wasn't that way at all.* It was only after the war that he decided to come back and study medicine and go into practice with his father.'

'Had Rod meant to?' Aunt Edna asked.

'I don't know,' my mother said slowly. 'I never felt I should ask Ewen that.'

Aunt Edna was gathering up the coffee things, for I could hear the clash of cups and saucers being stacked on the tray.

'You know what I heard her say to Vanessa once, Beth? *The MacLeods never tell lies.* Those were her exact words. Even then, I didn't know whether to laugh or cry.'

'Please, Edna—' my mother sounded worn out now. 'Don't.'

'Oh Glory,' Aunt Edna said remorsefully, 'I've got all the delicacy of a two-ton truck. I didn't mean Ewen, for heaven's sake. That wasn't what I meant at all. Here, let me plump up your pillows for you.'

Then the baby began to cry, so I could not hear anything more of interest. I took my bike and went out beyond Manawaka, riding aimlessly along the gravel highway. It was late summer, and the wheat had changed colour, but instead of being high and bronzed in the fields, it was stunted and desiccated, for there had been no rain again this year. But in the bluff where I stopped and crawled under the barbed wire fence and lay stretched out on the grass, the plentiful poplar leaves were turning to a luminous yellow and shone like church windows in the sun. I put my head down very close to the earth and looked at what was going on there. Grasshoppers with enormous eyes ticked and twitched around me, as though the dry air were perfect for their purposes. A ladybird laboured mightily to climb a blade of grass, fell off, and started all over again, seeming to be unaware that she possessed wings and could have flown up.

I thought of the accidents that might easily happen to a person—or, of course, might not happen, might happen to somebody else. I thought of the dead baby, my sister, who might as easily have been I. Would she, then, have been lying here in my place, the sharp grass making its small toothmarks on her brown arms, the sun warming her to the heart? I thought of the leatherbound volumes of Greek, and the six different kinds of iced cakes that used to be offered always in the MacLeod house, and the pictures of leopards and green seas. I thought of my brother, who had been born alive after all, and now had been given his life's name.

I could not really comprehend these things, but I sensed their strangeness, their disarray. I felt that whatever God might love in this world, it was certainly not order.

1970

James Reaney

b. 1926

Born on a farm near Stratford, Ont., James Reaney attended a nearby one-room school and then Stratford Collegiate before enrolling, in 1944, at Victoria College of the University of Toronto. While still an undergraduate, he began writing and publishing stories and poems in *Contemporary Verse, Northern Review, Canadian Forum,* and elsewhere. He received his BA in English in 1948 and an MA in 1949. In that same year he published his first collection of poems, *The Red Heart,* which won a Governor General's Award, bringing him early prominence at twenty-three.

In the fall of 1949 Reaney joined the English department at the University of Manitoba, remaining there until 1960, when he moved to the University of Western Ontario in London: his years in Manitoba were the only time he has lived outside Ontario. He took a leave from University of Manitoba in 1956–8 to return to University of Toronto in order to complete his doctoral degree, writing a thesis about Spenser's influence on Yeats. While engaged in this study, Reaney also created a playful imitation of *The Shepheardes Calender* entitled *A Suit of Nettles* (1958), in which he transformed Spenser's pastoral dialogues between shepherds tending their flocks into conversations among geese on an Ontario farm. Dense and witty, *A Suit of Nettles* won Reaney a second Governor General's Award.

Reaney also began to create pieces for performance. He composed a libretto for *Night-Blooming Cereus*—an opera by John Beckwith (performed on the CBC in 1959 and staged the next year)—and wrote several plays, including *The Killdeer and One-Man Masque* (both produced in 1960), as well as *The Sun and the Moon* (produced in 1965). In 1962, he published *The Killdeer and Other Plays* and *Twelve Letters to a Small Town* (a sequence of poems about Stratford, read on CBC radio); for these he was awarded a third Governor General's Award. The prolific output of drama that followed established him as the leading Canadian playwright of the 1960s. Many of the plays—including *Colours in the Dark* (1969) and *Listen to the Wind* (1972)—were eventually published. *The Killdeer* (in a revised version), *Three Desks*, and *The Easter Egg* were collected in *Masks of Childhood* (1972).

In the late sixties Reaney immersed himself in the exhaustive research, writing, and extensive revision that led to the creation of his best-known theatrical achievement, *The Donnellys*, a trilogy (*Sticks and Stones*, published in 1975; *The St Nicholas Hotel*, 1976; and *Handcuffs*, 1977) about an infamous, contumacious Irish family who lived near London, Ont., in the second half of the nineteenth century and who were massacred by a suspicious and intolerant community. (Reaney's account of his travels with *The Donnellys* national touring company was published in 1977 as *14 Barrels from Sea to Sea*.) Like all of Reaney's plays, *The Donnellys* subverts the formal conventions of realistic theatre in its poetic style and frequent departures from linear narrative.

Reaney's continued collaborations with Beckwith led to a second opera, *The Shivaree* (1978), as well as to a 'detective opera', *Crazy to Kill* (1989), that mixes live action with puppets. The chamber opera *Serinette* (1990), featuring Reaney's libretto and music by the late Harry Somers, tells the story of the Children of Peace, a pacifist and religious group that immigrated from the US after 1812; it was first produced in the octagonal Sharon Temple built by that group in Newmarket, Ont. Among Reaney's later theatrical successes is a stage adaptation of Lewis Carroll's *Alice through the Looking-Glass* (1994), performed at the Stratford Festival in 1994 and in 1996.

Reaney's prose includes two novels aimed at adolescent audiences—*The Boy with an R in His Hand: A Tale of the Type-Riot at William Lyon Mackenzie's Printing Office in 1886* (1965) and *Take the Big Picture* (1986)—and a collection of his short stories, which were written mostly in the 1940s and 1950s, *The Box Social and Other Stories* (1996). Several of the stories in this collection, particularly 'The Box Social', which scandalized Reaney's early readers, and 'The Bully', are examples of what has been called 'Southern Ontario Gothic', a tradition that also includes works by such writers as Margaret Atwood, Timothy Findley, and Alice Munro—fiction in which, as in American Southern Gothic, a strong sense of place is combined with macabre events.

In all of his writing Reaney has created a world in which local and regional merge with and reveal the mythic and universal. On the one hand, a great deal of his poetry and drama are intensely grounded in his experience of growing up in Perth County, Ont., and in the history of his region: he is so convinced of the need to know one's home place intimately that when he taught courses in Ontario culture and literature he began with a close consideration of the actualities of daily existence and a careful scrutiny of maps. On the other hand, Reaney regards myth and imagination as central to the construction and function of culture. His contact with Northrop Frye when he was an undergraduate and again when he worked on his doctoral thesis, which was directed by Frye, was an important influence that led him to consider the implications for writers of the theories contained in Frye's *Anatomy of Criticism*. It also led him to read other theorists on the mythic dimensions of the mind, such Carl Jung.

In an essay on *Alphabet*, the important literary magazine that Reaney founded and edited, Margaret Atwood discusses Reaney's goal of making a form that would be 'Documentary on one side and myth on the other: Life and Art'; she suggests that this tension between myth and documentary is not only central to Reaney's poetic vision but that it is peculiarly Canadian ('Eleven Years of "Alphabet"', *Canadian Literature*, No. 49, 1971). A special issue of the *University of Toronto Quarterly* published in 2001 on 'The Visionary Tradition in Canadian Writing' locates Reaney as a central figure in that tradition, along with Frye, Margaret Avison, P.K. Page, Atwood, Don McKay, and Michael Ondaatje.

The extent of Reaney's interest in the creative dimension and the power of the human mind is conveyed by the full title of his literary magazine: *Alphabet: A Semi-Annual Devoted to the Iconography of the Imagination* (1960–71). Begun the year Reaney moved from Manitoba to the University of Western Ontario, *Alphabet* was a significant influence on the Canadian literary scene. Not only did it serve, along with Frye's critical theories, to direct the attention of his contemporaries to myth as a resource, but it suggested—by the often arbitrary juxtaposition of its diverse contents to the mythic figure announced for each issue—that the presence of myth in a work is derived as much from the mind's quest for meaning as from anything inherent in individual stories and poems. At the same time, the title of Reaney's journal sets against the universalizing tendency of myth the particulars out of which language grows, the very letters themselves. (Before beginning to publish his magazine Reaney trained as a typesetter and for a time he typeset each issue himself.) One of the many emerging writers of the decade who appeared in *Alphabet* was bp Nichol, whose concrete poetry literally attempted to create art out of the alphabet by treating letters as things in themselves—an act that influenced Reaney in his later work.

Even while he was teaching, editing, and writing plays, Reaney never stopped working on his poetry. The sequence 'A Message to Winnipeg' (broadcast 1960) grew out of Reaney's decision to learn to read his new Western landscape in a way that made it as meaningful to him as that of his native Ontario. It was followed by *The Dance of Death at London, Ontario* (1963), a satiric sequence of poems about his new home town. The volume called simply *Poems* (1972), edited and with an introduction by Germaine Warkentin, is a large selection of Reaney's poetry. In that same year Reaney wrote an introduction to a new reprint of *The Collected Poems* of Isabella Valancy Crawford, whose early mythologizing of nature and its opposing forces had long interested him. In 1984 he published *Imprecations: The Art of Swearing*, in which he playfully explores the 'lost skill' of cursing. His *Performance Poems* (1990) is a collection of works written for performance, and arranged in a calendrical cycle from January to December.

Because Reaney is ultimately less interested in objective reality than in the imaginative structures into which the mind orders that reality—that is, not in what happens but in what we make of what happens—what he has most valued in his rural community are the examples of the power of words to transform reality into stories, song, folktales, nursery rhymes, and individual flights of fancy. Indeed, in 'The Alphabet' and 'Starling with a Split-Tongue', language itself seems a source of magic. Throughout Reaney's poetry, and in his plays, we sense a mind seeking to make the world comprehensible, but since both mind and world oscillate between innocence and experience, and between dreaming and waking—in ways that make it hard to say which is which—we also feel that comprehension remains elusive. The figure of the child, which recurs throughout Reaney's work, holds the secret truths that we as adults yearn for. It is to this child in all of us that Reaney, in his constant playfulness, is ultimately speaking.

The School Globe

Sometimes when I hold
Our faded old globe
That we used at school
To see where oceans were
And the five continents,
The lines of latitude and longitude,
The North Pole, the Equator and the South Pole—

Sometimes when I hold this
Wrecked blue cardboard pumpkin
I think: here in my hands
Rest the fair fields and lands
Of my childhood
Where still lie or still wander
Old games, tops and pets;
A house where I was little
And afraid to swear
Because God might hear and
Send a bear
To eat me up;
Rooms where I was as old
As I was high;
Where I loved the pink clenches,
The white, red and pink fists
Of roses; where I watched the rain
That Heaven's clouds threw down
In puddles and rutfuls
And irregular mirrors
Of soft brown glass upon the ground.
This school globe is a parcel of my past,
A basket of pluperfect[1] things.
And here I stand with it
Sometime in the summertime
All alone in an empty schoolroom
Where about me hang
Old maps, an abacus, pictures,
Blackboards, empty desks.
If I raise my hand
No tall teacher will demand
What I want.
But if someone in authority
Were here, I'd say
Give me this old world back
Whose husk I clasp
And I'll give you in exchange
The great sad real one
That's filled
Not with a child's remembered and pleasant skies
But with blood, pus, horror, death, stepmothers, and lies.

1949

1 More than perfect; in grammar the tense that denotes completed action (expressed in English by the auxiliary *had*).

The Lost Child

Long have I looked for my lost child.
I hear him shake his rattle
Slyly in the winter wind
In the ditch that's filled with snow.

He pinched and shrieked and ran away
At the edge of the November forest.
The hungry old burdock stood
By the dead dry ferns.

Hear him thud that ball!
The acorns fall by the fence.
See him loll in the St. Lucy sun,[1]
The abandoned sheaf in the wire.

Oh Life in Death! my bonny nursling
Merry drummer in the nut brown coffin,
With vast wings outspread I float
Looking and looking over the empty sea

And there! in the—on the rolling death
Rattling a dried out gourd
Floated the mysterious cradle
Filled with a source.

I push the shore and kingdom to you,
Oh winter walk with seedpod ditch:
I touch them to the floating child
And lo! Cities and gardens, shepherds and smiths.

1962[2]

1 St Lucy's Day, 13 December, was traditionally thought of as the shortest day of the year and the beginning of the winter solstice.

2 Originally the final poem in *One-Man Masque.*

The Alphabet

Where are the fields of dew?
I cannot keep them.
They quip and pun
The rising sun
Who plucks them out of view:
But lay down fire-veined jasper!

For out of my cloudy head
Come Ay Ee I Oh and U,
Five thunders shouted;
Drive in sardonyx!

And Ull Mm Nn Rr and hisSsings
Proclaim huge wings;
Pour in sea blue sapphires!

Through my bristling hair
Blows Wuh and Yuh
Puh, Buh, Phuh and Vuh,
The humorous air:
Lift up skies of chalcedony!

Huh, Cuh, Guh and Chuh
Grunt like pigs in my acorn mind:
Arrange these emeralds in a meadow!

Come down Tuh, Duh and Thuh!
Consonantly rain
On the windowpane
Of the shrunken house of the heart;
Lift up blood red sardius!

Lift up golden chrysolite!
Juh, Quuh, Zuh and X
Scribble heavens with light
Steeples take fright.

In my mouth like bread
Stands the shape of this glory;
Consonants and vowels
Repeat the story:
And sea-green beryl is carried up!

The candle tongue in my dark mouth
Is anguished with its sloth
And stung with self-scoff
As my eyes behold this treasure.
Let them bring up topaz now!

Dazzling chrysoprase!
Dewdrops tempt dark wick to sparkle.
Growl Spark! you whelp and cur,
Leap out of tongue kennel
And candle sepulchre.

I faint in the hyacinthine quarries!
My words pursue
Through the forest of time
The fading antlers of this dew.

A B C D E F G H I J K L M
Take captive the sun
Slay the dew quarry
Adam's Eve is morning rib
Bride and bridegroom marry
Still coffin is rocking crib
Tower and well are one
The stone is the wind, the wind is the stone
New Jerusalem[1]
N O P Q R S T U V W X Y Z!

1960, 1972

1 The final paradise after Armageddon according to Revelation; see Revelation 21–2, which is the source of the imagery of the poem.

Starling with a Split Tongue[1]

Some boys caught me
In the yard
And with a jackknife they
Split my tongue into speech

1 Folk belief holds that splitting the tongues of crows, ravens, and starlings makes it possible to teach them how to speak.

So in a phrenological[2] cage
Here in the garage I stay
And say
The cracklewords passersby taught.
I say I know not what
Though I pray I do not pray
Though I curse I do not curse
Though I talk I do not talk

'I thought that made it kinda nice'
I heard her say as she began slipping on the ice
The the I am   An a am I
I and am are the & a   Who is are? Who saw war?
I rock a little pronoun   It does instead of me
I rose as I   Nooned as you
Lay down as he or she   Begat we, you & they
My eggs are covered with commas

'Yuh remember when she fell down in a fit?'
Reveries Jake from the bottom of the pit.

Before beforeday   after St After's Massacre
While the while is on   Since since is since
Let's wait till till   Or until if you like
I come from from   to Whither Bay
Down Whence Road   but not To-day

As still as infinitives were the   Stones
Filled with adjectives were the   Trees
And with adverbs the   Pond
This all is a recorded announcement
This all is a recorded announcement
'I thought that made it kinda nice'
'Yuh remember . . . . in a fit?'
Darkness deep
Now fills the garage and its town
With wordless sleep.

Who split their tongues? I ask.
Of Giant Jackknife in the sky.
Who split their tongues into lie mask

2 That is, 'skull-like'; phrenology (literally the study of the mental faculties) is the pseudo-scientific theory that the shape of the skull gives evidence of personality and mental ability.

And lie face; split their hand
Into this way, that way, up and down,
Divided their love into restless hemispheres,
Split into two—one seeing left, one right
Their once one Aldebaran[3] all-seeing eye?
In the larger garage of the endless starlight
        Do they not croak as I?

1964, 1972

3 One of the brightest stars in the sky (actually a double star).

Phyllis Webb

b. 1927

Phyllis Webb was born in Victoria, BC, and grew up there and in Vancouver. In 1949 she received a BA in English and philosophy from the University of British Columbia. After an unsuccessful campaign as a CCF candidate for the BC legislature in 1949, Webb moved to Montreal, where she attended graduate school at McGill; during the fifties and sixties she spent extended periods in London, Paris, and San Francisco. After teaching at UBC for four years from 1960 to 1964, she moved to Toronto to accept a job with the CBC, for which she had been freelancing since 1955. There she created the ground-breaking radio program *Ideas*, serving from 1966 to 1969 as its executive producer. In 1969, she left full-time radio work and moved to BC to make her home on Saltspring Island. Over the years she has taught at the University of Victoria, UBC, and the Banff Centre, and has been writer-in-residence at the University of Alberta.

Webb's first book publication was in *Trio* (1954), a showcase for her work and that of two other new writers, Gael Turnbull and Eli Mandel. In the next eleven years she produced three poetry collections: *Even Your Right Eye* (1956), *The Sea Is Also a Garden* (1962), and *Naked Poems* (1965). The last of these marked a shift from the formal rhetorical style of her earlier work to a starker, more minimalist approach reflected in short lines of intense poetry. By the time Webb's *Selected Poems 1954–1965* was published in 1971, Webb had already entered a period of poetic silence that lasted until the publication of *Wilson's Bowl* (1980). The poems in this and subsequent volumes, though not so austere as the lyrics of *Naked Poems*, demonstrate Webb's characteristic economy of form. Since 1980 Webb has produced four more volumes of poetry: *Sunday Water: Thirteen Anti-Ghazals* (1982); *Selected Poems: The Vision Tree* (1982), a Governor General's Award winner that includes some new work; *Water and Light: Ghazals and Anti-ghazals* (1984); and *Hanging Fire* (1990). Webb has also written a number of essays on poetry and the creative process. These are gathered in two volumes: *Talking* (1982), which also includes scripts of some of her radio talks; and *Nothing but Brush Strokes: Selected Prose* (1995), which includes some of her photo-collages, reflecting her growing focus on visual art.

Though Webb's early poetry tends to be pessimistic, it is rarely morbid because it is always leavened with wit. Her concern with despair, suicide, and death is linked to a conscious existentialism—unusual in Canadian poetry—more like that of Kierkegaard and Gide. While investigating what she sees as a sterile, even meaningless, world she presents her readers with strategies for survival. The topics of break-up and break-down—of major importance since the Second World War to writers as diverse as John Berryman, Adrienne Rich, and Margaret Atwood—have led her to suggest that the individual must seek protective isolation and silence. In her own life she has found these in the silence of her native region: the beaches, water, and gardens of the Gulf Islands.

Webb's work displays a broad range of affinities—from the intricacies of metaphysical poetry techniques (as in 'Marvell's Garden') to the stylistic simplicity of the Black Mountain and San Francisco poetry movements (as in *Naked Poems*), as well as being responsive to the philosophy of Buddhism and the aesthetic forms of western Asia. Perhaps the most important aspect of her poetry—particularly from *Naked Poems* forward—has been her feminism and her need to create a poetics supportive of women's aesthetics and interests. Her wide familiarity with poetic traditions and her desire to find within them the tools she needs has made her last book, *Hanging Fire*, rewardingly rich in structure. She tries to obey what she calls

> *the physics of the poem. Energy/Mass. Waxy splendour, the massive quiet of the fallen tulip petals. So much depends upon: the wit of the syntax, the rhythm and speed of the fall, the drop, the assumption of a specific light, curved.* (*Talking*)

This curve is a line, that of the female body and that of the structure of poetry.

Marvell's Garden[1]

Marvell's garden, that place of solitude,[2]
is not where I'd choose to live
yet is the fixed sundial[3]
that turns me round
unwillingly
in a hot glade
as closer, closer I come to contradiction
to the shade green within the green shade.[4]

1 This poem contains many responses and allusions to 'The Garden' by the British poet Andrew Marvell (1621–78).

2 Marvell chooses to be solitary in the garden, declaring: 'Society is all but rude / To this delicious solitude'.

3 The sundial in Marvell's poem is equated with the garden itself; in the seventeenth century the sundial was often a symbol of a stable point against which to measure the illusions of experience.

4 In this stanza and the next, Webb refers to lines in Marvell's poem:

The mind, that ocean where each kind
Does straight its own resemblance find;
Yet it creates, transcending these,
Far other worlds, and other seas;
Annihilating all that's made
To a green thought in a green shade.

The garden where Marvell scorned love's solicitude[5]—
that dream—and played instead an arcane solitaire,
shuffling his thoughts like shadowy chance
across the shrubs of ecstasy,
and cast the myths away to flowering hours
as yes, his mind, that sea, caught at green
thoughts shadowing a green infinity.

And yet Marvell's garden was not Plato's
garden[6]—and yet—he *did* care more for the form
of things than for the thing itself—
ideas and visions,
resemblances and echoes,
things seeming and being
not quite what they were.

That was his garden, a kind of attitude
struck out of an earth too carefully attended,
wanting to be left alone.
And I don't blame him for that.
God knows, too many fences fence us out
and his garden closed in on Paradise.[7]

On Paradise! When I think of his hymning
Puritans in the Bermudas,[8] the bright oranges
lighting up that night! When I recall
his rustling tinsel hopes
beneath the cold decree of steel.[9]
Oh, I have wept for some new convulsion
to tear together this world and his.

5 Marvell rejects physical love, approving of the mythical stories in which young women escape seduction when they are transformed into flora.

6 Marvell, while affirming the Platonic concept of ideal forms, departed from most of his contemporary Neo-Platonists in his belief that man's mind (equated in 'The Garden' with the ocean, which was said to contain a parallel to every land-based thing) was superior to nature, and thus to the ideal reality, because it not only had a pre-existent knowledge of all the 'forms' of reality but also could imaginatively create new 'forms' that have never before existed. In this stanza Webb plays with the contradictory meanings suggested by the word 'form'.

7 Marvell equates his garden to Eden before the creation of Eve and the fall of man.

8 In the poem 'Bermudas', Marvell depicts religious dissenters rowing ashore to the Bermudas (celebrated by Europeans as a kind of earthly paradise), singing a hymn of praise to God that includes the lines: 'He hangs in shades the orange bright, / Like golden lamps in a green night'.

9 Marvell himself was twice exiled to the Bermudas as a result of ecclesiastical persecution. Throughout his life he sought a middle ground in the political strife of England, which was being torn by civil war.

But then I saw his luminous plumèd Wings[10]
prepared for flight,
and then I heard him singing glory
in a green tree,
and then I caught the vest he'd laid aside
all blest with fire.

And I have gone walking slowly in
his garden of necessity
leaving brothers, lovers, Christ
outside my walls
where they have wept without
and I within.

1956

10 In 'The Garden' the poet undergoes a spiritual transformation:

Casting the body's vest aside,
My soul into the boughs does glide:
There like a bird it sits, and sings,
Then whets and combs its silver wings.

To Friends Who Have Also Considered Suicide

It's still a good idea.
Its exercise is discipline:
to remember to cross the street without looking,
to remember not to jump when the cars side-swipe,
to remember not to bother to have clothes cleaned,
to remember not to eat or want to eat,
to consider the numerous methods of killing oneself,
that is surely the finest exercise of the imagination:
death by drowning, sleeping pills, slashed wrists,
kitchen fumes, bullets through the brain or through
the stomach, hanging by the neck in attic or basement,
a clean frozen death—the ways are endless.
And consider the drama! It's better than a whole season
at Stratford when you think of the emotion of your
family on hearing the news and when you imagine
how embarrassed some will be when the body is found.
One could furnish a whole chorus in a Greek play
with expletives and feel sneaky and omniscient
at the same time. But there's no shame

in this concept of suicide.
It has concerned our best philosophers
and inspired some of the most popular
of our politicians and financiers.
Some people swim lakes, others climb flagpoles,
some join monasteries, but we, my friends,
who have considered suicide take our daily walk
with death and are not lonely.
In the end it brings more honesty and care
than all the democratic parliaments of tricks.
It is the 'sickness unto death';[1] it is death;
it is not death; it is the sand from the beaches
of a hundred civilizations, the sand in the teeth
of death and barnacles our singing tongue:
and this is 'life' and we owe at least this much
contemplation to our western fact: to Rise,
Decline, Fall, to futility and larks,
to the bright crustaceans of the oversky.

1962

1 Phrase taken from *The Sickness unto Death* (1849) by the Danish philosopher and theologian Sören Kierkegaard (1813–55); for Kierkegaard, the 'sickness unto death' is despair.

From *Naked Poems*

Suite I

MOVING
to establish distance
between our houses.

It seems
I welcome you in.

Your mouth blesses me
all over.

There is room.

AND

here
and here and
here
and over   and
over   your mouth

TONIGHT

quietness.   In me
and the room.

I am enclosed
by a thought

and some walls.

THE BRUISE

Again you have left
your mark.

Or we
have.

Skins shuddered
secretly.

FLIES

tonight
in this room

two flies
on the ceiling
are making
love
quietly.   Or

so it seems
down here.

YOUR BLOUSE

I people
this room
with things, a
chair,   a lamp,   a
fly,   two books by
Marianne Moore.

I have thrown my
blouse on the floor.

Was it only
last night?

YOU
took

with so much
gentleness

my dark

Suite II

While you were away

I held you like this
in my mind.

It is a good mind
that can embody
perfection   with exactitude.

The sun comes through
plum curtains.

I said
the sun is gold

in your eyes.

It isn't the sun
you said.

On the floor your blouse.
The plum light
falls more golden

going down.

Tonight
quietness
in the room.

We knew.

Then you must go.
I sat cross-legged
on the bed.
There is no room
for self-pity
I said.

I lied.

In the gold darkening
light

you dressed.

I hid my face
in my hair.

The room that held you

is still here.

You brought me clarity.

Gift after gift
I wear.

Poems naked
in the sunlight

on the floor.

1965

Spots of Blood

I am wearing absent-minded red
slippers and a red vest—
spots of blood
to match the broken English
of Count Dracula being interviewed
on the radio in the morning sun.
I touch the holes in my throat
where the poppies bud—spots of blood
spots of womantime. '14,000 rats,'[1]
Dracula is saying, and the interviewer
echoes, '14,000 rats! So beautiful,'
he sighs, 'The Carpathian Mountains—
the photography, so seductive!' The Count
also loves the film; he has already seen it
several times. He tells in his dreamy voice
how he didn't need direction, didn't want
makeup, how he could have done it with his own
teeth. He glided in and out of this role
believing in reincarnation, in metamorphosis.
Yet 14,000 rats and the beleaguered
citizens of the Dutch town where those scenes
were shot (without him) are of no interest.
'And Hollywood?' the interviewer asks, himself
an actor, 'Hollywood next?' Who knows?
Who knows?

1 In *Nosferatu* (Germany, 1922), a film based on Bram Stoker's novel *Dracula* (1987), the vampire sets a plague of rats upon a city. The heroine, sacrificing her own life in an effort to save humankind, entices the vampire to her bed, where he remains until destroyed by the first rays of the morning sun.

The blood pounds at my temples.
The women of the world parade before me
in red slippers and red vests, back and
forth, back and forth, fists clenched.
My heart emerges from my breast for
14,000 rats and the citizens of Delft,
for the women of the world in their menses.
Yet I too imitate a crime of passion:
Look at these hands. Look at the hectic
red painting my cheekbones as I metamorphose
in and out of the Buddha's eye,[2] the *animus*
mundi.

In the morning sun Count Dracula leans
against my throat with his own teeth.
Breathing poppies. Thinking.

1980

2 Buddha is said to be the Eye of the World, the All-Seeing Eye in which all existence rests. *'Animus mundi'*: the world soul or mind, usually in the feminine form, *anima mundi*; here Webb refers to (i) the Buddhist notion of an Absolute Mind out of which the world emanates, and (ii) the Jungian principle of one's idealized sexual opposite. (Since the speaker is female, her ideal is male, *animus.*)

'Evensong'

(even song syllabics)

Tending toward music, the artist's
life tends toward solitary notes, slips
of the tongue, hand, eye, eerily like
intelligence of higher orders.
Hierarchical systems of dream
stuff, choirs of angelic lisps, minty
panpipes accompanying dawn, mist
rising from hills, green-splits, gold flecks, flicks
of day ascending. No one goes home.
They're out and about, lured by goat god[1]
music-food into noon sun hot rays,

1 The god Pan, of Greek mythology, conventionally represented with the horns, ears, and legs of a goat on a man's body, playing a shepherd's panpipe; a solitary figure haunting the high hills, his chief concern his flocks and herds. Typically Pan is, as here, thought of as satyr-like, taking on the qualities associated with half-man, half-goat followers of Dionysus and of his wild, drunken, and ecstatic religious rites that helped his worshippers loosen their inhibitions and become creative in music and poetry.

bothered, skewered on oily spit, fat
and famished; one note more, another
tugs them into laid-back afternoon,
lawlessness. Wine, sun sets their steps on
cool path's mythic return, labouring
all the way home. Quiet entrances,
doffed hats, feet on wood, stone, a chair, and
evensong's slim, uncanny sibilance.

1990

The Making of a Japanese Print

The first plate in the volume is the key block
giving the outline. It is easy to see how each
successive color is added by a separate block to
achieve the final result.

—from *The Making of a Japanese Print*

IMPRINT NO. 1

Eye contact, and it's forever.
The first circle.

And then the breast
the left or right.
So choice.
Or grab what is given.

Rosebud and at the
periphery / eyelash
dark sandals pass by.

Add a chair in the corner
with a white chemise.
This is the only way to go
—outward.

Door behind the mother
closing as father in blue
blows out.

White filled in, hatch-
crossings for negative space.
Decadent life.

Flesh tint laid on
with extreme caution.
All moves are dangerous:
open the door and wind pours in
with dust. Lift the head
of mother an inch
her attention goes
out the unseen window.

If baby sleeps
hand falling away from
the opening bud, rose
becomes dream, memory
a praise of distance.

Technique is all
a test of the artist's
sincerity. Oh
we are *sincere,* we go
for the blade, cut close
to the bone. The splotch
of red in the lower right-hand
corner, a sign of the happy
maker.

IMPRINT NO. 2

Knife. Chisel. Mallet.
Block of cherry wood.
Printing pad. Paper. Ink.

What does he think?

He floats a green
into the space
of its assignation.
A world divides
the view from an empty
chair shifts

a chair with a life of its own
an orange cushion.
Poppies arise from extinction
on the plane of the sun.

Harunobu,[1] your hand trembles.
You will die young and lucky.
Sit down in the chair you
yourself have provided.
The curved form is a fan
alarmingly pink.
Flutter the air.

Intaglio[2] for what you see best
the 'empty imprint'?
What you see best
is the ivory kimono
coming towards you.
It will stay in the same place
always, Harunobu, brocading[3]
the threat of advance.

A mere press of your hands
and your death flies
into a silken shadow.

Then washy blue three-quarters up.

IMPRINT NO. 3

A fake. There was no chair
no washy blue in the 'Heron Maid'.
I made it up for my own artistic
purposes. I was thinking of
Van Gogh, of myself sitting down
for the last time and getting
up again to make this confession.

1 Suzuki Harunobu (1724–70), Japanese artist, who was the first to use a wide range of colours effectively in printing. He is celebrated for his graceful female figures, idealized portraits of actors, courtesans, and young girls. In 1765 he created multicoloured calendar prints from wood blocks.

2 A design that is cut, etched, or engraved in a hard surface, such as metal or stone. When a print is made from an intaglio surface (here, wood), the colours are transferred to the negative space—that is, to the space *around* the objects being represented, rather than to the objects themselves.

3 The technique of weaving a raised pattern into silk. Here, Webb is suggesting a parallel with the layers created in the print as its different colours are added in.

Tree, shrubs, a turquoise stream
a Japanese woman dressed for cold
her parasol a shield against the
snow which we can't see falling.
One ear pokes out, too high up
from under her brown hood
yet all is harmonious.

In the floating world
she stands quite still
like the snowy heron
who is really always moving.
She is also winter and tells me
more about herself than Harunobu
wanted me to know.

IMPRINT NO. 4

The Heron Maid steps
on her wooden blocks
off the path
into summer.
She removes her winter
cloak, her sandals
dips her feet
in the turquoise stream.
What does she think
as she sits on the verge
this side of anonymous water?
She uncoils her hair
slips off her rings
imagines a different future.
She thinks of Harunobu
working away at his
butcher blocks
his famous seasons.

She'll have to change
habits and colors
wash off her fear.
Perhaps she'll look
for another job

cut her hair short
change her expression.
And, it's possible, die
some day in foreign arms
under the new dispensation.

Each block is laid on
with extreme caution
then set aside
out of harm's way.

A woman emerges at last
on the finest paper, cursing
his quest for the line
and this damned delicate fan
carved in her hand
to keep her forever cool
factitious,[4] apparently pleasing.

1990

4 False; inauthentic; artificial.

Robert Kroetsch

b. 1927

Despite growing up in the small northern Alberta community of Heisler amid the hardships that intense drought and the Depression brought prairie farmers in the thirties, Robert Kroetsch has become known for responding to his experiences with a sense of humour. It infuses his poetry, his critical essays, and especially his novels, which recall the wild and bawdy tall tales he would have heard in western beer halls. In retelling the stories of those who have lived in the Canadian west and north, Kroetsch has ranged widely for allusions—drawing on the Bible, on ancient tales from Mesopotamia such as the *Epic of Gilgamesh* and the myth of Marduk, on Homer and the Norse epic cycle, on the North American Native Trickster stories, and on a wide variety of literary texts including Conrad's *Heart of Darkness*, Joyce's *Ulysses*, and Mark Twain's *Huckleberry Finn*—to provide his readers with complexly intertextual works that parody as much as they recall their originals.

After earning a BA at the University of Alberta in 1948, Kroetsch journeyed to the Canadian north. In *A Likely Story: The Writing Life* (1995), he explains:

I went up North, not to discover gold in the Yukon or to find Sir John Franklin's bones, not even to get rich or to escape from home, but rather because I wanted to write a novel. . . . Insofar as the North carnivalizes given Canadian assumptions—turning upside-down assumptions about time, about direction, about urban ambition, about America—it seemed an escape from the authority of tradition and hierarchy, an escape that would allow me to become a storyteller.

Kroetsch spent time as a labourer on the Fort Smith Portage, worked on Mackenzie riverboats for two seasons, and held jobs for several years in Labrador. He then travelled to Montreal in order to study at McGill University under Hugh MacLennan. During his summers he attended the Bread Loaf School of English at Middlebury College, Vermont, where he completed an MA. In 1956 he entered the Writers' Workshop program at the University of Iowa, earning his Ph.D. in 1961 with the draft of a novel (an early version of *The Studhorse Man*). He remained in the US for the next fourteen years, teaching at the State University of New York at Binghamton, before returning to Canada in 1975. He taught for short periods at the Universities of Lethbridge and Calgary, and then, until retiring, was a member of the Department of English at the University of Manitoba.

While still at Binghamton, Kroetsch published *But We Are Exiles* (1965), the northern novel he had set out to write, about the crew of a riverboat on the Mackenzie. He turned, in his next five novels, to the history of his own province for material. In a trilogy—*The Words of My Roaring* (1966); *The Studhorse Man* (1969), for which he won a Governor General's Award; and *Gone Indian* (1973)—and then in *Badlands* (1975) and *What the Crow Said* (1978), he undertook what he had come to feel was the chief task of the western Canadian novelist: to write his environment into existence. In an often quoted line from a conversation with Margaret Laurence, he stressed the importance of this act: 'In a sense we haven't got an identity until somebody tells our story. The fiction makes us real' (*Creation*, 1970).

The 'Out West' trilogy (he calls it a 'triptych', a term referring to three interrelated paintings) forms an extended investigation of rural Alberta in the twentieth century: the political movements of the Depression thirties are followed by the social dislocations and changes in sexual mores that began after the Second World War, and then by the back-to-the-land pastoralism that sent Americans looking for utopias in Canada in the 1960s and 70s.

Badlands, which tells of river-rafting through the Alberta Badlands in quest of dinosaur bones, continues these investigations with reflections on a point earlier in the century and with suggestions of the prehistoric past, while Kroetsch's travel book, *Alberta* (1968), provides both a more personal and a more objective response to his native province.

In the early 1970s, at a time when the term 'postmodern' was just beginning to be used in the literary community, Kroetsch co-founded, with William Spanos, the Binghamton-based critical journal *Boundary 2: A Journal of Post-Modern Literature,* which became a shaping force in North American letters. Around that time, he also began to articulate his own theories of post-modernism in essays and in *Labyrinths of Voice* (1981), a book of conversations with Shirley Neuman and Robert Wilson—emphasizing the use of parody as a way of responding to inherited form and tradition; resistance to closure and to overriding unity in literary works; and a self-reflexivity that brings questions of textuality and process into the foreground of the reading experience, while undermining the authority of both writer and reader. Among his essays, 'Unhiding the Hidden', first published in 1974, served as a manifesto. Kroetsch no longer thought the Canadian writer's job was to name a new and previously unnamed country into existence. Instead, writers were burdened by cultural inheritances from elsewhere and needed to 'un-name' their surroundings—and even themselves.

In 1983, a special issue of *Open Letter* collected Kroetsch's essays. In 1989 several of these appeared in revised form along with newer critical writing as *The Lovely Treachery of Words.* The effect on his writing of Kroetsch's growing engagement with theory can be seen in the novel *What the Crow Said,* as well as in *Alibi* (1983) and its sequel *The Puppeteer* (1992), which show the influences of post-structuralism and deconstruction.

During the second half of the 1970s much of Kroetsch's creative energy was devoted to poetry. Increasingly fascinated by questions about form and structure in the modern long poem, he published the short poems he had written in the previous decade as *The Stone Hammer Poems* (1975), and then began, with *The Ledger* in 1975 and *Seed Catalogue* in 1977, a sequence of long poems. The poems that are reprinted below show Kroetsch's concern with un-naming—as in Frederick Philip Grove's creation of a new identity after first 'exfoliating' himself back to blankness ('F.P. Grove: The Finding'). 'Stone Hammer Poem', a work particularly important to Kroetsch, can be read as an investigation of the names we give things (is the object that sits on the poet's desk a stone or a hammer or a paperweight?) and a revelation of language as unstable. Like the glacier in 'Stone Hammer Poem', which is both 'retreating' and 'recreating', the poem can carry us away from the object of contemplation into larger meanings *and* at the same time move us into the history of that object to consider its ever-receding origins, and may even remind us that Europeans claimed what once belonged to the Native people by bringing European words and concepts into the New World.

In 1981 Kroetsch brought together the several parts of his long poems as *Field Notes.* 'Stone Hammer Poem' appears there as the prologue. At the end of the 1980s, he added several additional poems to this volume and published the whole as *Completed Field Notes: The Long Poems of Robert Kroetsch* (1989). Though he maintains that the book marks his farewell to poetry, he subsequently published *The Hornbooks of Rita K* (2001), in which a fictional 'archivist' gives an account of a Prairie poet (whose initials happen to be the same as Kroetsch's) and offers an extensive selection of 'her' poems. In 1998 Kroetsch returned to fiction with a similarly playful novel, *The Man from the Creeks,* which tells the 'untold' story behind Robert Service's popular poem of the Yukon gold rush, 'The Shooting of Dan McGrew'.

The Words of My Roaring

Kroetsch observed, after writing *But We Are Exiles,* that his first novel operated out of a tragic vision, with 'a sense of inevitability' that was, for him, no longer adequate to the second half of the twentieth century. What he found more satisfactory was a vision of a comic world with 'sheer chance and the kinds of absurdities which are neither logical nor rational'. *The Words of My Roaring,* with the absurd optimism and exuberant behaviour of J.J. Backstrom, its first-person narrator and protagonist, was Kroetsch's first exploration of such a comic world.

Backstrom's own high spirits are surprising in a period of desolating weather and devastating economic failure (the title comes from the opening verse of Psalm 22: 'My God, my God, why hast thou forsaken me? why art thou so far from helping me, and from the words of my roaring?'). But the novel is built around such paradoxes, the 'old dualities' as Backstrom calls them. Although *The Words of My Roaring* seems more tall tale than realist story, it has a historical basis: it is set during the 1935 Alberta General Election, which brought to power the world's first Social Credit government. Alberta Social Credit was an eccentric political party led by a charismatic radio evangelist whose attacks on eastern Canada and the federal government were part of a platform of apocalyptic warnings and wild promises based on an economic theory no one understood. That election may have changed western politics forever, but Backstrom—the undertaker of the small town of Notikeewin—has run for the Alberta Legislative Assembly only because he thinks it might bring him a steady salary.

A charismatic if unfocused man who describes himself as 'a heller with women', Backstrom feels he is engaged in a hopeless campaign against the incumbent, old Doc Murdoch, when, thirteen days before the vote, he makes the only campaign promise he can think of: 'I looked at the speaker and saw he was a farmer and I said "Mister, how would you like some rain?"' Challenged in the beer hall to which he retreats, Backstrom expands on his prophecy:

'When I say it's going to rain it's going to pour. And I say it's going to pour. So if I was in your boots I'd start shopping for a boat. You lazy pack of stubble-jumpers. I'd start building an ark.'

Finding that his idle promise has given the electorate the hope they were lacking and gambling that it *will* rain sometime in the next thirteen days, Backstrom launches into motion: using his hearse as his means of transportation, he tours his little community, campaigning madly.

The selection reprinted here, which comes at the midway point of the book and is the climax of Backstrom's campaign, suggests the serious side of Kroetsch's comedy. Set at the Notikeewin 'stampede', the annual fair and rodeo that permits release from the labour of farm life, the passage has at its centre the figure of the rodeo clown, whose job is to distract the bull from the rider after he has been thrown. Emblematic of the larger concerns of the novel, the clown shows us that, in making himself a figure of fun, an individual takes risks but also may provide the saving grace that others need.

Stone Hammer Poem

1

This stone
become a hammer
of stone, this maul

is the colour
of bone (no,
bone is the colour
of this stone maul).

The rawhide loops
are gone, the
hand is gone, the
buffalo's skull
is gone;

the stone is
shaped like the skull
of a child.

2

This paperweight on my desk

where I begin
this poem was

found in a wheatfield
lost (this hammer,
this poem).

Cut to a function,
this stone was
(the hand is gone—

3

Grey, two-headed,
the pemmican maul[1]

fell from the travois or
a boy playing lost it in
the prairie wool or
a squaw left it in
the brain of a buffalo or

1 That is, the hammer was used in the preparation of pemmican (preserved buffalo or caribou meat). 'Travois': Indian sledge made of a platform stretched between two shafts and pulled behind a horse.

It is a million
years older than
the hand that
chipped stone or
raised slough
water (or blood) or

4

This stone maul
was found.

In the field
my grandfather
thought
was his

my father
thought was his

5

It is a stone
old as the last
Ice Age, the
retreating/the
recreating ice,
the retreating
buffalo, the
retreating Indians

(the saskatoons bloom
white (infrequently
the chokecherries the
highbush cranberries the
pincherries bloom
white along the barbed
wire fence (the
pemmican   winter

6

This stone maul
stopped a plow
long enough for one
Gott im Himmel.

The Blackfoot (the
Cree?) not

finding the maul
cursed.

? did he curse
? did he try to
go back
? what happened
I have to/I want
to know (not know)
? WHAT HAPPENED

7

The poem
is the stone
chipped and hammered
until it is shaped
like the stone
hammer, the maul.

8

Now the field is
mine because
I gave it
(for a price)

to a young man
(with a growing son)
who did not

notice that the land
did not belong

to the Indian who
gave it to the Queen
(for a price) who
gave it to the CPR[2]
(for a price) which
gave it to my grandfather
(for a price) who
gave it to my father
(50 bucks an acre
Gott im Himmel I cut
down all the trees I
picked up all the stones) who

gave it to his son
(who sold it)

9

This won't
surprise you.

My grandfather
lost the stone maul.

10

My father (retired)
grew raspberries.
He dug in his potato patch.
He drank one glass of wine
each morning.
He was lonesome
for death.

He was lonesome for the
hot wind on his face, the smell
of horses, the distant
hum of a threshing machine,
the oilcan he carried, the weight
of a crescent wrench in his hind pocket.

2 In the Prairies the Canadian Pacific Railroad, which received land grants for their right-of-way when laying the tracks that connected the east with the west, sold the land along their right-of-way to prospective farmers and generally promoted settlement and development of the area as a way of encouraging rail commerce.

He was lonesome for his absent
sons and his daughters,
for his wife, for his own
brothers and sisters and
his own mother and father.

He found the stone maul
on a rockpile in the
north-west corner of what
he thought of
as his wheatfield.

He kept it (the
stone maul) on the railing
of the back porch in
a raspberry basket.

II

I keep it
on my desk
(the stone).

Sometimes I use it
in the (hot) wind
(to hold down paper)

smelling a little of cut
grass or maybe even of
ripening wheat or of
buffalo blood hot
in the dying sun.

Sometimes I write
my poems for that

stone hammer.

1975

F.P. Grove: The Finding[1]

I

Dreaming the well-born   hobo of yourself
against the bourgeois father[2]   dreaming Europe
if only to find   a place to be from

the hobo tragedian   pitching bundles
riding a freight   to the impossible city
the fallen archangel   of Brandon or Winnipeg

in all your harvesting   real
or imagined   did you really find
four aged stallions[3]   neigh

in your cold undertaking   on those trails north
in all the (dreamed) nights   in stooks
in haystacks   dreaming the purified dreamer

who lured you   to a new man (back
to the fatal earth)   inventing (beyond
America) a new world   did you find

did you dream   the French priest who hauled you
out of your *fleurs du mal*[4]   and headlong
into a hundred drafts   real

or imagined   of the sought form
(there are no models)   and always
(there are only models)   alone

1 This poem is constructed around references to three of Grove's books, *Over Prairie Trails* (1922), *A Search for America* (1927), and *In Search of Myself* (1946). See pp. 252–72.

2 In *In Search of Myself,* Grove describes his father as a wealthy Swedish landowner. In *A Search for America,* he recounts twenty years of wandering across North America as a tramp and a hobo. Both books were long thought of as autobiographical accounts but later discovered to be highly dramatized fictions.

3 In Chapter Five of *In Search of Myself,* Grove says, 'I was hired as a teamster, and I owed the job to one single fact, namely, that of not being afraid of handling any kind of horse, not even the team I was offered which consisted of four aged stallions.'

4 According to Chapter Six of *In Search of Myself,* Grove was persuaded to begin his teaching career by a chance encounter with a French priest who saw him reading Baudelaire's *Fleurs du mal* in a North Dakota train station.

2

alone in the cutter   in the blizzard[5]
two horses   hauling you into the snow
that buries the road   burying the forest

the layered mind   exfoliating[6]
back to the barren sea   (Greek to us,
Grove)   back to the blank sun

and musing snow to yourself   new
to the old rite of burial   the snow
lifting the taught man   into the coyote self

the silence of sight   'as if I were not myself
who yet am I'   riding the drifted snow
to your own plummeting   alone and alone

the *wirklichkeit*[7]   of the word itself
the name under the name   the sought
and calamitous edge   of the white earth

the horses   pawing the empty fall
the hot breath on the zero day   the man
seeing the new man so vainly   alone

we say with your waiting wife   (but she
was the world   before you invented it
old liar)   'You had a hard trip?'

1975

5 From here to the conclusion, the poem is based on the sketch 'Snow' from *Over Prairie Trails* (reprinted on pp. 254–72), which describes a particularly harrowing winter journey.

6 Grove says that the snow drifts he was crossing 'showed that curious appearance that we also find in the glaciated surfaces of granite rock and which, in them, geologists call exfoliation' (p. 259). Later Grove writes that as he looked at 'the infertile waste' around him, 'Unaccountably two Greek words formed on my lips: Homer's Pontos atrygetos—the barren sea' (p. 263).

7 Reality; actual fact (German).

From *The Words of My Roaring*

I went over to watch the wild-steer riding. A lot of the local boys were taking part in that event, not just the professional riders, so the whole community wanted to observe. It was the big event of the day for a lot of people, and I mean to tell you, there was more to look at than high-heeled boots and forty-dollar saddles. You should have seen the faces pressed to the hogwire that surrounded that pole corral.

They were having trouble in Chute Number Three. The animal wouldn't hold still long enough so that a rider could get down off the fence and onto its back. You could see that much through the big heavy gate on the chute. But all of a sudden a cowboy yanked open the gate and took one jump for the fence.

A boy came out on a monstrous black bull. That was one of the things that really got the crowd, having someone ride a young bull. It was more dangerous. And this bull didn't like the prick of spurs.

The boy riding him looked to be about sixteen, wearing yellow boots and a new green silk shirt; but he was good. Maybe he wasn't good; maybe he just needed the prize money. Or maybe he was showing off; I never found out. He took off his hat with his right hand and started fanning it, he hung onto the bellyband with his left hand, and his spurs were raking the bull from the shoulders to the flanks. The boy was a great crowd-pleaser. You could actually see the blood he drew.

And then the cowbell rang and the crowd started really cheering. The time was up. The rider had stuck it out, making points all the way for style. The judges up in the judges' booth were all writing notes.

But the bull wasn't finished. He kept bucking and turning. and the boy who had been riding so grandly suddenly looked scared. His hat was too new, that was a bad sign. He had got onto something and he didn't know how to get off. He'd planned on being bucked off, I suppose, and here he was riding the worst animal of the lot, and he wasn't losing. That was his trouble.

Two pick-up riders started out to try and crowd in on the bull from both sides and pick the boy off. He was using both hands now, pulling leather, and his hat was somewhere on the ground getting its first stains. But before those cowboys got to him he just let go of the bellyband and fell. That's when the bull turned.

The clown was there in a flash. He caught the bull's attention. That was his job. Whenever someone got thrown, especially a local boy, the clown would run out in front of the bull or steer in his gaudy outfit while the rider scrambled out of the dust and manure and hightailed it for the fence. The clown had a barrel he'd jump into. He was good at it; he would run and jump and never miss. Sometimes a really ornery steer would take a run at the barrel with its horns and send the barrel spinning and rolling and everybody had a good laugh. Especially when the clown's head would pop out of the barrel with that black derby on. He'd look around, always in the wrong direction, and then just in time he'd glance and spot the steer bearing down and he'd duck again and we'd have another laugh. Or a lot of people would have a laugh.

This clown was very exceptional. You don't often see a big clown. Not really big. This one—well, I might as well be honest—he was crowding six-three or six-four. He almost didn't fit into his barrel, which I suppose was part of the joke. I enjoy a good laugh as well as anybody else; but this was very painful for me to watch. For one thing, he was the funniest clown I've ever witnessed. I've always been attracted to clowns.

He stepped in between the boy and the bull, as I say, and turned and stuck out his rump. The boy was slow at getting up. The bull saw the clown's red-and-yellow behind and snorted. The crowd roared. The clown started his quick sidestep.

But he was just a split second late. The bull must have tossed him thirty feet in the air.

The funny thing was, the crowd all thought it was part of the act. They roared and applauded. They thought the clown would jump up and run for his barrel. But he didn't. He tried to get up but wasn't moving quite fast enough, and the bull was on him again.

I guess I closed my eyes for the next few seconds. But I was seeing it just the same. The body mangled and ripped by those gouging horns, the innocent figure mutilated, rolled and trampled in the stinking dust. The spirit struck into frantic despair; I saw it all right. Without so much as peeking, I saw and I saw.

When I opened my eyes one of the pick-up riders was crowding his horse between the clown and the bull. But the clown didn't get up. He was lying twisted. Two men ran out and bent over him; one of them signalled toward the chutes.

Don't ask me why, I simply took that high fence in one leap off the hood of a parked car; I raced for the centre of that arena. Three or four cowboys tried to stop me, greenhorn that they took me for, but with no success. One of them was knocked flat.

And then I was bending over the clown. His bulbous nose had come off, showing a human nose that wasn't painted or anything, except that blood was coming from it. He was bleeding pretty freely somewhere beneath his torn clown's costume; the red was stained a cleaner red.

I guess those cowboys wondered what hit them in the next two minutes. For as soon as I made it, a couple of hundred people did the same thing, boys and men and even women got into the corral. And nothing could stop us. We were all crowded around that clown lying motionless, and someone in the middle of things was shouting, 'Get back, folks. Let him have some air. Give him air.'

Other people took up the request. A dozen people, maybe, were repeating, 'Let him have some air, folks.'

But it didn't do any good. I can't explain why. That clown had captured all of us. We wouldn't move. Now someone had gone for a stretcher and they were hollering to ask if there was a doctor in the crowd. It was plain the clown couldn't be moved until a doctor looked at him.

Another thing I noticed, the clown was very thin. His costume was baggy and had billowed when he ran, but he was skin and bones. The only thing that moved on him now was his eyelids; they kept opening and staring in a sleepy confused way, and all the make-up, the white paint and the black and yellow, was smudged with sweat and dust and the blood from his nose. Then he tried to say something. His mouth moved small inside the smile that was painted on his face. He kept trying to say something to me, a perfect stranger, but he couldn't make it. He tried to raise a hand and point but couldn't and I wanted to point for him but didn't know where.

'The kid is all right,' I said. I thought maybe that was it. 'You saved him,' I said. 'Just a sprained ankle.'

But that wasn't it, apparently; he kept trying to point, kept trying to tell us all something.

Anyhow, to make a long story short, young Lipinski, the newest doctor in Notikeewin, happened to be on the stampede grounds. In a few minutes he had the clown lifted onto a stretcher and four cowboys went running with it toward the gate. They're used to things like that, I suppose.

But the whole crowd of us—we didn't move. Four hundred people by now. Or at least—everybody saw I didn't move and nobody was big enough to move me, so they stayed too. I was a leader right there. And that's when I made my speech, my first major speech. I'm not bragging when I say it was a good one. It was a great one. All my pain came out of me right there, and I spoke to a lot of people.

For one thing, it was a real scorcher of a day. And there in the corral it was simply blazing hot. No wind, nothing; not a breeze. We were all thinking about that clown who had stood up to a wild bull.

I didn't so much speak as roar. I raised my left hand.

'And I beheld another beast coming up out of the earth; and he had two horns like a lamb, and he spake as a dragon.' That must be from the Bible.[1] As I say, I nearly wore out my eyes on small print, sometimes against my will. But it stuck. Those words just came to my mind and I boomed them out. I have a fairly powerful voice when I'm wound up.

The crowd fell silent. They're mostly a bunch of Bible-pounders themselves around here. They knew what I was saying. 'Yes sir,' I said. 'A beast came out of the earth and that clown stood up to him.'

'Amen,' somebody said.

'He stood right up to that beast. And the rest of us ought to be paying attention.'

They were listening now. I heard somebody say, 'That's Johnnie Backstrom.' That little remark gave me confidence.

'The lesson is an easy one,' I said. 'We've got to stand up. For six years now we've been down on our knees, flat on our bellies; we've been shoved and mauled by the high-muckie-mucks.'

'Amen to that,' somebody said.

'By the plutocrat millionaires from the East. For six long cowardly years, we've grovelled in the dung and the dirt, the dirt and the dung.'

'Yea, yea,' somebody shouted.

'We've been pushed and shoved—and I'll tell you why. Because we haven't got the guts to stand up for our own rights and principles.' I raised both fists and shook them. The sun was just hammering down from the sky. 'If you *enjoy* sucking the hind tit, you prairie chickens, then close your ears. Pretend you didn't see that beast. Run over and suck on a bottle of Big Orange. If you still have a nickel—after six years of being rolled in the dirt and dung by the plutocrat millionaires.' I paused and licked the sweat off my lips. 'But if you *don't* enjoy it—then crowd a little closer. And don't be afraid to push and shove a little yourself.'

That made them sit up and take notice. I could have reached out and touched twenty different people without taking a step. There must have been five hundred people jammed into that corral, and more coming.

'I myself don't like this business of sucking the hind tit. I don't like slaving from morning till night for the big-money interests. The beast is upon us. The beast is here

1 Revelation 13: 11.

and charging. We are being gored and gouged by the charging mad beast. The big-money boys, the grabbers from the East. The high-muckie-mucks that never worked a day in their lives. Those high-muckie-muck gougers from Ontario that wouldn't know grade-one hard northern wheat from a bowl of corn flakes.' I paused again. 'Yet they harvest your crop. They do the harvesting, not you, you stubble-jumpers. Oh sure, sure—you get to do all the work. Lucky for you. All they do is the banking.'

People were crawling up on the corral rails to hear me better. They were standing on car fenders and car roofs, just to get a better look. Johnnie Backstrom was wound up and going. Even the cowboys were listening. The very bucking horses and the wild steers were listening, by the lovely Jesus.

'The Fifty Big Shots who milk the country dry,' I said. 'The grabbers from Toronto who never worked a day in their lives. They'd throw us in the jug for stealing a dollar: so they steal a million right out of our pockets—and then they get credit for being fine people. The cream of the crop. The top dogs. They throw big booze parties and tell each other what a dandy crew they are. Yes sir, believe me, folks, I paid a short visit to the East, and I know how you get to be a high-muckie-muck. By stealing and robbing, that's how. To hell with other people's rights and principles. Steal and rob, steal and rob. And to go on being a top dog you have to go on stealing and robbing. From the poor. From innocent bystanders. From the farmers and the hicks out West.'

There was a real roar from the crowd on that one, a deep growling roar.

'Oh sure,' I said. 'They send us a few apples and some salted codfish. And some of the apples are rotten to the core; and worms have beat us to the codfish. But show your gratitude. All they want in return is our farms. Our land and our businesses and our flesh and our tears and our blood. That's all.' I gave a big grin to show I was being sarcastic. I have this magnificent set of teeth. Everybody laughed. 'We'll get along swell with the mortgage owners. Just don't move their hands out of your pockets. Just be willing and grateful to go on sucking the hind tit.'

People were getting riled up. I saw it was time to drive home a few points.

'And now, folks, just so you can show them how grateful you really are, I have a special request to make. Remember this. Old Doc Murdoch, MD, is a friend of mine. I know him better than most of you will ever know him. I happen to know he comes from the East himself.' I paused to let that sink in. There was quite a bit of hooting and hollering; and some of it, I must confess, was in favour of the old Doc. 'And of course Easterners,' I said, 'being the fine square shooters that they are, given any kind of chance, will look after nothing but our own best interests.' I had to break into a grin. 'So I have this special request, folks. I want you all to vote come the election. Please get out and cast your votes—for the doctor from Ontario, Murdoch, MD.'

Well sir, I guess they rolled in the aisles. Or they would have, if anybody could have found room to lie down in that huge corral. There was one hell of a mob of people present. They were still crowding in, pushing and using their elbows. They were in stitches. They split their sides laughing.

I was wound up. I mentioned that the one thing worse than a high-muckie-muck is a minion of same. I guess there were a lot of Murdoch supporters in that crowd when I started. I mentioned a few more things about fine old Doc Murdoch, like his big white freshly painted house and how to afford a swanky car. 'What are you driving?' I said. I pointed to this man and that man. 'What are you driving? What are you driving? Don't tell me a swanky big Chevrolet.'

I was wound up and going. Those things came from my heart; they really did. I was mad. I said something about old Doc bringing you into this hellhole mess, but what was he doing to get you out of it? I worked up a sweat.

It was while I was mopping the sweat off my bare forehead that more of the Bible came to my mind. Just like that. 'And the fourth angel poured out his vial upon the sun; and power was given unto him to scorch men with fire.'[2] I shook my fists at that blazing hammering sky. And then I dropped my voice. I let the hush fall. 'We are afflicted,' I said. 'Afflicted and plagued, my friends. But remember. Let me repeat: remember. If you feel—if you feel in your heart and bowels that the heat can no longer be endured. If you know that the burning must cease. If you agree that we must have back our self-respect, our sense of decency, our hope, our pride—maybe then you should vote, my dear friends—you should vote for the clown.'

I blinked against that roaring blaze of sun. I was bareheaded. Hundreds of people were waiting, all quiet, all listening. Farmers and merchants, elevator men and truckers and men with no jobs at all. Men wanting work in the harvest fields. I have this strong profile; craggy. I swung my head this way, that way; I paused as if to listen to myself. 'Yes, my good friends. I'm the first to admit it. Johnnie Backstrom is a clown all right. I'm the first to admit it. But at least I can add this. I'm a penniless clown. I haven't been sitting up there in Parliament for twenty years, making clowns of my neighbours and friends.' I shook my head. 'I've been trying *earn* a living, like the rest of you. And I haven't done any great shakes of a job. Just ask my wife.'

The chuckles were intimate and warm, like those of old companions forgiving a foible. They understood about wives and foibles. Maybe that's what worked on me—that touch of intimacy. That little touch of genuine mercy.

'So I'll add something else,' I said. 'And a penniless man hates to say this. You'd be bigger clowns yourselves for voting for me—unless it rains by election day.'

I choked up in my throat. I've never been quite sure I intended to say that. I got carried away. Everybody kind of choked up. I guess they'd heard about me, word gets around. They'd all had a few laughs at my expense; and they could have another good laugh, if they wanted to, out there in that dusty hot corral where a clown had just been injured, gored by a mad bull.

Not a one of them could laugh, however. I let the silence hang for nearly a full minute. I was glad my wife wasn't present; she would have had to speak up. Then I said, 'My dear, dear friends, if I might call you that, I want you all to have a great time today. Because inside of one week from this moment you'll all have your noses to the grindstone, getting ready to harvest one Jesusly bumper of a crop.'

2 Revelation 16: 8. Backstrom's prophecies echo those he's heard just a few pages earlier in the novel while listening to the radio broadcasts of the leader of his party, John Applecart (a lightly fictionalized version of the politician William 'Bible Bill' Aberhart). Applecart preaches from St John of Patmos's Book of Revelation as a way of rallying his followers, emphasizing those portions of the Bible's closing book that prophesy a fiery end to the world and of inviting his listeners to make connections with the harsh climatic conditions they are experiencing.

That place just went wild. I'm a big man, standing nearly six-four in my stocking feet, but that crowd picked me up as if I was a bag of feathers. They carried me around inside the corral, shouting and whooping and throwing their hats or whatever came loose, and they busted through the corral gate and carried me out to where all the good food was piled up and the booths were set in rows. They threw me in the air and damned near broke every bone in my body when they couldn't hold me coming down; but they set me up on my feet and somebody whipped a micky out of the rags he called his trousers and said have some pain killer, and, may all teetotalers roast in hell, I had it. I was dying of thirst after all that talking. I was half-embarrassed to return the remains.

But I almost got knocked over again by people pushing more bottles at me.

'That hind-tit speech of yours', a fellow said, 'was the best speech I ever heard in my life.'

'Amen,' somebody said.

That's what they called it, my hind-tit speech. They all agreed it was a ripper.

Then the cowboys let a dozen wild cows into the corral and the milking contest was on, one man trying to hold a wild cow's head while another tried to get a little milk into a pail. Everything was getting into pails but the milk. There were some people caught in the corral along with the cows, and their big job was to get out alive. You might say all hell and damnation just busted loose.

'Follow me,' I shouted as loud as I could. Just those two words. That whisky was delicious. I was dying of thirst. I was standing there in the middle of a crowd that was so packed I couldn't budge an inch. 'Follow me,' I shouted.

'We're following,' somebody shouted back.

For some reason, people started handing me free food. I have no idea who got stuck for the bill. I was given a whole graham-wafer flapper pie, not a slice missing, which I lit into right on the spot. It was a tribute to me, a sign of affection. I couldn't resist. After that talk, I was starving. The whisky and the pie and the cobs of corn all went down together. I consumed. Yes sir, I consumed—pineapple squares and strawberry shortcake, Dutch apple pie and hot dogs with raw onions and whisky and ice cream and sour-cream raisin pie and affection and love and saskatoon pie and generosity and deference and admiration and adulation. I consumed and I consumed. I have a huge capacity, there was no filling me up; I was starving and I ate. I was bottomless. I devoured.

And let me tell you the saddest part—in the end it was the same old story once again.

1966

Adele Wiseman

1928–1992

Adele Wiseman was born in Winnipeg, Man., to Russian-Jewish parents who had emigrated from Ukraine in the 1920s. She began to write seriously while studying at the University of Manitoba, and, after receiving a BA in English and psychology, supported her early writing career by working such jobs as executive secretary (to the Royal Winnipeg Ballet), social worker (in England), and teacher (in Italy). Throughout most of the sixties Wiseman lived in Montreal, where she was married and had her daughter. In 1969 she and her family moved to Toronto. During the 1970s and 1980s Wiseman was writer-in-residence at several universities: University of Toronto, Trent, Western Ontario, Concordia, Prince Edward Island, and Windsor. From 1987 to 1991 she was head of the writing program at the Banff Centre until failing health forced her retirement. She died in 1992 of brain cancer.

Wiseman's writing focuses on her eastern European Jewish heritage, her upbringing in Winnipeg, and the experiences of twentieth-century Jewry. Her two novels, *The Sacrifice* (1956), which won the Governor General's Award, and *Crackpot* (1974), are mirror images of one other. One written in the tragic mode and one in the comic, each is a study of the experiences of Jewish immigrants in their new country, especially of the tension between old customs and new ways, and of the distance that develops between parents and their children as the first generation remains rooted in its Old World past while the next becomes part of the Canadian present. The familiar archetypical story of Abraham and Isaac is blended in *The Sacrifice* with other Biblical and mythical patterns, but the novel is also a firmly realistic narrative about immigrants who flee the pogroms of Europe to discover themselves in a new world that still requires sacrifice. Although Wiseman's Abraham tries to find his place in the Jewish community of an unnamed city that closely resembles Winnipeg, his story has the qualities of a Greek tragedy as well as of the pattern of testing and redemption of its Biblical counterpart. In the novel, Isaac is sacrificed not because God requires it of Abraham, a man who unthinkingly views his family as an extension of himself, but because he is pulled between a young man's need to gain autonomy and a good son's longing for paternal respect. On facing the truth of his own culpability in his son's fate, Abraham, driven mad, commits a murder (he delusionally sees it as an act of purification) and ends up in a mental hospital.

Set in a Jewish ghetto in what appears to be the north end of Winnipeg during the Depression, *Crackpot* is a comedy in form, structure, and tone, though it has its very dark tones as well. It is the story of Hoda, the ingenuous daughter of Russian Jewish immigrants, who turns to prostitution to support herself and her father after the death of her mother. Hoda's life is a series of tumultuous and absurd scenarios, reaching a climax when she must decide whether or not to commit incest in order to help her illegitimate son, whom she has not seen since birth, attain manhood. While the overtly mythic structure of *The Sacrifice* is not present in *Crackpot*, the two novels are in many ways parallel—except that events that bring tragic consequences in Wiseman's first novel have comic outcomes in the later book, as the tragic vision, with its emphasis on retributive justice and the timelessness of human trials and difficulties, is replaced by one that sees contemporary experience growing out of fragmentation and reconstruction into new patterns. Wiseman later remarked:

I wanted to create something . . . mixing Winnipeg and its 'muddy waters' with Hoda to see what would come out. 'Muddy waters' is the Indian name for Winnipeg but 'muddy waters' is that whole strange cultural mixture that we have in Canada, particularly in Winnipeg, where there are over thirty-one nationalities. Hoda should be the head of a new tribe which includes all the former ones. (*We Who Can Fly: Poems, Essays and Memories in Honour of Adele Wiseman*, 1997)

In addition to the novels that made her reputation, Wiseman published a collection of witty and sometimes biting personal essays: *Memoirs of a Book Molesting Childhood and Other Essays* (1987). It contains accounts of her reading habits, her family and friends, her trip to China, and her ongoing battle against bureaucracy. Her reminiscences of the Winnipeg Farmers Market accompany Joe Rosenthal's drawings in *Old Markets, New Worlds* (1964). She wrote several plays that were not produced: *Lovebound* (1960) and *Testimonial Dinner* (1978) were printed privately. She also wrote two children's books: *Kenji and the Cricket* (1988) and *Puccini and the Prowlers* (1992).

Wiseman's other full-length work, *Old Woman at Play* (1978), defies generic classification. A visual book filled with photographs, it is a chronicle of her mother's art, which took the form of elaborate folk dolls (and other creations based on the materials out of which garments are made). Into this she interweaves her parents' family stories, a record of her mother and her father speaking, her story as their child, and her own theory of art that governed her hard-won comic vision. Life-writing and life-viewing, it is a book of joy and sadness that draws aside a curtain to show a family talking. (The excerpt below begins with Wiseman talking about her trip to visit the Russian family that her parents left behind when they immigrated and with her parents' memories of family and home.)

In this work Wiseman uses the figure of her mother, the dollmaker, to show how the artist should value the past, even what seems its detritus. Just as her mother constructs new things of value from 'odds and ends of every kind of discard imaginable', so artists, in Wiseman's view, can use the shards of their culture, creating new order out of the scraps of the old.

From *Old Woman at Play*

That Russian visit remains an unforgettable kaleidoscope: of seven adults and two-year-old Tamara stuffing themselves into an eleven-person hotel elevator, and hoping the door will manage to close; of banqueting unbelievingly on cream puffs and Georgian champagne, courtesy of the Russian aunts and uncles; of my large, quiet uncle Josef getting up to make a toast, recalling that my mother had been the one who had matched him up with Rose, for whom she'd fancied him at first sight, and breaking down, finally, in the middle of expressions of affection and gratitude. 'What?' cries tartar Rose, 'you're crying? I've never seen him cry before!' And sitting quietly on the benches of a shaded boulevard in the afternoon, we talked, exchanging lives, and gazed at each other and briefly, unforgettably, permanently interlocked worlds, while wiry, lively uncle Shura, Polya's husband, played with the child, and I marvelled at the deep resemblance in the bone between my mother and Rose and between Polya and my Winnipeg aunt Sonia and between myself and them all.

You really saw my little sisters.

➢ *Yes mama. Look at the pictures.*

➢ *But Rose was a beauty. How could I ever come near her? When did she look so much like me? And Auntie Sonia and Polya. How do they come to look so alike? Little Shura. They were our neighbours on the same big yard. I remember only a dark, handsome little boy with big eyes and always a snot like a yoyo. Josef, the minute I saw him, I knew he was for Rose.*

➢ *Polya doesn't remember she didn't want Rose to be courted by Josef. When I reminded her of what you said about how she climbed up on the bake oven when he came the first time, and wouldn't come down to be introduced, she said she didn't remember any of it.*

➢ *And I remember to this day. She was just a youngster, but so proud, so haughty.*

➢ *She's not haughty any more, mama.*

My mother's face flushes. Her eyes seem to disappear. She weeps. *The years make fools of us all.*

Presently she asks, *And they told you what happened to our parents, to Chanaleh's husband, to my brother Sander?*

➢ *Yes.*

She weeps again. I wait for her to ask for details, knowing I will tell her, but hoping not to have to just yet. I won't refuse to share with my parents the truths, however painful, which they have always respected me enough to share with me. When they dedicated their years to earning, for their children, a choice of futures, we accepted it as our due and our destiny that we were to study and learn and become, and were convinced that not only our own lives, but life itself would be enhanced thereby. Our faith was the more acute for our awareness of the alternate, simultaneous fate of our helpless counterparts, the Jews of Europe. The gift of choice, under these circumstances, takes on an almost religious significance. I took my own destiny seriously, an attitude which retrospect always discovers to be more than slightly comic. Equally serious about the fate of our six million, I have found that time has left no leavener here. I know that I must pass on, eventually, both to parents and child, my few garnered details of the deaths of my grandparents, or deny the reality, the shape, the dignity, the great mystery of their so savagely truncated existence. But some endings are hard to lay on those you love.

Not that my parents are strangers to violence. What could I tell my mother that she has not already known in one form or another? Even her nostalgia sits childlike amid the rubble of human stupidity and destructiveness.

> *On the first day of the pogrom they razed a neighbour's shop. The next morning my friends and I slipped out of our family hiding places and got together to explore the ruins. There was only a deep pit left. But such treasures in that pit! Buttons and bits of glass and scraps of this and that. What more do little children need? Our parents finally found us down there hours later. By this time they were frantic. The pogrom was not yet over. At any moment the hooligans would be back.* Mama smiles reminiscently. *Such pretty bits of coloured glass.*

We are walking along the street. My arm hovers solicitously, in case she should need help, or want to lean, as an old woman may. Suddenly, she darts forward, stoops swiftly, straightens, holding a partly squashed tin button. 'I could use this somewhere,' she murmurs, tucking it away.

~

Since their children have grown up and have gone their various ways, my parents have been on a many years' routine of visits, often in response to emergency calls for help, from all around the continent. They have become quite sophisticated about railway stations and planes and airport limousines. In their absence, the little house on Burrows Ave. has been burglarized four times. Oh to have been a fly on the wall to watch even one of those felons, eager for the illicit profit of his form of free enterprise, as he rushed from room to room, wrenching open drawer after drawer, and turning out the zipper heads, the spools, the bottle tops, the springs, the plastic lemons and limes, the thousands of bits of gaily coloured cloth, of fur and leather, the buttons and sequins and ribbons and leather, the foam rubber, the shells and coral and stones and expended flash bulbs and thread and wool and junk jewellery and broken trinkets. I did, as it happened, arrive on one such occasion, on time to see her treasures littered about the house. What could that burglar's reaction have been to the carefully scrubbed and dried soup bones and fish spines and curiously shaped wood and dried leaves and odds and ends of every kind of discard imaginable? My mother's collection of treasure is enough to challenge a whole system of values at a far profounder level than any mere burglar can manage.

Nothing is wasted, nothing is cast aside to lead a used-up, fragmented, uncreated existence. Everything is suggestive; everything is potentially a part of something else.

> *Pieces of material when they lay around they bother me, because I want them to look like something.*

* * *

Redeemer of waste, champion of leftovers, saviour of non-biodegradables, apostle of continuous creation, she has this hunger to find and establish new relations between things, and so create new things. She knows that they too will disappear or be destroyed, but that is not her concern. She knows that somewhere there will still exist this hunger she shares, to make something else again.

> *The people should feel that even the doll is happy to be created, like I feel.*

Her values are impeccable if unorthodox. One of the first junk jewellery pictures she ever made consisted of figures made of sequins and buttons and jet and glass beads and other odds and ends, glistening on black velvet she'd sewn onto a piece of cardboard. The figures seem to come dancing out of the stars.

> *Mama,* I remarked, staring at the silver face of one of them. *Isn't that my Governor General's Medal?*
> *Yes,* she replied cheerfully. *Why should it just lie around the house?*

Even Emily Carr didn't do better when she got her friend to chuck her newly received medal at a dead bird she wanted to shift from the eaves facing the window she had to stare out of during the last few weeks of her life. That medal now makes sense.

More recently, when she heard that a cash prize goes with the medal now, she remarked, *What, they give you more than a button nowadays?*

* * *

My father was brought to meet his bride-to-be when she was twenty-three. People told him, 'Woo her? That one's a spark for the bellows!' He wooed her anyway, and won her with stories, romances from the vast, eclectic reading of a toil-enforced boyhood, the same stories, I imagine, which we kids used to wait so ardently in the hope he might be home on time to tell us at bedtime when we were little. From Jules Verne to *A Thousand and One Nights*, my father's repertoire was rich. 'I thought he made them all up himself,' my mother told me somewhat wryly, not long ago.

Some fifty-seven years later, he still looks at his prize askance at times. Occasionally, there is a confrontation of their private, unmatching realities which is baffling to them both, like trying to make one giant jigsaw puzzle out of two complex ones that are similar in shape and colour and have become hopelessly mixed together. The pieces seem to belong and yet they'll never quite make one coherent whole. But it would take another lifetime to sort and separate them, or perhaps another dimension to reveal their inherent unity. And so they remain, a puzzled but indissolubly married pair. From their occasional tensions of orbit they both retreat to habitual positions of tolerance, my mother murmuring the ancient irony of the dispersion, 'Well, it's lasted so long, let the diaspora continue,' and my father musing over the paradoxes of victory. Even their arguments confirm to him the wisdom of his choice of wife. For my father considers he did well in his marriage not only because she was the daughter of the relatively well-to-do wheel- and wagonwright of the sophisticated town and he the impecunious lad from the backward hamlet. Father's concept of upward mobility is rooted in a more ancient social structure. In the temple hierarchy my father is a mere Israeli, while my mother is the daughter of a Cohan, descendant of the priestly sons of Aaron.[1] Her volatile temperament is a matter of some pride. What could be more positive proof that she is a direct descendant of Moses, bringer and smasher and bringer again of the Holy Tablets? And who could be more suitable for a man whose given name, in Hebrew, is Pesach, Passover?

> *After we'd become engaged I walked over, one day, from my village, Oleskov, to see your mother. It was during revolutionary times, and I tramped across the fields to avoid the roaming bands.*
>
> *It was thirty-seven verst (thirty-odd miles), so naturally I was hot and thirsty by the time I reached the outskirts of Golta. There was a little shop there, where they sold*

1 The name 'Cohan' or 'Cohen' means 'priest' in Hebrew. In Jewish tradition, Aaron, Moses' brother, is identified as Israel's first high priest. The priesthood was hereditary, and in Leviticus 'the sons of Aaron' are shown as having authority over religious ceremonies.

drinks. I stopped and bought a glass of soda water. I was just raising it to my lips when SLAP! The glass was dashed from my hands, I didn't even get a taste. And she's standing there with her eyes flashing, 'Don't you dare drink!'

Daddy shakes his head, chuckling, and rocks to and from on his heels.

I was waiting for him. He was all sweated up. What was I supposed to do, let him get pneumonia and die on me, and disappoint my family?[2] *Do you know how many matches I'd laughed away before him? The eldest, and twenty-three already, and finicky yet.*

My grandmother was married by the time she was eleven. One day, when she was eight years old, just before Passover, she was down by the river with her little friends. Her father had a mill in a town called Piaterota, that means where the fifth regiment was stationed. The children were washing up the everyday dishes, to be packed away for the High Holidays.[3] *Her mother, my great-grandmother-to-be, came down the hill calling to her, 'Marjm Hannah, come home, you're a bride!' She started to cry. She didn't want to go. She wanted to stay and do her work and play with her friends. So her mother took her by the hand and brought her to meet her future father-in-law, who was a business acquaintance of her father's.*

As soon as my grandfather Sander reached adulthood, right after his Bar Mitzvah, they were married. He saw her for the first time when he raised her veil under the canopy.

Luckily, she was a pretty little thing, even as an old lady. They had eight children. My father was her youngest. But my zeida[4] *Sander died young. That's why my father had to learn a trade, which was a great blow to the family dignity. My grandmother lived with us for the last thirteen years of her life. She was such a delicate little creature, with her hair drawn up in a tiny little knot. When she arrived at our place, before I was born, she announced that she was eighty-seven years old. After that, no matter when you asked her, till the day she died, she remained eighty-seven years old. I don't know how long she'd been eighty-seven before she came. She must have been well over a hundred when she died. But she died so quietly. One day she was sitting and resting outdoors, and she called me to her and asked me to bring her a glass of varenieh, jam syrup. When we found her dead she was still sitting, leaning with the glass of varenieh in her open palm.*

When we returned from the holy field where they buried her, my father went to the rack where her clothes were hung, and he went down on his knees by her clothing and wept, 'I've lost my mother.'

Not that she had made life easy for my own mother. She was difficult, but my father honoured her, and my poor mother knew how to keep her own lips pressed together.

2 This folk belief—that drinking a cold beverage too soon after exercise can cause a potentially fatal illness—may be based on an analogy to the way horses, if run hard and allowed to drink water before being rested, can contract a fatal colic.

3 That is, the ten-day period beginning with Rosh Hashanah and ending with Yom Kippur.

4 Grandfather (Yiddish).

My dad has moved off. At the mention of death he moves out of range. It is a troubled topic between them. The great tug-of-war over my mother's dead body has been going on for years. Long ago, she began to warn us that she would not be with us in the flesh forever. I suppose she knew this was a necessary part of our education in reality. We responded by teasing her. Who wants to think of those things? 'Kicking the bucket again, are you?' was gradually abbreviated to 'kicking already?' or whatever variations sprang to mind to deflect a mood which I, for one, was not willing to entertain. But mama made plans. She did not intend to remain idly passive in the matter of the disposition of her remains. Young girls dream romantic dreams of handsome lovers, and mama's romantic dream simply evolved and changed according to her unerring intuition of seemliness. She wanted to continue to serve, she wanted to be needed, she wanted to be useful down to the last cell and corpuscle. Somewhere there must be a young medical student, poor but ardent to be of service to mankind. And what if he were too poor (she knew all about poverty) to be able to afford a cadaver of his own to dissect? How would he learn? How would he make his discoveries? What a team they would make!

When I die I want to donate my body to medical research.

➢ *Okay, mama.*

➢ *What's the use of lying around under a stone? You hear me, Peisy?* She raises her voice to catch my father, who paces the house, easing his troubled legs. *Peisy!* Her voice penetrates his deafness and he pauses enquiringly. She repeats her decision, explaining till his large dark eyes grow round and troubled. He shrugs his shoulders, and throwing her an astounded glance, resumes his pacing. *He doesn't like to hear about death,* she says. *Why?*

My father has returned and stands before me, a slight smile on his face.

➢ *When they first brought me to see her they warned me, 'Why, you won't even know how to carry her parasol to suit her.'* Chuckling, he wanders off again through the house. Soon he is warbling away, creakily, one of the favourite songs of his youth.

➢ *And afterwards I want to be cremated!* she calls after him. *He's afraid. What's he afraid of?* She tosses her head. *There's no forever.*

* * *

Never fear, she confides, he'll sign. He's afraid. On my deathbed I'll threaten to take him with me. He'll be terrified. He'll sign then. And if that's not enough I'll threaten to come back and haunt him. She glowers as daddy saunters by. *Afraid to endanger his precious little fur,* she growls. *Superstitious. He'll sign.*

I can tell that daddy knows that she is talking about him, and that she is not paying him compliments. But he's not sure of what she's saying, because at times like this he keeps on the move. Nevertheless he maintains a corner-of-the-eye awareness. His deafness has long since blunted his ability to slide accurately into a conversational topic already established. It has become his habit instead to launch himself on a stray word or phrase, heard or imagined, and swoop at an unexpected tangent into the conversation, where he will have his say on whatever biographically related topic is currently exercising him, though it may have taken place fifty or even five thousand years ago, for as long as he can manage to hold the floor. Disconcerting though this can sometimes be to the unwary, it is not really an unfair tactic, when you consider that he sometimes waits days in utter silence for the opportunity. He has materialized, now, during a momentary pause, and launches into a defensive reminiscence in his own tumbled English.

> *This man come to me, it's how you call depression times, I got laid off from my good job, I got no work. He say to me, 'Vizeman, come work for me, lotsa work in my shop, I'm very busy, you get plenty overtime.'*
>
> Mama mutters counterpoint, *Oi, he's here already with the overtime.*
>
> ➢ *So I say, 'I want a paper, what you call it an agreement, it should be written down.' So he say 'What for you need it an agreement? I need you more than you need me.'*
>
> ➢ *Here comes the bad wife,* mutters mama.
>
> ➢ *And the woman,* daddy inclines his head slightly motherward, *she say to me, 'What you want? You got it to trust the man, Peisy!'*
>
> ➢ *You'll hear how I spoiled for him the business,* murmurs mama.
>
> ➢ *So I go work for him. I try. I'm a good worker, forst class tailor-forrier, no what you call it by me fonny business. Face in the needle. Forst week come for my pay I see what, no overtime? He say 'Overtime we pay it altogedder later.' All right, he say so, the woman say trust, okay.'*
>
> ➢ *Again the woman. What would he do without the woman? Without the woman he wouldn't even know how to make a fool of himself.*
>
> ➢ *Come eleven months, I been work hard, lots overtime. I not see my wife, my famly; leave house it's dark, come home kids asleep. I never knew my kids they grow up.* Daddy pauses a little wistfully, eyeing me.
>
> ➢ *True,* mama nods. *Emes, can't take away the truth.*
>
> ➢ *All of a sudden, how you say? The business is down. 'There's no work,' he tell me, 'I have to let you go.' All right, no work, what can I do? 'But where's my overtime?' He say, 'What overtime? Who say I owe you overtime? You got it proof I owe you overtime? Go sue me.' That he say, 'You got it proof I owe you overtime go sue me with lawyers.'* My dad stamps his foot, rocks to and fro and laughs ruefully.
>
> *'You got to trust, Peisy.'* He throws my mother a glance and moves off, hands in pockets, secure that he has unassailably countered whatever accusations she might possibly have made against him.
>
> ➢ *So I trusted,* says mama. *My fault I trusted. He'll never forgive me I trusted. Who wants to live your whole life like you're surrounded by wild animals? Maybe we should have.*
>
> My father has returned.
>
> ➢ *I try with the lawyers, but they're all how you say it, bought and sold. They take my few dollars on this side, he stuffs them in the pockets from behind, and they*

say, 'Vizeman, it's notting to do. Again he throws a glance, not unmixed with despair, and moves off.

➢ *That's what it's been like, my whole life he throws up to me,* says mama. *'You're so lucky!' people tell me. 'You live together like two little turtle doves.' Just because we don't fight in the streets; nobody has to know what goes on in the bedroom behind closed doors. That's one thing we agreed on from the start. If it so happened we disagreed, the children didn't have to suffer from it, their eyes should grow big over us, and we shouldn't become a freeshow for the neighbours, either. Nobody,* adds mama impressively, *has to know what I suffered behind that closed door.*

It is true that I was nearly twenty before I witnessed, for the first time, an open quarrel between my parents. And I was shocked, my eyes no doubt as large and darkly stunned as I remember my kid brother's were as we stood helpless witness, neophytes to the darker side of familiar things. Probably, it was so shattering an experience because we saw our parents for the first time as separate people, separate from us and from each other, with their own private grievances against each other, and were forced to comprehend that there were whole areas of their lives from which we had been excluded or spared. It was a wrench to learn how little I knew about what I thought I knew, a salutary wrench in the long run, to learn not to presume on the familiar, where sometimes the greatest mysteries reside.

I have often thought, since then, at what cost my parents tried to make of themselves a compensatory garden of possibility for us, in a world of disappointment and threat. What enormous efforts of understanding and control and tolerance they had to call up, to overcome incompatibilities and resentments, and to show us only respect and affection and loyalty. In later years they might sometimes mutter at each other, or flare up, each in his or her own highly sensitized cell of self. But how grateful I am now both that they spared us our childhood, and that they did finally, though not deliberately, quarrel furiously before us. It was a coming of age.

Of course I had always known that there were facts of life still missing. There was a part of me that said even then, during the great parental quarrel, 'Ah, so that's it! How interesting! I wonder what else?' precisely as it had reacted to those other 'facts of life' for which I had so patiently and so trustingly waited so long. For distressed though I may be, I must admit to an objective interest in the phenomena of life which usually acts as a safety valve in times of stress. Under emotional pressure, it provides a kind of layer in my internal atmosphere, which filters the intense rays of feeling at a certain angle, deflecting the heat of events, somewhat, and analyzing their light. Artists, writers in particular, are sometimes accused of a lack of appropriate feeling when they respond in this way to significant events in their own lives. But surely a response which enables the making of public rainbows is a valid way of transforming the stuff of private scars.

So there was more than sex and the minty smell of oil-of-wintergreen from daddy's nightly body rub behind that closed bedroom door! Of course. There are mysteries behind closed doors, and closed doors behind mysteries, behind which more mysteries lurk in prelude to more closed doors and further revelations. This I had discovered in my own nature though I had not been able to ascertain whether the closed door led to the mystery or the mystery led to the closed door, for sometimes, as scientific thinkers have pointed out, the answer presents itself readily; the problem is to find the question which makes sense of the answer. I usually know what is going to happen at the end of a story I write. The revelation, or series of revelations, for me, is in the hows and whys, which give the whole the relevance it has hopefully achieved by the time one has reached the 'end'. The name we give to the created thing, the 'work', means not only that it is the result of someone's labour, but that it itself 'works'. It is, in a very important sense, alive. If you engage with it, it will work in you. The revelations of art are an attempt to capture the inner sense in the allusive suggestiveness of life, to penetrate its masks. We wrestle fragments of sensible form from flux, instants of inner sense from event, and if we're lucky, hallelujah, we've captured what? Little enough, it might seem, at most an instant in a fragment, but ALIVE, with its own separate, coherent vitality, its own resonance. And how it expands our own lives, if we allow it, our own consciousness of the possibilities of life! Creativity is an expression of vitality which strives for the enhancement of vitality.

My mother, when she begins to work, is often vague about what she is about to produce, and greets the creations of her own hands with exclamations of surprise. Nor is she rigid in defining her products.

Here's a little cat for you.
➢ *Mama, does that look like a little cat to you?*
➢ *All right, so it's a little pig.*

When I sit down, with that familiar excitement, compounded of what? expectation? yes, and fear, to the typewriter, and my head is utterly blank though I've been preoccupied, obsessed with certain themes and events which can not occur until they make the right kind of emotional sense. I know it is revelations I'm waiting for, revelations which will arise from that mulch of confused fragments, those other hints and revelations, welcome and otherwise, with which my life has already presented me. Most of us spend our lives tidying up unwanted feelings and contradictions and insights in the pursuit of the false ideal of antiseptic headspace. The artist, perhaps because of the intensity with which he has experienced them, knows that they contain vital energies to be harnessed, potent magic for the creation of worlds.

1978

Timothy Findley

1930–2002

Toronto-born Timothy Irving Frederick (Tiff) Findley grew up in and out of the city's wealthy community of Rosedale as his family's fortune ebbed and waned. When, at seventeen, he wanted to take ballet lessons, Findley had to leave high school and work in the foundry at the Massey-Harris factory in order to pay for them. After a back injury ended his dreams of being a dancer, he pursued a career in acting. He worked on stage and television—including a small role in a TV production of Leacock's *Sunshine Sketches of a Little Town*—and got his first real break while playing small parts in the Stratford Shakespeare Festival's first season. There Alec Guinness was so impressed with Findley that he sponsored him for further drama education in London, England. This training led to a small role in Thornton Wilder's *The Matchmaker*, which starred Ruth Gordon.

Gordon and Wilder both encouraged Findley to take seriously a long-held interest in writing. His debut as a writer came in 1956 with the story 'About Effie', published in the first issue of the Canadian literary magazine, *Tamarack Review*. When the Wilder play ended its tour in California, Findley remained in Hollywood in the hopes of a film-acting career and to try to develop a television play from one of his short stories. Unsuccessful at either, he returned to Toronto in 1958. Although he found work as a stage and television actor, he grew depressed about his lack of progress. After a brief marriage to actress Janet Reid, he met his life partner William Whitehead, a producer, actor, and writer. Together the two men retired from acting to focus on writing. In 1964 they purchased a farm near Cannington, Ontario, which they named Stone Orchard in homage to Chekhov's play, *The Cherry Orchard*, and from which they worked and lived until the late 1990s. Thereafter they lived in France and in Stratford, Ontario.

Though his first two novels, *The Last of the Crazy People* (1967) and *The Butterfly Plague* (1969), were rejected by Canadian publishers and published only in the US, the 1970s brought Findley recognition and success. He served as chief writer for *The Whiteoaks of Jalna* TV series (1971–4) and, with Whitehead, wrote the award-winning TV script about the building of the Canadian Pacific Railway, *The National Dream* (1974). Findley then became playwright-in-residence at the National Arts Centre in Ottawa (1974–5) and in 1977–8 the chairman of the Writers' Union of Canada, an organization of which he was also a co-founder. (He later served as president of the Canadian branch of PEN International.) Most importantly, recognition came to Findley around this time in the form of acclaim for his third novel, *The Wars* (1977), for which he received a Governor General's Award. (He wrote the script for the 1983 National Film Board adaptation).

The Wars began an extended period of creativity that included the novels *Famous Last Words* (1981), *Not Wanted on the Voyage* (1984), *The Telling of Lies* (1986), *Headhunter* (1993), *The Piano Man's Daughter* (1995), *Pilgrim* (1999), and *Spadework* (2001); the novella, *You Went Away* (1996); three short story collections, *Dinner Along the Amazon* (1984), *Stones* (1988), and *Dust to Dust* (1997); non-fiction, *Inside Memory: Pages from a Writer's Workbook* (1990) and *From Stone Orchard: A Collection of Memories* (1998); and five plays—including *The Stillborn Lover* (1993) and *Elizabeth Rex* (2000), which won a Governor General's Award. In recognition of his achievements Findley was made an Officer of the Order of Canada (1986), and was given the Trillium Award (for *Stones*) and the Chalmers Award (for *The Stillborn Lover*).

Although Findley's novels are marked by appalling acts of violence—fires, killings, wars—he was known as an individual deeply affected by the horrors of the contemporary world and was famous for his humanitarian causes and his love of animals. It was perhaps a reflection of his sensitivity that the fiercest struggles in his fiction and drama are waged internally by decent but isolated characters such as Everett Menlo in the story 'Dreams'—individuals who find it difficult to retain their grip on reality in an era that seems filled with pain.

Findley's narratives frequently suggest that the source of both individual and social breakdowns is mistaken idealism—whether it manifests itself at the personal level as the drive for individual perfection or at the social level in the longing for a completely regulated state. He challenges the notion of the perfect family in *The Last of the Crazy People* and of a perfect America in *The Butterfly Plague*; he suggests, in *The Wars*, that misplaced ideals of individual honour have produced global conflict, while in *Famous Last Words* he shows readers what happened when 'a shared ideal became a single man'.

Although war was a topic that often claimed Findley's attention, the elaborate narrative frames of works like *The Wars* and *Famous Last Words* (which treat the First and Second World Wars) provide a postmodern self-reflexivity that break his fiction out of the tradition of simple mimetic realism by calling attention to their existence as fictions while also demanding that the reader recognize their factual or historical nature. *Not Wanted on the Voyage* goes further in departing from realism by retelling the story of Noah's flood with a diverse cast of characters that includes the fallen Lucifer: in his rewriting of the original, it became Findley's protest against a God who would destroy his own creation (an anti-apocalyptic theme that appears in other of Findley's works). *Headhunter* similarly uses an earlier narrative, Conrad's *Heart of Darkness*, in a dark tale in which—as in *Famous Last Words*, told by Hugh Selwyn Mauberley, the eponymous hero of Ezra Pound's 1920 poem—the borderlines between art and life seem unexpectedly porous. In it Kurtz, Conrad's source of evil and imperialism, escapes the pages of his book to inhabit downtown Toronto. In works such as these, as in 'Dreams' where dreamlife and reality are inextricably mixed, a willingness to depart from conventions of realism was important to Findley's investigation of the contemporary era.

Dreams

Doctor Menlo was having a problem: he could not sleep and his wife—the other Doctor Menlo—was secretly staying awake in order to keep an eye on him. The trouble was that, in spite of her concern and in spite of all her efforts, Doctor Menlo—whose name was Mimi—was always nodding off because of her exhaustion.

She had tried drinking coffee, but this had no effect. She detested coffee and her system had a built-in rejection mechanism. She also prescribed herself a week's worth of Dexedrine to see if that would do the trick. *Five mg at bedtime*—all to no avail. And even though she put the plastic bottle of small orange hearts beneath her pillow and kept augmenting her intake, she would wake half an hour later with a dreadful start to discover the night was moving on to morning.

Everett Menlo had not yet declared the source of his problem. His restless condition had begun about ten days ago and had barely raised his interest. Soon, however, the time spent lying awake had increased from one to several hours and then, on Monday last, to all-night sessions. Now he lay in a state of rigid apprehension—his eyes wide open, arms above his head, his hands in fists—like a man in pain unable to shut it out. His neck, his back and his shoulders constantly harried him with cramps and spasms. Everett Menlo had become a full-blown insomniac.

Clearly, Mimi Menlo concluded, her husband was refusing to sleep because he believed something dreadful was going to happen the moment he closed his eyes. She had encountered this sort of fear in one or two of her patients. Everett, on the other hand, would not discuss the subject. If the problem had been hers, he would have said *such things cannot occur if you have gained control of yourself.*

Mimi began to watch for the dawn. She would calculate its approach by listening for the increase of traffic down below the bedroom window. The Menlos' home was across the road from The Manulife Centre—corner of Bloor and Bay streets. Mimi's first sight of daylight always revealed the high white shape of its terraced storeys. Their own apartment building was of a modest height and colour—twenty floors of smoky glass and polished brick. The shadow of the Manulife would crawl across the bedroom floor and climb the wall behind her, grey with fatigue and cold.

The Menlo beds were an arm's length apart, and lying like a rug between them was the shape of a large, black dog of unknown breed. All night long, in the dark of his well, the dog would dream and he would tell the content of his dreams the way that victims in a trance will tell of being pursued by posses of their nameless fears. He whimpered, he cried and sometimes he howled. His legs and his paws would jerk and flail and his claws would scrabble desperately against the parquet floor. Mimi—who loved this dog—would lay her hand against his side and let her fingers dabble in his coat in vain attempts to soothe him. Sometimes, she had to call his name in order to rouse him from his dreams because his heart would be racing. Other times, she smiled and thought: *at least there's one of us getting some sleep.* The dog's name was Thurber[1] and he dreamed in beige and white.

Everett and Mimi Menlo were both psychiatrists. His field was schizophrenia; hers was autistic children. Mimi's venue was the Parkin Institute at the University of Toronto; Everett's was the Queen Street Mental Health Centre. Early in their marriage they decided never to work as a team and not—unless it was a matter of financial life and death—to accept employment in the same institution. Both had always worked with the kind of physical intensity that kills, and yet they gave the impression this was the only tolerable way in which to function. It meant there was always a sense of peril in what they did, but the peril—according to Everett—made their lives worth living. This, at least, had been his theory twenty years ago when they were young.

Now, for whatever unnamed reason, peril had become his enemy and Everett Menlo had begun to look and behave and lose his sleep like a haunted man. But he refused to comment when Mimi asked him what was wrong. Instead, he gave the worst of all possible answers a psychiatrist can hear who seeks an explanation of a patient's silence: he said there was *absolutely nothing wrong.*

'You're sure you're not coming down with something?'

'Yes.'

'And you wouldn't like a massage?'

'I've already told you: no.'

1 The dog has been named after James Thurber (1894–1961), American humorist, short story writer, and cartoonist. Known for his work in *The New Yorker*, his most famous story is 'The Secret Life of Walter Mitty', in which a timid and mild-mannered man escapes repeatedly into adventuresome fantasies.

'Can I get you anything?'

'No.'

'And you don't want to talk?'

'That's right.'

'Okay, Everett . . .'

'Okay, what?'

'Okay, nothing. I only hope you get some sleep tonight.'

Everett stood up. 'Have you been spying on me, Mimi?'

'What do you mean by *spying*?'

'Watching me all night long.'

'Well, Everett, I don't see how I can fail to be aware you aren't asleep when we share this bedroom. I mean—I can hear you grinding your teeth. I can see you lying there wide awake.'

'When?'

'All the time. You're staring at the ceiling.'

'I've never stared at the ceiling in my whole life. I sleep on my stomach.'

'You sleep on your stomach *if* you sleep. But you have not been sleeping. Period. No argument.'

Everett Menlo went to his dresser and got out a pair of clean pyjamas. Turning his back on Mimi, he put them on.

Somewhat amused at the coyness of this gesture, Mimi asked what he was hiding.

'Nothing!' he shouted at her.

Mimi's mouth fell open. Everett never yelled. His anger wasn't like that; it manifested itself in other ways, in silence and withdrawal, never shouts.

Everett was staring at her defiantly. He had slammed the bottom drawer of his dresser. Now he was fumbling with the wrapper of a pack of cigarettes.

Mimi's stomach tied a knot.

Everett hadn't touched a cigarette for weeks.

'Please don't smoke those,' she said. 'You'll only be sorry if you do.'

'And you', he said, 'will be sorry if I don't.'

'But dear . . .' said Mimi.

'Leave me for Christ's sake alone!' Everett yelled.

Mimi gave up and sighed and then she said: 'all right. Thurber and I will go and sleep in the living-room. Good-night.'

Everett sat on the edge of his bed. His hands were shaking.

'Please,' he said—apparently addressing the floor. 'Don't leave me here alone. I couldn't bear that.'

This was perhaps the most chilling thing he could have said to her. Mimi was alarmed; her husband was genuinely terrified of something and he would not say what it was. If she had not been who she was—if she had not known what she knew—if her years of training had not prepared her to watch for signs like this, she might have been better off. As it was, she had to face the possibility the strongest, most sensible man on earth was having a nervous breakdown of major proportions. Lots of people have breakdowns, of course; but not, she had thought, the gods of reason.

'All right,' she said—her voice maintaining the kind of calm she knew a child afraid of the dark would appreciate. 'In a minute I'll get us something to drink. But first, I'll go and change. . . .'

Mimi went into the sanctum of the bathroom, where her nightgown waited for her—a portable hiding-place hanging on the back of the door. 'You stay there,' she said to Thurber, who had padded after her. 'Mama will be out in just a moment.'

Even in the dark, she could gauge Everett's tension. His shadow—all she could see of him—twitched from time to time and the twitching took on a kind of lurching rhythm, something like the broken clock in their living-room.

Mimi lay on her side and tried to close her eyes. But her eyes were tied to a will of their own and would not obey her. Now she, too, was caught in the same irreversible tide of sleeplessness that bore her husband backward through the night. Four or five times she watched him lighting cigarettes—blowing out the matches, courting disaster in the bedclothes—conjuring the worst of deaths for the three of them: a flaming pyre on the twentieth floor.

All of this behaviour was utterly unlike him: foreign to his code of principles and ethics; alien to everything he said and believed. *Openness, directness, sharing of ideas, encouraging imaginative response to every problem. Never hide troubles. Never allow despair* . . . These were his directives in everything he did. Now, he had thrown them over.

One thing was certain. She was not the cause of his sleeplessness. She didn't have affairs and neither did he. He might be ill—but whenever he'd been ill before, there had been no trauma; never a trauma like this one, at any rate. Perhaps it was something about a patient—one of his tougher cases; a wall in the patient's condition they could not break through; some circumstance of someone's lack of progress—a sudden veering towards a catatonic state, for instance—something that Everett had not foreseen that had stymied him and was slowly . . . what? Destroying his sense of professional control? His self-esteem? His scientific certainty? If only he would speak.

Mimi thought about her own worst case: a child whose obstinate refusal to communicate was currently breaking her heart and, thus, her ability to help. If ever she had needed Everett to talk to, it was now. All her fellow doctors were locked in a battle over this child; they wanted to take him away from her. Mimi refused to give him up; he might as well have been her own flesh and blood. Everything had been done—from gentle holding sessions to violent bouts of manufactured anger—in her attempt to make the child react. She was staying with him every day from the moment he was roused to the moment he was induced to sleep with drugs.

His name was Brian Bassett and he was eight years old. He sat on the floor in the furthest corner he could achieve in one of the observation-isolation rooms where all the autistic children were placed when nothing else in their treatment—nothing of love or expertise—had managed to break their silence. Mostly, this was a signal they were coming to the end of life.

There in his four-square, glass-box room, surrounded by all that can tempt a child if a child can be tempted—toys and food and story-book companions—Brian Bassett was in the process, now, of fading away. His eyes were never closed and his arms were restrained. He was attached to three machines that nurtured him with all that science can offer. But of course, the spirit and the will to live cannot be fed by force to those who do not want to feed.

Now in the light of Brian Bassett's utter lack of willing contact with the world around him—his utter refusal to communicate—Mimi watched her husband through the night. Everett stared at the ceiling, lit by the Manulife building's distant lamps, borne on his back further and further out to sea. She had lost him, she was certain.

When, at last, he saw that Mimi had drifted into her own and welcome sleep, Everett rose from his bed and went out into the hall, past the simulated jungle of the solarium, until he reached the dining-room. There, all the way till dawn, he amused himself with two decks of cards and endless games of Dead Man's Solitaire.

Thurber rose and shuffled after him. The dining-room was one of Thurber's favourite places in all his confined but privileged world, for it was here—as in the kitchen—that from time to time a hand descended filled with the miracle of food. But whatever it was that his master was doing up there above him on the table-top, it wasn't anything to do with feeding or with being fed. The playing cards had an old and dusty dryness to their scent and they held no appeal for the dog. So he once again lay down and he took up his dreams, which at least gave his paws some exercise. This way, he failed to hear the advent of a new dimension to his master's problem. This occurred precisely at 5:45 a.m. when the telephone rang and Everett Menlo, having rushed to answer it, waited breathless for a minute while he listened and then said: 'yes' in a curious, strangulated fashion. Thurber—had he been awake—would have recognized in his master's voice the signal for disaster.

For weeks now, Everett had been working with a patient who was severely and uniquely schizophrenic. This patient's name was Kenneth Albright, and while he was deeply suspicious, he was also oddly caring. Kenneth Albright loved the detritus of life, such as bits of woolly dust and wads of discarded paper. He loved all dried-up leaves that had drifted from their parent trees and he loved the dead bees that had curled up to die along the window-sills of his ward. He also loved the spiderwebs seen high up in the corners of the rooms where he sat on plastic chairs and ate with plastic spoons.

Kenneth Albright talked a lot about his dreams. But his dreams had become, of late, a major stumbling block in the process of his recovery. Back in the days when Kenneth had first become Doctor Menlo's patient, the dreams had been overburdened with detail: 'over-cast', as he would say, 'with characters' and over-produced, again in Kenneth's phrase, 'as if I were dreaming the dreams of Cecil B. de Mille.'

Then he had said: 'but a person can't really dream someone else's dreams. Or can they, Doctor Menlo?'

'No' had been Everett's answer—definite and certain.

Everett Menlo had been delighted, at first, with Kenneth Albright's dreams. They had been immensely entertaining—complex and filled with intriguing detail. Kenneth himself was at a loss to explain the meaning of these dreams, but as Everett had said, it wasn't Kenneth's job to explain. That was Everett's job. His job and his pleasure. For quite a long while, during these early sessions, Everett had written out the dreams, taken them home and recounted them to Mimi.

Kenneth Albright was a paranoid schizophrenic. Four times now, he had attempted suicide. He was a fiercely angry man at times—and at other times as gentle and as pleasant as a docile child. He had suffered so greatly, in the very worst moments of his disease, that he could no longer work. His job—it was almost an incidental detail in his life and had no importance for him, so it seemed—was returning reference books, in the Metro Library, to their places in the stacks. Sometimes—mostly late of an afternoon—he might begin a psychotic episode of such profound dimensions that he would attempt his suicide right behind the counter and even once, in the full view of everyone, while riding in the glass-walled elevator. It was after this last occasion that he was brought, in restraints, to be a resident patient at the Queen Street Mental Health Centre. He had slashed his wrists with a razor—but not before he had also slashed and destroyed an antique copy of *Don Quixote*, the pages of which he pasted to the walls with blood.

For a week thereafter, Kenneth Albright—just like Brian Bassett—had refused to speak or to move. Everett had him kept in an isolation cell, force-fed and drugged. Slowly, by dint of patience, encouragement and caring even Kenneth could recognize as genuine, Everett Menlo had broken through the barrier. Kenneth was removed from isolation, pampered with food and cigarettes, and he began relating his dreams.

At first there seemed to be only the dreams and nothing else in Kenneth's memory. Broken pencils, discarded toys and the telephone directory all had roles to play in these dreams but there were never any people. All the weather was bleak and all the landscapes were empty. Houses, motor cars and office buildings never made an appearance. Sounds and smells had some importance, the wind would blow, the scent of unseen fires was often described. Stairwells were plentiful, leading nowhere, all of them rising from a subterranean world that Kenneth either did not dare to visit or would not describe.

The dreams had little variation, one from another. The themes had mostly to do with loss and with being lost. The broken pencils were all given names and the discarded toys were given to one another as companions. The telephone books were the sources of recitations—hours and hours of repeated names and numbers, some of which—Everett had noted with surprise—were absolutely accurate.

All of this held fast until an incident occurred one morning that changed the face of Kenneth Albright's schizophrenia forever, an incident that stemmed—so it seemed—from something he had dreamed the night before.

Bearing in mind his previous attempts at suicide, it will be obvious that Kenneth Albright was never far from sight at the Queen Street Mental Health Centre. He was, in fact, under constant observation; constant, that is, as human beings and modern technology can manage. In the ward to which he was ultimately consigned, for instance, the toilet cabinet had no doors and the shower-rooms had no locks. Therefore, a person could not ever be alone with water, glass or shaving utensils. (All the razors were cordless automatics.) Scissors and knives were banned, as were pieces of string and rubber bands. A person could not even kill his feet and hands by binding up his wrists or ankles. Nothing poisonous was anywhere available. All the windows were barred. All the double doors between this ward and the corridors beyond were doors with triple locks and a guard was always near at hand.

Still, if people want to die, they will find a way. Mimi Menlo would discover this to her everlasting sorrow with Brian Bassett. Everett Menlo would discover this to his everlasting horror with Kenneth Albright.

On the morning of April 19th, a Tuesday, Everett Menlo, in the best of health, had welcomed a brand-new patient into his office. This was Anne Marie Wilson, a young and brilliant pianist whose promising career had been halted mid-flight by a schizophrenic incident involving her ambition. She was, it seemed, no longer able to play and all her dreams were shattered. The cause was simple, to all appearances: Ann Marie had a sense of how, precisely, the music should be and she had not been able to master it accordingly. 'Everything I attempt is terrible,' she had said—in spite of all her critical accolades and all her professional success. Other doctors had tried and failed to break the barriers in Anne Marie, whose hands had taken on a life of their own, refusing altogether to work for her. Now it was Menlo's turn and hope was high.

Everett had been looking forward to his session with this prodigy. He loved all music and had thought to find some means within its discipline to reach her. She seemed so fragile, sitting there in the sunlight, and he had just begun to take his first notes when the door flew open and Louise, his secretary, said: 'I'm sorry, Doctor Menlo. There's a problem. Can you come with me at once?'

Everett excused himself.

Anne Marie was left in the sunlight to bide her time. Her fingers were moving around in her lap and she put them in her mouth to make them quiet.

Even as he'd heard his secretary speak, Everett had known the problem would be Kenneth Albright. Something in Kenneth's eyes had warned him there was trouble on the way: a certain wariness that indicated all was not as placid as it should have been, given his regimen of drugs. He had stayed long hours in one position, moving his fingers over his thighs as if to dry them on his trousers; watching his fellow patients come and go with abnormal interest—never, however, rising from his chair. An incident was on the horizon and Everett had been waiting for it, hoping it would not come.

Louise had said that Doctor Menlo was to go at once to Kenneth Albright's ward. Everett had run the whole way. Only after the attendant had let him in past the double doors, did he slow his pace to a hurried walk and wipe his brow. He didn't want Kenneth to know how alarmed he had been.

Coming to the appointed place, he paused before he entered, closing his eyes, preparing himself for whatever he might have to see. *Other people have killed themselves: I've seen it often enough*, he was thinking, *I simply won't let it affect me.* Then he went in.

The room was small and white—a dining-room—and Kenneth was sitting down in a corner, his back pressed out against the walls on either side of him. His head was bowed and his legs drawn up and he was obviously trying to hide without much success. An intern was standing above him and a nurse was kneeling down beside him. Several pieces of bandaging with blood on them were scattered near Kenneth's feet and there was a white enamel basin filled with pinkish water on the floor beside the nurse.

'Morowetz,' Everett said to the intern. 'Tell me what has happened here.' He said this just the way he posed such questions when he took the interns through the wards at examination time, quizzing them on symptoms and prognoses.

But Morowetz the intern had no answer. He was puzzled. What had happened had no sane explanation.

Everett turned to Charterhouse, the nurse.

'On the morning of April 19th, at roughly ten-fifteen, I found Kenneth Albright covered with blood,' Ms Charterhouse was to write in her report. 'His hands, his arms, his face and his neck were stained. I would say the blood was fresh and the patient's clothing—mostly his shirt—was wet with it. Some—a very small amount of it—had dried on his forehead. The rest was uniformly the kind of blood you expect to find free-flowing from a wound. I called for assistance and meanwhile attempted to ascertain where Mister Albright might have been injured. I performed this examination without success. I could find no source of bleeding anywhere on Mr Albright's body.

Morowetz concurred.

The blood was someone else's.

'Was there a weapon of any kind?' Doctor Menlo had wanted to know.

'No, sir. Nothing,' said Charterhouse.

'And was he alone when you found him?'

'Yes, sir. Just like this in the corner.'

'And the others?'

'All the patients in the ward were examined,' Morowetz told him.

'And?'

'Not one of them was bleeding.'

Everett said: 'I see.'

He looked down at Kenneth.

'This is Doctor Menlo, Kenneth. Have you anything to tell me?'

Kenneth did not reply.

Everett said: 'When you've got him back in his room and tranquillized, will you call me, please?'

Morowetz nodded.

The call never came. Kenneth had fallen asleep. Either the drugs he was given had knocked him out cold, or he had opted for silence. Either way, he was incommunicado.

No one was discovered bleeding. Nothing was found to indicate an accident, a violent attack, an epileptic seizure. A weapon was not located. Kenneth Albright had not a single scratch on his flesh from stem, as Everett put it, to gudgeon. The blood, it seemed, had fallen like the rain from heaven: unexplained and inexplicable.

Later, as the day was ending, Everett Menlo left the Queen Street Mental Health Centre. He made his way home on the Queen streetcar and the Bay bus. When he reached the apartment, Thurber was waiting for him. Mimi was at a goddamned meeting.

That was the night Everett Menlo suffered the first of his failures to sleep. It was occasioned by the fact that, when he wakened sometime after three, he had just been dreaming. This, of course, was not unusual—but the dream itself was perturbing. There was someone lying there, in the bright white landscape of a hospital dining-room. Whether it was a man or a woman could not be told, it was just a human body, lying down in a pool of blood.

Kenneth Albright was kneeling beside this body, pulling it open the way a child will pull a Christmas present open—yanking at its strings and ribbons, wanting only to see the contents. Everett saw this scene from several angles, never speaking, never being spoken to. In all the time he watched—the usual dream eternity—the silence was broken only by the sound of water dripping from an unseen tap. Then, Kenneth Albright rose and was covered with blood, the way he had been that morning. He stared at Doctor Menlo, looked right through him and departed. Nothing remained in the dining-room but plastic tables and plastic chairs and the bright red thing on the floor that once had been a person. Everett Menlo did not know and could not guess who this person might have been. He only knew that Kenneth Albright had left this person's body in Everett Menlo's dream.

Three nights running, the corpse remained in its place and every time that Everett entered the dining-room in the nightmare he was certain he would find out who it was. On the fourth night, fully expecting to discover he himself was the victim, he beheld the face and saw it was a stranger.

But there are no strangers in dreams; he knew that now after twenty years of practice. *There are no strangers; there are only people in disguise.*

Mimi made one final attempt in Brian Bassett's behalf to turn away the fate to which his other doctors—both medical and psychiatric—had consigned him. Not that, as a group, they had failed to expend the full weight of all they knew and all they could do to save him. One of his medical doctors—a woman whose name was Juliet Bateman—had moved a cot into his isolation room and stayed with him twenty-four hours a day for over a week. But her health had been undermined by this and when she succumbed to the Shanghai flu she removed herself for fear of infecting Brian Bassett.

The parents had come and gone on a daily basis for months in a killing routine of visits. But parents, their presence and their loving, are not the answer when a child has fallen into an autistic state. They might as well have been strangers. And so they had been advised to stay away.

Brian Bassett was eight years old—*unlucky eight*, as one of his therapists had said—and in every other way, in terms of physical development and mental capability, he had always been a perfectly normal child. Now, in the final moments of his life, he weighed a scant thirty pounds, when he should have weighed twice that much.

Brian had not been heard to speak a single word in over a year of constant observation. Earlier—long ago as seven months—a few expressions would visit his face from time to time. Never a smile—but often a kind of sneer, a passing of judgment, terrifying in its intensity. Other times, a pinched expression would appear—a signal of the shyness peculiar to autistic children, who think of light as being unfriendly.

Mimi's militant efforts in behalf of Brian had been exemplary. Her fellow doctors thought of her as *Bassett's crazy guardian angel.* They begged her to remove herself in order to preserve her health. Being wise, being practical, they saw that all her efforts would not save him. But Mimi's version of being a guardian angel was more like being a surrogate warrior: a hired gun or a samurai. Her cool determination to thwart the enemies of silence, stillness and starvation gave her strengths that even she had been unaware were hers to command.

Brian Bassett, seated in his corner on the floor, maintained a solemn composure that lent his features a kind of unearthly beauty. His back was straight, his hands were poised, his hair was so fine he looked the very picture of a spirit waiting to enter a newborn creature. Sometimes Mimi wondered if this creature Brian Bassett waited to inhabit could be human. She thought of all the animals she had ever seen in all her travels and she fell upon the image of a newborn fawn as being the most tranquil and the most in need of stillness in order to survive. If only all the natural energy and curiosity of a newborn beast could have entered into Brian Bassett, surely, they would have transformed the boy in the corner into a vibrant, joyous human being. But it was not to be.

On the 29th of April—one week and three days after Everett had entered into his crisis of insomnia—Mimi sat on the floor in Brian Bassett's isolation room, gently massaging his arms and legs as she held him in her lap.

His weight, by now, was shocking—and his skin had become translucent. His eyes had not been closed for days—for weeks—and their expression might have been carved in stone.

'Speak to me. Speak,' she whispered to him as she cradled his head beneath her chin. 'Please at least speak before you die.'

Nothing happened. Only silence.

Juliet Bateman—wrapped in a blanket—was watching through the observation glass as Mimi lifted up Brian Bassett and placed him in his cot. The cot had metal sides—and the sides were raised. Juliet Bateman could see Brian Bassett's eyes and his hands as Mimi stepped away.

Mimi looked at Juliet and shook her head. Juliet closed her eyes and pulled her blanket tighter like a skin that might protect her from the next five minutes.

Mimi went around the cot to the other side and dragged the IV stand in closer to the head. She fumbled for a moment with the long plastic lifelines—anti-dehydrants, nutrients—and she adjusted the needles and brought them down inside the nest of the cot where Brian Bassett lay and she lifted up his arm in order to insert the tubes and bind them into place with tape.

This was when it happened—just as Mimi Menlo was preparing to insert the second tube.

Brian Bassett looked at her and spoke.

'No,' he said. 'Don't.'

Don't meant death.

Mimi paused—considered—and set the tube aside. Then she withdrew the tube already in place and she hung them both on the IV stand.

All right, she said to Brian Bassett in her mind, *you win.*

She looked down then with her arm along the side of the cot—and one hand trailing down so Brian Bassett could touch if he wanted to. She smiled at him and said to him: 'not to worry. Not to worry. None of us is ever going to trouble you again.' He watched her carefully. 'Goodbye, Brian,' she said. 'I love you.'

Juliet Bateman saw Mimi Menlo say all this and was fairly sure she had read the words on Mimi's lips just as they had been spoken.

Mimi started out of the room. She was determined now there was no turning back and that Brian Bassett was free to go his way. But just as she was turning the handle and pressing her weight against the door—she heard Brian Bassett speak again.

'Goodbye,' he said.

And died.

Mimi went back and Juliet Bateman, too, and they stayed with him another hour before they turned out his lights. 'Someone else can cover his face,' said Mimi. 'I'm not going to do it.' Juliet agreed and they came back out to tell the nurse on duty that their ward had died and their work with him was over.

On the 30th of April—a Saturday—Mimi stayed home and made her notes and she wondered if and when she would weep for Brian Bassett. Her hand, as she wrote, was steady and her throat was not constricted and her eyes had no sensation beyond the burning itch of fatigue. She wondered what she looked like in the mirror, but resisted that discovery. Some things could wait. Outside it rained. Thurber dreamed in the corner. Bay Street rumbled in the basement.

Everett, in the meantime, had reached his own crisis and because of his desperate straits a part of Mimi Menlo's mind was on her husband. Now he had not slept for almost ten days. *We really ought to consign ourselves to hospital beds*, she thought. Somehow, the idea held no persuasion. It occurred to her that laughter might do a better job, if only they could find it. The brain, when over-extended, gives us the most surprisingly simple propositions, she concluded. *Stop*, it says to us. *Lie down and sleep.*

Five minutes later, Mimi found herself still sitting at the desk with her fountain pen capped and her fingers raised to her lips in an attitude of gentle prayer. It required some effort to re-adjust her gaze and re-establish her focus on the surface of the window glass beyond which her mind had wandered. Sitting up, she had been asleep.

Thurber muttered something and stretched his legs and yawned, still asleep. Mimi glanced in his direction. *We've both been dreaming*, she thought, *but his dream continues.*

Somewhere behind her, the broken clock was attempting to strike the hour of three. Its voice was dull and rusty, needing oil.

Looking down, she saw the words *BRIAN BASSETT* written on the page before her and it occurred to her that, without his person, the words were nothing more than extrapolations from the alphabet—something fanciful we call a 'name' in the hope that, one day, it will take on meaning.

She thought of Brian Bassett with his building blocks—pushing the letters around on the floor and coming up with more acceptable arrangements: *TINA STERABBS . . . IAN BRETT BASS . . . BEST STAB the RAIN*: a sentence. He had known all along, of course, that *BRIAN BASSETT* wasn't what he wanted because it wasn't what he was. He had come here against his will, was held here against his better judgment, fought against his captors and finally escaped.

But where was here to Ian Brett Bass? Where was here to Tina Sterabbs? Like Brian Bassett, they had all been here in someone else's dreams, and had to wait for someone else to wake before they could make their getaway.

Slowly, Mimi uncapped her fountain pen and drew a firm, black line through Brian Bassett's name. *We dreamed him,* she wrote, that's all. *And then we let him go.*

Seeing Everett standing in the doorway, knowing he had just returned from another Kenneth Albright crisis, she had no sense of apprehension. All this was only as it should be. Given the way that everything was going, it stood to reason Kenneth Albright's crisis had to come in this moment. If he managed, at last, to kill himself then at least her husband might begin to sleep again.

Far in the back of her mind a carping, critical voice remarked that any such thoughts were *deeply unfeeling and verging on the barbaric.* But Mimi dismissed this voice and another part of her brain stepped forward in her defence. *I will weep for Kenneth Albright,* she thought, *when I can weep for Brian Bassett. Now, all that matters is that Everett and I survive.*

Then she strode forward and put out her hand for Everett's briefcase, set the briefcase down and helped him out of his topcoat. She was playing wife. It seemed to be the thing to do.

For the next twenty minutes Everett had nothing to say, and after he had poured himself a drink and after Mimi had done the same, they sat in their chairs and waited for Everett to catch his breath.

The first thing he said when he finally spoke was: 'finish your notes?'

'Just about,' Mimi told him. 'I've written everything I can for now.' She did not elaborate. 'You're home early,' she said, hoping to goad him into saying something new about Kenneth Albright.

'Yes,' he said. 'I am.' But that was all.

Then he stood up—threw back the last of his drink and poured another. He lighted a cigarette and Mimi didn't even wince. He had been smoking now three days. The atmosphere between them had been, since then, enlivened with a magnetic kind of tension. But it was a moribund tension, slowly beginning to dissipate.

Mimi watched her husband's silent torment now with a kind of clinical detachment. This was the result, she liked to tell herself, of her training and her discipline. The lover in her could regard Everett warmly and with concern, but the psychiatrist in her could also watch him as someone suffering a nervous breakdown, someone who could not be helped until the symptoms had multiplied and declared themselves more openly.

Everett went into the darkest corner of the room and sat down hard in one of Mimi's straight-backed chairs: the ones inherited from her mother. He sat, prim, like a patient in a doctor's office, totally unrelaxed and nervy; expressionless. Either he had come to receive a deadly diagnosis, or he would get a clean bill of health.

Mimi glided over to the sofa in the window, plush and red and deeply comfortable; a place to recuperate. The view—if she chose to turn only slightly sideways—was one of the gentle rain that was falling onto Bay Street. Sopping wet pigeons huddled on the window-sill; people across the street in the Manulife building were turning on their lights.

A renegade robin, nesting in their eaves, began to sing.

Everett Menlo began to talk.

'Please don't interrupt,' he said at first.

'You know I won't,' said Mimi. It was a rule that neither one should interrupt the telling of a case until they had been invited to do so.

Mimi put her fingers into her glass so the ice-cubes wouldn't click. She waited.

Everett spoke—but he spoke as if in someone else's voice, perhaps the voice of Kenneth Albright. This was not entirely unusual. Often, both Mimi and Everett Menlo spoke in the voices of their patients. What was unusual, this time, was that, speaking in Kenneth's voice, Everett began to sweat profusely—so profusely that Mimi was able to watch his shirt front darkening with perspiration.

'As you know,' he said, 'I have not been sleeping.'

This was the understatement of the year. Mimi was silent.

'I have not been sleeping because—to put it in a nutshell—I have been afraid to dream.'

Mimi was somewhat startled by this. Not by the fact that Everett was afraid to dream, but only because she had just been thinking of dreams herself.

'I have been afraid to dream, because in all my dreams there have been bodies. Corpses. Murder victims.'

Mimi—not really listening—idly wondered if she had been one of them.

'In all my dreams, there have been corpses,' Everett repeated. 'But I am not the murderer. Kenneth Albright is the murderer, and, up to this moment, he has left behind him fifteen bodies: none of them people I recognize.'

Mimi nodded. The ice-cubes in her drink were beginning to freeze her fingers. Any minute now, she prayed, they would surely melt.

'I gave up dreaming almost a week ago,' said Everett, 'thinking that if I did, the killing pattern might be altered; broken.' Then he said tersely, 'it was not. The killings have continued. . . .'

'How do you know the killings have continued, Everett, if you've given up your dreaming? Wouldn't this mean he had no place to hide the bodies?'

In spite of the fact she had disobeyed their rule about not speaking, Everett answered her.

'I know they are being continued because I have seen the blood.'

'Ah, yes. I see.'

'No, Mimi. No. You do not see. The blood is not a figment of my imagination. The blood, in fact, is the only thing not dreamed.' He explained the stains on Kenneth Albright's hands and arms and clothes and he said: 'It happens every day. We have searched his person for signs of cuts and gashes—even for internal and rectal bleeding. Nothing. We have searched his quarters and all the other quarters in his ward. His ward is locked. His ward is isolated in the extreme. None of his fellow patients was ever found bleeding—never had cause to bleed. There were no injuries—no self-inflicted wounds. We thought of animals. Perhaps a mouse—a rat. But nothing. Nothing.

Nothing . . . We also went so far as to strip-search all the members of the staff who entered that ward and I, too, offered myself for this experiment. Still nothing. Nothing. No one had bled.'

Everett was now beginning to perspire so heavily he removed his jacket and threw it on the floor. Thurber woke and stared at it, startled. At first, it appeared to be the beast that had just pursued him through the woods and down the road. But, then, it sighed and settled and was just a coat; a rumpled jacket lying down on the rug.

Everett said: 'we had taken samples of the blood on the patient's hands—on Kenneth Albright's hands and on his clothing and we had these samples analyzed. No. It was not his own blood. No, it was not the blood of an animal. No, it was not the blood of a fellow patient. No, it was not the blood of any members of the staff. . . .'

Everett's voice had risen.

'Whose blood was it?' he almost cried. 'Whose the hell was it?'

Mimi waited.

Everett Menlo lighted another cigarette. He took a great gulp of his drink.

'Well . . .' He was calmer now; calmer of necessity. He had to marshal the evidence. He had to put it all in order—bring it into line with reason. 'Did this mean that—somehow—the patient had managed to leave the premises—do some bloody deed and return without our knowledge of it? That is, after all, the only possible explanation. Isn't it?'

Mimi waited.

'Isn't it?' he repeated.

'Yes,' she said. 'It's the only possible explanation.'

'Except there is no way out of that place. There is absolutely no way out.'

Now, there was a pause.

'But one,' he added—his voice, again, a whisper.

Mimi was silent. Fearful—watching his twisted face.

'Tell me,' Everett Menlo said—the perfect innocent, almost the perfect child in quest of forbidden knowledge. 'Answer me this—be honest: is there blood in dreams?'

Mimi could not respond. She felt herself go pale. Her husband—after all, the sanest man alive—had just suggested something so completely mad he might as well have handed over his reason in a paper bag and said to her, *burn this.*

'The only place that Kenneth Albright goes, I tell you, is into dreams,' Everett said. 'That is the only place beyond the ward into which the patient can or does escape.'

Another—briefer—pause.

'It is real blood, Mimi. Real. And he gets it all from dreams. My dreams.'

They waited for this to settle.

Everett said: 'I'm tired. I'm tired. I cannot bear this any more. I'm tired. . . .'

Mimi thought, *good. No matter what else happens, he will sleep tonight.*

He did. And so, at last, did she.

Mimi's dreams were rarely of the kind that engender fear. She dreamt more gentle scenes with open spaces that did not intimidate. She would dream quite often of water and of animals. Always, she was nothing more than an observer; roles were not assigned her; often, this was sad. Somehow, she seemed at times locked out, unable to participate. These were the dreams she endured when Brian Bassett died: field trips to see him in some desert setting; underwater excursions to watch him floating amongst the seaweed. He never spoke, and indeed, he never appeared to be aware of her presence.

That night, when Everett fell into his bed exhausted and she did likewise, Mimi's dream of Brian Bassett was the last she would ever have of him and somehow, in the dream, she knew this. What she saw was what, in magical terms, would be called a disappearing act. Brian Bassett vanished. Gone.

Sometime after midnight on May Day morning, Mimi Menlo awoke from her dream of Brian to the sound of Thurber thumping the floor in a dream of his own.

Everett was not in his bed and Mimi cursed. She put on her wrapper and her slippers and went beyond the bedroom into the hall.

No lights were shining but the street lamps far below and the windows gave no sign of stars.

Mimi made her way past the jungle, searching for Everett in the living-room. He was not there. She would dream of this one day; it was a certainty.

'Everett?'

He did not reply.

Mimi turned and went back through the bedroom.

'Everett?'

She heard him. He was in the bathroom and she went in through the door.

'Oh,' she said, when she saw him. 'Oh, my God.'

Everett Menlo was standing in the bathtub, removing his pyjamas. They were soaking wet, but not with perspiration. They were soaking wet with blood.

For a moment, holding his jacket, letting its arms hang down across his belly and his groin, Everett stared at Mimi, blank-eyed from his nightmare.

Mimi raised her hands to her mouth. She felt as one must feel, if helpless, watching someone burn alive.

Everett threw the jacket down and started to remove his trousers. His pyjamas, made of cotton, had been green. His eyes were blinded now with blood and his hands reached out to find the shower taps.

'Please don't look at me,' he said. 'I . . . Please go away.'

Mimi said: 'no.' She sat on the toilet seat. 'I'm waiting here,' she told him, 'until we both wake up.'

1988

Alice Munro

b. 1931

Born Alice Laidlaw, Alice Munro grew up in Wingham, Ont., before moving, at nineteen, to nearby London to attend the University of Western Ontario. After two years there she married Jim Munro and settled with him in British Columbia. She lived in Vancouver and Victoria for more than twenty years, writing, helping her husband manage a bookstore, and raising three daughters. In 1972 she returned to southwestern Ontario and now lives in Clinton, not far from Wingham, with her second husband.

Munro began writing early—her first published work appeared in UWO's undergraduate literary magazine in 1950—and by 1960, when 'The Peace of Utrecht' was read over CBC radio and published in *The Tamarack Review*, her writing was beginning to gain acceptance. But she did not publish her first collection of stories, *Dance of the Happy Shades*, until 1968. (The extraordinarily accomplished level of this first book was recognized when Munro was awarded the first of her three Governor General's Awards for fiction.) Munro has since produced nine more books: seven further collections of short fiction—*Something I've Been Meaning to Tell You* (1974); *The Moons of Jupiter* (1982); *The Progress of Love* (1986; Governor General's Award); *Friend of My Youth* (1990), *Open Secrets* (1994), *The Love of a Good Woman* (1998), and *Hateship, Friendship, Courtship, Loveship, Marriage* (2001)—and two linked story-sequences sometimes described as novels, *Lives of Girls and Women* (1971) and *Who Do You Think You Are?* (1978; Governor General's Award). Her *Selected Stories*, published in 1996, contains twenty-eight stories chosen by Munro herself. For many years now most of her new stories—like those of Mavis Gallant—have appeared first in *The New Yorker*.

Munro's narrative structures are frequently developed through the use of oppositions, which may take the form of contrasting characters (such as the sisters Marietta and Beryl in 'The Progress of Love') or of dialectics between 'female' and 'male' worlds or between rural and urban cultures. It is especially evident in the playing off of *then* against *now* that gives her stories a complex movement back and forth across time (which may be reflected in a play of tenses) and that reproduces the act of the mind in recovering and reassessing the past in all its layers.

Critics have often used building metaphors to describe the intricate structure of these stories. In fact, Munro herself, in suggesting that her way of writing stories can be explained by how she reads those written by other people, speaks of fiction as if were something to explore, even to inhabit:

> *I can start reading anywhere; from beginning to end, from end to beginning, from any point in between in either direction. So obviously I don't take up a story and follow it as if it were a road, taking me somewhere, with views and neat diversions along the way. I go into it, and move back and forth and settle here and there, and stay in it for a while. It's more like a house.* (*Making It New: Contemporary Canadian Stories,* edited by John Metcalf, 1982)

Munro furnishes her fictional houses meticulously. She is often thought of as a regionalist, in that she usually sets her stories in recognizable small-town Ontario, working with material she knows personally and evoking fully realized milieus; yet beneath the ordinariness of the world she creates, the apparent reality may prove deceptive, because disaster often lurks or is longed for, and secrets are glimpsed but remain untold. Many of her stories read as if they are on the verge of becoming full-length mystery novels; however, they resist neat solutions, leaving their readers instead with what the narrator of 'The Progress of Love' calls 'the old puzzles you can't resist or solve'.

Describing Munro's achievements, the American short story writer Mona Simpson wrote:

Her genius, like Chekhov's, is quiet and particularly hard to describe, because it has the simplicity of the best naturalism, in that it seems not translated from life but, rather, like life itself. . . . Like the highest practitioners of any craft, Alice Munro seems, in her four most recent collections, to have left old forms behind, or to have broken them open, so that she is now writing not short stories or novellas but something altogether new. . . symphonic, large, architecturally gorgeous. (The Atlantic Monthly, Dec. 2001)

The stories in *The Progress of Love* mark the beginning of this new stage in Munro's writing. Where earlier she had created beautifully written narratives about the complexities of the individual life, her later stories emphasize the power of perception and memory in shaping those lives. Although memory and the way one tells the story of the past were already important themes in Munro's fiction, increasingly these stories have become kaleidoscopic, suggesting that a shifting array of understandings unfold from every event. The chronology of Munro's stories is broken to suggest that there is no one story, only fragments of memory and the retellings of events that help characters make sense of one another and of themselves. The 'deceptive realism' that characterized her earlier fiction, where unexpected uncertainties and irresolution lie beneath apparently stable surfaces, has yielded to stories in which surfaces themselves are uncertain, both for the reader and for the characters—a way of telling that allows readers to share the disorientation of her characters.

Narrated by a woman called Fame, 'The Progress of Love' tells a story of loss, particularly of the loss of equilibrium. While this loss begins with the death of her mother, physical death may not prove as serious as the death of love. Fame and the women from whom she is descended have experienced—and caused—a 'progress' of love, one that Fame hopes not to pass on to her sons. The other stories in that collection, and indeed much of the body of Munro's work, might be thought of as similarly tracing out this ever-changing progress of love over the course of several generations.

The Progress of Love

I got a call at work, and it was my father. This was not long after I was divorced and started in the real-estate office. Both of my boys were in school. It was a hot enough day in September.

My father was so polite, even in the family. He took time to ask me how I was. Country manners. Even if somebody phones up to tell you your house is burning down, they ask first how you are.

'I'm fine,' I said. 'How are you?'

'Not so good, I guess,' said my father, in his old way—apologetic but self-respecting. 'I think your mother's gone.'

I knew that *gone* meant *dead*. I knew that. But for a second or so I saw my mother in her black straw hat setting off down the lane. The word *gone* seemed full of nothing but a deep relief and even an excitement—the excitement you feel when a door closes and your house sinks back to normal and you let yourself loose into all the free space around you. That was in my father's voice too—behind the apology, a queer sound like a gulped breath. But my mother hadn't been a burden—she hadn't been sick a day—and far from feeling relieved at her death, my father took it hard. He never got used to living alone, he said. He went into the Netterfield Country Home quite willingly.

He told me how he found my mother on the couch in the kitchen when he came in at noon. She had picked a few tomatoes, and was setting them on the windowsill to ripen; then she must have felt weak, and lain down. Now, telling this, his voice went wobbly—meandering, as you would expect—in his amazement. I saw in my mind the couch, the old quilt that protected it, right under the phone.

'So I thought I better call you,' my father said, and he waited for me to say what he should do now.

My mother prayed on her knees at midday, at night, and first thing in the morning. Every day opened up to her to have God's will done in it. Every night she totted up what she'd done and said and thought, to see how it squared with Him. That kind of life is dreary, people think, but they're missing the point. For one thing, such a life can never be boring. And nothing can happen to you that you can't make use of. Even if you're wracked by troubles, and sick and poor and ugly, you've got your soul to carry through life like a treasure on a platter. Going upstairs to pray after the noon meal, my mother would be full of energy and expectation, seriously smiling.

She was saved at a camp meeting[1] when she was fourteen. That was the same summer that her own mother—my grandmother—died. For a few years, my mother went to meetings with a lot of other people who'd been saved, some who'd been saved over and over again, enthusiastic old sinners. She could tell stories about what went on at those meetings, the singing and hollering and wildness. She told about one old man getting up and shouting, 'Come down, O Lord, come down among us now! Come down through the roof and I'll pay for the shingles!'

She was back to being just an Anglican, a serious one, by the time she got married. She was about twenty-five then, and my father was thirty-eight. A tall good-looking couple, good dancers, good cardplayers, sociable. But serious people—that's how I would try to describe them. Serious the way hardly anybody is anymore. My father was not religious in the way my mother was. He was an Anglican, an Orangeman, a Conservative, because that's what he had been brought up to be. He was the son who got left on the farm with his parents and took care of them till they died. He met my mother, he waited for her, they married; he thought himself lucky then to have a family to work for. (I have two brothers, and I had a baby sister who died.) I have a feeling that my father never slept with any woman before my mother, and never with her until he married her. And he had to wait, because my mother couldn't get married until she had paid back to her own father every cent he had spent on her since her mother died. She had kept track of everything—board, books, clothes—so that she could pay it back. When she married, she had no nest egg, as teachers usually did, no hope chest, sheets, or dishes. My father used to say, with a sombre, joking face, that he had hoped to get a woman with money in the bank. 'But you take money in the bank, you have to take the face that goes with it,' he said, 'and sometimes that's no bargain.'

The house we lived in had big, high rooms, with dark-green blinds on the windows. When the blinds were pulled down against the sun, I used to like to move my head

1 An evangelical religious rally (in Ontario, usually Methodist), held outdoors or in a tent, and characterized by enthusiastic worship and altar calls; for many individuals, such camp meetings were accompanied by the tremendous emotional release that followed a conversion experience.

and catch the light flashing through the holes and cracks. Another thing I liked looking at was chimney stains, old or fresh, which I could turn into animals, people's faces, even distant cities. I told my own two boys about that, and their father, Dan Casey, said, 'See, your mom's folks were so poor, they couldn't afford TV, so they got these stains on the ceiling—your mom had to watch the stains on the ceiling!' He always liked to kid me about thinking poor was anything great.

When my father was very old, I figured out that he didn't mind people doing new sorts of things—for instance, my getting divorced—as much as he minded them having new sorts of reasons for doing them.

Thank God he never had to know about the commune.

'The Lord never intended,' he used to say. Sitting around with the other old men in the Home, in the long, dim porch behind the spirea bushes, he talked about how the Lord never intended for people to tear around the country on motorbikes and snowmobiles. And how the Lord never intended for nurses' uniforms to be pants. The nurses didn't mind at all. They called him 'Handsome', and told me he was a real old sweetheart, a real old religious gentleman. They marvelled at his thick black hair, which he kept until he died. They washed and combed it beautifully, wet-waved it with their fingers.

Sometimes, with all their care, he was a little unhappy. He wanted to go home. He worried about the cows, the fences, about who was getting up to light the fire. A few flashes of meanness—very few. Once, he gave me a sneaky, unfriendly look when I went in; he said, 'I'm surprised you haven't worn all the skin off your knees by now.'

I laughed. I said, 'What doing? Scrubbing floors?'

'Praying?' he said, in a voice like spitting.

He didn't know who he was talking to.

I don't remember my mother's hair being anything but white. My mother went white in her twenties, and never saved any of her young hair, which had been brown. I used to try to get her to tell me what colour brown.

'Dark.'

'Like Brent, or like Dolly?' Those were two workhorses we had, a team.

'I don't know. It wasn't horsehair.'

'Was it like chocolate?'

'Something like.'

'Weren't you sad when it went white?'

'No. I was glad.'

'Why?'

'I was glad that I wouldn't have hair anymore that was the same colour as my father's.'

Hatred is always a sin, my mother told me. Remember that. One drop of hatred in your soul will spread and discolour everything like a drop of black ink in white milk. I was struck by that and meant to try it, but knew I shouldn't waste the milk.

All these things I remember. All the things I know, or have been told, about people I never even saw. I was named Euphemia, after my mother's mother. A terrible name, such as nobody has nowadays. At home they called me Phemie, but when I started to work, I called myself Fame. My husband, Dan Casey, called me Fame. Then in the bar of the Shamrock Hotel, years later, after my divorce, when I was going out, a man said to me, 'Fame, I've been meaning to ask you, just what is it you are famous for?'

'I don't know,' I told him. 'I don't know, unless it's for wasting my time talking to jerks like you.'

After that I thought of changing it altogether, to something like Joan, but unless I moved away from here, how could I do that?

In the summer of 1947, when I was twelve, I helped my mother paper the downstairs bedroom, the spare room. My mother's sister, Beryl, was coming to visit us. These two sisters hadn't seen each other for years. Very soon after their mother died, their father married again. He went to live in Minneapolis, then in Seattle, with his new wife and his young daughter, Beryl. My mother wouldn't go with them. She stayed on in the town of Ramsay, where they had been living. She was boarded with a childless couple who had been neighbours. She and Beryl had met only once or twice since they were grown up. Beryl lived in California.

The paper had a design of cornflowers on a white ground. My mother had got it at a reduced price, because it was the end of a lot. This meant we had trouble matching the pattern, and behind the door we had to do some tricky fitting with scraps and strips. This was before the days of pre-pasted wallpaper. We had a trestle table set up in the front room, and we mixed the paste and swept it onto the back of the paper with wide brushes, watching for lumps. We worked with the windows up, screens fitted under them, the front door open, the screen door closed. The country we could see through the mesh of screens and the wavery old window glass was all hot and flowering—milkweed and wild carrot in the pastures, mustard rampaging in the clover, some fields creamy with the buckwheat people grew then. My mother sang. She sang a song she said her own mother used to sing when she and Beryl were little girls.

'I once had a sweetheart, but now I have none.
He's gone and he's left me to weep and to moan.
He's gone and he's left me, but contented I'll be,
For I'll get another one, better than he!'

I was excited because Beryl was coming, a visitor, all the way from California. Also because I had gone to town in late June to write the Entrance Examinations,[2] and was hoping to hear soon that I had passed with honours. Everybody who had finished Grade 8 in the country schools had to go into town to write those examinations. I loved that—the rustling sheets of foolscap, the important silence, the big stone high-school building, all the old initials carved in the desks, darkened with varnish. The first burst of summer outside, the green and yellow light, the townlike chestnut trees, and honeysuckle. And all it was was this same town, where I have lived now more than half

2 Examinations used throughout Ontario for entrance into secondary school, they divided students up into vocational and academic streams.

my life. I wondered at it. And at myself, drawing maps with ease and solving problems, knowing quantities of answers. I thought I was so clever. But I wasn't clever enough to understand the simplest thing. I didn't even understand that examinations made no difference in my case. I wouldn't be going to high school. How could I? That was before there were school buses; you had to board in town. My parents didn't have the money. They operated on very little cash, as many farmers did then. The payments from the cheese factory were about all that came in regularly. And they didn't think of my life going in that direction, the high-school direction. They thought that I would stay at home and help my mother, maybe hire out to help women in the neighbourhood who were sick or having a baby. Until such time as I got married. That was what they were waiting to tell me when I got the results of the examinations.

You would think my mother might have a different idea, since she had been a schoolteacher herself. But she said God didn't care. God isn't interested in what kind of job or what kind of education anybody has, she told me. He doesn't care two hoots about that, and it's what He cares about that matters.

This was the first time I understood how God could become a real opponent, not just some kind of nuisance or large decoration.

My mother's name as a child was Marietta. That continued to be her name, of course, but until Beryl came I never heard her called by it. My father always said Mother. I had a childish notion—I knew it was childish—that Mother suited my mother better than it did other mothers. Mother, not Mama. When I was away from her, I could not think what my mother's face was like, and this frightened me. Sitting in school, just over a hill from home, I would try to picture my mother's face. Sometimes I thought that if I couldn't do it, that might mean my mother was dead. But I had a sense of her all the time, and would be reminded of her by the most unlikely things—an upright piano, or a tall white loaf of bread. That's ridiculous, but true.

Marietta, in my mind, was separate, not swallowed up in my mother's grown-up body. Marietta was still running around loose up in her town of Ramsay, on the Ottawa River. In that town, the streets were full of horses and puddles, and darkened by men who came in from the bush on weekends. Loggers. There were eleven hotels on the main street, where the loggers stayed, and drank.

The house Marietta lived in was halfway up a steep street climbing from the river. It was a double house, with two bay windows in front, and a wooden trellis that separated the two front porches. In the other half of the house lived the Sutcliffes, the people Marietta was to board with after her mother died and her father left town. Mr Sutcliffe was an Englishman, a telegraph operator. His wife was German. She always made coffee instead of tea. She made strudel. The dough for the strudel hung down over the edges of the table like a fine cloth. It sometimes looked to Marietta like a skin.

Mrs Sutcliffe was the one who talked Marietta's mother out of hanging herself.

Marietta was home from school that day, because it was Saturday. She woke up late and heard the silence in the house. She was always scared of that—a silent house—and as soon as she opened the door after school she would call, 'Mama! Mama!' Often her mother wouldn't answer. But she would be there. Marietta would hear with relief the rattle of the stove grate or the steady slap of the iron.

That morning, she didn't hear anything. She came downstairs, and got herself a slice of bread and butter and molasses, folded over. She opened the cellar door and called. She went into the front room and peered out the window, through the bridal fern. She saw her little sister, Beryl, and some other neighbourhood children rolling down the bit of grassy terrace to the sidewalk, picking themselves up and scrambling to the top and rolling down again.

'Mama?' called Marietta. She walked through the house to the back yard. It was late spring, the day was cloudy and mild. In the sprouting vegetable gardens, the earth was damp, and the leaves on the trees seemed suddenly full-sized, letting down drops of water left over from the rain of the night before.

'Mama?' calls Marietta under the trees, under the clothesline.

At the end of the yard is a small barn, where they keep firewood, and some tools and old furniture. A chair, a straight-backed wooden chair, can be seen through the open doorway. On the chair, Marietta sees her mother's feet, her mother's black laced shoes. Then the long, printed cotton summer work dress, the apron, the rolled-up sleeves. Her mother's shiny-looking white arms, and neck, and face.

Her mother stood on the chair and didn't answer. She didn't look at Marietta, but smiled and tapped her foot, as if to say, 'Here I am, then. What are you going to do about it?' Something looked wrong about her, beyond the fact that she was standing on a chair and smiling in this queer, tight way. Standing on an old chair with back rungs missing, which she had pulled out to the middle of the barn floor, where it teetered on the bumpy earth. There was a shadow on her neck.

The shadow was a rope, a noose on the end of a rope that hung down from a beam overhead.

'Mama?' says Marietta, in a fainter voice. 'Mama. Come down, please.' Her voice is faint because she fears that any yell or cry might jolt her mother into movement, cause her to step off the chair and throw her weight on the rope. But even if Marietta wanted to yell she couldn't. Nothing but this pitiful thread of a voice is left to her—just as in a dream when a beast or a machine is bearing down on you.

'Go and get your father.'

That was what her mother told her to do, and Marietta obeyed. With terror in her legs, she ran. In her nightgown, in the middle of a Saturday morning, she ran. She ran past Beryl and the other children, still tumbling down the slope. She ran along the sidewalk, which was at that time a boardwalk, then on the unpaved street, full of last night's puddles. The street crossed the railway tracks. At the foot of the hill, it intersected the main street of the town. Between the main street and the river were some warehouses and the buildings of small manufacturers. That was where Marietta's father had his carriage works. Wagons, buggies, sleds were made there. In fact, Marietta's father had invented a new sort of sled to carry logs in the bush. It had been patented. He was just getting started in Ramsay. (Later on, in the States, he made money. A man fond of hotel bars, barbershops, harness races, women, but not afraid of work—give him credit.)

Marietta did not find him at work that day. The office was empty. She ran out into the yard where the men were working. She stumbled in the fresh sawdust. The men laughed and shook their heads at her. No. Not here. Not a-here right now. No. Why don't you try upstreet? Wait. Wait a minute. Hadn't you better get some clothes on first?

They didn't mean any harm. They didn't have the sense to see that something must be wrong. But Marietta never could stand men laughing. There were always places she hated to go past, let alone into, and that was the reason. Men laughing. Because of that, she hated barbershops, hated their smell. (When she started going to dances later on with my father, she asked him not to put any dressing on his hair, because the smell reminded her.) A bunch of men standing out on the street, outside a hotel, seemed to Marietta like a clot of poison. You tried not to hear what they were saying, but you could be sure it was vile. If they didn't say anything, they laughed and vileness spread out from them—poison—just the same. It was only after Marietta was saved that she could walk right past them. Armed by God, she walked through their midst and nothing stuck to her, nothing scorched her; she was safe as Daniel.[3]

Now she turned and ran, straight back the way she had come. Up the hill, running to get home. She thought she had made a mistake leaving her mother. Why did her mother tell her to go? Why did she want her father? Quite possibly so that she could greet him with the sight of her own warm body swinging on the end of a rope. Marietta should have stayed—she should have stayed and talked her mother out of it. She should have run to Mrs Sutcliffe, or any neighbour, not wasted time this way. She hadn't thought who could help, who could even believe what she was talking about. She had the idea that all families except her own lived in peace, that threats and miseries didn't exist in other people's houses, and couldn't be explained there.

A train was coming into town. Marietta had to wait. Passengers looked out at her from its windows. She broke out wailing in the faces of those strangers. When the train passed, she continued up the hill—a spectacle, with her hair uncombed, her feet bare and muddy, in her nightgown, with a wild, wet face. By the time she ran into her own yard, in sight of the barn, she was howling. 'Mama!' she was howling. 'Mama!'

Nobody was there. The chair was standing just where it had been before. The rope was dangling over the back of it. Marietta was sure that her mother had gone ahead and done it. Her mother was already dead—she had been cut down and taken away.

But warm, fat hands settled down on her shoulders, and Mrs Sutcliffe said, 'Marietta. Stop the noise. Marietta. Child. Stop the crying. Come inside. She is well, Marietta. Come inside and you will see.'

Mrs Sutcliffe's foreign voice said, 'Mari-et-cha', giving the name a rich, important sound. She was as kind as could be. When Marietta lived with the Sutcliffes later, she was treated as the daughter of the household, and it was a household just as peaceful

3 Daniel was a Hebrew prophet who spent his life as a captive in the court of Babylon but who refrained from partaking of the Babylonian king's bounty so that he 'would not defile himself'. The Book of Daniel recounts two stories of God's protecting those who are faithful to him: first, when Daniel's compatriots Shadrach, Meshach, and Abednego escape unscathed from a fiery furnace to which they are consigned for refusing to worship gods they do not believe in; and then when Daniel himself is delivered from the lions' den into which he had been thrown for his faithful observance of his religious customs.

and comfortable as she had imagined other households to be. But she never felt like a daughter there.

In Mrs Sutcliffe's kitchen, Beryl sat on the floor eating a raisin cookie and playing with the black-and-white cat, whose name was Dickie. Marietta's mother sat at the table, with a cup of coffee in front of her.

'She was silly,' Mrs Sutcliffe said. Did she mean Marietta's mother or Marietta herself? She didn't have many English words to describe things.

Marietta's mother laughed, and Marietta blacked out. She fainted, after running all that way uphill, howling, in the warm, damp morning. Next thing she knew, she was taking black, sweet coffee from a spoon held by Mrs Sutcliffe. Beryl picked Dickie up by the front legs and offered him as a cheering present. Marietta's mother was still sitting at the table.

Her heart was broken. That was what I always heard my mother say. That was the end of it. Those words lifted up the story and sealed it shut. I never asked, Who broke it? I never asked. What was the men's poison talk? What was the meaning of the word *vile*?

Marietta's mother laughed after not hanging herself. She sat at Mrs Sutcliffe's kitchen table long ago and laughed. Her heart was broken.

I always had a feeling, with my mother's talk and stories, of something swelling out behind. Like a cloud you couldn't see through, or get to the end of. There was a cloud, a poison, that had touched my mother's life. And when I grieved my mother, I became part of it. Then I would beat my head against my mother's stomach and breasts, against her tall, firm front, demanding to be forgiven. My mother would tell me to ask God. But it wasn't God, it was my mother I had to get straight with. It seemed as if she knew something about me that was worse, far worse, than ordinary lies and tricks and meanness; it was a really sickening shame. I beat against my mother's front to make her forget that.

My brothers weren't bothered by any of this. I don't think so. They seemed to me like cheerful savages, running around free, not having to learn much. And when I just had the two boys myself, no daughters, I felt as if something could stop now—the stories, and griefs, the old puzzles you can't resist or solve.

Aunt Beryl said not to call her Aunt. 'I'm not used to being anybody's aunt, honey. I'm not even anybody's momma. I'm just me. Call me Beryl.'

Beryl had started out as a stenographer, and now she had her own typing and bookkeeping business, which employed many girls. She had arrived with a man friend, whose name was Mr Florence. Her letter had said she would be getting a ride with a friend, but she hadn't said whether the friend would be staying or going on. She hadn't even said if it was a man or woman.

Mr Florence was staying. He was a tall, thin man with a long, tanned face, very light-coloured eyes, and a way of twitching the corner of his mouth that might have been a smile.

He was the one who got to sleep in the room that my mother and I had papered, because he was the stranger, and a man. Beryl had to sleep with me. At first we thought that Mr Florence was quite rude, because he wasn't used to our way of talking and we weren't used to his. The first morning, my father said to Mr Florence, 'Well, I hope you got some kind of a sleep on that old bed in there?' (The spare-room bed was heavenly, with a feather tick.[4]) This was Mr Florence's cue to say that he had never slept better.

Mr Florence twitched. He said, 'I slept on worse.'

His favourite place to be was in his car. His car was a royal-blue Chrysler, from the first batch turned out after the war. Inside it, the upholstery and floor covering and roof and door padding were all pearl grey. Mr Florence kept the names of those colours in mind and corrected you if you said just 'blue' or 'grey'.

'Mouse skin is what it looks like to me,' said Beryl rambunctiously. 'I tell him it's just mouse skin!'

The car was parked at the side of the house, under the locust trees. Mr Florence sat inside with the windows rolled up, smoking, in the rich new-car smell.

'I'm afraid we're not doing much to entertain your friend,' my mother said.

'I wouldn't worry about him,' said Beryl. She always spoke about Mr Florence as if there was a joke about him that only she appreciated. I wondered long afterward if he had a bottle in the glove compartment and took a nip from time to time to keep his spirits up. He kept his hat on.

Beryl herself was being entertained enough for two. Instead of staying in the house and talking to my mother, as a lady visitor usually did, she demanded to be shown everything there was to see on a farm. She said that I was to take her around and explain things, and see that she didn't fall into any manure piles.

I didn't know what to show. I took Beryl to the icehouse, where chunks of ice the size of dresser drawers, or bigger, lay buried in sawdust. Every few days, my father would chop off a piece of ice and carry it to the kitchen, where it melted in a tin-lined box and cooled the milk and butter.

Beryl said she had never had any idea ice came in pieces that big. She seemed intent on finding things strange, or horrible, or funny.

'Where in the world do you get ice that big?'

I couldn't tell if that was a joke.

'Off of the lake,' I said.

'Off of the lake! Do you have lakes up here that have ice on them all summer?'

I told her how my father cut the ice on the lake every winter and hauled it home, and buried it in sawdust, and that kept it from melting.

Beryl said, 'That's amazing!'

'Well, it melts a little,' I said. I was deeply disappointed in Beryl.

'That's really amazing.'

Beryl went along when I went to get the cows. A scarecrow in white slacks (this is what my father called her afterward), with a white sun hat tied under her chin by a flaunting red ribbon. Her fingernails and toenails—she wore sandals—were painted to match the ribbon. She wore the small, dark sunglasses people wore at that time. (Not the people I knew—they didn't own sunglasses.) She had a big red mouth, a loud laugh, hair of an unnatural colour and a high gloss, like cherry wood. She was so noisy

4 Mattress.

and shiny, so glamorously got up, that it was hard to tell whether she was good-looking, or happy, or anything.

We didn't have any conversation along the cowpath, because Beryl kept her distance from the cows and was busy watching where she stepped. Once I had them all tied in their stalls, she came closer. She lit a cigarette. Nobody smoked in the barn. My father and other farmers chewed tobacco there instead. I didn't see how I could ask Beryl to chew tobacco.

'Can you get the milk out of them or does your father have to?' Beryl said. 'Is it hard to do?'

I pulled some milk down through the cow's teat. One of the barn cats came over and waited. I shot a thin stream into its mouth. The cat and I were both showing off.

'Doesn't that hurt?' said Beryl. 'Think if it was you.'

I had never thought of a cow's teat as corresponding to any part of myself, and was shaken by this indecency. In fact, I could never grasp a warm, warty teat in such a firm and casual way again.

Beryl slept in a peach-coloured rayon nightgown trimmed with écru lace. She had a robe to match. She was just as careful about the word *écru* as Mr Florence was about his royal blue and pearl grey.

I managed to get undressed and put on my nightgown without any part of me being exposed at any time. An awkward business. I left my underpants on, and hoped that Beryl had done the same. The idea of sharing my bed with a grownup was a torment to me. But I did get to see the contents of what Beryl called her beauty kit. Hand-painted glass jars contained puffs of cotton wool, talcum powder, milky lotion, ice-blue astringent. Little pots of red and mauve rouge—rather greasy-looking. Blue and black pencils. Emery boards, a pumice stone, nail polish with an overpowering smell of bananas, face powder in a celluloid box shaped like a shell, with the name of a dessert—Apricot Delight.

I had heated some water on the coal-oil stove we used in summertime. Beryl scrubbed her face clean, and there was such a change that I almost expected to see makeup lying in strips in the washbowl, like the old wallpaper we had soaked and peeled. Beryl's skin was pale now, covered with fine cracks, rather like the shiny mud at the bottom of puddles drying up in early summer.

'Look what happened to my skin,' she said. 'Dieting. I weighed a hundred and sixty-nine pounds once, I took it off too fast and my face fell in on me. Now I've got this cream, though. It's made from a secret formula and you can't even buy it commercially. Smell it. See, it doesn't smell all perfumy. It smells serious.'

She was patting the cream on her face with puffs of cotton wool, patting away until there was nothing to be seen on the surface.

'It smells like lard,' I said.

'Christ almighty, I hope I haven't been paying that kind of money to rub lard on my face. Don't tell your mother I swear.'

She poured clean water into the drinking glass and wet her comb, then combed her hair wet and twisted each strand around her finger, clamping the twisted strand to her head with two crossed pins. I would be doing the same myself, a couple of years later.

'Always do your hair wet, else it's no good doing it up at all,' Beryl said. 'And always roll it under even if you want it to flip up. See?'

When I was doing my hair up—as I did for years—I sometimes thought of this, and thought that of all the pieces of advice people had given me, this was the one I had followed most carefully.

We put the lamp out and got into bed, and Beryl said, 'I never knew it could get so dark. I've never known a dark that was as dark as this.' She was whispering. I was slow to understand that she was comparing country nights to city nights, and I wondered if the darkness in Netterfield County could really be greater than that in California.

'Honey?' whispered Beryl. 'Are there any animals outside?'

'Cows,' I said.

'Yes, but wild animals? Are there bears?'

'Yes,' I said. My father had once found bear tracks and droppings in the bush, and the apples had all been torn off a wild apple tree. That was years ago, when he was a young man.

Beryl moaned and giggled. 'Think if Mr Florence had to go out in the night and he ran into a bear!'

Next day was Sunday. Beryl and Mr Florence drove my brothers and me to Sunday school in the Chrysler. That was at ten o'clock in the morning. They came back at eleven to bring my parents to church.

'Hop in,' Beryl said to me. 'You too,' she said to the boys. 'We're going for a drive.'

Beryl was dressed up in a satiny ivory dress with red dots, and a red-lined frill over the hips, and red high-heeled shoes. Mr Florence wore a pale-blue summer suit.

'Aren't you going to church?' I said. That was what people dressed up for, in my experience.

Beryl laughed. 'Honey, this isn't Mr Florence's kind of religion.'

I was used to going straight from Sunday school into church, and sitting for another hour and a half. In summer, the open windows let in the cedary smell of the graveyard and the occasional, almost sacrilegious sound of a car swooshing by on the road. Today we spent this time driving through country I had never seen before. I had never seen it, though it was less than twenty miles from home. Our truck went to the cheese factory, to church, and to town on Saturday nights. The nearest thing to a drive was when it went to the dump. I had seen the near end of Bell's Lake, because that was where my father cut the ice in winter. You couldn't get close to it in summer; the shoreline was all choked up with bulrushes. I had thought that the other end of the lake would look pretty much the same, but when we drove there today, I saw cottages, docks and boats, dark water reflecting the trees. All this and I hadn't known about it. This too was Bell's Lake. I was glad to have seen it at last, but in some way not altogether glad of the surprise.

Finally, a white frame building appeared, with verandas and potted flowers, and some twinkling poplar trees in front. The Wildwood Inn. Today the same building is covered with stucco and done up with Tudor beams and called the Hideaway. The poplar trees have been cut down for a parking lot.

On the way back to the church to pick up my parents, Mr Florence turned in to the farm next to ours, which belonged to the McAllisters. The McAllisters were Catholics. Our two families were neighbourly but not close.

'Come on, boys, out you get,' said Beryl to my brothers. 'Not you,' she said to me. 'You stay put.' She herded the little boys up to the porch, where some McAllisters were watching. They were in their raggedy home clothes, because their church, or Mass, or whatever it was, got out early. Mrs McAllister came out and stood listening, rather dumbfounded, to Beryl's laughing talk.

Beryl came back to the car by herself. 'There,' she said. 'They're going to play with the neighbour children.'

Play with McAllisters? Besides being Catholics, all but the baby were girls.

'They've still got their good clothes on,' I said.

'So what? Can't they have a good time with their good clothes on? I do!'

My parents were taken by surprise as well. Beryl got out and told my father he was to ride in the front seat, for the legroom. She got into the back, with my mother and me. Mr Florence turned again onto the Bell's Lake road, and Beryl announced that we were all going to the Wildwood Inn for dinner.

'You're all dressed up, why not take advantage?' she said. 'We dropped the boys off with your neighbours. I thought they might be too young to appreciate it. The neighbours were happy to have them.' She said with a further emphasis that it was to be their treat. Hers and Mr Florence's.

'Well, now,' said my father. He probably didn't have five dollars in his pocket. 'Well, now. I wonder do they let the farmers in?'

He made various jokes along this line. In the hotel dining room, which was all in white—white tablecloths, white painted chairs—with sweating glass water pitchers and high, whirring fans, he picked up a table napkin the size of a diaper and spoke to me in a loud whisper, 'Can you tell me what to do with this thing? Can I put it on my head to keep the draft off?'

Of course he had eaten in hotel dining rooms before. He knew about table napkins and pie forks. And my mother knew—she wasn't even a country woman, to begin with. Nevertheless this was a huge event. Not exactly a pleasure—as Beryl must have meant it to be—but a huge, unsettling event. Eating a meal in public, only a few miles from home, eating in a big room full of people you didn't know, the food served by a stranger, a snippy-looking girl who was probably a college student working at a summer job.

'I'd like the rooster,' my father said. 'How long has he been in the pot?' It was only good manners, as he knew it, to joke with people who waited on him.

'Beg your pardon?' the girl said.

'Roast chicken,' said Beryl. 'Is that okay for everybody?'

Mr Florence was looking gloomy. Perhaps he didn't care for jokes when it was his money that was being spent. Perhaps he had counted on something better than ice water to fill up the glasses.

The waitress put down a dish of celery and olives, and my mother said, 'Just a minute while I give thanks.' She bowed her head and said quietly but audibly, 'Lord, bless this food to our use, and us to Thy service, for Christ's sake. Amen.' Refreshed, she sat up straight and passed the dish to me, saying, 'Mind the olives. There's stones in them.'

Beryl was smiling around at the room.

The waitress came back with a basket of rolls.

'Parker House!' Beryl learned over and breathed in their smell. 'Eat them while they're hot enough to melt the butter!'

Mr Florence twitched, and peered into the butter dish. 'Is that what this is—butter? I thought it was Shirley Temple's curls.'

His face was hardly less gloomy than before, but it was a joke, and his making it seemed to convey to us something of the very thing that had just been publicly asked for—a blessing.

'When he says something funny', said Beryl—who often referred to Mr Florence as 'he' even when he was right there—'you notice how he always keeps a straight face? That reminds me of Mama. I mean of our mama, Marietta's and mine. Daddy, when he made a joke you could see it coming a mile away—he couldn't keep it off his face—but Mama was another story. She could look so sour. But she could joke on her deathbed. In fact, she did that very thing. Marietta, remember when she was in bed in the front room the spring before she died?'

'I remember she was in bed in that room,' my mother said. 'Yes.'

'Well, Daddy came in and she was lying there in her clean nightgown, with the covers off, because the German lady from next door had just been helping her take a wash, and she was still there tidying up the bed. So Daddy wanted to be cheerful, and he said, "Spring must be coming. I saw a crow today." This must have been in March. And Mama said quick as a shot, "Well, you better cover me up then, before it looks in that window and gets any ideas!" The German lady—Daddy said she just about dropped the basin. Because it was true, Mama was skin and bones; she was dying. But she could joke.'

Mr Florence said, 'Might as well when there's no use to cry.'

'But she could carry a joke too far, Mama could. One time, one time, she wanted to give Daddy a scare. He was supposed to be interested in some girl that kept coming around to the works. Well, he was a big good-looking man. So Mama said, "Well, I'll just do away with myself, and you can get on with her and see how you like it when I come back and haunt you." He told her not to be so stupid, and he went off downtown. And Mama went out to the barn and climbed on a chair and put a rope around her neck. Didn't she, Marietta? Marietta went looking for her and she found her like that!'

My mother bent her head and put her hands in her lap, almost as if she was getting ready to say another grace.

'Daddy told me all about it, but I can remember anyway. I remember Marietta tearing off down the hill in her nightie, and I guess the German lady saw her go, and she came out and was looking for Mama, and somehow we all ended up in the barn—me too, and some kids I was playing with—and there was Mama up on a chair preparing to give Daddy the fright of his life. She'd sent Marietta after him. And the German lady starts wailing, "Oh, missus, come down missus, think of your little *kindren*"—"*kindren*" is the German for "*children*"—"think of your *kindren*," and so on. Until it was me standing there—I was just a little squirt, but I was the one noticed that rope. My eyes followed that rope up and up and I saw it was just hanging over the beam, just flung there—it wasn't tied at all! Marietta hadn't noticed that, the German lady hadn't noticed it. But I just spoke up and said, "Mama, how are you going to manage to hang yourself without that rope tied around the beam?"'

Mr Florence said, 'That'd be a tough one.'

'I spoiled her game. The German lady made coffee and we went over there and had a few treats, and, Marietta, you couldn't find Daddy after all, could you? You could hear Marietta howling, coming up the hill, a block away.'

'Natural for her to be upset,' my father said.

'Sure it was. Mama went too far.'

'She meant it,' my mother said. 'She meant it more than you give her credit for.'

'She meant to get a rise out of Daddy. That was their whole life together. He always said she was a hard woman to live with, but she had a lot of character. I believe he missed that, with Gladys.'

'I wouldn't know,' my mother said, in that particularly steady voice with which she always spoke of her father. 'What he did say or didn't say.'

'People are dead now,' said my father. 'It isn't up to us to judge.'

'I know,' said Beryl. 'I know Marietta's always had a different view.'

My mother looked at Mr Florence and smiled quite easily and radiantly. 'I'm sure you don't know what to make of all these family matters.'

The one time that I visited Beryl, when Beryl was an old woman, all knobby and twisted up with arthritis, Beryl said, 'Marietta got all Daddy's looks. And she never did a thing with herself. Remember her wearing that old navy-blue crêpe dress when we went to the hotel that time? Of course, I know it was probably all she had, but did it have to be all she had? You know, I was scared of her somehow. I couldn't stay in a room alone with her. But she had outstanding looks.' Trying to remember an occasion when I had noticed my mother's looks, I thought of the time in the hotel, my mother's pale-olive skin against the heavy white, coiled hair, her open, handsome face smiling at Mr Florence—as if he was the one to be forgiven.

I didn't have a problem right away with Beryl's story. For one thing, I was hungry and greedy, and a lot of my attention went to the roast chicken and gravy and mashed potatoes laid on the plate with an ice-cream scoop and the bright diced vegetables out of a can, which I thought much superior to those fresh from the garden. For dessert, I had a butterscotch sundae, an agonizing choice over chocolate. The others had plain vanilla ice cream.

Why shouldn't Beryl's version of the same event be different from my mother's? Beryl was strange in every way—everything about her was slanted, seen from a new angle. It was my mother's version that held, for a time. It absorbed Beryl's story, closed over it. But Beryl's story didn't vanish; it stayed sealed off for years, but it wasn't gone.

It was like the knowledge of that hotel and dining room. I knew about it now, though I didn't think of it as a place to go back to. And indeed, without Beryl's or Mr Florence's money, I couldn't. But I knew it was there.

The next time I was in the Wildwood Inn, in fact, was after I was married. The Lions Club had a banquet and dance there. The man I had married, Dan Casey, was a Lion. You could get a drink there by that time. Dan Casey wouldn't have gone anywhere you couldn't. Then the place was remodelled into the Hideaway, and now they have strippers every night but Sunday. On Thursday nights, they have a male stripper. I go there with people from the real estate office to celebrate birthdays or other big events.

The farm was sold for five thousand dollars in 1965. A man from Toronto bought it, for a hobby farm or just an investment. After a couple of years, he rented it to a commune. They stayed there, different people drifting on and off, for a dozen years or so. They raised goats and sold the milk to the health-food store that had opened up in town. They painted a rainbow across the side of the barn that faced the road. They hung tie-dyed sheets over the windows, and let the long grass and flowering weeds reclaim the yard. My parents had finally got electricity in, but these people didn't use it. They preferred oil lamps and the woodstove, and taking their dirty clothes to town. People said they wouldn't know how to handle lamps or wood fires, and they would burn the place down. But they didn't. In fact, they didn't manage badly. They kept the house and barn in some sort of repair and they worked a big garden. They even dusted their potatoes against blight—though I heard that there was some sort of row about this and some of the stricter members left. The place actually looked a lot better than many of the farms round about that were still in the hands of the original families. The McAllister son had started a wrecking business on their place. My own brothers were long gone.

I knew I was not being reasonable, but I had the feeling that I'd rather see the farm suffer outright neglect—I'd sooner see it in the hands of hoodlums and scroungers—than see that rainbow on the barn, and some letters that looked Egyptian painted on the wall of the house. They seemed a mockery. I even disliked the sight of those people when they came to town—the men with their hair in ponytails, and with holes in their overalls that I believed were cut on purpose, and the women with long hair and no makeup and their meek, superior expressions. What do you know about life, I felt like asking them. What makes you think you can come here and mock my father and mother and their life and their poverty? But when I thought of the rainbow and those letters, I knew they weren't trying to mock or imitate my parent's life. They had displaced that life, hardly knowing it existed. They had set up in its place these beliefs and customs of their own, which I hoped would fail them.

That happened, more or less. The commune disintegrated. The goats disappeared. Some of the women moved to town, cut their hair, put on makeup, and got jobs as waitresses or cashiers to support their children. The Toronto man put the place up for sale, and after about a year it was sold for more than ten times what he had paid for it. A young couple from Ottawa bought it. They have painted the outside a pale grey with oyster trim, and have put in skylights and a handsome front door with carriage lamps on either side. Inside, they've changed it around so much that I've been told I'd never recognize it.

I did get in once, before this happened, during the year that the house was empty and for sale. The company I work for was handling it, and I had a key, though the house was being shown by another agent. I let myself in on a Sunday afternoon. I had a man with me, not a client but a friend—Bob Marks, whom I was seeing a lot at the time.

'This is that hippie place,' Bob Marks said when I stopped the car. 'I've been by here before.'

He was a lawyer, a Catholic, separated from his wife. He thought he wanted to settle down and start up a practice here in town. But there already was one Catholic lawyer. Business was slow. A couple of times a week, Bob Marks would be fairly drunk before supper.

'It's more than that,' I said. 'It's where I was born. Where I grew up.' We walked through the weeds, and I unlocked the door.

He said that he had thought, from the way I talked, that it would be farther out.

'It seemed farther then.'

All the rooms were bare, and the floors swept clean. The woodwork was freshly painted—I was surprised to see no smudges on the glass. Some new panes, some old wavy ones. Some of the walls had been stripped of their paper and painted. A wall in the kitchen was painted a deep blue, with an enormous dove on it. On a wall in the front room, giant sunflowers appeared, and a butterfly of almost the same size.

Bob Marks whistled. 'Somebody was an artist.'

'If that's what you want to call it,' I said, and turned back to the kitchen. The same woodstove was there. 'My mother once burned up three thousand dollars,' I said. 'She burned three thousand dollars in that stove.'

He whistled again, differently, 'What do you mean? She threw in a cheque?'

'No, no. It was in bills. She did it deliberately. She went into town to the bank and she had them give it all to her, in a shoebox. She brought it home and put it in the stove. She put it in just a few bills at a time, so it wouldn't make too big a blaze. My father stood and watched her.'

'What are you talking about?' said Bob Marks. 'I thought you were so poor.'

'We were. We were very poor.'

'So how come she had three thousand dollars? That would be like thirty thousand today. Easily. More than thirty thousand today.'

'It was her legacy,' I said. 'It was what she got from her father. Her father died in Seattle and left her three thousand dollars, and she burned it up because she hated him. She didn't want his money. She hated him.'

'That's a lot of hate,' Bob Marks said.

'That isn't the point. Her hating him, or whether he was bad enough for her to have a right to hate him. Not likely he was. That isn't the point.'

'Money,' he said. 'Money's always the point.'

'No. My father letting her do it is the point. To me it is. My father stood and watched and he never protested. If anybody had tried to stop her, he would have protected her. I consider that love.'

'Some people would consider it lunacy.'

I remember that that had been Beryl's opinion, exactly.

I went into the front room and stared at the butterfly, with its pink-and-orange wings. Then I went into the front bedroom and found two human figures painted on the wall. A man and a woman holding hands and facing straight ahead. They were naked, and larger than life size.

'It reminds me of that John Lennon and Yoko Ono picture,' I said to Bob Marks, who had come in behind me. 'That record cover, wasn't it?' I didn't want him to think that anything he had said in the kitchen had upset me.

Bob Marks said, 'Different colour hair.'

That was true. Both figures had yellow hair painted in a solid mass, the way they do it in comic strips. Horsetails of yellow hair curling over their shoulders and little pigtails of yellow hair decorating their not so private parts. Their skin was a flat beige pink and their eyes a staring blue, the same blue that was on the kitchen wall.

I noticed that they hadn't quite finished peeling the wallpaper away before making this painting. In the corner, there was some paper left that matched the paper on the other walls—a modernistic design of intersecting pink and grey and mauve bubbles. The man from Toronto must have put that on. The paper underneath hadn't been stripped off when this new paper went on. I could see an edge of it, the cornflowers on a white ground.

'I guess this was where they carried on their sexual shenanigans,' Bob Marks said, in a tone familiar to me. That thickened, sad, uneasy, but determined tone. The not particularly friendly lust of middle-aged respectable men.

I didn't say anything. I worked away some of the bubble paper to see more of the cornflowers. Suddenly I hit a loose spot, and ripped away a big swatch of it. But the cornflower paper came too, and a little shower of dried plaster.

'Why is it?' I said. 'Just tell me, why is it that no man can mention a place like this without getting around to the subject of sex in about two seconds flat? Just say the words *hippie* or *commune* and all you guys can think about is screwing! As if there wasn't anything at all behind it but orgies and fancy combinations and non-stop screwing! I get so sick of that—it's all so stupid it just makes me sick!'

In the car, on the way home from the hotel, we sat as before—the men in the front seat, the women in the back. I was in the middle, Beryl and my mother on either side of me. Their heated bodies pressed against me, through cloth; their smells crowded out the smells of the cedar bush we passed through, and the pockets of bog, where Beryl exclaimed at the water lilies. Beryl smelled of all those things in pots and bottles. My mother smelled of flour and hard soap and the warm crêpe of her good dress and the kerosene she had used to take the spots off.

'A lovely meal,' my mother said. 'Thank you, Beryl. Thank you, Mr Florence.'

'I don't know who is going to be fit to do the milking,' my father said. 'Now that we've all ate in such style.'

'Speaking of money,' said Beryl—though nobody actually had been—'do you mind my asking what you did with yours? I put mine in real estate. Real estate in California—you can't lose. I was thinking you could get an electric stove, so you wouldn't have to bother with a fire in summer or fool with that coal-oil thing, either one.'

All the other people in the car laughed, even Mr Florence.

'That's a good idea, Beryl,' said my father. 'We could use it to set things on till we get the electricity.'

'Oh, Lord,' said Beryl. 'How stupid can I get?'

'And we don't actually have the money, either,' my mother said cheerfully, as if she was continuing the joke.

But Beryl spoke sharply. 'You wrote me you got it. You got the same as me.'

My father half turned in his seat. 'What money are you talking about?' he said. 'What's this money?'

'From Daddy's will,' Beryl said. 'That you got last year. Look, maybe I shouldn't have asked. If you had to pay something off, that's still a good use, isn't it? It doesn't matter. We're all family here. Practically.'

'We didn't have to use it to pay anything off,' my mother said. 'I burned it.'

Then she told how she went into town in the truck, one day almost a year ago, and got them to give her the money in a box she had brought along for the purpose. She took it home, and put it in the stove and burned it.

My father turned around and faced the road ahead.

I could feel Beryl twisting beside me while my mother talked. She was twisting, and moaning a little, as if she had a pain she couldn't suppress. At the end of the story, she let out a sound of astonishment and suffering, an angry groan.

'So you burned up money!' she said. 'You burned up money in the stove.'

My mother was still cheerful. 'You sound as if I'd burned up one of my children.'

'You burned their chances. You burned up everything the money could have got for them.'

'The last thing my children need is money. None of us need his money.'

'That's criminal,' Beryl said harshly. She pitched her voice into the front seat: 'Why did you let her?'

'He wasn't there,' my mother said. 'Nobody was there.'

My father said, 'It was her money, Beryl.'

'Never mind,' Beryl said. 'That's criminal.'

'Criminal is for when you call in the police,' Mr Florence said. Like other things he had said that day, this created a little island of surprise and a peculiar gratitude.

Gratitude not felt by all.

'Don't you pretend this isn't the craziest thing you ever heard of,' Beryl shouted into the front seat. 'Don't you pretend you don't think so! Because it is, and you do. You think just the same as me!'

My father did not stand in the kitchen watching my mother feed the money into the flames. It wouldn't appear so. He did not know about it—it seems fairly clear, if I remember everything, that he did not know about it until that Sunday afternoon in Mr Florence's Chrysler, when my mother told them all together. Why, then, can I see the scene so clearly, just as I described it to Bob Marks (and to others—he was not the first)? I see my father standing by the table in the middle of the room—the table with the drawer in it for knives and forks, and the scrubbed oilcloth on top—and there is the box of money on the table. My mother is carefully dropping the bills into the fire. She holds the stove lid by the blackened lifter in one hand. And my father, standing by, seems not just to be permitting her to do this but to be protecting her. A solemn scene, but not crazy. People doing something that seems to them natural and necessary. At least, one of them is doing what seems natural and necessary, and the other believes that the important thing is for that person to be free, to go ahead. They understand that other people might not think so. They do not care.

How hard it is for me to believe that I made that up. It seems so much the truth it is the truth; it's what I believe about them. I haven't stopped believing it. But I have stopped telling that story. I never told it to anyone again after telling it to Bob Marks. I don't think so. I didn't stop just because it wasn't, strictly speaking, true. I stopped because I saw that I had to give up expecting people to see it the way I did. I had to give up expecting them to approve of any part of what was done. How could I even say that I approved of it myself? If I had been the sort of person who approved of that, who could do it, I wouldn't have done all I have done—run away from home to work in a restaurant in town when I was fifteen, gone to night school to learn typing and bookkeeping, got into the real-estate office, and finally become a licensed agent. I wouldn't be divorced. My father wouldn't have died in the county home. My hair would be white, as it has been naturally for years, instead of a colour called Copper Sunrise. And not one of these things would I change, not really, if I could.

Bob Marks was a decent man—good-hearted, sometimes with imagination. After I had lashed out at him like that, he said, 'You don't need to be so tough on us.' In a moment, he said, 'Was this your room when you were a little girl?' He thought that was why the mention of the sexual shenanigans had upset me.

And I thought it would be just as well to let him think that. I said yes, yes, it was my room when I was a little girl. It was just as well to make up right away. Moments of kindness and reconciliation are worth having, even if the parting has to come sooner or later. I wonder if those moments aren't more valued, and deliberately gone after, in the setups some people like myself have now, than they were in those old marriages, where love and grudges could be growing underground, so confused and stubborn, it must have seemed they had forever.

1996

Mordecai Richler

1931–2001

Born in Montreal at the beginning of the Depression, Mordecai Richler's experience of growing up in the working-class neighbourhood around St Urbain Street, and of attending Baron Byng, the predominantly Jewish high school nearby, is recorded in several of his novels and in the semi-autobiographical sketches collected in *The Street* (1969). Richler matured during the conflicts provoked by Fascism—the Spanish Civil War and the Second World War—and in his writing he has often expressed regret that his generation was too young to take part in that heroic struggle. The anti-Semitism that brought such horrifying consequences in Germany and that Richler himself encountered growing up has been a concern within his fiction.

As a student at Sir George Williams College (now part of Concordia University), Richler made friends with the veterans who were returning from the European conflicts; after they graduated he dropped out and, using savings from a life-insurance policy, left Canada. He spent his next two years in Europe, chiefly in Paris. While there he devoured the works of André Malraux, Ernest Hemingway, Louis Ferdinand Céline, Jean-Paul Sartre, and Albert Camus, and became part of a group of aspiring expatriate writers who would gather in the cafés to try out their wit and irony on each other: he has said that Paris 'was, in the truest sense, my university. St Germain des Prés was my campus, Montparnasse my frat house'.

Returning to Canada in 1952, Richler worked briefly for the CBC. In 1954 his first novel, *The Acrobats*—about Spain after the Spanish Civil War and written while Richler was in Europe—was published in England. An apprenticeship work, Richler later disavowed it and would not allow it back into print during his lifetime. (It was reprinted the year after his death, with an afterword by Richler's old friend Ted Kotcheff.)

Like many North Americans of his generation, Richler was convinced that he had to return to Europe to fulfill his literary ambitions, and he moved to England after *The Acrobats* appeared. The following year he published *Son of a Smaller Hero* (1955): an account of a young Jew's struggle to free himself from the restrictions of family, ghetto, and North American society in general, it ends with its protagonist's decision to leave Canada. His treatment of Montreal Jewry in that novel and his later ironic portrayal of the London expatriate writers and filmmakers who had taken refuge from American McCarthyism in *A Choice of Enemies* (1957) revealed Richler's willingness to expose for critical examination those communities of which he was a member—something that didn't always earn him the gratitude of those he scrutinized.

Although he did not return to Montreal until 1972, Richler continued to write about his Montreal past, and in 1959 he published the novel that established his reputation, *The Apprenticeship of Duddy Kravitz*, a morally ambiguous story about a bumptious young hustler who will go to any lengths to achieve his goals. In this novel and in *St. Urbain's Horseman* (1971), as well as in *Joshua Then and Now* (1980) and *Barney's Version* (1998), Richler shows one of the qualities that has won him readers: his impressive ability to create fully developed characters and to locate them in authentic and densely textured milieus. The two novels that Richler published in the sixties—*The Incomparable Atuk* (1963) and *Cocksure* (1968)—are works of a very different sort and show Richler's other great strength: his ability to create sharply aimed satires that discomfit the complacent. Indeed, these mordant and surreal fables marked him as the most vitriolic satirist of his generation, and the savage and frequently bawdy humour of *Cocksure* (one of Richler's own favourites) made it an object of controversy when it was chosen for a Governor General's Award.

Richler won a second Governor General's Award for *Saint Urbain's Horseman*, a story of Canadian expatriate film director Jake Hersh (he first appears in *The Apprenticeship of Duddy Kravitz*; Duddy reappears in this novel). Jake, all but overwhelmed by the 'competing mythologies' of the modern world and haunted by the catastrophe of the Holocaust, synthesizes a new mythic figure, a justice-bringer he calls 'the horseman', to suit his own needs—and must come to terms with the myth he has created.

Although Richler enjoyed making fun of the pretensions and limitations of the cultural nationalism that bloomed in the 1960s and 1970s, in *Solomon Gursky Was Here* (1989) he created his own version of the Canadian epic—a sprawling narrative that takes over (and sends up) the multi-generational family saga. Dealing with four generations and spanning over one hundred and thirty-eight years of Canadian history, it chronicles the fabulous and sometimes mysterious Gursky clan whose history makes Jews the fourth of the founding peoples of Canada. The novel plays with various historical events—the Franklin expedition gets an extended treatment—and individuals—including the early fur-trader Ezekiel Solomons, the entire Bronfman family (who built their giant liquor company out of Prohibition-era bootlegging), and the poet A.M. Klein—a figure who had always troubled Richler because of his employment as the Bronfmans' 'poet laureate'.

Barney's Version, Richler's valedictory novel and winner of the Giller Prize, is the story of a television producer, sixty-eight-year-old Barney Panofsky, a curiously loveable curmudgeon who, in response to an old rival's account of him as a poseur, a lecher, and a drunk, is writing out a version of his own life. As well as providing another occasion for Richler to direct his barbs at mass media and at a number of his other favourite targets, *Barney's Version* allowed him at the end of his life, to reflect on the way one consults memory and constructs, in age, a version of the story of that life.

In the 1990s, Richler, increasingly troubled by Quebec separatism, went on the attack, assuming the role of the most prominent public defender of Quebec's anglophones. Clearly enjoying the controversy he was provoking, he expanded his journalistic polemics into a book-length diatribe, *Oh Canada! Oh Quebec! Requiem for a Divided Country* (1992), in which he further disturbed Québécois nationalists by pointing to French Quebec's history of anti-Semitism. At the time of his death, Richler was working on another non-fiction work, this one about a private passion—the game of snooker. *On Snooker* was published posthumously in 2002.

Richler helped finance his career as a novelist and filled the time between novels by working as a freelance journalist and acerbic newspaper columnist. His journalism has been collected in *Hunting Tigers under Glass* (1968); *Shovelling Trouble* (1972); *The Great Comic Book Heroes and Other Essays* (1978); *Home Sweet Home: My Canadian Album* (1981); and *Broadsides: Reviews and Opinions* (1990). The many short pieces he has written over the years about sporting events were gathered in 2002 as *Dispatches from the Sporting Life*. Richler is the author of two popular children's books, *Jacob Two-Two Meets the Hooded Fang* (1975) and *Jacob Two-Two and the Dinosaur* (1987), and of the text of a travel book, *Images of Spain* (1977); he edited two anthologies: *Canadian Writing Today* (1970) and *The Best of Modern Humour* (1983).

For a time Richler supplemented his income by working as a scriptwriter for radio, television, and films (he scripted *Life at the Top*, 1965, and collaborated on several other films, including *Room at the Top*, 1959; *The Young and the Willing*, 1962; and *Fun with Dick and Jane*, 1977). He also wrote the scripts for adaptations of several of his own works, including *The Apprenticeship of Duddy Kravitz* (1974) and *Joshua Then and Now* (1985), both of which were directed by Ted Kotcheff. His experiences working in the film and TV industries are frequently refracted in his fiction—as in the biting depiction of European film community career politics and pretentious egoism in 'Playing Ball on Hampstead Heath' reprinted here. (Originally published separately in 1966, this story reappeared in revised form as a comic set piece midway through *St. Urbain's Horseman*; it also appears as the final selection in *Dispatches from the Sporting Life*)

From *St. Urbain's Horseman*

PLAYING BALL ON HAMPSTEAD HEATH

Sunday morning softball on Hampstead Heath in summer was unquestionably the fun thing to do. It was a ritual.

Manny Gordon tooled in all the way from Richmond, stowing a fielder's mitt and a thermos of martinis in the boot, clapping a sporty tweed cap over his bald head and strapping himself and his starlet of the night before into his Aston-Martin at nine a.m. C. Bernard Farber started out from Ham Common, picking up Al Levine, Bob Cohen, Jimmy Grief and Myer Gross outside Mary Quant's on the King's Road. Moey Hanover had once startled the staff at the Connaught by tripping down the stairs on a Sunday morning, wearing a peak cap and T-shirt and blue jeans, carrying his personal Babe Ruth bat in one hand and a softball in the other. Another Sunday Ziggy Alter had flown in from Rome, just for the sake of a restorative nine innings.

Frankie Demaine drove in from Marlow-on-Thames in his Maserati. Lou Caplan, Morty Calman, and Cy Levi usually brought their wives and children. Monty Talman, ever mindful of his latest twenty-one-year-old girlfriend, always cycled to the Heath from St. John's Wood. Wearing a maroon track suit, he usually lapped the field eight or nine times before anyone else turned up.

Jake generally strolled to the Heath, his tattered fielder's mitt and three enervating bagels filled with smoked salmon concealed under the *Observer* in his shopping bag. Some Sundays, like this one, possibly his last for a while, Nancy brought the kids along to watch.

The starting line-up on Sunday, June 28, 1963 was:

AL LEVINE'S TEAM	LOU CAPLAN'S BUNCH
Manny Gordon, ss.	Bob Cohen, 3b.
C. Bernard Farber, 2b.	Myer Gross, ss.
Jimmy Grief, 3b.	Frankie Demaine, lf.
Al Levine, cf.	Morty Calman, rf.
Monty Talman, 1b.	Cy Levi, 2b.
Ziggy Alter, lf.	Moey Hanover, c.
Jack Monroe, rf.	Johnny Roper, cf.
Sean Fielding, c.	Jason Storm, 1b.
Alfie Roberts, p.	Lou Caplan, p.

Jake, like five or six others who had arrived late and hung over (or who were unusually inept players), was a sub. A utility fielder, Jake sat on the bench with Lou Caplan's Bunch. It was a fine, all but cloudless morning, but looking around Jake felt there were too many wives, children, and kibitzers about. Even more ominous, the Filmmakers' First Wives Club or, as Ziggy Alter put it, the Alimony Gallery, was forming, seemingly relaxed but actually fulminating, on the grass behind home plate.

First Al Levine's Team and then Lou Caplan's Bunch, both sides made up mostly of men in their forties, trotted out, sunken bellies quaking, discs suddenly tender, hemorrhoids smarting, to take a turn at fielding and batting practice.

Nate Sugarman, once a classy shortstop, but since his coronary the regular umpire, bit into a digitalis pill, strode onto the field, and called, 'Play ball!'

'Let's go, boychick.'

'We need a hit,' Monty Talman, the producer, hollered.

'*You* certainly do,' Bob Cohen, who only yesterday had winced through a rough cut of Talman's latest fiasco, shouted back snidely from the opposite bench.

Manny, hunched over the plate cat-like, trying to look menacing, was knotted with more than his usual fill of anxiety. If he struck out, his own team would not be too upset because it was early in the game, but Lou Caplan, pitching for the first time since his Mexican divorce, would be grateful, and flattering Lou was a good idea because he was rumoured to be ready to go with a three-picture deal for Twentieth; and Manny had not been asked to direct a big-budget film since *Chase. Ball one, inside.* If, Manny thought, I hit a single I will be obliged to pass the time of day with that stomach-turning queen Jason Storm, 1b., who was in London to make a TV pilot film for Ziggy Alter. *Strike one, called.* He had never hit a homer, so that was out, but if come a miracle he connected for a triple, what then? He would be stuck on third sack with Bob Cohen, strictly second featuresville, a born loser, and Manny didn't want to be seen with Bob, even for an inning, especially with so many producers and agents about. K-NACK! *Goddammit, it's a hit! A double, for Chrissake!*

As the players on Al Levine's bench rose to a man, shouting encouragement—

'Go, man. Go.'

'Shake the lead out, Manny. Run!'

—Manny, conscious only of Lou Caplan glaring at him ('It's not my fault, Lou.'), scampered past first base and took myopic, round-shouldered aim on second, wondering should he say something shitty to Cy Levi, 2b., who he suspected was responsible for getting his name on the blacklist[1] years ago.

Next man up to the plate, C. Bernie Farber, who had signed to write Lou Caplan's first picture for Twentieth, struck out gracefully, which brought up Jimmy Grief. Jimmy swung on the first pitch, lifting it high and foul, and Moey Hanover, c., called for it, feeling guilty because next Saturday Jimmy was flying to Rome and Moey had already arranged to have lunch with Jimmy's wife on Sunday. Moey made the catch, which brought up Al Levine, who homered, bringing in Manny Gordon ahead of him. Monty Talman grounded out to Gross, ss., retiring the side.

Al Levine's Team, first inning: two hits, no errors, two runs.

Leading off for Lou Caplan's Bunch, Bob Cohen smashed a burner to centre for a single and Myer Gross fanned, bringing up Frankie Demaine and sending all the

1 A reference to the individuals in the motion picture industry who, as a result of the American government's anti-Communist 'witch hunts' of the 1950s led by US senator Joseph McCarthy, were blacklisted and unable to find further employment in Hollywood. Careers were ruined without evidence. Many who found themselves on the blacklist became expatriates and continued their work in film in Europe.

outfielders back, back, back. Frankie whacked the third pitch long and high, an easy fly had Al Levine been playing him deep left instead of inside right, where he was able to flirt hopefully with Manny Gordon's starlet, who was sprawled on the grass there in the shortest of possible Pucci prints. Al Levine was the only man on either team who always played wearing shorts—shorts revealing an elastic bandage which began at his left kneecap and ran almost as low as the ankle.

'Oh, you poor darling,' the starlet said, making a face at Levine's knee.

Levine, sucking in his stomach, replied, 'Spain,' as if he were the tossing the girl a rare coin.

'Don't tell me,' she squealed. 'The beach at Torremolinos. Ugh!'

'No, no,' Levine protested. 'The civil war, for Chrissake. Shrapnel. Defence of Madrid.'[2]

Demaine's fly fell for a homer, driving in a panting Bob Cohen.

Lou Caplan's Bunch, first inning: one hit, one error, two runs.

Neither side scored in the next two innings, which were noteworthy only because Moey Hanover's game began to slip badly. In the second Moey muffed an easy pop fly and actually let C. Bernie Farber, still weak on his legs after a cleansing, all but foodless, week at Forest Mere Hydro, steal a base on him. The problem was clearly Sean Fielding, the young RADA[3] graduate whom Columbia had put under contract because, in profile, he looked like Peter O'Toole. The game had only just started when Moey Hanover's wife, Lilian, had ambled over to Al Levine's bench and stretched herself out on the grass, an offering, beside Fielding, and the two of them had been giggling together and nudging each other ever since, which was making Moey nervy. Moey, however, had not spent his young manhood at a yeshiva[4] to no avail. Not only had he plundered the Old Testament for most of his winning *Rawhide* and *Bonanza* plots, but now that his Lilian was obviously in heat again, his hard-bought Jewish education, which his father had always assured him was priceless, served him splendidly once more. Moey remembered his *David ha'Melech*:[5] *And it came to pass in the morning, that David wrote a letter to Joab, and sent it by the hand of Uriah. And he wrote in the letter, saying, Set Uriah in the forefront of the hottest battle, and retire ye from him, that he may be smitten, and die.*

Amen.

2 A reference to the Spanish Civil War (1936–9), fought between Nationalist forces and Republicans. In the military uprising against the leftist Republican Popular Front government, the Nationalists, led by General Francisco Franco, repeatedly tried to capture the Spanish capital, Madrid; their success in early 1939 marked the end for the Republic. Franco established a Fascist dictatorship that lasted until his death in 1975. In its aftermath the Spanish Civil War came to be seen as a testing ground for Fascism before Hitler's aggression led the world into World War II: those from outside Spain who volunteered to fight on the Republican side—which included Ernest Hemingway and André Malraux (the war was a great chapter in the careers of each)—gained special heroic status. Torremolinos is a popular Mediterranean resort town on the Costa del Sol in southern Spain.

3 The Royal Academy of Dramatic Art, a government-subsidized acting school (est. 1904) in London, England.

4 An Orthodox Jewish school or seminary.

5 King David (Hebrew). The Biblical passage that follows is from 2 Samuel 11, which tells the story of how David, King of Israel, adulterously impregnates Bathsheba while her husband is away fighting, then arranges with Joab, the leader of his forces, to have her husband die in battle.

Lou Caplan yielded two successive hits in the third and Moey Hanover took off his catcher's mask, called for time, and strode to the mound, rubbing the ball in his hands.

'I'm all right,' Lou said. 'Don't worry. I'm going to settle down now.'

'It's not that. Listen, when do you start shooting in Rome?'

'Three weeks tomorrow. You heard something bad?'

'No.'

'You're a friend now, remember. No secrets.'

'No. It's just that I've had second thoughts about Sean Fielding. I think he's very exciting. He's got lots of appeal. He'd be a natural to play Domingo.'

As the two men began to whisper together, players on Al Levine's bench hollered, 'Let's go, gang.'

'Come on. Break it up, Moey.'

Moey returned to the plate, satisfied that Fielding was as good as in Rome already. May he do his own stunts, he thought.

'Play ball,' Nate Sugarman called.

Alfie Roberts, the director, ordinarily expected soft pitches from Lou, as he did the same for him, but today he wasn't so sure, because on Wednesday his agent had sent him one of Lou's properties to read and—Lou's first pitch made Alfie hit the dirt. That settles it, he thought, my agent already told him it doesn't grab me. Alfie struck out as quickly as he could. Better be put down for a rally-stopper than suffer a head fracture.

Which brought up Manny Gordon again, with one out and runners on first and third. Manny dribbled into a double play, retiring the side.

Multi-coloured kites bounced in the skies over the Heath. Lovers strolled on the tow paths and locked together on the grass. Old people sat on benches, sucking in the sun. Nannies passed, wheeling toddlers with titles. The odd baffled Englishman stopped to watch the Americans at play.

'Are they air force chaps?'

'Filmmakers, actually. It's their version of rounders.'

'Whatever is that enormous thing that woman is slicing?'

'Salami.'

'*On the Heath?*'

'Afraid so. One Sunday they actually set up a bloody folding table, right over there, with cold cuts and herrings and mounds of black bread and a whole bloody side of smoked salmon. *Scotch. Ten and six a quarter, don't you know?*'

'On the Heath?'

'Champagne *in paper cups*. Mumm's. One of them had won some sort of award.'

Going into the bottom of the fifth, Al Levine's Team led 6–3, and Tom Hunt came in to play second base for Lou Caplan's Bunch. Hunt, a Negro actor, was in town shooting *Othello X* for Bob Cohen.

Moey Hanover lifted a lazy fly into left field, which Ziggy Alter trapped rolling over and over on the grass until—just before getting up—he was well placed to look up Natalie Calman's skirt. Something he saw there so unnerved him that he dropped the ball, turning pale and allowing Hanover to pull up safely at second.

Johnny Roper walked. Which brought up Jason Storm, to the delight of a pride of British fairies who stood with their dogs on the first base line, squealing and jumping. Jason poked a bouncer through the infield and floated to second, obliging the fairies and their dogs to move up a base.

With two out and the score tied 7–7 in the bottom half of the sixth, Alfie Roberts was unwillingly retired and a new pitcher came in for Al Levine's Team. It was Gordie Kaufman, a writer blacklisted for years, who now divided his time between Madrid and Rome, asking a hundred thousand dollars a spectacular. Gordie came in to pitch with the go-ahead run on third and Tom Hunt stepping up to the plate for the first time. Big black Tom Hunt, who had once played semi-pro ball in Florida, was a militant. If he homered, Hunt felt he would be put down for another buck nigger, good at games, but if he struck out, which would call for rather more acting skill than was required of him on the set of *Othello X*, what then? He would enable a bunch of fat, foxy, sexually worried Jews to feel big, goysy.[6] Screw them, Hunt thought.

Gordie Kaufman had his problems too. His stunning villa on Mallorca was run by Spanish servants, his two boys were boarding at a reputable British public school, and Gordie himself was president, sole stockholder, and the only employee of a company that was a plaque in Liechtenstein. And yet—and yet—Gordie still subscribed to the *Nation*;[7] he filled his Roman slaves with anti-apartheid dialogue and sagacious Talmudic sayings; and whenever the left-wing *pushke* was passed around he came through with a nice cheque. I must bear down on Hunt, Gordie thought, because if he touches me for even a scratch single I'll come off a patronizing ofay. If he homers, God forbid, I'm a shitty liberal. And so with the count 3 and 2, and a walk, the typical social-democrat's compromise, seemingly the easiest way out for both men, Gordie gritted his teeth, his proud Trotskyite past getting the best of him, and threw a fast ball right at Hunt, bouncing it off his head. Hunt threw away his bat and started for the mound, fist clenched, but not so fast that players from both sides couldn't rush in to separate the two men, both of whom felt vindicated, proud, because they had triumphed over impersonal racial prejudice to hit each other as individuals on a fun Sunday on Hampstead Heath.

Come the crucial seventh, the Filmmakers' First Wives Club grew restive, no longer content to belittle their former husbands from afar, and moved in on the baselines and benches, undermining confidence with their heckling. When Myer Gross, for instance, came to bat with two men on base and his teammates shouted, 'Go, man. Go,' one familiar grating voice floated out over the others. 'Hit, Myer. Make your son proud of you, *just this once*.'

6 Goy-like; that is, not like a Jew.

7 An American weekly journal of opinion, then considered the leading voice of the North American political left. The Talmud is the collection of ancient Rabbinic writings constituting the basis of religious authority in Orthodox Judaism; a pushke is a charity or collection box (Yiddish); 'ofay': a mildly derogatory term used by blacks for whites.

What a reproach the first wives were. How steadfast! How unchanging! Still Waiting for Lefty after all these years.[8] Today maybe hair had greyed and chins doubled, necks had gone pruney, breasts drooped and stomachs dropped, but let no man say these crones had aged in spirit. Where once they had petitioned for the Scotsboro Boys, broken with their families over mixed marriages, sent their boy friends off to defend Madrid, split with old comrades over the Stalin-Hitler Pact, fought for Henry Wallace, demonstrated for the Rosenbergs, and never, never yielded to McCarthy . . . today they clapped hands at China Friendship Clubs, petitioned for others to keep hands off Cuba and Vietnam, and made their sons chopped liver sandwiches and sent them off to march to Aldermaston.

The wives, alimonied but abandoned, had known the early struggling years with their husbands, the self-doubts, the humiliations, the rejections, the cold-water flats, and the blacklist, but they had always remained loyal. They hadn't altered, their husbands had.

Each marriage had shattered in the eye of its own self-made hurricane, but essentially the men felt, as Ziggy Alter had once put it so succinctly at the poker table, 'Right, wrong, don't be silly, it's really a question of who wants to grow old with Anna Pauker when there are so many juicy little things we can now afford.'

So there they were, out on the grass chasing fly balls on a Sunday morning, short men, overpaid and unprincipled, all well within the coronary and lung cancer belt, allowing themselves to look ridiculous in the hope of pleasing their new young wives and girlfriends. There was Ziggy Alter, who had once written a play 'with content' for the Group Theater. Here was Al Levine, who had used to throw marbles under horses' legs at demonstrations and now raced two horses of his own at Epsom. On the pitcher's mound stood Gordie Kaufman, who had once carried a banner that read *No Pasarán*[9] through the streets of Manhattan and now employed a man especially to keep Spaniards off the beach at his villa on Mallorca. And sweating under a catcher's mask there was Moey Hanover, who had studied at a yeshiva, stood up to the committee, and was now on a sabbatical from Desilu.

Usually the husbands were able to avoid their used-up wives. They didn't see them in the gaming rooms at the White Elephant or in the Mirabelle or Les Ambassadeurs. But come Brecht to Shaftesbury Avenue and without looking up from the second row centre they could feel them squatting in their cotton bloomers in the second balcony, burning holes in their necks.

8 An allusion to Clifford Odets's 1935 play *Waiting for Lefty*. This agitprop classic ends with the revelation that Lefty will never come—as the result of an injustice that is meant to stir the audience to social activism. The Scotsboro Boys were nine black youths found guilty by an all-white jury in Scotsboro, Alabama, in 1931 on charges of raping two white women—a decision that sparked outrage outside the US South, particularly among Northern liberal and radical groups. Henry Wallace (1836–1916): American agricultural pioneer and statesman, vice president of the US during Franklin D. Roosevelt's third term (1941–5); he epitomized the 'common man' philosophy of 'New Deal' Democrats. In 1948 he broke with the party and ran for president as leader of the new left-wing Progressive party, which he helped form. The Rosenbergs: Julius (1918–53) and Ethel Rosenberg (1915–53) were found guilty of passing military secrets to Soviet intelligence agents and were executed, though at the time many felt they were victims of America's anti-Communist Cold War hysteria. Aldermaston: a village near Reading in southern England, site of the Atomic Weapons Research Establishment.

9 'They shall not pass'. In the Spanish Civil War, a slogan of the Republicans in their opposition to the Nationalists; subsequently used generally for resistance.

And count on them to turn up on a Sunday morning in summer on Hampstead Heath just to ruin a game of fun baseball. Even homering, as Al Levine did, was no answer to the drones.

'It's nice for him, I suppose', a voice behind Levine on the bench observed, 'that on the playing field, with an audience, if you know what I mean, he actually appears virile.'

The game dragged on. In the eighth inning Jack Monroe had to retire to his Mercedes-Benz for his insulin injection and Jake Hersh, until now an embarrassed sub, finally trotted onto the field. Hersh, thirty-three, one-time relief pitcher for Room 41, Fletcher's Field High (2–7), moved into right field, mindful of his disc condition and hoping he would not be called on to make a tricksy catch. He assumed a loose-limbed stance on the grass, waving at his wife, grinning at his children, when without warning a sizzling line drive came right at him. Jake, startled, did the only sensible thing: he ducked. Outraged shouts and moans from the bench reminded Jake where he was, in a softball game, and he started after the ball.

'Fishfingers.'

'*Putz!*'

Runners on first and third started for home as Jake, breathless, finally caught up with the ball. It had rolled to a stop under a bench where a nanny sat watching over an elegant perambulator.

'Excuse me,' Jake said.

'Americans,' the nurse said.

'I'm a Canadian,' Jake protested automatically, fishing the ball out from under the bench.

Three runs scored. Jake caught a glimpse of Nancy, unable to contain her laughter. The children looked ashamed of him.

In the ninth inning with the score tied again, 11–11, Sol Peters, another sub, stepped cautiously to the plate for Lou Caplan's Bunch. The go-ahead run was on second and there was only one out. Gordie Kaufman, trying to prevent a bunt, threw right at him and Sol, forgetting he was wearing his contact lenses, held the bat in front of him to protect his glasses. The ball hit the bat and rebounded for a perfectly laid down bunt.

'Run, you shmock.'

'Go, man.'

Sol, terrified, ran, carrying the bat with him.

Monty Talman phoned home.

'Who won?' his wife asked.

'We did. 13–12. But that's not the point. We had lots of fun.'

'How many you bringing back for lunch?'

'Eight.'

'*Eight?*'

'I couldn't get out of inviting Johnny Roper. He knows Jack Monroe is coming.'

'I see.'

'A little warning. Don't, for Chrissake, ask Cy how Marsha is. They're separating. And I'm afraid Manny Gordon is coming with a girl. I want you to be nice to her.'

'*Anything else?*'

'If Gershon phones from Rome while the guys are there please remember I'm taking the call upstairs. And please don't start collecting glasses and emptying ashtrays at four o'clock. It's embarrassing. Bloody Jake Hersh is coming and it's just the sort of incident he'd pick on and joke about for months.'

'I never coll—'

'All right, all right. Oh, shit, something else. Tom Hunt is coming.'

'The actor?'

'Yeah. Now listen, he's very touchy, so will you please put away Sheila's doll.'

'Sheila's doll?'

'If she comes in carrying that bloody golliwog[10] I'll die. Hide it. Burn it. Hunt gets script approval these days, you know.'

'All right, dear.'

'See you soon.'

1971

10 Dolls based on caricatures of the American minstrel show portrayal of black males, they became the most popular doll in Europe in the first half of the twentieth century.

Alden Nowlan

1933–1983

The sympathy for victims of emotional and economic poverty that is often expressed in the writing of Alden Nowlan derives from personal experience. Nowlan grew up near Nova Scotia's Annapolis Valley, in a small 'thin-soil' settlement that he described as little touched by the Depression because it was already impoverished. Although he quit school in grade five, eventually going to work in nearby lumber mills and on farms, he continued his education by reading whatever he could find. At nineteen he took a position on the Hartland *Observer* in New Brunswick. In his ten years as a journalist and editor at the *Observer* and later at the Saint John *Telegraph-Journal* he developed a simple, direct style that may be seen in the poetry and short fiction he began writing in the mid-1950s. In 1957 he met Maritime poet and educator Fred Cogswell, whose encouragement led to the publication of Nowlan's first collection of poems, *The Rose and the Puritan* (1958).

During his lifetime Nowlan published ten more volumes of poetry, including *Bread, Wine and Salt* (1967), which won a Governor General's Award; *The Mysterious Naked Man* (1969); *Playing the Jesus Game: Selected Poems* (1970); *Smoked Glass* (1977); and *I Might Not Tell Everybody This* (1982). He also wrote short stories—collected in *Miracle at Indian River* (1968)—that depict the brutal cultural trap in which his fellow Maritimers are caught. *Double Exposure*, a collection of his journalistic pieces, was published in 1978. Nowlan's novel *Various Persons Named Kevin O'Brien* (1973) is essentially an autobiographical account of his difficult boyhood. Another novel, *The Wanton Troopers* (1988), which was found in Nowlan's papers and published after his death, provides further details of the autobiographical character Kevin O'Brien. Six more collections of his work have been published posthumously: *Early Poems* (1983); *Will Ye Let the Mummers In?* (1984), a book of short stories; *An Exchange of Gifts: Poems New and Selected* (1985); *The Best of Alden Nowlan* (1993), edited by Allison Mitcham; *Selected Poems* (1995), edited by Patrick Lane and Lorna Crozier; and *White Madness* (1996), a selection of some of Nowlan's *Telegraph-Journal* columns, edited by Robert Gibbs.

From 1969 on, Nowlan was associated with the University of New Brunswick while working as a writer and freelance journalist. In the 1970s he collaborated with Walter Learning in the writing of three plays; two of them focus on popular figures—Frankenstein (in *Frankenstein: The Man Who Became God*, 1974) and Sherlock Holmes (in *The Incredible Murder of Cardinal Tosca*, 1978).

In his poetry, as in his stories, Nowlan is a chronicler—he called himself a 'witness'—of a rural Maritime way of life that has remained virtually unchanged for centuries. Nowlan pictures a Maritimes landscape (as in 'On the Barrens' and 'Canadian January Night') that seems primitive even in comparison with those seen in such famous nineteenth-century poems as Roberts' 'Tantramar Revisited' and Carman's 'Low Tide on Grand Pré'. He once observed that when he moved to small-town New Brunswick, he also moved from the eighteenth century into the twentieth because he left behind a boyhood home that had 'no furnace, no plumbing, no electricity, no refrigerator, no telephone . . . [a home, where] we used kerosene lamps and on the coldest winter nights water froze in the bucket in the kitchen'.

The tone of Nowlan's poems is notable for the way he presents not the picturesque but the commonplace. Never a detached observer telling his audience about a region, he is a part of his milieu and its reporter—a dual role that he often found uncomfortable. The harsh, uncompromising realism of his poetry prevents it from becoming mundane or seeming naive. The sentimentality that might have been implicit in focusing on the crippling effects of the guilt and repression that Nowlan saw as his cultural heritage ('I am a product of a culture that fears any display of emotion and attempts to repress any true communication') is regularly undercut by an ironic humour that suggests imagination is man's only real escape from adversity and deprivation.

Temptation

The boy is
badgering the man
to lower him down the
face of the cliff
to a narrow shelf
about eight feet
below:
'Your hands are strong,
and I'm not afraid.
The ledge is wide enough,
I won't hurt myself
even if you let go.'

'Don't be a fool.
You'd break every bone
in your body.
Where in God's name
do you get such ideas?
It's time we went home.'

But there is no
conviction in the
man's voice and
the boy persists;
nagging his wrists,
dragging him nearer.
Their summer shirts
balloon in the wind.

While devils whisper
what god-like sport
it would be
to cling to the
edge of the world
and gamble
one's only son
against the wind
and rocks
and sea.

1967

Country Full of Christmas

Country full of Christmas,
the stripped, suspicious elms
groping for the dun sky—
what can I give my love?

The remembrance—mouse hawks
scudding on the dykes, above
the wild roses; horses and cattle
separate in the same field.
It is not for my love.

Do you know that foxes
believe in nothing
but themselves—everything
is a fox disguised: men, dogs and rabbits.

1969

Canadian January Night

Ice storm: the hill
a pyramid of black crystal
down which the cars
slide like phosphorescent beetles
while I, walking backwards in obedience
to the wind, am possessed
of the fearful knowledge
my compatriots share
but almost never utter:
this is a country
where a man can die
simply from being
caught outside.

1971

The Broadcaster's Poem

I used to broadcast at night
alone in a radio station
but I was never good at it,
partly because my voice wasn't right
but mostly because my peculiar
metaphysical stupidity
made it impossible
for me to keep believing
there was somebody listening
when it seemed I was talking
only to myself in a room no bigger
than an ordinary bathroom.

I could believe it for a while
and then I'd get somewhat
the same feeling as when you
start to suspect you're the victim
of a practical joke.
So one part of me
was afraid another part
might blurt out something
about myself so terrible
that even I had never until
that moment suspected it.
This was like the fear
of bridges and other
high places: Will I take off my glasses
and throw them
into the water, although I'm
half-blind without them?
Will I sneak up behind
myself and push?
Another thing:
as a reporter
I covered an accident in which a train
ran into a car, killing
three young men, one of whom
was beheaded. The bodies looked
boneless, as such bodies do.
More like mounds of rags.
And inside the wreckage
where nobody could get at it
the car radio
was still playing.
I thought about places
the disc jockey's voice goes
and the things that happen there
and of how impossible it would be for him
to continue if he really knew.

1974

On the Barrens

'Once when we were hunting cattle
on the barrens,'
so began many of the stories they told,
gathered in the kitchen, a fire still
the focus of life then,
the teapot on the stove as long as
anyone was awake,
mittens and socks left to thaw on
the open oven door,
chunks of pine and birch piled
halfway to the ceiling,
and always a faint smell of smoke
like spice in the air,
the lamps making their peace with
the darkness,
the world not entirely answerable
to man.

They took turns talking, the listeners
puffed their pipes,
he whose turn it was to speak used his
as an instrument,
took his leather pouch from a pocket
of his overalls,
gracefully, rubbed tobacco between
his rough palms
as he set the mood, tamped it into
the bowl
at a moment carefully chosen, scratched
a match when it was necessary
to prolong the suspense. If his pipe
went out it was no accident,
if he spat in the stove it was done
for a purpose.
When he finished he might lean back
in his chair so that it stood
on two legs; there'd be a short silence.

The barrens were flat clay fields,
twenty miles from the sea
and separated from it by dense woods
and farmlands.

They smelled of salt and the wind
 blew there
constantly as it does on the shore
 of the North Atlantic.

There had been a time, the older men
 said, when someone had owned
the barrens but something had happened
long ago and now anyone who wanted to
 could pasture there.
The cattle ran wild all summer,
sinewy little beasts, ginger-coloured
 with off-white patches,
grazed there on the windswept barrens
 and never saw a human
until fall when the men came to round
 them up,
sinewy men in rubber boots and tweed caps
 with their dogs beside them.

Some of the cattle would by now have
 forgotten
there'd been a time before they'd
 lived on the barrens.
They'd be truly wild, dangerous, the
 men would loose the dogs on them,
mongrel collies, barn dogs with the
 dispositions of convicts
who are set over their fellows,
 the dogs would go for the nose,
sink their teeth in the tender flesh,
 toss the cow on its side,
bleating, hooves flying, but shortly
 tractable.
There were a few escaped,
 it was said, and in a little while
they were like no other cattle—
 the dogs feared them,
they roared at night and the men
 lying by their camp-fires
heard them and moaned in their sleep,
 the next day tracking them
found where they'd pawed the moss,

where their horns had scraped
bark from the trees—all the stories
agreed
in this: now there was nothing to do
but kill them.

1977

Leonard Cohen

b. 1934

Born and raised in Montreal, Leonard Cohen attended McGill, receiving his BA in 1955. His first collection of poetry, *Let Us Compare Mythologies,* written while he was still an undergraduate and published in 1956, shows the influences of the American Beat movement, which rejected the structures of society for the ideal of personal freedom, and embraced, in a romantic fascination with self-destruction, a bohemian way of life associated with drugs, sexual permissiveness, and social experimentation. *Let Us Compare Mythologies* also takes as its forefathers two generations of Montreal Jewish poets, A.M. Klein and Irving Layton; its title acknowledges Cohen's attempts to come to terms with his Jewish identity in a culture in which other and competing forms of belief, such as the working-class Catholic values he experienced in French Montreal, are important ways of organizing the individual's relationship to the world.

Cohen's interest in this question of how mythologies govern our lives is continued in his later work (and was important in the work of several other Canadian writers just then emerging or soon to emerge). It marked the beginning of Cohen's career as a spiritual seeker, a man who, having concluded that the myths and systems of belief he grew up with were no longer adequate, has spent his life trying to construct a satisfactory alternative by synthesisizing divergent, even hostile, traditions.

Cohen briefly attended graduate school at Columbia University before deciding to return to Montreal and become a professional writer. In 1961 he published a second poetry collection, *The Spice-Box of Earth,* in which his preoccupation with eroticism and sensuality announces itself. In Cohen's larger body of work the combination of spirituality and sensuality is a distinctive quality. It is writing in which erotic experiences can sometimes seem not so much a union between two people as a means of saintly purification.

In 1963 he published the first of his two novels, *The Favorite Game.* This story of growing up Jewish in Montreal is indebted to Joyce's *Portrait of the Artist as a Young Man,* as well as to an emerging tradition of North American-Jewish writing. Like Joyce's novel—and like Mordecai Richler's *Son of a Smaller Hero* (1955)—*The Favorite Game* shows the need for the artist and intellectual to break free of all conventional values and milieus. In the year it appeared, Cohen left Canada to begin a period of expatriation, for a time basing himself on the Greek Island of Hydra.

Cohen's next book of poetry, *Flowers for Hitler* (1964)—the first of his works intended to alienate the reader and his most explicit piece of social criticism—blends death, violence, and eroticism, employing rhetoric that allies it with the protest poetry beginning to appear in the mid-sixties. The novel that followed, *Beautiful Losers* (1966), showed his increasing willingness to take risks as a writer and to experiment with new forms. Called pornographic in its day and criticized for being self-indulgent, *Beautiful Losers* brings together all the important elements of Cohen's writing. It is a dazzling tour-de-force, the novel as stylistic exhibition: in it, Eros meets Thanatos and myths and images collide in what Cohen has called 'a model of sainthood'—a self-destructive Dionysiac madness. This wild fragmentary fantasy, which has gained a cult following even while it continues to leave some readers deeply offended, focuses on the question of beatification by telling of a narrator who takes inspiration from the story of Kateri Tekakwitha, the Mohawk woman who was made a saint by the Roman Catholic Church. The novel raises important questions about prejudice based on colour and race, and joins Cohen's explorations of mythology with his fascination with the eternal feminine when a woman being made love to identifies herself—in untranslated Greek—as Isis, one of the most powerful of ancient goddesses.

Cohen later reprinted several selections from *Beautiful Losers*—including 'What Is a Saint'—in *Stranger Music: Selected Poems and Songs* (1993), treating them there as prose poems. 'We are now at the heart', the second selection from the novel reprinted below, comes from a long, hallucinatory letter written by the other narrator of the novel, a man known only as 'F'. In F's writing, Cohen's interest in altered states of consciousness is apparent, as is his growing fascination with pop culture and its effects. In this passage, F enters the 'System Theatre' to discover that film genres have become unstable and that the newsreel, usually shown between film features, no longer remains separate from the main feature. In *Beautiful Losers* fact and fantasy, fiction and history, similarly blend and become impossible to distinguish.

Cohen's interest in pop culture seems to have left him dissatisfied with the conventional role of the poet around this time. Returning for a while to North America to be near Nashville, he started setting his poems to music and writing song lyrics. In 1966, the popular folk singer Judy Collins began to record Cohen's songs on her albums. One of these, 'Suzanne'—a portrait of a secular saint that was also published that year in a slightly different form as 'Suzanne Takes You Down' (in *Parasites of Heaven*, Cohen's fourth book of poetry)—became the most recorded song of the period. In 1967 Cohen made an appearance at the Newport Folk Festival. Early in 1968 *Songs of Leonard Cohen*, his first album as a performer, appeared.

As a result of his success as poet, novelist, songwriter, and performer, Cohen had become a media personality by the end of the 1960s—the artist-hero who was his own creation, playing out the role of sacrificial victim. He was given to grand gestures (such as refusing a Governor General's Award for his *Selected Poems*, 1968), as he assumed the pose of an ageless, wandering rebel, a brooding, mysterious figure whose first task was to investigate his own experiences and to exhibit his own pain. As Michael Ondaatje observed, 'Cohen's dreamworlds, Cohen and death, Cohen and love, the legend of Cohen—no matter what the topic is, Cohen is at the centre of the story' (*Leonard Cohen*, 1967). In 1969, after releasing *Songs from a Room*, Cohen began touring North America and Europe; for the next twenty-five years his career as a musician remained the most important of his activities. As of 2002, he has produced fourteen record albums, including *Various Positions* (1985), *I'm Your Man* (1988), *The Future* (1992), and, with Sharon Robinson, *Ten New Songs* (2001).

Even after songwriting and performing had become his chief preoccupation, Cohen continued to write for the page. In 1972 he published *The Energy of Slaves*, a nihilistic and grim collection of poems based on the themes of suicide and artistic burnout. In 1978 *Death of a Lady's Man* mixed poetry, prose-poems, and prose in the form of excerpts from a longer work, 'My Life in Art', and accompanied these with running commentaries and extensive quotations from notebook sources. The conflict in *Death of a Lady's Man* between redemption and desire became more explicit in the poetic meditations of *Book of Mercy* (1984); it is also apparent in the songs on Cohen's later albums.

The psalm-like poems of *Book of Mercy* show that Cohen remained on a spiritual quest, and in the years that followed, he increasingly turned to Zen Buddhism, withdrawing for considerable periods of time to the Zen Center of Mount Baldy, near Los Angeles. After releasing *The Future*, he withdrew from the world entirely and lived at the Center for the rest of the 1990s as the Zen monk Jikan, meditating, working on the Zen riddles known as koans, and cooking for his teacher, Sasaki Roshi. In his late writing, his religious vision has been revitalized (as has his interest in political structures), though his expectations of the future, expressed in songs such as 'The Future' and 'Closing Time', remain at best grimly jocular. Though Cohen continues to reflect back to us a world largely without faith in the divine—indeed, without faith in any secular authority, or even in the individual self—his recent work suggests that while suffering may be necessary for salvation, acceptance of things as they are has become not only possible but increasingly important. Martyrdom no longer seems an end in itself.

In 1997, Cohen began to make use of the Internet as a way of becoming less private. Contributing to a Web site called 'The Leonard Cohen Files', he posted sketches, paintings, drawings and computer art from his extensive notebooks and published, on a part of the Web site designated 'Blackening Pages', poetic work-in-progress from a manuscript he calls 'The Book of Longing'. Cohen also added early archival material, writing, 'I want to send, among other things, the first manuscript scratchings for Suzanne and other early songs. I'd like to make the process clear, or at least throw some light on the mysterious activity of writing.'

You Have the Lovers

You have the lovers,
they are nameless, their histories only for each other,
and you have the room, the bed and the windows.
Pretend it is a ritual.
Unfurl the bed, bury the lovers, blacken the windows,
let them live in that house for a generation or two.
No one dares disturb them.
Visitors in the corridor tiptoe past the long closed door,
they listen for sounds, for a moan, for a song:
nothing is heard, not even breathing.
You know they are not dead,
you can feel the presence of their intense love.
Your children grow up, they leave you,
they have become soldiers and riders.
Your mate dies after a life of service.
Who knows you? Who remembers you?
But in your house a ritual is in progress:
it is not finished: it needs more people.
One day the door is opened to the lover's chambers.
The room has become a dense garden,
full of colours, smells, sounds you have never known.
The bed is smooth as a wafer of sunlight,
in the midst of the garden it stands alone.
In the bed the lovers, slowly and deliberately and silently,
perform the act of love.

Their eyes are closed,
as tightly as if heavy coins of flesh lay on them.
Their lips are bruised with new and old bruises.
Her hair and his beard are hopelessly tangled.
When he puts his mouth against her shoulder
she is uncertain whether her shoulder
has given or received the kiss.
All her flesh is like a mouth.
He carries his fingers along her waist
and feels his own waist caressed.
She holds him closer and his own arms tighten around her.
She kisses the hand beside her mouth.
It is his hand or her hand, it hardly matters,
there are so many more kisses.
You stand beside the bed, weeping with happiness,
you carefully peel away the sheets
from the slow-moving bodies.
Your eyes are filled with tears, you barely make out the lovers.
As you undress you sing out, and your voice is magnificent
because now you believe it is the first human voice
heard in that room.
The garments you let fall grow into vines.
You climb into bed and recover the flesh.
You close your eyes and allow them to be sewn shut.
You create an embrace and fall into it.
There is only one moment of pain or doubt
as you wonder how many multitudes are lying beside your body,
but a mouth kisses and a hand soothes the moment away.

1961

Suzanne

Suzanne takes you down
to her place near the river
you can hear the boats go by
you can spend the night beside her
And you know that she's half crazy
but that's why you want to be there
and she feeds you tea and oranges
that come all the way from China
And just when you mean to tell her

that you have no love to give her
she gets you on her wavelength
and she lets the river answer
that you've always been her lover
And you want to travel with her
you want to travel blind
and you know that she can trust you
for you've touched her perfect body
with your mind

And Jesus was a sailor
when he walked upon the water[1]
and he spent a long time watching
from his lonely wooden tower
and when he knew for certain
only drowning men could see him
he said All men will be sailors then
until the sea shall free them
but he himself was broken
long before the sky would open
forsaken, almost human
he sank beneath your wisdom like a stone
And you want to travel with him
you want to travel blind
and you think maybe you'll trust him
for he's touched your perfect body
with his mind

Now Suzanne takes your hand
and she leads you to the river
she is wearing rags and feathers
from Salvation Army counters
And the sun pours down like honey
on our lady of the harbour
And she shows you where to look
among the garbage and the flowers
There are heroes in the seaweed
there are children in the morning
they are leaning out for love
they will lean that way forever
while Suzanne holds the mirror

1 The account of Jesus' walking on the wave-tossed sea to his disciples on a ship can be found in Matthew 14: 22–33. Peter tried to emulate him but lost faith and began to sink.

And you want to travel with her
you want to travel blind
and you know that you can trust her
for she's touched your perfect body
with her mind

1966

How to Speak Poetry

Take the word butterfly. To use this word it is not necessary to make the voice weigh less than an ounce or equip it with small dusty wings. It is not necessary to invent a sunny day or a field of daffodils. It is not necessary to be in love, or to be in love with butterflies. The word butterfly is not a real butterfly. There is the word and there is the butterfly. If you confuse these two items people have the right to laugh at you. Do not make so much of the word. Are you trying to suggest that you love butterflies more perfectly than anyone else, or really understand their nature? The word butterfly is merely data. It is not an opportunity for you to hover, soar, befriend flowers, symbolize beauty and frailty, or in any way impersonate a butterfly. Do not act out words. Never act out words. Never try to leave the floor when you talk about flying. Never close your eyes and jerk your head to one side when you talk about death. Do not fix your burning eyes on me when you speak about love. If you want to impress me when you speak about love put your hand in your pocket or under your dress and play with yourself. If ambition and the hunger for applause have driven you to speak about love you should learn how to do it without disgracing yourself or the material.

What is the expression which the age demands? The age demands no expression whatever. We have seen photographs of bereaved Asian mothers. We are not interested in the agony of your fumbled organs. There is nothing you can show on your face that can match the horror of this time. Do not even try. You will only hold yourself up to the scorn of those who have felt things deeply. We have seen newsreels of humans in the extremities of pain and dislocation. Everyone knows you are eating well and are even being paid to stand up there. You are playing to people who have experienced a catastrophe. This should make you very quiet. Speak the words, convey the data, step aside. Everyone knows you are in pain. You cannot tell the audience everything you know about love in every line of love you speak. Step aside and they will know what you know because they know it already. You have nothing to teach them. You are not more beautiful than they are. You are not wiser. Do not shout at them. Do not force a dry entry. That is bad sex. If you show the lines of your genitals, then deliver what you promise. And remember that people do not really want an acrobat in bed. What is our need? To be close to the natural man, to be close to the natural woman. Do not pretend that you are a beloved singer with a vast loyal audience which has followed the ups and downs of your life to this very moment. The bombs, flame-throwers, and all the shit have destroyed more than just the trees and villages. They have also destroyed the stage. Did you think that your profession would escape the general destruction? There is no more stage. There are no more footlights. You are among the people. Then be modest. Speak the words, convey the data, step aside. Be by yourself. Be in your own room. Do not put yourself on.

This is an interior landscape. It is inside. It is private. Respect the privacy of the material. These pieces were written in silence. The courage of the play is to speak them. The discipline of the play is not to violate them. Let the audience feel your love of privacy even though there is no privacy. Be good whores. The poem is not a slogan. It cannot advertise you. It cannot promote your reputation for sensitivity. You are not a stud. You are not a killer lady. All this junk about the gangsters of love. You are students of discipline. Do not act out the words. The words die when you act them out, they wither, and we are left with nothing but your ambition.

Speak the words with the exact precision with which you would check out a laundry list. Do not become emotional about the lace blouse. Do not get a hard-on when you say panties. Do not get all shivery just because of the towel. The sheets should not provoke a dreamy expression about the eyes. There is no need to weep into the handkerchief. The socks are not there to remind you of strange and distant voyages. It is just your laundry. It is just your clothes. Don't peep through them. Just wear them.

The poem is nothing but information. It is the Constitution of the inner country. If you declaim it and blow it up with noble intentions then you are no better than the politicians whom you despise. You are just someone waving a flag and making the cheapest appeal to a kind of emotional patriotism. Think of the words as science, not as art. They are a report. You are speaking before a meeting of the Explorers' Club of the National Geographic Society. These people know all the risks of mountain climbing. They honour you by taking this for granted. If you rub their faces in it that is an insult to their hospitality. Tell them about the height of the mountain, the equipment you used, be specific about the surfaces and the time it took to scale it. Do not work the audience for gasps and sighs. If you are worthy of gasps and sighs it will not be from your appreciation of the event but from theirs. It will be in the statistics and not the trembling of the voice or the cutting of the air with your hands. It will be in the data and the quiet organization of your presence.

Avoid the flourish. Do not be afraid to be weak. Do not be ashamed to be tired. You look good when you're tired. You look like you could go on forever. Now come into my arms. You are the image of my beauty.

1978

From *Book of Mercy*

In the Eyes of Men

In the eyes of men he falls, and in his own eyes too. He falls from his high place, he trips on his achievement. He falls to you, he falls to know you. It is sad, they say. See his disgrace, say the ones at his heel. But he falls radiantly toward the light to which he falls. They cannot see who lifts him as he falls, or how his falling changes, and he himself bewildered till his heart cries out to bless the one who holds him in his falling. And in his fall he hears his heart cry out, his heart explains why he is falling, why he had to fall, and he gives over to the fall. Blessed are you, clasp of the falling. He falls into the sky, he falls into the light, none can hurt him as he falls. Blessed are you, shield of the falling. Wrapped in his fall, concealed within his fall, he finds the place, he is gathered in. While his hair streams back and his clothes tear in the wind, he is held up, comforted, he enters into the place of his fall. Blessed are you, embrace of the falling, foundation of the light, master of the human accident.

When I Have Not Rage

When I have not rage or sorrow, and you depart from me, then I am most afraid. When the belly is full, and the mind has its sayings, then I fear for my soul; I rush to you as a child at night breaks into its parents' room. Do not forget me in my satisfaction. When the heart grins at itself, the world is destroyed. And I am found alone with the husks and the shells. Then the dangerous moment comes: I am too great to ask for help. I have other hopes. I legislate from the fortress of my disappointments, with a set jaw. Overthrow this even terror with a sweet remembrance: when I was with you, when my soul delighted you, when I was what you wanted. My heart sings of your longing for me, and my thoughts climb down to marvel at your mercy. I do not fear as you gather up my days. Your name is the sweetness of time, and you carry me close into the night, speaking consolations, drawing down lights from the sky, saying, See how the night has no terror for one who remembers the Name.

It Is All Around Me

It is all around me, the darkness. You are my only shield. Your name is my only light. What love I have, your law is the source, this dead love that remembers only its name, yet the name is enough to open itself like a mouth, to call down the dew, and drink. O dead name that through your mercy speaks to the living name, mercy harkening to the will that is bent toward it, the will whose strength is its pledge to you—O name of love, draw down the blessings of completion on the man you have cut in half to know you.

Holy Is Your Name

Holy is your name, holy is your work, holy are the days that return to you. Holy are the years that you uncover. Holy are the hands that are raised to you, and the weeping that is wept to you. Holy is the fire between your will and ours, in which we are refined. Holy is that which is unredeemed, covered with your patience. Holy are the souls lost in your unnaming. Holy, and shining with a great light, is every living thing, established in this world and covered with time, until your name is praised forever.

Not Knowing Where to Go

Not knowing where to go, I go to you. Not knowing where to turn, I turn to you. Not knowing what to hold, I bind myself to you. Having lost my way, I make my way to you. Having soiled my heart, I lift my heart to you. Having wasted my days, I bring the heap to you. The great highway covered with debris, I travel on a hair to you. The wall smeared with filth, I go through a pinhole of light. Blocked by every thought, I fly on the wisp of a remembrance. Defeated by silence, here is a place where the silence is more subtle. And here is the opening in defeat. And here is the clasp of the will. And here is the fear of you. And here is the fastening of mercy. Blessed are you, in this man's moment. Blessed are you, whose presence illuminates outrageous evil. Blessed are you who brings chains out of the darkness. Blessed are you, who waits in the world. Blessed are you, whose name is in the world.

1984

Everybody Knows[1]

Everybody knows that the dice are loaded. Everybody
rolls with their fingers crossed. Everybody knows the
war is over. Everybody knows the good guys lost. Everybody knows the fight was fixed: the poor stay poor, the
rich get rich. That's how it goes. Everybody knows.

Everybody knows that the boat is leaking. Everybody
knows the captain lied. Everybody got this broken
feeling like their father or their dog just died. Everybody
talking to their pockets. Everybody wants a box of
chocolates and a long-stem rose. Everybody knows.

1 Written with Sharon Robinson.

Everybody knows that you love me, baby. Everybody knows that you really do. Everybody knows that you've been faithful, give or take a night or two. Everybody knows you've been discreet but there were so many people you just had to meet without your clothes. And everybody knows.

Everybody knows that it's now or never. Everybody knows that it's me or you. Everybody knows that you live forever when you've done a line or two. Everybody knows the deal is rotten: Old Black Joe's still picking cotton for your ribbons and bows.[2] Everybody knows.

Everybody knows that the Plague is coming. Everybody knows that it's moving fast. Everybody knows that the naked man and woman—just a shining artifact of the past. Everybody knows the scene is dead, but there's going to be a metre on your bed that will disclose what everybody knows.

Everybody knows that you're in trouble. Everybody knows what you've been through, from the bloody cross on top of Calvary to the beach at Malibu. Everybody knows it's coming apart: take one last look at this Sacred Heart before it blows. And everybody knows.

1993 (recorded 1988)

2 Old Black Joe, the title character of a song by Stephen Foster (1826–64), served for a time as a sentimentalized personification of the 'happy slave' on pre-Civil War plantations. Written in 1860, when slavery was still an institution in the American South, the song begins with the verse, 'Gone are the days when my heart was young and gay, / Gone are my friends from the cotton fields away, / Gone from the earth to a better land I know, / I hear their gentle voices calling "Old Black Joe".'

The Future

Give me back my broken night
my mirrored room, my secret life
It's lonely here,
there's no one left to torture
Give me absolute control
over every living soul
And lie beside me, baby,
that's an order!

Give me crack and anal sex
Take the only tree that's left
and stuff it up the hole
in your culture
Give me back the Berlin Wall
give me Stalin and St Paul
I've seen the future, brother:
it is murder.

Things are going to slide in all directions
Won't be nothing
Nothing you can measure any more
The blizzard of the world
has crossed the threshold
and it has overturned
the order of the soul
When they said REPENT
I wonder what they meant

You don't know me from the wind
you never will, you never did
I'm the little jew
who wrote the bible
I've seen the nations rise and fall
I've heard their stories, heard them all
but love's the only engine of survival

Your servant here, he has been told
to say it clear, to say it cold:
It's over, it ain't going
any further
And now the wheels of heaven stop
you feel the devil's riding crop
Get ready for the future:
it is murder.

Things are going to slide in all directions

There'll be the breaking
of the ancient western code
Your private life will suddenly explode
There'll be phantoms
there'll be fires on the road
and the white man dancing

You'll see your woman
hanging upside down
her features covered by her fallen gown
and all the lousy little poets
coming round
trying to sound like Charlie Manson

Give me back the Berlin Wall
give me Stalin and St Paul
Give me Christ
or give me Hiroshima
Destroy another fetus now
We don't like children anyhow
I've seen the future, baby:
it is murder.

Things are going to slide in all directions
Won't be nothing
Nothing you can measure any more
The blizzard of the world
has crossed the threshold
and it has overturned
the order of the soul
When they said REPENT
I wonder what they meant

1993 (recorded 1992)

Closing Time

So we're drinking and we're dancing
and the band is really happening
and the Johnny Walker wisdom running high
And my very sweet companion
she's the Angel of Compassion
and she's rubbing half the world against her thigh
Every drinker, every dancer
lifts a happy face to thank her
and the fiddler fiddles something so sublime
All the women tear their blouses off
and the men they dance on the polka-dots
and it's partner found and it's partner lost

and it's hell to pay when the fiddler stops
It's closing time

We're lonely, we're romantic
and the cider's laced with acid
and the Holy Spirit's crying, 'Where's the beef?'
And the moon is swimming naked
and the summer night is fragrant
with a mighty expectation of relief
So we struggle and we stagger
down the snakes and up the ladder
to the tower where the blessed hours chime
And I swear it happened just like this:
a sigh, a cry, a hungry kiss
the Gates of Love they budged an inch
I can't say much has happened since
but closing time

I loved you for your beauty
but that doesn't make a fool of me—
you were in it for your beauty too
I loved you for your body
there's a voice that sounds like G-d to me
declaring that your body's really you
I loved you when our love was blessed
and I love you now there's nothing left
but sorrow and a sense of overtime
And I miss you since our place got wrecked
I just don't care what happens next
looks like freedom but it feels like death
it's something in between, I guess
it's closing time

And I miss you since the place got wrecked
by the winds of change and the weeds of sex
looks like freedom but it feels like death
it's something in between, I guess
it's closing time

We're drinking and we're dancing
but there's nothing really happening
the place is dead as Heaven on a Saturday night
and my very close companion
gets me fumbling, gets me laughing
she's a hundred but she's wearing something tight

And I lift my glass to the Awful Truth
which you can't reveal to the Ears of Youth
except to say it isn't worth a dime
And the whole damn place goes crazy twice
and it's once for the Devil and it's once for Christ
but the Boss don't like these dizzy heights—
we're busted in the blinding lights
of closing time

1993 (recorded 1992)

From *Beautiful Losers*

WHAT IS A SAINT

What is a saint? A saint is someone who has achieved a remote human possibility. It is impossible to say what that possibility is. I think it has something to do with the energy of love. Contact with this energy results in the exercise of a kind of balance in the chaos of existence. A saint does not dissolve the chaos; if he did the world would have changed long ago. I do not think that a saint dissolves the chaos even for himself, for there is something arrogant and warlike in the notion of a man setting the universe in order. It is a kind of balance that is his glory. He rides the drifts like an escaped ski. His course is a caress of the hill. His track is a drawing of the snow in a moment of its particular arrangement with wind and rock. Something in him so loves the world that he gives himself to the laws of gravity and chance. Far from flying with the angels, he traces with the fidelity of a seismograph needle the state of the solid bloody landscape. His house is dangerous and finite, but he is at home in the world. He can love the shapes of human beings, the fine and twisted shapes of the heart. It is good to have among us such men, such balancing monsters of love.

[WE ARE NOW IN THE HEART]

We are now in the heart of the last feature in the System Theatre. Within severe limits, like smoke in a chimney, the dusty projection beam above our hair twisted and changed. Like crystals rioting in a test-tube suspension, the unstable ray changed and changed in its black confinement. Like battalions of sabotaged parachutists falling from the training tower straight down in various contortions, the frames streamed at the screen, splashing into contrast colour as they hit, just as the bursting cocoons of arctic camouflage spread colourful organic contents over the snow as the divers disintegrate, one after the other. No, it was more like a ghostly white snake sealed in an immense telescope. It was a serpent swimming home, lazily occupying the entire sewer which irrigated the auditorium. It was the first snake in the shadows of the original garden, the albino orchard snake offering our female memory the taste of—everything! As it floated and danced and writhed in the gloom over us, I often raised my eyes to consult the projection beam rather than the story it carried. Neither of you noticed me. Sometimes I conceded surprising territories of the armrest so as to distract your pleasure. I studied the snake and he made me greedy for everything. In the midst of this heady contemplation, I am invited to formulate the question which will torment me most. I formulate the question and it begins to torment me immediately: *What will happen when the newsreel escapes into the Feature?* What will happen when the newsreel occurs at its own pleasure or accident in any whatever frame of the Vistavision, willy nilly? The newsreel lies between the street and the Feature like Boulder Dam, vital as a border in the Middle East—breach it (so I thought), and a miasmal mixture will imperialize existence by means of its sole quality of total corrosion. So I thought! The newsreel lies between the street and the Feature: like a tunnel on the Sunday drive it ends quickly and in creepy darkness joins the rural mountains to the slums. It took courage! I let the newsreel escape, I invited it to walk right into plot, and they merged in aweful originality, just as trees and plastic synthesize new powerful landscapes in those districts of the highway devoted to motels. Long live motels, the name, the motive, the success! Here is my message, old lover of my heart. Here is what I saw: here is what I learned:

Sophia Loren Strips For A Flood Victim
THE FLOOD IS REAL AT LAST

1966

Rudy Wiebe
b. 1934

Born in a Mennonite farming community in northern Saskatchewan, near Fairholme, to parents who came to Canada from the Soviet Union in 1930, Rudy Wiebe grew up in a polyglot environment in which the Low German dialect was the language of everyday life, English that of school, and High German that of religion. After receiving his primary and secondary education in Saskatchewan and Alberta, where his family moved in 1947, Wiebe graduated from the University of Alberta in 1966. He then continued his studies at the University of Tübingen, West Germany, and completed his MA back at the University of Alberta. (His thesis was the manuscript of his first novel.) After earning a teaching certificate at the University of Manitoba and a Bachelor of Theology degree from the Mennonite Brethren Bible College, Wiebe worked for a year and a half for the *Mennonite Brethren Herald*, a weekly church publication. He resigned following a controversy over the details about Mennonite life revealed in *Peace Shall Destroy Many* (1962), his first novel, about the crisis a young man faces when he must choose between pursuing Mennonite pacifism and aligning himself with the general social atmosphere of Canada during the Second World War. He took a job teaching English at a Mennonite college in Indiana, where he remained until 1967, when he accepted a position in the English department of the University of Alberta. (Since 1992 he has been professor emeritus.)

Wiebe's second novel, *First and Vital Candle* (1966), describes a crisis of faith for a young man who, displaced from modern society, cannot find a satisfactory alternative among the Native peoples in the North. His next three books—*The Blue Mountains of China* (1970), a complex, panoramic history of the Mennonites; *The Temptations of Big Bear* (1973, Governor General's Award), an account of the disintegration of Aboriginal culture that resulted from the growth of the Canadian nation; and *The Scorched-Wood People* (1977), the related story of Louis Riel's struggle to establish recognition for the Métis—are all epic stories of minority peoples who fight to maintain the integrity of their communities. *The Mad Trapper* (1980) chronicles the struggle between sharpshooter Albert Johnson, an isolated individual who has turned to violence and self-destruction, and the members of the Northern community who must hunt him.

Wiebe reflected on the pursuit of history that characterizes his fiction in *My Lovely Enemy* (1983), a love story set against an account of a historian's struggle to make sense of the past and of his own relationship to history. *A Discovery of Strangers* (1994), a novel about the first Franklin expedition, draws on his collection of essays on early exploration and contemporary life in the North—*Playing Dead: A Contemplation Concerning the Arctic* (1989)—by interweaving the story of the expedition with passages from the journals kept by John Richardson and Robert Hood; the novel earned him a second Governor General's Award. His most recent novel is *Sweeter than All the World* (2001), about a man who, when his marriage and family life begin to collapse, looks back on his Mennonite ancestry, tracing four centuries of his family history from the Netherlands in the sixteenth century through Russia and South America, to the Alberta homestead where he was born in 1935.

Wiebe's short fiction was first collected in *Where is the Voice Coming From?* (1974); he later provided stories for *Alberta / A Celebration* (1979). Stories from both books were republished in *The Angel of the Tar Sands and Other Stories* (1982). *River of Stone: Fiction and Memories* (1995) combines some of Wiebe's short fiction with personal narratives and memoirs. Wiebe has also written a play, *Far as the Eye Can See* (1977), and edited a number of anthologies, some focusing on the western Canadian short story, and others, such as *The Storymakers* (1970), placing the Canadian short story in an international context. His book for children, *Chinook Christmas* (1992), with illustrations by David More, looks at southern Alberta Christmas traditions.

The single most important feature of Wiebe's writing is the moral vision that derives from his religious background. Central to Mennonite belief is the rejection of worldly loyalties and values, particularly those associated with the state, in favour of commitment to a Christian community. (Revolutionary pacifists, Mennonites fled Germany and the Netherlands in the eighteenth and nineteenth centuries, going to Russia and the Americas, as much in an effort to preserve their community as to avoid the persecution and violence they had frequently encountered.) Wiebe believes that today this close, nonconformist community is no longer functioning as it should: he sees the Mennonites in North America as having accepted middle-class values and goals and become part of the modern, urban culture. Still, even though much of the original vitality of the community has been replaced by a reverence for heritage—which offers no free choices for the individual—and the once revolutionary new ways have become rituals, Wiebe considers these eroded communities better than none at all. Wiebe addresses these concerns and his own role as an artist in his essays and interviews in *A Voice in the Land* (1981).

Wiebe does not see the loss of community and the alienation of the individual as unique to the Mennonites. In particular he sees affinities between the Mennonite community in Canada and Canada's First Nations—about whom he has written extensively—who, like the Mennonites, exist on the margin of contemporary society. Having already written a novel on Big Bear, Wiebe met the Cree chief's great-great-granddaughter, Yvonne Johnson, in 1991—at that time imprisoned in the Kingston Federal Prison for Women—and over the next seven years helped her record her memoirs. These were published as *Stolen Life: The Journey of a Cree Woman* (1998).

Wiebe's fiction confronts problems of alienation of the individual in larger contexts as well. In his three major novels he outlines what he sees as the obligatory human action: remaining true to one's beliefs while attempting to build, maintain, or re-establish a community—a spiritual collectivity that gains its identity from the antagonism of the outside world and from the martyrdom its leaders freely seek. The spiritual ideals that Wiebe's heroes wish to maintain are those that are reinforced by a historical consciousness—an ongoing involvement with, and devotion to, the past.

While Wiebe's interest in uniting the present with historical events is visible in many other Canadian writers as well, the extent of his faith in the redemptive value of a revitalized history is striking. His method of reclaiming the forgotten past by adding imagined details of daily life and individual perceptions to material available in documents is an attempt to provide his readers with the texture of a spiritual community that is otherwise unavailable to them. In a way that is parallel to his belief that communities must be almost inaccessible to those outside them, Wiebe makes entry into his fictional worlds difficult, through the use of unfamiliar dialects, a sometimes opaque style, complex time shifts, and meticulous detail. It is as if he writes his novels for an audience that already shares his views, or is at least willing to be converted or tested.

'Where is the Voice Coming From?'—one of Wiebe's best-known stories—dramatizes his interest in the complex relationship of document, history, and fiction. In this examination of the tragic confrontation between Kah-kee-say-mane-too-wayo ('Voice of the Great Spirit' or 'Almighty Voice', 1874–97) and the North-West Mounted Police, an event that has been the subject of conflicting accounts, Wiebe gives powerful expression to a paradox that he shares with many of his contemporaries—a sense that while the act of turning events into stories may be falsifying, it is also may be our only way of experiencing the past.

Where Is the Voice Coming From?

The problem is to make the story.

One difficulty of this making may have been excellently stated by Teilhard de Chardin:[1] 'We are continually inclined to isolate ourselves from the things and events which surround us . . . as though we were spectators, not elements, in what goes on.' Arnold Toynbee does venture, 'For all that we know, Reality is the undifferentiated unity of the mystical experience,' but that need not here be considered. This story ended long ago; it is one of the finite acts, of orders, of elemental feelings and reactions, of obvious legal restrictions and requirements.

Presumably all the parts of the story are themselves available. A difficulty is that they are, as always, available only in bits and pieces. Though the acts themselves seem quite clear, some written reports of the acts contradict each other. As if these acts were, at one time, too well known; as if the original nodule of each particular fact had from somewhere received non-factual accretions; or even more, as if, since the basic facts

1 Pierre Teilhard de Chardin (1881–1955), French Jesuit philosopher whose unorthodox views included the concept of the 'noosphere', a kind of evolving collective consciousness formed by humanity's mental activity. Arnold Toynbee (1889–1975), the English historian best known for his twelve-volume *Study of History* (1934–61), believed that history exhibited unitary order, which was evidence of a cosmic design.

were so clear perhaps there were a larger number of facts than any one reporter, or several, or even any reporter had ever attempted to record. About facts that are still simply told by this mouth to that ear, of course, even less can be expected.

An affair seventy-five years old should acquire some of the shiny transparency of an old man's skin. It should.

Sometimes it would seem that it would be enough—perhaps more than enough—to hear the names only. The grandfather One Arrow; the mother Spotted Calf; the father Sounding Sky; the wife (wives rather, but only one of them seems to have a name, though their fathers are Napaise, Kapahoo, Old Dust, The Rump)—the one wife named, of all things, Pale Face; the cousin Going-Up-To-Sky; the brother-in-law (again, of all things) Dublin. The names of the police sound very much alike; they all begin with Constable or Corporal or Sergeant, but here and there an Inspector, then a Superintendent and eventually all the resonance of an Assistant Commissioner echoes down. More. Herself: Victoria, by the Grace of God etc., etc., QUEEN, defender of the Faith, etc., etc.; and witness 'Our Right Trusty and Right Well-beloved Cousin and Councillor the Right Honorable Sir John Campbell Hamilton-Gordon, Earl of Aberdeen; Viscount Formartine, Baron Haddo, Methlic, Tarves and Kellie, in the Peerage of Scotland; Viscount Gordon of Aberdeen, County of Aberdeen, in the Peerage of the United Kingdom; Baronet of Nova Scotia, Knight Grand Cross of Our Most Distinguished Order of Saint Michael and Saint George, etc., Governor General of Canada'. And of course himself: in the award proclamation named 'Jean-Baptiste' but otherwise known only as Almighty Voice.

But hearing cannot be enough; not even hearing all the thunder of A Proclamation: 'Now Hear Ye that a reward of FIVE HUNDRED DOLLARS will be paid to any person or persons who will give such information as will lead . . . (etc., etc.) this Twentieth day of April, in the year of Our Lord one thousand eight hundred and ninety-six, and the Fifty-ninth year of Our Reign . . .' etc. and etc.

Such hearing cannot be enough. The first item to be seen is the piece of white bone. It is almost triangular, slightly convex—concave actually as it is positioned at this moment with its corners slightly raised—graduating from perhaps a strong eighth to a weak quarter of an inch in thickness, its scattered pore structure varying between larger and smaller on its perhaps polished, certainly shiny surface. Precision is difficult since the glass showcase is at least thirteen inches deep and therefore an eye cannot be brought as close as the minute inspection of such a small, though certainly quite adequate, sample of skull would normally require. Also, because of the position it cannot be determined whether the several hairs, well over a foot long, are still in some manner attached or not.

The seven-pounder cannon can be seen standing almost shyly between the showcase and the interior wall. Officially it is known as a gun, not a cannon, and clearly its bore is not large enough to admit a large man's fist. Even if it can be believed that this gun was used in the 1885 Rebellion and that on the evening of Saturday, May 29, 1897 (while the nine-pounder, now unidentified, was in the process of arriving with the police on the special train from Regina), seven shells (all that were available in Prince Albert at that time) from it were sent shrieking into the poplar bluffs as night fell, clearly such shelling could not and would not disembowel the whole earth. Its carriage is now nicely lacquered, the perhaps oak spokes of its petite wheels (little higher than a knee) have been recently scraped, puttied and varnished; the brilliant burnish of its brass breeching testifies with what meticulous care charmen and women have used nationally-advertised cleaners and restorers.

Though it can also be seen, even a careless glance reveals that the same concern has not been expended on the one (of two) .44 calibre 1866 model Winchesters apparently found at the last in the pit with Almighty Voice. It also is preserved in a glass case; the number 1536735 is still, though barely, distinguishable on the brass cartridge section just below the brass saddle ring. However, perhaps because the case was imperfectly sealed at one time (though sealed enough not to warrant disturbance now), or because of simple neglect, the rifle is obviously spotted here and there with blotches of rust and the brass itself reveals discolorations almost like mildew. The rifle bore, the three long strands of hair themselves, actually bristle with clots of dust. It may be that this museum cannot afford to be as concerned as the other; conversely, the disfiguration may be something inherent in the items themselves.

The small building which was the police guardroom at Duck Lake, Saskatchewan Territory, in 1895 may also be seen. It had subsequently been moved from its original place and used to house small animals, chickens perhaps, or pigs—such as a woman might be expected to have under her responsibility. It is, of course, now perfectly empty, and clean so that the public may enter with no more discomfort than a bend under the doorway and a heavy encounter with disinfectant. The door-jamb has obviously been replaced; the bar network at one window is, however, said to be original; smooth still, very smooth. The logs inside have been smeared again and again with whitewash, perhaps paint, to an insistent point of identity-defying characterlessness. Within the small rectangular box of these logs not a sound can be heard from the streets of the, probably dead, town.

Hey Injun you'll get hung for stealing that steer
Hey Injun for killing that government cow you'll get three
weeks on the woodpile Hey Injun

The place named Kinistino seems to have disappeared from the map but the Minnechinass Hills have not. Whether they have ever been on a map is doubtful but they will, of course, not disappear from the landscape as long as the grass grows and the rivers run. Contrary to general report and belief, the Canadian prairies are rarely, if ever, flat and the Minnechinass (spelled five different ways and translated sometimes as 'The Outside Hill', sometimes as 'Beautiful Bare Hills') are dissimilar from any other of the numberless hills that everywhere block out the prairie horizon. They are bare; poplars lie tattered along their tops, almost black against the straw-pale grass and sharp green against the grey soil of the plowing laid in half-mile rectangular blocks upon their western slopes. Poles holding various wires stick out of the fields, back down the bend of the valley; what was once a farmhouse is weathering into the cultivated earth. The poplar bluff where Almighty Voice made his stand has, of course, disappeared.

The policemen he shot and killed (not the ones he wounded, of course) are easily located. Six miles east, thirty-nine miles north in Prince Albert, the English Cemetery. Sergeant Colin Campbell Colebrook, North West Mounted Police Registration Number 605, lies presumably under a gravestone there. His name is seventeenth in a very long 'list of non-commissioned officers and men who have died in the service since the inception of the force'. The date is October 29, 1895, and the cause of death is anonymous: 'Shot by escaping Indian prisoner near Prince Albert.' At the foot of this grave are two others: Constable John R. Kerr, No. 3040, and Corporal C.H.S. Hockin, No. 3106. Their cause of death on May 28, 1897 is even more anonymous, but the place is relatively precise: 'Shot by Indians at Min-etch-inass Hills, Prince Albert District.'

The gravestone, if he has one, of the fourth man Almighty Voice killed is more difficult to locate. Mr Ernest Grundy, postmaster at Duck Lake in 1897, apparently shut his window the afternoon of Friday, May 28, armed himself, rode east twenty miles, participated in the second charge into the bluff at about 6:30 p.m., and on the third sweep of that charge was shot dead at the edge of the pit. It would seem that he thereby contributed substantially not only to the Indians' bullet supply, but his clothing warmed them as well.

The burial place of Dublin and Going-Up-To-Sky is unknown, as is the grave of Almighty Voice. It is said that a Métis named Henry Smith lifted the latter's body from the pit in the bluff and gave it to Spotted Calf. The place of burial is not, of course, of ultimate significance. A gravestone is always less evidence than a triangular piece of skull, provided it is large enough.

Whatever further evidence there is to be gathered may rest on pictures. There are, presumably, almost numberless pictures of the policemen in the case, but the only one with direct bearing is one of Sergeant Colebrook, who apparently insisted on advancing to complete an arrest after being warned three times that if he took another step he would be shot. The picture must have been taken before he joined the force; it reveals him a large-eared young man, hair brush-cut and ascot tie, his eyelids slightly drooping, almost hooded under thick brows. Unfortunately a picture of Constable R.C. Dickson, into whose charge Almighty Voice was apparently committed in that guardroom and who after Colebrook's death was convicted of negligence, sentenced to two months hard labour and discharged, does not seem to be available.

There are no pictures to be found of either Dublin (killed early by rifle fire) or Going-Up-To-Sky (killed in the pit), the two teenage boys who gave their ultimate fealty to Almighty Voice. There is, however, one said to be of Almighty Voice, Junior. He may have been born to Pale Face during the year, two hundred and twenty-one days that his father was a fugitive. In the picture he is kneeling before what could be a tent, he wears striped denim overalls and displays twin babies whose sex cannot be determined by the double-laced dark bonnets they wear. In the supposed picture of Spotted Calf and Sounding Sky, Sounding Sky stands slightly before his wife; he wears a white shirt and a striped blanket folded over his left shoulder in such a manner that the arm in which he cradles a long rifle cannot be seen. His head is thrown back; the rim of his hat appears as a black half-moon above eyes that are pressed shut in, as it were, profound concentration; above a mouth clenched thin in a downward curve.

Spotted Calf wears a long dress, a sweater which could also be a man's dress coat, and a large fringed and embroidered shawl which would appear distinctly Doukhobor[2] in origin if the scroll patterns on it were more irregular. Her head is small and turned slightly towards her husband so as to reveal her right ear. There is what can only be called a quizzical expression on her crumpled face; it may be she does not understand what is happening and that she would have asked a question, perhaps of her husband, perhaps of the photographers, perhaps even of anyone, anywhere in the world if such questioning were possible for an Indian lady.

There is one final picture. That is one of Almighty Voice himself. At least it is purported to be of Almighty Voice himself. In the Royal Canadian Mounted Police Museum on the Barracks Grounds just off Dewdney Avenue in Regina, Saskatchewan, it lies in the same showcase, as a matter of fact immediately beside, that triangular piece of skull. Both are unequivocally labelled, and it must be assumed that a police force with a world-wide reputation would not label *such* evidence incorrectly. But here emerges an ultimate problem in making the story.

There are two official descriptions of Almighty Voice. The first reads: 'Height about five feet, ten inches, slight build, rather good looking, a sharp hooked nose with a remarkably flat point. Has a bullet scar on the left side of his face about 1½ inches long running from near corner of mouth towards ear. The scar cannot be noticed when his face is painted but otherwise is plain. Skin fair for an Indian.' The second description is on the Award Proclamation: 'About twenty-two years old, five feet ten inches in height, weight about eleven stone, slightly erect, neat small feet and hands; complexion inclined to be fair, wavy dark hair to shoulders, large dark eyes, broad forehead, sharp features and parrot nose with flat tip, scar on left cheek running from mouth towards ear, feminine appearance.'

So run the descriptions that were, presumably, to identify a well-known fugitive in so precise a manner that an informant could collect five hundred dollars—a considerable sum when a police constable earned between one and two dollars a day. The nexus of the problems appears when these supposed official descriptions are compared to the supposed official picture. The man in the picture is standing on a small rug. The fingers of his left hand touch a curved Victorian settee, behind him a photographer's backdrop of scrolled patterns merges to vaguely paradisiacal trees and perhaps a sky. The moccasins he wears make it impossible to deduce whether his feet are 'neat small'. He may be five feet, ten inches tall, may weigh eleven stone, he certainly is 'rather good looking' and, though it is a frontal view, it may be that the point of his long and flaring nose could be 'remarkably flat'. The photograph is slightly over-illuminated and so the unpainted complexion could be 'inclined to be fair'; however, nothing can be seen of a scar, the hair is not wavy and shoulder-length but hangs almost to the waist in two thick straight braids worked through with beads, fur, ribbons and cords. The right hand that holds the corner of the blanket-like coat in position is large and, even in the high illumination, heavily veined. The neck is concealed under coiled beads and the forehead seems more low than 'broad'.

2 Member of a Russian Christian sect, many members of which migrated to western Canada in 1899 after persecution for refusing military service.

Perhaps, somehow, these picture details could be reconciled with the official description if the face as a whole were not so devastating.

On a cloth-backed sheet two feet by two-and-one-half feet in size, under the Great Seal of the Lion and the Unicorn, dignified by the names of the Deputy of the Minister of Justice, the Secretary of State, the Queen herself and all the heaped detail of her 'Right Trusty and Right Well Beloved Cousin', this description concludes: 'feminine appearance'. But the pictures: any face of history, any believed face that the world acknowledges as *man*—Socrates, Jesus, Attila, Genghis Khan, Mahatma Gandhi, Joseph Stalin—no believed face is more *man* than this face. The mouth, the nose, the clenched brows, the eyes—the eyes are large, yes, and dark, but even in this watered-down reproduction of unending reproductions of that original, a steady look into those eyes cannot be endured. It is a face like an ax.

It is not evident that the de Chardin statement quoted at the beginning has relevance only as it proves itself inadequate to explain what has happened. At the same time, the inadequacy of Aristotle's much more famous statement becomes evident: 'The true difference [between the historian and the poet] is that one relates what *has* happened, the other what *may* happen.' These statements cannot explain the storyteller's activity, since, despite the most rigid application of impersonal investigation, the elements of the story have now run me aground. If ever I could, I can no longer pretend to objective, omnipotent disinterestedness. I am no longer *spectator* of what *has* happened or what *may* happen: I am become *element* in what is happening at this very moment.

For it is, of course, I myself who cannot endure the shadows on that paper which are those eyes. It is I who stand beside this broken veranda post where two corner shingles have been torn away, where barbed wire tangles the dead weeds on the edge of this field. The bluff that sheltered Almighty Voice and his two friends has not disappeared from the slope of the Minnechinass, no more than the sound of Constable Dickson's voice in that guardhouse is silent. The sound of his speaking is there even if it has never been recorded in an official report:

hey injun you'll get
hung
for stealing that steer
hey injun for killing that government
cow you'll get three
weeks on the woodpile hey injun

The unknown contradictory words about an unprovable act that move a boy to defiance, an implacable Cree warrior long after the three-hundred-and-fifty-year war is ended, a war already lost the day the Cree watch Cartier hoist his gun ashore at Hochelaga[3] and they begin the long retreat west; these words of incomprehension, of threatened incomprehensible law are there to be heard just as the unmoving tableau of the three-day siege is there to be seen on the slopes of the Minnechinass. Sounding Sky

3 Former Native village, located at the present-day site of Montreal, where Jacques Cartier arrived in the fall of 1535.

is somewhere not there, under arrest, but Spotted Calf stands on a shoulder of the Hills a little to the left, her arms upraised to the setting sun. Her mouth is open. A horse rears, riderless, above the scrub willow at the edge of the bluff, smoke puffs, screams tangle in rifle barrage, there are wounds, somewhere. The bluff is so green this spring, it will not burn and the ragged line of seven police and two civilians is staggering through, faces twisted in rage, terror, and rifles sputter. Nothing moves. There is no sound of frogs in the night; twenty-seven policemen and five civilians stand in cordon at thirty-yard intervals and a body also lies in the shelter of a gully. Only a voice rises from the bluff:

We have fought well
You have died like braves
I have worked hard and am hungry
Give me food

but nothing moves. The bluff lies, a bright green island on the grassy slope surrounded by men hunched forward rigid over their long rifles, men clumped out of rifle-range, thirty-five men dressed as for fall hunting on a sharp spring day, a small gun positioned on a ridge above. A crow is falling out of the sky into the bluff, its feathers sprayed as by an explosion. The first gun and the second gun are in position, the beginning and end of the bristling surround of thirty-five Prince Albert Volunteers, thirteen civilians, and fifty-six policemen in position relative to the bluff and relative to the unnumbered whites astride their horses, standing up in their carts, staring and pointing across the valley, in position relative to the bluff and the unnumbered Indians squatting silent along the higher ridges of the Hills, motionless mounds, faceless against the Sunday morning sunlight edging between and over them down along the tree tips, down into the shadows of the bluff. Nothing moves. Beside the second gun the red-coated officer has flung a handful of grass into the motionless air, almost to the rim of the red sun.

And there is a voice. It is an incredible voice that rises from among the young poplars ripped of their spring bark, from among the dead somewhere lying there, out of the arm-deep pit shorter than a man; a voice rises over the exploding smoke and thunder of guns that reel back in their positions, worked over, serviced by the grimed motionless men in bright coats and glinting buttons, a voice so high and clear, so unbelievably high and strong in its unending wordless cry.

The voice of 'Gitchie-Manitou Wayo'—interpreted as 'voice of the Great Spirit'—that is, The Almighty Voice. His death chant no less incredible in its beauty than in its incomprehensible happiness.

I say 'wordless cry' because that is the way it sounds to me. I could be more accurate if I had a reliable interpreter who would make a reliable interpretation. For I do not, of course, understand the Cree myself.

1982

George Bowering

b. 1935

A playful sense of humour has led George Bowering to add, to the substantial body of work under his own name, so many poems and reviews under various pseudonyms that his bibliographers may never straighten out all the questions of authorship. He has similarly confused his biographers by such acts as naming at least three different towns in the Okanagan Valley of British Columbia as his birthplace: Penticton, Osoyoos, and Oliver. ('A very slow birth in a fast-moving car' is how he once explained this.) He was actually born in the first of these. He left to become an aerial photographer for the RCAF (1954–7). After his service, he enrolled at the University of British Columbia, where he earned a BA in history (1960) and an MA in English (1963).

At UBC Bowering studied creative writing under Earle Birney, as well as with visiting professor Robert Creeley (who was Bowering's MA thesis adviser), and became part of a group of aspiring poets that included Frank Davey, Fred Wah, Daphne Buckle (Daphne Marlatt), and Lionel Kearns. From UBC professor Warren Tallman they learned about contemporary American movements, especially the aesthetic theories and poetic practices current on the American west coast, which were then under the sway of the poetics of William Carlos Williams and the Black Mountain movement (an influential school of poetry begun at Black Mountain College in North Carolina by Charles Olson, Robert Duncan, and Creeley), and about avant-garde writers such as Jack Spicer and Beat poet Allen Ginsberg. These young BC poets were inspired by a 1961 visit to Vancouver by Duncan—who discussed both Black Mountain theories and the importance of 'little magazines' for new poetry movements—to launch their own literary periodical, *Tish*, a monthly poetry 'newsletter' that patterned itself in part after such magazines as *Origin* in the US and Louis Dudek's *Delta* in Canada.

The writers associated with the magazine came to be known as the '*Tish* group'. They were greatly influenced by the Black Mountain movement's spare style (an inheritance from the imagist tradition and from Williams), as well as its use of a loose poetic line based on the rhythms and pauses of colloquial speech, its emphasis on local and regional aspects of experience, and its belief in the communal nature of writing. Especially interested in the long poem (in the tradition of Williams' *Patterson*) and in the serial poem (as developed by Spicer), they rejected the lyric mode associated with what they decried as the 'humanism' and 'romanticism' of poetry from eastern Canada and the eastern US. Following Olson, they called for a poetry of essentials that would be accurate and objective, created by writers who, as Bowering later said, 'turned their attention upon the factual things that make up the world' (*Tish*, No. 20, 1963).

Although *Tish* lasted for eight years (forty-five issues), its founders left after issue No. 19 to pursue other interests. Bowering accepted a teaching position at the University of Calgary, then went to the University of Western Ontario for further graduate studies before becoming writer-in-residence, and subsequently professor, at Sir George Williams University (now part of Concordia). In 1971 he returned to BC to teach English and creative writing at Simon Fraser University. (He is now a professor emeritus.) He remained committed to little-magazine publishing in Canada, first founding and editing *Imago* (1964–74) and then becoming contributing editor for Frank Davey's influential literary and critical journal *Open Letter* (begun in 1965).

The most prolific member of the *Tish* group, Bowering has published more than thirty books of poetry, mostly with small presses. His first book, *Sticks & Stones* (with a preface by Creeley), appeared in 1963. He received a Governor General's Award in 1969 for the two books of poetry he published that year: *Rocky*

Mountain Foot and *The Gangs of Kosmos*. Among his later books are *Touch: Selected Poems 1960–70* (1971); *Selected Poems: Particular Accidents* (1980), and *Seventy-one Poems for People* (1985). *George Bowering Selected: Poems 1961–1992* (1993) brings together a substantial sample of his work. Like other poets of the *Tish* group, Bowering tends to avoid rhetorical devices and metaphor, preferring a language and style close to common speech. (Some of Bowering's long works—such as *Autobiology*, 1972, and *A Short Sad Book*, 1977—straddle the borderline between prose and poetry.) His poetry is saved from prosiness by a subtle musical quality in the diction and rhythms, and from slackness by its sharply etched observations.

Since 1970 Bowering's most important poetry has taken the form of loosely unified long poems; several of these are reprinted in *The Catch* (1976) and in *West Window* (1982). The best known of these is the book-length poem *Kerrisdale Elegies* (1985), a meditative sequence modelled on Rainer Maria Rilke's *Duino Elegies* (1923), recast in contemporary terms and set in a contemporary Vancouver neighbourhood. Bowering's fascination with baseball—visible in several of his earlier poems (as in the chapbook *Poem and Other Baseballs*, 1976)—leads him to use a game of softball as an organizing device in Elegy Five.

Bowering's most recent book of poetry, *His Life: A Poem* (2000), is a sequence drawing on personal experiences from 1958 to 1988. Of the way he has often drawn from his life in his books, he observed in *Errata* (1988):

> *I never wanted to write an autobiography. I think that certain works I have done with what looks like my life story should be called biotext. . . . Autobiography replaces the writer. Biotext is an extension of him.*

Bowering is also the author of a number of important prose works. His short stories have been collected as *Flycatcher & Other Stories* (1974); *Protective Footwear: Stories and Fables* (1978); *A Place to Die* (1983); and *The Rain Barrel and Other Stories* (1994). He is the author of a novella, *Concentric Circles* (1977); and of five novels: *A Mirror on the Floor* (1967); *Burning Water* (1980), which won Bowering his second Governor General's Award; *Harry's Fragments*, a parody thriller (1990); and two mock-westerns, *Caprice* (1987) and *Shoot!* (1994), a metafiction about the McLean boys, a notorious gang of outlaws in BC.

Although he has written critical pieces throughout his career, in the eighties Bowering turned to criticism with particular intensity, publishing four collections of essays: *A Way with Words* (1982); *The Mask in Place: Essays on Fiction in North America* (1983); *Craft Slices* (1985); and *Imaginary Hand* (1988). Several of his prose works, such as *Errata*, combine critical and personal meditations.

Bowering has also written two books of history: *Bowering's B.C.: A Swashbucking History* (1996) and *Egoists and Autocrats: The Prime Ministers of Canada* (1999), in which he draws on his sense of humour and talents as a storyteller to offer fresh—but not objective—accounts of their subjects. Like that of other members of the *Tish* group, all of Bowering's writing, even this, strives to communicate a sense of a work that is not finished but in *process*. This quality is conveyed by dramatizing the writer in the text—the author embodied in the act of writing—and locating the work within the subjectivities that surround the act of creation. Such writing is postmodern in its rejection of the modernist doctrine of the artist as a detached maker of impersonal, objective, and permanent artifacts.

It is the poet's developing awareness in *Kerrisdale Elegies* that gives immediacy to his larger subject—that of loss. The dramatization of the poem's speaker (as in the opening of Elegy Two) works particularly well in an elegiac work, in which writers traditionally, by mourning and expressing personal bereavement, become mediators for their readers' griefs. Because Bowering's poem deals in part with a loss of culture and identity, it has a special place in a Canadian context, which has seen a number of laments for lost ideals or heritages. But Bowering's poem also occupies a place within the larger elegiac mode, in which the poet reminds us of the inevitability of mortality and grieves for the passing away of that which we have known and loved.

From *Kerrisdale Elegies*

ELEGY TWO

Dead poets' voices I have heard in my head
are not terrifying.
They tell me like lovers
we are worth speaking to,
I am a branch
a singing bird will stand on for a moment.[1]

Like a singing branch I call out in return. How
do otherwise?
Rather that than couple
with a swan on 41st Avenue.
When Hilda[2]
appeared in my dream, she did not visit, she
walked by, into the other room,
and I didn't fall
in fear, but in love.

Inside.

Out there was the fortunate fall,[3] mountains
glistening with creation,
a glacier between them,
flowing bright out of the working god's fingers,
first orchards rising from the melt, light
shaped on crest and cut,
the roll of storms
shaking new trees, flattening the grass,
quick lakes
a scatter of mirrors, clouds in them, all
favour, all breathing side to side, all
being outside,
all blossom.

1 In keeping with a poem about hearing 'dead poets' voices', Elegy Two is filled with echoes and resonances of poems and songs. Here Bowering is playing with a line from W.B. Yeats's 'Byzantium', in which the golden bird, which serves Yeats as a metaphor for the way a poem outlives the poet, is described as 'Planted on the star-lit golden bough', beyond 'all complexities of mire or blood'. A few lines later Bowering recalls Yeats's 'Leda and the Swan'.

2 Hilda Doolittle (1886–1961), the American poet who signed her work H.D., was a contemporary of Pound's and one of the central figures of the Imagist movement.

3 The Christian doctrine of the Fortunate Fall (the idea that Adam and Eve's fall from grace into sin was fortunate because it permitted God to provide humanity with the sacrifice of his son) is central to Milton's Renaissance epic *Paradise Lost.*

As for us, we dissolve into hungers,
                                        our breath
disappears every minute,
                              our skin flakes off
and lies unseen on the pavement.
                                        She says
I've got you under my skin, yes, she says
you walk with me wherever I go,
                                        you are
the weather.
            I reply with a call for help,
I'm disappearing,
                  there's a change in the weather.

In love we have a secret language we dont remember.
We catch a word or two,
                              as the wind passes,
we turn an ear to the cool,
                              it's gone. The trees
shake their leaves to say look,
                                  we're alive
The house you've sat in for years remains
against all odds,
                 a part of the earth.

We are wisps,
              we flit invisible
around all that wood.
                          They dont even hear us,
they may be waiting for us to say something important.

Late night on 37th Avenue I see lovers
on each other in a lamplit Chevrolet.

Do their hands know for certain that's skin
they glide over?
                I have rubbed my neck in exhaustion,
and almost believe I've touched something.

Is that a reason to look forward to next year?
Still, being dead
is no bed of roses.

Half the beautiful ones I have known are gone,
what's the hurry?
                    On this street the school girls
grow up and disappear into kitchens,
                                        a breeze
shakes the blossoms from my cherry tree,
there's cat hair all over the rug.
                                    What happened
to that smile that was on your face
a minute ago?
                God, there goes another breath,
and I go with it,
                    I was further from my grave
two stanzas back, I'm human.
                                    Will the universe
notice my unattached molecules drifting thru?

Will the dead poets notice our lines appearing among them,
or are their ears filled with their own music?

Will their faces look as blank as these I pass
on 41st Avenue?
                    I'm not talking about
making that great anthology,
                                    I am recalling that god
who said excuse me, I wasnt listening, sorry.

Yet if they see the morning,
                                    safe from their first
rough sea,
            if they smooth each other's hair,
talk about their weekend shopping—are they
what they were?
                    Are they as far from time?

Do they kiss, and try to kiss again, and say
inside, yes I remember this?
                                    Does a mask
feel the touch of a mask;
                                does the face
beneath the mask feel the mask?

Did you see ancient Fred and whitened Ginger[4]
in the morning paper,
June 25, 1982? Now
each time we see them glide by each other's
garments in black & white youth, we stand
amazed.
How light that touch, how quick,
how foreign to the dull surge of our own passion,
we thought.
They generated enormous energy, yet
met like eyelashes.
They were exactly like us.
God, if he choose,
can press us into
sausage patties,
he can flatten a car,
furl up a street,
tuck us into our own shoes.

But the moony flesh in the sedan
turns like the firmament,
he is entangled
in legs and gearshift,
she likely says yes
and grows to meet his growth,
dumb imitation
of the burgeoning garden in the nearby yard.

I grow more frail as they fill the car,
already disappearing,
should I ask them
whether I exist?

Si me soubmectz, leur serviteur
En tout ce que puis faire et dire,
A les honnorer de bon cuer[5]

I know they put their hands there and there
because their early fancy now arrives,
an island

4 Fred Astaire (1899–1987) and Ginger Rogers (1911–95), American actors and dancers, who starred together in a number of film musicals and were noted for their grace and sophistication.

5 These lines come from stanza CIX of *Le Grand Testament* (1461), a collection of bequests to friends and enemies interspersed with ballads and rondeaux (including 'Ballade des Dames du Temps Jadis') written by French poet François Villon (1431–*c.*63).

risen from a placid sea.
An actual breast, a leg
that does not disappear below conflicting pictures.

But the ones who have touched me have
disintegrated into seraphs and books.

These half-undressed in the front seat
have nearly slipped from time,
elastic hours
making Pleiades of the street.

We step out of cars, finally,
movies come to an end,
we need a place at last that will fit us,
we need a cabin, a creek, a few trees,
maybe a typewriter and a sink.
We are evaporating
as our heroes did.
We cannot pursue our fragments
as they separate into earth and stars.

ELEGY FIVE

The white ball acts upon them as a stone in a pool
They run, they bend, they leap, they fall
to the patchy green carpet,
walled away from the factory city.

The eye up high for a moment catches
a soft human Diamond,
a star
twinkt in a moment by the hurl, the ex-
stacy of the thing among them.
The giant at first
leaps then tumbles,
his feet quick to return
to artificial earth.
What holds him there
is not anywhere.

The crowd opens,
rises like a row of poppies,

and subsides,
            scattering peanut shells like petals.

They surround the never-dying game,
a stem that feeds their seeming boredom,
the late innings,
            the mom at home
basting a roast.
            Children stray thru the stands,
faces away from the centre.

A thin fine play in the eighth
draws a flutter of hands.

The wrinkled neck of the third base coach
mocks his uniform,
            or vice versa.
He wears no spikes,
            but shoes like slippers.
His stomach falls over his double-knit belt.

His statistics lie like the skeleton of another man
in yearbooks out of print.

He never stands in the coach's box, as if
afraid it might be a grave.

*

Beauty is the first prod of fear,
            the young
shortstop knows it but does not say it.
            Tobacco
bulges his cheek,
            his movement speaks
of his parentage,
            a swan and a gangster.

He is simple for three hours.

He knows the ground between his feet.

You play thru your injuries,
            you play

hurt,
        you knew it was waiting for you,
you remember your first bad arm,
it said your pension would be full of pain.

You hit the ground every day,
knocked over in the middle of your grace,
a green apple hitting every branch
on the way to the sun-beaten orchard floor;

your team-mates' play called it into being,
                                                                          your fall
seen a hundred times on the screen,
a way down, and out.
                                        You bounce up
without a smile,
                                but the crowd says 'ahh,'
and you look quick at your manager,
                                                              dad,
were you watching me.

                                            He is looking in his book,
but your sore body grins
all the way back to the dugout,
unaware of your steps over the grave.

Already the stands are noisy
with the call for some hitting,
                                                the home half
cuts the pain from your knees,
                                                your heart
hides in the shade,
                                hoping the pitcher
will serve unwritten fate,
                                            your wooden friend
will find a fatness,
                                you will run
to throw yourself to earth again,
                                                let me in.

*

Baseball angel,
                        it's early summer,

accept him,
lighten the air,
open the infield,
give him
one white rainbow today,
set him on second,
the lovely red dirt all over his flannel.

Extra
basis.

And shine bright shadows on the tan skin
of that sweetheart with the odd designation:
ball girl.

I watch her blossom these years,
call her Debbie though I dont know her;

she sits in a simple folding chair next to the stands,
glove on her hand,
blonde hair spilling from her cap,
long tan thighs,
tall white sox.

She is not baseball at all,
but a harmless grace here,
a tiny joy
glimpsed one time each inning,
when she bends
and, oh God give us extra innings,
picks up the ball.
We applaud, and nature
is good.

Les humains savent tant de jeux l'amour la mourre
L'amour jeu des nombrils ou jeu de la grande oie
La mourre jeu de nombre illusoire des doigts
Seigneur faites Deigneur qu'on jour je m'enamoure[1]

1 These lines are based on 'L'ermite', in the collection *Les Alcools* (1913) by French poet Guillaume Apollinaire (1880–1918), who coined the term *surrealist* and was acknowledged by the surrealist poets as their precursor.

Watching the game of work,
I wonder at the big owe[2]
how dark in my heart is the place where we all
could not make the play,
fell to earth crooked,
swung a bat too late,
threw far over the fielder's head,
cringed in fear of the hardness,
or the coach who scorned our fear.

Here is the fancied green of our wishes,
here where I still think the ballplayers are older than I,
this is where they are unreasonably adept,
where our failure is turned inside out,
by quick hands and an always white ball.

I sit in section nine and sometimes wonder why,
but know I am at ground zero
where art is made,
where there is no profit,
no loss.

The planet lies perfect in its orbit.
Diamonds,
this green diamond at Little Mountain,[3]
where these younger than we leap and run and fall
like our older brothers,
where we shout inanities
from our high wall,
our wit echoes loudly
from the right-field fence.

This is not
poetry,
neither is it play;
it is life
whether you like it or not,
money
changes hands,
the sun goes purple and gold

2 A punning reference to the 'big O', as the Montreal Olympic Stadium, home of the Expos, is familiarly known.
3 Nat Bailey Stadium, home to professional baseball in Vancouver, situated on Little Mountain, a 150-metre granite outcropping and the city's highest point.

behind the trees,
                    the lights come on bright,
the ball is white,
                    and someone
has to pay for it.

Dear spooks:
                if there were a domed stadium between the stars
upon whose astroturf athletic lovers
made plays beyond the hearts of these heroes,
daring ozone catches in deepest centre,
                                        stolen base
in a cloud of crystal,
                        delightful silent hand-shakes
at home plate—

                    and if they could arouse the crowd
of long-ghosted millions to a standing ovation,
a thunder-clap around the park,

                                  would that throng
cast blossoms of immortality over nine heads,
bring at last a satisfied smile to the face
between these shoulders here on earth,
                                        on the road,
in last place?

1984

Joy Kogawa

b. 1935

Born in Vancouver, Joy Kogawa and her family were evacuated to a 'shack' in Slocan, BC, and then to 'a smaller shack' in Coaldale, Alta, as a result of the 1941 attack on Pearl Harbor—which bore terrible consequences for many Japanese Canadians living on the West Coast because they were separated by the Canadian government from homes and possessions and interned for the duration of the Second World War. Deeply affected by this unjust treatment of Japanese Canadians, Kogawa has used literature as an instrument of social action, making these events the subject of much of her poetry and fiction, including the short story 'Obasan', which grew into the novel *Obasan* (1981) and also served as the basis for *Naomi's Road* (1986), a children's book that has been used as a school text in Japan. All three versions tell the story of Naomi, who is a child of the time of the evacuation.

A political activist, Kogawa worked to bring about legal reparations for those Japanese Canadians who were adversely affected by government policies during the Second World War. The daughter of an Anglican clergyman, she studied theology in Toronto, as well as music at the Royal Conservatory. She worked as an elementary school teacher for a time, then as a writer in the Prime Minister's Office (1974–6). In 1978 she was writer-in-residence at the University of Ottawa. She has lived in Vancouver, Grand Forks, Moose Jaw, Saskatoon, and Ottawa.

In Kogawa's poetry—collected in *The Splintered Moon* (1967), *A Choice of Dreams* (1974), *Jericho Road* (1977), and *Woman in the Woods* (1985)—specific events and images evoke larger philosophical issues often in an epigrammatic or allegorical fashion. She works in a way that might be compared to that of the Japanese craftsman (Naomi's grandfather) mentioned in 'Obasan', who uses a plane requiring a *pulling* motion rather than a *pushing* one ('a fundamental difference in workmanship')—avoiding didacticism by striving to elicit the reader's feelings rather than imposing conclusions. Even in her longer poems about the internment (such as 'What do I Remember of the Evacuation' and 'Road Building by Pick Axe'), significance lies not so much in their collection of facts, figures, and personal memories as in the implications conveyed.

In *Obasan* the family's silence about the forced evacuation of the Japanese compels Naomi to gather information for herself from documents that have been responsible for changing her life. The novel itself becomes another document, one that exposes the inadequacies of 'historical truth' by challenging the accounts of 'the Japanese threat' with a different version—Naomi's—of the internment. Naomi learns that her family's story is constructed not only from events and versions of reality but also from the silence that surrounds the experience. In the story 'Obasan' we see the compassion that Naomi gains from her search: behind easy judgments and the discovery that society's injustice is the sum of lesser evils, she finds the love and understanding that made it possible for the family's honour and values to survive during the war. This discovery is echoed by Kogawa in 'What do I Remember of the Evacuation':

> *I remember how careful my parents were*
> *Not to bruise us with bitterness.*

Obasan was followed by a sequel, *Itsuka* (1992), which traces the adult life of Naomi as she moves from the Prairies to Toronto and becomes involved in the fight for redress for those Japanese Canadians who were evacuated. Kogawa's third novel, *The Rain Ascends* (1995), is the story of how a young woman struggles to come to terms with the discovery that her father, a well-liked and respected minister whom she has always worshipped, was also a child molester. Kogawa's most recent work is

A Song of Lilith (2000), featuring illustrations by Lilian Broca, a long poem retelling the story of the woman who, according to Talmudic legend, was created with Adam to be his wife and equal partner but was exiled from Eden when she rejected her subordinate position.

Where There's a Wall

Where there's a wall
there's a way through a
gate or door. There's even
a ladder perhaps and a
sentinel who sometimes sleeps.
There are secret passwords you
can overhear. There are methods
of torture for extracting clues
to maps of underground passages.
There are zeppelins, helicopters,
rockets, bombs, battering rams,
armies with trumpets whose
all at once blast shatters
the foundations.

Where there's a wall there are
words to whisper by loose bricks,
wailing prayers to utter, birds
to carry messages taped to their feet.
There are letters to be written—
poems even.

Faint as in a dream
is the voice that calls
from the belly
of the wall.

1985

Road Building by Pick Axe

The Highway

Driving down the
highway from Revelstoke—
the road built by

forced labour—all the
Nisei[1] having no
choice etcetera etcetera
and mentioning this in
passing to this Englishman
who says when he
came to Canada from
England he wanted to
go to Vancouver too but
the quota for professors
was full so he was
forced to go to Toronto.

1 Pronounced 'knee-say', a name for second-generation Japanese-Canadians; 'Issei' means first-generation, 'Sansei' third-generation.

Found Poem

Uazusu Shoji
who was twice wounded
while fighting with the Princess Pats
in World War I
had purchased nineteen acres of land
under the Soldiers Settlement Act
and established a chicken farm.

His nineteen acres
a two-storied house
four chicken houses
and electric incubator
and 2,500 fowl
were sold for $1,492.59.

After certain deductions
for taxes and sundries were made
Mr Shoji received a cheque
for $39.32.

The Day After

The day after Sato-sensei
received the Order of Canada
he told some of us Nisei
the honour he received

was our honour, our glory
our achievement.

And one Nisei remembered
the time Sensei went to Japan
met the emperor
and was given a rice cake
how Sensei brought it back to Vancouver
took the cake to a baker and
had it crushed into powder
so that each pupil might
receive a tiny bit.

And someone suggested
he take the Order of Canada medal
and grind it to bits
to share with us.

Memento

Trapped in
a clear plastic
hockey-puck
paperweight
is a blank ink sketch
of a jaunty outhouse.

Slocan Reunion—
August 31, 1974
Toronto.

May 3, 1981

I'm watching the flapping
green ferry flag on the
way to Victoria—
the white dogwood flower
centred by a yellow dot.

A small yellow dot
in a BC ferry boat—

In the Vancouver Daily Province
a headline today reads

'Western Canada Hatred
Due to Racism.'

Ah my British
British Columbia, my
first brief home.

For Issei in Nursing Homes

Beneath the waiting
in the garden in
late autumn—how
the fruit falls without
a thud, the white
hoary hair falls and
falls and strangers
tread the grey walk ways
of the concrete garden.

How without vegetation how
without touch the old ones
lie in their slow days.

With pick axe then
or dynamite

that in their last breaths, a
green leaf, yes, and
grandchild bringing gifts.

1985

Minerals from Stone

For many years
androgynous with truth
I molded fact and fantasy
and where they met
made the crossroads home.

Here the house built
by lunatic limbs
fashioning what is not
into what might be—

a palace cave
for savage saints with
hunting knife still moist.

Bring me no longer
your spoils.
I have a house in the
shadows now and have
learned to eat minerals
straight from stone.

1985

Obasan

She is sitting at the kitchen table when I come in. She is so deaf now that my knocking does not rouse her and when she sees me she is startled.

'O,' she says, and the sound is short and dry as if there is no energy left to put any inflection into her voice. She begins to rise but falters and her hands, outstretched in greeting, fall to the table. She says my name as a question.

I put my shoulder bag down, remove the mud-caked books and stand before her.

'Obasan,' I say loudly and take her hands. My aunt is not one for hugs and kisses.

She peers into my face. 'O,' she says again.

I nod in reply. We stand for a long time in silence. I open my mouth to ask, 'Did he suffer very much?' but the question feels pornographic.

'Everyone dies some day,' she says eventually. She tilts her head to the side as if it's all too heavy inside.

I hang my jacket on a coat peg and sit beside her.

The house is familiar but has shrunk over the years and is even more cluttered than I remember. The wooden table is covered with a plastic table cloth over a blue and white cloth. Along one edge are African violets in profuse bloom, salt and pepper shakers, a soya sauce bottle, an old radio, a non-automatic toaster, a small bottle full of toothpicks. She goes to the stove and turns on the gas flame under the kettle.

'Everyone dies some day,' she says again and looks in my direction, her eyes unclear and sticky with a gum-like mucus. She pours the tea. Tiny twigs and bits of popcorn circle in the cup.

When I last saw her nine years ago, she told me her tear ducts were clogged. I have never seen her cry. Her mouth is filled with a gummy saliva as well. She drinks warm water often because her tongue sticks to the roof of her false plate.

'Thank you,' I say, taking the cup in both hands.

Uncle was disoriented for weeks, my cousin's letter told me. Towards the end he got dizzier and dizzier and couldn't move without clutching things. By the time they got him to the hospital, his eyes were rolling.

'I think he was beginning to see everything upside down again,' she wrote, 'the way we see when we are born.' Perhaps for Uncle, everything had started reversing and he was growing top to bottom, his mind rooted in an upstairs attic of humus and memory, groping backwards through cracks and walls to a moist cellar. Down to water. Down to the underground sea.

Back to the fishing boat, the ocean, the skiff moored off Vancouver Island where he was born. Like Moses, he was an infant of the waves, rocked to sleep by the lap lap and '*Nen, nen, korori*', his mother's voice singing the ancient Japanese lullaby. His father, Japanese craftsman, was also a son of the sea which had tossed and coddled his boatbuilding ancestors for centuries. And though he had crossed the ocean from one island as a stranger coming to an island of strangers, it was the sea who was his constant landlord. His fellow tenants, the Songhee Indians of Esquimalt, and the fishermen, came from up and down the BC coast to his workshop in Victoria, to watch, to barter and to buy.

In the framed family photograph hanging above the sideboard, Grandfather sits on a chair with his short legs not quite square on the floor. A long black cape hangs from his shoulders. His left hand clutches a pair of gloves and the top of a cane. On a pedestal beside him is a top hat, open end up. Uncle stands slightly to his right, and behind, with his hand like Napoleon's in his vest. Sitting to their left is Grandmother in a lace and velvet suit with my mother in her arms. They all look in different directions, carved and rigid with their expressionless Japanese faces and their bodies pasted over with Rule Britannia. There is not a ripple out of place.

And then there is the picture, not framed, not on display, showing Uncle as a young man smiling and proud in front of an exquisitely detailed craft. Not a fishing boat, not an ordinary yacht—a creation of many years and many winter evenings—a work of art. Uncle stands, happy enough for the attention of the camera, eager to pass on the message that all is well. That forever and ever all is well.

But many things happen. There is the voice of the RCMP officer saying 'I'll keep that one,' and laughing as he cuts through the water. 'Don't worry, I'll make good use of her.' The other boats are towed away and left to rot. Hundreds of Grandfather's boats belonging to hundreds of fishermen.

The memories are drowned in a whirlpool of protective silence. 'For the sake of the children,' it is whispered over and over. '*Kodomo no tame.*'

And several years later, sitting in a shack on the edge of a sugar beet field in southern Alberta, Obasan is watching her two young daughters with their school books doing homework in the light of a coal oil lamp. Her words are the same, '*Kodomo no tame.*' For their sakes, they will survive the dust and the wind, the gumbo, the summer oven sun. For their sakes, they will work in the fields, hoeing, thinning acres of sugar beets, irrigating, topping, harvesting.

'We must go back,' Uncle would say on winter evenings, the ice thick on the windows. But later, he became more silent.

'*Nen nen.*' Rest, my dead uncle. The sea is severed from your veins. You have been cut loose.

They were feeding him intravenously for two days, the tubes sticking into him like grafting on a tree. But Death won against the medical artistry.

'Obasan, will you be all right?' I ask.

She clears her throat and wipes dry skin off her lips but does not speak. She rolls a bit of dried up jam off the table cloth. She isn't going to answer.

The language of grief is silence. She knows it well, its idioms, its nuances. She's had some of the best tutors available. Grief inside her body is fat and powerful. An almighty tapeworm.

Over the years, Grief has roamed like a highwayman down the channels of her body with its dynamite and its weapons blowing up every moment of relief that tried to make its way down the road. It grew rich off the unburied corpses inside her body.

Grief acted in mysterious ways, its melancholy wonders to perform. When it had claimed her kingdom fully, it admitted no enemies and no vengeance. Enemies belonged in a corridor of experience with sense and meaning, with justice and reason. Her Grief knew nothing of these and whipped her body to resignation until the kingdom was secure. But inside the fortress, Obasan's silence was that of a child bewildered.

'What will you do now?' I ask.

What choices does she have? Her daughters, unable to rescue her or bear the silent rebuke of her suffering have long since fled to the ends of the earth. Each has lived a life in perpetual flight from the density of her inner retreat—from the rays of her inverted sun sucking in their lives with the voracious appetite of a dwarf star.[1] Approaching her, they become balls of liquid metal—mercurial—unpredictable in their moods and sudden departures. Especially for the younger daughter, departure is as necessary as breath. What metallic spider is it in her night that hammers a constant transformation, lacing open doors and windows with iron bars.

'What will you do?' I repeat.

She folds her hands together. I pour her some more tea and she bows her thanks. I take her hands in mine, feeling the silky wax texture.

'Will you come and stay with us?' Are there any other words to say? Her hands move under mine and I release them. Her face is motionless. 'We could leave in a few days and come back next month.'

'The plants . . .'

'Neighbours can water them.'

'There is trouble with the house,' she says. 'This is an old house. If I leave . . .'

'Obasan,' I say nodding, 'it is your house.'

She is an old woman. Every homemade piece of furniture, each pot holder and child's paper doily, is a link in her lifeline. She has preserved in shelves and in cupboards, under layers of clothing in closets—a daughter's rubber ball, colouring books, old hats,

1 A white dwarf, a star in an advanced state of stellar evolution, is created when the star finally exhausts all of its possible sources of fuel for thermonuclear fusion, at which point it collapses under its own gravity into a dense, compressed mass.

children's dresses. The items are endless. Every short stub pencil, every cornflake box stuffed with paper bags and old letters is of her ordering. They rest in the corners of the house like parts of her body, hair cells, skin tissue, food particles, tiny specks of memory. This house is now her blood and bones.

She is all old women in every hamlet in the world. You see her on a street corner in a village in southern France, in her black dress and her black stockings. She is squatting on stone steps in a Mexican mountain village. Everywhere she stands as the true and rightful owner of the earth, the bearer of love's keys to unknown doorways, to a network of astonishing tunnels, the possessor of life's infinite personal details.

'I am old,' she says.

These are the words my grandmother spoke that last night in the house in Victoria. Grandmother was too old then to understand political expediency, race riots, the yellow peril. I was too young.

She stands up slowly. 'Something in the attic for you,' she says.

We climb the narrow stairs one step at a time carrying a flashlight with us. Its dull beam reveals mounds of cardboard boxes, newspapers, magazines, a trunk. A dead sparrow lies in the nearest corner by the eaves.

She attempts to lift the lid of the trunk. Black fly corpses fall to the floor. Between the wooden planks, more flies fill the cracks. Old spider webs hang like blood clots, thick and black from the rough angled ceiling.

Our past is as clotted as old webs hung in dark attics, still sticky and hovering, waiting for us to adhere and submit or depart. Or like a spider with its skinny hairy legs, the past skitters out of the dark, spinning and netting the air, ready to snap us up and ensnare our thoughts in old and complex perceptions. And when its feasting is complete, it leaves its victims locked up forever, dangling like hollowed out insect skins, a fearful calligraphy, dry reminders that once there was life flitting about in the weather.

But occasionally a memory that refuses to be hollowed out, to be categorized, to be identified, to be explained away, comes thudding into the web like a giant moth. And in the daylight, what's left hanging there, ragged and shredded is a demolished fly trap, and beside it a bewildered eight-legged spinning animal.

My dead refuse to bury themselves. Each story from the past is changed and distorted, altered as much by the present as the present is shaped by the past. But potent and pervasive as a prairie dust storm, memory and dream seep and mingle through cracks, settling on furniture, into upholstery. The attic and the living room encroach onto each other, deep into their invisible places.

I sneeze and dust specks pummel across the flashlight beam. Will we all be dust in the end—a jumble of faces and lives compressed and powdered into a few lines of statistics—fading photographs in family albums, the faces no longer familiar, the clothing quaint, the anecdotes lost?

I use the flashlight to break off a web and lift the lid of the trunk. A strong whiff of mothballs assaults us. The odour of preservation. Inside, there are bits of lace and fur, a 1920s nightgown, a shoe box, red and white striped socks. She sifts through the contents, one by one.

'That's strange,' she says several times.

'What are you looking for?' I ask.

'Not here. It isn't here.'

She turns to face me in the darkness. 'That's strange,' she says and leaves her questions enclosed in silence.

I pry open the folds of a cardboard box. The thick dust slides off like chocolate icing sugar—antique pollen. Grandfather's boat building tools are wrapped in heavy cloth. These are all he brought when he came to this country wearing a western suit, western shoes, a round black hat. Here is the plane with a wooden handle which he worked by pulling it towards him. A fundamental difference in workmanship—to pull rather than push. Chisels, hammer, a mallet, a thin pointed saw, the handle extending from the blade like that of a kitchen knife.

'What will you do with these?' I ask.

'The junk in the attic', my cousin's letter said, 'should be burned. When I come there this summer, I'll have a big bonfire. It's a fire trap. I've taken the only things that are worth keeping.'

Beneath the box of tools is a pile of *Life* magazines dated the 1950s. A subscription maintained while the two daughters were home. Beside the pile is another box containing shoe boxes, a metal box with a disintegrating elastic band, several chocolate boxes. Inside the metal box are pictures, duplicates of some I have seen in our family albums. Obasan's wedding photo—her mid-calf dress hanging straight down from her shoulders, her smile glued on. In the next picture, Uncle is a child wearing a sailor suit.

The shoe box is full of documents.

Royal Canadian Mounted Police, Vancouver, BC, March 4, 1942. A folded mimeographed paper authorizes Uncle as the holder of a numbered Registration Card to leave a Registered Area by truck for Vernon where he is required to report to the local Registrar of Enemy Aliens, not later than the following day. It is signed by the RCMP superintendant.

Uncle's face, young and unsmiling looks up at me from the bottom right hand corner of a wallet size ID card. 'The bearer whose photograph and specimen of signature appear hereon, has been duly registered in compliance with the provisions of Order-in-Council PC 117.' A purple stamp underneath states 'Canadian Born'. His thumb print appears on the back with marks of identification specified—scar on back of right hand.

There is a letter from the Department of the Secretary of State. Office of the Custodian. Japanese Evacuation Section. 506 Royal Bank Bldg. Hastings and Granville. Vancouver, BC.

Dear Sir.

Dear Uncle. With whom were you corresponding and for what did you hope? That the enmity would cease? That you could return to your boats? I have grown tired, Uncle, of seeking the face of the enemy hiding in the thick forests of the past. You were not the enemy. The police who came to your door were not the enemy. The men who rioted against you were not the enemy. The Vancouver alderman who said 'Keep BC

White' was not the enemy. The men who drafted the Order-in-Council were not the enemy. He does not wear a uniform or sit at a long meeting table. The man who read your timid letter, read your polite request, skimmed over your impossible plea, was not your enemy. He had an urgent report to complete. His wife was ill. The phone rang all the time. The senior staff was meeting in two hours. The secretary was spending too much time over coffee breaks. There were a billion problems to attend to. Injustice was the only constant in a world of flux. There were moments when expedience demanded decisions which would later be judged unjust. Uncle, he did not always know what he was doing. You too did not have an all compassionate imagination. He was just doing his job. I am just doing my work, Uncle. We are all just doing our jobs.

My dear dead Uncle. Am I come to unearth our bitterness that our buried love too may revive?

'Obasan, what shall we do with these?'

She has been waiting at the top of the stairs, holding the railing with both hands. I close the shoe box and replace the four interlocking flaps of the cardboard box. With one hand I shine the flashlight and with the other, guide her as I precede her slowly down the stairs. Near the bottom she stumbles and I hold her small body upright.

'Thank you, thank you,' she says. This is the first time my arms have held her. We walk slowly through the living room and back to the kitchen. Her lips are trembling as she sits on the wooden stool.

Outside, the sky of the prairie spring is painfully blue. The trees are shooting out their leaves in the fierce wind, the new branches elastic as whips. The sharp-edged clarity is insistent as trumpets.

But inside, the rooms are muted. Our inner trees, our veins, are involuted, cocooned, webbed. The blood cells in the trunks of our bodies, like tiny specks of light, move in a sluggish river. It is more a potential than an actual river—an electric liquid—the current flowing in and between us, between our generations. Not circular, as in a whirlpool, or climactic and tidal as in fountains or spray—but brooding. Bubbling. You expect to hear barely audible pip-pip electronic tones, a pre-concert tuning up behind the curtains in the darkness. Towards the ends of our branches and fingertips, tiny human-shaped flames or leaves break off and leap towards the shadows. My arms are suffused with a suppressed urge to hold.

At the edges of our flesh is a hint of a spiritual osmosis, an eagerness within matter, waiting to brighten our dormant neurons, to entrust our stagnant cells with movement and dance.

Obasan drinks her tea and makes a shallow scratching sound in her throat. She shuffles to the door and squats beside the boot tray. With a putty knife, she begins to scrape off the thick clay like mud that sticks to my boots.

[1978], 1984

Carol Shields

b. 1935

Born in Oak Park, Illinois, outside Chicago, Carol Warner earned a BA at Hanover College, Indiana, and then married the Canadian engineer Donald Hugh Shields in 1957, moving with him to Ottawa. She received an MA in English at the University of Ottawa in 1975. (A revision of her master's thesis was published as *Susanna Moodie: Voice and Vision.*) She has since taught literature and writing at the University of Ottawa, the University of British Columbia, and from 1980 at the University of Manitoba. In 1996, she became chancellor of the University of Winnipeg. In 1999 she retired with her husband to Victoria.

Responding to her sense that, for all their gains, women are still not sufficiently visible in our culture, Shields has, during a rich and varied career, created a body of work that features probing examinations of ordinary women's lives and friendships. Although best known for her novels, she at first wrote poetry, collected in *Others* (1972) and *Intersect* (1974). Once she decided her creative instincts were better served by fiction, she produced in quick succession *Small Ceremonies* (1976), *The Box Garden* (1977), *Happenstance* (1980), and *A Fairly Conventional Woman* (1982). She has since described these novels as 'quite traditional', saying that it was only later that she realized how 'elastic' and 'commodious' the form of the novel could actually be, and how much one could do within it.

These early novels were followed by Shields' first collection of short stories, *Various Miracles* (1985). The small intense explorations of individual perspectives that the short story afforded her seems to have corresponded to her growing sense of the possibilities of the novel, which is first visible in *Swann: A Mystery* (1987). There, four voices come together in their attempts to unearth a fifth, a silent voice—that of Mary Swann, a rural Canadian poet—in a narrative that suggests the impossibility of understanding a life through the linear structure of traditional biography with its unifying point of view.

While *Swann* brought Shields critical recognition, the short story remained important for her: a second collection, *The Orange Fish* (1989), contains portraits of characters who—like the widow in 'Hazel', trying to find her way in life—seem outwardly ordinary and unremarkable but who reveal surprising depths. These are narratives that demonstrate Shields' preoccupation not just with the interactions between specific characters but also with the social prejudices, restrictions, and habits that define such interactions.

After her next novel, *The Republic of Love* (1992)—a succinct examination of two individuals in need of love and in need of understanding what love is—Shields returned to poetry with *Coming to Canada* (1992). Published the year after she became a Canadian citizen, it contains new poems in addition to reprinting selections from her two earlier books.

Shields achieved national and international fame when *The Stone Diaries* (1993) won both a Governor General's Award and the Pulitzer Prize (an unprecedented feat made possible by her dual citizenship). This novel, which was also shortlisted for both the Booker Prize and the IMPAC Dublin Literary Award, traces the life of its female protagonist, Daisy, from her birth to her death eighty years later, examining the factors that form and define the individual life of a woman. (The title plays on Margaret Laurence's *The Stone Angel.*) While never a stereotype, Daisy fulfills the traditional roles of women—daughter, wife, mother, mistress, and grandmother—in an arc of experience marked by her constant physical and spiritual need to discover an inherent, female self. *The Stone Diaries* continues the examination begun in *Swann* of multiple voices and viewpoints, but now filters all of these through Daisy's consciousness. The sense that a web of human relationships defines the individual is complemented by what are ostensibly photographs of these characters (from which Daisy is missing), a gesture that gives a kind of verisimilitude to the deeply human portraiture of the book even while affirming the unreliability and necessary subjectivity of its observations.

Shields' 1997 novel, *Larry's Party*, also garnered laurels, winning the British Orange Prize, the National Book Critics Circle Award in the US, and the Prix de Lire in France. (In 2001, it was adapted as a musical for the Canadian Stage Company.) While *Larry's Party* resembles *The Stone Diaries*, in that it is an extended examination of the life of an ordinary individual, it focuses on a male protagonist. Not attempting to plumb a man's physical experience the way *The Stone Diaries* does a woman's, the novel examines the individual's attempts to order a life that seems nothing but a series of accidents. Larry's desire to make sense of his own identity is reflected in his preoccupation with mazes (inspired by the Hampton Court maze, he becomes a successful designer of garden mazes). The maze serves as a metaphor for the ways in which narrative can both create and evoke an understanding of that self. Just as mazes 'make perfect sense when you look down on them from above', lives require the distance achieved by narrative to be comprehended. In the party that concludes the book, one guest observes that 'at the center of the maze there's an encounter with oneself' that permits 'a sense of rebirth'.

In 2000, Shields published a third book of stories, *Dressing Up for the Carnival*. In that collection 'Soupe du Jour' articulates most clearly her fundamental interest in the extraordinary potential of the ordinary: 'there's no stone, shrub, chair or door that doesn't offer arrows of implicit reasoning or promises of epiphany.' In her return to criticism the following year with *Jane Austen*, she provides an appreciation of a writer with whom she clearly feels deep affinity. Like Austen, Shields has often been termed a miniaturist, but as in Austen's fiction, the small moments of human interaction, like those apparently ordinary objects, can yield revelation of great significance.

Shields' most recent novel, *Unless* (2002), shows again her interest in unearthing the 'truth' of the psychology of a particular character by locating it within the social, geographical, and historical context that helps define that character, even while reminding us of the ultimate impossibility of ever fully defining that truth. It tells the story of a translator and fiction writer ('I wanted to write about the overheard and the glimpsed') who, in her forties and alienated from one of her daughters, tries to understand her own life as if it were one of her books ('How did this part of the narrative happen?'). This novel was published as Shields confronted her imminent death from cancer.

In addition to being a prolific writer of novels and short stories, Shields found time for dramatic writing as well. In *Thirteen Hands* (1993), the best known of her plays, she captures the relationship between life and the game of bridge. About this play she wrote: 'For many years I've been interested in the lives of women, particularly those lives which have gone unrecorded, . . . the so called "blue rinse set", the "ladies of the club", the bridge club "biddies".' Shields has also edited an anthology of women's writing, *Dropped Threads* (2001).

Shields holds a number of honorary doctorates from universities in Canada and the United States, is a member of the Royal Society of Canada, and was inducted as a Member of the Order of Canada in 1999. In 2000 the government of France appointed her as a Chevalier de l'Ordre des Arts et des Lettres.

Hazel

After a man has mistreated a woman he feels a need to do something nice which she must accept.

In line with this way of thinking, Hazel has accepted from her husband, Brian, sprays of flowers, trips to Hawaii, extravagant compliments on her rather ordinary cooking, bracelets of dull-coloured silver and copper, a dressing gown in green tartan wool, a second dressing gown with maribou trim around the hem and sleeves, dinners in expensive revolving restaurants and, once, a tender kiss, tenderly delivered, on the instep of her right foot.

But there will be no more such compensatory gifts, for Brian died last December of heart failure.

The heart failure, as Hazel, even after all these years, continues to think of it. In her family, the family of her girlhood that is, a time of gulped confusion in a place called Porcupine Falls, all familiar diseases were preceded by the horrific article: *the* measles, *the* polio, *the* rheumatism, *the* cancer, and—to come down to her husband Brian and his final thrashing with life—*the* heart failure.

He was only fifty-five. He combed his uncoloured hair smooth and wore clothes made of gabardinelike materials, a silky exterior covering a complex core. It took him ten days to die after the initial attack, and during the time he lay there, all his minor wounds healed. He was a careless man who bumped into things, shrubbery, table legs, lighted cigarettes, simple curbstones. Even the making of love seemed to him a labour and a recovery, attended by scratches, bites, effort, exhaustion and, once or twice, a mild but humiliating infection. Nevertheless, women found him attractive. He had an unhurried, good-humoured persistence about him and could be kind when he chose to be.

The night he died Hazel came home from the hospital and sat propped up in bed till four in the morning, reading a trashy, fast-moving New York novel about wives who lived in spacious duplexes overlooking Central Park, too alienated to carry on properly with their lives. They made salads with rare kinds of lettuce and sent their apparel to the dry cleaners, but they were bitter and helpless. Frequently they used the expression 'fucked up' to describe their malaise. Their mothers or their fathers had fucked them up, or jealous sisters or bad-hearted nuns, but mainly they had been fucked up by men who no longer cared about them. These women were immobilized by the lack of love and kept alive only by a reflexive bounce between new ways of arranging salad greens and fantasies of suicide. Hazel wondered as she read how long it took for the remembered past to sink from view. A few miserable tears crept into her eyes, her first tears since Brian's initial attack, that shrill telephone call, that unearthly hour. Impetuously she wrote on the book's flyleaf the melodramatic words 'I am alone and suffering unbearably.' Not her best handwriting, not her usual floating morning-glory tendrils. Her fingers cramped at this hour. The cheap ball-point pen held back its ink, and the result was a barely legible scrawl that she nevertheless underlined twice.

By mid-January she had taken a job demonstrating kitchenware in department stores. The ad in the newspaper promised on-the-job training, opportunities for advancement, and contact with the public. Hazel submitted to a short, vague, surprisingly painless interview, and was rewarded the following morning by a telephone call telling her she was to start immediately. She suspected she was the sole applicant, but nevertheless went numb with shock. Shock and also pleasure. She hugged the elbows of her dressing gown and smoothed the sleeves flat. She was fifty years old and without skills, a woman who had managed to avoid most of the arguments and issues of the world. Asked a direct question, her voice wavered. She understood nothing of the national debt or the situation in Nicaragua, nothing. At ten-thirty most mornings she was still in her dressing gown and had the sense to know this was shameful. She possessed a softened, tired body and rubbed-looking eyes. Her posture was only moderately good. She often touched her mouth with the back of her hand. Yet someone, some person with a downtown commercial address and an official letterhead and a firm telephone manner had seen fit to offer her a job.

Only Hazel, however, thought the job a good idea.

Brian's mother, a woman in her eighties living in a suburban retirement centre called Silver Oaks, said, 'Really, there is no need, Hazel. There's plenty of money if you live reasonably. You have your condo paid for, your car, a good fur coat that'll last for years. Then there's the insurance and Brian's pension, and when you're sixty-five—now don't laugh, sixty-five will come, it's not that far off—you'll have your social security. You have a first-rate lawyer to look after your investments. There's no need.'

Hazel's closest friend, Maxine Forestadt, a woman of her own age, a demon bridge player, a divorcée, a woman with a pinkish powdery face loosened by too many evenings of soft drinks and potato chips and too much cigarette smoke flowing up toward her eyes, said, 'Look. You're not the type, Hazel. Period. I know the type and you're not it. Believe me. All right, so you feel this urge to assert yourself, to try to prove something. I know, I went through it myself, wanting to show the world I wasn't just this dipsy pushover and hanger-oner. But this isn't for you, Haze, this eight-to-five purgatory, standing on your feet, and especially *your* feet, your arches act up just shopping. I know what you're trying to do, but in the long run, what's the point?'

Hazel's older daughter, Marilyn, a pathologist, and possibly a lesbian, living in a women's co-op in the east end of the city, phoned and, drawing on the sort of recollection that Hazel already had sutured, said, 'Dad would not have approved. I know it, you know it. I mean, Christ, flogging pots and pans, it's so public. People crowding around. Idle curiosity and greed, a free show, just hanging in for a teaspoon of bloody quiche lorraine or whatever's going. Freebies. People off the street, bums, anybody. Christ. Another thing, you'll have to get a whole new wardrobe for a job like that. Eye shadow so thick it's like someone's given you a punch. Just ask yourself what Dad would have said. I know what he would have said, he would have said thumbs down, nix on it.'

Hazel's other daughter, Rosie, living in British Columbia, married to a journalist, wrote: 'Dear Mom, I absolutely respect what you're doing and admire your courage. But Robin and I can't help wondering if you've given this decision enough thought. You remember how after the funeral, back at your place with Grandma and Auntie Maxine and Marilyn, we had that long talk about the need to lie fallow for a bit and not rush headlong into things and making major decisions, just letting the grieving process take its natural course. Now here it is, a mere six weeks later, and you've got yourself involved with these cookware people. I just hope you haven't signed anything. Robin says he never heard of Kitchen Kult and it certainly isn't listed on the boards. We're just anxious about you, that's all. And this business of working on commission is exploitative to say the least. Ask Marilyn. You've still got your shorthand and typing and, with a refresher course, you probably could find something, maybe Office

Overload would give you a sense of your own independence and some spending money besides. We just don't want to see you hurt, that's all.'

At first, Hazel's working day went more or less like this: at seven-thirty her alarm went off; the first five minutes were the worst; such a steamroller of sorrow passed over her that she was left as flat and lifeless as the queen-size mattress that supported her. Her squashed limbs felt emptied of blood, her breath came out thin and cool and quiet as ether. What was she to do? How was she to live her life? She mouthed these questions to the silky blanket binding, rubbing her lips frantically back and forth across the stitching. Then she got up, showered, did her hair, made coffee and toast, took a vitamin pill, brushed her teeth, made up her face (going easy on the eye shadow), and put on her coat. By eight-thirty she was in her car and checking her city map.

Reading maps, the tiny print, the confusion, caused her headaches. And she had trouble with orientation, turning the map first this way, then that, never willing to believe that north must lie at the top. North's natural place should be toward the bottom, past the Armoury and stockyards where a large cold lake bathed the city edges. Once on a car trip to the Indian River country early in their married life, Brian had joked about her lack of map sense. He spoke happily of this failing, proudly, giving her arm a squeeze, and then had thumped the cushioned steering wheel. Hazel, thinking about the plushy thump, wished she hadn't. To recall something once was to remember it forever; this was something she had only recently discovered, and she felt that the discovery might be turned to use.

The Kitchen Kult demonstrations took her on a revolving cycle of twelve stores, some of them in corners of the city where she'd seldom ventured. The Italian district. The Portuguese area. Chinatown. A young Kitchen Kult salesman named Peter Lemmon broke her in, *familiarizing* her as he put it with the Kitchen Kult product. He taught her the spiel, the patter, the importance of keeping eye contact with customers at all times, how to draw on the mood and size of the crowd and play, if possible, to its ethnic character, how to make Kitchen Kult products seem like large beautiful toys, easily mastered and guaranteed to win the love and admiration of friends and family.

'That's what people out there really want,' Peter Lemmon told Hazel, who was surprised to hear this view put forward so undisguisedly. 'Lots of love and truckloads of admiration. Keep that in mind. People can't get enough.'

He had an aggressive pointed chin and ferocious red sideburns, and when he talked he held his lips together so that the words came out with a soft zitherlike slur. Hazel noticed his teeth were discoloured and badly crowded, and she guessed that this accounted for his guarded way of talking. Either that or a nervous disposition. Early on, to put him at his ease, she told him of her small-town upbringing in Porcupine Falls, how her elderly parents had never quite recovered from the surprise of having a child. How at eighteen she came to Toronto to study stenography. That she was now a widow with two daughters, one of whom she suspected of being unhappily married and one who was undergoing a gender crisis. She told Peter Lemmon that this was her first real job, that at the age of fifty she was out working for the first time. She talked too much, babbled in fact—why? She didn't know. Later she was sorry.

In return he confided, opening his mouth a little wider, that he was planning to have extensive dental work in the future if he could scrape the money together. More than nine thousand dollars had been quoted. A quality job cost quality cash, that was the long and short of it, so why not take the plunge. He hoped to go right to the top with Kitchen Kult. Not just sales, but the real top, and that meant management. It was a company, he told her, with a forward-looking sales policy and sound product.

It disconcerted Hazel at first to hear Peter Lemmon speak of the Kitchen Kult product without its grammatical article, and she was jolted into the remembrance of how she had had to learn to suppress the article that attached to bodily ailments. When demonstrating product, Peter counselled, keep it well in view, repeating product's name frequently and withholding product's retail price until the actual demo and tasting has been concluded.

After two weeks Hazel was on her own, although Peter Lemmon continued to meet her at the appointed 'sales venue' each morning, bringing with him in a company van the equipment to be demonstrated and helping her 'set up' for the day. She slipped into her white smock, the same one every day, a smooth permapress blend with grommets down the front and Kitchen Kult in red script across the pocket, and stowed her pumps in a plastic bag, putting on the white crepe-soled shoes Peter Lemmon had recommended. 'Your feet, Hazel, are your capital.' He also produced, of his own volition, a tall collapsible stool on which she could perch in such a way that she appeared from across the counter to be standing unsupported.

She started each morning with a demonstration of the Jiffy-Sure-Slicer, Kitchen Kult's top seller, accounting for some sixty per cent of total sales. For an hour or more, talking to herself, or rather to the empty air, she shaved hillocks of carrots, beets, parsnips and rutabagas into baroque curls or else she transformed them into little star-shaped discs or elegant matchsticks. The use of cheap root vegetables kept the demo costs down, Peter Lemmon said, and presented a less threatening challenge to the average shopper, Mrs Peas and Carrots, Mrs Corn Niblets.

As Hazel warmed up, one or two shoppers drifted toward her, keeping her company—she learned she could count on these one or two who were elderly women for the most part, puffy of face and bulgy of eye. Widows, Hazel decided. The draggy-hemmed coats and beige tote bags gave them away. Like herself, though perhaps a few years older, these women had taken their toast and coffee early and had been driven out into the cold in search of diversion. 'Just set the dial, ladies and gentlemen,' Hazel told the discomfited two or three voyeurs, 'and press gently on the Jiffy lever. Never requires sharpening, never rusts.'

By mid-morning she generally had fifteen people gathered about her, by noon as many as forty. No one interrupted her, and why should they? She was free entertainment. They listened, they exchanged looks, they paid attention, they formed a miniature, temporary colony of good will and consumer seriousness waiting to be instructed, initiated into Hazel's rituals and promises.

At the beginning of her third week, going solo for the first time, she looked up to see Maxine in her long beaver coat, gawking. 'Now this is just what you need, madam,' Hazel sang out, not missing a beat, an uncontrollable smile on her face. 'In no time you'll be making more nutritious, appealing salads for your family and friends and for those bridge club get-togethers.'

Maxine had been offended. She complained afterward to Hazel that she found it embarrassing being picked out in a crowd like that. It was insulting, especially to mention the bridge club as if she did nothing all day long but shuffle cards. 'It's a bit thick, Hazel, especially when you used to enjoy a good rubber yourself. And you know I only play cards as a form of social relaxation. You used to enjoy it, and don't try to tell me otherwise because I won't buy it. We miss you, we really do. I know perfectly well it's not easy for you facing Francine. She was always a bit of a you-know-what, and Brian was, God knows, susceptible, though I have to say you've put a dignified face on the whole thing. I don't think I could have done it, I don't have your knack for looking the other way, never have had, which is why I'm where I'm at, I suppose. But who are you really cheating, dropping out of the bridge club like this? I think, just between the two of us, that Francine's a bit hurt, she thinks you hold her responsible for Brian's attack, even though we all know that when our time's up, it's up. And besides, it takes two.'

In the afternoon, after a quick pick-up lunch (leftover grated raw vegetables usually or a hardboiled egg), Hazel demonstrated Kitchen Kult's all-purpose non-stick fry pan. The same crowds that admired her julienne carrots seemed ready to be mesmerized by the absolute roundness of her crepes and omelets, their uniform gold edges and the ease with which they came pulling away at a touch of her spatula. During the early months, January, February, Hazel learned just how easily people could be hypnotized, how easily, in fact, they could be put to sleep. Their mouths sagged. They grew dull-eyed and immobile. Their hands went hard into their pockets. They hugged their purses tight.

Then one afternoon a small fortuitous accident occurred: a crepe, zealously flipped, landed on the floor. Because of the accident, Hazel discovered how a rupture in routine could be turned to her advantage. 'Whoops-a-daisy,' she said that first day, stooping to recover the crepe. People laughed out loud. It was as though Hazel's mild exclamation had a forgotten period fragrance to it. 'I guess I don't know my own strength,' she said, shaking her curls and earning a second ripple of laughter.

After that she began, at least once or twice a day, to misdirect a crepe. Or overcook an omelet. Or bring herself to a state of comic tears over her plate of chopped onions. 'Not my day,' she would croon. Or 'good grief' or 'sacred rattlesnakes' or a shrugging, cheerful, 'who ever promised perfection on the first try'. Some of the phrases that came out of her mouth reminded her of the way people talked in Porcupine Falls back in a time she could not possibly have remembered. Gentle, unalarming expletives calling up wells of good nature and neighbourliness. She wouldn't have guessed she had this quality of rubbery humour inside her.

After a while she felt she could get away with anything as long as she kept up her line of chatter. That was the secret, she saw—never to stop talking. That was why these crowds gave her their attention: she could perform miracles (with occasional calculated human lapses) and keep right on talking at the same time. Words, a river of words. She had never before talked at such length, as though she were driving a wedge of air ahead of her. It was easy, easy. She dealt out repetitions, little punchy pushes of emphasis, and an ever growing inventory of affectionate declarations directed toward her vegetable friends. 'What a devil!' she said, holding aloft a head of bulky cauliflower. 'You darling radish, you!' She felt foolish at times, but often exuberant, like a semi-retired, slightly eccentric actress. And she felt, oddly, that she was exactly as strong and clever as she need be.

But the work was exhausting. She admitted it. Every day the crowds had to be wooed afresh. By five-thirty she was too tired to do anything more than drive home, make a sandwich, read the paper, rinse out her Kitchen Kult smock and hang it over the shower rail, then get into bed with a thick paperback. Propped up in bed reading, her book like a wimple at her chin, she seemed to have flames on her feet and on the tips of her fingers, as though she'd burned her way through a long blur of a day and now would burn the night behind her too. January, February, the first three weeks of March. So this was what work was: a two-way bargain people made with the world, a way to reduce time to rubble.

The books she read worked braids of panic into her consciousness. She'd drifted toward historical fiction, away from Central Park and into the Regency courts of England. But were the queens and courtesans any happier than the frustrated New York wives? Were they less lonely, less adrift? So far she had found no evidence of it. They wanted the same things more or less: abiding affection, attention paid to their moods and passing thoughts, their backs rubbed and, now and then, the tender grateful application of hands and lips. She remembered Brian's back turned toward her in sleep, well covered with flesh in his middle years. He had never been one for pyjamas, and she had often been moved to reach out and stroke the smooth mound of flesh. She had not found his extra weight disagreeable, far from it.

In Brian's place there remained now only the rectangular softness of his allergy-free pillow. Its smooth casing, faintly puckered at the corners, had the feel of mysterious absence.

'But why does it always have to be one of my *friends!*' she had cried out at him once at the end of a long quarrel. 'Don't you see how humiliating it is for me?'

He had seemed genuinely taken aback, and she saw in a flash it was only laziness on his part, not express cruelty. She recalled his solemn promises, his wet eyes, new beginnings. She fondly recalled, too, the resonant pulmonary sounds of his night breathing, the steep climb to the top of each inhalation and the tottery stillness before the descent. How he used to lull her to sleep with this nightly music! Compensations. But she had not asked for enough, hadn't known what to ask for, what was owed her.

It was because of the books she read, their dense complications and sharp surprises, that she had applied for a job in the first place. She had a sense of her own life turning over page by page, first a girl, then a young woman, then married with two young daughters, then a member of a bridge club and a quilting club, and now, too soon for symmetry, a widow. All of it fell into small childish paragraphs, the print over-large and blocky like a school reader. She had tried to imagine various new endings or turnings for herself—she might take a trip around the world or sign up for a course in ceramics—but could think of nothing big enough to fill the vacant time left to her—except perhaps an actual job. This was what other people did, tucking in around the edges those little routines—laundry, meals, errands—that had made up her whole existence.

'You're wearing yourself out,' Brian's mother said when Hazel arrived for an Easter Sunday visit, bringing with her a double-layered box of chocolate almond bark and a bouquet of tulips. 'Tearing all over town every day, on your feet, no proper lunch arrangements. You'd think they'd give you a good hour off and maybe a lunch voucher, give you a chance to catch your breath. It's hard on the back, standing. I always feel my tension in my back. These are delicious, Hazel, not that I'll eat half of them, not with my appetite, but it'll be something to pass round to the other ladies. Everyone shares here, that's one thing. And the flowers, tulips! One or the other would have more than sufficed, Hazel, you've been extravagant. I suppose now that you're actually earning, it makes a difference. You feel differently, I suppose, when it's your own money. Brian's father always saw that I had everything I needed, wanted for nothing, but I wouldn't have minded a little money of my own, though I never said so, not in so many words.'

One morning Peter Lemmon surprised Hazel, and frightened her too, by saying, 'Mr Cortland wants to see you. The big boss himself. Tomorrow at ten-thirty. Downtown office. Headquarters. I'll cover the venue for you.'

Mr Cortland was the age of Hazel's son-in-law, Robin. She couldn't have said why, but she had expected someone theatrical and rude, not this handsome curly-haired man unwinding himself from behind a desk that was not really a desk but a gate-legged table, shaking her hand respectfully and leading her toward a soft brown easy chair. There was genuine solemnity to his jutting chin and a thick brush of hair across his quizzing brow. He offered her a cup of coffee. 'Or perhaps you would prefer tea,' he said, very politely, with a shock of inspiration.

She looked up from her shoes, her good polished pumps, not her nurse shoes, and saw a pink conch shell on Mr Cortland's desk. It occurred to her it must be one of the things that made him happy. Other people were made happy by music or flowers or bowls of ice cream—enchanted, familiar things. Some people collected china, and when they found a long-sought piece, *that* made them happy. What made *her* happy was the obliteration of time, burning it away so cleanly she hardly noticed it. Not that she said so to Mr Cortland. She said, in fact, very little, though some dragging filament of intuition urged her to accept tea rather than coffee, to forgo milk, to shake her head sadly over the proffered sugar.

'We are more delighted than I can say with your sales performance,' Mr Cortland said. 'We are a small but growing firm and, as you know'—Hazel did not know, how could she?—'we are a family concern. My maternal grandfather studied commerce at McGill and started this business as a kind of hobby. Our aim, the family's aim, is a reliable product, but not a hard sell. I can't stress this enough to our sales people. We are anxious to avoid a crude hectoring approach or tactics that are in any way manipulative, and we are in the process of developing a quality sales force that matches the quality of our product line. This may surprise you, but it is difficult to find people like yourself who possess, if I may say so, your gentleness of manner. People like yourself transmit a sense of trust to the consumer. We've heard very fine things about you, and we have decided, Hazel—I do hope I may call you Hazel—to put you on regular salary, in addition of course to an adjusted commission. And I would like also to present you with this small brooch, a glazed ceramic K for Kitchen Kult, which we give each quarter to our top sales person.'

'Do you realize what this means?' Peter Lemmon asked later that afternoon over a celebratory drink at Mr Duck's Happy Hour. 'Salary means you're on the team, you're a Kitchen Kult player. Salary equals professional, Hazel. You've arrived, and I don't think you even realize it.'

Hazel thought she saw flickering across Peter's guarded, eager face, like a blade of sunlight through a thick curtain, the suggestion that some privilege had been carelessly allocated. She pinned the brooch on the lapel of her good spring coat with an air of bafflement. Beyond the simple smoothness of her pay cheque, she perceived dark squadrons of planners and decision makers who had brought this teasing irony forward. She was being rewarded—a bewildering turn of events—for her timidity, her self-effacement, for what Maxine called her knack for looking the other way. She was a shy, ineffectual, untrained, neutral looking woman, and for this she was being kicked upstairs, or at least this was how Peter translated her move from commission to salary. He scratched his neck, took a long drink of his beer, and said it a third time, with a touch of belligerence it seemed to Hazel, 'a kick upstairs'. He insisted on paying for the drinks, even though Hazel pressed a ten-dollar bill into his hand. He shook it off.

'This place is bargain city,' he assured her, opening the orange cave of his mouth, then closing it quickly. He came here often after work, he said, taking advantage of the two-for-one happy hour policy. Not that he was tight with his money, just the opposite, but he was setting aside a few dollars a week for his dental work in the summer. The work was mostly cosmetic, caps and spacers, and therefore not covered by Kitchen Kult's insurance scheme. The way he saw it, though, was as an investment in the future. If you were going to go to the top, you had to be able to open your mouth and project. 'Like this brooch, Hazel, it's a way of projecting. Wearing the company logo means you're one of the family and that you don't mind shouting it out.'

That night, when she whitened her shoes, she felt a sort of love for them. And she loved, too, suddenly, her other small tasks, rinsing out her smock, setting her alarm, settling into bed with her book, resting her head against Brian's little fiber-filled pillow with its stitched remnant of erotic privilege and reading herself out of her own life, leaving behind her cut-out shape, so bulky, rounded and unimaginably mute, a woman who swallowed her tongue, got it jammed down her throat and couldn't make a sound.

Marilyn gave a shout of derision on seeing the company brooch pinned to her mother's raincoat. 'The old butter-up trick. A stroke here, a stroke there, just enough to keep you going and keep you grateful. But at least they had the decency to get you off straight commission, for that I have to give them some credit.'

'Dear Mother,' Rosie wrote from British Columbia. 'Many thanks for the waterless veg cooker which is surprisingly well made and really very attractive too, and Robin feels that it fulfills a real need, nutritionally speaking, and also aesthetically.'

'You're looking better,' Maxine said. 'You look as though you've dropped a few pounds, have you? All those grated carrots. But do you ever get a minute to yourself? Eight hours on the job plus commuting. I don't suppose they even pay for your gas, which adds up, and your parking. You want to think about a holiday, people can't be buying pots and pans three hundred and sixty-five days a year. JoAnn and Francine and I are thinking seriously of getting a cottage in Nova Scotia for two weeks. Let me know if you're interested, just tell those Kitchen Kult moguls you owe yourself a little peace and quiet by the seaside, ha! Though you do look more relaxed than the last time I saw you, you looked wrung out, completely.'

In early May Hazel had an accident. She and Peter were setting up one morning, arranging a new demonstration, employing the usual cabbage, beets and onions, but adding a few spears of spring asparagus and a scatter of chopped chives. In the interest of economy she'd decided to split the asparagus length-wise, bringing her knife first through the tender tapered head and down the woody stem. Peter was talking away about a new suit he was thinking of buying, asking Hazel's advice—should he go all out for a fine summer wool or compromise on wool and viscose? The knife slipped and entered the web of flesh between Hazel's thumb and forefinger. It sliced further into the flesh than she would have believed possible, so quickly, so lightly that she could only gaze at the spreading blood and grieve about the way it stained and spoiled her perfect circle of cucumber slices.

She required twelve stitches and, at Peter's urging, took the rest of the day off. Mr Cortland's secretary telephoned and told her to take the whole week off if necessary. There were insurance forms to sign, but those could wait. The important thing was—but Hazel couldn't remember what the important thing was; she had been given some painkillers at the hospital and was having difficulty staying awake. She slept the afternoon away, dreaming of green fields and a yellow sun, and would have slept all evening too if she hadn't been wakened around eight o'clock by the faint buzz of her doorbell. She pulled on a dressing gown, a new one in flowered seersucker, and went to the door. It was Peter Lemmon with a clutch of flowers in his hand. 'Why Peter,' she said, and could think of nothing else.

The pain had left her hand and moved to the thin skin of her scalp. Its remoteness as much as its taut bright shine left her confused. She managed to take Peter's light jacket—though he protested, saying he had only come for a moment—and steered him toward a comfortable chair by the window. She listened as the cushions subsided under him, and hurried to put the flowers, already a little limp, into water, and to offer a drink—but what did she have on hand? No beer, no gin, and she knew better than to suggest sherry. Then the thought came: what about a glass of red wine?

He accepted twitchily. He said, 'You don't have to twist my arm.'

'You'll have to uncork it,' Hazel said, gesturing at her bandaged hand. She felt she could see straight into his brain where there was nothing but rags and old plastic. But where had *this* come from, this sly, unpardonable superiority of hers?

He lurched forward, nearly falling. 'Always happy to do the honours.' He seemed afraid of her, of her apartment with its settled furniture, lamps and end tables and china cabinet, regarding these things first with a strict, dry, inquiring look. After a few minutes, he resettled in the soft chair with exaggerated respect.

'To your career,' Peter said, raising his glass, appearing not to notice how the word career entered Hazel's consciousness, waking her up from her haze of painkillers and making her want to laugh.

'To the glory of Kitchen Kult,' she said, suddenly reckless. She watched him, or part of herself watched him, as he twirled the glass and sniffed its contents. She braced herself for what would surely come.

'An excellent vin—' he started to say, but was interrupted by the doorbell.

It was only Marilyn, dropping in as she sometimes did after her self-defense course. 'Already I can break a collarbone,' she told Peter after a flustered introduction, 'and next week we're going to learn how to go for the groin.'

She looked surprisingly pretty with her pensive, wet, youthful eyes and dusty lashes. She accepted some wine and listened intently to the story of Hazel's accident, then said, 'Now listen, Mother, don't sign a release with Kitchen Kult until I have Edna look at it. You remember Edna, she's the lawyer. She's sharp as a knife; she's the one who did our lease for us, and it's airtight. You could develop blood poisoning or an infection, you can't tell at this point. You can't trust these corporate entities when it comes to—'

'Kitchen Kult', Peter said, twirling his glass in a manner Hazel found silly, 'is more like a family.'

'Balls.'

'We've decided', Maxine told Hazel a few weeks later, 'against the cottage in Nova Scotia. It's too risky, and the weather's only so-so according to Francine. And the cost of air fare and then renting a car, we just figured it's too expensive. My rent's going up starting in July and, well, I took a look at my bank balance and said, Maxine kid, you've got to tighten the old belt. As a matter of fact, I thought—now this may surprise you—I'm thinking of looking for a job.'

Hazel set up an interview for Maxine through Personnel, and in a week's time Maxine did her first demonstration. Hazel helped break her in. As a result of a dimly perceived office shuffle, she had been promoted to Assistant Area Manager, freeing Peter Lemmon for what was described as 'Creative Sales Outreach'. The promotion worried her slightly and she wondered if she were being compensated for the nerve damage in her hand, which was beginning to look more or less permanent. 'Thank God you didn't sign the release,' was all Marilyn said.

'Congrats,' Rosie wired from British Columbia after hearing about the promotion. Hazel had not received a telegram for some years. She was surprised that this austere printed sheet went by the name of telegram. Where was the rough gray paper and the little pasted together words? She wondered who had composed the message, Robin or Rosie, and whose idea it had been to abbreviate the single word and if thrift were involved. *Congrats.* What a hard little hurting pellet to find in the middle of a smooth sheet of paper.

'Gorgeous,' Brian's mother said of Hazel's opal-toned silk suit with its scarf of muted pink pearl and lemon. Her lips moved appreciatively. 'Ah, gorgeous.'

'A helluva improvement over a bloody smock,' Maxine sniffed, looking sideways.

'Most elegant!' said Mr Cortland, who had called Hazel into his office to discuss her future with Kitchen Kult. 'The sort of image we hope and try to project. Elegance and understatement.' He presented her with a small box in which rested, on a square of textured cotton, a pair of enameled earrings with the flying letter K for Kitchen Kult.

'Beautiful,' said Hazel, who never wore earrings. The clip-on sort hurt her, and she had never got around to piercing her ears. 'For my sake,' Brian had begged her when he was twenty-five and she was twenty and about to become his wife, 'don't ever do it. I can't bear to lose a single bit of you.'

Remembering this, the tone of Brian's voice, its rushing, foolish sincerity, Hazel felt her eyes tingle. 'My handbag,' she said, groping blindly.

Mr Cortland misunderstood. He leaped up, touched by his own generosity, a Kleenex in hand. 'We simply wanted to show our appreciation,' he said, or rather sang.

Hazel sniffed, more loudly than she intended, and Mr Cortland pretended not to hear. 'We especially appreciate your filling in for Peter Lemmon during his leave of absence.'

At this Hazel nodded. Poor Peter. She must phone tonight. He was finding the aftermath of his dental surgery painful and prolonged, and she had been looking, every chance she had, for a suitable convalescent card, something not too effusive and not too mocking—Peter took his teeth far too seriously. Perhaps she would just send one of her blurry impressionistic hasty notes, or better yet, a jaunty postcard saying she hoped he'd be back soon.

Mr Cortland fingered the pink conch shell on his desk. He picked it up between his two hands and rocked it gently to and fro, then said, 'Mr Lemmon will not be returning. We have already sent him a letter of termination and, of course, a generous severance settlement. It was decided that his particular kind of personality, though admirable, was not quite in line with the Kitchen Kult approach, and we feel that you yourself have already demonstrated your ability to take over his work and perhaps even extend the scope of it.'

'I don't believe you're doing this,' Marilyn shouted over the phone to Hazel. 'And Peter doesn't believe it either.'

'How do you know what Peter thinks?'

'I saw him this afternoon. I saw him yesterday afternoon. I see him rather often if you want to know the truth.'

Hazel offered the Kitchen Kult earrings to Maxine who snorted and said, 'Come off it, Hazel.'

Rosie in Vancouver sent a short note saying, 'Marilyn phoned about your new position, which is really marvelous, though Robin and I are wondering if you aren't getting in deeper than you really want to at this time.'

Brian's mother said nothing. A series of small strokes had taken her speech away and also her ability to leave her bed. Nothing Hazel brought her aroused her interest, not chocolates, not flowers, not even the fashion magazines she used to love.

Hazel phoned and made an appointment to see Mr Cortland. She invented a pretext, one or two ideas she and Maxine had worked out to tighten up the demonstrations. Mr Cortland listened to her and nodded approvingly. Then she sprang. She had been thinking about Peter Lemmon, she said, how much the sales force missed him, missed his resourcefulness and his attention to details. He had a certain imaginative flair, a peculiar usefulness. Some people had a way of giving energy to others, it was uncanny, it was a rare gift. She didn't mention Peter's dental work; she had some sense.

Mr Cortland sent her a shrewd look, a look she would not have believed he had in his repertoire. 'Well, Hazel,' he said at last, 'in business we deal in hard bargains. Maybe you and I can come to some sort of bargain.'

'Bargain?'

'That insurance form, the release. The one you haven't got round to signing yet. How would it be if you signed it right now on the promise that I find some slot or other for Peter Lemmon by the end of the week? You are quite right about his positive attributes, quite astute of you, really, to point them out. I can't promise anything in sales though. The absolute bottom end of management might be the best we can do.'

Hazel considered. She stared at the conch shell for a full ten seconds. The office lighting coated it with a pink, even light, making it look like a piece of unglazed pottery. She liked the idea of bargains. She felt she understood them. 'I'll sign,' she said. She had her pen in her hand, poised.

On Sunday, a Sunday at the height of the summer in early July, Hazel drives out to Silver Oaks to visit her ailing mother-in-law. All she can do for her now is sit by her side for an hour and hold her hand, and sometimes she wonders what the point is of these visits. Her mother-in-law's face is impassive and silken, and occasionally driblets of spittle, thin and clear as tears, run from the corners of her mouth. It used to be such a strong, organized face with its firm mouth and steady eyes. But now she doesn't recognize anyone, with the possible exception of Hazel.

Some benefit appears to derive from these handholding sessions, or so the nurses tell Hazel. 'She's calmer after your visits,' they say. 'She struggles less.'

Hazel is calm too. She likes sitting here and feeling the hour unwind like thread from a spindle. She wishes it would go on and on. A week ago she had come away from Mr Cortland's office irradiated with the conviction that her life was going to be possible after all. All she had to do was bear in mind the bargains she made. This was an obscene revelation, but Hazel was excited by it. Everything could be made accountable, added up and balanced and fairly, evenly, shared. You only had to pay attention and ask for what was yours by right. You could be clever, dealing in sly acts of surrender, but holding fast at the same time, negotiating and measuring and tying up your life in useful bundles.

But she was wrong. It wasn't true. Her pride had misled her. No one has that kind of power, no one.

She looks around the little hospital room and marvels at the accident of its contents, its bureau and tumbler and toothbrush and folded towel. The open window looks out on to a parking lot filled with rows of cars, all their shining roofs baking in the light. Next year there will be different cars, differently ordered. The shrubs and trees, weighed down with their millions of new leaves, will form a new dark backdrop.

It is an accident that she should be sitting in this room, holding the hand of an old, unblinking, unresisting woman who had once been sternly disapproving of her, thinking her countrified and clumsy. 'Hazel!' she had sometimes whispered in the early days. 'Your slip strap! Your salad fork!' Now she lacks even the power to wet her lips with her tongue; it is Hazel who touches the lips with a damp towel from time to time, or applies a bit of Vaseline to keep them from cracking. But she can feel the old woman's dim pulse, and imagines that it forms a code of acknowledgment or faintly telegraphs certain perplexing final questions—how did all this happen? How did we get here?

Everything is an accident, Hazel would be willing to say if asked. Her whole life is an accident, and by accident she has blundered into the heart of it.

1989

Alistair MacLeod

b. 1936

Born in North Battleford, Sask., Alistair MacLeod lived in various small prairie settlements in Saskatchewan and Alberta until 1946, when his parents moved back to the family farm in Cape Breton, NS. He graduated from high school there and worked to support himself in a variety of jobs (salesman, editor, logger, truck driver, public-relations man, miner, and teacher). He put himself through Nova Scotia Teachers' College and, during the 1960s, earned degrees at St Francis Xavier University (BA, B.Ed.), the University of New Brunswick (MA), and the University of Notre Dame (Ph.D., 1968). He taught at the University of Indiana for three years before taking a position at the University of Windsor in 1969, where he taught courses in nineteenth-century British literature and creative writing. He retired in 2000.

MacLeod began to publish in journals in Canada and the United States while he was still a graduate student. His output has been small—his two collections of short stories, *The Lost Salt Gift of Blood* (1976) and *As Birds Bring Forth the Sun* (1986), along with two additional stories, are contained in the just over 400 pages of *Island: The Collected Stories* (2000)—but he has gained a considerable reputation as a meticulous craftsman, whose accounts have great resonance and enduring power. In all of his writing, the traditional life of the small Maritime communities, though austere and even dangerous, provides a sense of stability and tradition that seems to be vanishing elsewhere.

In 1999 MacLeod published a novel, *No Great Mischief*, the product of over ten years of careful writing. Through reminiscences and anecdotes the book chronicles the family history of the Cape Breton MacDonalds from 1779—when the first of the clan came to Cape Breton from Scotland following the defeat, at Culloden, of the Highlanders supporting Bonny Prince Charlie—to the present. Out of these chronicles emerges a presiding narrative that blends stories from a mythic and heroic past with the theme of loss, often violent or tragic—both of the clan's family members and of their Gaelic heritage. *No Great Mischief* won the IMPAC Dublin Award.

MacLeod has remarked: 'I'm one of those writers who believes storytelling is older than literacy and I think of myself as a storyteller.' Certainly a story like 'As Birds Bring Forth the Sun'—which is most often MacLeod's choice when he reads aloud from his work—feels oral as much as written, as the narrator tells of how he and his family have been haunted by a spectre from their past. Like all of MacLeod's fiction it speaks of a Celtic inheritance and of a world rich in memory, one still alive in tales that, however old, retain their pertinence and immediacy. For MacLeod, as for many contemporary Canadian writers, fiction is a meeting place where the everyday world and the mythic realm of the fable or folk-tale come together.

As Birds Bring Forth the Sun

Once there was a family with a Highland name who lived beside the sea. And the man had a dog of which he was very fond. She was large and grey, a sort of staghound from another time. And if she jumped up to lick his face, which she loved to do, her paws would jolt against his shoulders with such force that she would come close to knocking him down and he would be forced to take two or three backward steps before he could regain his balance. And he himself was not a small man, being slightly over six feet and perhaps one hundred and eighty pounds.

She had been left, when a pup, at the family's gate in a small handmade box and no one knew where she had come from or that she would eventually grow to such a size. Once, while still a small pup, she had been run over by the steel wheel of a horse-drawn cart which was hauling kelp from the shore to be used as fertilizer. It was in October and the rain had been falling for some weeks and the ground was soft. When the wheel of the cart passed over her, it sunk her body into the wet earth as well as crushing some of her ribs; and apparently the silhouette of her small crushed body was visible in the earth after the man lifted her to his chest while she yelped and screamed. He ran his fingers along her broken bones, ignoring the blood and urine which fell upon his shirt, trying to soothe her bulging eyes and her scrabbling front paws and her desperately licking tongue.

The more practical members of his family, who had seen run-over dogs before, suggested that her neck be broken by his strong hands or that he grasp her by the hind legs and swing her head against a rock, thus putting an end to her misery. But he would not do it.

Instead, he fashioned a small box and lined it with woollen remnants from a sheep's fleece and one of his old and frayed shirts. He placed her within the box and placed the box behind the stove and then he warmed some milk in a small saucepan and sweetened it with sugar. And he held open her small and trembling jaws with his left hand while spooning in the sweetened milk with his right, ignoring the needle-like sharpness of her small teeth. She lay in the box most of the remaining fall and into the early winter, watching everything with her large brown eyes.

Although some members of the family complained about her presence and the odour from the box and the waste of time she involved, they gradually adjusted to her; and as the weeks passed by, it became evident that her ribs were knitting together in some form or other and that she was recovering with the resilience of the young. It also became evident that she would grow to a tremendous size, as she outgrew one box and then another and the grey hair began to feather from her huge front paws. In the spring she was outside almost all of the time and followed the man everywhere; and when she came inside during the following months, she had grown so large that she would no longer fit into her accustomed place behind the stove and was forced to lie beside it. She was never given a name but was referred to in Gaelic as *cù mòr glas*, the big grey dog.

By the time she came into her first heat, she had grown to a tremendous height, and although her signs and her odour attracted many panting and highly aroused suitors, none was big enough to mount her and the frenzy of their disappointment and the longing of her unfulfilment were more than the man could stand. He went, so the story goes, to a place where he knew there was a big dog. A dog not as big as she was, but still a big dog, and he brought him home with him. And at the proper time he took the *cù mòr glas* and the big dog down to the sea where he knew there was a hollow in the rock which appeared only at low tide. He took some sacking to provide footing for the male dog and he placed the *cù mòr glas* in the hollow of the rock and knelt beside her and steadied her with his left arm under her throat and helped position the male dog above her and guided his blood-engorged penis. He was a man used to working with the breeding of animals, with the guiding of rams and bulls and stallions and often with the funky smell of animal semen heavy on his large and gentle hands.

The winter that followed was a cold one and ice formed on the sea and frequent squalls and blizzards obliterated the offshore islands and caused the people to stay near their fires much of the time, mending clothes and nets and harness and waiting for the change in season. The *cù mòr glas* grew heavier and even more large until there was hardly room for her around the stove or even under the table. And then one morning, when it seemed that spring was about to break, she was gone.

The man and even his family, who had become more involved than they cared to admit, waited for her but she did not come. And as the frenzy of spring wore on, they busied themselves with readying their land and their fishing gear and all of the things that so desperately required their attention. And then they were into summer and fall and winter and another spring which saw the birth of the man and his wife's twelfth child. And then it was summer again.

That summer the man and two of his teenaged sons were pulling their herring nets about two miles offshore when the wind began to blow off the land and the water began to roughen. They became afraid that they could not make it safely back to shore, so they pulled in behind one of the offshore islands, knowing that they would be sheltered there and planning to outwait the storm. As the prow of their boat approached the gravely shore, they heard a sound above them, and looking up they saw the *cù mòr glas* silhouetted on the brow of the hill which was the small island's highest point.

'*M'eudal cù mòr glas*' shouted the man in his happiness—*m'eudal* meaning something like dear or darling; and as he shouted, he jumped over the side of his boat into the waist-deep water, struggling for footing on the rolling gravel as he waded eagerly and awkwardly towards her and the shore. At the same time, the *cù mòr glas* came hurtling down towards him in a shower of small rocks dislodged by her feet; and just as he was emerging from the water, she met him as she used to, rearing up on her hind legs and placing her huge front paws on his shoulders while extending her eager tongue.

The weight and speed of her momentum met him as he tried to hold his balance on the sloping angle and the water rolling gravel beneath his feet, and he staggered backwards and lost his footing and fell beneath her force. And in that instant again, as the story goes, there appeared over the brow of the hill six more huge grey dogs hurtling down towards the gravelled strand. They had never seen him before; and seeing him stretched prone beneath their mother, they misunderstood, like so many armies, the intention of their leader.

They fell upon him in a fury, slashing his face and tearing aside his lower jaw and ripping out his throat, crazed with blood-lust or duty or perhaps starvation. The *cù mòr glas* turned on them in her own savagery, slashing and snarling and, it seemed, crazed by their mistake; driving them bloodied and yelping before her, back over the brow of the hill where they vanished from sight but could still be heard screaming in the distance. It all took perhaps little more than a minute.

The man's two sons, who were still in the boat and had witnessed it all, ran sobbing through the salt water to where their mauled and mangled father lay; but there was little they could do other than hold his warm and bloodied hands for a few brief moments. Although his eyes 'lived' for a small fraction of time, he could not speak to them because his face and throat had been torn away, and of course there was nothing they could do except to hold and be held tightly until that too slipped away and his eyes glazed over and they could no longer feel his hands holding theirs. The storm increased and they could not get home and so they were forced to spend the night huddled beside their father's body. They were afraid to try to carry the body to the rocking boat because he was so heavy and they were afraid that they might lose even what little of him remained and they were afraid also, huddled on the rocks, that the dogs might return. But they did not return at all and there was no sound from them, no sound at all, only the moaning of the wind and the washing of the water on the rocks.

In the morning they debated whether they should try to take his body with them or whether they should leave it and return in the company of older and wiser men. But they were afraid to leave it unattended and felt that the time needed to cover it with protective rocks would be better spent in trying to get across to their home shore. For a while they debated as to whether one should go in the boat and the other remain on the island, but each was afraid to be alone and so in the end they managed to drag and carry and almost float him towards the bobbing boat. They lay him facedown and covered him with what clothes there were and set off across the still-rolling sea. Those who waited on the shore missed the large presence of the man within the boat and some of them waded into the water and others rowed out in skiffs, attempting to hear the tearful message called out across the rolling waves.

The *cù mòr glas* and her six young dogs were never seen again, or perhaps I should say they were never seen again in the same way. After some weeks, a group of men circled the island tentatively in their boats but they saw no sign. They went again and again but found nothing. A year later, and grown much braver, they beached their boats and walked the island carefully, looking into the small sea caves and hollows at the base of the wind-ripped trees, thinking perhaps that if they did not find the dogs, they might at least find their whitened bones; but again they discovered nothing.

The *cù mòr glas*, though, was supposed to be sighted here and there for a number of years. Seen on a hill in one region or silhouetted on a ridge in another or loping across the valleys or glens in the early morning or the shadowy evening. Always in the area of the half perceived. For a while she became rather like the Loch Ness Monster or the Sasquatch on a smaller scale. Seen but not recorded. Seen when there were no cameras. Seen but never taken.

The mystery of where she went became entangled with the mystery of whence she came. There was increased speculation about the handmade box in which she had been found and much theorizing as to the individual or individuals who might have left it. People went to look for the box but could not find it. It was felt she might have been part of a *buidseachd* or evil spell cast on the man by some mysterious enemy. But no one could go much farther than that. All of his caring for her was recounted over and over again and nobody missed any of the ironies.

What seemed literally known was that she had crossed the winter ice to have her pups and had been unable to get back. No one could remember ever seeing her swim; and in the early months at least, she could not have taken her young pups with her.

The large and gentle man with the smell of animal semen often heavy on his hands was my great-great-great-grandfather, and it may be argued that he died because he was too good at breeding animals or that he cared too much about their fulfilment and well-being. He was no longer there for his own child of the spring who, in turn, became my great-great-grandfather, and he was perhaps too much there in the memory of his older sons who saw him fall beneath the ambiguous force of the *cù mòr glas.* The youngest boy in the boat was haunted and tormented by the awfulness of what he had seen. He would wake at night screaming that he had seen the *cù mòr glas a'bhàis*, the big grey dog of death, and his screams filled the house and the ears and minds of the listeners, bringing home again and again the consequences of their loss. One morning, after a night in which he saw the *cù mòr glas a'bhàis* so vividly that his sheets were drenched with sweat, he walked to the high cliff which faced the island and there he cut his throat with a fish knife and fell into the sea.

The other brother lived to be forty, but, again so the story goes, he found himself in a Glasgow pub one night, perhaps looking for answers, deep and sodden with the whiskey which had become his anaesthetic. In the half darkness he saw a large, grey-haired man sitting by himself against the wall and mumbled something to him. Some say he saw the *cù mòr glas a'bhàis* or uttered the name. And perhaps the man heard the phrase through ears equally affected by drink and felt he was being called a dog or a son of a bitch or something of that nature. They rose to meet one another and struggled outside into the cobblestoned passageway behind the pub where, most improbably, there were supposed to be six other large, grey-haired men who beat him to death on the cobblestones, smashing his bloodied head into the stone again and again before vanishing and leaving him to die with his face turned to the sky. The *cù mòr glas a'bhàis* had come again, said his family, as they tried to piece the tale together.

This is how the *cù mòr glas a'bhàis* came into our lives, and it is obvious that all of this happened a long, long time ago. Yet with succeeding generations it seemed the spectre had somehow come to stay and that it had become *ours*—not in the manner of an unwanted skeleton in the closet from a family's ancient past but more in the manner of something close to a genetic possibility. In the deaths of each generation, the grey dog was seen by some—by women who were to die in childbirth; by soldiers who went forth to the many wars but did not return; by those who went forth to feuds or dangerous love affairs; by those who answered mysterious midnight messages; by those who swerved on the highway to avoid the real or imagined grey dog and ended in masses of crumpled steel. And by one professional athlete who, in addition to his ritualized athletic superstitions, carried another fear or belief as well. Many of the man's descendants moved like careful hemophiliacs, fearing that they carried unwanted possibilities deep within them. And others, while they laughed, were like members of families in which there is a recurrence over the generations of repeated cancer or the diabetes which comes to those beyond middle age. The feeling of those who may say little to others but who may say often and quietly to themselves, 'It has not happened to me,' while adding always the cautionary '*yet*.'

I am thinking all of this now as the October rain falls on the city of Toronto and the pleasant, white-clad nurses pad confidently in and out of my father's room. He lies quietly amidst the whiteness, his head and shoulders elevated so that he is in that hospital position of being neither quite prone nor yet sitting. His hair is white upon his pillow and he breathes softly and sometimes unevenly, although it is difficult ever to be sure.

My five grey-haired brothers and I take turns beside his bedside, holding his heavy hands in ours and feeling their response, hoping ambiguously that he will speak to us, although we know it may tire him. And trying to read his life and ours into his eyes when they are open. He has been with us for a long time, well into our middle age. Unlike those boys in that boat of so long ago, we did not see him taken from us in our youth. And unlike their youngest brother who, in turn, became our great-great-grandfather, we did not grow into a world in which there was no father's touch. We have been lucky to have this large and gentle man so deep into our lives.

No one in this hospital has mentioned the *cù mòr glas a'bhàis*. Yet as my mother said ten years ago, before slipping into her own death as quietly as a grownup child who leaves or enters her parents' house in the early hours, 'It is hard to not know what you do know.'

Even those who are most skeptical, like my oldest brother who has driven here from Montreal, betray themselves by their nervous actions. 'I avoided the Greyhound bus stations in both Montreal and Toronto,' he smiled upon his arrival, and then added, 'Just in case.'

He did not realize how ill our father was and has smiled little since then. I watch him turning the diamond ring upon his finger, knowing that he hopes he will not hear the Gaelic phrase he knows too well. Not having the luxury, as he once said, of some who live in Montreal and are able to pretend they do not understand the 'other' language. You cannot not know what you do know.

Sitting here, taking turns holding the hands of the man who gave us life, we are afraid for him and for ourselves. We are afraid of what he may see and we are afraid to hear the phrase born of the vision. We are aware that it may become confused with what the doctors call 'the will to live' and we are aware that some beliefs are what others would dismiss as 'garbage'. We are aware that there are men who believe the earth is flat and that the birds bring forth the sun.

Bound here in our own peculiar mortality, we do not wish to see or see others see that which signifies life's demise. We do not want to hear the voice of our father, as did those other sons, calling down his own particular death upon him.

We would shut our eyes and plug our ears, even as we know such actions to be of no avail. Open still and fearful to the grey hair rising on our necks if and when we hear the scrabble of the paws and the scratching at the door.

1986

Jack Hodgins

b. 1938

Raised in the small farming and logging town of Merville, BC—in which, according to Hodgins, everyone was either a relative or a friend—Jack Hodgins attended the University of British Columbia, studying creative writing under Earle Birney. After receiving a B.Ed. in 1961, he took a job teaching high school English in Nanaimo. In the late 1960s Hodgins began to publish his first short stories, set in the Comox Valley where he grew up. These were collected in 1976 as *Spit Delaney's Island.* The sense that all of Hodgins' fiction not only emerges out of the communities of northern Vancouver Island but exists in an imaginative continuum is reinforced by the fact that some of the eccentric characters introduced in that first collection (such as the seven daughters of the Barclay family in 'Other People's Troubles') have continued to reappear in later work.

The following year saw the publication of Hodgins' first novel, *The Invention of the World* (1977), a hyperbolic account of life on Vancouver Island that blends tales he heard growing up with Vancouver Island history and legend. When his second novel, *The Resurrection of Joseph Bourne* (1979), won a Governor General's Award, that gave him the confidence to resign his job as school teacher and devote himself to his writing. He became writer-in-residence and then a creative writing instructor at the University of Ottawa, and spent a year in Australia as a result of winning the Canada-Australia Literary Prize, completing a second collection of stories, *The Barclay Family Theatre,* in 1981. In 1983 he returned to Vancouver Island to teach creative writing at the University of Victoria. He retired in 2002.

In his early work Hodgins established a characteristic style of storytelling, one that combines the anecdotal feeling of the back-country yarn with an extravagance of telling that gives to his creations the magical quality of myth. His novels in particular are flamboyant and fantastic epics that seem naturally to arise from innocently corrupt island communities. Unlike the planned settlements of the mainland, these Edens gone to seed have evolved haphazardly—founded by a madman in *The Invention of the World,* restored by a dead man in *The Resurrection of Joseph Bourne,* confronted by a homecomer in *The Honorary Patron* (1987). In their ingrown state, normality and eccentricity exist in comfortable symbiosis.

Hodgins' next two novels, *Innocent Cities* (1990) and *The Macken Charm* (1995), explore the ways in which local island communities are challenged by contact with the outside world—and with outsiders. In the first, the protagonist, a nineteenth-century architect who wants to transform Victoria into a world-class city, finds his city altered by the arrival of a mysterious stranger—a widow from Australia. In the second, Rusty Macken, who looks beyond rural Vancouver Island to an exciting cosmopolitan world, finds that his plans to leave the island are pre-empted by the death and funeral of a glamorous city girl, Glory.

Hodgins' most recent novel, *Broken Ground* (1998), is a departure from the generally extravagant and comedic style of his earlier fiction. Set on the 'soldier's settlement' of Portuguese Creek on Vancouver Island in 1922, this dark novel portrays a community struggling to recover from tragic personal losses suffered in the First World War. Compounding—and echoing—the devastating horrors of war, a forest fire threatens to sweep down upon the tiny settlement.

Between those last two novels, Hodgins published two non-fiction works. His colourful account of his return to Australia in *Over 40 in Broken Hill* (1992) is a description of a tour he made of the outback. His *Passion for Narrative: A Guide for Writing Fiction* (1993; expanded and with a new afterword in 2001) is a highly successful guide for apprentice writers. He begins it by quoting the Russian-American novelist Vladimir Nabokov: 'A major writer combines . . . storyteller, teacher, enchanter—but it is the enchanter in him that predominates and makes him a major writer.' It is clear that Hodgins has aspired to be such an enchanter.

Drawing on the power of the tall tale as he often does, Hodgins locates his fiction in the tradition of westerners like W.O. Mitchell and Robert Kroetsch. But Hodgins' fictional world differs from that of Prairie novelists: where their landscapes are wide and empty, his are filled and lush—and confined. Even when his characters go abroad (as Philip Desmond has, in 'The Lepers' Squint', travelled to Ireland to understand his Celtic inheritance), their experiences of their own island life continues to shape their being. Unsure how to respond to the half-familiar yet discomfitingly unfamiliar world he finds in Ireland, Philip holds himself apart, remaining 'islanded' in his own isolation.

The Lepers' Squint

Today, while Mary Brennan may be waiting for him on that tiny island high in the mountain lake called Gougane Barra,[1] Philip Desmond is holed up in the back room of this house at Bantry Bay, trying to write his novel. A perfect stack of white paper, three black nylon-tipped pens, and a battered portable typewriter are set out before him on the wooden table. He knows the first paragraph already, has already set it down, and trusts that the rest of the story will run off the end of it like a fishing line pulled by a salmon. But it is cold, it is so cold in this house, even now in August, that he presses both hands down between his thighs to warm them up. It is so cold in this room that he finds it almost impossible to sit still, so damp that he has put on the same clothes he would wear if he were walking out along the edge of that lagoon, in the spitting rain and the wind. Through the small water-specked panes of the window he can see his children playing on the lumpy slabs of rock at the shore, beyond the bobbing branches of the fuchsia hedge. Three children; three red quilted jackets; three faces flushed up by the steady force of the cold wind; they drag tangled clots of stinking seaweed up the slope and, crouching, watch a family of swans explore the edges of a small weedy island not far out in the lagoon.

A high clear voice in his head all the while insists on singing to him of some girl so fair that the ferns uncurl to look at her. The voice of an old man in a mountain pub, singing without accompaniment, stretched and stiff as a rooster singing to the ceiling

1 In a park just north of Bantry Bay, Ireland, on the road to Killarney.

and to the crowd at the bar and to the neighbours who sit around him. *The ferns uncurled to look at her, so very fair was she, with her hair as bright as the seaweed that floats in from the sea.* But here at Ballylickey the seaweed is brown as mud and smells so strong your eyes water.

Mrs O'Sullivan is in the next room, Desmond knows, in her own room, listening. If he coughs she will hear. If he sings. She will know exactly the moment he sets down his next word on that top sheet of paper. Mrs O'Sullivan is the owner of this house, which Desmond rented from home through the Borde Failte[2] people before he discovered that she would live in it with them, in the centre of the house, in her two rooms, and silently listen to the life of his family going on around her. She is a tall dry-skinned old woman with grey finger-waves caged in blue hair net, whose thick fingers dig into the sides of her face in an agony of desire to sympathize with everything that is said to her. 'Oh I know I know I know,' she groans. Last night when Desmond's wife mentioned how tired she was after the long drive down from Dublin, her fingers plucked at her face, her dull eyes rolled up to search for help along the ceiling: 'Oh I know I know I know.' There is no end to her sympathy, there is nothing she doesn't already know. But she will be quiet as a mouse, she promised, they won't know she is here.

'Maybe she's a writer,' Desmond's wife whispered to him, later in bed. 'Maybe she's making notes on us. Maybe she's writing a book called *North Americans I Have Eaves-dropped On*.'

'I can't live with someone listening to me breathe,' Desmond said. 'And I can't write with someone sitting waiting.'

'Adjust,' his wife said, and flicked at his nose. She who could adjust to anything, or absorb it.

On this first day of his novel Desmond had been abandoned by his wife, Carrie, who early this morning drove the car in to Cork. There are still, apparently, a few Seamus Murphy[3] statues she hasn't seen, or touched. 'Keep half an eye on the kids,' she said before she left. Then she came back and kissed him and whispered, 'Though if you get busy it won't matter. I'm sure Mrs O'Sullivan won't miss anything.' To be fair, to be really fair, he knows that his annoyance is unjustified. He didn't tell her he intended to work today, the first day in this house. She probably thinks that after travelling for six weeks through the country he'll rest a few more days before beginning; she may even believe that he is glad to be rid of her for the day, after all those weeks of unavoidable closeness. She certainly knows that with Mrs O'Sullivan in the house no emergency will be overlooked, no crisis ignored.

Desmond, now that his hands have warmed a little, lifts one of the pens to write, though silently as possible, as if what he is about to do is a secret perversion from which the ears of Mrs O'Sullivan must be protected. But he cannot, now, put down any new words. Because if the novel, which has been roaring around in his head all summer and much longer, looking for a chance to get out, should not recognize in the opening words the crack through which it is to spring forth, transformed into a string of words like a whirring fish line, then he will be left with all that paper to stare at, and

2 Tourist board (Irish).
3 (1907–75), a sculptor from Cork.

an unmoving pen, and he is not ready to face that. Of course he knows the story, has seen it all in his mind a hundred times as if someone else had gone to the trouble of writing it and producing it as a movie just for him. But he has never been one for plunging into things, oceans or stories, and prefers to work his way in gently. That opening paragraph, though, is only a paragraph after all and has no magic, only a few black lifeless lines at the top of the paper. So he writes his title again, and under it his name: Barclay Philip Desmond. Then he writes the opening paragraph a second time, and again under that, and again, hoping that the pen will go on by itself to write the next words and surprise him. But it does not happen, not now. Instead, he discovers he is seeing two other words which are not there at all, as if perhaps they are embedded, somehow, just beneath the surface of the paper.

Mary Brennan.

Desmond knows he must keep the name from becoming anything more than that, from becoming a face too, or the pale scent of fear. He writes his paragraph again, over and over until he has filled up three or four pages. Then, crumpling the papers in his hand, he wonders if this will be one of those stories that remain forever in their authors' heads, driving them mad, refusing to suffer conversion into words.

It's the cold, he thinks. Blame it on the bloody weather. His children outside on the rocky slope have pulled the hoods of their jackets up over their heads. Leaves torn from the beech tree lie soaked and heavy on the grass. At the far side of the lagoon the family of swans is following the choppy retreating tide out through the gap to the open bay; perhaps they know of a calmer inlet somewhere. The white stone house with red window frames in its nest of bushes across the water has blurred behind the rain, and looks more than ever like the romantic pictures he has seen on postcards. A thin line of smoke rises from the yellowish house and the gate sign *Carrigdhoun.*[4]

But it is easier than writing, far easier, to allow the persistent daydreams in, and memory. That old rooster-stiff man, standing in the cleared-away centre of the bar in Ballyvourney to pump his song out to the ceiling, his hands clasping and unclasping at his sides as if they are responsible for squeezing those words into life. The ferns uncurled to see her, he sings, so very fair was she. Neighbours clap rhythm, or stamp their feet. Men six-deep at the bar-counter continue to shout at each other about sheep, and the weather. With hair as bright as the seaweed that floats in from the sea.

' 'Tis an island of singers sure!' someone yells in Desmond's ear. 'An island of saints and paupers and bloody singers!'

But Desmond thinks of Mary Brennan's hot apple-smelling breath against his face: 'Islands do not exist until you have loved on them.' The words are a Caribbean poet's,[5] she explains, and not her own. But the sentiment is adaptable. The ferns may not uncurl to see the dark brown beauty of her eyes, but Desmond has seen men turn at her flash of hair the reddish-brown of gleaming kelp. Turn, and smile to themselves. This day while he sits behind the wooden table, hunched over his pile of paper, he knows that she is waiting for him on a tiny hermitage island in a mountain lake not

4 Brown rock (Irish). (This is also the name of the Irish village in *The Invention of the World.*)

5 Derek Walcott, from the poem 'Islands' in *In a Green Night* (1962); the original lines are: 'But islands can only exist / If we have loved in them'.

far away, beneath the branches of the crowded trees. Islands, she had told him, do not exist until you've loved on them.

Yesterday, driving south from Dublin across the Tipperary farmland, they stopped again at the Rock of Cashel so that Carrie could prowl a second time through that big roofless cathedral high up on the sudden limestone knoll and run her hands over the strange broken form of St Patrick's Cross. The kings of Munster lived there once, she told him, and later turned it over to the church. St Patrick himself came to baptize the king there, and accidentally pierced the poor man's foot with the point of his heavy staff.

'There's all of history here, huddled together,' she said, and catalogued it for him. 'A tenth-century round tower, a twelfth-century chapel, a thirteenth-century cathedral, a fourteenth-century tower, a fifteenth-century castle, and . . .' she rolled her eyes, 'a twentieth-century tourist shop.'

But it was the cross itself that drew her. Originally a cross within a frame, it was only the central figure of a man now, with one arm of the cross and a thin upright stem that held that arm in place. Rather like a tall narrow pitcher. There was a guide this second time, and a tour, and she pouted when he insisted they stick to the crowd and hear the official truths instead of making guesses or relying on the brief explanations on the backs of postcards. She threw him a black scowl when the guide explained the superstition about the cross: that if you can touch hand to hand around it you'll never have another toothache as long as you live. Ridiculous, she muttered; she'd spent an hour the last time looking at that thing, marvelling at the beautiful piece of sculpture nature or time or perhaps vandals had accidentally made of it, running her hands over the figures on the coronation stone at its base and up the narrow stem that supported the remaining arm of the cross.

He was more curious, though, about the round swell of land which could be seen out across the flat Tipperary farms, a perfect green hill crowned with a circle of leafy trees. The guide told him that after one of the crusades a number of people returned to Ireland with a skin disease which was mistaken for leprosy and were confined to that hill, inside that circle, and forbidden to leave it. They were brought across to Mass here on Sundays, she said, before leading him back inside the cathedral to show a small gap in the stones far up one grey wall of the empty Choir. 'The poor lepers, a miserable lot altogether as you can imagine, were crowded into a little room behind that wall,' she said, 'and were forced to see and hear through that single narrow slit of a window. It's called the Lepers' Squint, for obvious reasons.'

Afterwards, when the crowd of nuns and priests and yellow-slickered tourists had broken up to walk amongst the graves and the Celtic crosses or to climb the stone steps to the round tower, Desmond would like to have spoken to one of the priests, perhaps the short red-faced one, to say, 'What do you make of all this?' or 'Is it true what she told us about that fat archbishop with all his wives and children?' But he was intimidated by the black suit, that collar, and by the way the priest seemed always to be surrounded by nuns who giggled like schoolgirls at the silly jokes he told, full of words Desmond couldn't understand. He would go home without ever speaking to a single member of the one aristocracy this country still permitted itself.

But while he stood tempted in the sharp wind that howled across the high hump of rock the guide came over the grass to him. ' 'Tis certain that you're not American as I thought at first,' she said, 'for you speak too soft for that. Would you be from England then?'

'No,' he said. And without thinking: 'We're from Vancouver Island.'

'Yes?' she said, her eyes blank. 'And where would that be now?'

'A long way from here,' he said. 'An island, too, like this one, with its own brand of ruins.

'There's a tiny island off our coast', he said, 'where they used to send the lepers once, but the last of them died a few years ago. It's a bare and empty place they say now, except for the wind. There are even people who believe that ghosts inhabit it.'

But then there were people, too, who said he was crazy to take the children to this uneasy country. It's smaller than you think, they said. You'll hear the bombs from above the border when you get there. What if war breaks out? What if the IRA decides that foreign hostages might help their cause? What about that bomb in the Dublin department store?

Choose another country, they said. A warmer safer one. Choose an island where you can lie in the sun and be waited on by smiling blacks. Why pick Ireland?

Jealousy, he'd told them. Everyone else he knew seemed to have inherited an 'old country', an accent, a religion, a set of customs, from parents. His family fled the potato famine in 1849 and had had five generations in which to fade out into Canadians. 'I don't know what I've inherited from them,' he said, 'but whatever it is has gone too deep to be visible.'

They'd spent the summer travelling; he would spend the fall and winter writing.

His search for family roots, however, had ended down a narrow hedged-in land: a half-tumbled stone cabin, stony fields, a view of misty hills, and distant neighbours who turned their damp hay with a two-tined fork and knew nothing at all of the cabin's past.

'Fled the famine did they?' the old woman said. ' 'Twas many a man did that and was never heard from since.'

The summer was intended as a literary pilgrimage too, and much of it was a disappointment. Yeats's castle tower near Coole had been turned into a tourist trap as artificial as a wax museum, with cassette recorders to listen to as you walk through room to room, and a souvenir shop to sell you books and postcards; Oliver Goldsmith's village was not only deserted, it had disappeared, the site of the little schoolhouse nothing more than a potato patch and the parsonage just half a vine-covered wall; the James Joyce museum only made him feel guilty that he'd never been able to finish *Ulysses*, though there'd been a little excitement that day when a group of women's libbers crashed the male nude-bathing beach just behind the tower.

A man in Dublin told him there weren't any live writers in this country. 'You'll find more of our novelists and poets in America than you'll find here,' he said. 'You're wasting your time on that.'

With a sense almost of relief, as though delivered from a responsibility (dead writers, though disappointing, do not confront you with flesh, as living writers could, or with demands), he took the news along with a handful of hot dogs to Carrie and the kids, who had got out of the car to admire a statue. Watching her eat that onion and pork sausage 'hot dog' he realized that she had become invisible to him, or nearly invisible. He hadn't even noticed until now that she'd changed her hair, that she was pinning it back; probably because of the wind. In the weeks of travel, in constant too-close confinement, she had all but disappeared, had faded out of his notice the way his own limbs must have done, oh, thirty years ago.

If someone had asked, 'What does your wife look like?' he would have forgotten to mention short. He might have said dainty but that was no longer entirely true; sitting like that she appeared to have rounded out, like a copper Oriental idol: dark and squat and yet fine, perhaps elegant. He could not have forgotten her loud, almost masculine laugh of course, but he had long ago ceased to notice the quality of her speaking voice. Carrie, his Carrie, was busy having her own separate holiday, almost untouched by his, though they wore each other like old comfortable unnoticed and unchanged clothes.

'A movie would be nice,' he said. 'If we could find a babysitter.'

But she shook her head. 'We can see movies at home. And besides, by the evenings I'm tired out from all we've done, I'd never be able to keep my eyes open.'

After Cashel, on their way to the Bantry house, they stopped a while in the city of Cork. And here, he discovered, here after all the disappointments, was a dead literary hero[6] the tourist board hadn't yet got ahold of. He forgot again that she even existed as he tracked down the settings of the stories he loved: butcher shops and smelly quays and dark crowded pubs and parks.

The first house, the little house where the famous writer was born, had been torn down by a sports club which had put a high steel fence around the property, but a neighbour took him across the road and through a building to the back balcony to show him the Good Shepherd Convent where the writer's mother had grown up, and where she returned often with the little boy to visit the nuns. 'If he were still alive,' Desmond said, 'if he still lived here, I suppose I would be scared to come, I'd be afraid to speak to him.' The little man, the neighbour, took off his glasses to shine them on a white handkerchief. 'Ah, he was a shy man himself. He was back here a few years before he died, with a big crew of American fillum people, and he was a friendly man, friendly enough. But you could see he was a shy man too, yes. 'Tis the shy ones sometimes that take to the book writing.'

Carrie wasn't interested in finding the second house. She had never read the man's books, she never read anything at all except art histories and museum catalogues. She said she would go to the park, where there were statues, if he'd let her off there. She said if the kids didn't get out of the car soon to run off some of their energy they would drive her crazy, or kill each other. You could hardly expect children to be interested in

6 Frank O'Connor (1903–66), pseudonym of Michael O'Donovan; born in Cork, O'Connor was involved with the Irish revolution and later became director of the Abbey Theatre; he emigrated and lived the rest of his life in America, where he became famous as a writer of short stories with Irish settings.

old dead writers they'd never heard of, she said. It was no fun for them.

He knew as well as she did that if they were not soon released from the backseat prison they would do each other damage. 'I'll go alone,' he said.

'But don't be long. We've got a good ways to do yet if we're going to make it to that house today.'

So he went in search of the second house, the house the writer had lived in for most of his childhood and youth and had mentioned in dozens of his stories. He found it high up the sloping streets on the north side of the river. Two rows of identical homes, cement-grey, faced each other across a bare sloping square of dirt, each row like a set of steps down the slope, each home just a gate in a cement waist-high wall, a door, a window. Somewhere in this square was where the barefoot grandmother had lived, and where the lady lived whose daughter refused to sleep lying down because people died that way, and where the toothless woman lived who between her sessions in the insane asylum loved animals and people with a saintly passion.

The house he was after was half-way up the left hand slope and barely distinguishable from the others, except that there was a woman in the tiny front yard, opening the gate to come out.

'There's no one home,' she said when she saw his intentions. 'They weren't expecting me this time, and presumably they weren't expecting you either.'

'Then it *is* the right house?' Desmond said. Stupidly, he thought. Right house for what?

But she seemed to understand. 'Oh yes. It's the right house. Some day the city will get around to putting a plaque in the wall but for the time being I prefer it the way it is. My name, by the way,' she added, 'is Mary Brennan. I don't live here but I stop by often enough. The old man, you see, was one of my teachers years ago.

She might have been an official guide, she said it all so smoothly. Almost whispering. And there was barely a trace of the musical tipped-up accent of the southern counties in her voice. Perhaps Dublin, or educated. Her name meant nothing to him at first, coming like that without warning. 'There would be little point in your going inside anyway, even if they were home,' she said. 'There's a lovely young couple living there now but they've redone the whole thing over into a perfectly charming but very modern apartment. There's nothing at all to remind you of him. I stop by for reasons I don't begin to understand, respect perhaps, or inspiration, but certainly not to find anything of him here.'

In a careless, uneven way, she was pretty. Even beautiful. She wore clothes—a yellow skirt, a sweater—as if they'd been pulled on as she'd hurried out the door. Her coat was draped over her arm, for the momentary blessing of sun. But she was tall enough to get away with the sloppiness and had brown eyes which were calm, calming. And hands that tended to behave as if they were helping deliver her words to him, stirring up the pale scent of her perfume. He would guess she was thirty, she was a little younger than he was.

'Desmond,' he said. 'Uh, Philip Desmond.'

She squinted at him, as if she had her doubts. Then she nodded, consenting.

'You're an American,' she said. 'And probably a writer. But I must warn you. I've been to your part of the world and you just can't do for it what he did for this. It isn't the same. You don't have the history, the sense that everything that happens is happening on top of layers of things which have already happened. Now I saw you drive up in a motor car and I arrived on a bus so if you're going back down to the city centre I'll thank you for a ride.'

Mary Brennan, of course. Why hadn't he known? There were two of her books in the trunk of his car. Paperbacks. Desmond felt his throat closing. Before he'd known who she was she hadn't let him say a word, and now that she seemed to be waiting to hear what he had to offer, he was speechless. His mind was a blank. All he could think of was *Mary Brennan* and wish that she'd turned out to be only a colourful eccentric old lady, something he could handle. He was comfortable with young women only until they turned out to be better than he was at something important to him. Then his throat closed. His mind pulled down the shades and hid.

All Desmond could think to say, driving down the hill towards the River Lee, was: 'A man in Dublin told me there was no literature happening in this country.' He could have bitten off his tongue. This woman *was* what was happening. A country that had someone like her needed no one else.

She would not accept that, she said, not even from a man in Dublin. And she insisted that he drive her out to the limestone castle restaurant at the mouth of the river so she could buy him a drink there and convince him Dublin was wrong. Inside the castle, though, while they watched the white ferry to Swansea slide out past their window, she discovered she would rather talk about her divorce, a messy thing which had been a strain on everyone concerned and had convinced her if she needed convincing that marriage was an absurd arrangement. She touched Desmond, twice, with one hand, for emphasis.

Oh, she was a charming woman, there was no question. She could be famous for those eyes alone, which never missed a detail in that room (a setting she would use, perhaps, in her next novel of Irish infidelity and rebellion?) and at the same time somehow returned to him often enough and long enough to keep him frozen, afraid to sneak his own glances at the items she was cataloguing for herself. 'Some day,' she said, 'they will have converted all our history into restaurants and bars like this one, just as I will have converted it all to fiction. Then what will we have?'

And when, finally, he said he must go, he really must go, the park was pretty but didn't have all that much in it for kids to do, she said, 'Listen, if you want to find out what is happening here, if you really do love that old man's work, then join us tomorrow. There'll be more than a dozen of us, some of the most exciting talent in the country, all meeting up at Gougane Barra . . . you know the place, the lake in the mountains where this river rises . . . it was a spot he loved.'

'Tomorrow,' he said. 'We'll have moved in by then, to the house we've rented for the winter.'

'There's a park there now,' she said. 'And of course the tiny hermitage island. It will begin as a picnic but who knows how it will end.' The hand, a white hand with unpainted nails, touched him again.

'Yes,' he said. 'Yes. We've been there. There's a tiny church on the island, he wrote a story[7] about it, the burial of a priest. And it's only an hour or so from the house, I'd guess. Maybe. Maybe I will.'

'Oh you must,' she said, and leaned forward. 'You knew, of course, that they called it Deep-Valleyed Desmond[8] in the songs.' She drew back, biting on a smile.

But when he'd driven her back to the downtown area, to wide St Patrick's Street, she discovered she was not quite ready yet to let him go. 'Walk with me', she said, 'for just a while,' and found him a parking spot in front of the Munster Arcade where dummies dressed as monks and Vikings and Celtic Warriors glowered at him from behind the glass.

'This place exists', she said, 'because he made it real for me. He and others, in their stories. I could never write about a place where I was the first, it would panic me. I couldn't be sure it really existed or if I were inventing it.'

She led him down past the statue of sober Father Matthew[9] and the parked double-decker buses to the bridge across the Lee. A wind, coming down the river, brought a smell like an open sewer with it. He put his head down and tried to hurry across.

'If I were a North American, like you,' she said, 'I'd have to move away or become a shop girl. I couldn't write.'

He was tempted to say something about plastering over someone else's old buildings, but thought better of it. He hadn't even read her books yet, he knew them only by reputation, he had no right to comment. He stopped, instead, to lean over the stone wall and look at the river. It was like sticking his head into a septic tank. The water was dark, nearly black, and low. Along the edges rats moved over humps of dark shiny muck and half-buried cans and bottles. Holes in the stone wall dumped a steady stream of new sewage into the river. The stories, as far as he could remember, had never mentioned this. These quays were romantic places where young people met and teased each other, or church goers gathered to gossip after Mass, or old people strolled. None of them, apparently, had noses.

Wind in the row of trees. Leaves rustling. Desmond looked at her hands. The perfect slim white fingers lay motionless along her skirt, then moved suddenly up to her throat, to touch the neck of her sweater. Then the nearer one moved again, and touched his arm. Those eyes, busy recording the street, paused to look at him; she smiled. Cataloguing me too? he thought. Recording me for future reference? But she didn't know a thing about him.

'I've moved here to work on a book,' he said.

Her gaze rested for a moment on the front of his jacket, then flickered away. 'Not about *here*,' she said. 'You're not writing about *this* place?' She looked as if she would protect it from him, if necessary, or whisk it away.

'I have my own place,' he said. 'I don't need to borrow his.'

She stopped, to buy them each an apple from an old black-shawled woman who sat up against the wall by her table of fruit. Ancient, gypsy-faced, with huge earrings

7 'The Moss Island' in *A Set of Variations* (1969).

8 'Desmond' is the ancient name for the south of Munster province, in which Cork and Gougane Barra are located.

9 (1790–1838), a famous leader of the Irish Temperance movement.

hanging from those heavy lobes. Black Spanish eyes. Mary Brennan flashed a smile, counted out some silver pieces, and picked over the apples for two that were red and clear. The hands that offered change were thick and wrinkled, with crescents of black beneath the nails. They disappeared again beneath the shawl. Desmond felt a momentary twinge about biting into the apple; vague memories of parental warnings. You never know whose hands have touched it, they said, in a voice to make you shudder in horror at the possibilities and scrub at the skin of fruit until it was bruised and raw.

Mary Brennan, apparently, had not been subjected to the same warnings. She bit hugely. 'Here,' she said, at the bridge, 'here is where I'm most aware of him. All his favourite streets converge here, from up the hill. Sunday's Well, over there where his wealthy people lived. And of course Blarney Lane. If you had the time we could walk up there, I could show you. Where his first house was, and the pub he dragged his father home from.

'I've seen it,' Desmond said, and started across the bridge. She would spoil it all for him if he let her.

But she won him again on the way back down the other side with her talk of castles and churches. Did he know, she asked, the reason there was no roof on the cathedral at Cashel? Did he know why Blackrock Castle where they'd been a half hour before was a different style altogether than most of the castles of Ireland? Did he know the origin of the word 'blarney'?

No he did not, but he knew that his wife would be furious if he didn't hurry back to the park. They passed the noise of voices haggling over second-hand clothes and old books at the Coal Market, they passed the opera house, a tiny yellow book store. She could walk, he saw, the way so many women had forgotten how to walk after high-heeled shoes went out, with long legs and long strides, with some spring in her steps as if there were pleasure in it.

'Now you'll not forget,' she said at his car, in his window. 'Tomorrow, in Deep-Valleyed Desmond where the Lee rises.' There was the scent of apple on her breath. Islands, she leaned in to say, do not exist until you've loved on them.

But today, while Mary Brennan waits on that tiny island for him, Philip Desmond is holed up in the back room of this house at Bantry Bay, trying to write his novel. His wife has taken the car to Cork. When she returns, he doesn't know what he will do. Perhaps he'll get into the car and drive up the snaking road past the crumbling O'Sullivan castle into the mountains, and throw himself into the middle of that crowd of writers as if he belongs there. Maybe he will make them think that he is important, that back home he is noticed in the way Mary Brennan is noticed here, that his work matters. And perhaps late at night, when everyone is drunk, he will lead Mary Brennan out onto the hermitage island to visit the oratory, to speak in whispers of the stories which had happened there, and to lie on the grass beneath the trees, by the quiet edge of the lake. It is not, Desmond knows, too unthinkable. At a distance.

The piece of paper in front of him is still blank. Mrs O'Sullivan will advertise the laziness of writers, who only pretend they are working when they are actually dreaming. Or sleeping. She will likely be able to tell exactly how many words he has written, though if he at the end of this day complains of how tired he is, she will undoubtedly go into her practised agony. He wonders if she too, from her window, has noticed that the tide has gone out, that the lagoon is empty of everything except brown shiny mud and seaweed, and that the nostril-burning smell of it is penetrating even to the inside of the house, even in here where the window hasn't been opened, likely, in years. He wonders, too, if she minds that the children, who have tired of their sea-edge exploring, are building a castle of pebbles and fuchsia branches in the middle of her back lawn. The youngest, Michael, dances like an Indian around it; maybe he has to go to the bathroom and can't remember where it is. While his father, who could tell him, who could take him there, sits and stares at a piece of paper.

For a moment Desmond wonders how the medieval masses in the cathedral at Cashel must have appeared to the lepers crowded behind that narrow hole. Of course he has never seen a Mass of any kind himself, but still he can imagine the glimpses of fine robes, the bright colours, the voices of a choir singing those high eerie Latin songs, the voice of a chanting priest, the faces of a few worshippers. It was a lean world from behind that stone wall, through that narrow hole. Like looking through the eye of a needle. The Mass, as close as they were permitted to get to the world, would be only timidly glimpsed past other pressed straining heads. For of course Desmond imagines himself far at the back of the crowd.

('Yes?' the guide said. 'And where would that be now?'

'A long way from here,' he said. 'An island, too, like this one, with its own brand of ruins. You've never heard of it though it's nearly the size of Ireland?'

'I have, yes. And it's a long way you've come from home.'

'There's a tiny island just off our coast where they used to send the lepers, but the last of them died there a few years ago. It's a bare and empty place they say now, except for the wind. There are even people who believe that ghosts inhabit it.')

What does the world look like to a leper, squinting through that narrow hole? What does it feel like to be confined to the interior of a circle of trees, at the top of a hill, from which everything else can be seen but not approached? Desmond likes to think that he would prefer the life of that famous fat archbishop, celebrating Mass in the cathedral and thinking of his hundred children.

Somewhere in the house a telephone rings. Desmond hasn't been here long enough to notice where the telephone is, whether it is in her part of the house or theirs. But he hears, beyond the wall, the sudden rustling of clothes, the snap of bones, the sound of feet walking across the carpet. Why should Mrs O'Sullivan have a phone? There are so few telephones in this country that they are all listed in one book. But her footsteps return, and he hears behind him the turning of his door handle, the squeal of the hinge. Then her voice whispering: 'Mr Desmond? Is it a bad time to interrupt?'

'Is it my wife?'

No it is not. And of course Desmond knows who it is. Before he left the castle-restaurant she asked for his address, for Mrs O'Sullivan's name, for the name of this village.

'I'm sorry, Mrs O'Sullivan,' he said. 'Tell her, tell them I'm working, they'll understand. Tell them I don't want to be disturbed, not just now anyway.'

He doesn't turn to see how high her eyebrows lift. He can imagine. Working, she's thinking. If that's working. But when she has closed the door something in him relaxes a little—or at least suspends its tension for a while—and he writes the paragraph again at the top of the page and then adds new words after it until he discovers he has completed a second. It is not very good; he decides when he reads it over that it is not very good at all, but at least it is something. A beginning. Perhaps the dam has been broken.

But there is a commotion, suddenly, in the front yard. A car horn beeping. The children run up the slope past the house. He can hear Carrie's voice calling them. There is a flurry of excited voices and then one of the children is at the door, calling, 'Daddy, Daddy, come and see what Mommy has!'

What Mommy has, he discovers soon enough, is something that seems to be taking up the whole back seat, a grey lumpy bulk. And she, standing at the open door, is beaming at him. 'Come help me get this thing out!' she says. There is colour in her face, excitement. She has made another one of her finds.

It is, naturally, a piece of sculpture. There is no way Desmond can tell what it is supposed to be and he has given up trying to understand such things long ago. He pulls the figure out, staggers across to the front door, and puts it down in the hall.

'I met the artist who did it,' she says. 'He was in the little shop delivering something. We talked, it seemed, for hours. This is inspired by the St Patrick's Cross, he told me, but he abstracted it even more to represent the way art has taken the place of religion in the modern world.'

'Whatever it represents,' Desmond says, 'we'll never get it home.'

Nothing, to Carrie, is a problem. 'We'll enjoy it here, in this house. Then before we leave we'll crate it up and ship it home.' She walks around the sculpture, delighted with it, delighted with herself.

'I could have talked to him for hours,' she says, 'we got along beautifully. But I remembered you asked me to have the car home early.' She kisses him, pushes a finger on his nose. 'See how obedient I am?'

'I said that?'

'Yes,' she says. 'Right after breakfast. Some other place you said you wanted to go prowling around in by yourself. I rushed home down all that long winding bloody road for you. On the wrong side, I'll never get used to it. Watching for radar traps, for heaven's sake. Do you think the gardai[10] have radar traps here?'

But Desmond is watching Mrs O'Sullivan, who has come out into the hall to stare at the piece of sculpture. Why does he have this urge to show her his two paragraphs? Desmond doesn't even show Carrie anything until it is finished. Why, he wonders, should he feel just because she sits there listening through the wall that she's also waiting for him to produce something? She probably doesn't even read. Still, he wants to say, 'Look. Read this, isn't it good? And I wrote it in your house, only today.'

Mrs O'Sullivan's hand is knotting at her throat. The sculpture has drawn a frown, a heavy sulk. ' 'Tis a queer lot of objects they've been making for the tourists, and none of them what you could put a name to.'

10 Police (Irish).

'But oh,' Carrie says, 'he must be nearly the best in the country! Surely. And this is no tourist souvenir. I got it from an art shop in Cork.'

Mrs O'Sullivan's hand opens and closes, creeps closer to her mouth. 'Oh,' she says. 'Cork.' As if a lot had been explained. 'You can expect anything at all from a city. Anything at all. There was people here staying in this house, 'twas last year yes, came back from Cork as pleased as the Pope with an old box of turf they had bought. They wanted to smell it burning in my fire if you don't mind. What you spend your money on is your own business, I told them, but I left the bogs behind years ago, thank you, and heat my house with electricity. Keep the turf in your car so.'

Carrie is plainly insulted. Words struggle at her lips. But she dismisses them, apparently, and chooses diversion. 'I'll make a pot of tea. Would you like a cup with us, Mrs O'Sullivan? The long drive's made me thirsty.'

And Mrs O'Sullivan, whose role is apparently varied and will shift for any occasion, lets her finger pluck at her face. 'Oh I know I know I know!' Her long brown-stockinged legs move slowly across the patterned carpet. 'And Mr Desmond, too, after his work. I was tempted to take him a cup but he shouldn't be disturbed I know.'

'Work?' Carrie says. 'Working at what?'

'I started the novel,' Desmond says.

'You have? Then that's something we should celebrate. Before you go off wherever it is you think you're going.'

'It's only a page,' Desmond says. 'And it's not very good at all, but it's a start. It's better than the blank paper.'

Like some children, he thinks, he's learned to make a virtue out of anything. Even a page of scribble. When he'd be glad to give a thousand pages of scribble for the gift of honesty. Or change. Or even blindness of a sort. What good is vision after all if it refuses to ignore the dark?

Because hasn't he heard, somewhere, that artists—painters—deliberately create frames for themselves to look through, to sharpen their vision by cutting off the details which have no importance to their work?

He follows the women into the kitchen, where cups already clatter onto saucers. 'Maybe after tea,' he says, 'I'll get a bit more done.'

Pretending, perhaps, that the rest of the world sits waiting, like Mrs O'Sullivan, for the words he will produce. Because his tongue, his voice, has made the decision for him. Desmond knows that he may only sit in front of that paper for the rest of that day, that he may only play with his pen—frustrated—until enough time has gone by to justify his coming out of the room. To read one of the books he's bought. To talk with Carrie about her shopping in Cork, about her sculptor. To play with the children perhaps, or take them for a walk along the road to look for donkeys, for ruins. Desmond knows that the evening may be passed in front of the television set, where they will see American movies with Irish commercials, and will later try to guess what *an naught*[11] is telling them about the day's events, and that he will try very hard not to think of Mary Brennan or of the dozen Irish writers at Gougane Barra or of the tiny

11 The news (Irish).

hermitage island which the famous writer loved. Deep-Valleyed Desmond. He knows that he could be there with them, through this day and this night, celebrating something he'd come here to find; but he acknowledges, too, the other. That words, too, were invented perhaps to do the things that stones can do. And he has come here, after all, to build his walls.

1981

Margaret Atwood

b. 1939

Since winning a Governor General's Award at twenty-seven (for *The Circle Game*, her first full-length book), Margaret Atwood has created a substantial body of writing—poetry, short stories, novels, and criticism—that has gained her an international reputation. She has also been active in the publishing and writing community: in her early role as an editor for the House of Anansi Press she was, with Dennis Lee, David Godfrey, Graham Gibson, and others, part of the energetic small press scene that emerged at the end of the 1960s and that played a vital role in the vigorous growth of Canadian literature. A member of Anansi's board in the 1970s, Atwood — who also served as the president of the Writers' Union in 1982–3, the editor of *The New Oxford Book of Canadian Verse* (1982) and of *The Oxford Book of Canadian Short Stories* (with Robert Weaver; 1986)—has been a tireless promoter of Canadian literary culture, lecturing about Canadian writers as well as reading from her own work in Canada, in the US, in the UK and the rest of Europe, in Russia, and in Australia.

Born in Ottawa, Atwood grew up there, in Sault Ste Marie, and in Toronto. As a result of her father's entomological research, she spent extended periods of her childhood with her family in the northern Ontario and Quebec bush and did not attend a full year of formal school until grade eight. In 1957 she entered Victoria College, University of Toronto, where her teachers included Northrop Frye and the poet Jay Macpherson, with whom she became friends. She completed her BA in 1961, publishing a slim book of poems, *Double Persephone*, that year. Enrolling in graduate studies at Harvard, she took a master's degree in 1962 and began a doctoral thesis on 'the English metaphysical romances' of George MacDonald and H. Rider Haggard. She worked briefly as a market researcher in Toronto; then, between 1964 and 1973, she taught English or was writer-in-residence at Sir George Williams University (now part of Concordia) in Montreal (1967–8), at the University of Alberta (1969–70), at York University (1971–2), and at the University of Toronto (1972–3). Since then she has accepted occasional residencies but has chiefly been a full-time writer, living first on a farm near Alliston, Ont., and, since 1980, in Toronto. She continues to travel widely, and has spent extended periods in France, Italy, Germany, the US, and Australia.

Atwood's writing can be separated into two main periods. The poems collected in *The Circle Game* (1966), *The Animals in That Country* (1968), *Procedures for Underground* (1970), and *You Are Happy* (1974)—as well as those in the book-length sequences *The Journals of Susanna Moodie* (1970) and *Power Politics* (1973)—share the tone and themes of her novels of this period: *The Edible Woman* (1969), *Surfacing* (1972), and *Lady Oracle* (1976). Utilizing a stark and unemotional style, this is writing that can startle readers out of conventional expectations and into new ways of perceiving—as in the very short poem that opens *Power Politics*:

> *You fit into me*
> *like a hook into an eye*
>
> *a fish hook*
> *an open eye.*

Frequently told from the point of view of alienated individuals (sometimes on the verge of breakdown), her poetry and fiction express a distrust of the everyday world, finding it a place of deceptive appearances and emotional shallowness—in part because contemporary society is driven by commercial interests and dominated by mass media and consumerism. To this world and its concerns Atwood opposes the claims made by dreams, hallucinations, and visions, showing her readers that it is through descents into the psyche and the rediscovery of the primitive and mythic dimensions of both mind and world that one can experience wholeness. (Her interest in myth runs through the body of her work and reappears in her current project, a libretto for an opera called 'Inanna's Journey', based on a Sumerian tale that predates *The Epic of Gilgamesh*. The Canadian Opera Company expects to mount the finished work in the 2005–6 season.)

Both a nationalist and a feminist, Atwood finds the problem of inauthenticity—a concern for many contemporary writers—especially associated with women, as in *Power Politics* and *The Edible Woman*, and with Canadians, as in *Surfacing* and *The Journals of Susanna Moodie*. In the afterword to that sequence of poems, she wrote:

> *If the national mental illness of the United States is megalomania, that of Canada is paranoid schizophrenia. Mrs Moodie is divided down the middle: she praises the Canadian landscape but accuses it of destroying her; she dislikes the people already in Canada but finds in people her only refuge from the land itself; she preaches progress and the march of civilization while brooding elegiacally upon the destruction of the wilderness. . . . She claims to be an ardent Canadian patriot while all the time she is standing back from the country and criticizing it as though she were a detached observer, a stranger. Perhaps that is the way we still live. We are all immigrants to this place even if we were born here: the country is too big for anyone to inhabit completely, and in the parts unknown to us we move in fear, exiles and invaders. This country is something that must be chosen—it is so easy to leave—and if we do choose it we are still choosing a violent duality.*

Atwood has written on the dangers of a colonial mentality, and the consequent lack of Canadian identity, not only in her poetry and her fiction but also in *Survival: A Thematic Guide to Canadian Literature* (1972). Atwood built this polemical work of literary criticism, which both came out of and helped fuel the cultural nationalism of its day, on Northrop Frye's 'garrison' thesis. Accepting Frye's idea that, in contrast to the powerful vitalizing effect of the frontier in American history, Canadian development was given its shape by an early settlement that took the form of isolated garrisons constructed as a defence against a difficult or hostile environment, Atwood argued that Canadian literature was a record of a people who were alienated from their environment and who, having existed in a colonial relationship first to England and then to America, had come to think of themselves as powerless victims. Although her reading of the Canadian literary tradition has been criticized as one-sided and subjective, this study proved popular and stimulated a valuable debate, in part because it seemed to many to reveal a previously unrecognized coherence in Canadian culture.

Survival also sheds light on Atwood's own work: her early fiction and poetry develop out of the tradition she describes and are intended as a corrective to it. ('This above all, to refuse to be a victim' is the final lesson learned by the protagonist of *Surfacing*.) In 1982 Atwood published *Second Words*, a large selection of reviews, lectures, and essays, some of which complement or comment on *Survival*. In moving towards the post-colonial society that Atwood desires, she assigns to the writer a special function:

Frye's push towards naming, towards an interconnected system, seems to me a Canadian reaction to a Canadian situation. Stranded in the midst of a vast space which nobody has made sense out of for you, you settle down to map-making, charting the territory, the discovery of where things are in relation to each other, the extraction of meaning. ('Northrop Frye Observed')

The publication in 1976 and 1977 of two compilations of earlier work, *Selected Poems* and *Dancing Girls* (her first collection of short stories), marked the end of a phase in Atwood's writing career. In her work since the late seventies—the poetry of *Two-Headed Poems* (1978), *True Stories* (1981), *Interlunar* (1984), and *Morning in the Burned House* (1995); the stories in *Bluebeard's Egg* (1983) and *Wilderness Tips* (1991); and the novels *Life Before Man* (1979), *Bodily Harm* (1981), *The Handmaid's Tale* (1985), *Cat's Eye* (1988), *The Robber Bride* (1993), *Alias Grace* (1996), and *The Blind Assassin* (2000), which won the Booker Prize—Atwood does not abandon the concerns of her earlier writing, but she does employ a greater range of style and topics. She is by turns more lyrical and personal, and more satirical and political. For the first time, she portrays her family relationships in her poems (as in 'Spelling', or in the elegiac series of meditations on the death of her father in *Morning in the Burned House*), and she now finds comfort rather than conflict in human relationships. The characters in her novels are more fully drawn and more varied (in *Life Before Man* she uses a male viewpoint for the first time), while in a poem such as 'Variation on the Word *Sleep*' she can write without irony of a woman's love for a man.

At the same time politics assumes a new importance, one that allows her to engage in matters more specific than her previous large concerns about imperialism. *Two-Headed Poems* takes its title from a sequence about Canada's division between two cultures. (The title also recalls the preoccupation with doubleness and duality that runs through Atwood's work.) Elsewhere in that book, as well as the sequence in *True Stories* called 'Notes Towards a Poem That Cannot Be Written', Atwood, protesting against torture as an instrument of political repression, adopts a global perspective that reflects her association with Amnesty International. The sense that Canada must now look beyond its own borders is also evident in *Bodily Harm*, a tale of a Canadian travel writer's naive involvement in a political coup in the Caribbean, and in *The Handmaid's Tale*, a futuristic dystopian fable about a repressive American society governed by right-wing religious fundamentalists. *The Handmaid's Tale* won Atwood a second Governor General's Award.

From the multiple viewpoints of *The Robber Bride* to the layered narrative structure of *The Blind Assassin*—which features excerpts from a work of science fiction within a novella within the novel—to the historical setting of *Alias Grace*, about the mid-nineteenth-century murder case of Grace Marks, Atwood's most recent novels demonstrate a wide range of concerns and narrative techniques, often coupled with greater movement across eras. In 'The Age of Lead', for example, she presents a complex ecological fable through elaborate counterpoint between the narrator's developing understanding of the past, which comes to her in the form of a television show about fate of the last Franklin Expedition (for details, see the headnote for John Franklin and Dr John Richardson), and her own social relationships. The explorations led by Franklin seem to the narrator to correspond to a larger drive in the Canadian psyche to go North, to find 'somewhere, somewhere mapless, off into the unknown', but the mapless future she finds herself venturing into holds unexpected terrors, because in it: 'People were dying. They were dying too early.'

Until 1984, Atwood remained equally divided between her roles as poet and fiction writer. Since the 1986 publication of *Selected Poems II*, a volume that drew together poems from the previous ten years and new work, she has published only one further collection of poems. About an eighth of that 1986 book is made up of prose poetry ('Strawberries', below, is an example), an indication of Atwood's growing interest in this form—which abandons the poetic line while maintaining other qualities of the lyric poem. Her earlier collection, *Murder in the Dark* (1983), made up entirely of short prose pieces, was identified in its subtitle as 'short fictions and prose poems'. Atwood's use of such 'short fictions' can be associated with contemporary 'minimalist' writing, which seeks to reduce narrative to a few essentials. (*Murder in the Dark* was later published together with *Good Bones*, 1992—ironic recastings of traditional forms such as the parable, the monologue, and the fairy tale—as *Good Bones and Simple Murders*, 2001).

Atwood's most recent book, *Negotiating with the Dead: A Writer on Writing* (2002), a moving set of meditations about the role of the writer, is based on the Empson Lectures she delivered at the University of Cambridge in 2000. From *Lady Oracle* to *The Blind Assassin*, writers have figured largely in her fiction, which often engages in metafictional and self-reflexive mirroring. In all her work—whether fiction, non-fiction, or poetry—Atwood takes very seriously the writer's duty to society and the power of the written word. As a passage in *Murder in the Dark* suggests, writing is an act of great consequence, and so, therefore, is reading:

> . . . *Beneath the page is a story. Beneath the page is everything that has ever happened, most of which you would rather not hear about.*
>
> *Touch the page at your peril: it is you who are blank and innocent, not the page. Nevertheless you want to know, nothing will stop you. You touch the page, it's as if you've drawn a knife across it, the page has been hurt now, a sinuous wound opens, a thin incision. Darkness wells through.* ('The Page')

This is a Photograph of Me

It was taken some time ago.
At first it seems to be
a smeared
print: blurred lines and grey flecks
blended with the paper;

then, as you scan
it, you see in the left-hand corner
a thing that is like a branch: part of a tree
(balsam or spruce) emerging
and, to the right, halfway up
what ought to be a gentle
slope, a small frame house.

In the background there is a lake,
and beyond that, some low hills.

(The photograph was taken
the day after I drowned.

I am in the lake, in the center
of the picture, just under the surface.

It is difficult to say where
precisely, or to say

how large or small I am:
the effect of water
on light is a distortion

but if you look long enough,
eventually
you will be able to see me.)

1966

Progressive Insanities of a Pioneer

i

He stood, a point
on a sheet of green paper
proclaiming himself the centre,

with no walls, no borders
anywhere; the sky no height
above him, totally un-
enclosed
and shouted:

Let me out!

ii

He dug the soil in rows,
imposed himself with shovels.
He asserted
into the furrows, I
am not random.

The ground
replied with aphorisms:

a tree-sprout, a nameless
weed, words
he couldn't understand.

iii

The house pitched
the plot staked
in the middle of nowhere

At night the mind
inside, in the middle
of nowhere

The idea of an animal
patters across the roof.

In the darkness the fields
defend themselves with fences
in vain:
    everything
    is getting in.

iv

By daylight he resisted.
He said, disgusted
with the swamp's clamourings and the outbursts
of rocks.
    This is not order
    but the absence
    of order

He was wrong, the unanswering
forest implied:

    It was
    an ordered absence

v

For many years
he fished for a great vision,
dangling the hooks of sown
roots under the surface
of the shallow earth.

It was like
enticing whales with a bent
pin. Besides he thought

in that country
only the worms were biting.

vi

If he had known unstructured
space is a deluge
and stocked his log house-
boat with all the animals

even the wolves,

he might have floated.

But obstinate he
stated, The land is solid
and stamped,

watching his foot sink
down through stone
up to the knee.

vii

Things
refused to name themselves; refused
to let him name them.

The wolves hunted
outside.

On his beaches, his clearings,
by the surf of under-
growth breaking
at his feet, he foresaw
disintegration
                    and in the end
through eyes

made ragged by his
effort, the tension
between subject and object,

the green
vision, the unnamed
whale invaded.

1968

From *The Journals of Susanna Moodie*[1]

FROM JOURNAL I, 1832–1840

Disembarking at Quebec

Is it my clothes, my way of walking,
the things I carry in my hand
—a book, a bag with knitting—
the incongruous pink of my shawl

this space cannot hear

or is it my own lack
of conviction which makes
these vistas of desolation,
long hills, the swamps, the barren sand, the glare
of sun on the bone-white
driftlogs, omens of winter,
the moon alien in day-
time a thin refusal

The others leap, shout

Freedom![2]

1 In this book Atwood uses the historical Susanna Moodie (1803–85) as the speaker in poems inspired by her two narratives of settlement, *Roughing It in the Bush* (1852) and *Life in the Clearings* (1853). Most of the people and events alluded to in the poems reprinted here may be found in the selections from *Roughing It in the Bush*, pp. 94–122.

2 In Chapter 2 of *Roughing It*, Moodie says she was 'not a little amused at the extravagant expectations entertained by some of our steerage passengers. . . . In spite of the remonstrances of the captain and the dread of the cholera, they all rushed on shore to inspect the land of Goshen, and to endeavour to realize their absurd anticipations.'

The moving water will not show me
my reflection.

The rocks ignore.

I am a word
in a foreign language.

Further Arrivals

After we had crossed the long illness
that was the ocean, we sailed up-river

On the first island
the immigrants threw off their clothes
and danced like sandflies[1]

We left behind one by one
the cities rotting with cholera,
one by one our civilized
distinctions

and entered a large darkness.

It was our own
ignorance we entered.

I have not come out yet

My brain gropes nervous
tentacles in the night, sends out
fears hairy as bears,
demands lamps; or waiting

1 In the first chapter of *Roughing It* the Moodies visited Grosse Isle for an afternoon while their ship stood off shore following an inspection by health officers (Quebec was then experiencing a cholera epidemic): 'Never shall I forget the extraordinary spectacle that met our sight. . . . A crowd of many hundred Irish emigrants had been landed . . . and all this motley crew—men, women, and children— . . . were employed in washing clothes. . . . The men and boys were in the water, while the women, with their scanty garments tucked above their knees, were tramping their bedding in tubs or in holes in the rocks. Those [not washing] were running to and fro, screaming and scolding in no measured terms . . . all accompanying their vociferations with violent and extraordinary gestures, quite incomprehensible to the uninitiated.'

for my shadowy husband, hears
malice in the trees' whispers.

I need wolf's eyes to see
the truth.

I refuse to look in a mirror.

Whether the wilderness is
real or not
depends on who lives there.

FROM JOURNAL II, 1840–1871

Death of a Young Son by Drowning

He, who navigated with success
the dangerous river of his own birth
once more set forth

on a voyage of discovery
into the land I floated on
but could not touch to claim.

His feet slid on the bank,
the currents took him;
he swirled with ice and trees in the swollen water

and plunged into distant regions,
his head a bathysphere;
through his eyes' thin glass bubbles

he looked out, reckless adventurer
on a landscape stranger than Uranus
we have all been to and some remember.

There was an accident; the air locked,
he was hung in the river like a heart.
They retrieved the swamped body,

cairn of my plans and future charts,
with poles and hooks
from among the nudging logs.

It was spring, the sun kept shining, the new grass
lept to solidity;
my hands glistened with details.

After the long trip I was tired of waves.
My foot hit rock. The dreamed sails
collapsed, ragged.

        I planted him in this country
        like a flag.

Dream 2: Brian the Still-Hunter[1]

The man I saw in the forest
used to come to our house
every morning, never said anything;
I learned from the neighbours later
he once tried to cut his throat.

I found him at the end of the path
sitting on a fallen tree
cleaning his gun.

There was no wind;
around us the leaves rustled.

He said to me:
I kill because I have to

but every time I aim, I feel
my skin grow fur
my head heavy with antlers
and during the stretched instant
the bullet glides on its thread of speed
my soul runs innocent as hooves.

1 A 'still-hunter' is one who hunts stealthily on foot. In Chapter 10 of *Roughing It* Moodie describes her friendship with Brian, a man once subject to such fits of depression that he had tried to commit suicide. Brian tells her a vivid story of watching a 'noble deer' pulled down by a pack of wolves, concluding:

> *At that moment he seemed more unfortunate even than myself, for I could not see in what manner he had deserved his fate. All his speed and energy, his courage and fortitude, had been exerted in vain. I had tried to destroy myself; but he, with every effort vigorously made for self-preservation, was doomed to meet the fate he dreaded! Is God just to his creatures?*

Moodie ends the chapter by saying:

> *We parted with the hunter as an old friend; and we never met again. His fate was a sad one. After we left that part of the country, he fell into a moping melancholy, which ended in self-destruction.*

Is God just to his creatures?

I die more often than many.

He looked up and I saw
the white scar made by the hunting knife
around his neck.

When I woke
I remembered: he has been gone
twenty years and not heard from.

FROM JOURNAL III, 1871–1969

Thoughts from Underground[1]

When I first reached this country
I hated it
and I hated it more each year:

in summer the light a
violent blur, the heat
thick as a swamp,
the green things fiercely
shoving themselves upwards, the
eyelids bitten by insects

In winter our teeth were brittle
with cold. We fed on squirrels.
At night the house cracked.
In the mornings, we thawed
the bad bread over the stove.

Then we were made successful
and I felt I ought to love
this country.
I said I loved it
and my mind saw double.

1 This poem is spoken by Moodie after her death.

I began to forget myself
in the middle
of sentences. Events
were split apart

I fought. I constructed
desperate paragraphs of praise, everyone
ought to love it because

and set them up at intervals

    due to natural resources, native industry, superior
    penitentiaries
    we will all be rich and powerful

flat as highway billboards

    who can doubt it, look how
    fast Belleville is growing

(though it is still no place for an english gentleman)

1970

Tricks with Mirrors

i

It's no coincidence
this is a used
furniture warehouse.

I enter with you
and become a mirror.

Mirrors
are the perfect lovers,

that's it, carry me up the stairs
by the edges, don't drop me,

that would be bad luck,
throw me on the bed

reflecting side up,
fall into me,

it will be your own
mouth you hit, firm and glassy,

your own eyes you find you
are up against   closed   closed

ii

There is more to a mirror
than you looking at

your full-length body
flawless but reversed,

there is more than this dead blue
oblong eye turned outwards to you.

Think about the frame.
The frame is carved, it is important,

it exists, it does not reflect you,
it does not recede and recede, it has limits

and reflections of its own.
There's a nail in the back

to hang it with; there are several nails,
think about the nails,

pay attention to the nail
marks in the wood,

they are important too.

iii

Don't assume it is passive
or easy, this clarity

with which I give you yourself.
Consider what restraint it

takes: breath withheld, no anger
or joy disturbing the surface

of the ice.
You are suspended in me

beautiful and frozen, I
preserve you, in me you are safe.

It is not a trick either.
it is a craft:

mirrors are crafty.

iv

I wanted to stop this,
this life flattened against the wall,

mute and devoid of colour,
built of pure light,

this life of vision only, split
and remote, a lucid impasse.

I confess: this is not a mirror,
it is a door

I am trapped behind.
I wanted you to see me here,

say the releasing word, whatever
that may be, open the wall.

Instead you stand in front of me
combing your hair.

v

You don't like these metaphors.
All right:

Perhaps I am not a mirror.
Perhaps I am a pool.

Think about pools.

1974

Siren Song[1]

This is the one song everyone
would like to learn: the song
that is irresistible:

the song that forces men
to leap overboard in squadrons
even though they see the beached skulls

the song nobody knows
because anyone who has heard it
is dead, and the others can't remember.

Shall I tell you the secret
and if I do, will you get me
out of this bird suit?

I don't enjoy it here
squatting on this island
looking picturesque and mythical

with these two feathery maniacs,
I don't enjoy singing
this trio, fatal and valuable.

I will tell the secret to you,
to you, only to you.
Come closer. This song

1 In Greek mythology three sirens, half-women and half-birds, used their enchanting songs to lure sailors to their island in the Mediterranean Sea where, deprived of their will-power, they wasted away, leaving the beach strewn with their whitening bones.

is a cry for help: Help me!
Only you, only you can,
you are unique

at last. Alas
it is a boring song
but it works every time.

1974

Spelling

My daughter plays on the floor
with plastic letters,
red, blue & hard yellow,
learning how to spell,
spelling,
how to make spells

*

and I wonder how many women
denied themselves daughters,
closed themselves in rooms,
drew the curtains
so they could mainline words.

*

A child is not a poem,
a poem is not a child.
There is no either/or.
However.

*

I return to the story
of the woman caught in the war
& in labour, her thighs tied
together by the enemy
so she could not give birth.

Ancestress: the burning witch,
her mouth covered by leather
to strangle words.

A word after a word
after a word is power.

*

At the point where language falls away
from the hot bones, at the point
where the rock breaks open and darkness
flows out of it like blood, at
the melting point of granite
when the bones know
they are hollow & the word
splits & doubles & speaks
the truth & the body
itself becomes a mouth.

This is a metaphor.

*

How do you learn to spell?
Blood, sky & the sun,
your own name first,
your first naming, your first name,
your first word.

1981

Strawberries

The strawberries when I first remember them are not red but blue, that blue flare, before the whitehot part of the wire, sun glancing from the points of waves. It was the heat that made things blue like that, rage, I went into the waste orchard because I did not want to talk to you or even see you, I wanted instead to do something small and useful that I was good at. It was June, there were mosquitoes, I stirred them up as I pushed aside the higher stems, but I didn't care, I was immune, all that adrenalin kept them away, and if not I was in the mood for minor lacerations. I don't get angry like that any more. I almost miss it.

I'd like to say I saw everything through a haze of red; which is not true. Nothing was hazy. Everything was clear, clearer than usual, my hands with the stained nails, the sunlight falling on the ground through the apple-tree branches, each leaf, each white five petalled yellow centred flower and conical fine-haired dark red multi-seeded dwarf berry rendering itself in dry flat two dimensional detail, like background foliage by one of the crazier Victorian painters, just before the invention of the camera; and at some time during that hour, though not for the whole hour, I forgot what things were called and saw instead what they are.

1983

Down

i.

They were wrong about the sun.
It does not go down into
the underworld at night.
The sun leaves merely
and the underworld emerges.
It can happen at any moment.

It can happen in the morning,
you in the kitchen going through
your mild routines.
Plate, cup, knife.
All at once there's no blue, no green,
no warning.

ii.

Old thread, old line
of ink twisting out into the clearness
we call space
where are you leading me this time?

Past the stove, past the table,
past the daily horizontal
of the floor, past the cellar,
past the believable,
down into the darkness
where you reverse and shine.

iii.

At first you think they are angels,
these albino voices, these voices
like the unpainted eyes of statues,
these mute voices like gloves
with no hands in them,
these moth voices fluttering
and baffled around your ears,
trying to make you hear them.

What do they need?

You make a cut in yourself,
a little opening
for the pain to get in.
You set loose three drops of your blood.

iv.

This is
the kingdom of the unspoken,
the kingdom of the unspeaking:

all those destroyed by war
all those who are starving
all those beaten to death
and buried in pits, those slit apart
for reasons of expediency or money
all those howling
in locked rooms, all sacrificed
children, all murdered brides,
all suicides.

They say:
Speak for us (to whom)
Some say: *Avenge us* (on whom)
Some say: *Take our place.*
Some say: *Witness.*

Others say (and these are women):
Be happy for us.

v.

There is the staircase,
there is the sun.
There is the kitchen,
the plate with toast and strawberry jam,
your subterfuge,
your ordinary mirage.

You stand red-handed.
You want to wash yourself
in earth, in rocks and grass

What are you supposed to do
with all this loss?

1995

The Age of Lead

The man has been buried for a hundred and fifty years. They dug a hole in the frozen gravel, deep into the permafrost, and put him down there so the wolves couldn't get to him. Or that is the speculation.

When they dug the hole the permafrost was exposed to the air, which was warmer. This made the permafrost melt. But it froze again after the man was covered up, so that when he was brought to the surface he was completely enclosed in ice. They took the lid off the coffin and it was like those maraschino cherries you used to freeze in ice-cube trays for fancy tropical drinks: a vague shape, looming through a solid cloud.

Then they melted the ice and he came to light. He is almost the same as when he was buried. The freezing water has pushed his lips away from his teeth into an astonished snarl, and he's a beige colour, like a gravy stain on linen, instead of pink, but everything is still there. He even has eyeballs, except that they aren't white but the light brown of milky tea. With these tea-stained eyes he regards Jane: an indecipherable gaze, innocent, ferocious, amazed, but contemplative, like a werewolf meditating, caught in a flash of lightning at the exact split second of his tumultuous change.

Jane doesn't watch very much television. She used to watch it more. She used to watch comedy series, in the evenings, and when she was a student at university she would watch afternoon soaps about hospitals and rich people, as a way of procrastinating. For a while, not so long ago, she would watch the evening news, taking in the disasters with her feet tucked up on the chesterfield, a throw rug over her legs, drinking a hot milk and rum to relax before bed. It was all a form of escape.

But what you can see on the television, at whatever time of day, is edging too close to her own life; though in her life, nothing stays put in those tidy compartments, comedy here, seedy romance and sentimental tears there, accidents and violent deaths in thirty-second clips they call *bites*, as if they were chocolate bars. In her life, everything is mixed together. *Laugh, I thought I'd die*, Vincent used to say, a very long time ago, in a voice imitating the banality of mothers; and that's how it's getting to be. So when she flicks on the television these days, she flicks it off again soon enough. Even the commercials, with their surreal dailiness, are beginning to look sinister, to suggest meanings behind themselves, behind their façade of cleanliness, lusciousness, health, power, and speed.

Tonight she leaves the television on, because what she is seeing is so unlike what she usually sees. There is nothing sinister behind this image of the frozen man. It is entirely itself. *What you sees is what you gets*, as Vincent also used to say, crossing his eyes, baring his teeth at one side, pushing his nose into a horror-movie snout. Although it never was, with him.

The man they've dug up and melted was a young man. Or still is: it's difficult to know what tense should be applied to him, he is so insistently present. Despite the distortions caused by the ice and the emaciation of his illness, you can see his youthfulness, the absence of toughening, of wear. According to the dates painted carefully onto his nameplate, he was only twenty years old. His name was John Torrington. He was, or is, a sailor, a seaman. He wasn't an able-bodied seaman though; he was a petty officer, one of those marginally in command. Being in command has little to do with the ableness of the body.

He was one of the first to die. This is why he got a coffin and a metal nameplate, and a deep hole in the permafrost—because they still had the energy, and the piety, for such things, that early. There would have been a burial service read over him, and prayers. As time went on and became nebulous and things did not get better, they must have kept the energy for themselves; and also the prayers. The prayers would have ceased to be routine and become desperate, and then hopeless. The later dead ones got cairns of piled stones, and the much later ones not even that. They ended up as bones, and as the soles of boots and the occasional button, sprinkled over the frozen stony treeless relentless ground in a trail heading south. It was like the trails in fairy tales, of bread crumbs or seeds or white stones. But in this case nothing had sprouted or lit up in the moonlight, forming a miraculous pathway to life; no rescuers had followed. It took ten years before anyone knew even the barest beginnings of what had been happening to them.

All of them together were the Franklin Expedition. Jane has seldom paid much attention to history except when it has overlapped with her knowledge of antique furniture and real estate—'19th c. pine harvest table', or 'Prime location Georgian centre hall, impeccable reno'—but she knows what the Franklin Expedition was. The two ships with their bad-luck names have been on stamps—the *Terror*, the *Erebus*. Also she took it in school, along with a lot of other doomed expeditions. Not many of those explorers seemed to have come out of it very well. They were always getting scurvy, or lost.

What the Franklin Expedition was looking for was the Northwest Passage, an open seaway across the top of the Arctic, so people, merchants, could get to India from England without going all the way around South America. They wanted to go that way because it would cost less and increase their profits. This was much less exotic than Marco Polo or the headwaters of the Nile;[1] nevertheless, the idea of exploration appealed to her then: to get onto a boat and just go somewhere, somewhere mapless, off into the unknown. To launch yourself into fright; to find things out. There was something daring and noble about it, despite all of the losses and failures, or perhaps because of them. It was like having sex, in high school, in those days before the Pill, even if you took precautions. If you were a girl, that is. If you were a boy, for whom such a risk was fairly minimal, you had to do other things: things with weapons or large amounts of alcohol, or high-speed vehicles, which at her suburban Toronto high school, back then at the beginning of the sixties, meant switchblades, beer, and drag races down the main streets on Saturday nights.

Now, gazing at the television as the lozenge of ice gradually melts and the outline of the young sailor's body clears and sharpens, Jane remembers Vincent, sixteen and with more hair then, quirking one eyebrow and lifting his lip in a mock sneer and saying, 'Franklin, my dear, I don't give a damn.' He said it loud enough to be heard, but the history teacher ignored him, not knowing what else to do. It was hard for the teachers to keep Vincent in line, because he never seemed to be afraid of anything that might happen to him.

He was hollow-eyed even then; he frequently looked as if he'd been up all night. Even then he resembled a very young old man, or else a dissipated child. The dark circles under his eyes were the ancient part, but when he smiled he had lovely small white teeth, like the magazine ads for baby foods. He made fun of everything, and was adored. He wasn't adored the way other boys were adored, those boys with surly lower lips and greased hair and a studied air of smouldering menace. He was adored like a pet. Not a dog, but a cat. He went where he liked, and nobody owned him. Nobody called him Vince.

Strangely enough, Jane's mother approved of him. She didn't usually approve of the boys Jane went out with. Maybe she approved of him because it was obvious to her that no bad results would follow from Jane's going out with him: no heartaches, no heaviness, nothing burdensome. None of what she called *consequences*. Consequences: the weightiness of the body, the growing flesh hauled around like a bundle, the tiny frill-framed goblin head in the carriage. Babies and marriage, in that order. This was how she understood men and their furtive, fumbling, threatening desires, because Jane herself had been a consequence. She had been a mistake, she had been a war baby. She had been a crime that had needed to be paid for, over and over.

1 Marco Polo (*c.* 1254–*c.* 1324): Italian traveller whose book recounting his travels to China and the court of Kublai Khan via central Asia gave considerable impetus to the European quest to discover the riches of the East. The source of the Nile was a mystery and the subject of fascinated debate and speculation for centuries, and attracted considerable attention among explorers in the eighteenth and nineteenth centuries. The Scottish explorer James Bruce eventually identified Lake Tana as the source of the Blue Nile (1770); the English explorer John Speke is credited with identifying Lake Victoria and Ripon Falls as the source of the White Nile (1861–2).

By the time she was sixteen, Jane had heard enough about this to last her several lifetimes. In her mother's account of the way things were, you were young briefly and then you fell. You plummeted downwards like an overripe apple and hit the ground with a squash; you fell, and everything about you fell too. You got fallen arches and a fallen womb, and you hair and teeth fell out. That's what having a baby did to you. It subjected you to the force of gravity.

This is how she remembers her mother, still: in terms of a pendulous, drooping, wilting motion. Her sagging breasts, the downturned lines around her mouth. Jane conjures her up: there she is, as usual, sitting at the kitchen table with a cup of cooling tea, exhausted after her job clerking at Eaton's department store, standing all day behind the jewellery counter with her bum stuffed into a girdle and her swelling feet crammed into the mandatory medium-heeled shoes, smiling her envious, disapproving smile at the spoiled customers who turned up their noses at pieces of glittering junk she herself could never afford to buy. Jane's mother sighs, picks at the canned spaghetti Jane has heated up for her. Silent worlds waft out of her like stale talcum powder: *What can you expect*, always a statement, never a question. Jane tries at this distance for pity, but comes up with none.

As for Jane's father, he'd run away from home when Jane was five, leaving her mother in the lurch. That's what her mother called it—'running away from home'—as if he'd been an irresponsible child. Money arrived from time to time, but that was the sum total of his contribution to family life. Jane resented him for it, but she didn't blame him. Her mother inspired in almost everyone who encountered her a vicious desire for escape.

Jane and Vincent would sit out in the cramped backyard of Jane's house, which was one of the squinty-windowed little stuccoed wartime bungalows at the bottom of the hill. At the top of the hill were the richer houses, and the richer people: the girls who owned cashmere sweaters, at least one of them, instead of the Orlon and lambswool so familiar to Jane. Vincent lived about halfway up the hill. He still had a father, in theory.

They would sit against the back fence, near the spindly cosmos flowers that passed for a garden, as far away from the house itself as they could get. They would drink gin, decanted by Vincent from his father's liquor hoard and smuggled in an old military pocket flask he'd picked up somewhere. They would imitate their mothers.

'I pinch and scrape and I work my fingers to the bone, and what thanks do I get?' Vincent would say peevishly. 'No help from you, Sonny Boy. You're just like your father. Free as the birds, out all night, do as you like and you don't care one pin about anyone else's feelings. Now take out that garbage.'

'It's love that does it to you,' Jane would reply, in the resigned, ponderous voice of her mother. 'You wait and see, my girl. One of these days you'll come down off your devil-may-care high horse.' As Jane said this, and even though she was making fun, she could picture love, with a capital L, descending out of the sky towards her like a huge foot. Her mother's life had been a disaster, but in her own view an inevitable disaster, as in songs and movies. It was Love that was responsible, and in the face of Love, what could be done? Love was like a steamroller. There was no avoiding it, it went over you and you came out flat.

Jane's mother waited, fearfully and uttering warnings, but with a sort of gloating relish, for the same thing to happen to Jane. Every time Jane went out with a new boy her mother inspected him as a potential agent of downfall. She distrusted most of these boys; she distrusted their sulky, pulpy mouths, their eyes half-closed in the up-drifting smoke of their cigarettes, their slow, sauntering manner of walking, their clothing that was too tight, too full: too full of their bodies. They looked this way even when they weren't putting on the sulks and swaggers, when they were trying to appear bright-eyed and industrious and polite for Jane's mother's benefit, saying goodbye at the front door, dressed in their shirts and ties and their pressed heavy-date suits. They couldn't help the way they looked, the way they were. They were helpless; one kiss in a dark corner would reduce them to speechlessness; they were sleepwalkers in their own liquid bodies. Jane, on the other hand, was wide awake.

Jane and Vincent did not exactly go out together. Instead they made fun of going out. When the coast was clear and Jane's mother wasn't home, Vincent would appear at the door with his face painted bright yellow, and Jane would put her bathrobe on back to front and they would order Chinese food and alarm the delivery boy and eat sitting cross-legged on the floor, clumsily, with chopsticks. Or Vincent would turn up in a threadbare 30-year-old suit and a bowler hat and a cane, and Jane would rummage around in the cupboard for a discarded church-going hat of her mother's, with smashed cloth violets and a veil, and they would go downtown and walk around, making loud remarks about the passers-by, pretending to be old, or poor, or crazy. It was thoughtless and in bad taste, which was what they both liked about it.

Vincent took Jane to the graduation formal, and they picked out her dress together at one of the second-hand clothing shops Vincent frequented, giggling at the shock and admiration they hoped to cause. They hesitated between a flame-red with falling-off sequins and a backless hip-hugging black with a plunge front, and chose the black, to go with Jane's hair. Vincent sent a poisonous-looking lime-green orchid, the colour of her eyes, he said, and Jane painted her eyelids and fingernails to match. Vincent wore white tie and tails, and a top hat, all frayed Sally-Ann issue and ludicrously too large for him. They tangoed around the gymnasium, even though the music was not a tango, under the tissue-paper flowers, cutting a black swath through the sea of pastel tulle, unsmiling, projecting a corny sexual menace, Vincent with Jane's long pearl necklace clenched between his teeth.

The applause was mostly for him, because of the way he was adored. Though mostly by the girls, thinks Jane. But he seemed to be popular enough among the boys as well. Probably he told them dirty jokes, in the proverbial locker room. He knew enough of them.

As he dipped Jane backwards, he dropped the pearls and whispered into her ear, 'No belts, no pins, no pads, no chafing.' It was from an ad for tampons, but it was also their leitmotif. It was what they both wanted: freedom from the world of mothers, the world of precautions, the world of burdens and fate and heavy female constraints upon the flesh. They wanted a life without consequences. Until recently, they'd managed it.

The scientists have melted the entire length of the young sailor now, at least the upper layer of him. They've been pouring warm water over him, gently and patiently; they don't want to thaw him too abruptly. It's as if John Torrington is asleep and they don't want to startle him.

Now his feet have been revealed. They're bare, and white rather then beige; they look like the feet of someone who's been walking on a cold floor, on a winter day. That is the quality of the light that they reflect: winter sunlight, in early morning. There is something intensely painful to Jane about the absence of socks. They could have left him his socks. But maybe the others needed them. His big toes are tied together with a strip of cloth; the man talking says this was to keep the body tidily packaged for burial, but Jane is not convinced. His arms are tied to his body, his ankles are tied together. You do that when you don't want a person walking around.

This part is almost too much for Jane; it is too reminiscent. She reaches for the channel switcher, but luckily the show (it is only a show, it's only another show) changes to two of the historical experts, analyzing the clothing. There's a close-up of John Torrington's shirt, a simple, high-collared, pin-striped white-and-blue cotton, with mother-of-pearl buttons. The stripes are a printed pattern, rather than a woven one; woven would have been more expensive. The trousers are grey linen. Ah, thinks Jane. Wardrobe. She feels better: this is something she knows about. She loves the solemnity, the reverence, with which the stripes and buttons are discussed. An interest in the clothing of the present is frivolity, an interest in the clothing of the past is archaeology; a point Vincent would have appreciated.

After high school, Jane and Vincent both got scholarships to university, although Vincent had appeared to study less, and did better. That summer they did everything together. They got summer jobs at the same hamburger heaven, they went to movies together after work, although Vincent never paid for Jane. They still occasionally dressed up in old clothes and pretended to be a weird couple, but it no longer felt careless and filled with absurd invention. It was beginning to occur to them that they might conceivably end up looking like that.

In her first year at university Jane stopped going out with other boys: she needed a part-time job to help pay her way, and that and the schoolwork and Vincent took up all her time. She thought she might be in love with Vincent. She thought that maybe they should make love, to find out. She had never done such a thing, entirely; she had been too afraid of the untrustworthiness of men, of the gravity of love, too afraid of consequences. She thought, however, that she might trust Vincent.

But things didn't go that way. They held hands, but they didn't hug; they hugged, but they didn't pet; they kissed, but they didn't neck. Vincent liked looking at her, but he liked it so much he would never close his eyes. She would close hers and then open them, and there would be Vincent, his own eyes shining in the light from the streetlamp or the moon, peering at her inquisitively as if waiting to see what odd female thing she would do next, for his delighted amusement. Making love with Vincent did not seem altogether possible.

(Later, after she had flung herself into the current of opinion that had swollen to a river by the late sixties, she no longer said 'making love'; she said 'having sex'. But it amounted to the same thing. You had sex, and love got made out of it whether you liked it or not. You woke up in a bed or more likely on a mattress, with an arm around you, and found yourself wondering what it might be like to keep on doing it. At that point Jane would start looking at her watch. She had no intention of being left in any lurches. She would do the leaving herself. And she did.)

Jane and Vincent wandered off to different cities. They wrote each other postcards. Jane did this and that. She ran a co-op food store in Vancouver, did the financial stuff for a diminutive theatre in Montreal, acted as managing editor for a small publisher, ran the publicity for a dance company. She had a head for details and for adding up small sums—having to scrape her way through university had been instructive—and such jobs were often available if you didn't demand much money for doing them. Jane could see no reason to tie herself down, to make any sort of soul-stunting commitment, to anything or anyone. It was the early seventies; the old heavy women's world of girdles and precautions and consequences had been swept away. There were a lot of windows opening, a lot of doors: you could look in, then you could go in, then you could come out again.

She lived with several men, but in each of the apartments there were always cardboard boxes, belonging to her, that she never got around to unpacking; just as well, because it was that much easier to move out. When she got past thirty she decided it might be nice to have a child, some time, later. She tried to figure out a way of doing this without becoming a mother. Her own mother had moved to Florida, and sent rambling, grumbling letters, to which Jane did not often reply.

Jane moved back to Toronto, and found it ten times more interesting than when she'd left it. Vincent was already there. He'd come back from Europe, where he'd been studying film; he'd opened a design studio. He and Jane met for lunch, and it was the same: the same air of conspiracy between them, the same sense of their own potential for outrageousness. They might still have been sitting in Jane's garden, beside the cosmos flowers, drinking forbidden gin and making fun.

Jane found herself moving in Vincent's circles, or were they orbits? Vincent knew a great many people, people of all kinds; some were artists and some wanted to be, and some wanted to know the ones who were. Some had money to begin with, some made money; they all spent it. There was a lot more talk about money, these days, or among these people. Few of them knew how to manage it, and Jane found herself helping them out. She developed a small business among them, handling their money. She would gather it in, put it away safely for them, tell them what they could spend, dole out an allowance. She would note with interest the things they bought, filing their receipted bills: what furniture, what clothing, which *objets*. They were delighted with their money, enchanted with it. It was like milk and cookies for them, after school. Watching them play with their money, Jane felt responsible and indulgent, and a little matronly. She stored her own money carefully away, and eventually bought a townhouse with it.

All this time she was with Vincent, more or less. They'd tried being lovers but had not made a success of it. Vincent had gone along with this scheme because Jane had wanted it, but he was elusive, he would not make declarations. What worked with other men did not work with him: appeals to his protective instincts, pretences at jealously, requests to remove stuck lids from jars. Sex with him was more like a musical work-out. He couldn't take it seriously, and accused her of being too solemn about it. She thought he might be gay, but was afraid to ask him; she dreaded feeling irrelevant to him, excluded. It took them months to get back to normal.

He was older now, they both were. He had thinning temples and a widow's peak, and his bright inquisitive eyes had receded even further into his head. What went on between them continued to look like a courtship, but was not one. He was always bringing her things: a new, peculiar food to eat, a new grotesquerie to see, a new piece of gossip, which he would present to her with a sense of occasion, like a flower. She in her turn appreciated him. It was like a yogic exercise, appreciating Vincent; it was like appreciating an anchovy, or a stone. He was not everyone's taste.

There's a black-and-white print on the television, then another: the nineteenth century's version of itself, in etchings. Sir John Franklin, older and fatter than Jane had supposed; the *Terror* and the *Erebus*, locked fast in the crush of the ice. In the high Arctic, a hundred and fifty years ago, it's the dead of winter. There is no sun at all, no moon; only the rustling northern lights, like electronic music, and the hard little stars.

What did they do for love, on such a ship, at such a time? Furtive solitary gropings, confused and mournful dreams, the sublimation of novels. The usual, among those who have become solitary.

Down in the hold, surrounded by the creaking of the wooden hull and the stale odours of men far too long enclosed, John Torrington lies dying. He must have known it; you can see it on his face. He turns towards Jane his tea-coloured look of puzzled reproach.

Who held his hand, who read to him, who brought him water? Who, if anyone, loved him? And what did they tell him about whatever it was that was killing him? Consumption, brain fever, Original Sin. All those Victorian reasons, which meant nothing and were the wrong ones. But they must have been comforting. If you are dying, you want to know why.

In the eighties, things started to slide. Toronto was not so much fun anymore. There were too many people, too many poor people. You could see them begging on the streets, which were clogged with fumes and cars. The cheap artists' studios were torn down or converted to coy and upscale office space; the artists had migrated elsewhere. Whole streets were torn up or knocked down. The air was full of windblown grit.

People were dying. They were dying too early. One of Jane's clients, a man who owned an antique store, died almost overnight of bone cancer. Another, a woman who was an entertainment lawyer, was trying on a dress in a boutique and had a heart attack. She fell over and they called the ambulance, and she was dead on arrival. A theatrical producer died of AIDS, and a photographer; the lover of the photographer shot himself, either out of grief or because he knew he was next. A friend of a friend died of emphysema, another of viral pneumonia, another of hepatitis picked up on a tropical vacation, another of spinal meningitis. It was as if they had been weakened by some mysterious agent, a thing like a colourless gas, scentless and invisible, so that any germ that happened along could invade their bodies, take them over.

Jane began to notice news items of the kind she'd once skimmed over. Maple groves dying of acid rain, hormones in the beef, mercury in the fish, pesticides in the vegetables, poison sprayed on the fruit, God knows what in the drinking water. She subscribed to a bottled spring-water service and felt better for a few weeks, then read in the paper that it wouldn't do her much good, because whatever it was had been seeping into everything. Each time you took a breath, you breathed some of it in. She thought about moving out of the city, then read about toxic dumps, radioactive waste, concealed here and there in the countryside and masked by the lush, deceitful green of waving trees.

Vincent has been dead for less than a year. He was not put into the permafrost or frozen in ice. He went into the Necropolis, the only Toronto cemetery of whose general ambience he approved; he got flower bulbs planted on top of him, by Jane and others. Mostly by Jane. Right now John Torrington, recently thawed after a hundred and fifty years, probably looks better than Vincent.

A week before Vincent's forty-third birthday, Jane went to see him in the hospital. He was in for tests. Like fun he was. He was in for the unspeakable, the unknown. He was in for a mutated virus that didn't even have a name yet. It was creeping up his spine, and when it reached his brain it would kill him. It was not, as they said, responding to treatment. He was in for the duration.

It was white in his room, wintry. He lay packed in ice, for the pain. A white sheet wrapped him, his white thin feet poked out the bottom of it. They were so pale and cold. Jane took one look at him, laid out on ice like a salmon, and began to cry.

'Oh Vincent,' she said. 'What will I do without you?' This sounded awful. It sounded like Jane and Vincent making fun, of obsolete books, obsolete movies, their obsolete mothers. It also sounded selfish: here she was, worrying about herself and her future, when Vincent was the one who was sick. But it was true. There would be a lot less to do, altogether, without Vincent.

Vincent gazed up at her; the shadows under his eyes were cavernous. 'Lighten up,' he said, not very loudly, because he could not speak very loudly now. By this time she was sitting down, leaning forward; she was holding one of his hands. It was thin as the claw of a bird. 'Who says I'm going to die?' He spent a moment considering this, revised it. 'You're right,' he said, 'They got me. It was the Pod People from outer space. They said, "All I want is your poddy." '

Jane cried more. It was worse because he was trying to be funny. 'But what *is* it?' she said. 'Have they found out yet?'

Vincent smiled his ancient, jaunty smile, his smile of detachment, of amusement. There were his beautiful teeth, juvenile as ever. 'Who knows?' he said. 'It must have been something I ate.'

Jane sat with the tears running down her face. She felt desolate: left behind, stranded. Their mothers had finally caught up to them and been proven right. There were consequences after all; but they were the consequences to things you didn't even know you'd done.

The scientists are back on the screen. They are excited, their earnest mouths are twitching, you could almost call them joyful. They know why John Torrington died; they know, at last, why the Franklin Expedition went so terribly wrong. They've snipped off pieces of John Torrington, a fingernail, a lock of hair, they've run them through machines and come out with the answers.

There is a shot of an old tin can, pulled open to show the seam. It looks like a bomb casing. A finger points: it was the tin cans that did it, a new invention back then, a new technology, the ultimate defence against starvation and scurvy. The Franklin Expedition was excellently provisioned with tin cans, stuffed full of meat and soup and soldered together with lead. The whole expedition got lead-poisoning. Nobody knew it. Nobody could taste it. It invaded their bones, their lungs, their brains, weakening them and confusing their thinking, so that at the end those that had not yet died in the ships set out in an idiotic trek across the stony, icy ground, pulling a lifeboat laden down with toothbrushes, soap, handkerchiefs, and slippers, useless pieces of junk. When they were found ten years later, they were skeletons in tattered coats, lying where they'd collapsed. They'd been heading back towards the ships. It was what they'd been eating that had killed them.

Jane switches off the television and goes into her kitchen—all white, done over the year before last, the outmoded butcher-block counters from the seventies torn out and carted away—to make herself some hot milk and rum. Then she decides against it; she won't sleep anyway. Everything in here looks ownerless. Her toaster oven, so perfect for solo dining, her microwave for the vegetables, her espresso maker—they're sitting around waiting for her departure, for this evening or forever, in order to assume their final, real appearances of purposeless objects adrift in the physical world. They might as well be pieces of an exploded spaceship orbiting the moon.

She thinks about Vincent's apartment, so carefully arranged, filled with the beautiful or deliberately ugly possessions he once loved. She thinks about his closet, with its quirky particular outfits, empty now of his arms and legs. It has all been broken up now, sold, given away.

Increasingly the sidewalk that runs past her house is cluttered with plastic drinking cups, crumpled soft-drink cans, used take-out plates. She picks them up, clears them away, but they appear again overnight, like a trail left by an army on the march or by the fleeing residents of a city under bombardment, discarding the objects that were once thought essential but are now too heavy to carry.

1991

Patrick Lane

b. 1939

Born in Nelson, BC, Patrick Lane grew up near Vernon, in the British Columbia interior. Although he has travelled extensively—as a young man he wandered through North and South America, working at manual jobs such as logger and miner—he has based himself in western Canada most of his life. He began to write poetry in his early twenties, and in 1966 he helped found, with the poets bill bissett and Seymour Mayne, Very Stone House, a small press that published a number of important poetry books including Lane's *Letters from the Savage Mind* in 1966. (The press was later called Very Stone House in Transit, 1971–80, an allusion to Lane's moving from place to place.)

Over the course of a long career, Lane has continued to write steadily, producing a number of broadsheets, pamphlets, and books of poetry, among which are *Beware the Months of Fire* (1974); *Unborn Things* (1975); *Albino Pheasant* (1977); *Poems New and Selected* (1978), which won a Governor General's Award; *The Measure* (1980); *Old Mother* (1982); *A Linen Crow, a Caftan Magpie* (1984); *Selected Poems* (1987), which contains a section of new work; *Winter* (1990); *Mortal Remains* (1991); *Too Spare, Too Fierce* (1995); and *The Bare Plum of Winter Rain* (2000). A children's book, *Milford and Me,* appeared in 1989, and in 1992 twenty of his stories were gathered in *How Do You Spell Beautiful?* Several sections from an autobiography in progress have appeared in the literary magazine *Geist* and elsewhere.

In 1978 he began a relationship with the poet Lorna Crozier, which they celebrated in the book *No Longer Two People* (1979), a series of poems set in dialogue. Among other joint projects, the two wrote the radio script 'Chile', which won the National Radio Award for best public radio program in 1987. From 1986 to 1991 they shared (with the fiction writer David Carpenter) an appointment in the English department at the University of Saskatchewan. Lane has also taught creative writing, or been a writer-in-residence, at Concordia University and the Universities of Notre Dame at Nelson, Manitoba, Ottawa, Alberta, Toronto, and Victoria.

Lane initially became known for a signature style distinguished by the qualities suggested in the title of *Too Spare, Too Fierce.* While it is a poetry of anecdotal narrative, it is expressed in a haunting, pared-down lyricism that, in poems such as 'Because I Never Learned', 'Too Spare, Too Fierce', and 'The Far Field', frequently has at its centre violence—casual acts of brutality, and a reckless self-destructiveness. These poems are tough-minded investigations of the male ethos, joined to an awareness of the world's pain, an intense response to nature, and an attachment to the land.

Lane's interest in the shaping force of the environment receives extended treatment in *Winter*, an investigation of the experience of the North that is more allusive and meditative than his earlier poetry. He writes in the afterword: 'Winter is at once both symbol and metaphor, unique and ubiquitous. Alden Nowlan said once that we live in country where simply to go outside is to die. I agree.' *Winter* ends with Lane's retelling of the story of Albert Johnson, the 'Mad Trapper', whose ability to elude the Mounties by fleeing through incredibly harsh northern conditions became legendary. Describing Johnson as an individual who has gone into the 'heart of winter', the sequence's final image is of

> *Him walking, head down, shoulders hunched,*
> *moving*
> *toward his own quick death, his breath*
> *breaking sharp and hard,*
> *entering,*
> *leaving.*

In a poem such as 'Too Spare, Too Fierce' and in creating the characters in the short story 'Honey', Lane writes out of his own personal knowledge of alcohol addiction. In 2001, he and Crozier co-edited *Addicted: Notes from the*

Belly of the Beast, a collection to which a number of prominent figures from Canadian cultural life (including the poet John Newlove, the novelist David Adams Richards, and the CBC radio personality Peter Gzowski—who died of emphysema soon after) contributed essays about the experience of addiction. Lane's own essay, 'Counting the Bones', is a frank account of his own struggles with alcohol. His afterword to the book was written from the treatment centre in which he spent Christmas, 2000. He remains sober.

Because I Never Learned

for John

Because I never learned how
to be gentle and the country
I lived in was hard with dead
animals and men I didn't question
my father when he told me
to step on the kitten's head
after the bus had run over
its hind quarters.

Now, twenty years later,
I remember only:
the silence of the dying
when the fragile skull collapsed
under my hard bare heel,
the curved tongue in the dust
that would never cry again
and the small of my father's back
as he walked tall away.

1974

Stigmata[1]

for Irving Layton[2]

What if there wasn't a metaphor
and the bodies were only bodies
bones pushed out in awkward fingers?

1 Marks corresponding to the crucifixion wounds of Christ.

2 See pp. 459–70; compare particularly 'Butterfly on Rock' (where the poet crushes the butterfly under his hand) with the conclusion of this poem.

Waves come to the seawall, fall away,
children bounce mouths against the stones
man has carved to keep the sea at bay
and women walk with empty wombs
proclaiming freedom to the night.
Through barroom windows rotten with light
eyes of men open and close like fists.

I bend beside a tidal pool and take a crab from the sea.
His small green life twists helpless in my hand
the living bars of bone and flesh
a cage made by the animal I am.
This thing, the beat, the beat of life
now captured in the darkness of my flesh
struggling with claws as if it could tear its way
through my body back to the sea.
What do I know of the inexorable beauty,
the unrelenting turning of the wheel I am inside me?
Stigmata. I hold a web of blood.

I dream of the scrimshawed[3] teeth of endless whales,
the oceans it took to carve them. Drifting ships
echo in fog the wounds of Leviathan[4]
great grey voices giving cadence to their loss.
The men are gone
who scratched upon white bones their destiny.
Who will speak of the albatross in the shroud of the man,
the sailor who sinks forever in the Mindanao Deep?[5]
I open my hand. The life leaps out.

1977

3 Intricately carved; scrimshaw is usually made from whale ivory, bone, or shells.
4 Biblical sea monster; a whale.
5 Deepest point in oceans.

The Witnesses

To know as the word is known, to know little
or less than little, nothing, to contemplate
the setting sun and sit for hours, the world
turning you into the sun as day begins again

To remember words, to remember nothing
but words and make out of nothing the past,
to remember my father, the McLeod Kid
carrying the beat, riding against time

On the rodeo circuit of fifty years ago
the prairie, stretched wet hide
scraped by a knife, disappearing everywhere
to know the McLeod Kid was defeated

To know these things
to climb into the confusions
which are only words, to climb into desire
to ride in the sun, to ride against time

The McLeod Kid raking his spurs on the mare
the cheers from the wagon-backs
where the people sit to watch the local
boy ride against the riders from Calgary

To spit melon seeds into the dust
to roll cigarettes, to leave them hanging
from the lip, to tip your hat back and grin
to laugh or not laugh, to climb into darkness

Below the stands and touch Erla's breast
to eat corn or melons, to roll cigarettes
to drink beer, bottles hidden in paper bags
to grin at the RCMP, horseless, dust on their boots

To watch or not to watch, to surround the spectacle
horses asleep in their harness, tails switching
bees swarming on melon rinds, flys buzzing
and what if my words are their voices

What if I try to capture an ecstasy that is not
mine, what if these are only words saying
this was or this was not, a story told to me
until I now no longer believe it was told to me

The witnesses dead, what if I create a past
that never was, make out of nothing
a history of my people whether in pain
or ecstasy, my father riding in the McLeod Rodeo

The hours before dawn when in the last of darkness
I make out of nothing a man riding against time
and thus my agony, the mare twisted sideways
muscles bunched in knots beneath her hide

Her mane, black hair feathered in the wind
that I believe I see, caked mud in her eyes
the breath broken from her body and the McLeod Kid
in the air, falling, the clock stopped.

1978

The Long Coyote Line

for Andy Suknaski

The long coyote line crosses the pure
white and the prairie is divided
again by hunger. The snowshoe hare
thin as January creates a running
circle encompassing a moon of snow
as the lean lope of the coyote
cuts in a curving radius
bringing escape down to a single terror.
It is the long line, coyote, and the man
who stands in your small disturbance
counting the crystals of blood and bone:
three by three, coyote, hare and the howl
where the true prairie begins.

1980

CPR Station—Winnipeg

You sit and your hands are folded in
upon you. The coffee is bleak, black. This
catacomb is lighted with the pale death
our fathers called marble in their pride.
This is an old song. This country.

This country was still a hope.
It is the CPR Station in Winnipeg,
11:30 and no one is leaving again.
The trains are late. The passengers wait
for the passing freight of the nation.

The people have turned to stone, cannot be
moved. The coffee is black. The night is far
above us. Steel passes over in the rumbling
called destinations. The gates are dark.
There is no passing here.

There is no desire to pass. Someone with
a lantern hesitates and moves on.
The river of white marble swirls cold
beneath us. It is worn, worn by the feet
of a nation. Your heavy hands. Your

fingers are huge, swollen with the
freight of years. This country has
travelled through you. The man with the
lantern sits in the far corner, waiting,
If you could lift your head I could go

out into the night with grace. O hell,
you are old. Winter is above us. Steel
wheels. If you could lift your head.
Bleak black. White marble.
And the trains, the trains pass over.

1980

A Red Bird Bearing on His Back an Empty Cup

for Lorna

It was almost night when I asked the land
to hold in the folds of her bright skin
my body, save me from the wind. But I
have asked for abstinence before. The sun
broke against the land, its death
a witness to the thing I found:

a red bird bearing on his back an empty cup.
His eyes were blind. This is not fear.
I have spoken of prophecy before.
Silence is not the end.

I was walking the long hills in search
of forgiveness. I found the red bird
though all the signs warned me to be gone.
There was a rising moon. It was then
I disturbed your troubled sleep.
And then the grey dog, thin, and you
beside me, sick, grieving for innocence.
The dog carried with him the foreleg
of a deer; the hoof, the flesh still
hanging from the bone, the tired flesh.

Forgive me, I am almost old.
I was dreaming of my father in the garden
when winter was upon us, his rueful laugh.
The years have been long for us too, and winter.
It was finding the blind bird and his cup.
His burden seemed a consolation. He was why
I lifted you from sleep and led you
through the fences and scrub willow.
Perhaps there is a perfect detachment.
God knows, I want to believe in things.

I will list here what occurred: the bird
bearing on his back an empty cup, the dog,
the foreleg of the deer, your sleeping
and your rising, the pain I feel
when you are sick to death, my father,
all the things that swing into the mind
when I am tired of praise. It will always be now
when you read this poem. It will be new
and you and the nights and the long day gone.
Perhaps to name is excellence enough.

I will not speak again of death, though
I want death. There are many ceremonies
I have not come through yet there is
a quietness. It is not for nothing we love.
Even though winter is upon us and all
the signs warned me to be gone, though

my trespass will be called to account,
it is no matter. We are here to praise
the occurrences, the moment when a red bird
bears upon his back for us an empty cup.

1982

From *Winter*

Winter 1

The generosity of snow, the way it forgives
transgression, filling in the many betrayals
and leaving the world
exactly as it was. Imagine a man
walking endlessly and finding his tracks,
knowing he has gone in a circle. Imagine
his disappointment. See how he strikes out again
in a new direction, hoping this way
will lead him out. Imagine how much
happier he will be this time with the wind
all around him, the wind filling in his tracks.

He is thinking of that man,
of what keeps him going.
The thought of snow,
small white grains sifting
into the holes where his feet went,
filling things in,
leaving no room for despair.

Winter 4

He is thinking of the end of Oedipus,
not the beginning, not the part
where Oedipus chooses by giving the answer
to the beast at the Gate of Thebes.
No, it is the end he likes. The part

just after he puts out his eyes
and stands, suddenly
in that certain darkness, decided.[1]

It is not a story of winter
but of the sun, the ceaseless
perfection of the desert in Africa.

How different it would be
had it taken place here, he thinks.
Here the critical moment
would be putting the eyes back
in their sockets, that first shock
exactly the same as in the other story
only the beginning would have
to be different, all the roles
reversed.

1 In the Greek myth, Oedipus, who, because of an oracle, was abandoned on a hillside and raised in a distant land, establishes his powers when, as a young man on the way to Thebes, he gives the correct solution to a riddle posed by the Sphinx (a winged monster with the body of a lioness and the head of a woman). Oedipus later fails, however, to use his mental powers to realize that the stranger he has killed on the way was his father and that the woman he meets and marries is his mother. In Sophocles' famous tragedy, once all has been revealed to him, Oedipus puts out his eyes.

Winter 7

It is the bare bone of winter
he holds in his hand, a wisp of ice
slender as a fifteenth-century Spanish knife
fashioned in Cordova. A woman's knife
to be hidden in a sleeve when meeting
a false lover. It is delicately curved,
a small floating rib, just right
to slip into the heart as they embrace.
He looks at the thing in his hand
as it transforms itself, changing,
melting into a thin pool of water. He is
almost afraid to return it to its element.

Winter 16

Everything moves without change. The trees
without leaves dance sadly, allowing
nothing to get in their way. Not sorrow,
not snow under snow, but a slow forgetting.
The old moon sleeps with the young moon in her arms.[1]
Words like that are like reaching out
in the darkness, wanting
to sleep and not being able to. Reaching out
to find nothing at the end of the hand but cold.
Wondering at flesh, its need, as the trees
who do not remember leaves, dance sadly
with a steady dumb grief, their dark moving
a monotonous music in the snowy night.

1 A folk expression referring to the fact that in the first phases of a new moon, the darker part of the moon is also often visible (because of light reflected from the earth)—hence it seems to be held in an embrace by the illuminated portion.

Winter 22

There is almost no air left
in the white balloon blowing across the snow.
It is wrinkled and barely lifts from the drifts.
If you could read the crinkled writing on its side
it would say: *Save the Whales*,
a temporary greed he loves,
the wish to preserve without regret.
He loves it in the way he loves
all those old poems about Byzantium,
cages full of gilded mechanical birds,
that impossible dream of beauty
while everything blows away.[1]

1 The Irish poet William Butler Yeats (1865–1939) wrote two poems, 'Sailing to Byzantium' and 'Byzantium', expressing his ideas about the immortality of art. In the first of these, to suggest the way poems outlive the poet, he uses the metaphor of mechanical birds made 'of hammered gold', which go on singing long after their creators have died.

Winter 31

What the child finds in snow is what a ship finds
in the sea, a wake left behind, a froth
that sinks back into itself, everyone else
waiting for the return, the full hold,
the grain come again, the hosannas
which are prayers to plenty. The child knows
nothing of this. He has been sent out to play
and has discovered misery.

He is learning that the footsteps he finds in snow
are his and his alone. How sweet is his lament,
this silence in the negative world of cold.
It is a kind of perfect mutiny, everyone waiting
and him knowing there will be no return.
If he were a priest he would say:
This is the end of the first lesson.[1]

1 In the Catholic mass there are two (or more) 'lessons', or readings from scripture. This line is the formula said by the priest to signal the conclusion of the first of these.

Winter 33

The brightness which is the light seen from a tomb
and which is what the dead see when they gaze
with their marble eyes from the dark rooms they are
laid in. This is a whole city this snow.

Winter 35

One is about the man who walks out into the storm
and is never seen again. We all know that one.
It is the story about grief and music,
where all the dancing is an escape
from virtue, everyone shaken by a higher crime,
the emptiness that follows completion,
the one the body knows

in the formal gentleness of suffering, everything gone,
everything forgiven in the land East of Eden.[1]

Then there is the other story, the one
where the man enters out of the storm,
ice melting from his beard, his huge hands
moving over the fire, the fear of what will follow,
the women quiet, filling his cup and bowl
with all the food there is in hope it will be
enough, in hope he will be satisfied only with that,
and knowing he won't, knowing
this is the part of the story the reader will call
the middle, and hoping for an alternative, another
beginning, and ending it
before the mind reaches the end
with everyone crying out, everyone
saying things like: *Lie down in sorrow!*
or: *This is the burden of Babylon!*[2]

There is another story, there always is.
The one about . . .
of course, of course.
How cold it is with only a lamp in this small room.

1 According to the account in Genesis, for their disobedience, Adam and Eve are banished from the garden to the land East of Eden.

2 Two allusions to the Book of Isaiah. The first is to the warning of the outcome for sinners found in Isaiah 50: 11: 'Behold, all ye that kindle a fire, that compass yourselves about with sparks: walk in the light of your fire, and in the sparks that ye have kindled. This shall ye have of mine hand; ye shall lie down in sorrow.' The second is an allusion to Isaiah 13: 1 ('The burden of Babylon, which Isaiah the son of Amoz did see'), which is the beginning of a passage foretelling an apocalyptic heavenly vengeance that will free the Israelites from Babylonian captivity.

Winter 40

She is a northern woman, barely more
than a child, one who has walked through the drifts
to find her dream vision. Her eyes are
covered by a blade of bone, a thin slit
cut in it so the light does not blind her.
The man she has found is not one of the four
possibilities: father, brother, lover, son.
He is the dream man, given to her by the snow.

He has wandered far from the sea,
his crew dead, his ship broken in the ice.
If there were someone there to translate his song
it would start with the words: *At last.*
But only she is there.
As he sings she cuts off his fingers,
only these small bones and the twenty-six
teeth for her necklace.

They will be her medicine, something
to shake over the bellies of women
in childbirth, the heads of men
who have returned empty from hunting,
their minds become snow.

How like a real man he is, she thinks.
How real this dream, the blood on the ice.
How thin he is, how much like the snow is his flesh.

Winter 42

It comes after the return, after
everything has been won and the body
feasts. It comes just after that.
That is what the story is all about,
the crashing through the door,
the shouts, the lamentation after
when the hero leaves all his dead behind
to find anything that terrible.

1990

The Far Field

We drove for more than an hour, my father's hands
on the truck's wheel, taking us farther and farther
into the hills, both of us watching
the sagebrush and spare pines drift
past, both of us silent. He did not know

what to do with me. I think he thought of
my death, as a man will whose son has chosen
to destroy. I think that's why he drove
so long, afraid to stop for fear
of what he'd do. My mother had cried
when we left, her hands over her mouth,
saying through her splayed fingers
my father's name, speaking
that word as if it were a question. I
sat there peaceful with him,
knowing for these hours he was wholly mine.

He stripped me naked in the last hour of day
and made me stand with my back to him, my bare
feet in the dust, my back and buttocks to him,
a naked body, hands braced upon the hood,
staring across the metal at the hills.

I remember the limb of the tree falling
upon me, the sound of the white wood crying
as it hurt the air, and the flesh of my body
rising to him as I fell to the ground and rose
only to fall again. I don't remember pain,
remember only what a body feels
when it is beaten, the way it resists
and fails, and the sound of my flesh.

I rose a last time, my father dropping
the last limb of the tree beside me.
I stood there in my bones wanting it not to be
over, wanting what had happened to continue, to go
on and on forever, my father's hands on me.

It was as if to be broken was love, as if
the beating was a kind of holding, a man
lifting a child in his huge hands and throwing him
high in the air, the child's wild laughter
as he fell a question spoken into both their lives,
the blood they shared pounding in their chests.

1991

Too Spare, Too Fierce

When the dawn is large enough
you will go out into that stiff blue and find a cat's paw
in the bird bath, a gift from the crow to morning.
There was a moment last night when you started walking
the iron rail in your bare feet on the bridge above the river
and you believed you wouldn't fall. Now, this morning
you shake so badly you can't hold the glass,
lowering your face to it, your tongue
a thick grey muscle trying to drown.
Outside, mosquito larvae dance
among the claws and the little red cords
where the birds come to bathe. Old crow,
I will come as soon as I can.

1995

Held Water

I have discovered I cannot bear to be
with people anymore. Even the querulous love of old friends
defeats me and I turn away, my face staring
at the hard sleet
scraping at what little is left of the trees
in early spring. The bellied pods of the wisteria hold
my face, upside down
in minute mirrors of held water. Ice falls from the eaves.
The telephone rings and like a monk I chant to myself
the many names of whatever gods I can find
in the temple bells of the hidden voices. I know
under the rotting snow there are small flowers
like insistent girls giggling in narrow attic beds,
and yes,
I know the flowers are not girls, just as
I know what resemblance there is
is lost in the ordinary crying
we think we will release and don't.
The furred pods of the wisteria crack open
dropping the mirrors from their blue hands.
Ice slides from the roof and for a moment the air is torn.

If I wasn't afraid
I could play back the sounds of my friends,
the measure of their voices
almost steady in the hard wind out of the north.
Little flawed bells.
If I didn't hear them I could almost listen.

1995

Breaking

Who will break me now that I am broken?

Black wings rest inside my arms.
The bodies they remember leave their songs
in my chest, hard beaks,
their cries as small as sound.

Little bird, little sweet one?

Where is the angel with black wings
who came to my tired arms?
There is a song in the cage of my ribs.
Forgive me when you see her.

Tell her the night comes on.

1995

Honey

Johnny and Carl were friends and so were their wives, Madge and Mabel. Mabel and Madge. They all used to laugh at that, the way the names sounded together. Carl even made a little poem about it. One Friday night when they'd been drinking and playing cards, he tipped his head back and said in that crazy way:

Madge and Mabel,
They're both able.

He and Johnny nearly killed themselves laughing. Madge and Mabel, they're both able. They repeated it like it was some kind of chant, their voices saying it together, Carl pounding on the table with his fist and Johnny sagging against the chair he was laughing so hard. Madge said she didn't think it was that funny, which made them both laugh even harder.

Mabel didn't say anything. She just sat there with her cards in her hand and a funny look on her face. The cat, who'd been sitting on her lap, jumped off and went over to the couch. It climbed up and sat on the back of it, hunched over its white paws.

'Look,' Madge said, 'you even scared the cat.'

Carl said, 'C'mon, honey, it's just a joke.'

'Well,' Madge said, 'it may be funny to you two, but it makes us both sound, oh, I don't know, loose or something.'

Carl and Johnny started laughing again, Carl saying the word loose between his laughing and Johnny finally slipping off his chair and lying on the floor saying. 'Stop it, you're killing me.'

Madge looked at Mabel and said, 'C'mon, why don't you give me a hand in the kitchen. I think it's time we made some coffee for these two.'

Mabel nodded her head and they left the room, Johnny lying on the floor, his face all red, and Carl with his fist making the glasses on the table bounce around. Finally he stopped pounding and reached for the bottle of Seagram's and poured himself another drink. 'Hey, Johnny,' he said, still gulping for air, 'get up and have a drink.'

Johnny groaned and then uncurled himself and crawled back into his chair. He watched Carl pour him a drink and said, 'Carl, you've got to be the funniest guy I ever met. I mean it. There isn't anybody who can make me laugh as hard as you.'

Carl agreed, saying he didn't know how he did it. 'They just come out of me,' he said. He reached out and picked up his cards. They'd been lying in the spilled drinks. 'Jesus,' he said. 'Look at the mess.' He started wiping the cards off on the sleeve of his shirt.

Johnny yelled, 'Hey, Mabel, bring a cloth or something. There's drinks spilled in here and the cards are all wet.'

'Who was your slave last year?' Madge hollered back.

'Women,' Carl said to that. 'What're you supposed to do?'

'Well, I'll be go to hell,' Johnny said. He was pouring more whisky into his glass while he said it. 'She's your old lady, isn't she?'

Carl said, 'It's just a fucking joke. Can't they take a joke for Christ's sake?'

Johnny took a drink from his glass. 'Jesus, I'm getting drunk. Where the hell are they? I'd like to play some more cards. Hell, I was winning until you broke us all up.'

When Carl just kept wiping the cards on his shirt, Johnny got up and went into the kitchen. The girls were standing by the stove waiting for the coffee to start perking. 'Hey,' he said.

He went over to his wife and put his arms around her, and she tried to push him away. She said, 'I agree with Madge, you know. It wasn't all that funny once you think of it.'

Johnny fought her arms away and picked her up off the floor. He swirled her around the kitchen. 'Who's my pretty girl?' he said. 'Let's dance. You know I like dancing.'

Mabel put her arms around his neck, trying to hold on as her feet swept in circles about a foot off the floor. Johnny looked over her small dark head at Madge and told her to go out and be nice to Carl. 'We didn't mean it,' he said. 'Go on. Be nice to him. Hell, we're friends and this's a party, isn't it?'

The coffee had started burping on the stove and Madge turned it down so it wouldn't boil over. 'Go on,' she heard Johnny say again, and so she did. On the way past the fridge she jerked a dish towel from the handle.

'It never ends,' she said.

By the time she was out of the room, Johnny had stopped swinging Mabel. They stood in the middle of the kitchen and Johnny held her up so she wouldn't fall down.

'I think I'm going to be sick,' Mabel said.

'No, you're not,' Johnny said. 'The best think to stop yourself being sick, is to have another drink.' While he was saying this he was trying to slip his hand inside the back of Mabel's skirt.

'Don't,' Mabel said. 'I mean it, Johnny. I really think I might be sick.'

Johnny just laughed and kept trying to get his hand in. When he finally did, Mabel twisted away and two of the buttons on her skirt popped off and bounced crazily across the floor.

'Now see what you did,' Mabel said. She got down on her hands and knees and tried to find the buttons. One of them she found right away, but the other had rolled under the fridge and she couldn't reach it. 'It's under the fridge,' she said to Johnny. 'Help me get it. I'll never find a matching button anywhere else.'

'What did you say?'

Mabel looked up over her shoulder. 'Under the fridge,' she said.

'Hey,' Johnny said.

He was grinning when he stepped over to the fridge. Mabel was on her hands and knees on the floor and Johnny put his legs on either side of her and, bracing himself, pushed the fridge so it was tilted up on its side. 'Reach under and get it,' he said.

Mabel hesitated. 'You won't drop it, will you?'

Johnny grunted. 'For Christ's sake,' he said. 'What do you think?'

She looked up at him for a moment and then she leaned her head down and peered under.

'It's way at the back,' she said.

'Well, get it,' said Johnny. 'Hurry up. I can't hold this fridge here all night.'

Mabel put her arm under and reached for the button, but it was still too far, so she eased her head under. As she did, Johnny lowered the fridge, bracing it with one shoulder so it rested lightly on the top of her head.

Mabel screamed.

When Carl and Madge ran into the room, Johnny was slapping Mabel on the rear end with his free hand. Not hard, just regular little slaps so it sounded like someone playing patty-cake. 'Jesus, Johnny,' Madge said. She punched him on the arm and told him to lift the fridge so Mabel could get out from under it.

'Don't bump me,' he said, 'or I might drop it.' When Madge hesitated, he flipped Mabel's skirt up.

Madge reached out and pulled the skirt down. She got down on her knees and, putting her arms around Mabel, pulled her out from under. Johnny lowered the fridge back onto the floor. 'Whoof,' he said. 'That bugger was heavy.' Carl grinned as if he didn't know what else to do, then followed Johnny into the living room.

Madge and Mabel sat on the floor beside each other. Mabel had her hand open in her lap and was looking at the button in it. 'At least I got my button,' she said.

Madge said, 'That Johnny.'

'He scares me,' said Mabel. 'He could've dropped it on me.'

Madge giggled. 'You sure looked funny with your bum up in the air.'

'It didn't feel funny,' Mabel said, and then she started to cry. She was trying to hitch her skirt around so she could see if it was ripped.

'Don't cry,' Madge said. 'He didn't mean it. He was just having fun.' She put her arm around Mabel's shoulder. 'C'mon,' she said, 'we've just got ourselves two really crazy guys, that's all. He wouldn't have dropped that fridge on your head. You know that.' But Mabel kept on crying and trying to turn her skirt around so she could see it.

'Now what's the matter?' Johnny yelled from the living room. 'Is Mabel crying, for Christ's sake? Hey, Mabel,' he called, 'quit that and c'mon in here and play some cards. You're being a real party-pooper.'

Madge finally got Mabel up off the floor. She got a safety pin from the windowsill and pinned Mabel's skirt together. The waist was torn. 'Now don't worry,' Madge said, 'It isn't torn too badly. You can fix it easy.' Mabel had stopped crying by this time. She was holding a dish towel up to her face.

'You go on to the bathroom and fix up your face,' Madge said. 'After, we can go and play some more cards. It'll be fun, honest. You know Johnny. You know how he likes to fool around. He's just like Carl,' she said.

Carl had his arm around Johnny's shoulder, trying to hold him up as they walked home. Mabel was behind them. It was dark with heavy clouds and a strong hard wind. Johnny was staggering and Carl was having trouble holding him up. Every few steps Johnny would stop and sway on the side of the dirt road leading back to their cabin. When he did, Carl swayed with him, the two of them weaving back and forth, almost falling together. 'Don't let him fall down,' she said to Carl. 'He hates falling down.'

Johnny sang, 'Madge and Mabel, they're both able.'

'If you fall down I'll just leave you there,' Carl said to Johnny. 'I'll just leave you in the ditch if you do, so don't.' He was laughing as he said it. 'I mean it, you bugger. I'll just leave you right there in the ditch and I'll take Mabel home instead of you.'

'Don't say that,' Mabel said behind him.

Johnny stopped again and spread his arms in the air. 'Carl's my best friend,' he slurred. 'Did you know that? Cause that's what he is. He's my best friend in the whole fucking world.'

'I know, I know,' Mabel said. 'Please, Carl,' she said. 'Let's go. We're almost home.'

'My best friend,' Johnny kept mumbling as Carl steered him up the road. 'That Carl. He's my best friend.'

When they got him into the cabin, Carl took him to the back and let him fall on the bed. He looked down the hall to the living room. 'Do you want me to help get him undressed?' he called to Mabel.

She didn't answer him.

Carl undid Johnny's shoes, took them off, and then stripped off his socks. He tried to get the pants off. He got them to where they were just below the knees and then they got tangled in the blankets. 'Shit,' Carl said, and fell sideways, landing on the floor. He looked across the bed at his friend. Johnny's arms were folded across his chest, his hands clenched into fists. He looks like he's ready to fight or something, Carl thought.

The heavy gold ring on Johnny's left hand shone dully in the light reflecting from the hall. Carl decided he should try to take off Johnny's shirt. He got up off the floor and, balancing himself, tried to undo the top button. Johnny jerked his arm and hit Carl hard on the chest.

'Fuck it,' Carl said. His chest hurt where Johnny had hit him. 'You bugger,' Carl said, and then realized he was talking to himself. 'Hey, I'm talking to myself,' he said. 'Hey Johnny, can you hear me? I'm talking to myself.' He got up and leaned heavily against the wall. 'Take her easy, buddy,' he said.

While Carl was trying to get Johnny undressed and into bed, Mabel stood by the stove. She turned the front element on and turned it off again. She pulled her skirt around, undoing the safety pin Madge had loaned her, and dropped her skirt and slip to the floor. She stepped out of them and then rolled her stockings down and off. She walked unsteadily over to the long mirror beside the kitchen table and looked at herself. She started at her toes and worked herself all the way up to her face and then back down again. Taking her face in her hands, she moved it from side to side and looked at it. 'You're too damned pretty,' she said to the mirror. 'Nobody should be as pretty as you.'

She dropped her hands away from her face and, twisting her arms behind her, undid the buttons on her blouse and slowly peeled it off as if she were a stripper in a bar. She mumbled a song to herself and did an awkward bump-and-grind in front of the mirror.

When she heard Carl behind her, she didn't turn around. She kept moving slowly, looking out of the mirror. Carl just stood there, swaying in the doorway.

Carl felt a little bewildered. He shook his head and tried to smile. 'Well, looky here,' he said.

Mabel didn't say anything for a moment. She just kept moving. After she'd done another bump or two she said, 'I'm practising. It's Johnny's dance. I don't do it very well. I try. But I don't.'

'I got Johnny into bed,' Carl said.

'Where's Johnny?' she asked suddenly.

Her eyes were very wide and her voice sounded funny. Carl stared. He couldn't keep his eyes off her. She's almost totally naked, he thought.

Mabel put her hands on her hips and did another bump-and-grind, falling against the table and then onto the floor. She sprawled there with her hands between her legs, her palms flat on the floor.

'I'm his pretty girl, Johnny says.'

'Johnny's my best friend,' Carl finally said. He looked at the dark bruises on her breasts and sides. There were bruises on her legs as well. Some were almost black while others were blue, fading at the edges to a soft yellow green.

'I'm the prettiest girl in this whole town, that's what Johnny says. Only sometimes I don't dance just right.' She put her hands up to her face and turned it from side to side. 'Johnny's sleeping, isn't he?'

'Yeah,' Carl said.

'I want him to be sleeping,' Mabel said. 'Will you stay here until he's for sure sleeping? I don't want you to go if he isn't. He's sleeping, isn't he? Is he?'

'I gotta be going,' Carl said.

When Mabel said, 'Please stay,' Carl put his hands into his pockets.

'So, I guess I'd better go,' he said. 'I guess we got Johnny home all right.' Mabel sat on the floor and kept touching her skin. Carl turned around and went out the door, leaving her sitting there in front of the mirror.

Carl fell down twice while he was walking home. The second time he fell he looked up at the sky. There weren't any stars. As he lay there he could see her again with her head under the fridge and Johnny standing there slapping her. He thought of the sounds Johnny's hands made. He couldn't seem to get them out of his mind.

He lay there and held up his hands and looked at them. He clapped them together, loud in the night. He did it again and then again. He liked his hands clapping hard against each other. 'Madge and Mabel, they're both able,' he sang out loud. He smacked his hands to the rhythm of the words, repeating them over and over. Then he felt sick.

He got as far as the doorstep before he threw up. When he was finished he staggered into the house. Madge had gone to bed and the house was quiet. He walked into the living room. The table was still covered with glasses and cards. The cat stared at him from under a chair and Carl said, 'Hey, cat.' The cat didn't move, just looked at him warily as he tried pouring himself a whisky. Some of the liquor spilled on the floor and some into his glass. He lifted what was there and drank it. The next one was harder, most of the liquor spilling onto the floor. He went down the hall into the bedroom, balancing himself by leaning against the wall, the glass held far out in front of him.

It took a long time to get there.

Standing in the doorway, he looked at Madge lying in their bed. 'Honey,' he said. 'Honey? There's something crazy.'

Madge stirred and pulled the blankets around her shoulders.

Carl sat heavily on the edge of the bed. Madge's brown hair had fallen across her face so all he could see was her arm where it stuck out from under the blanket. It looked white. He stared at it. It didn't look like it belonged to anybody. It just looked like an arm somebody had left in his bed, an arm with some brown hair beside it.

He wanted to reach out and pull the blanket down a bit to see if Madge was really there. His drink was spilling and he tried to put it down on the night table. He couldn't reach, so he dropped the glass on the floor.

'Madge,' he said, 'Madge, are you there?'

When he didn't get an answer, he lifted the blanket and crawled under. He reached out and touched her and then he pulled himself closer and put his arms around her, pulling her to him, her body folded into his, his arms around her holding her there.

Madge groaned. 'What is it?' she asked, struggling in his arms. 'What's the matter?' She rolled over and faced him. 'Carl,' she said, 'you've still got your clothes on.'

He put his face in her hair and kept it there. 'Put your arms around me honey,' he said. 'Hold onto me.'

'You,' she said. She wrapped her arms around him. 'Between you and Johnny, a girl's got her hands full.'

'Hold on,' he said. It was all he could think of to say, so he said it again. 'Hold on.'

'I'm holding you,' Madge said. 'I've got you.'

He lay there with her arms around him and his face in her hair. 'I saw your arm,' he said. 'Everything's so crazy. Everything's crazy.'

She stroked his head as he stared into the darkness of her hair. 'I know, I know,' he heard her say.

The bed began to turn slowly.

He closed his eyes, the bed turning, and Madge murmuring something he couldn't hear. This's what we're doing, he thought, his eyes wet, his body shaking. 'You've got me,' he said.

'Oh, honey,' said Madge. 'What is it? What's the matter? Is it Johnny and Mabel? Is it our friends?'

'Hold on,' Carl said, the bed turning faster and faster until he felt like he was in the centre of a big dark wheel with the only thing saving him, Madge. 'Hold on,' he yelled. He pulled her body to him, wrapping his legs with hers, his arms around her, her skin in his hands.

He lay there in the centre of the dark world of their bed, the two of them getting smaller and smaller. Both of them were falling somewhere. 'Carl,' he heard her say. 'What is it? What's gone wrong?'

'I don't know where we're going, honey,' he called out, hoping she would hear him over the sound of the wheel as it kept spinning and they kept falling, faster and faster.

1992

Fred Wah

b. 1939

Born in Swift Current, Sask., Fred Wah grew up in Trail and in Nelson, BC. In high school his interest in music led him to play trumpet in a band called the Kampus Kings. (Lionel Kearns, who would also later become a poet associated with the *Tish* group, was the saxophonist.) Wah left the Kootenay region in 1959 to pursue music at the University of British Columbia; there he also turned to poetry, joining Daphne Marlatt, George Bowering, and others in the incipient *Tish* movement.

Wah became one of the founders of the periodical, *Tish*, from which the group took its name—the first of his many associations with literary magazines. After completing a BA in music and English literature at UBC, he began graduate studies with the American poet Robert Creeley at the University of New Mexico. Wah followed Creeley when he moved to the State University of New York at Buffalo: there he met and studied with Charles Olson as well. Creeley was associated with the Black Mountain school, and Olson was the major theorist of Black Mountain poetics. Their emphasis on a poetry of simple syntax, concreteness, and organic literary forms and on a poetic line felt to be an expression of the poet's breath—ideas already important to the *Tish* poets—now became central to Wah's own writing.

In 1965 Wah published his first book of poetry, *Lardeau*; in 1967 he followed it with *Mountain*. After completing an MA that year, he returned to the Kootenays to teach at Selkirk College in Castlegar. When the David Thomson University Centre was created in Nelson he became head of the creative writing program there. He published four books of poetry during the 1970s, including *Among* (1972), which contains work from earlier books, and *Pictograms from the Interior of B.C.* (1975). His 1980 volume of selected poems, *Loki is Buried at Smoky Creek*, edited by George Bowering, shows him as a poet working in a spare imagistic style to create short poems concerned with the experiences of everyday life. In that same year Wah also edited *Net Work*, a selection of Daphne Marlatt's poetry.

The book he published the following year, *Breathin' My Name With a Sigh* (1981), explores sound as well as imagery as a resource for the poet, evincing Wah's continuing love of music. In particular, the playful connection he makes there between the sound of his name and the sound of air being exhaled recalls the Black Mountain concern for breath as an influence on poetry. Among the several other books he wrote in that decade are *Waiting for Saskatchewan* (1985), which won a Governor General's Award, and *Music at the Heart of Thinking* (1987).

In 1989 Wah accepted an appointment at the University of Calgray and moved, with his wife, Pauline Butling, to Alberta. In Alberta he continued his associations with the *Tish* group, serving on the editorial board of *Open Letter*—having been a contributing editor ever since that journal succeeded *Tish* in 1965 as a forum for discussions of contemporary writing and experimental poetics—and he maintained his West Coast affiliations as an editor of the journal *West Coast Line*. He co-edited, with Roy Miki, a special issue of that journal in 1994: *Colour. An Issue*. In 1999 he and Miki edited a collection of essays about bp Nichol.

While Wah had always, like other *Tish* poets, been interested in the poet's connections with place, *Waiting for Saskatchewan* began new investigations of both how personal history was grounded within place and how genealogy transcended place. It contains a sequence of prose poems, 'Elite', which takes its name from the family café in Swift Current and deals with a return Wah made to the Prairies and with his desire to understand the influence of his father, whose presence dominates the book. This new direction in his work is continued in the extended investigations of his past in what he calls, following George Bowering, 'biotexts', culminating in *Diamond Grill* (1996), and in a series of essays (collected in 2000 as *Faking It—Poetics and Hybridity: Critical Writing 1984–1999*) in which he examines his mixed heritage and the questions arising from it—such as how 'ethnic writing' has come to be perceived in Canada.

In one of those essays, called 'Half-Bred Poetics', Wah writes that *Diamond Grill* 'interrogates the roots of my own anger as racial—genetically and culturally':

> *The site of poetics for me, and many other multi-racial and multi-cultural writers, is the hyphen, that marked (or unmarked) space that both binds and divides. . . . Though the hyphen is in the middle it is not in the centre. It is a property marker, a boundary post, a borderland, a bastard, a railroad, a last spike, a stain, a cipher, a rope, a knot, a chain (link), a foreign word, a warning sign, a head tax, a bridge, a no-man's land, a nomadic, floating magic carpet, now you see it now you don't.*

Like its author, *Diamond Grill* is a complex mixture: it seems to be a sequence of short prose poems, it uses the form of the memoir, it has occasional footnotes that recall the academic essay, and it has won an award for short fiction. Part autobiographical narrative, part a series of self-reflexive meditations, the work as a whole is a record of an individual recording the dynamics and difficulties of self-identification and self-representation that arise when his heritage and his experience of being 'Canadian' is inherently multiple. The fact that Canada is a country with an official policy of multiculturalism might suggest that it is prepared to recognize the individual whose racial and cultural origins are mixed, but we learn otherwise in Wah's fluid autobiographical account—the story of a man born in Canada to a Swedish mother and a half-Chinese, half-Scots-Irish father—as he traces out the way he is asked to choose between a single 'non-white' identity or life lived 'in the hyphen'.

Examining the limitations of hyphenated representation in *Diamond Grill*, partly by using food imagery and its preparation in his family restaurant as a metaphor for questions of ethnic identity, Wah recognizes that although he *does* strongly identify with his Chinese background, he has never been entirely comfortable in the Chinese community—in part because members of that group do not see him as one of them. The fact that English is his first language is itself a barrier to that community, but the influence of the Chinese language has affected Wah's way of speaking that English and has given him a sense of language that is distinct from that of other English Canadians with whom he comes into contact.

From the very beginning *Diamond Grill* makes us aware of the mixed nature of language. As we read on we see that in that mixture lies the history of Wah's family and of his nations, both old and new. One word in particular, *muckamuck*, comes to represent this complexity. Wah associates the word with his Chinese grandfather and assumes it is Chinese in origin; as he learns better he comes to understand the confusions caused by his mixtures of genealogies and languages. *Diamond Grill* thus becomes a reflection on the ways in which one's personal history is often obscured, and it dramatizes the realization for Wah that identity can never be adequately expressed.

From *Diamond Grill*

IN THE DIAMOND, AT THE END OF A

long green vinyl aisle between booths of chrome, Naugahyde, and Formica, are two large swinging wooden doors, each with a round hatch of face-sized window. Those kitchen doors can be kicked with such a slap they're heard all the way up to the soda fountain. One the other side of the doors, hardly audible to the customers, echoes a jargon of curses, jokes, and cryptic orders. Stack a hots! Half a dozen fry! Hot beef san! Fingers and tongues all over the place jibe and swear You mucka high!—Thloong you!

And outside, running through and around the town, the creeks flow down to the lake with, maybe, a spring thaw. And the prairie sun over the mountains to the east, over my family's shoulders. The journal journey tilts tight-fisted through the gutter of the book, avoiding a place to start—or end. Maps don't have beginnings, just edges. Some frayed and hazy margin of possibility, absence, gap. Shouts in the kitchen. Fish an! Side a fries! Over easy! On brown! I pick up an order and turn, back through the doors, whap! My foot registers more than its own imprint, starts to read the stain of memory.

Thus: a kind of heterocellular recovery reverberates through the busy body, from the foot against the kitchen door on up the leg into the torso and hands, eyes thinking straight ahead, looking through doors and languages, skin recalling its own reconnaissance, cooked into the steamy food, replayed in the folds of elsewhere, always far away, tunneling through the centre of the earth, mouth saying can't forget, mouth saying what I want to know can feed me, what I don't can bleed me.

MIXED GRILL IS AN ENTRÉE
AT THE DIAMOND

and, as in most Chinese-Canadian restaurants in western Canada, is your typical improvised imitation of Empire cuisine. No kippers or kidney for the Chinese cafe cooks, though. They know the authentic mixed grill alright. It is part of their colonial cook's training, learning to serve the superior race in Hong Kong and Victoria properly, mostly as chefs in private elite clubs and homes. But, as the original lamb chop, split lamb kidney, and pork sausage edges its way onto every town cafe menu, its ruddy countenance has mutated into something quick and dirty, not grilled at all, but fried.

Shu composes his mixed grill on top of the stove. He throws on a veal chop, a rib-eye, a couple of pork sausages, bacon, and maybe a little piece of liver or a few breaded sweetbreads if he has those left over from the special. While the meat's sizzling he adds a handful of sliced mushrooms and a few slices of tomato to sauté alongside. He shovels it all, including the browned grease, onto the large oblong platters used only for this dish and steak dinners, wraps the bacon around the sausages, nudges on a scoop of mashed potatoes, a ladle of mixed steamed (actually canned and boiled) vegetables, a stick of celery, and sometimes a couple of flowered radishes. As he lifts the finished dish onto the pickup counter he wraps the corner of his apron around his thumb and wipes the edge of the platter clean, pushes a button that rings a small chime out front, and shouts loudly into the din of the kitchen, whether there's anyone there or not, *mixee grill*!

* * *

YET LANGUAGELESS. MOUTH ALWAYS
A GAUZE, WORDS LOCKED

behind tongue, stopped in and out, what's she saying, what's she want, why's she mad, this woman-silence stuck, struck, stopped—there and back, English and Chinese churning ocean, her languages caught in that loving angry rip tide of children and coercive tradition and authority. Yet.

Grampa Wah's marriage to Florence Trimble is a surprise to most of the other Chinamen in the cafes around southern Saskatchewan, but not to his wife back in China. Kwan Chung-keong comes to Canada in 1892, returns to his small village in Hoiping County in 1900, and stays just long enough to marry a girl from his village and father two daughters and a son. When he returns to Canada in 1904 he has to leave his family behind because the head tax has, in his absence, been raised to five hundred dollars (two years' Canadian wages).[1] He realized he'll never be able to get his family over here so, against the grain for Chinamen, he marries a white woman (Scots-Irish from Trafalgar, Ontario), the cashier in his cafe. They have three boys and four girls and he never goes back to China again.

I don't know how Grampa Wah talks her into it (maybe he doesn't) but somehow Florence lets two of her children be sent off to China as recompense in some patriarchal deal her husband has with his Chinese wife. He rationalizes to her the Confucian idea that a tree may grow as tall as it likes but its leaves will always return to the ground. Harumph, she thinks, but to no avail.

Fred and his older sister are suddenly one day in July 1916 taken to the train station in Swift Current, their train and boat tickets and identities pinned to their coats in an envelope. My grandfather had intended to send number one son but when departure day arrives Uncle Buster goes into hiding. Grampa grabs the next male in line, four-year-old Fred, and, because he is so young, nineteen-year-old Ethel as well, to look after him. He has the word of the conductor that the children will be delivered safely to the boat in Vancouver and from there the connections all the way to Canton have been arranged. Fred, Kwan Foo-Lee, and Ethel, Kwan An-wa, spend the next eighteen years, before returning to Canada, being raised by their Chinese step-mother alongside two half-sisters and a half-brother.

Yet, in the face of this patrimonial horse-trading it is the women who turn it around for my father and Aunty Ethel. Back in Canada my grandmother, a deeply religious lady, applies years of Salvation Army morality to her heathen husband to bring her children home. But he is a gambler and, despite his wife's sadness and Christian outrage, he keeps gambling away the money that she scrapes aside for the kid's return passage.

Meanwhile, the remittance money being sent from Canada to the Chinese wife starts to dwindle when the depression hits. She feels the pinch of supporting these two half-ghosts and, besides, she reasons with my grandfather, young Foo-lee is getting dangerously attracted to the opium crowd. As a small landholder she sells some land to help buy his way back to Canada.

Aunty Ethel's situation is different. She is forced to wait while, back in Canada, Fred convinces his father to arrange a marriage for her with a Chinaman in Moose Jaw. She doesn't get back to Canada until a year later, 1935.

1 In 1885 the Act to Restrict and Regulate Chinese Immigration into Canada was passed, requiring that all Chinese immigrants entering Canada pay a 'head tax' (originally $50 per person). In 1903 the amount was raised to $500.

Yet the oceans of women migrant-tongued words in a double-bind of bossy love and wary double-talk forced to ride the waves of rebellion and obedience through a silence that shutters numb the traffic between eye and mouth and slaps across the face of family, yet these women forced to spit, out of bound-up feet and torsoed hips made-up yarns and foreign scripts unlucky colours zippered lips—yet, to spit, when possible, in the face of the father the son the holy ticket safety-pinned to his lapel—the pileup of twisted curtains intimate ink pious pages partial pronouns translated letters shore-to-shore Pacific jetsam pretending love forgotten history braided gender half-breed loneliness naive voices degraded miscourse racist myths talking gods fact and fiction remembered faced different brothers sisters misery tucked margins whisper zero criss-cross noisy mothers absent fathers high muckamuck husbands competing wives bilingual I's their unheard sighs, their yet still-floating lives.

DIRTY HEATHENS, GRANNY ERICKSON
THINKS OF THE CHINESE,

the whole bunch of them, in their filthy cafes downtown. Just because that boy dresses up and has a little money, she throws herself at him. She and those other girls, they're always horsing around, looking for fun, running off to Gull Lake for a basketball game, a bunch of little liars, messing around in those cars, I know, not getting home until late at night, all fun and no work. I know what they're doing, they can't fool me, oof dah, that Coreen, she'll ruin herself, you wait and see, she'll be back here for help soon enough. Well she can look out for herself, she's not going to get any more of my money, she can just take her medicine, now that she's living with that Chinaman, nobody'll speak to her, the little hussy.

* * *

HIS MOTHER'S FAMILY ARE STERN AND
RELIGIOUS SCOTS/IRISH

railroad people from Ontario. His in-laws, when he marries Coreen Erickson in 1938, are post-WWI economic refugees from Sweden. While he and Ethel have been in China, their brothers and sisters have negotiated particular identities for themselves through the familiarity of a white European small prairie town commonality (albeit colonial democracy). Though he arrives back to everyone struggling through the thirties, they all have their place. They're part of the reputed latest Pleistocene migration staged to the middle of Canada. And they are, then, him and then his and her, and then me and so on, given the impediment, authority and, above all, the possibility of place. He thinks, after he and Ethel's intimidation as half-ghosts in China, that this Petri dish of hope and plenty is a great opportunity through which (and with which) he and his kind can go on, away from, hopefully, the fragmented diaspora, but always with some tag of chance that will continually fire a brand-spanking new trajectory into what has been, after all, an unrelentingly foreign world. Hybridize or disappear; family *in* place.

* * *

Famous Chinese Restaurant
is the name of a

small, strip-mall Chinese cafe a friend of mine eats at once in awhile. We laugh at the innocent pretentiousness of the name, Famous.

But then I think of the pride with which my father names the Diamond Grill. For him, the name is neither innocent nor pretentious. The Diamond, he proudly regales the banquet at the grand opening, is the most modern, up-to-date restaurant in the interior of BC. The angled design of the booths matches the angles of a diamond and the diamond itself stands for good luck. We hope this new restaurant will bring good luck for all our families and for this town. Eat! Drink! Have a good time!

Almost anything in Chinese stands for good luck, it seems. You're not supposed to use words that might bring bad luck. Aunty Ethel is very upset when we choose a white casket for my father's funeral. She says, that no good! White mean death, bad luck!

So I understand something of the dynamics of naming and desire when I think of the names of some Chinese cafes in my family's history. The big one, of course, is the Elite, which we, with no disrespect for the Queen's English, always pronounce the eee-light. In fact, everyone in town pronounces it that way. My dad works in an Elite in Swift Current and that's what he names his cafe in Trail when we move out to BC. Elite is a fairly common Chinese cafe name in the early fifties, but not any more. I see one still on Edmonton Trail in Calgary and I know of one in Revelstoke. I like the resonant undertone in the word *élite*: the privilege to choose. In the face of being denied the right to vote up until 1949,[2] I smile a little at the recognition by the Chinese that choice is, indeed, a privilege.

Other names also play on the margins of fantasy and longing. Grampa Wah owns the Regal in Swift Current and just around the corner are the Venice and the Paris. Just as Chiang escapes to Taiwan my father gets into the New Star in Nelson.[3]

During the fifties and sixties, coincidental with the rise of Canadian nationalism, we find small-town cafes with names like the Canadian, Canada Chinese Take-Out, and, in respect of Hockey Night in Canada, the All Star. Along the border: American-Canadian Cafe and the Ambassador.

One could read more recent trends such as Bamboo Terrace, Heaven's Gate, Pearl Seafood Restaurant, and the Mandarin as indicative of both the recognized exoticization in orientalism as well as, possibly, a slight turn, a deference, pride and longing for the homeland.

Perhaps we might regard more concretely what resonates for us when we walk into places like White Dove Cafe and Hotel in Mossbank Saskatchewan or the even-now famous Disappearing Moon Cafe, 50 East Pender Street, Vancouver, BC.[4]

* * *

2 Prior to 1949 the British Columbia Qualifications of Voters Act of 1872 denied the Chinese and First Nations peoples the right to vote in provincial elections.

3 After the Nationalist government, which took a blue and white star design as its emblem, was defeated by the communists in China in 1949, Chiang Kai-shek fled the mainland with more than one million followers and established a government in exile on Taiwan.

4 Famous because of Sky Lee's novel, *Disappearing Moon Cafe* (1990).

THE RACE TRACK? SWEDISH, CHINESE,
SCOTTISH, IRISH, CANADIAN.

You bet. But somewhere in that stable the purebreds dissolve into paints. The starting gate opens as my father's face implanted on my scowly brow, body rigid. Parts folding into body after body. His father Lucky Jim on the porch singing old Chinese nursery rhymes, tears but a gold-toothed smile always. My mother a smiler too, then her father sour, her mother more sour yet. Temper. The Teacher telling us who we get to be, to write down what our fathers are. Race, race, race. English, German, Doukhobor, Italian. But not Canadian, there's a difference between a race and a country. No matter what, you're what your father is, was, forever. After school. Chink, Limy, Kraut, Wop, Spik. The whole town. Better than the Baker street nickel millionaires[5] my dad calls them. Race makes you different, nationality makes you the same. Sameness is purity. Not the same anything when you're half Swede, quarter Chinese, and quarter Ontario Wasp. The Salvation Army my granny marches with, into the parade of other grannies, uncles, aunts, cousins, half quarter full and distant, all waiting for Saskatchewan to appear for them. Stuttered inventive, invective process. The domain of this track is an ordered fiction, a serious intervention. Until we now know the only fiction here has to be the reader. You know, relative.

* * *

BETTER WATCH OUT FOR THE
CRAW, BETTER WATCH

out for the goat. That's the mix, the breed, the half-breed, metis, quarter-breed, trace-of-a-breed true demi-semi-ethnic polluted rootless living technicolour snarl to complicate the underbelly panavision of racism and bigotry across this country. I know, you're going to say, that's just being Canadian. The only people who call themselves Canadian live in Ontario and have national sea-to-shining-sea twenty-twenty CPR vision.

When I was in elementary school we had to fill out a form at the beginning of each year. The first couple of years I was really confused. The problem was the blank after Racial Origin. I thought, well, this is Canada, I'll put down Canadian. But the teacher said no Freddy, you're Chinese, your racial origin is Chinese, that's what your father is. Canadian isn't a racial identity. That's turned out to be true. But I'm not really Chinese either. Nor were some of the other kids in my class *real* Italian, Doukhobor, or British.

Quite a soup. Heinz 57 Varieties. There's a whole bunch of us who've grown up as resident aliens, living in the hyphen. Like the Chinese kids who came over after 1949 couldn't take me into their confidence. I always ended up playing on the other team, against them, because they were foreign and I was white enough to be on the winning team. When I visited China and I told the guide of our tour group that I was Chinese he just laughed at me. I don't blame him. He, for all his racial purity so characteristic

5 That is, those who act as if they have a million dollars but really only have a million nickels.

of mainland Chinese, was much happier thinking of me as a Canadian, something over there, white, Euro. But not Chinese.

That could be the answer in this country. If you're pure anything you can't be Canadian. We'll save that name for all the mixed bloods in this country and when the cities have Heritage Days and ethnic festivals there'll be a group that I can identify with, the Canadians. When the government gives out money for cultural centres we'll get ours too. These real Canadians could gain a legitimate marginalized position. The French-Canadians would have to be Québécois, the Mennonites Mennonite, Brits Brit. And if you're a Scot from Hamilton or a Jew from Winnipeg, then be that; I don't care.

But stop telling me what I'm not, what I can't join, what I can't feel or understand. And don't whine to me about maintaining your ethnic ties to the old country, don't explain the concept of time in terms of a place called Greenwich, don't complain about not being able to find Tootsie Rolls or authentic Mexican food north of the 49th.

Sometimes I'd rather be left alone.

* * *

SITKUM DOLLAH GRAMPA WAH
LAUGHS AS HE FLIPS

a shiny half-dollar coin into the air. I say tails and he laughs too bad Freddy and shows me the head of King George the sixth. Then he puts a quarter into my hand, closes his brown and bony hand over mine, pinches my cheek while he says you good boy Freddy, buy some candy!

Whenever I hear grampa talk like that, high muckamuck, sitkum dollah, I think he's sliding Chinese words into English words just to have a little fun. He has fun alright, but I now realize he also enjoys mouthing the dissonance of encounter, the resonance of clashing tongues, his own membership in the diasporic and nomadic intersections that have occurred in northwest North America over the past one hundred and fifty years.

I don't know, then, that he's using Chinook jargon, the pidgin vocabulary of colonial interaction, the code-switching talkee-talkee of the contact zone.[1]

6 Mary Louise Pratt describes this as the practice of

> *code-switching*, in which speakers switch spontaneously and fluidly between two languages. . . . In the context of fiercely monolingual dominant cultures like that of the United States, code-switching lays claim to a form of cultural power: the power to own but not be owned by the dominant language. Aesthetically, code-switching can be a source of great verbal subtlety and grace as speech dances fluidly and strategically back and forth between two languages and two cultural systems. Code-switching is a rich source of wit, humour, puns, word play, and games of rhythm and rhyme. '"Yo soy la Malinche"', in *Twentieth Century Poetry: From Text to Context*, edited by Peter Verdonk, London: Routledge, 1993: 177.

Pratt's description of the 'contact zone' is equally useful in considering the dynamics of foreignicity:

> The space of colonial encounters, the space in which peoples geographically and historically separated come into contact with each other and establish ongoing relations, usually involving conditions of coercion, radical inequality, and intractable conflict. . . . 'Contact zone' . . . is often synonymous with 'colonial frontier'. But while the latter term is grounded within a European expansionist perspective (the frontier is a frontier only with respect to Europe), 'contact zone' is an attempt to invoke the spatial and temporal copresence of subjects previously separated by geographic and historical disjunctures, and whose trajectories now intersect. By using the

The term grampa uses most is high muckamuck (from *hyu muckamuck*, originally among First Nations meaning plenty to eat and then transformed, through the contact zone, into big shot, big-time operator). He exclaims high muckamuck whenever he sees us get into our best clothes for Sunday school. Or, even sometimes when he gets all spiffed up, arranging his hanky to pouf out of the breast pocket of his suit, angling his tie into a full Windsor, fixing his diamond cuff-links and shaking his arms so the shirt-sleeves will fill out smooth, sticking the gold nugget tie pin through the layers of tie and shirt, brushing some lint off of his trouser leg as he stands to reach up for his best felt hat, and then walking out the door with a twinkle in his eyes chuckling high muckamuck.

Though my grandfather seems to say the phrase with a kind of humorous and testy tone, my father translates high muckamuck into a term of class derision. He doesn't like pretension and, though he certainly works hard to raise our family up a middle-class notch, he'll sideswipe anyone he sees putting on airs or using class advantage.

Don't think you're such a high muckamuck, my dad said to me after my brother Ernie ratted on my driving down Baker Street in Dad's Monarch with my right arm around a girl. It's not class itself, really, but how you use it.

For example, he tears into one of the Baker Street nickel millionaires who picks up a tip from a booth that hasn't been cleaned yet. We all know the tip's there; it's at least a bill because you can see it sticking out from under the plate. As the guy's looking through the menu my dad goes up to him and says jesus christ Murphy what do you think you're doing lifting the girls' tips. They work hard for that money and you got more'n you know what to do with. You think you're such a high muckamuck. You never leave tips yourself and here you are stealing small change. I want you to get out of here and don't come into this cafe again. The guy leaves, cursing at my dad, saying he doesn't know why anyone'd wanna eat this Chink food anyway. He never does come back. A pipsqueak trying to be high muckamuck.

And I only realize, right here on this page, when the cooks in the kitchen swear You mucka high! at me, they've transed the phrase out of their own history here. I thought they were swearing in Chinese.

Whenever my mother uses the term she adds a syllable by saying high mucketymuck.

> term 'contact', I aim to foreground the interactive, improvisational dimensions of colonial encounters so easily ignored or suppressed by diffusionist accounts of conquest and domination. A 'contact' perspective emphasizes how subjects are constituted in and by their relations among colonizers and colonized . . . not in terms of separateness or apartheid, but in terms of copresence, interaction, interlocking understandings and practices, often within radically asymmetrical relations of power. *Imperial Eyes: Travel Writing and Transculturation.* London: Routledge, 1992: 6–7.

See also Monica Kin Gagnon's catalogue essay on Henry Tsang's installation 'Utter Jargon':

> Chinook Jargon was developed initially as a pidgin language amongst west coast First Nations peoples. Used primarily for trade purposes, Chinook Jargon's (roughly) five-hundred word vocabulary can be more specifically traced to the dialect of the Columbia River Chinook with further influences from English, French and Nuu-chah-nulth (a language group located predominantly on the west coast of Vancouver Island). At the height of its usage, Chinook Jargon had an estimated one hundred thousand speakers throughout a region stretching from northern California to Alaska, and from the Rockies to the Pacific Ocean. As Tsang notes, the jargon was unable to resist the dominance of English, and fell out of use during the first half of the 1900s. *Dual Cultures,* Kamloops Art Gallery: Kamloops, 1993: 9. [Wah's note]

* * *

I'M JUST A BABY, MAYBE
SIX MONTHS (.5%)

old. One of my aunts is holding me on her knee. Sitting on the ground in front of us are her two daughters, 50% Scottish. Another aunt, the one who grew up in China with my father, sits on the step with her first two children around her. They are 75% Chinese. There is another little 75% girl cousin, the daughter of another 50% aunt who married a 100% full-blooded Chinaman (full-blooded, from China even). At the back of the black-and-white photograph is my oldest boy cousin; he's 25% Chinese. His mother married a Scot from North Battleford and his sisters married Italians from Trail. So there, spread out on the stoop of a house in Swift Current, Saskatchewan, we have our own little western Canadian multicultural stock exchange.

We all grew up together, in Swift Current, Calgary, Trail, Nelson and Vancouver (27% of John A.'s nation) and only get together now every three years (33%) for a family reunion, to which between 70% and 80% of us show up. Out of fifteen cousins only one (6.6%) married a 100% pure Chinese.

The return on these racialized investments has produced colourful dividends and yielded an annual growth rate that now parallels blue-chip stocks like Kodak and Fuji, though current global market forces indicate that such stocks, by their volatile nature, will be highly speculative and risky. Unexpected developments (like Immigration Acts) could knock estimates for a loop. Always take future projections with either a grain of salt or better still a dash of soy.

* * *

ON THE EDGE OF CENTRE.
JUST OFF MAIN.

Chinatown. The cafes, yes, but further back, almost hidden, the ubiquitous Chinese store—an unmoving stratus of smoke, dusky and quiet, clock ticking. Dark brown wood paneling, some porcelain planters on the windowsill, maybe some goldfish. Goldfish for Gold Mountain men.[7] Not so far, then, from the red carp of their childhood ponds. Brown skin stringy salt-and-pepper beard polished bent knuckles and at least one super-long fingernail for picking. Alone and on the edge of their world, far from the centre, no women, no family. This kind of edge in race we only half suspect as edge. A gap, really. Hollow.

I wander to it, tagging along with my father or with a cousin, sent there to get a jar of some strange herb or balm from an old man who forces salted candies on us or digs for a piece of licorice dirtied with grains of tobacco from his pocket, the background of old men's voices sure and argumentative within this grotto. Dominoes clacking. This store, part of a geography, mysterious to most, a migrant haven edge of

7 Because emigration from China in the second half of the nineteenth century was largely in response to gold rushes in California, British Columbia, and the Yukon, North America came to be referred to as Gold Mountain.

outpost, of gossip, bavardage,[8] foreign tenacity. But always in itself, on the edge of some great fold.

In a room at the back of the Chinese store, or above, like a room fifteen feet over the street din in Vancouver Chinatown, you can hear, amplified through the window, the click-clacking of mah-jong pieces being shuffled over the table tops. The voices from up there or behind the curtain are hot-tempered, powerful, challenging, aggressive, bickering, accusatory, demeaning, bravado, superstitious, bluffing, gossipy, serious, goading, letting off steam, ticked off, fed up, hot under the collar, hungry for company, hungry for language, hungry for luck, edgy.

* * *

AND YOU, OLD, MUMBLING TO
YOURSELF SWEDISH GRAMPA,

what madnesses of northern Europe in 1922 drove you across an ocean to Saskatchewan? Uprooted, lost or new? What are you doing up there, silent on a wooden height in the sun and wind, nailing grain elevator after grain elevator. What sour images immigrated with you to that horizon, that languagelessness? His answer full of angst and sadness.

No. They weren't sour. Up here nailing nailing, the pictures of Uppsala and Vastmanland, my father cutting cordwood in the forest, the old city, streets and friends, this is erased slowly and softly, empty prairie wind whipped into the corners of my eyes, my mind, memory hammered into, day after day on the scaffold. But to hell with it, it's work.

This sky is the world now.

I know no one except for a few others on this job. On Saturday we'll have a few beers, relax a bit. Not like back home. Too much church.

After the war, lots of work. My brother got a good job in Göteborg, in the shipyards. He suggested we move there, he could get me on easily he said. But really, it was the same old thing. I wanted something different.

This sky is different: larger, bluer, farther. Maybe it will be different here. Maybe I will be different.

Smell this pine we're working with, still wet and bleeding pitch, turpentine. They say all our wood here comes from the mountains to the west. I believe it. You can smell that hot summer wind blowing pine bite through the forests anywhere, everywhere, over this prairie, over this ocean.

* * *

ANOTHER CHIP ON MY SHOULDER
IS THE APPROPRIATION

of the immigrant identity. I see it all over the place. Even one of the country's best-known writers has said We are all immigrants to this place even if we were born

8 French term for 'prattle' or 'chatter'.

here.[9] Can't these people from *central* leave anything to itself? Why deny the immigrant his or her real world? Why be in such a rush to dilute? Those of us who have already been genetically diluted need our own space to figure it out. I don't want to be inducted into someone else's story, or project. Particularly one that would reduce and usurp my family's residue of ghost values to another status quo. Sorry, but I'm just not interested in this collective enterprise erected from the sacrosanct great railway imagination dedicated to harvesting a dominant white cultural landscape. There's a whole forest of us out here who don't like clear-cut, suspect the mechanical purity of righteous, clear, shining, Homelite Americas, chainsaws whining, just across the valley.

No way I'll let these chips fall where they may.

* * *

I HARDLY EVER GO INTO KING'S
FAMILY RESTAURANT

because, when it comes to Chinese cafes and Chinatowns, I'd rather be transparent. Camouflaged enough so they know I'm there but can't see me, can't get to me. It's not safe. I need a clear coast for a getaway. Invisible. I don't know who I am in this territory and maybe don't want to. Yet I love to wander into Toronto's Chinatown and eat tofu and vegetables at my favourite barbecue joint and then meander indolently through the crowds listening to the tones and watching the dark eyes, the black hair. Sometimes in a store, say, I'm picking up a pair of new Kung-fu sandals and the guy checks my Mastercard as I sign and he says Wah! You Chinese? heh heh heh! because he knows I'm not. Physically, I'm racially transpicuous and I've come to prefer that mode.

I want to be there but don't want to be seen being there. By the time I'm ten I'm only white. Until 1949 the only Chinese in my life are relatives and old men. Very few Chinese kids my age. After '49, when the Canadian government rescinds its Chinese Exclusion Act, a wave of young Chinese immigrate to Canada. Nelson's Chinese population visibly changes in the early fifties. In a few years there are enough teenage Chinese kids around to not only form an association, the Nelson Chinese Youth Association, but also a basketball team. And they're good, too. Fast, smart. I play on the junior high school team and when the NYCA team comes to play us, I know a lot of the Chinese guys. But my buddies at school call them Chinks and geeks and I feel a little embarrassed and don't talk much with the Chinese kids. I'm white enough to get away with it and that's what I do.

But downtown, working in the cafe, things are different. Some of the young guys start working at our cafe and my dad's very involved with helping them all settle into their new circumstances. He acts as an interpreter for a lot of the legal negotiations. Everyone's trying to reunite with long-lost relatives. Anyway, I work alongside some of these new Chinese and become friends.

Shu brings his son over around 1953 and Lawrence is in the cafe business for the rest of his working life. Lawrence and I work together in the Diamond until I leave small-town Nelson for university at the coast. We're good friends. Even today, as

9 See Margaret Atwood, page 777.

ageing men, we always exchange greetings whenever we meet on the street. But I hardly ever go into his cafe.

So now, standing across the street from King's Family Restaurant, I know I'd love to go in there and have a dish of beef and greens, but he would know me, he would have me clear in his sights, not Chinese but stained enough by genealogy to make a difference. When Lawrence and I work together, him just over from China, he's a boss's son and I'm a boss's son. His pure Chineseness and my impure Chineseness don't make any difference to us in the cafe. But I've assumed a dull and ambiguous edge of difference in myself; the hyphen always seems to demand negotiation.

I decide, finally, to cross the street. I push myself through the door and his wife, Fay, catches me with the corner of her eye. She doesn't say anything and I wonder if she recognizes me. The white waitress takes my order and I ask if Lawrence is in the kitchen. He is, she says.

I go through Lawrence's kitchen door like I work there. I relish the little kick the door is built to take. He's happy to see me and stops slicing chicken on the chopping block, wipes his hands on his apron and shakes my hand. How's your mother? Whatchyou doing here? How's Ernie and Donnie? Family, that's what it is. The politics of the family.

He says something to the cook, a young guy. Then he turns to me and says hey Freddy, did you know this is your cousin? He's from the same area near Canton. His name is Quong. Then in Chinese, he gives a quick explanation to Quong; no doubt my entire Chinese family history. Lawrence smiles at me like he used to when were kids: he knows something I don't. I suffer the negative capability[10] of camouflage.

How many cousins do I have, I wonder. Thousands maybe. How could we recognize one another? Names.

The food, the names, the geography, the family history—the filiated dendrita[11] of myself displayed before me. I can't escape, and I don't want to, for a moment. Being there, in Lawrence's kitchen, seems one of the surest places I know. But then after we've exchanged our mutual family news and I've eaten a wonderful dish of tofu and vegetables, back outside, on the street, all my ambivalence gets covered over, camouflaged by a safety net of class and colourlessness—the racism within me that makes and consumes that neutral (white) version of myself, that allows me the sad privilege of being, in this white white world, not the target but the gun.

* * *

I'M NOT AWARE IT'S CALLED
TOFU UNTIL AFTER

I leave home. It's one of those ingredients that are transparent to me in the multitude of Cantonese dishes I grow up eating. So, until my dad tells me what that white stuff

10 A term coined by the English Romantic poet John Keats (1795–1821); he defined it as the ability to entertain 'uncertainties, Mysteries, doubts, without any irritable reaching after fact and reason'.

11 That is, the related threads of Wah's inheritance that he sees before him; the phrase 'filiated dendrita' combines the idea of familial relationships (specifically, paternal acknowledgement of a son) with the image of treelike branches of mineral crystals or nerve cells.

is called, I'm unable to order it during my forays into Vancouver Chinatown. Even when I first try it out on a waitress, she looks puzzled and says something in Chinese to her father who's hanging out by the till. She comes back to my booth and says o.k., you mean dow-uw foo, bean curd!

But over the past forty years, tofu has come into its own in North America, taking a choice place among the burgeoning macrobiotic and cholesterol-conscious diet fads. Available at any supermarket. If I'd been smart in the sixties I would have invested in soybean futures. There's even a little hippie tofu industry that has sprung up to supply the organic craze marketed through local co-ops. I wear my Kootenay Tofu T-shirt with pride.

This is all to my delight because tofu is, after rice, basic to my culinary needs. I've rendered this custard-like cake from pureed soybeans; I've pressed it, frozen it, mashed it, and cubed it; I've boiled, steamed, fried and maintained it; I even use Tofunaise as a substitute for mayonnaise. One summer I planted soybeans with some improbably fantasy of building my own tofu from the ground up. My attraction to this food is more than belief; it's a deep need, obsessive.

My basic all-time favourite dish is braised bean curd with vegetables. Cut each cake of tofu into one-inch cubes and very gently stir-fry along with some chopped green onion until the outer surface is lightly browned and the cake holds together without crumbling. Add some sliced vegetables: bok choy, carrots, green or red pepper, whatever you have around. Black Chinese mushrooms and water chestnuts are a nice option. As the dish is finishing, stir in a couple tablespoons of soy sauce and then some cornstarch mixed in water for thickening. This tasty and nutritious melange is spooned over steamed rice and washed down with oolong tea. There. That's a lunch.

* * *

JUST ANOTHER TIGHT LIPPED HIGH
MUCKAMUCK RECEPTION LISTENING

to the whining groans of an old-fart pink-faced investor worried about the Hong Kong real estate takeover, a wincing glance as he moans that UBC has become the University of a Billion Chinks, tense shoulder scrunch as I'm introduced, with emphasis on the Wah, to his built-and-fought-for-inheritor-of-the-country arrogant, raised-eyebrow, senior executive entrepreneur boss pig business associate—so that sometimes my cast of frown-furled brow looks right on past a bent nail, eyes screwed over the lake, into some trees, the tangle of bush impenetrable before they clear cut birch bark pocked crop settin' chokers'd break yer ass so fast you wouldn't even wanna look at a goddamned tree let alone cut through the crap backoff this Havoc old Hav Ok will stuff it in your cry this magic leaping tree will never be the apple of anyone else's eye because this is the last stand which for you is just a weekend pick-em-up truck so fuck the Husky Tower hustle and the Sleepy R train games this rusty nail has been here forever in fact the real last spike is yet to be driven.

* * *

HIS HALF-DREAM IN THE STILL-
DARK BREATHING SILENCE IS

the translation from the bitter-green cloudiness of the winter melon soup in his dream to the sweet-brown lotus root soup he knows Shu will prepare later this morning for the Chinese staff in the cafe. He moves the taste of the delicate nut-like lotus seeds through minor degrees of pungency and smokiness to the crunchy slices of lotus root suspended in the salty-sweet beef broth. This silent rehearsal of the memory of taste moves into his mind so that the first language behind his closed eyes is a dreamy play-by-play about making beef and lotus root soup. Simple: a pound of short ribs and a pound of lotus root in a small pot of water with some soy sauce and salt, a little sliced ginger, maybe a few red Chinese dates. Shu will surely touch it with a piece of dried tangerine peel because it's close to Christmas. He feels his tongue start to move as his mouth waters at the palpable flavour of words.

* * *

HE USUALLY PARKS BEHIND THE
CAFE. COMING DOWN

the hill he crosses Baker street, turns left behind Wood Vallance Hardware, drives halfway down the alley, manoeuvres around some garbage cans, and noses into his parking spot by a loading dock.

Fred Wah
Diamond Grill
Private

is painted on the dirty cement wall. He climbs the wooden steps to the back door of the cafe and holds open the spring-hinged screen door with his left foot while he unlocks both the dead bolt and a padlock. The smoky glass in the top half of this door is covered by a heavy metal grill and, as he jars it open with a slight body-check, the door clangs and rattles a noisy hyphen between the muffled winter outside and the silence of the warm and waiting kitchen inside.

1996

Maria Campbell

b. 1940

Métis writer Maria Campbell was born in northern Saskatchewan and raised in a 'road-allowance' community—a settlement built on a public right-of-way that has been set aside for the construction of roads. In *Halfbreed* (1973), her autobiographical account of growing up in northern Saskatchewan as the eldest child in a large Métis family, Campbell explains how, after the defeat of the Métis in the Northwest Rebellion cost them the open lands they had historically held and after their once abundant game was no longer available, they settled illegally on such road allowances, each generation becoming more defeated and poorer than the last.

The Métis culture out of which Campbell comes is warm and close-knit, but the stability of her own family was disrupted by her mother's early death. At fifteen, trying to find some way to keep her siblings from being dispersed by social agencies, Campbell made a disastrous marriage that eventually left her in Vancouver with no secondary education and no job, the single mother of an infant. Placing her child in the care of nuns, she became a prostitute, an alcoholic, a drug addict, and a mule for cross-border smugglers. Although she tried to overcome her addictions in Vancouver and later when she was living in the Calgary area, she was not able to break free until she joined Alcoholics Anonymous and became an activist in Métis, Native, and women's affairs.

Campbell's adult life has been divided into three areas: working as an activist, teaching, and writing. She has been writer-in-residence at the Universities of Alberta and Saskatchewan, as well as at the Whitehorse, Prince Albert, and Regina Public Libraries, and has been playwright-in-residence at the Persephone Theatre in Saskatoon. She has taught literature, Native studies, and drama at Athabasca University and Brandon University and at the Banff School of Fine Arts. She currently teaches at the University of Saskatchewan. Her numerous awards include the National Aboriginal Achievement Award, the Gabriel Dumont Medal of Merit, a Dora Mavor Moore Award, and the Chief Crowfoot Award. She has been given honorary degrees by the Universities of Athabasca, York, and Regina.

Halfbreed, which Campbell is said to have begun writing as a letter to herself and not for publication, is a landmark in North American Native literature. It became a bestseller in Canada, and, making its way onto school and university reading lists, it called attention to the new wave of Native writing that was emerging in Canadian literature. Campbell has since written three children's books as a way of preserving aspects of Métis culture and heritage. Two of these, *People of the Buffalo* (1975) and *Riel's People* (1978), describe aspects of the culture of the Canadian Plains people and tell how the arrival of white settlers adversely affected traditional life on the prairies. *Little Badger and the Fire Spirit* (1977) is a literary folktale set within a contemporary framework: in it, she tells the story of a blind boy who attempts a perilous journey to acquire fire for his people.

Campbell has also written four plays, the best known of which is *Jessica*, a semi-autobiographical story of a Métis woman's journey of self-discovery, which she co-wrote with Linda Griffiths. It opened in 1986 in Toronto and won the Dora Mavor Moore Award for outstanding new play that year. The play is reprinted in *The Book of Jessica: A Theatrical Transformation* (1989), where it is framed by an interwoven dialogue between Campbell and Griffiths that describes the story of the play's creation and shows the difficulties that emerged in this cross-cultural project, especially when questions arose about who had control over the story to be told.

Stories of the Road-Allowance People (1995), illustrated by Sherry Farrell Racette, is a collection of eight stories Campbell translated from the Cree-Mitchif language spoken by the Plains Métis. In order to tell these stories of 'dem peoples dat belong in dah old days' and how 'Dere starting to come back again / tank dah God for dat', she cast them in English as spoken by the Métis of her community. To reflect the rhythms of this dialect the stories are set as lines of verse rather than as continuous prose.

Jacob

Mistupuch he was my granmudder.
He come from Muskeg
dat was before he was a reservation.
My granmudder he was about twenty-eight when he
marry my granfawder.
Dat was real ole for a woman to marry in dem days
But he was an Indian doctor
I guess dats why he wait so long.

Ooh he was a good doctor too
All the peoples dey say dat about him.
He doctor everybody dat come to him
an he birt all dah babies too.
Jus about everybody my age
my granmudder he birt dem.

He marry my granfawder around 1890.
Dat old man he come to him for doctoring
and when he get better
he never leave him again.

Dey get married dah Indian way
an after dat my granfawder
he help him with all hees doctoring.
Dats dah way he use to be a long time ago.
If dah woman he work
den dah man he help him an if dah man he work
dah woman he help.
You never heerd peoples fighting over whose job he was
dey all know what dey got to do to stay alive.

My granfawder his name he was Kannap
but dah whitemans dey call him Jim Boy
so hees Indian name he gets los.
Dats why we don know who his peoples dey are.

We los lots of our relations like dat.
Dey get dah whitemans name
den no body
he knows who his peoples dey are anymore.

Sometimes me
I tink dats dah reason why we have such a hard time
us peoples.
Our roots dey gets broken so many times.
Hees hard to be strong you know
when you don got far to look back for help.

Dah whitemans
he can look back tousands of years
cause him
he write everything down.
But us peoples
we use dah membering
an we pass it on by telling stories an singing songs.
Sometimes we even dance dah membering.

But all dis trouble you know
he start after we get dah new names
cause wit dah new names
he come a new language an a new way of living.
Once a long time ago
I could 'ave told you dah story of my granfawder Kannap
an all his peoples but no more.
All I can tell you now
is about Jim Boy
an hees story hees not very ole.

Well my granmudder Mistupuch
he never gets a whitemans name an him
he knowed lots of stories.
Dat ole lady
he even knowed dah songs.
He always use to tell me
one about an ole man call Jacob.

Dat old man you know
he don live to far from here.
Well hees gone now
but dis story he was about him when he was alive.

Jacob him
he gets one of dem new names when dey put him in dah
residential school.
He was jus a small boy when he go
an he don come home for twelve years.

Twelve years!
Dats a long time to be gone from your peoples.
He can come home you know
cause dah school he was damn near two hundred miles
away.
His Mommy and Daddy dey can go and see him
cause deres no road in dem days
an dah Indians dey don gots many horses
'specially to travel dat far.

Dats true you know
not many peoples in dem days dey have horses.
Its only in dah comic books an dah picture shows dey
gots lots of horses.
He was never like dat in dah real life.

Well Jacob him
he stay in dat school all dem years an when he come
home he was a man.
While he was gone
his Mommy and Daddy dey die so he gots nobody.
And on top of dat
nobody he knowed him cause he gots a new name.
My granmudder
he say dat ole man he have a hell of time.
No body he can understand dat
unless he happen to him.

Dem peoples dat go away to dem schools
an come back you know dey really suffer.
No matter how many stories we tell
we'll never be able to tell
what dem schools dey done to dah peoples
an all dere relations.

Well anyways
Jacob he was jus plain pitiful
He can talk his own language

He don know how to live in dah bush.
It's a good ting da peoples dey was kine
cause dey help him dah very bes dey can.
Well a couple of summers later
he meet dis girl
an dey gets married.

Dat girl he was kine
an real smart too.
He teach Jacob how to make an Indian living.

Dey have a good life togedder an after a few years
dey have a boy.
Not long after dat
dey raise two little girls dat was orphans.

Jacob and his wife dey was good peoples
Boat of dem dey was hard working
an all dah peoples
dey respec dem an dey come to Jacob for advice.

But dah good times dey was too good to las
cause one day
dah Preeses
dey comes to dah village with dah policemans.
Dey come to take dah kids to dah school.

When dey get to Jacob hees house
he tell dem dey can take his kids.

Dah Prees he tell him
he have to lets dem go cause dats the law.
Well dah Prees
he have a big book
an dat book he gots dah names
of all dah kids
an who dey belongs to.

He open dat book an ask Jacob for his name
an den he look it up.
'Jacob' he say
'you know better you went to dah school an you know
dah edjication hees important.'

My granmudder Mistupuch
he say Jacob he tell that Prees
'Yes I go to dah school
an dats why I don wan my kids to go.
All dere is in dat place is suffering.'

Dah Prees he wasn happy about dat
an he say to Jacob
'But the peoples dey have to suffer Jacob
cause dah Jesus he suffer.'

'But dah Jesus he never lose his language an
hees peoples' Jacob tell him.
'He stay home in hees own land and he do hees
suffering.'

Well da Prees him
he gets mad
an he tell him its a sin to tink like dat
an hees gonna end up in purgatory for dem kind of
words.

But Jacob he don care
cause far as hees concern
purgatory
he can be worse den the hell he live with trying to
learn hees language and hees Indian ways.

He tell dat Prees
he don even know who his people dey are.
'Dah Jesus he knowed his Mommy and Daddy'
Jacob he tell him
'and he always knowed who his people dey are.'

Well
dah Prees he tell him
if he wans to know who hees people dey are
he can tell him dat
an he open in dah book again.

'Your Dad hees Indian name he was Awchak'
dah prees he say
'I tink dat means Star in your language.
He never gets a new name cause he never become a
Christian.'

Jacob he tell my granmudder
dat when da Prees he say hees Dad hees name
his wife he start to cry real hard.

'Jacob someday you'll tank the God we done dis.'
dah Prees he tell him
an dey start loading up dah kids on dah big wagons.
All dah kids dey was crying an screaming
An dah mudders
dey was chasing dah wagons.

Dah ole womans
dey was all singing dah det song
an none of the mans
dey can do anyting.
Dey can
cause the policemans dey gots guns.

When dah wagons dey was all gone
Jacob he look for hees wife but he can find him no place.
An ole woman he see him an he call to him
'Pay api noosim'
'Come an sit down my granchild I mus talk to you.
Hees hard for me to tell you dis but dat Prees
hees book he bring us bad news today.
He tell you dat Awchak he was your Daddy.
My granchild
Awchak he was your wife's Daddy too.'

Jacob he tell my granmudder
he can cry when he hear dat.
He can even hurt inside.
Dat night he go looking
an he fine hees wife in dah bush
Dat woman he kill hisself.

Jacob he say
dah ole womans
dey stay wit him for a long time
an dey sing healing songs an dey try to help him
But he say he can feel nutting.
Maybe if he did
he would have done dah same ting.

For many years Jacob he was like dat
just dead inside.

Dah peoples dey try to talk wit him
but it was no use.
Hees kids dey growed up
an dey come home an live wit him.
'I made dem suffer' he tell my granmudder.
'Dem kids dey try so hard to help me.'

Den one day
his daughter he get married an he have a baby.
He bring it to Jacob to see.
Jacob he say
he look at dat lil baby
an he start to cry and he can stop.
He say he cry for himself an his wife
an den he cry for his Mommy and Daddy.
When he was done
he sing dah healing songs dah ole womans
dey sing to him a long time ago.

Well you know
Jacob he die when he was an ole ole man.
An all hees life
he write in a big book
dah Indian names of all dah Mommies and Daddies.
An beside dem
he write dah old names and
dah new names of all dere kids.

An for dah res of hees life
he fight dah government to build schools on the
reservation.
'The good God he wouldn of make babies come
from Mommies and Daddies'
he use to say
'if he didn want dem to stay home
an learn dere language
an dere Indian ways.'

You know
dat ole man was right.
No body he can do dat.

Take all dah babies away. Hees jus not right.
Long time ago
dah old peoples dey use to do dah naming
an dey do dah teaching too.

If dah parents dey have troubles
den dah aunties and dah uncles
or somebody in dah family
he help out till dah parents dey gets dere life work
out.
But no one
no one
he ever take dah babies away from dere peoples.

You know my ole granmudder
Mistupuch
he have lots of stories about people like Jacob.
Good ole peoples
dat work hard so tings will be better for us.
We should never forget dem ole peoples.

1995

Gwendolyn MacEwen

1941–1987

Born in Toronto and raised there and in Winnipeg, Gwendolyn MacEwen published her first poem at seventeen in the *Canadian Forum* and left school a year later to become a writer. By the time she was twenty she had privately published two chapbooks, *Sela* (1961) and *The Drunken Clock* (1961). Two years later she had her first commercial publication with *The Rising Fire*. She subsequently produced eight more poetry collections: *A Breakfast for Barbarians* (1966); *The Shadow-Maker* (1969); *The Armies of the Moon* (1972); *The Fire Eaters* (1976); *The T.E. Lawrence Poems* (1982), a sequence about the man known as Lawrence of Arabia; and *Afterworlds* (1987), which—like *The Shadow-Maker*—received a Governor General's Award. In addition, there are two volumes of selected poetry: *Magic Animals* (1975), which also contains a few new poems; and *Earthlight* (1982). Two volumes of *The Poetry of Gwendolyn MacEwen*, edited by Margaret Atwood and Barry Callaghan, appeared posthumously: *Vol. 1: The Early Years* (1993) and *Vol. 2: The Later Years* (1994).

As well as writing poetry, MacEwen worked with a number of other literary forms. She wrote plays and dramatic documentaries for CBC radio, one of which, 'Terror and Erebus' (a poetic drama about the Franklin expedition), is reprinted in *Afterworlds*. She created a new version of Euripides' play *The Trojan Women*, and with Greek singer Nikos Tsingos, to whom she was married for six years, translated two long poems by the Greek poet Yannis Ritsos (the play and translations appear in *Trojan Women*, 1981). Her modern adaptation of Aristophanes' *The Birds* appeared in 1983.

MacEwen wrote two novels, *Julian the Magician* (1963) and *King of Egypt, King of Dreams* (1971), which reflected her interest in the richness of myth and history from a variety of periods and cultures. (The Mediterranean and the Middle East were of particular interest to her, and she travelled extensively in those areas; *Mermaids and Ikons: A Greek Summer*, 1978, is a memoir of one journey.) Even her two collections of short stories, *Noman* (1972) and *Noman's Land* (1985), although set in 'Kanada', exhibit her predisposition for the foreign and the fantastic. MacEwen's imaginative world can also be seen in three children's books—*The Chocolate Moose* (1979), *The Honeydrum: Seven Tales from Arab Lands* (1983), and *Dragon Sandwiches* (1987).

The diverse blend of mythologies that MacEwen locates beneath the engaging surfaces of her work mix with commonplace Canadian experience (as in 'The Portage') or with the bizarre romance of war (in *The T.E. Lawrence Poems*) or with the mysteries of the ancient past (as in *King of Egypt, King of Dreams*). Out of these juxtapositions, MacEwen creates paired oppositions, such as spirit and flesh, the magical and the mundane, father and son, male and female. Such contraries were central in her world view, in which the occult and the everyday world exist together in harmonious simultaneity, and one must learn to move between them with ease.

Inhabiting these realms is a recurrent figure that Margaret Atwood identified as MacEwen's male muse, or animus, ('MacEwen's Muse' in *Second Words*, 1982). Sometimes a god incarnate, sometimes man in divine transmutation, this figure can ascend to universal levels or fall into the commonplace specifics of life and death. He appears as Icarus, Manzini, Julian, Noman, Akhenaton (the Egyptian pharaoh), and T.E. Lawrence.

MacEwen often used these figures as oracular I-narrators, and through a humorous blend of incantatory diction and the casual cadences of speech, she both affirms their vitality and undercuts their heroic dimensions. As the poet-critic D.G. Jones observed, MacEwen was a poet who could 'say then what most will not, that we are ambiguous, that our exorbitant hungers and satisfactions are both erotic and holy, that their incestuous relations may spawn a bestial phantasmagoria or project an angelic visitation' (Introduction to *Earthlight*).

MacEwen's life was a highly creative one, though brief and difficult (she struggled with and for a long time conquered her problems with alcohol, and her relationships with men, including a brief marriage to the poet Milton Acorn, were troubled ones); it has been the subject of two stage plays.

Icarus[1]

Feather and wax, the artful wings
bridge a blue gulf between
the stiff stone tower
and its languid god, fat sky.

1 Character from Greek mythology who with his father, Daedalus (the master craftsman and inventor), escaped the island of Crete by means of wings made of wax and feathers. Forgetful of Daedalus's warning not to fly too close to the sun, which might melt the wax, Icarus soared too high and fell to his death.

The boy, bent to the whim of wind,
the blue, and the snarling sun
form a brief triumvirate
—flesh, feather, light—
locked in the jaws of the noon
they rule with fleeting liberty.

These are the wings, then,
a legacy of hollow light—
feathers, a quill to write
white poetry across the sky.

Through the mouth of the air, the boy
sees his far father, whose muscled flight
is somehow severed from his own.
Two blinking worlds, and Daedalus'
unbound self is a thing apart.

You, bound for that other area
know that this legacy of mindflight
is all you have to leave me.

The boy, Icarus, twists the threads of his throat
and his eyes argue with the sun
on a flimsy parallel, and
the mouth of the sun eager, eager,
smuggles a hot word to the boy's ear.

But flying, locked in dark dream,
I see Queen Dream, Queen Flight,
the last station of the poet
years above my brow, and

Something, something in the air,
in the light's flight, in the vaguely
voluptuous arc of the wings
drives a foreign rhythm into his arms
his arms which are lean, white willows.

Icarus feels his blood race to his wrist
in a marathon of red light. Swifter,
swift, he tears away the slow veil
from his tendons; the playful biceps
sing; they wish new power to the beautiful
false wings

and the boy loops up into tall cobalt.
His hair is a swirl of drunken light,
his arms are wet blades; wings wed with arms.

You knew
I would get drunk on beauty.
The famous phantom quill
would write me, pull me
through the eye
of needle noon.

Crete is a huge hump of a black whore beneath him.
Her breasts, two wretched mountains
tremble under his eye.
All is black, except the sun in slow explosion;
a great war strangles his vision
and knots his flying nerve.
Black, and fire, and the boy.

You and your legacy!
You knew I would try to
slay the sunlight.

Look, Icarus has kissed the sun
and it sucks the wax,
feathers and wax.
The wings are melting!

The boy Icarus is lean and beautiful.
His body grows limp and falls.
It is cruel poetry set
to the tempo of lightning; it is too swift,
this thin descent.

On the lips of the Aegean:
globules of wax,
strands of wet light,

the lean poem's flesh
tattered and torn
by a hook
of vengeful fire . . .

Combustion of brief feathers

1961

Manzini:[1] Escape Artist

now there are no bonds except the flesh; listen—
there was this boy, Manzini, stubborn with
gut stood with black tights and a turquoise
leaf across his sex

and smirking while the big
brute tied his neck arms legs, Manzini
naked waist up and white with sweat

struggled. Silent, delinquent, he
was suddenly all teeth and knee, straining slack
and excellent with sweat, inwardly

wondering if Houdini would take as long
as he; fighting time and the drenched
muscular ropes, as though his tendons were worn
on the outside—

as though his own guts were the ropes
encircling him; it was beautiful; it was thursday; listen—
there was this boy, Manzini

finally free, slid as snake from
his own sweet agonized skin, to throw his entrails
white upon the floor
with a cry of victory—

now there are no bonds except the flesh,
but listen, it was thursday, there was this boy,
Manzini—

1966

1 Manzini was an American magician whom MacEwen met in the 1960s. As an escape artist, he worked in the tradition of the famous early twentieth-century magician Harry Houdini (born Ehrich Weiss, 1874–1926), who was known for the rapidity of his dramatic escapes from chains, ropes, jail cells, and straitjackets.

The Portage

We have travelled far with ourselves
and our names have lengthened;
    we have carried ourselves
on our backs, like canoes
in a strange portage, over trails,
insinuating leaves
and trees dethroned like kings,
    from water-route to
    water-route
seeking the edge, the end,
the coastlines of this land.

On earlier journeys we
were master ocean-goers
going out, and evening always found us
spooning the ocean from our boat,
    and gulls, undiplomatic
    couriers brought us
cryptic messages from shore
till finally we sealords vowed
we'd sail no more.

Now under a numb sky, sombre
cumuli weigh us down;
the trees are combed for winter
and bears' tongues have melted
all the honey;
    there is a lourd[1]
suggestion of thunder;
subtle drums under
the candid hands of Indians
are trying to tell us
why we have come.

But now we fear movement
and now we dread stillness;
we suspect it was the land
that always moved, not our ships;

1 Sluggish, dull.

we are in sympathy with the fallen
trees; we cannot relate
    the causes of our grief.
We can no more carry
our boats our selves
over these insinuating trails.

1969

Dark Pines under Water

This land like a mirror turns you inward
And you become a forest in a furtive lake;
The dark pines of your mind reach downward,
You dream in the green of your time,
Your memory is a row of sinking pines.

Explorer, you tell yourself this is not what you came for
Although it is good here, and green;
You had meant to move with a kind of largeness,
You had planned a heavy grace, an anguished dream.

But the dark pines of your mind dip deeper
And you are sinking, sinking, sleeper
In an elementary world;
There is something down there and you want it told.

1969

The Real Enemies[1]

In that land where the soul aged long before the body,
My nameless men, my glamorous bodyguards,
                                        died for me.
My deadly friends with their rouged lips and pretty eyes
        died for me; *my bed of tulips* I called them,
        who wore every color but the white
        that was mine alone to wear.

1 The narrative voice of this poem, and of the other poems in *The T.E. Lawrence Poems* is that of Thomas Edward Lawrence (1888–1935), known as Lawrence of Arabia. Author, archaeologist, and soldier, Lawrence led a successful rebellion of the Arabs against the Turks during the First World War and became a near-legendary figure. He subsequently assumed the name T.E. Shaw and retired to self-imposed obscurity to write *The Seven Pillars of Wisdom* (1926), his account of his Arabian adventure.

But they could not guard me against the real enemies—
Omnipotence, and the Infinite—
those beasts the soul invents
and then bows down before.
The real enemies were not the men of Fakhri Pasha,[2] nor
Were they even of this world.
One could never conquer them,
Never. Hope was another of them. Hope, most brutal of all.

For those who thought clearly, failure was the only goal.
Only failure could redeem you, there where the soul aged
long before the body.
You failed at last, you fell into the delicious light
and were free.

And there was much honor in this;
it was a worthy defeat.
Islam is surrender—the passionate surrender of the self,
the puny self, to God.
We declared a Holy War upon Him and were victors as He won.

1982

2 The leader of the Turkish forces.

The Death of the Loch Ness Monster

Consider that the thing has died before we proved it ever lived
and that it died of loneliness, dark lord of the loch,
fathomless Worm, great Orm,[1] this last of our mysteries—
haifend ane meikill fin on ilk syde
with ane taill and ane terribill heid—
and that it had no tales to tell us, only that it lived there,
lake-locked, lost in its own coils,
waiting to be found; in the black light of midnight
surfacing, its whole elastic length unwound,
and the sound it made as it broke the water
was the single plucked string of a harp—

1 Dragon, serpent, worm (Middle English).

this newt or salamander, graceful as a swan,
this water-snake, this water-horse, this water-dancer.

Consider him tired of pondering the possible existence of man
whom he thinks he has sighted sometimes on the shore,
and rearing up from the purple churning water,
weird little worm head swaying from side to side,
he denies the vision before his eyes;
his long neck, swan of Hell, a silhouette against the moon,
his green heart beating its last,
his noble, sordid soul in ruins.

Now the mist is a blanket of doom, and we pluck from the depths
a prize of primordial slime—
the beast who was born from some terrible ancient kiss,
lovechild of unspeakable histories,
this ugly slug, half blind no doubt, and very cold,
his head which is horror to behold
no bigger than our own;
whom we loathe, for his kind ruled the earth before us,
who died of loneliness in a small lake in Scotland,
and in his mind's dark land,
where he dreamed up his luminous myths, the last of which was man.

1987

Polaris

or, Gulag Nightscapes[1]

At midnight in this foreign country
in the vivid snow as cold as vodka
you stand watching constellations which are ever
so slowly turning
and the great bear of Russia is ever so slowly turning
round and round in the forest behind you.

1 The Gulag was the system of forced labour camps under the Soviet regime in Russia from 1919, made infamous in Alexander Solzhenitsyn's memoirs of his imprisonment, which were published in English in the 1970s. This poem, responding to enduring Cold War tensions, plays with the fact that 'Polaris' was—as well as the name of the North Star, the fixed point by which mariners once found their way—the name given to one of the first of the ballistic missiles, deployed by the US via submarines and targeted at the USSR in the event of nuclear war.

You ask yourself are you
the fixed centre of this scene
and you will stand here forever witnessing
the movement of stars, politics of the northern sky,
kinesis of snow?

You begin with freedom as a word,
freedom in its bleakest, purest form
and proceed through crazy stations of the compass
to this kingdom of snow where
freedom is a prison; it is
Russia or America or the republic of your mind
where governments and constellations are endlessly rotating
and everything is a lie; there is no governing body,
there is nothing to direct you
on your course, there
is no right course, there is no guiding star.

Yet

Everything points to Polaris—
endlessly still star, endlessly unturning,
Alpha in Ursa Minor,
first letter in the alphabet of midnight, and
America like a giant crystal
is ever so slowly turning, deflecting starlight,
the real and imagined missiles of real and imagined enemies.

If you consult the polestar for the truth
of your present position, you will learn that you have no
position, position is illusion (consider this
endlessly still self, endlessly turning);
this prison is actually your freedom, and
it is you, it is you, you
are the only thing in this frozen night which is really moving.

1987

Don McKay

b. 1942

Born in Owen Sound, Ont., Don McKay grew up in Cornwall, Ont. After attending Bishop's University and the University of Western Ontario, where he received an MA in 1966, he travelled to Wales to complete his Ph.D. at the University College of Swansea. He has taught at the University of Western Ontario and at the University of New Brunswick, where from 1991 to 1996 he edited *The Fiddlehead*, Canada's longest-lived literary magazine. After teaching for twenty-seven years, McKay retired early to write and edit poetry full-time. He now resides in BC with his partner, Jan Zwicky.

McKay is the author of nine books of poetry: *Air Occupies Space* (1973); the long poem *Long Sault* (1975); *Lependu* (1978); *Lightning Ball Bait* (1980); *Birding, or Desire* (1983); *Sanding Down This Rocking Chair on a Windy Night* (1987); *Night Field* (1991); *Apparatus* (1997); and *Another Gravity* (2000). He won a Governor General's Award for *Night Field* and a second for *Another Gravity*.

His intense responses to the natural world in these books have brought him a reputation as an ecological poet, but it is more than just a depth of appreciation for nature that gives power to his writing. In one of the essays published in *Vis à Vis: Fieldnotes on Poetry and Wilderness* (2001), he writes:

By 'wilderness' I want to mean, not just a set of endangered spaces, but the capacity of all things to elude the mind's appropriations. . . . To what degree do we own our houses, hammers, dogs? Beyond that line lies wilderness. We probably experience its presence most often in the negative as dry rot in the basement, a splintered handle, or shit on the carpet. But there is also the sudden angle of perception, the phenomenal surprise which constitutes the sharpened moments of haiku *and imagism. The coat hanger asks a question; the armchair is suddenly crouched: in such defamiliarizations, often arranged by art, we encounter the momentary circumvention of the mind's categories to glimpse some thing's autonomy—its rawness, its* duende [magnetism]*, its alien being.* ('Baler Twine: Thoughts on Ravens, Home, and Nature Poetry')

This drive towards visionary moments means that MacKay's interest in nature extends both to and beyond such things as the literal birds and the imagery of flight found in so many of his poems: their occurrences constitute an urge to understand the meanings those birds convey, the mysterious significance flight holds for the human mind. That idea of flight is seen not only in the arc of a bird's wing gracefully moving on a thermal draft or in the retelling of the mythic tale of Icarus, but also in the metaphorical flights of a hockey skate cutting the ice, of a musical sound entering the ear, and of the precise descent of the blade that the sushi chef swings to slice a morsel of fish.

Birding, or Desire is the book that established McKay's reputation as a master of his craft, a poet's poet. One lyric in particular from that book, 'Kestrels'—which became a signature poem for McKay—provides a good example of the special union he finds between world and art. There the lively and vigorous beat of the kestrel's wings can be heard in musical terms, 'con brio', and the pulsing movements of the bird remind the poet of the 'sprung rhythm' in Gerard Manley Hopkins' poetry. That nod to Hopkins is more than casual, because 'Kestrels' is responsive to literature as well as to nature: McKay is aware that Hopkins, in 'The Windhover', has written about the kestrel under another of its names, and he draws on resonances with one of the most famous poets in the language to give additional depth to his own observations of the bird. Moreover, as is so often the case in McKay's writing, 'Kestrels' also reaches beyond both nature and art towards a visionary realm, that 'frontier of nothing' that appears in its closing lines.

The richness of 'Kestrels' is characteristic of McKay's poetry in general. It is filled with finely drawn pictures and elegant lines that emerge from an informed mind, one in which the close observations of a naturalist (sometimes turned onto the human world) and the wealth of tradition created by his precursors (his 'Icarus', for example, invites a reading against W.H. Auden's 'Musée des Beaux Arts', among many other retellings of that Greek myth) are brought together by a probing curiosity that seeks to know more about the things we can know—and the things we cannot.

Kestrels

'The name "Sparrow hawk" is unfair to this handsome
and beneficial little falcon.'

—*The Birds of Canada*

1.

unfurl from the hydro wire, beat
con brio out across the field and
hover, marshalling the moment, these
gestures of our slender hostess,
ushering her guests into the dining room

2.

sprung rhythm and
surprises, enharmonic change directions simply
step outside and let the earth turn
underneath, trapdoors, new lungs, missing bits
of time, plump familiar pods go
pop in your mind you learn not
principles of flight but how to fall, you learn
pity for that paraplegic bird, the heart

3.

to watch by the roadside singing *killy killy killy*,
plumaged like a tasteful parrot,
to have a repertoire of moves so clean their edge is
the frontier of nothing
to be sudden to send
postcards of distance which arrive in nicks of time

to open letters with a knife

1983

Twinflower

What do you call
the muscle we long with? Spirit?
I don't think so. Spirit is a far cry. This
is a casting outward which
unwinds inside the chest. A hole
which complements the heart.
The ghost of a chance.

*

Then God said, ok let's get this show
on the road, boy, get some names
stuck on these critters, and Adam,
his head on the ground in a patch of tiny
pink-white flowers, said
mmn, just a sec.
He was, let's say,
engrossed in their gesture,
the two stalks rising, branching, falling back
into nodding bells, the fading arc
that would entrance Pre-Raphaelites[1] and basketball.
Maybe he browsed among the possibilities of elves.
Maybe he was blowing on the blossoms,
whispering whatever came into his head, I have
no way of knowing what transpired
as Adam paused, testing his parent's
limit, but I know
it matters.

*

Through the cool woods of the lower
slopes, where the tall
Lodgepole Pine point
into the wild blue while they supervise
the shaded space below, I walk,
accompanied by my binoculars and field guides.
I am working on the same old problem,

1 Among the aims of the Pre-Raphaelite Brotherhood—a group of English artists, poets, and critics who banded together in 1848 in reaction against what they considered the unimaginative, overly sentimental, and artificial historical painting of the Royal Society and who sought to express a new moral sincerity and simplicity in their works—was fidelity to nature, manifested in detailed first-hand observation of flora.

how to be both
knife and spoon, when there they are, and maybe have been
all along, covering the forest floor: a creeper, a shy
hoister of flags, a tiny lamp to read by, one
word at a time.
Of course, having found them, I'm about
to find them in the field guide, and the bright
reticulated snaps of system will occur
as the plant is placed, so, among the honeysuckles,
in cool dry northern woods from June to August.
But this is not, despite the note of certainty,
the end. Hold the book open,
leaf to leaf. Listen now,
Linnaea Borealis, while I read of how
you have been loved—
with keys and adjectives and numbers, all the teeth
the mind can muster. How your namer,
Carolus Linnaeus, gave you his[2]
to live by in the system he devised.
How later, it was you,
of all the plants he knew and named,
he asked to join him in his portrait.
To rise in your tininess,
to branch and nod beside him
as he placed himself in that important
airless room.

1997

2 Carolus Linnaeus is the Latinized name of Swedish botanist Carl von Linné (1707–78), who devised an authoritative classification system for flowering plants involving binomial Latin names. Linnaeus, who often named new genera after his friends and colleagues, used his own name in choosing the taxonomic name of his favourite flower, *Linnaea Borealis,* an evergreen trailing plant with small trumpet-shaped pink flowers, commonly known as the twinflower. In portraits, Linnaeus is often holding this flower.

Goldeneye, Diving

A smooth unhurried
gulp: and the lake
has swallowed the duck
Being left
so suddenly, without benefit of flight paths teaching
distance to the eye, stretching the muscle

it drinks with, you tend to think of crossings-over,
metamorphoses, you tend to hold your breath,
which is a bad idea. In the *Kalevala*, this
is ocean's last eternal moment, during which the Goldeneye
brings bottom to the top,[1] the mirror
puckers up and speaks, and land,
with its metabolism of true-life adventure,
starts.
Absence makes the heart grow.
And the reappearance,
always expected, always,
like a burp
          surprises.
                    There it is
beside the reed bed, wearing the same
misshapen moon, the gold eye glaring.
Was it stricken by a glimpse
of something awful on the other side? Or,
unbeknownst to us, or to the *Kalevala*, has some hot star
seized upon that lens to stare into our atmosphere, furious
with envy at this tissue of betweens, this braid of breathings
which is air, from its own point,
fixed at the beginning, or the end?

1997

1 The opening cantos of the *Kalevala* (a collection of Finnish legends transmitted orally before being collected and published in the nineteenth century and now regarded as the Finnish national epic) describe the creation of the world, which begins when a duck's eggs sink to the depths of the primeval waters and break on the ocean floor. The legend is an example of the 'earth-diver' narrative found in the creation myths of several cultures (such as the Nahathaway tale related by David Thompson, pp. 40–1), in which an animal dives into the primeval waters to find mud or clay with which to form land.

Black Box

So, you are saying, it comes
to this—the end of voice, swan songs
in the can:
          all that singing in the shower,
          all that palaver, sweet talk, sales pitch, I-don't-
          want-to-walk-without-you-
          babies; pillow talk's soft
          husky bottoms, phone calls breaking talk down

into particles which
blossom in the ear, the mike
like a svengali saying *be*
voluptuous, be public; and the quick
soprano silver that was glance,
was wing, that would turn transparent air
into a mirror, and transcend the phlegm—to this,
you say,
this heaviness
this mute weight in your hands.

Now you hope, having combed,
as the expression goes, the slopes,
and spent enough to underwrite a middle-sized crusade,
for evidence: catches, flaws,
the return of surly bonds—the facts
which can only add up.
But think of your inklings,
how they grew, inking in whole
corners. How Frankie loved Johnny.
Think of that shade behind the beat,
the jazz lag which,
by being barely place, is most so:
the patch of anonymous ground where all our failures meet
to grow alliterative with rust, where the voice
keeps its desire to eat dirt.
To every thing

there was a season. To every melody a door
at which we pause and want to stay paused—surely your hand
has rested on the latch?
Now think of us as falling,
as dusk does, sideways, and not through that door
but into it—
the butts of slapstick.
That was the lick we never knew.
That was the horse laugh lurking in the surface.

1997

Short Fat Flicks

(i) *He rides into town*

already perfect, already filled with nothing. His music is a hawk scream which has been crossed with a machine, perhaps eternity's lathe, and fashioned into a horse. His hat-brim is horizon. It is all over. Only the unspeakable trauma which erased his name concerns him. Now it concerns the townsfolk as they scuttle, gutless, behind shopfronts. Two minutes ago their houses were three-dimensional and contained kitchens, not to mention closets. Now the houses, the general store, livery and sheriff's office are so obviously props that the townsfolk have stopped believing in them before the curtains twitch back into place. Now they are cover awaiting shootout, and the townsfolk are extras waiting to fall, aaargh, from their roofs, and crash, spratinkle tinkle tinkle, through their windows. He rides into town from another genre, from the black star that sucks the depth from everything, a soundless bell tolling. *You should have changed your life*, it says, *done, done, done.* Doesn't even consider that you fixed up the den and took that night class in creative writing.

(ii) *Their eyes meet*

ah, and there is a satisfying drag on the sprockets, as though the celluloid were suddenly too heavy to turn, as though the projector were sleepy. One violin has been stricken and starts, legato, a drugged smoke alarm, to troll the theme, which the camera catches, tracking left (always left) to take in a quiver of lips. Close-up, close-up, two-shot, their four eyes have begun to unbutton and bud, the strings now ahum, vibrato, zoom zoom zoom they shed the depth of field. Who needs it? The darkness is inhabited, the popcorn is buttered. Their lips approach like shy cats. Her eyes have decided to skinny-dip in his and his in hers: one more microzoom and they dive, leaving the rest of their faces behind to nuzzle and rub, attempting to smudge the irregular line between them. And the eyes? Are swimming with us, dolphins, in the darkness, which is rich and viscous, the lake of tears we've been waiting for.

(iii) *We take our seats*

and settle into our bodies, waiting for the lights to dim so we can feel ourselves falling, this is the best part, feel ourselves falling into a safer kind of sleep, an elaborate parkland of carefully prepared surprises. As the curtains begin to part, *lingerie*, we can see through them to the screen, which has begun to flicker into being. Will the plot matter? Of course not. Movies have been sent to us to make up for the bathroom mirror, with its rigid notion of representation, and the family, with its chain-link semantic net. Here we feel ideas wriggle into costume and images reach toward us out of light. Soon their logos will appear—the winged horse in the symmetrical cosmos, perhaps, or shifting constellations that swirl into an O. Everything will be incarnate, *in camera*,[1] anything can be a star.

1997

1 In private (Latin).

To Danceland

'No one is ever happier than when they're dancing.'

—Margaret McKay

South through bumper crops we are driving to Danceland,
barley
oats, canola, wheat, thick as a beaver pelt, but late, she said,
late, since June had been so cold already we were deep
in August and still mostly green so it was nip
and tuck with frost and somewhere between Nipawin and
Tisdale finally
I found the way to say, um, I can't dance
you know, I can't dance don't ask me
why I am driving like a fool to Danceland having flunked it
twenty-seven years ago in the kitchen where my mother,
bless her, tried to teach me while I passively resisted,
doing the jerk-step while she tried to slow, slow, quick quick
slow between the table and the fridge, her face fading
like someone trying to start a cranky Lawnboy
nevertheless,
step by sidestep
we are driving down the grid, Swainson's hawks occurring
every
thirty hydro poles, on average
to Danceland
where the dancefloor floats on rolled horsehair
and the farmers dance with their wives even though it is not
Chicago
where the mirror ball blesses everyone with flecks from
another, less rigorous, dimension
where the Westeel granary dances with the weathervane,
the parent with the child, the John Deere with the mortgage
where you may glimpse occasional coyote lopes and

gopher hops
where the dark may become curious and curl one long arm
around us
as we pause for a moment, and I think about my mother
and her
wishes in that kitchen, then
we feed ourselves to the world's most amiable animal,
in Danceland.

1997

Homing

That things should happen
twice, and place
share the burden of remembering. Home,
the first cliché. We say it
with aspiration as the breath
opens to a room of its own (a bed,
a closet for the secret self), then closes
on a hum. Home. Which is the sound of time
braking a little, growing slow and thick as the soup
that simmers on the stove. Abide,
abode. Pass me that plate,
the one with the hand-painted *habitant*
sitting on a log. My parents bought it
on their honeymoon—see? Dated on the bottom,
1937. He has paused to smoke his pipe, the tree
half cut and leaning. Is he thinking where
to build his cabin or just idling his mind
while his pipe smoke mingles with the air? A bird,
or something (it is hard to tell), hangs overhead.
Now it's covered by your grilled cheese sandwich.

Part two, my interpretation. The leaning tree
points home, then
past home into real estate and its innumerable
Kodak moments: kittens, uncles,
barbecues. And behind those scenes the heavy
footstep on the stair, the face locked
in the window frame, things that happen
and keep happening, reruns

of family romance. And the smudged bird? I say it's
a Yellow Warbler who has flown
from winter habitat in South America to nest here
in the clearing. If we catch it, band it,
let it go a thousand miles away it will be back
within a week. How?
Home is what we know
and know we know, the intricately
feathered nest. Homing
asks the question.

2000

Icarus[1]

isn't sorry. We do not find him
doing penance, writing out the golden mean for all
eternity, or touring its high schools to tell student bodies
not to do what he done
done. Over and over he rehearses flight
and fall, tuning his moves, entering
with fresh rush into the mingling of the air
with spirit. This is his practice
and his prayer: to be translated into air, as air
with each breath enters lungs,
then blood. He feels resistance gather in his stiff
strange wings, angles his arms to shuck the sweet lift
from the drag, runs the full length
of a nameless corridor, his feet striking the paving stones
less and less heavily, then
they're bicycling above the ground,
a few shallow beats and he's up,
he's out of the story and into the song.

At the melting point of wax, which now he knows
the way Doug Harvey knows the blue line,[2]
he will back-beat to create a pause, hover for maybe fifty
hummingbird heartbeats and then
lose it, tumbling into freefall, shedding feathers

1 See p. 852, note 1.
2 Doug Harvey (1924–89), who played hockey for the Montreal Canadiens from 1947–61, is generally considered the best defenceman of his time.

like a lover shedding clothes. He may glide
in the long arc of a Tundra Swan or pull up sharp
to Kingfisher into the sea which bears his name.[3] Then,
giving it the full Ophelia, drown.

On the shore
the farmer ploughs his field, the dull ship
sails away, the poets moralize about our
unsignificance. But Icarus is thinking tremolo and
backflip, is thinking
next time with a half-twist
and a tuck and isn't
sorry.

*

Repertoire, technique. The beautiful contraptions bred from ingenuity and practice, and the names by which he claims them, into which—lift-off, loop-the-loop—they seem to bloom. Icarus could write a book. Instead he will stand for hours in that musing half-abstracted space, watching. During fall migrations he will often climb to the edge of a north-south running ridge where the soaring hawks find thermals like naturally occurring laughter, drawing his eyebeam up an unseen winding stair until they nearly vanish in the depth of sky. Lower down, Merlins[4] slice the air with wings that say crisp crisp, precise as sushi chefs, while Sharp-shins alternately glide and flap, hunting as they go, each line break poised, ready to pivot like a point guard or Robert Creeley.[5] Icarus notices how the Red-tails and Broadwings separate their primaries[6] to spill a little air, giving up just enough lift to break their drag up into smaller trailing vortices. What does this remind him of? He thinks of the kind of gentle teasing that can dissipate a dark mood so it slips off as a bunch of skirmishes and quirks. Maybe that. Some little gift to acknowledge the many claims of drag and keep its big imperative at bay. Icarus knows all about that one.

In the spring he heads for a slough and makes himself a blind out of wolf willow and aspen, then climbs inside to let the marsh-mind claim his thinking. The soft splashdowns of Scaup and Bufflehead, the dives which are simple shrugs and vanishings; the Loon's wing, thin and sharp for flying in the underwater world, and the broad wing of the Mallard, powerful enough to break the water's grip with one sweep, a guffaw which

3 The Icarian Sea, an ancient name for the southern part of the Aegean Sea around the island of Ikaria, between the Cyclades and Turkey, where Icarus is said to have fallen.

4 A type of small falcon; Sharp-shins, Red-tails, and Broadwings are all varieties of hawk. The flight patterns of these birds—graceful, protracted sailing and circling with the ability to change direction suddenly and break into sharp descent—is contrasted with the deft diving and powerful swimming abilities of the water birds mentioned later in this section—the scaup, bufflehead, mallard, and loon.

5 That is, the agility of the birds recalls that of a point guard—usually the quickest and most skilled player on a basketball team—or of the American poet Robert Creeley, known for his facility of expression and technical precision.

6 The main flight feathers projecting along the outer edge of the bird's wing.

lifts it straight up into the air. Icarus has already made the mistake of trying this at home, standing on a balustrade in the labyrinth and fanning like a manic punkah,[7] the effort throwing him backward off his perch and into a mock urn which the Minotaur[8] had, more than once, used as a pisspot. Another gift of failure. Now his watching is humbler, less appropriative, a thoughtless thinking amid fly drone and dragonfly dart. Icarus will stay in the blind until his legs cramp up so badly that he has to move. He is really too large to be a foetus for more than an hour. He unbends creakily, stretches, and walks home, feeling gravity's pull upon him as a kind of wealth.

*

Sometimes Icarus dreams back into his early days with Daedalus in the labyrinth. Then he reflects upon the Minotaur, how seldom they saw him—did they ever?—while they shifted constantly from no-place to no-place, setting up false campsites and leaving decoy models of themselves. Sometimes they would come upon these replicas in strange postures, holding their heads in their laps or pointing to their private parts. Once they discovered two sticks stuck like horns in a decoy's head, which Daedalus took to be the worst of omens. Icarus was not so sure.

For today's replay he imagines himself sitting in a corridor reflecting on life as a Minotaur (*The* Minotaur) while waiting for his alter ego to come bumbling by. They were, he realizes, both children of technology—one its *enfant terrible*, the other the rash adolescent who, they will always say, should never have been given a pilot's licence in the first place. What will happen when they finally meet? Icarus imagines dodging like a Barn Swallow, throwing out enough quick banter to deflect his rival's famous rage and pique his interest. How many Minotaurs does it take to screw in a light bulb? What did the queen say to the machine? Should he wear two sticks on his head, or save that for later? He leaps ahead to scenes out of the Hardy Boys and Tom Sawyer. They will chaff and boast and punch each other on the arm. They will ridicule the weird obsessions of their parents. As they ramble, cul-de-sacs turn into secret hideouts and the institutional corridors take on the names of birds and athletes. They discover some imperfections in the rock face, nicks and juts which Daedalus neglected to chisel off, and which they will use to climb, boosting and balancing each other until they fall off. Together they will scheme and imagine. Somehow they will find a way to put their brute heads in the clouds.

2000

7 A fan, usually a large cloth fan on a frame suspended from the ceiling, moved backwards and forwards by pulling on a cord.

8 A creature, half-man and half-bull, who was the offspring of Pasiphaë and a bull with whom she fell in love. King Minos of Crete, Pasiphaë's husband, commissioned Daedalus to build the labyrinth to confine the beast, and fed it children sent from Athens as part of an annual tribute. Learning that Daedalus had helped Pasiphaë in her amours, Minos imprisoned him in the labyrinth with his son Icarus. Pasiphaë released them from it; Daedalus then devised wings for himself and his son when they still found it difficult to escape the Island of Crete.

Daphne Marlatt

b. 1942

Born Daphne Buckle in Melbourne, Australia, to English parents who had been evacuated from Malaya before the Japanese occupation, Marlatt spent her early childhood in Penang, a northern Malaysian island, before coming to Vancouver in 1951. She entered the University of British Columbia in 1960 and studied there with Warren Tallman, Robert Creeley, and Earle Birney. She also became closely involved with the *Tish* group (which included George Bowering and Fred Wah). Interested in writing about their specific locality, these western writers gained inspiration from the 1963 Vancouver Poetry Conference, which was attended by Charles Olson, Robert Duncan, Robert Creeley, Allen Ginsberg, Denise Levertov, Margaret Avison, and Philip Whalen. In 1964 Marlatt moved to Bloomington, Indiana, where she took an MA in comparative literature at Indiana University. While she was in the US, she met the poet and computer programmer d alexander, who not only introduced her to the new kinds of poetry he was publishing in the little magazine *Odda Tala* but encouraged her to find in speech patterns a source and structure for her own writing. Marlatt's interest in the patterns of speech and thought led her to explore a range of forms in her poetry and prose, beginning with her earliest collections of poetry, *Frames of a Story* (1968) and *Leaf leaf/s* (1969).

After separating from her husband in 1970, Marlatt returned to British Columbia with her son. Although the West Coast has remained her home, she has served as writer-in-residence at such universities as the University of Alberta and the University of Western Ontario; she has also taught at the University of Victoria. In 1989–90 she was the Ruth Wynn Woodward Professor in Women's Studies at Simon Fraser University. She currently lives in Vancouver.

After her return to Canada, Marlatt published four books of poetry—*Rings* (1971), *Our Lives* (1975), *The Story, She Said* (1977), and *What Matters* (1980)—as well as a prose work, *Zócalo* (1977). She also produced four books that focus on the Vancouver area: two books of poetry—*Vancouver Poems* (1972) and *Steveston* (1974), a long poem about the Japanese fishing village at the mouth of the Fraser River—and two non-fiction works—*Steveston Recollected: A Japanese-Canadian History* (1975) and *Opening Doors: Vancouver's East End* (1980), oral histories Marlatt constructed with the help of the BC Provincial Archives. (Several poems originally written for but not included in *Steveston* appear in Marlatt's 1991 poetry collection *Salvage.*)

In her poems of this period Marlatt abandons 'the textbook notion of sentence as the container for a completed thought' and the idea of the poetic line as a 'box for a certain measure of words'. Instead the line becomes for her 'a moving step in the process of thought'. Thus, each of a series of lines may add something to the preceding one—questioning, qualifying, or commenting upon it—without actually completing it. These poems are examples of what Charles Olson called 'proprioceptive' writing, which, as Fred Wah points out in his introduction to Marlatt's *Selected Writing: Net Work* (1980), aims to 'accurately reflect the condition of the writer at the moment of the writing'. Marlatt invites her readers to participate in the creation of meaning: more than thinking about the poem, readers must hear and feel the poem's 'movement toward, and against, conclusion'. As in 'listen' (below), this is a poetry that seeks to convey to readers the sense that an emotion he or she had felt had been 'named at last', was being named 'even as he read, the shape of what he felt to be his own, recognized at last in words coming through him from the page, coming to her through his emphatic & stirred voice'.

Marlatt has edited a number of literary journals, including *The Capilano Review.* She was a founding member of the Canadian feminist editorial collective *tessera* and a founding co-editor of its journal. She helped organize the important 1983 conference Women and Words / *Les femmes et les mots* and was a founding member of its collective. A feminist perspective is also evident in Marlatt's creative work of this period: *Here and There* (1981); *How Hug a Stone* (1983); and *Touch to My Tongue* (1984), the last of which comprises a series of lyrical love poems addressed to poet Betsy Warland and a meditation on the feminist theories of Julia Kristeva and Mary Daly. Marlatt collaborated with Warland on *Double Negative* (1988), a long poem about two lesbians crossing the Australian desert, and *Two Women in a Birth* (1994), which contains earlier work by both writers.

Marlatt's novel *Ana Historic* (1988) deals with the need to reject male-dominated historical accounts and to write women into the historical record. These themes, found earlier in *Double Negative*, are expanded upon in *Ghost Works* (1993) and in the novel *Taken* (1996), which features characters who strongly resemble Marlatt's own parents. She also gave final shape to *Mothertalk: Life Stories of Mary Kiyoshi Kiyooka* (1997), a work by the late poet and artist Roy Kiyooka, her partner for some years, who had recorded his mother's conversations. (It is Kiyooka to whom the brief sequence of poems 'winter/ rice/ tea strain' is addressed and who appears as the reader in 'listen'.) In 1998, Marlatt published *Readings from the Labyrinth* (1998), a collection of new and previously published essays on subjects ranging from the immigrant imagination to women's autobiography and feminism. In 2001 she brought together *This Tremor Love Is*, a collection of her love poems.

Ana Historic

Ana Historic is the story of Annie, the wife of a historian who, when she discovers the journal of an 1870s school teacher, abandons her work as her husband's research assistant and begins to write a novel about the journal's author. Parallel to Annie's act of creating a history for a forgotten woman is Marlatt's act of telling Annie's story. Marlatt gives to Annie the shape of her own childhood: growing up in the Pacific Rim, living through the brutal environment of the Second World War, and moving into 1950s Vancouver and its Cold War environment. Both are disoriented by cultural change and social expectations of gender. In the selection below, the opening of *Ana Historic*, the fear of the unknown, the possibility of a threatening male presence, and the threat of Communism fuses into a universal enemy so local he may be under one's bed. Annie, in an attempt to resist the limitations society has placed on women and to face her own demons, seeks role models in the narratives she has read but finds that she must reshape them (just as she later reshapes the journal writer's story) to provide a feminine source of strength.

listen

he was reading to her, standing on the other side of the kitchen counter where she was making salad for supper, tender orange carrot in hand, almost transparent at its tip, slender, & she was wondering where such carrots came from in winter. he was standing in the light reading to her from a book he was holding, her son behind him at the table where amber light streamed from under a glass shade she had bought for its warm colour midwinter, though he had called it a cheap imitation of the real thing.

in its glow her son was drawing red Flash & blue Superman into a comic he was making, painstakingly having stapled the pages together & now with his small & definite hand trying to draw exact images of DC Superstars & Marvel heroes none of them had ever seen except in coloured ink.

but he was reading to her about loss, excited, because someone had named it at last, was naming even as he read, the shape of what he felt to be his own, recognized at last in words coming through him from the page, coming to her through his emphatic & stirred voice stumbling over the rough edges of terms that weren't his, even as he embraced them. lost, how their dancing had lost touch with the ring dance which was a collective celebration, he said.

she was standing with the grater in one hand, carrot in the other, wondering if the grating sound would disturb him. she wanted to hear what had stirred him. she wanted to continue the movement of making salad which, in the light & the löwenbrau they shared, was for once coming so easily, almost was spring stirring around the corner of the house in a rhythm of rain outside she was moving in, had moved, barely knowing it was rain beyond the wetness of walking home—

hand in hand, he was saying, a great circle like the circle of the seasons, & now people barely touch, where at least with the waltz they used to dance in couples, then with rock apart but *to* each other, whereas now, he caught her eye, the dances we've been to you can see people dancing alone, completely alone with the sound.

lifting the carrot to the grater, pressing down, watching flakes of orange fall to the board, she felt accused in some obscure way, wanted to object (it was her generation after all), thought up an obscure argument about how quadrilles[1] could be called collective in ballrooms where privileged guests took their assigned places in the dance. but now, & she recalled the new year's eve party they'd been to, almost a hundred people, strangers, come together, & people don't know each other in the city the way they used to in a village. but that only glanced off what the book was saying about husbandry & caring for the soil as a collective endeavour.

the whole carrot was shrinking into a thousand flakes heaped & scattered at once, the whole carrot with its almost transparent sides shining in the light, had ground down to a stump her fingers clutched close to the jagged pockets of tin that scraped them, she saw her fingers, saw blood flying like carrot flakes, wondered why she imagined blood as part of the salad . . .

listen, he was saying, this is where he's really got it. & he read a long passage about their imprisonment in marriage, all the married ones with that impossible ideal of confining love to one—*one cannot love a particular woman unless one loves womankind,* he read. listen, he said, & he read her the passage about the ring dance, about the participation of couples in one great celebration, the *amorous feast that joins them to all living things.* he means fertility, she said, thinking, oh no, oh back to that, woman's one true function. he means the fertility of the earth, he said, he means our lives aware of seasonal growth & drawing nourishment from that instead of material

1 Square dances performed typically by four couples.

acquisition & exploitation. listen, he read a passage about sexual capitalism, about the crazy images of romance that fill people's heads, sexual freedom & skill & the me-generation on all the racks of all the supermarket stores.

using her palms like two halves of a split spoon, she scooped up the heap of carrot flakes & dropped them onto a plate of lettuce, dark because it was romaine torn into pieces in the wooden bowl with other green things. dance. in & out. she watched the orange flakes glisten in their oil of skin, touch the surface of green she tossed with real spoons, each flake dipping into the dark that lay at the heart of, what, their hearts, as they had, the other night, sunk into bed at the end of the party, drunk & floating, their laughter sifting in memory through conversations, wrapt in the warmth of what everyone had said & how they had moved away & toward each other & loved in very obscure ways, slowly they had made love to everyone they loved in each other, falling through & away from their separate bodies—listen, she said, as the rain came up & she set the salad on the wooden table underneath the lamp.

1980; rev. 2001

winter/ rice/ tea strain

ocha[1] words

—well into the winter, we stir up out of what, what dreams, what
cause of communion, names, odd stirrings-up of the past as
honey pours, *your dream was* this & this reading, this poem
pouring this cup of tea proposes (your favourite word)

days stream down any one of the window panes i press my nose against/
you—start & drop the book, your books, all over the floor *so much*
depends begin again, pressing these days into pages as if, paged
we could pull out any one to savour—this one so young, these

nouns i want to call out to you winter/ rice/ tea strain, unlikely
sweet tongue, a green hope i bury my face into, steam's slip, & you
overheard, breathing yourself into sound

1 Green tea.

touch

the music rice makes, rice on the tongue in our tea, tea & trout, while outside
rain's quintet batters our ears   hardly the bitterest month, sweet steep, sweet
infusion of green   tipping our lips at the smallest ordinary then   crescendo light
through dark your eye
                                        stares i stare, in step, the skin of your foot so smooth it
startles, quick

                    trout where the darkness lies

                                                                        unformed its leap mere shine
ichthyic, from the base of the spinal column's chorded ascent (rippling
through the lines of what was planned, unplanned, undone—nothing
to catch our lines haphazard lie

                                                            gen mai cha[2] grain
                                                            between the teeth, still i see

you eye luminant, luminous wonder my eye wanders, amazed & touching
touched with *astony*, love, the thunder of it inflorescent you said   a downpour
trout weave through as you described yourself so slow to leap

                                                                                            out in what is

clearly the wonder of budding, leaves, scales of the old
miraculous, adart in the air as a friend would say *among*

bachi[3]

sea bush, 'small tree'   fruit-bearing, salt-sprung   fights your big wood
making a world—*poiein*[4]—to its own description   these drenched leaves
straining toward the light, spume, drift of repeated observation drawn
to shore

          you offer tea, wipe the wood of the table clearing sea wrack, surface
grit   we sip to a murmuring of visions, yours, mine, inter-inflected

2 Japanese green tea mixed with roasted rice. It has a mild nutty flavour with a sweet finish.
3 Japanese, a basin or bowl.
4 Greek, 'to make'; the etymological root of the word poetry.

yet to break
our description of the world & thence to see *the dreamer & the dreamed* who's
dreaming who? you asked

wind buffets the windowpane words incessant as rain fall hear what slips
between this tea we bring to our different lips, this space where nouns unfold

leaf
by leaf

bits on the floor of the pot we disappear

2000

retrieving madrone[1]

take, take the

arbutus, crazy-woman tree, she said, does
everything at the wrong time, sheds last year's leaves mid-
summer, yellow, out of new green, sheds ochre bark at the
end of summer when

you'd think she'd hang onto it

the way
light catches in the curled edges of her

skin, it's only
paper, thin enough to let light, as the words of this world
impinge, turn me out of mine. i throw off words, leave outgrown images of myself

crazy-waving-in-air ma-
drone this murmur you make, a stir of bright
leaves hitting home, the sound of *geta*, his
name for the thongs he wears against sharp
things on his path underfoot: a name, a use

1 An arbutus tree with white flowers, red berries, and glossy leaves, native to western North America. Its bark peels naturally from the trunk, giving the tree a naked appearance.

overhead, over my head, i listen to slippery
woman, word peeler, leaf weaver, hear the slur
of a different being approach

leaf lingua love-
tongue
turning me
inside out

2001

(is love enough?)

Salt through the earth conduct the sea

— Olga Broumas

such green glistening, a sparrow preening a far-stretched wing, light full of pleasure-chirping, feathered bodies at home in earth's soft voltage & newness written over your face waking from dream, each blade, each leaf encased still in the wet from last night's rain

is love enough when the breast milk a mother jets in the urgent mouth of her baby is laced with PCBs?

hungry you said, for love, for light, armfulls of daffodils we refuse to gather standing luminous, pale ears listening, ochre trumpets at the heart darkness pools, & the radio, as we sit on a paint-blistered deck in brilliant sun reports that snow, whiter than chalk on the highest shelf of the Rockies is sedimented with toxins

the dead, the dying—we imprint our presence everywhere on every wall & rock

what is love in the face of such loss?

since dawn, *standing by my bed*, she wrote, *in gold sandals . . . that very/ moment* half-awake in a whisper of light her upturned face given to presence, a woman involved, a circle of women she taught how to love, how to pay a fine attention raising simply & correctly the fleeting phases of what is, arrives

we get these glimpses, you said, grizzlies begging at human doorways, two cubs & a mother so thin her ribs showed prominent under ratty fur, shot now that our salmon rivers run empty, rivers that were never ours to begin with—

& the sea, the sea goes out a long way in its unpublished killing ground

this webwork—what we don't know about the body, what we don't know may well be killing us—well : spring : stream : river, these powerful points you set your fingers on, drawing current through blockages, moving inward, not out, to see

chi[1] equally in
the salt sea and fields thick with bloom
inner channels & rivers

a sea full of apparent islands, no jetting-off point, no airborne leap possible

without the body all these bodies
interlaced

2001

1 Circulating life force whose existence and properties are the basis of much Chinese philosophy and medicine.

From *Ana Historic*

Who's There? she was whispering. knock knock. in the dark. only it wasn't dark had woken her to her solitude, conscious alone in the night of his snoring more like snuffling dreaming elsewhere, burrowed into it, under the covers against her in animal sleep. he was dreaming without her in some place she had no access to and she was awake. now she would have to move, shift, legs aware of themselves and wanting out. a truck gearing down somewhere. the sound of a train, in some yard where men already up were working signals, levers, lamps. she turned the clock so she could see its blue digital light like some invented mineral glowing, radium 4:23. it was the sound of her own voice had woken her, heard like an echo asking,

who's there?

echoes from further back, her fear-defiant child voice carried still in her chest, stealing at night into the basement with the carving knife toward those wardrobes at the bottom of the staircase. wardrobes. wardrobes. warding off what? first the staircase with its star scrawled on the yellow wall and COMRADE, an illicit word never heard upstairs but known from Major Hoople's[1] talk about those sleazy reds who were always infiltrating from some foreign underworld and threatening to get under or was it into the bed. nobody ever erased or painted over the scrawl and nobody seemed to see it but her, like some signal blinking every time she had to go downstairs with the knife. Comrade / would she really kill? she who was only a girl but even so the

1 Major Amos B. Hoople, the pompous, conservative windbag of the syndicated comic strip *Our Boarding House* (1921–81) created by Gene Ahern, was given to long discourses and tirades.

oldest in her family recently settled in cold-war Vancouver of the Fifties—a cold country, Canada, her mother said, people don't care. would she kill if she had to? after all she was responsible for her younger sisters sleeping innocent above while she, their guardian on those nights (babysitter wasn't quite the word), conscious and awake, unable NOT to hear, tiptoed after those suspicious noises—what if he were hungry, starved even, and so desperately from outside he would kill to get what he wanted, as afraid even as she, to get what he needed, while she who had her needs met, secure (was she really?) in her parents' house, trembling and bare-armed (in nightie even), she was merely in his way—no, he was in the wrong if he were there at all he meant to do them harm, and she would resist, righteously. she stood in front of the darkest of the six-foot wardrobes, teak, too big to place upstairs, big enough to hide Frankenstein, stood feeling her fear, her desperate being up against it, that other breathing on the other side of the door she could almost hear, would take him by surprise, her only real weapon, kick it open flashlight weaving madly yelling (don't let me see! don't let me!)
Who's There?

empty. it always was. though every time she believed it might not be. relief, adrenalin shaking her legs. she had chosen the darkest first and must go to each in turn, confronting her fear (for what if he were there, in one of the others, waiting til she had her back turned, absorbed and vulnerable and never thinking he would leap on her from behind?). wishing, even, that what she knew could be there would be there and she be taken, lost, just to show them. who? her parents who went out leaving her alone to defend the house. her mother who . . .

my mother (who) . . . voice that carries through all rooms, imperative, imperious. don't be silly. soft breast under blue wool dressing gown, tea breath, warm touch . . . gone. I-na (the long drawn calling out at night for a drink of water, one more story, one last hug, as i experimented with attracting your attention, Mum-my, Mom-eee, Mah-mee . . .)

I-na, I-no-longer, i can't turn you into a story. there is this absence here, where the words stop. (and then i remember—

i was two perhaps, you told me often enough, hurry up Annie, we have to go now, while i went on playing, paying no attention, Annie, hurry up! i'm going now! playing with your attention, delaying, and then there was silence, the whole house filled with it. Mummy, i cried, Mummy? and you said in a low distant voice i didn't recognize (i did but i knew i wasn't meant to): your Mummy's gone. i burst into tears. don't be silly, darling, i'm here, you see how silly you are—as if *saying* it makes it so. but it does, it did. you had gone in the moment you thought to say it, separating yourself even as you stood there, making what wasn't, what couldn't be, suddenly real.

and now you've made your words come true, making it so by an act of will (despair). gone. locked up in a box. frozen in all the photographs Harald took. the worst is that you will never reappear with that ironic smile, don't be silly, darling. pulling through.

the worst is that it's up to me to pull you through. this crumbling apart of words. 'true, real.' you who is you or me. she. a part struck off from me. apart. separated.

she, my Lost Girl, because i keep thinking, going back to that time with you (and why weren't there Lost Girls in Never-Never Land, only Lost Boys and Wendy who had to mother them all, mother or nurse—of course they fought the enemy, that's what boys did) and what i did when i was she who did not feel separated or split, her whole body trembling with one intent behind the knife. and it was defense (as they say in every war). no, it was trespassing across an old boundary, exposing my fear before it could paralyse me—before i would end up as girls were meant to be.

who did my Lost Girl think might be there in that house on the side of a mountain on the edge of a suburb surrounded by private laurels? what did she think would come staggering out of the woods? those woods men worked in, building powerlines and clearing land for subdivision. those woods the boys on the rest of the block had claimed as theirs.

except for that part directly behind the garden, that part she and her sisters called the Old Wood, moulted and softened with years of needle drift, tea brown, and the cedar stump hollow in the middle where they nestled in a womb, exchanging what if's, digging further with their fingers, sniffing the odour of tree matter become a stain upon their hands like dried blood.

what if the boys came down from their fort in the Green Wood with slingshots and air gun? would their own string bows and crookedly peeled arrows hold them off? standing on the rockery for practice, shooting at the bull's-eye in the field (a stone in an empty lot), she despaired of herself, her sister-archers, her camarades—their arrows fell off the string, plopped on the dirt like so many cowpies. who cares? they said. they hurt their thumbs, they got tired, they went off to read Little Lulu (not even Sheba, Queen of the Jungle). but what if the boys . . . what if the men tried to bulldoze their woods? so what could *we* do? her little sister shrugged.

do, do. she my Lost Girl, my Heroine, wanted something to do not something that might be done to them. the refrain of a rainy afternoon: there's nothing to do! do something useful, her mother said, clean up you room. but she wanted out, in the fresh wet smell of cedar and rain.

tomboy, her mother said. tom, the male of the species plus boy. double masculine, as if girl were completely erased. a girl, especially a young girl, who behaves like a spirited boy—as if only boys could be spirited. who read Robin Hood, wore scarlet, identified with Lancelot and the boy who wanted to join the knights of St John (all trespassers, law-breakers in the guise of saviours. what did 'useful' mean to them?)

the trouble was you gave me a sense of justice—your 'fair play', Ina, your mother's instinct distributing things equally between us. but you would never admit it wasn't 'fair' that girls weren't allowed to do the things boys did. escape the house, 'home-free'—not home, but free in the woods to run, nameless in the split-second manoeuvre of deadfalls, bush blinds, ghost stumps glowing in the twilight. spirit(ed), filled with it, the world of what was other than us, tom as in thrum as in bullfrog sound, or the sudden awful drumming of a grouse.

it wasn't tom, or boy, it wasn't hoyden, minx, baggage, but what lay below names—barely even touched by them.

* * *

i learned to stay in the house as a good girl should. i am still in the house i move around in all day in the rain, the kids in school, Richard at it, at school as he calls the campus, reducing it to the scale of Mickey's elementary, why? they all do it, all the faculty, as if belittling, and maybe it is, the forced rote of teaching the same course year after year. when i go there i see library, see centuries of hidden knowledge, wealth, see romance—like you in this, Ina, how you used to enter the North Van library as if entering a medieval cloister, sssh, you warned, as if trespassing, pulling me into the smell of dust, of breath bated between plastic covers, heading immediately for the shelf of historical novels, family history with its lurid stretches shaping the destiny of a nation. consoled by this, that the familial, the mundane, could actually have historic proportions? kings and queens in bed with you of an afternoon. rain, rain.

you might as well learn some history, you said, handing me *The Old Curiosity Shoppe* (both volumes), *The Scarlet Pimpernel*, drawing distinctions between trash and literature. you might as well learn, you said, and blamed me later for becoming a 'bluestocking—I can't even *talk* to you,' when i got my degree (BA only, mind you, ending my graduate career by getting pregnant and marrying Richard). 'i'm marrying my history prof,' i said, hoping to shock you. but you were pleased. trained to exhibit a 'good mind', but only 'within reason'—reason being utilitarian, education as part of 'attractiveness' leading to marriage—i ended up doing what i was meant to, i followed the plotline through, the story you had me enact.

and now you're dead, Ina, the story has abandoned me. i can't seem to stay on track, nor can my sentence, even close its brackets. you didn't teach me about asides, you never told me the 'right track' is full of holes, pot-holes of absence (sleeping pills and social smiles, 'i'm fine, fine,' hanging on.) i don't even want to 'pull yourself together,' as Richard urges (myself? yourself? theirself), 'after all, grieving can't bring her back, you've got your own life to lead, you've got us.' true. (that reasonable word again.) but something isn't.

i've been moving around the house all day in the rain, in the growing dark outside, far from leading my own life or my life leading anywhere (goodbye, hero), i feel myself in you, irritated at the edges where we overlap. it occurs to me you died of reason (thunder far off on the edges of town and always i think it's missiles going off): i mean explanation, justification, normal mental state—that old standard.

the dictionary, your immigrant weapon, Ina, saves me when the words stop, when the names stick . . . real? you said, what is 'real cute'? Canadians don't know how to speak proper English. real is an adjective, look, and you showed me in the dictionary: true, actual. true cute? it doesn't make sense. You can say it's either true or cute, but not both. too true.

was dying a way of stopping all those words, all those variable terms, true or not? because it's hopeless ('hopeless,' you said, 'you'll never learn'), this task of trying to muffle them to one. true: exactly conforming to a rule, standard, or pattern; trying to sing true. by whose standard or rule? and what do you do when the true you feel inside sounds different from the standard?

i want to talk to you. (now? now when it's too late?) i want to say something. tell you something about the bush and what you were afraid of, what i escaped to: anonymous territory where names faded to a tiny hubbub, lost in all that other noise—the soughing, sighing of bodies, the cracks and chirps, odd rustles, something like breath escaping, something inhuman i slipped through. in communion with trees, following the migratory routes of bugs, the pathways of water, the warning sounds of birds, i was native, i was the child who grew up with wolves, original lost girl, elusive, vanished from the world of men . . .

but you, a woman, walked with the possibility of being seen, ambushed in the sudden arms of bears or men. 'never go into the woods with a man,' you said, 'and don't go into woods alone.'

we knew about bears. sometimes they would raid our garbage cans at night and the phones would ring all up and down the block, there's a bear at the Potts', keep the dogs and kids inside. excitement, peering through the windows out at street-light pooling gravel. so they were real then? shambling shadows, garbage-eaters, only a little larger than the Newfoundland next door. but with something canny in them, resistant to attempts to scare them off, looking over their shoulders with contempt, four-footed men in shaggy suits intent on a meal.

'if a man talks to you on the street, don't answer him,' you said. 'but what if he wants directions? what if he wants a dime?' we asked. 'just keep walking,' you said. but we saw you fish for quarters when the men shambled up to you on the street outside department stores, we watched you in your trim black coat, well-tailored, your little hat, we watched you scrambling around in your purse for change, and it was true, you didn't say a word, though you did respond, awkward and flushed. when we asked if that's what you meant, you said it wasn't that.

skid row was a name we learned. rape was a word that was hidden from us. 'but what would he do?' 'bad things you wouldn't like.'

our bodies were ours as far as we knew and we knew what we liked, laughing exhausted and sweaty in our fort or wiping bloody knees with leaves and creek water. without history we squatted in needle droppings to pee, flung our bodies through the trees—we would have swung on vines if there had been any, as it was we swung on vine maples. always we imagined we were the first ones there, the first trespassers—

if you go down in the woods today you'd better go in disguise. It was bears' territory we entered, or cedars'. it was the land of skunk cabbage. it was not ours and no one human, no man preceded us.

1988

Michael Ondaatje

b. 1943

Born in Sri Lanka (then Ceylon), the youngest of four siblings, Michael Ondaatje grew up speaking both English and Singhalese. His parents separated when he was an infant and he saw little of the father he describes in 'Letters & Other Worlds', a poem he has said was difficult to write. He lived with relatives until he joined his mother in England, where he received his secondary schooling at Dulwich College boarding school. In 1962 he followed his brother Christopher to Canada, which became his permanent home. He enrolled in Bishop's University, where the poet and critic D.G. Jones, then a professor at Bishop's, encouraged Ondaatje as a writer and acquainted him with the contemporary Canadian literary milieu. Ondaatje moved to Toronto after his third year, completing his BA at the University of Toronto in 1965. After taking an MA at Queen's in 1967, he taught English at the University of Western Ontario before joining the faculty of Glendon College, York University, in 1970.

Ondaatje's first book of poems, *The Dainty Monsters*, appeared in 1967. In 1969, Ondaatje—attracted from an early point in his career to the 'documentary' mode that Dorothy Livesay has identified as important for Canadian writers—published *The Man with Seven Toes*, a unified sequence of poems based on the experience of a woman shipwrecked off the Queensland coast of Australia. In the following year he employed a collage form, joining his own prose and poetry to such things as a jail-house interview with Billy, a bit of an old pulp western, and historical photographs and period illustrations to fashion *The Collected Works of Billy the Kid*, a chronicle of the American outlaw and of Pat Garrett's pursuit of him. It won a Governor General's Award but caused problems for the judges, who were accustomed to giving prizes for fiction, poetry, and non-fiction. (They created a special 'prose and poetry' category for that year only.)

Ondaatje's interest in building narratives around historical events and individuals remains evident in many of his later works. His 1976 novel, *Coming through Slaughter*, set in the Storyville area of New Orleans, is based on the life of, and makes use of documents about, the influential early jazz musician Buddy Bolden. Like *Billy the Kid*, it is a portrait of an outsider driven to violence and self-destruction both by society and by himself. Ondaatje's later blend of history and fiction in *In the Skin of a Lion* (1987) recalls the construction of two important edifices of twentieth-century Toronto, the Bloor Street Viaduct and the city's first water filtration plant. Two characters introduced in this novel—Hana, the daughter of the protagonist Patrick Lewis, and the thief Caravaggio—return in *The English Patient* (1992), which focuses on people brought together in the final days of the Second World War. They are joined by Kip, a Sikh bomb-disposal expert, who comes to understand empire and his place in it; and by the 'English patient', a man badly burned in a plane crash, whose mysterious identity and background are at the centre of the story. *The English Patient* earned Ondaatje another Governor General's Award and the prestigious Booker Prize—the first time the prize had been awarded to a Canadian—and was made into a highly successful Hollywood film (it won the Oscar for best picture in 1997).

Although he has turned increasingly to narrative forms, Ondaatje has never abandoned the lyric poem. His second book of short poems, *Rat Jelly*, appeared in 1973. In 1979 his book of selected and new poetry, *There's a Trick with a Knife I'm Learning to Do: Poems 1963–1978*, won a Governor General's Award. He has since published a second book of selected poems, *The Cinnamon Peeler* (1992). In sharp contrast to his fiction, Ondaatje's poems often draw on very personal material, such as the old scars of 'A Time Around Scars' or the deep feelings of a father for his growing daughter in 'To a Sad Daughter'.

In the 1980s Ondaatje published two autobiographical works—*Running in the Family* (1982) and the poem sequence *Secular Love* (1984). *Running in the Family* combines interrelated prose sketches, poems, and photographs as Ondaatje constructs a narrative version of his family history. The more ostensibly autobiographical *Secular Love*, while containing poems—such as 'To a Sad Daughter'—that can be read in isolation, is organized like a verse journal, with repetitions and echoes unifying the whole. It traces the poet's life from his near breakdown after the collapse of his first marriage through his recovery.

Ondaatje's increased willingness to explore autobiographical material coincides with a investigation of his Sri Lankan background. He used the money he received for the Booker Prize to inaugurate the Gratiaen Award—named in honour of his mother's family—as an annual literary prize for Sri Lankan writers, and in 1998 he published *Handwriting*, a book of poems focused mostly on the country in which he was born. In 2000 he set a novel in Sri Lanka for the first time: *Anil's Ghost*, for which he won a fourth Governor General's Award. The story of Anil Tissera, a forensic anthropologist, who returns to Sri Lanka under the sponsorship of the Centre for Human Rights in Geneva to document the source of organized campaigns of murder plaguing her homeland, this novel, like the poetry in *Handwriting*, is set against a background of strife and civil war. Dramatizing the relationship of international observers to the people who continue to live amid unending terror, it reflects Ondaatje's concerns about the situation there.

In the 1970s Ondaatje joined the Coach House Press editorial collective, and in 1985 he became, with his second wife, Linda Spalding, one of the editors of the literary journal *Brick*. His work for Coach House and for *Brick*, which has frequently meant energetic support for new and emerging writers, and as the editor of various anthologies speaks to his long-standing commitment to Canadian writing. He has edited two short-story collections—*Personal Fictions* (1977) and the compendious *From Ink Lake* (1992), and the *Long Poem Anthology* (1979)—which helped call attention to the continuing importance of the long poem in Canada. In 2000, he helped compile (with Michael Redhill, Esta Spalding, and Linda Spalding) *Lost Classics*, a collection of eighty essays (thirty-two of which had previously appeared in a special issue of *Brick*) by writers such as Margaret Atwood, Russell Banks, and John Irving about their favourite forgotten works of literature.

Ondaatje has also been interested in forms of expression for media other than that of the page. He has adapted his works—*The Man with Seven Toes*, *Billy the Kid*, and *Coming Through*

Slaughter—for the stage. In the early seventies he made three films, including one on bp Nichol (*The Sons of Captain Poetry*, 1970) and another on Theatre Passe Muraille's 'The Farm Show' (*The Clinton Special*, 1972). His interest in film is also evident in *The Conversations: Walter Murch and the Art of Film Editing* (2002), a collection of stories, observations, and information about film editing and the writing of literature based on Ondaatje's conversations with master film and sound editor Walter Murch, whom he met on the set of *The English Patient*.

Ondaatje's engagement in visual forms is not surprising: his work is filled with carefully realized physical images. The contrast between the warmth and familiarity that arises out of his sharply etched depictions of everyday events and the reticent, at times coolly objective, voice that sometimes seems to hold both reader and narrator at distance from his characters can create a sense of being off balance and produce dramatic emotional intensity.

Ondaatje's poetry and fiction records a world that is rich but dangerous. Whether he writes of family and friends or of historical figures, he weaves a web of interrelations and juxtapositions and traces out its complexities in an intensely sensory language.

In the Skin of a Lion

The blend of fact and fiction in this novel brings to life the people who helped shape Toronto in the 1920s and 1930s. The book is centred around Patrick Lewis, a young man from an isolated part of rural Ontario who arrives in Toronto in 1923 as a 21-year-old. Becoming involved in the famous search for the missing business tycoon Ambrose Small, he meets two women with whom he falls in love: Small's lover, Clara Dickens, and her friend Alice Gull. Interwoven with Patrick's story are scenes dealing with the construction of early twentieth-century Toronto and stories of the immigrants who, though they played crucial roles in the building of the city, have been omitted from the city's recorded history.

The book's title, an allusion to the *Epic of Gilgamesh*, refers to the importance of telling one's story as a means of self-affirmation; it is further explained in the following passage:

Alice had once described a play to him in which several actresses shared the role of the heroine. After half an hour the powerful matriarch removed her large coat from which animal pelts dangled and she passed it, along with her strength, to one of the minor characters. In this way even a silent daughter could put on the cloak and be able to break through her chrysalis into language. Each person had their moment when they assumed the skins of wild animals, when they took responsibility for the story.

Drawing on research in the Toronto archives, Ondaatje used the construction of the Bloor Street Viaduct and the digging of the two-mile tunnel that brought fresh water into the city as structural elements in a tale that gives to Toronto the kind of mythic aura possessed by Paris, London, and New York. The bridge that links Danforth Avenue to the centre of Toronto represents a powerful symbol of growth—a connection between the old city and its newer immigrant communities, and between past and future—and the novel transforms its continuing existence into an emblem of the indispensable role played by the city's forgotten immigrants.

The selection reprinted here, a version of which first appeared in *The New Yorker* before the novel's publication, is the second chapter in its entirety. It introduces Nicholas Temelcoff, a Macedonian immigrant whose daring efforts, as he swings amid tons of metal and wood, play a crucial role in bringing the bridge into existence.

The Time Around Scars

A girl whom I've not spoken to
or shared coffee with for several years
writes of an old scar.
On her wrist it sleeps, smooth and white,
the size of a leech.
I gave it to her
brandishing a new Italian penknife.
Look, I said turning,
and blood spat onto her shirt.

My wife has scars like spread raindrops
on knees and ankles,
she talks of broken greenhouse panes
and yet, apart from imagining red feet,
(a nymph out of Chagall[1])
I bring little to that scene.
We remember the time around scars,
they freeze irrelevant emotions
and divide us from present friends.
I remember this girl's face,
the widening rise of surprise.

And would she
moving with lover or husband
conceal or flaunt it,
or keep it at her wrist
a mysterious watch.
And this scar I then remember
is medallion of no emotion.

I would meet you now
and I would wish this scar
to have been given with
all the love
that never occurred between us.

1967

1 Marc Chagall (1887–1985), Russian-born French artist whose paintings often have a quality of fairytale fantasy.

Letters & Other Worlds

'for there was no more darkness for him and, no doubt
like Adam before the fall, he could see in the dark'[1]

My father's body was a globe of fear
His body was a town we never knew
He hid that he had been where we were going
His letters were a room he seldom lived in
In them the logic of his love could grow

My father's body was a town of fear
He was the only witness to its fear dance
He hid where he had been that we might lose him
His letters were a room his body scared

He came to death with his mind drowning.
On the last day he enclosed himself
in a room with two bottles of gin, later
fell the length of his body
so that brain blood moved
to new compartments
that never knew the wash of fluid
and he died in minutes of a new equilibrium.
His early life was a terrifying comedy
and my mother divorced him again and again.
He would rush into tunnels magnetized
by the white eye of trains
and once, gaining instant fame,
managed to stop a Perahara[2] in Ceylon
—the whole procession of elephants dancers
local dignitaries—by falling
dead drunk onto the street.

As a semi-official, and semi-white at that,
the act was seen as a crucial
turning point in the Home Rule Movement
and led to Ceylon's independence in 1948.

1 Translation from Alfred Jarry's *La Dragonne* (1943), cited in *The Banquet Years* by Roger Shattuck (1955).
2 Religious ceremony celebrated by a parade.

(My mother had done her share too—
her driving so bad
she was stoned by villagers
whenever her car was recognized)

For 14 years of marriage
each of them claimed he or she
was the injured party.
Once on the Colombo docks
saying goodbye to a recently married couple
my father, jealous
at my mother's articulate emotion,
dove into the waters of the harbour
and swam after the ship waving farewell.
My mother pretending no affiliation
mingled with the crowd back to the hotel.

Once again he made the papers
though this time my mother
with a note to the editor
corrected the report—saying he was drunk
rather than broken hearted at the parting of friends.
The married couple received both editions
of *The Ceylon Times* when their ship reached Aden.[3]

And then in his last years
he was the silent drinker,
the man who once a week
disappeared into his room with bottles
and stayed there until he was drunk
and until he was sober.

There speeches, head dreams, apologies,
the gentle letters, were composed.
With the clarity of architects
he would write of the row of blue flowers
his new wife had planted,
the plans for electricity in the house,
how my half-sister fell near a snake
and it had awakened and not touched her.
Letters in a clear hand of the most complete empathy
his heart widening and widening and widening

3 International port in Yemen and a stop on the trip from Ceylon through the Suez Canal on the way to Europe.

to all manner of change in his children and friends
while he himself edged
into the terrible acute hatred
of his own privacy
till he balanced and fell
the length of his body
the blood screaming in
the empty reservoir of bones
the blood searching in his head without metaphor

1973

Pig Glass

Bonjour.   This is pig glass
a piece of cloudy sea

nosed out of the earth by swine
and smoothed into pebble
run it across your cheek
it will not cut you

and this is my hand   a language
which was buried for years   touch it
against your stomach

                    The pig glass
I thought
was the buried eye of Portland Township
slow faded history
waiting to be grunted up
There is no past until you breathe
on such green glass
                    rub it
over your stomach and cheek

The Meeks family used this section
years ago to bury tin
crockery forks dog tags
and each morning
pigs ease up that ocean
redeeming it again

into the possibilities of rust
one morning I found a whole axle
another day a hand crank

but this is pig glass
tested with narrow teeth
and let lie. The morning's green present
Portland Township jewelry.

There is the band from the ankle of a pigeon
a weathered bill from the Bellrock Cheese Factory
letters in 1925 to a dead mother I
disturbed in the room above the tractor shed.
Journals of family love
servitude to farm weather
a work glove in a cardboard box
creased flat and hard like a flower.

A bottle thrown
by loggers out of a wagon
past midnight
explodes against rock.
This green fragment has behind it
the booomm when glass
tears free of its smoothness

now once more smooth as knuckle
a tooth on my tongue.
Comfort that bites through skin
hides in the dark afternoon of my pocket.
Snake shade.
Determined histories of glass.

1979

The Cinnamon Peeler

If I were a cinnamon peeler[1]
I would ride your bed
and leave the yellow bark dust
on your pillow.

1 One who peels the cinnamon bark, the source of the spice, from the trees.

Your breasts and shoulders would reek
you could never walk through markets
without the profession of my fingers
floating over you. The blind would
stumble certain of whom they approached
though you might bathe
under rain gutters, monsoon.

Here on the upper thigh
at this smooth pasture
neighbour to your hair
or the crease
that cuts your back. This ankle.
You will be known among strangers
as the cinnamon peeler's wife.

I could hardly glance at you
before marriage
never touch you
—your keen nosed mother, your rough brothers.
I buried my hands
in saffron, disguised them
over smoking tar,
helped the honey gatherers . . .

When we swam once
I touched you in water
and our bodies remained free,
you could hold me and be blind of smell.
You climbed on the bank and said
                    this is how you touch other women
the grass cutter's wife, the lime burner's daughter.
And you searched your arms
for the missing perfume
                              and knew

                    what good is it
to be the lime burner's daughter
left with no trace
as if not spoken to in the act of love
as if wounded without the pleasure of a scar.

You touched
your belly to my hands
in the dry air and said
I am the cinnamon
peeler's wife. Smell me.

1982

To a Sad Daughter

All night long the hockey pictures
gaze down at you
sleeping in your tracksuit.
Belligerent goalies are your ideal.
Threats of being traded
cuts and wounds
—all this pleases you.
O my god! you say at breakfast
reading the sports page over the Alpen
as another player breaks his ankle
or assaults the coach.

When I thought of daughters
I wasn't expecting this
but I like this more.
I like all your faults
even your purple moods
when you retreat from everyone
to sit in bed under a quilt.
And when I say 'like'
I mean of course 'love'
but that embarrasses you.
You who feel superior to black and white movies
(coaxed for hours to see *Casablanca*)
though you were moved
by *Creature from the Black Lagoon.*

One day I'll come swimming
beside your ship or someone will
and if you hear the siren

listen to it.[1] For if you close your ears
only nothing happens. You will never change.

I don't care if you risk
your life to angry goalies
creatures with webbed feet.
You can enter their caves and castles
their glass laboratories. Just
don't be fooled by anyone but yourself.

This is the first lecture I've given you.
You're 'sweet sixteen' you said.
I'd rather be your closest friend
than your father. I'm not good at advice
you know that, but ride
the ceremonies
until they grow dark.

Sometimes you are so busy
discovering your friends
I ache with a loss
—but that is greed.
And sometimes I've gone
into *my* purple world
and lost you.

One afternoon I stepped
into your room. You were sitting
at the desk where I now write this.
Forsythia outside the window
and sun spilled over you
like a thick yellow miracle
as if another planet
was coaxing you out of the house
—all those possible worlds!—
and you, meanwhile, busy with mathematics.

I cannot look at forsythia now
without loss, or joy for you.
You step delicately
into the wild world

1 For the myth of the sirens and their dangerous song, see page 791, note 1. Ondaatje's line here recalls the story of Odysseus, who, when he passed by the Sirens' island, had the ears of his crew stopped up to keep the ship safe but was himself lashed to the mast with his ears unstopped that he might hear their song.

and your real prize will be
the frantic search.
Want everything. If you break
break going out not in.
How you live your life I don't care
but I'll sell my arms for you,
hold your secrets forever.

If I speak of death
which you fear now, greatly,
it is without answers,
except that each
one we know is
in our blood.
Don't recall graves.
Memory is permanent.
Remember the afternoon's
yellow suburban annunciation.
Your goalie
in his frightening mask
dreams perhaps
of gentleness.

1984

The Medieval Coast

A village of stone-cutters. A village of soothsayers.
Men who burrow into the earth in search of gems.

Circus in-laws who pyramid themselves into trees.

Home life. A fear of distance along the southern coast.

Every stone-cutter has his secret mark, angle of his chisel.

In the village of soothsayers
bones of a familiar animal
guide interpretations.

This wisdom extends no more than thirty miles.

1998

Wells

i

The rope jerked up
so the bucket flies
into your catch

pours over you

its moment
of encasement

standing in sunlight
wanting more,
another poem please

and each time
recognition and caress,
the repeated pleasure

of finite things.
Hypnotized by lyric.
This year's kisses

like diving a hundred times
from a moving train
into the harbour

like diving a hundred times
from a moving train
into the harbour

ii

The last Sinhala word I lost
was *vatura.*
The word for water.
Forest water. The water in a kiss. The tears
I gave to my ayah[1] Rosalin on leaving
the first home of my life.

1 Nursemaid.

More water for her than any other
that fled my eyes again
this year, remembering her,
a lost almost-mother in those years
of thirsty love.

No photograph of her, no meeting
since the age of eleven,
not even knowledge of her grave.

Who abandoned who, I wonder now.

iii

In the sunless forest
of Ritigala[2]

heat in the stone
heat in the airless black shadows

nine soldiers on leave
strip uniforms off
and dig a well

to give thanks
for surviving this war

A puja[3] in an unnamed grove
the way someone you know
might lean forward
and mark the place
where your soul is
—always, they say,
near to a wound.

In the sunless forest
crouched by a forest well

pulling what was lost
out of the depth.

1998

2 Ancient city of Sri Lanka, site of a Buddhist monastery.
3 Ceremonial offering.

From *In the Skin of a Lion*

The Bridge

A truck carries fire at five a.m. through central Toronto, along Dundas Street and up Parliament Street, moving north. Aboard the flatbed three men stare into passing darkness—their muscles relaxed in this last half-hour before work—as if they don't own the legs or the arms jostling against their bodies and the backboard of the Ford.

Written in yellow over the green door is DOMINION BRIDGE COMPANY. But for now all that is visible is the fire on the flatbed burning over the three-foot by three-foot metal dish, cooking the tar in a cauldron, leaving this odour on the streets for anyone who would step out into the early morning and swallow the air.

The truck rolls burly under the arching trees, pauses at certain intersections where more workers jump onto the flatbed, and soon there are eight men, the fire crackling, hot tar now and then spitting onto the back of a neck or an ear. Soon there are twenty, crowded and silent.

The light begins to come out of the earth. They see their hands, the textures on a coat, the trees they had known were there. At the top of Parliament Street the truck turns east, passes the Rosedale fill, and moves towards the half-built viaduct.

The men jump off. The unfinished road is full of ruts and the fire and the lights of the truck bounce, the suspension wheezing. The truck travels so slowly the men are walking faster, in the cold dawn air, even though it is summer.

Later they will remove coats and sweaters, then by eleven their shirts, bending over the black rivers of tar in just their trousers, boots, and caps. But now the thin layer of frost is everywhere, coating the machines and cables, brittle on the rain puddles they step through. The fast evaporation of darkness. As light emerges they see their breath, the clarity of the air being breathed out of them. The truck finally stops at the edge of the viaduct, and its lights are turned off.

The bridge goes up in a dream. It will link the east end with the centre of the city. It will carry traffic, water, and electricity across the Don Valley. It will carry trains that have not even been invented yet.

Night and day. Fall light. Snow light. They are always working—horses and wagons and men arriving for work on the Danforth side at the far end of the valley.

There are over 4,000 photographs from various angles of the bridge in its time-lapse evolution. The piers sink into bedrock fifty feet below the surface through clay and shale and quicksand—45,000 cubic yards of earth are excavated. The network of scaffolding stretches up.

Men in a maze of wooden planks climb deep into the shattered light of blond wood. A man is an extension of hammer, drill, flame. Drill smoke in his hair. A cap falls into the valley, gloves are buried in stone dust.

Then the new men arrive, the 'electricals', laying grids of wire across the five arches, carrying the exotic three-bowl lights, and on October 18, 1918 it is completed. Lounging in mid-air.

The bridge. The bridge. Christened 'Prince Edward'. The Bloor Street Viaduct.

* * *

During the political ceremonies a figure escaped by bicycle through the police barriers. The first member of the public. Not the expected show car containing officials, but this one anonymous and cycling like hell to the east end of the city. In the photographs he is a blur of intent. He wants the virginity of it, the luxury of such space. He circles twice, the string of onions that he carries on his shoulder splaying out, and continues.

But he was not the first. The previous midnight the workers had arrived and brushed away officials who guarded the bridge in preparation for the ceremonies the next day, moved with their own flickering lights—their candles for the bridge dead—like a wave of civilization, a net of summer insects over the valley.

And the cyclist too on his flight claimed the bridge in that blurred movement, alone and illegal. Thunderous applause greeted him at the far end.

On the west side of the bridge is Bloor Street, on the east side is Danforth Avenue. Originally cart roads, mud roads, planked in 1910, they are now being tarred. Bricks are banged into the earth and narrow creeks of sand are poured in between them. The tar is spread. *Bitumiers, bitumatori*, tarrers, get onto their knees and lean their weight over the wooden block irons, which arc and sweep. The smell of tar seeps through the porous body of their clothes. The black of it is permanent under the nails. They can feel the bricks under their kneecaps as they crawl backwards towards the bridge, their bodies almost horizontal over the viscous black river, their heads drunk within the fumes.

Hey, Caravaggio!

The young man gets up off his knees and looks back into the sun. He walks to the foreman, lets go of the two wooden blocks he is holding so they hang by the leather thongs from his belt, bouncing against his knees as he walks. Each man carries the necessities of his trade with him. When Caravaggio quits a year later he will cut the thongs with a fish knife and fling the blocks into the half-dry tar. Now he walks back in a temper and gets down on his knees again. Another fight with the foreman.

All day they lean over tar, over the twenty yards of black river that has been spread since morning. It glistens and eases in sunlight. Schoolkids grab bits of tar and chew them, first cooling the pieces in their hands then popping them into their mouths. It concentrates the saliva for spitting contests. The men plunk cans of beans into the blackness to heat them up for their lunch.

In winter, snow removes the scent of tar, the scent of pitched cut wood. The Don River floods below the unfinished bridge, ice banging at the feet of the recently built piers. On winter mornings men fan out nervous over the whiteness. Where does the earth end? There are flares along the edge of the bridge on winter nights—worst shift of all—where they hammer the nails in through snow. The bridge builders balance on a strut, the flares wavering behind them, aiming their hammers towards the noise of a nail they cannot see.

* * *

The last thing Rowland Harris, Commissioner of Public Works, would do in the evenings during its construction was have himself driven to the edge of the viaduct, to sit for a while. At midnight the half-built bridge over the valley seemed deserted—just lanterns tracing its outlines. But there was always a night shift of thirty or forty men. After a while Harris removed himself from the car, lit a cigar, and walked onto the bridge. He loved this viaduct. It was his first child as head of Public Works, much of it planned before he took over but he had bullied it through. It was Harris who envisioned that it could carry not just cars but trains on a lower trestle. It could also transport water from the east-end plants to the centre of the city. Water was Harris's great passion. He wanted giant water mains travelling across the valley as part of the viaduct.

He slipped past the barrier and walked towards the working men. Few of them spoke English but they knew who he was. Sometimes he was accompanied by Pomphrey, an architect, the strange one from England who was later to design for Commissioner Harris one of the city's grandest buildings—the water filtration plant in the east end.

For Harris the night allowed scope. Night removed the limitations of detail and concentrated on form. Harris would bring Pomphrey with him, past the barrier, onto the first stage of the bridge that ended sixty yards out in the air. The wind moved like something ancient against them. All men on the bridge had to buckle on halter ropes. Harris spoke of his plans to this five-foot-tall Englishman, struggling his way into Pomphrey's brain. Before the real city could be seen it had to be imagined, the way rumours and tall tales were a kind of charting.

One night they had driven there at eleven o'clock, crossed the barrier, and attached themselves once again to the rope harnesses. This allowed them to stand near the edge to study the progress of the piers and the steel arches. There was a fire on the bridge where the night workers congregated, flinging logs and other remnants onto it every so often, warming themselves before they walked back and climbed over the edge of the bridge into the night.

They were working on a wood-facing for the next pier so that concrete could be poured in. As they sawed and hammered, wind shook the light from the flares attached to the side of the abutment. Above them, on the deck of the bridge, builders were carrying huge Ingersoll-Rand air compressors and cables.

An April night in 1917. Harris and Pomphrey were on the bridge, in the dark wind. Pomphrey had turned west and was suddenly stilled. His hand reached out to touch Harris on the shoulder, a gesture he had never made before.

—Look!

Walking on the bridge were five nuns.

Past the Dominion Steel castings wind attacked the body directly. The nuns were walking past the first group of workers at the fire. The bus, Harris thought, must have dropped them off near Castle Frank and the nuns had, with some confusion at that hour, walked the wrong way in the darkness.

They had passed the black car under the trees and talking cheerfully stepped past the barrier into a landscape they did not know existed—onto a tentative carpet over the piers, among the night labourers. They saw the fire and the men. A few tried to wave them back. There was a mule attached to a wagon. The hiss and jump of the machines made the ground under them lurch. A smell of creosote. One man was washing his face in a barrel of water.

The nuns were moving towards a thirty-yard point on the bridge when the wind began to scatter them. They were thrown against the cement mixers and steam shovels, careering from side to side, in danger of going over the edge.

Some of the men grabbed and enclosed them, pulling leather straps over their shoulders, but two were still loose. Harris and Pomphrey at the far end looked on helplessly as one nun was lifted up and flung against the compressors. She stood up shakily and then the wind jerked her sideways, scraping her along the concrete and right off the edge of the bridge. She disappeared into the night by the third abutment, into the long depth of air which held nothing, only sometimes a rivet or a dropped hammer during the day.

Then there was no longer any fear on the bridge. The worst, the incredible, had happened. A nun had fallen off the Prince Edward Viaduct before it was even finished. The men covered in wood shavings or granite dust held the women against them. And Commissioner Harris at the far end stared along the mad pathway. This was his first child and it had already become a murderer.

The man in mid-air under the central arch saw the shape fall towards him in that second knowing his rope would not hold them both. He reached to catch the figure while his other hand grabbed the metal pipe edge above him to lessen the sudden jerk on the rope. The new weight ripped the arm that held the pipe out of its socket and he screamed, so whoever might have heard him up there would have thought the scream was from the falling figure. The halter thulked, jerking his chest up to his throat. The right arm was all agony now—but his hand's timing had been immaculate, the grace of the habit, and he found himself a moment later holding the figure against him dearly.

He saw it was a black-garbed bird, a girl's white face. He saw this in the light that sprayed down inconstantly from a flare fifteen yards above them. They hung in the halter, pivoting over the valley, his broken arm loose on one side of him, holding the woman with the other. Her body was in shock, her huge eyes staring into the face of Nicholas Temelcoff.

Scream, please, Lady, he whispered, the pain terrible. He asked her to hold him by the shoulders, to take the weight off his one good arm. A sway in the wind. She could not speak though her eyes glared at him bright, just staring at him. *Scream, please.* But she could not.

During the night, the long chutes through which wet concrete slid were unused and hung loose so the open spouts wavered a few feet from the valley floor. The tops of these were about ten feet from him now. He knew this without seeing them, even though they fell outside the scope of light. If they attempted to slide the chute their weight would make it vertical and dangerous. They would have to go further—to reach the lower-deck level of the bridge where there were structures built for possible water mains.

We have to swing. She had her hands around his shoulders now, the wind assaulting them. The two strangers were in each other's arms, beginning to swing wilder, once more, past the lip of the chute which had tempted them, till they were almost at the lower level of the rafters. He had his one good arm free. Saving her now would be her responsibility.

She was in shock, her face bright when they reached the lower level, like a woman with a fever. She was in no shape to be witnessed, her veil loose, her cropped hair open to the long wind down the valley. Once they reached the catwalk she saved him from falling back into space. He was exhausted. She held him and walked with him like a lover along the unlit lower parapet towards the west end of the bridge.

Above them the others stood around the one fire, talking agitatedly. The women were still tethered to the men and not looking towards the stone edge where she had gone over, falling in darkness. The one with that small scar against her nose . . . she was always falling into windows, against chairs. She was always unlucky.

The Commissioner's chauffeur slept in his car as Temelcoff and the nun walked past, back on real earth away from the bridge. Before they reached Parliament Street they cut south through the cemetery. He seemed about to faint and she held him against a gravestone. She forced him to hold his arm rigid, his fist clenched. She put her hands underneath it like a stirrup and jerked upwards so he screamed out again, her whole body pushing up with all of her strength, groaning as if about to lift him and then holding him, clutching him tight. She had seen the sweat jump out of his face. *Get me a shot. Get me. . . .* She removed her veil and wrapped the arm tight against his side. *Parliament and Dundas . . . few more blocks.* So she went down Parliament Street with him. Where she was going she didn't know. On Eastern Avenue she knocked at the door he pointed to. All these abrupt requests—scream, swing, knock, get me. Then a man opened the door and let them into the Ohrida Lake Restaurant. *Thank you, Kosta. Go back to bed, I'll lock it.* And the man, the friend, walked back upstairs.

She stood in the middle of the restaurant in darkness. The chairs and tables were pushed back to the edge of the room. Temelcoff brought out a bottle of brandy from under the counter and picked up two small glasses in the fingers of the same hand. He guided her to a small table, then walked back and, with a switch behind the zinc counter, turned on a light near her table. There were crests on the wall.

She still hadn't said a word. He remembered she had not even screamed when she fell. That had been him.

* * *

Nicholas Temelcoff is famous on the bridge, a daredevil. He is given all the difficult jobs and he takes them. He descends into the air with no fear. He is a solitary. He assembles ropes, brushes the tackle and pulley at his waist, and falls off the bridge like a diver over the edge of a boat. The rope roars alongside him, slowing with the pressure of his half-gloved hands. He is burly on the ground and then falls with terrific speed, grace, using the wind to push himself into corners of abutments so he can check driven rivets, sheering valves, the drying of the concrete under bearing plates and padstones. He stands in the air banging the crown pin into the upper cord and then shepherds the lower cord's slip-joint into position. Even in archive photographs it is difficult to find him. Again and again you see vista before you and the eye must search along the wall of sky to the speck of burned paper across the valley that is him, an exclamation mark, somewhere in the distance between bridge and river. He floats at the three hinges of the crescent-shaped steel arches. These knit the bridge together. The moment of cubism.[1]

He is happiest at daily chores—ferrying tools from pier down to trestle, or lumber that he pushes in the air before him as if swimming in a river. He is a spinner. He links everyone. He meets them as they cling—braced by wind against the metal they are riveting or the wood sheeting they hammer into—but he has none of their fear. Always he carries his own tackle, hunched under his ropes and dragging the shining pitons behind him. He sits on a coiled seat of rope while he eats his lunch on the bridge. If he finishes early he cycles down Parliament Street to the Ohrida Lake Restaurant and sits in the darkness of the room as if he has had enough of light. Enough of space.

His work is so exceptional and time-saving he earns one dollar an hour while the other bridge workers receive forty cents. There is no jealousy towards him. No one dreams of doing half the things he does. For night work he is paid $1.25, swinging up into the rafters of a trestle holding a flare, free-falling like a dead star. He does not really need to see things, he has charted all that space, knows the pier footings, the width of the crosswalks in terms of seconds of movement—281 feet and 6 inches make up the central span of the bridge. Two flanking spans of 240 feet, two end spans of 158 feet. He slips into openings on the lower deck, tackles himself up to bridge level. He knows the precise height he is over the river, how long his ropes are, how many seconds he can free-fall to the pulley. It does not matter if it is day or night, he could be blindfolded. Black space is time. After swinging for three seconds he puts his feet up to link with the concrete edge of the next pier. He knows his position in the air as if he is mercury slipping across a map.

* * *

A South River parrot hung in its cage by the doorway of the Ohrida Lake Restaurant, too curious and interested in the events of the night to allow itself to be blanketed. It

1 Early twentieth-century movement in art, especially painting, in which perspective with a single viewpoint was abandoned for a multiple way of seeing; wholes were reduced to components by the use of simple geometric shapes, interlocking planes, and, later, collage. In emphasizing the two-dimensional surface of the picture plane, Cubists often portrayed three-dimensional objects as fragmented, with several sides showing at once. The bridge, in this passage, is described as though its joined crescent-shaped arches are actually four sides of a three-dimensional object, unfolded. (The phrase 'The moment of cubism' is taken from the title of a book by the English novelist and art critic John Berger, whose writing also supplied Ondaatje with the epigraph for *In the Skin of a Lion*: 'Never again will a single story be told as though it were only one.')

watched the woman who stood dead centre in the room in darkness. The man turned on one light behind the counter. Nicholas Temelcoff came over to the bird for a moment's visit after getting the drinks. 'Well, Alicia, my heart, how are you?' And walked away not waiting for the bird's reply, the fingers of his left hand delicately holding the glasses, his arm cradling the bottle.

He muttered as if continuing his conversation with the bird, in the large empty room. From noon till two it was full of men, eating and drinking. Kosta the owner and his waiter performing raucous shows for the crowd—the boss yelling insults at the waiter, chasing him past customers. Nicholas remembered the first time he had come there. The dark coats of men, the arguments of Europe.

He poured a brandy and pushed it over to her. 'You don't have to drink this but you can if you wish. Or see it as a courtesy.' He drank quickly and poured himself another. 'Thank you,' he said, touching his arm curiously as if it were the arm of a stranger.

She shook her head to communicate it was not all right, that it needed attention.

'Yes, but not now. Now I want to sit here.' There was a silence between them. 'Just to drink and talk quietly. . . . It is always night here. People step in out of sunlight and must move slow in the darkness.'

He drank again. 'Just for the pain.' She smiled. 'Now music.' He stood up free of the table as he spoke and went behind the counter and turned the wireless on low. He spun the dial till there was bandstand. He sat down again opposite her. 'Lot of pain. But I feel good.' He leaned back in his chair, holding up his glass. 'Alive.' She picked up her glass and drank.

'Where did you get that scar?' He pointed his thumb to the side of her nose. She pulled back.

'Don't be shy . . . talk. You must talk.' He wanted her to come out to him, even in anger, though he didn't want anger. Feeling such ease in the Ohrida Lake Restaurant, feeling the struts of the chair along his back, her veil tight on his arm. He just wanted her there near him, night all around them, where he could look after her, bring her out of the shock with some grace.

'I got about twenty scars,' he said 'all over me. One on my ear here.' He turned and leaned forward so the wall-light fell onto the side of his head. 'See? Also this under my chin, that also broke my jaw. A coiling wire did that. Nearly kill me, broke my jaw. Lots more. My knees. . . .' He talked on. Hot tar burns on his arm. Nails in his calves. Drinking up, pouring her another shot, the woman's song on the radio. She heard the lyrics underneath Temelcoff's monologue as he talked and half mouthed the song and searched into her bright face. Like a woman with a fever.

This is the first time she has sat in a Macedonian bar, in any bar, with a drinking man. There is a faint glow from the varnished tables, the red checkered tablecloths of the day are folded and stacked. The alcove with its serving counter has an awning hanging over it. She realizes the darkness represents a Macedonian night where customers sit outside at their tables. Light can come only from the bar, the stars, the clock dressed in its orange and red electricity. So when customers step in at any time, what they are entering is an old courtyard of the Balkans. A violin. Olive trees.

Permanent evening. Now the arbour-like wallpaper makes sense to her. Now the parrot has a language.

He talked on, slipping into phrases from the radio songs which is how he learned his words and pronunciations. He talked about himself, tired, unaware his voice split now into two languages, the woman hearing everything he said and trying to remember it all. He could see her eyes were alive, interpreting the room. He noticed the almost-tap of her finger to the radio music.

The blue eyes stayed on him as he moved, leaning his head against the wall. He drank, his breath deep into the glass so the fumes would hit his eyes and the sting of it keep him awake. Then he looked back at her. How old was she? Her brown hair so short, so new to the air. He wanted to coast his hand through it.

'I love your hair,' he said. 'Thank you . . . for the help. For taking the drink.'

She leaned forward earnestly and looked at him, searching out his face now. Words just on the far side of her skin, about to fall out. Wanting to know his name which he had forgotten to tell her. 'I love your hair.' His shoulder was against the wall and he was trying to look up. Then his eyes were closed. So deeply asleep he would be gone for hours. She could twist him around like a puppet and he wouldn't waken.

She felt as if she were the only one alive in this building. In such formal darkness. There was a terrible taste from that one drink still on her tongue, so she walked behind the zinc counter, turning on the tap to wash out her mouth. She moved the dial of the radio around a bit but brought it back securely to the same station. She was looking for that song he had half sung along with earlier, the voice of the singer strangely powerful and lethargic. She saw herself in the mirror. A woman whose hair was showing, caught illicit. She did what he had wanted to do. She ran her hand over her hair briefly. Then turned from her image.

Leaning forward, she laid her face on the cold zinc, the chill there even past midnight. Upon her cheek, her eyelid. She let her skull roll to cool her forehead. The zinc was an edge of another country. She put her ear against the grey ocean of it. Its memory of a day's glasses. The spill and the wiping cloth. Confessional. Tabula Rasa.

At the table she positioned the man comfortably so he would not fall on his arm. *What is your name?* she whispered. She bent down and kissed him, then began walking around the room. This orchard. Strangers kiss softly as moths, she thought.

* * *

In certain weather, when fog fills the valley, the men stay close to each other. They arrive for work and walk onto a path that disappears into whiteness. What country exists on the other side? They move in groups of three or four. Many have already died during the building of the bridge. But especially on mornings like this there is a prehistoric fear, a giant bird lifting one of the men into the air. . . .

Nicholas has removed his hat, stepped into his harness, and dropped himself off the edge, falling thirty feet down through fog. He hangs under the spine of the bridge.

He can see nothing, just his hands and the yard of pulley-rope above him. Six in the morning and he's already lost to that community of men on the bridge who are also part of the fairy tale.

He is parallel to the lattice-work of hanging structures. Now he enters the cages of steel and wood like a diver entering a sunken vessel that could at any moment tip over into deeper fracture zones of the sea floor. Nicholas Temelcoff works as the guy derricks raise and lower the steel—assembling it further out towards the next pier. He directs the steel through the fog. He is a fragment at the end of the steel bone the derrick carries on the end of its sixty-foot boom. The steel and Nicholas are raised up to a temporary track and from there the 'travellers' handle it. On the west end of the viaduct a traveller is used to erect the entire 150-foot span. The travellers are twin derricks fitted with lattice-work booms that can lift twelve tons into any position, like a carrot off the nose of the most recently built section of the bridge.

Nicholas is not attached to the travellers, his rope and pulleys link up only with the permanent steel of a completed section of the bridge. Travellers have collapsed twice before this and fallen to the floor of the valley. He is not attaching himself to a falling structure. But he hangs beside it, in the blind whiteness, slipping down further within it until he can shepherd the new ribs of steel onto the end of the bridge. He bolts them in, having to free-fall in order to use all of his weight for the final turns of the giant wrench. He allows ten feet of loose rope on the pulley, attaches the wrench, then drops onto the two-foot handle, going down with it, and jars with the stiffening of the bolt, falling off into the air, and jars again when he reaches the end of the rope. He pulleys himself up and does it again. After ten minutes every bone feels broken—the air he stops in feels hard as concrete, his spine aching where the harness pulls him short.

He rises with the traveller from the lower level, calling out numbers to the driver above him through the fog, alongside the clattering of the woodwork he holds onto, the creaks and bends of the lattice drowning out his call of *one—two—three—four* which is the only language he uses. He was doing this once when a traveller collapsed at night—the whole structure—the rope shredding around him. He let go, swinging into the darkness, *anywhere* that might be free of the fifteen tons of falling timber which crashed onto the lower level and then tumbled down into the valley, rattling and banging in space like a trolley full of metal. And on the far end of the swing, he knew he had escaped the timber, but not necessarily the arm-thick wires that were now uncoiling free, snaking powerfully in every direction through the air. On his return swing he curled into a ball to avoid them, hearing the wires whip laterally as they completed the energy of the break. His predecessor had been killed in a similar accident, cut, the upper half of his body found an hour later, still hanging in the halter.

By eight a.m. the fog is burned up and the men have already been working for over two hours. A smell of tar descends to Nicholas as workers somewhere pour and begin to iron it level. He hangs waiting for the whistle that announces the next journey of the traveller. Below him is the Don River, the Grand Trunk, the CN and CP railway tracks, and Rosedale Valley Road. He can see the houses and work shacks, the beautiful wooden sheeting of the abutment which looks like a revival tent. Wind dries the sweat on him. He talks in English to himself.

* * *

She takes the first step out of the Ohrida Lake Restaurant into the blue corridor—the narrow blue lane of light that leads to the street. What she will become she becomes in that minute before she is outside, before she steps into the six-a.m. morning. The parrot Alicia regards her departure and then turns its attention back to the man asleep in the chair, one arm on the table, palm facing up as if awaiting donations, his head against the wall beside a crest. He is in darkness now, the open palm callused and hard. Five years earlier or ten years into the future the woman would have smelled the flour in his hair, his body having slept next to the dough, curling around it so his heat would make it rise. But now it was the hardness of his hands, the sound of them she would remember like wood against glass.

* * *

Commissoner Harris never speaks to Nicholas Temelcoff but watches often as he hooks up and walks at the viaduct edge listening to the engineer Taylor's various instructions. He appears abstracted but Harris knows he listens carefully. Nicholas never catches anyone's eye, as if he must hear the orders nakedly without seeing a face around the words.

His eyes hook to objects. Wood, a railing, a rope clip. He eats his sandwiches without looking at them, watching instead a man attaching a pulley to the elevated railings or studying the expensive leather on the shoes of the architects. He drinks water from a corked green bottle and his eyes are focused a hundred feet away. He never realizes how often he is watched by others. He has no clue that his gestures are extreme. He has no portrait of himself. So he appears to Harris and the others as a boy: say, a fanatic about toy cars, some stage they all passed through years ago.

Nicholas strides the parapet looking sideways at the loops of rope and then, without pausing, steps into the clear air. Now there is for Harris nothing to see but the fizzing rope, a quick slither. Nicholas stops twenty feet down with a thud against his heart. Sometimes on the work deck they will hear him slowly begin to sing various songs, breaking down syllables and walking around them as if laying the clauses out like tackle on a pavement to be checked for worthiness, picking up one he fancies for a moment then replacing it with another. As with sight, because Nicholas does not listen to most conversations around him, he assumes no one hears him.

For Nicholas language is much more difficult than what he does in space. He loves his new language, the terrible barriers of it. *'"Does she love me?—Absolutely! Do I love her?—Positively!"'* Nicholas sings out to the forty-foot pipe he ferries across the air towards the traveller. *He* knows Harris. He *knows* Harris by the time it takes him to walk the sixty-four feet six inches from sidewalk to sidewalk on the bridge and by his expensive tweed coat that cost more than the combined week's salaries of five bridge workers.

The event that will light the way for immigration in North America is the talking picture. The silent film brings nothing but entertainment—a pie in the face, a fop being dragged by a bear out of a department store—all events governed by fate and timing, not language and argument. The tramp never changes the opinion of the policeman. The truncheon swings, the tramp scuttles through a corner window and disturbs the fat lady's ablutions. These comedies are nightmares. The audience emits horrified laughter as Chaplin, blindfolded, rollerskates near the edge of the unbalconied mezzanine. No one shouts to warn him. He cannot talk or listen. North America is still without language, gestures and work and bloodlines are the only currency.

But it was a spell of language that brought Nicholas here, arriving in Canada without a passport in 1914, a great journey made in silence. Hanging under the bridge, he describes the adventure to himself, just as he was told a fairy tale of Upper America by those who returned to the Macedonian village, those first travellers who were the judas goats[2] to the west.

Daniel Stoyanoff had tempted them all. In North America everything was rich and dangerous. You went in as a sojourner and came back wealthy—Daniel buying a farm with the compensation he had received for losing an arm during an accident in a meat factory. Laughing about it! Banging his other hand down hard onto the table and wheezing with laughter, calling them all fools, sheep! As if his arm had been a dry cow he had fooled the Canadians with.

Nicholas had been stunned by the simplicity of the contract. He could see Stoyanoff's body livid on the killing floor—standing in two inches of cow blood, screaming like nothing as much as cattle, his arm gone, his balance gone. He had returned to the village of Oschima, his sleeve flapping like a scarf, and with cash for the land. He had looked for a wife with two arms and settled down.

In ten years Daniel Stoyanoff had bored everyone in the village with his tall tales and he couldn't wait for children to grow up and become articulate so he could thrill them with his sojourner's story of Upper America. What Daniel told them was that he had in fact lost both arms in the accident, but he happened to be rooming with a tailor who was out of work and who had been, luckily, on the killing floors of Schnaufer's that morning. Dedora the tailor had pulled gut out of a passing cat, stitched Daniel's right arm back on, and then turned for the other but a scrap dog had run off with it, one of those dogs that lounged by the doorway. Whenever you looked up from cutting and slicing the carcasses you would see them, whenever you left work at the end of the day in your blood-soaked overalls and boots they followed you, licking and chewing your cuffs.

Stoyanoff's story was told to all children of the region at a certain age and he became a hero to them. Look, he would say, stripping off his shirt in the Oschima high street, irritating the customers of Petroff's outdoor bar once more, *look at what a good tailor Dedora was—no hint of stitches.* He drew an imaginary line around his good shoulder and the kids brought their eyes up close, then went over to his other shoulder and saw the alternative, the grotesque stump.

Nicholas was twenty-five years old when war in the Balkans began. After his village was burned he left with three friends on horseback. They rode one day and a whole night

2 Here, a person who lures others into temptation. (A judas goat is used to lead sheep to slaughter.)

and another day down to Trikala, carrying food and a sack of clothes. Then they jumped on a train that was bound for Athens. Nicholas had a fever, he was delirious, needing air in the thick smoky compartments, wanting to climb up onto the roof. In Greece they bribed the captain of a boat a napoleon each to carry them over to Trieste. By now they all had fevers. They slept in the basement of a deserted factory, doing nothing, just trying to keep warm. There had to be no hint of illness before trying to get into Switzerland. They were six or seven days in the factory basement, unaware of time. One almost died from the high fevers. They slept embracing each other to keep warm. They talked about Daniel Stoyanoff's America.

On the train the Swiss doctor examined everyone's eyes and let the four friends continue over the border. They were in France. In LeHavre they spoke to the captain of an old boat that carried animals. It was travelling to New Brunswick.

Two of Nicholas's friends died on the trip. An Italian showed him how to drink blood in the animal pens to keep strong. It was a French boat called *La Siciliana.* He still remembered the name, remembered landing in Saint John and everyone thinking how primitive it looked. How primitive Canada was. They had to walk half a mile to the station where they were to be examined. They took whatever they needed from the sacks of the two who had died and walked towards Canada.

Their boat had been so filthy they were covered with lice. The steerage passengers put down their baggage by the outdoor taps near the toilets. They stripped naked and stood in front of their partners as if looking into a mirror. They began to remove the lice from each other and washed the dirt off with cold water and a cloth, working down the body. It was late November. They put on their clothes and went into the Customs sheds.

Nicholas had no passport, he could not speak a word of English. He had ten napoleons, which he showed them to explain he wouldn't be dependent. They let him through. He was in Upper America.

He took a train for Toronto, where there were many from his village; he would not be among strangers. But there was no work. So he took a train north to Copper Cliff, near Sudbury, and worked there in a Macedonian bakery. He was paid seven dollars a month with food and sleeping quarters. After six months he went to Sault Ste Marie. He still could hardly speak English and decided to go to school, working nights in another Macedonian bakery. If he did not learn the language he would be lost.

The school was free. The children in the class were ten years old and he was twenty-six. He used to get up at two in the morning and make dough and bake till 8:30. At nine he would go to school. The teachers were all young ladies and were very good people. During this time in the Sault he had translation dreams—because of his fast and obsessive studying of English. In the dreams trees changed not just their names but their looks and character. Men started answering in falsettos. Dogs spoke out fast to him as they passed him on the street.

When he returned to Toronto all he needed was a voice for all this language. Most immigrants learned their English from recorded songs or, until the talkies came, through mimicking actors on stage. It was a common habit to select one actor and follow him throughout his career, annoyed when he was given a small part, and seeing each of his plays as often as possible—sometimes as often as ten times during a run. Usually by the end of an east-end production at the Fox or Parrot Theatres the actors' speeches would be followed by growing echoes as Macedonians, Finns, and Greeks repeated the phrases after a half-second pause, trying to get the pronunciation right.

This infuriated the actors, especially when a line such as 'Who put the stove in the living room, Kristin?'—which had originally brought the house down—was now spoken simultaneously by at least seventy people and so tended to lose its spontaneity. When the matinee idol Wayne Burnett dropped dead during a performance, a Sicilian butcher took over, knowing his lines and his blocking meticulously, and money did not have to be refunded.

Certain actors were popular because they spoke slowly. Lethargic ballads, and a kind of blues where the first line of a verse is repeated three times, were in great demand. Sojourners walked out of their accent into regional American voices. Nicholas, unfortunately, would later choose Fats Waller[3] as his model and so his emphasis on usually unnoticed syllables and the throwaway lines made him seem high-strung or dangerously anti-social or too loving.

But during the time he worked on the bridge, he was seen as a recluse. He would begin sentences in his new language, mutter, and walk away. He became a vault of secrets and memories. Privacy was the only weight he carried. None of his cohorts really knew him. This man, awkward in groups, would walk off and leave strange clues about himself, like a dog's footprints on the snowed roof of a garage.

* * *

Hagh! A doctor attending his arm, this is what woke him, brought him out of his dream. *Hah!* It was six hours since he had fallen asleep. Kosta was there. He saw that the veil and his shirt had been cut open by the doctor. Somehow, they said, he had managed to get his arm back into the socket.

He jerked his hand to the veil, looking at it closely.

She had stayed until Kosta came down in the early morning. She talked to him about the arm, to get a doctor, she had to leave. She spoke? Yes yes. What did she sound like? Hah? What more did Kosta know about her? He mentioned her black skirt. Before he left, Nicholas looked around the bar and found strips of the black habit she had cut away to make a skirt for the street.

When he walks into the fresh air outside the Ohrida Lake Restaurant, on the morning after the accident on the bridge, he sees the landscape as something altered, no longer so familiar that it is invisible to him. Nicholas Temelcoff walks now seeing Parliament Street from the point of view of the woman—who had looked through his belt-satchel while he slept, found his wide wire shears, and used them to cut away the black lengths

3 (1904–43), American jazz pianist, singer, and composer, known for an eccentric performance style that combined intricate playing, with a gravelly but flirtatious voice, dignity and buffoonery, and a wildly free spirit.

of her habit. When he walks out of the Ohrida Lake Restaurant that morning it is her weather he grows aware of. He knows he will find her.

There are long courtships which are performed in absence. This one is built perhaps on his remark about her hair or her almost-silent question as he was falling off some tower or bridge into sleep. The verge of sleep was always terrifying to Nicholas so he would drink himself into it blunting out the seconds of pure fear when he could not use his arms, would lie there knowing he'd witness the half-second fall before sleep, the fear of it greater than anything he felt on the viaduct or any task he carried out for the Dominion Bridge Company.

As he fell, he remembers later, he felt a woman's arm reaching for him, curious about his name.

He is aware of her now, the twin. What holds them together is not the act which saved her life but those moments since. The lost song on the radio. His offhand and relaxed flattery to a nun with regard to her beauty. Then he had leaned his head back, closed his eyes for too long, and slept.

A week later he rejoins the flatbed truck that carries the tar and fire, jumps on with the other men, and is back working at the bridge. His arm healed, he swings from Pier D to Pier C, ignores the stories he hears of the nun who disappeared. He lies supine on the end of his tether looking up towards the struts of the bridge, pivoting slowly. He knows the panorama of the valley better than any engineer. Like a bird. Better than Edmund Burke, the bridge's architect, or Harris, better than the surveyors of 1912 when they worked blind through the bush. The panorama revolves with him and he hangs in this long silent courtship, her absence making him look everywhere.

In a year he will open up a bakery with the money he has saved. He releases the catch on the pulley and slides free of the bridge.

1988

Thomas King

b. 1943

Thomas King, of Cherokee and Greek descent, was born and raised in Roseville, California, near Sacramento. King left university after his first year and took a series of jobs before travelling to New Zealand and Australia, where he worked as a photojournalist. In 1967 he returned to the US and to university, completing his BA in 1970 and his MA two years later at Chico State University (now California State University, Chico). King subsequently taught at the University of Minnesota, where he was chair of the American Indian Studies Program; after immigrating to Canada in 1980, he held a faculty position at the University of Lethbridge before moving to the University of Guelph, where he currently teaches Native literature and creative writing. He briefly returned to the US for Ph.D. studies at the University of Utah, which he completed in 1986.

King has been an important voice in Aboriginal studies in essays such as 'Godzilla vs. Postcolonial' (1990), in which he rejected the post-colonial approach as inappropriate to American Native literature and culture—because of its assumption that the European occupation of the Americas has been the single most important reference point for Native peoples. (He concludes that essay by emphasizing his continual desire to 'cross the lines that definitions—no matter how loose—create'.) King has also edited two important books concerning First Nations and Canadian literature: *The Native in Literature: Canadian and Comparative Perspectives* (1987), a book of essays by various critics; and *All My Relations: An Anthology of Contemporary Canadian Native Fiction* (1990). The latter appeared in the same year as King's first novel, *Medicine River*. This novel (which was made into a 1993 CBC movie for which King wrote the screenplay) is a humorous and ironic account of a Métis photographer's return to his home town on the prairies and to the nearby reservation. Unlike the fiction that followed, *Medicine River* is told in a traditional realist mode.

Although King had begun studying oral narrative and had already been thinking about how it could be used in fiction, it was his encounter early in 1990 with the work of Harry Robinson that transformed his storytelling technique:

I read those stories and they just sort of turned things around for me. I could see what he had done and how he worked it and I began to try to adapt it to my own fiction. It was inspirational.

King's new way of writing is evident in a work that first appeared as a children's book, *A Coyote Columbus Story* (1992). (King has written two other children's books, *Coyote Sings to the Moon*, 1998, and *Coyote's Suit*, 1999.) King republished 'A Coyote Columbus Story', along with a number of similarly-told stories, in his adult short story collection, *One Good Story, That One* (1993). In this book King uses oral patterns of narration ('You know, I hear this story up north,' the first page announces) to break free of the established conventions of the story. As well, in keeping with Coyote's trickiness, he keeps changing the rules of the tale, thereby challenging the reader's preconceptions.

This shiftiness extends even to King's own use of oral materials: for example, though we may think of Coyote, the Plains Natives' mythic trickster figure, as singular and contained within a mythic narrative located in its own time and space, King treats his Coyote as multiple, as existing both in and out of time, and as having not only been here before Europeans came to the Americas but as remaining with us still. King's coyotes can change gender; can become other characters; can change their traits, beliefs, and actions; and seem to lack the usual sense of character motivation that has been central to the traditional short story. King explains that Coyote has been important to Native writers because the 'trickster . . . allows us to create a particular kind of world in which the Judeo-Christian concern with good and evil and order and disorder is replaced with the more Native concern for balance and harmony'.

King's wildly comic second novel, *Green Grass, Running Water* (1993), combines some of the realism of *Medicine River* with these oral storytelling techniques and with this coyote sense of the instability of time and space to produce a fabulist and often surreal narrative. It brings together stories of the contemporary Native community, domestic life, and political activism with a range of allusions to the Bible, myth, literature, and popular narratives and icons, all framed by coyote stories about the creation of the world.

King's third novel, *Truth and Bright Water* (1999), seems to occupy a middle ground between the straightforward telling of his first novel and the freeplay of *Green Grass, Running Water*, but it is no less complex than the fiction that preceded it. A narrative about Truth and Bright Water, neighbouring Native communities separated by the Canada–US border, it brings together myths from the Native tradition and stories about the Cherokee past to tell of the displacement of a people. The novel, filled with twinning, reminds us that borders are European constructions that Native peoples can transcend. Central to the novel is the 'famous Indian artist' Monroe Swimmer, an enigmatic figure who announces that 'realism will only take you so far' and that his art will make magic work to help restore what has been lost.

King has also done extensive work in broadcast and film: he was story editor for 'Four Directions,' a CBC television series about First Nation people, and he contributed several scripts for the CBC series 'North of 60' in the early 1990s and adapted a number of the stories in *One Good Story, That One* for radio and television. He created, wrote, and co-starred in a satirical series for CBC radio, 'The Dead Dog Café Comedy Hour' (1996–2001), about Native peoples and Aboriginal affairs told from a First Nations perspective.

In many ways, King himself is Coyote, always at play, always having fun. In 2002, under the pseudonym Hartley GoodWeather, King ventured into a new genre, the comic mystery. *Dreadful Water Shows Up*—a novel about Thumps DreadfulWater, an ex-cop, now photographer, from California who is trying to fit into Chinook, a reservation trying to support itself with a tourist resort and casino—is the first of what King plans as a series of detective novels.

A Coyote Columbus Story

You know, Coyote came by my place the other day. She was going to a party. She had her party hat and she had her party whistle and she had her party rattle.

I'm going to a party, she says.

Yes, I says, I can see that.

It is a party for Christopher Columbus, says Coyote. That is the one who found America. That is the one who found Indians.

Boy, that Coyote is one silly Coyote. You got to watch out for her. Some of Coyote's stories have got Coyote tails and some of Coyote's stories are covered with scraggy Coyote fur but all of Coyote's stories are bent.

Christopher Columbus didn't find America, I says. Christopher Columbus didn't find Indians, either. You got a tail on that story.

Oh no, says Coyote. I read it in a book.

Must have been a Coyote book, I says.

No, no, no, no, says Coyote. It was a history book. Big red one. All about how Christopher Columbus sailed the ocean blue looking for America and the Indians.

Sit down, I says. Have some tea. We're going to have to do this story right. We're going to have to do this story now.

It was all Old Coyote's fault, I tell Coyote, and here is how the story goes. Here is what really happened.

So.

Old Coyote loved to play ball, you know. She played ball all day and all night. She would throw the ball and she would hit the ball and she would run and catch the ball. But playing ball by herself was boring, so she sang a song and she danced a dance and she thought about playing ball and pretty soon along came some Indians. Old Coyote and the Indians became very good friends. You are sure a good friend, says those Indians. Yes, that's true, says Old Coyote.

But, you know, whenever Old Coyote and the Indians played ball, Old Coyote always won. She always won because she made up the rules. That sneaky one made up the rules and she always won because she could do that.

That's not fair, says the Indians. Friends don't do that.

That's the rules, says Old Coyote. Let's play some more. Maybe you will win the next time. But they don't.

You keep changing the rules, says those Indians.

No, no, no, no, says Old Coyote. You are mistaken. And then she changes the rules again.

So, after a while, those Indians find better things to do.

Some of them go fishing.

Some of them go shopping.

Some of them go to a movie.

Some of them go on a vacation.

Those Indians got better things to do than play ball with Old Coyote and those changing rules.

So, Old Coyote doesn't have anyone to play with.

So, she has to play by herself.

So, she gets bored.

When Old Coyote gets bored, anything can happen. Stick around. Big trouble is coming, I can tell you that.

Well. That silly one sings a song and she dances a dance and she thinks about playing ball. But she's thinking about changing those rules, too, and she doesn't watch what she is making up out of her head. So pretty soon, she makes three ships.

Hmmmm, says Old Coyote, where did those ships come from?

And pretty soon, she makes some people on the beach with flags and funny-looking clothes and stuff.

Hooray, says Old Coyote. You are just in time for the ball game.

Hello, says one of the men in silly clothes and red hair all over his head. I am Christopher Columbus. I am sailing the ocean blue looking for China. Have you seen it?

Forget China, says Old Coyote. Let's play ball.

It must be around here somewhere, says Christopher Columbus. I have a map.

Forget the map, says Old Coyote. I'll bat first and I'll tell you the rules as we go along.

But that Christopher Columbus and his friends don't want to play ball. We got work to do, he says. We got to find China. We got to find things we can sell.

Yes, says those Columbus people, where is the gold?

Yes, they says, where is that silk cloth?

Yes, they says, where are those portable colour televisions?

Yes, they says, where are those home computers?

Boy, says Old Coyote, and that one scratches her head. I must have sung that song wrong. Maybe I didn't do the right dance. Maybe I thought too hard. These people I made have no manners. They act as if they have no relations.

And she is right. Christopher Columbus and his friends start jumping up and down in their funny clothes and they shout so loud that Coyote's ears almost fall off.

Boy, what a bunch of noise, says Coyote. What bad manners. You guys got to stop jumping and shouting or my ears will fall off.

We got to find China, says Christopher Columbus. We got to become rich. We got to become famous. Do you think you can help us?

But all Old Coyote can think about is playing ball.

I'll let you bat first, says Old Coyote.

No time for games, says Christopher Columbus.

I'll let you make the rules, cries Old Coyote.

But those Columbus people don't listen. They are too busy running around, peeking under rocks, looking in caves, sailing all over the place. Looking for China. Looking for stuff they can sell.

I got a monkey, says one.

I got a parrot, says another.

I got a fish, says a third.

I got a coconut, says a fourth.

That stuff isn't worth poop, says Christopher Columbus. We can't sell those things in Spain. Look harder.

But all they find are monkeys and parrots and fish and coconuts. And when they tell Christopher Columbus, that one he squeezes his ears and he chews his nose and grinds his teeth. He grinds his teeth so hard, he gets a headache, and, then, he gets cranky.

And then he gets an idea.

Say, says Christopher Columbus. Maybe we could sell Indians.

Yes, says his friends, that's a good idea. We could sell Indians, and they throw away their monkeys and parrots and fish and coconuts.

Wait a minute, says the Indians, that is not a good idea. That is a bad idea. That is a bad idea full of bad manners.

When Old Coyote hears this bad idea, she starts to laugh. Who would buy Indians, she says, and she laughs some more. She laughs so hard, she has to hold her nose on her face with both her hands.

But while that Old Coyote is laughing, Christopher Columbus grabs a big bunch of Indian men and Indian women and Indian children and locks them up in his ships.

When Old Coyote stops laughing and looks around, she sees that some of the Indians are missing. Hey, she says, where are those Indians? Where are my friends?

I'm going to sell them in Spain, says Christopher Columbus. Somebody has to pay for this trip. Sailing over the ocean blue isn't cheap, you know.

But Old Coyote still thinks that Christopher Columbus is playing a trick. She thinks it is a joke. That is a good joke, she says, trying to make me think that you are going to sell my friends. And she starts to laugh again.

Grab some more Indians, says Christopher Columbus.

When Old Coyote sees Christopher Columbus grab some more Indians, she laughs even harder. What a good joke, she says. And she laughs some more. She does this four times and when she is done laughing, all the Indians are gone. And Christopher Columbus is gone and Christopher Columbus's friends are gone, too.

Wait a minute, says Old Coyote. What happened to my friends? Where are my Indians? You got to bring them back. Who's going to play ball with me?

But Christopher Columbus didn't bring the Indians back and Old Coyote was real sorry she thought him up. She tried to take him back. But, you know, once you think things like that, you can't take them back. So you have to be careful what you think.

So. That's the end of the story.

Boy, says Coyote. That is one sad story.

Yes, I says. It's sad alright. And things don't get any better, I can tell you that.

What a very sad story, says Coyote. Poor Old Coyote didn't have anyone to play ball with. That one must have been lonely. And Coyote begins to cry.

Stop crying, I says. Old Coyote is fine. Some blue jays come along after that and they play ball with her.

Oh, good, says Coyote. But what happened to the Indians? There was nothing in that red history book about Christopher Columbus and the Indians.

Christopher Columbus sold the Indians, I says, and that one became rich and famous.

Oh, good, says Coyote. I love a happy ending. And that one blows her party whistle and that one shakes her party rattle and that one puts her party hat back on her head. I better get going, she says, I'm going to be late for the party.

Okay, I says. Just remember how that story goes. Don't go messing it up again. Have you got it straight, now?

You bet, says Coyote. But if Christopher Columbus didn't find America and he didn't find Indians, who found these things?

Those things were never lost, I says. Those things were always here. Those things are still here today.

By golly, I think you are right, says Coyote.

Don't be thinking, I says. This world had enough problems already without a bunch of Coyote thoughts with tails and scraggy fur running around bumping into each other.

Boy, that's the truth. I can tell you that.

1993

bp Nichol

1944–1988

Born in Vancouver, Barrie Phillip Nichol was raised there and in Winnipeg and Port Arthur (now part of Thunder Bay). He began writing poetry in the early sixties while attending the University of British Columbia, where he became acquainted with the work of Earle Birney, bill bissett, and the poets of the *Tish* movement. Unhappy with the conventional lyrics he was writing, Nichol found himself attracted to recent visual experiments of Birney's and bissett's. After teaching grade four (in Port Coquitlam, BC) for part of a year, he left to settle in Toronto. While employed at the University of Toronto library, he began to create 'concrete', or visual, poetry. In 1964 he started *Ganglia* magazine and Ganglia press with David Aylward; during the magazine's two-year existence it served as an outlet for West Coast writers who did not have Toronto publishers. In 1967 Nichol began *grOnk*, a newsletter devoted to visual poetry.

Having met lay-analyst Lea Hindley-Smith in 1963, Nichol joined her therapy-learning group and in 1967 became part of Therafields, a therapeutic community, where he lived and worked as a lay-therapist. Throughout the 1980s he continued his work as an editor (for Coach House Press, Underwhich Editions, and Frank Davey's *Open Letter* magazine), while teaching creative writing at York University.

Nichol published a large array of broadsides, pamphlets, chapbooks, and full-length books. His first 'book' of poems was *Journeying & the Returns* (1967; also entitled *bp*), a cardboard package that contains a record, a lyrical sequence, an envelope of visual poems, and a flip book or animated poem. In 1970 he won a Governor General's Award for the four publications that appeared that year: *Still Water*; *The Cosmic Chef*, an anthology of concrete poetry; *Beach Head*, a sequence of lyrics; and *The True Eventual Story of Billy the Kid*, a prose piece. In 1972 he formed, with poet and theorist Steve McCaffery, the 'Toronto Research Group' (TRG). In statements appearing in *Open Letter*, TRG introduced new developments in European theory as a way of opposing trends in Canadian literary criticism, such as the search for national identity in literature. (McCaffery brought the project to an official close in 1992 with the publication of *Rational Geomancy: The Kids of the Book Machine. The Collected Research Reports of the Toronto Research Group 1973–1982*.)

Nichol's *Selected Writing: As Elected*, which includes some previously unpublished work, appeared in 1980. *Zygal: A Book of Mysteries and Translations* (1985) provides a good indication of Nichol's breadth: it contains poems that range from the traditional, such as 'lament', to experimental and Dadaist work in what he and Steve McCaffery called 'pataphysics (after the term coined by the eccentric nineteenth-century French author Alfred Jarry)—which Nichol defined as 'the science of imaginary solutions'. Some of Nichol's other 'pataphysical works can be found in *Art Facts* (1990) and *Truth: A Book of Fictions* (1993). Nichol also experimented with a wide range of unconventional prose narratives, including *Two Novels* (1969) and the essay collection *Craft Dinner* (1978). *An H in the Heart: bp Nichol, a Reader* (1994) contains prose work selected by George Bowering and Michael Ondaatje.

Although Nichol's interests varied widely, he is best known for his work in concrete poetry (such as *ABC: The Aleph Beth Book*, 1971, and *LOVE: A Book of Remembrances*, 1974); his multivolume poem *The Martyrology* (the first books of which appeared in 1972, the most recent of which appeared posthumously; Book 9 was published in 2000); and his involvement in the sound poetry movement. By experimenting with visual and sound poetry while maintaining an interest in traditional forms in which syntax continues to function as a carrier of meaning, Nichol sought to synthesize new modes of poetry and prose. For his first visual poems he employed typed arrangements of words and letters to produce concrete poetry (letters, phonemes, words, and graphic figures arranged on a page pictorially rather than verbally or syntactically); later he introduced graphic designs—drawings combined with letters or words. After the mid-1970s Nichol's visual poetry moved more and more towards pure graphics, particularly the cartoon.

Nichol's experiments with sound poetry—in contrast to visual poetry, with its concern for graphic form—seek to recover the emotional possibilities of speech and human sound that were originally part of the oral tradition. Through the use of homonyms, unusual cadences and emphases, and (in group performance) the overlay of one utterance upon another, sound poems free the rich oral qualities of poetry from the silence of the page. Although he also gave solo performances, Nichol was most often seen and recorded as a member of The Four Horsemen, a performance poetry group that he helped to found and that performed improvisational 'readings' ranging from pieces made entirely of non-verbal sounds to complex contrapuntal verbal sequences. (Its other members, Steve McCaffery, Paul Dutton, and Rafael Barreto-Rivera, have continued to perform occasionally, as 'The Horsemen', since Nichol's death.) Michael Ondaatje's film *The Sons of Captain Poetry* (1970) catches Nichol's dynamic presence as a performer; the Four Horsemen can be seen in a brief appearance in Ron Mann's movie *Poetry in Motion* (1982).

The Martyrology, Nichol's most ambitious and important work, unites the visual and oral aspects of his writing with its narrative and personal dimensions and shows his relationship to postmodern and post-structuralist interests: in its volumes he deconstructs literary forms and language, uses parody both to criticize and to affirm, and works at several levels of intertextuality to invite many possible readings of this work. The opening volumes of this long poem build up a mythology that accounts for the structure of the universe through the existence of 'saints' created from broken up or 'deconstructed' words (for example, 'storm' becomes 'St Orm'). As the focus in later books turned from the saints' stories to a more general examination of language itself, his interest in linguistic deconstruction gave way to playful recombination: words become the means of examining sound, and ideas cause new words to be formed. (For instance, in Book 5, Chain 8, the neologism 'eyear' combines 'eye' and 'ear', while functioning also as the sound equivalent of 'a year'.)

This reordering and restructuring of language, visual image, sound, and form invites questions about the boundaries of art, and about the point at which the poem ceases to be a literary form and becomes mere sound or mere visual effect. Nichol created a body of work that demands that readers reconsider distinctions between content and form and question their definitions of art.

From *The Martyrology*

FROM BOOK 1: 'THE SORROWS OF SAINT ORM'

my lady my lady

this is the day i want to cry for you
but my eyes are dry

somewhere i'm happy

not like the sky
outside this window
gone grey

---

this is the line between reality
when i hold your body
enter the only way i am

saint orm
keep her from harm

this ship journey safely

quick as it can

saint orm you were a stranger
came to me out of the dangerous alleys &
the streets

                lived in
that dirty room on
comox avenue

                          me &
my friends
                          playing what lives we had to
the end

              i want to tell you a story
in the old way
                              i can't

haven't the words or
the hands to reach you

& this circus   this noise in
my brain
               makes it hard to explain
my sorrow

you were THE DARK WALKER
stood by my side as a kid

i barely remember

except the heaven i dreamt of
was a land of clouds
you moved at your whim

knowing i walked
the bottom of a sea

that heaven was up there
on that world in the sky

that this was death

that i would go there
when i came to life

how do you tell a story?

saint orm you were the one

you saw the sun rise
knew the positions of the stars

how far we had to go
before the ultimate destruction

as it was prophesied in REVELATIONS[1]
nations would turn away from god & be destroyed

told me the difference between now & then
when i could no longer tell the beasts from men

1 See especially Revelation 11: 18 and 16. Revelation also predicts that before the final destruction of the world it will be ruled by a man known as 'the beast' (13: 11ff).

saint orm
grant me peace

days i grow sick of seeing

bring my lady
back from that sea she's crossed
tossed in a grey world of
her own

there is no beauty in madness

no sinlessness
in tossing the first stone

make her sea calm

bring her safe to
my arms

* * *

1972

FROM BOOK 3, SECTION VIII.

* * *

last take

late february 73

dave & i look out towards the lion's gate[1]

years mass
events
we made it out between the lion's paws
rear shocks gone
swerving to avoid the bumps
spell of spelling cast around us
tiny ripples in the blood stream the brain stem's rooted in
a body place &
time
the lion's month before us the lamb's born in
the door
you are not permitted to open again
enter thru the lion's mouth the man's root gets planted in
not to be consumed
as tho the use of lips weren't speech
a doorway into the woman's soul intelligence comes out of
SCREAMING
a complete thot
born from the dialogue between you

or what comes forth from my mouth
born from the woman in me
handed down thru my grandma ma & lea
is what marks me most a man
that i am finally this we
this one & simple thing
my father Leo
my mother Cancer
she births herself
the twin mouths of women
w's omen
it turns over & reverses itself
the mirrors cannot trick us

1 The Lions Gate Bridge—connecting Vancouver with North and West Vancouver—is a mile-long suspension bridge that is flanked by two stone lions at either end.

our words are spun within the signs our fathers left
the sibilance of s
the cross of t
there are finally no words for you father
too many letters multiply the signs
you are the one
the unifying
no signifier when we cannot grasp the signified[2]
saints in between
the world of men
women
the sign complete
the w & the circle turning
add the E
the three levels
linked by line
or the two fold vision
H to I
the saints returned to this plane

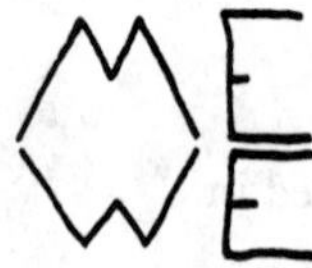

the emblems were there when i began
seven years to understand
the first letter/level of
martyrdom

CODA: Mid-Initial Sequence

faint edge of sleep
a literal fuzzing in the mind
as tho the edge of
what was held clearly
became less defined
the penalty paid &
your father recognized
for what he is

for W

HA!

the is

2 Structuralists divide the 'signs' we use to communicate—the most prominent of which are words—into 'signifiers' (the arbitrary conveyors of meaning, such as the combinations of letters or sounds) and 'signified' (the underlying sense, the meaning intended).

orange

the vague light
closing the eye

's lid

home plate

the late P
destroyed
leaving only b
& n

beginning again

b n a[3]

all history there

t here

opposed against the suffering
we have yet to bear

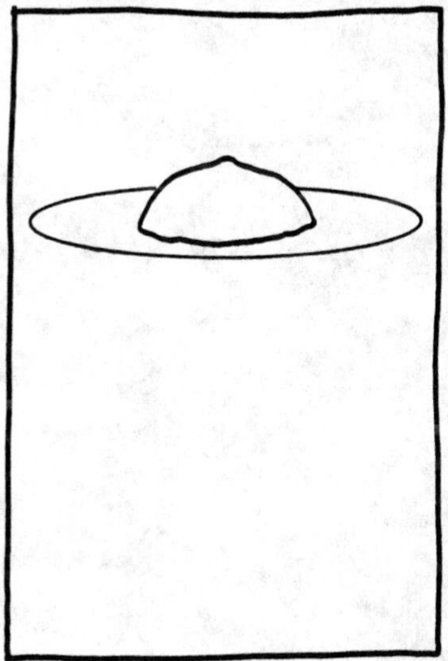

3 The BNA Act, or British North America Act, is the name of the act passed by the British Parliament in 1867 to bring the Dominion of Canada into existence.

last note

no t
no e

I as no

I body
I where
I w here

no w
for w's sake

no is
        e
against the silent sleep

bushes

dawn

the r rises
brushes drawn
the whole scene

the w hole
into which the world
disappears

d is a p
pear shaped

dear H
a p edges
into the sea

sun

the unenviable s

there is no desire for speech

there is no desire to spell

each gesture
against the chaos
must be made well

there is stillness in the heart of the power
as there is stillness in the heart of the storm

between the w & the d
the in side of
the mind/
/’s a quiet place
from which the power unwinds

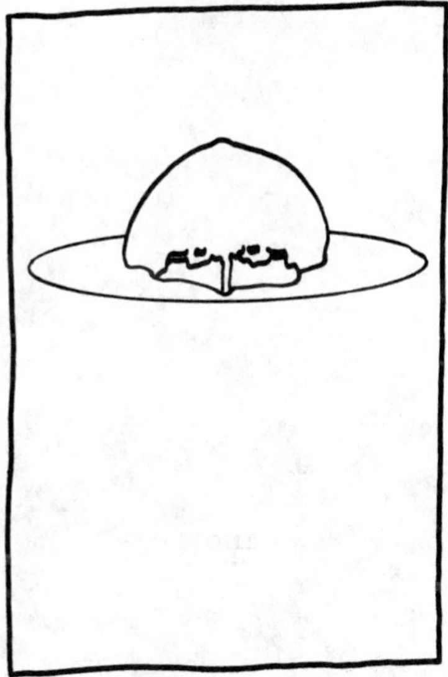

in vocation
i am
a singer

every letter
invokes a spell
ing is
the power
letters have
over me 2100

word shaping

addition of the l

within the difference
if exists

tensions a
polarity

who is moved or moves
a distinction a disparity

a.d. a.d.
history's spoken in 2110
the first four letters

all e to z
outside the head's
measure of our kind

man's time

1976

FROM BOOK 5, CHAIN 8

out of the west the best rises
out of the east the beast
Leviathan[1]
        Utnapishtim's potential nemesis
a cloud of dust &
cliché in its sashay with the day-to-day
conversea in ation minor
variation
        recapitulation of
a to z themes

t hem e
        or e a
thrd yrs
        a vow the e makes with the l or a
capitulation
riddle read for writers: cap it!
what?
    —ulation—
    ululation of its wake

roused from depths the deep
double e threads our speech
full power of the beast noise
voice
we cling to   silence

Thunder Bay   roar & crash the storms made
echoed off the cliffs
so loud you thot the giant'd wake[2]
slept over the lake
millenia
        trees had covered him
earth filled his pores
my mother'd hide in dread
took me to bed with her
protector from the storm

1 A mythical sea monster, sometimes identified with Satan (Isaiah 27: 1), 'Utnapishtim': in Assyro-Babylonian mythology, the Noah-like figure (prominent in the *Epic of Gilgamesh*, *c.* 2000 BCE) who, as the only human to know of the impending worldwide deluge, built a boat to house his family and the earth's animal life. After the flood, Utnapishtim and his wife became immortal.

2 The Sleeping Giant, a rock formation in Thunder Bay harbour, is identified in Ojibwa legend with Nanabozho, the famous trickster; he is expected to wake in the future and come to the aid of his people.

St Orm we've not forgotten you
you speak with voice of wind
power to bend the limbs of trees & man
blow down anything stands in the way of your word's truth
spoke with force
against the coarse lie we call our 'civilization'

so i sing
stupefied by speech
brought under the spell eyear can bring
  ought e e ing
thought she sleeps thing
emerges from the deep
the faceless dream
dreamt dreamer ter or
entered world of shifting imagery
we try to freeze
make shiftless
because we feel less than
stored imagery's full weight

torn apart too often
that divisiveness
an isolation to protect the feared for work
valued as self is valued
defended as you would your life
'he laid it down for art'
does art thank us?

Noel Coward[3] in the 1950's
'why must the show go on?'
the 'noble soul in torment' one does grow bored with
recognizing the romanticization
self-aggrandisement of one's own pain
we all fall prey to

you address the problems as they rise
prize what is most human as
worth the struggle
                                the will to better
your self & others
hate that poverty of spirit ignorance breeds

3 (1899–1973); English dramatist, actor, and composer. Noted for his sophisticated songs and plays that were wittily critical of society, Coward was less popular in the fifties when the theatre was dominated by realistic drama; during this period he became a commercially successful cabaret performer.

Hannah Arendt[4] speaking of Eichmann
'the face of evil is ordinary'

we build it up
look for it in cops & robbers morality plays
ignore its presence in the day-to-day
out of our own naivete

the distortion or ignoring of what is obvious
(that structural scale must remain human)
leads to monumentalization
whatever the political belief
the ordinary man or woman is forgotten
because they are not known
sentimentalized or swept aside
noone takes the time to talk to them

noone t   t   t   t t   t t
seven crosses for our lack of humanity
        (akes)
seven crosses for our arrogance & pride
                (he ime)
seven crosses for our lack of humility
                            (o alk o)
seven crosses for the people swept aside
                                        (hem
'd in then

am id St Noise
the voices
ignorance
such lack of knowing
starts there

a beginning only
a tentative law or
exception
lets the self reveal itself
we claim despite our fear

* * *

1982

4 (1906–75), German-Jewish philosopher and political theorist who escaped the Nazis and settled in the United States; in *Eichmann in Jerusalem: A Report on the Banality of Evil* (1961) Arendt argues that Adolf Eichmann (1906–62), the Nazi leader who was in charge of the execution of the Jews, represents the modern figure of evil: the rational, pragmatic bureaucrat who accepts immoral commands as part of life's banal routine.

landscape: I

alongthehorizongrewanunbrokenlineoftrees

1986

lament[1]

cruelty   the land was
harsh   as is told you
a barren island marguerite de roberval was marooned on
in the mouth of the saint lawrence river
by her uncle
viceroy of canada
for having fallen in love with
a poor man
                he escaped the ship &
swam to join her

this is the first european family we know of
one child is born to them
there on the isle of demons
so called because the wind howled over the rocks
drowned in sound the three of them

1 This poem retells the story of Marguerite de Roberval, the niece of French lieutenant-general Jean-Francois de La Rocque de Roberval (1500–60), viceroy of Canada, Newfoundland, and Labrador from 1540. Accompanying her uncle on his expedition to the colony in 1542–3, she incurred his wrath by becoming involved with a poor cavalier. The 'Isle of Demons' to which she was banished is thought to be Quirpon Island, off the coast of Labrador. Her lover, managing to escape his guards, jumped ship and swam ashore to join her.

later she is rescued
returned to france
her husband & her child dead of famine
rode out the storm her mind broken
by such cruelty as should never come again
out of this land to haunt us

•

innocence
          in a sense
begins on   the outcrop

that we had it & lost it (maybe)
that we never had it (closer to the truth)
that we could all be to this day
marguerite de roberval's fantasy of company
alone on the isle of demons
dreaming of a country full of people
a land you could grow food in
starving to death
human howling in the elemental grief

1986

Bronwen Wallace

1945–1989

In her poetry and her short stories Bronwen Wallace explored connections between people and places—and between the immediacies of her own life in the Kingston, Ont., area (where her family has lived for the past 200 years) and the larger issues of her postwar generation. Born in Kingston and educated at Queen's University (BA, 1967; MA, 1969), Wallace, a committed political activist who was shaped by the political events and social ferment of the 1960s, moved to Windsor in 1970 and became associated with groups dealing with workers' and with women's issues. While there she also co-founded a women's bookstore and worked with local unionists on an oral history of the Union of Auto Workers in Windsor. In 1977 she returned permanently to Kingston: there, remaining committed to working for social change, she became involved with Interval House, a shelter for abused women and children. She also taught at St Lawrence College and at Queen's and wrote a weekly column for the Kingston *Whig-Standard.* (A collection of these columns, and other essays and talks, was published posthumously as *Arguments with the World,* 1992.) In 1988 she was writer-in-residence at the University of Western Ontario.

Wallace's first book of poetry, *Marrying into the Family* (it was published, in a single volume, with Mary di Michele's *Bread and Chocolate* in 1980 and republished separately in 1994) showed her interest in the complex relationships between the individual and community, a subject she explored further in subsequent poetry collections: *Signs of the Former Tenant* (1983), *Common Magic* (1985), *The Stubborn Particulars of Grace* (1987), and a posthumous collection of prose poems inspired by the country and western singer Emmylou Harris, *Keep That Candle Burning Bright and Other Poems* (1991). With her partner, Chris Whynot, Wallace made two films: *All You Have To Do* (1982), about the death from cancer of a friend (an experience that also gave rise to her sequence called 'The Cancer Poems', which now seems all too predictive of her own early death from cancer), and *That's Why I'm Talking* (1984), about her fellow poets Mary di Michele, Pier Giorgio di Cicco, Carolyn Smart, and Robert Priest. A collection of short stories Wallace completed shortly before her death was published posthumously as *People You'd Trust Your Life To* (1990).

Most of Wallace's poetry is narrative. It is always accessible: she writes in a colloquial manner that captures the rhythms of spoken language. Her easygoing style has given rise to comparisons with her fellow eastern Ontario poet Al Purdy—though her voice is far more introspective than Purdy's and less engaged in public history. 'One of the challenges for me as a writer is to put some of what is missing, some of the messy details by which most of us live our lives, finally, on the page,' she wrote in an essay called 'The Contemplative Life: A Necessity as Well as a Limitation for the Writer'. In her chatty, almost rambling style, Wallace gave voice and clarity to the odd bits of experience contained within memory, as if trying to find an elusive narrative shape for life could restore its lost magnitude and redeem experience from the depths of time.

Her interest in the personal dimensions of the past meant that in her poetry, as much as in her fiction, stories become the currency of human exchange: 'My stories are my wealth,' a woman says in 'Testimonies': 'all I have to give / my children.' Memories, anecdotes, and inherited tales crowd together in poems that examine the complex roles women play or the difficulty of understanding human frailties. Wallace engages the reader in the *process* of narratives, drawing on a welter of remembered details, from the first rainbow she saw as she walked home one day at the age of five to the small incidents that give meaning to past relationships.

Titles such as *Common Magic* and *The Stubborn Particulars of Grace* speak to Wallace's sense of the world. Both her poetry and her fiction are marked by a sense that the miraculous can emerge from the often overlooked minutiae of daily life: her writing therefore raises events, perceptions, and ideas that might be deemed banal to a level of experience bordering on the mystical. She draws no easy conclusions, but the connections we are invited to make in poems such as 'The Watermelon Incident' affirm what Wallace called the 'grace' of everyday existence. She depicts the private, yet common, features of human experience: the fear of death and failure, the need for love and belonging. The woman paralysed in 'the middle of her spotless kitchen' in 'The Woman in this Poem' captures these anxieties: 'we stop in the middle / of an ordinary day and / like the woman in this poem / begin to feel / our own deaths / rising slowing within us.' But in contrast, Wallace also gives us, in poems such as 'Joseph MacLeod Daffodils', the heroism of living, loving, and accepting not only those around us but ourselves.

In the last year of her life Wallace turned naturally to short-story writing, expanding in her fiction on her familiar themes of love and female relationships. The stories in *People You'd Trust Your Life To* are portraits of individuals who are seeking to transcend the ordinary, not discarding it but embracing it in search of the miraculous qualities inherent in life itself. The opening of 'An Easy Life' recalls the clear, journalistic expression and attention to detail already present in 'The Woman in this Poem' as it introduces Marion, the woman with the 'easy life'. By the end of the story we learn that standing in this scene of domestic order and contentment—signified by the gleaming kitchen and pulsing crocuses in the garden—is a woman feeling both 'anger and tenderness', a woman whose life is much more complicated, and richer, than it appears.

The Woman in this Poem

The woman in this poem
lives in the suburbs
with her husband and two children
each day she waits for the mail and
once a week receives
a letter from her lover
who lives in another city
writes of roses   warm patches
of sunlight on his bed
Come to me he pleads
I need you and the woman
reaches for the phone
to dial the airport
she will leave this afternoon
her suitcase packed
with a few light clothes

But as she is dialing
the woman in this poem
remembers the pot-roast
and the fact that it is Thursday
she thinks of how her husband's face

will look when he reads her note
his body curling sadly toward
the empty side of the bed

She stops dialing and begins
to chop onions for the pot-roast
but behind her back the phone
shapes itself insistently
the number for airline reservations
chants in her head
in an hour her children will be
home from school and after that
her husband will arrive
to kiss the back of her neck
while she thickens the gravy
and she knows that
all through dinner
her mouth will laugh and chatter
while she walks with her lover
on a beach somewhere

She puts the onions in the pot
and turns toward the phone
but even as she reaches
she is thinking of
her daughter's piano lessons
her son's dental appointment

Her arms fall to her side
and as she stands there
in the middle of her spotless kitchen
we can see her growing
old like this
and wish for something   anything
to happen   we could have her go
mad perhaps and lock herself
in the closet   crouch there
for days her dresses withering
around her like cast-off skins
or maybe she could take
to cruising the streets at night
in her husband's car
picking up teenage boys
and fucking them in the back seat

we can even imagine
finding her body
dumped in a ditch somewhere
on the edge of town

The woman in this poem offends us
with her useless phone and the persistent
smell of onions we regard her as we do
the poorly calculated overdose
who lies in a bed somewhere
not knowing how her life drips
through her drop by measured drop
we want to think of death
as something sudden
stroke or the leap
that carries us over the railing
of the bridge in one determined arc
the pistol aimed precisely
at the right part of the brain
we want to hate this woman

but mostly we hate knowing
that for us too it is
moments like this
our thoughts stiff fingers
tear at again and again
when we stop in the middle
of an ordinary day and
like the woman in this poem
begin to feel
our own deaths
rising slow within us

1987

Joseph Macleod Daffodils

for Isabel Huggan

'I'm planting perennials this year,' you tell me,
'because I'm scared and it's the only way I know
to tell myself I'm going to be here,

years from now, watching them come up.'
Maybe it's a phase we're going through,
since I'm at it too; lily of the valley,
under the back hedge, thinking *when Jeremy*
is old enough to drive, I'll have to divide these,
put some under the cedars there; by the time
he leaves home, they'll be thick as grass,
and at the same time saying
'God, we're parodies of ourselves,
sixties children, still counting on flowers,
for chrissake, to get us through.'
Knowing you'll see it that way too,
your snort of laughter
the index of my love and the wisdom
of George Eliot's[1] observation that
'a difference of taste in jokes
is a great strain on the affections.'
(Another thing we share, our delight
in quotations like that, exactly what you'd expect
from girls who grew up wearing glasses
into women who read everything;
your bathroom so much like mine,
a huge bin of books by the toilet
and on the shelves, all the bottles
turned label side out.
'The contents of somebody's bathroom',
Diane Arbus[2] said, 'is like reading their biography.')

This doesn't help much, does it?
You're laughing, but your hands stay
clenched in your lap, still forcing
the tight, dumb bulbs into the ground
as if you could force your life
to a pattern as serene as theirs,
a calm that flourishes in darkness
to the pull of the sun.
Still, I keep on talking.
It's the only wisdom that I've got.
How about this one: you know those
big, yellow daffodils—they're called
Joseph MacLeods—well, the way they got their name
was that the man who developed them

1 Pseudonym of Mary Ann Evans (1819–80), a British novelist known for her depiction of provincial life.
2 American photographer (1923–71) known for her striking and bizarre pictures of people.

always kept a radio on in the greenhouse
and the day the first one bloomed, in 1942,
was the day he got the news
of the Allied victory, against Rommel,
at El Alamein, and the announcer who read the news
was Joseph MacLeod. Which shows a sense of history
I can appreciate; no *El Alamein Glorias* or
Allied Victory Blooms for this guy, you can be sure.
It's like the story my mother always tells
about joining the crowds on V-E day,[3] swollen with me,
but dancing all night, thinking *now*
she can be born any time.

What I love
is how these stories try to explain
the fit of things, though I can see
your mood's for something more sinister.
Like the reason Diane Arbus gave
for photographing freaks, maybe?
'Aristocrats,' she called them,
'they've already passed their test in life.'
Being born with their trauma, that is,
while the rest of us must sit around, dreading it.
Meaning you and me. *Normal.* Look at us,
practically wizened with worry, hunched
over coffee cups, whispering of cancer and divorce,
something happening to one of the kids, our lives
spread between us like those articles you read
about Mid-Life Crisis or Identity Anxiety,
Conflict of Role Expectations in Modern Marriages,
the kind that tell you you can fix all that
with less red meat and more exercise,
the ones that talk as if the future's
something you decide about,
though what it all comes down to, every time,
is making do. You can call it a choice
if you want, but that doesn't change
what we learn to rely on,
the smaller stratagems. Whatever works.
The socks in their neat balls, tucked on the right
side of the drawer, the iris coming up each summer

3 8 May 1945, the date of Germany's surrender to the Allied forces, which ended the Second World War. ('V-E' stands for 'victory in Europe'.)

in the south bed. 'Be sincere and don't fuss.'
'Noble deeds and hot baths
are the best cures for depression.'

It's what I love in you, Isabel.
How you can stand here saying
'Brave and kind. I want to get through this
being brave and kind,' squaring your shoulders
like a heroine in those movies our mothers watched
where people knew their problems
didn't amount to a hill of beans
in this crazy world and let it go at that,
fitting themselves to the shape
a life makes for itself without meaning to.
I love your grin from the end of my sidewalk
as you head for home, posed like a photograph.
'Perfectly Ordinary Woman on Suburban Street.'
'A secret about a secret,' Arbus called this kind,
'the more it tells you,
the less you know.'

1987

Testimonies

for Julie Cruickshank

As the cadence in an old woman's voice
becomes the line that will lead others
into the territory her people saw,
you make me see
the importance of your work, the long hours
taping these languages which only a few
of the elders speak now. 'My stories are my wealth,'
one woman tells you, 'all I have to give
my children,' and you help create the alphabet
that takes them there. Linguistic anthropology,
the science of making language
into maps. The crazy detours
it can take you on, that story
of the parrot up in Carcross, NWT,
a bird someone brought over the pass

during the gold-rush and left at the Caribou Hotel
where it lived for another sixty years
entertaining customers by singing
nineteenth-century bar-room ballads
in a cockney accent. The voice of a dead miner
kept on in a brain the size of an acorn,
all the countries of his lifetime, contracted
to its bright, improbable presence
amid men who figure they've seen
just about everything now,
so that their sitting there, listening like that
becomes part of the story too,
just as I am added when I tell it,
as anyone will be, each version
a journey that carries us all along,
as the shards of pottery, carefully labelled
and carried up through layered villages
flesh out more hands
than the two that made them.

How can any of us know
what will speak for us or who
will be heard? We who are never
satisfied, eager for the evidence
no matter how it comes, slowing the car down
as we pass the accident, to see
what's pulled from the wreckage, crowding
the ones who were at the scene, the cop
or the ambulance driver, the survivors
stepping forward for their moment, blessed
by our terrible need to know everything.
Even those women we dread
sitting next to on buses or trains,
their bodies swelling with messy secrets,
the odour of complaint on their breath,
may be prophets. Whether we listen or not
won't stop them from telling
our story in their own.

Not far from where I live, a man ploughs
someone's skull up in his cornfield
and the next spring, four more, a family maybe
though no one knows even that,

their being there at all,
and longer, the only claim that's offered.
Like the farms themselves, their few rich fields
the chance deposits of a glacier.
Even the ones that I keep looking for,
wading through goldenrod to a house
where just inside the door, the trunk of old clothes
or the chair that didn't make it
to the load on back of the truck
bears witness to those smaller choices
we all have to make
about the future
and what can be wisely carried into it.

What your work brings you to, I see now,
not the past. Each site, a threshold
into this slow discovery,
the random testimony gathered
as best we can, each of us down
to essentials, as the failed are
and the dead, who bear us forward
in their fine, accurate arms.

1987

The Watermelon Incident

It was during this same summer,
in the back seat of another
speeding car, that I nearly
cut my finger off, slicing watermelon
with a jack-knife. We were all laughing
when the knife went in
to the bone, when it sucked out
one of those silences through which
blood spurted over my hand and onto the
watermelon, onto my other hand, my
knees, staining my new black and white
checked pedal-pushers which my mother said
were too tight anyway, made me look
cheap, like the peroxide streaks

Lorraine and I put in our hair when she
was babysitting at the Neilsons', onto
the grey plush seat and down to my
ankle socks, to my white sandals, onto
the floor, until Lorraine said 'Jesus
H. Christ,' and the car pulled over
rolled to a stop where we all got out
and stared. Two miles away,
the city bristled with hospitals,
antiseptic, doctors, cat-gut,
parents and tetanus shots, but we
were Beyond All That. Immortal.
And it's because I mean this
literally
that the bleeding stopped
that the end of my finger hung,
by a strand, from the rest of it
that Lorraine found some bandaids
she'd stuffed in her purse in case
her new shoes gave her blisters
that they held
that my mother was cooking dinner
when I got home
that my brother poked me in the ribs
and chewed with his mouth full
that nobody asked
that it was after the sun went down
(and in that sudden way a sunburn
will) that the pain surfaced.
Through my sleep, my hand
the size of a boxing glove
as if all the blood still in my body
pushed to that spot
where the bandaids held me together
and on whatever cool square
of sheet or pillow
I could find for it
kept it up: *pound-pound, pound-pound*
pound-pound, pound-pound,
until I knew for sure
it'd wake my parents
sleeping in the next room.

I'm one of those people
who believe that we remember
everything, though we may not know it.
Just the other day, in fact, I read
that even though we forget what we learn
when we're drunk, it'll all come back
sometime, when we're drunk again.
And that made me think
of the guy who lived in the apartment next
to the place I had before my son was born,
one of those buildings where so much
has passed from one room to another
that the walls thin out,
like those spots in an old shirt
where grease or sweat's been scrubbed at
so that the skin shines through,
so that every Friday night, when this guy
got drunk, I could hear the bottles
dropping, empty, to the table top
and by the tenth, maybe, the twelfth,
he'd be on to his mother, how he'd
disappointed her, he'd start wailing
and pounding the walls. Most of the time
I hated him, this old fart, sobbing
in his beer for Mama. I'd turn
the TV up or go for a walk,
but other nights, I guess, he must have
got in with my own sounds, somehow,
like those bits of dreams you never
quite let go, until this thing
I read on drunkenness and memory
opens the door for him and he sings there,
fiercely, in the midst of all the other stuff
about the watermelon and the knife
missing it, the blood and Lorraine's face,
the pain pounding out from my finger
to my wrist to my chest to my throat, my teeth
clenched over it, my parents
sleeping, soundly, on.

1983

An Easy Life

Right now, Marion is giving her kitchen its once-a-year major cleaning, right down to that little crack where the gunk builds up between the counter and the metal edge of the sink. She's going at it with Comet and an old toothbrush, singing along to the Talking Heads on her Walkman, having a great time. She smoked a joint with her coffee before she started this morning. It helps. She's already done the fridge, the stove, *and* the oven, wiped down the walls. Just the counters and drawers to go, really. Then the floor. Marion does a little dance over to the cupboard for the Lysol.

It's a beautiful day. The patio door is half open and the air that blows in is real spring air without that underscent of snow. Crocuses glow in creamy pools of purple and gold, all along the stone path to the garden. Soon, there'll be daffodils, tulips. And hyacinths, Marion's favourite, their sweet, heavy scent filling the kitchen, outrageous, it always seems to Marion, like the smell of sex.

Marion has thick auburn hair and the fine, almost translucent complexion that often goes with it. These days, she's got it cut short with longer wisps over her forehead and at the back of her neck. She has always been beautiful, not in any regular, classic way, certainly, but because she has the kind of bone structure that can give a face movement. At forty-two, her beauty seems deeper, more complex than it ever was, as if it's just beginning to discover all its possibilities. Everyone who knows Marion acknowledges how beautiful she is. The other thing they say is that she seems to have a very easy life.

She was born Marion Patterson, the youngest of three, the only daughter of a Home Economics teacher and a high school principal. Her health was always excellent, her teeth straight. She watched 'Howdy Doody' and 'Father Knows Best' and saw the first-time appearances on 'The Ed Sullivan Show' of both Elvis Presley and The Beatles. In school she was one of those people who manage to get high marks without being a browner and at the same time is pretty, popular, and good at sports.

All of this had its predictable effect when she entered university. After her first class, English 101, Marion walked directly to the centre of the campus where a long-haired boy with deep-set, deep-brown eyes was handing out leaflets. END CANADIAN COMPLICITY IN VIETNAM, they said. Below that was the time and place of a meeting. Marion took a leaflet. She also went to the meeting.

By Christmas she was spending most of her time in the coffee shop reading *Ramparts* and *I.F. Stone's Biweekly*,[1] and talking to anyone who would listen about what she read. She wore short skirts, fishnet stockings, and turtleneck sweaters in dark colours. Her hair was long then, straight down her back, almost to her waist, and her face was sharper than it is now, vibrant in an almost aggressive way that some men found intimidating.

One man who was not intimidated was Carl Walker, a second-year art student who spent his afternoons in the coffee shop smoking and sketching. Marion had one of the strongest profiles he'd ever seen. In April, Carl and Marion were arrested at a demonstration outside the US Embassy in Toronto.

1 In the 1960s the most important magazines of the radical left.

That summer they were married. Marion wore a long, red Indian cotton skirt, a tie-dyed T-shirt, and a crown of daisies and black-eyed Susans. Carl wore blue jeans, a loose white shirt, and a button that said, L.B.J. L.B.J. HOW MANY KIDS DID YOU KILL TODAY? Back at school, their tiny apartment was the favourite hangout of campus politicos. Carl made huge pots of chili, Marion rolled the joints, and everyone argued with their mouths full. Over the stereo was a poster showing the profiles of Karl Marx, Mao Tse Tung, and Ho Chi Minh. SOME PEOPLE TALK ABOUT THE WEATHER, it said above the profiles. And below, in larger letters, WE DON'T.

When Marion got pregnant, she and Carl decided to quit university and find a place in the country. They could grow their own food, Carl would continue painting, Marion would read.

'Who needs a degree?' Marion said.

'Just you wait,' replied Marion's women friends, among whom feminism (or Women's Lib as it was then called) was making rapid advances. 'Wait'll you have a colicky baby and it's thirty below outside. Carl'll go on painting the great male masterpiece and you'll be up to your elbows in shit.'

Not so, however. Jason Dylan Walker was rapidly followed by Benjamin Joplin and Joshua Guthrie. All of Marion's labours were short, the boys were born undrugged, screaming red and perfectly formed. Carl was always there. He was—and still is—an enthusiastic parent, willing to do his share. He also kept on painting and managed to mount two highly acclaimed shows in six years. His paintings began to sell for very respectable prices.

Both Marion and Carl took pride in their organic vegetable garden and were keenly involved in a protest that stopped Ontario Hydro from building transmitter towers through a strip of choice farmland in their community. Marion raised chickens, Carl baked bread, and they both spent hours taking the boys for walks in the woods around their farm. When Josh was five, Marion decided to go back to school. Carl's growing reputation got him an excellent faculty position in the art department of a small community college, they moved into the city, and Marion got her Masters in Psychology and Education. For the last five years, she has been a guidance counsellor at Centennial Secondary School. She is good at what she does. Not only do most of the kids like her, they sometimes listen to some of what she has to say. What's more, some of what she has to say is actually relevant to their lives as they see them.

Of course, Marion and Carl argue, who doesn't. And sometimes they both wonder what it would have been like if they'd waited a while, met other people, maybe travelled a little, if they hadn't been, well, so *young.* On the other hand, they also believe you have to go with what's happening at the time. Surprising as it may seem, this attitude still works for them.

Or so Marion says.

'Oh, Marion,' her friends reply, only half-laughing. 'Wake up. Look around. The sixties are over.'

Marion knows what they're getting at, of course. For every Marion Walker, married at eighteen and having three kids bang, bang, bang, who ends up cleaning her spacious kitchen in her tasteful house on her tasteful street, a little stoned and more beautiful than she was twenty years ago, there are thousands of others with their teeth rotted and their bodies gone to flab on Kraft Dinner and Wonder Bread, up to their eyeballs in shit. Women whose husbands left them (as, in fact, Marion's own brother, Jeff, left his first wife, Sandra, with a three year old and a set of twins, with no degree because she'd worked to put him through med school and with support payments based on his last year as a resident rather than his present salary as a pediatrician), or, worse yet, women whose husbands are still around, taking it out on them, women who are beaten, whose kids end up in jail or ruined by drugs or . . .

Or take Tracey Harper, for example. She's just come home from her Saturday afternoon shift at Harvey's. The kitchen is scrupulously clean, as it always is, and on the table, in exactly the same spot as last Saturday and the Saturday before and every day after school for as long as she can remember, is a note in her mother's thick, wavery writing: '*Your supper's in the fridge. Just heat and eat. Love, Leslie.*'

In the living room, the television is on full-blast, as always, 'Wheel of Fortune' is half over, and Leslie is sprawled on the couch, sound asleep, mouth open, snoring. On the table beside her, in a row, is a bottle of Maalox, a bottle of Coke, a bottle of rum, an empty glass, and an empty package of Export 'A's. If Leslie were still awake, which would be unusual, she would light a cigarette, take two drags, put it in the ashtray, take two sips of rum and Coke, a sip of Maalox, two more drags of her cigarette, and so on, never breaking her pattern until she ran out or passed out, whichever came first. It's by the same rigorous adherence to a system that she manages to keep her kitchen clean and food on the table for her daughter.

In so doing, she has done one helluva lot better—and she would be the first to tell you this—than her own mother. Like Tracey, Leslie came home to her mother passed out on the couch and the television blaring. Where Tracey stands in the doorway and watches men and women win glamorous merchandise and large sums of money on 'Wheel of Fortune', Leslie would stand and watch women's wildest dreams come true, right there, on 'Queen For a Day'. What's changed (besides the television shows, of course) is that Tracey comes home to a clean kitchen and a meal, whereas Leslie came home to a shithole and nothing to eat. The other thing that's changed is that she, Leslie, has managed to keep her boyfriends out of Tracey's bed, which is more than her mother ever did for her.

What hasn't changed (besides the idea that winning something will improve your life): Tracey's eyes and her way of standing in the doorway, both of which are exactly like her mother's. Already she has the look and posture of someone whose parents abandoned her early. It doesn't matter to what—drugs, alcohol, violence, madness, or death—she has that look. That particular sadness which starts in the eyes and goes bone-deep, displacing all traces of the child she was, leaving the shoulders stiff and thin, all their suppleness and softness gone for good. The softness that some of us are allowed to carry (that Marion Walker carries, for example) a good distance into our lives.

So Tracey is standing in the doorway of the living room, waiting for her supper to heat up, watching her mother sleep. Her mother is only seventeen years older than she is, which makes her thirty-four, but she looks about sixty. Her belly bloats out over the waistband of her jeans and the skin that shows, in the space between her jeans and her T-shirt, is grey and puckered. If statistics are anything to live by (and surely they're as reliable as game shows), Leslie will be dead in five to ten years. *How* is still being decided by her cells. Will it be her stomach, where the ulcer has already made its presence known? Her heart or her lungs, whose complaints she hears but manages to ignore? Right now, her cells are deciding her future.

As indeed Tracey's cells are deciding hers. If she goes back to her boyfriend Kevin's tonight after the movies, as she usually does, she will get pregnant. Everything in her body (the delicate balance of hormones controlled by her pituitary gland, the ripened ovum swimming in her right fallopian tube) is ready. In one sense, her pregnancy has already been decided. Statistically, it's almost inevitable. If it actually occurs, then, given that course of events which are so usual as to seem almost natural, Tracey may replace Leslie in a few years, exactly as she is—passed out, bloated on the couch.

Lately, though, Tracey is beginning to think that maybe it isn't such a great idea after all, dropping out of school and living together, which is what she and Kevin are planning to do as soon as he gets on at Petro-Can.

What she is hearing, under the chatter of the TV and her mother's snoring and the sausages hissing in the pan behind her and her own confused thoughts, is the voice of her guidance counsellor at school, Mrs Walker, who is one of the weirdest people Tracey has ever met. Sometimes they don't even talk, for fuck sake, they go to the mall and try on clothes. Seriously.

But what Mrs Walker is saying now inside Tracey's head is: *Well, really, Tracey, your marks aren't that bad, you know. And you've got more experience of life than most kids your age. What you've gotta decide is how you're going to use that to your advantage. Any ideas?*

And then Tracey is amazed to hear her own voice, there, inside her head. As amazed as she was last Wednesday, when she heard herself say: *Well, I always thought I might like to be a physiotherapist.*

Physiotherapist. Yeah, right. She'd just read it on one of those stupid pamphlets they have outside the guidance office.

That's not a bad idea, Tracey, Mrs Walker is saying now, *I think you'd be really good at that. In some ways working with people who've been injured might be a little like helping your mom. Now you'd have to go to university, so we're going to have to figure out some money schemes but I . . .*

And then she goes on, laying it all out like it's possible, and now Tracey sometimes thinks that maybe it just is. She walks over to the TV, turns it off, goes to the couch and picks up the empty glass and the cigarette pack, butts the last cigarette, which is stinking up the ashtray. She takes the glass, the full ashtray, and the empty pack to the kitchen counter, comes back and eases her mother's body gently along the couch a little ways so that her neck isn't cramped over the arm like that. Then she gets her sausages and macaroni from the stove and heads for her room.

Already, she's thinking she might tell Kevin she doesn't want to go out tonight, though it's hard to imagine having the nerve to actually say that to him. Right now, it's just sort of there, like a buzzy place, inside her head. Right now, she's just going to eat her supper and study for her math exam. Then she'll see.

Marion fills the sink with hot water, adds detergent and a few drops of Javex, and dumps in the contents of the left-hand middle drawer, the one where she keeps all the stuff she hardly ever uses. Tea strainers, pie servers, cookie cutters, two ice picks, and a couple of those things you use to make little scoops of melon for fruit salads.

'Melon ballers', the boys call them.

Outside, she can see Ben and Josh sorting stuff for a garage sale tomorrow, hauling everything into the driveway and organizing it into piles. Hockey sticks and skates, a huge box of Lego. Jason's old ten-speed, a bunch of flippers and some diving masks, tennis racquets, a badminton set, ski poles. They lift and carry the awkward bundles with ease, competent and serious. Even Josh is almost past the gangly stage, almost completely at home in the body he'll live in for the rest of his life.

A body that seems so much like a stranger's to Marion these days, even as she watches him, his every movement familiar. It's hard to believe she used to take it so for granted. All of it. The rooting motions their mouths made when she picked them up to nurse. The ease with which she oiled and powdered their bums, handling their penises as casually as she'd handle her own breasts, pushing back their foreskins to check for redness, helping them aim over the potty when she was training them. It doesn't seem possible.

Marion wipes out the drawer with a damp cloth, empties the sink, starts drying the stuff and putting it back, automatically, still watching the boys. Sometimes she doesn't know and it scares her. She can feel it, inside, what she doesn't know. It's like when she miscarried between Jason and Ben and how, even before the blood came, from the very beginning, she knew something was wrong, terribly wrong and there was nothing she could do about it even though it was there, right there, inside her own body. She can feel the cold sweat of it, the way she felt it then, all over her.

And no one else seems to notice, that's what really gets to her, they seem to see her as, well, *finished*, somehow. Carl and the boys. Or the kids she sees at work, other people's kids, as precious and impossible as her own. That she should be expected, should get *paid*, to sit in an office and tell other people's kids what to do with their lives seems crazy to her sometimes. Crazier that they listen.

Ben and Josh turn suddenly and see her in the window. They wave vigorously and Ben gets onto his old skateboard, mouthing something Marion can't hear with the Walkman on and the window between them. She shakes her head, but he keeps on, tilting the skateboard wildly, his arms waving a crazy semaphore, insisting on her attention. It reminds her of when they were little, all crowded around her, and she'd send them outside, just long enough for a coffee or to talk to Carl for a few minutes. How every two seconds they'd be at the door, wanting her to watch something or do something.

It used to drive her crazy sometimes. Still does. Even now as she waves, shaking her head again, vigorously this time, she can feel that familiar pulse of irritation at her temples, quick and absolute as the swell of love that comes with it.

Anger and tenderness. That she can feel so many conflicting things, that she can know so little about anything she feels and still manage to appear a competent adult. Sometimes it scares her. Knowing there's no end to feeling like this, ever.

The best Tracey Harper can do right now is to crouch behind the chest of drawers in her bedroom and listen as Kevin bangs and bangs and bangs on the door to the apartment. Before, it was the phone ringing and ringing and ringing. Her mother has slept through it all, which, even for her, is amazing.

'All right, bitch. I know you're in there.' Kevin gives the door a kick.

Silence.

Then Tracey hears him stomp down the stairs, she hears the outer door bang shut. In a few minutes his car squeals off down the street. Tracey can see it perfectly, the dark blue, rusted-out '78 Firebird and Kevin inside, his knuckles white around the steering wheel, really fuckin' pissed off.

For a minute she thinks of getting up, going out, trying to find him. It would be a lot easier than this is. She wishes she'd never met that fucking bitch Walker. Now she's going to have to spend her time avoiding Kevin, who will be on her ass every goddamn minute. Phoning her at all hours, following her to and from school. All she'll be able to do is ignore him and keep on walking.

Even when he grabs her arm, hard, next Friday afternoon and pulls her towards him. Even when she has to kick him, she won't speak, she'll just get the fuck out of there and keep on going. It's all she can do.

And it isn't Kevin's fault, either. Though he's acting like a jerk right now, he's an okay guy. Next week he'll get on at Petro-Can, and had he and Tracey gone through with their plan, everything might have worked out fine for them, statistics be damned.

As it is, Tracey will spend the next three weeks sitting silent in Marion Walker's office, not even looking at her, arms clamped around her chest as if it takes her whole strength to hold its contents in.

She will look a lot the way she looks now, crouching against the wall of her bedroom, hugging her knees to her chest as if the effort of keeping them from jumping up, running into the hallway and never stopping till she finds Kevin, wherever he is, takes everything she's got.

Which it does.

Drawers and counters done, Marion goes to the cupboard for the pail and sponge mop, but before she starts the floors, she fills the coffeemaker and turns it on so that it will be ready when she is. She puts a new tape—*Patsy Cline's Greatest Hits*—into the Walkman and gets down on her knees to do the tough spots near the sink and under the edge of the stove. A whiff of Lysol stings her nose. Once the hard stuff's loosened, she does the rest with the mop, singing again, having a great time.

Sometimes what Marion thinks is simply that she's lucky to have such an easy life. 'Karma' some of their friends used to call it, hanging out at the farm, smoking black hash, letting the boys run naked through the fields.

Other times she knows damn well it's because of Carl and their double income, her education, her parents' double income even, everything that's made her luck possible. Political, not spiritual, and she should damn well face up to what that means. Whatever that means.

Sometimes she just doesn't know, and it scares her.

Besides, who knows what will happen next, even in an easy life. In five minutes, for example, Jason will be driving in from the mall where he works part-time as a clerk at Music World, speeding, already late to pick up his girlfriend, Karen. While in an apartment nearby, someone else knocks back his last beer and climbs into his car to go get more before his friends show up. Two cars, both driven by teenage boys, hurtle towards each other, like sonar blips on a great map of possibilities, like cells gone haywire. Marion's own death ticks in her cells as it does in anybody's. Anything can happen, any time.

Still crouching behind her dresser, Tracey Harper has fallen asleep. She is dreaming. In the dream she is in a red Corvette convertible, moving very fast along a highway which is like a highway in a cartoon show, with flowers springing up on all sides, and birds and rainbows filling the sky. Mrs Walker is driving and the two of them are laughing and eating triple-scoop French chocolate ice-cream cones from Baskin-Robbins. The dream is so vivid that Tracey can taste the cold chocolate on her tongue and feel the wind in her hair. She can hear herself laughing and laughing, and in the dream she reaches over and puts her hand, just there, for a moment, on Mrs Walker's arm. In the dream, she has no idea where they are going.

Meanwhile, a few blocks away, Jason pulls up in front of Karen's place, gets out of the car and goes around to the back porch where she is waiting for him in brand-new acid-washed jeans and a yellow sweatshirt, one of her mother's daffodils stuck behind her ear.

Meanwhile, Marion's kitchen gleams, the sun shines through the window, the crocuses pulse and shimmer as the afternoon wanes. Marion pushes the mop and pail into the corner and tiptoes around the edge of the floor to the coffeemaker, pours herself a cup, and tiptoes back towards the patio door.

The breeze feels wonderful on her hot face. She wipes the sweat off her forehead with the back of her hand as she steps out, and that for some reason makes her think of the day she took Tracey Harper to the mall because she couldn't think of anything else to do and how they'd tried on clothes and makeup in The Bay. Tracey wanted to do Marion's face and she let her though she never wears makeup. Now, she can feel Tracey's fingertips again on her eyelids and her cheeks. They stick slightly, pulling at her skin, as if Tracey is pressing too hard, exasperated with something she sees there, something she can't erase or alter. And at the same time, they flutter and soothe, almost as a lover's would.

Anger and tenderness. From nowhere, Marion feels the tears start. On the Walkman Patsy Cline is singing one of those songs that someone sings when they've been ditched, trying to cram a lifetime of pain into every note.

And so Marion just stands there, on her patio, with a cup of coffee in her hand, crying like an idiot. Partly because of the song. Partly because it's finally spring and she's a little stoned. Because of her kids and her job. Because she's like that, Marion, soft and open, in her easy life.

But not only because.

1990

Robert Bringhurst

b. 1946

About his peripatetic background Robert Bringhurst once wrote that, before settling in British Columbia, he had lived:

Elsewhere, elsewhen. Born to migrant parents in the forties, nomadic without animals, and continued thoughtlessly but happily in the tradition for 25 years.

Bringhurst began his life in Los Angeles, California, the only child of Canadian parents, and grew up chiefly in the Canadian Rockies from the 1950s. He also lived in Montana, Utah, and Wyoming. In his early years he held a variety of jobs, one of which was as jazz drummer.

During the ten years he spent as an itinerant undergraduate, he studied architecture, physics, and linguistics at the Massachusetts Institute of Technology (1963–4; 1970–1), philosophy and oriental languages at the University of Utah, and comparative literature at Indiana University, where he completed his BA in 1973. By the time he entered the writing program at the University of British Columbia he had already published two books of poetry: *The Shipwright's Log* (1972) and *Cadastre* (1973). He received a Master of Fine Arts degree in creative writing from UBC in 1975 and taught there from 1975–80 and then at Simon Fraser University for a year (1983–4). He has been poet-in-residence and writer-in-residence at several universities in North America and Europe, including the School of Fine Arts at the Banff Centre (1983), the University of Edinburgh (1989–90), and the University of Western Ontario (1998–9), and has been a Guggenheim Fellow in poetry (1988–9) and the Philips Fund Resident Research Fellow at the American Philosophical Society Library in Philadelphia (2000).

As well as having established a reputation as an important poet, Bringhurst has played a significant role as a typographer and pressman. In the 1970s his small Kanchenjunga Press became well known among Canadian poets for its fine editions and chapbooks. He is the author of *Elements of Typographic Style* (1992; revised and expanded, 1997): the premier text in the field, it has been described as the 'Bible' of typography and is a beautiful book in its own right.

A polymath who has touched on art history, Native history, and the history of the book, Bringhurst has travelled in and lived in the Middle East, Europe, Asia, and Latin America. He reads and translates from at least half a dozen ancient and modern languages. He has published literary translations and commentaries on works in Arabic, Greek, French, Spanish, Navajo, and Haida, and, since 1985, has been engaged in an intensive study of the indigenous languages and cultures of British Columbia.

Bringhurst has published many poetry chapbooks, several he designed and printed himself, as well as more than a dozen full-length books of highly dramatic and informed poetry that draws on a variety of cultural sources, ranging from the Italian Renaissance and contemporary North American writing through Japanese Zen, the Bible, and North American Aboriginal material. In his poems Bringhurst often makes use of dramatic monologue (as in 'The Stonecutter's Horse'). As 'Conversations with a Toad' shows, he also experiments with polyphony to give the impression of 'several speakers speak[ing] at the same time though they have different things to say'—which he sees as a metaphor for 'the cultural plurality of the world in which I live'. He won the CBC poetry competition for *Blue Roofs of Japan*, which features complexly layered voices. (A CD with a performance of that work and of *New World Suite*, a new Bringhurst poem for three voices, has recently been released.) His books of poetry include *Bergschrund* (1975); *Tzuhalem's Mountain* (1982); *The Beauty of the Weapons: Selected Poems, 1972–82* (1982); *Pieces of Map, Pieces of Music* (1986), which includes an autobiographical 'meditation' and an interview on his working methods; and *The Calling: Selected Poems 1970–1995* (1995).

Bringhurst frequently speaks of his dislike for the contemporary age, which he has characterized as dominated by a 'cult of personality and power, and the religion of money' and filled with 'ersatz information': never sentimental or confessional in his writing, he celebrates the bodies of knowledge the twentieth and twenty-first centuries have inherited. Though his poems sometimes indulge—readily and unfashionably—in high rhetoric (as, for example, in 'These Poems, She Said'), Bringhurst has said that one use of poetry is 'to sing thought back into being, to personify it, state it, locate it, to clear the haze'. The use of an elevated voice in poems such as 'Essay on Adam' and 'Leda and the Swan' seems appropriate as a way of recalling and asking readers to reconsider events from the mythic past.

It is the importance he places on this past that has fuelled Bringhurst's interest in North American mythology. His several books on Aboriginal culture include an influential collection of Haida trickster stories, *The Raven Steals the Light* (1984), which he produced in collaboration with his friend the late Haida artist Bill Reid, and a study of Haida art and culture, *The Black Canoe: Bill Reid and the Spirit of Haida Gwaii* (1991), now considered one of the classics in the field of Native American art history. His monumental *A Story as Sharp as a Knife: The Classical Haida Mythtellers and Their World* (1999) includes myths, stories, and songs in the Haida language (gathered from those recorded by American anthropologist and linguist John Swanton in 1901–2). In that book he writes evocatively of the way he understands myth:

A mythology is not a fixed body of stories; it is an open set. It is a narrative ecology, a watershed, a forest, a community of stories that are born and die and breed with one another and with stories from outside.

The mythteller's calling differs little from the scientist's. It is to elucidate the structure and workings of the world. . . . It is a kind of science in narrative form. . . . Both science and mythology aspire to be true, and both for that reason are perpetually under revision for as long as they are alive.

Bringhurst followed *A Story as Sharp as a Knife*—which exuberantly celebrated the nineteenth-century storytellers Ghandl of the Qayahl Llaanas and Skaay of the Qquuna Qiighawaay—with *Nine Visits to the Mythworld* (2000), featuring nine of Ghandl's tales, and *Being in Being: The Collected Works of a Master Haida Mythteller* (2002), featuring three of Skaay's stories. Bringhurst's translations in these volumes are cast in a spare free verse that owes as much to contemporary interpreters of Homer as to the Native mode of storytelling recorded either in Swanton's transcriptions or in other transcriptions of Native tales such as Wendy Wickwire's rendering of Harry Robinson (see 'Captive in an English Circus' in this volume).

A Story as Sharp as a Knife aroused controversy among some of the Haida and scholars of the Haida language, who disputed Bringhurst's right to translate—especially without permission of the Council of Haida Nations—a literature that is considered sacred. As well, some readers felt that Bringhurst distorted the texts by imposing on them a different kind of oral poetics. The issues here are complex—involving not only the difficulties of translating artistic works, but also questions about the nature of sacred texts; about Bringhurst's treatment of the tales as works of individual genius comparable to Homer's *Odyssey* rather than products of communal transmission; and more generally questions of appropriation, exclusion, inclusion, and cross-cultural communication. Although these topics will continue to be argued about in many contexts, Bringhurst's versions of these Haida tales are powerful evocations of a culture and a mythology and they make an important argument for these works as profound poems.

Essay on Adam

There are five possibilities. One: Adam fell.
Two: he was pushed. Three: he jumped. Four:
he only looked over the edge, and one look silenced him.
Five: nothing worth mentioning happened to Adam.

The first, that he fell, is too simple. The fourth,
fear, we have tried and found useless. The fifth,
nothing happened, is dull. The choice is between:
he jumped or was pushed. And the difference between these

is only an issue of whether the demons
work from the inside out or from the outside
in: the one
theological question.

1975

The Stonecutter's Horses[1]

Sepe de eo mecum cogitans de quo nemo nimis
pauci satis cogitant. . . .[2]

¶ Pavia, 4 April 1370:

Francesco Petrarca (1304–1374)[3]

[Francesca], *his illegitimate daughter*

Franceschino da Brossano, *in law Petrarca's adopted son, but in actuality his son-in-law*

I, Francesco, this April day . . .
death stirs like a bud in the sunlight, and Urban
has got off his French duff and re-entered Rome[4]
and for three years running has invited me to Rome . . .
over the bright hills and down the Cassia,
back through Arezzo one more time . . .
my age sixty-five and my birthday approaching,
the muggers on the streets in broad daylight in Rome,
the hawks and the buzzards. . . .
Take this down.

1 This is in some measure the story of Francesco Petrarca, who was a gentleman, and a scholar, and a brilliant poet, and a good Roman Catholic, and the father of an illegitimate daughter whom he loved very deeply and whose illegitimacy was, for him, a source of incurable pain. His feelings concerning himself and his daughter grew so intense that for years he would not speak her name in public, though he pronounced it often enough and lovingly enough in private. After her marriage he sought to simplify his affairs and his explanations by adopting as his foster son the man he might have called his son-in-law: his daughter's husband Brossano. With him and few others, Petrarca shared the story of his precious wound.

On the morning of 4 April 1370, in one of the upper rooms of his house in Padova, in the north of Italy, Francesco Petrarca summoned his secretary, to whom he dictated in simple Italian the first draft of his last will and testament. A later version of this document—the dry and guarded Latin rewrite which Petrarca considered suitable for public disclosure—still survives. Only an occasional flash in the Latin suggests the rough glint of its predecessor. The close, for instance, reads: *Ego Franciscus Petrarca scripsi qui testamentum aliud fecissem si essem dives ut vulges insanem putat.* 'I, Francesco Petrarca, have written this. I would have made a different testament if I were rich, as the lunatic public believes me to be.' The Italian original would, I believe, have begun with a meditative wail: *Io, Francesco, io, io . . .* [Bringhurst's note]

2 'Thinking often about what no one considers very much and few enough . . .'

3 The Italian poet, scholar, and humanist best known as Petrarch (the Latinized form of his name). His poetic sequence *Canzoniere* (*c.* 1351–3), written in praise of Laura, had a profound impact on the lyric poetry of the Renaissance. Its love sonnets were much imitated throughout Europe, and it helped establish the use of the vernacular languages (as opposed to medieval Latin) as appropriate for literary writing.

4 With the appointment of a French pope, Clement V in 1305, the seat of the papacy was moved to Avignon and fell under the control of the French monarchy until 1378. Pope Urban V made an unsuccessful attempt to bring the papacy from Avignon to Rome (1367–70), a move Petrarch had long supported.

No one has thought too deeply of death.
So few have left anything toward or against it.
Peculiar, since thinking of death can never be
wasted thinking, nor can it be come to
too quickly. A man carries his death with him
everywhere, waiting, but seldom thinking
of waiting. Death is uncommonly like the soul.

What I own other than that ought to fall
of its own weight and settle. But beggars and tycoons
and I are concerned with our possessions,
and a man with a reputation for truth
must have one also for precision.
                                        I leave
my soul to my saviour, my corpse to the earth.
And let it be done without any parades.
I don't care very much where I'm buried,
so it please God and whoever is digging.
Still, you will ask. You will badger me.
If I am dead you will badger each other.
But don't lug my bones through the public streets
in a box to be gabbled at and gawked at and followed.
Let it be done without any parades.

If I die here in Padova, bury me here
near the friend who is dead who invited me here.
If I die on my farm, you can use the chapel
I mean to build there, if I ever build it.
If not, try the village down the road.

If in Venezia, near the doorway.
If in Milano, next to the wall.
In Pavia, anywhere. Or if in Rome—
if in Rome, in the centre, of course, if there's room.
These are the places I think I might die in
in Italy.
          Or if I happen to be in Parma,
there is the cathedral, of which for some reason
I am the archdeacon. But I will avoid
going to Parma. It would scarcely be possible,
I suppose, in Parma, not to have a parade.

At any rate, put what flesh I have left
in a church. A Franciscan church if there is one.

I don't want it feeding a tree from which
rich people's children swipe apples.

Two hundred ducats go to the church in which
I am buried, with another hundred to be given
out in that parish to the poor, in small doses.
The money to the church, let it buy a piece of land
and the land be rented and the rental from the land
pay for an annual mass in my name.
I will be fitter company in that sanctuary
then, present in spirit and name only,
than this way, muttering to the blessed virgin
through my hemorrhoids and bad teeth. I should be glad
to be rid of this sagging carcass.
Don't write that.

I have cleared no fields of their stones. I have built
no barns and no castles. I have built a name
out of other men's voices by banging my own
like a kitchen pan. My name to the Church
with the money it takes to have it embalmed.

Very few other things. My Giotto[5] to the Duke.
Most men cannot fathom its beauty. Those
who know painting are stunned by it. The Duke
does not need another Giotto, but the Duke knows painting.

To Dondi,[6] money for a plain ring to remind him
to read me.
To Donato—what? I forgive him
the loan of whatever he owes me. And I
myself am in debt to della Seta. Pay
that, if I haven't paid it. And give him
my silver cup. Della Seta drinks
water. Damned metal ruins the wine.

To Boccaccio,[7] I am unworthy to leave
anything, and have nothing worthy to leave.

5 That is, a work by innovative Florentine painter Giotto di Bondone (*c.* 1267–1337).

6 Giovanni Dondi (*c.* 1318–1389), a noted humanist and friend of Petrarch's, a professor of medicine, mathematics, and philosophy. 'Donato' is Donato degli Albanzani da Pratovecchio, who translated Petrarch's *De viris illustribus*—a series of biographies of figures from antiquity (begun *c.* 1338)—into Italian. Lombardo della Seta assisted Petrarch in the writing of this work.

7 Giovanni Boccaccio (1313–74), the famous Italian poet and storyteller best known for *The Decameron* (1351–3); his work was influenced by Petrarch, and they were lifelong friends from the time of their initial meeting in 1350. His old age was troubled by poverty and ill health.

Money then, for a coat to keep himself warm
when he works after dark, as he frequently does,
while the river wind stutters and bleats at his window,
and his hand-me-down cordwood fizzles and steams.

My lute to Tommaso.[8] I hope he will play it
for God and himself and not to gain fame
for his playing.
These are such trivial legacies.

Money to Pancaldo, but not for the card table.
Money to Zilio—at least his back salary.
Money to the other servants. Money to the cook.
Money to their heirs if they die before I do.

Give my Bible back to the Church.
And my horses . . .
my horses.
Let a few of my friends, if they wish to,
draw lots for my horses. Horses
are horses. They cannot be given away.

The rest to my heir and executor, Brossano,
who knows he is to split it, and how he is to split it,
and the names I prefer not to put into this
instrument. Names of no other importance.
Care for them. Care for them here in this house
if you can. And don't sell off the land to get money
in any case. Selling the earth without cause
from the soul is simony,[9] Brossano. Real-estate
hucksters are worse than funeral parades.
I have lived long enough in quite enough
cities, notwithstanding the gifts
of free lodging in some of them, long enough, Brossano,
to know the breath moves underfoot in the clay.
The stone quarried and cut and reset
in the earth is a lover's embrace, not an overlay.

The heart splits like a chinquapin pod,
spilling its angular seed on the ground.

8 The poet Tommaso Caloiro, also known as Tomasso da Messina, was a friend and correspondent of Petrarch's. 'Pancaldo': Like Zilio, one of Petrarch's servants.

9 The buying or selling of ecclesiastical privileges, such as pardons or benefices.

Though we ride to Rome and back aboard animals,
nothing ever takes root on the move.
I have seen houses and fields bartered
like cargo on shipboard. But nothing takes root
without light in the eye and earth in the hand.

The land is our solitude and our silence.
A man should hoard what little silence
he is given and what little solitude he can get.

Just the one piece over the mountains
ought, I think, to be given away. Everything
I have ever done that has lasted began there.
And I think my heir will have no need to go there.

If Brossano die before I do,
look to della Seta. And for his part, let him
look into that cup. He will know my mind.

A man who can write as I can ought not
to talk of such things at such length. Keep this
back if you can. Let the gifts speak
for themselves if you can, small though they are.
But I don't like the thought of what little there is
spilling into the hands of lawyers through lawsuits.
The law is no ritual meant to be practised
in private by scavengers. Law is the celebration
of duty and the ceremony of vengeance. The Duke's
law has nothing to do with my death
or with horses.
                    Done.
                              Ask the notary to come over
precisely at noon. I will rewrite it
and have it to sign by the time he arrives.

1979

Leda and the Swan[1]

Before the black beak reappeared
like a grin from in back of a drained cup,
letting her drop,
she fed at the sideboard of his thighs,
the lank air tightening in the sunrise,
yes. But no, she put on no knowledge
with his power. And it was his power alone
that she saved of him for her daughter.
Not his knowledge.
No.
He was the one who put on knowledge.
He was the one who looked down out of heaven
with a dark croak, knowing more
than he had ever known before,
and knowing he knew it:

knowing the xylophone of her bones,
the lute of her back and the harp of her belly,
the flute of her throat,
woodwinds and drums of her muscles,
knowing the organ pipes of her veins;

knowing her as a man knows mountains he has hunted
naked and alone in—
knowing the fruits, the roots and the grasses,
the tastes of the streams
and the depths of the mosses,

1 According to Greek myth, Zeus came to Leda in the form of a swan and mated with her; Leda also had sex with her husband that night. Four children were conceived from these unions: Helen, whose abduction was the cause of the Trojan War; Clytemnestra, whose husband, King Agamemnon, organized the Greeks to fight the war, and whom she killed on his return; and the twins Castor and Pollux, part of the Greek contingent that sacked Troy and rescued Helen. The Irish poet William Butler Yeats wrote a famous poem called 'Leda and the Swan' (1923), to which Bringhurst is here responding in detail. Yeats's poem concludes:

How can those terrified vague fingers push
The feathered glory from her loosening thighs?
And how can body, laid in that white rush,
But feel the strange heart beating where it lies?

A shudder in the loins engenders there
The broken wall, the burning roof and tower
And Agamemnon dead.
Being so caught up,
So mastered by the brute blood of the air,
Did she put on his knowledge with his power
Before the indifferent beak could let her drop?

knowing as he moves in the darkness he is also
resting at noon in the shade of her blood—
leaving behind him in the sheltered places
glyphs meaning mineral and moonlight and mind
and possession and memory,
leaving on the outcrops signs meaning mountain
and sunlight and lust and rest and forgetting.

Yes. And the beak that opened to croak
of his knowing that morning creaked like a rehung
door and said nothing, felt nothing. The past
is past. What is known is as lean
as the day's edge and runs
one direction. The truth floats
down, out of fuel,
indigestible, like a feather. The lady
herself, though—whether
or not she was truth or untruth, or both, or was neither—
she dropped through the air like a looped rope,
a necklace of meaning, remembering
everything forward and backward—
the middle, the end, the beginning—
and lit like a fishing skiff gliding aground.

That evening, of course, while her husband, to whom
she told nothing, strode like the king
of Lakonia through the orchestra
pit of her body, touching
this key and that string in his passing,
she lay like so much
green kindling,
fouled tackle and horse harness under his hands
and said nothing, felt
nothing, but only
lay thinking
not flutes, lutes and xylophones,
no: thinking soldiers
and soldiers and soldiers and soldiers
and daughters,
the rustle of knives in his motionless wings.

1982

These Poems, She Said

These poems, these poems,
these poems, she said, are poems
with no love in them. These are the poems of a man
who would leave his wife and child because
they made noise in his study. These are the poems
of a man who would murder his mother to claim
the inheritance. These are the poems of a man
like Plato, she said, meaning something I did not
comprehend but which nevertheless
offended me. These are the poems of a man
who would rather sleep with himself than with women,
she said. These are the poems of a man
with eyes like a drawknife,[1] with hands like a pickpocket's
hands, woven of water and logic
and hunger, with no strand of love in them. These
poems are as heartless as birdsong, as unmeant
as elm leaves, which if they love love only
the wide blue sky and the air and the idea
of elm leaves. Self-love is an ending, she said,
and not a beginning. Love means love
of the thing sung and not of the song or the singing.
These poems, she said . . . .
You are, he said,
beautiful.
That is not love, she said rightly.

1982

1 Woodworker's tool with a handle at each end of the blade, used to shave off surfaces.

The Reader

. . . der da mit seinem Schatten / getränktes liest

—Rainer Maria Rilke[1]

Who reads her while she reads? Her eyes slide
under the paper, into another world
while all we hear of it
or see is the slow surf of turning pages.

1 From Rilke's '*Der Leser*' ('The Reader'), which Bringhurst is recasting here. The epigraph is from lines 5–6: 'immersed in his shadow / he reads'.

Her mother might not recognize her,
soaked to the skin as she is in her own shadow.
How could you then? You with your watch and tongue
still running, tell me: how much does she lose

when she looks up? When she lifts
the ladles of her eyes, how much
flows back into the book, and how much
spills down the walls of the overflowing world?

Children, playing alone, will sometimes
come back suddenly, seeing what it is
to be here, and their eyes are altered. Hers too. Words
she's never said reshape her lips forever.

1986

Conversations with a Toad

I

Not for the toad, no, but for us,
In this poem a man talks
as a prologue only: two
to a toad. The toad may listen
legends. One. *That a three-legged*
or he may not. That, perhaps,
crow with vermilion feathers
is not the man's concern.
nests in the sun; in the restless
I suppose it is not the toad's concern
moon, a rabbit, a willow tree, a toad.
either. I am convinced, though,
Two. *Near water, a rock. Where a toad*
that the silences of the toad
had been sitting, an old woman sits.
are the most important—I mean
She is deaf, dumb and blind. But she hears
the most meaningful—parts of the poem,
through the soles of her feet, speaks
filling the dark shells

from under her skirt, and sees
of the man's ears and the spaces
through the holes in the palms of her hands.
between his sentences,

What do they mean, these
filling his syllables, filling the wrinkled,
images? I cannot tell you.
stretched and invisible skins of his words,
I learned them here and there
filling his eyes wherever he looks
among the Tsimshian[1] *and the immigrants—*
and his lungs whenever he breathes.
Celts and Chinese—who don't know
So the silences of the toad would appear
anything anymore except whatever it is
to be nothing but empty space
that everybody knows, and how
if the poem were printed, but
to keep silent—

who carry their other knowledge
the man in the poem would not know
shrivelled into undeciphered images,
how to speak it without them.
symbols, souvenirs. I lied then, didn't I,
In this poem a man talks
when I said these legends were for us?
to a toad. He tries, at first,
They don't have much to do
talking to us, but not very hard.
with us, with me, with you. They are true
It seems that he really wants
stories. I should, instead,
to talk to the toad instead.
have told them to the toad.
And so he does.

1 A group of Native peoples living in coastal and interior northern BC. Remains of early Tsimshian villages date back as far as five thousand years, making theirs one of the oldest continuous cultural heritages in the New World.

II

So few bones, toad, you must know
how to count them and give them away.
You can swallow your own skin, and pluck dinner,
still living, out of the air without lifting a hand.
And you let in the weather, taking
your temperature from the world.

A toothless carnivore, an unarmed hunter. Your tongue
hinged at the lip like a swallowed reflection.
Like one who in preference to speaking
is spoken. Like one who *uneats*
bits of the world—or the whole world: whatever
is already eaten. Who unthinks what others have thought,
unreads what is read, unwrites what is written.

Nevertheless, toad, like us, you have traded
a tail for elbows and pelvis and fingers
and toes, and one mouth for another, the smooth
for the angular: traded the long
hug of the water for the abstemious,
pontifical kiss of the air.

III

Behind you: the owl, whose eyes
have no corners: the owl with her quick
neck, who faces whatever she sees.
The raven, with voices like musselshell, wellwater, wood.
The dippers with voices like water on water.
The ruffed grouse drumming in the Douglas-fir.
And the heron flying in whole notes,
the kingfisher crossing in dotted eighths
and in quarters—both silent; much later,
two voices like washboards:
one bass, coarser than gravel,
one mezzo, crushed gravel and sand.

Their beauty bites into the truth.
One way to fail to be is to be merely
pretty. But that beauty: it feeds on you; we
feed on it. As you feed on this

moth, toad, or may: he met yet be
your dinner: his hazelnut tonsure,
the face like a goat's but clean,
and the mane like brown cornsilk.
Nerves spring from his forehead like fernfronds,
like feathers. He too is transformed.
This is the last life, toad.
Those who eat will be eaten. That
is the one resurrection.

We who kill not to eat but to mark
our domain—to build and breed, in place
of what is, what we choose to create—
have reduced by that much the population of heaven.

IV

The mind is the other. The mind
is a long complication of water. The mind
is time, space and all creatures. The mind
is the world. What we keep in the head,
with its dark facets, this jewel,
is a small, disproportional model.

What we are not is all we can think with.
In the leaking cup of the skull
we dip up the other. Daily we trade it
for money, for comfort, for power. But what we are not
is all we can think with. To hold and let go
is all we can do with whatever we are.

V

My people no longer stare into water
and fire for clues to the future. We no longer
read even the signs in our faces and hands.
Instead we grind lenses and mirrors
to sop up the spilled light of the stars. We decipher
the rocks that we walk on, too, while we loot them.

Toad, as we level the future we make
topographical maps of the past.

But the mirrors say at the edges
of what we can see, things are leaving
and taking their light with them, flying away
at six hundred million miles an hour—
or were when the light that is reaching us now
was just leaving them, ten billion years ago.

Ten billion years seems
long to us, toad, though to you
it is little: a few dozen times
the age of your ancestors' graves
in these rocks. Only two or three times
the age of the oldest rocks we have found.

What is is too quick for our fingers
and tongues to keep up with. The light
outmanoeuvres us. Time and space close over us, toad.
The lock of the sky will turn but not open.
We are where we are and have been here
forever. Longer, that is, than we can remember.

VI

Your ancestors, toad, were kings
in a world of trilobites, fish, bryozoans.
Do you know any stories, toad, of a species
determined, as mine is, to cease to have meaning?
Is it really so onerous, toad, to live
and to die at less distance from being?

My people have named a million species of insects.
They tell me that millions more are unnamed—
tens of millions among the living
and hundreds of millions among the dead.

It is good news, toad: that no one can list
what exists in the world. But not good enough.
Named or unnamed, if it lives, we can kill it.
We owe to the stones
that many chances and that many means
to kill us.

In the blank rock of Precambrian time
the earliest creatures, too soft to leave fossils,
too light to leave footprints, have left us
old proteins and sugars as signatures. We will leave
chronicles filled with our griefs and achievements,
a poetry spoken by locusts as they descend.

VII

Woodlice breed in the fallen alder.
Toad, the varied thrush is a beautiful bird.
And the red-shafted flickers, who feed there.
Uses will form for us too in the end.

What is is the truth. What precedes it
is meaning. We will not destroy
being, toad. We will not. But I think
we will overreligiously clean it.

Yet the voices still seep through us too. Even
through us, who have long since forgotten:
to pray does not mean to send messages
to the gods; to pray means to listen.

VIII

We have barely stopped binding the feet
of the women, toad. Is it true we ought to be binding
the hands of the men? Or weighting them
back into frequent touch with the ground?
Like eyes, the hands open and close, squeeze and release.
The feet, like the ears, are always wide open.

Toad, on the rocks near the stream
are the pictures of dreamers, and where the head
of the dreamer should be, there is a summary
of the dream. Close your eyes, say the rocks,
and dream of things seen in the darkness.
Open your eyes and dream of the sun.

The mind is a body, with shinbones and wrists
and roots, milkteeth and wings,

ankles and petals, fins,
feathers and dewclaws, leafstalks and lungs.
It is larva, pupa, imago, sea urchin,
tree. Ripening ideas drop from its limbs.

IX

Toad, all the roads from a man to a woman,
a man to a man, woman to man, woman to woman
lead through the nonhuman. This
is the reason, toad, for musicians.
In this poem a man talks
We speak to each other by means
to a toad. The toad may listen
of the bones and the horns and the bodies
or he may not. That
and bowels of dead animals, plucking
is not the man's concern.
their gutstrings, thumping their bellies, plinking
I suppose it is not the toad's concern
their evened teeth laid out in a row.
either. I believe,
The animals give us our speech and the means
nevertheless, that the silences
of our thinking, just as the dreamers'
of the toad are the most important—
masks open the doors of our dreams.
I mean the most meaningful—
The voice is a face. The face is a vision.
parts of the poem.

How could the man in the poem find
his own silence without them?

X

In winter the mountain goats think.
In summer they gather. Thought
equals solitude. Toad, is there no other
answer? Thought is the mind walking
the ridges and edges of being, not
the tuned instruments crooning their perfect routines.

That smoothness is blasphemy. Thought
is the mute breaking through in the voice.
Like ice going out in the spring,
the voice giving way.
The language dug up by the roots
where thought has been speaking.

Leap, toad. Our invincible
greed, a dead silence, an absolute
absence of meaning, is closing.

1987

Bone Flute Breathing

They say that a woman with steel-gray
eyes has lived for a thousand years
in these mountains. They say that the music
you almost hear in the level blue light
of morning and evening is music she played
in these mountains many years ago
on a flute she'd cut from the cannon bone
of a mule deer buck she'd tracked and wrestled
to the ground.
They say that at the first few notes
she played, her sisters started giggling, because,
instead of listening, they were watching
the change that came over her face.
She stalked off in anger, and for years thereafter
only in darkness did anyone ever hear
the flute. Day after day
it lay silent on the mountain,
half hidden under a whitebark pine.
No one else was permitted to touch it,
much less to watch her while she played.

But a man came by one day from another
country, they say, who had never heard either
the flute or the story, and he found the flute
on the ground, under the pine tree, where it lay.
As soon as he put it to his lips, it played.
It breathed her music when he breathed,

and his hands began to find new
tunes between the tunes it played.

Angry once again at this intrusion,
the woman who lives in these mountains
complained about the stranger to her brother,
who lived on the other side of the world.
That very afternoon, her brother built
an elk's skull and antlers and a mountain cat's
intestines into a guitar, and as
he walked here, he taught himself to play.

Coming over the hills that way,
without a name, one stranger to another,
he challenged the stranger with the flute to a musical
duel to be judged by the woman who lives
in these mountains.
                                It may be the stranger, as many people say,
was simply unwary. It may be
the sun slivered his eyes that day
in such a way that he could see only
one choice. In any case, everyone
says that he consented to the contest.

They played night and day, and the stranger,
while he listened, watched the eyes,
and when they wandered, watched the lips
of the woman who lives in these mountains.
Sister, said the eyes: *sister of the other*
who is playing the guitar. But the lips said, *Music*
of the breath, music of the bone. And the breath
of the woman, whether she willed it to or no,
kept moving in the flute whenever the stranger
played. After seven nights and days,
everyone knew the stranger was the winner.

That was when the man with the guitar said,
Stranger, can you sing? Stranger, can you sing us
a song along with the music you play?
Listen, said the man with the guitar,
and I will show you what I mean.
And while the woman and the stranger watched
and listened, the man with the guitar stared
hard into the air, and his hands like water spiders

flickered over the guitar, and a song slid
out between his teeth and flowed
through the music he played.

The stranger in his turn stared
hard into the air and far into the eyes
of the woman who lives in these mountains.
And the eyes stared back, and the eyes said, *These
are the eyes of the sister of the other*, and the stranger
played and the stranger played, and no word
came. He stared long at her lips,
and the lips said, *Bone*. The lips said,
Wordless breath in the bone. And breathe
as he would, he could not
sing through the music he played.

So it was that the woman with the steel-gray
eyes, gazing into the whitebark
pine behind both of them, quietly declared
the man with the guitar to be the winner.

She reached for the flute,
but her brother stepped in front of her.
He picked up the flute and the guitar
and smacked them one against the other and against
the rocks until both of them shattered.

Then, taking the stranger by the throat,
he threw him flat against the ground.
And taking a splinter from the flute,
and moving swiftly, like a crouching
dancer, he peeled the living flesh
away from the stranger's feet and hands.
He peeled his face and hips and ribs
and neatly filleted each of his limbs.

One by one he extracted the stranger's
bones, and one by one he replaced them
with the splinters of the deerbone flute
and the shattered skull and antlers
that had been his own guitar.

He stitched the splinters into the stranger's
fingers, into his head and chest

and limbs with the mountain cat's intestines,
and set him on his feet, and propped the last splinter
of the bone flute upright in his hand,
and walked off, stopping to scrub
his own hands in a shrinking bank
of spring snow, never uttering a sound.

The stranger stood there motionless
for years—but they say that the music you almost
hear in the level blue light of morning
and evening, now, is the sound of the stranger
moving, walking back toward his own country,
one step at a time.

1995

Lorna Crozier

b. 1948

Born and raised in Swift Current, Saskatchewan, Lorna Crozier says that her family never had books around the house, and that she's not sure how she developed her love of reading and writing, but that she always had an itch to put words down on paper. Although discouraged from going on beyond high school, she earned a BA at the University of Saskatchewan and then taught high school English for ten years. During that time, having discovered her interest in and aptitude for poetry, she began attending the Saskatchewan Summer School of the Arts. She published her first book, *Inside the Sky*, in 1976, and soon followed it with *Crow's Black Joy* (1979) and *Humans and Other Beasts* (1980; these books were written under her married name, Lorna Uher). In 1980 she took an MA at the University of Alberta.

In the decade that followed, *The Weather* (1983) and *The Garden Going On Without Us* (new and selected work; 1985) brought Crozier's poetry to general attention for its intense response to her prairie milieu, for its addresses of the abuses of power in the contemporary world, for its witty and humorous meditations, as seen in 'Poem about Nothing', and for its feisty monologues like 'This One's for You'. Crozier began teaching creative writing and was an instructor at several western schools, including the Saskatchewan Summer School of the Arts and the Banff School of Fine Arts. From 1986 to 1991 she shared an appointment in the English department at the University of Saskatchewan with the poet Patrick Lane and the fiction writer David Carpenter. During that time she edited *A Sudden Radiance* (1987), an anthology of poetry by Saskatchewan writers. In 1988 *Angels of Flesh, Angels of Silence* won a Governor General's Award and solidified her reputation for frank and passionate writing of emotional intensity. One sequence in that book, 'The Penis Poems', like 'The Sex Lives of Vegetables' in the volume that preceded it, earned her a reputation for ribald humour.

In 1991 Crozier moved to Victoria, BC, to become a full-time member of the creative writing department at the University of

Victoria, where she is currently the chair. In 1992 she published *Inventing the Hawk*, which shows her exploring longer forms, as in 'Time to Praise'. Like many of Crozier's poems, it recalls the stories she heard growing up. That sense that we are hearing the oral stories of a small community being retold is also strong in a poem like 'The Old Order' from *Everything Arrives at the Light* (1995). (A passing reference in 'Poem about Nothing' to the event described in 'The Old Order' shows that this particular story had long haunted Crozier.) In 1996 Crozier investigated another aspect of her Saskatchewan heritage in *A Saving Grace*, a series of poems responding to Sinclair Ross's classic of prairie fiction, *As for Me and My House*, written in the voice of its protagonist Mrs Bentley.

Crozier has lived with Patrick Lane since 1978, and aspects of their relationship have frequently provided her with material for her poems, as in 'The Other Woman', which appeared in *What the Living Won't Let Go* (1999). In 1981 Lane and Crozier co-authored a series of poems set in dialogue, *No Longer Two People*, and she later wrote two essays about their life together: 'Changing into Fire', which is contained in a book she edited in 1999, *Desire in Seven Voices*; and 'Breathing under Ice', which appears in a volume she edited with Lane, *Addicted: Notes from the Belly of the Beast* (2001). In that latter piece she talks frankly about her experiences growing up as the daughter of an alcoholic father and about the pain of living with Lane during his struggle with his alcohol addiction; she ends by expressing her hopes for a better future.

Crozier has always interwoven vignettes of daily life with myths as well as with old stories. In particular, she has returned many times to the imagery of her religious inheritance—of a garden of lost innocence, of angels of various kinds, and of a God who created the world out of nothing. Recalling 'Sunday school days in the United Church when we got rewards for memorizing [Bible] passages', she once observed:

> *I have gone back to those, in Psalms, Isaiah, and some of the prophetic books. A lot of this is very close to prairie experience—the droughts and barren wastes and the plagues of locusts.*

Often she employs considerable humour in her handling of this material, which not infrequently involves a contemporary or a feminist revisionism. For example, in her 1992 poem 'On the Seventh Day' she imagines the large-sky prairie landscape having been the result of an absent-minded God, whose more alert wife has to remind him to put some soil underneath all the light he is busily creating. Playing, in her title, with the idea of the Apocrypha (sacred texts that were not accepted into the official canon of biblical books but that are still often reprinted with them), Crozier published *Apocrypha of Light* in 2002, building an entire collection around her sometimes comic, sometimes profound reconsiderations of religious themes and Biblical stories, of the human understanding of God, and finally of the need to praise. 'I praise', the last poem in that book ends, 'this waking into wind's / slow change of seasons, / wings lifting under the great / glittering belly of the Bear.'

This One's for You

Hey, big hummer,
who can strut like you?
Crotch-tight jeans, boots
shiny as pool balls, heels
pounding stars into pavement
you call sky.

Hey, big rooster,
who can cockadoodledo
like you do? You raise the
bloody sun from his corner
your voice, brass
bell in the ring.

Hey, prize fighter,
who can screw like you?
Women howl your name,
say no man will take
your place, buzz them
like an electric drill.
You spin the world
on the end of your cock.

Hey, big talker,
waited all my life
for a man like you.
Come my way, I'll blow
the fuses in your big machine,
short all your circuits.
I'll break the balls
you rack on the table,
I'll bust your pool cue.

1980

Poem about Nothing

Zero is the one we didn't understand
at school. Multiplied by anything
it remains nothing.

When I ask my friend
the mathematician who studies rhetoric
if zero is a number, he says *yes*
and I feel great relief.

If it were a landscape
it would be a desert.
If it had anything to do

with anatomy, it would be
a mouth, a missing limb,
a lost organ.

Ø

Zero worms its way
between one and one
and changes everything.
It slips inside the alphabet.
It is the vowel on a mute tongue,
the pupil in a blind man's eye,
the image
of the face
he holds on his fingertips.

Ø

When you look up
from the bottom of a dry well
zero is what you see,
the terrible blue of it.

It is the rope
you knot around your throat
when your heels itch for wings.

Icarus[1] understood zero
as he caught the smell
of burning feathers
and fell into the sea.

Ø

If you roll zero down a hill
it will grow,
swallow the towns, the farms,
the people at their tables
playing tic-tac-toe.

1 See page 852, note 1.

Ø

When the Cree chiefs
signed the treaties on the plains
they wrote *X*
beside their names.

In English, *X* equals zero.

Ø

I ask my friend
the rhetorician who studies mathematics
What does zero mean and keep it simple.

He says *Zip*.

Ø

Zero is the pornographer's number.
He orders it through the mail
under a false name. It is the number
of the last man on death row,
the number of the girl who jumps
three stories to abort.

Zero starts and ends
at the same place. Some compare it
to driving across the Prairies all day
and feeling you've gone nowhere.

Ø Ø Ø

In the beginning God made zero.

1985

Forms of Innocence

The girl can tell you exactly
where and when her innocence
took flight,
how it soared from the window
beating its wings
high above the stubble field.

A strange shape for innocence
when you think of Leda[1]
but this girl insists
it was a swan, black
not white as you might expect.
From its head no bigger than her fist
a beak blossomed red as if wings
pumped blood up the long neck
to where the bird split the sky.

She watched this through the windshield,
lying on her back, the boy's breath
breaking above her in waves, the swan's
dark flight across the snow so beautiful
she groaned and the boy groaned with her,
not understanding the sound she made.

When she tells this story now, she says
thought it was winter, she knows the swan
made it all the way to Stanley Park,[2]
a place she's never been, just seen
in the room where no one
ever touches anything
in the book her mother keeps
open on the coffee table,
one black swan swimming
endless circles among the white.

1985

1 See p. 962, note 1.
2 A wilderness park in Vancouver.

Getting Pregnant

You can't get pregnant
if it's your first time.

You can't get pregnant
if you do it standing up,
if you don't French kiss,
if you pretend
you won't let him
but just can't stop.

You can't get pregnant
if you go to the bathroom
right after,
if you ride a horse
bareback, if you jump
up and down on one leg,
if you lie in the snow
till your bum feels numb,
if you do it in the shower,
if you eat garlic,
if you wear a girdle,
if it's only your second time.

You can't get pregnant
if he keeps his socks on,
if he's captain of the football team,
if he says he loves you,
if he comes quickly,
if you don't come at all,
if it's only your third time.

You can't get pregnant
if he tells you
you won't.

1992

From 'Time to Praise'

I

Jack. My mother's brother
The one I never knew.
Grandmother in mid-morning
kneading the bread when she heard
the horses at the gate. Something wrong.
Grandfather tall and stern in the wagon
didn't wait for her as he always did,
but got down himself (*My God, what's wrong?*),
opened the gate,
opened the gate then drove the horses through.
Didn't get down again, didn't loop the wire
over the post, but drove past the barn
up to the house, a small red bundle
beside him in the wagon seat.
Grandmother at the window,
perfectly still,
except for her hands. They twisted
her apron round and round as if they wanted
to tie themselves up, stop her fingers
from tearing out her eyes. (*Don't look!*)
Her boy Jack.
Dead.
Crushed by the wagon wheels.
Giving to the land a son
as if the land demanded it.
The hollow thud of earth
on the wooden box like a cannon shot,
changing forever
the history of the heart.

* * *

4

Or—
Grandmother ran to the gate
when she heard the horses,
ran as she always did, drying her hands
on her apron, Grandfather sitting
tall and imperial on the wagon seat,

the reins of the horses wrapped around
his wrists. And beside him Jack,
the smallest of the boys, the one
who brought laughter into the house
and music, on a tin flute, so my mother says.
Grandmother closed the gate,
closed the gate, Grandfather and Jack
by now at the barn, unhitching the horses
with names like Tony, and Mae and Maude.

Jack was my favourite uncle, O,
he was nimble, he was quick.
He knew the homeplace
as the others didn't,
taking me to see
the fox's den, the small coulee
where herons built their nests,
the buffalo stone. In winter
showing me, the city kid,
what walked before us in the snow.

This was the land to him,
not just what was broken,
the acres the other uncles fought over
when Grandfather died,
but the wild places and the creatures
who lived there, places where
the spirits of the earth,
if they still exist,
might dwell.

* * *

6

The fox has been poisoned
(to save the chickens in the yard),
the herons were never there
(I remember them from another place)
but the buffalo stone remains
on the hill above the alkali lake
where my mother used to swim,
her skin and hair turning stiff
as if she'd been held by the heels
and dipped in starch.

Not Uncle Jack but she
took me there to her childhood place,
a huge white rock covered with lichens—
crab nebulae exploding
in brilliant orange,
their light reaching us
across a billion years of space. Still
you could see the depression
where the buffalo
rubbed their huge foreheads,
their matted backs,
walking round and round
as if they were turning
a granite wheel
grinding the sky,
the machine of their destruction
bearing down.

Mom showed me
how she used the buffalo stone
for a slide, it was smooth
as glass, and I slid too,
neither of us children then,
but loving this rock
(as it was, as it is,
as it will be) where
the animals gathered.

Below, the hill itself
sliding on wind-slickened grass
into the past,
up to the white-crusted
lips of the silent lake.

* * *

9

Where the wire loop
slides over the gate post
there is a depression in the wood,
the grain smooth as satin.

The gate left open.
Nothing leaves

but someone walks through
from then to now,
walks into the yard
and what lies ahead.

Will he close the gate behind him?
Will he leave it open?

What must he atone for
before the land takes him in?

10

My grandparents dead
but the house remains within
the semi-circle of caraganas
Grandpa planted by hand
to break the wind. No matter
how long I look
nothing is written
on the walls, inside or out.

My uncle,
the youngest son who never left,
still lives there in the summers
with his wife, both of them
years older now
than the man who bore the body of a boy
through the gate, the woman who watched.

If my mother were to read this poem,
she'd probably say I'd made too much
of Jack, too much of signs,
the afternoon I spent with her
at the buffalo stone
unreadable
though I finally swam in the lake below,
wanting to feel what she felt
as a child, my skin growing tight,
my mouth closed to the terrible taste
of alkali on my tongue.

For me the farm has always been
her stories. Where I take up the telling,
where I begin and she stops,
I no longer know. There are only
a few things I am sure of
and these I set down here:

it is not the land
that spells the end of things.

From the bones we lay
forever in the earth,
at the urging of sun and wind
something grows,
something rises to the light
and has its say.

My mother had a brother,
Jack.

1992

Teaching a Crow to Talk[1]

Nobody's moon. The crow
with the split tongue
hops through the grass,
searching for his lost feather.

When I call *Who's there?*
he cries *Nobody*, using only one
of his many voices. Nobody
drops a black eye-patch
on my doorstep, a dead
wren on my pillow.
Nobody drags his shadow
like a tired broom across the snow
leaving the trail an animal leaves
when it crawls away from pain.

1 Compare Reaney's 'Starling with a Split Tongue', pages 601–3, and note 1.

I am not the one, I say out loud,
the crow calling three times
in his harsh, anonymous voice.

In the middle of my life
I am sitting without anyone,
holding a torn feather
between my fingers. I drag it
across my breasts, my belly,
over my own downy dark.

Out of the sounds I make
comes Nobody, his wings wet
and glistening. As crows do
when they travel on the ground,
he bobs and bobs his head,
saying *yes* to everything
in all his voices.

1992

The Old Order

A fear so huge
it pushed the girl from the window
three storeys up.

Thirteen years on earth
                    and suddenly
she knew the air, a daring
graceful thing, then grass
hard as clay.

Her three older sisters
watched her jump without a sound
then picked her up
and carried her to bed.

They didn't call the doctor
until her cramps
and bleeding stopped,

what would have been a child
scooped into a bowl,
thrown in the furnace
in those days of coal and fire.

Imagine the afternoon they waited
in that tall Victorian house
for their father to come home,
demanding reverence, embroidery and hours
of sitting, ankles crossed,
sips of lukewarm tea.

Every Sunday in the parlour
the dead Queen watched them
from above the mantle, beside her
the painting of the Morgan stud
their father broke in Tennessee.
His eyes followed their skirts
whispering on dusty rugs,
their small buttoned shoes.

When their mother spoke
she called him *Sir*,
and sometimes stayed inside
her room for days, indisposed,
until her 'unnatural colour' went away.

The younger one
fell down the stairs,
that's what her sisters said,
tripped on her skirts
(she always moved too fast),
leg snapping like willow sticks,
one, two, three.
Silly as any girls
dying to tell a story
yet her sisters kept the secret.

They didn't know
she could have bled to death
or lay forever broken
like the thing inside their mother
that would not heal.

Two months later
she could run on crutches
beside them on the grass
and laugh like a child
at the tricks they played.

She was the one who came back
to nurse him
when their mother died,
twenty years since she'd leapt
from the window, belly
heavy as a stone.

In the room she'd never entered
as a child, she found his name
written in a young man's hand
across the first page of the Bible
that never left his bedside stand.
                A common name
she said out loud and it held
no fear

        imagine
the look on her face
as she changed him in that bed,
he who was so tall and fierce,
who begat and begat—
under her hands
                his flesh
hot as a baby's
burned in coal.

1995

At the Millstone

Two women shall be grinding at the mill; the one shall be taken, and the other left.

—Matthew 24: 41[1]

She saw her sister spill her bowl,
then rise toward a cloud
as she'd seen her many times
stretch on tiptoes
to reach the hides of lambs
drying cleanly in the sun, morning
heavy with the scent of lanolin.

If the villagers had known their god
would choose between these two,
they could have guessed. The smaller
sister seemed all spirit, no rounded hips
or belly, no waxing breasts that made up
what a woman was. Hardly anything
to lift to heaven.

Not knowing what else to do,
the one left behind
began to grind the corn,
hands covered with golden dust
like pollen or what a soul might
leave when it ascends.
She hoped there still was time
before the second coming,
the plagues and conflagration,
time to grind enough to make a loaf,
a last one for her lover.

She could see his shepherd's hands,
breaking the bread in half,
steam rising from its heart
like her body's heat
when they lay together in dirty straw

1 One of the passages in the New Testament on which the concept of a 'secret rapture' is based—the idea that as the end of the world approaches, faithful Christians will be, without warning, taken up to Heaven and the unfaithful left behind to endure the 'tribulation' during the reign of the antichrist and prior to the second coming of Christ.

far from her father's terrible eyes,
he who loved her sister
as fathers often loved the girl
but not the woman she'd become.

The last thing she saw of her,
rising out of sight,
was the bottom of her feet
which had never worn shoes,
suddenly unlined,
and from the cloud that seemed to carry her
they wore the shine of flesh
lit up from loving.

The sister left on earth
couldn't help but think
she might be the chosen one,
her bare feet gripping the muscles
in his calves once more,
above her his belly rippling
like rows of ripened barley.

Even now as the sky darkened
over the houses of the village
was she not blessed? The millstone
turning one thing into another
before her eyes.

1995

From *A Saving Grace: The Collected Poems of Mrs. Bentley*[1]

Two Eternal Things

Early summer, the land wanting
colour—sienna, gamboge,
burnt umber—Philip[2] says,
making a joke of it,
he'll paint a thistle
against a rock.

Two eternal things
in this godforsaken place:
rock—what the drought
cannot destroy,
thistle—what the grasshoppers
will not eat.

Call it *Hope*, I say.
Despair, he replies.

1 'I met Mrs Bentley of Sinclair Ross's *As For Me and My House* when I was in my mid-twenties. She was the first literary character I'd encountered who inhabited the landscape where I was born. In some ways, I knew her instantly. Her ability to see the severe beauty of a countryside turned into desert was pure prairie; her sensibilities were shaped by wind, dust, and sky. One of the most enigmatic and controversial figures in Canadian literature, she has remained with me, particularly during the last ten years as I was writing these poems. The voice in her journals has been as hard to dispel from my imagination as a caragana rooted in soil.' [from Crozier's afterword]

2 Mrs Bentley's withdrawing husband Philip is an amateur painter as well as the town minister. 'Gamboge' is a dark yellow or mustard-coloured pigment used by oil painters.

Wind

We have all seen it here—
its ribs pressed into snow
and drifts of topsoil
smothering the fence lines.

It never passes by
but prowls outside the house,
an animal
come down from hunger.

It's what drives the women crazy
especially on the farms
it never stops.

It can strip a roof,
clap a barn to the ground,
crack a windmill like a wishbone.
You have to tilt to walk into it,
your body lists. All your words
are nothing in its mouth.

Some days it stops you dead
and suddenly
you've run out of time,
your life swept behind you
and the wind in front
not letting you
take another step.

Wilderness

Like Mrs Moodie I could say
the wilderness moved inside me[1]
but where there is no bush,
the wilderness is different.

It's really space that rushes at you
in spite of fences, the grid roads
laid in graphs across the earth.

A space not as empty as
you might imagine, it's a thing itself
minus details you can't separate
the whole into any parts.
The worst is

                    it doesn't need you.
It goes on and on whether the land
is broken or not, whether a town makes
its small exclamation mark or flattens out.

1 For Moodie, see pp. 93–122. This line also recalls Atwood's recreation of Moodie in *The Journals of Susanna Moodie*; compare her 'Departure from the Bush', in which Moodie says: 'In time the animals / arrived to inhabit me / . . . / I was not ready to be moved into'.

What's most like the prairie
is the mind of God, the huge way
he must have of looking at the world.
That's why I feel small and scared
inside myself, and yet at times
full of wonder.

Calm

When the wind stops,
how strange it is—
everything as still
as the end of a concert
before applause
ripples the air.

The birds reel in
their singing.
The few dry leaves
settle into stillness.
Used to the keening of the wind
those of us on Main Street
pause, heads tilted,
as if trying to hear
someone softly speaking
in another room.

For one moment before
the dust grows wings,
I think of Paradise,
how this must feel
something like it.

Serene and at rest,
I seem to gleam
in my skin, waiting
on the other side of light
for the new
life to begin.

1996

The Other Woman

Nearly twenty years ago and finally
I can think of her. She used to dial,
put the older of the two boys on the line.
Only four, *Daddy*, he'd say,
when are you coming home? till his father
clicked the receiver down. He'd left them
$10,000 and a yellow truck, came to me
with more than his pockets empty.

We struck out across the prairies,
wind roaring through the car, the road
hurtling us into the sky like a midway ride.
Every night a bottle of wine, a cheap motel,
we went so far we came back animal
and wild. No child could hold us.

The first time he visited his sons
she wore clothes he'd never seen before,
hair shampooed and newly permed.
Stay the night, she said, *save the price of a room.*
Home with me his hands stammered
down my belly in a language they'd forgotten,
one with several words for guilt and pain.
I almost lost him then.

Now it's she who phones
late at night, the boys grown up.
When I answer, she doesn't ask for him.
There's a silence, both of us breathing,
and I think of her mouth almost touching
the phone—as close as we have come.
Sometimes the next morning I keep quiet.
In twenty years I've never seen her face.

Nineteen seventy-eight, the end of summer
is a snapshot I never took—
the first time I see him with the boys.
In Okanagan Lake he holds around the waist
his younger son, pale legs kicking.
So beautiful together, it's an ache
I've carried since, something small and shining.
A stranger, from the shore I observe
the other boy thrash towards the raft.

She may be standing in the trees, invisible,
watching. She should have been.

If the child had been drowning,
if his father had turned to me
and the little one, free,
kicked into deeper water,
I couldn't have moved,
couldn't have saved them,
so fierce I was
holding on to my new life.

1999

The Sacrifice of Abraham[1]

Imagine the boy a goat,
pupils horizontal,
his laugh a bleating
wind shepherds through the grass.

I still count those seconds
when I raised the knife:

sunlight blinking
on his belly. God's terrible
desire to see the heart fly out.

Everything after
comes from this.

2002

1 Abraham is, in the Hebrew Scriptures, the founding patriarch of Judaism, the man with whom, according to Genesis 12, God makes a covenant promising him a land of his own and the progeny to make 'a great nation'. Although Abraham eventually has one son by his wife's handmaid Hagar, the promise of offspring for him and his wife, Sarah, seems unfulfilled until, when he is a hundred years old and Sarah is ninety, God promises that they shall have a son, an idea that provokes Sarah to laughter. When Sarah does then bear a son to Abraham, she names him Isaac, which means 'he laughed'. This poem and the paired one that follows are based on Genesis 22, the famous trial of Abraham's faith, which begins: *'God did tempt [test] Abraham, and said unto him, Abraham . . . Take now thy son, thine only son Isaac, whom thou lovest, and get thee into the land of Moriah; and offer him there for a burnt offering. . . .'* Abraham makes all of the necessary preparations and is about to slay Isaac when the angel of the Lord calls to him, saying: *'Lay not thine hand upon the lad, neither do thou any thing unto him: for now I know that thou fearest God, seeing thou hast not withheld thy son, thine only son from me. And Abraham lifted up his eyes, and looked, and behold behind him a ram caught in a thicket by his horns: and Abraham went and took the ram, and offered him up for a burnt offering in the stead of his son.'* Later interpreters have seen this event as a foundational story about perfect obedience to God, not only for Judaism but also for the two religions (Christianity and Islam) that descend from it.

The Sacrifice of Isaac

I bind my breasts with hide. Eat a jackal's heart
and ride in dust to the mountains of Moriah.
Three nights I sit with what they cannot see
beyond their fires. Though I'm close enough
to touch his cheek, I will my hands to stillness.
Before dawn, our last day on the road, a caravan
stutters by, heavy with its load like something
from the past. I am too old for them to trouble me
though a boy rides up, tips his goatskin
and offers me a drink. He drops his eyes
when I unveil my mouth, the darkness there.
I swallow his breath with water from his father's well,
mumble a blessing though I do not know
his gods, their indifference or their lust.
When the groan of wheels fades, I hear
my child's laugh ringing through the grass
like bells tied to the morning wind.
He is climbing. Bent double under wood,
he bears his fire upon his back.
I wait by a thicket, tufts of ram's wool
on the brambles, knife cold against my thigh,
until the altar's built, Isaac asking,
Father, where's the lamb?
then I step into the open, fists on fire,
above my swinging arm
the bare throat of my husband's
Lord opening in a flood of crimson light.

2002

John Steffler

b. 1947

Born in Toronto, John Steffler grew up in a rural community north of the city. He attended the University of Toronto, completing a BA in English in 1971, and took an MA from the University of Guelph in 1974 before moving to Newfoundland in that year. In 1975 he became a member of the Department of English at Sir Wilfred Grenfell College (the Corner Brook campus of the Memorial University of Newfoundland). Except for serving as writer-in-residence at Concordia University and at the University of New Brunswick, he has made his home in Newfoundland ever since.

Steffler began his writing career as a lyric poet, publishing *An Explanation of Yellow* in 1980. His other volumes of lyrics are *The Wreckage of Play* (1988), *That Night We Were Ravenous* (1998), and *Helix: New and Selected Poems* (2002). There is a considerable range of topics in the poems that make up these volumes, but their unifying concern is suggested in the opening lines of the 1998 poem 'Eclipse Again': 'So hard to parcel an event / without lying. A flood running out / in every direction, including up and down.'

Steffler's book-length sequence *The Grey Islands: A Journey* (1985) shows the writer finding one way to understand that flood of meaning an event brings. He records a range of emerging responses in the form of a journal, mixing poetry and prose and including some found documents—such as a small essay on Newfoundlanders (it seems to the protagonist of this book so terribly falsifying that he burns it), a census, even a snatch of song. Out of these fragments emerges the story of an individual who, having moved to Newfoundland from Ontario, is trying to make a connection with his new landscape by retreating to the solitude of an island off the coast of Newfoundland. Acclaimed as a classic of Canadian wilderness writing, *The Grey Islands*' intense response to its milieu was an early sign of the recent and extraordinary interest in artistic re-creations of the landscape, folklore, and history of this rocky island province. What has been described as a 'Newfoundland Renaissance' has become visible both in works by Newfoundlanders, such as Wayne Johnson's *Colony of Unrequited Dreams* (1998), and in works written by visitors to the province, such as Annie Proulx's *The Shipping News* (1993).

Steffler's 1992 novel, *The Afterlife of George Cartwright*, which won the Books in Canada First Novel Award and the Thomas Raddall Atlantic Fiction Award, also looks at the difficulty of understanding, and of narrating, events. Told by the ghost of George Cartwright (an actual representative of the British Empire, an eighteenth-century soldier, adventurer, and trader), the novel traces out Cartwright's struggle to understand, long after his death, the meaning of his life—particularly his experiences in Labrador and with the Native people he met, as well as the consequences of his actions. In Steffler's telling, Cartwright becomes an emblem for the way the Newfoundland landscape carries within itself both the European encounter with the New World and the way this encounter must eventually be resolved.

Indeed, in *The Afterlife of George Cartwright*, as well as in *The Grey Islands* and in some of the short poems, the relationship between person and geography becomes a dominant theme. Steffler has observed that:

> *Different landscapes have different characters just as various kinds of animals do. Partly for this reason I've always been interested in the long-term interaction between people and the place they inhabit. This process is especially striking in Newfoundland where nature is rowdy and naked. . . . A place holds an impression of everything that has ever happened there. The human past lives on in its physical setting, even in the air, in the local light. The past is alive all around us; it belongs to us and gives us an extra range of feelings and insights, if we let it.*

In addition to his poetry and fiction, Steffler published a children's book in 1987, *Flights of Magic*, which was illustrated by his wife, the painter Shawn Steffler. Interested in the interplay between music and writing, he has also written the libretto for *The Visitor*, a one-act chamber opera that was commissioned to celebrate the Viking Millennium and performed in Newfoundland in 2001. (The music was created by Michael Parker.) He describes it as about the search for a place to call home.

The Grey Islands

This mixture of prose and poetry describing a pilgrimage to the islands that lie off the east coast of Newfoundland's northern peninsula is the story of an individual seeking solitude: 'A way to corner myself is what I want,' he explains on the first page; 'Some blunt place I can't go beyond. Where excuses stop.' Steffler does not romanticize this retreat to a pre-technological world: once the narrator begins his journey he realizes he will have to live with 'the brutal mechanics of having a wish come true'—and after he has been on the island for some time he senses himself becoming 'spear point narrowing line this place is paring me to'.

In addition to the narrator, a central but unseen figure in the book is Carm Denny, who was the island's last resident before leaving it and who seems to have gone mad. Though the protagonist never meets Denny, he is constantly aware of his spectral presence, and he tries to imagine the hardships Denny experienced in living on the island—and to comprehend his willingness to endure unending isolation and the nature of the bond he must have formed with his difficult environment. While the protagonist, alone on the island, is the dominant speaker in the book, the voices of other Newfoundlanders do emerge, most often in the act of telling tales—especially ghost stories—of the place to which he's come. In his mind the narrator also hears the voice of Carm Denny, his absent but ineradicable presence having become a part of the island.

The selection that follows, which involves some reordering, is one suggested by Steffler.

From *The Grey Islands*

scoured sky. wind
and open miles.
all morning we climb the bright
hills cresting across our course,
pitching us up, sledding us sideways
down, wallowing, walled in water.
                        quick. near us
and gone,
            slim birds flit low, banking,
twisting, skimming the closing troughs,
and I feel it,
                know it a laughing
fact: the harder your hungry eyes bite
into the world (the island cliffs pencilled
in blue haze, and there, Nels pointing:
whale spray!

huge flukes kicking at the sun), the more
you spread your arms to hug it in,
the less you mind the thought of diving under,

eyes flooded. gulping dark.

•

The unfamiliarity of the sounds of the sea combined with the fact that I'm alone here and always half expecting someone to come to the cabin makes me uneasy at night and keeps me from sleeping. An apartment above a busy street would be no worse. I expected the sea to lull me, not keep me awake.

I hear the sound in too much detail. Whole groups and tiers and ranges of sound within and behind the obvious slap and slosh, wash, thump, gurgle and slurp. I hear knocks and hisses and crackles. At times last night it sounded as though the cabin was being hit by a stream of tiny weightless particles—powdered sand in the wind or pellets of snow. I thought it could almost be the sound of fire starting, and got out of bed to look around.

•

what can we do in such elements?

rock hills only recently
softened with green, some moss
and boggy hollows

vast migration of cloud

the wind an invisible glacier
wearing the island down

I keep warm burning
bits of a house

the work of people who tried to live here.

•

This morning two fishermen came ashore to get drinking water from the spring. I stepped outside to meet them, and they set their tall buckets down, willing to chat. Cyril Wellon, the skipper, a short thick man with spattered spectacles, was full of talk. His brother, Ambrose, nodded and grinned. I invited them in for tea, and they shifted and shuffled at first, caught in the midst of the day's work, threatened with hospitality. As they came in the door they ducked and smoothed their hair and seemed to think of their dirty hands and rubber clothes, as though expecting something fancy or foreign. Lace doilies. China cups. The sight of the tools and decoys put them at ease, and they took a good look around, praising the cozy nook I had for myself.

They wanted to know what I was doing of course, and I asked about their work—three cod traps in the island's coves—and about catches, the price of fish, the number of trips they make. They drank one mug of tea each then had to go, their brothers on the ship no doubt wondering where they'd gotten to.

•

not man's time here.
sun's time.
rock's time.
I begin to feel it.

days blink by—light
and cold flowing over—tide
breathing smoothly, evenly, I

slip between half-seconds, flash
light-beam pinball-style, do
ten thousand vanishing things
in a breath.

•

The coarse grass growing around the cabin draws its life from a layer of black peat three or four inches deep at the most. Below that are stones and pure sand. I cut squares of turf with an old splitting knife, stab, claw the tangled wads free. The smell that rises is raw and sour—faint bog fumes, wet minerals—the end of some slow process having little to do with the history of animals. I tear the clumped roots, examining them. Prod the exposed earth, turning the grains with my knife. No bugs or grubs. Nothing wriggling or digging or scampering. The few worms I find are thin match-sized things, anemic, nearly white. Not enough to go over a hook.

I look in various places—high spots, wet spots, under moss, under weeds—I lift stones and pieces of wood, all the fisherman's tricks. At one of the fallen houses I guess where the door would have been and dig, imagining kitchen scraps, dogs, people pissing, serenading the stars, the whole fertile trail of life. But whatever there was to eat here has been eaten long ago and the worms have starved or moved on. Resettled like everyone else. My only hope is the house most recently used. I straighten my back, take my knife and jar and walk the half mile to Carm Denny's shack.

And here, before Carm's door, under the first plank I turn: blood-brown worms, fat, quickly contracting like tendons suddenly laid bare. I move fast too, getting most of them.

Bent, I circle the building grubbing and rooting. Every shingle and stick I lift yields bait. Things Carm ate and didn't eat, turned to worms. A kind of organic shadow of the man. A lingering aura of his heat and movements stirring in the sod. The worms feeding under his window at night when he was here, curling and drawing themselves through years of what he had thrown away, sliding into the sound of his humming, his lonely talk, into and out of the warm rectangle of light that lay in the grass.

And I feel a bond of brotherhood with Carm, as though I am touching some extended parts of him, veins that had spread from his body taking root in the land from which he had never divided himself. I move swiftly, borrowing his life, his island's life, feeling it coiling, pulsing under my hands.

•

jagged island
island of noise.
the sea serious as ever, breaking
all that it touches.
wind tearing itself to pieces
pounces with all its weight, stops, flattens
grass again. tramples the waves.

the mountains cinder grey
cinder jagged
handsome as animals
hunt the passing clouds.
gathering trouble.

•

Was on the water most of the day with the Weltons. Cyril asked three days ago if I'd ever seen a cod trap being pulled, said they'd be by to get me next trip out. I heard their boat at seven this morning and jumped out of bed, no time to eat, went out the door pulling my sweater on and that was the start. Even now, ten at night, the cabin is flowing and tipping, the floor like a breathing belly. I close my eyes and: codfish, body to body, eyes, mouths gaping. Walls of stirring life.

•

these *birds* again. skimming
the water gullies all their lives

dodging the grabbing waves until
they can't.

and that's okay.

slipping into the only thing
they ever looked at

the thing they were only ever
an inch above.

•

I decided to move into Carm's cabin yesterday. His place is closer to good fishing and has a roof without leaks and a better stove. Devoted the day to carrying things here and tidying up—though surprisingly little of that to do: some bean tins and candle ends left by visitors. I already feel completely at home. The building and location make more sense, the windows take in all the shore and bay.

It's like standing inside the head of someone who knows the place.

•

clear day
island summit under my feet. sea spreads
curves up all round turning to
space: blue
field of the sun.

most ancient
most simple sight.
I stand on the first letter of earth's alphabet.
tower of stone and air.
nothing behind this bull's eye of power.
nothing higher.

eagle god.
wind's first eyes.

the green lands drift
at my feet.

•

I use Carm's brook only for fresh water now, having learned to fish straight from the sea. I find the sea-run trout always thick off the point for some reason and eager to take the lure. The water I get for drinking is clear brown, nearly as dark as tea, and it tastes of the island, the rock and peat, years underground.

•

warm sounds: the gas lamp's
loud hiss

the stove snaps and flutters

outside
the wind
the cold wash of gravel and sea

1985

Jane Urquhart

b. 1949

Born Jane Quinn, in the small mining community of Little Long Lac in northern Ontario, Jane Urquhart moved with her family to Toronto when she was five. She earned two BAs at the University of Guelph, one in English literature in 1971 and another in art history in 1975. She met the artist Tony Urquhart while completing the second; since marrying they have made their permanent home in Wellesley, a small village outside Waterloo, Ontario.

Urquhart began writing in the late 1970s and published three poetry collections in the early eighties: *False Shuffles* (1982), *I am Walking in the Garden of His Imaginary Palace* (1982; with illustrations by her husband), and *The Little Flowers of Madame de Montespan* (1983). These last two books have been reissued, bound together, as *Some Other Garden* (2000). In that poetry and in *Storm Glass,* a collection of short prose and prose poetry pieces that appeared in 1987, Urquhart showed an ability to render precise and contained, yet emotionally evocative, images.

The imagism and re-creation of historical moments so evident in her poetry can also be found in Urquhart's first novel, *The Whirlpool* (1986; a French translation of that book won France's prestigious Prix de Meilleur Livre Étranger in 1992). Set in late nineteenth-century Niagara Falls, the novel comprises three interconnected stories linked not only by events but also by images, such as the whirlpool of the title.

Fully felt as a literal presence in the novel, that whirlpool also becomes a complex metaphor: on the one hand, as part of the Niagara Gorge it is emblematic of the way the national borderline has real power over one's destiny and may be risky to cross; on the other hand, its constant revolutions resemble those of a history that seems to be 'moving nowhere and endlessly repeating itself' (a circular motion reiterated in the way Urquhart's own narratives move forward and back along their historical continuums).

In her second novel, *Changing Heaven* (1990), Urquhart extends her investigation of the nineteenth century as a formative age that flows forward into our own time: this tale marries fantasy and realism to show how the great writers of the Romantic and the Victorian eras go on haunting our contemporary imaginations. Urquhart's third novel, *Away* (1993), also set in the nineteenth century, draws on Celtic myth and oral history as the novel's Irish-Canadian narrator, Esther O'Malley, recounts the story of her family's emigration during the Irish potato famine of the 1840s and their settlement as pioneers in Ontario. *Away* received considerable critical acclaim and also set a record for number of weeks on the *Globe and Mail* bestseller list. It received the Trillium Award and was nominated for the IMPAC Dublin Literary Award.

Urquhart's fourth novel, *The Underpainter* (1997), which won a Governor General's Award, is the story of Austin Fraser, a well-known landscape painter from upstate New York who has returned to Davenport, a town on the Canadian side of Lake Ontario where he spent his boyhood summers. Now in his eighties, Austin, a cold man who has lived a life of surfaces, reflects on that life and on its web of relationships—with his old friend George; with his mentor, Robert Henri, a New York painter; with his friend and fellow painter Rockwell Kent; and with Sara, his model and lover—but he finds that the underlying designs that have given it meaning still elude him.

Given the Marian Engel Award for an outstanding body of prose written by a Canadian woman in 1994, Urquhart was named in 1996 to France's Order of Arts and Letters. She has also served as a writer-in-residence at the Universities of Ottawa and Toronto and at Memorial University of Newfoundland.

The Stone Carvers

The concern for the artist and the creative process in *The Underpainter* is also central to *The Stone Carvers* (2001) and its investigation of human relationships and the redemptive qualities of art. To her earlier considerations of literature and painting Urquhart adds sculpture and architecture, and here it is the influence of the First World War and its aftermath on the modern age that Urquhart investigates—along with further consideration of the early settling of rural Ontario. The novel tells the story of three Canadians: Klara Becker, the inheritor of her grandfather's talent for carving and sculpting; her brother Tilman, the inheritor of a Bavarian wanderlust; and Walter Allward, a historical figure who was a self-taught master architect and sculptor. A story of various kinds of carving—that of a village out of the wilderness; of a church out of mad fantasies; of a monument out of a battlefield that continues to explode with death and the unburied; and of a life out of the wreckage of war—*The Stone Carvers* takes as its central event the construction of the Vimy Memorial, itself the product of a dream Walter Allward had that changed the direction of his work and his life. The selection reprinted below tells Allward's story.

The Great War in Canadian Literature and Art

The Great War of 1914–8, now usually called the First World War, has been an important topic for English-Canadian writers: it is central to Hugh MacLennan's *Barometer Rising*, to Timothy Findley's *The Wars*, and to Jack Hodgins' *Broken Ground*, and its presence is powerfully felt in many other literary works, such as Robertson Davies' *Fifth Business*. Obviously that war at the beginning of the modern period transformed not just Canada but the entire world: while wars of modern weaponry, and the awful casualties and damages that such wars can inflict, had already begun to take place, the scope and horror of the First

World War was unanticipated. Its effects were immense: it changed not only those directly touched by it but altered forever the larger understandings of war, politics, and international relations. It left in its wake a worldwide sense of lost innocence—and a sense that a gaping wound had been opened and was not healing. Its political aftermath was felt in the Second World War and the Cold War that followed it, and it still resonates in many of today's conflicts.

Although Canada was not a theatre of war, the nation felt its effects with particular intensity: not only were Canada's losses very high, but it was a youthful nation—only fifty-one years a dominion and not yet a completely independent country—and it was a country that lacked the history of revolution and civil bloodshed that may have helped to buffer the experience for its neighbour to the south. In Canada more than 65,000 young men were lost, about 1 per cent of the nation's total population at the beginning of the war. The many more who served and returned, often wounded or emotionally traumatized, had witnessed horrors that, especially in an age without today's electronic media, those who waited at home could not conceive of.

In every country touched by the First World War, writers responded with poems and narratives: Wilfred Owen, Siegfried Sassoon, Erich Maria Remarque, and Ernest Hemingway were among the first. Contemporary writers have gone on trying to articulate the meaning of this devastating experience. (Recently, Pat Barker in England has written a distinguished trilogy.) Urquhart's examination of the creation of the Vimy Memorial in *The Stone Carvers* is perhaps characteristic of the way Canadians have responded, which is to deal with the trauma of war more than with the conflict itself.

The 1917 Battle of Vimy Ridge was a major turning point in the Allied war effort. The Vimy Memorial, situated in a ninety-one hectare park, was built by Canada at the cost of $1.5 million (over $20 million in current dollars) and required eleven years of work. It is architectural as well as sculptural in design, which is appropriate because there was much about the battle itself that was architectural—in its careful planning as well as in its execution, which involved elaborate 'subways' and tunnels into no man's land.

In constructing the Vimy Memorial, the Canadian sculptor Walter Seymour Allward (1876–1955) created a work of art that responded to a personal vision: 'I dreamed I was in a great battlefield,' he wrote in 1921: 'I saw our men going in by the thousands and being mowed down by the sickles of death. . . . Suddenly . . . I saw thousands marching to the aid of our armies. They were the dead. . . . Without the dead we were helpless. So I have tried to show this in this monument to Canada's fallen, what we owed them and we will forever owe them.' Allward's monument, which is located on land set aside by France for Canada's use in perpetuity, is constructed on a grand scale, meant not only to be seen from a distance but itself to look out onto the surrounding villages (with their graveyards in which those Canadian soldiers who could be identified were buried after the battle) and over the Douai Plain—once arable farmland but now mostly no longer useable. (It remains dangerous as a result of the live bombs and shells that fell there nearly a century ago—and it is felt to be hallowed because remains of the many who died there continue to be found.)

The monument, like the war itself, is a meeting of nineteenth- and twentieth-century sensibilities. The figures are characteristic of the symbolist art of the prewar period, but the architecture that frames these figures—two abstract pylons representing Canada and France, extending up from an austere platform largely without adornment—is modernist. The stone figures look as if they mounted these skyscraper-like extensions sometime after the latter came into existence. On the main level of the structure, which is a stark plane, stands a personification of Canada: alone and looking down at an abstract tomb, she mourns the losses of her children, particularly those who lie unburied in this vast grassy field. Carved into the white stone of the outside walls of the monument are the names of 11,285 soldiers whose bodies were never found.

The experience of the monument is a very powerful one, as riveting today as when it was unveiled in 1936. As well as engaging the visitor in the architecture of the stone structure itself and inviting contemplation of the twenty symbolic and affecting statues, it involves one in the landscape on which it sits. It is a work that takes those who visit into the experience of the losses suffered in war in general, not just on the field of battle at Vimy, and it helps those who come to reflect on such losses. By writing a novel that takes the redemptive power of this extraordinary piece of art as central to its narrative, Urquhart locates her own work within that humanistic conception of art's function.

From *The Stone Carvers*

It turned out that for a man with such an uncompromising nature, Walter Allward had served a fragmented, yet fortunate and by times lyrical apprenticeship. His exhausted mother, able for a few startling moments to look past the chaos of her seven children toward what even she recognized as precocious marks on paper, sent him off for Saturday drawing classes at the Toronto School of Art. There he showed more interest in line than in colour, and more interest in pencil and charcoal when the opportunity to sample paint was given to him. His father, a carpenter, taught him the mechanics of wood construction: the care and use of tools, the importance of measurement, plumb bobs, and spirit levels. Indeed, some of his earliest memories concerned the trapped, quivering bubble of the latter instrument. He might have become a carpenter like his father, but his need, his desire, to control what should be built (and what should not) led him to spend five years of his youth as an apprentice draughtsman in the offices of an architect, until one day he realized that he would never be permitted to draught anything other than brick row houses were he to remain there permanently—a price he felt was far too high to pay for a limited amount of security.

There was a fissure in the brick city of Toronto, where he grew up, a deep, branching wound caused by a river and its tributaries endeavouring to scrape out channels to Lake Ontario and creating, after centuries of effort, a series of interconnecting ravines known as the Don Valley. The nineteenth century had left in its wake a smattering of mills and factories, breweries and tanneries in the valley—some of which were abandoned by the dawn of the twentieth century—but little else had been coaxed out of the wild. Smaller enterprises flourished there in Allward's time: market gardens, orchards, and apiaries. And here and there one might discover the huts of nature-loving hermits lending to its green depths in summer the feel of Pliny's country home, or Yeats' imagined Innisfree.[1]

After leaving the architect, the young Allward descended each day into this unlikely verdant and humming world in order to work for the Don Valley Brickworks, where he had been employed to design and model the terracotta bas-reliefs that decorated the outside walls of the homes of the wealthy in the world above. This he did happily for a few years, using his wages to set up a studio in the city core. Eventually, the incoming commissions for statues of dead young women, elderly statesmen, and various allegorical figures freed him from the brickworks. He climbed out of the

1 In his Epistles, the Roman statesman Pliny the Younger (*c.* 62–*c.* 112) celebrates his country home in Tuscany ('The summers are exceedingly temperate and continually attended with refreshing breezes'); in his 1892 poem 'The Lake Isle of Innisfree', the Irish poet W.B. Yeats imagines an idyllic refuge where 'peace comes dropping slow' and 'the cricket sings'.

gorgeously blossoming valley on an evening in June and never glanced back. Except that it entered his dreams sometimes as a kind of alternative deep space that one could gaze into as if looking from a cliff above water while birds swam in an ocean of air. In some far and as yet uninvestigated room in his mind he had learned much from the valley about vantage points, about edges, about depths. He had learned that a valley can be used by industry, or can be used as a peaceful answer to industry, that it can provide shelter for several species of plants that would not have been able to survive in the congestion and exposure of the upper world, and that much of that which thrives in congestion and exposure would have languished near, or would have itself been killed by the music of nature. And then there was the question of whether any or all of this was worth preserving, worth protecting or fighting for. In his dreams sometimes the little orchards of the valley that he had walked through on his last ascent to the world above darkened with sudden armies.

During the first half of the war years, Allward walked to his studio like a ghost from the past who has no knowledge or interest in the present, fixed images of bronze figures in his mind, his preoccupation with casting larger and larger objects blocking his view of the carnage in the papers and the mourning of his neighbours. As if he were an arctic navigator determined to find the Northwest Passage, he was frozen into his own discoveries, unable to stop commemorating the might of the empire. Commissions had for some time been arriving at his door: a statue of Sir Oliver Mowat, the Alexander Bell Memorial, the memorial to the Boer War. His wife presided over his domestic life with efficiency and pride. He was a great man, still young, and yet too old to go overseas. Their children were, thankfully, simply too young to think about the war at all.

Who knows who or what shattered his indifference, or why, but the last years of the war came to him as a great awakening that let all the horror in, and he dreamed the Great Memorial well before the government competition was announced. He saw the huge twin pillars commemorating those who spoke French and those who spoke English, the allegorical figures with downcast or uplifted faces, and in the valley beneath the work of art, the flesh and bones and blood of the dead stirring in the mud. And then the dead themselves emerged like terrible naked flowers, pleading for a memorial to the disappeared, the vanished ones . . . those who were unrecognizable and unsung. The ones earth had eaten, as if her appetite were insatiable, as if benign nature had developed a carnal hunger, a yawning mouth, a sinkhole capable of swallowing, forever, one-third of those who had fallen. A messy burial without a funeral, without even a pause in the frantic slaughter.

Who were these boys with their clear eyes and their long bones, their unscarred skin and their educated muscle? How was it possible that they were destined to be soldiers? In what rooms had they stood? In what shafts of sunlight? Prairie grasses quivering beyond the old watery glass of farm windows. Snow falling softly on small uncertain cities, or into the dark lakes of the north. And all the footsteps they left in the white winter of 1914 would be gone by spring. The boys themselves gone the following autumn.

Nothing about the memorial was probable, even possible. Allward wanted white, wanted to recall the snow that fell each year on coast and plains and mountains, the disappeared boys' names preserved forever, unmelting on a vast territory of stone that was as white as the frozen winter lakes of the country they had left behind. Or he wanted granite, like the granite in the shield of rock that bled down from the north toward the Great Lakes. So sad and unyielding, so terrible and fierce in the face of the farmer.

The memorial was to be built in France, at the site of the great 1917 battle of Vimy Ridge, won with huge losses by the Canadians who had lived for weeks in tunnels they had carved themselves out of the chalky soil before bursting out of these tunnels on April 9 into a hell of mud and shrapnel. It was to stand near the Ypres salient on the crest of Hill 62, looking across the Douai Plain toward the coveted coal fields in the east and what were once lush fields belonging to peasant farmers to the west. After the war the French, in an act of reckless gratitude, had given one hundred hectares of the battleground to Canada in perpetuity, one hundred hectares of landscape that looked like it had been victimized by a terrible disease boiling through the earth's system to its surface. Almost a century later there would still be territorial restrictions on this land as active mines and grenades would occasionally ignite. And in the tunnels below, helmets and entrenching tools would continue to smoulder in the slow, relentless fire of rust.

Allward had watched the citizens of the provincial capital of Toronto stroll or hurry past his Queen's Park sculptures of colonial founding fathers without a glance; in fact, he had not once seen a passerby pause to examine the bronze faces of these men who had so successfully imposed Europe's questionable order on what had been their personal definition of chaos. After the brief ceremonies of installation, these statues in frock coats had become as easy to ignore as trees, fire hydrants, or lampposts. This would not—could not—happen with the memorial. It would be so monumental that, forty miles away, far across the Douai Plain, people would be moved by it, large enough that strong winds would be put off course by it, and perfect enough that it would seem to have been built by a vanished race of brilliant giants.

After he received the commission, Allward moved his family to a studio at Maida Vale in London, England, assuming that from there he would be able to travel easily back and forth to France in order to oversee the engineering of the project. He auditioned models for the figures of defenders, mourners, torchbearers, for the figures of peace and justice, truth and knowledge, often abandoning or substituting these individuals before the plaster models were cast or sometimes later, when he would change his mind throughout the night. He made hundreds of drawings of swords and wreaths, of pylons and of walls, always with the lead of his pencil sharpened like a weapon. In the end it was the imposing front wall of the memorial that obsessed him, the wall that would carry on its surface the names of the eleven thousand no one ever saw again.

In 1923, he began his investigation into dimension stone, his tour of the great quarries of Europe, his search for flawlessness. It was as if in his mind he had decided that the stone he chose must carry within it no previous history of organic life, that no fossil could have been trapped in it, no record of the earth's hot centre or the long periods of cold retreat that had crept across its surfaces in the form of ice ages or floods.

An undisturbed constituent, innocent since its own birth, of any transient event, so that the touch of the chisel cutting out the names would be its first caress.

Nothing pleased him, not the warm stone used by medieval architects for the great cathedrals, not the cold stone used centuries later for great public buildings. He visited quarries in France, Spain, Italy, England; he investigated the possibilities of Canadian quarries, American quarries; he sent his emissaries off to distant corners of the world, rejecting their suggestions over and over until they quit his employment in despair. Two years passed, a sizeable portion of the money had been spent on the quest. *I have been eating and sleeping stone for so long it has become an obsession with me,* he wrote in response to queries on the part of the concerned War Graves Commission in Canada, *and incidentally, a nightmare.*

Eventually, news came to him of a vast quarry near Split in Yugoslavia whence the Emperor Diocletian had procured the stone for his baths and palaces.[2] It was opened for the first time in centuries so that Allward could inspect it in the company of his engineers. Like the negative imprint of a great architectural complex, the deep outdoor rooms of the quarry shone with a blinding whiteness in the sun. Exhausted after months of travel, and after a full day of scrutinizing the face of the stone, a day in which he spoke not one word to those who accompanied him, Allward placed his hand and then his forehead against the quarry wall and wept. 'At last,' he is said to have whispered, 'at last.'

Before the stone could be shipped to France, a road leading from the Route Nationale on the Douai Plain to the site of the memorial had to be built. During the two years that passed in this employment Chinese workers young enough to have but scant knowledge of the European war were killed by mines hidden in mud, the noise of the fatal explosion like an insistent letter of reminder from the past. A rabbit warren of tunnels had to be closed and filled beneath the spot, a sunken rectangle had to be dug, and concrete had to be poured where the enormous foundation was to be installed. Body parts and clothing, bibles, family snapshots, letters, buttons, bones, and belt buckles were unearthed daily, and under the plot of earth from which the central staircase would someday rise, the fully uniformed skeletal remains of a German general were disinterred. In the seven years since the battle, several poplars had made a valiant attempt to take root on the battlefield, and some were now taller than a man. In almost every case when they were removed to make way for the road, bits of stained cloth and human hair and bones were found entangled in the roots. Once, a mine a half a mile away exploded, unearthing a young oak tree and the carcass of a horse, intact, activated, it would seem, by the fractional movement of the underground growth of roots.

While this was going on, Allward worked on plaster figures in his London studio or travelled to the continent to audition Italian carvers for the making of the great on-site sculptures—the male and female nudes that were to be executed on the base or high on each of the pylons. He made several voyages back to Yugoslavia to supervise the extraction of the stone at Split. Crossing the water to the white marble island of

2 Diocletian, emperor of the Roman Empire (284–305), built one of the most famous palaces in the Mediterranean region, using white local limestone from the nearby island of Brac.

Brac, he entered a white stone world where men worked all day in white quarries, departing at night for villages composed so entirely of white marble it was as if they lived in their own mausolea. Back on the mainland, he spent days watching stonecutters ease the limestone from the earth with such gentleness they might have been handling bone china. When it came time to move the massive pieces for the pylons to waiting ships, the wagons used in the process were so heavy they broke the ancient bridge at Trau over which stone for palaces and parliaments had passed without incident for almost two millennia. Work had to be halted until another bridge was built. Time passed.

And then more time passed. The stone was coaxed from the earth, permitted to slide in a controlled manner down the mountainside. It then was taken—with great difficulty—over the Adriatic Sea, across Italy, and up from the south to the north of France. Eighteen thousand tons. Load after load. The final several tons were interred in the wrecked earth of Vimy for safekeeping against repairs, for Allward always anticipated breakage and ruin. And each minute of every day Allward's ambition rolled heavily, turgidly through his mind, as something he would have to work with since it could neither be buried nor moved.

Angry letters arrived from Ottawa demanding dates of completion, and then more letters arrived filled with threats of cutting back the funds. Allward replied with rage, claiming that no one but he was intimate with the memorial, knew what it meant, what it would be. I will be emptied, he thought, when this is over. I will have put every drop of my life's blood into this already blood-soaked place. The anatomy of everything—natural or built—obsessed him. Stems became pedestals for that which must be supported to survive. Rivers became carving tools scouring curved banks, acting on the earth through which they passed in the same way as a sculptor's gouge moved through stone. Human beings too were either an extension, a manifestation of his own skills, his own vision, or they were not. If they were not, he wasn't interested. If he thought they were, and they proved otherwise, he felt first betrayed, then furious. The personal couldn't hold his attention, he was driven by the idea of the monument. A sentence that did not make reference to its construction was a sentence he could neither hear nor respond to.

When more than ten years had passed, an increasingly hysterical government in Canada sent out emissaries to lure him home. The depression in the country had deepened, the tax base was shrinking. Allward kept none of the appointments these bureaucrats made with him. If they were in France, he was in England and vice versa. They eventually went back to Canada to report that the memorial was too advanced to stop now, that to suspend operations would be a diplomatic error impossible to overcome.

Visible from a distance of forty miles, the two massive, irregular pylons stretching toward the sky like white bone needles or remarkable stalagmites, even the skeleton of the memorial had become a feature of the French landscape. The Italian carvers were beginning to work on the figures Allward had cast in plaster in his London studio. The names of the eleven thousand missing men were being collected and the complicated mathematics necessary to fit these names into the space available on the base was being undertaken. The most recent set of figures had suggested that it would likely take four stone carvers two years to chisel the hundreds of thousands of characters into the stone. Lines, circles, and curves corresponding to a cherished, remembered sound called over fields at summer dusk from a back porch door, shouted perhaps in anger or whispered in passion, or in prayer, in the winter dark. All that remained of torn faces, crushed bone, scattered limbs.

* * *

Allward returned to a country he hardly recognized. The war had been over for twenty years; few people wanted to discuss the monument. Each day he walked through the bright rooms of his Toronto house, the memorial a fact in his brain, its white stone echoed by snow in winter, a cumulus cloud with a flat base in summer. He could not disengage.

Designs for further monuments were attempted by him—he wanted to move forward, wanted to re-enter his life. But like a strong love affair that had ended in sorrow, the Vimy Memorial would not relinquish the large space it had occupied in his heart. He wouldn't let it go, and traces of its brooding presence entered every drawing he made. In the end the government was uninterested in his proposals, his efforts to document the past. And his reputation preceded him; his memorials took too long, cost too much money. The military bureaucracy wanted nothing more to do with him. Besides, it was too busy preparing for a violent future to wallow in a nostalgia for a violent past.

When the Second World War broke out in 1939, less than three years after he had returned to Canada, Allward reacted with panic and rage. He deluged the Department of National Defence with telegrams begging for reports and demanding that the memorial be sandbagged against aerial bombardment. As the weeks passed and he received no replies, he retreated into an inner landscape of great bleakness, pacing the house in the middle of the night, imagining the worst. He accepted no invitations, withdrew emotionally from his family, sat for hours by windows staring at falling snow or at a winter moon the colour of white stone. Sometimes he wept silently, tears falling over the now creased and folded skin of his large face.

With sharp coloured pencils he began a series of small, secretive drawings, each one more violent, more angry than the last. Tangled bodies littered torn landscapes, burning clots of brimstone rained down from a savage sky. And, in the background, tiny, almost insignificant in the drama, the wreckage of the monument. He shared these works with no one, carried them around in his pockets or sometimes crumpled and twisted under his hat. He knew he would never exhibit these records of anguish, wanted to keep his despair private, close to his head, his heart.

The drawings seemed to feed his belief in catastrophe, his certainty that there was absolutely nothing on earth not subject to vicious attack. In his imagination, and on the rice paper he used, the allegorical figures of his sculptures stepped away from their fixed positions to engage in appalling dramas. Always with the ruins of the memorial smoking in the distance, he drew embracing lovers impaled by a single sword, cairns composed of lifeless bodies, a naked man straddling the torn, prone torso of a woman from whose chest he had snatched her bleeding heart. Allward knew, even before he had completed this particular drawing, that it was his own heart the man held aloft, a trophy steaming in his desperate hands.

He had spent fifteen years of his life obsessed by perfection and permanence, had used verbal descriptions such as 'the impregnable wall of defence on the clean slice of the ridge' to describe the base of his memorial. He had believed that he was making memory solid, indestructible, that its perfect stone would stand against the sky forever. With this certainty threatened, his world collapsed.

Ironically, although the memorial survived the Second World War, the psyche of its creator did not. Allward remained a kind, courteous man who walked slowly through the city streets in a grey coat. Sometimes, especially in winter, when he was more likely to be alone, he visited the bronze sculptures he had created so many years ago for the park in front of the provincial legislature. He liked the way the gestures of dark statues that had first established his reputation were made explicit by the whiteness of the surrounding snow. But in this land so famous for winter, the knowledge of Allward's genius was quickly forgotten by the very nation that had commissioned the memorial where he was most able to demonstrate this genius. Even those Canadians who would later make the trip to France and who would admire the monument would rarely take the trouble to ask the sculptor's name.

2001

Anne Carson

b. 1950

Anne Carson's work challenges the reader because, like Carson herself, it is hard to categorize. Carson first established her reputation as a classical scholar but her scholarly works (the title of her first book is *Eros the Bittersweet*, 1986) read more like poems. She is an acclaimed poet whose first book of poems are called 'talks' and are set as prose, and whose later poems have titles that identify them as essays, as a novel, or even as tangos. She is a writer who is fiercely intellectual but who is also drawn to the realms of the physical and the metaphysical—and who in the poem called 'God's Work' (from a sequence called 'The Truth about God') shows herself attracted to the Buddhist doctrine of 'no-mind'. While her writing suggests a bookish person, she is said to be fascinated by volcanoes and to seek them out in order to paint them erupting. Generally thought of as reticent and impersonal (her extraordinarily brief biographical notes on her books say simply, 'Anne Carson lives in Canada'), she often writes of erotic desire, creating works that both mask and unmask the immediate and personal dimensions of the poem and that challenge assumptions of sexual roles and gender definitions—as in her recent tale of tension between two women, a classics professor and a student, in 'Irony Is Not Enough: Essay on My Life as Catherine Deneuve' (in *Men in the Off Hours*, 2000). Despite the fact that referring to her Canadian residency is the way she identifies herself on her book jackets, her poetry does not seem particularly 'Canadian' in topic, theme, or style: not sharing much with her Canadian predecessors or contemporaries, it looks back to the classics and out to an international community for its inspiration, including early American modernists such as T.S. Eliot and Ezra Pound. With some of her poems carrying titles that describe them as 'first draft' or 'second draft' even after they've been published, her texts often convey a sense of instability, and of ongoing process. In short, all of Carson's texts pose problems: they provoke and puzzle readers; they both invite and resist interpretation.

Born in Toronto, Carson was educated at the University of Toronto, where she earned a BA in 1974, an MA in 1975, and a Ph.D. in 1980. She began her academic career teaching classics at the University of Calgary; since 1988, she has been a professor of classics at McGill University—though she typically spends one term of each academic year as a visiting professor at an American university. (These have included Princeton, Emory, and Berkeley.)

In 2001, Carson published a new translation of Sophocles' *Electra*. Perhaps because part of the activity of a classicist is translation (she describes the experience of translating as the 'mutual undoing of each language into the other'), she shows herself in her own poetry aware of the way language governs what cannot—as well as what can be—said, and sometimes calls attention to the histories and etymologies of the words she uses, playing with the layers of meaning that each carries or returning them to their early forms to remind her readers of what has been lost 'in translation'. In *Glass, Irony, and God* (1995), for example, she concludes 'The Book of Isaiah' by suggesting that there is a good deal of significance in the fact that there are two words in Hebrew for righteousness, a masculine and a feminine form: 'Isaiah could not be expected to untie this / hard knot himself.'

Because many poets and fiction writers of the contemporary age have based themselves at universities, there has been some debate about whether an academic milieu is good for creative writers. But for Carson, scholarship is integral to her creative writing—because for her, scholarship is as creative as any other form of writing:

> *To explain what I do is simple enough. A scholar is someone who takes a position. From which position, certain lines become visible. You will at first think I am painting the lines myself; it's not so I merely know where to stand to see the lines that are there. And the mysterious thing, it is a very mysterious thing, is how these lines do paint themselves. Before there were any edges or angles or virtue—who was there to ask the questions?* (Introduction to 'The Life of Towns', in *Plainwater: Essays and Poetry,* 1995)

Carson's profession as a teacher and a scholar of classics brings her into constant contact with what she has called the 'haunted old phrases' of classical texts and makes her aware of how those texts go on speaking in the works of later writers and of how the concerns and preoccupations of the ancient world continue to illuminate our own. Her wide knowledge of ancient literature infuses her writing, which sets historical and contemporary events on an equal plane: the worlds of mythic, Biblical, and literary creations blend with pop song and present reality; the past and the imagined events of poetry and fiction carry the same importance as today's news. Thus, in poems such as 'TV Men: Hektor' (various characters, including Sappho, Lazarus, Antigone, and Tolstoy, have appeared in 'TV Men' poems in her books), not only does Homer's story of Hektor become newly relevant to contemporary experience but elements of the present world, such as television, look as strange as if they were archaic.

The prose poems in *Short Talks,* published in 1992, are scattered with allusions to artists of all kinds: among them, Seurat, Prokofiev, Kafka, Ovid, Van Gogh, Rembrandt, Sylvia Plath, and the Brontës. Many reappear in Carson's subsequent work: 'The Glass Essay' in *Glass, Irony, and God,* for example, is a long poem that tells of a woman who, in the aftermath of a love affair, begins to inhabit the world created by the Brontës. The fact that Kafka, in particular, is often alluded to in Carson's work suggests that Carson feels a particular affinity for that twentieth-century writer who treated dream and reality as indistinguishable, an affinity that can also be heard in the voice that introduces *Short Talks,* which begins 'Early one morning words were missing. Before that, words were not. Facts were, faces were.'

The poems in *Short Talks* resemble riddles: their titles announce a topic (as those reprinted here say they are about 'rectification' or 'waterproofing'), which is followed by a short piece that often has no obvious connection to that title. But riddles are only sometimes jokes; they can also be *koans*—enigmas that provide occasions for meditation—and much of Carson's writing has the feeling of meditation. She dramatizes the mind in the act of investigating or puzzling over a topic, and the full meaning always remains to be discovered.

The meditative riddle is not the only form that is apparent in Carson's writing. *The Beauty of the Husband,* the book of poetry Carson published in 2001, is subtitled *A Fictional Essay in 29 Tangos,* and the tango also appears in *Autobiography of Red: A Novel in Verse* (1998), which recasts the Greek myth of the winged monster Geryon as a story of spurned love. The tango as a form has its own significance: it is a difficult dance with a set of highly formal conventions that must be mastered, yet it also associated, perhaps more than any other dance, with the expression of intense passion. The great tango dancer therefore seems both to employ extraordinary technique and to be caught up in a frenzy of expressive motion dictated by desire.

Carson's other works include *Economy of the Unlost* (1999) and a 2001 libretto created for 'an opera installation', with music by the US composer Guillermo Galindo, called *Decreation: Fight Cherries*: it is based on the life and thought of the French philosopher Simone Weil (1909–43). For this body of work, Carson has received numerous honours and prizes, including a Guggenheim Fellowship (1998). The Griffin Poetry Prize and the T. S. Eliot Prize in 2001 followed the prestigious MacArthur Foundation 'genius' grant in 2000, which brought her $500,000 over five years in support of any projects she wants to pursue.

Short Talk on Rectification

Kafka[1] liked to have his watch an hour and a half fast. Felice kept setting it right. Nonetheless for five years they almost married. He made a list of arguments for and against marriage, including inability to bear the assault of his own life (for) and the sight of the nightshirts laid out on his parents' beds at 10:30 (against). Hemorrhage saved him. When advised not to speak by doctors in the sanatorium, he left glass sentences all over the floor. Felice, says one of them, had too much nakedness left in her.

1992

1 The Prague-born Jewish fiction writer Franz Kafka (1883–1924), whose work portrays an enigmatic and nightmarish reality about lonely, perplexed, and threatened individuals. Kafka met Felice Bauer (1887–1960) in 1912, and the two became engaged to be married; each was filled with doubts, and they broke it off, then became engaged again. After writing up his list of reasons for and against marriage in 1916, Kafka separated from Felice permanently in 1917. In that same year he was diagnosed with tuberculosis after a hemorrhage and began spending long periods of time in sanatoriums.

Short Talk on Waterproofing

Franz Kafka was Jewish. He had a sister, Ottla, Jewish.[1] Ottla married a jurist, Josef David, not Jewish. When the Nuremburg laws[2] were introduced to Bohemia-Moravia in 1942, quiet Ottla suggested to Josef David that they divorce. He at first refused. She spoke about sleep shapes and property and their two daughters and a rational approach. She did not mention, because she did not yet know the word, Auschwitz, where she would die in October 1943. After putting the apartment in order she packed a rucksack and was given a good shoeshine by Josef David. He applied a coat of grease. Now they are waterproof, he said.

1992

1 Ottla Kafka (1892–1943), the youngest of Franz Kafka's three sisters and the family member closest to him, was killed in Auschwitz, the infamous Nazi concentration and extermination camp in Poland.
2 Passed by the Nazi party in 1935, but not introduced to Bohemia-Moravia until seven years later, these laws were created to protect the 'purity' of the German race: they made Jews second-class citizens, ineligible for German citizenship, and denied them the right to vote or hold political office; in addition, Jews had to abide by a curfew, and many public spaces became off-limits to them. Germans were no longer allowed to marry Jews and were discouraged from having social or business interactions with them.

Short Talk on the Total Collection

From childhood he dreamed of being able to keep with him all the objects in the world lined up on his shelves and bookcases. He denied lack, oblivion or even the likelihood of a missing piece. Order streamed from Noah in blue triangles and as the pure fury of his classifications rose around him, engulfing his life they came to be called waves by others, who drowned, a world of them.

1992

Short Talk on Who You Are

I want to know who you are. People talk about a voice calling in the wilderness.[1] All through the Old Testament a voice, which is not the voice of God but which knows what is on God's mind, is crying out. While I am waiting, you could do me a favour. Who are you?

1992

1 In the Gospels, John the Baptist is described as 'he that was spoken of by the prophet Esaias [Isaiah], saying, The voice of one crying in the wilderness, Prepare ye the way of the Lord, make his paths straight' (Matthew 3: 3; also Mark 1: 3; Luke 3: 4; John 1: 23). The reference is to the verse in the Book of Isaiah (in the Old Testament), which describes the speaker as hearing 'The voice of him that crieth in the wilderness, Prepare ye the way of the LORD, make straight in the desert a highway for our God' (40: 3).

God's Work

Moonlight in the kitchen is a sign of God.
The kind of sadness that is a black suction pipe extracting you
from your own navel and which the Buddhists call

'no mindcover' is a sign of God.
The blind alleys that run alongside human conversation
like lashes are a sign of God.

God's own calmness is a sign of God.
The surprisingly cold smell of potatoes or money.
Solid pieces of silence.

From these diverse signs you can see
how much work remains to do.
Put away your sadness, it is a mantle of work.

1995

Book of Isaiah[1]

I.

Isaiah awoke angry.

Lapping at Isaiah's ears black birdsong no it was anger.

God had filled Isaiah's ears with stingers.

Once God and Isaiah were friends.

God and Isaiah used to converse nightly, Isaiah would rush into the
garden.

1 The Book of Isaiah, attributed to an eighth-century-BCE prophet, begins: 'The vision of Isaiah the son of Amoz, which he saw concerning Judah and Jerusalem. . . . Ah sinful nation, a people laden with iniquity, a seed of evil-doers, children that are corrupters: they have forsaken the LORD, they have provoked the Holy One of Israel unto anger, they are gone away backward.' The most cited of the prophetic books in the Hebrew Scriptures (or Old Testament), in it, Isaiah like the other Hebrew prophets, sternly rebukes the Jews for their unrighteous behaviour. In the last part of the Book of Isaiah there are promises of redemption and restoration for the nation following reform.

They conversed under the Branch,[2] night streamed down.

From the sole of the foot to the head God would make Isaiah ring.

Isaiah had loved God and now his love was turned to pain.

Isaiah wanted a name for the pain, he called it sin.

Now Isaiah was a man who believed he was a nation.[3]

Isaiah called the nation Judah and the sin Judah's condition.

Inside Isaiah God saw the worldsheet burning.

Isaiah and God saw things differently, I can only tell you their actions.

Isaiah addressed the nation.

Man's brittleness! cried Isaiah.

The nation stirred in its husk and slept again.

Two slabs of bloody meat lay folded on its eyes[4] like wings.

Like a hard glossy painting the nation slept.

Who can invent a new fear?

Yet I have invented sin, thought Isaiah, running his hand over the knobs.

And then, because of a great attraction between them—

which Isaiah fought (for and against) for the rest of his life—

2 Although the line suggests a literal 'branch', Carson is responding to a metaphor in the Book of Isaiah in which 'branch' refers to the restored community of Israel (Isa. 4: 2), and particularly to the descendants of the house of King David (Isa. 11: 1).

3 See Isa. 65: 1: 'Behold me, behold me, unto a nation that was not called by my name.'

4 Various images of blindness—in particular that of a nation that has shut or covered its eyes—run through the Book of Isaiah. Regarding the nation's hands as 'bloody slabs of meat', see Isa. 1: 15: 'And when ye spread forth your hands, I will hide mine eyes from you: yea, when ye make many prayers, I will not hear: your hands are full of blood.' That the nation's eyes are covered by something like 'wings' gives it an ironic resemblance to the seraphim described in Isaiah (see note 6).

God shattered Isaiah's indifference.

God washed Isaiah's hair in fire.

God took the stay.[5]

From beneath its meat wings the nation listened.

You, said Isaiah.

No answer.

I cannot hear you, Isaiah spoke again under the Branch.

Light bleached open the night camera.

God arrived.

God smashed Isaiah like glass through every socket of his nation.

Liar! said God.

Isaiah put his hands on his coat, he put his hand on his face.

Isaiah is a small man, said Isaiah, but no liar.

God paused.

And so that was their contract.

Brittle on both sides, no lying.

Isaiah's wife came to the doorway, the doorposts had moved.[6]

What's that sound? said Isaiah's wife.

The fear of the Lord, said Isaiah.

He grinned in the dark, she went back inside.

5 See Isa. 3: 1: 'For, behold, the Lord, the LORD of hosts, doth take away from Jerusalem and from Judah the stay and the staff, the whole stay of bread, and the whole stay of water.'

6 In Chapter 6, Isaiah describes a vision in which he saw 'the LORD sitting upon a throne, high and lifted up, and his train filled the temple. Above it stood the seraphims: each one had six wings; with twain he covered his face, and with twain he covered his feet, and with twain he did fly. And one cried unto another, and said, Holy, holy, holy, is the LORD of hosts: the whole earth is full of his glory. And the posts of the door moved at the voice of him that cried, and the house was filled with smoke.'

II.

There is a kind of pressure in humans to take whatever is most
beloved by them
and smash it.

Religion calls the pressure *piety* and the smashed thing *a sacrifice to God.*

Prophets question these names.

What is an idol?

An idol is a useless sacrifice, said Isaiah.

But how do you know which ones are useless? asked the nation in its genius.

Isaiah pondered the various ways he could answer this.

Immense chunks of natural reality fell out of a blue sky
and showers of light upon his mind.

Isaiah chose the way of metaphor.

Our life is a *camera obscura*, said Isaiah, do you know what that is?[7]

Never heard of it, said the nation.

Imagine yourself in a darkened room, Isaiah instructed.

Okay, said the nation.

The doors are closed, there is a pinhole in the black wall.

A pinhole, the nation repeated.

Light shoots through the pinhole and strikes the opposite wall.

7 Isaiah's metaphor of the *camera obscura* is not Biblical but it does owe a great deal to Plato's allegory of the cave, found in Book IV of *The Republic.* There Plato suggests that most people mistakenly believe the everyday world is real when reality lies on a higher plane; he compares that situation to the kind of error that would be made by individuals in a fire-lit cave if they were unable to turn their heads to see the real world and could only judge it by the flickering shadows real things cast on the cave wall.

The nation was watching Isaiah, bored and fascinated at once.

You can hold up anything you like in front of that pinhole, said Isaiah,
and worship it on the opposite wall.

Why worship an image? asked the nation.

Exactly, said Isaiah.

The nation chewed on that for a moment.

Then its genius spoke up.

So what about Isaiah's pinhole?

Ah, said Isaiah.

A memory fell through him as clear heat falls on herbs.

Isaiah remembered the old days, conversing with God under the Branch

and like an old butler waking in an abandoned house the day the revolution began,

Isaiah bent his head.

A burden[8] was upon Isaiah.

Isaiah opened his mouth.

A sigh came from Isaiah's mouth, the sigh grew into a howl.[9]

8 This and the lines that follow are indebted to Isaiah's prophecy in 19: 1–9: 'The burden [a prophecy] of Egypt. Behold, the LORD rideth upon a swift cloud, . . . and they shall seek to the idols, and to the charmers, and to them that have familiar spirits, and to the wizards. . . . And they shall turn the rivers far away; and the brooks of defence shall be emptied and dried up: the reeds and flags shall wither. The paper reeds by the brooks, by the mouth of the brooks, and every thing sown by the brooks, shall wither, be driven away, and be no more. The fishers also shall mourn, and all they that cast angle into the brooks shall lament, and they that spread nets upon the waters shall languish. Moreover they that work in fine flax, and they that weave networks, shall be confounded.'

9 Compare Isa. 65: 13–14: 'Therefore thus saith the LORD God, Behold, my servants shall eat, but ye shall be hungry: behold, my servants shall drink, but ye shall be thirsty: behold, my servants shall rejoice, but ye shall be ashamed: Behold, my servants shall sing for joy of heart, but ye shall cry for sorrow of heart, and shall howl for vexation of spirit.'

The howl ran along the brooks to the mouth of the brooks

and tore the nets of the fishers who cast angle into the brooks

and confounded the workers in fine flax who weave networks

and broke their purpose.

The howl rolled like a rolling thing past slain men and harvests and
spoils

and stopped in a ditch between two walls.[10]

Then Isaiah unclamped his mouth from the howl.

Isaiah let his mouth go from the teat.

Isaiah turned, Isaiah walked away.

Isaiah walked for three years naked and barefoot with buttocks
uncovered
to the shame of the nation.

All night you could see the Branch roaming against the sky like a
soul.

III.

Isaiah walked for three years in the valley of vision.

In his jacket of glass he crossed deserts and black winter mornings.

The icy sun lowered its eyelids against the glare of him.

God stayed back.

Now Isaiah had a hole in the place where his howl had broken off.

All the while Isaiah walked, Isaiah's heart was pouring out the hole.

10 Recalling Isa. 22: 11: 'Ye made also a ditch between the two walls for the water of the old pool: but ye have not looked unto the maker thereof, neither had respect unto him that fashioned it long ago.'

One day Isaiah stopped.

Isaiah put his hand on the amputated place.

Isaiah's heart is small but in a way sacred, said Isaiah, I will save it.

Isaiah plugged the hole with millet and dung.

God watched Isaiah's saving action.

God was shaking like an olive tree.[11]

Now or never, whispered God.

God reached down and drew a line on the floor of the desert in front of Isaiah's feet.

Silence began.

Silence roared down the canals of Isaiah's ears into his brain.

Isaiah was listening to the silence.

Deep under it was another sound Isaiah could hear miles down.

A sort of ringing.

Wake up Isaiah! said God from behind Isaiah's back.[12]

Isaiah jumped and spun around.

Wake up and praise God! said God smiling palely.

Isaiah spat.

God thought fast.

11 An echo of a stern warning found in Isa. 24, telling how 'the LORD maketh the earth empty, and maketh it waste, and turneth it upside down, and scattereth abroad the inhabitants thereof. . . . In the city is left desolation, and the gate is smitten with destruction. When thus it shall be in the midst of the land among the people, there shall be as the shaking of an olive tree, and as the gleaning grapes when the vintage is done. They shall lift up their voice, they shall sing for the majesty of the LORD, they shall cry aloud from the sea. Wherefore glorify ye the LORD in the fires, even the name of the LORD God of Israel in the isles of the sea.'

12 The Book of Isaiah ends with several injunctions for the people to awake: see, for example, 51: 9: 'Awake, awake, put on strength, O arm of the LORD.'

The nation is burning![13] God cried pointing across the desert.

Isaiah looked.

All the windows of the world stood open and blowing.

In each window Isaiah saw a motion like flames.

Behind the flames he saw a steel fence lock down.

Caught between the flames and the fence was a deer.

Isaiah saw the deer of the nation burning all along its back.

In its amazement the deer turned and turned and turned

until its own shadow lay tangled around its feet like melted wings.

Isaiah reached out both his hands, they flared in the dawn.

Poor flesh! said Isaiah.

Your nation needs you Isaiah, said God.

Flesh breaks, Isaiah answered. Everyone's will break. There is
nothing we can do.

I tell you Isaiah you can save the nation.

The wind was rising, God was shouting.

You can strip it down, start over at the wires, use lions! use thunder!
use what you see—

Isaiah was watching sweat and tears run down God's face.

Okay, said Isaiah, so I save the nation. What do *you* do?

God exhaled roughly.

13 See, for example, Isa. 10: 16–18: 'Therefore shall the Lord, the Lord of hosts, send among his fat ones leanness; and under his glory he shall kindle a burning like the burning of a fire. And the light of Israel shall be for a fire, and his Holy One for a flame: and it shall burn and devour his thorns and his briers in one day; And shall consume the glory of his forest, and of his fruitful field, both soul and body: and they shall be as when a standard-bearer fainteth.'

I save the fire, said God.

Thus their contract continued.

IV.

When Isaiah came back in from the desert centuries had passed.

There was nothing left of Isaiah but a big forehead.

The forehead went rolling around the nation and spoke to people
who leapt to their feet
and fled.

If the nation had taken Isaiah to court he could have proven his
righteousness.

But they met in secret and voted to cut him off.

Shepherds! Chosen ones! Skinny dogs! Blood of a dog! Watchmen
all! said Isaiah.

Isaiah withdrew to the Branch.

It was a blue winter evening, the cold bit like a wire.

Isaiah laid his forehead on the ground.

God arrived.

Why do the righteous suffer? said Isaiah.

Bellings of cold washed down the Branch.

Notice whenever God addresses Isaiah in a feminine singular verb
something dazzling is
about to happen.

Isaiah what do you know about women? asked God.

Down Isaiah's nostrils bounced woman words:

Blush. Stink. Wife. Fig. Sorceress—

God nodded.

Isaiah go home and get some sleep, said God.

Isaiah went home, slept, woke again.

Isaiah felt sensation below the neck, it was a silk and bitter sensation.

Isaiah looked down.

It was milk forcing the nipples open.

Isaiah was more than whole.

I am not with you I am *in* you, said the muffled white voice of God.

Isaiah sank to a kneeling position.

New pain! said Isaiah.

New contract! said God.

Isaiah lifted his arms, milk poured out his breasts.

Isaiah watched the milk pour like strings.

It poured up the Branch and across history and down into people's lives and time.

The milk made Isaiah forget about righteousness.

As he fed the milk to small birds and animals Isaiah thought only about their little lips.

God meanwhile continued to think about male and female.

After all there are two words for righteousness, Isaiah could not be expected to untie this
hard knot himself.

First the masculine word TSDQ, a bolt of justice that splits the oak in two.

Then in the empty muscle of the wood, mushrooms and maggots and monkeys set up a
livelihood:

here is (the feminine word) TSDQH.

God grave the two words on Isaiah's palms.

God left it at that.

And although it is true Isaiah's prophecies continued to feature
eunuch cylinders and
clickfoot woman shame.

And although it is true Isaiah himself knew several wives and begot a bastard son.

Still some nights through his dreams slipped a river of milk.

A river of silver, a river of pity.

He slept, the asters in the garden unloaded their red thunder into the dark.

1995

TV Men: Hektor[1]

I.

TV is hardhearted, like Lenin.[2]
TV is rational, like mowing.
TV is wrong, often, a worry.
TV is ugly, like the future.
TV is a classic example.

Hektor's family members found themselves engaged in exciting acts,
and using excited language, which they knew derived from TV.

1 This poem responds to Homer's *Iliad* (Carson has called it the one work she would take to a desert island), which tells the story of the Greek siege of Troy during the Trojan War. Hektor, the eldest son of King Priam and Queen Hekabe, is the commander of the Trojan army, his prowess in battle second only to that of Achilles, the hero of the Greek army. Much of the poem focuses on Book 22 of the *Iliad*, in which the two meet in a climactic battle that ends with Hektor's defeat.

2 Vladimir Ilyich Lenin (1870–1924), the founder of Marxism-Leninism, was the principal figure in the Russian Revolution and, from 1918 to 1924, the first premier of the Soviet Union. By 1922 (six years after the rise of Communism in Russia), five million people had perished through famine; in response to strikes and uprisings against the Communist regime, Lenin began show trials with executions of dissidents.

A classic example of what.

A classic example of a strain of cruelty.

II.

Hektor was born to be a prince of Troy not a man of TV,
hence his success.
Wrong people look good on TV, they are so obviously
a soul divided[3]

and we all enjoy the pathos of that.
Let us join Hektor
on the eve of the Death Valley shoot.[4]
Hektor lies

on the motel bed in his armour observing himself and his red lips
high overhead.
The ceiling is mirrored in divine fire.
Your Law has got hold

of my entrails,[5] he murmurs. His lipstick grins at him
upside down.
Out the window he can see a horizon of low brown mountains
laid end to end.

They make a hissing sound. O prince of Troy!
Butter and honey
shall you eat, that you may know to refuse the evil
and choose the good.[6]

TV is inherently cynical. It speaks to the eye, but the mind has no eye.

3 Perhaps an allusion to Plato's theory that the soul is divided into three components—reason, will, and appetite—and that in some individuals the lack of balance among the parts of the soul is apparent as they clash with one another.

4 Carson playfully imagines this scene for television as being shot on location in Death Valley, California—where many Hollywood westerns were made—probably for the associations the name evokes, including that of the Greek underworld, to which Hektor is said to depart after his death in the *Iliad*.

5 This line may allude to the fate that those killed in battle may face, as when Achilles spears Hektor's younger brother Polydorus, and Hektor watches him die holding his entrails; or it may reflect the fear, expressed by Hektor as he dies at Achilles' hands, of the dishonour of being left after death for dogs and vultures to devour. As well, this line may also be intended to echo the phrase 'the law on entrails', as old laws governing the earth's resources (or 'entrails') are called. For the connection Carson makes between Hektor's name and 'hold', see note 7.

6 See Isaiah 7: 14–16: 'Therefore the Lord himself shall give you a sign; Behold, a virgin shall conceive, and bear a son, and shall call his name Immanuel. Butter and honey shall he eat, that he may know to refuse the evil, and choose the good. For before the child shall know to refuse the evil, and choose the good, the land that thou abhorrest shall be forsaken of both her kings.'

. III.

Hektor's name is from the ancient verb 'to hold'.[7]
Hold.
Hold on.
Hold out.
Hold up.
Hold off.
Hold in.
Hold together.
Hektor's name is the antithesis
of those temporary constructions on the shore
(Greek army)
that
stood—
from opening kills to the day Troy was razed—
a mere ten years.

Head down against a thin winter wind
Hektor paces the floor of Death Valley,
repeating his line.
I have learned to be brave.[8]
The light-hole pulls away on every side.

TV is dull, like the block of self in each of us.

IV.

Salt particle by salt particle the desert grows luminous at dawn.
It is the second day of the Death Valley shoot.
Hektor is alone in the light-hole.

The walkie-talkie taped to the small of his back is cold as a slab of
meat.
It crackles alive and the director's voice
crawls up his spine like a bee.

7 Although the etymology of the Greek *Hektōr* is uncertain, Carson here accepts the possibility that it may derive from the Greek verb *echō*, to hold, making 'Hektor' the equivalent of 'holder'— and she calls attention to the implied contrast, in the *Iliad*, between Hektor's firm 'hold', as a bulwark protecting his city, with what she describes as the 'temporary constructions' of the Greeks — i.e. the tents and huts in which the Greek army has continued to live during their years of besieging Troy.

8 An allusion to a speech Hektor makes at the beginning of Book 22 to his wife, Andromache, after she tries to persuade him to remain within the walls of the city: 'My heart bids me not to [stay inside], since I have learned to be brave always and to fight among the front lines of the Trojans, winning great glory for my father and for myself there.'

Places please! Helicopter five minutes away!
Hektor hunkers down close to the sand.
The eunuch winter sun

stains him in a blind place. Cracks appear. And the silence—
a silence that starts so deep
under the rock

he can hear it ringing. Man is a slave and a sombre being.
Who does not know enough to lick the salt
off the low bushes at dawn.

TV is loud, yet we do not awake.

V.

TV wastes nothing, like a wife.

While Hektor was out making war, his wife heated water on the fire
for a bath when he returned wearied of killing.
Later that night

they brought news of his death. She puts away the water
and uses the fire to burn all his clothes.
Since they will be no benefit to you,

nor will you wear them, she says. Looking out over the parapet
to the arc-lit battlefield where men
with string

were measuring the distance from Hektor's darkening nipple
to the camera's eye.
She saw men on their knees.

VI.

From the helicopter Death Valley looks like an entrail.
Vast coiling cracks of gold and grey lunge endlessly across it—
Run Hektor![9]

9 Hektor runs away from Achilles in their final encounter, though he had resolved to stand to meet him. Achilles chases him three times around the city walls.

rasps the director from the walkie-talkie
as the helicopter goes squalling past Hektor's head
and the downdraft

knocks him flat. Plunged into the depths of encircling walls
an animal will lose its tuning knob.
Hektor was

for Troy a source of food, a cause for exultation in prayer[10]
a likeness of God,
a human glory.

He had constructed throughout Troy a system of gutters,
which ran along both sides of every street,
squared with stone

in alternating blocks of polished and unpolished agate.
Waters ran quietly out of Troy.
Now Hektor worries

that stains on the back of his clothing will be visible
from the helicopter as he turns
to run.

TV is made of light, like shame.[11]

VII.

As the bottom of a sea, which it once was, Death Valley is perpetually
in motion.
A thin
silver
pressure rakes the dunes from north to west forming parallel grooves
miles

10 Carson is here reworking Hekabe's lament for Hektor after his death:
My child, ah woe is me! How shall I live in my sore anguish, now thou art dead?—thou that wast my boast night and day in the city, and a blessing to all, both to the men and women of Troy throughout the town, who ever greeted thee as a god; for verily thou wast to them a glory exceeding great, while yet thou livedst; but now death and fate are come upon thee. (Trans. A.T. Murray)

In referring to Hektor here as a 'source of food', Carson is playing with the Greek word *oneiar*, translated above as 'blessing'. (In its plural, *oneiata*, the word can mean good things to eat.) Her phrase 'Cause for exultation in prayer' is an exact translation of the Greek *euchōlē*, translated above as 'boast'.

11 Carson is apparently playing with the fact that the Greek word for shame, *aidōs*, contains *-id-*, the root of various words for 'see' and 'know. (In Book 22 of the *Iliad*, being seen and being shamed are connected for Hektor—who doesn't want his reputation to be stained by being seen to be a coward.)

wide
that vanish in half an hour and vanish again, tarrying and driving on,
marking,
blanking.
As the kings of Troy comb out their hair before battle
into
patterns
no one can remember after, Hektor is running
the
length
of a gravel groove heading straight for Troy.

He
can
just see his wife on the parapet waving a piece of clothing.[12]
He
waves
too. He will never reach her. Under his feet the sand is shifting,
its
slight
incomprehensible ball bearings carrying him ever more west
and
south
toward the unclocked clarity of his last and inland sea.

TV is a condition of weightless balance, like a game.
But TV is not a game.[13]

VIII.

TV comes out of the dark, like Hektor's prayer verbs.

To blue.
To tear from the midpoint.
To lay bare crystals.
To lay bare a sky.
To ash.
To put silence over it.

12 After Achilles' victory over Hektor, Andromache rushes from her house to the walls to find out why everyone is screaming: seeing Hektor's slain body being dragged behind Achilles' chariot, she grows faint and tears off her veil.

13 An echo of a passage in Book 22 that notes the way Hektor's attempt to escape resembles a sporting competition: 'They were running very quickly, since they were not competing for a sacrificial animal or an ox-hide shield, the kinds of things that are prizes for men's feet, but they were running for the life of Hektor.'

To not desist.
To inmost.
To mount smoke (of a soul).

IX.

TV has a glare to it, like Hektor's prayer.

YOU PART. ENDANGERED WE.
HANG.
PERSONS OF ASH.

ASHED.

X.

Late each night in his motel room Hektor puts on a headset
to shut out the noise of the keno lounge next door
and sits down to write a postcard to his wife.

VERY COLD IN THE DESERT WE SHOOT FROM DAWN TO DUSK
MILITARY JETS CAVORTING OVERHEAD THE DIRECTOR RED
WITH RAGE NO TIME FOR LUNCH *THE LIGHT IS GOING!* YOU
WOULD LIKE MY COSTUME IT IS SILK THANK YOU FOR THE
~~T~~EARS THEY TASTE LIKE HOME
P

Then he takes out a big red notebook from the desk drawer
and puts on a sweater and sits again. Staring hard.
DIARY FOR MYSELF ALONE says the cover.

Today Hektor fought like a boulder going downhill.[14]
Torn from the rockface it bounds and flies, treetops
roar past underneath,
nothing can stop it—
hits the plain!
There he was stabbing away at a wall of skirmishers.
Like a flashing snowpeak he moved,
like a wave exploding foam, like a giant breaker
boiling toward the beach—

14 Here Hektor's 'diary' entries assimilate and recast various passages and similes from the *Iliad.*

By now morning fires are being kindled throughout the motel.
Dawn pots are banging.
Hektor works on,

while behind him, the long blades of his spars and harpoons
stand propped on the wall
beside the TV—

there he was
testing the enemy line at every point
to see where it would give!
The deaf day moved toward ox-time.[15]
Truth
rolled away from him
under the cannon-bones of the night.

TV uses for 'grave' the word 'sign', like Homer.[16]

XI.

TV is presocial, like Man.

On the last day of the Death Valley shoot
driving through huge slow brown streaks of mountain
towards the light-hole,

Hektor feels his pits go dry.

Clouds drop their lines down the faces of the rock
as if marking out a hunting ground.
Hektor, whose heart

walked ahead of him always,

ran ahead like a drunk creature
to lick salt particles off the low bushes
as if they were butter or silver honey,

whose heart Homer compared to a lion

15 As can be seen in Book 23 of the *Iliad* (when Achilles' friend Patroclus is being buried while Hektor lies dead and dishonoured), ancient funerals featured the ritual slaughter of oxen.

16 The Greek word *sēma* can mean grave or tomb (in Book 24 it is used to refer to the tomb of Hektor), but it also has the more general meaning of 'sign'.

turning in a net of dogs and men and
whichever way the lion lunges the men and dogs give way
yet the net keeps contracting—

Hektor trembles.

The human way includes two kinds of knowledge.
Fire and Night. Hektor has been to the Fire
in conditions of experimental purity.

It is 6:53 AM when his Night unhoods itself.

Hektor sees that he is lying at the centre of a vast metal disc.
A dawn clot of moon dangles oddly above
and this realization comes coldly through him:

the disc is tilting.

Very slowly the disc attains an angle of thirty degrees.
Dark blue signal is flowing steadily
from the centre to the edge

as Hektor starts to slide.

It takes but an instant to realize you are mortal.
Troy reared up on its hind legs
and a darkness of life flowed through the town

from purple cup to purple cup.

Toes to the line please, says the assistant camera man,
slapping two pieces of yellow tape
on the surface of the disc

just in front of Hektor's feet.

Dashing back to the camera he raises his slate.
Places everyone, calls the director as a thousand wasps
come stinging out of the arc lamp[17]

and the camera is pouring its black butter,

17 In Book 16, when the forces of Achilles, the Myrmidons, rush into battle behind Patroclus, they are compared to wasps pouring out to attack someone who has disturbed them.

its bitter honey,
straight into Hektor's eye.
Hektor steps to the line.

War has always interested me,[18] he begins.

1995

18 An echo of a passage in Book 6: before Hektor leaves Andromache to return to battle, he tells her, 'war will be a concern to all of the men, but especially to me.'

David Adams Richards

b. 1950

David Adams Richards was born and raised in Newcastle (now part of Miramichi), NB, where his father owned and operated the local movie theatres. While attending St Thomas University, he joined an informal writers' workshop in Fredericton known as the 'Ice House Gang' (it met weekly in the McCord Hall Ice House), which included established writers such as Alden Nowlan—whom he cites as an important literary influence—and Fred Cogswell. Known now as a novelist, Richards began his career by publishing short stories in journals (they were eventually collected in 1978 as *Dancers at Night*) and, in 1972, two poetry chapbooks: *One Step Inside* and *Small Heroics*. In this early work, the dark forests, the desolate landscapes, and the run-down dwellings that will form the settings of his novels are already visible.

The Coming of Winter (1974), Richards' first novel, exhibits the strengths that have served him well: a fine ear for Maritime speech patterns and an eye for the telling details that give a scene its texture. A moralist who describes Tolstoy and Dostoevsky as the novelists he most admires and a writer fascinated by those who are losing out in life, Richards is a social realist who tells dark and sometimes grim stories that show how economic hardship and emotional deprivation determine the lives of his working-class characters. He gives special attention to the rural poor: 'I think rural men and women in our society are losing a battle,' he has remarked. 'I think they're extremely condescended to and misunderstood so much of the time.'

Richards published nine further novels: *Blood Ties* (1976); *Lives of Short Duration* (1981); *Road to the Stilt House* (1985); a trilogy formed by the Governor General's Award–winning *Nights Below Station Street* (1988), *Evening Snow Will Bring Such Peace* (1990), and *For Those Who Hunt the Wounded Down* (1993); *Hope in the Desperate Hour* (1996); *The Bay of Love and Sorrows* (1998); and *Mercy among the Children* (2000), which won the Giller Prize. He has also published three books of non-fiction: *A Lad from Brantford* (1994), which is a collection of short personal reflections; *Hockey Dreams: Memories of a Man Who Couldn't Play* (1996), which combines memories of his childhood passion for the sport with reflections on the current state of the game; and a book about fly-fishing, *Lines on the Water: A Fisherman's Life on the Miramichi* (1998), which won a Governor General's Award for non-fiction. Richards has been writer-in-residence at universities in New Brunswick, Ottawa, Alberta, and Virginia.

Richards' novels are unified by recurring characters and by references in later books to events that occurred in earlier ones. But most of all, his entire body of work is drawn together by what the prologue to *Mercy among the Children* describes as 'the great Miramichi River, which flowed out of the heavy forests into the Northumberland Strait, north of the western tip of Prince Edward Island'. That river runs through all of Richards' writing, unifying the community and serving as the source of a natural world that provides some respite for his characters.

The fact that Richards gives so much importance to landscape in his fiction has established him in the minds of many as a regionalist—but it is a term that makes Richards uncomfortable because he wants readers to be most aware of the universal elements of his fiction. He has said that his real concern is with individuals who have 'a sense of an inexorable spiritual duty', a statement that calls our attention to the way his novels focus on spiritual needs and show how that dimension of his characters' lives carries them beyond their restrictions.

Mercy among the Children

Mercy among the Children is the story of the Hendersons, whose strong family bond is their only protection against the abuses of power that so often distort the lives of characters in Richards' fiction. In fashioning his narrative, Lyle Henderson reconstructs and tries to understand the interrelated lives of three generations—his own; that of his father, Sydney; and that of Roy, his grandfather. The opening chapter of the book, reprinted here, is the first story Lyle tells as he circles around events that shaped Sydney as an adolescent boy. We realize these incidents have also had a powerful effect on Lyle, who has witnessed the trials his father endures and their tragic repercussions. Because he is unable to believe, as his father does, that Providence will ultimately punish wrongdoers and reward virtue, Lyle will have to learn how to live in a world of betrayal and tragedy and find his own way to peace.

From *Mercy among the Children*

The small Catholic churches here are all the same, white clapboard drenched with snow or blistering under a northern sun, their interiors smelling of confessionals and pale statues of the Madonna. Our mother, Elly Henderson, took us to them all along our tract of road—thinking that solace would come.

In November the lights shone after seven o'clock on the stained-glass windows. The windows show the crucifixion or one of the saints praying. The hills where those saints lived and dropped their blood look soft, distant and blue; the roads wind like purple ribbons toward the Mount of Olives. It is all so different from *real* nature with its roaring waters over valleys of harsh timber where I tore an inch and a half of skin from my calves. Or Miramichi bogs of cedar and tamarack and the pungent smell of wet moosehide as the wounded moose still bellows in the dark wood. I often wanted to enter the world of the stained glass—to find myself walking along the purple road, with the Mount of Olives behind me. I suppose because I wanted to be good, and my mother wanted goodness for me. I wanted too to escape the obligation I had toward my own destiny, my family, my sister and brother who were more real to me than a herd of saints.

My father's name was Sydney Henderson. He was born in a shack off Highway 11, a highway only Maritimers could know—a strip of asphalt through stunted trees and wild dead fields against the edge of a cold sky.

He did poorly in school but at church became the ward of Father Porier. He was given the job of washing Porier's car and cleaning his house. He was an altar boy who served mass every winter morning at seven. He did this for three years, from the age of eight to eleven.

Then one day there was a falling-out, an 'incident', and Father Porier's Pontiac never again came down the lane to deliver him home, nor did Father ever again trudge off to the rectory to clean the priest's boots. Nor did he know that his own father would take the priest's side and beat him one Sunday in front of most of the parishioners on the church steps. This became Father's first disobedience, not against anything but the structure of things. I have come to learn, however, that this is not at all a common disobedience.

Back then, harsh physical labour seemed the only thing generations of Canadians like my grandfather considered work. So by thirteen my father wore boots and checked jackets, and quit school to work in the woods, in obligation to his father. He would spend days with little to comfort him. He was to need this strength, a strength of character, later on. He had big hands like a pulpcutter, wore thick glasses, and his hair was short, shaved up the side of his head like a zek[1] in some Russian prison camp.

He worked crossing back and forth over that bleak highway every day; when the June sky was black with no-see-ums, or all winter when the horse dung froze as it hit the ground. He was allergic to horses, yet at five in the morning had to bring the old yellow mare to the front of the barn—a mare denied oats and better off dead.

My grandfather bought a television in 1962, and during the last few years of his life would stare at it all evening, asking Sydney questions about the world far away. The light of the television brought into that dark little house programs like *The Honeymooners, The Big Valley, Have Gun Will Travel*, and *The Untouchables*; and glowed beyond the silent window into the yard, a yard filled with desolate chips of wood.

My grandfather Roy Henderson would ask Dad why people would act in a movie if they knew they were going to be shot. He would not be completely convinced by my father's explanation about movie scripts and actors, and became more disheartened and dangerous the clearer the explanation was.

'But they die—I seen them.'

'No they don't, Dad.'

'Ha—lot you know, Syd—lot you know—I seen blood, and blood don't lie, boy—blood don't lie. And if ya think blood lies I'll smash yer mouth, what I'll do.'

As a teen my father sat in this TV-lightened world; a shack in the heat of July watching flies orbit in the half dark. He hid there because his father tormented him in front of kids his own age.

I have learned that because of this torment, Father became a drunk by the age of fifteen.

1 Inmate (informal).

People did not know (and what would it matter if they had known?) that by the time he was fifteen, my father had read and could quote Stendhal and Proust. But he was trapped in a world of his own father's fortune, and our own fortune became indelibly linked to it as well.

In the summer of 1964 my grandfather was asked by his employer, Leo Alphonse McVicer, to take two Americans fishing for salmon at the forks at Arron Brook. Roy did not want to go; first, because it was late in the year and the water low, and secondly, because if they did not get a fish he might be blamed. Still, he was obligated.

'Get them a fish,' Leo said, rooting in the bowl of his pipe with a small knife and looking up with customary curtness. Roy nodded, as always, with customary willingness. He took the men this certain hot day in August to a stretch of the river at the mouth of the brook, where the fish were pooled. He took his boy, Sydney, with him, to help pole the canoe up river and make the men comfortable. Then in the heat of midday, he sent Sydney north in the canoe to scout other pools for fish while he spent his time rigging the lines and listening to the men as they spoke about places as diverse as Oregon and Honolulu, while being polite enough to have no opinion when they spoke of the quality of Leo McVicer's wood and his mill.

Sydney poled back down river later that afternoon, looking in the water, and saying the fish had gone far up but that four salmon rested here, taking the oxygen from the cool spring, lying aside the boulders at the upper edge of the rip.

These men were important. They had been instrumental in helping Leo McVicer and Leo wanted to amuse them the way Maritimers do—by pretending a rustic innocence under obligation to *real* human beings who have travelled from *real* places to be entertained.

So after three hours, Roy whispered to my father: 'It would be better for Leo if they caught something—if they are here to help finance the new barker for his mill.'

And with those words, and with his shirt covered in patches of sweat and dust, and with his neck wrinkled in red folds from a life under lash to sun and snow, with his blackened teeth crooked and broken, showing the smile not of a man but of a tobacco-plug-chewing child, and with all the fiery sinewy muscles of his long body, he set in motion the brutal rural destiny of our family. Asking one of the men to give him a rod, he tied a three-pronged jig hook to it, had Sydney pole above them and then drift silently down through the pool without pole in the water, to point out where the salmon were lying. He threw the jig where the pool joined the spring and jerked upwards. All of a sudden the line began to sing, and away ran the fifteen-pound salmon jigged in the belly. After twenty-five minutes he hauled the spent cock fish in, killed it, and hooked another. The Americans were laughing, patting Roy on his bony back, not knowing what Sydney and Roy and the wardens watching them knew—that this exercise was illegal. The wardens watching stepped out, confiscated the rods, and seized the men's brand-new Chevrolet truck.

Leo McVicer heard of this at seven o'clock, when he got back from the mill. He paced all night in quiet almost completive fury. My grandfather went back to work early that Monday, willing to explain. But Leo fired him on the spot, even though Roy had sought to please him. For that I was to learn was Leo McVicer. Never minding either that the great Leo McVicer had often poached salmon for New Brunswick cabinet members and the occasional senator from Maine who partied at his house. This of course my grandfather did not know. He was kept from knowledge of the decisions of his great friend, as he was kept out of the dark rooms of his gigantic house.

To be fired after years of faith and work broke him, and he sat, as my own father once said, 'like some poor sad rustic angel confined to hell'.

Still, there was a chance—if only one—to work his way back into the fold. That summer Leo's men were unsatisfied and twice threatened a wildcat walkout. Finally McVicer beat them to it, and locked the sawmill's gate.

For the next two weeks things existed at a simmer between Leo and his men. They milled about the yard like atoms bouncing off each other, collecting and separating, collecting again, in pools of dusty, loitering brown-shirted figures, caught up at times in wild gestures, at other times almost grief-strickenly subdued. And within these two states there was talk of sabotage and revenge. No trucks or wood moved on or off McVicer property, and they stood firm when a welders' supply truck tried to enter, howling to each other and holding it back with their bodies, knowing little in life except what bodies were for, to be bent and shoved and twisted and gone against. At the end, the welders' truck was defeated. With a jubilant shout from the men into the empty September heat, the driver turned back and a lone truck of herbicide was left unloaded in the yard.

Finally Roy Henderson asked my father's advice. What could he do to make things better for Leo, and regain his job?

There was one thing my father advised: 'Go to the men.' My father at fourteen stated, 'Convince them to end their walkout.' He added that Leo would be grateful—the contracts filled, the herbicide unloaded, and Roy would be considered instrumental in this.

Roy headed into the woods on a warm September afternoon, with the pungent smell of spruce trees waving in the last of the summer heat. Just before he arrived onsite three men cut the locks to the gate. They stormed the truck and rolled the hundred barrels of herbicide off it, busted the barrels open with axes, and dumped them all, along with forty barrels of pesticide from the warehouse, into the upper edges of Little Arron Brook. The new barker was sabotaged, a flare was lighted to engage the men in more hellery, and a fire raged.

All of this was documented by a local reporter. A picture was taken that day long ago. Unfortunately, standing on the hulking ruin of smouldering machinery, a half-crazed drunken smile on his face, was my grandfather. It made the front pages of the provincial papers. He had not exactly done what my father had advised him to. In fact he looked like a vigilante from the deep south stomping the ruins of innocence. It was how *they* wanted him to look.

I have this picture still. As faded as it might be, the image is strikingly familiar, savage and gleeful, as if in one moment of wilful revenge Roy had forgotten the reason for his journey that afternoon.

Grandfather told Dad that he had tried to stop, not start, the conflagration. But his picture, even faded to yellow in an old archival room, shows him a rather willing participant in the mayhem. As if his grin leering from a newspaper at me, a grandson he never knew, was his only moment of bright majesty, caught in the splendid orb of a flashbulb, which signalled our doom for the next thirty years.

All others there that day got away when the police arrived but grandfather, too drunk to run, fell from the machine he was prancing on, and crawled on his knees to the police car to sleep.

The fire burned eleven hundred acres of Leo McVicer's prime soft timber land; timber subcontracted to the large paper mill. After my grandfather's picture was published, this fire became known locally as the 'Henderson horror'.

'Roy is bad—his son is mad,' the saying rose from the lips of everyone.

Meanwhile Roy Henderson, illiterate and frightened of people who weren't illiterate, had to go to court and pay a lawyer to defend him on both counts; that is, of poaching and the destruction of the barker. My father described Roy as he stood in court in a grey serge suit. He had lost his beloved television. He was confronted by a menacing prosecutor. He shook and cried. He was sentenced to three years. People teased him on the way out of court.

Sydney, at fourteen, would make him biscuits and hitchhike to Dorchester to visit. But Roy, who had never been in jail in his life, refused to eat.

'Tell Leo I will not eat unless he forgives me,' he said, sniffing, and sitting with his hands on his knees. His hair was turning grey and grey hair stuck out of his ears; his eyes were as deep set, his brow as wide, as some rustic prophet. But Sydney knew he was no prophet. He gave Sydney this message, as the sunlight came in on his prison trousers:

'Tell him that my life is in his hands—and then see what he has to say. Tell him that the biscuits are hard now, and gettin' harder. Go on, fella—get goin'—'

My father left the prison, in his old red coat and torn gumboots, and ran all the way to Moncton—thirty-seven miles. He caught the train, went to Leo—not to the house, but to the office in McVicer's store that had served our community for years. The store was a monument to the class of people it served, where calendars of halter-topped blonde and blue-eyed girls shining Fords with Turtle Wax were hidden by Leo under the counter, and where diversified products were unknown but Humphrey work pants and boots, and corduroys for children, were sold, along with erasers and scribblers and pencils for school.

'I just lost me a hundred-thousand-dollar barker—and a million-dollar lot,' Leo said, without looking at Dad but looking through some invoices of clothing that he believed he had not ordered. 'Now I have to clean up the barrels that got into the brook,' Leo said, flipping the pages. 'Everyone—' flip, 'the Sheppards—' flip, 'the Pits—' flip, 'the Poriers—' flip, flip, 'and everyone else said it was yer dad—*yer* and no other dad—and what do you want me to do?'

'Go visit him so he'll eat.'

'Go visit him and cheer him up so he'll eat a good breakfast—well, damn him.'

My father went back to jail to see his dad. It was close to Christmas and snow had fallen and covered the cities and towns, the long raw southern New Brunswick hills were slick with ice.

My father pitied Roy yet could do nothing to rouse him. At first Roy did not believe that Leo, whom he had known since he was sixteen, wouldn't come to see him. He stood with his hands on the bars of the holding cell they had brought him to, looking out expectantly, like a child. He addressed his own child as if he was another species, a strange creature that one day had appeared in his little cabin, someone Roy himself never knew what to do with. And that is why often as not he addressed Sydney as 'fella'.

'Yer saying he won't come to see me, fella.'

'That's what I'm saying, Dad. I'm saying that he won't come to see you.'

'Let's just get this straight—not that he's busy and might come to see me some other time—or something like that there?'

'He won't come, Dad.'

Roy's look was one of incomprehensible vacancy, as if from some faraway land he was listening to some strange music. Then his eyes caught his son's and became cognizant of what had been said, and perhaps also for the very first time who his son was, and what grace his son held. And realizing this he was shocked, and broken even more.

'Well I pity him then—for doin' that—is all I can say,' Roy whispered. And he refused on principle—perhaps the only one he had left (and to prove, just once, grandeur to his son)—to eat.

A few weeks later, ill with pneumonia, Roy Henderson was taken to hospital on the Miramichi. He died there, and was buried in an old graveyard downriver, leaving my father alone.

I always said *I* would have done more. But my father felt he had done what he could. He never left his father alone. He walked 230 miles of road, appealing to McVicer to forgive. He fasted as his father did. He broke his fast only to take communion. He remained with his father to the end, even though it was a solitary vigil. But he would never seek revenge. Revenge, my father believed in his fertile brilliance, was anathema to justice.

After Roy's death Dad lived a primitive life, for what contact would he have with others? He would be teased whenever he went out to a dance; girls would string him along as a joke. He began to drink every day whatever he could find; to forget, as Sam Johnson has said, and I once found underlined in a book my father owned, 'the pain of being a man'.

The pain of being a man, or simply being cold or wet or tired. The old barn was long gone. His house was built of plywood and tarpaper. Its walls were insulated by cardboard boxes. It was fifteen by twelve and sixteen feet high—so it looked like a shoebox standing on end. That is something that I like to remember. Most of his life was lived principally here.

He lived three years alone hiding from people who might do something *for* him—I mean send him to foster care. But no one expressed any concern whatsoever on his behalf. Except for one man: Jay Beard, who lived in a trailer up on the main road and hired Dad to cut wood. At one time Dad got a job (as illegal as it must have been) planting dynamite to blow boulders at a construction site. He was not afraid and he was also nimble. He earned what was a good deal of money for him, and with it he bought both his mother's and father's graves their stones.

At eighteen he was coming home from a long hot day in a lobster boat on the bay, where he worked helping bait traps. His skin was burned by the sun and saltwater and his hands were blistered by the rope and the traps. But that day he met Jay Beard, who was selling off many of his books, books Jay had inherited from his dead brother and had himself never read. Beard was actually looking for my father to sell these books to. My father bought three hundred paperbacks and old faded hardcovers, the whole lot for twenty dollars, and brought them home by wheelbarrow.

Then in early fall of that same year Sydney, who in reading these books had given up drink, went to Chatham to see a professor about the chance at a university education. The professor, Daivid Scone, a man who had gone to the University of Toronto, disliked the Maritimes while believing he knew of its difficulties and great diversity. Looking at my father sitting in his old bib overalls and heavy woollen shirt proved what he felt. And he commented that it might be better for Dad to find a trade. This was not at all contradictory to Dr Scone's sense of himself as a champion of people just like Father. In fact, being a champion of them meant, in his mind, he knew them well enough to judge them. And something he saw in my father displeased him.

'Yes, I know you have come here with your heart set on a lofty education—but look in another direction. A carpenter—how is that?—you seem like a man who would know angles.' And then he whispered, as people do who want to show how lightly they take themselves, 'It would not be as difficult for you as some things in here, philosophy and theology and all of that—'

Scone smiled, with a degree of naive self-infatuation seen only in those with an academic education, shook his head at the silliness of academia, while knowing that his tenure was secure and every thought he had ever had was manifested as safe by someone else before him. My father never had such a luxury. There was a time my father would have been beaten by his own father if it was known that he read. Knowing this, tell me the courage of Dr David Scone.

My father said that being a carpenter might be nice and he liked carpentry but that he liked books more. Outside, the huge Irish Catholic church rested against the horizon, the sun gleaming from its vast windows and its cavernous opened doors; its steps swept clean, its roof reflecting the stains of sunlight, while on the faraway hills across the river the trees held the first sweet tinges of autumn.

'Well, then—you want to be a scholar, do you. So what books have you read, Sydney? Mystery—science fiction—Ray *Bradbury*—well, there's nothing wrong with that at all, is there?' He smiled. My father was about to answer. Dr Scone was about to listen but he was called away by the head of the department, a rather rotund priest with thick downy cheeks and a bald spot on the top of his head. Father stood and nodded at Scone as he left. Then he walked home from Saint Michael's University and sat in his kitchen. He did not know how to go about qualifying for university. It had taken him five weeks to find the courage to do what he had done. Now he felt that the man had condescended to him. What surprised him was the fact that an educated man would ever do this. He had been innocent enough to assume that the educated had excised all prejudice from themselves and would never delight in injury to others—that is, he believed that they had easily attained the goal he himself was struggling toward.

He did not know that this goal—which he considered the one truthful goal man should strive toward—was often not even considered a goal by others, educated or not.

He had by that evening discovered his gross miscalculation. He was angry and decided to write a letter, and sat down in the kitchen and started to write to this professor, in pencil on an old lined sheet. But when the words came he realized a crime had taken place. (This is how he later described it to my mother.) The crime was that he had set out in a letter to injure someone else. He was ashamed of himself for this and burned the letter in the stove, sank on his bed with his face to the wall.

Later I came to hate that he did not send it, but it was noble. And what was most noble about it was that it would never be known as such. Nor did that in itself alleviate his suffering over what the professor had said, or his memory of the professor's self-infatuated smile when he said it. That is, like most spoken injuries, Father had to sample it not only at the time it had taken place but for days and even weeks after, and again each time this well-known professor was interviewed in the paper about Maritime disparage or his lifelong fight on behalf of First Nations rights. (Which became a lifelong fight at the same time it became a lifelong fight among his intellectual class, most of them ensconced in universities far away from any Native man or woman.)

The fact that my father not only was a part of the demographic this professor was supposedly expert upon but had worked since he was a boy, and had his own ideas from years of violence and privation, made the sting ever sharper and fresher each time he heard Dr David Scone lauded for his *utter decency* by our many gifted announcers on the CBC.

Yet by his honour—my father's honour—he could and did say nothing. Even when Dr David Scone tried to influence my mother against him.

I know now it was because of an incident that happened when my father was a child of twelve. One day he and another boy were shovelling snow from the slanted church roof. The boy had robbed Dad's molasses sandwich and Dad pushed him. The boy fell fifty feet, and lay on his back, blood coming from his nose and snow wisping down over his face.

My father, perched high upon the roof next to the base of the steeple, was certain the boy had died. He did not believe in anything, had hated the priest after that certain incident, that falling-out I mentioned. But still he whispered that if the boy lived he would never raise his hand or his voice to another soul, that he would attend church every day. *Every damn day.* What is astounding is, as soon as he made this horrible pact, the boy stood up, wiped his face, laughed at him, and walked away. That boy was Connie Devlin.

I don't believe Devlin was ever hurt. I believe my father only thought he was. The bloody nose came when the boy fell, but was nothing to be upset over, and the boy liked the attention that happens when people think you are dead. I told my father this when I heard of his pact years later. I said, 'Dad, you never touched the boy—so therefore God tricked you into this masochistic devotion. God has made you His slave because of your unnatural self-condemnation.'

My father never answered; he just turned and walked away.

Connie Devlin was to plague Father all his life. And it was from that day forward my father's true life started. After that day, things happened *to* his life that showed, or proved to him at least, other forces.

What my father believed from the time his own father died was this: whatever pact you make with God, God *will* honour. You may not think He does, but then do you really know the pact you have actually made? Understand the pact you have made, and you will understand how God honours it.

2000

Tomson Highway

b. 1951

The first years of Tomson Highway's life were spent with his parents and many siblings in the area around the remote northern Manitoba Brochet Reserve. His father was a hunter, fisher, and trapper, and the whole family lived in tents, spoke only Cree, and followed the seasons and the game. An idyllic if difficult existence, it ended for Highway when he was six and was required by law to go to a church-run residential school. He was luckier than many Native children in that he was able to maintain contact with his family and in that the education he received encouraged his considerable musical talent, but he also experienced traumatic abuse by the priests in the Roman Catholic school in The Pas.

At fifteen, Highway was sent to high school in Winnipeg, where he boarded in non-Native homes and learned English. Although he had been studying music since he was thirteen, he had only limited access to pianos before entering the University of Manitoba. There he found support for his talents and spent a year abroad, studying piano in London, England, and travelling in Europe. He completed his education at the University of Western Ontario, taking a Bachelor of Music degree in 1975. Having discovered his interest in literature while at Western, he remained there for an additional year earning a BA in English. He recalls that it was while at Western that he became interested in drama as a result of attending a play by Michel Tremblay and studying with James Reaney.

After university, Highway served as a social worker for seven years, involved with political and cultural groups in Native communities across Canada. It was in this context that he first began to write and stage plays, such as *A Ridiculous Spectacle in One Act.* In 1986 he became artistic director of Native Earth Performing Arts, a professional Aboriginal theatre company. That same year Highway's first play staged for a general audience, *The Rez Sisters,* opened—co-produced by Native Earth and the Theatre Pass Muraille collective. That play and its sequel three years later, *Dry Lips Oughta Move to Kapuskasing,* brought Highway to considerable national prominence. Each won him Dora Mavor Moore and Floyd S. Chalmers Awards, and both were nominated for Governor General Awards. Highway has written and produced several other plays, including *Aria; New Song . . . New Dance; The Sage, the Dancer and the Fool; Annie and the Old One;* and *Rose.* In addition, he has written one novel, *Kiss of the Fur Queen* (1998), and two children's books, *Caribou Song* (2001) and *Dragonfly Kites* (2002).

A writer-in-residence at several universities, he has been awarded honorary doctorates from the Universities of Winnipeg, Brandon, and Western Ontario. In 1994, he was made a Member of the Order of Canada.

Highway's work blends Native (and also Biblical) mythologies with the often harsh realities of Native experience, and he shows the spirit world and the human one as existing on the same plane. In *Kiss of the Fur Queen*, for example, the aspects of a number of supernatural Cree beings are visible in human form: Weetigo, the cannibal spirit who feasts on the flesh of the young; Weesageechak ('the clown who bridges humanity and God—a God who laughs, a God who's here, not for guilt, not for suffering, but for a good time'); fox woman, who in the Cree epic tale of the Son of Ayash gives the hero magical gifts; and the Pawakan, which is an individual's guardian spirit. (As well, the birth stories recall the belief in 'acahkos', or little souls.)

In contrast to the European tradition of employing myth as an enriching layer that universalizes the realistic level of the text, Highway's narratives let the human characters take on symbolic meaning. Thus, in *Dry Lips*, when a woman is raped with a crucifix, the victim becomes an allegorical figure, standing for many things: all those who have been victimized by the church; the Native people in their encounter with European Christianity; even matriarchal religion being overcome by a patriarchal one.

The Roman Catholic Church, which Highway has called 'a beautiful idea that went wrong', has been an important nexus in his writing. The abuse he suffered was experienced by his brother Rene as well. Rene, the family member Tomson Highway was closest to, became a talented and successful dancer and choreographed some of his brother's plays, but was led by his anger over his own experience of abuse into a life of sex and drugs. He died of AIDS in 1990.

Tomson Highway's response in his writing to the abuse that he and his brother suffered in the residential school has been to challenge patriarchal institutions and to construct works that blur gender. Reasoning that since the Cree language lacks grammatical gender, he feels Cree gods can be female as well as male. Because of his drive to cross boundaries and challenge codes and limits, he sees the Native trickster figure as central to his art—and, in *Dry Lips*, he portrays Trickster as a woman.

The selection below forms the first two chapters of *Kiss of the Fur Queen*. The novel, which deals in part with the effects of sexual abuse on two Cree brothers, opens before the birth of either with their future father racing to triumph in the Millington Cup World Championship Dog Derby (Highway's own father was a champion musher). His win leads him to an encounter with the Fur Queen—who, though she at first seems an ordinary beauty contest winner, has many mythical aspects. This encounter in turn sets into motion his first son's birth, which begins a narrative that takes place both inside and outside the ordinary limits of time and space, a tale that shows how individuals' lives are both bound to and ultimately free from the constraints of this world.

From *Kiss of the Fur Queen*

CHAPTER ONE

'*Mush!*' the hunter cried into the wind. Through the rising vapour of a northern Manitoba February, so crisp, so dry, the snow creaked underfoot, the caribou hunter Abraham Okimasis drove his sled and team of eight grey huskies through the orange-rose tinted dusk. His left hand gripping handlebar of sled, his right snapping moose-hide whip above his head, Abraham Okimasis was urging his huskies forward.

'*Mush!*' he cried, '*mush.*' The desperation in his voice, like a man about to sob, surprised him.

Abraham Okimasis could see, or thought he could, the finish line a mile away. He could also see other mushers, three, maybe four. Which meant forty more behind him. But what did these forty matter? What mattered was that, so close to the end, he was not leading. What mattered was that he was not going to win the race.

And he was so tired, his dogs beyond tired, so tired they would have collapsed if he was to relent.

'*Mush!*' the sole word left that could feed them, dogs and master both, with the will to travel on.

Three days. One hundred and fifty miles of low-treed tundra, ice-covered lakes, all blanketed with at least two feet of snow—fifty miles per day—a hundred and fifty miles of freezing temperatures and freezing winds. And the finish line mere yards ahead.

The shafts of vapour rising from the dogs' panting mouths, the curls of mist emerging from their undulating backs, made them look like insubstantial wisps of air.

'*Mush!*' the hunter cried to his lead dog. 'Tiger-Tiger, *mush*.'

He had sworn to his dear wife, Marieses Okimasis, on pain of separation and divorce, unthinkable for a Roman Catholic in the year of our Lord 1951, that he would win the world championship just for her: the silver cup, that holy chalice was to be his twenty-first-anniversary gift to her. With these thoughts racing through his fevered mind, Abraham Okimasis edged past musher number 54—Jean-Baptiste Ducharme of Cranberry Portage. Still not good enough.

Half a mile to the finish line—he could see the banner now, a silvery white with bold black lettering, though he couldn't make out the words.

Mushers numbers 32 and 17, so close, so far: Douglas Ballantyne of Moosoogoot, Saskatchewan, at least twenty yards ahead, and Jackson Butler of Flin Flon, Manitoba, another ten ahead of that.

'*Mush!*' the sound a bark into the wind.

'Please, please, God in heaven, let me win this race,' a voice inside the caribou hunter's body whispered, 'and I will thank you with every deed, every touch, every breath for the rest of my long life, for hallowed be thy name . . .' The prayer strung itself, word by word, like a rosary, pulling him along, bead by bead by bead, 'Thy kingdom come, thy will be done on Earth . . .'

Less than half a prayer and already God the Father was answering. Wasn't that his voice Abraham Okimasis could hear in the northwest wind? Less than a quarter of a mile to go, he was sure of it, and already he had passed musher number 32, Douglas Ballantyne of Moosoogoot. And now, not forty yards away, the banner hovered over the finish line like the flaming sword of the angel guarding paradise—'The World Championship Dog Derby, Trappers' Festival, Oopaskooyak, Manitoba, February 23–25, 1951!' And now musher number 21, Abraham Okimasis of Eemanapiteepitat, Manitoba, was only ten feet behind musher number 17, Jackson Butler of Flin Flon, the finish line not thirty yards away. Twenty-five. Twenty. Fifteen. Ten . . .

The screams of children, of women, of men, the barking of dogs, the blare of loudspeakers crashed over the hunter, submerging him, drowning him. A sudden darkness knocked the breath clean of his lungs, the vision from his eyes. And in his blindness, all he could sense was a small white flame, as if perceived through a long, dark tunnel, fluttering and waving like a child's hand, beckoning him. All he knew was that he wanted to lie down and sleep forever, and only the waving flame was preventing him.

When Abraham Okimasis surfaced, he found hands reaching for him, other hands clutching at his arms, his shoulder, his back, manoeuvring him through a mass of human flesh. Cameras, microphones were aimed at him. Men with notepads and pencils, women with pens and large red moving mouths, prying, babbling in this language of the Englishman, hard, filled with sharp, jagged angles.

Then the caribou hunter felt himself levitating towards a platform. Wings must have been attached to his shoulders by guardian angels posing as minions of the festival, Abraham would reason some days later. And on the platform a man like a white balloon, so large, so pale, his voice thunderous and huge.

'Boom,' the voice went, 'boom, boom.' Something about 'Abraham Okimasis, forty-three years old, caribou hunter, fur trapper, fisherman, boom, boom'. Something about 'Abraham Okimasis, musher, from the Eemanapiteepitat Indian reserve, northwestern Manitoba, boom'. Something having to do with 'Abraham Okimasis, winner of the 1951 Millington Cup World Championship Dog Derby, boom, boom'. Something about 'Mr Okimasis, first Indian to win this gruelling race in its twenty-eight-year history . . .'. The syllables became one vast, roiling rumble.

Whereupon another darkness came over the Cree hunter. And in his blindness, all he could sense was the long, black tunnel, the small white flame so far, far away, flickering and fluttering, waving and swaying—a child's hand? a spirit?—beckoning, summoning.

A mile away, on a makeshift stage at one end of the high-ceilinged temple of ice hockey, seven fresh-faced, fair-haired women stood blinking under glaring lights. The youngest was eighteen, the eldest no more than twenty-three. Across the stage, a banner read: 'The Fur Queen Beauty Pageant, Trappers' Festival, 1951, Oopaskooyak, Manitoba.'

A panel of judges had sized up these seven finalists from every angle conceivable: height, width, weight, posture, deportment, quality of face, length of neck, circumference of leg, sway of hip, length of finger, quality of tooth, lip, nose, ear, eye, and eyebrow, down to the last dimple, mole, visible hair. The women had been prodded, poked, photographed, interviewed, felt, watched, paraded around the town for the entire three days of the Trappers' Festival, for the delectation of audiences from as far afield as Whitehorse, Yellowknife, Labrador, and even Germany, it had been reported in the *Oopaskooyak Times*. These seven beauties had cut ribbons, sliced cakes, unveiled snow sculptures, made pronouncements, announcements, proclamations. They had given out prizes at the muskrat-skinning contest, the trap-setting contest, the beard-growing contest, the dreaded Weetigo look-alike contest, the bannock-baking and tea-boiling contests. They had coddled babies, kissed schoolchildren, shaken hands with the mayor and his wife, danced with lonely strangers whose sole desire it was to pass one fleeting minute of their lives in the arms of a Fur Queen finalist. And now, the judges were about to reveal the most graceful, the most intelligent, the most desirable, the most beautiful. The Fur Queen.

All puffed out in timber-wolf-lined top hat and tuxedo, the mayor, who had graciously volunteered as chairman of the judges' panel, stepped up to the microphone at centre stage, cleared his throat, thumped his chest, opened his mouth, and trumpeted the entrance into the arena of the brave and daring men who had risked life and limb to take part in the Millington Cup World Championship Dog Derby. The crowd roared.

The chairman again cleared his throat, thumped his chest, opened his mouth, and boomed into the microphone.

'Results of the 1951 Fur Queen Beauty Pageant, for which the decision of the judges is final. Third runner-up, Miss Linda Hawkins, Silver Lake, Manitoba.' A young woman burst into a tearful smile and stepped up to the chairman to receive her cash award and a bouquet of yellow roses, had her upper body draped by the two other judges with a yellow satin sash, and was photographed a hundred times until all she could see was showers of stars. The crowd roared.

'Second runner-up, Miss Olivia Demchuk, Eematat, Manitoba,' boomed the chairman's voice. And a second young woman burst into a tearful smile, stepped up to the chairman to receive her cash award and a bouquet of pink roses, had her upper body draped with a pink satin sash, and was photographed a hundred times until all she could see was showers of stars. The crowd roared louder.

'First runner-up, Miss Catherine Shaw, Smallwood Lake, Manitoba,' boomed the chairman's voice. And a third young woman burst into a tearful smile, stepped up to the chairman to receive her cash award and a bouquet of crimson roses, had her upper body draped with a crimson satin sash, and was photographed a hundred times until she was blinded by the light. The crowd roared. And roared again.

Then the chairman of the judges' panel cleared his throat, thumped his chest, opened his mouth, and boomed into the microphone: 'And the Fur Queen for the year 1951 is . . .' One could hear the ticking of watches, the buzzing of incandescent lights, the hum of loudspeakers. 'Miss Julie Pembrook, Wolverine River, Manitoba. Miss Julie Pembrook!' The young woman burst into a blissful smile, stepped up to the chairman to receive her cash award and a bouquet of white roses. The radiant Miss Pembrook was draped not only with a white satin sash but with a floor-length cape fashioned from the fur of arctic fox, white as day. She had her head crowned with a fox-fur tiara ornamented with a filigree of gold and silver beads, and was photographed a thousand times until all she could see was stars and showers of stars. And the crowd roared until the very ceiling of the building threatened to rise up and float off towards the planet Venus.

In the thick of this raucous, festive throng, Abraham Okimasis stood, Cree gentleman from Eemanapiteepitat, Manitoba, caribou hunter without equal, grand champion of the world, unable to move, barely remembering to breathe. Because of the stars exploding in his own eyes, all he could see was bits and pieces of the scene before him interspersed with the vision of his lead dog Tiger-Tiger, panting out his puffs and clouds of vapour, striving for the finish line. And before the hunter could collect himself, a third darkness came upon him, the roaring in his ears gigantic. And at the far end of this new darkness appeared again the small white flame, flickering on the platform. Floating, whispering sibilance and hush, blooming into a presence, the white flame began to hum, a note so pure human ears could never have been meant to hear it. Then the presence began to take on shape—the caribou hunter could just discern a flowing cape seemingly made from fold after fold of white, luxuriant fur, swelling like the surface of a lake. The caribou hunter thought he saw a crown made of the same white fur, hovering above this cape. And the crown sparkled and flashed with what could have been a constellation. Then Abraham Okimasis saw the sash, white, satin, draped across the upper body of a young woman so fair her skin looked chiselled out of arctic frost, her teeth pearls of ice, lips streaks of blood, eyes white flames in a pitch-black night, eyes that appeared to see nothing but the caribou hunter alone. And then the caribou hunter and the woman in white fur began floating towards each other, as if powerless to stay apart. And as the two moved closer, Abraham Okimasis could decipher the message printed across her sash, syllable by syllable, letter by letter: 'The Fur Queen, 1951'.

Then he became aware—he must have been dreaming, surely—that this creature of unearthly beauty, the Fur Queen, was wafting towards him with something in her arms, something round and made of silver, carrying the object at waist level, like a sacred vessel, a heart perhaps, a lung, a womb? The goddess stopped in front of him, her face not half a foot away, her eyes burning into his, her person sending off ripples of warm air redolent of pine needles and fertile muskeg and wild fireweed. He couldn't look away, not even when he felt something falling gently, almost imperceptibly, into his hands.

When the queen turned for one fleeting second to smile at the screaming throngs below, Abraham looked down at his hands. There lay the large silver bowl, the Millington Cup, the coveted first prize of the World Championship Dog Derby, and, in the bowl, a cheque in the amount of one thousand dollars.

He had won. He was the king of all the legions of dog-mushers, the champion of the world! All realization, all sense, all time suddenly became entangled in some invisible glue. Abraham pulled his stunned gaze from the silver bowl to the Fur Queen's brilliant smile, where it became imprisoned once again.

And then the Fur Queen's lips began descending. Down they came, fluttering like a leaf from an autumn birch, until they came to rest on Abraham's left cheek. There.

After what seemed like years to Abraham Okimasis, she removed her lips from his cheek, expelling a jet of ice-cold vapour that mushroomed into a cloud. Her lips, her eyes, the gold and silver beads of her tiara sparkled one last time and then were swallowed by the billowing mist.

The next thing Abraham knew, or so he would relate to his two youngest sons years later, the goddess floated up to a sky fast fading from pink-and-purple dusk to the great blackness of night, then became one with the northern sky, became a shifting, nebulous pulsation, the seven stars of the Great Bear ornamenting her crown. And when she extended one hand down towards the hunter on Earth, a silver wand appeared in it, as simple as magic. Now a fairy-tale godmother glimmering in the vastness of the universe, the Fur Queen waved the wand. Her white fur cape spread in a huge shimmering arc, becoming the aurora borealis. As its galaxies of stars and suns and moons and planets hummed their way across the sky and back, the Fur Queen smiled enigmatically, and from the seven stars on her tiara burst a human fetus, fully formed, opalescent, ghostly.

The Fur Queen disappeared, leaving her cape and crown, and the ghost child drifting in the womb of space, the wisps of winter cloud its amniotic fluid, turning and turning, with a speed as imperceptible yet certain as the rhythm of the spheres. And slowly, ever so slowly, the ghost baby tumbled, head over heels over head, down, down to Earth.

CHAPTER TWO

The pinewood sled and eight grey huskies glided, free of gravity, among the northern Manitoba stars, or so Abraham Okimasis would relate to his youngest sons years later. Occasionally, a stray beam from the frosty midwinter moon became entangled in the ornate surface of the World Championship Dog Derby trophy, and needles of silver light shot out.

For by the time he had rested a day and a night in an Oopaskooyak hotel and then set off on his journey north—and home—the northwest wind had been replaced by a kinder, gentler wind from the south. Still, the caribou hunter knew only too well how suddenly these winter storms could pounce upon the northern traveller. The evenings were so unseasonably balmy that he drove on well past dusk, for he couldn't wait to see his wife and children.

The six nights he spent bedded down by his campfire, under a lean-to of spruce boughs, became one long night. The six days he spent crossing ice-covered lake after ice-covered lake, island upon island—the snow, soft and pure, covering their stands of spruce and pine and tamarack—these six days melded into one. In the grip of the moment when he crossed the finish line, the moment of the Fur Queen's kiss, he wasn't even aware that he had entered the southern end of Mistik Lake until he was well on his way across the first great bay. The snow was so white, the sun so warm, the spruce so aromatic, the north so silent; and the moon, drifting from passing cloud to passing cloud, seemed to howl, backed up by a chorus of distant wolves.

And all the while, among the stars and wisps of cloud, the silvery fetal child tumbled down, miles, light years above the caribou hunter's dream-filled head.

At dusk on the sixth day, the hunter caught sight of the Chipoocheech Point headland and his heart swelled, as it always did when he knew Eemanapiteepitat would be coming into view within the next half hour. Chipoocheech Point was a mere five miles south of where his wife awaited him patiently. When he rounded the point and the toy-like buildings began to glimmer in the distance, his heart jumped and his mouth flew open to yodel in a falsetto clear and rich as the love cry of a loon—*'Weeks'chiloowew!'*—a yodel that always spurred his faithful team of huskies onto even more astonishing feats.

Before he could count to one hundred, Abraham Okimasis was racing past the lopsided log cabin of Black-eyed Susan Magipom and her terrible husband, Happy Doll. Black-eyed Susan Magipom boldly thrust her spindly thorax out the door, gazing ardently at Abraham as though Happy Doll Magipom didn't exist.

'Mush!' the hunter yelled out to Tiger-Tiger, *'mush, mush!'*

Before he could count to a hundred and ten, Abraham Okimasis was racing past the red-tiled roof of Choggylut McDermott and his wife, Two-Room; the lonely shack of Bad Robber Gazandlaree and his dog, Chuksees; the house of the widow Jackfish Head Lady, who once had a near-death encounter with the cannibal spirit Weetigo just off Tugigoom Island; the silver crucifix crowning the steeple of the church that had killed Father Cheepootat when its brick wall collapsed on him during confession; the dark-green rectory where Father Cheepootat's successor, Father Eustache Bouchard, received the faithful, for everything from marriage counselling to hemorrhoid examinations, and passed out raisins to small children on Easter Sunday mornings. And then Abraham Okimasis, for the very first time in three weeks, saw the little pine-log cabin he had built for his wife, the lovely Mariesis Adelaide Okimasis, and their five surviving children.

He was only vaguely aware that people were gathering: stragglers trundling home from the store at the north end of Eemanapiteepitat hill, young men sawing firewood in front of old log cabins, laughing children romping in the snow with barking dogs, even Crazy Salamoo Oopeewaya arguing with God from a rooftop; all had abandoned their current pursuit and rushed after Abraham's sled as it raced up the hill towards the Okimasis cabin. Their gesticulating arms, their babbling voices were indecipherable to the tired though elated hunter. His only two scraps of thought were that this ragtag bunch was ready for a party such as it had never had, and that it was clearly Jane Kaka McCrae's enormous new radio that had spread the news of his triumph throughout the reserve; for there was Jane Kaka, the most slovenly woman in Eemanapiteepitat, braying like a donkey to a gaggle of women with mouths and eyes as wide as bingo cards.

Before he could alight from his sled, Annie Moostoos, his wife's addled fifty-five-year-old cousin, renowned throughout the north for the one tooth left in her head, was dancing among the woodchips in the front yard, round and round the sawhorse, wearing Abraham's silver trophy on her head, like a German soldier's helmet. How the skinny four-foot widow got the trophy Abraham never did find out, for when he turned to ask, who should be standing there holding out Abraham's battered old accordion, his face as pink as bubblegum, but his own crusty, half-crazed fifty-five-year-old cousin, Kookoos Cook, renowned throughout the north for having chopped a juvenile caribou in the left hindquarter with a miniature axe and having been whisked off to the horizon by the terrified animal because Kookoos Cook had refused to let go of his only axe. Before Abraham could say '*Weeks'chiloowew*', Kookoos Cook had shoved the ratty old instrument into the musher's hands.

'Play my dead wife's favourite jig, play "*Kimoosoom Chimasoo*" or I'll never talk to you again.'

So the caribou hunter pumped and pulled his screechy old accordion, playing '*Kimoosoom Chimasoo*' like it had never been played, which is how Mariesis Okimasis first saw her husband after three whole weeks: through her kitchen window, her apron bloodied by the shank of caribou she was wrestling with, Mariesis Okimasis, forty years of age, black-haired, brown-eyed, lovely as a willow tree in spring. Her bloodied butcher knife missing Jane Kaka's left breast by half an inch, she zoomed through the door and flew into her husband's arms.

A mere two hundred yards south of the Okimasis cabin, one could have seen the priest in his study, a nail in one hand, a hammer in the other, poised to nail a brand-new crucifix into a wall. No good Catholic danced on Sundays, Father Eustache Bouchard had told his flock repeatedly. He considered marching over to tell the revellers to go home to supper and do their dancing some other day. His hammer came down, very hard, on his left thumb.

One trillion miles above the Aboriginal jamboree, the ghostly fetus continued its airy descent towards Earth. And only medicine women, shamans, artists, and visionaries were aware that a star-born child would soon be joining their dance.

Mariesis Okimasis had once won a contest for which the prize had been to have her picture taken by an itinerant British anthropologist who had claimed that never in all his travels had he seen cheekbones such as hers.

'That guy never did send us a copy of the picture,' moaned Mariesis into her husband's tingling ear as she slipped under him, he over her, their mountainous, goose-down-filled sleeping robe shifting like an earthquake in slow motion. Mariesis could see the left side of her husband's face, and for this she was glad, for nothing in life gave her more pleasure than the sight of his thick, sensuous lips.

The moonlight drifting in the little window over their bed made them look like large ripe fruit.

'That's all right,' the large ripe fruit breathed into her ear as she struggled with her white flannel slip. 'I don't need a picture when I have the real thing.' He slid out of his underwear.

The moonlight led Mariesis's eyes to the floor beside the bed where her sleeping children lay, those four still at home; she listened to their delicate snores wheeze their way in and out of her husband's heavy breathing, a sweet kitten's purr floating up to her. Then the light took them to the dresser top, where sat the trophy her champion of the world had brought for her from the distant south. Beside it stood a photograph: Abraham cradling in his arms the silver bowl, his cheek being kissed by the young woman radiant in her white fur cape and her silver-beaded fur tiara: 'The Fur Queen,' he had explained, 'the most beautiful woman in the world. Except for Mariesis Okimasis,' of course.

Suddenly, the light was coming from the Fur Queen's eyes. Mariesis half-closed hers and let this moment take her, out the little window above the bed, out past the branch of the young spruce tree bending under its weight of snow, out to millions of stars, to the northern lights: the ancestors of her people, ten thousand generations, to the beginning of time. Dancing.

And somewhere within the folds of this dance, Mariesis saw, through tears of an intense joy—or did ecstasy inflict hallucinations on its victims?—a sleeping child, not yet born but fully formed, naked, curled up inside the womb of night, tumbling down towards her and her husband.

The ancestors—the women—moaned and whispered. Mariesis could hear among them her mother, who had left this Earth mere months after Mariesis had become a bride, one among many to have succumbed to tuberculosis. And though barely audible where she lay in her pool of perspiration, the women's voices said to her: 'And *K'si mantou*, the Great Spirit, held the baby boy by his big toe and dropped him from the stars . . .'

And that was all she remembered.

Poof! he went on his bum, smack into the most exquisite mound of snow in the entire forest, making crystals of silver spray shoot up to join the stars. He disappeared into the mound and would have stayed down there indefinitely if it hadn't been for his bouncy baby flesh and his supple newborn bones.

'If you throw them on the floor', one-toothed Annie Moostoos would brag about her nine brown babies to all who cared to listen, 'they'll bounce right back into your arms—it's true. Why would I lie to you?'

And the baby boy came shooting out of the mound of snow in two seconds flat and landed on his feet, right beside a small spruce tree that happened to be sleeping there. The little spruce tree opened one drowsy eye to see who could have made the whispering bump in the night and just managed to catch the tail-end of a spirit baby sprinting off into the darkness. There being nothing left to see but the little whirlwind in the baby's wake, the spruce tree went back to sleep.

The spirit baby ran through the forest, and ran and ran and ran. Hunch led him on, guided him, something having to do with warmth, he knew, something to do with hunger, with appeasing that hunger, something to do with love hunger, with appeasing that hunger, something to do with the length of string that led from the middle of his belly, a string almost invisible, so refined it could have been a strand of spider's web. This string and hunch. That was all.

Bang! The baby tripped, falling flat on his face, with a shriek more of surprise than of pain, in front of a cave. Growling like an ill-tempered bitch, a large, hairy animal lumbered out of the cave, admonished the prostrate child for having roused him from his winter sleep, and give him a swift kick in the bum. The baby yelped, jumped up, and dashed away from the cave and its cantankerous occupant through the forest towards a tent standing on the shore of a lake.

Then the child bumped into a rabbit, who took pity on him, for, by this time, the naked child was shivering. The rabbit slipped off his coat and wrapped it around the child's shivering, plump midsection. The as-yet-unborn infant made his gratitude clear to the rabbit, who turned out to be a writer of lyric rabbit poetry, and the travelling baby and the now naked, shivering animal would be friends for life.

Finally emerging from the forest, glinting with crystals of snow and frost, the child ran around the tent by the lake, across the pile of woodchips strewn at the entrance, just missing getting sliced in half by a man flailing away with an axe, and burst through the tent flap like a comet.

The tent interior glowed golden warm from the kerosene lamp. Moaning and whimpering and crying softly, Mariesis Okimasis lay on a bed of spruce boughs, a minuscule and very ancient woman hovering over her like the branch of an old pine tree: Misty Marie Gazandlaree, Chipewyan, ninety-three years of age and one of the most respected midwives in the north at that time. The silver baby scooted under the old woman's left arm, took a little hop, two small skips, one dive and half a pirouette, and landed square on top of Mariesis Okimasis's firm round belly: 5:00 a.m., Saturday, December 1, 1951.

He lay puffing and panting, when the man with the flailing weapon entered the tent, his arms piled high with firewood, his eyes aglow at the sight of the child. And the last thing the child remembered, until he was to read about it years later, was shutting his eyes and seeing up in the dome of his miniature skull a sky filled with a million stars, the northern lights pulsating, and somewhere in the web of galaxies, a queen waving a magic wand.

The baby boy was floating in the air, his skin no longer silver blue but pinkish brown. As he floated, he turned and turned and laughed and laughed. Until, lighter than a tuft of goose-down, he fell to Earth, his plump posterior landing neatly in a bowl of silver.

'*Ho-ho!* My victory boy!' the fun-loving caribou hunter trumpeted to whatever audience he could get, which, at the moment, was his wife. '*Ho-ho!* My champion boy!'

'Down! Put him down, or his little bum will freeze!' cried Mariesis Okimasis, though she couldn't help but laugh and, with her laughing, love this man for all his unpredictable bouts of clownishness. Jumping up and down, the short Mariesis was trying to get the tall Abraham to put his World Championship Dog Derby trophy down so she could put their baby back into the warmth and safety of his cradle-board. This was, after all, a tent, not a palace, not even a house, and this was, after all, mid-December and not July, in a region so remote that the North Pole was rumoured to be just over that next hill. In fact, if it hadn't been for the curl of smoke from its tin chimney, the little canvas shelter would have been invisible, that's how much snow there was when Champion Okimasis was born.

1998

Guy Vanderhaeghe

b. 1951

Like the central character of his short story 'Man on Horseback', reprinted here, or the dramatized narrator of his award-winning novel *The Englishman's Boy* (1996), Guy Vanderhaeghe comes from Saskatchewan (he was born in Esterhazy in 1951) and has a career that has involved him with history. He earned a BA in 1972 and an MA in 1975 studying history at the University of Saskatchewan. He later took a B.Ed. at the University of Regina in 1978 and, before turning to writing, taught high school and worked as an archivist and researcher.

The short stories Vanderhaeghe began publishing in journals in the late 1970s were brought together in the early 1980s to form two collections that immediately established his reputation as a major writer: *Man Descending* (1982), which won him the Faber Prize and the first of his Governor General's Awards, and *The Trouble with Heroes and Other Stories* (1983). A third collection of short stories, *Things as They Are* appeared in 1992.

Vanderhaeghe has also been honoured for his novels. *My Present Age*, published in 1984, was shortlisted for the Booker Prize. He has since published *Homesick* (1989), *The Englishman's Boy* (which won a Governor General's Award and was shortlisted for both the IMPAC Dublin and the Booker Prizes), and *Mr. Moses* (2002). He has also written several plays that have been produced, and two of these have been published: *I Had a Job I Liked. Once.* (1992) and *Dancock's Dance* (1996). He has served as writer-in-residence at the Saskatoon Public Library (1993–4) and the University of Ottawa (1985). Since 1993, he has been a visiting professor at Saint Thomas More College in Saskatoon.

If history is important to Vanderhaeghe, so is his sense of the local. *Homesick* suggests that the kind of rural and small-town world he grew up in is a difficult one, but that it is more difficult to leave it behind. He demythologizes this west (explicitly so in *The Englishman's Boy*, which is partly about the dangerous narrative that the American western movie offers), but he also sees the west as shaping the values and way of life of those who live there. He depicts the culture clash that results when the values that come out of the traditional western, agrarian way of life meet other or more contemporary ways of living and understanding.

As is also true with other writers of prairie fiction, such as Sinclair Ross and Robert Kroetsch, Vanderhaeghe is particularly interested in how the North American west has played (and goes on playing) a powerful role in the construction of manhood, and how the west's masculine ethos affects every aspect of men's behaviour, influencing the relationships between men and men, between men and women, and between fathers and their children.

At the same time, while region is a powerful presence in his writing, Vanderhaeghe is also keenly interested in the larger implications of his stories: a moralist with an abiding awareness of moral ambiguities, he writes about justice and the difficulty of finding it, about all the ways in which power can be abused, and about the need for human dignity.

Man on Horseback

Following his father's death, Joseph Kelsey discovered, in his bereavement, a passion for horses. Joseph's passion for horses was not of the same character as the old man's had been; Joseph's was searching, secretive, concerned with lore, confined to books. It was not love. When his wife asked him what he was doing, staying up so late night after night, he said he was working on an article. Joseph was a professor of history.

The article was a lie. He was reading about horses.

A good horse sholde have three propyrtees of a man, three of a woman, three of a foxe, three of a hare, and three of an asse.[1]

Joseph was born in a poor, backward town to a couple reckoned to be one of the poorest and most backward. It was a world of outhouses, chicken coops in backyards, eyeglasses purchased from Woolworth's, bad teeth that never got fixed. On the afternoon of October 29, 1949, when his mother's water broke his father ran down the lane to get Pepper Carmichael to drive them to the hospital. Rupert Kelsey didn't own an automobile, not even a rusted collection of rattles like Pepper's.

What Rupert Kelsey owned was seven horses. Horses slipped and slid through his fingers like quicksilver. When he was flush he bought more, when funds ran low he sold off one or two. Horses came and horses went in a continual parade, bays and sorrels, blacks and greys, chestnuts and roans, pintos and piebalds. His wife was jealous of them.

There was trouble with Joseph's birth right from the start. The hospital, staffed mostly by nuns, was tiny and antiquated, as backward as the town. Rupert Kelsey sat in the waiting room for an hour, and then a sister came out and told him they had telephoned everywhere but the doctor couldn't be found. It was understood what that meant. The doctor was either drunk—not an uncommon occurrence—or was off playing poker somewhere without having left a number where he could be reached. Rupert nodded solemnly and the nun left, face as starchy as her wimple.

The duty nurse behind the reception desk, a gossip, watched him closely, intrigued to see how he would take the news. He could sense her curiosity clear across the room and he was careful not to give away anything he was feeling. He had a country boy's wilful, adamant sense of what was private, the conviction that people in towns had no notion of what was their business and what wasn't.

Because this was his wife's first baby he knew that labour would likely be prolonged and hard. For three hours he sat, alternately studying the scuffed toes of his boots and the clock on the wall, his face held gravely polite against the duty nurse's

1 A fifteenth-century definition found in *Brewer's Dictionary of Phrase and Fable.* The other passages in italics that appear throughout have been created by Vanderhaeghe from several different sources.

inspection. The nurse was working a double shift because the woman who was to relieve her had called in at the last minute sick. She was bored and Rupert Kelsey was the only item of even mild interest in what was going to be a very long night. To the nurse he looked thirty, but seemed much older. Maybe it was the old-fashioned haircut which made his ears stand out like jug handles, maybe it was the way he shyly hid his dirty hands and cracked nails underneath the cap lying in his lap, maybe it was the bleak rawness of a face shaved with a blade sharpened that morning in a water glass, maybe it was the sum of all of these things or maybe it was none of these things which lent him that air of steadfast dignity she associated with men her father's age. He appeared to have nothing to do with her generation.

No one came out from the ward to tell Rupert Kelsey how matters stood. The Kelseys were not the sort of people that those in authority felt it necessary to make reports and explanations to. When the hands of the clock swung around to eleven he found it impossible to sustain a pose of calm any longer. Rupert got abruptly to his feet and started for the entrance.

The young nurse behind the desk spoke sharply to him. 'Mr Kelsey, Mr Kelsey, where are you going?' In her opinion this was not the way a father-to-be with a wife in the pangs of childbirth ought to behave.

'I'll be back,' he said, shouldering through the door.

It was cold, unusually cold for the end of October. The little town was dark, only its main street boasted streetlamps. Scarcely a window showed a light at this hour; in the days before television arrived, people here retired early, to sleep or entertain themselves in bed.

The barn where Kelsey stabled his horses was on the other side of town, but the other side of town was less than a ten-minute walk away. Just stepping into the heavy, crowded warmth of jostling bodies and freshly dropped dung, the ammoniac reek of horse piss, the dusty smell of hay and oats, the tang of sweat-drenched leather, made him hate that lifeless, sinister waiting room all the more.

He saddled the mare, led her into the yard, swung up on her back, and trotted through the town. The dirt roads were dry and packed and thudded crisply under the iron shoes. Like strings of firecrackers, dogs began to go off, one after another, along the streets he and his horse travelled. The mare carried her head high, neck twisted to the dogs howling out of the blackness, answering them with startled, fearful snorts. Easy and straight as a chair on a front porch, Rupert Kelsey rode her through the uproar and beyond the town limits.

It was a clear night, the sky pitilessly high, strewn faintly with bright sugary stars. Where the curtain of sky brushed the line of the horizon, poplar bluffs bristled. Beneath this cold sky Rupert Kelsey released his horse, let her fear of dogs and night bear human fear wild down the empty road, reins slack along her neck, hands knotted in the mane, braced for the headlong crash, the capsize into darkness. Her belly groaned hollowly between his legs, her breath tore in her chest. For three miles she fled, a runaway panicked.

At the bridge, the sudden glide of water, the broken shimmer unexpectedly intersecting the road caused the mare to shy, and as she broke stride he fought to turn her, striking back ruthlessly on the left rein, dragging her around open-mouthed like a hooked fish, swinging her back in the direction from which she had come, his heels drumming her through the turn, urging her, stretching her out flat down the road, back to the hospital.

By the time they reached the town the mare galloped on her last legs. On the planked railway crossing she stumbled, plunged, but kept her feet. Rupert whipped her the last five hundred yards to the hospital, reining her back on her haunches before the glass doors through which he could see the nurse as he had left her, at the desk. The nurse looked at him from where she sat and he looked at her. The mare trembled with exhaustion, a faint steam rising from wet flanks and neck. The nurse, finally realizing he was not about to dismount, got to her feet, came to the door, and pushed out into the night.

'Anything yet?' he asked.

She shook her head.

'The doctor come?'

She shook her head again.

He wheeled the horse around and was gone. For several moments the nurse stood straining for a glimpse of him, pink sweater draped over her shoulders, arms wrapped around herself against the piercing cold. Everything was swallowed up in darkness but the tattoo of hooves. She turned and went inside.

Back at the barn Kelsey pulled the bridle, blanket, and saddle off the mare and flung them on a four-year-old gelding, leaving the winded horse where she stood. Once again unseen dogs gave tongue, their wavering voices lifting along the streets. He rode hard into the countryside, the taste of a cold dark wind in his mouth.

The story was a favourite of the nurse's for a long time. 'Three times he rode up to the hospital and asked after his wife and then rode away again. Different horse every time. Looked drunker every time too. They usually are. Last time it was just after the sun came up, around eight in the morning that I told him she had finally delivered a boy. You know what he said? Said, "Tell the wife I'll be up to see her as soon as I can. I got some horses to look after." Imagine. And that woman came near dying too. It was a near thing if she'd lost any more blood.'

Joseph's mother always said to him. 'You, you little bastard, you wore out three horses and one woman getting born. It's got to be a record.'

Wolf Calf of the Blackfoot first received horse medicine. It was given to him in a dream by a favourite horse which he had always treated respectfully and kindly. This horse appeared to him and said, 'Father, I am grateful for your kindness to me. Now I give you the sacred dance of the horses which will be your secret. I give you the power to heal horses and to heal people. In times of trouble I will always be near you.'

Horse Medicine Men could accomplish miracles. Not only could they cure sick horses and sick people, they could influence the outcome of races, causing horses to leave the course, buck, or refuse to run. Pursued by enemies, they would rub horse medicine on a quirt, point it at the pursuer and drop the quirt in the path of the foe's horse, causing the animal to falter.

All Horse Medicine Men recognized taboos. Rib bones and shin bones were not to be broken in the lodge of a Horse Medicine Man. No child should ride a wooden stick horse in a lodge in the presence of a Horse Medicine Man. If he did, misfortune and bad luck would befall that child.

Before a vet arrived in the district, if a horse was sick or badly injured, its owner summoned Rupert Kelsey. Usually his father took Joseph along on these visits, although the boy wished he wouldn't. When Joseph was four a stud bit him on the shoulder. His mother told him that he had screamed bloody blue murder, screamed like a stuck pig. The purple, apple-green bruise lasted for weeks and if he hadn't been wearing a heavy parka, which had blunted the horse's teeth, the damage could have been a lot more severe. Years later Joseph would suppose that the sudden crushing pain, the breath hot on his neck and face, the mad glare of the eyes must have been the root of what, in a son of his father's, was an unnatural, shameful fear of horses. But he couldn't be sure. He had no memory of the incident. Envying his father's courage, he did all he could to conceal and dissemble his cowardice.

Once, when Joseph was eleven, a woman telephoned his father with horse trouble. Her husband was away from home working on the rigs[2] and his horse had hurt itself. The woman said she was afraid her husband would blame her for what had happened to the horse, accuse her of carelessness and neglect as he had a habit of doing whenever anything went wrong. This man was infamous for his hot, ungovernable temper. His wife had been seen in the grocery store, eyes blackened, looking like a racoon. Rupert agreed to come at once to see what he could do to help the horse and, by implication, her.

He and Joseph drove out to her place and found the horse pacing a corral, a long jagged gash on its chest dangling a piece of hide shaped like an envelope flap, an animal tormented, driven half-mad by pain and relentless clouds of flies. Joseph was ready to bet his father was going to get killed trying to catch this crazy horse. To start with, it tried to escape, clambered up six feet of fence rails, grunting and pawing, toppled over on its hind quarters, and collapsed in a whirl of slashing legs. Then it scrambled to its feet and came straight at his father, squealing, wriggling, kicking, teeth bared. His father broke the charge, made the horse veer away at the last possible second by flogging it across the face and eyes with the stock whip he carried. Joseph, clinging to the fence, begged and shouted at his father to come out of there, leave that horse be, but he wouldn't listen. Around and around the corral the two went, horse and man. The dust hung in the lowering evening light like a fine, golden powder. As it settled on his father's clothes and hair it turned from gold to grey, turning him into a ghost.

2 That is, working in the oil fields as wells are being dug. (A rig is the tall apparatus used for drilling oil wells.)

At last his father lassoed the horse and snubbed him down[3] as tight as he could to a post. Next he fashioned himself a makeshift twitch out of a bit of rope and stick and performed the dangerous sleight of hand of slipping the loop on the horse's nose and cranking it up like a tourniquet. The horse braced itself on widely splayed legs, mad eyes rolling, strong yellow teeth bared, slobber slopping off its bottom lip. But now his father had the son of a bitch, had him good. When he called Joseph to come and take the twitch, the boy came with no more protest than if God Almighty himself had ordered him out from behind the fence of poplar poles to keep a jug-headed man-killer squeezed into submission with a twist of hemp and dry wood. He was safe because his father was near, patiently sponging Creolin[4] into the raw mouth of the laceration, painstakingly picking slivers and dirt from the butcher-flesh. His father was there talking quietly and matter-of-factly to both horse and boy. 'Now when I pull this splinter loose, look out. Get set. He's going to breathe fire. Aren't you going to breathe fire, you no-nuts son of a bitch?' Nothing could go amiss or awry with his father there, speaking so calmly.

The wound was clean, there was nothing left to do but stitch the cut. Fishing through shirt pockets his father began to swear. Somehow his needle and thread had gone missing and he would have to borrow what he needed from the woman. Joseph was to hold the horse until he got back. 'He won't be going anywheres on you if you keep that twitch tight. Just keep the twitch tight,' his father reiterated and was gone before the boy could manufacture an excuse why he shouldn't leave him.

Over his shoulder, Joseph watched his father amble to the house, knock and disappear into the porch when the door was answered. He turned back to the horse. The wound was bleeding, dripping slow, fat drops of blood into the dust. It was like watching the second hand of a clock. He counted the drops, watched three hundred fall. Three hundred drops equalled five minutes. Five minutes ought to be enough time to scare up a needle and thread. He glanced nervously toward the house to see if his father was returning. There was no sign of him. The boy swayed with panic. What was keeping him? Where was his father? How long was he supposed to stand holding this horse? He imagined the sun setting, his father still missing and night falling, alone with this glassy-eyed, devil horse, both rooted to this spot of ground by a twitch. Joseph's palms were slick with sweat. He thought of the stick slipping in his hands, the sudden blur of unwinding. The unwinding and springing of the fear twisted up inside him and the fear twisted up on a stick.

He began to count the drops of blood again. He would count another three hundred before he permitted himself to look again to see if his father was coming. Five minutes more. There were flies gathering at the growing puddle of black blood thickening on the ground. There were flies on Joseph. He could feel them crawling in his ears and at the corners of his eyes. He didn't dare swat them, he might lose his grip on the stick. One slip and that crazy horse might get him.

3 That is, severely restricted the horse's movement by wrapping the rope around its neck and then around a corral post. The horse is further restricted by the twitch—a cord looped around a stick and then the horse's mouth and upper lip—that can be tightened by twisting the stick.

4 A brand name for a disinfectant.

'Hurry up,' he said aloud and the horse laid back its ears at the sound of his voice, changing the shape of its head, giving it a snake's sleekness. 'Hurry up, please,' he said. He was still counting in his head, the numbers very loud. He got mixed up. Started counting flies, not tears of blood. He began over. Once again three hundred. He looked back at the dead calm of the yard soaked in evening light; everything motionless except for the swallows swooping and flitting above the peaked roof of the house. In the final flight of these birds before the coming darkness he experienced his own desertion. There was no logic to it, except the logic of association. Somehow he understood he would never be his father. It was that simple. He could never be a man like his father. The realization left him bereft, made him cry.

He was still crying when he heard the scrape of boots on the fence rails. His father wanted to know what had happened. Joseph couldn't explain. When his father came nearer and repeated the question, Joseph smelled the whisky on his breath. Now he felt entitled to his anger at his father's failure to understand.

'You been drinking!' he said. The shrillness of his voice was a clue, if not an explanation.

'She gave me a drink,' his father said. 'I had to have a drink for coming out. She wouldn't have it any other way.' He couldn't figure what was behind this. 'I was only gone fifteen minutes,' he said. 'Did he come at you? Take a jump? Scare you? Is that it? I told you to hold tight.'

'Tell me another one. Fifteen minutes,' Joseph said sullenly, trying to rub the tears on his cheek into the shoulder of his shirt.

'Okay, twenty minutes,' said his father. 'At the outside.' He threaded the needle and set about stitching the wound. The light was failing, he didn't have much time. Each time the needle penetrated the skin, the horse shivered, its hide rippled with a life of its own.

'You ought to think,' said Joseph.

'Think about what?' said his father. 'You tell me what to think about and I'll think about it.'

'Just think.' *Think about me*, he meant.

'Wait until you're my age,' his father said. 'Then you'll know what thinking is.'

Think about what'd happen if I let go of this stick. Joseph watched the poised needle. *You'd be sorry then.*

His father tied the thread in a neat surgical knot. He had a book of knots at home, there wasn't one he didn't know.

'Turn him loose,' he said to the boy. His father was getting angry. What was he supposed to apologize for? 'And another thing,' he added, 'just so you know who calls the shots in this outfit—get yourself ready for another fifteen-minute wait because the lady asked me in for another drink and I'm going to have it.'

Joseph refused to go into the house with his father.

'Pout if you want,' his father said. 'It's no skin off my ass.'

Joseph prowled around the house, chucking handfuls of gravel up under the eaves to drive the swallows out of their nests and into bursts of edgy flight to test the truth of his earlier feeling. He continued doing this until his father came roaring and raving outside, shouting enough was enough, he'd had all he could stand of this carry-on. Show some respect for other people's property or he'd get the worst jeezly licking of his life.

Another taboo broken.

After France's defeat at the hands of the Prussians in 1870 and the annexation of Alsace-Lorraine, the humiliated nation cried out for revenge, for a saviour. The eyes of Frenchmen turned to the handsome General Georges Boulanger, The Man on Horseback. No one knew that The Man on Horseback had only learned to ride, to cut such a captivating figure, by the most diligent application. Boulanger after all was an infantry man, not a cavalry officer full of careless dash and daring. His riding school was an abandoned chapel which stood beside his house. Each morning at six o'clock the General would spur his horse through the doorway of the chapel and commence bouncing about in the sacral, coloured morning light falling through the stained-glass windows. The General was not a stupid man. Although he frequently toppled off his horse and took many embarrassing tumbles, he was careful to see to it that there were no witnesses to his hilarious accidents. His mistakes were made in private.

General Boulanger had an infallible sense of publicity. Everyone remembers the names of the horses of truly great generals. Alexander the Great and Bucephalus, Napoleon and the white stallion Marengo, General Lee and Traveller, Stonewall Jackson and Little Sorrel. But no general owed as much to a horse as General Boulanger did to Tunis. The General did not choose his horse himself, he left the choice of his mount to an expert, someone who knew his business. The man who picked Tunis for the General chose well. Tunis was a beautiful black which gleamed in the sunshine. Despite being a considerable age, the horse looked strong and had a striking carriage. He moved and pranced elegantly, with great elan, with great presence. Perhaps most important for a general who had only recently become an equestrian, sitting on Tunis was as comfortable as sitting in his own armchair beside his own fire. The horse's disposition was tested by trumpeting bugles in his ear and discharging rifle volleys under his nose. The animal didn't turn a hair, didn't startle. There would be no unfortunate and mortifying surprises for The Man on Horseback.

On July 14, 1886, the anniversary of the Fall of the Bastille, General Boulanger introduced Tunis to the public in a military review at Longchamps. By three o'clock in the afternoon a crowd of one hundred thousand had gathered on the field to view the parade. Gunfire and military tunes announced the arrival of a squad of spahis[5] *followed by fifteen generals, hundreds of officers and the military attachés of all the embassies. When they had passed, a solitary figure made his entrance on a black horse; General Boulanger garbed in turquoise dolman with gold epaulettes, pink trousers and black boots.*

The crowd went wild. Cries of Vive Boulanger! *drowned out the weak smattering of applause which greeted those dowdy, drab politicians, the Prime Minister and the President of France. While those two fussily took their seats in the presidential box, General Boulanger and Tunis capered about the field looking strenuously military, the eyes of the crowd fastened adoringly upon them.*

5 French army cavalry units, usually of Algerian and Senegalese riders (originally Ottoman troops, composed of Turkish and Arab soldiers).

When the review began, many of the common soldiers broke protocol by saluting General Boulanger rather than the President of the Republic. Thousands of voices thundered 'Vive Boulanger!' *again and again. As the last troops departed, the hysterical crowd burst through the police and onto the field, men shouting frantically, women weeping. Only with the greatest reluctance did the overwhelming mob permit their darling to canter off on his beautiful black horse. For hours, like jilted brides and forsaken bridegrooms, they wandered about Longchamps, disconsolate. That night every restaurant and café in Paris was full, the streets were jammed with people shouting for Boulanger.*

The striking figure he had cut on Tunis insured Boulanger's popularity and led to a ubiquitous celebrity. Over three hundred popular songs were composed in his honour. Photographs of his striking features sold out issues of eight hundred thousand. There were pottery statuettes of the General and cheap clay pipes with their bowls fashioned in the likeness of The Man on Horseback. You could scrub yourself with Boulanger soap and eat your dinner from a Boulanger plate. His office in the Ministry of War was flooded with letters from the women of France offering their bodies to him with fervent, erotic patriotism. France gave its heart to Boulanger, but Boulanger's was pledged to his mistress, the Vicomtesse Marguerite de Bonnemains, lover, advisor, and administerer of ever increasing doses of morphine to alleviate the pain of an old war wound of the General's.

On January 27, 1887, General Boulanger was elected to the constituency of the Seine by a stunning majority of 80,000 votes. That night France was his for the taking, virtually without opposition he could have established his dictatorship. In the Restaurant Durand, where he awaited election results throughout the evening, an enthusiastic mob was kept at bay with the iron shutters closed over the windows. Admirers urged him to act, to seize the government. Workingmen, students from Montmartre, aristocrats chanted 'A l'Elysée! A l'Elysée!' *in the streets. Boulanger withdrew to a private room in the restaurant and consulted Marguerite. When he returned he issued orders that nothing was to be done.*

Sensing indecision and weakness on his part, the government set in train steps to arrest The Man on Horseback and General Boulanger fled wife and France accompanied by his mistress. A brief period of fashionable acclaim in English society followed, but the General was a spent force, an article for the shelf. In exile on the isle of Jersey, Marguerite fell ill while the General sat in front of a large portrait of Tunis.

The unhappy couple removed themselves to Belgium. There Marguerite died on July 16, two days after the date of the General's greatest triumph on the field of Longchamps. Several months later The Man on Horseback shot himself on his lover's grave. A large photograph of Marguerite which he carried under his shirt was so firmly pasted to the skin of his chest with dried blood that it had be torn to be removed.

A horse can carry a man only so far and no farther.

Joseph Kelsey left home at the age of seventeen. For four years he attended the University of Saskatchewan, supporting himself with part-time jobs and scholarships. A Woodrow Wilson Fellowship took him to the University of Wisconsin. From there he went on to the University of Chicago and a Ph.D. in modern French history. While in Chicago, he met and married Catherine Bringhurst, a medical student and a native of the Windy City. In 1974 Catherine completed her medical degree, Joseph took a job teaching history at Carleton, and they moved to Ottawa.

Each of these steps removed Joseph Kelsey a little further from his father, geographically and emotionally. Distance made visits more expensive and more infrequent. The world he lived and worked in now made the one he had departed seem impossible, at the very least improbable. Whenever he told Catherine stories of his childhood, of life in a shacky house, of a father and mother who never read a book, he felt self-dramatizing and false. The stories were true but in the alchemy of Catherine's imagination they were transformed and he became located in an unreal world of glamorous destitution. In rare moments of self-knowledge, Joseph Kelsey knew that this had always been his intention—to make his origins as romantic to her as hers were to him. His goal was a reciprocity of envy, something conceivable, given the mood of the sixties. Raised in an affluent suburb of Chicago by a doctor father and a psychiatrist mother, whom she addressed as Claude and Amelia, Catherine seemed inconceivably exotic to her young husband.

Joseph and his new wife made trips back to Sastatchewan twice in the years between 1974 and 1977. On both occasions they stayed in the local hotel at Catherine's insistence. Because Joseph's parents' house was so small, she didn't want Rupert and Mary disturbed by Andrew, a fussing baby on their first visit and, on their second, a small child in the throes of the terrible twos. Joseph didn't tell his wife that her middle-class consideration was interpreted by his parents as high and mightiness, a distaste for ordinary people and plain living. Overhearing his mother refer to Catherine as 'Dr Bringhurst' confirmed for her son that it was a sore point with his mother that his spouse had retained her maiden name.

How Catherine reacts to this, or doesn't react to this—she is oblivious in the way the protected, privileged so often are, they cannot conceive of opinions except the proper ones, *theirs*—makes Joseph swell with a mild, chafing contempt. *She has no idea.* For her the man with the prematurely, fiercely lined face and the woman with the home permanent and tough, callused hands are salt of the earth idealizations; honest, kindly peasants like the ones first encountered in a suburban fairy tale, Chicago-style. Deep in her heart she assumes that they must admire her because that is what peasants do with princesses. (Catherine would be shocked and hurt if Joseph accused her of such an attitude.) But Joseph knows what his parents think of women who give their boy child a doll to play with, or hang on to their maiden names, or put up in hotels on family visits. Hoity-toity bitch, is what they think. So his son turns five before Joseph can bring himself to pay another visit home, before he and Catherine, his mother and Andrew find themselves standing in the IGA parking lot, watching the local Canada Day parade assemble. This year, like each of the fifteen before, his father, on horseback, is going to lead the parade and bear the flag.

It is not a good day for a parade. The morning is woolly and grey with a fine, misty rain, which recalls for Joseph the barely perceptible spray suspended in the air above the observation railings at Niagara Falls. He wishes it would piss or get off the pot. The day has the feel of a sodden Kleenex about to shred in his hands. He doesn't know why he should feel this, but he does. Maybe it's because Andrew, holding Catherine's hand and delightedly awaiting the commencement of the parade in a brilliantly yellow raincoat and sou'wester, seems to his father the only genuine patch of brightness on the scene, a patch of brightness soon to be eclipsed by disappointment. It's Joseph's guess that the boy expects a parade of pomp and magnitude, an Ottawa parade like he's used to. Andrew doesn't understand that all he is going to get is what is already collected in the parking lot.

That's the local high-school band whose uniform consists of the high-school jacket, nothing splashier, showier, or more elaborate. Also the local Credit Union, which has resurrected its perennial float, a six-foot-high papier mâché globe spotted with cardboard Credit Union flags to illustrate the international nature of credit unionism. The owner and parts man of the John Deere dealership are drunk and in clown costumes. The owner will drive a John Deere riding mower pulling a child's wagon in which the two-hundred-and-fifty-pound parts man will hunker, honking a horn and tossing wrapped candies to the children. The few remaining parade entries are of a similar calibre. Meanwhile the hapless drizzle continues, making everything fuzzier and murkier, wilting the pastel tissue paper flowers on the floats, frizzing the hair of the high-school queen and her attendants, painting a pearly film of moisture on the hoods, roofs, fenders of parked cars.

Buried in Joseph is the nagging realization that it is wrong to assign the feel of the day, the foreboding that it is about to fall apart in his hands, to any possible disappointment on Andrew's part. The real problem is his, adult disappointment. Because, ever since they arrived, grandson and grandfather have been stuck to one another like a new wooden rung glued into an old wooden chair. Joseph knows it is the horses. How can he compete with horses? Despite Catherine anxiously forbidding her father-in-law to carry Andrew wedged between his belly and the pommel of the saddle the way he once carried Joseph as a toddler, Joseph knows that hasn't stopped the old man when he's out of her sight: no woman is going to tell him what to do. And disobeying her has won him a friend for life.

Just now Andrew, all shining yellow, is standing riveted with admiration to the shining black asphalt of the parking lot, watching his grandfather show off for him on his horse.

There is no other word for what the old fool is doing but showing off and the performance leaves Joseph faintly disgusted. The pretence is that he is putting his mount through its paces, a sort of pre-parade disciplining, but in Joseph's books it is purely, simply, transparently, a pathetic ploy to impress a five year old.

The old man backs up the gelding across the parking lot, toes pointing outward in his stirrups, urging it backward with the pressure of his legs and firm tucks of the reins. Then he jumps it forward suddenly, swings it to the right in a tight, tail-chasing circle, the drooping standard shaking itself out from the flag pole in shuddering billows. Abruptly he throws the horse's head left, reversing the direction of the turn, rippling the flag with counter-spin. The slither of the gelding's hooves, the awkward, comic scramble of its back legs as they fight for purchase on the slippery pavement kick high-pitched laughter and skittish, excited hops out of Andrew. He's delighted with this cartoon.

Suddenly, in the midst of a spin, the horse's legs slip on the rain-slick pavement with a sound like a spoon scraping the bottom of a pot and shoot stiffly out, the horse going down, landing heavily on the old man's left leg, pinning him to the wet asphalt. For a moment, everyone except Andrew freezes. The boy, unable to judge the seriousness of the situation, continues laughing in shrill appreciation of the new trick until a squeal of terror from the fallen horse shocks him into silence.

Joseph runs through the rain. He sees the muscular arching of the horse's neck, the legs thrashing the air and pavement for a footing, his father clinging to the horn and heeling the horse hard with his free boot, urging it to its feet with shouts of 'Hup! Hup! Hup!', the horse whinnying, straining to rise with this dead weight, this sack of guts and bone unbalancing it.

As Joseph reaches out to seize the bridle and help lift the head, the horse heaves, heaves desperately again, scrambles to its feet snorting and jerking, the old man sticking on for dear life, slung precariously from the saddle like a sidecar, bouncing and pitching with each convulsion of the powerful body, fighting to pull himself upright. Which he does, the horse dancing a nervous side-step across the parking lot, one rein dragging, the old man leaning forward, snatching for it and calling out, 'Whoa! Whoa! Whoa, you son of a bitch!'

At last he grabs the rein and regains some control of the horse which stands blowing, snuffling, trembling, cornered eyes wary. People begin to crowd near, now that the danger is over. 'I'm going to walk him out', says the old man to Joseph, ignoring the others, 'to see he didn't bugger his legs.' Horse and rider slowly circle the parking lot. Andrew leans against his father, bumps his head on Joseph's hip, and cries. Now that it is over, now that he has absorbed what has happened, the boy is finally frightened. As the old man passes them on his second circuit he calls out to his grandson, 'Grandpa's okay, see? Look, Andy, Grandpa's okay.' He grins hugely and strikes his chest dramatically with his fist to demonstrate his soundness. Grandpa making a joke on himself, Grandpa beating his chest wildly in this funny way, pitches the boy into no man's land, leaves him gulping tears, sucking back snot but also smiling with relief. Grandpa's all right. Grandpa's okay. He says so. However, a certain grim tightening about the mouth, the way the old man gingerly shifts his seat in the saddle contradict Grandpa's claim.

Reassured as to the horse's fitness, the old man asks Joseph to hand him the flag he dropped in the wreck. His son tries to talk him out of continuing but he'll hear none of that. Joseph knows it's injured pride, the shame of the apple cart upset in front of witnesses which prevents his father from withdrawing from the parade. Long ago he had said to Joseph, 'Just like a box of Crackerjacks, there's a surprise in every horse.' What went without saying was that Rupert Kelsey could handle any of those surprises. Now he is not going to let this surprise get the better of him, not with his grandson, his son, his daughter-in-law as onlookers.

Catherine is incredulous that Joseph won't stop him. 'He ought to have medical attention! He's sixty-five,' she says.

'You tell him he's sixty-five. You tell him he ought to have medical attention. You're the doctor, not me,' says Joseph and walks away from her.

His father troops the parade all around the town with a grinning face as grey and wan as the day itself, then leads it back again to the parking lot. When he tries to dismount he discovers his left leg, the one crushed under the horse, can't bear his weight and he has to suffer the indignity of having Joseph support him while he bails out on the right side of the horse, the wrong side, like some know-nothing dude ranch cowboy. The left leg is, of course, broken and has swollen to fill his riding boot like sausage meat stuffed tight in its casing. When they cut the cowboy boot off him in the hospital he keeps sadly remarking, 'Those are my show boots. Lizard skin. Expensive as all get out.'

Joseph knows the difficulty of unlearning the things you were taught as a kid—he's been trying to do it for nearly twenty years. Still he backslides, caught in the current of his father's assumptions like a rudderless boat. Take the question of toughness, grit, physical courage. Joseph Kelsey's colleagues condescend to any such notions as the last refuge of the pitiably stupid and primitive, the resort of macho Neanderthals with brains the size of peas and exaggerated testosterone levels—football players or men like Oliver North and Gordon Liddy.[6] They prefer moral courage, the variety of bravery on which intellectuals have a corner of the market.

Joseph has to concede that physical courage *is* inferior to moral courage. Nevertheless he often feels the need to play the devil's advocate, the devil prompting this reaction being his rooster-tough old man. Joseph wants to argue: But isn't physical courage sometimes a precondition of moral courage? Was moral courage in Hitler's Germany or Stalin's Russia possible without physical courage, without the guts to face the piano wire, the fist in the face, the boot in the groin, worse? When smug self-congratulation is in full spate in the faculty club lounge he is tempted to say, 'Let's remember that it wasn't Heidegger who tried to blow up Adolf Hitler, it was army officers.'[7]

Nineteenth-century explorers reported of the bare-back riding Ankwe of the Kwalla district of northern Nigeria that they ensured themselves a sticky, adhesive seat on their horses by cutting a strip of hide out of the centre of the animal's back approximately eight inches long and several inches wide. On this raw, bloody surface the rider settled, gluing himself to his beast. The scab was scraped off and the sore freshened up with a knife whenever the horse's owner intended to go for a gallop.

6 Two individuals who refused to give evidence against their leader when called before US congressional hearings and questioned about their roles in aiding US presidents in breaking the law: Lt. Col. Oliver North was connected to Ronald Reagan's 'Iran-Contra' activities (which involved the covert sale of US armaments to Iran); G. Gordon Liddy, known for aggressive and belligerent behaviour, was a leader in the criminal activities associated with the Watergate break-in and the subsequent scandal that drove Richard Nixon from office.

7 Despite being one of the most profound philosophers of his day, Martin Heidegger supported Hitler. Professional officers in Hitler's army attempted to assassinate him on several occasions. The most well-known attempt on Hitler's life occurred on 20 July 1944; Hitler survived the attempt and executed all the conspirators or forced them to poison themselves.

Life went on. Joseph and Andrew paid annual visits to Saskatchewan; sometimes Catherine accompanied them, more frequently she did not. Her family medicine practice had grown to such an extent that it was difficult for her to get away. When she took time off, it was to see her own parents, both now retired and living in Florida. It was no secret that she wasn't missed by her in-laws.

The summer he turned fifteen Andrew trotted out a typical teenager's complaint. It was cruel and unusual punishment to be separated from his girlfriend and his buddies, trapped for ten days in a boring, geeky town where he didn't know a soul. Could he stay home this year? Joseph didn't put any pressure on Andrew to visit his grandparents because secretly he was glad that his son had proved to be as inconstant and disloyal as he had himself.

This was the August Joseph came home to find that his father had cancer. His mother was the one who broke the news to him, not the old man. That night, after supper was finished, the two men sat alone at the kitchen table with a bottle of rye between them while Mary Kelsey watched television in the living room. His father was not a drinking man, it was unusual for him to get drunk, but that night he did. For a long time neither Rupert Kelsey nor his son said anything. Joseph held himself sober, expecting the old man to raise the topic present in both their minds, but when his father did finally speak, it was to claim his innocence of crimes with which he had never been charged.

'One goddamn thing nobody could ever say about me was that I mistreated a horse,' he suddenly said. 'I never mistreated a horse. Am I right or am I wrong?'

Joseph looked at him with surprise. He said he was right. Nobody could ever accuse him of cruelty to a horse.

His father nodded to himself. 'Every horse I ever owned was fat and happy. Nobody can say otherwise. I had horses that died of old age on this place because I wouldn't sell them to the likes of those that wanted to buy them. Died, mind you, *of old age and natural causes.*'

'Yes,' said Joseph quietly.

'So, nobody, *nobody*', the old man repeated with stark emphasis, as if challenging his son to dare deny it, 'can say that Rupert Kelsey didn't do right by any goddamn horse he ever owned. And if they say he did—why they're goddamn liars. When there was money for nothing else around here, I saw to it my horses had oats. And nobody can say different. I never neglected a horse in my life!'

He continued on in a similar vein, justifying himself, offering evidence of his goodness, his kindness, his concern. Joseph wanted him to stop. It made painful listening. It put an ache in Joseph's chest, the kind that managed at one and the same time to feel heavy and sharp, the kind he hadn't carried around in him since he was a boy. It made him want to cry, the most inappropriate thing he could do in front of his father.

'Who's saying you did?' said Joseph. 'Nobody's saying you did.'

Rupert Kelsey picked up his glass with the calculated steadiness of the far gone in drink. 'There's some,' he said, 'who I won't name, who would like to paint me in a certain light. They're wrong. I was never cruel. I never mistreated a horse in my life.'

Joseph could not fathom what any of this struggled to express.

The following morning Joseph's father invited him to come for a ride. Because of the circumstances, Joseph couldn't see how he could refuse. It had been more than a dozen years since he had sat a horse and he felt ridiculous dragging himself aboard, feeling his ligaments tighten and burn alarmingly, his joints creak dryly as the horse plodded along.

His father led him down a little-travelled country lane, which was no more than the scar of old tire tracks. On either side of them the black poplars swirled masses of glittering leaves in the early morning breeze as birds hopped and sang noisily in the branches. A number of wrecked cars had been towed here to rust into the margins of the bush, shards of broken windshield grinning in the jaws of the frames with savage glass teeth. A woodpecker slashed by their horses' noses in the level, swift flight plan of its kind.

His father began to talk, not about his cancer, but in a different fashion from the night before.

He said, 'You won't believe it but I had the same idea as you once—about getting out of here. I thought about going to South America, one of those countries there. Argentina. I saw this book with pictures, all open country, no fences, lots of cattle. Lots of horses. They live on the backs of horses there. I was twenty-one. I thought about going. But then the war came along.' He paused. Joseph saw that in the morning light his father's face looked drawn, that in the light of day he looked sicker than he had in the electric light of the night before. 'Who knows?' his father said to himself. 'It doesn't matter. I likely wouldn't have gone. What do they speak there anyway? Mexican?'

'Yes,' said Joseph, restraining pedantry.

'I wouldn't have been one for learning Mexican,' said his father. 'I didn't learn nothing much in my time.'

They went along a little further in silence. The trail had dwindled away from lack of use. Chokecherry, pincherry, cranberry, and saskatoon bushes crowded in upon them. Tall grass, which had overgrown the tracks, feather-dusted their horses' bellies. The men were constantly fending off branches that threatened their faces, only a narrow channel of washed blue sky snaked above them. It felt to Joseph as if he were being swallowed up in a green dream.

His father said, 'I had another chance to get away when you were about ten—you wouldn't know this. A fellow who was up here from Texas buying horses said I should come down to Houston and break horses for him. He had this operation outside the city where he sold saddle horses to doctors and lawyers and businessmen, rich people. Then he stabled the horses for them, got them coming and going, got them twice. He said to me, "You can't live in Texas unless you own a horse. I got Jew dentists, come down from up north, never seen a horse in their lives, and even they end up owning horses. If they don't have to have one, their kids do. It's a fucking gold mine. You ought to throw in with me." I ought to have. He needed a horse-breaker. He was offering good wages.'

'And why didn't you?'

'Your mother didn't want to go some place strange.' His father laughed. 'You could have grown up a Texan.'

'Just in time for Vietnam,' said Joseph.

The grove of poplar was thinning, they came out into an opening in the bush, into the garish glare of prairie light unsifted by leaves overhead, rousting two large, rusty-brown hawks off the ground where they were tearing at a rabbit. The birds flapped into the air with harsh, indignant screams, inched up the sky steadily, one wing beat at a time, and disappeared from sight.

'I think we better turn back,' said his father.

'You don't have to go back for me,' said Joseph. 'I'll pay for it in stiffness later, but I'm okay for now. You want to go on, go on.'

'I ain't comfortable on a horse much any more,' his father said. 'I got this thing in my belly, after twenty or thirty minutes up on a horse, it hurts like a fucker. I been twenty minutes here. I got twenty minutes back. I don't have another twenty minutes in me.'

To Joseph this was the only direct reference his father made to his cancer. Ever.

It takes him two more years to die. There are inexorable advances of the disease and inexplicable remissions. Joseph is there for the last and final stage, by his bedside. His father is unrecognizable, all the deft grace and assured power of the horseman has been wasted, worn away against the grindstone of illness.

His father has a recurring dream that he recounts to Joseph repeatedly. In the dream it is spring, early April by the look of it, patches of melting snow on bare ground, water running in the gutters, a persistent, pushing spring wind. He is enjoying the warmth, the returning sap of life, when a nagging disquiet surfaces to spoil his pleasure. There is something important he meant to do, has forgotten. Then he remembers. Last fall he'd failed to bring the horses in from the pasture, they have spent the entire winter out, endured blizzards and bitter cold without food and shelter.

The horses are waiting for him at the gate, where they have waited all winter. Skeletons with ribs like barrel hoops under the long matted hair of their winter coats, feeble legs with swollen knees bulging like coconuts, cracked hooves planted in the cold trampled mud, pleading necks stretched across the barbed wire, dull eyes staring.

Joseph tells his father that dreams like this are common, mean nothing. Yet in the last hours of semi-consciousness, in the delirious prelude to death, his father makes him promise, again and again, that he will save the winter horses. 'Save the winter horses,' is his last appeal, to anyone. 'Save the winter horses,' he beseeches.

Nine months after his father's death when it is late at night, very late at night, and Joseph is sitting in his study supposedly working on his fictitious article about Charles Maurras and the Action Française[8] but really reading books on horses, he locates a memory, or a memory locates him. The yellow lamplight loses its harshness, softens and deepens, signalling this is a memory situated in late afternoon, sometime around the supper hour. He is a small boy riding with his father, tucked behind the saddle

8 A radical right-wing party in France, the Action Française, founded by Charles Maurras, promoted violent anti-Semitic and anti-Republican views.

horn in the way not so long ago his father used to carry Andrew, half-hypnotized by the horse's head nodding up and down against the sky in the regular rhythm of a metronome, tick tock, tick tock, lulled by the rolling gait. Full of a child's floating torpor, he is adrift, the tired, fumble-footed shamble of the horse rocking him, rocking him, his heavy-lidded eyes blearing the long grass rippling around him in a vibrant smear of endless green. The heat of the sun burns on his face and chest, the horse burns beneath him, the curve of his father's belly burns on his back. Golden, burning, he is carried off in what direction, where, he doesn't know. In his child's heart this journey is forever, this hour is a day, this day a week, this week a month, this is infinite, this is everything. He falls back against his father and he sleeps.

In Christian art the horse is held to represent courage and generosity. It is the companion of St Martin, St Maurice, St George, and St Victor, all of whom are pictured on horseback. In the catacombs it was, with the fish and the cross, a common symbol. No one is absolutely certain what its meaning was, although it is assumed it represents the swift, fleeting, and transitory character of life.

1992

Rohinton Mistry

b. 1952

Born in Bombay, India, Rohinton Mistry studied mathematics and economics at the University of Bombay before immigrating to Toronto in 1975. He supported himself by working in a bank while taking night courses in English and philosophy at the University of Toronto. When the university instituted an annual short-story contest in 1983, he entered and won. After winning the contest again in the following year (one of the judges was Mavis Gallant, who singled out his story for its excellence), as well as a *Canadian Fiction Magazine* contributor's prize, he began writing full-time. The stories he wrote during this period were collected as *Tales from Firozsha Baag* (1987).

A writer of humane social realism and a creator of intricately realized worlds that recall those of the great nineteenth-century novelists, Mistry focuses his fiction on India's Parsi community from which he himself emerged. Parsis are Zoroastrians who, centuries ago, immigrated to India from Persia (now Iran) to escape persecution. Having become increasingly marginalized in India, many, like Mistry, have left for other countries. *Tales from Firozsha Baag* is a series of linked stories that takes as its subject matter that community and that possibility of departure. It tells of a group of individuals living in one apartment complex in Bombay, some of whom consider emigrating, some of whom actually travel to Toronto. Mistry documents the divided consciousness experienced by those who do depart (as in 'Lend Me Your Light', with its protagonist who feels himself 'throbbing between two lives, the one in Bombay and the one to come in Toronto'); and in the story 'Squatter', he humorously embodies the culture shock that comes from the way even small and commonplace things are done differently in a new environment. (In it, Sarosh comes back home defeated by his inability to adjust to sitting down on western toilets instead of using the squatting posture to which he is accustomed.) 'Squatter' exemplifies the interwoven quality of this collection: Nariman Hansotia, the teller of this tale, appears as a character elsewhere, and his story resolves the enigma that surrounded Sarosh's return when it was mentioned in an earlier story told from the point of view of his aunt.

'Swimming Lessons', anthologized here, is the last story in the collection and serves as a coda to the book. A self-reflexive narrative, it is told by an I-narrator who has written a book of stories that corresponds to *Tales from Firozsha Baag*. Thus, when what seems to be the book we are reading arrives back in Firozsha Baag, where the narrator's parents still live, we share our reading experience with them and listen as they discuss the relationship between art and life. ('Squatter' is similarly self-reflexive: Nariman is said to be the storyteller of Firozsha Baag, and one of his auditors appreciates and comments on his storytelling technique.) A complex and nuanced story, 'Swimming Lessons' suggests the need, experienced by every new immigrant, for the 'lessons' that keep one afloat in an unfamiliar culture—the kind of lessons that enable one to identify the objects of the new environment (as, at the beginning of the story, the narrator has learned to recognize the maple leaf) and that instruct one in the rules of daily life (which govern even things as simple as the protocol of using shared washing machines). But learning such lessons involves making generalizations, and we become aware of the dangers of the general when the narrator encounters the ugly stereotypes that fuel racism and prejudice. Still, he goes on trying to learn from his experiences: we cannot simply dispense with generalizations. And because this story's narrator is also a writer, he thinks about how to 'read' the symbolism and allegorical implications of his own life, and he wonders about its narrative shape, a reminder that the move from the specific to the general is also the basic technique of literature, which uses concrete details to get at larger truths.

Mistry's first novel, *Such a Long Journey* (1991), won a Governor General's Award and a Commonwealth Writers Prize and was shortlisted for the Booker Prize. Set in Bombay in 1971 against the chaotic political backdrop of India's military intervention in the Bangladesh War, it is the story of the kind yet hapless Gustad Noble and his circle of family and friends, whose misfortunes and betrayals are both entangled with and paralleled by the volatile politics and financial intrigues of Indira Gandhi's India. For Mistry's protagonist, the workings of history, political circumstance, and government ineptitude prove to be corrupting forces that threaten the microcosmic order of family life.

Mistry's Giller Prize–winning second novel, *A Fine Balance* (1995), also made the Booker shortlist. Similarly set amid the turmoil of India in the mid-1970s, with backward glances to the monumental events surrounding India's 1947 move to independence, it is about the desperate bonds that develop, in defiance of class and religious barriers, between four unlikely people brought together in a small apartment: Dina, a middle-aged Parsi widow forced to work as a seamstress to maintain her independence; two tailors (whom Dina at first considers 'untouchable') seeking refuge from caste-based government violence that has destroyed their home; and a young Parsi student exiled from his childhood home and alienated from his family. Their hardships, humiliations, and disillusionment play out against a background of a government-declared state of emergency, religious and ethnic violence, and political assassination. The 'balance' to which the title alludes is one that weighs resignation against fortitude, prejudice against acceptance, fear of weakness against the need for compassion, and the corrosive effects of atrocity against the restorative power of the world's beauty.

The dynamics and meaning of family, visible in all of Mistry's fiction, remain central in his most recent novel, *Family Matters* (2002), which is again set in Bombay. Its ailing protagonist, seventy-nine-year-old Nariman Vakeel, tests the limits of filial devotion after he breaks his ankle in a fall and becomes dependent on his overburdened daughter, Roxana, who takes him in when his more affluent stepchildren force him from his own apartment. Nariman's decline—he also has Parkinson's disease—and the strain it puts on Roxana's family parallels that of India and its people, and raises questions about the resiliency of personal identity and the efficacy of emigration. Like all of Mistry's fiction, this novel combines lyric detail with an epic vision that locates the intersections of the public and the personal. Elaborately plotted, his novels create a sense of grand scale that, combined with the deeply mythic level of Indian experience they make visible, gives to every character, no matter how poor or weak, a significant place in a larger whole.

Swimming Lessons

The old man's wheelchair is audible today as he creaks by in the hallway: on some days it's just a smooth whirr. Maybe the way he slumps in it, or the way his weight rests has something to do with it. Down to the lobby he goes, and sits there most of the time, talking to people on their way out or in. That's where he first spoke to me a few days ago. I was waiting for the elevator, back from Eaton's with my new pair of swimming trunks.

'Hullo,' he said. I nodded, smiled.

'Beautiful summer day we've got.'

'Yes,' I said, 'it's lovely outside.'

He shifted the wheelchair to face me squarely. 'How old do you think I am?'

I looked at him blankly, and he said, 'Go on, take a guess.'

I understood the game; he seemed about seventy-five although the hair was still black, so I said, 'Sixty-five?' He made a sound between a chuckle and a wheeze: 'I'll be seventy-seven next month.' Close enough.

I've heard him ask that question several times since, and everyone plays by the rules. Their faked guesses range from sixty to seventy. They pick a lower number when he's more depressed than usual. He reminds me of Grandpa as he sits on the sofa in the lobby, staring out vacantly at the parking lot. Only difference is, he sits with the stillness of stroke victims, while Grandpa's Parkinson's disease would bounce his thighs and legs and arms all over the place. When he could no longer hold the *Bombay Samachar* steady enough to read, Grandpa took to sitting on the veranda and staring emptily at the traffic passing outside Firozsha Baag. Or waving to anyone who went by in the compound: Rustomji, Nariman Hansotia in his 1932 Mercedes-Benz, the fat ayah Jaakaylee with her shopping-bag, the kuchrawalli with her basket and long bamboo broom.

The Portuguese woman across the hall has told me a little about the old man. She is the communicator for the apartment building. To gather and disseminate information, she takes the liberty of unabashedly throwing open the door when newsworthy events transpire. Not for Portuguese Woman the furtive peerings from thin cracks or spyholes. She reminds me of a character in a movie, *Barefoot in The Park* I think it was, who left empty beer cans by the landing for anyone passing to stumble and give her the signal. But PW does not need beer cans. The gutang-khutang of the elevator opening and closing is enough.

The old man's daughter looks after him. He was living alone till his stroke, which coincided with his youngest daughter's divorce in Vancouver. She returned to him and they moved into this low-rise in Don Mills. PW says the daughter talks to no one in the building but takes good care of her father.

Mummy used to take good care of Grandpa, too, till things became complicated and he was moved to the Parsi General Hospital. Parkinsonism and osteoporosis laid him low. The doctor explained that Grandpa's hip did not break because he fell, but he fell because the hip, gradually growing brittle, snapped on that fatal day. That's what osteoporosis does, hollows out the bones and turns effect into cause. It has an unusually high incidence in the Parsi community, he said, but did not say why. Just one of those mysterious things. We are the chosen people where osteoporosis is concerned. And divorce. The Parsi community has the highest divorce rate in India. It also claims to be the most westernized community in India. Which is the result of the other? Confusion again, of cause and effect.

The hip was put in traction. Single-handed, Mummy struggled valiantly with bedpans and dressings for bedsores which soon appeared like grim spectres on his back. *Mamaiji*, bent double with her weak back, could give no assistance. My help would be enlisted to roll him over on his side while Mummy changed the dressing. But after three months, the doctor pronounced a patch upon Grandpa's lungs, and the male ward of Parsi General swallowed him up. There was no money for a private nursing home. I went to see him once, at Mummy's insistence. She used to say that the blessings of an old person were the most valuable and potent of all, they would last my whole life long. The ward had rows and rows of beds; the din was enormous, the smells nauseating, and it was just as well that Grandpa passed most of his time in a less than conscious state.

But I should have gone to see him more often. Whenever Grandpa went out, while he still could in the days before parkinsonism, he would bring back pink and white sugar-coated almonds for Percy and me. Every time I remember Grandpa, I remember that; and then I think: I should have gone to see him more often. That's what I also thought when our telephone-owning neighbour, esteemed by all for that reason, sent his son to tell us the hospital had phoned that Grandpa died an hour ago.

The postman rang the doorbell the way he always did, long and continuous; Mother went to open it, wanting to give him a piece of her mind but thought better of it, she did not want to risk the vengeance of postmen, it was so easy for them to destroy letters; workers nowadays thought no end of themselves, strutting around like peacocks, ever since all this Shiv Sena agitation about Maharashtra for Maharashtrians, threatening strikes and Bombay bundh *all the time, with no respect for the public; bus drivers and conductors were the worst, behaving as if they owned the buses and were doing favours to commuters, pulling the bell before you were in the bus, the driver purposely braking and moving with big jerks to make the standees lose their balance, the conductor so rude if you did not have the right change.*

But when she saw the airmail envelope with a Canadian stamp her face lit up, she said wait to the postman, and went in for a fifty paisa piece, a little baksheesh *for you, she told him, then shut the door and kissed the envelope, went in running, saying my son has written, my son has sent a letter, and Father looked up from the newspaper and said, don't get too excited, first read it, you know what kind of letters he writes, a few lines of empty words, I'm fine, hope you are all right, your loving son—that kind of writing I don't call letter-writing.*

Then Mother opened the envelope and took out one small page and began to read silently, and the joy brought to her face by the letter's arrival began to ebb; Father saw it happening and knew he was right, he said read aloud, let me also hear what our son is writing this time, so Mother read: My dear Mummy and Daddy, Last winter was terrible, we had record-breaking low temperatures all through February and March, and the first official day of spring was colder than the first official day of winter had been, but it's getting warmer now. Looks like it will be a nice warm summer. You asked about my new apartment. It's small, but not bad at all. This is just a quick note to let you know I'm fine, so you won't worry about me. Hope everything is okay at home.

After Mother put it back in the envelope, Father said everything about his life is locked in silence and secrecy, I still don't understand why he bothered to visit us last year if he had nothing to say; every letter of his has been a quick note so we won't worry—what does he think we worry about, his health, in that country everyone eats well whether they work or not, he should be worrying about us with all the black market and rationing, has he forgotten already how he used to go to the ration-shop and wait in line every week; and what kind of apartment description is that, not bad at all; and if it is a Canadian weather report I need from him, I can go with Nariman Hansotia from A Block to the Cawasji Framji Memorial Library and read all about it, there they get newspapers from all over the world.

The sun is hot today. Two women are sunbathing on the stretch of patchy lawn at the periphery of the parking lot. I can see them clearly from my kitchen. They're wearing bikinis and I'd love to take a closer look. But I have no binoculars. Nor do I have a car to saunter out to and pretend to look under the hood. They're both luscious and gleaming. From time to time they smear lotion over their skin, on the bellies, on the inside of the thighs, on the shoulders. Then one of them gets the other to undo the string of her top and spread some there. She lies on her stomach with the straps undone. I wait. I pray that the heat and haze make her forget, when it's time to turn over, that the straps are undone.

But the sun is not hot enough to work this magic for me. When it's time to come in, she flips over, deftly holding up the cups, and reties the top. They arise, pick up towels, lotions, and magazines, and return to the building.

This is my chance to see them closer. I race down the stairs to the lobby. The old man says hullo. 'Down again?'

'My mailbox,' I mumble.

'It's Saturday,' he chortles. For some reason he finds it extremely funny. My eye is on the door leading in from the parking lot.

Through the glass panel I see them approaching. I hurry to the elevator and wait. In the dimly lit lobby I can see their eyes are having trouble adjusting after the bright sun. They don't seem as attractive as they did from the kitchen window. The elevator arrives and I hold it open, inviting them in with what I think is a gallant flourish. Under the fluorescent glare in the elevator I see their wrinkled skin, aging hands, sagging bottoms, varicose veins. The lustrous trick of sun and lotion and distance has ended.

I step out and they continue to the third floor. I have Monday night to look forward to, my first swimming lesson. The high school behind the apartment building is offering, among its usual assortment of macramé and ceramics and pottery classes, a class for non-swimming adults.

The woman at the registration desk is quite friendly. She even gives me the opening to satisfy the compulsion I have about explaining my non-swimming status.

'Are you from India?' she asks. I nod. 'I hope you don't mind my asking, but I was curious because an Indian couple, husband and wife, also registered a few minutes ago. Is swimming not encouraged in India?'

'On the contrary,' I say. 'Most Indians swim like fish. I'm an exception to the rule. My house was five minutes walking distance from Chaupatty beach in Bombay. It's one of the most beautiful beaches in Bombay, or was, before the filth took over. Anyway, even though we lived so close to it, I never learned to swim. It's just one of those things.'

'Well,' says the woman, 'that happens sometimes. Take me, for instance. I never learned to ride a bicycle. It was the mounting that used to scare me, I was afraid of falling.' People have lined up behind me. 'It's been very nice talking to you,' she says, 'hope you enjoy the course.'

The art of swimming had been trapped between the devil and the deep blue sea. The devil was money, always scarce, and kept the private swimming clubs out of reach; the deep blue sea of Chaupatty beach was grey and murky with garbage, too filthy to swim in. Every so often we would muster our courage and Mummy would take me there to try and teach me. But a few minutes of paddling was all we could endure. Sooner or later something would float up against our legs or thighs or waists, depending on how deep we'd gone in, and we'd be revulsed and stride out to the sand.

Water imagery in my life is recurring. Chaupatty beach, now the high-school swimming pool. The universal symbol of life and regeneration did nothing but frustrate me. Perhaps the swimming pool will overturn that failure.

When images and symbols abound in this manner, sprawling or rolling across the page without guile or artifice, one is prone to say, how obvious, how skilless; symbols, after all, should be still and gentle as dewdrops, tiny, yet shining with a world of meaning. But what happens when, on the page of life itself, one encounters the ever-moving, all-engirdling sprawl of the filthy sea? Dewdrops and oceans both have their rightful places; Nariman Hansotia certainly knew that when he told his stories to the boys of Firozsha Baag.

The sea of Chaupatty was fated to endure the finales of life's everyday functions. It seemed that the dirtier it became, the more crowds it attracted: street urchins and beggars and beachcombers, looking through the junk that washed up. (Or was it the crowds that made it dirtier?—another instance of cause and effect blurring and evading identification.)

Too many religious festivals also used the sea as repository for their finales. Its use should have been rationed, like rice and kerosene. On Ganesh Chaturthi, clay idols of the god Ganesh, adorned with garlands and all manner of finery, were carried in processions to the accompaniment of drums and a variety of wind instruments. The music got more frenzied the closer the procession got to Chaupatty and to the moment of immersion.

Then there was Coconut Day, which was never as popular as Ganesh Chaturthi. From a bystander's viewpoint, coconuts chucked into the sea do not provide as much of a spectacle. We used the sea, too, to deposit the leftovers from Parsi religious ceremonies, things such as flowers, or the ashes of the sacred sandalwood fire, which just could not be dumped with the regular garbage but had to be entrusted to the care of Avan Yazad, the guardian of the sea. And things which were of no use but which no one had the heart to destroy were also given to Avan Yazad. Such as old photographs.

After Grandpa died, some of his things were flung out to sea. It was high tide; we always checked the newspaper when going to perform these disposals; an ebb would mean a long walk in squelchy sand before finding water. Most of the things were probably washed up on shore. But we tried to throw them as far out as possible, then waited a few minutes; if they did not float back right away we would pretend they were in the permanent safekeeping of Avan Yazad, which was a comforting thought. I can't remember everything we sent out to sea, but his brush and comb were in the parcel, his *kusti,* and some Kemadrin pills, which he used to take to keep the parkinsonism under control.

Our paddling sessions stopped for lack of enthusiasm on my part. Mummy wasn't too keen either, because of the filth. But my main concern was the little guttersnipes, like naked fish with little buoyant penises, taunting me with their skills, swimming underwater and emerging unexpectedly all around me, or pretending to masturbate—I think they were too young to achieve ejaculation. It was embarrassing. When I look back, I'm surprised that Mummy and I kept going as long as we did.

I examine the swimming-trunks I bought last week. Surf King, says the label, Made in Canada–Fabriqué Au Canada. I've been learning bits and pieces of French from bilingual labels at the supermarket too. These trunks are extremely sleek and streamlined hipsters, the distance from waistband to pouch tip the barest minimum. I wonder how everything will stay in place, not that I'm boastful about my endowments. I try them on, and feel the tip of my member lingers perilously close to the exit. Too close, in fact, to conceal the exigencies of my swimming lesson fantasy: a gorgeous woman in the class for non-swimmers, at whose sight I will be instantly aroused, and she, spying the shape of my desire, will look me straight in the eye with her intentions; she will come home with me, to taste the pleasures of my delectable Asian brown body whose strangeness has intrigued her and unleashed uncontrollable surges of passion inside her throughout the duration of the swimming lesson.

I drop the Eaton's bag and wrapper in the garbage can. The swimming-trunks cost fifteen dollars, same as the fee for the ten weekly lessons. The garbage bag is almost full. I tie it up and take it outside. There is a medicinal smell in the hallway; the old man must have just returned to his apartment.

PW opens her door and says, 'Two ladies from the third floor were lying in the sun this morning. In bikinis.'

'That's nice,' I say, and walk to the incinerator chute. She reminds me of Najamai in Firozsha Baag, except that Najamai employed a bit more subtlety while going about her life's chosen work.

PW withdraws and shuts her door.

Mother had to reply because Father said he did not want to write to his son till his son had something sensible to write to him, his questions had been ignored long enough, and if he wanted to keep his life a secret, fine, he would get no letters from his father.

But after Mother started the letter he went and looked over her shoulder, telling her what to ask him, because if they kept on writing the same questions, maybe he would understand how interested they were in knowing about things over there; Father said go on, ask him what his work is at the insurance company, tell him to take some courses at night school, that's how everyone moves ahead over there, tell him not to be discouraged if his job is just clerical right now, hard work will get him ahead, remind him he is a Zoroastrian: manashni, gavashni, kunashni, *better write the translation also: good thoughts, good words, good deeds—he must have forgotten what it means, and tell him to say prayers and do* kusti *at least twice a day.*

Writing it all down sadly, Mother did not believe he wore his sudra *and* kusti *anymore, she would be very surprised if he remembered any of the prayers; when she had asked him if he needed new* sudras *he said not to take any trouble because the Zoroastrian Society of Ontario imported them from Bombay for their members, and this sounded like a story he was making up, but she was leaving it in the hands of God, ten thousand miles away there was nothing she could do but write a letter and hope for the best.*

Then she sealed it, and Father wrote the address on it as usual because his writing was much neater than hers, handwriting was important in the address and she did not want the postman in Canada to make any mistake; she took it off to the post office herself, it was impossible to trust anyone to mail it ever since the postage rates went up because people just tore off the stamps for their own use and threw away the letter, the only safe way was to hand it over the counter and make the clerk cancel the stamp before your own eyes.

Berthe, the building superintendent, is yelling at her son in the parking lot. He tinkers away with his van. This happens every fine-weathered Sunday. It must be the van that Berthe dislikes because I've seen mother and son together in other quite amicable situations.

Berthe is a big Yugoslavian with high cheekbones. Her nationality was disclosed to me by PW. Berthe speaks a very rough-hewn English, I've overheard her in the lobby scolding tenants for late rents and leaving dirty lint screens in the dryers. It's exciting to listen to her, her words fall like rocks and boulders, and one can never tell where or how the next few will drop. But her Slavic yells at her son are a different matter, the words fly swift and true, well-aimed missiles that never miss. Finally, the son slams down the hood in disgust, wipes his hands on a rag, accompanies mother Berthe inside.

Berthe's husband has a job in a factory. But he loses several days of work every month when he succumbs to the booze, a word Berthe uses often in her Slavic tirades on those days, the only one I can understand, as it clunks down heavily out of the tight-flying formation of Yugoslavian sentences. He lolls around in the lobby, submitting passively to his wife's tongue-lashings. The bags under his bloodshot eyes, his stringy moustache, stubbled chin, dirty hair are so vulnerable to the poison-laden barbs (poison works the same way in any language) emanating from deep within the powerful watermelon bosom. No one's presence can embarrass or dignify her into silence.

No one except the old man who arrives now. 'Good morning,' he says, and Berthe turns, stops yelling, and smiles. Her husband rises, positions the wheelchair at the favourite angle. The lobby will be peaceful as long as the old man is there.

It was hopeless. My first swimming lesson. The water terrified me. When did that happen, I wonder, I used to love splashing at Chaupatty, carried about by the waves. And this was only a swimming pool. Where did all that terror come from? I'm trying to remember.

Armed with my Surf King I enter the high school and go to the pool area. A sheet with instructions for the new class is pinned to the bulletin board. All students must shower and then assemble at eight by the shallow end. As I enter the showers three young boys, probably from a previous class, emerge. One of them holds his nose. The second begins to hum, under his breath: Paki Paki, smell like curry. The third says to the first two: pretty soon all the water's going to taste of curry. They leave.

It's a mixed class, but the gorgeous woman of my fantasy is missing. I have to settle for another, in a pink one-piece suit, with brown hair and a bit of a stomach. She must be about thirty-five. Plain-looking.

The instructor is called Ron. He gives us a pep talk, sensing some nervousness in the group. We're finally all in the water, in the shallow end. He demonstrates floating on the back, then asks for a volunteer. The pink one-piece suit wades forward. He supports her, tells her to lean back and let her head drop in the water.

She does very well. And as we all regard her floating body, I see what was not visible outside the pool: her bush, curly bits of it, straying out at the pink Spandex V. Tongues of water lapping against her delta, as if caressing it teasingly, make the brown hair come alive in a most tantalizing manner. The crests and troughs of little waves, set off by the movement of our bodies in a circle around her, dutifully irrigate her; the curls alternately wave free inside the crest, then adhere to her wet thighs, beached by the inevitable trough. I could watch this forever, and I wish the floating demonstration would never end.

Next we are shown how to grasp the rail and paddle, face down in the water. Between practising floating and paddling, the hour is almost gone. I have been trying to observe the pink one-piece suit, getting glimpses of her straying pubic hair from various angles. Finally, Ron wants a volunteer for the last demonstration, and I go forward. To my horror he leads the class to the deep end. Fifteen feet of water. It is so blue, and I can see the bottom. He picks up a metal hoop attached to a long wooden stick. He wants me to grasp the hoop, jump in the water, and paddle, while he guides me by the stick. Perfectly safe, he tells me. A demonstration of how paddling propels the body.

It's too late to back out; besides, I'm so terrified I couldn't find the words to do so even if I wanted to. Everything he says I do as if in a trance. I don't remember the moment of jumping. The next thing I know is, I'm swallowing water and floundering, hanging on to the hoop for dear life. Ron draws me to the rails and helps me out. The class applauds.

We disperse and one thought is on my mind: what if I'd lost my grip? Fifteen feet of water under me. I shudder and take deep breaths. That is it. I'm not coming next week. This instructor is an irresponsible person. Or he does not value the lives of non-white immigrants. I remember the three teenagers. Maybe the swimming pool is the hangout of some racist group, bent on eliminating all non-white swimmers, to keep their waters pure and their white sisters unogled.

The elevator takes me upstairs. Then gutang-khutang. PW opens her door as I turn the corridor of medicinal smells. 'Berthe was screaming loudly at her husband tonight,' she tells me.

'Good for her', I say, and she frowns indignantly at me.

The old man is in the lobby. He's wearing thick wool gloves. He wants to know how the swimming was, must have seen me leaving with my towel yesterday. Not bad, I say.

'I used to swim a lot. Very good for the circulation.' He wheezes. 'My feet are cold all the time. Cold as ice. Hands too.'

Summer is winding down, so I say stupidly, 'Yes, it's not so warm any more.'

The thought of the next swimming lesson sickens me. But as I comb through the memories of that terrifying Monday, I come upon the straying curls of brown pubic hair. Inexorably drawn by them, I decide to go.

It's a mistake, of course. This time I'm scared even to venture in the shallow end. When everyone has entered the water and I'm the only one outside, I feel a little foolish and slide in.

Instructor Ron says we should start by reviewing the floating technique. I'm in no hurry. I watch the pink one-piece pull the swim-suit down around her cheeks and flip back to achieve perfect flotation. And then reap disappointment. The pink Spandex triangle is perfectly streamlined today, nothing strays, not a trace of fuzz, not one filament, not even a sign of post-depilation irritation. Like the airbrushed parts of glamour magazine models. The barrenness of her impeccably packaged apex is a betrayal. Now she is shorn like the other women in the class. Why did she have to do it?

The weight of this disappointment makes the water less manageable, more lung-penetrating. With trepidation, I float and paddle my way through the remainder of the hour, jerking my head out every two seconds and breathing deeply, to continually shore up a supply of precious, precious air without, at the same time, seeming too anxious and losing my dignity.

I don't attend the remaining classes. After I've missed three, Ron the instructor telephones. I tell him I've had the flu and am still feeling poorly, but I'll try to be there the following week.

He does not call again. My Surf King is relegated to an unused drawer. Total losses: one fantasy plus thirty dollars. And no watery rebirth. The swimming pool, like Chaupatty beach, has produced a stillbirth. But there is a difference. Water means regeneration only if it is pure and cleansing. Chaupatty was filthy, the pool was not. Failure to swim through filth must mean something other than failure of rebirth—failure of symbolic death? Does that equal success of symbolic life? death of a symbolic failure? death of a symbol? What is the equation?

The postman did not bring a letter but a parcel, he was smiling because he knew that every time something came from Canada his baksheesh *was guaranteed, and this time because it was a parcel Mother gave him a whole rupee, she was quite excited, there were so many stickers on it besides the stamps, one for Small Parcel, another Printed Papers, a red sticker saying Insured; she showed it to Father, and opened it, then put both hands on her cheeks, not able to speak because the surprise and happiness was so great, tears came to her eyes and she could not stop smiling, till Father became impatient to know and finally got up and came to the table.*

When he saw it he was surprised and happy too, he began to grin, then hugged Mother saying our son is a writer, and we didn't even know it, he never told us a thing, here we are thinking he is still clerking away at the insurance company, and he has written a book of stories, all these years in school and college he kept his talent hidden, making us think he was just like one of the boys in the Baag, shouting and playing the fool in the compound, and now what a surprise; then Father opened the book and began reading it, heading back to the easy chair, and Mother so excited, still holding his arm, walked with him, saying it was not fair him reading it first, she wanted to read it too, and they agreed that he would read the first story, then give it to her so she could also read it, and they would take turns in that manner.

Mother removed the staples from the padded envelope in which he had mailed the book, and threw them away, then straightened the folded edges of the envelope and put it away safely with the other envelopes and letters she had collected since he left.

The leaves are beginning to fall. The only ones I can identify are maple. The days are dwindling like the leaves. I've started a habit of taking long walks every evening. The old man is in the lobby when I leave, he waves as I go by. By the time I'm back, the lobby is usually empty.

Today I was woken up by a grating sound outside that made my flesh crawl. I went to the window and saw Berthe raking the leaves in the parking lot. Not in the expanse of patchy lawn on the periphery, but in the parking lot proper. She was raking the black tarred surface. I went back to bed and dragged a pillow over my head, not releasing it till noon.

When I return from my walk in the evening, PW, summoned by the elevator's gutang-khutang, says, 'Berthe filled six big black garbage bags with leaves today.'

'Six bags!' I say. 'Wow!'

Since the weather turned cold, Berthe's son does not tinker with his van on Sundays under my window. I'm able to sleep late.

Around eleven, there's a commotion outside. I reach out and switch on the clock radio. It's a sunny day, the window curtains are bright. I get up, curious, and see a black Olds Ninety-Eight in the parking lot, by the entrance to the building. The old man is in his wheelchair, bundled up, with a scarf wound several times round his neck as though to immobilize it, like a surgical collar. His daughter and another man, the car-owner, are helping him from the wheelchair into the front seat, encouraging him with words like: that's it, easy does it, attaboy. From the open door of the lobby, Berthe is shouting encouragement too, but hers is confined to one word: yah, repeated at different levels of pitch and volume, with variations on vowel-length. The stranger could be the old man's son, he has the same jet black hair and piercing eyes.

Maybe the old man is not well, it's an emergency. But I quickly scrap that thought—this isn't Bombay, an ambulance would have arrived. They're probably taking him out for a ride. If he is his son, where has he been all this time, I wonder.

The old man finally settles in the front seat, the wheelchair goes in the trunk, and they're off. The one I think is the son looks up and catches me at the window before I can move away, so I wave, and he waves back.

In the afternoon I take down a load of clothes to the laundry room. Both machines have completed their cycles, the clothes inside are waiting to be transferred to dryers. Should I remove them and place them on top of a dryer, or wait? I decide to wait. After a few minutes, two women arrive, they are in bathrobes, and smoking. It takes me a while to realize that these are the two disappointments who were sunbathing in bikinis last summer.

'You didn't have to wait, you could have removed the clothes and carried on, dear,' says one. She has a Scottish accent. It's one of the few I've learned to identify. Like maple leaves.

'Well,' I say, 'some people might not like strangers touching their clothes.'

'You're not a stranger, dear,' she says, 'you live in this building, we've seen you before.'

'Besides, your hands are clean,' the other one pipes in. 'You can touch my things any time you like.'

Horny old cow. I wonder what they've got on under their bathrobes. Not much, I find, as they bend over to place their clothes in the dryers.

'See you soon,' they say, and exit, leaving me behind in an erotic wake of smoke and perfume and deep images of cleavages. I start the washers and depart, and when I come back later, the dryers are empty.

PW tells me, 'The old man's son took him out for a drive today. He has a big beautiful black car.'

I see my chance, and shoot back: 'Olds Ninety-Eight.'

'What?'

'The car,' I explain, 'it's an Oldsmobile Ninety-Eight.'

She does not like this at all, my giving her information. She is visibly nettled, and retreats with a sour face.

Mother and Father read the first five stories, and she was very sad after reading some of them, she said he must be so unhappy there, all his stories are about Bombay, he remembers every little thing about his childhood, he is thinking about it all the time even though he is ten thousand miles away, my poor son, I think he misses his home and us and everything he left behind, because if he likes it over there why would he not write stories about that, there must be so many new ideas that his new life could give him.

But Father did not agree with this, he said it did not mean that he was unhappy, all writers worked in the same way, they used their memories and experiences and made stories out of them, changing some things, adding some, imagining some, all writers were very good at remembering details of their lives.

Mother said, how can you be sure that he is remembering because he's a writer, or whether he started to write because he is unhappy and thinks of his past, and wants to save it all by making stories of it; and Father said that is not a sensible question, anyway, it is now my turn to read the next story.

The first snow has fallen, and the air is crisp. It's not very deep, about two inches, just right to go for a walk in. I've been told that immigrants from hot countries always enjoy the snow the first year, maybe for a couple of years more, then inevitably the dread sets in, and the approach of winter gets them fretting and moping. On the other hand, if it hadn't been for my conversation with the woman at the swimming registration desk, they might now be saying that India is a nation of non-swimmers.

Berthe is outside, shovelling the snow off the walkway in the parking lot. She has a heavy, wide pusher which she wields expertly.

The old radiators in the apartment alarm me incessantly. They continue to broadcast a series of variations on death throes, and go from hot to cold and cold to hot at will, there's no controlling their temperature. I speak to Berthe about it in the lobby. The old man is there too, his chin seems to have sunk deeper into his chest, and his face is a yellowish grey.

'Nothing, not to worry about anything,' says Berthe, dropping rough-hewn chunks of language around me. 'Radiator no work, you tell me. You feel cold, you come to me, I keep you warm,' and she opens her arms wide, laughing. I step back, and she advances, her breasts preceding her like the gallant prows of two ice-breakers. She looks at the old man to see if he is appreciating the act: 'You no feel scared, I keep you safe and warm.'

But the old man is staring outside, at the flakes of falling snow. What thoughts is he thinking as he watches them? Of childhood days, perhaps, and snowmen with hats and pipes, and snowball fights, and white Christmases, and Christmas trees? What will I think of, old in this country, when I sit and watch the snow come down? For me, it is already too late for snowmen and snowball fights, and all I will have is thoughts about childhood thoughts and dreams, built around snowscapes and winter-wonderlands on the Christmas cards so popular in Bombay; my snowmen and snowball fights and Christmas trees are in the pages of Enid Blyton's books, dispersed amidst the adventures of the Famous Five, and the Five Find-Outers, and the Secret Seven. My snowflakes are even less forgettable than the old man's, for they never melt.

It finally happened. The heat went. Not the usual intermittent coming and going, but out completely. Stone cold. The radiators are like ice. And so is everything else. There's no hot water. Naturally. It's the hot water that goes through the rads and heats them. Or is it the other way around? Is there no hot water because the rads have stopped circulating it? I don't care, I'm too cold to sort out the cause and effect relationship. Maybe there is no connection at all.

I dress quickly, put on my winter jacket, and go down to the lobby. The elevator is not working because the power is out, so I take the stairs. Several people are gathered, and Berthe has announced that she has telephoned the office, they are sending a man. I go back up the stairs. It's only one floor, the elevator is just a bad habit. Back in Firozsha Baag they were broken most of the time. The stairway enters the corridor outside the old man's apartment, and I think of his cold feet and hands. Poor man, it must be horrible for him without heat.

As I walk down the long hallway, I feel there's something different but can't pin it down. I look at the carpet, the ceiling, the wallpaper: it all seems the same. Maybe it's the freezing cold that imparts a feeling of difference.

PW opens her door: 'The old man had another stroke yesterday. They took him to the hospital.'

The medicinal smell. That's it. It's not in the hallway any more.

In the stories that he'd read so far Father said that all the Parsi families were poor or middle-class, but that was okay; nor did he mind that the seeds for the stories were picked from the sufferings of their own lives; but there should also have been something positive about Parsis, there was so much to be proud of: the great Tatas and their contribution to the steel industry, or Sir Dinshaw Petit in the textile industry who made Bombay the Manchester of the East, or Dadabhai Naoroji in the freedom movement, where he was the first to use the word swaraj, *and the first to be elected to the British Parliament where he carried on his campaign; he should have found some way to bring some of these wonderful facts into his stories, what would people reading these stories think, those who did not know about Parsis—that the whole community was full of cranky, bigoted people; and in reality it was the richest, most advanced and philanthropic community in India, and he did not need to tell his own son that Parsis had a reputation for being generous and family-oriented. And he could have written something also about the historic background, how Parsis came to India from Persia because of Islamic persecution in the seventh century, and were the descendants of Cyrus the Great and the magnificent Persian Empire. He could have made a story of all this, couldn't he?*

Mother said what she liked best was his remembering everything so well, how beautifully he wrote about it all, even the sad things, and though he changed some of it, and used his imagination, there was truth in it.

My hope is, Father said, that there will be some story based on his Canadian experience, that way we will know something about our son's life there, if not through his letters then in his stories; so far they are all about Parsis and Bombay, and the one with a little bit about Toronto, where a man perches on top of the toilet, is shameful and disgusting although it is funny at times and did make me laugh, I have to admit, but where does he get such an imagination from, what is the point of such a fantasy; and Mother said that she would also enjoy some stories about Toronto and the people there; it puzzles me, she said, why he writes nothing about it, especially since you say that writers use their own experience to make stories out of.

Then Father said this is true, but he is probably not using his Toronto experience because it is too early; what do you mean, too early, asked Mother and Father explained it takes a writer about ten years time after an experience before he is able to use it in his writing, it takes that long to be absorbed internally and understood, thought out and thought about, over and over again, he haunts it and it haunts him if it is valuable enough, till the writer is comfortable with it to be able to use it as he wants; but this is only one theory I read somewhere, it may or may not be true.

That means, said Mother, that his childhood in Bombay and our home here is the most valuable thing in his life just now, because he is able to remember it all to write about it, and you were so bitterly saying he is forgetting where he came from; and that may be true, said Father, but that is not what the theory means, according to the theory he is writing of these things because they are far enough in the past for him to deal with objectively, he is able to achieve what critics call artistic distance, without emotions interfering; and what do you mean emotions, said Mother, you are saying he does not feel anything for his characters, how can he write so beautifully about so many sad things without any feelings in his heart?

But before Father could explain more, about beauty and emotion and inspiration and imagination, Mother took the book and said it was her turn now and too much theory she did not want to listen to, it was confusing and did not make as much sense as reading the stories, she would read them her way and Father could read them his.

My books on the windowsill have been damaged. Ice has been forming on the inside ledge, which I did not notice, and melting when the sun shines in. I spread them in a corner of the living room to dry out.

The winter drags on. Berthe wields her snow pusher as expertly as ever, but there are signs of weariness in her performance. Neither husband nor son is ever seen outside with a shovel. Or anywhere else, for that matter. It occurs to me that the son's van is missing, too.

The medicinal smell is in the hall again, I sniff happily and look forward to seeing the old man in the lobby. I go downstairs and peer into the mailbox, see the blue and magenta of an Indian aerogramme with Don Mills, Ontario, Canada in Father's flawless hand through the slot.

I pocket the letter and enter the main lobby. The old man is there, but not in his usual place. He is not looking out through the glass door. His wheelchair is facing a bare wall where the wallpaper is torn in places. As though he is not interested in the outside world any more, having finished with all that, and now it's time to see inside. What does he see inside, I wonder? I go up to him and say hullo. He says hullo without raising his sunken chin. After a few seconds his grey countenance faces me. 'How old do you think I am?' His eyes are dull and glazed; he is looking even further inside than I first presumed.

'Well, let's see, you're probably close to sixty-four.'

'I'll be seventy-eight next August.' But he does not chuckle or wheeze. Instead, he continues softly, 'I wish my feet did not feel so cold all the time. And my hands.' He lets his chin fall again.

In the elevator I start opening the aerogramme, a tricky business because a crooked tear means lost words. Absorbed in this while emerging, I don't notice PW occupying the centre of the hallway, arms folded across her chest: 'They had a big fight. Both of them have left.'

I don't immediately understand her agitation. 'What . . . who?'

'Berthe. Husband and son both left her. Now she is all alone.'

Her tone and stance suggest that we should not be standing here talking but do something to bring Berthe's family back. 'That's very sad,' I say, and go in. I picture father and son in the van, driving away, driving across the snow-covered country, in the dead of winter, away from wife and mother; away to where? how far will they go? Not son's van nor father's booze can take them far enough. And the further they go, the more they'll remember, they can take it from me.

All the stories were read by Father and Mother, and they were sorry when the book was finished, they felt they had come to know their son better now, yet there was much more to know, they wished there were many more stories; and this is what they mean, said Father, when they say that the whole story can never be told, the whole truth can never be known; what do you mean, they say, asked Mother, who they, and Father said writers, poets, philosophers. I don't care what they say, said Mother, my son will write as much or as little as he wants to, and if I can read it I will be happy.

The last story they liked the best of all because it had the most in it about Canada, and now they felt they knew at least a little bit, even if it was a very little bit, about his day-to-day life in his apartment; and Father said if he continues to write about such things he will become popular because I am sure they are interested there in reading about life through the eyes of an immigrant, it provides a different viewpoint; the only danger is if he changes and becomes so much like them that he will write like one of them and lose the important difference.

The bathroom needs cleaning. I open a new can of Ajax and scour the tub. Sloshing with mug from bucket was standard bathing procedure in the bathrooms of Firozsha Baag, so my preference now is always for a shower. I've never used the tub as yet; besides, it would be too much like Chaupatty or the swimming pool, wallowing in my own dirt. Still, it must be cleaned.

When I've finished, I prepare for a shower. But the clean gleaming tub and the nearness of the vernal equinox give me the urge to do something different today. I find the drain plug in the bathroom cabinet, and run the bath.

I've spoken so often to the old man, but I don't know his name. I should have asked him the last time I saw him, when his wheelchair was facing the bare wall because he had seen all there was to see outside and it was time to see what was inside. Well, tomorrow. Or better yet, I can look it up in the directory in the lobby. Why didn't I think of that before? It will only have an initial and a last name, but then I can surprise him with: hullo Mr Wilson, or whatever it is.

The bath is full. Water imagery is recurring in my life: Chaupatty beach, swimming pool, bathtub. I step in and immerse myself up to the neck. It feels good. The hot water loses its opacity when the chlorine, or whatever it is, has cleared. My hair is still dry. I close my eyes, hold my breath, and dunk my head. Fighting the panic, I stay under and count to thirty. I come out, clear my lungs and breathe deeply.

I do it again. This time I open my eyes under water, and stare blindly without seeing, it takes all my will to keep the lids from closing. Then I am slowly able to discern the underwater objects. The drain plug looks different, slightly distorted; there is a hair trapped between the hole and the plug, it waves and dances with the movement of the water. I come up, refresh my lungs, examine quickly the overwater world of the washroom, and go in again. I do it several times, over and over. The world outside the water I have seen a lot of, it is now time to see what is inside.

The spring session for adult non-swimmers will begin in a few days at the high school. I must not forget the registration date.

The dwindled days of winter are now all but forgotten; they have grown and attained a respectable span. I resume my evening walks, it's spring, and a vigorous thaw is on. The snowbanks are melting, the sound of water on its gushing, gurgling journey to the drains is beautiful. I plan to buy a book of trees, so I can identify more than the maple as they begin to bloom.

When I return to the building, I wipe my feet energetically on the mat because some people are entering behind me, and I want to set a good example. Then I go to the board with its little plastic letters and numbers. The old man's apartment is the one on the corner by the stairway, that makes it number 201. I run down the list, come to 201, but there are no little white plastic letters beside it. Just the empty black rectangle with holes where the letters would be squeezed in. That's strange. Well, I can introduce myself to him, then ask his name.

However, the lobby was empty. I take the elevator, exit at the second floor, wait for the gutang-khutang. It does not come, the door closes noiselessly, smoothly. Berthe has been at work, or has made sure someone else has. PW's cue has been lubricated out of existence.

But she must have the ears of a cockroach. She is waiting for me. I whistle my way down the corridor. She fixes me with an accusing look. She waits till I stop whistling, then says: 'You know the old man died last night.'

I cease groping for my key. She turns to go and I take a step towards her, my hand still in my trouser pocket. 'Did you know his name?' I ask, but she leaves without answering.

Then Mother said, the part I like best in the last story is about Grandpa, where he wonders if Grandpa's spirit is really watching him and blessing him, because you know I really told him that, I told him helping an old suffering person who is near death is the most blessed thing to do, because that person will ever after watch over you from heaven, I told him this when he was disgusted with Grandpa's urine-bottle and would not touch it, would not hand it to him even when I was not at home.

Are you sure, said Father, that you really told him this, or you believe you told him because you like the sound of it, you said yourself the other day that he changes and adds and alters things in the stories but he writes it all so beautifully that it seems true, so how can you be sure; this sounds like another theory, said Mother, but I don't care, he says I told him and I believe now I told him, so even if I did not tell him then it does not matter now.

Don't you see, said Father, that you are confusing fiction with facts, fiction does not create facts, fiction can come from facts, it can grow out of facts by compounding, transposing, augmenting, diminishing, or altering them in any way; but you must not confuse cause and effect, you must not confuse what really happened with what the story says happened, you must not loose your grasp on reality, that way madness lies.

Then Mother stopped listening because, as she told Father so often, she was not very fond of theories, and she took out her writing pad and started a letter to her son; Father looked over her shoulder, telling her to say how proud they were of him and were waiting for his next book, he also said, leave a little space for me at the end, I want to write a few lines when I put the address on the envelope.

1987

Dionne Brand

b. 1953

In the anthology *A Caribbean Dozen* (1996), Dionne Brand writes:

I was born deep in the south of Trinidad in a village called Guayguayare. . . . It is the place I remember and love the most. I now live in Toronto, Canada, but each time I go back to Trinidad I always go to Guayguayare just to see the ocean there, to breathe in the smell of copra drying and wood burning and fish frying. In the Sixties when I was in elementary and high schools, none of the books we studied were about Black people's lives; they were about Europeans, mostly the British. But I felt that Black people's experiences were as important and as valuable, and needed to be written down and read about. This is why I became a writer. . . . I went to a girls' high school where I was taught that girls could use their intellect to live a full life. My teachers and friends there helped me to see that women should enjoy the same rights and freedoms as men. When I moved to Canada in 1970 I joined the civil rights, feminist and socialist movements. I was only seventeen but I already knew that to live freely in the world as a Black woman I would have to involve myself in political action as well as writing.

After coming to Canada, Brand completed a BA at the University of Toronto in 1975; she later entered graduate studies at the Ontario Institute of Studies in Education, taking an MA in 1988. During the 1970s and 1980s she performed community social work in such capacities as counsellor at the Immigrant Women's Centre and at the Black Youth Hotline; facilitator for the Ontario Federation of Labour Women's Committee and the Metro Labour Council Anti-Racism Conference; and board member of a Toronto shelter for battered immigrant women. She was an information officer in Grenada in 1983 when the US invaded that island nation. She now lives north of Toronto.

She has taught English literature and creative writing at the Universities of Guelph and Toronto, at York University, and at the Humber School of Writing, and has been writer-in-residence at the University of Toronto and the Halifax City Regional Library. She has worked as a writer and editor for a number of alternative journals, including *Spear*, *Fuse*, and *Our Lives*, and was guest editor for *Fireweed*'s issues on Women of Colour (1983) and Canadian Women Poets (1986). In everything she writes, she is concerned with the damaging effects of discrimination and particularly with the repression that continues to exist in Canada despite the country's reputation for tolerance. Poet, fiction writer, essayist, and social historian, Brand has produced a large body of work intensely grounded in her own personal experience—as an immigrant, as someone of a racial minority, and as a lesbian.

Her 1990 book of poems, *No Language Is Neutral*, portrays the divided experience of the immigrant—the dislocation that produces an imagined and nostalgic life lived 'in another place not here': 'Dumbfounded I walk as if these sidewalks are a place I'm visiting. . . . it's fiction what I remember, only mornings took a long time to come, I became more secretive, language seemed to split in two, one branch fell silent, the other argued hotly for going home.' Brand explores immigrant alienation further in her first novel, *In Another Place, Not Here* (1996), where 'everyone is from someplace else but this city does not give them a chance to say this; it pushes their confusion underground'—but she shows that a return home seems impossible. In the collection of poems published a year later, *Land to Light On* (1997), which further investigates the state of immigrant exile, she writes of her despair at finding any refuge in a world dominated by brutal global politics and crushing multinational capitalism. (*Land to Light On* won a Governor General's Award for Poetry and a Trillium Award for Literature.)

In 2002 she published *Thirsty*, a long poem that acutely dramatizes the paradox that a big city in a new country represents for its newcomers. Describing Toronto as a place where one may at first feel that 'This city is beauty / unbreakable and amorphous as eyelids', and may experience its intensity ('That polychromatic murmur, the dizzying / waves, the noise of it'), she unveils its shadowy side, and shows us its potential for tragic consequences:

All the hope gone hard. That is a city.
The blind houses, the cramped dirt, the broken
air, the sweet ugliness, the blissful and tortured
flowers, the misguided clothing, the bricked lies
the steel lies, all the lies seeping from flesh
falling in rain and snow, the weeping buses,
the plastic throats, the perfumed garbage, the
needled sky, the smogged oxygen, the deathly clerical
gentlemen cleaning their fingernails at the stock
exchange, the dingy hearts in the newsrooms, that is
a city, the feral amnesia of us all.

For Brand, the immigrant condition cannot be separated from the festering sore that is racism. However, in the short stories in *Sans Souci and Other Stories* (1988) and elsewhere Brand suggests that the experience of prejudice and related violence is not limited to the immigrant. Her female protagonists may discover that they are 'in enemy territory' even if they remain in the Caribbean (where sexism may lead to violence against women) as well as in their transplanted homes in Canada. Immigration may seem a necessary act, and those from the Caribbean become part of a larger Black diaspora that seeks a home throughout the world. In Brand's second novel, *At the Full and Change of the Moon* (1999), the descendants of Bola—a young girl who was the only survivor of a mass suicide, a protest against slavery led by her mother, Marie Ursule, on a sugar-cane plantation in Trinidad in 1824—are traced through several generations as they move out through the Americas and Europe. This multigenerational chronicle becomes an affirmation of the strength and endurance of a race spread across a globe filled with tragedy and suffering:

In another century without knowing of her, because centuries are forgetful places, Marie Ursule's great-great-grandchildren would face the world too. But even that forgetfulness Marie Ursule had accounted for. Forgetfulness is true speech if anyone listens. This is the plain arrangement of the world, they would think, even if they knew different, even if they could have remembered Marie Ursule. They would say: This is the plain arrangement of the world, this I have suffered, this I have eaten, this I have loved.

The forgetfulness and loss that pervades Brand's work frequently manifests itself at the level of language, and of naming. In a work of non-fiction prose, *A Map to the Door of No Return: Notes to Belonging* (2001), Brand shows her readers why such losses matter.

My grandfather said he knew what people we came from. I reeled off all the names I knew. Yoruba? Ibo? Ashanti? Mandingo? He said no to all of them, saying that he would know it if he heard it. I was thirteen. I was anxious for him to remember. . . . Then I stopped asking. He was disappointed. I was disappointed. We lived after that in this mutual disappointment. It was a rift between us. It gathered into a kind of estrangement. . . .

Having no name to call was having no past; having no past pointed to the fissure between the past and the present. That fissure is represented in the Door of No Return: that place where our ancestors departed one world for another; the Old World for the New. The place where all names were forgotten and all beginnings recast. In some desolate sense it was the creation place of Blacks in the New World Diaspora at the same time that it signified the end of traceable beginnings. Beginnings that can be noted through a name or a set of family stories that extend farther into the past than five hundred or so years, or the kinds of beginnings that can be expressed in a name which in turn marked out territory or occupation. I am interested in exploring this creation place—the Door of No Return, a place emptied of beginnings—as a site of belonging or unbelonging.

The question of language is important in other ways in Brand's work as well. She has returned several times to the insight expressed in the title of *No Language Is Neutral* (the phrase comes from a poem by the Caribbean poet and playwright Derek Walcott)—which speaks to her awareness that language is inherently political and must always be examined skeptically for its ideological baggage. But because language often fails entirely she also suggests that the body must be allowed to speak in its own way. For example, in an essay called 'This Body for Itself', Brand writes of attending a symposium of Caribbean women writers and feeling that 'what is missing' from their discussions is 'the sexual body':

In a world where Black women's bodies are so sexualised, avoiding the body as sexual is a strategy. . . . I know that not talking about the sexual Black female self at all is as much an anti-colonial strategy as armed struggle. But what a trap. Often when we talk about the wonderful Black women in our lives, their valour, their emotional strength, their psychic endurance overwhelm our texts so much that we forget that apart from learning the elegant art of survival from them, we also learn in their gestures the art of sensuality, the fleshy art of pleasure and desire. (*Bread Out of Stone: Recollections, Sex, Recognitions, Race, Dreaming, Politics*, 1994)

As a lesbian, Brand has also experienced discrimination based on sexual orientation, and she must find, in her poems and fiction, a language that is not constrained by the expectations of heterosexuality or male desire, as in the sequence of poems called 'hard against the soul', reprinted here.

Although aware of the problems within Canadian society and wanting to find ways to correct them, Brand seeks to draw in her writing on a larger pan-African tradition and to respond to a global as much as to a national culture. In the mixture of reportage, critical commentary, journal entries, and polemics that forms *A Map to the Door of No Return*, for example, she draws on her African background, her childhood experiences in the Caribbean, and her travels across the Canadian physical and cultural landscape to meditate on the nature of identity in a culturally diverse society; and she discusses a wide variety of writers, including J.M. Coetzee, Paul Theroux, Toni Morrison, and V.S. Naipaul—observing: 'It is not the job of writers to lift our spirits. Books simply do what they do. They sometimes confirm the capricious drama of a childhood living room. When you think you are in the grace of a dance, you come upon something hard.'

From *No Language Is Neutral*

hard against the soul

X

Then it is this simple. I felt the unordinary romance of
women who love women for the first time. It burst in
my mouth. Someone said this is your first lover, you
will never want to leave her. I had it in mind that I
would be an old woman with you. But perhaps I
always had it in mind simply to be an old woman,
darkening, somewhere with another old woman,
then, I decided it was you when you found me in that
apartment drinking whisky for breakfast. When I came
back from Grenada and went crazy for two years, that
time when I could hear anything and my skin was
flaming like a nerve and the walls were like paper
and my eyes could not close. I suddenly sensed you
at the end of my room waiting. I saw your back arched
against this city we inhabit like guerillas, I brushed my
hand, conscious, against your soft belly, waking up.

I saw this woman once in another poem, sitting,
throwing water over her head on the rind of a country
beach as she turned toward her century. Seeing her
no part of me was comfortable with itself. I envied her,
so old and set aside, a certain habit washed from her
eyes. I must have recognized her. I know I watched
her along the rim of the surf promising myself, an old
woman is free. In my nerves something there
unravelling, and she was a place to go, believe me,
against gales of masculinity but in that then, she was
masculine, old woman, old bird squinting at the
water's wing above her head, swearing under her
breath. I had a mind that she would be graceful in me
and she might have been if I had not heard you
laughing in another tense and lifted my head from her
dry charm.

You ripped the world open for me. Someone said this
is your first lover you will never want to leave her. My
lips cannot say old woman darkening anymore, she
is the peace of another life that didn't happen and

couldn't happen in my flesh and wasn't peace but flight into old woman, prayer, to the saints of my ancestry, the gourd and bucket carrying women who stroke their breasts into stone shedding offspring and smile. I know since that an old woman, darkening, cuts herself away limb from limb, sucks herself white, running, skin torn and raw like a ball of bright light, flying, into old woman. I only know now that my longing for this old woman was longing to leave the prisoned gaze of men.

It's true, you spend the years after thirty turning over the suggestion that you have been an imbecile, hearing finally all the words that passed you like air, like so much fun, or all the words that must have existed while you were listening to others. What would I want with this sentence you say flinging it aside . . . and then again sometimes you were duped, poems placed deliberately in your way. At eleven, the strophe[1] of a yellow dress sat me crosslegged in my sex. It was a boy's abrupt birthday party. A yellow dress for a tomboy, the ritual stab of womanly gathers at the waist. *She look like a boy in a dress*, my big sister say, a lyric and feminine correction from a watchful aunt, *don't say that, she look nice and pretty.* Nice and pretty, laid out to splinter you, so that never, until it is almost so late as not to matter do you grasp some part, something missing like a wing, some fragment of your real self.

Old woman, that was the fragment that I caught in your eye, that was the look I fell in love with, the piece of you that you kept, the piece of you left, the lesbian, the inviolable, sitting on a beach in a time that did not hear your name or else it would have thrown you into the sea, or you, hear that name yourself and walked willingly into the muting blue. Instead you sat and I saw your look and pursued one eye until it came to the end of itself and then I saw the other, the blazing fragment.

1 In ancient Greek drama, the strophe was a turn in dancing.

Someone said this is your first lover, you will never
want to leave her. There are saints of this ancestry
too who laugh themselves like jamettes[2] in the
pleasure of their legs and caress their sex in mirrors.
I have become myself. A woman who looks
at a woman and says, here, I have found you,
in this, I am blackening in my way. You ripped the
world raw. It was as if another life exploded in my
face, brightening, so easily the brow of a wing
touching the surf, so easily I saw my own body, that
is, my eyes followed me to myself, touched myself
as a place, another life, terra. They say this place
does not exist, then, my tongue is mythic. I was here
before.

1990

2 Prostitutes; by extension women of loose morals, living in a slum area (Caribbean English).

From *Land to Light On*

I Have Been Losing Roads

I i

Out here I am like someone without a sheet
without a branch but not even safe as the sea,
without the relief of the sky or good graces of a door.
If I am peaceful in this discomfort, is not peace,
is getting used to harm. Is giving up, or misplacing
surfaces, the seam in grain, so standing
in a doorway I cannot summon up the yard,
familiar broken chair or rag of cloth on a blowing line,
I cannot smell smoke, something burning in a pit,
or gather air from far off or hear anyone calling.
The doorway cannot bell a sound, cannot repeat
what is outside. My eyes is not a mirror.

I ii

If you come out and you see nothing recognizable,
if the stars stark and brazen like glass,
already done decide you cannot read them.
If the trees don't flower and colour refuse to limn
when a white man in a red truck on a rural road
jumps out at you, screaming his exact hatred
of the world, his faith extravagant and earnest
and he threatens, something about your cunt,
you do not recover, you think of Malcolm[1]
on this snow drifted road, you think,
'Is really so evil they is then
that one of them in a red truck can split your heart
open, crush a day in fog?'

I iii

I lift my head in the cold and I get confuse.
It quiet here when is night, and is only me
and the quiet. I try to say a word but it fall. Fall
like the stony air. I stand up there but nothing
happen, just a bank of air like a wall. I could swear
my face was touching stone. I stand up but
nothing happen, nothing happen or I shouldn't say
nothing. I was embarrassed, standing like a fool,
the pine burdened in snow, the air fresh, fresh
and foreign and the sky so black and wide I did not
know which way to turn except to try again, to find
some word that could be heard by the something
waiting. My mouth could not find a language.
I find myself instead, useless as that. I sorry.
I stop by the mailbox and I give up.

I iv

I look at that road a long time.
It seem to close.
Yes, is here I reach
framed and frozen on a shivered

1 Malcolm X (1925–65), American black activist.

country road instead of where I thought
I'd be in the blood
red flame of a revolution.
I couldn't be farther away.
And none of these thoughts
disturb the stars or the pine
or the road or the red truck
screeching cunt along it.

I v

All I could do was turn and go back to the house
and the door that I can't see out of.
My life was supposed to be wider, not so forlorn
and not standing out in this north country bled
like maple. I did not want to write poems
about stacking cords of wood, as if the world
is that simple, that quiet is not simple or content
but finally cornered and killed. I still need the revolution
bright as the blaze of the wood stove in the window
when I shut the light and mount the stairs to bed.

II i

Out here, you can smell indifference driving
along, the harsh harsh happiness of winter
roads, all these roads heading nowhere, all
these roads heading their own unknowing way,
all these roads into smoke, and hoarfrost, friezed
and scrambling off in drifts, where is this
that they must go anytime, now, soon, immediately
and gasping and ending and opening in snow dust.
Quiet, quiet, earfuls, brittle, brittle ribs of ice
and the road heaving under and the day lighting up,
going on any way.

II ii

I have to think again what it means that I am here,
what it means that this, harsh as it is and without
a name, can swallow me up. I have to think how I

am here, so eaten up and frayed, a life that I was
supposed to finish by making something of it
not regularly made, where I am not this woman
fastened to this ugly and disappointing world.
I wanted it for me, to burst my brain and leap a distance
and all I have are these hoarse words that still owe
this life and all I'll be is tied to this century and waiting
without a knife or courage and still these same words
strapped to my back

II iii

I know as this thing happens, a woman
sucks her teeth, walks into a shop on an island
over there to stretch a few pennies across another
day, brushes a hand over her forehead and leaves,
going into the street empty-handed. Her certainty
frighten me. 'Is so things is,' she muse, reading
the shopkeeper's guiltless eyes, this hot hope the skin
tames to brooding, that particular advice, don't expect
nothing good. Quite here you reach and you forget.

II iv

no wonder I could get lost here, no wonder
in this set of trees I lose my way, counting
on living long and not noticing a closing,
no wonder a red truck could surprise me
and every night shape me into a crouch
with the telephone close by and the doors
checked and checked, all night. I can hear
everything and I can hear birds waking up
by four a.m. and the hours between three
and five last a whole day. I can hear wood
breathe and stars crackle on the galvanized
steel, I can hear smoke turn solid and this
house is only as safe as flesh. I can hear the
gate slam, I can hear wasps in my doorway,
and foraging mice, there's an old tree next
to my car and I can hear it fall, I can hear
the road sigh and the trees shift. I can
hear them far away from this house late, late

waiting for what this country is to happen,
I listen for the crunch of a car on ice or gravel,
the crush of boots and something coming

II v

A comet, slow and magnificent, drapes the north sky
but I cannot see it, cannot allow it, that would be
allowing another sign. And songs, songs to follow.
What songs can sing this anyway, what humming
and what phrase will now abandon me, what woman
with a gun and her fingers to her lips draw us to another
territory further north, further cold, further on,
into the mouth of the Arctic.
I'm heading to frost, to freezing,
how perhaps returning south heads to fever,
and what I'm saving for another time is all our good,
good will, so not listening, not listening
to any dangling voice or low, lifting whistle.
All the sounds gone out, all the wind died away,
I won't look, won't look at the tail of lighted dust.

III i

In the middle of afternoons driving north
on 35, stopping for a paper and a coffee,
I read the terrifying poetry of newspapers. I
notice vowels have suddenly stopped their
routine, their alarming rooms are shut,
their burning light collapsed

the wave of takeovers, mergers and restructuring
. . . swept the world's . . . blue chips rally in New York
. . . Bundesbank[2] *looms . . . Imperial Oil increases dividends*
. . . tough cutbacks build confidence

Your mouth never opens to say all this.
The breathful air of words are taken. Swept, yes.
You feel your coffee turn asphalt, you look around
and your eyes hit the dirty corners of the windy store,

2 The central bank of the Federal Republic of Germany and an integral component of the European system of the central banks.

stray paper, stray cups, stray oil, stray fumes of gas.
Your mouth never opens, your keys look unfamiliar.

is Microsoft a rapacious plunderer . . . or a benign
benevolent giant . . . rough road ahead

Rough road ahead they say so I leave the gas
station, leaving the paper on the counter,
not listening to the woman calling me back,
my mouth full and tasteless

III ii

Where is this. Your tongue, gone cold, gone
heavy in this winter light.
On a highway burrowing north don't waste your breath.
This winter road cannot hear it and will swallow it
whole. Don't move.
This detail then, when grass leans in certain light.
In other days, blue. This, every week no matter what grows
worse you cannot say you are on the same road, green darkens
or yellows or snows or disappears. Leave me there then,
at 2 p.m. rounding 35 to the 121 hoping
never to return here.

I should have passed, gone my way.

You come to think
the next house one kilometre away might as well
be ten, it so far from love, and shouting would produce
no blood. If I believe anything it will not matter though.
Life is porous, unimaginable in the end, only substance
burning in itself, lit by the heat of touching. It's good
how we melt back into nothing.

III iii

Look, let me be specific. I have been losing roads
and tracks and air and rivers and little thoughts
and smells and incidents and a sense of myself
and fights I used to be passionate about
and don't remember. And once I lost the mechanics, no,

the meaning of dancing, and
I have been forgetting everything, friends, and pain.
The body bleeds only water and fear when you survive
the death of your politics, but why don't I forget.
That island with an explosive at the beginning of its name[3]
keeps tripping me and why don't I recall my life
in detail because I was always going somewhere else
and what I was living was unimportant for the while

Rough Road Ahead

let me say that all the classrooms should be burned
and all this paper abandoned like dancing and the gas
stations heading north, and all the independents
who wasted time arguing and being superior, pulling out
dictionaries and refereed journals,[4] new marxists, neo-marxists,
independent marxists, all of us loving our smartness, oh jeez,
the arguments filling auditoriums and town halls with
smartness, taking our time with smartness for serious study,
committing suicide blowing saxophones of smartness, going
home, which windy night on Bloor Street knowing full well and
waking up shaky until smartness rings the telephone with
another invitation and postmortem about last night's meeting.
Then I lost, well, gave up the wherewithal

III iv

One gleeful headline drives me to the floor, kneeling,
and all paint turns to gazette paper and all memory
collides into photographs we could not say happened,
that is us, that's what we did. When you lose you become
ancient but this time no one will rake over those bodies
gently collecting their valuables, their pots, their hearts
and intestines, their papers and what they could bury.
This civilization will be dug up to burn all its manifestos.
No tender archaeologist will mend our furious writings
concluding, 'They wanted sweat to taste sweet, that is all,
some of them played music for nothing, some of them
wrote poems to tractors, rough hands, and rough roads,
some sang for no reason at all to judge by their condition.'

3 Grenada, which, because it is pronounced with a long a, sounds like 'grenade'.

4 Journals in which scholarly essays are published are said to be 'refereed' because each submission is sent out to two or three experts in the field for review and suggestions before it can be accepted.

III v

After everything I rely on confusion. I listen for
disaster, a storm in the Gulf of Mexico, arctic air
wreathing the whole of this unblessed continent,
mud slides burying the rich in California and the
devil turned in on himself in Oklahoma.[5] And others,
and more than my desire reminding me that someone
used to say when I was a child don't wish for bad
you might get it, your own face might be destroyed,
you will call trouble on yourself and on your own house.
How I watch, like someone without a being, the whole
enterprise come to zero and my skin not even able
to count on itself. Still, with snow coming, counting
by the slate sky, I hope for cars and hands to freeze,
lines and light to fall, since what I've learned,
the lie of it, is no amount of will can change it. There
are whole countries exhausted for it, whole villages,
whole arms, whole mornings and whole hearts burning.
And what I wish for is natural and accidental

5 A reference to the bombing of the Murrah Federal Building in Oklahoma City in 1995, an act of domestic terrorism.

Land to Light On

V i

Maybe this wide country just stretches your life to a thinness
just trying to take it in, trying to calculate in it what you must
do, the airy bay at its head scatters your thoughts like someone
going mad from science and birds pulling your hair, ice invades
your nostrils in chunks, land fills your throat, you are so busy
with collecting the north, scrambling to the Arctic so wilfully, so
busy getting a handle to steady you to this place you get blown
into bays and lakes and fissures you have yet to see, except
on a map in a schoolroom long ago but you have a sense that
whole parts of you are floating in heavy lake water heading for
what you suspect is some other life that lives there, and you, you
only trust moving water and water that reveals itself in colour. It
always takes long to come to what you have to say, you have to
sweep this stretch of land up around your feet and point to the

signs, pleat whole histories with pins in your mouth and guess
at the fall of words

V ii

But the sight of land has always baffled you,
there is dirt somewhere older than any exile
and try as you might, your eyes only compose
the muddy drain in front of the humid almond
tree, the unsettling concrete sprawl of the housing
scheme, the stone your uncle used to smash his name
into another uncle's face, your planet is your hands,
your house behind your eyebrows and the tracing
paper over the bead of islands of indifferent and
reversible shapes, now Guadeloupe is a crab pinched
at the waist, now Nevis' borders change by mistake
and the carelessness of history, now sitting in Standard
Five,[1] the paper shifting papery in the sweat of your
fingers you come to be convinced that these lines will
not matter, your land is a forced march on the bottom
of the Sargasso,[2] your way tangled in life

V iii

I am giving up on land to light on, it's only true, it is only
something someone tells you, someone you should not trust
anyway. Days away, years before, a beer at your lips and the view
from Castara,[3] the ocean as always pulling you towards its bone
and much later, in between, learning to drive the long drive
to Burnt River, where the land is not beautiful, braised
like the back of an animal, burnt in coolness, but the sky is,
like the ocean pulling you toward its bone, skin falling away
from your eyes, you see it without its history of harm, without
its damage, or everywhere you walk on the earth there's harm,
everywhere resounds. This is the only way you will know
the names of cities, not charmed or overwhelmed, all you see is

1 That is, the speaker is recalling sitting in class at school ('Standard Five' is a grade level in the Caribbean), tracing out the shapes of the islands as an exercise.

2 The Sargasso Sea is a region of the western Atlantic Ocean between the Azores and the Caribbean, so called because of the prevalence in it of floating and thickly matted sargasso seaweed. This sea was seen, in the days of sailing, as a danger to ships, which could become trapped in the massed vegetation.

3 A fishing village situated on the northwestern coast of Tobago.

museums of harm and metros full, in Paris, walls inspected
crudely for dates, and Amsterdam, street corners full of
druggists, ashen with it, all the way from Suriname, Curaçao,
Dutch and German inking their lips, pen nibs of harm blued in
the mouth, not to say London's squares, blackened in statues,
Zeebrugge,[4] searching the belly of fish, Kinshasa, through an
airplane window the dictator cutting up bodies grips the plane
to the tarmac and I can't get out to kiss the ground

V iv

This those slaves must have known who were my mothers, skin
falling from their eyes, they moving toward their own bone,
'so thank god for the ocean and the sky all implicated, all
unconcerned,' they must have said, 'or there'd be nothing to
love.' How they spent a whole lifetime undoing the knot
of a word and as fast it would twirl up again, spent
whole minutes inching their eyes above sea level only
for latitude to shift, only for a horrible horizon to list, thank god
for the degrees of the chin, the fooling plane of a doorway, only
the mind, the not just simple business of return and turning,
that is for scholars and indecisive frigates, circling and circling,
stripped in their life, naked as seaweed, they would have sat
and sunk but no, the sky was a doorway, a famine and a jacket,
the sea a definite post

V v

I'm giving up on land to light on, slowly, it isn't land,
it is the same as fog and mist and figures and lines
and erasable thoughts, it is buildings and governments
and toilets and front door mats and typewriter shops,
cards with your name and clothing that comes undone,
skin that doesn't fasten and spills and shoes. It's paper,
paper, maps. Maps that get wet and rinse out, in my hand
anyway. I'm giving up what was always shifting, mutable
cities' fluorescences, limbs, chalk curdled blackboards
and carbon copies, wretching water, cunning walls. Books
to set it right. Look. What I know is this. I'm giving up.

4 A seaport on the coast of Belgium; 'Kinshasa': the capital of the Democratic Republic of Congo (Zaire), which was ruled by the dictator Mobutu from 1965 to 1997.

No offence. I was never committed. Not ever, to offices
or islands, continents, graphs, whole cloth, these sequences
or even footsteps

V vi

Light passes through me lightless, sound soundless,
smoking nowhere, groaning with sudden birds. Paper
dies, flesh melts, leaving stockings and their useless vanity
in graves, bodies lie still across foolish borders.
I'm going my way, going my way gleaning shade, burnt
meridians, dropping carets,[5] flung latitudes, inattention,
screeching looks. I'm trying to put my tongue on dawns
now, I'm busy licking dusk away, tracking deep twittering
silences. You come to this, here's the marrow of it, not
moving, not standing, it's too much to hold up, what I
really want to say is, I don't want no fucking country, here
or there and all the way back, I don't like it, none of it,
easy as that. I'm giving up on land to light on, and why not,
I can't perfect my own shadow, my violent sorrow, my
individual wrists.

1997

5 A caret is a mark [^] used by writers and proofreaders to indicate that something is inserted; on maps a line of carets is sometimes used to indicate routes. In this section, as in V. iv, the instability of these carets, as of latitudes, meridians, and horizon, recalls the difficult shipboard journeys of 'those slaves . . . who were my mothers' and who were taken across the Atlantic, away from their homes and homelands—a historical context that reminds the reader that their 'land to light on' would be one of brutal servitude.

Aritha van Herk

b. 1954

Born to Dutch immigrant parents, Aritha van Herk spent the first eighteen years of her life on a pig farm near Edberg, Alta, a few miles from the Battle River. Although her writing often deals with travel, she has remained based in and is strongly identified with her home province of Alberta—and both the geography of the home place and the history associated with that geography play important roles in her writing. A fictional version of her pig farm is the setting of her first novel, *Judith* (1978), and she returns to investigate her home town of Edberg in the first of what she calls the *geografictiones* that make up *Places Far from Ellesmere* (1990). She has also edited five volumes of stories by writers from Alberta and the Prairies; in 2001 she published *Mavericks: An Incorrigible History of Alberta*.

Judith, which won a Seal Books Canadian First Novel Award, was an expansion of van Herk's master's thesis, 'When Pigs Fly', which she wrote while studying at the University of Alberta (BA, 1977; MA, 1978). Rich in textual allusion, it employs—in addition to the story of Judith (found in the Catholic Bible), a woman who saved her people by entering the military camp of an attacking enemy and beheading its general—extensive allusions to the tale of Circe, the enchantress from Greek myth who turned men into pigs. It became the first of a series of works in which van Herk explores powerful female myths in modern terms.

In addition to her concern with the west, van Herk shifts her geographical orientation to the north—which serves as a space not yet filled with preconceptions about women—in several of her works, beginning with her second novel, *The Tent Peg* (1981). Like *Judith*, *The Tent Peg* takes a Biblical story as its presiding myth: its central character, a woman named Ja-el, shares her name with the Biblical heroine who, in the Book of Judges, drives a tent peg through the head of an enemy general. In van Herk's retelling of the story, a western woman seeking identity disguises herself as a man known as J.L., and—moving north to work as a cook for a geological camp, where she learns to shoot a gun—finds the freedom to be the woman she wants to be.

In her third novel, *No Fixed Address* (1986), van Herk sends another female protagonist travelling—Arachne, whose name is that of the woman in Greek myth who, because she thinks her skills as a weaver exceed those of the Goddess Athena, is turned into a spider and spends her days crossing and recrossing a web of her own making, spun from silk she extrudes from her own belly. Van Herk's Arachne moves back and forth across the west, a travelling saleswoman who sells a line of 'Ladies' Comfort panties' and a parody of the inherited male figures—the picaro who is the European source of the novel, the travelling salesman of North American folklore and humour, and Kroetsch's mythic studhorse man as an Albertan archetypal figure—that have defined her inherited tradition, recreating them all in female terms.

Van Herk's next narrative, *Places Far from Ellesmere*, departs from the relatively conventional form of her first three novels: it is an exploration—the book itself as trip—in four parts, one for each of the places important in her life. The first part explores her years growing up on her home ground of Edberg; the second part, reprinted here, tells of her time in Edmonton, the city in which she received her education; the third part explores Calgary, where she has taught (at the University of Calgary) since 1983; the final section is another journey to the north, an imagined trip to Ellesmere Island, the far northern island that in van Herk's account becomes a utopian home for dislocated women. There she allows Tolstoy's character Anna Karenina, who has been travelling with her as she has moved from city to city, to rewrite the tragic ending of her famous narrative and to find freedom by escaping the fate that her original, male, author established for her. In its experiments with genre, *Places Far from Ellesmere* reconstructs the idea of life writing, creating places from the author's memory maps, and restructures van Herk's life into that of a character whose connections to places rather than experience of events form her identity.

In its rewriting of the mystery thriller and its inverting of the form of the travel narrative, van Herk's most recent work of fiction, *Restlessness* (1998), continues her revisionist practice. It is the record of a trip that moves not through geography but through time as its narrator, Dorcas—who suffers from placelessness, a homesickness she cannot cure by travelling in space—chooses to becomes stationary and decides to bring herself to the end of her own time by hiring an assassin who will kill her. She finds, however, she cannot stay within the conventions of her own script because she is unable to stop telling stories long enough to die.

Van Herk has also published two collections of essays. Both, like her fiction, blur the boundaries of their genres, becoming what she calls 'ficto-criticism'. The first of these, *In Visible Ink: Crypto-Frictions* (1991), responds to a wide variety of Canadian texts and authors. Several of the essays in the second, *A Frozen Tongue* (1992), discuss the tension she experienced between the language of her parents' past and that of her Canadian homeland, and the effect that has had on her writing.

From *Places Far from Ellesmere*

EDMONTON, LONG DIVISION

The North Saskatchewan cutting the town in half: north/south; business/pleasure; government/learning. The few bridges incidental to separation and the high brows of the river banking their own domain. Here is the city that will divide you from the country, that will wean you from Edberg, its wide streets and narrow alleys leading toward seduction. This is the quandary you face, your problem in long division: north/south.

And what's to be expected of a fort(ress) set up to trade/skin Indians. The Hudson's Bay Company holding its own centuries later, Edmonton House but one dot of many stringing the North Saskatchewan, so long under the tyrannical eye of John Rowand ('We know only two powers—God and the Company!'), Chief Factor (1823–1854) whose bones were boiled to make his bread, still haunting the upper reaches of the north bank, where the Château Lacombe and Edmonton House turn themselves round. You can see him at dusk strutting his girth above the city he thinks he invented, the flats below him remodelling their green gardens.

You know Paul Kane's story[1] of Christmas dinner in Edmonton (1847), with its dried moose noses, feasting and plenty and the dancing that stormed its steps through the endless night, and you imagine you too will feast after your long forbidding, after your incestuous waiting to be free to taste those delicacies, those impossible erotics never found in Edberg, only dreamed about listening to the radio in the late bloom of summer, the voice of the DJ in its husky promisement.

1 Paul Kane is remembered today both as one of the first European artists of North American Native life and for his published journal, *Wanderings of an Artist among the Indians of North America from Canada to Vancouver Island and Oregon through the Hudson's Bay Company Territory and Back Again* (1859), an account of the painter's 1847–8 sketching trip through western Canada.

If you can only get to Edmonton in one piece, you now the Indian coming with your skin, your fresh eyes up from the Battle River country, through the Gwynne Outwash Channel, looking for a trade, something of use in the long winter ahead.

Long division: what you were never good at, had to concentrate for, practice. What choices are there? You set up the equation, begin with a thick-stemmed landlady who rustles through your closets when you are in classes, who insists you are amoral because you resist falling in love: not yet, not just yet. This city caught in its own nebulous prairie history: a fort(ress) to be stormed. Love must subtract a difference.

Edmonton: here the world rests outside the glass of cold, winter speculations.

> CITY OF EDMONTON
>
> situated at the head of navigation on the North Saskatchewan River; the centre of the Gold, Coal, Timber and Mineral region of the Great North-West, and surrounded by the richest wheat-producing country in the world.
>
> The four great highways leading from Winnipeg, the great Bow River grazing country, the Peace River country and British Columbia via the Jasper Pass, centre on the Town Site.
>
> It is the terminus of the CP telegraph line, the North-West mail route, and the projected Saskatchewan branch of the CPR.
>
> The Hudson's Bay Co. offer for sale 1,000 lots on the above town site at low prices and on reasonable terms. All information can be had by applying at the HB Co. Offices in Winnipeg or Montréal,
>
> R. McGinn, Agent, Edmonton — C.J. Brydges, Commissioner

Just what you need, in 1882, a bare ninety years before your arrival, not entirely accurate in its projections but close, close enough. Although the CPR line went south to Calgary, and gold was in the eye of the beholder, the telegraph line was real enough, encoding Methodists and temperatures, local threshings and silver foxes. Toronto is full of expelled Jesuits and stern-chinned Presbyterians; landslides and murders the same as everywhere. You might as well start here.

How do you start a life in Edmonton? You buy a frying pan, a kettle, a teapot. Two bowls, two cups, two plates, a knife, a fork. Some towels. You lay the clothes you sewed out in your drawers, hang your dresses in your closet. They seem frumpy, not quite up-to-date. Is there any store (beyond the HBC) in which to purchase future? If Frank Oliver's were still going you could search there for the answer to your long division.

> (fourth door east of Methodist Church) has on hand a full stock of GROCERIES, comprising Black and Green Teas, Crushed Sugar, Coffee, Myrtle Navy Tobacco, Raisins, Currents, Rice, Oatmeal; Beans, Dried and Evaporated Apples, California Fruit, etc.; HARDWARE, comprising Grain Shovels, Miner's Shovels, Hay and Manure Forks, Ox Bows and Yoke Staples, Strap Hinges, Gold Pans, Quicksilver, 3–4, 5–8 and 3–8 Manger

> Rope, Canadian Axes and Handles, Large Mirror, Butter Bowls, Bread pans, Ready-Made Stove Pipe and Elbows, etc.; BOOTS & SHOES, Men's and Women's Wear; and DRY GOODS, comprising Seamless Bags, and a few pair of extra good Overalls, Shirts, Drawers and Stocks.

You need a large mirror, manger rope, crushed sugar, a gold pan, quicksilver. You will need to learn to play pool, to read in the dark, to elope.

You want to fall in love with a racer, a man with his hands firmly on the reins, Jim Campbell with his highstepper challenging any horse within fifty miles. You need a horse: the walk to university is long division itself, and the walk between the buildings, from class to class, a disorienting race, despite maps and registration schedules, despite Tuberculin Tests and Library Instruction. You try to pace days, promise yourself you will sink in, settle down, but the autumn is impossibly crisp, and you feel yourself staggering between adjustment and desire.

Why go to Edmonton if not to fall in love?

You do fall in love, with the thin insect legs of entomology, with the zealous musings of philosophy, the incessant novels of literature, the moustache of Maurice Legris as he chews you through *Huckleberry Finn* and *Portrait of the Artist.* If lovers cannot be found in Edmonton, they can be found in books. But where are the dances, the marriages, the murder trials? In hiding, in retrospect.

You blur from one class to the next, one antecedent to another. You need to be ferried from the south to the north side, the city still un/read as you evade its gold/coal/timber mines and dream of reading secret dyings. You have left your Edberg murders behind and although red roses walk to your door, you guard your own bank account and find a forester. Races and footraces, elopements and amputations, will succeed. 11438–79 Avenue. The room overlooking the back alley and the garage still suggests occupation, but the landlady is surely vanished with her amputations of tenants and rules, her shrill commands while poor-relation Anna did the bent-head and lifeless-eyes work. The last time you avoided the landlady she had pitilessly stroked herself into the hospital. Probably better than what you stroked yourself into?

Here in this archaic, bottomed-out glacial lake, the bowl of city held in the hand of geological (10,000 years) time, only the river's incisement to remember division over melting. Legal fences and dis/legal fires incite rebellions, women are at a premium and should be allowed free, the turning of leaves into their own crumbling lights, the late afternoons of the city's burn when you walk heavy-footed home with your books and your bag of solitary groceries. You live on toast and tea; you want to go dancing; you slog through classes, papers (on Body Language, on Mark Twain, on existentialism, on the mandibles of grasshoppers); the heads of the young men all bent quietly away. The engineer in Philosophy class, the would-be singer and road construction worker in English with his November 9th Bastille day stormings of the body. Phone numbers etched in memory (465-6327, 429-8749) although estranged now, have changed owners, succumbed to answering machines and the ravages of push-tone dialling.

Long division: attainable in this outwash city overlooking its own autumns. Your landlady accuses that you work too hard, you read too much: she knocks on your door at all hours seeking to distract you (she teaches you to despise distraction), while you only want to return to words, the neat enlistments of notes, the swollen pages of portentous papers. Edmonton is a reading, an act of text, an open book. Beyond the door it crouches in lanes of leaves, and walking through its crackle you dream fire, river water, frozen breath, summerfallow, never suspicioning that you will turn south, eventually, to the beautifully groomed cemetery lawns of Calgary.

There are no silk handkerchiefs to steal, the insane are kept out of the city, heart attacks rage. You encircle books in your arms, a lovering persistent, although your purse has no revenue, your future has no kiss. But you remember every movie you saw: *Junior Bonner, Alice's Restaurant, Gone With the Wind, On the Buses, The Last Waltz, Pete and Tillie, Slaughterhouse Five, Love Story, The Last Picture Show, Fiddler on the Roof, Ryan's Daughter, Man of La Mancha, Travels with My Aunt, The Godfather, The Effect of Gamma Rays on the Man-in-the-Moon Marigolds, Brother Sun, Sister Moon, Jesus Christ Superstar, A Clockwork Orange, Class of '44, The Emigrants,* the dreaming screen.

Long division: pay up. Prospects superior, as long as you keep company with books. The Northcote might ply, winter might never arrive. Temperatures and ice thicknesses no longer measured, but winter comes nevertheless and your coat hopelessly inadequate, your legs always cold. Over-heated buildings flush the blood while the pages still insist on turning themselves over and over in the crowded and hustling library, the studious bent studiously and the restless restless. Rutherford is the wrong place for long division: potential for church but not passion. Starvation pay for love. You work at diminishing your innocence, you en/tangle yourself with students who seem unlikely to do more than turn pages.

And Russia is looming, luring, lurking, Anna's quick step on the platforms of desire reaches all the way to Edmonton.

> The Czar of Russia, who lost his wife a short time ago, is married again. He had not been blown up for several days and was feeling lonesome.

The world at large and Edmonton its stagnation point: how to get from this place farther, how to reach the reaches of the world, and maybe Russia. Are seductions to Arctic Islands possible? Do they read themselves a future, a presence on a map? You want to go there, Nova Zembla, its trembling promise, its unrailwayed joining.

> The Russian Government is trying to cause an emigration to Nova Zembla, an island within the Arctic Circle, by giving 350 roubles and five years' freedom from taxes to every able-bodied man who will emigrate there. They have a simpler and cheaper way of encouraging emigration to Siberia.

Bulletin opinion. The curved beauty of Nova Zembla drifts past the imaginations of Edmonton: long division.

Squatter's rights in Edmonton: the city waiting for you to unbend yourself in a basement room with a man who may or may not be worth unbending your good knees for. Who dares to fall in love with murderers at large? You go to more movies, you read more novels, your professor is astonished at what you remember from the bleached pages. Love does that; sexual attraction brings every hair to attention. You try to temper your initiations, but fall persists while the city dreams itself around you and the snow blots wet through your thin boots. Your coat is too short, your hair too unruly to be helpful, your hands red and chapped. Edmonton winters are not made for love or fondness, even for declarations or seductions. Outside the basement room, children shout as they run home through the snow, the school buzzer an echo of Edberg's, a start of guilt, of remindering.

Still, you've been abstemious enough, have yet to see the inside of a hotel, either historical or contemporary.

> EDMONTON HOTEL
>
> The Pioneer House of Entertainment West of Portage la Prairie Pemmican and dried buffalo meat has long been a stranger at the table, and its place has been taken by substantials more in keeping with the onward march of civilization.
>
> A cosy billiard room, where the Edmonton coal can be seen burning to advantage.
>
> Good stabling attached.
>
> Donald Ross, Proprietor

Good stabling attached.

Long division: temperance. A new meaning to the old missionary. These are the bars you drink at: the Corona, the Riviera, the Park, the King Eddie, the Cap; the Embers, Ernie's. A way of breaking free of books, sharpening your peripheral vision, tensing your wrist muscles.

> It appears from exchanges that the name 'coffin varnish', used at Edmonton last winter to denote a villainous compound swallowed by some of our thirsty fellow citizens for the purpose of producing a temporary exhiliaration, has travelled a long distance from home without having had its significance or usefulness impaired. It is now the popular name of the popular drink in Laramie, Wyoming, and various other classic localities. It is altogether appropriate that 'coffin varnish' should be succeeded by 'sudden death' which rejoices the hearts of the boys . . .

You drink: beer, Chanté Rose, Baby Duck, Sangre de Torro, awful stuff. You survive a few hangovers, a couple of horror shows, you enjoy a genuinely inebriate time (once or twice, between implacable sobriety). But the grand division of sons of temperance will call a convention in order to discuss whether the time has not arrived to press for total prohibition. On all passions.

You have not yet read *Anna Karenin*, but she is waiting to be read, to remind you of what to expect of books, of love affairs and their killings. It is reported that the Czar of Russia was assassinated. Still later it is reported that the czar is all right yet.

Somewhere within the orbit of the Arctic Circle you deduce the potential of lost Shanghai pigs, of census takers as recording angels, of attacks of quinsy. You avoid the crime of deserting employment, of bones and tambourine, of eight-day clocks, which you are certainly circling. The czar is afraid to appear in public, even at religious ceremonies and the Herzegovians are making it hot for their rulers.

Dances exert their magnetic field: their follow-up reports, bring their own applause:

> The Masonic ball on Tuesday evening last in McDougall's Hall was undoubtedly the best affair of the season . . . Not the least remarkable feature was the number of ladies—sixteen—the largest number that has been got together at any affair of the kind in Edmonton within the memory of man, or of which there is any authentic record. As our fashion reporter is away we are unable to speak critically of the toilets of the ladies or the costumes of the gentlemen, suffice it to say that although only one gentleman appeared in a clawhammer coat there was more lace, frilling, kid gloves, black cloth, starched linen and store clothes generally, not forgetting a few police uniforms, were at this hall than could have been collected in any previous year in the whole Saskatchewan country.

Sixteen ladies and a clawhammer coat. Keep a record of the ladies that come dancing. Your wear short skirts, baggy checked pants, you buy a pink corduroy suit and a black blazer. But you always look slightly wrong, not quite as matched as the rich city girls who sit (Sociology) in front of you, whose neatly pressed flowered blouses vaunt cashmere cardigans, and whose perfectly straight teeth shine.

Through the maze of your books you try to read this place, this once-fort, Hudson's Bay Company stronghold, this ferried and rivered city. How to cross from one side to the other? The High Level[8] trembles in the brisk north wind, its black lattice a crib of threat. From here the Mackenzie brigade went overland to Athabasca Landing and Fort Assiniboine on the Athabasca River. From here you will launch yourself north and west, south and east.

The street names (Jasper Avenue, McKay, Hardisty, Saskatchewan, Calgary, McLeod, Walsh) have altered themselves to numbers, but the ice in the river still grafts a thin skin in November, still grinds itself against the divided banks in an ecstatic breaking, an April canticle that springs winter free the same as it always did. Edmonton still a wooded valley up from White Mud Creek, Black Mud Creek, still the site of glacial long division, the self caught between origins and destinations: body and cemetery.

The cemetery questions persists, demands consideration. High time the citizens of Edmonton arranged for a public cemetery. Delay causes increased trouble and expense: the long trek to bury outside the skirts of the city, the winter does not keep bodies nearly so well or so long, and death will proliferate, will insist. Edmonton funereal, where death is enacted but never finished. There are more ways to hang a cat than by choking it with butter.

But that high and hanging valley that traced you a faint outline for walking under the impossible brilliance of the northern lights still divides. The whole sky a vast teepee, the greater part white, but the lower portion towards the south and east a dark and spectacular red. If Calgary is famous for its endless and potent light, Edmonton is a city that you learned best through its darkness, never going to bed until dawn streaked five-thirty, and then sleeping through the day. Edmonton: still the darkness of winter and of buildings, of enclosured cold.

Despite passing, you spend a summer driving the tractor for your father, buy your own bed and find a landladyless apartment, erect shelves of bricks and boards, accelerate your reading. You avoid the football evenings with your classmates, you avoid the temptation to enter law, you avoid baking cookies into your professor's favour. While others divide and swyve,[2] hunt life partners and missionary intent, you read, entext yourself a city of pages, their sybarite answers.

The jobs you take are yours, the hours you spend as typing temp for the government; ushering legs in the Paramount theatre (you saw *Butch Cassidy and the Sundance Kid* two hundred and forty times that summer, but it bought your wedding dress and a set of dishes); reading and marking for the blind professor of Religious Studies while around you engagements break and resettle, around you buzz LSATs and B.ED.'s after degree. The others seem to need no jobs, they go to church, have children and a social life, buy furnishings, while you turn desperate time to an eight-day clock on high speed reading. Six years engaged in long division, and without having ever put down your book, you are degreed, married, authored, even public and published, and out of there.

Swearing you will never return to your sites of seduction and rage, to the baffling problem of an eternal long division of the self, this Edmonton, still glazed with ice, pretends to be another place than it pretends to be.

You meet them now, Heidi (shy and still gap-toothed) at a reading in Spruce Grove, Len (who *did* work—in his father's bakery) suddenly around a corner in the stacks of MacKimmie, confiding alterations.

Dis/criminate these absent words: your brevities of Edmonton. Six years fore/shortened, refuse to be re/read. Conversion/metamorphosis/seduction. The criminal conversations of burial consigned to a potential desert woman, an island sublimination.

You visit Edmonton, longing for the foothills with their knowing cemeteries, their monuments to resurrection. Still you know, walking the quandam streets that walked you, here was long division and this the abacus.

1990

2 Have sex (archaic); 'sybarite': sensual, luxurious.

Erin Mouré

b. 1955

Erin Mouré was born and raised in Calgary. She began her post-secondary education at the University of Calgary, then moved in 1974 to Vancouver, where she attended the University of British Columbia before going to work. She was employed for several years by the Canadian National Railway, where she became the first woman to manage trains, while producing her first collections of poetry: *Empire, York Street* (1979), the chapbook *The Whisky Vigil* (1981), *Wanted Alive* (1983), and *Domestic Fuel* (1985).

Mouré's career can be divided into two distinct phases. In her early writing she saw the artist as a 'focal point' for the thoughts, feelings, and concerns of ordinary people. Wanting to integrate her work life with her writing life, Mouré became an active member of 'The Vancouver Industrial Writers' Union', a group formed in 1979 to support and promote creative writing about the workplace. This conception of the poet's role is apparent in a book like *Wanted Alive,* with its lines about how 'the end of a city is still / a field, ordinary persons live there, a frame house, & occasionally— / a woman comes out to hang the washing', and with the way she draws on her job experience in descriptions of 'Workers awake half the night / in the closed kitchens drinking beer / Sliding arms around each other / Lovers of humans, of steel diesel trains' ('Seven Rail Poems').

In 1984 Mouré took a job with VIA Rail. Moving to their Montreal offices in 1985, she wrote their handbooks to make them clearer and more effective, and began writing their monthly newsletter. Since 1996 she has worked in Montreal as a full-time writer, freelance translator, and communications specialist. As can be seen in the progress charted in *The Green World: Selected Poems 1973–1992* (1994), the political, theoretical, and cultural dynamics she encountered in Montreal, which brought her into contact with individuals such as the novelist and critic Gail Scott, and the personal growth she experienced as a result, profoundly changed the direction of her poetry. An exchange of letters between Mouré and Bronwen Wallace that took place around this time on the subject of women and language has been published as *Two Women Talking: Correspondence 1985–97.* It tracks Mouré's move into a kind of politics that, while it shared many of the goals that Wallace embraced, shows the two of them conceiving of different ways of achieving those goals.

In terms of content, Mouré was now, as she writes in 'Blindness', ready to investigate those 'desires . . . known only on the floor / of oceans'. Responding to the feminist politics she found in Montreal, she began to focus on the relationship between language and identity, including the way some representations can be dangerous. In poems such as 'Miss Chatelaine', she rejects the image of women as it is defined in the media and writes about how hard it is to free language from male dominance. In *Sudden Miracles,* a 1991 anthology of women poets edited by Rhea Tregebov, Mouré discusses the way language can be manipulated to affect perception and our understanding of reality:

> *Sounds and words attract each other, and ideas, and worries. And dreams. . . . The world is imbued with language and linguistic possibility, with bad and good expression, with hopefulness, with manipulation and trickery as well, with rationalizations and silence and gaps that alter, slowly, the structures of thought in the head. And poetry laughs at all of this at the same time as it confronts it, because poetry is entirely useless and owes no debts. . . .*

After 1985 there is a progressively radical alteration in Mouré's way of writing as well. Her later collections, which include *Furious* (1988, Governor General's Award); *WSW (West South West)* (1989); *Sheepish Beauty, Civilian Love* (1992); *Search Procedures* (1996); *A Frame of the Book,* a.k.a. *The Frame of a Book* (1999); and *Pillage Laud* (1999), show Mouré abandoning the traditional poetics of a lyrical representation of felt experience that was apparent in her first books for a poetry that is influenced by postmodern and deconstructive theory and by the American L=A=N=G=U=A=G=E movement, which has called into question the idea that language is transparent, neutral, or innocent—in part by creating texts (such as 'The Splendour') with disrupted narrative and syntax, poems that are non-linear and deliberately disjunctive. Many of her poems become self-consciously experimental, sometimes resulting in mysterious texts, such as those in *Pillage Laud*, which is subtitled *Cauterizations, Vocabularies, Cantigas, Topiary, Prose* and which was created by selecting 'from pages of computer-generated sentences to produce lesbian sex poems, by pulling their certain found vocabularies, relying on context: boy plug vagina library fate tool doctrine bath discipline belt beds pioneer book ambition finger fist flow'.

In the poems reprinted here, Mouré's desire to destabilize her texts can be seen in the way she pairs the prose poem 'The Beauty of Furs', which looks back to the kind of poetry of personal experience she once wrote, with 'The Beauty of Furs: A Site Glossary', which becomes a meta-commentary on the poem and asks (seriously or playfully?) that we read it in a new and more psychoanalytic way. Similarly, she refuses to allow her poem about her experience of surgery, 'Dream of the Towns', to remain bounded, by adding to it not only a sketch of the post-operative scar, but also her own footnotes, becoming a scholar-critic of her poem before others can do that job for her.

Her sense of the importance of language, its mercurial quality, and the way a poet playfully grapples with it are all suggested by the fact that in 2002 the poet who had previously signed her books Erin Mouré used two other forms of her name: Erín Moure (for *O Cidadán*, a collection of new poems) and Eirin Moure (for *Sheep's Vigil by a Fervent Person*, an extremely free 'translation'—she calls it a 'transelation'—of *O Guardador de Rebanhos*, a poem by the Portuguese poet Fernando Pessoa, 1888–1935, published under the name Alberto Caeiro, one of his many 'heteronyms').

In addition to writing her own poetry, Mouré has crafted English translations of a number of foreign-language texts, including those of the Quebec feminist theorist and poet Nicole Brossard. She has conducted poetry workshops across North America and in Europe and has been writer-in-residence at Concordia University, University of Calgary, and University of Toronto.

It Is Only Me

Say there is a woman
in the locked-up cornfield.
She is making a desert for herself, not me.
Like the poet said:[1] Fumbling the sky's queer wires,
asking for
mercy, abstract collusion, a kind of awe;
she hikes across the frozen furrows in mid-November
ready to observe nearly anything,
self-consciously, as if the turned dirt
would see her singing,
would answer with arguments on Kandinsky[2] & Klee.

1 Al Purdy; in lines 4–6 Mouré alludes to his poem 'Wilderness Gothic' (see pp. 552–3).
2 Wassily Kandinsky (1866–1944), Russian painter and pioneer of expressionism; Kandinsky and the Swiss abstract painter Paul Klee (1899–1940) were members in Germany of the *Blue Rider* group of artists and colleagues on the Bauhaus faculty.

At least she can't hear
the saxophone playing scales in the next room,
taking the colours out of the air;
they become discordant sounds & no longer answer.
The words stay silent on the page, their usual selves,
picking lice from under their collars,
not yet torn, or interested, or censored,
or even free.
There are never enough groceries, does the woman
know this in the strange field?
Probably she has thought of it before, a few minutes,
but now the long furrows
are turning her over & over, like a leaf
in the wind.

Never mind the sound,
the saxophonist is in another country, its mountains
stop him from reaching her.
It is only me, with my bad language, my long distance whisky:
I see her far away, it is very cold, I am
calling her out of her field.

1983

Blindness

Some of our desires are known only on the floor
of oceans, the nets dragged thru,
a light beyond colour we can't imagine, where we live now,
people of the surface,
whose foetuses still bear gills for a few days
& lose them, our kinship,
the water inside women,
water where we form & grow.

The halibut frozen whole, a sheet of memory,
held up, thawed, cut into slices
across the body, the central location of the spine,
our shared spine,
small bone hands of its vertebrae,
evolved away from us.

To feed us, first & lastly, taste
of white flakes upon the tongue,
soft resistance to the teeth & jaw;
our body is water &
the fish burn in it like fuel.

The flatfish that begins like any other,
swims upright
buoyant in the water, one eye on each side
of the head.
Then adolescent, feeling the body stagger
& list, gone sideways, one eye
migrates across the forehead or
thru the skull
to the right or left side, depending on the species.

Some of our desires are known only here,
are only now being let loose & admitted,
have only this moment stopped being
ashamed,
ashamed of the shape our bodies took & stayed on land
when the fish said No & went back
into the water,
mistake, mistake, fuck the lungs, some of our desires
are known only on the ocean floor, in the head

of the flatfish, halibut lying on its left side,
the eye that migrated across its skull
staring upward with the other.
At rest with it, patient.
Some of us have lungs that suffocate in the air.
The human body, two eyes fixed in the skull,
a third eye that presses on the forehead
& gets nowhere, presses & lives,
its silence the silence under oceans,
in the deep water of the body,
its blind side facing the brain

1985

Miss Chatelaine

In the movie, the horse almost dies.
A classic for children, where the small girl pushes a thin
knife into the horse's side.
Later I am sitting in brightness with the women
I went to high school with in Calgary,
fifteen years later we are all feminist, talking of the girl
in the film.
The horse who has some parasite & is afraid of the storm,
& the girl who goes out to save him.
We are in a baggage car on VIA Rail around a huge table,
its varnish light & cold,
as if inside the board rooms of the corporation;
the baggage door is open
to the smell of dark prairie,
we are fifteen years older, serious
about women, these images:
the girl running at night between the house & the barn,
& the noise of the horse's fear mixed in with the rain.

Finally there are no men between us.
Finally none of use are passing or failing according to
Miss Chatelaine.
I wish I could tell you how much I love you,
my friends with your odd looks, our odd looks,
our nervousness with each other,
the girl crying out as she runs in the darkness,
our decoration we wore, so many years ago, high school
boys watching from another table.

Finally I can love you.
Wherever you have gone to, in your secret marriages.
When the knife goes so deeply into the horse's side, a
few seconds & the rush of air.
In the morning, the rain is over.
The space between the house & barn is just a space again.
Finally I can meet with you & talk this over.
Finally I can see us meeting, & our true tenderness, emerge.

1988

The Beauty of Furs

At lunch with the girls, the younger ones are talking about furs, & what looks good with certain hair colours. Red fox looks no good with my hair, says one. White fox looks snobbish, beautiful but snobbish, says another one. They talk about the pronunciation of coyote. I think of my brother catching muskrat. I think of pushing the drown-set into the weeds, the freezing water of the Elbow, the brown banks & snow we lived with, soft smell of aspen buds not yet coming out on the trees, & us in our nylon coats in the back-yards of Elbow Park Estates, practically downtown, trapping. *Coy-oh-tea*, the women say. In some places they say *Ky-oot* or *Ky-oht*, I say, thinking of the country where my brother now lives, the moan of coyotes unseen, calling the night sky. & me caught in the drown-set so deeply, my breath snuffled for years. & then it comes. They are talking about the beauty of furs, and how so-and-so's family is in the business. I remember, I say, I remember my mother had a muskrat coat, & when she wore it & you grabbed her too hard by the arm, fur came out. Eileen, fifteen years older than me, starts to laugh, & puts her hand on my shoulder, laughing. We both start laughing. I start to explain to her that it was old; my mother wore it to church on Sunday & got upset if we grabbed her arm. We're laughing so hard, now the young ones are looking at us, together we are laughing, in our house there was a beaver coat like that Eileen said, then suddenly we are crying, crying for those fur coats & the pride of our mothers, our mothers' pride, smell of the coat at church on Sunday, smell of the river, & us so small, our hair wet, kneeling in that smell of fur beside our mothers

The Beauty of Furs: A Site Glossary

Later you realize it is a poem about being born, the smell of the fur is your mother birthing you & your hair is wet not slicked back but from the wetness of womb, the fur coat the hugest fur of your mother the cunt of your mother from which you have emerged & you cower in this smell The fur coat the sex of women reduced to decoration, & the womb the place of birth becomes the church in which you are standing, the womb reduced to decoration, where women are decoration, where the failure of decoration is the humiliation of women, to wear these coats, these emblems of their own bodies, in church on Sunday, children beside them The church now the place of birth & rebirth, they say *redemption*, everyone knows what this signifies & the mother is trying to pay attention, all the mothers, my mother, & we are children, I am children, a child with wet hair cowlick slicked down perfect, no humiliation, the site still charged with the smell of the river, the coat smell of the river, smell of the birth canal, caught in the drown-set is to be stopped from being born, is to be clenched in the water unable to breathe or see the night sky, the *coyohts* calling me upward, as if in these circumstances, so small beside my mother, I could be born now, but cannot, can I, because we are inside this hugest womb which has already denied us, in which we are decoration, in which men wear dresses & do the cooking, & the slicked hair is not the wet hair of birth but the hair of decoration, as if I could be born now, I am born, my snout warm smelling the wet earth of my mother's fur

1989

Absalom[1]

& if she called her daughter Absalom
her raised hand crying out the word

in the beginning a stickler for promises
'les promesses, les prometteurs'

holding up one hand when she was speaking
this was 'motherly'

& her daughter ran out into the trees
feeling the cold air on her face & forehead

the cold air on her arms
September

a rattling in the leaves calling down the stars
& winter

the sound of the party inside the building
from which a yellow light

& the daughter grown up alone
catching up to herself like a latch or hinge

thinking
she called me Absalom

when really there was only a promise
in which the trees had whispered

in which the sap was gathered with a spoon to rub
onto the lash or sore

when really there was none of this
her mother restless & shifting forward

1 In the Bible, Absalom, the son of King David, had his half-brother Amnon killed for the rape of his sister and later led an unsuccessful revolt against his father.

sitting up in bed like the leaves
calling her

1996

Dream of the Towns

I've been getting over a shaved pudenda
I've been playing the bagpipe of the intestines
& what have I learned
apocrypha

Then, I was in a hospital window high over Montréal
I called it my penthouse & lay in the horizon six days, for six days
they helped me rise up
& commit to memory my vital signs

Now I am just left of the alley where the weedy tree blooms its blossomy
leaves, sleeping face-down in shadowy afternoons
I thank you everyone for your dream of the towns
where you saw me, running wildly

Valença do Minho, Chlebowicz, Duga Res[1]

As for me I am abstinent awhile yet

The tremour still here

    (the slice in me

May 17, 1994

1996

1 Notes:

1) Valença do Minho is a northern Portuguese border town, directly across the Minho (Miño) from Tuy, in Pontevedra province, Galicia, España.
2) Chlebowicz is the birthplace in Poland, now in the Ukraine, of the author's mother. It may have a different name now.
3) The residents of the town of Duga Res in Croatia in 1992 or 1993 cut down a wood of 88 trees they themselves had planted to honour Marshall Tito's 88th birthday, saying they were removing 'the last remnants of the communist regime'. [Mouré's notes]

The Splendour

Is it rigour or is it patchwork
Riding, alone, the engine of economy

A splendour
(or is it)

Trying to be as curious
Trying to forge an upset frame of reference
Pulling the window thru the door,
her blue sweater gradually emerges
or rocks where she had crossed

the Elbow River
A splendour (is it)
Following 'Louise's' laugh
An economic dwelling where we all have been spilled or tarnished

Alone, but as such
I connote her arm where once no art was possible
A true life

we have been seeking
is it seekable

or 'stake in'

2

What it is, we wait
as once we did
Await the father's anger which we knew as love
Tools & soil inhabit us

(it is so difficult not to be bitter
as such
Communicáte or icon, a slick rock she once did slip on
in the Colorado River, falling)

Because it is such difficulty names us . . .
I 'admit'

3

A zone where tremors do inhabit
We are at ease here
Our heart shocks us every moment

A respite is what we long for
To be honest
I remain

4

Where keys of doors & doors of poetry
An insistent anecdote brings up her smile
Last seen in June (it is November)

As such, time passes
we refuse it
Kale, mimosa, milk & resin

Time passes
Poems recuperate, but do not solve
We refuse it

do not obey
or chastise

pulsate

5

The realm here is
irremediable

Thus in my act I do remember
what is memory
If not

aberrant splendour

6

I insist upon (falling into the fall or river, shoes wet)

to pulsate[1]

1999

1 imagine [Mouré's note]

Jan Zwicky

b. 1955

Born in Calgary in 1955, Jan Zwicky grew up on the Prairies but spent extended periods of her adult life in other regions of Canada and now lives, with the poet Don McKay, in Victoria, BC. This experience of varied landscapes informs the environmental and ecological concerns in her writing, while her backgrounds as professional violinist and philosopher guide the interdisciplinary explorations that also characterize her poems. Zwicky received a BA from the University of Calgary (1976) and an MA (1977) and Ph.D. (1981) in philosophy from the University of Toronto. Before joining the philosophy department at the University of Victoria in 1996, she taught philosophy—and, on occasion, creative writing, English, and the humanities—at Princeton University and the Universities of Waterloo and New Brunswick. Her books include *Where Have We Been* (1982); *Wittgenstein Elegies* (1986); *The New Room* (1989); *Lyric Philosophy* (1992); *Songs for Relinquishing the Earth* (1996); and *21 Small Songs* (2000). With Brad Cran, she edited an anthology (accompanied by a 13-song CD) of blues poems by Canadian and American poets: *Why I Sing the Blues* (2001).

Lyric Philosophy is a cross-generic work investigating the relationship between the truth that philosophy can express and the truth expressed by poetry, and it suggests that we need both analytic and poetic ways of thinking. This belief 'that lyric poetry and philosophy are not mutually exclusive', and Zwicky's general interest in creating a poetry of ideas, can also be seen in an early book like *Wittgenstein Elegies*, which is made up of five polyphonic sequences responding to the life and teachings of the Austrian-born philosopher of language and meaning, the Cambridge don Ludwig Wittgenstein (1889–1951). Her third collection, *The New Room*, shows the other side of Zwicky's writing in its personal lyrics that deal with the details of memory and daily life as a way of investigating exile; home; and the relationship between place, objects, and the perceiving mind. The title poem shows how these ideas come together in the simple acts of living inside a room, and of furnishing and taking care of it.

Songs for Relinquishing the Earth won a Governor General's Award for work the jury described as a masterful blend of 'narrative and association, the colloquial and the elegant, metaphor and discourse, the conceptual and the sensuous'. It began life in 1996 as a handmade book, 'each copy individually sewn for its reader in response to a request'—Zwicky's way of affirming the close personal connection she felt existed between a poet and her reader. When she found she couldn't keep pace with demand, an edition was published in 1998 by Brick Books. The desire to draw meaningful connections between individuals, places, and ways of thinking is apparent throughout the collection in poems that Zwicky describes as meditations ranging 'in subject matter from Kant, Hegel, and Pythagoras to Beethoven, Bruckner, and Hindemith, unified by questions about the nature of home and our responsibilities to it'. For Zwicky, 'home' expands to take in the whole environment, the whole phenomenological world of visible details—along with, in 'Driving Northwest', the light itself that makes them visible. Elsewhere in the book the art of music—which, in the poem 'Open Strings', includes the conventional EADG tuning of the violin—serves as another language, just as in 'Bill Evans: "Here's That Rainy Day"' the piece of jazz seems to be telling a story to the listener at the end of a long day.

The collection closes with a prose poem, '*Trauermusik*', that focuses on modernist composer Paul Hindemith's masterpiece by that name. There Zwicky employs music theory to show how we must listen for that which we cannot hear, and how we hear that which we expect, even when it is not present. To read Zwicky is to experience Horace's ideal: hers is a poetry that both teaches and delights.

The New Room

Find we don't notice
seams where we pieced, bubbles
subsiding like lymph pockets
over rotten plaster. (Christ,
not one square corner in the place.)
Wallpaper repeats
        repeats
that faded denim stripe
forever to the ceiling. Space is
vertical, smooth
as the touch of sun through glass,
the beds of women
past the reach of love.

Empty now. A last skiff
of light drifts in across
flat seas of corn. Lines of loss
simple as a window.
We will fill this room
as if we owned them: bleached armchair,
the gouge-topped desk, those objects
waiting outside, motionless.

        Their essence
is their loyalty. Their lives
are the accumulations
of our absence, bounded
by the moments when we draw them
into time. Their surfaces, defenceless
against incursions of our whimsy are
displaced, abandoned, taken
for granted. Here, we can
see them for an instant as they are,
all the mute axes of our lives
stretched behind them, racing away from us
row on row on row.

1978

Open Strings

E, laser of the ear, ear's
vinegar, bagpipes
in a tux, the sky's blue, pointed;

A, youngest of the four, cocksure
and vulnerable, the white kid
on the basketball team—immature,
ambitious, charming,
indispensable; apprenticed
to desire;

D is the tailor
who sewed the note 'I shall always love you'
into the hem of the village belle's wedding dress,
a note not discovered until ten years later in New York
where, poor and abandoned, she was ripping up the skirt
for curtains, and he came,
and he married her;

G, cathedral of the breastbone,
oak-light, earth;

it's air they offer us,
but not the cool draught of their half-brothers
the harmonics, no,
a bigger wind, the body
snapped out like a towel, air
like the sky above the foothills,
like the desire to drown,
a place of worship,
a laying down of arms.
Open strings
are ambassadors from the republic of silence.
They are the name of that moment when you realize
clearly, for the first time,
you will die. After illness,
the first startled breath.

1998

Bill Evans[1]: 'Here's That Rainy Day'

On a bad day, you come in from the weather
and lean your back against the door.
This time of year it's dark by five.
Your armchair, empty in its pool of light.

That arpeggio[2] lifts, like warmth, from the fifth of B minor,
offers its hand—*let me*
tell you a story . . . But in the same breath,
semitones falling to the tonic:
you must believe and not believe;
that door you came in
you must go out again.

In the forest, the woodcutter's son
sets the stone down from his sack and speaks to it.
And from nothing, a spring wells
falling as it rises, spilling out
across the dark green moss.
There is sadness in the world, it says,
past telling. Learn stillness
if you would run clear.

1998

1 (1929–80), solo jazz pianist, who also played with Miles Davis; his innovations in playing and composition influenced the shape of jazz. The song 'Here's That Rainy Day' appeared on his 1968 album *Bill Evans Alone.*

2 An arpeggio is a chord in which the notes are played separately in rapid succession. Here the notes of the B-minor chord (i.e. BDF#) are played ascending, beginning with the chord's 'fifth' (F#), while Evans also plays semitones (black and white keys on the piano such as C and C# are one semitone apart in the standard scale) that descend to the tonic or keynote of the scale, B.

Musicians

I pass a bunch of musicians in the street.
It's about 12:30, rehearsal just over, they're
standing around outside the side door of the church.
A good rehearsal; and it's April. They're laughing,
horsing around, talking about shoes, or taxes, where
to go for lunch, anything
except what their heads are full of.

It's a kind of helplessness, you can see
they're still breathing almost in unison, like people
the searchlight has passed over
and spared, their attention
lifts, swerves, settles; even
the gravel dust stuttering at their feet
is coherent.

1998

Transparence

Do not drink
the darkness, said Pythagoras,
the soul cannot become pure darkness.

—Robert Bringhurst

I would reply to Pythagoras[1]
nor can the soul
become pure light.

Or if it does, the experience,
unless you are freakishly lucky—like
that woman, thrown from her car, her car
rolling and bouncing up one side of the embankment and then
back down, to land on top of her, except
the roof had been dented by the guardrail
and it came down with the hollow
over her and she escaped
unscathed—will kill you.

So we are caught stumbling
in between, longing for home.

*

Things we leave behind: the belief
that nothing else will matter as much again,
and this: if we could learn
to let go without leaving then
our real lives might begin.

1 (*c.* 569–*c.* 475 BCE), pre-Socratic mathematician, philosopher, and mystic, who saw the world in terms of numbers and sought out balances of qualities including darkness and light.

Where do we hang our hats? Up the long slope
we are always running to in dreams?

Or here, in the confused kitchen of paychecks
and good intentions, one black one
double-double, make that to go? Meaning
is a measure of resistance: to that hand
shoving you out over the cliff of your future,
to the thought of your own hands
gulping for the substance of the familiar. And
nothing *will* matter as much
as those back stairs, that red bench,
the Matisse drawing cut from a calendar
years ago, left curling on the garage wall
after the yard sale, remembered suddenly
with vividness just west of Oshawa.
Something not a bone
but like a bone—just here, behind the clutter
in your chest—broken so many times
it's ground to dust; and you bend, resistless,
to shoulder every absence.

*

Light lives
everywhere: no legs, no breath,
no need for shoes. Its unmoorings
effortless, nothing
in tow. No need
for hands: it does not take itself
to be responsible. Light
carries nothing, and the place
it thinks, it is.

*

Morning after rain, the mind wakes
dewy, tender—bad news, miscalculations
piled behind it like a shelf of badly-folded blankets.
Only in fairy tales,
or given freakish luck, does the wind
rise suddenly and set you down where everything
is safe and loved and in its place. The mind
does not expect it. But the heart,
the heart—

the heart keeps looking for itself.
It knows and does not know
where it belongs. It quivers
like a compass, taut with anticipation,
the sweep thump
of arrival. The heart,
a solid thing, is dark
like turf, and it believes
luck is a talent, or a form of light—
at least, its due for service—
and refuses to be schooled.

*

Dust from the eighteen-wheeler
whipping in to the Dryden Husky as we
step out of the restaurant—it looks like fog—
and I'm reminded of the morning river-mists
in the scrub parkland where I grew up,
walking through them how they'd swirl,
evaporate, the dampness on the grass
sighed into sky. Here in August,
northern Ontario, evening,
grit sticks to my face and neck, sits in my lungs.
Out of sight, the rig door slams and someone laughs.
I spill my coffee as I struggle with the lid.
As we pull away
the dust's still there, sun
catching it, and being caught,
exactly: a lightness you can see
right through, suspended
in the night-blue air.

1998

Driving Northwest

Driving Northwest in July before
the long twilight that stretches into
the short summer dark, despite the sun
the temperature is dropping, air
slips by the truck, like diving,

diving,
        and you are almost blind
with light: on either side of you
it floats across the fields, young barley
picking up the gold, oats white,
the cloudy bruise of alfalfa
along the fencelines, the air itself
tawny with haydust, and the shadows of the willows
in the draw miles long, oh it is lovely
as a myth, the touch of a hand on your hair,
and you need, like sleep, to lie down now
and rest, but you are almost
blind with light, the highway
stretched across the continent
straight at the sun: visor,
dark glasses, useless against its gonging,
the cab drowns in it, shuddering, you cannot tell,
you might be bleeding or suffocating, shapes
fly out of it so fast there's no time to swerve:
but there is no other path, there is no other bed,
it is the only way home you know.

1998

Trauermusik

In 1936, on the occasion of the death of King George V, Paul Hindemith, who was in London at the time giving a series of concerts, wrote a chamber work scored for string orchestra with viola solo.[1] The fourth of its brief movements is a setting of the chorale 'Vor deinen Thron tret' ich hiermit', known to most Lutherans as 'Herr Gott, dich loben alle wir', and to most English-speaking church-goers as 'Old Hundredth'.[2]

1 *Trauermusik* (literally, 'mourning music'), a composition by the German-American composer Paul Hindemith (1895–1963), combined traditional music, particularly that based on folk melodies or poetry, with experimental techniques that moved away from the European keys or scales.

2 Although the words vary, the melodic line of Hindemith's fourth movement has a long history, dating back to the *Genevan Psalter* (1562), a collection of psalms set to music, of which this was the One Hundredth, and known as 'Herr Gott, dich loben alle wir' ('Lord God, we all praise Thee'), and before that to *Souter Liedekens*, a 1540 collection of Dutch rhymed versions of the Psalms with roots in folk music. Johann Sabastian Bach (1685–1750) wrote a cantata based on the psalm and also a choral variation of the tune: 'Vor deinen Thron tret' ich hierrmit' ('Before Thy Throne Do I Come Now'); earlier Johann Pachelbel (1653–1706) used it as the basis for a choral prelude. Zwicky's poem explains how, in *Trauermusik*, Hindemith created a chord setting for this melody that leads one to expect, but does not employ, a closing cadence in which the chord is resolved through the leading note (which is the seventh of the eight notes in an octave). The ear hears the absence of the leading note, and thus longs for it (an appropriate feeling to have when listening to *Trauermusik*).

The melody is indeed old, among those Louis Bourgeois composed for the Genevan psalter in the mid-sixteenth century: its roots reach back, through the Dutch *Souter Liedekens*, into folksong. In Bach's harmonizations, as in Pachelbel's and others', the closing cadence is what music theorists call a perfect or authentic cadence—one in which a chord built on the fifth of the scale resolves to a chord built on the tonic. In a move you won't find described let alone recommended in the theory books, Hindemith, by contrast, writes a cadence that turns on an inverted triad on the sixth—and thereby manages to avoid sounding what musicians call the leading note. What is remarkable about this is not that there aren't plenty of standard cadences in which the leading note doesn't occur; it's that here, none of those standard cadences are available. The melody—that simple descending scale in the last two bars—together with the rules of classical harmony conspire to give the composer little leeway: they make a cadence that includes the leading note so overwhelmingly obvious that deciding not to use it is a bit like not using the Lion's Gate Bridge when you're in Stanley Park and want to get home to North Vancouver.

Those who have seen Ansel Adams' early photographs of the Golden Gate before its own bridge was built[3] may have encountered a similar effect: although the landscape in those photographs is breathtakingly beautiful, and intact, and although that is surely the point, the imagination, conditioned by years of photographs since the bridge, senses that something is missing. The bridge, less necessary to what the Golden Gate *is* than the headlands of either the San Francisco or Marin Peninsulas, has nonetheless become definitive: it embodies one shape of human desire.

So, too, the leading note—the seventh in the eight-note scale. It gets it name because, more than any other, it tends to be followed by the tonic. But it leads not only by proximity, it leads because its emotional gaze, more than that of any other note, is directed home: the seventh is the interval most coloured by desire, the point at which the key is stretched to its limit, at which the demand for return is most intense.

Grief, too, has to do with homesickness; and in the closing measures of *Trauermusik* we are told a little of what this is. A cadence in which the leading note is not included—but in which our ear must detect its absence—says that mourning requires an acknowledgement that death is the absence of desire, that death moves with the indifference of the sunlight in these sunlit blocks of chords.

And, it tells us, in the relinquishing that is the end of mourning, we must pass through—as through a ghost—that absence in ourselves.

1998

3 Ansel Adams (1902–84) was a photographer and conservationist who took pictures of western landscapes to help Americans understand the necessity of preserving their natural treasures. Among these were photographs of the Golden Gate Strait (the entrance from the Pacific Ocean to San Francisco Bay) taken before the bridge crossing the strait was built. (He later took many famous photographs of the Golden Gate Bridge itself.)

Anne Michaels

b. 1958

Anne Michaels was born in Toronto, where her father ran a small record store. She and her three brothers grew up with books, classical music, and parents who loved discussions. She studied piano and violin and grew interested in poetry even before attending university. After receiving her BA in English from the University of Toronto in 1980, she taught creative writing, and worked as an arts administrator, a freelance writer, an editor, and a composer of music for theatre.

Although born long after the Holocaust, she found that the story of characters touched by that horrific event in history began to haunt her imagination. That led her to spend ten years in researching and writing the novel that became *Fugitive Pieces*. A central thesis of that novel—in which the first of its narrators says 'I was transfixed by the way time buckled; met itself in pleats and folds'—is that what is important is not a record of the past but how we respond to that past: 'History is amoral: events occurred. But memory is moral; what we consciously remember is what our conscience remembers.' Published in 1996, *Fugitive Pieces* brought Michaels international acclaim and won a number of awards, among them the *Books in Canada* First Novel Award, the Trillium Award, the Guardian Fiction Award, the Lannan Literary Award for Fiction, and the Orange Prize for Fiction.

Michaels began her literary career as a highly regarded poet. Her first collection of poems, *The Weight of Oranges* (1986), won a Commonwealth Prize; her second collection, *Miner's Pond* (1991), was shortlisted for the Governor General's and Trillium Awards. Her most recent volume of poems, *Skin Divers*, appeared in 1999, following the reissue in 1997 of her first two collections of poetry as a single volume.

While some of her poems are personal and immediate, many show that her writing has often turned around large questions about memory and the past. The long poem reprinted here, 'Lake of Two Rivers' (it makes up the first of the three sections of *The Weight of Oranges*), investigates the way 'We do not descend, but rise from our histories'. In it the child's memory of being six and travelling to the Two Rivers campground in Algonquin Park with her parents blends with the stories her father told on those trips about the discovery of the wonderful land of Shangri-La (in the movie *Lost Horizon*) and about his own crossing of Poland in 1931, stories that later cause her to 'fall through' her reading of a history text when the fate of his family in the Holocaust becomes embedded in the facts she now learns from a book.

Others among Michaels' poems deal with a more distant past through the form of the dramatic monologue. In these, historical figures turn their vision inward to examine the complexities of their own lives and struggle to make the connection between language and experience. In 'Ice House', for example, Michaels provides a fresh perspective on a famous story by dramatizing the voice of the sculptor Kathleen Scott, the wife of the explorer Robert F. Scott, whose final trip to the Antarctic to make scientific observations and to travel by land to the South Pole ended in disastrously.

Fugitive Pieces

The selection reprinted here, from the novel's first chapter, is spoken by Jakob Beer, the first of the book's two narrators. Having witnessed the murder of his family at the hands of the Germans in Poland during the Second World War, the boy survives by burying himself alive in a swampy bog that holds the remains of a 2000-year-old village, moving only by night, and avoiding all other human beings. Unearthed by the archaeologist Athos Roussos, he is taken to live on an Island in Greece, where he is taught about art, poetry, botany, and cartography. After the war, he immigrates with Athos to Toronto: there he falls in love and becomes a poet, only to die in a traffic accident. In the second part of the book, told after his death, a Canadian professor named Ben attempts, with the help of the poet's journals, to excavate Beer's life. Ben's efforts and the effect that his discoveries about Beer have on his own life support Michaels' contention that 'an idea recorded will become an idea resurrected'.

Critics have commented on how *Fugitive Pieces* needs to find a way to speak about the unspeakable in order to bear witness to the Holocaust and its continuing effects. Looking back to such precursors as Theodore Adorno, Primo Levi, and Walter Benjamin, who each struggled with the question of how to respond to such horror with something other than silence, Michaels provides a voice for those lost to memory and to history, and at the same time seeks redemption for our pasts.

Lake of Two Rivers

1

Pull water, unhook its seam.

Lie down in the lake room,
in the smell of leaves still sticky from their birth.

Fall to sleep the way the moon falls
from earth: perfect lethargy of orbit.

2

Six years old, half asleep,
a traveller. The night car mysterious
as we droned past uneasy twisting fields.

My father told two stories on these drives.
One was the plot of 'Lost Horizon',
the other: his life.
This speeding room, dim in the dashboard's green emission,
became the hijacked plane carrying Ronald Colman to Tibet,
or the train carrying my father across Poland in 1931.

Spirit faces crowded the windows of a '64 Buick.
Unknown cousins surrounded us, arms around each other,
a shawl of sleeves.

The moon fell into our car from Grodno.
It fell from Chaya-Elke's village,
where they stopped to say goodbye.

His cousin Mashka sat up with them
in the barn, while her face
floated down the River Neman in my father's guitar.
He watched to remember
in the embalming moonlight.

3

Sensate weather, we are your body,
your memory. Like a template,
branch defines sky, leaves
bleed their gritty boundaries,
corrosive with nostalgia.

Each year we go outside to pin it down,
light limited, light specific,
light like a name.

*

For years my parents fled at night,
loaded their children in the back seat,
a tangle of pyjamas anxious to learn the stars.

I watched the backs of their heads
until I was asleep, and when I woke
it was day, and we were in Algonquin.

I've always known this place,
familiar as a room in our house.

The photo of my mother, legs locked in water,
looking into the hills where you and I stand—

only now do I realize
it was taken before I was born.

*

Purple mist, indefinite hills.

At Two Rivers, close as branches.
Fish scatter, silver pulses with their own electric logic.

Milky spill of moon over the restless lake,
seen through a sieve of foliage.

In fields to the south
vegetables radiate underground,
displace the earth.
While we sit, linked by firelight.

4

The longer you look at a thing
the more it transforms.

My mother's story is tangled,
overgrown with lives of parents and grandparents
because they lived in one house and among them
remembered hundreds of years of history.

This domestic love is plain, hurts
the way light balancing objects in a still life hurts.

The heart keeps body and spirit in suspension,
until density pulls them apart.
When she was my age
her mother had already fallen through.

Pregnant, androgynous with man,
she was afraid. When life goes out,
loss gets in, wedging a new place.

Under dark lanes of the night sky
the eyes of our skin won't close,
we dream in desire.

Love wails from womb, caldera,[1] home.
Like any sound, it goes on forever.

*

The dissolving sun turns Two Rivers into skin.
Our pink arms, slightly fluorescent,
hiss in the dusky room, neon tubes bending
in the accumulated dark.

1 A crater formed by a volcanic explosion or collapse.

Night transforms the lake into a murmuring solid.
Naked in the eerie tremor of leaves rubbing stars,
in the shivering fermata[2] of summer,
in the energy of stones made powerful by gravity,
desire made powerful by the seam between starlight and skin,
we join, moebius ribbon in the night room.

5

We do not descend, but rise from our histories.
If cut open memory would resemble
a cross-section of the earth's core,
a table of geographical time.
Faces press the transparent membrane
between conscious and genetic knowledge.
A name, a word, triggers the dilatation.
Motive is uncovered, sharp overburden in a shifting field.

*

When I was twenty-five I drowned in the River Neman,
fell through when I read that bone-black from the ovens
was discarded there.[3]

Like a face pressed against a window,
part of you waits up for them,
like a parent, you wait up.

*

A family now, we live each other's life
without the details.

The forest flies apart, trees are shaken loose
by my tears,

by love that doesn't fall to earth
but bursts up from the ground, fully formed.

1985

2 The prolongation of a note or chord beyond its marked time value. 'Moebius ribbon': a band fastened into a loop after being twisted once, causing what seem opposing sides of its flat surface to double-back on themselves and become continuous; it is an unusual physical object in that it has both two-dimensional and three-dimensional qualities.

3 The River Neman is the main river in Lithuania; when the Axis powers overran the area (Lithuania was then part of the Soviet Union), its banks were home to many Jewish families and settlements; more than 10,000 were killed by the Nazis, many cremated alive in the ovens of Axis concentration camps.

Flowers

There's another skin inside my skin
that gathers to your touch, a lake to the light;
that looses its memory, its lost language
into your tongue,
erasing me into newness.

Just when the body thinks it knows
the ways of knowing itself,
this second skin continues to answer.

In the street—café chairs abandoned
on terraces; market stalls emptied
of their solid light,
though pavement still breathes
summer grapes and peaches.
Like the light of anything that grows
from this newly-turned earth,
every tip of me gathers under your touch,
wind wrapping my dress around our legs,
your shirt twisting to flowers in my fists.

1991

There Is No City That Does Not Dream

There is no city that does not dream
from its foundations. The lost lake
crumbling in the hands of brickmakers,
the floor of the ravine where light lies broken
with the memory of rivers. All the winters
stored in that geologic
garden. Dinosaurs sleep in the subway
at Bloor and Shaw, a bed of bones
under the rumbling track. The storm
that lit the city with the voltage
of spring, when we were eighteen
on the clean earth. The ferry ride in the rain,
wind wet with wedding music and everything that
sings in the carbon of stone and bone
like a page of love, wind-lost from a hand, unread.

1999

Ice House[1]

'I regret nothing but his suffering.'
—Kathleen Scott

Wherever we cry,
it's far from home.

*

At Sandwich, our son pointed
persistently to sea.
I followed his infant gaze,
expecting a bird or a boat
but there was nothing.
How unnerving,
as if he could see you
on the horizon,
knew where you were
exactly:
at the edge of the world.

*

You unloaded the ship at Lyttleton[2]
and repacked her:

'thirty-five dogs
five tons of dog food
fifteen ponies
thirty-two tons of pony fodder
three motor-sledges
four hundred and sixty tons of coal
collapsible huts
an acetylene plant
thirty-five thousand cigars
one guinea pig
one fantail pigeon

1 'Kathleen Scott was a sculptor, and the wife of the Antarctic explorer Robert Falcon Scott. They had been married two years, with an eleven-month-old son, when Scott went south to the Pole. Upon parting in New Zealand, they made a pact to keep a daily journal for each other. Scott perished on the return journey from the Pole, and when his body and the bodies of his companions were found in the spring, his diary was brought back to England. On the inside cover, Scott had written "Send this diary to my wife." Then Scott drew a line through the word "wife" and wrote instead, "widow".' [Michaels' note]

2 Kathleen recalls their trip to New Zealand, where they stayed in Lyttleton with friends (the Kinseys, mentioned later in the poem).

three rabbits
one cat with its own hammock, blanket and pillow
one hundred and sixty-two carcasses of mutton and
an ice house'

*

Men returned from war
without faces, with noses lost
discretely as antique statues,
accurately as if eaten
by frostbite.
In clay I shaped their
flesh, sometimes
retrieving a likeness
from photographs.
Then the surgeons copied
nose, ears, jaw
with molten wax and metal plates
and horsehair stitches;
with borrowed cartilage,
from the soldiers' own ribs,
leftovers stored under the skin
of the abdomen. I held the men down
until the morphia
slid into them.
I was only sick
afterwards.

Working the clay, I remembered
mornings in Rodin's studio,[3]
his drawerfuls of tiny hands and feet,
like a mechanic's tool box.
I imagined my mother in her blindness
before she died, touching my face,
as if still she could
build me with her body.

At night, in the studio
I took your face in my hands and your fine
arms and long legs, your small waist,
and loved you into stone.

3 As a young woman, Kathleen worked in the studio of the sculptor Auguste Rodin (1840–1917), who was famous for his evocative portrayals of the human figure.

The men returned from France
to Ellerman's Hospital.
Their courage
was beautiful.
I understood the work at once:
To use scar tissue to advantage.
To construct through art,
one's face to the world.
Sculpt what's missing.

*

You reached furthest south,
then you went further.

In neither of those forsaken places
did you forsake us.

*

At Lyttleton the hills unrolled,
a Japanese scroll painting;
we opened the landscape with our bare feet.
So much learned by observation.
We took in brainfuls of New Zealand air
on the blue climb over the falls.

Our last night together we slept
not in the big house but
in the Kinseys' garden.
Belonging only
to each other.
Guests of the earth.

*

Mid-sea, a month out of range
of the wireless;
on my way to you. Floating
between landfalls,
between one hemisphere and another.
Between the words
'wife' and 'widow'.

*

Newspapers, politicians
scavenged your journals.

But your words
never lost their way.

*

We mourn in a place no one knows;
it's right that our grief be unseen.

I love you as if you'll return
after years of absence.
As if we'd invented
moonlight.

*

Still I dream
of your arrival.

1999

From *Fugitive Pieces*

Time is a blind guide.

Bog-boy, I surfaced into the miry streets of the drowned city. For over a thousand years, only fish wandered Biskupin's[1] wooden sidewalks. Houses, built to face the sun, were flooded by the silty gloom of the Gasawka River. Gardens grew luxurious in subaqueous silence; lilies, rushes, stinkweed.

No one is born just once. If you're lucky, you'll emerge again in someone's arms; or unlucky, wake when the long tail of terror brushes the inside of your skull.

I squirmed from the marshy ground like Tollund Man, Grauballe Man,[2] like the boy they uprooted in the middle of Franz Josef Street while they were repairing the

1 Biskupin, in north-central Poland, is the site of an ancient wooden village (700–550 BCE), built over a peat bog; it was probably once located on an island in the lake of the same name that was flooded somewhere around 500 BCE. Archaeological excavation was begun on the site in 1934. The Nazis used the extensive remains of the village as 'evidence' to support Hitler's theories about race. The nearby Gasawka River feeds the lake.

2 Tollund Man and Grauballe Man are the names given two 2,000-year-old bog-preserved bodies discovered in the 1950s near Bjeldskovdal, Denmark. Like many such bog people, they seemed to have been placed in the peat swamp after death.

road, six hundred cockleshell beads around his neck, a helmet of mud. Dripping with the prune-coloured juices of the peat-sweating bog. Afterbirth of earth.

I saw a man kneeling in the acid-steeped ground. He was digging. My sudden appearance unnerved him. For a moment he thought I was one of Biskupin's lost souls, or perhaps the boy in the story, who digs a hole so deep he emerges on the other side of the world.

Biskupin had been carefully excavated for almost a decade. Archaeologists gently continued to remove Stone and Iron Age relics from soft brown pockets of peat. The pure oak causeway that once connected Biskupin to the mainland had been reconstructed, as well as the ingenious nail-less wooden houses, ramparts, and the high-towered city gates. Wooden streets, crowded twenty-five centuries before with traders and craftsmen, were being raised from the swampy lake bottom. When the soldiers arrived they examined the perfectly preserved clay bowls; they held the glass beads, the bronze and amber bracelets, before smashing them on the floor. With delighted strides, they roamed the magnificent timber city, once home to a hundred families. Then the soldiers buried Biskupin in sand.

My sister had long outgrown the hiding place. Bella was fifteen and even I admitted she was beautiful, with heavy brows and magnificent hair like black syrup, thick and luxurious, a muscle down her back. 'A work of art,' our mother said, brushing it for her while Bella sat in a chair. I was still small enough to vanish behind the wallpaper in the cupboard, cramming my head sideways between choking plaster and beams, eyelashes scraping.

Since those minutes inside the wall, I've imagined that the dead lose every sense except hearing.

The burst door. Wood ripped from hinges, cracking like ice under the shouts. Noises never heard before, torn from my father's mouth. Then silence. My mother had been sewing a button on my shirt. She kept her buttons in a chipped saucer. I heard the rim of the saucer in circles on the floor. I heard the spray of buttons, little white teeth.

Blackness filled me, spread from the back of my head into my eyes as if my brain had been punctured. Spread from stomach to legs. I gulped and gulped, swallowing it whole. The wall filled with smoke. I struggled out and stared while the air caught fire.

I wanted to go to my parents, to touch them. But I couldn't, unless I stepped on their blood.

The soul leaves the body instantly, as if it can hardly wait to be free: my mother's face was not her own. My father was twisted with falling. Two shapes in the flesh-heap, his hands.

I ran and fell, ran and fell. Then the river: so cold it felt sharp.

The river was the same blackness that was inside me; only the thin membrane of my skin kept me floating.

From the other bank, I watched darkness turn to purple-orange light above the town; the colour of flesh transforming to spirit. They flew up. The dead passed above me, weird haloes and arcs smothering the stars. The trees bent under their weight. I'd never been alone in the night forest, the wild bare branches were frozen snakes. The ground tilted and I didn't hold on. I strained to join them, to rise with them, to peel from the ground like paper ungluing at its edges. I know why we bury our dead and mark the place with stone, with the heaviest, most permanent thing we can think of: because the dead are everywhere but the ground. I stayed where I was. Clammy with cold, stuck to the ground. I begged: If I can't rise, then let me sink, sink into the forest floor like a seal into wax.

Then—as if she'd pushed the hair from my forehead, as if I'd heard her voice—I knew suddenly my mother was inside me. Moving along sinews, under my skin the way she used to move through the house at night, putting things away, putting things in order. She was stopping to say goodbye and was caught, in such pain, wanting to rise, wanting to stay. It was my responsibility to release her, a sin to keep her from ascending. I tore at my clothes, my hair. She was gone. My own fast breath around my head.

I ran from the sound of the river into the woods, dark as the inside of a box. I ran until the first light wrung the last greyness out of the stars, dripping dirty light between the trees. I knew what to do. I took a stick and dug. I planted myself like a turnip and hid my face with leaves.

My head between the branches, bristling points like my father's beard. I was safely buried, my wet clothes cold as armour. Panting like a dog. My arms tight against my chest, my neck stretched back, tears crawling like insects into my ears. I had no choice but to look straight up. The dawn sky was milky with new spirits. Soon I couldn't avoid the absurdity of daylight even by closing my eyes. It poked down, pinned me like the broken branches, like my father's beard.

Then I felt the worst shame of my life: I was pierced with hunger. And suddenly I realized, my throat aching without sound—Bella.

I had my duties. Walk at night. In the morning dig my bed. Eat anything.

My days in the ground were a delirium of sleep and attention. I dreamed someone found my missing button and came looking for me. In a glade of burst pods leaking their white stuffing, I dreamed of bread; when I woke, my jaw was sore from chewing the air. I woke terrified of animals, more terrified of men.

In this day-sleep, I remembered my sister weeping at the end of novels she loved; my father's only indulgence—Romain Rolland[3] or Jack London. She wore the

3 (1866–1944), French writer and Nobelist, known for his pacifism and idealism; he attacked fascism and saw art as part of the struggle against tyranny and as a source of enlightenment. Jack London (1876–1916): prolific American fiction writer now chiefly remembered for his animal adventure tales, *The Call of the Wild* and *White Fang*.

characters in her face as she read, one finger rubbing the edge of the page. Before I learned to read, angry to be left out, I strangled her with my arms, leaning over with my cheek against hers, as if somehow to see in the tiny black letters the world Bella saw. She shrugged me off or, big-hearted, she stopped, turned the book over in her lap, and explained the plot . . . the drunken father lurching home . . . the betrayed lover waiting vainly under the stairs . . . the terror of wolves howling in the Arctic dark, making my own skeleton rattle in my clothes. Sometimes at night, I sat on the edge of Bella's bed and she tested my spelling, writing on my back with her finger and, when I'd learned the word, gently erasing it with a stroke of her smooth hand.

I couldn't keep out the sounds: the door breaking open, the spit of buttons. My mother, my father. But worse than those sounds was that I couldn't remember hearing Bella at all. Filled with her silence, I had no choice but to imagine her face.

The night forest is incomprehensible: repulsive and endless, jutting bones and sticky hair, slime and jellied smells, shallow roots like ropy veins.

Draping slugs splash like tar across the ferns; black icicles of flesh.

During the day I have time to notice lichen like gold dust over the rocks.

A rabbit, sensing me, stops close to my head and tries to hide behind a blade of grass.

The sun is jagged through the trees, so bright the spangles turn dark and float, burnt paper, in my eyes.

The white nibs of grass get caught in my teeth like pliable little fishbones. I chew fronds into bitter, stringy mash that turns my spit green.

Once, I risk digging my bed close to pasture, for the breeze, for relief from the dense damp of the forest. Buried, I feel the shuddering dark shapes of cattle thudding across the fields. In the distance, their thrusting heads make them look as if they're swimming. They gallop to a stop a few feet from the fence then drift towards me, their heads swinging like slow church bells with every glory step of their heavy flanks. The slender calves quiver behind, fear twitching their ears. I'm also afraid—that the herd will bring everyone from miles away to where I'm hiding—as they gather to rest their massive heads on the fence and stare down at me with rolling eyes.

I fill my pockets and my hands with stones and walk into the river until only my mouth and nose, pink lilies, skim the air. Muck dissolves from my skin and hair, and it's satisfying to see floating like foam on the surface the fat scum of lice from my clothes. I stand on the bottom, my boots sucked down by the mud, the current flowing around me, a cloak in a liquid wind. I don't stay under long. Not only because of the cold, but because with my ears under the surface, I can't hear. This is more frightening to me than darkness, and when I can't stand the silence any longer, I slip out of my wet skin, into sound.

Someone is watching from behind a tree. I stare from my hiding place without moving, until my eyeballs harden, until I'm no longer sure he's seen me. What's he waiting for? In the last possible moment before I have to run, light coming fast, I discover I've been held prisoner half the night by a tree, its dead, dense bole carved by moonlight.

Even in daylight, in the cold drizzle, the tree's faint expression is familiar. The face above a uniform.

The forest floor is speckled bronze, sugar caramelized in the leaves. The branches look painted onto the onion-white sky. One morning I watch a finger of light move its way deliberately towards me across the ground.

I know, suddenly, my sister is dead. At this precise moment, Bella becomes flooded ground. A body of water pulling under the moon.

A grey fall day. At the end of strength, at the place where faith is most like despair, I leaped from the streets of Biskupin; from underground into air.

I limped towards him, stiff as a golem,[4] clay tight behind my knees. I stopped a few yards from where he was digging—later he told me it was as if I'd hit a glass door, an inarguable surface of pure air—'and your mud mask cracked with tears and I knew you were human, just a child. Crying with the abandonment of your age.'

He said he spoke to me. But I was wild with deafness. My peat-clogged ears.

So hungry. I screamed into the silence the only phrase I knew in more than one language, I screamed it in Polish and German and Yiddish, thumping my fists on my own chest: dirty Jew, dirty Jew, dirty Jew.

1996

4 (Hebrew); in Jewish medieval folklore, an artificially created human being animated by a charm (usually a word placed under the creature's tongue), often brought to life to right a wrong.

George Elliott Clarke
b. 1960

George Elliott Clarke comes from what he calls 'Africadia', a word he coined to suggest the way he was formed by the combined inheritances of Africa and Acadia. He was born at Windsor Plains, NS, a seventh-generation descendant of black Loyalists who came to Nova Scotia from the US, and he grew up in Halifax, in a house he has described as filled with 'television, radio, magazines, art and music'. Studying marine topology at the University of Waterloo he found himself interested in poetry and the blues, and he published a book of poems, *Saltwater Spirituals and Deeper Blues*, in 1983, while still an undergraduate. After returning to Nova Scotia and taking a job as a community development worker in the Annapolis Valley for the Black United Front of Nova Scotia, he realized that he was hearing the language of his region in a new way, recognizing that it was innately poetic. He took an MA at Dalhousie University, writing a thesis on Michael Ondaatje's work, then moved in 1987 to Ottawa, where he worked as a parliamentary aide. While there, he completed the book that brought his work to attention—what he has described as a 'poem-novel', *Whylah Falls* (1990), about an imagined Black community in Nova Scotia that, in the preface, he describes as a 'snowy, northern Mississippi, with blood spattered, not on magnolias, but on pines, lilacs, and wild roses'.

In *Whylah Falls* Clarke draws on a variety of Africadian experiences and mixes poems and prose with archival photographs of the region and clippings from a fictional newspaper ('The Whylah Moon') to create a series of portraits of the inhabitants of his landscape that provide the reader with a powerful sense of a group of people living together in vital if difficult circumstances. The book marries the sound of blues music ('black train cry, black train wail; / It don't matter / I'm close to home / Highway howl in rain and gale; / It don't matter, I'm close to home') with verse forms and rhythms that are drawn from the whole tradition of English literature to create a free-flowing fusion of idiomatic and traditional. In a new introduction to the book for a tenth-anniversary edition Clarke writes:

> Whylah Falls *was born in the blues, the philosophy of the* cry. *Indeed, I was trying to find the emotion of song, to rediscover the Four Muses—Eros, Death, Intellect and Spirit. I attempted to worry the line, each verse line, like a blues guitarist using a piece of glass to alter notes. You see, you have to understand improvisation, how a standard reference can become something else.*

In 1993 Clarke completed a Ph.D. at Queen's University. In the following year he published *Lush Dreams, Blue Exile: Fugitive Poems 1978–93*, a collection of lyrics that declare 'I yearn to be Ulyssean, to roam / foaming oceans or wrest / a wage from tough, mad adventure. / For now I labour language.' They show him not only engaged in further investigations of the black Nova Scotian experience but also entering into larger engagements with history. The use of the word 'lush' in the title calls attention to Clarke's willingness to break out of the stripped and spare style of writing characteristic of many of his Canadian contemporaries. Clarke joined the faculty of Duke University that year. Feeling that he would be happier based in Canada, he spent a year in 1998 as the Seagram Visiting Chair in Canadian studies at McGill University and then joined the Department of English at the University of Toronto in 1999.

Clarke's enormous energies are suggested by his literary productivity in 1999. That year saw the publication of his verse-play *Beatrice Chancy* (1999), which uses Percy Bysshe Shelley's 1819 lyric verse-tragedy *The Cenci* (itself based on the history of a sixteenth-century Italian family) to frame a tragic story, set in the Annapolis Valley in 1801, about slavery in Canada. Interested in the many ways words and music can interact, Clarke turned the play into an opera libretto. Set to music by James Rolfe, that opera premiered in 1999. (It has been performed in Toronto, Halifax, and elsewhere, and was broadcast on CBC Television.) Clarke's interest in dramatic writing can also be seen in the fact that he turned *Whylah Falls* into a play (also published in 1999), which was first performed for CBC radio and then on stage; he has also written a feature-film screenplay, *One Heart Broken into Song*, which was broadcast on CBC-TV that year.

In 2001 Clarke published two new books of poetry. *Blue* expands his investigation into contemporary Black identity (as in the poem addressed to Derek Walcott: 'composing lines blustery, yet tender / your voice your own (Auden in the margins, / Eliot, Yeats, and Pound in the dungeon / . . . / extracting black blues from a yellowed Oxford'). *Execution Poems*, which won a Governor General's Award, is a sequence of poems based on an event from Clarke's family history—the execution in 1949 of two of Clarke's cousins for the murder of a Fredericton, NB, taxi driver. He has since completed a novel retelling that story in fiction.

Clarke has edited two anthologies: *Fire on the Water: An Anthology of Black Nova Scotian Writing* (1991) and *Eyeing the North Star: Directions in African-Canadian Literature* (1997). In 2002 he extended his investigations of black Canadian identity in *Odysseys Home: Mapping African-Canadian Literature*, a collection of critical essays that offer thoughtful examinations of African-Canadian writing in the context of both African diasporic and Canadian studies. Rejecting both those in Canada who may think 'whiteness is equal to Canadianness' and those American reviewers who speak of him as an 'African-American writer', Clarke emphasizes his sense of himself as a fusion of Black and Canadian. He has described the goal of all of his work as calling attention to a neglected history:

> *As a writer of African descent who's also Canadian, I have this need to continue to reach out to my fellow and sister Canadians and educate them at the same time that I also need to speak to members of my own racial and regional community or communities.*

From The Adoration of Shelley,[1] *Whylah Falls*

The Argument

Crows trumpet indigo dawn. The rose sun blossoms. A paddlewheel steamer, spilling blues, country, and flamenco guitar, churns the still Sixhiboux River. Simultaneously, a dark blue engine steams into Whylah station—a white marble phantasm. Garbed in baroque motley, a theatre troupe disembarks. One actor, blurred completely in white, brandishes an oily shotgun. Another player, a poet, bears a satchel full of letters and seven books of the elegant verse that perished in the slaughter of The Great War. His black suit, tie, shirt, shoes, melt into the dark dawn. A comet streak of rose flames on one lapel. Thin as any dreamer, this Mandinga-M'ikmaq[2] wears circle lenses on his earthen face. A slow clock, Xavier Zachary turns, his hands crying rose petals, and wheels upward into the high, blue hills above Whylah.

1 The title of the first (and, later in the volume, of the seventh) of the seven parts of the book; the phrase 'The Adoration of Shelley' echoes the title of several famous religious paintings from the middle ages and the Renaissance (*The Adoration of the Magi, The Adoration of the Shepherds*), all of which are about the birth of Christ and emphasize the manifestation of a divine presence into the world.

2 That is, descended from both the West African Mandinga tribe and the M'ikmaqs, a Native people of eastern Canada.

Wooooooo! The train howls into steam and vanishes.

Shelley Adah Clemence, eighteen Aprils old, awakens, stretches in her brass bed. The train moans. She wonders, 'Is this trouble?' Small, slender, she rises, tossing back the covers like a spurned wave. She resembles Rousseau's Yadwigha.[3] Same almond-shaped eyes, same sloe-coloured hair. She peers into her diary, a garden of immortelles[4] and printed sunflowers. Then, Shelley opens her warm Bible and copies verses from The Song of Solomon[5] into her own book. A radio awakens, croons a Ma Rainey song rich with regretful guitars, and she crafts a song with Hebrew lyrics and a Coptic melody:

Snow softly, silently, settles
White petals upon white petals.

She buttons her long, ivory nightdress down to her thin, brown ankles and angles carefully down steep steps to the kitchen, a bath of yellow light. Her ma, Cora, is pulling fire from the woodstove. Othello, her brother, rests his guitar-troubled fingers on a mug of coffee. They suspect that X will arrive shortly, after five years of exile, to court Shelley with words that she will know have been pilfered from literature. Smooth lines come from Castiglione.[6] Shelley vows she'll not be tricked. She be wisdom.

Outside, Whylah shimmers. Sunshine illumines the mirage of literature, how everyone uses words to create a truth he or she can trust and live within.

3 In the painting *Le Rêve* (1910) by Henri Rousseau (1844–1910)—originally known as *Yadwigha's Dream*—a nude woman reclines on a red couch in the middle of a surreal jungle.

4 Dried flowers.

5 The Song of Solomon is unusual among the books of the Bible in that it is a work of love poetry without religious content. 'Ma Rainey' (1889–1939): black American singer (born Gertrude Pridgett), known as the Mother of the Blues.

6 That is, from *The Courtier* (1528), the famous Renaissance treatise on courtly behaviour and Neo-Platonic theories of love by Baldassare Castiglione (1478–1529).

The River Pilgrim: A Letter

At eighteen, I thought the Sixhiboux wept.
Five years younger, you were lush, beautiful
Mystery; your limbs—scrolls of deep water.
Before your home, lost in roses, I swooned,
Drunken in the village of Whylah Falls,
And brought you apple blossoms you refused,
Wanting Hank Snow[1] woodsmoke blues and dried smelts,
Wanting some milljerk's dumb, unlettered love.

1 (1914–99); white Nova Scotian country music singer.

That May, freights chimed xylophone tracks that rang
To Montréal. I scribbled postcard odes,
Painted *le fleuve Saint-Laurent comme la Seine*—
Sad watercolours for Negro exiles
In France, and dreamt Paris white with lepers,
Soft cripples who finger pawns under elms,
Drink blurry into young debauchery,
Their glasses clear with Cointreau, rain, and tears.
You hung the moon backwards, crooned crooked poems
That no voice could straighten, not even O
Who stroked guitars because he was going
To die with a bullet through his stomach.
Innocent, you curled among notes—petals
That scaled glissando from windows agape,
And remained in southwest Nova Scotia,
While I drifted, sad and tired, in the east.
I have been gone four springs. This April, pale
Apple blossoms blizzard. The garden flutes
E-flats of lilacs, *G*-sharps of lilies.
Too many years, too many years, are past . . .
Past the marble and pale flowers of Paris,
Past the broken, Cubist guitars of Arles,[2]
Shelley, I am coming down through the narrows
Of the Sixhiboux River. I will write
Beforehand. Please, please come out to meet me
As far as Beulah Beach.

2 Arles was the base for the painters Pablo Picasso and Braque while they were creating many of their early cubist paintings, several of which feature cubist representations of guitars.

Rose Vinegar

In his indefatigable delirium of love, Xavier wires rugosa rose blossoms to Shelley. Deluded by his quixotic romanticism, he cannot yet appreciate the practical necessities of friendship. But, Shelley trusts in reason; thus, though she admires the blossoms for their truthfulness to themselves, she does not hesitate to distill a delicate and immortal vinegar from what she considers the ephemeral petals of X's desire. An ornament becomes an investment. She fills a cup with the fresh rose petals; then, stripping off their heels (the white part), she pours the petals into a quart sealer and adds two cups of white vinegar. Then, she seals the jar and places it on the sunny livingroom windowsill for sixteen days, seven hours, and nine minutes. When the vinegar is ready, she strains it through a sieve and then pours it back into the bottle.

Rose vinegar. It's especially good on salads.

Bees' Wings

This washed-out morning, April rain descants,
Weeps over gravity, the broken bones
Of gravel and graveyards, and Cora puts
Away gold dandelions to sugar
And skew into gold wine, then discloses
That Pablo gutted his engine last night
Speeding to Beulah Beach under a moon
As pocked and yellowed as aged newsprint.
Now, Othello, famed guitarist, heated
By rain-clear rum, voices transparent notes
Of sad, anonymous heroes who hooked
Mackerel and slept in love-pried-open thighs
And gave out booze in vain crusades to end
Twenty centuries of Christianity.
His voice is simple, sung air: without notes,
There's nothing. His unknown, imminent death
(The feel of iambs ending as trochees
In a slow, decasyllabic death-waltz;
His vertebrae trellised on his stripped spine
Like a xylophone or keyboard of nerves)
Will also be nothing: the sun pours gold
Upon Shelley, his sis', light as bees' wings,
Who roams a garden sprung from rotten wood
And words, picking green nouns and fresh, bright verbs,
For there's nothing I will not force language
To do to make us one—whether water
Hurts like whisky or the sun burns like oil
Or love declines to weathered names on stone.

Blank Sonnet

The air smells of rhubarb, occasional
Roses, or first birth of blossoms, a fresh,
Undulant hurt, so body snaps and curls
Like flower. I step through snow as thin as script,
Watch white stars spin dizzy as drunks, and yearn
To sleep beneath a patchwork quilt of rum.
I want the slow, sure collapse of language
Washed out by alcohol. Lovely Shelley,

I have no use for measured, cadenced verse
If you won't read. Icarus-like,[1] I'll fall
Against this page of snow, tumble blackly
Across vision to drown in the white sea
That closes every poem—the white reverse
That cancels the blackness of each image.

1 See page 852, note 1.

The Wisdom of Shelley

You come down, after
five winters, X,
bristlin' with roses
and words words words,
brazen as brass.
Like a late blizzard,
You bust in our door,
talkin' April and snow and rain,
litterin' the table
with poems—
as if we could trust them!

I can't.
I heard pa tell ma
how much and much he
loved loved loved her
and I saw his fist
fall so gracefully
against her cheek,
she swooned.

Roses
got thorns.
And words
do lie.

I've seen love
die.

Each Moment Is Magnificent

Othello practises *White Rum*, his scale of just music, and clears the love song of muddying his morals. He sets his glass down lovingly, a whole chorus of molecules sloshing in harmony. He vows he will not, he will not be a dead hero, no way, suffering a beautiful sleep, trimmed with ochre, hazelnut, dressed in mahogany, smelling of last-minute honey and tears, regrets rained upon him too late in the guise of wilted, frail flowers. Instead, he will sleep right now, while he still can, up to his thighs in thighs, gnaw dried, salty smelts, and water song with rum. *Sweet Sixhiboux, run softly till I end my song.*

Wearing the lineaments of ungratified desire, Selah sashays from the livingroom, watches dusk bask in the River Sixhiboux. She tells Othello to shut up because Jericho's where she's gonna go[1] when she falls in love. Yep, when that someday man come out the blue to Whylah Falls, Beauty Town, to serenade her and close his wings around her, she'll be in Jericho at last like the fortune-teller says. She'll jump the broom[2] and cross the Nile.

I stroll outside with strange music in my skull. Here's the Sixhiboux River, tossed tinfoil, crinkling along the ground, undistracted by all the grave lovers it attracts, all those late Romantics who spout Lake Poet Wordsworth, 'The world is too much with us, late and soon,' and brood upon the river's shimmering bliss before tossing themselves within, pretending to be Percy Bysshe Shelley at Lerici.[3] I've thought of the Sixhiboux in those erotic ways, dreamt it as being midnight-thick, voluptuous, folding—like a million moths, furry with a dry raininess—over one. No matter where you are in Sunflower County, you can hear it pooling, milling in a rainstorm, or thundering over a hapless town. Even now, I can hear its shining roar pouring over Shelley's house, polishing the roses that nod, drunken, or spring—petalled crude—from earth. All I hear is an old song, her voice, lilting, 'Lover Man.'

She's absent, far from here. My blood moves angry through its rooms; rain washes all my tears to the sea. My pain will never end unless I can sleep beside my love, pluck the ripe moon, halve it, and share its sweet milk between us: *Hear me, oh moon, hear my song:*

> *I am like that road that slinks to your door*
> *Like a married lover, sneaking around*
> *To curve his ribaldry about your form.*
> *Shelley, that's how much, that's how much, I feel.*

1990

1 In the Book of Joshua, the conquest of Jericho permits the Israelites to gain possession of the Promised Land.
2 Get married without a minister or priest.
3 The Romantic poet Shelley died on 8 July 1822, when his schooner sank on his return voyage from Livorno to Lerici, where he was staying in Italy.

Primitivism

He could not escape
the wilderness. Bark
encrusted his wine bottles.
His pencils grew fur
and howled. Sentences
became wild eagles
that flew predatory patterns,
swooping out of a white sky-
page to tear apart field
mice-images, scurrying
for meaning. A carcass-
manuscript rotted on a shelf
or a hillside. He could
not tell the difference.
A bear-trap of ideas
snared him: he could
not poeticize
the country
and not become it;
his poems filling
with neanderthal nudes,
prowling punctuation,
snarling sounds, guttural.

1994

Violets for Your Furs

I still dream the steamed blackness, witness, of you in rain;
I talk about that—pouring living fire on guitar strings,
And suffer Cointreau's blues aftertaste of burnt orange,
The torturous bitter flavour of the French in Africa,
The crisis of your long black hair assaulting your waist,
Your small, troubling breasts not quite spoken for,
Your spontaneous mouth unconsummated with kisses,
'Cos you cashed in your pretty *Négritude* and gone.

Ah, you were a living *S*, all Coltrane or Picasso swerves;
Your hair stranded splendid on the gold beach of your face,
So sweet, I moaned black rum, black sax, black moon,
The black trace of your eyelash like lightning,

The sonorous blackness of your skin after midnight—
The sadness of loving you glimmering in Scotch.
Now, this sheet darkens with the black snow of words;
In my sheets, a glimpse of night falls, then loneliness.

I can't sleep—haunted by sad sweetness outside the skull,
The hurtful perfume you bathed in by the yellow lamp,
Three-quarters drunk, your rouged kiss branding my neck,
The orange cry of my mouth kindling your blue night skin.
The night blossoms ugly, I down gilded damnation.
I've been lovin' you—more than words—too long to stop now.
What will happen next? I can't know, you should know:
The moon tumbles, caught in fits of grass, seizures of leaves.

1994

Peggy's Cove

In pitched night fog, I stagger upon *Fear*—
Cabals of rock, wreckage, sobs of wet death,
Caterwauled epics of drowning, a salt
Nightmare—this dun, Expressionist Stonehenge
Of hunched and broken anarchic boulders
Heaped against the fierce, mad, dark Atlantic
By homicidal force that drove them there
In dumb, impaling anger. I tremble;
A blind roar suffocates the stars, a black
Hatred lathers this grotesque beach and howls.
I hear groanings like bones being smashed—and cries
Like infants hurled head-first against brick walls.

1994

From *Execution Poems*

The Killing

Rue: I ingratiated the grinning hammer
with Silver's not friendless, not unfriendly skull.
Behind him like a piece of storm, I unleashed a frozen glinting—
a lethal gash of lightning.

His soul leaked from him in a Red Sea, a Dead Sea,
churning his clothes to lava.

Geo: No, it didn't look like real blood,
but something more like coal, that inched from his mouth.

Rue: It was a cold hit in the head. A hurt unmassageable.
Car seat left stinking of gas and metal and blood.
And reddening violently.
A rhymeless poetry scrawled his obituary.

Geo: It was comin on us for awhile, this here misery.
We'd all split a beer before iron split Silver's skull.
Silver's muscles still soft and tender. That liquor killed him.
The blood like shadow on his face, his caved-in face.
Smell of his blood over everything.

Rue: Iron smell of the hammer mingled with iron smell of blood
and chrome smell of snow and moonlight.

Geo: He had two hundred dollars on him; bootleg in him.
We had a hammer on us, a spoonful of cold beer in us.

The taxi-driver lies red in the alabaster snow.
His skeleton has taken sick and must be placed in the ground.

This murder is 100 per cent dirt of our hands.

Rue: Twitchy, my hand was twitchy, inside my jacket.
The hammer was gravity: everything else was jumpy.
I wondered if Silver could hear his own blood thundering,
vermilion, in his temples, quickened, twitchy, because of beer;
jumpy molecules infecting his corpuscles, already nervous.

The hammer went in so far that there was no sound—
just the slight mushy squeak of bone.

Silver swooned like the leaden Titanic.
Blood screamed down his *petit-bourgeois* clothes.

Geo: Can we cover up a murder with snow?
With white, frosty roses?

Rue: Here's how I justify my error:
The blow that slew Silver came from two centuries back.
It took that much time and agony to turn a white man's whip
into a black man's hammer.

Geo: No, we needed money,
so you hit the So-and-So,
only much too hard.
Now what?

Rue: So what?

2000

Nu(is)ance

for Wayde Compton

Jabbering double-crossing doubletalk,
Pale-assed poetasters void my 'blues-caucused,
Raucous lyrics'—too Negroid and rowdy,
While sable, sassy poets preach I ink
Too blankly, *comme les blancs,* my bleached-out verse
Bleating too whitey-like—worse—in they ears.
What can I say?
All this blather about
'Black' and 'white' verse is blackmail and white noise.
Cripes! English—fallacious—be finished here!
I'd rather stutter a bastard's language
Only spoken in gutters, a broken,
Vulgar, Creole screech, loud with bawling, slurring,
Balderdash, cussing, and caterwauling,
A corrupt palaver that bankrupts all meeching speech
Because it be literal, guttural *Poetry,*
I.e. *Hubbub.*

2001

Stephanie Bolster

b. 1969

Stephanie Bolster, born and raised in Vancouver, attended the University of British Columbia, receiving a Bachelor of Fine Arts in Creative Writing in 1991 and a Master of Fine Arts in 1994. After university, she moved to Ottawa, where she worked as an editor of *Vernissage* magazine at the National Gallery of Canada and taught creative writing for the Ottawa-Carleton District School Board. She now teaches creative writing at Concordia University and lives in Montreal.

Bolster has won a number of awards, including the Bronwen Wallace Award (given to the most promising Canadian poet under thirty-five who has not yet published a book) in 1996 and the *Malahat Review* Long Poem Prize in 1997. Her first full-length book of poetry, *White Stone: The Alice Poems* (1998), won both a Governor General's Award and a Gerald Lampert Award. Her second collection, *Two Bowls of Milk* (1999), won the Archibald Lampman Award and was a finalist for the Trillium Award. Her third collection, *Pavilion*, was published in 2002.

As a poet Bolster clearly enjoys responding to the art of others. As well as creating a book about the Alice books, she has frequently responded to the work of visual artists, as in poems such as '*Le Far-West* (1955)' from *Two Bowls of Milk*. In these poems, distinctions between the work of art and its beholder are blurred: she imagines herself into the work, passing beyond the frame, becoming another character, as may be seen in her discussion of her responses to Vermeer's work in her third book, *Pavilion*:

Much of my poetry is focussed (pun intended) on photography, on paintings, on various types of frames, whether they belong to mirrors or windows. What is inside the frame is a selected part of the whole. Just in the way that, when I look at myself or someone I love in a mirror, I see only the surface, so when I look at a painting by Vermeer I see a woman in a room with dim corridors leading off into who knows what other rooms. . . . my dual identity as watcher and watched makes me identify with both the painted woman and (here's where gender comes in) the male painter. In his famous 'Head of a Young Girl', it's myself I see there, turbaned, my pearl earring catching the light, turning my head both knowingly towards my watching self and painfully away. This particular painting fascinates me because the girl, by the turning movement of her head and the nature of her wise and grief-struck gaze, is, like me, both watcher and watched.

Like the fictional Alice, readers are drawn through a looking glass in Bolster's poems such as 'Window' and 'Train Windows', while in 'Room' she peels back the layers of the wallpaper to find the earlier states that lie beneath.

White Stone: The Alice Poems

White Stone intertwines four stories (three of which are represented in the selections reprinted here): the relationship between the author of *Alice in Wonderland* and *Through the Looking Glass*, and Alice Liddell, the little girl for whom they were written; the relationship of Liddell and Julia Margaret Cameron, a Victorian portrait photographer; the experiences of Liddell as an adult, interacting with the world; and the relationship of author of *White Stone* to the individuals and events in Alice's life. Bolster includes the following background note to her sequence:

Alice Pleasance Liddell Hargreaves (1852–1934) was the daughter of . . . the Dean of Christ Church College, Oxford, where Charles Lutwidge Dodgson (1832–1898; also known as Lewis Carroll) was a Mathematics don. Known for his affinity for children, Dodgson befriended Alice and her sisters Lorina and Edith in the Deanery garden on 25 April 1856. During the ensuing years, he spent an increasing amount of time photographing Alice and her siblings and telling them stories. On a boating trip down the Thames on 4 July 1862, he began the tale that became Alice's Adventures in Wonderland.

Details of a mysterious break between Dodgson and the Liddells, which occurred the following year (Alice was eleven), were lost after his death. . . . In any case, Dodgson would probably have lost contact with Alice around this time, as he typically abandoned—or more frequently, was abandoned by—his child friends once they began to grow up. After this point, Alice's contact with Dodgson mainly involved small pleasantries and news of the Alice books. He took his final photograph of her in 1870.

In 1872, the noted photographer Julia Margaret Cameron . . . photographed Alice, who was vacationing wit her family near Cameron's home on the Isle of Wight. . . . The same year, Queen Victoria's youngest son, Prince Leopold, came to study at Oxford. According to many sources, he and Alice became romantically involved, but marriage would have been forbidden by both sets of parents because of the discrepancy in social class. The prince, a haemophiliac, married in 1882, named his daughter . . . Alice, [and] was godfather to Alice Liddell Hargreaves' son, Leopold. . . . On 15 September 1880, in Westminster Abbey, Alice married Reginald Hargreaves, a cricket player from a wealthy and respected family, whom most considered her intellectual inferior, and who apparently idolized her. They had three sons (Leopold, Reginald and Caryl), the first two of whom died in World War I. . . . In 1932, Alice, Caryl, and Alice's sister, Rhoda, visited the United States for a large celebration in which Alice received an honorary degree at Columbia University. . . . Several years before her death, she wrote in a letter: 'Poor little Alice, I am quite tired of that little lady, slightly ungrateful on my part, I admit.'

From *White Stone:*[1] *The Alice Poems*

Dark Room

We're here, the three of us, lit by one candle.
Dodgson's wrist dips into solutions;
he nudges a glass plate to make her be there

sooner. Standing on a box, Alice peers down—
when will she appear in the slow mirror
that is not a mirror? A flame wavers, kept far away

so it won't burn, kept small so it won't ruin her
development. Two faces wait above the vat
where Alice will loom little, stopped.

But not: already hair has fallen in her eyes.
He tucks it back behind her ear, flourishes
the cleaner of his hand. *Now?* she asks.

1 Regarding 'white stone', Bolster notes: 'The expression originates in Catullus' "*Lapide candidiore diem notare*...", which translates as "to mark with an especially white stone the lucky day". The English version was quite commonly used in Victorian times.'

She tugs his cuff. They don't seem to know
I'm here, poet on the corner stool, watching
a kind of homecoming. As a child I reached

to shift myself in chemicals, wanting my image
perfect in that reddish light and tang.
But the me who darkened with such grace

was ordinary once appeared, and stayed
that way. Alice gasps as she comes into view.
He hands the bathed girl to her, dripping,

says she's lovely in those rags. She laughs—
then looks a long time at her beggar self.
Although it's dim, I think I can say with near

assurance he does not attempt
to unlatch her collar. It's time for tea.
He draws back the curtain and she leaves,

he follows. This room is long and narrow, full
of longing. Outside, cups clink. Here I steep,
emulsified. Her milky shoulders start to dry.

Thames

The ongoing story has briefly paused.
Three Liddell girls fidget as Dodgson gazes
at rushes edging the banks, oaks bending over them.

Please! Alice squeezes from her throat and he's back
in the story: a small doorway, a garden.
Her mouth opens, each distant lily nodding to her gaze,

but he says she's too tall to get in and her lips clamp shut.
He knows she's too young to be kept out of gardens.
He's gone too far, he's lost. As he drifts, searching,

words swim up through him toward her waiting eyes:
Alice fell, Alice found, Alice cried. Her foot just an inch
from his, her sisters nestled there alike as eggs in cups.

And me: where do I fit? Do I sit on that bank a hundred
years beyond his reach; am I the fish that flits as Alice
dips her oar? I am her eyes that shy from his

and look again when he can't see; I watch
his halting mouth and think *how smart he is, how big,*
how funny that this man likes me. I am his need

to make a story good enough to hold her
like no photograph, his hope that her foot will stay close
and his knowledge that it won't; her fear that he'll

stop the tale now or that it will not end,
ever. On that river, my pole lodges in stones and I
lose my grip. My punt slips away with me on it.

No one notices. The river flows only one way—
away. Sick for home but too old to admit it,
I watch the oaks they watched. I am hours on that river

hovering above myself, too close, not close enough.

In Which Alice Is in Love with Queen Victoria's Youngest Son, 1873

Somewhere under her vast skirts, Victoria
put down her foot. Your mother followed suit.
And you, Children of Victoria, you cloaked
carved legs of furniture to save yourselves
the bother of the body. Against all rules
Prince Leopold's blood ran. His mother
praised him as a fine bruised grape.

You were too common for his haemophilia.
So small your tightly woven bones,
you were the girl fat women yelled at.
Your head would have to go. Be hands
to hold aloft a cup of tea, be waist.
Don't call them all a pack of cards or they'll stomp
heel to spade, dig a hole and force you into it.

After the Wedding, 1880

You measure the distance of your husband's sleep, watch his eyes twitch under their lids as he plays cricket in a field wide with fresh-cut grass. You would like to tell him of the one you were, how others deemed the prince you loved too pure to mingle with your blood. How you wish he had turned mute in his grief and become a pair of hands that gathered from your brush all remnants of your hair to make some keepsake ornament, as Dodgson must have framed that strand you mailed him as a child. He sent a Christ Church watercolour for your wedding at Westminster Abbey, site of royal marriages and funerals. From the prince: good wishes, a pearl horseshoe brooch.

There is nothing you can utter to the recess of Reginald's ear. Your heart beats. You chose this. Your mother nodded as you said your vows and, under paper showers, tossed your smiles. Somewhere the cake's becoming dry and hard under iced red roses.

In this bed you cannot lie. Best to watch him at his matches and applaud, best to hope to bear a child so your love will have somewhere to aim for. You cannot even ask who wrote you into this, who dropped that stone into your wedding glass of wine. You raised it, drank it down.

Two Deaths in January, 1898

Those flowers you sent to Dodgson's funeral
took your place in the crowd. Beside his stone
a perfumed heap of lilies and gentleness
of babies' breath, your name on the white card
still a child's. You spared mourners
your real face: fallen, etched with lines.

At Father's service you wore black as required,
let tears roll serenely down your cheeks, let
Reginald's husbandly elbow hook around your own.
Condolences blurred to the letter o, hollow
disbelief, *so sorry—and this on top of*
the other. You nodded at appropriate times.

For months your griefs brushed past each other,
draped and faceless as the men who left them.
On a wall inside the Deanery appeared a spreading
damp the servants covered with a chair
and wouldn't let you see. It seemed the profile of a man.

Then one morning, alone in your husband's unused
study, you found in a whiff of ink the word *father*
and your ears buzzed, stars spun you

into darkness. Your orphaned body rocked
as on a boat down a river one ancient, golden
afternoon, but no one to tell the stories, no one to row.

Close Your Eyes and Think of England

Did you follow that advice
while your husband strained for sons?
Or only once the eldest two were dead

in the Great War, and you guessed
what sodden nights had all along
been for? Your country is no mother.

Your children's country was in books,
a small and tangled patch

Dodgson planted years before—
your hand hazy in warm green water,
his words like dragonflies by your ear.

His words the children who lived
beyond all expectation. Your sons

lie broken underneath a land of stones
and bones and mud. England recovers,
Wonderland flourishes. Alice keeps on

cheating: she closes her eyes,
goes underground, comes back.

In Which Alice Receives an Honorary Doctorate from Columbia University, 1932

The Waldorf-Astoria can't match old York Minister's restraint and manageable grandeur. Amidst these towers you've shrunk to mere inches, the height of your ankle in England. 'Woman with famous name becomes grasshopper.' Your giant son won't laugh at your quips but clarifies the spelling of his name—not Carroll—for reporters.

Flashes capture you. But that ancient face in a crease between columns of praise cannot be yours. It's Alice whom they wish to set a square black cap upon, a girl.

And yet you're here: crowned, tassel dangling before one eye. The rising crowd becomes a field of tiger lilies mocking your white petals. *You are old*, they chant. Again he's done it, set your place at a tea party too large and empty to include you. You're here at one end of the table, and far across its length—wavering like that Atlantic you heaved your way across—she sits, a child, in England. *Hello, my dear*, you call. She's looking elsewhere, at him in those white gloves behind his tripod. She's beautiful—you never knew. You'd forgotten her open eyes, remembered only the shut Alice in books.

Hands clap somewhere. A professor stands to analyze the Alice texts as allegory. Too late—the girl is gone. Poor little Alice, her empty chair. Caryl passes you a handkerchief. You are his mother. He believes you happy at last.

Visitor from Overseas

I received an envelope from England, somewhat torn,
postage two pounds, cancellation stamped across a queen's face.
Inside brown paper, an ironmonger's plastic bag gasped
like my childhood rabbit just before it died. Unsealed,

Alice crawled out small and scraggly, arms stuck to her sides
and starved. I had no crumpets so fed her large Canadian
muffins instead, which she nibbled with admirable restraint.

Overnight while I slept she swelled, spurted in height until
I woke and found her crouched against the ceiling, learning
how to curse. I offered the entire contents of my fridge
but nothing shrank her back again, nothing until I told her

she was beautiful, her legs burnished as arbutus limbs. Curious,
she reduced herself to doorframe size, followed me to find
a land she'd never seen. There on a Pacific beach remembered:

rowing under shapely willows with a man three times her size,
who liked her little, who kept her between pages, sent her
wrapped over the Atlantic so as not to mar the idea of her
he kept under glass, scalloped like a fancy cake.

1998

Come to the edge of the barn the property really begins there[1]

Come to the edge of the barn the property really begins there,
you see things defining themselves, the hoofprints left by sheep,
the slope of the roof, each feather against each feather on each goose.
You see the stake with the flap of orange plastic that marks

the beginning of real. I'm showing you this because
I'm sick of the way you clutch the darkness with your hands,
seek invisible fenceposts for guidance, accost spectres.
I'm coming with you because I fear you'll trip

over the string that marks the beginning, you'll lie across the border
and with that view—fields of intricate grain and chiselled mountains,
cold winds already lifting the hairs of your arm—you'll forget your feet,
numb in straw and indefinite dung, and be unable to rise, to walk farther.

My fingers weave so close between yours because I've been there
before, I know the relief of everything, how it eases the mind to learn
shapes it hasn't made, how it eases the feet to know the ground
will persist. See those two bowls of milk, just there,

on the other side of the property line, they're for the cats
that sometimes cross over and are seized by thirst, they're
to wash your hands in. Lick each finger afterwards. That will be
your first taste, and my finger tracing your lips will be the second.

1999

1 A line from '37 Haiku', a poem by the American poet John Ashbery.

Many have written poems about blackberries

But few have gotten at the multiplicity of them, how each berry
composes itself of many dark notes, spherical,
swollen, fragile as a world. A blackberry is the colour of a painful
bruise on the upper arm, some internal organ
as yet unnamed. It is shaped to fit
the tip of the tongue, to be a thimble, a dunce cap
for a small mouse. Sometimes it is home to a secret green worm
seeking safety and the power of surprise. Sometimes it plunks
into a river and takes on water.
Fishes nibble it.

The bushes themselves ramble like a grandmother's sentences,
giving birth to their own sharpness. Picking the berries
must be a tactful conversation
of gloved hands. Otherwise your fingers will bleed
the berries' purple tongue; otherwise thorns
will pierce your own blank skin. Best to be on the safe side,
the outside of the bush. Inside might lurk
nests of yellowjackets; rabid bats; other,
larger hands on the same search.

The flavour is its own reward, like kissing the whole world
at once, rivers, willows, bugs and all, until your swollen
lips tingle. It's like waking up
to discover the language you used to speak
is gibberish, and you have never really
loved. But this does not matter because you have
married this fruit, mellifluous, brutal, and ripe.

1999

Assonance

Hurt bird in dirt[1]—she writes
for sound, and a sparrow

that hit the window of her childhood
too hard. Because of how the ear

takes words in and holds them
to itself, how they strike

those bones: *hammer, anvil*
and *stirrup.* Words that conjure

machinery, weight,
horses, that morning her leg

caught and the mare dragged her
for miles. From the first,

1 'The line "Hurt bird in dirt" was adapted from an unpublished poem by Christopher Patton.' [Bolster's note]

each word she'd learned
a hoof just missing her

temple. It is all pain,
the reddish shell the side

of the head cups, and hears
itself, hears itself.

1999

Poems for the Flood

Hills are islands, waiting. Mountains
will wait longer. This valley

was once a lake, until we made it land. See how the rain
against the windshield turns to fishes.

Each puddle a premonition. The woman's face
is clearer there. When I peer in,

the trees shift. The sky is bluer
than the sky and when I look deeper there is the sun.

Any rain is enough to make all the colours
come out. The fuchsias sting my eyes

and the bees shine. The lawn teems with drops
that might be diamonds, might be frogs.

The first time I ran inside and shut my house. The second
I let it all wash over me. The third time I went looking

where the clouds were and weeks later
waded back with minnows in my boots.

Between storms: a segment of train track. A red
block with the letter O. A mouse the colour

of bread mould. An ace of spades. Three steps going down
and who knows how many underwater.

I keep a canoe on the back porch just in case.
Each morning I listen for the lap against the bedposts.

Each morning I imagine my legs floating down the steps,
my hair seeping back from my face.

Watering the garden, I call the earth thirsty
and then cringe at what I've said. The way things are

is simpler and more difficult to understand. My throat
and the columbines open for the same water differently.

Closed rose petals, a sky not scrawled with cloud,
the small of the back, these are lesser. Beauty is the red

rectangle of a barn surrounded by flood.
The white chicken on the rooftop testing its wings.

When the first drop falls, she is there
to meet it. The underside of her arm is a fish's belly,

her mouth a rain gauge. She is the watermark
and the water rising.

Her rusted car. Where the road was, a river the colour of asphalt.
A rag doll is growing heavier beside her boat. Beneath,

a catfish looms. Farther down, street signs
and streets, yellow lines down the centre.

Two thirds of the earth is composed of water,
not counting floods. I'm more water than this world is.

Maybe that explains the shift of my organs
during sleep, the glass beside my bed.

The curve of the boat's hold
is the shape my hand makes

when it wants something. How quickly
my palm fills when I stop asking.

1999

Le Far-West (1955)[1]

A few acres of snow.[2] In a Montréal
December I come upon your few feet

of west, a tawny field grazed on
by some animals. They might be

antelope and this some view of
Africa—or cows and Idaho? What

cowboy hat do you imagine
my umbrella is? You have not gone

far enough, your English Bay a mouth
drawn shut, its trees cowering

under an enormous Québec
sky I cannot write, my words

1 A painting by Jean Paul Lemieux (1904–90).

2 A reference to Voltaire's famous dismissal of Canada (in 1759): 'These two nations [France and England] are at war for a few acres of snow.'

small glimpses between
this branch of fir and that. How west

must have threatened to open
you. My pages nearly white

these days, I'm shutting up.
That 'I' I write no longer me

but you, alone in the midst of what
I call nothing and you home.

1999

Window

This is the window I grew up inside.
This is the Japanese maple that grew beyond it
and still does, obscuring the view. It is
the view. These are the leaves of the Japanese
split-leafed maple, red except
when autumn puckers them to rust.
This is the glass: between branches the small
patch of lawn we owned, and the sidewalk,
and the house across the street, and farther
houses. Fogged in winter, it made ethereal
the place I didn't call suburb until after
it took three hours
for the boat to circle Manhattan.
The frame of the retina
cracked. When I returned,
the view had flattened to a stamp.
This is the stamp I kept when I left,
the stamp to which I sent my letters.
Stuck every night under eyelids.
These are the roots that extend
from the tree outside the window I grew up
inside. When I left, they kept on growing
into the foundations.

2002

Room

Not really *there* yet. Peel back
latex to find the wild rose paper
underneath. Pin-ups appear there, men whose lips
urge my lips toward their sheen. Their faces
fall away. Posters of kittens come and go.
Unchosen, each glued sheet loosens, leaves
a stretch of pink. Print small hands
across it, trying out edges. That colour
the world entire. A brush retracts it.
Yellow walls, ungendered. Someone
else's objects gather. Now
the walls are boards with gaps,
now gaps, and now a forest
encloses. Who knows where it goes.

2002

Train Windows

The first train came to me
like this: unstoppable force.
I stood aside at Fredericton Junction
and let the speed and flare approach.
Wind flailed my hair, the gathered dark

dispersed. I found my room
of pull-out bed and pull-up blind.
A solitude so rare, uncracked, I
couldn't sleep. Morning: I tugged

the shade and empty ponds appeared.
We were that close to something;
the surface still rippled.
We were late for Montréal, New York,

for the years that would come, were gone,
were here. Years of blurred views through
windows. The engine approached,
I was alone, I held my breath

and didn't let it out, and haven't.

2002

Acknowledgements

MARGARET ATWOOD. 'This is a photograph of me' from *The Circle Game* copyright © Margaret Atwood 1968, 1998, reprinted by permission of House of Anansi Press. Used by permission of Oxford University Press: 'Progressive Insanities of a Pioneer', 'Disembarking at Quebec', 'Further Arrivals,' 'Death of a Young Son by Drowning', 'Dream 2: Brian the Still-Hunter', 'Thoughts from Underground', 'Tricks with Mirrors', and 'Siren Song' from *Selected Poems 1966–1984* © Margaret Atwood 1990; 'Spelling' from *True Stories* © Margaret Atwood 1981. Used by permission of McClelland & Stewart Ltd *The Canadian Publishers*: 'The Age of Lead' from *Wilderness Tips* by Margaret Atwood; 'Down' from *Morning in the Burned House* by Margaret Atwood; 'Strawberries' from *Murder in the Dark: Short Fictions and Prose Poems* by Margaret Atwood.

MARGARET AVISON. 'Cycle of Community' from *Concrete and Wild Carrot* (Brick Books, 2002), reprinted by permission. 'asap; etc.', 'Music Was in the Wind', and 'In Season and Out of Season' from *Not Yet But Still* (Lancelot Press, 1997; distributed by Brick Books), reprinted by permission. 'Neverness', 'The Butterfly', 'Perspective', 'Snow', 'Butterfly Bones; or Sonnet Against Sonnets', 'Light (I)', and 'A Thief in the Night' from *Selected Poems* (Oxford University Press, 1991) © Margaret Avison 1991, reprinted by permission.

EARLE BIRNEY. Used by permission of McClelland & Stewart Ltd *The Canadian Publishers*: 'Anglosaxon Street' from *Selected Poems* by Earle Birney; 'Vancouver Lights', 'The Ebb Begins from Dream', 'Pacific Door', 'Bushed', 'Can. Lit.', and 'El Greco: Espolio' from *Ghost in the Wheels* by Earle Birney.

STEPHANIE BOLSTER. 'Dark Room', 'Thames', 'In Which Alice is in Love with Queen Victoria's Youngest Son, 1873', 'After the Wedding, 1880', 'Two Deaths in January, 1898', 'Close Your Eyes and Think of England', 'In Which Alice Receives an Honorary Degree from Columbia University, 1932', and 'Visitor from Overseas' from *White Stone: The Alice Poems* (Véhicule Press: Signal Editions, 1998), used by permission. Used by permission of McClelland & Stewart Ltd *The Canadian Publishers*: 'Window', 'Room', and 'Train Windows' from Pavilion by Stephanie Bolster; '*Come to the edge of the barn the property really begins there*', 'Many Have Written Poems about Blackberries', 'Assonance', 'Poems for the Flood', and '*Le Far-West* (1955)' from *Two Bowls of Milk* by Stephanie Bolster.

GEORGE BOWERING. 'Elegy Two' and 'Elegy Five' from *Kerrisdale Elegies* (Coach House Press, 1984), reprinted by permission of the author.

DIONNE BRAND. Used by permission of McClelland & Stewart Ltd *The Canadian Publishers*: 'I Have Been Losing Roads' and 'Land to Light On' from *Land to Light On* by Dionne Brand; 'Hard Against the Soul' from *No Language Is Neutral* by Dionne Brand.

ROBERT BRINGHURST. Used by permission of McClelland & Stewart Ltd *The Canadian Publishers*: 'Essay on Adam' and 'These Poems, She Said' from *The Beauty of Weapons: Selected Poems* by Robert Bringhurst; 'Conversations with a Toad', 'The Stonecutter's Horses', 'Leda and the Swan', 'Bone Flute Breathing', and 'The Reader' from *The Calling: Selected Poems 1970–1995* by Robert Bringhurst.

MORLEY CALLAGHAN. 'Watching and Waiting' from *Morley Callaghan's Stories* (Macmillan of Canada, 1959), reprinted by permission of the Estate of Morley Callaghan.

MARIA CAMPBELL. 'Jacob' from *Stories of the Road Allowance People* (Theytus Books, 1995), used by permission of the author.

ANNE CARSON. 'Short Talk on Rectification', 'Short Talk on Waterproofing', 'Short Talk on the Total Collection', and 'Short Talk on Who You Are' from *Short Talks* (Brick Books, 1992), reprinted by permission. Reprinted by permission of New Directions Publishing Corp.: 'God's Work' from *Glass, Irony, and God* copyright © Anne Carson 1995; 'Book of Isaiah' and 'TV Men: Hektor' from *Glass, Irony, and God* copyright © Anne Carson 1995.

GEORGE ELLIOTT CLARKE. Reprinted by permission of Raincoast Books: 'Nu(is)ance' from *Blue* by George Elliott Clarke (Polestar Books Publishers, an imprint of Raincoast Books, 2001); 'The Argument', 'The River Pilgrim: A Letter', 'Rose Vinegar', 'Bees' Wings', 'Blank Sonnett', 'The Wisdom of Shelley', and 'Each Moment is Magnificent' from *Whylah Falls* by George Elliott Clarke (Polestar Book Publishers, an imprint of Raincoast Books, 1990). 'Primitivism', 'Violets for Your Furs', and 'Peggy's Cove' from *Lush Dreams, Blue Exile* (Pottersfield Press, 1994), reprinted by permission of the author. 'The Killing' from *Execution Poems* © George Elliott Clarke, reprinted by permission of Gaspereau Press.

LEONARD COHEN. Used by permission of McClelland & Stewart Ltd *The Canadian Publishers*: 'We Are Now in the Heart' from *Beautiful Losers* by Leonard Cohen; 'You Have the Lovers', 'Suzanne', 'How to Speak Poetry', 'In the Eyes of Men', 'When I Have Not Rage', 'It Is All Around Me', 'Holy Is Your Name', 'Not Knowing Where To Go', 'Everybody Knows', 'The Future', 'Closing Time', and 'What Is a Saint?' from *Stranger Music: Selected Poems and Songs* by Leonard Cohen.

LORNA CROZIER. Used by permission of McClelland & Stewart Ltd *The Canadian Publishers*: 'Poem about Nothing', 'Forms of Innocence', and 'This One's for You' from *The Garden Going On Without Us* by Lorna Crozier; 'The Other Woman' from *What the Living Won't Let Go* by Lorna Crozier; 'Two Eternal Things', 'Wind', 'Wilderness', 'Calm', and 'Afterword' from *A Saving Grace* by Lorna Crozier; 'The Old Order' and 'At the Millstone' from *Everything Arrives at the Light* by Lorna Crozier; 'Getting Pregnant', 'Time to Praise' (sections 1, 4, 6, 9, and 10), and 'Teaching a Crow to Talk' from *Inventing the Hawk* by Lorna Crozier; 'The Sacrifice of Abraham' and 'The Sacrifice of Isaac' from *Apocrypha of Light* by Lorna Crozier.

ROBERTSON DAVIES. Excerpt from *World of Wonders* copyright © Robertson Davies 1975, reprinted by permission of Macmillan Canada, an imprint of CDG Books Canada, Inc.

TIMOTHY FINDLEY. 'Dreams' from *Stones* by Timothy Findley. Copyright © Pebble Productions 1988, reprinted by permission of Penguin Books Canada Limited.

MAVIS GALLANT. 'Varieties of Exile' copyright © Mavis Gallant 1981. Originally appeared in *The New Yorker*, reprinted by permission of Georges Borchardt, Inc.

TOMSON HIGHWAY. Excerpt from *Kiss of the Fur Queen* (Doubleday Canada, 1998) reprinted by permission of the author.

JACK HODGINS. 'The Leper's Squint' from *The Barclay Family Theatre* (Macmillan, 1981), used by permission of the author.

THOMAS KING. 'A Coyote Columbus Story' from *One Good Story, That One* (HarperCollins, 1993). Copyright © Dead Dog Café Productions Inc. 1993, reprinted by permission of the author.

A.M. KLEIN. 'Reb Levi Yitschok Talks to God', 'Heirloom', 'Psalm XXXVI: A Psalm Touching Genealogy', 'The Rocking Chair', 'Political Meeting', 'Portrait of the Poet as Landscape', and 'Autobiographical' from *A.M. Klein: Complete Poems*, ed. Zailig Pollock, reprinted by permission of University of Toronto Press.

JOY KOGAWA. 'Where There's a Wall', 'Road Building by Pick Axe', and 'Minerals from Stone' from *Woman in the Woods*, reprinted by permission of Mosaic Press. 'Obasan' © Joy Kogawa, reprinted by permission of the author.

ROBERT KROETSCH. 'Stone Hammer Poem', copyright © Robert Kroetsch 1989, from *Completed Field Notes: The Long Poems of Robert Kroetsch* (originally published by McClelland & Stewart, now available from University of Alberta Press), reprinted by permission. 'F.P. Grove: The Finding' from *Stone Hammer Poems* (Oolichan Books, 1975) copyright © Robert Kroetsch 1975, reprinted by permission. Excerpt from *The Words of My Roaring* (The Macmillan Company of Canada Ltd) copyright © Robert Kroetsch 1966, reprinted by permission.

PATRICK LANE. Reprinted by permission of the author: 'Because I Never Learned', 'Stigmata', 'The Witnesses', and 'The Long Coyote Line'; 'Honey' from *How Do You Spell Beautiful?* (Fifth House, 1992); 'Too Spare, Too Fierce' from *Too Spare, Too Fierce* (Harbour Publishing, 1995); 'CPR Station—Winnipeg', 'A Red Bird Bearing on His Back an Empty Cup', 'Winter 1', 'Winter 4', 'Winter 7', 'Winter 16', Winter 22', 'Winter 31', 'Winter 33', 'Winter 35', 'Winter 40', 'Winter 42', 'The Far Field', 'Held Water', and 'Breaking' from *Selected Poems 1977–1997* (Harbour Publishing, 1997).

MARGARET LAURENCE. 'To Set Our House in Order' from *A Bird in the House* by Margaret Laurence, used by permission of McClelland & Stewart Ltd *The Canadian Publishers.*

IRVING LAYTON. 'The Birth of Tragedy', 'The Cold Green Element', 'The Fertile Muck', 'Whatever Else, Poetry is Freedom', 'Keine Lazarovitch 1870–1959', 'Butterfly on Rock', and 'A Tall Man Executes a Jig' from *A Wild Peculiar Joy: Selected Poems 1945–1989* by Irving Layton, used by permission of McClelland & Stewart Ltd *The Canadian Publishers.*

DOROTHY LIVESAY. Reprinted by permission of Jay Stewart, literary executrix for the Estate of Dorothy Livesay: 'Green Rain', 'The Difference', 'Day and Night', 'Bartok and the Geranium', 'The Three Emilys', and 'The Artefacts: West Coast' from *Collected Poems: The Two Seasons of Dorothy Livesay* (McGraw-Hill Ryerson, 1972); 'The Secret Doctrine of Women' from *A Room of One's Own* 5, 1–2 (1979): 117–9.

GWENDOLYN MACEWEN. 'The Real Enemies' from *The T.E. Lawrence Poems*, reprinted by permission of Mosaic Press. Reprinted by permission of the author's family: 'Icarus', 'Manzini: Escape Artist', 'The Portage', and 'Dark Pines under Water' from *Magic Animals: Selected Poetry of Gwendolyn MacEwen* (Stoddart, 1984); 'The Death of the Loch Ness Monster' and 'Polaris' from *Afterworlds* (McClelland & Stewart, 1987).

DON MCKAY. 'Kestrels' from *Birding, or Desire* (McClelland & Stewart, 1983), reprinted by permission of the author. Used by permission of McClelland & Stewart Ltd *The Canadian Publishers*: 'Twinflower', 'Goldeneye, Diving', 'Black Box', 'Short Fat Flicks', and 'To Danceland' from *Apparatus* by Don McKay; 'Homing' and 'Icarus' from *Another Gravity* by Don McKay.

HUGH MACLENNAN. Excerpt from *Barometer Rising* (McClelland & Stewart, 1989), reprinted by permission of McGill-Queen's University Press.

ALISTAIR MACLEOD. 'As Birds Bring Forth the Sun' from *Islands* by Alistair MacLeod, used by permission of McClelland & Stewart Ltd *The Canadian Publishers.*

DAPHNE MARLATT. 'winter/ rice/ tea strain', 'listen', 'retrieving madrone', and '(is love enough?)' from *This Tremor Love Is*, reprinted by permission of Talon Books Ltd. Excerpt from *Ana Historic* © Daphne Marlatt, originally published by Coach House Press, 1988, reprinted by permission of House of Anansi Press.

ANNE MICHAELS. Used by permission of McClelland & Stewart *The Canadian Publishers*: excerpt from *Fugitive Pieces*; 'There is No City That Does Not Dream' and 'Ice House' from Skin Divers by Anne Michaels; 'Lake of Two Rivers' and 'Flowers' from *The Weight of Oranges/Miner's Pond* by Anne Michaels.

ROHINTON MISTRY, 'Swimming Lessons' from *Tales from Firozsha Baag* by Rohinton Mistry, used by permission of McClelland & Stewart Ltd *The Canadian Publishers.*

W.O. MITCHELL. 'Saint Sammy' from *Who Has Seen the Wind* by W.O. Mitchell, used by permission of McClelland & Stewart Ltd *The Canadian Publishers.*

ERIN MOURÉ. Reprinted by permission of House of Anansi Press: 'It Is Only Me' from *Wanted Alive* © 1983; 'Blindness' from *Domestic Fuel* © 1985; 'Miss Chatelaine' from *Furious* © 1988; 'Absalom' and 'Dream of the Towns' from *Search Procedures* © 1996; 'The Splendour' from *Frame of the Book* © 1999. 'The Beauty of Furs' and 'The Beauty of Furs: A Site Glossary' from *WSW (West South West)* (Véhicule Press, 1989), used by permission.

ALICE MUNRO. 'The Progress of Love' from *Selected Stories* by Alice Munro, used by permission of McClelland & Stewart Ltd *The Canadian Publishers.*

bp NICHOL. Reprinted by permission of the Estate of bp Nichol: 'landscape: I' and 'lament' from *Zygal: A Book of Mysteries and Translations* by bp Nichol (Coach House Books, 2000); excerpts from 'Book 1', 'Book 3', and 'Book 5' of *The Martyrology* by bp Nichol (Coach House Press).

ALDEN NOWLAN. 'Temptation' from *Bread, Wine and Salt* (Clarke, Irwin, 1967), reprinted by permission of the Estate of Alden Nowlan. 'Country Full of Christmas', 'Canadian January Night', 'The Broadcaster's Poem', and 'On the Barrens' copyright © Irwin Publishing Inc. 1969, 1971, 1974, 1977, reprinted by permission of House of Anansi Press.

MICHAEL ONDAATJE. Reprinted by permission of the author: 'The Time Around Scars', 'Letters & Other Worlds', 'Pig Glass', 'The Cinnamon Peeler', 'To a Sad Daughter', 'The Medieval Coast', and 'Wells'; 'The Bridge' from *In the Skin of a Lion* (Toronto: McClelland & Stewart, 1987).

P.K. PAGE. 'Stories of Snow', 'Photos of a Salt Mine', 'Cry Ararat!', 'Arras', 'Unless the Eye Catch Fire', 'The Gold Sun', 'Poor Bird', and 'Kaleidoscope' from *The Hidden Room: Collected Poems* (2 vols), reprinted by permission of The Porcupine's Quill.

E.J. PRATT. 'The Shark', 'Newfoundland', 'Silences', 'Come Away, Death', 'The Truant', and excerpts from *Towards the Last Spike* from *E.J. Pratt: The Complete Poems*, ed. Sandra Djwa and R.G. Moyles, reprinted by permission of University of Toronto Press.

AL PURDY. 'The Country North of Belleville', 'Trees at the Arctic Circle', 'Wilderness Gothic', 'Lament for the Dorsets', 'Roblin's Mills (2)', 'A Handful of Earth', 'Elegy for a Grandfather', 'The Dead Poet', 'For Steve McIntyre', 'Red Leaves', 'On the Flood Plain', 'Grosse Isle', and 'Say the Names' from *Beyond Remembering: The Collected Poems of Al Purdy*, ed. Sam Solecki, reprinted by permission of Harbour Publishing.

JAMES REANEY. 'The School Globe', 'The Lost Child', 'The Alphabet', and 'Starling with a Split Tongue' from *Poems* (New Press, 1972), reprinted by permission of Livingston Cooke, Inc.

DAVID ADAMS RICHARDS. Excerpt from *Mercy Among the Children* by David Adams Richards. Copyright © David Adams Richards 2000, reprinted by permission of Doubleday Canada, a division of Random House of Canada Limited.

MORDECAI RICHLER. 'Playing Ball on Hampstead Heath' from *St. Urbain's Horseman* by Mordecai Richler, used by permission of McClelland & Stewart Ltd *The Canadian Publishers.*

HARRY ROBINSON. 'Captive in an English Circus' from *Write It On Your Heart*, comp. and ed. Wendy Wickwire, reprinted by permission of Talon Books Ltd.

SINCLAIR ROSS. 'The Runaway' from *The Lamp at Noon and Other Stories* by Sinclair Ross, used by permission of McClelland & Stewart Ltd *The Canadian Publishers.*

F.R. SCOTT. 'The Canadian Authors Meet', 'Trans Canada', 'Lakeshore', 'Poetry', 'All the Spikes but the Last', and 'W.L.M.K.' from *Collected Poems* (McClelland & Stewart, 1981), reprinted by permission of William Toye, literary executor for the Estate of F.R. Scott.

CAROL SHIELDS. 'Hazel' from *Orange Fish* by Carol Shields. Copyright © Carol Shields 1989, reprinted by permission of Random House Canada, a division of Random House of Canada Limited.

J.G. SIME. 'Munitions!' from *Sister Woman* (The Tecumseh Press, 1992).

A.J.M. SMITH. 'The Lonely Land', 'Far West', 'Sea Cliff', and 'The Wisdom of Old Jelly Roll' from *The Classic Shade* (McClelland & Stewart, 1978), reprinted by permission of William Toye, literary executor for the Estate of A.J.M. Smith.

JOHN STEFFLER. Selections from *The Grey Islands* copyright © John Steffler 1985, 2000. First published by McClelland & Stewart, reprinted by permission of the author and Brick Books.

JANE URQUHART. Excerpt from *The Stone Carvers*, used by permission of McClelland & Stewart Ltd *The Canadian Publishers.*

ARITHA VAN HERK. 'Edmonton, Long Division' from *Places Far from Ellesmere*, reprinted by permission of the author and Red Deer Press.

GUY VANDERHAEGHE. 'Man on Horseback' from *Things As They Are?* by Guy Vanderhaeghe, used by permission of McClelland & Stewart Ltd *The Canadian Publishers.*

FRED WAH. Excerpt from *Diamond Grill* (1996) by Fred Wah, reprinted by permission of NeWest Publishers Ltd.

BRONWEN WALLACE. 'An Easy Life' from *People You'd Trust Your Life To* by Bronwen Wallace, used by permission of McClelland & Stewart Ltd *The Canadian Publishers*. 'Joseph Macleod Daffodils', 'Testimonies', and 'The Watermelon Incident' from *The Stubborn Particulars of Grace* (McClelland & Stewart, 1987), reprinted by permission of the Estate of Bronwen Wallace. 'The Woman in this Poem' by Bronwen Wallace from *Signs of the Former Tenant*, reprinted by permission of Oberon Press.

SHEILA WATSON. Excerpt from *The Double Hook* by Sheila Watson, used by permission of McClelland & Stewart Ltd *The Canadian Publishers*.

PHYLLIS WEBB. Reprinted by permission of Talon Books Ltd: 'Marvell's Garden', 'To Friends Who Have Also Considered Suicide', 'Suite I', and 'Suite II' from *Selected Poems: The Vision Tree*; 'Evensong' and 'The Making of a Japanese Print' from *Hanging Fire*.

RUDY WIEBE. 'Where Is the Voice Coming From?' from *River of Stone* (Vintage Books, 1995), reprinted by permission of the author.

ETHEL WILSON. 'The Window' from *Mrs. Golightly and Other Stories* copyright © Ethel Wilson 1961, reprinted by permission of Macmillan Canada, an imprint of CDG Books Canada, Inc.

ADELE WISEMAN. Excerpt from *Old Woman at Play* by Adele Wiseman, reprinted by permission of Tamara Stone. Copyright © Adele Wiseman 1978, © Tamara Stone 1992.

JAN ZWICKY. Reprinted by permission of the author: 'Open Strings', 'Bill Evans: "Here's That Rainy Day"', 'Musicians', 'Transparence', '*Trauermusik*', and 'Driving Northwest' from *Songs for Relinquishing the Earth* (Brick Books, 1998); 'The New Room' from *The New Room* (Coach House Press, 1989).

Every effort has been made to contact copyright owners. In the case of any omissions, the publisher will be pleased to make suitable acknowledgement in future editions.

Index